LITERATURE

EXPERIENCE
AND
MEANING

MARTHA McGOWAN
University of Lowell

HBJ

Harcourt Brace Jovanovich, Publishers

San Diego   New York   Chicago   Austin   Washington, D.C.
London   Sydney   Tokyo   Toronto

PREFACE

Literature: Experience and Meaning is intended for introductory-level literature courses, which typically include students from various academic disciplines along with prospective English or other literature majors. One aim is to acquaint this general student population with a challenging range of literature in three genres—short fiction, poetry, and drama—compassable in a single semester. The organization and editorial content of this anthology are also meant to encourage students to become more actively responsive readers of literature, understood here as requiring a dynamic interaction between readers and texts.

The selections span a period from the fifth century B.C. to the present. Works from the English tradition, in addition to Greek and Continental drama in English translation, represent older literature of permanent significance. More than half the selections are from the twentieth century. Its diversity of voices, with the growing strength of female and black writers in America, is an important and exciting phenomenon. The works chosen here stimulate interest in this vital area of our literary culture.

The broadest organization of the selections is thematic, with works presented in five main sections: "Innocence Recalled," "Self and Society," "Complexities of Love," "Sustaining Visions," and "Life's Conclusions." Within these sections, works in each genre are grouped together and arranged chronologically by the writer's year of birth, with a few exceptions for more effective placement.

But the thematic organization is most obvious and meant to be the most operative. The thematic headings under which selections are presented are deliberately broad: intended to prompt reflection but never to limit perspectives upon individual works. Readers may grumble over decisions made here, since many works might well have been placed under two or more headings. Nevertheless, this general organization should help students make connections between their own experience and works read. In other texts, theme often appears as merely another "element" in works grouped to illustrate various poetic devices or techniques of the fiction writer or dramatist. The organization here recalls the universally human concerns that recur in most writers' works and that have always led readers to literature.

The organization of this text avoids isolating any element of literary form. Students, indeed most readers, are less likely to respond at once to matters of literary craft than to a sense of what a whole work means in relation to their personal and other literary experience. Obviously, some appreciation of technique and an understanding of literary conventions form part of the process of reading actively and well. Recognizing all a literary text may offer helps clarify and enlarge a reader's response to it. Therefore, the essential terms of literary discourse for each genre are introduced into the editorial content (and defined in a glossary) in ways meant to ease the student into their use. But the emphasis is upon the customary and convenient, rather than upon the need for a specialized terminology.

An introduction describes the process of reading literature generally, with attention given to the reading experience for each genre. Meaning is defined in each case as resulting in part from the reader's responses—the literary texts being the origin, guide, and final touchstone for these. In the light of recent reader/response theory, this approach is conservative; but instructors will find here, as elsewhere, enough flexibility for special emphases they may wish to bring to the course.

Questions appear after nearly half the selections. The first questions after a work often require analysis of the reader's initial, or primary response. Subsequent questions move toward more objective considerations and the integration of perceptions and analyses into a sense of the whole work and its meanings. All questions attempt to be nontendentious. Those after individual works may provide topics for course papers, as may the additional questions at the end of each section, which often ask students to consider two or more works together.

The Appendix on "Writing about Literature" aims to persuade students of the value of written expression as a way of clarifying and sharing their experiences as readers. Ways of selecting a topic, the nature of literary evidence, and the conventions of literary papers are all discussed with a view to eliciting written responses adequate to the creative writer's imagination and intelligence.

Many colleagues have encouraged me and provided various sorts of help while I worked on this book. I particularly wish to thank William Hersey, Mary D. Kramer, and Gerard O'Connor of the University of Lowell and John L. Mahoney of Boston College.

I am deeply indebted also to the many people at Harcourt Brace Jovanovich who assisted in the preparation and production of the text. My thanks go especially to Bill McLane, Eleanor Garner, Julia Ann Ross, Diane Pella, and Mandy Van Dusen for their insights, professionalism, and good humor.

Martha McGowan

CONTENTS

III COMPLEXITIES OF LOVE   369

IV SUSTAINING VISIONS   607

FICTION

POETRY

DRAMA

INTRODUCTION

The Literary Experience

If you have ever thought studying literature in college has disadvantages, you were right. It may seem odd to say so here in a college textbook which you probably were required to buy, perhaps for a course also required of you. Studying literature in a college situation does have real advantages and possible pleasures not easily duplicated elsewhere. More of that later. Let us admit at the outset that an academic environment is in some ways the worst for experiencing literature—an art in which ideas, feelings, values, visions of humanity and of the world surrounding us are expressed by the creative intelligence and imagination through language.

Requiring literary study of someone, like requiring someone else to assign grades for credits, has a slightly chilling effect on what should be an encounter prompted only by interest. You also study literature under adverse conditions of class scheduling and time pressures. During the week you may find the mere logistics of getting from one class to another a challenge, given the time allowed. Your course subjects, the sizes of your classes, and the way they are run may all be quite different. Then on a weekend you may find yourself having to complete 80 pages for Psychology, 120 for United States History, several formidable chapters for Chemistry, along with, perhaps, a play due to be discussed Monday morning. So you may never have thought about a vital distinction that sets your reading of literature apart from the other reading you are expected to do.

You read material for most other disciplines primarily for informational or practical purposes, much as you read, say, newspapers, magazine articles, or instructional booklets outside of school. True, academic reading generally emphasizes ideas and focuses on details. But except in your literature class, no one expects you to linger much over the way details are relayed, to be struck by a word or turn of phrase, to be moved emotionally, or to reflect upon your personal experience as an essential activity for understanding the text. When reading literature, you are expected to do or be all these things, perhaps not all at once but in close enough sequence to make a uniquely complicated process. That is, if you are reading literature as it is meant to be read and reading the kinds of literature, represented in this book, that make special demands on you.

"Serious," or "real" literature is sometimes distinguished from types of popular literature you may enjoy—such as science fiction, mysteries, or romances—as

1

offering deeper, more genuine enjoyment and enlightenment, along with intellectual challenge.

Literature of the "serious" kinds is usually more troublesome, however, than such descriptions acknowledge. You may be able to cite any number of difficulties you have already encountered in studying literature in school or while reading works on your own, such as the huge and now partially antiquated vocabulary used by Shakespeare, the eccentric capitalization and punctuation in Emily Dickinson, or a setting in another period and unfamiliar locale in a writer such as James Joyce. "Serious" literature is certainly not always solemn, but even in a comic mode it may be unsettling. You may find yourself tempted to dismiss what puzzles and disturbs you as simply not enjoyable, if not "depressing."

The essential difference between "serious" and "popular" literature may seem to be the work each requires of you. Actually, a main difference *is* the degree to which each engages you. Serious literature demands your openness to and participation in an experience offered—which may involve joy, pain, or one of the countless other feelings. Popular literature entertains precisely by not demanding so much and so continually from you.

Consider detective stories that treat a reader to the darker side of the human psyche, their plots typically strewing bodies about in grotesque ways. The detective hero may be beaten bloody, have a friend murdered, face disillusionment, or suffer otherwise in his or her attempt to complete a job, see justice done, avenge the friend, or whatever a variant of the basic formula dictates. It is the presence of this basic formula, an expected pattern of certain prescribed sorts of events, that you, as reader, find satisfying. Such fiction rolls you along pleasantly, although at times you may feel the slightly uncomfortable tension of suspense. That is also expected as part of the formula.

As in reading serious fiction, you do need to contribute imaginatively. You contribute quite a lot, in fact, although you may think of yourself as reading merely to relax or "escape." You must put together characters, often from only a few clues in the text. You assume imaginatively that they walk, eat, sleep, and so on (unless they are the murder victims) even during those parts of the story where they do not appear. You must also imagine time passing and construct from relatively few words the places where the story occurs. You imagine setting as space—at once real and a kind of moral terrain through which the hero journeys. Doing just this much should relieve you of possibly feeling slow-witted for not outsmarting the hero by first reaching the correct conclusion about the identity of the murderer. In any case, probably the formula will not permit you to do so.

But the challenges of serious literature, called simply literature after this, differ in kind as well as degree. Each of the major types, or genres, does have certain conventions governing length and form, and so do recognized subtypes of drama, poetry, and short fiction. For example, the number of acts customary in plays in a given period is a matter of convention, as is the number of lines in a sonnet, or the number of incidents suitable to a short story. Distinctive conventions of style may also serve to identify work written in a particular period. In our century, for example, poets, dramatists, and writers of fiction all use language like that of everyday speech. In earlier centuries poets were especially apt to use archaisms or other unusual diction to "elevate" their art and emphasize its distinctiveness. The more you read, the more you will be able to recognize and appreciate such different conventions. But you will find also that conventions impose less sense of the expected upon a whole work than formulas do. When reading a work based on a formula, you are satisfied and entertained by its variation upon some familiar pattern. In reading literature you encounter, instead, the demands of particularity—or of what may truly be called originality. You must surrender expectations of relativity easy entertainment. You enter an imaginative world with virtually as much challenge to sort specific data and as much potential for an essentially new experience as you may meet in daily life.

You may well have a stronger sense of challenge. Actively reading a powerful work heightens our awareness of life, as the patterns of an ordinary day may fail to do. As you read a short story, for example, you sense that it demands more of you than imaginative belief in the characters' existence or in the places and time through which they move. Plot or external action may be minimal. You may realize that what is really important is occurring instead within the characters. You may receive direct information about this or need to infer it from details of their actions or speech. In either case, you become aware of a voice conveying the information of the text. Again no formula pleases by its near-predictability. The voice of the narrator may or may not be that of a character in the story. The voice may be more or less assertive, or its tone may suggest some attitude towards what it relates. All these possible situations present you with more details to process. In all such processing, you must use your imagination, intelligence, and experience.

Other literature you have read is part of your experience. Nonliterary experience includes other kinds of reading and, most generally, all your living thus far. So it is a deep reservoir upon which you can draw. More to the point, you cannot help drawing from it, even if you do not consciously search your brain as you read for relevant thoughts or memories. Even if you tried, you could not read even the first sentence of a story or first line of a poem as though you yourself were a blank page. Sometimes you may feel almost that you are, when you have "drawn a blank" after reading a short poem, perhaps, for the first time. That little poem of a scant few lines may leave you at first feeling numb, as you search for a clue to it. Be assured that a person—even an English professor—who reads poetry regularly may experience much the same reaction after a first reading. Most likely you and the professor have already begun to make some progress, however. You have used, among other things, your understanding of the language, its words, grammar, and normal syntax. You have stored various bits of information from the poem to process with data retrieved both consciously and unconsciously from your memory.

Being human, you do not draw upon the same memory, just as you individually do not have the exact same combination of characteristics as anyone else. Your experience—like your temperament, intelligence, or set of values—is also uniquely yours. It would not be easy even for you to say of just what the uniqueness of your experience consists, since the latter involves both external events and a deeply inward development. Yet evidence of how experience accumulates will appear as you read through that same troublesome little poem a second and third time. Better, return to it in a week or month, or three or thirteen years from now. You will notice that it gives you back more and, very possibly, different things each time. A growth process that can only be part of your growth has occurred. (Someone else, who has once read the poem with you and with similar results, will have grown differently.)

Perhaps you have brought to each rereading a special, increasing sensitivity to the sounds of words or of verse, or a stronger ability to see objects, colors, or whatever the words of the poem lead you to visualize. Other reading and learning and more knowledge of people, including yourself, will have had an effect on you. Possibly you have met an insult like that in Countee Cullen's poem "Incident." If you once swung on birches, growing older may have enabled you to understand more clearly what Robert Frost describes in his not-so-little poem. You may have come to question beliefs held since childhood. If so, William Blake's "Tyger," with all its questions, will seem less strange to you than it did once.

Whatever the case, the passage of time in itself will not have clarified the poem for you; nor do you wait passively for time to help you to understand any work— at least, not if you read it again. Whenever reading occurs, it may look to an observer like a passive activity but really is otherwise. Walt Whitman once wrote that "the process of reading is not a half-sleep, but in the highest sense, an exercise, a gymnast's struggle . . . the reader is to do something for himself, must be on the alert, must himself or herself construct indeed the poem" or (he went on) whatever is "the text furnishing the hints, the clue, the start or frame-work." You may or may not be attracted by the mental picture of such intense activity as Whitman's analogy evokes. But unless you just quit cold on that poem, or reject your own experience and understanding as though not possibly worth anything, the process going on as you read is as active and energetic as Whitman suggests. Reading engages you in a complicated exchange, an interaction as potentially absorbing as an intimate conversation, or, perhaps, an intricate dance.

All such vital engagement with a literary work is always in the interest of *meaning*. What this is not is fairly easy to say. Meaning is not a simple moral, such as the Duchess in *Alice in Wonderland* sought to tag onto every event, insisting "and the moral of *that* is . . ." True, sometimes a poem or story or play may contain a cautionary message. In *The Misanthrope* you may see in Alceste's increasingly angry isolation a warning about the perils of too much self-involvement or about the punishment for refusing to accept human frailty. You may read Charlotte Perkins Gilman's "The Yellow Wall-Paper" as a horrifying illustration of what can result from the stifling of female energies. Or Edward Arlington Robinson's "Richard Cory" as a reminder that things are not always as they appear or that the rich share the human lot. If you reduce any literary work to a simplistic lesson, however, you do both the work and yourself a disservice. You do so also if, by paraphrasing a poem or summarizing the plot of a story or play, you suppose you have done any more than that.

A statement of theme, or a thematic heading such as you find in this book, is not meaning, although it may point you in a helpful direction. Meaning is not something you look up in a "study guide" bought off a bookstore rack. Meaning is not a secret your instructor is keeping while trying to draw you out in class discussion.

Rather, meaning is what you make as you interact with a literary text. All your responses—emotional, intellectual, linguistic—help shape meaning. Your uniquely individual contribution helps. What troubles you in a work and compels you to focus on a detail or wrestle with your reaction is likely to yield meaning, or understanding, if you stay with it. A work's meaning is first of all very personal: its meaning for you. That meaning may change, as you bring greater experience of other kinds to your experience of the work over a period of time. You may find the work's meaning for you to be very different from what it is for somebody else, even a person you think is quite like you. Its meaning for you may also differ from an apparently general consensus about the work in published interpretive essays and books.

So you may wonder whether the meaning you have found in the work has any validity or value beyond yourself. Can it stand as a reading, in the sense of an interpretation? You may ask further what makes one reading, or interpretation, better than another, when the two are compared. Perhaps you will hear someone confuse the issue by speaking about a reading of a work as though only personal opinion were involved. This person may argue stubbornly—and with the defiance of a patriot—that one reading is as good as another in a democratic society. Another common suggestion is that, beyond all individual interpretations, there is only one true meaning of any work. According to this view, this true meaning is what the poet or author intended—assuming you might discover that.

Meaning and the Text

Generally speaking, democratic principles have nothing to do with the merits of a reading. Living writers are, moreover, notoriously unhelpful about explaining their intentions, even when questioned directly about their works. For example, Joyce Carol Oates has remarked in an interview that "every person dreams . . . and every dreamer is a kind of artist. The formal artist is one who arranges his dreams into a shape that can be experienced by other people." She added that "there is no guarantee that art will be understood, not even by the artist; it is not meant to be understood but to be experienced." Ernest Hemingway once commented more pointedly that it was not his business to act as tour guide through his fictional country.

Good writers refuse to do more than their share to communicate through their art. We need to respect that attitude and appreciate the writer's concern for the independent life of his or her art.

It is texts that make this art available. Literary texts really are the "primary sources" we often call them as a text provides literally the first and last word on the author's intentions. Curiously enough, not all writers have been committed to providing "set" or "finished" texts, such as you find in this anthology. As the best (or worst) example, Shakespeare apparently cared little about leaving to posterity fair manuscript or printed copies of *Hamlet,* the *Shrew,* and the rest, exactly as he had conceived them. The history of Shakespeare's texts, like that of other authors' less dramatically, is of debts we owe to those who guarded, transcribed, or saw to publication works they recognized as too precious to be lost. Without this care for texts, many more works would have succumbed to "death and all-oblivious enmity"—as the voice in Shakespeare's Sonnet 55 boasts grandly it shall not.

Even the greatest literary work begins as a fragile, perishable thing; but however we have it, a literary text is curious because, while only a collection of markings on relatively flimsy paper (in this lingering age of print), it seems like an object or force to be reckoned with. Just how a text does exist, beyond the obvious, has become in fact a matter of some current debate. Literary critics have long regarded literary texts as very much like objects, or complex structures, component parts of which may be analyzed. The "structure" that they discuss really is based on a metaphor, but the strong implication of this figure of speech is that a work occupies its own space in reality, as other substantial, free-standing objects do.

In recent years, literary theorists have questioned this view increasingly. Some argue that a literary work does not exist in any meaningful way except in a reader's mind. According to these theorists, the reader creates the work in the process of reading it. His or her responses become, in effect, the poem, play, short story, or novel. No real evidence of the work's existence, including the text, occurs outside a reader's response to it.

This second position owes much to modern philosophical theories of perception. To some it may also recall Bishop George Berkeley, an eighteenth-century Irish philosopher admired by the poet W. B. Yeats for having "proved all things a dream." Berkeley believed that no reality could be verified beyond the ideas of it in the mind. A famous anecdote concerns the reaction to this belief by Dr. Samuel Johnson, the leading English man of letters of the mideighteenth century. Johnson was practical-minded and somewhat curmudgeonly. His biographer, James Boswell, recalls remarking to him that it was "impossible" to refute Berkeley's doctrine. Then Boswell adds, "I shall never forget the alacrity with which Johnson answered, striking his foot with might against a large stone, till he rebounded from it,—'I refute it *thus'*."

The smarting foot Johnson no doubt suffered speaks for the merits of common sense. Of course, the kick did not really do justice to Berkeley's philosophy. The quarrel over the nature of reality predates either man and will go on long after our own time. The present quarrel over the way a literary work exists may also. As a student, you need not evaluate finally the position of either side. But being practical-minded, you should note that your instructor very probably leans towards the curmudgeonly. For most instructors, as for most readers of literature, the presence of the text, considered as existing in itself, provides welcome guidance and a source of reference for those responses the work evokes.

Recall the earlier analogies of the conversation or dance, and consider how much more agreeable such activities are than being shut up in one's own head. Recall Whitman's comparison of the reader and gymnast, and consider how meaningless even one's personal best becomes without some standard outside the self. The literary text is a means by which we extend ourselves by adding to our personal experience. The otherness of the text relieves an overinvolvement with self and furnishes bases upon which we can communicate with other people concerning it.

You may still question whether a work has only one "true" meaning, to which individual readers come more or less close. A text remains the same, although its meaning may change—and not only for you—over time. A story, poem, or play may seem to change, to gain or lose meaning, when read by generations of readers over a long period. Such apparent alteration occurs especially when broad intellectual or social changes take place within a culture, such as have occurred in America in little more than one generation. These changes have altered the way we experience the portrayal of women and black people in literature. For readers with sensitivity, many older works containing racial or gender stereotypes now pose new problems of meaning. Some works seem drained of their earlier force. Others have rapidly gained new significance.

How can such changes occur, while texts still remain the same? The answer lies, once again, in the dynamic interaction of texts and readers, or of a text and an individual reader, that is central to all literary experience.

As one reader, you may find that a particular work, or a scene, character, or line in it has aroused an unusually strong response in you. You may wonder why your reaction to the scene or line, or your perception of the character, is so different from that of someone else, or why that voice you hear in the work has such an appealing tone. So you find yourself returning to the text, trying to put your finger (sometimes literally) upon the problem or, more positively, the source of your response. You may develop a view of the whole work as the result of examining the text in this way. You may revise that view later, as further acquaintance with the work puts into different perspective the details that stand out as significant. You may well feel that each rereading of the text brings you closer to some one "true" meaning. You may also find that you have come to agree with an apparent consensus among other readers concerning it. There is no problem at all if you do, and this is not a contradiction of what has been said earlier.

You may read some works differently from everyone else; but do not expect that every literary text will yield widely divergent readings—and do not assume that it should. A work's most vital quality may be the way it speaks with force and simplicity to our common experience. Understanding such a work may require little analysis, perhaps only a definition of an unfamiliar word or the identification of a reference. Probably most readers understand and value John Donne's "Death Be Not Proud" in a similar way, for example. Readers who have planted bulbs in the fall will experience Robert Herrick's "Divination by a Daffodil" only a little differently—maybe with a bit more pleasure—from those who have not.

By contrast to either poem, Emily Dickinson's "Because I could not stop for Death" is likely to arouse more varied responses. Each reader may point to different details in the text to explain what the poem means. Some works are indeed so rich as to afford multiple readings, each distinct and each of which may be supported by textual detail. *Hamlet* is preeminently such a work, having been read (and interpreted on stage) in a variety of ways over the centuries. Even the best-known poems in the language still have surprises in store and may appear new and fresh, as new readers consider them. A good short story, whether only a few pages long or many, provides enough complexity for a considerable diversity of responses.

To move from your private experience of a work to any situation permitting comparison of your views with others' is usually instructive. You will need, simply, to return often to the text. Your reading and someone else's may seem equally valid in the long run, but both must be grounded equally in details, the importance of which each of you can explain. Otherwise you may be accused of "reading into" the work or of being arbitrary or irrelevant. A reading that loses sight of the text may be interesting and provocative, but it tells others more about the reader's preoccupations than about the work supposedly considered. What is being discussed will have shifted.

Literary Discourse

Like texts, other people serve as good controls for our reading experiences. So communicating about literature, either in discussion or writing, can be as challenging in its way as the experience that leads to it. In some ways it can be more so, since a response to a work may be so deeply felt that articulating it may seem difficult and perhaps even distorting. Reluctance to discuss a work may therefore involve more than shyness. The person who complains in class about having to "tear everything apart" may really be pleading to leave what feels like a full, if silent, response to it undisturbed. The more deeply moved a person is by a work, all the more silence may seem the proper homage to offer it. Smiles, that rare laughter-out-loud over a page, or tears that amaze you by their un-likelihood are other worthy signs of responses that, had you written the work arousing them, you would no doubt find satisfactory.

In a classroom situation, however, your instructor inevitably will want a verbal expression of what you have made of the work, what meaning it has for you that you can share to promote an exchange of views. Whatever the limitations of the academic study of literature, the classroom and work done for a literature course provide valuable opportunities to engage in literary discourse. (At other times in your life, you may even wish for the challenge of provocative opinion, lively disagreement, or another reader's helpful insight into a work you have read in solitude.) In class you will feel yourself shifting gears as you move from a very personal, private experience of a work to an open discussion of it. Submitting yourself to all the surprises, demands, tensions, or ambiguities of a work, as you read well, puts you in a different relation to it than you need to establish now. You feel yourself moving, in effect, from within the work to a position outside or standing back from it.

The work will seem more like an object, and one requiring analysis even of the appreciation you experience. The strictly personal, or responses too private to share, must be filed away. So the change in your relation to the text feels like a loss at first. Expressing your views is also, as always, to feel yourself (or your *self*) at some risk. Why not just say you liked the poem, disliked the play, or thought the short story "really weird," and leave it at that? You know you are being drawn into talk of a sort that you would never start over lunch in the cafeteria. You may feel uncomfortable using words you would never speak in an intimate conversation with someone you hoped to impress.

Literary discourse tends to be analytic and relatively formal with respect to the language used. Much of the language is actually about form, or the so-called "formal elements" of the different types of literature, in an introductory-level course. This last is generally a misnomer, by the way, since undoubtedly you have been introduced to literature and some of the analytic terms proper to it already. You probably know that you can discuss narrative fiction, novels as well as short stories, in terms of characterization, setting, plot, and point of view. Except for the last, the same terms are applied also to drama, with some refinements in discussing plot (rising action, climax, *dénouement,* and so on) added. A few more exotic terms (tragic flaw, catharsis) are peculiar to a specific type of drama—in this case, to tragedy.

Poetry employs terms both with and without overlap with the other kinds of literature. Symbol is one overlap term. You may find symbols throughout literature, and something so common should not worry you. Irony also occurs often in poetry, in fiction, and, you may remember, is a major effect of Greek tragedy. In poetry, however, special attention is paid to imagery, figurative language, diction, and syntax. It is not enough to learn that odd little "Morse code" for scanning lines of verse for the meter. Different meters (metrical feet, as they are also called) have names. So do the subtypes of poetry in a classification scheme that includes narrative and lyric poetry, dramatic monologues and elegies, ballads and odes. Scorn all these for the sonnet, and you still need to recall quatrains and couplets, the division of lines into an octave and sestet, and the Italian, or Petrarchan sonnet, as distinct from the English, or Shakespearean.

Ars long vita brevis, as the Latin poet Horace wrote: "Life so short, the craft so long to learn." He was speaking as a poet but might have been sighing over all the terms needed to discuss literature formally. To assist you, an ample glossary is appended to this text. Refer to it at need. Remember while you do that literature is no different in this demand on you from other subjects that have become specialized disciplines. Here, as elsewhere, a basic terminology makes communication easier. You share in a consensus as to what elements of your subject are the essential ones. You should not be overwhelmed by the terms of the trade but use them for your purposes. In particular, you should realize that such terms do not replace your experience of a work but should help you express that.

Point of view is important in fiction, for instance, and so the term is useful. Yet it is hardly meaningful without your experience of the narrator in a specific work. Having read *Sonny's Blues,* by James Baldwin, you may say readily that the story is told from a first-person, participant, major-character viewpoint. You can easily identify the narrator and describe what he does and tells you about himself. But your important experience of the story involves this narrator's voice, your sense of his nature and of what troubles and sustains his relationship with his brother. You may draw upon your experience of siblings, of "straight" types, perhaps of Harlem, or of how it feels to be confronted by addiction or by a rare talent. Perhaps you know already how hard it is to love someone whose pain you might almost prefer not to understand. You will consider the narrator from your own moral viewpoint. Probably you will relate emotionally to both him and Sonny. When you begin to speak with others about the story, all such involvement should inform your comments in some way.

You will not succeed in being wholly objective in your analysis. Try as hard and in much the same way as you do in daily life; but no terms you use should prevent your hearing—in this most human of arts—the sounds of the human voice. When you read the poems in this book, listen first for that voice, or more accurately, the sounds of those different voices. You should know the terms *speaker* and its alternate, *persona.* Use either to distinguish between the poet's personal identity, his or her whole existence, and that voice created through the use of language as art. The created voice, the speaker or persona, is nevertheless a presence to which you respond as to another person in the "real world." The voice you hear in a poem may sound as real, engaging, or assertive as any voice you have ever heard.

Read Shakespeare's Sonnet 73, and forget for the moment that figurative language (metaphors and personification) elaborates what is first said in rich, somber imagery. Do see those November trees, that brief glow in the west after sunset, and that low, smoldering fire in the grate. You cannot help noting how the three quatrains repeat basically the same thought with increasing precision, painstakingly delicate. If you will, notice how monosyllabic the couplet is. Bare of images, it refers back in simple words to what has been said before. Note all this and, if you like, think of that old a b a b, and so on, rhyme scheme. If you must, mark mentally or on the page those short smiling accents and lazy long ones that denote iambic pentameter. But first and last listen to that voice. Catch its drift, the inflection of its tone, and whom (before you) it addresses. Listen attentively to the speaker, letting the voice guide you through the poem. Then its other elements will assume their proper relation to the meaning you find in it.

When analyzing any work, trust your experience. The terms you have learned will not be equally important as you examine a specific text and consider its elements. Not all poems have striking imagery, for example, nor do they all have sound effects that beg to be heard and analyzed. Setting is not essential in the same way in every short story. You should also not expect to find characterization equally interesting, even in two stories that themselves interest you equally. Moreover, you may sometimes question the usefulness or validity of a term you have been led to suppose always applies to some type of work. When you read drama, for instance, you may assume that every tragic protagonist must have a *tragic flaw* and an *antagonist.* Then read *Antigone,* and consider whether both these terms fit that tragedy or apply to it usefully. Perhaps you will conclude that they do, but possibly you will feel that they suggest too neat a scheme for this particular work. Terms like tragic flaw and antagonist derive from others' reading experiences. No such terms are incised in marble. They are disputable in ways that your experience of the text and its details are not.

Literature that makes strong claims on you makes questionable all formulas. Literary experience does not rely on theorems. No computations yield correct answers. The kind of simplicity that elsewhere is elegant here is irrelevant. For another example from drama, you may expect the neat management of plot that the terms *exposition, complication, climax,* and *resolution* imply. While reading a play, probably you will feel increasing tension, but your attention may be engaged more by the characters than by any actions. You may not experience the plot line as symmetry. Perhaps it seems and, when analyzed, is more a continuous movement in one direction than a climb up and down two equal slopes. Some readers have experienced *Oedipus,* for instance, as the progress of its protagonist further and further down a narrowing cul-de-sac. And the term resolution suggests a calm settling of issues that the horrors of Oedipus's fate may not let you feel.

Be ready to question terminology as well as your own and others' views. Literary discourse begins with questions, posed by you or by someone else. It proceeds with more questioning and interaction between you and texts and you and others, either in person or in such relation as a written response to a literary work makes possible. A chapter at the end of this book discusses writing about literature in a way intended to help you, as you pull thoughts together for an essay examination or course paper. The advice given should be supplemented always by your understanding of what any reader of or about literature wants. He or she wants new insight, *your* insight. People may have written about a given literary work over centuries. Still, your response may illuminate it anew—even for an experienced instructor.

People choose the advanced study and professional teaching of literature because they enjoy reading. They want an exchange of responses and ideas, and they take pleasure in realizing that literature both provides experience and becomes part of it. At some levels of literary scholarship, specialists talk most easily and maybe most happily with other specialists; but at the "introductory" level, where basic terms apply, you can go far also with plain language. This is a common ground, where uncommon opportunities for good talk and writing exist. Whatever his or her special interests, your instructor is prepared to enjoy meeting on this ground. Despite all the pressures you feel, you should be also.

PART ONE

INNOCENCE RECALLED

The works in this first section, like those in the sections following, not only range widely in time but display a variety of subjects and styles within the three genres. You will find considerable scope for new literary experience here. You also have challenging opportunities for analysis, whether you read through all the works or limit your attention to a selection from them.

Some works may recall incidents from your personal experience and therefore have the most immediate appeal. Recollection may take you back to some golden time and a place loved in childhood, or a work may bring back a painful realization about life that marked your passage into the more complicated world you now inhabit as an adult. In either case, some shadow will undoubtedly fall on your memory. Innocence is a state we recognize always as in the past or as it passes. Its loss, however painful, is required for growth. You will notice that some works present the coming-to-terms with this growth amidst loss. Others focus upon the loss and accompanying sense of bewilderment, sadness, or tragedy.

The word *tragedy* applies most strictly to Sophocles's dramatization of the Oedipus story. Like several other works in this section, it may cause you to feel some loss of innocence even as you read. With *Oedipus*, Richard Wright's story of Big Boy, or William Blake's invocation of the "Tyger," you may have the troubling sense of finding your assumptions about justice, human nature, or the polarities of good and evil suddenly insufficient.

In contrast, John Keats's poem "On First Looking into Chapman's Homer" records the exhilaration of finding one's inner world, indeed one's universe, abruptly expanded by a voice speaking "loud and bold" from the pages of a book.

Often you must wait for this sense of growth as you meet the demands of a text new to you. The questions following about half the works here are meant to assist you in this process but not to direct you towards some one conclusion. Feel free to ask other questions that your reading suggests. Additional questions appear at the end of this section. These do not exhaust the possibilities either, but may be helpful as topics as you consider a single work or two or more works together.

FICTION

Nathaniel Hawthorne (1804–1864)
YOUNG GOODMAN BROWN

Young Goodman Brown came forth at sunset into the street at Salem village; but put his head back, after crossing the threshold, to exchange a parting kiss with his young wife. And Faith, as the wife was aptly named, thrust her own pretty head into the street, letting the wind play with the pink ribbons of her cap while she called to Goodman Brown.

"Dearest heart," whispered she, softly and rather sadly, when her lips were close to his ear, "prithee put off your journey until sunrise and sleep in your own bed to-night. A lone woman is troubled with such dreams and such thoughts that she's afeard of herself sometimes. Pray tarry with me this night, dear husband, of all nights in the year."

"My love and my Faith," replied young Goodman Brown, "of all nights in the year, this one night must I tarry away from thee. My journey, as thou callest it, forth and back again, must needs be done 'twixt now and sunrise. What, my sweet, pretty wife, dost thou doubt me already, and we but three months married?"

"Then God bless you!" said Faith, with the pink ribbons; "and may you find all well when you come back."

"Amen!" cried Goodman Brown. "Say thy prayers, dear Faith, and go to bed at dusk, and no harm will come to thee."

So they parted; and the young man pursued his way until, being about to turn the corner by the meeting-house, he looked back and saw the head of Faith still peeping after him with a melancholy air, in spite of her pink ribbons.

"Poor little Faith!" thought he, for his heart smote him. "What a wretch am I to leave her on such an errand! She talks of dreams, too. Methought as she spoke there was trouble in her face, as if a dream had warned her what work is to be done tonight. But no, no; 't would kill her to think it. Well, she's a blessed angel on earth; and after this one night I'll cling to her skirts and follow her to heaven."

With this excellent resolve for the future, Goodman Brown felt himself justified in making more haste on his present evil purpose. He had taken a dreary road, darkened by all the gloomiest trees of the forest, which barely stood aside to let the narrow path creep through, and closed immediately behind. It was all as lonely as could be; and there is this peculiarity in such a solitude, that the traveller knows not who may be concealed by the innumerable trunks and the thick boughs overhead; so that with lonely footsteps he may yet be passing through an unseen multitude.

"There may be a devilish Indian behind every tree," said Goodman Brown to himself; and he glanced fearfully behind him as he added, "What if the devil himself should be at my very elbow!"

His head being turned back, he passed a crook of the road, and, looking forward again, beheld the figure of a man, in grave and decent attire, seated at the foot of an old tree. He arose at Goodman Brown's approach and walked onward side by side with him.

"You are late, Goodman Brown," said he. "The clock of the Old South was striking as I came through Boston, and that is full fifteen minutes agone."

"Faith kept me back a while," replied the young man, with a tremor in his voice, caused by the sudden appearance of his companion, though not wholly unexpected.

It was now deep dusk in the forest, and deepest in that part of it where these two were journeying. As nearly as could be discerned, the second traveller was about fifty years old, apparently in the same rank of life as Goodman Brown, and bearing a considerable resemblance to him, though perhaps more in expression than features. Still they might have been taken for father and son. And yet, though the elder person was as simply clad as the younger, and as simple in manner too, he had an indescribable air of one who knew the world, and who would not have felt abashed at the governor's dinner table or in King William's court, were it possible that his affairs should call him thither. But the only thing about him that could be fixed upon as remarkable was his staff, which bore the likeness of a great black snake, so curiously wrought that it might almost be seen to twist and wriggle itself like a living serpent. This, of course, must have been an ocular deception, assisted by the uncertain light.

"Come, Goodman Brown," cried his fellow-traveller, "this is a dull pace for the beginning of a journey. Take my staff, if you are so soon weary."

"Friend," said the other, exchanging his slow pace for a full stop, "having kept covenant by meeting thee here, it is my purpose now to return whence I came. I have scruples touching the matter thou wot'st of."

"Sayest thou so?" replied he of the serpent, smiling apart. "Let us walk on, nevertheless, reasoning as we go; and if I convince thee not thou shalt turn back. We are but a little way in the forest yet."

"Too far! too far!" exclaimed the goodman, unconsciously resuming his walk. "My father never went into the woods on such an errand, nor his father before him. We have been a race of honest men and good Christians since the days of the martyrs; and shall I be the first of the name of Brown that ever took this path and kept"—

"Such company, thou wouldst say," observed the elder person, interpreting his pause. "Well said, Goodman Brown! I have been as well acquainted with your family as with ever a one among the Puritans; and that's no trifle to say. I helped your grandfather, the constable, when he lashed the Quaker woman so smartly through the streets of Salem; and it was I that brought your father a pitch-pine knot, kindled at my own hearth, to set fire to an Indian village, in King Philip's war. They were my good friends, both; and many a pleasant walk have we had along this path, and returned merrily after midnight. I would fain be friends with you for their sake."

"If it be as thou sayest," replied Goodman Brown, "I marvel they never spoke of these matters; or, verily, I marvel not, seeing that the least rumor of the sort would have driven them from New England. We are a people of prayer, and good works to boot, and abide no such wickedness."

"Wickedness or not," said the traveller with the twisted staff, "I have a very general acquaintance here in New England. The deacons of many a church have drunk the communion wine with me; the selectmen of divers towns make me their chairman; and a majority of the Great and General Court are firm supporters of my interest. The governor and I, too—But these are state secrets."

"Can this be so?" cried Goodman Brown, with a stare of amazement at his undisturbed companion. "Howbeit, I have nothing to do with the governor and council; they have their own ways, and are no rule for a simple husbandman like me. But, were I to go on with thee, how should I meet the eye of that good old man, our minister, at Salem village? Oh, his voice would make me tremble both Sabbath day and lecture day."

Thus far the elder traveller had listened with due gravity; but now burst into a fit of irrepressible mirth, shaking himself so violently that his snake-like staff actually seemed to wriggle in sympathy.

"Ha! ha! ha!" shouted he again and again; then composing himself, "Well, go on, Goodman Brown, go on; but, prithee, don't kill me with laughing."

"Well, then, to end the matter at once," said Goodman Brown, considerably nettled, "there is my wife, Faith. It would break her dear little heart; and I'd rather break my own."

"Nay, if that be the case," answered the other, "e'en go thy ways, Goodman Brown. I would not for twenty old women like the one hobbling before us that Faith should come to any harm."

As he spoke he pointed his staff at a female figure on the path, in whom Goodman Brown recognized a very pious and exemplary dame, who had taught him his catechism in youth, and was still his moral and spiritual adviser, jointly with the minister and Deacon Gookin.

"A marvel, truly, that Goody Cloyse should be so far in the wilderness at nightfall," said he. "But with your leave, friend, I shall take a cut through the woods until we have left this Christian woman behind. Being a stranger to you, she might ask whom I was consorting with and whither I was going."

"Be it so," said his fellow-traveller. "Betake you the woods and let me keep the path."

Accordingly the young man turned aside, but took care to watch his companion, who advanced softly along the road until he had come within a staff's length of the old dame. She, meanwhile, was making the best of her way, with singular speed for so aged a woman, and mumbling some indistinct words—a prayer, doubtless—as she went. The traveller put forth his staff and touched her withered neck with what seemed the serpent's tail.

"The devil!" screamed the pious old lady.

"Then Goody Cloyse knows her old friend?" observed the traveller, confronting her and leaning on his writhing stick.

"Ah, forsooth, and is it your worship indeed?" cried the good dame. "Yea, truly is it, and in the very image of my old gossip, Goodman Brown, the grand-father of the silly fellow that now is. But—would your worship believe it?—my broomstick hath strangely disappeared, stolen, as I suspect, by that unhanged witch, Goody Cory, and that, too, when I was all anointed with the juice of smallage, and cinquefoil, and wolf's bane"—

"Mingled with fine wheat and the fat of a new-born babe," said the shape of old Goodman Brown.

"Ah, your worship knows the recipe," cried the old lady, cackling aloud. "So, as I was saying, being all ready for the meeting, and no horse to ride on, I made up my mind to foot it; for they tell me there is a nice young man to be taken into communion to-night. But now your good worship will lend me your arm, and we shall be there in a twinkling."

"That can hardly be," answered her friend. "I may not spare you my arm, Goody Cloyse; but here is my staff, if you will."

So saying, he threw it down at her feet, where, perhaps, it assumed life, being one of the rods which its owner had formerly lent to the Egyptian magi. Of this fact, however, Goodman Brown could not take cognizance. He had cast up his eyes in astonishment, and, looking down again, beheld neither Goody Cloyse nor the serpentine staff, but this fellow-traveller alone, who waited for him as calmly as if nothing had happened.

"That old woman taught me my catechism," said the young man; and there was a world of meaning in this simple comment.

They continued to walk onward, while the elder traveller exhorted his companion to make good speed and persevere in the path, discoursing so aptly that his arguments seemed rather to spring up in the bosom of his auditor than to be suggested by himself. As they went, he plucked a branch of maple to serve for a walking stick, and began to strip it of the twigs and little boughs, which were wet with evening dew. The moment his fingers touched them they became strangely withered and dried up as with a week's sunshine. Thus the pair proceeded, at a good free pace, until suddenly, in a gloomy hollow of the road, Goodman Brown sat himself down on the stump of a tree and refused to go any farther.

"Friend," said he, stubbornly, "my mind is made up. Not another step will I budge on this errand. What if a wretched old woman do choose to go to the devil when I thought she was going to heaven: is that any reason why I should quit my dear Faith and go after her?"

"You will think better of this by and by," said his acquaintance, composedly. "Sit here and rest yourself a while; and when you feel like moving again, there is my staff to help you along."

Without more words, he threw his companion the maple stick, and was as speedily out of sight as if he had vanished into the deepening gloom. The young man sat a few moments by the roadside, applauding himself greatly, and thinking with how clear a conscience he should meet the minister in his morning walk, nor shrink from the eye of good old Deacon Gookin. And what calm sleep would be his that very night, which was to have been spent so wickedly, but so purely and sweetly now, in the arms of Faith! Amidst these pleasant and praiseworthy meditations, Goodman Brown heard the tramp of horses along the road, and deemed it advisable to conceal himself within the verge of the forest, conscious of the guilty purpose that had brought him thither, though now so happily turned from it.

On came the hoof tramps and the voices of the riders, two grave old voices, conversing soberly as they drew near. These mingled sounds appeared to pass along the road, within a few yards of the young man's hiding-place; but, owing doubtless to the depth of the gloom at that particular spot, neither the travellers nor their steeds were visible. Though their figures brushed the small boughs by the wayside, it could not be seen that they intercepted, even for a moment, the faint gleam from the strip of bright sky athwart which they must have passed. Goodman Brown alternately crouched and stood on tiptoe, pulling aside the branches and thrusting forth his head as far as he durst without discerning so much as a shadow. It vexed him the more, because he could have sworn, were such a thing possible, that he recognized the voices of the minister and Deacon Gookin, jogging along quietly, as they were wont to do, when bound to some ordination or ecclesiastical council. While yet within hearing, one of the riders stopped to pluck a switch.

"Of the two, reverend sir," said the voice like the deacon's, "I had rather miss an ordination dinner than to-night's meeting. They tell me that some of our community are to be here from Falmouth and beyond, and others from Connecticut and Rhode Island, besides several of the Indian powwows, who, after their fashion, know almost as much deviltry as the best of us. Moreover, there is a goodly young woman to be taken into communion."

"Mighty well, Deacon Gookin!" replied the solemn old tones of the minister. "Spur up, or we shall be late. Nothing can be done, you know, until I get on the ground."

The hoofs clattered again; and the voices, talking so strangely in the empty air, passed on through the forest, where no church had ever been gathered or solitary Christian prayed. Whither, then, could these holy men be journeying so deep into the heathen wilderness? Young Goodman Brown caught hold of a tree for support, being ready to sink down on the ground, faint and overburdened with the heavy sickness of his heart. He looked up to the sky, doubting whether there really was a heaven above him. Yet there was the blue arch, and the stars brightening in it.

"With heaven above and Faith below, I will yet stand firm against the devil!" cried Goodman Brown.

While he still gazed upward into the deep arch of the firmament and had lifted his hands to pray, a cloud, though no wind was stirring, hurried across the zenith and hid the brightening stars. The blue sky was still visible, except directly overhead, where this black mass of cloud was sweeping swiftly northward. Aloft in the air, as if from the depths of the cloud, came a confused and doubtful sound of voices. Once the listener fancied that he could distinguish the accents of towns-people of his own, men and women, both pious and ungodly, many of whom he had met at the communion table, and had seen others rioting at the tavern. The next moment, so indistinct were the sounds, he doubted whether he had heard aught but the murmur of the old forest, whispering without a wind. Then came a stronger swell of those familiar tones, heard daily in the sunshine at Salem village, but never until now from a cloud of night. There was one voice, of a young woman, uttering lamentations, yet with an uncertain sorrow, and entreating for some favor, which, perhaps, it would grieve her to obtain; and all the unseen multitude, both saints and sinners, seemed to encourage her onward.

"Faith!" shouted Goodman Brown, in a voice of agony and desperation; and the echoes of the forest mocked him, crying, "Faith! Faith!" as if bewildered wretches were seeking her all through the wilderness.

The cry of grief, rage, and terror was yet piercing the night, when the unhappy husband held his breath for a response. There was a scream, drowned immediately in a louder murmur of voices, fading into far-off laughter, as the dark cloud swept away, leaving the clear and silent sky above Goodman Brown. But something fluttered lightly down through the air and caught on the branch of a tree. The young man seized it, and beheld a pink ribbon.

"My Faith is gone!" cried he, after one stupefied moment. "There is no good on earth; and sin is but a name. Come, devil; for to thee is this world given."

And, maddened with despair, so that he laughed loud and long, did Goodman Brown grasp his staff and set forth again, at such a rate that he seemed to fly along the forest path rather than to walk or run. The road grew wilder and drearier and more faintly traced, and vanished at length, leaving him in the heart of the dark wilderness, still rushing onward with the instinct that guides mortal man to evil. The whole forest was peopled with frightful sounds—the creaking of the trees, the howling of wild beasts, and the yell of Indians; while sometimes the wind tolled like a distant church bell, and sometimes gave a broad roar around the traveller, as if all Nature were laughing him to scorn. But he was himself the chief horror of the scene, and shrank not from its other horrors.

"Ha! ha! ha!" roared Goodman Brown when the wind laughed at him. "Let us hear which will laugh loudest. Think not to frighten me with your deviltry. Come witch, come wizard, come Indian powwow, come devil himself, and here comes Goodman Brown. You may as well fear him as he fear you."

In truth, all through the haunted forest there could be nothing more frightful than the figure of Goodman Brown. On he flew among the black pines, brandishing his staff with frenzied gestures, now giving vent to an inspiration of horrid blasphemy, and now shouting forth such laughter as set all the echoes of the forest laughing like demons around him. The fiend in his own shape is less hideous than when he rages in the breast of man. Thus sped the demoniac on his course, until, quivering among the trees, he saw a red light before him, as when the felled trunks and branches of a clearing have been set on fire, and throw up their lurid blaze against the sky, at the hour of midnight. He paused, in a lull of the tempest that had driven him onward, and heard the swell of what seemed a hymn, rolling solemnly from a distance with the weight of many voices. He knew the tune; it was a familiar one in the choir of the village meetinghouse. The verse died heavily away, and was lengthened by a chorus, not of human voices, but of all the sounds of the benighted wilderness pealing in awful harmony together. Goodman Brown cried out, and his cry was lost to his own ear by its unison with the cry of the desert.

In the interval of silence he stole forward until the light glared full upon his eyes. At one extremity of an open space, hemmed in by the dark wall of the forest, arose a rock, bearing some rude, natural resemblance either to an altar or a pulpit, and surrounded by four blazing pines, their tops aflame, their stems untouched, like candles at an evening meeting. The mass of foliage that had overgrown the summit of the rock was all on fire, blazing high into the night and fitfully illuminating the whole field. Each pendent twig and leafy festoon was in a blaze. As the red light arose and fell, a numerous congregation alternately shone forth, then disappeared in shadow, and again grew, as it were, out of the darkness, peopling the heart of the solitary woods at once.

"A grave and dark-clad company," quoth Goodman Brown.

In truth they were such. Among them, quivering to and fro between gloom and splendor, appeared faces that would be seen next day at the council board of the province, and others which, Sabbath after Sabbath, looked devoutly heavenward, and benignantly over the crowded pews, from the holiest pulpits in the land. Some affirm that the lady of the governor was there. At least there were high dames well known to her, and wives of honored husbands, and widows, a great multitude, and ancient maidens, all of excellent repute, and fair young girls, who trembled lest their mothers should espy them. Either the sudden gleams of light flashing over the obscure field bedazzled Goodman Brown, or he recognized a score of the church members of Salem village famous for their especial sanctity. Good old Deacon Gookin had arrived, and waited at the skirts of that venerable saint, his revered pastor. But, irreverently consorting with these grave, reputable, and pious people, these elders of the church, these chaste dames and dewy virgins, there were men of dissolute lives and women of spotted fame, wretches given over to all mean and filthy vice, and suspected even of horrid crimes. It was strange to see that the good shrank not from the wicked, nor were the sinners abashed by the saints. Scattered also among their pale-faced enemies were the Indian priests, or powwows, who had often scared their native forest with more hideous incantations than any known to English witchcraft.

"But where is Faith?" thought Goodman Brown; and, as hope came into his heart, he trembled.

Another verse of the hymn arose, a slow and mournful strain, such as the pious love, but joined to words which expressed all that our nature can conceive of sin, and darkly hinted at far more. Unfathomable to mere mortals is the lore of fiends. Verse after verse was sung; and still the chorus of the desert swelled between like the deepest tone of a mighty organ; and with the final peal of that dreadful anthem there came a sound, as if the roaring wind, the rushing streams, the howling beasts, and every other voice of the unconcerted wilderness were mingling and according with the voice of guilty man in homage to the prince of all. The four blazing pines threw up a loftier flame, and obscurely discovered shapes and visages of horror on the smoke wreaths above the impious assembly. At the same moment the fire on the rock shot redly forth and formed a glowing arch above its base, where now appeared a figure. With reverence be it spoken, the figure bore no slight similitude, both in garb and manner, to some grave divine of the New England churches.

"Bring forth the converts!" cried a voice that echoed through the field and rolled into the forest.

At the word, Goodman Brown stepped forth from the shadow of the trees and approached the congregation, with whom he felt a loathful brotherhood by the sympathy of all that was wicked in his heart. He could have well-nigh sworn that the shape of his own dead father beckoned him to advance, looking downward from a smoke wreath, while a woman, with dim features of despair, threw out her hand to warn him back. Was it his mother? But he had no power to retreat one step, nor to resist, even in thought, when the minister and good old Deacon Gookin seized his arms and led him to the blazing rock. Thither came also the slender form of a veiled female, led between Goody Cloyse, that pious teacher of the catechism, and Martha Carrier, who had received the devil's promise to be queen of hell. A rampant hag was she. And there stood the proselytes beneath the canopy of fire.

"Welcome, my children," said the dark figure, "to the communion of your race. Ye have found thus young your nature and your destiny. My children, look behind you!"

They turned; and flashing forth, as it were, in a sheet of flame, the fiend worshippers were seen; the smile of welcome gleamed darkly on every visage.

"There," resumed the sable form, "are all whom ye have reverenced from youth. Ye deemed them holier than yourselves, and shrank from your own sin, contrasting it with their lives of righteousness and prayerful aspirations heavenward. Yet here are they all in my worshipping assembly. This night it shall be granted you to know their secret deeds: how hoary-bearded elders of the church have whispered wanton words to the young maids of their households; how many a woman, eager for widows' weeds, has given her husband a drink at bedtime and let him sleep his last sleep in her bosom; how beardless youths have made haste to inherit their fathers' wealth; and how fair damsels—blush not, sweet ones—have dug little graves in the garden, and bidden me, the sole guest, to an infant's funeral. By the sympathy of your human hearts for sin ye shall scent out all the places—whether in church, bed-chamber, street, field, or forest—where crime has been committed, and shall exult to behold the whole earth one stain of guilt, one mighty blood spot. Far more than this. It shall be yours to penetrate, in every bosom, the deep mystery of sin, the fountain of all wicked arts, and which inexhaustibly supplies more evil impulses than human power—than my power at its utmost—can make manifest in deeds. And now, my children, look upon each other."

They did so; and, by the blaze of the hell-kindled torches, the wretched man beheld his Faith, and the wife her husband, trembling before that unhallowed altar.

"Lo, there ye stand, my children," said the figure, in a deep and solemn tone, almost sad with its despairing awfulness, as if his once angelic nature could yet mourn for our miserable race. "Depending upon one another's hearts, ye had still hoped that virtue were not all a dream. Now are ye undeceived. Evil is the nature of mankind. Evil must be your only happiness. Welcome again, my children, to the communion of your race."

"Welcome," repeated the fiend worshippers, in one cry of despair and triumph.

And there they stood, the only pair, as it seemed, who were yet hesitating on the verge of wickedness in this dark world. A basin was hollowed, naturally, in the rock. Did it contain water, reddened by the lurid light? or was it blood? or, perchance, a liquid flame? Herein did the shape of evil dip his hand and prepare to lay the mark of baptism upon their foreheads, that they might be partakers of the mystery of sin, more conscious of the secret guilt of others, both in deed and thought, than they could now be of their own. The husband cast one look at his pale wife, and Faith at him. What polluted wretches would the next glance show them to each other, shuddering alike at what they disclosed and what they saw!

"Faith! Faith!" cried the husband, "look up to heaven, and resist the wicked one."

Whether Faith obeyed he knew not. Hardly had he spoken when he found himself amid calm night and solitude, listening to a roar of the wind which died heavily away through the forest. He staggered against the rock, and felt it chill and damp; while a hanging twig, that had been all on fire, besprinkled his cheek with the coldest dew.

The next morning young Goodman Brown came slowly into the street of Salem village, staring around him like a bewildered man. The good old minister was taking a walk along the graveyard to get an appetite for breakfast and meditate his sermon, and bestowed a blessing, as he passed, on Goodman Brown. He shrank from the venerable saint as if to avoid an anathema. Old Deacon Gookin was at domestic worship, and the holy words of his prayer were heard through the open window. "What God doth the wizard pray to?" quoth Goodman Brown. Goody Cloyse, that excellent old Christian, stood in the early sunshine at her own lattice, catechizing a little girl who had brought her a pint of morning's milk. Goodman Brown snatched away the child as from the grasp of the fiend himself. Turning the corner by the meeting-house, he spied the head of Faith, with the pink ribbons, gazing anxiously forth, and bursting into such joy at sight of him that she skipped along the street and almost kissed her husband before the whole village. But Goodman Brown looked sternly and sadly into her face, and passed on without a greeting.

Had Goodman Brown fallen asleep in the forest and only dreamed a wild dream of a witch-meeting?

Be it so if you will; but, alas! it was a dream of evil omen for young Goodman Brown. A stern, a sad, a darkly meditative, a distrustful, if not a desperate man did he become from the night of that fearful dream. On the Sabbath day, when the congregation were singing a holy psalm, he could not listen because an anthem of sin rushed loudly upon his ear and drowned all the blessed strain. When the minister spoke from the pulpit with power and fervid eloquence, and, with his hand on the open Bible, of the sacred truths of our religion, and of saint-like lives and triumphant deaths, and of future bliss or misery unutterable, then did Goodman Brown turn pale, dreading lest the roof should thunder down upon the gray blasphemer and his hearers. Often, awaking suddenly at midnight, he shrank from the bosom of Faith; and at morning or eventide, when the family knelt down at prayer, he scowled and muttered to himself, and gazed sternly at his wife, and turned away. And when he had lived long, and was borne to his grave a hoary corpse, followed by Faith, an aged woman, and children and grandchildren, a goodly procession, besides neighbors not a few, they carved no hopeful verse upon his tombstone, for his dying hour was gloom.

QUESTIONS

1. Have any previous ideas or information about Salem or colonial New England influenced your reading of this story? Explain.
2. How did you respond to the names Goodman Brown and Faith when these were first introduced into the story? How have the names of the characters influenced your reading of it?
3. What sort of voice have you heard telling the story? Note specific passages that create a certain tone in the narrative.
4. How much sympathy do you feel with Goodman Brown? What details concerning his character or situation were most important in shaping your response?
5. Is Goodman an innocent man betrayed by the wickedness of all those around him? Explain.

Sherwood Anderson (1876–1941)

I WANT TO KNOW WHY

We got up at four in the morning, that first day in the east. On the evening before we had climbed off a freight train at the edge of town, and with the true instinct of Kentucky boys had found our way across town and to the race track and the stables at once. Then we knew we were all right. Hanley Turner right away found a nigger we knew. It was Bildad Johnson who in the winter works at Ed Becker's livery barn in our home town, Beckersville. Bildad is a good cook as almost all our niggers are and of course he, like everyone in our part of Kentucky who is anyone at all, likes the horses. In the spring Bildad begins to scratch around. A nigger from our country can flatter and wheedle anyone into letting him do most anything he wants. Bildad wheedles the stable men and trainers from the horse farms in our country around Lexington. The trainers come into town in the evening to stand around and talk and maybe get into a poker game. Bildad gets in with them. He is always doing little favors and telling about things to eat, chicken browned in a pan, and how is the best way to cook sweet potatoes and corn bread. It makes your mouth water to hear him.

When the racing season comes on and the horses go to the races and there is all the talk on the streets in the evenings about the new colts, and everyone says when they are going over to Lexington or to the spring meeting at Churchill Downs or to Latonia, and the horsemen that have been down to New Orleans or maybe at the winter meeting at Havana in Cuba come home to spend a week before they start out again, at such a time when everything talked about in Beckersville is just horses and nothing else and the outfits start out and horse racing is in every breath of air you breathe, Bildad shows up with a job as cook for some outfit. Often when I think about it, his always going all season to the races and working in the livery barn in the winter where horses are and where men like to come and talk about horses, I wish I was a nigger. It's a foolish thing to say, but that's the way I am about being around horses, just crazy. I can't help it.

Well, I must tell you about what we did and let you in on what I'm talking about. Four of us boys from Beckersville, all whites and sons of men who live in Beckersville regular, made up our minds we were going to the races, not just to Lexington or Louisville, I don't mean, but to the big eastern track we were always hearing our Beckersville men talk about, to Saratoga. We were all pretty young then. I was just turned fifteen and I was the oldest of the four. It was my scheme. I admit that and I talked the others into trying it. There was Hanley Turner and Henry Rieback and Tom Tumberton and myself. I had thirty-seven dollars I had earned during the winter working nights and Saturdays in Enoch Myer's grocery. Henry Rieback had eleven dollars and the others, Hanley and Tom had only a dollar or two each. We fixed it all up and laid low until the Kentucky spring meetings were over and some of our men, the sportiest ones, the ones we envied the most, had cut out—then we cut out too.

I won't tell you the trouble we had beating our way on freights and all. We went through Cleveland and Buffalo and other cities and saw Niagara Falls. We bought things there, souvenirs and spoons and cards and shells with pictures of the falls on them for our sisters and mothers, but thought we had better not send any of the things home. We didn't want to put the folks on our trail and maybe be nabbed.

We got into Saratoga as I said at night and went to the track. Bildad fed us up. He showed us a place to sleep in hay over a shed and promised to keep still. Niggers are all right about things like that. They won't squeal on you. Often a white man you might meet, when you had run away from home like that, might appear to be all right and give you a quarter or a half dollar or something, and then go right and give you away. White men will do that, but not a nigger. You can trust them. They are squarer with kids. I don't know why.

At the Saratoga meeting that year there were a lot of men from home. Dave Williams and Arthur Mulford and Merry Myers and others. Then there was a lot from Louisville and Lexington Henry Rieback knew but I didn't. They were professional gamblers and Henry Rieback's father is one too. He is what is called a sheet writer and goes away most of the year to tracks. In the winter when he is home in Beckersville he don't stay there much but goes away to cities and deals faro. He is a nice man and generous, is always sending Henry presents, a bicycle and a gold watch and a boy scout suit of clothes and things like that.

My own father is a lawyer. He's all right, but don't make much money and can't buy me things and anyway I'm getting so old now I don't expect it. He never said nothing to me against Henry, but Hanley Turner and Tom Tumberton's fathers did. They said to their boys that money so come by is no good and they didn't want their boys brought up to hear gamblers' talk and be thinking about such things and maybe embrace them.

That's all right and I guess the men know what they are talking about, but I don't see what it's got to do with Henry or with horses either. That's what I'm writing this story about. I'm puzzled. I'm getting to be a man and want to think straight and be O.K., and there's something I saw at the race meeting at the eastern track I can't figure out.

I can't help it, I'm crazy about thoroughbred horses. I've always been that way. When I was ten years old and saw I was growing to be big and couldn't be a rider I was so sorry I nearly died. Harry Hellinfinger in Beckersville, whose father is Postmaster, is grown up and too lazy to work, but likes to stand around in the street and get up jokes on boys like sending them to a hardware store for a gimlet to bore square holes and other jokes like that. He played one on me. He told me that if I would eat a half a cigar I would be stunted and not grow any more and maybe could be a rider. I did it. When father wasn't looking I took a cigar out of his pocket and gagged it down some way. It made me awful sick and the doctor had to be sent for, and then it did no good. I kept right on growing. It was a joke. When I told what I had done and why most fathers would have whipped me but mine didn't.

Well, I didn't get stunted and didn't die. It serves Harry Hellinfinger right. Then I made up my mind I would like to be a stable boy, but had to give that up too. Mostly niggers do that work and I knew father wouldn't let me go into it. No use to ask him.

If you've never been crazy about thoroughbreds it's because you've never been around where they are much and don't know any better. They're beautiful. There isn't anything so lovely and clean and full of spunk and honest and everything as some race horses. On the big horse farms that are all around our town Beckersville there are tracks and the horses run in the early morning. More than a thousand times I've got out of bed before daylight and walked two or three miles to the tracks. Mother wouldn't of let me go but father always says, "Let him alone." So I got some bread out of the bread box and some butter and jam, gobbled it and lit out.

At the tracks you sit on the fence with men, whites and niggers, and they chew tobacco and talk, and then the colts are brought out. It's early and the grass is covered with shiny dew and in another field a man is plowing and they are frying things in a shed where the track niggers sleep, and you know how a nigger can giggle and laugh and say things that make you laugh. A white man can't do it and some niggers can't but a track nigger can every time.

And so the colts are brought out and some are just galloped by stable boys, but almost every morning on a big track owned by a rich man who lives maybe in New York, there are always, nearly every morning, a few colts and some of the old race horses and geldings and mares that are cut loose.

It brings a lump up into my throat when a horse runs. I don't mean all horses but some. I can pick them nearly every time. It's in my blood like in the blood of race track niggers and trainers. Even when they just go slop-jogging along with a little nigger on their backs I can tell a winner. If my throat hurts and it's hard for me to swallow, that's him. He'll run like Sam Hill when you let him out. If he don't win every time it'll be a wonder and because they've got him in a pocket behind another or he was pulled or got off bad at the post or something. If I wanted to be a gambler like Henry Rieback's father I could get rich. I know I could and Henry says so too. All I would have to do is to wait 'til that hurt comes when I see a horse and then bet every cent. That's what I would do if I wanted to be a gambler, but I don't.

When you're at the tracks in the morning—not the race tracks but the training tracks around Beckersville—you don't see a horse, the kind I've been talking about, very often, but it's nice anyway. Any thoroughbred, that is sired right and out of a good mare and trained by a man that knows how, can run. If he couldn't what would he be there for and not pulling a plow?

Well, out of the stables they come and the boys are on their backs and it's lovely to be there. You hunch down on top of the fence and itch inside you. Over in the sheds the niggers giggle and sing. Bacon is being fried and coffee made. Everything smells lovely. Nothing smells better than coffee and manure and horses and niggers and bacon frying and pipes being smoked out of doors on a morning like that. It just gets you, that's what it does.

But about Saratoga. We was there six days and not a soul from home seen us and everything came off just as we wanted it to, fine weather and horses and races and all. We beat our way home and Bildad gave us a basket with fried chicken and bread and other eatables in, and I had eighteen dollars when we got back to Beckersville. Mother jawed and cried but Pop didn't say much. I told everything we done except one thing. I did and saw that alone. That's what I'm writing about. It got me upset. I think about it at night. Here it is.

At Saratoga we laid up nights in the hay in the shed Bildad had showed us and ate with the niggers early and at night when the race people had all gone away. The men from home stayed mostly in the grandstand and betting field, and didn't come out around the places where the horses are kept except to the paddocks just before a race when the horses are saddled. At Saratoga they don't have paddocks under an open shed as at Lexington and Churchill Downs and other tracks down in our country, but saddle the horses right out in an open place under trees on a lawn as smooth and nice as Banker Bohon's front yard here in Beckersville. It's lovely. The horses are sweaty and nervous and shine and the men come out and smoke cigars and look at them and the trainers are there and the owners, and your heart thumps so you can hardly breathe.

Then the bugle blows for post and the boys that ride come running out with their silk clothes on and you run to get a place by the fence with the niggers.

I always am wanting to be a trainer or owner, and at the risk of being seen and caught and sent home I went to the paddocks before every race. The other boys didn't but I did.

We got to Saratoga on a Friday and on Wednesday the next week the big Mullford Handicap was to be run. Middlestride was in it and Sunstreak. The weather was fine and the track fast. I couldn't sleep the night before.

What had happened was that both these horses are the kind it makes my throat hurt to see. Middlestride is long and looks awkward and is a gelding. He belongs to Joe Thompson, a little owner from home who only has a half dozen horses. The Mullford Handicap is for a mile and Middlestride can't untrack fast. He goes away slow and is always way back at the half, then he begins to run and if the race is a mile and a quarter he'll just eat up everything and get there.

Sunstreak is different. He is a stallion and nervous and belongs on the biggest farm we've got in our country, the Van Riddle place that belongs to Mr. Van Riddle of New York. Sunstreak is like a girl you think about sometimes but never see. He is hard all over and lovely too. When you look at his head you want to kiss him. He is trained by Jerry Tillford who knows me and has been good to me lots of times, lets me walk into a horse's stall to look at him close and other things. There isn't anything as sweet as that horse. He stands at the post quiet and not letting on, but he is just burning up inside. Then when the barrier goes up he is off like his name, Sunstreak. It makes you ache to see him. It hurts you. He just lays down and runs like a bird dog. There can't anything I ever see run like him except Middlestride when he gets untracked and stretches himself.

Gee! I ached to see that race and those two horses run, ached and dreaded it too. I didn't want to see either of our horses beaten. We had never sent a pair like that to the races before. Old men in Beckersville said so and the niggers said so. It was a fact.

Before the race I went over to the paddocks to see. I looked a last look at Middlestride, who isn't such a much standing in a paddock that way, then I went to see Sunstreak.

It was his day. I knew when I seen him. I forgot all about being seen myself and walked right up. All the men from Beckersville were there and no one noticed me except Jerry Tillford. He saw me and something happened. I'll tell you about that.

I was standing looking at that horse and aching. In some way, I can't tell how, I knew just how Sunstreak felt inside. He was quiet and letting the niggers rub his legs and Mr. Van Riddle himself put the saddle on, but he was just a raging torrent inside. He was like the water in the river at Niagara Falls just before it goes plunk down. That horse wasn't thinking about running. He don't have to think about that. He was just thinking about holding himself back 'til the time for the running came. I knew that. I could just in a way see right inside him. He was going to do some awful running and I knew it. He wasn't bragging or letting on much or prancing or making a fuss, but just waiting. I knew it and Jerry Tillford his trainer knew. I looked up and then that man and I looked into each other's eyes. Something happened to me. I guess I loved the man as much as I did the horse because he knew what I knew. Seemed to me there wasn't anything in the world but that man and the horse and me. I cried and Jerry Tillford had a shine in his eyes. Then I came away to the fence to wait for the race. The horse was better than me, more steadier, and now I know better than Jerry. He was the quietest and he had to do the running.

Sunstreak ran first of course and he busted the world's record for a mile. I've seen that if I never see anything more. Everything came out just as I expected. Middlestride got left at the post and was way back and closed up to be second, just as I knew he would. He'll get a world's record too some day. They can't skin the Beckersville country on horses.

I watched the race calm because I knew what would happen. I was sure. Hanley Turner and Henry Rieback and Tom Tumberton were all more excited than me.

A funny thing had happened to me. I was thinking about Jerry Tillford the trainer and how happy he was all through the race. I liked him that afternoon even more than I ever liked my own father. I almost forgot the horses thinking that way about him. It was because of what I had seen in his eyes as he stood in the paddocks beside Sunstreak before the race started. I knew he had been watching and working with Sunstreak since the horse was a baby colt, had taught him to run and be patient and when to let himself out and not to quit, never. I knew that for him it was like a mother seeing her child do something brave or wonderful. It was the first time I ever felt for a man like that.

After the race that night I cut out from Tom and Hanley and Henry. I wanted to be by myself and I wanted to be near Jerry Tillford if I could work it. Here is what happened.

The track in Saratoga is near the edge of town. It is all polished up and trees around, the evergreen kind, and grass and everything painted and nice. If you go past the track you get to a hard road made of asphalt for automobiles, and if you go along this for a few miles there is a road turns off to a little rummy-looking farm house set in a yard.

That night after the race I went along that road because I had seen Jerry and some other men go that way in an automobile. I didn't expect to find them. I walked for a ways and then sat down by a fence to think. It was the direction they went in. I wanted to be as near Jerry as I could. I felt close to him. Pretty soon I went up the side road—I don't know why—and came to the rummy farm house. I was just lonesome to see Jerry, like wanting to see your father at night when you are a young kid. Just then an automobile came along and turned in. Jerry was in it and Henry Rieback's father, and Arthur Bedford from home, and Dave Williams and two other men I didn't know. They got out of the car and went into the house, all but Henry Rieback's father who quarreled with them and said he wouldn't go. It was only about nine o'clock, but they were all drunk and the rummy looking farm house was a place for bad women to stay in.

That's what it was. I crept up along a fence and looked through a window and saw.

It's what gave me the fantods. I can't make it out. The women in the house were all ugly mean-looking women, not nice to look at or be near. They were homely too, except one who was tall and looked a little like the gelding Middlestride, but not clean like him, but with a hard ugly mouth. She had red hair. I saw everything plain. I got up by an old rose bush by an open window and looked. The women had on loose dresses and sat around in chairs. The men came in and some sat on the women's laps. The place smelled rotten and there was rotten talk, the kind a kid hears around a livery stable in a town like Beckersville in the winter but don't ever expect to hear talked when there are women around. It was rotten. A nigger wouldn't go into such a place.

I looked at Jerry Tillford. I've told you how I had been feeling about him on account of his knowing what was going on inside of Sunstreak in the minute before he went to the post for the race in which he made a world's record.

Jerry bragged in that bad woman house as I know Sunstreak wouldn't never have bragged. He said that he made that horse, that it was him that won the race and made the record. He lied and bragged like a fool. I never heard such silly talk.

And then, what do you suppose he did! He looked at the woman in there, the one that was lean and hard-mouthed and looked a little like the gelding Middlestride, but not clean like him, and his eyes began to shine just as they did when he looked at me and at Sunstreak in the paddocks at the track in the afternoon. I stood there by the window—gee!—but I wished I hadn't gone away from the tracks, but had stayed with the boys and the niggers and the horses. The tall rotten looking woman was between us just as Sunstreak was in the paddocks in the afternoon.

Then, all of a sudden, I began to hate that man. I wanted to scream and rush in the room and kill him. I never had such a feeling before. I was so mad clean through that I cried and my fists were doubled up so my finger nails cut my hands.

And Jerry's eyes kept shining and he waved back and forth, and then he went and kissed that woman and I crept away and went back to the tracks and to bed and didn't sleep hardly any, and then next day I got the other kids to start home with me and never told them anything I seen.

I been thinking about it ever since. I can't make it out. Spring has come again and I'm nearly sixteen and go to the tracks mornings same as always, and I see Sunstreak and Middlestride and a new colt named Strident I'll bet will lay them all out, but no one thinks so but me and two or three niggers.

But things are different. At the tracks the air don't taste as good or smell as good. It's because a man like Jerry Tillford, who knows what he does, could see a horse like Sunstreak run, and kiss a woman like that the same day. I can't make it out. Darn him, what did he want to do like that for? I keep thinking about it and it spoils looking at horses and smelling things and hearing niggers laugh and everything. Sometimes I'm so mad about it I want to fight someone. It gives me the fantods. What did he do it for? I want to know why.

QUESTIONS

1. Did you find it easy or difficult to respond to the central character and the setting of this story? What in your experience or in the text most influenced your response?
2. Were you disturbed by the narrator's comments about "niggers"? How important was the use of the word to your reading of the story as a whole?
3. Did anything recalled from your own adolescence help you to understand why the narrator is so troubled? Explain.
4. If you are a female, how bothered were you by the references to the "bad women" and the way the narrator describes them?
5. What sort of innocence is involved in this story?

Katherine Anne Porter (1890–1980)
THE FIG TREE

Old Aunt Nannie had a habit of gripping with her knees to hold Miranda while she brushed her hair or buttoned her dress down the back. When Miranda wriggled, Aunt Nannie squeezed still harder, and Miranda wriggled more, but never enough to get away. Aunt Nannie gathered up Miranda's scalp lock firmly, snapped a rubber band around it, jammed a freshly starched white chambray bonnet over her ears and forehead, fastened the crown to the lock with a large safety pin, and said: "Got to hold you still someways. Here now, don't you take this off your head till the sun go down."

"I didn't want a bonnet, it's too hot, I wanted a hat," said Miranda.

"You not goin' to get a hat, you goin' to get just what you got," said Aunt Nannie in the bossy voice she used for washing and dressing time, "and mo'over some of these days I'm goin' to *sew* this bonnet to your topknot. Your daddy says if you get freckles he blame me. Now, you're all ready to set out."

"Where are we going, Aunty?" Miranda could never find out about anything until the last minute. She was always being surprised. Once she went to sleep in her bed with her kitten curled on the pillow purring, and woke up in a stuffy tight bed in a train, hugging a hot-water bottle; and there was Grandmother stretched out beside her in her McLeod tartan dressing-gown, her eyes wide open. Miranda thought something wonderful had happened. "My goodness, Grandmother, where are we going?" And it was only for another trip to El Paso to see Uncle Bill.

Now Tom and Dick were hitched to the carry-all standing outside the gate with boxes and baskets tied on everywhere. Grandmother was walking alone through the house very slowly, taking a last look at everything. Now and then she put something else in the big leather portmoney on her arm until it was pretty bulgy. She carried a long black mohair skirt on her other arm, the one she put on over her other skirt when she rode horseback. Her son Harry, Miranda's father, followed her saying: "I can't see the sense in rushing off to Halifax on five minutes' notice."

Grandmother said, walking on: "It's five hours exactly." Halifax wasn't the name of Grandmother's farm at all, it was Cedar Grove, but Father always called it Halifax. "Hot as Halifax," he would say when he wanted to describe something very hot. Cedar Grove was very hot, but they went there every summer because Grandmother loved it. "I went to Cedar Grove for fifty summers before you were born," she told Miranda, who remembered last summer very well, and the summer before a little. Miranda liked it for watermelons and grasshoppers and the long rows of blooming chinaberry trees where the hounds flattened themselves out and slept. They whined and winked their eyelids and worked their feet and barked faintly in their sleep, and Uncle Jimbilly said it was because dogs always dreamed they were chasing something. In the middle of the day when Miranda looked down over the thick green fields towards the spring she could simply see it being hot: everything blue and sleepy and the mourning doves calling.

"Are we going to Halifax, Aunty?"

"Now just ask your dad if you wanta know so much."

"Are we going to Halifax, Dad?"

Her father twitched her bonnet straight and pulled her hair forward so it would show. "You mustn't get sunburned. No, let it alone. Show the pretty curls. You'll be wading in Whirlypool before supper this evening."

Grandmother said, "Don't say Halifax, child, say Cedar Grove. Call things by their right names."

"Yes, ma'am," said Miranda. Grandmother said again, to her son, "It's five hours, exactly, and your Aunt Eliza has had plenty of time to pack up her telescope, and take my saddle horse. She's been there three hours by now. I imagine she's got the telescope already set up on the hen-house roof. I hope nothing happens."

"You worry too much, Mammy," said her son, trying to conceal his impatience.

"I am not worrying," said Grandmother, shifting her riding skirt to the arm carrying the portmoney. "It will scarcely be any good taking this," she said; "I might in fact as well throw it away for this summer."

"Never mind, Mammy, we'll send to the Black Farm for Pompey, he's a good easy saddler."

"You may ride him yourself," said Grandmother. "I'll never mount Pompey while Fiddler is alive. Fiddler is my horse, and I hate having his mouth spoiled by a careless rider. Eliza never could ride, and she never will. . . ."

Miranda gave a little skip and ran away. So they were going to Cedar Grove. Miranda never got over being surprised at the way grown-up people simply did not seem able to give anyone a straight answer to any question, unless the answer was "No." Then it popped out with no trouble at all. At a little distance, she heard her grandmother say, "Harry, have you seen my riding crop lately?" and her father answered, at least maybe he thought it was an answer, "Now, Mammy, for God's sake let's get this thing over with." That was it, exactly.

Another strange way her father had of talking was calling Grandmother "Mammy." Aunt Jane was Mammy. Sometimes he called Grandmother "Mama," but she wasn't Mama either, she was really Grandmother. Mama was dead. Dead meant gone away forever. Dying was something that happened all the time, to people and everything else. Somebody died, and there was a long string of carriages going at a slow walk over the rocky ridge of the hill towards the river while the bell tolled and tolled, and that person was never seen again by anybody. Kittens and chickens and specially little turkeys died much oftener, and sometimes calves, but hardly ever cows or horses. Lizards on rocks turned into shells, with no lizard inside at all. If caterpillars all curled up and furry didn't move when you poked them with a stick, that meant they were dead—it was a sure sign.

When Miranda found any creature that didn't move or make a noise, or looked somehow different from the live ones, she always buried it in a little grave with flowers on top and a smooth stone at the head. Even grasshoppers. Everything dead had to be treated this way. "This way and no other!" Grandmother always said when she was laying down the law about all kinds of things. "It must be done *this* way, and no other!"

Miranda went down the crooked flat-stone walk hopping zigzag between the grass tufts. First there were pomegranate and cape jessamine bushes mixed together; then it got very dark and shady and that was the fig grove. She went to her favorite fig tree where the deep branches bowed down level with her chin, and she could gather figs without having to climb and skin her knees. Grandmother hadn't remembered to take any figs to the country the last time, she said there were plenty of them at Cedar Grove. But the ones at Cedar Grove were big soft greenish white ones, and these at home were black and sugary. It was strange that Grandmother did not seem to notice the difference. The air was sweet among the fig trees, and chickens were always getting out of the run and rushing there to eat the figs off the ground. One mother hen was scurrying around scratching and clucking. She would scratch around a fig lying there in plain sight and cluck to her children as if it was a worm and she had dug it up for them.

"Old smarty," said Miranda, "you're just pretending."

When the little chickens all ran to their mother under Miranda's fig tree, one little chicken did not move. He was spread out on his side with his eyes shut and his mouth open. He was yellow fur in spots and pinfeathers in spots, and the rest of him was naked and sunburned. "Lazy," said Miranda, poking him with her toe. Then she saw that he was dead.

Oh, and in no time at all they'd be setting out for Halifax. Grandmother never went away, she always set out for somewhere. She'd have to hurry like anything to get him buried properly. Back into the house she went on tiptoe hoping not to be seen, for Grandmother always asked: "Where are you going child? What are you doing? What is that you're carrying? Where did you get it? Who gave you permission?" and after Miranda had explained all that, even if there turned out not to be anything wrong in it, nothing ever seemed so nice any more. Besides it took forever to get away.

Miranda slid open her bureau drawer, third down, left-hand side where her new shoes were still wrapped in tissue paper in a nice white box the right size for a chicken with pinfeathers. She pushed the rustling white folded things and the lavender bags out of the way and trembled a little. Down in front the carry-all wheels screeched and crunched on the gravel, with Old Uncle Jimbilly yelling like a foghorn, "Hiyi, thar, back up, you steeds! Back up thar, you!" and of course, that meant he was turning Tom and Dick around so they would be pointing towards Halifax. They'd be after her, calling and hurrying her, and she wouldn't have time for anything and they wouldn't listen to a word.

It wasn't hard work digging a hole with her little spade in the loose dry soil. Miranda wrapped the slimpsy chicken in tissue paper, trying to make it look pretty, laid it in the box carefully, and covered it up with a nice mound, just like people's. She had hardly got it piled up grave shape, kneeling and leaning to smooth it over, when a strange sound came from somewhere, a very sad little crying sound. It said Weep, weep, weep, three times like that slowly, and it seemed to come from the mound of dirt. "My goodness," Miranda asked herself aloud, "what's that?" She pushed her bonnet off her ears and listened hard. "Weep, weep," said the tiny sad voice. And People began calling and urging her, their voices coming nearer. She began to clamor, too.

"Yes, Aunty, wait a minute, Aunty!"

"You come right on here this minute, we're goin'!"

"You *have* to wait, Aunty!"

Her father was coming along the edge of the fig trees. "Hurry up, Baby, you'll get left!"

Miranda felt she couldn't bear to be left. She ran all shaking with fright. Her father gave her the annoyed look he always gave her when he said something to upset her and then saw that she was upset. His words were kind but his voice scolded: "Stop getting so excited, Baby, you know we wouldn't leave you for anything." Miranda wanted to talk back: "Then why did you say so?" but she was still listening for that tiny sound: "Weep, weep." She lagged and pulled backward, looking over her shoulder, but her father hurried her towards the carry-all. But things didn't make sounds if they were dead. They couldn't. That was one of the signs. Oh, but she had heard it.

Her father sat in front and drove, and old Uncle Jimbilly didn't do anything but get down and open gates. Grandmother and Aunt Nannie sat in the back seat, with Miranda between them. She loved setting out somewhere, with everybody smiling and settling down and looking up at the weather, with the horses bouncing and pulling on the reins, the springs jolting and swaying with a creaky noise that made you feel sure you were traveling. That evening she would go wading with Maria and Paul and Uncle Jimbilly, and that very night she would lie out on the grass in her nightgown to cool off, and they would all drink lemonade before going to bed. Sister Maria and Brother Paul would already be burned like muffins because they were sent on ahead the minute school was out. Sister Maria had got freckled and Father was furious. "Keep your bonnet on," he said to Miranda, sternly. "Now remember. I'm not going to have that face ruined, too." But oh, what had made that funny sound? Miranda's ears buzzed and she had a dull round pain in her just under her front ribs. She had to go back and let him out. He'd never get out by himself, all tangled up in tissue paper and that shoebox. He'd never get out without her.

"Grandmother, I've got to go back. Oh, I've got to go back!"

Grandmother turned Miranda's face around by the chin and looked at her closely, the way grown folks did. Grandmother's eyes were always the same. They never looked kind or sad or angry or tired or anything. They just looked, blue and still. "What is the matter with you, Miranda, what happened?"

"Oh, I've got to go back—I forg-got something important."

"Stop that silly crying and tell me what you want."

Miranda couldn't stop. Her father looked very anxious. "Mammy, maybe the Baby's sick." He reached out his handkerchief to her face. "What's the matter with my honey? Did you eat something?"

Miranda had to stand up to cry as hard as she wanted to. The wheels went grinding round in the road, the carry-all wobbled so that Grandmother had to take her by one arm, and her father by the other. They stared at each other over Miranda's head with a moveless gaze that Miranda had seen often, and their eyes looked exactly alike. Miranda blinked up at them, waiting to see who would win. Then Grandmother's hand fell away, and Miranda was handed over to her father. He gave the reins to Uncle Jimbilly, and lifted her over the top of the seat. She sprawled against his chest and knees as if he were an armchair and stopped crying at once. "We can't go back just for notions," he told her in the reasoning tone he always talked in when Grandmother scolded, and held the muffly handkerchief for her. "Now, blow hard. What did you forget, honey? We'll find another. Was it your doll?"

Miranda hated dolls. She never played with them. She always pulled the wigs off and tied them on the kittens, like hats. The kittens pulled them off instantly. It was fun. She put the doll clothes on the kittens and it took any one of them just half a minute to get them all off again. Kittens had sense. Miranda wailed suddenly, "Oh, I want my doll!" and cried again, trying to drown out the strange little sound, "Weep, weep"—

"Well now, if that's all," said her father comfortably, "there's a raft of dolls at Cedar Grove, and about forty fresh kittens. How'd you like that?"

"Forty?" asked Miranda.

"About," said Father.

Old Aunt Nannie leaned and held out her hand. "Look, honey, I toted you some nice black figs."

Her face was wrinkled and black and it looked like a fig upside down with a white ruffled cap. Miranda clenched her eyes tight and shook her head.

"Is that a pretty way to behave when Aunt Nannie offers you something nice?" asked Grandmother in her gentle reminding tone of voice.

"No, ma'am," said Miranda meekly. "Thank you, Aunt Nannie." But she did not accept the figs.

Great-Aunt Eliza, half way up a stepladder pitched against the flat-roofed chicken house, was telling Hinry just how to set up her telescope. "For a fellow who never saw or heard of a telescope," Great-Aunt Eliza said to Grandmother, who was really her sister Sophia Jane, "he doesn't do so badly so long as I tell him."

"I do wish you'd stop clambering up stepladders, Eliza," said Grandmother, "at your time of life."

"You're nothing but a nervous wreck, Sophia, I declare. When did you ever know me to get hurt?"

"Even so," said Grandmother tartly, "there is such a thing as appropriate behavior at your time of . . ."

Great-Aunt Eliza seized a fold of her heavy brown pleated skirt with one hand, with the other she grasped the ladder one rung higher and ascended another step. "Now Hinry," she called, "just swing it around facing west and leave it level. I'll fix it the way I want when I'm ready. You can come on down now." She came down then herself, and said to her sister: "So long as you can go bouncing off on that horse of yours, Sophia Jane, I s'pose I can climb ladders. I'm three years younger than you, and *at your time of life* that makes all the difference!"

Grandmother turned pink as the inside of a seashell, the one on her sewing table that had the sound of the sea in it; Miranda knew that she had always been the pretty one, and she was pretty still, but Great-Aunt Eliza was not pretty now and never had been. Miranda, watching and listening—for everything in the world was strange to her and something she had to know about—saw two old women, who were proud of being grandmothers, who spoke to children always as if they knew best about everything and children knew nothing, and they told children all day long to come here, go there, do this, do not do that, and they were always right and children never were except when they did anything they were told right away without a word. And here they were bickering like two little girls at school, or even the way Miranda and her sister Maria bickered and nagged and picked on each other and said things on purpose to hurt each other's feelings. Miranda felt sad and strange and a little frightened. She began edging away.

"Where are you going, Miranda?" asked Grandmother in her everyday voice.

"Just to the house," said Miranda, her heart sinking.

"Wait and walk with us," said Grandmother. She was very thin and pale and had white hair. Beside her, Great-Aunt Eliza loomed like a mountain with her grizzled iron-colored hair like a curly wig, her steel-rimmed spectacles over her snuff-colored eyes, and snuff-colored woollen skirts billowing about her, and her smell of snuff. When she came through the door she quite filled it up. When she sat down the chair disappeared under her, and she seemed to be sitting solidly on herself from her waistband to the floor.

Now with Grandmother sitting across the room rummaging in her work basket and pretending not to see anything, Great-Aunt Eliza took a small brown bottle out of her pocket, opened it, took a pinch of snuff in each nostril, sneezed loudly, wiped her nose with a big white starchy-looking handkerchief, pushed her spectacles up on her forehead, took a little twig chewed into a brush at one end, dipped and twisted it around in the little bottle, and placed it firmly between her teeth. Miranda had heard of this shameful habit in women of the lower classes, but no lady had been known to "dip snuff," and surely not in the family. Yet here was Great-Aunt Eliza, a lady even if not a very pretty one, dipping snuff. Miranda knew how her grandmother felt about it; she stared fascinated at Great-Aunt Eliza until her eyes watered. Great-Aunt Eliza stared back in turn.

"Look here, young one, d'ye s'pose if I gave you a gumdrop you'd get out from underfoot?"

She reached in the other pocket and took out a roundish, rather crushed-looking pink gumdrop with the sugar coating pretty badly crackled. "Now take this, and don't let me lay eyes on you any more today."

Miranda hurried away, clenching the gumdrop in her palm. When she reached the kitchen it was oozing through her fingers. She went to the tap and held her hand under the water and tried to wash off the snuffy smell. After this crime she did not really dare go near Great-Aunt Eliza again soon. "What did you do with that gumdrop so quickly, child?" she could almost hear her asking.

Yet Miranda almost forgot her usual interests, such as kittens and other little animals on the place, pigs, chickens, rabbits, anything at all so it was a baby and would let her pet and feed it, for Great-Aunt Eliza's ways and habits kept Miranda following her about, gazing, or sitting across the dining-table, gazing, for when Great-Aunt Eliza was not on the roof before her telescope, always just before daylight or just after dark, she was walking about with a microscope and a burning glass, peering closely at something she saw on a tree trunk, something she found in the grass; now and then she collected fragments that looked like dried leaves or bits of bark, brought them in the house, spread them out on a sheet of white paper, and sat there, poring, as still as if she were saying her prayers. At table she would dissect a scrap of potato peeling or anything else she might be eating, and sit there, bowed over, saying, "Hum," from time to time. Grandmother, who did not allow the children to bring anything to the table to play with and who forbade them to do anything but eat while they were there, ignored her sister's manners as long as she could, then remarked one day, when Great-Aunt Eliza was humming like a bee to herself over what her microscope had found in a raisin, "Eliza, if it is interesting save it for me to look at after dinner. Or tell me what it is."

"You wouldn't know if I told you," said Great-Aunt Eliza, coolly, putting her microscope away and finishing off her pudding.

When at last, just before they were all going back to town again, Great-Aunt Eliza invited the children to climb the ladder with her and see the stars through her telescope, they were so awed they looked at each other like strangers, and did not exchange a word. Miranda saw only a great pale flaring disk of cold light, but she knew it was the moon and called out in pure rapture, "Oh, it's like another world!"

"Why, of course, child," said Great-Aunt Eliza, in her growling voice, but kindly, "other worlds, a million other worlds."

"Like this one?" asked Miranda, timidly.

"Nobody knows, child. . . ."

"Nobody knows, nobody knows," Miranda sang to a tune in her head, and when the others walked on, she was so dazzled with joy she fell back by herself, walking a little distance behind Great-Aunt Eliza's swinging lantern and her wide-swinging skirts. They took the dewy path through the fig grove, much like the one in town, with the early dew bringing out the sweet smell of the milky leaves. They passed a fig tree with low hanging branches, and Miranda reached up by habit and touched it with her fingers for luck. From the earth beneath her feet came a terrible, faint troubled sound. "Weep weep, weep weep . . ." murmured a little crying voice from the smothering earth, the grave.

Miranda bounded like a startled pony against the back of Great-Aunt Eliza's knees, crying out, "Oh, oh, oh, wait . . ."

"What on earth's the matter, child?"

Miranda seized the warm snuffy hand held out to her and hung on hard. "Oh, there's something saying 'weep weep' out of the ground!"

Great-Aunt Eliza stooped, put her arm around Miranda and listened carefully, for a moment. "Hear them?" she said. "They're not in the ground at all. They are the first tree frogs, means it's going to rain," she said, "weep weep—hear them?"

Miranda took a deep trembling breath and heard them. They were in the trees. They walked on again, Miranda holding Great-Aunt Eliza's hand.

"Just think," said Great-Aunt Eliza, in her most scientific voice, "when tree frogs shed their skins, they pull them off over their heads like little shirts, and they eat them. Can you imagine? They have the prettiest little shapes you ever saw—I'll show you one some time under the microscope."

"Thank you, ma'am," Miranda remembered finally to say through her fog of bliss at hearing the tree frogs sing, "Weep weep . . ."

Kay Boyle (b. 1903)
WINTER NIGHT

There is a time of apprehension which begins with the beginning of darkness, and to which only the speech of love can lend security. It is there, in abeyance, at the end of every day, not urgent enough to be given the name of fear but rather of concern for how the hours are to be reprieved from fear, and those who have forgotten how it was when they were children can remember nothing of this. It may begin around five o'clock on a winter afternoon when the light outside is dying in the windows. At that hour the New York apartment in which Felicia lived was filled with shadows, and the little girl would wait alone in the living room, looking out at the winter-stripped trees that stood black in the park against the isolated ovals of unclean snow. Now it was January, and the day had been a cold one; the water of the artificial lake was frozen fast, but because of the cold and the coming darkness, the skaters had ceased to move across its surface. The street that lay between the park and the apartment house was wide, and the two-way streams of cars and busses, some with their headlamps already shining, advanced and halted, halted and poured swiftly on to the tempo of the traffic signals' altering lights. The time of apprehension had set in, and Felicia, who was seven, stood at the window in the evening and waited before she asked the question. When the signals below would change from red to green again, or when the double-decker bus would turn the corner below, she would ask it. The words of it were already there, tentative in her mouth, when the answer came from the far end of the hall.

"Your mother," said the voice among the sound of kitchen things, "she telephoned up before you came in from nursery school. She won't be back in time for supper. I was to tell you a sitter was coming in from the sitting parents' place."

Felicia turned back from the window into the obscurity of the living room, and she looked toward the open door, and into the hall beyond it where the light from the kitchen fell in a clear yellow angle across the wall and onto the strip of carpet. Her hands were cold, and she put them in her jacket pockets as she walked carefully across the living-room rug and stopped at the edge of light.

"Will she be home late?" she said.

For a moment there was the sound of water running in the kitchen, a long way away, and then the sound of the water ceased, and the high, Southern voice went on:

"She'll come home when she gets ready to come home. That's all I have to say. If she wants to spend two dollars and fifty cents and ten cents' carfare on top of that three or four nights out of the week for a sitting parent to come in here and sit, it's her own business. It certainly ain't nothing to do with you or me. She makes her money, just like the rest of us does. She works all day down there in the office, or whatever it is, just like the rest of us works, and she's entitled to spend her money like she wants to spend it. There's no law in the world against buying your own freedom. Your mother and me, we're just buying our own freedom, that's all we're doing. And we're not doing nobody no harm."

"Do you know who she's having supper with?" said Felicia from the edge of dark. There was one more step to take, and then she would be standing in the light that fell on the strip of carpet, but she did not take the step.

"Do I know who she's having supper with?" the voice cried out in what might have been derision, and there was the sound of dishes striking the metal ribs of the drainboard by the sink. "Maybe it's Mr. Van Johnson, or Mr. Frank Sinatra, or maybe it's just the Duke of Wincers for the evening. All I know is you're having soft-boiled egg and spinach and applesauce for supper, and you're going to have it quick now because the time is getting away."

The voice from the kitchen had no name. It was as variable as the faces and figures of the women who came and sat in the evenings. Month by month the voice in the kitchen altered to another voice, and the sitting parents were no more than lonely aunts of an evening or two who sometimes returned and sometimes did not to this apartment in which they had sat before. Nobody stayed anywhere very long any more, Felicia's mother told her. It was part of the time in which you lived, and part of the life of the city, but when the fathers came back, all this would be miraculously changed. Perhaps you would live in a house again, a small one, with fir trees on either side of the short brick walk, and Father would drive up every night from the station just after darkness set in. When Felicia thought of this, she stepped quickly into the clear angle of light, and she left the dark of the living room behind her and ran softly down the hall.

The drop-leaf table stood in the kitchen between the refrigerator and the sink, and Felicia sat down at the place that was set. The voice at the sink was speaking still, and while Felicia ate it did not cease to speak until the bell of the front door rang abruptly. The girl walked around the table and went down the hall, wiping her dark palms in her apron, and, from the drop-leaf table, Felicia watched her step from the angle of light into darkness and open the door.

"You put in an early appearance," the girl said, and the woman who had rung the bell came into the hall. The door closed behind her, and the girl showed her into the living room, and lit the lamp on the bookcase, and the shadows were suddenly bleached away. But when the girl turned, the woman turned from the living room too and followed her, humbly and in silence, to the threshold of the kitchen. "Sometimes they keep me standing around waiting after it's time for me to be getting on home, the sitting parents do," the girl said, and she picked up the last two dishes from the table and put them in the sink. The woman who stood in the doorway was a small woman, and when she undid the white silk scarf from around her head, Felicia saw that her hair was black. She wore it parted in the middle, and it had not been cut, but was drawn back loosely into a knot behind her head. She had very clean white gloves on, and her face was pale, and there was a look of sorrow in her soft black eyes. "Sometimes I have to stand out there in the hall with my hat and coat on, waiting for the sitting parents to turn up," the girl said, and, as she turned on the water in the sink, the contempt she had for them hung on the kitchen air. "But you're ahead of time," she said, and she held the dishes, first one and then the other, under the flow of steaming water.

The woman in the doorway wore a neat black coat, not a new-looking coat, and it had no fur on it, but it had a smooth velvet collar and velvet lapels. She did not move, or smile, and she gave no sign that she had heard the girl speaking above the sound of water at the sink. She simply stood looking at Felicia, who sat at the table with the milk in her glass not finished yet.

"Are you the child?" she said at last, and her voice was low, and the pronunciation of the words a little strange.

"Yes, this here's Felicia," the girl said, and the dark hands dried the dishes and put them away. "You drink up your milk quick now, Felicia, so's I can rinse your glass."

"I will wash the glass," said the woman. "I would like to wash the glass for her," and Felicia sat looking across the table at the face in the doorway that was filled with such unspoken grief. "I will wash the glass for her and clean off the table," the woman was saying quietly. "When the child is finished, she will show me where her night things are."

"The others, they wouldn't do anything like that," the girl said, and she hung the dishcloth over the rack. "They wouldn't put their hand to housework, the sitting parents. That's where they got the name for them," she said.

Whenever the front door closed behind the girl in the evening, it would usually be that the sitting parent who was there would take up a book of fairy stories and read aloud for a while to Felicia; or else would settle herself in the big chair in the living room and begin to tell the words of a story in drowsiness to her, while Felicia took off her clothes in the bedroom, and folded them, and put her pajamas on, and brushed her teeth, and did her hair. But this time, that was not the way it happened. Instead, the woman sat down on the other chair at the kitchen table, and she began at once to speak, not of good fairies or bad, or of animals endowed with human speech, but to speak quietly, in spite of the eagerness behind her words, of a thing that seemed of singular importance to her.

"It is strange that I should have been sent here tonight," she said, her eyes moving slowly from feature to feature of Felicia's face, "for you look like a child that I knew once, and this is the anniversary of that child."

"Did she have hair like mine?" Felicia asked quickly, and she did not keep her eyes fixed on the unfinished glass of milk in shyness any more.

"Yes, she did. She had hair like yours," said the woman, and her glance paused for a moment on the locks which fell straight and thick on the shoulders of Felicia's dress. It may have been that she thought to stretch out her hand and touch the ends of Felicia's hair, for her fingers stirred as they lay clasped together on the table, and then they relapsed into passivity again. "But it is not the hair alone, it is the delicacy of your face, too, and your eyes the same, filled with the same spring lilac color," the woman said, pronouncing the words carefully. "She had little coats of golden fur on her arms and legs," she said, "and when we were closed up there, the lot of us in the cold, I used to make her laugh when I told her that the fur that was so pretty, like a little fawn's skin on her arms, would always help to keep her warm."

"And did it keep her warm?" asked Felicia, and she gave a little jerk of laughter as she looked down at her own legs hanging under the table, with the bare calves thin and covered with a down of hair.

"It did not keep her warm enough," the woman said, and now the mask of grief had come back upon her face. "So we used to take everything we could spare from ourselves, and we would sew them into cloaks and other kinds of garments for her and for the other children. . . ."

"Was it a school?" said Felicia when the woman's voice had ceased to speak.

"No," said the woman softly, "it was not a school, but still there were a lot of children there. It was a camp—that was the name the place had; it was a camp. It was a place where they put people until they could decide what was to be done with them." She sat with her hands clasped, silent a moment, looking at Felicia. "That little dress you have on," she said, not saying the words to anybody, scarcely saying them aloud. "Oh, she would have liked that little dress, the little buttons shaped like hearts, and the white collar—"

"I have four school dresses," Felicia said. "I'll show them to you. How many dresses did she have?"

"Well, there, you see, there in the camp," said the woman, "She did not have any dresses except the little skirt and the pullover. That was all she had. She had brought just a handkerchief of her belongings with her, like everybody else—just enough for three days away from home was what they told us, so she did not have enough to last the winter. But she had her ballet slippers," the woman said, and her clasped fingers did not move. "She had brought them because she thought during her three days away from home she would have the time to practice her ballet."

"I've been to the ballet," Felicia said suddenly, and she said it so eagerly that she stuttered a little as the words came out of her mouth. She slipped quickly down from the chair and went around the table to where the woman sat. Then she took one of the woman's hands away from the other that held it fast, and she pulled her toward the door. "Come into the living room and I'll do a pirouette for you," she said, and then she stopped speaking, her eyes halted on the woman's face. "Did she—did the little girl—could she do a pirouette very well?" she said.

"Yes, she could. At first she could," said the woman, and Felicia felt uneasy now at the sound of sorrow in her words. "But after that she was hungry. She was hungry all winter," she said in a low voice. "We were all hungry, but the children were the hungriest. Even now," she said, and her voice went suddenly savage, "when I see milk like that, clean, fresh milk standing in a glass, I want to cry out loud, I want to beat my hands on the table, because it did not have to be . . ." She had drawn her fingers abruptly away from Felicia now, and Felicia stood before her, cast off, forlorn, alone again in the time of apprehension. "That was three years ago," the woman was saying, and one hand was lifted, as in weariness, to shade her face. "It was somewhere else, it was in another country," she said, and behind her hand her eyes were turned upon the substance of a world in which Felicia had played no part.

"Did—did the little girl cry when she was hungry?" Felicia asked, and the woman shook her head.

"Sometimes she cried," she said, "but not very much. She was very quiet. One night when she heard the other children crying, she said to me, 'You know, they are not crying because they want something to eat. They are crying because their mothers have gone away.'"

"Did the mothers have to go out to supper?" Felicia asked, and she watched the woman's face for the answer.

"No," said the woman. She stood up from her chair, and now that she put her hand on the little girl's shoulder, Felicia was taken into the sphere of love and intimacy again. "Shall we go into the other room, and you will do your pirouette for me?" the woman said, and they went from the kitchen and down the strip of carpet on which the clear light fell. In the front room, they paused hand in hand in the glow of the shaded lamp, and the woman looked about her, at the books, the low tables with the magazines and ash trays on them, the vase of roses on the piano, looking with dark, scarcely seeing eyes at these things that had no reality at all. It was only when she saw the little white clock on the mantelpiece that she gave any sign, and then she said quickly: "What times does your mother put you to bed?"

Felicia waited a moment, and in the interval of waiting the woman lifted one hand and, as if in reverence, touched Felicia's hair.

"What time did the little girl you knew in the other place go to bed?" Felicia asked.

"Ah, God, I do not know, I do not remember," the woman said.

"Was she your little girl?" said Felicia softly, stubbornly.

"No," said the woman. "She was not mine. At least, at first she was not mine. She had a mother, a real mother, but the mother had to go away."

"Did she come back late?" asked Felicia.

"No, ah, no, she could not come back, she never came back," the woman said, and now she turned, her arm around Felicia's shoulders, and she sat down in the low soft chair. "Why am I saying all this to you, why am I doing it?" she cried out in grief, and she held Felicia close against her. "I had thought to speak of the anniversary to you, and that was all, and now I am saying these other things to you. Three years ago today, exactly, the little girl became my little girl because her mother went away. That is all there is to it. There is nothing more."

Felicia waited another moment, held close against the woman, and listening to the swift, strong heartbeats in the woman's breast.

"But the mother," she said then in the small, persistent voice, "did she take a taxi when she went?"

"This is the way it used to happen," said the woman, speaking in hopelessness and bitterness in the softly lighted room. "Every week they used to come into the place where we were and they would read a list of names out. Sometimes it would be the names of children they would read out, and then a little later they would have to go away. And sometimes it would be the grown people's names, the names of the mothers or big sisters, or other women's names. The men were not with us. The fathers were somewhere else, in another place."

"Yes," Felicia said. "I know."

"We had been there only a little while, maybe ten days or maybe not so long," the woman went on, holding Felicia against her still, "when they read the name of the little girl's mother out, and that afternoon they took her away."

"What did the little girl do?" Felicia said.

"She wanted to think up the best way of getting out so that she could go find her mother," said the woman, "but she could not think of anything good enough until the third or fourth day. And then she tied her ballet slippers up in the handkerchief again, and she went up to the guard standing at the door." The woman's voice was gentle, controlled now. "She asked the guard please to open the door so that she could go out. 'This is Thursday,' she said, 'and every Tuesday and Thursday I have my ballet lessons. If I miss a ballet lesson, they do not count the money off, so my mother would be just paying for nothing, and she cannot afford to pay for nothing. I missed my ballet lesson on Tuesday,' she said to the guard, 'and I must not miss it again today.'"

Felicia lifted her head from the woman's shoulder, and she shook her hair back and looked in question and wonder at the woman's face.

"And did the man let her go?" she said.

"No, he did not. He could not do that," said the woman. "He was a soldier and he had to do what he was told. So every evening after her mother went, I used to brush the little girl's hair for her," the woman went on saying. "And while I brushed it, I used to tell her the stories of the ballets. Sometimes I would begin with *Narcissus*," the woman said, and she parted Felicia's locks with her fingers, "so if you will go and get your brush now, I will tell it while I brush your hair."

"Oh, yes," said Felicia, and she made two whirls as she went quickly to the bedroom. On the way back, she stopped and held on to the piano with the fingers of one hand while she went upon her toes. "Did you see me? Did you see me standing on my toes?" she called the woman, and the woman sat smiling in love and contentment at her.

"Yes, wonderful, really wonderful," she said. "I am sure I have never seen anyone do it so well." Felicia came spinning toward her, whirling in pirouette after pirouette, and she flung herself down in the chair close to her, with her thin bones pressed against the woman's soft, wide hip. The woman took the silver-backed, monogrammed brush and the tortoise-shell comb in her hands, and now she began to brush Felicia's hair. "We did not have any soap at all and not very much water to wash in, so I never could fix her as nicely and prettily as I wanted to," she said, and the brush stroked regularly, carefully down, caressing the shape of Felicia's head.

"If there wasn't very much water, then how did she do her teeth?" Felicia said.

"She did not do her teeth," said the woman, and she drew the comb through Felicia's hair. "There were not any toothbrushes or tooth paste, or anything like that."

Felicia waited a moment, constructing the unfamiliar scene of it in silence, and then she asked the tentative question.

"Do I have to do my teeth tonight?" she said.

"No," said the woman, and she was thinking of something else, "you do not have to do your teeth."

"If I am your little girl tonight, can I pretend there isn't enough water to wash?" said Felicia.

"Yes," said the woman, "you can pretend that if you like. You do not have to wash," she said, and the comb passed lightly through Felicia's hair.

"Will you tell me the story of the ballet?" said Felicia, and the rhythm of the brushing was like the soft, slow rocking of sleep.

"Yes," said the woman. "In the first one, the place is a forest glade with little pale birches growing in it, and they have green veils over their faces and green veils drifting from their fingers, because it is the springtime. There is the music of a flute," said the woman's voice softly, softly, "and creatures of the wood are dancing—"

"But the mother," Felicia said as suddenly as if she had been awaked from sleep. "What did the little girl's mother say when she didn't do her teeth and didn't wash at night?"

"The mother was not there, you remember," said the woman, and the brush moved steadily in her hand. "But she did send one little letter back. Sometimes the people who went away were able to do that. The mother wrote it in a train, standing up in a car that had no seats," she said, and she might have been telling the story of the ballet still, for her voice was gentle and the brush did not falter on Felicia's hair. "There were perhaps a great many other people standing up in the train with her, perhaps all trying to write their little letters on the bits of paper they had managed to hide on them, or that they had found in forgotten corners as they traveled. When they had written their letters, then they must try to slip them out through the boards of the car in which they journeyed, standing up," said the woman, "and these letters fell down on the tracks under the train, or they were blown into the fields or onto the country roads, and if it was a kind person who picked them up, he would seal them in envelopes and send them to where they were addressed to go. So a letter came back like this from the little girl's mother," the woman said, and the brush followed the comb, the comb the brush in steady pursuit through Felicia's hair. "It said good-by to the little girl, and it said please to take care of her. It said: 'Whoever reads this letter in the camp, please take good care of my little girl for me, and please have her tonsils looked at by a doctor if this is possible to do.'"

"And then," said Felicia softly, persistently, "what happened to the little girl?"

"I do not know. I cannot say," the woman said. But now the brush and comb had ceased to move, and in the silence Felicia turned her thin, small body on the chair, and she and the woman suddenly put their arms around each other. "They must all be asleep now, all of them," the woman said, and in the silence that fell on them again, they held each other closer. "They must be quietly asleep somewhere, and not crying all night because they are hungry and because they are cold. For three years I have been saying 'They must all be asleep, and the cold and the hunger and the seasons or night or day or nothing matters to them—'"

It was after midnight when Felicia's mother put her key in the lock of the front door, and pushed it open, and stepped into the hallway. She walked quickly to the living room, and just across the threshold she slipped the three blue foxskins from her shoulders and dropped them, with her little velvet bag, upon the chair. The room was quiet, so quiet that she could hear the sound of breathing in it, and no one spoke to her in greeting as she crossed toward the bedroom door. And then, as startling as a slap across her delicately tinted face, she saw the woman lying sleeping on the divan, and Felicia, in her school dress still, asleep within the woman's arms.

QUESTIONS

1. At what point could you identify the period of the story? What previous knowledge of it was helpful to you as you read? What new impressions of the period did you gain—for instance, from the fact that Felicia's mother works all day?

2. What details of the story's particular setting—the apartment on this winter night— gave you a sense of Felicia's situation? What mood is created by this setting?
3. How did you respond to the "sitting parent" on her first appearance in the story? If your sense of her changed as she spoke to Felicia, explain how it did.
4. Did you make comparisons between Felicia and her mother and the mother and child from the camp? If you did, how did these comparisons influence the way you read the last paragraph of the story?
5. How important to the story's meaning is the way the sitter answers Felicia's last question about the little girl?

Richard Wright (1908–1960)
BIG BOY LEAVES HOME

I

Yo mama don wear no drawers . . .
Clearly, the voice rose out of the woods, and died away. Like an echo another voice caught it up:
Ah seena when she pulled em off . . .
Another, shrill, cracking, adolescent:
N she washed 'em in alcohol . . .
Then a quartet of voices, blending in harmony, floated high above the tree tops:
N she hung 'em out in the hall . . .
Laughing easily, four black boys came out of the woods into cleared pasture. They walked lollingly in bare feet, beating tangled vines and bushes with long sticks.
"Ah wished Ah knowed some mo lines t tha song."
"Me too."
"Yea, when yuh gits t where she hangs em out in the hall yuh has t stop."
"Shucks, whut goes wid *hall*?"
"*Call.*"
"*Fall.*"
"*Wall.*"
"*Quall.*"
They threw themselves on the grass, laughing.
"Big Boy?"
"Huh?"
"Yuh know one thing?"
"Whut?"
"Yuh sho is crazy!"
"Crazy?"

"Yeah, yuh crazys a bed-bug!"

"Crazy bout whut?"

"Man, whoever hearda *quall*?"

"Yuh said yuh wanted something to go wid *hall*, didn't yuh?"

"Yeah, but whuts a *quall*?"

"Nigger, a *qualls* a *quall*."

They laughed easily, catching and pulling long green blades of grass with their toes.

"Waal, ef a *qualls* a *quall*, whut IS a *quall*?"

"Oh, Ah know."

"Whut?"

"Tha ol song goes something like this:

> Yo mama don wear no drawers,
>   Ah seena when she pulled em off,
> N she washed em in alcohol,
>   N she hung em out in the hall,
> N then she put em back on her QUALL!"

They laughed again. Their shoulders were flat to the earth, their knees propped up, and their faces square to the sun.

"Big Boy, yuhs CRAZY!"

"Don ax me nothin else."

"Nigger, yuhs CRAZY!"

They fell silent, smiling, dropping the lids of their eyes softly against the sunlight.

"Man, don the groun feel warm?"

"Jus lika bed."

"Jeeesus, Ah could stay here ferever."

"Me too."

"Ah kin feel tha ol sun goin all thu me."

"Feels like mah bones is warm."

In the distance a train whistled mournfully.

"There goes number fo!"

"Hittin on all six!"

"Highballin it down the line!"

"Bound fer up Noth, Lawd, bound fer up Noth!"

They began to chant, pounding bare heels in the grass.

> Dis train bound fo Glory
> Dis train, Oh Hallelujah
> Dis train bound fo Glory

> *Dis train, Oh Hallelujah*
> *Dis train bound fo Glory*
> *Ef yuh ride no need fer fret er worry*
> *Dis train, Oh Hallelujah*
> *Dis train . . .*
> *Dis train don carry no gambler*
> *Dis train, Oh Hallelujah*
> *Dis train don carry no gambler*
> *Dis train, Oh Hallelujah*
> *Dis train don carry no gambler*
> *No fo day creeper er midnight rambler*
> *Dis train, Oh Hallelujah*
> *Dis train . . .*

When the song ended they burst out laughing, thinking of a train bound for Glory.

"Gee, thas a good ol song!"

"Huuuuummmmmmmmman . . ."

"Whut?"

"Geeee whiiiiiiz . . ."

"Whut?"

"Somebody done let win! Das whut!"

Buck, Bobo and Lester jumped up. Big Boy stayed on the ground, feigning sleep.

"Jeeesus, tha sho stinks!"

"Big Boy!"

Big Boy feigned to snore.

"Big Boy!"

Big Boy stirred as though in sleep.

"Big Boy!"

"Hunh?"

"Yuh rotten inside!"

"Rotten?"

"Lawd, cant yuh smell it?"

"Smell whut?"

"Nigger, yuh mus gotta bad col!"

"*Smell whut?*"

"NIGGER, YUH BROKE WIN!"

Big Boy laughed and fell back on the grass, closing his eyes.

"The hen whut cackles is the hen whut laid the egg."

"We ain no hens."

"Yuh cackled, didnt yuh?"

The three moved off with noses turned up.

"C mon!"

"Where yuh-all goin?"

"T the creek fer a swim."

"Yeah, les swim."

"Naw buddy naw!" said Big Boy, slapping the air with a scornful palm.

"Aa, c mon! Don be a heel!"

"N git *lynched?* Hell naw!"

"He ain gonna see us."

"How yuh know?"

"Cause he ain."

"Yuh-all go on. Ahma stay right here," said Big Boy.

"Hell, let im stay! C mon, les go," said Buck.

The three walked off, swishing at grass and bushes with sticks. Big Boy looked lazily at their backs.

"Hey!"

Walking on, they glanced over their shoulders.

"Hey, niggers!"

"C mon!"

Big Boy grunted, picked up his stick, pulled to his feet, and stumbled off.

"Wait!"

"C mon!"

He ran, caught up with them, leaped upon their backs, bearing them to the ground.

"Quit, Big Boy!"

"Gawddam, nigger!"

"Git t hell offa me!"

Big Boy sprawled in the grass beside them, laughing and pounding his heels in the ground.

"Nigger, whut yuh think we is, hosses?"

"How come yuh awways hoppin on us?"

"Lissen, wes gonna doubt-team on yuh one of these days n beat yo ol ass good."

Big Boy smiled.

"Sho nough?"

"Yeah, don yuh like it?"

"We gonna beat yuh sos yuh cant walk!"

"N dare yuh t do nothin erbout it!"

Big Boy bared his teeth.

"C mon! Try it now!"

The three circled around him.

"Say, Buck, yuh grab his feets!"

"N yuh git his head, Lester!"

"N Bobo, yuh get berhin n grab his arms!"

Keeping more than arm's length, they circled round and round Big Boy.

"C mon!" said Big Boy, feinting at one and then the other.

Round and round they circled, but could not seem to get any closer. Big Boy stopped and braced his hands on his hips.

"Is all three of yuh-all scareda me?"

"Les git im some other time," said Bobo, grinning.

"Yeah, we kin ketch yuh when yuh ain thinkin," said Lester.

"We kin trick yuh," said Buck.

They laughed and walked together.

Big Boy belched.

"Ahm hongry," he said.

"Me too."

"Ah wished Ah hada big hot pota belly-busters!"

"Cooked wid some good ol saltry ribs . . ."

"N some good ol egg cornbread . . ."

"N some buttermilk . . ."

"N some hot peach cobbler swimmin in juice . . ."

"Nigger, hush!"

They began to chant, emphasizing the rhythm by cutting at grass with sticks.

> *Bye n bye*
> *Ah wanna piece of pie*
> *Pies too sweet*
> *Ah wanna piece of meat*
> *Meats too red*
> *Ah wanna piece of bread*
> *Breads too brown*
> *Ah wanna go t town*
> *Towns too far*
> *Ah wanna ketch a car*
> *Cars too fas*
> *Ah falln break mah ass*
> *Ahll understan it better bye n bye . . .*

They climbed over a barbed-wire fence and entered a stretch of thick woods. Big Boy was whistling softly, his eyes half-closed.

"LES GIT IM!"

Buck, Lester, and Bobo whirled, grabbed Big Boy about the neck, arms, and legs, bearing him to the ground. He grunted and kicked wildly as he went back into weeds.

"Hol im tight!"

"Git his arms! Git his arms!"

"Set on his legs so he cant kick!"

Big Boy puffed heavily, trying to get loose.

"WE GOT YUH NOW, GAWDDAMMIT, WE GOT YUH NOW!"

"Thas a Gawddam lie!" said Big Boy. He kicked, twisted, and clutched for a hold on one and then the other.

"Say, yuh-all hep me hol his arms!" said Bobo.

"Aw, we got this bastard now!" said Lester.

"Thas a Gawddam lie!" said Big Boy again.

"Say, yuh-all hep me hol his arms!" called Bobo.

Big Boy managed to encircle the neck of Bobo with his left arm. He tightened his elbow scissors-like and hissed through his teeth:

"Yuh got me, ain yuh?"

"Hol im!"

"Les beat this bastard's ass!"

"Say, hep me hol his *arms!* Hes got aholda mah *neck!*" cried Bobo.

Big Boy squeezed Bobo's neck and twisted his head to the ground.

"Yuh got me, ain yuh?"

"Quit, Big Boy, yuh chokin me! Yuh hurtin mah neck!" cried Bobo.

"Turn me loose!" said Big Boy.

"Ah ain got yuh! Its the others whut got yuh!" pleaded Bobo.

"Tell them others t git t hell offa me or Ahma break yo neck," said Big Boy.

"Ssssay, yyyuh-al gggit ooooffa Bbig Boy. Hhhes got me," gurgled Bobo.

"Cant yuh hol im?"

"Nnaw, hhes ggot mmah nneck . . ."

Big Boy squeezed tighter.

"N Ahma break it too les yuh tell em t git t hell offa me!"

"Ttturn mmmeee llloose," panted Bobo, tears gushing.

"Cant yuh hol im, Bobo?" asked Buck.

"Nnaw, yuh-all tturn im lloose; hhhes got mah nnneck . . ."

"Grab his neck, Bobo . . ."

"Ah cant; yugurgur . . ."

To save Bobo, Lester and Buck got up and ran to a safe distance. Big Boy released Bobo, who staggered to his feet, slobbering and trying to stretch a crick out of his neck.

"Shucks, nigger, yuh almos broke mah neck," whimpered Bobo.

"Ahm gonna break yo ass nex time," said Big Boy.

"Ef Bobo coulda hel yuh we woulda had yuh," yelled Lester.

"Ah waznt gonna let im do that," said Big Boy.

They walked together again, swishing sticks.

"Yuh see," began Big Boy, "when a ganga guys jump on yuh, all yuh gotta do is put the heat on one of them n make im tell the others t let up, see?"

"Gee, thas a good idee!"

"Yeah, thas a good idee!"

"But yuh almos broke mah neck, man," said Bobo.

"Ahma smart nigger," said Big Boy, thrusting out his chest.

II

They came to the swimming hole.

"Ah ain goin in," said Bobo.

"Done got scared?" asked Big Boy.

"Naw, Ah ain scared . . ."

"How come yuh ain goin in?"

"Yuh know ol man Harvey don erllow no niggers t swim in this hole."

"N jus las year he took a shot at Bob fer swimming in here," said Lester.

"Shucks, ol man Harvey ain studyin bout us niggers," said Big Boy.

"Hes at home thinking about his jelly-roll," said Buck.

They laughed.

"Buck, yo mins lowern a snakes belly," said Lester.

"Ol man Harveys too doggone ol t think erbout jelly-roll," said Big Boy.

"Hes dried up; all the saps done lef im," said Bobo.

"C mon, les go!" said Big Boy.

Bobo pointed.

"See tha sign over yonder?"

"Yeah."

"Whut it say?"

"NO TRESPASSIN," read Lester.

"Know whut tha mean?"

"Mean ain no dogs n niggers erllowed," said Buck.

"Waal, wes here now," said Big Boy. "Ef he ketched us even like this thered be trouble, so we just as waal go on in . . ."

"Ahm wid the nex one!"

"Ahll go ef anybody else goes!"

Big Boy looked carefully in all directions. Seeing nobody, he began jerking off his overalls.

"LAS ONE INS A OLD DEAD DOG!"

"THAS YO MA!"

"THAS YO PA!"

"THAS BOTH YO MA N YO PA!"

They jerked off their clothes and threw them in a pile under a tree. Thirty seconds later they stood, black and naked, on the edge of the hole under a sloping embankment. Gingerly Big Boy touched the water with his foot.

"Man, this waters col," he said.

"Ahm gonna put mah cloes back on," said Bobo, withdrawing his foot.

Big Boy grabbed him about the waist.

"Like hell yuh is!"

"Git outta the way, nigger!" Bobo yelled.

"Thow im in!" said Lester.

"Duck im!"

Bobo crouched, spread his legs, and braced himself against Big Boy's body. Locked in each other's arms, they tussled on the edge of the hole, neither able to throw the other.

"C mon, les me n yuh push em in."

"O.K."

Laughing, Lester and Buck gave the two locked bodies a running push. Big

Boy and Bobo splashed, sending up silver spray in the sunlight. When Big Boy's head came up he yelled:

"Yuh bastard!"

"Tha wuz yo ma yuh pushed!" said Bobo, shaking his head to clear the water from his eyes.

They did a surface dive, came up and struck out across the creek. The muddy water foamed. They swam back, waded into shallow water, breathing heavily and blinking eyes.

"C mon in!"

"Man, the water's fine!"

Lester and Buck hesitated.

"Les wet em," Big Boy whispered to Bobo.

Before Lester and Buck could back away, they were dripping wet from handfuls of scooped water.

"Hey, quit!"

"Gawddam, nigger; tha waters col!"

"C mon in!" called Big Boy.

"We just as waal go on in now," said Buck.

"Look n see ef anybody's comin."

Kneeling, they squinted among the trees.

"Ain nobody."

"C mon, les go."

They waded in slowly, pausing each few steps to catch their breath. A desperate water battle began. Closing eyes and backing away, they shunted water into one another's faces with the flat palms of hands.

"Hey, cut it out!"

"Yeah, Ahm bout drownin!"

They came together in water up to their navels, blowing and blinking. Big Boy ducked, upsetting Bobo.

"Look out, nigger!"

"Don holler so loud!"

"Yeah, they kin hear yo ol big mouth a mile erway."

"This waters too col fer me."

"Thas cause it rained yistiddy."

They swam across and back again.

"Ah wish we hada bigger place t swim in."

"The white folks got plenty swimming pools n we ain got none."

"Ah useta swim in the ol Missippi when we lived in Vicksburg."

Big Boy put his head under the water and blew his breath. A sound came like that of a hippopotamus.

"C mon, les be hippos."

Each went to a corner of the creek and put his mouth just below the surface and blew like a hippopotamus. Tiring, they came and sat under the embankment.

"Look like Ah gotta chill."

"Me too."

"Les stay here n dry off."

"Jeeesus, Ahm col!"

They kept still in the sun, suppressing shivers. After some of the water had dried off their bodies they began to talk through clattering teeth.

"Whut would yuh do ef ol man Harveyd come erlong right now?"

"Run like hell!"

"Man, Ahd run so fas hed thinka black streaka lightnin shot pass im."

"But spose he hada gun?"

"Aw, nigger, shut up!"

They were silent. They ran their hands over wet, trembling legs, brushing water away. Then their eyes watched the sun sparkling on the restless creek.

Far away a train whistled.

"There goes number seven!"

"Headin fer up Noth!"

"Blazin it down the line!"

"Lawd, Ahm goin Noth some day."

"Me too, man."

"They say colored folks up Noth is got ekual rights."

They grew pensive. A black winged butterfly hovered at the water's edge. A bee droned. From somewhere came the sweet scent of honeysuckles. Dimly they could hear sparrows twittering in the woods. They rolled from side to side, letting sunshine dry their skins and warm their blood. They plucked blades of grass and chewed them.

"Oh!"

They looked up, their lips parting.

"Oh!"

A white woman, poised on the edge of the opposite embankment, stood directly in front of them, her hat in her hand and her hair lit by the sun.

"Its a woman!" whispered Big Boy in an underbreath. "A *white* woman!"

They stared, their hands instinctively covering their groins. Then they scrambled to their feet. The white woman backed slowly out of sight. They stood for a moment, looking at one another.

"Les git outta here!" Big Boy whispered.

"Wait till she goes erway."

"Les run, theyll ketch us here naked like this!"

"Mabbe theres a man wid her."

"C mon, les git our cloes," said Big Boy.

They waited a moment longer, listening.

"What t hell! Ahma git mah cloes," said Big Boy.

Grabbing at short tufts of grass, he climbed the embankment.

"Don run out there now!"

"C mon back, fool!"

Bobo hesitated. He looked at Big Boy, and then at Buck and Lester.

"Ahm goin wid Big Boy n git mah cloes," he said.

"Don run out there naked like tha, fool!" said Buck. "Yuh don know whos out there!"

Big Boy was climbing over the edge of the embankment.

"C mon," he whispered.

Bobo climbed after. Twenty-five feet away the woman stood. She had one hand over her mouth. Hanging by fingers, Buck and Lester peeped over the edge.

"C mon back; that womans scared," said Lester.

Big Boy stopped, puzzled. He looked at the woman. He looked at the bundle of clothes. Then he looked at Buck and Lester.

"C mon, les git our cloes!"

He made a step.

"Jim!" the woman screamed.

Big Boy stopped and looked around. His hands hung loosely at his side. The woman, her eyes wide, her hand over her mouth, backed away to the tree where their clothes lay in a heap.

"Big Boy, come back here n wait till shes gone!"

Bobo ran to Big Boy's side.

"Les go home! Theyll ketch us here," he urged.

Big Boy's throat felt tight.

"Lady, we wanna git our cloes," he said.

Buck and Lester climbed the embankment and stood indecisively. Big Boy ran toward the tree.

"Jim!" the woman screamed. "Jim! Jim!"

Black and naked, Big Boy stopped three feet from her.

"We wanna git our cloes," he said again, his words coming mechanically.

He made a motion.

"You go away! You go away! I tell you, you go away!"

Big Boy stopped again, afraid. Bobo ran and snatched the clothes. Buck and Lester tried to grab theirs out of his hands.

"You go away! You go away! You go away!" the woman screamed.

"Les go!" said Bobo, running toward the woods.

CRACK!

Lester grunted, stiffened, and pitched forward. His forehead struck a toe of the woman's shoes.

Bobo stopped, clutching the clothes. Buck whirled. Big Boy stared at Lester, his lips moving.

"Hes gotta gun; hes gotta gun!" yelled Buck, running wildly.

CRACK!

Buck stopped at the edge of the embankment, his head jerked backward, his body arched stiffly to one side; he toppled headlong, sending up a shower of bright spray to the sunlight. The creek bubbled.

Big Boy and Bobo backed away, their eyes fastened fearfully on a white man who was running toward them. He had a rifle and wore an army officer's uniform. He ran to the woman's side and grabbed her hand.

"You hurt, Bertha, you hurt?"

She stared at him and did not answer.

The man turned quickly. His face was red. He raised the rifle and pointed it at Bobo. Bobo ran back, holding the clothes in front of his chest.

"Don shoot me, Mistah, don shoot me . . ."

Big Boy lunged for the rifle, grabbing the barrel.

"You black sonofabitch!"

Big Boy clung desperately.

"Let go, you black bastard!"

The barrel pointed skyward.

CRACK!

The white man, taller and heavier, flung Big Boy to the ground. Bobo dropped the clothes, ran up, and jumped onto the white man's back.

"You black sonsofbitches!"

The white man released the rifle, jerked Bobo to the ground, and began to batter the naked boy with his fists. Then Big Boy swung, striking the man in the mouth with the barrel. His teeth caved in, and he fell, dazed. Bobo was on his feet.

"C mon, Big Boy, les go!"

Breathing hard, the white man got up and faced Big Boy. His lips were trembling, his neck and chin wet with blood. He spoke quietly.

"Give me that gun, boy!"

Big Boy leveled the rifle and backed away.

The white man advanced.

"Boy, I say give me that gun!"

Bobo had the clothes in his arms.

"Run, Big Boy, run!"

The man came at Big Boy.

"Ahll kill yuh; Ahll kill yuh" said Big Boy.

His fingers fumbled for the trigger.

The man stopped, blinked, spat blood. His eyes were bewildered. His face whitened. Suddenly, he lunged for the rifle, his hands outstretched.

CRACK!

He fell forward on his face.

"Jim!"

Big Boy and Bobo turned in surprise to look at the woman.

"Jim!" she screamed again, and fell weakly at the foot of the tree.

Big Boy dropped the rifle, his eyes wide. He looked around. Bobo was crying and clutching the clothes.

"Big Boy, Big Boy . . ."

Big Boy looked at the rifle, started to pick it up, but didn't. He seemed at a loss. He looked at Lester, then at the white man; his eyes followed a thin stream of blood that seeped to the ground.

"Yuh done killed im," mumbled Bobo.

"Les go home!"

Naked, they turned and ran toward the wood. When they reached the barbed-wire fence they stopped.

"Les git our cloes on," said Big Boy.

They slipped quickly into overalls. Bobo held Lester's and Buck's clothes.

"Whut we gonna do wid these?"

Big Boy stared. His hands twitched.

"Leave em."

They climbed the fence and ran through the woods. Vines and leaves switched their faces. Once Bobo tripped and fell.

"C mon!" said Big Boy.

Bobo started crying, blood streaming from his scratches.

"Ahm scared!"

"C mon! Don cry! We wanna git home fo they ketches us!"

"Ahm scared!" said Bobo again, his eyes full of tears.

Big Boy grabbed his hand and dragged him along.

"C mon!"

III

They stopped when they got to the end of the woods. They could see the open road leading home, to ma and pa. But they hung back, afraid. The thick shadows cast from the trees were friendly and sheltering. But the wide glare of sun stretching out over the fields was pitiless. They crouched behind an old log.

"We gotta git home," said Big Boy.

"Theys gonna lynch us," said Bobo, half-questioningly.

Big Boy did not answer.

"Theys gonna lynch us," said Bobo again.

Big Boy shuddered.

"Hush!" he said. He did not want to think of it. He could not think of it; there was but one thought, and he clung to that one blindly. He had to get home, home to ma and pa.

Their heads jerked up. Their ears had caught the rhythmic jingle of a wagon. They fell to the ground and clung flat to the side of a log. Over the crest of the hill came the top of a hat. A white face. Then shoulders in a blue shirt. A wagon drawn by two horses pulled into full view.

Big Boy and Bobo held their breath, waiting. Their eyes followed the wagon till it was lost in dust around a bend of the road.

"We gotta git home," said Big Boy.

"Ahm scared," said Bobo.

"C mon! Les keep t the fields."

They ran till they came to the cornfields. Then they went slower, for last year's corn stubbles bruised their feet.

They came in sight of a brickyard.

"Wait a minute," gasped Big Boy.

They stopped.

"Ahm goin on t mah home n yuh better go on t yos."

Bobo's eyes grew round.

"Ahm scared!"

"Yuh better go on!"

"Lemme go wid yuh; theyll ketch me . . ."

"Ef yuh kin git home mabbe yo folks kin hep yuh t git erway."

Big Boy started off. Bobo grabbed him.

"Lemme go wid yuh!"

Big Boy shook free.

"Ef yuh stay here theys gonna lynch yuh!" he yelled, running.

After he had gone about twenty-five yards he turned and looked; Bobo was flying through the woods like the wind.

Big Boy slowed when he came to the railroad. He wondered if he ought to go through the streets or down the track. He decided on the tracks. He could dodge a train better than a mob.

He trotted along the ties, looking ahead and back. His cheek itched, and he felt it. His hand came away smeared with blood. He wiped it nervously on his overalls.

When he came to his back fence he heaved himself over. He landed among a flock of startled chickens. A bantam rooster tried to spur him. He slipped and fell in front of the kitchen steps, grunting heavily. The ground was slick with greasy dishwater.

Panting, he stumbled through the doorway.

"Lawd, Big Boy, whuts wrong wid yuh?"

His mother stood gaping in the middle of the floor. Big Boy flopped wordlessly onto a stool, almost toppling over. Pots simmered on the stove. The kitchen smelled of food cooking.

"Whuts the matter, Big Boy?"

Mutely, he looked at her. Then he burst into tears. She came and felt the scratches on his face.

"Whut happened t yuh, Big Boy? Somebody been botherin yuh?"

"They after me, Ma! They after me . . ."

"Who!"

"Ah . . . Ah . . . We . . ."

"Big Boy, whuts wrong wid yuh?"

"He killed Lester n Buck," he muttered simply.

"Killed!"

"Yessum."

"Lester n Buck!"

"Yessum, Ma!"

"How killed?"

"He shot em, Ma!"

"Lawd Gawd in Heaven, have mercy on us all! This is mo trouble, mo trouble," she moaned, wringing her hands.

"An Ah killed im, Ma . . ."

She stared, trying to understand.

"Whut happened, Big Boy?"

"We tried t git our cloes from the tree . . ."

"Whut tree?"

"We wuz swimmin, Ma. N the white woman . . ."

"*White* woman? . . ."

"Yessum. She wuz at the swimmin hole . . ."

"Lawd have mercy! Ah knowed yuh boys wuz gonna keep on till yuh got into somethin like this!"

She ran into the hall.

"Lucy!"

"Mam?"

"C mere!"

"Mam?"

"C mere, Ah say!"

"Whutcha wan, Ma? Ahm sewin."

"Chile, will yuh c mere like Ah ast yuh?"

Lucy came t the door holding an unfinished apron in her hands. When she saw Big Boy's face she looked wildly at her mother.

"Whuts the matter?"

"Wheres Pa?"

"He's out front, Ah reckon."

"Get im, quick!"

"Whuts the matter, Ma?"

"Go git yo Pa, Ah say!"

Lucy ran out. The mother sank into a chair, holding a dish rag. Suddenly, she sat up.

"Big Boy, Ah thought yuh wuz at school?"

Big Boy looked at the floor.

"How come yuh didn't go t school?"

"We went t the woods."

She signed.

"Ah done done all Ah kin fer yuh, Big Boy. Only Gawd kin help yuh now."

"Ma don let em git me; don let em git me . . ."

His father came into the doorway. He stared at Big Boy, then at his wife.

"Whuts Big Boy inter now?" he asked sternly.

"Saul, Big Boys done gone n got inter trouble wid the white folks."

The old man's mouth dropped, and he looked from one to the other.

"Saul, we gotta git im erway from here."

"Open yo mouth n talk! Whut yuh been doin" The old man gripped Big Boy's shoulders and peered at the scratches on his face.

"Me n Lester n Buck n Bobo wuz out on ol man Harveys place swimmin . . ."

"Saul, its a *white* woman!"

Big Boy winced. The old man compressed his lips and stared at his wife. Lucy gaped at her brother as though she had never seen him before.

"Whut happened? Cant yuh all talk?" the old man thundered, with a certain helplessness in his voice.

"We wuz swimmin," Big Boy began, "n then a white woman comes up t the

hole. We got up right erway to git our cloes sos we could git erway, n she started
screamin. Our cloes wuz right by the tree where she wuz standin, n when we
started t git em she jus screamed. We told her we wanted our cloes . . . Yuh
see, Pa she was standin' right *by* our cloes; n when we went t git em she jus
screamed . . . Bobo got the cloes, n then he shot Lester . . ."

"*Who* shot Lester?"

"The white man."

"Whut white man?"

"Ah dunno, Pa. He wuz a soljer, n he had a rifle."

"A soljer?"

"Yessuh."

"A *soljer*?"

"Yessuh, Pa. A soljer."

The old man frowned.

"N then what yuh-all do?"

"Waal, Buck said, 'Hes gotta gun!' N we started runnin. N then he shot Buck,
n he fell in the swimmin hole. We didn't see im no mo . . . He wuz close on us
then. He looked at the white woman n then he started t shoot Bobo. Ah grabbed
the gun, n we started fightin. Bobo jumped on his back. He started beatin Bobo.
Then Ah hit im wid the gun. Then he started at me n Ah shot im. Then we
run . . ."

"Who seen?"

"Nobody."

"Wheres Bobo?"

"He went home."

"Anybody run after yuh-all?"

"Nawsuh."

"Yuh see anybody?"

"Nawsuh. Nobody but a white man. But he didnt see us."

"How long fo yuh-all lef the swimmin hole?"

"Little while ergo."

The old man nervously brushed his hand across his eyes and walked to the
door. His lips moved, but no words came.

"Saul, whut we gonna do?"

"Lucy," began the old man, "go t Brother Sanders n tell im Ah said c mere;
n go to Brother Jenkins n tell im Ah said c mere; n go to Elder Peters n tell im
Ah said c mere. N don say nothin t nobody but whut Ah tol yuh. N when yuh
git thu come straight back. Now go!"

Lucy dropped her apron across the back of a chair and ran down the steps.
The mother bent over, crying and praying. The old man walked slowly over to
Big Boy.

"Big Boy?"

Big Boy swallowed.

"Ahm talkin t yuh!"

"Yessuh."

"How come yuh didnt go t school this mawnin?"

"We went t the woods."

"Didnt yo ma send yuh t school?"

"Yessuh."

"How come yuh didnt go?"

"We went t the woods."

"Don yuh know thas wrong?"

"Yessuh."

"How come yuh go?"

Big Boy looked at his fingers, knotted them, and squirmed in his seat.

"AHM TALKIN T YUH!"

His wife straightened up and said reprovingly:

"Saul!"

The old man desisted, yanking nervously at the shoulder straps of his overalls.

"How long wuz the woman there?"

"Not long."

"Wuz she young?"

"Yessuh. Lika gal."

"Did yuh-all say anythin t her?"

"Nawsuh. We jes said we wanted our cloes."

"N what she say?"

"Nothin, Pa. She jus backed erway t the tree n screamed."

The old man stared, his lips trying to form a question.

"Big Boy, did yuh-all bother her?"

"Nawsuh, Pa. We didnt *touch* her."

"How long fo the white man come up?"

"Right erway."

"Whut he say?"

"Nothin. He jus cussed us."

Abruptly the old man left the kitchen.

"Ma, cant Ah go fo they ketches me?"

"Sauls doin whut he kin."

"Ma, Ma, Ah don want em t ketch me . . ."

"Sauls doin what he kin. Nobody but the good Lawd kin hep us now."

The old man came back with a shotgun and leaned it in a corner. Fascinatedly, Big Boy looked at it.

There was a knock at the front door.

"Liza, see whos there."

She went. They were silent, listening. They could hear her talking.

"Whos there?"

"Me."

"Who?"

"Me, Brother Sanders."

"C mon in. Sauls waitin fer yuh."

Sanders paused in the doorway, smiling.

"Yuh sent fer me, Brother Morrison?"

"Brother Sanders, wes in deep trouble here."

Sanders came all the way into the kitchen.

"Yeah?"

"Big Boy done gone n killed a white man."

Sanders stopped short, then came forward, his face thrust out, his mouth open. His lips moved several times before he could speak.

"A *white* man?"

"They gonna kill me; they gonna kill me!" Big Boy cried, running to the old man.

"Saul, cant we git im erway somewhere?"

"Here now, take it easy; take it easy," said Sanders, holding Big Boy's wrists.

"They gonna kill me; they gonna lynch me!"

Big Boy slipped to the floor. They lifted him to a stool. His mother held him closely, pressing his head to her bosom.

"Whut we gonna do?" asked Sanders.

"Ah done sent fer Brother Jenkins n Elder Peters."

Sanders leaned his shoulders against the wall. Then, as the full meaning of it came to him, he exclaimed:

"Theys gonna git a mob! . . ." His voice broke off and his eyes fell on the shotgun.

Feet came pounding on the steps. They turned toward the door. Lucy ran in crying. Jenkins followed. The old man met him in the middle of the room, taking his hand.

"Wes in bad trouble here, Brother Jenkins. Big Boy's done gone n killed a white man. Yuh-alls gotta hep me . . ."

Jenkins looked hard at Big Boy.

"Elder Peters says hes comin," said Lucy.

"When all this happen?" asked Jenkins.

"Near bout a hour ergo, now," said the old man.

"Whut we gonna do?" asked Jenkins.

"Ah wanna wait till Elder Peters come," said the old man helplessly.

"But we gotta work fas ef we gonna do anythin," said Sanders. "We'll git in trouble jus standin here like this."

Big Boy pulled away from his mother.

"Pa, lemma go now! Lemma go now!"

"Be still, Big Boy!"

"Where kin yuh go?"

"Ah could ketch a freight!"

"Thas *sho* death!" said Jenkins. "They'll be watchin em all!"

"Kin yuh-all hep me wid some money?" the old man asked.

They shook their heads.

"Saul, whut kin we do? Big Boy cant stay here."

There was another knock at the door.

The old man backed stealthily to the shotgun.

"Lucy, go!"

Lucy looked at him, hesitating.

"Ah better go," said Jenkins.

It was Elder Peters. He came in hurriedly.

"Good evenin, everybody!"

"How yuh, Elder?"

"Good evenin."

"How yuh today?"

Peters looked around the crowded kitchen.

"Whuts the matter?"

"Elder, wes in deep trouble," began the old man. "Big Boy n some mo boys . . ."

". . . Lester n Buck n Bobo . . ."

". . . wuz over on ol man Harveys place swimmin . . ."

"N he don like us niggers *none*," said Peters emphatically. He widened his legs and put his thumbs in the armholes of his vest.

". . . n some white woman . . ."

"Yeah?" said Peters, coming closer.

". . . comes erlong n the boys tries t git their cloes where they done lef em under a tree. Waal, she started screamin n all, see? Reckon she thought the boys wuz after her. Then a white man in a soljers suit shoots two of em . . ."

". . . Lester n Buck. . ."

"Huummm," said Peters. "Tha wuz old man Harveys son."

"Harveys son?"

"Yuh mean the one that wuz in the Army?"

"Yuh mean Jim?"

"Yeah," said Peters. "The papers said he wuz here fer a vacation from his regiment. N tha woman the boys saw wuz jus erbout his wife . . ."

They stared at Peters. Now that they knew what white person had been killed, their fears became definite.

"N whut else happened?"

"Big Boy shot the man . . ."

"Harveys *son?*"

"He had t, Elder. He wuz gonna shoot im ef he didnt . . ."

"Lawd!" said Peters. He looked around and put his hat back on.

"How long ergo wuz this?"

"Mighty near an hour, now, Ah reckon."

"Do the white folks know yit?"

"Don know, Elder."

"Yuh-all better git this boy outta here right now," said Peters. "Cause ef yuh don theres gonna be a lynchin . . ."

"Where kin Ah go, Elder?" Big Boy ran up to him.

They crowded around Peters. He stood with his legs wide apart, looking up at the ceiling.

"Mabbe we kin hide im in the church till he kin git erway," said Jenkins.

Peters' lips flexed.

"Naw, Brother, thall never do! Theyll git im there sho. N anyhow, ef they ketch im there itll ruin us all. We gotta git the boy outta town . . ."

Sanders went up to the old man.

"Lissen," he said in a whisper. "Mah son, Will, the one whut drives fer the Magnolia Express Comny, is takin a truck o goods t Chicawgo in the mawnin. If we kin hide Big Boy somewhere till then, we kin put him on the truck . . ."

"Pa, please, lemme go wid Will when he goes in the mawnin," Big Boy begged.

The old man stared at Sanders.

"Yuh reckon thas safe?"

"Its the only thing yuh *kin* do," said Peters.

"But where we gonna hide im till then?"

"Whut time yo boy leavin out in the mawnin?"

"At six."

They wer quiet, thinking. The water kettle on the stove sang.

"Pa, Ah knows where Will passes erlong wid the truck out on Bullards Road. Ah kin hide in one of them ol kilns . . ."

"Where?"

"In one of them kilns we built . . ."

"But they'll git yuh there," wailed the mother.

"But there ain no place else fer im t go."

"Theres some holes big enough fer me t git in n stay till Will comes erlong," said Big Boy. "Please, Pa, lemme go fo they ketches me . . ."

"Let im go!"

"Please, Pa . . ."

The old man breathed heavily.

"Lucy, git his things!"

"Saul, theyll git im out there!" wailed the mother, grabbing Big Boy.

Peters pulled her away.

"Sister Morrison, ef yuh don let im go n git erway from here hes gonna be caught shos theres a Gawd in Heaven!"

Lucy came running with Big Boy's shoes and pulled them on his feet. The old man thrust a battered hat on his head. The mother went to the stove and dumped the skillet of corn pone into her apron. She wrapped it, and unbuttoning Big Boy's overalls, pushed it into his bosom.

"Heres something fer yuh t eat; n pray, Big Boy, cause thas all anybody kin do now . . ."

Big Boy pulled to the door, his mother clinging to him.

"Let im go, Sister Morrison!"

"Run fas, Big Boy!"

Big Boy raced across the yard, scattering the chickens. He paused at the fence and hollered back:

"Tell Bobo where Ahm hidin n tell im t c mon!"

IV

He made for the railroad, running straight toward the sunset. He held his left hand tightly over his heart, holding the hot pone of corn bread there. At times he stumbled over the ties, for his shoes were tight and hurt his feet. His throat burned from thirst; he had had no water since noon.

He veered off the track and trotted over the crest of a hill, following Bullard's Road. His feet slipped and slid in the dust. He kept his eyes straight ahead, fearing every clump of shrubbery, every tree. He wished it were night. If he could only get to the kilns without meeting anyone. Suddenly a thought came to him like a blow. He recalled hearing the old folks tell tales of blood-hounds, and fear made him run slower. None of them had thought of that. Spose blood-houns wuz put on his trail? Lawd! Spose a whole pack of em, foamin n howlin, tore im t pieces? He went limp and his feet dragged. Yeah, thas whut they wuz gonna send after im, blood-houns! N then thered be no way fer im t dodge! Why hadnt Pa let im take tha shotgun? He stopped. He oughta go back n git tha shotgun. And then when the mob came he would take some with him.

In the distance he heard the approach of a train. It jarred him back to a sharp sense of danger. He ran again, his big shoes sopping up and down in the dust. He was tired and his lungs were bursting from running. He wet his lips, wanting water. As he turned from the road across a plowed field he heard the train roaring at his heels. He ran faster, gripped in terror.

He was nearly there now. He could see the black clay on the sloping hillside. Once inside a kiln he would be safe. For a little while, at least. He thought of the shotgun again. If he only had something! Someone to talk to . . . Thas right! Bobo! Bobod be wid im. Hed almost fergot Bobo. Bobod bringa gun; he knowed he would. N tergether they could kill the whole mob. Then in the mawning theyd git inter Will's truck n go far erway, t Chicawgo . . .

He slowed to a walk, looking back and ahead. A light wind skipped over the grass. A beetle lit on his cheek and he brushed it off. Behind the dark pines hung a red sun. Two bats flapped against that sun. He shivered, for he was growing cold; the sweat on his body was drying.

He stopped at the foot of the hill, trying to choose between two patches of black kilns high above him. He went to the left, for there lay the ones he, Bobo, Lester, and Buck had dug only last week. He looked around again; the landscape was bare. He climbed the embankment and stood before a row of black pits sinking four and five feet deep into the earth. He went to the largest and peered in. He stiffened when his ears caught the sound of a whir. He ran back a few steps and poised on his toes. Six foot of snake slid out of the pit and went into coil. Big Boy looked around wildly for a stick. He ran down the slope, peering into the grass. He stumbled over a tree limb. He picked it up and tested it by striking it against the ground.

Warily, he crept back up the slope, his stick poised. When about seven feet from the snake he stopped and waved the stick. The coil grew tighter, the whir sounded louder, and a flat head reared to strike. He went to the right, and the flat head followed him, the blue-black tongue darting forth; he went to the left, and the flat head followed him there too.

He stopped, teeth clenched. He had to kill this snake. Jus had t kill im! This wuz the safest pit on the hillside. He waved the stick again, looking at the snake before, thinking of a mob behind. The flat head reared higher. With stick over shoulder, he jumped in, swinging. The stick sang through the air, catching the snake on the side of the head, sweeping him out of coil. There was a brown writhing mass. Then Big Boy was upon him, pounding blows home, one on top of the other. He fought viciously, his eyes red, his teeth bared in a snarl. He beat till the snake lay still; then he stomped it with his heel, grinding its head into the dirt.

He stopped, limp, wet. The corners of his lips were white with spittle. He spat and shuddered.

Cautiously, he went to the hole and peered. He longed for a match. He imagined whole nests of them in there waiting. He put the stick into the hole and waved it around. Stooping, he peered again. It mus be awright. He looked over the hillside, his eyes coming back to the dead snake. Then he got to his knees and backed slowly into the hole.

When inside he felt there must be snakes about him, ready to strike. It seemed he could see and feel them there, waiting tensely in coil. In the dark he imagined long, white fangs ready to sink into his neck, his side, his legs. He wanted to come out, but kept still. Shucks, he told himself, ef there wuz any snakes in here they sho woulda done bit me by now. Some of his fear left, and he relaxed.

With elbows on ground and chin on palms, he settled. The clay was cold to his knees and thighs, but his bosom was kept warm by the hot pone of corn bread. His thirst returned and he longed for a drink. He was hungry, too. But he did not want to eat the corn pone. Naw, not now. Mabbe after erwhile, after Bobo came. Then theyd both eat the corn pone.

The view from his hole was fringed by the long tufts of grass. He could see all the way to Bullard's Road, and even beyond. The wind was blowing, and in the east the first touch of dusk was rising. Every now and then a bird floated past, a spot of wheeling black printed against the sky. Big Boy sighed, shifted his weight, and chewed at a blade of grass. A wasp droned. He heard number nine, far away and mournful.

The train made him remember how they had dug these kilns on long hot summer days, how they had made boilers out of big tin cans, filled them with water, fixed stoppers for steam, cemented them in holes with wet clay and built fires under them. He recalled how they had danced and yelled when a stopper blew out of a boiler, letting out a big spout of steam and a shrill whistle. There were times when they had the whole hillside blazing and smoking. Yeah, yuh see, Big Boy wuz Casey Jones n wuz speedin it down the gleamin rails of the Southern Pacific. Bobo had number two on the Santa Fe. Buck wuz on the Illinoy Central. Lester the Nickel Plate. Lawd, how they sheveled the wood in! The boiling water would almost jar the cans loose from the clay. More and more pine-knots and dry leaves would be piled under the cans. Flames would grow so tall they would have to shield their eyes. Sweat would pour off their faces. Then, suddenly, a peg would shoot high into the air, and

Pssseeeezzzzzzzzzzzzzzzzz . . .

Big Boy sighed and stretched out his arm, quenching the flames and scattering the smoke. Why didnt Bobo c mon? He looked over the fields; there was nothing but dying sunlight. His mind drifted back to the kilns. He remembered the day when Buck, jealous of his winning, had tried to smash his kiln. Yeah, that ol sonofabitch! Naw, Lawd! He didnt go t say tha! Whut wu he thinkin erbout? Cussin the dead! Yeah, po ol Buck wuz dead now. N Lester too. Yeah, it wuz awright fer Buck t smash his kiln. Sho. N he wished he hadnt socked ol Buck so hard tha day. He wuz sorry fer Buck now. N he sho wished he hadnt cussed po ol Bucks ma, neither. Tha wuz sinful! Mabbe Gawd would git im fer that? But he didnt go t do it! Po Buck! Po Lester! Hed never treat anybody like tha ergin, never. . .

Dusk was slowly deepening. Somewhere, he could not tell exactly where, a cricket took up a fitful song. The air was growing soft and heavy. He looked over the fields, longing for Bobo . . .

He shifted his body to ease the cold damp of the ground, and thought back over the day. Yeah, hed been damn right erbout not wantin t go swimmin. N ef hed followed his right min hed neverve gone n got inter all this trouble. At first hed said naw. But shucks, somehow hed just went on wid the res. Yeah he shoulda went on t school tha mawnin, like Ma told im t do. But, hell, who wouldnt git tireda awways drivin a guy t school! Tha wuz the big trouble awways drivin a guy t school! He wouldnt be in all this trouble now if it wuznt fer that Gawddam school! Impatiently, he took the grass out of his mouth and threw it away, demolishing the little red school house . . .

Yeah, if they had all kept still n quiet when tha ol white woman showed-up, mabbe shedve went on off. But yuh never kin tell erbout these white folks. Mabbe she wouldntve went. Mabbe tha white man woulda killed all of em! All *fo* of em! Yeah, yuh never kin tell erbout white folks. Then, ergin, mabbe tha white woman woulda went on off n laffed. Yeah, mabbe tha white man woulda said: *Yuh nigger bastards git t hell outta here! Yuh know Gawdam well yuh don berlong here!* N then they woulda grabbed their cloes n run like all hell . . . He blinked the white man away. Where wuz Bobo? Why didnt he hurry up n c mon?

He jerked another blade and chewed. Yeah, ef Pa had only let im have tha shotgun! He could stan off a whole mob wid a shotgun. He looked at the ground as he turned a shotgun over in his hands. Then he leveled it at an advancing white man. *Boooom!* The man curled up. Another came. He reloaded quickly, and let him have what the other had got. He too curled up. Then another came. He got the same medicine. Then the whole mob swirled around him, and he blazed away, getting as many as he could. They closed in; but, by Gawd, he had done his part, hadnt he? N the newspapersd say: NIGGER KILLS DOZEN OF MOB BEFO LYNCHED! Er mabbe theyd say: TRAPPED NIGGER SLAYS TWENTY BEFO KILLED! He smiled a little. Tha wouldnt be so bad, would it?

Blinking the newspaper away, he looked over the fields. Where wuz Bobo? Why didnt he hurry up n c mon?

He shifted, trying to get a crick out of his legs. Shucks, he wuz gettin tireda this. N it wuz almos dark now. Yeah, there wuz a little bittie star way over yonder in the eas. Mabbe tha white man wuznt dead? Mabbe they wuznt even lookin fer im? Mabbe he could go back home now? Naw, better wait erwhile. Thad be bes. But, Lawd, ef he only had some water! He could hardly swallow, his throat was so dry. Gawddam them white folks! Thas all they wuz good fer, t run a nigger down lika rabbit! Yeah, they git yuh in a corner n then they let yuh have it. A thousan of em! He shivered, for the cold of the clay was chilling his bones. Lawd, spose they found im here in this hole? N wid nobody t help im? . . . But ain no use in thinkin erbout tha; wait till trouble come fo yuh start fightin it. But if tha mob came one by one hed wipe em all out. Clean up the whole bunch. He caught one by the neck and choked him long and hard, choked him till his tongue and eyes popped out. Then he jumped upon his chest and stomped him like he had stomped that snake. When he had finished with one, another came. He choked him too. Choked till he sank slowly to the ground, gasping . . .

"Hoalo!"

Big Boy snatched his fingers from the white man's neck and looked over the fields. He saw nobody. Had someone spied him? He was sure that somebody had hollered. His heart pounded. But, shucks, nobody couldn't see im here in this hole . . . But mabbe theyd seen im when eh wuz comin n had laid low n wuz now closin in on im! Praps they wuz signalin fer the others? Yeah, they wuz creepin up on im! Mabbe he oughta git up n run . . . Oh! Mabbe tha wuz Bobo! Yeah, Bobo! He oughta clim out n see if Bobo wuz lookin fer im . . . He stiffened.

"Hoalo!"

"Hoalo!"

"Wheres yuh?"

"Over here on Bullards Road!"

"C mon over!"

"Awright!"

He heard footsteps. Then voices came again, low and far away this time.

"Seen anybody?"

"Naw. Yuh?"

"Naw."

"Yuh reckon they got erway?"

"Ah dunno. Its hard t tell."

"Gawddam them sonofabitchin niggers!"

"We oughta kill every black bastard in this country!"

"Waal, Jim got two of em, anyhow."

"But Bertha said there wuz *fo!*"

"Where in hell they hidin?"

"She said one of em wuz named Big Boy, or somethin like tha."

"We went t his shack lookin fer im."

"Yeah?"

"But we didnt fin im."

"These niggers stick tergether; they don never tell on each other."

"We looked all thu the shack n couldnt fin hide ner hair of im. Then we drove the ol woman n man out n set the shack on fire . . ."

"Jeesus! Ah wished Ah coulda been there!"

"Yuh shoulda heard the ol nigger woman howl . . ."

"Hoalo!"

"C mon over!"

Big Boy eased to the edge and peeped. He saw a white man with a gun slung over his shoulder running down the slope. Wuz they gonna search the hill? Lawd, there wuz no way fer im t git erway now; he wuz caught! He shoulda knowed theyd git im here. N he didnt hava thing, notta thing t fight wid. Yeah, soon as the blood-houns came theyd fin im. Lawd, have mercy! Theyd lynch im right here on the hill . . . Theyd git im n tie im t a stake n burn im erlive! Lawd! Nobody but the good Lawd could hep im now, nobody . . .

He heard more feet running. He nestled deeper. His chest ached. Nobody but the good Lawd could hep now. They wuz crowdn all round im n when they hada big crowd theyd close in on im. Then itd be over . . . The good Lawd would have t hep im, cause nobody could hep im now, nobody . . .

And then he went numb when he remembered Bobo. Spose Bobod come now? Hed be caught sho! Both of em would be caught! Theyd make Bobo tell where he wuz! Bobo oughta not try to come now. Somebody oughta tell im . . . But there wuz nobody; there wuz no way . . .

He eased slowly back to the opening. There was a large group of men. More were coming. Many had guns. Some had coils of rope slung over shoulders.

"Ah tell yuh they still here, somewhere . . ."

"But we looked all over!"

"What t hell! Wouldnt do t let em git erway!"

"Naw. Ef they git erway notta woman in this town would be safe."

"Say, whuts tha yuh got?"

"Er pillar."

"Fer whut?"

"Feathers, fool!"

"Chris! Thisll be hot if we kin ketch them niggers!"

"Ol Anderson said he wuz gonna bringa barrela tar!"

"Ah got some gasolin in mah car if yuh need it."

Big Boy had no feelings now. He was waiting. He did not wonder if they were coming after him. He just waited. He did not wonder about Bobo. He rested his cheek against the cold clay, waiting.

A dog barked. He stiffened. It barked again. He balled himself into a knot at the bottom of the hole, waiting. Then he heard the patter of dog feet.

"Look!"

"Whuts he got?"

"Its a snake!"

"Yeah, the dogs foun a snake!"

"Gee, its a big one!"

"Shucks, Ah wish he could fin one of them sonofabitchin niggers!"

The voices sank to low murmurs. Then he heard number twelve, its bell tolling and whistle crying as it slid along the rails. He flattened himself against the clay. Someone was singing:

We'll hang ever nigger t a sour apple tree . . .

When the song ended there was hard laughter. From the other side of the hill he heard the dog barking furiously. He listened. There was more than one dog now. There were many and they were barking their throats out.

"Hush. Ah hear them dogs!"

"When theys barkin like tha theys foun somethin!"

"Here they come over the hill!"

"WE GOT IM! WE GOT IM!"

There came a roar. Tha must be Bobo; tha mus be Bobo . . . In spite of his fear, Big Boy looked. The road, and half of the hilside across the road, were covered with men. A few were at the top of the hill, stenciled against the sky. He could see dark forms moving up the slopes. They were yelling.

"By Gawd, we got im!"

"C mon!"

"Where is he?"

"Theyre bringin im over the hill!"

"Ah got a rope fer im!"

"Say, somebody go n git the others!"

"Where is he? Cant we see im, Mister?"

"They say Berthas comin, too."

"Jack! Jack! Don leave me! Ah wanna see im!"

"Theyre bringin im over the hill, sweetheart!"

"AH WANNA BE THE FIRS T PUT A ROPE ON THA BLACK BASTARDS NECK!"

"Les start the fire!"

"Heat the tar!"

"Ah got some chains t chain im."

"Bring im over this way!"

"Chris, Ah wished Ah hada drink . . ."

Big Boy saw men moving over the hill. Among them was a long dark spot. Tha must be Bobo; tha mus be Bobo theys carryin . . . Theyll git im here. He oughta git up n run. He clamped his teeth and ran his hand across his forehead, bringing it away wet. He tried to swallow, but could not; his throat was dry.

They had started the song again:

We'll hang ever nigger t a sour apple tree . . .

There were women singing now. Their voices made the song round and full. Song waves rolled over the top of pine trees. The sky sagged low, heavy with clouds. Wind was rising. Sometimes cricket cries cut surprisingly across the mob song. A dog had gone to the utmost top of the hill. At each lull of the song his howl floated full into the night.

Big Boy shrank when he saw the first flame light the hillside. Would they see im here? Then he remembered you could not see into the dark if you were standing in the light. As flames leaped higher he saw two men rolling a barrel up the slope.

"Say, gimme a han here, will yuh?"

"Awright, heave!"

"C mon! Straight up! Git t the other end!"

"Ah got the feathers here in this pillar!"

"BRING SOME MO WOOD!"

Big Boy could see the barrel surrounded by flames. The mob fell back, forming a dark circle. Theyd fin im here! He had a wild impulse to climb out and fly across the hills. But his legs would not move. He stared hard, trying to find Bobo. His eyes played over a long, dark spot near the fire. Fanned by wind, flames leaped higher. He jumped. That dark spot had moved. Lawd, thas Bobo; thas Bobo . . .

He smelt the scent of tar, faint at first, then stronger. The wind brought it full into his face, then blew it away. His eyes burned and he rubbed them with his knuckles. He sneezed.

"LES GET SOURVINEERS!"

He saw the mob close in around the fire. Their faces were hard and sharp in the light of the flames. More men and women were coming over the hill. The long, dark spot was smudged out.

"Everybody git back!"

"Look! Hes gotta finger!"

"C MON! GIT THE GALS BACK FROM THE FIRE!"

"He's got one of his ears, see?"

"Whuts the matter!"

"A woman fell out! Fainted, Ah reckon . . ."

The stench of tar permeated the hillside. The sky was black and the wind was blowing hard.

"HURRY UP N BURN THE NIGGER FO IT RAINS!"

Big Boy saw the mob fall back, leaving a small knot of men about the fire. Then, for the first time, he had a full glimpse of Bobo. A black body flashed in the light. Bobo was struggling, twisting; they were binding his arms and legs.

When he saw them tilt the barrel he stiffened. A scream quivered. He knew the tar was on Bobo. The mob fell back. He saw a tar-drenched body glistening and turning.

"THE BASTARDS GOT IT!"

There was a sudden quiet. Then he shrank violently as the wind carried, like a flurry of snow, a widening spiral of white feathers into the night. The flames leaped tall as the trees. The scream came again. Big Boy trembled and looked. The mob was running down the slopes, leaving the fire clear. Then he saw a writhing white mass cradled in yellow flame, and heard screams, one on top of the other, each shriller and shorter than the last. The mob was quiet now, standing still, looking up the slopes at the writhing white mass gradually growing black, growing black in a cradle of yellow flame.

"PO ON MO GAS!"

"Gimme a lif, will yuh!"

Two men were struggling, carrying between them a heavy can. They set it down, tilted it, leaving it so that the gas would trickle down to the hollowed earth around the fire.

Big Boy slid back into the hole, his face buried in clay. He had no feelings now, no fears. He was numb, empty, as though all blood had been drawn from him. Then his muscles flexed taut when he heard a faint patter. A tiny stream of cold water seeped to his knees, making him push back to a drier spot. He looked up; rain was beating in the grass.

"It's rainin!"

"C mon, les git t town!"

". . . don worry, when the fire git thu wid im hell be gone . . ."

"Wait, Charles! Don leave me; its slippery here . . ."

"Ahll take some of yuh ladies back in mah car. . ."

Big Boy heard the dogs barking again, this time closer. Running feet pounded past. Cold water chilled his ankles. He could hear raindrops steadily hissing.

Now a dog was barking at the mouth of the hole, barking furiously, sensing a presence there. He balled himself into a knot and clung to the bottom, his knees and shins buried in water. The bark came louder. He heard paws scraping and felt the hot scent of dog breath on his face. Green eyes glowed and grew nearer as the barking, muffled by the closeness of the hole, beat upon his eardrums. Backing till his shoulders pressed against the clay, he held his breath. He pushed out his hands, his fingers stiff. The dog yawped louder, advancing, his bark rising sharp and thin. Big Boy rose to his knees, his hands before him. Then he flattened out still more against the bottom, breathing lungsful of hot dog scent, breathing it slowly, hard, but evenly. The dog came closer, bringing hotter dog scent. Big Boy could go back no more. His knees were slipping and slopping in the water. He braced himself, ready. Then, he never exactly knew how—he never knew whether he had lunged or the dog had lunged—they were together, rolling in the water. The green eyes were beneath him, between his legs. Dognails bit into his arms. His knees slipped backward and he landed full on the dog; the dog's breath left in a heavy gasp. Instinctively, he fumbled for the throat as he felt the dog twisting between his knees. The dog snarled, long and low, as though gathering strength. Big Boy's hands traveled swiftly over the dog's back, groping for the throat. He felt dognails again and saw green eyes, but his fingers had found the throat. He choked, feeling his fingers sink; he choked, throwing back his head and stiffening his arms. He felt the dog's body heave, felt dognails digging into his loins. With strength flowing from fear, he closed his fingers, pushing his full weight on the dog's throat. The dog heaved again, and lay still . . . Big Boy heard the sound of his own breathing filling the hole, and heard shouts and footsteps above him going past.

For a long time he held the dog, held it long after the last footstep had died out, long after the rain had stopped.

V

Morning found him still on his knees in a puddle of rainwater, staring at the stiff body of a dog. As the air brightened he came to himself slowly. He held still for a long time, as though waking from a dream, as though trying to remember.

The chug of a truck came over the hill. He tried to crawl to the opening. His knees were stiff and a thousand needlelike pains shot from the bottom of his feet to the calves of his legs. Giddiness made his eyes blur. He pulled up and looked. Through brackish light he saw Will's truck standing some twenty-five yards away, the engine running. Will stood on the running board, looking over the slopes of the hill.

Big Boy scuffled out, falling weakly in the wet grass. He tried to call to Will, but his dry throat would make no sound. He tried again.

"Will!"

Will heard, answering:

"Big Boy, c mon!"

He tried to run, and fell. Will came, meeting him in the tall grass.

"C mon," Will said, catching his arm.

They struggled to the truck.

"Hurry up!" said Will, pushing him onto the runningboard.

Will pushed back a square trapdoor which swung above the back of the driver's seat. Big Boy pulled through, landing with a thud on the bottom. On hands and knees he looked around in the semi-darkness.

"Wheres Bobo?"

Big Boy stared.

"Wheres Bobo?"

"They got im."

"When?"

"Las night."

"The mob?"

Big Boy pointed in the direction of a charred sapling on the slope of the opposite hill. Will looked. The trapdoor fell. The engine purred, the gears whined, and the truck lurched forward over the muddy road, sending Big Boy on his side.

For a while he lay as he had fallen, on his side, too weak to move. As he felt the truck swing around a curve he straightened up and rested his back against a stack of wooden boxes. Slowly, he began to make out objects in the darkness. Through two long cracks fell thin blades of daylight. The floor was of smooth steel, and cold to his thighs. Splinters and bits of sawdust danced with the rumble of the truck. Each time they swung around a curve he was pulled over the floor;

he grabbed at corners of boxes to steady himself. Once he heard the crow of a rooster. It made him think of home, of ma and pa. He thought he remembered hearing somewhere that the house had burned, but could not remember where . . . It all seemed unreal now.

He was tired. He dozed, swaying with the lurch. Then he jumped awake. The truck was running smoothly, on gravel. Far away he heard two short blasts from the Buckeye Lumber Mill. Unconsciously, the thought sang through his mind: Its six erclock . . .

The trapdoor swung in. Will spoke through a corner of his mouth.

"How yuh comin?"

"Awright."

"How they git Bobo?"

"He wuz comin over the hill."

"Whut they do?"

"They burnt im . . . Will, Ah wan some water; mah throats like fire . . ."

"Well git some when we pas a fillin station."

Big Boy leaned back and dozed. He jerked awake when the truck stopped. He heard Will get out. He wanted to peep through the trapdoor, but was afraid. For a moment, the wild fear he had known in the hole came back. Spose theyd search n fin im? He quieted when he heard Will's footsteps on the running board. The trapdoor pushed in. Will's hat came through, dripping.

"Take it, quick!"

Big Boy grabbed, spilling water into his face. The truck lurched. He drank. Hard cold lumps of brick rolled into his hot stomach. A dull pain made him bend over. His intestines seemed to be drawing into a tight knot. After a bit it eased, and he sat up, breathing softly.

The truck swerved. He blinked his eyes. The blades of daylight had turned brightly golden. The sun had risen.

The truck sped over the asphalt miles, sped northward, jolting him, shaking out of his bosom the crumbs of corn bread, making them dance with the splinters and sawdust in the golden blades of sunshine.

He turned on his side and slept.

John Cheever (1912–1982)

THE FOURTH ALARM

I sit in the sun drinking gin. It is ten in the morning. Sunday. Mrs. Uxbridge is off somewhere with the children. Mrs. Uxbridge is the housekeeper. She does the cooking and takes care of Peter and Louise.

It is autumn. The leaves have turned. The morning is windless, but the leaves fall by the hundreds. In order to see anything—a leaf or a blade of grass—you have, I think, to know the keenness of love. Mrs. Uxbridge is sixty-three, my wife is away, and Mrs. Smithsonian (who lives on the other side of town) is seldom in the mood these days, so I seem to miss some part of the morning as if the hour had a threshold or a series of thresholds that I cannot cross. Passing a football might do it but Peter is too young and my only football-playing neighbor goes to church.

My wife, Bertha, is expected on Monday. She comes out from the city on Monday and returns on Tuesday. Bertha is a good-looking young woman with a splendid figure. Her eyes, I think, are a little close together and she is sometimes peevish. When the children were young she had a peevish way of disciplining them. "If you don't eat the nice breakfast Mummy has cooked for you before I count three," she would say, "I will send you back to bed. One. Two. *Three. . . .*" I heard it again at dinner. "If you don't eat the nice dinner Mummy has cooked for you before I count three I will send you to bed without any supper. One. Two. Three. . . ." I heard it again. "If you don't pick up your toys before Mummy counts three Mummy will throw them all away. One. Two. Three. . . ." So it went on through the bath and bedtime and one two three was their lullaby. I sometimes thought she must have learned to count when she was an infant and that when the end came she would call a countdown for the Angel of Death. If you'll excuse me I'll get another glass of gin.

When the children were old enough to go to school, Bertha got a job teaching social studies in the sixth grade. This kept her occupied and happy and she said she had always wanted to be a teacher. She had a reputation for strictness. She wore dark clothes, dressed her hair simply, and expected contrition and obedience from her pupils. To vary her life she joined an amateur theatrical group. She played the maid in *Angel Street* and the old crone in *Desmonds Acres*. The friends she made in the theatre were all pleasant people and I enjoyed taking her to their parties. It is important to know that Bertha does not drink. She will take a Dubonnet politely but she does not enjoy drinking.

Through her theatrical friends, she learned that a nude show called *Ozamanides II* was being cast. She told me this and everything that followed. Her teaching contract gave her ten days' sick leave, and claiming to be sick one day she went into New York. *Ozamanides* was being cast at a producer's office in midtown, where she found a line of a hundred or more men and women waiting to be interviewed. She took an unpaid bill out of her pocketbook, and waving this as if it were a letter she bucked the line saying, "Excuse me please, excuse me, I have an appointment. . . ." No one protested and she got quickly to the head of the line, where a secretary took her name, Social Security number, etc. She was told to go into a cubicle and undress. She was then shown into an office where there were four men. The interview, considering the circumstances, was very circumspect. She was told that she would be nude throughout the performance. She would be expected to simulate or perform copulation twice during the performance and participate in a love pile that involved the audience.

I remember the night when she told me all of this. It was in our living room. The children had been put to bed. She was very happy. There was no question about that. "There I was naked," she said, "but I wasn't in the least embarrassed. The only thing that worried me was that my feet might get dirty. It was an old-fashioned kind of place with framed theatre programs on the wall and a big photograph of Ethel Barrymore. There I sat naked in front of these strangers and I felt for the first time in my life that I'd found myself. I found myself in nakedness. I felt like a new woman, a better woman. To be naked and unashamed in front of strangers was one of the most exciting experiences I've ever had. . . ."

I didn't know what to do. I still don't know, on this Sunday morning, what I should have done. I guess I should have hit her. I said she couldn't do it. She said I couldn't stop her. I mentioned the children and she said this experience would make her a better mother. "When I took off my clothes," she said, "I felt as if I had rid myself of everything mean and small." Then I said she'd never get the job because of her appendicitis scar. A few minutes later the phone rang. It was the producer offering her a part. "Oh, I'm so happy," she said. "Oh, how wonderful and rich and strange life can be when you stop playing out the roles that your parents and their friends wrote out for you. I feel like an explorer."

The fitness of what I did then or rather left undone still confuses me. She broke her teaching contract, joined Equity, and began rehearsals. As soon as *Ozamanides* opened she hired Mrs. Uxbridge and took a hotel apartment near the theatre. I asked for a divorce. She said she saw no reason for a divorce. Adultery and cruelty have well-marked courses of action but what can a man do when his wife wants to appear naked on the stage? When I was younger I had known some burlesque girls and some of them were married and had children. However, they did what Bertha was going to do only on the midnight Saturday show, and as I remember their husbands were third-string comedians and the kids always looked hungry.

A day or so later I went to a divorce lawyer. He said a consent decree was my only hope. There are no precedents for simulated carnality in public as grounds for divorce in New York State and no lawyer will take a divorce case without a precedent. Most of my friends were tactful about Bertha's new life. I suppose most of them went to see her, but I put it off for a month or more. Tickets were expensive and hard to get. It was snowing the night I went to the theatre, or what had been a theatre. The proscenium arch had been demolished, the set was a collection of used tires, and the only familiar features were the seats and the aisles. Theatre audiences have always confused me. I suppose this is because you find an incomprehensible variety of types thrust into what was an essentially domestic and terribly ornate interior. There were all kinds there that night. Rock music was playing when I came in. It was that deafening old-fashioned kind of rock they used to play in places like Arthur. At eight-thirty the houselights dimmed, and the cast—there were fourteen—came down the aisles. Sure enough, they were all naked excepting Ozamanides, who wore a crown.

I can't describe the performance. Ozamanides had two sons, and I think he murdered them, but I'm not sure. The sex was general. Men and women embraced one another and Ozamanides embraced several men. At one point a stranger, sitting in the seat on my right, put his hand on my knee. I didn't want to reproach him for a human condition, nor did I want to encourage him. I removed his hand and experienced a deep nostalgia for the innocent movie theatres of my youth. In the little town where I was raised there was one—the Alhambra. My favorite movie was called *The Fourth Alarm*. I saw it first one Tuesday after school and stayed on for the evening show. My parents worried when I didn't come home for supper and I was scolded. On Wednesday I played hooky and was able to see the show twice and get home in time for supper. I went to school on Thursday but I went to the theatre as soon as school closed and sat partway through the evening show. My parents must have called the police, because a patrolman came into the theatre and made me go home. I was forbidden to go to the theatre on Friday, but I spent all Saturday there, and on Saturday the picture ended its run. The picture was about the substitution of automobiles for horsedrawn fire engines. Four fire companies were involved. Three of the teams had been replaced by engines and the miserable horses had been sold to brutes. One team remained, but its days were numbered. The men and the horses were sad. Then suddenly there was a great fire. One saw the first engine, the second, and the third race off to the conflagration. Back at the horse-drawn company, things were very gloomy. Then the fourth alarm rang—it was their summons—and they sprang into action, harnessed the team, and galloped across the city. They put out the fire, saved the city, and were given an amnesty by the Mayor. Now on the stage Ozamanides was writing something obscene on my wife's buttocks.

Had nakedness—its thrill—annihilated her sense of nostalgia? Nostalgia—in spite of her close-set eyes—was one of her principal charms. It was her gift gracefully to carry the memory of some experience into another tense. Did she, mounted in public by a naked stranger, remember any of the places where we had made love—the rented houses close to the sea, where one heard in the sounds of a summer rain the prehistoric promises of love, peacefulness, and beauty? Should I stand up in the theatre and shout for her to return, return, return in the name of love, humor, and serenity? It was nice driving home after parties in the snow, I thought. The snow flew into the headlights and made it seem as if we were going a hundred miles an hour. It was nice driving home in the snow after parties. Then the cast lined up and urged us—commanded us in fact—to undress and join them.

This seemed to be my duty. How else could I approach understanding Bertha? I've always been very quick to get out of my clothes. I did. However, there was a problem. What should I do with my wallet, wristwatch, and car keys? I couldn't safely leave them in my clothes. So, naked, I started down the aisle with my valuables in my right hand. As I came up to the action a naked young man stopped me and shouted—sang—"Put down your lendings. Lendings are impure."

"But it's my wallet and my watch and the car keys," I said.

"Put down your lendings," he sang.

"But I have to drive home from the station," I said, "and I have sixty or seventy dollar in cash."

"Put down your lendings."

"I can't, I really can't. I have to eat and drink and get home."

"Put down your lendings."

Then one by one they all, including Bertha, picked up the incantation. The whole cast began to chant: "Put down your lendings, put down your lendings."

The sense of being unwanted has always been for me acutely painful. I suppose some clinician would have an explanation. The sensation is reverberative and seems to attach itself as the last link in a chain made up of all similar experience. The voices of the cast were loud and scornful, and there I was, buck naked, somewhere in the middle of the city and unwanted, remembering missed football tackles, lost fights, the contempt of strangers, the sound of laughter from behind shut doors. I held my valuables in my right hand, my literal identification. None of it was irreplaceable, but to cast if off would seem to threaten my essence, the shadow of myself that I could see on the floor, my name.

I went back to my seat and got dressed. This was difficult in such a cramped space. The cast was still shouting. Walking up the sloping aisle of the ruined theatre was powerfully reminiscent. I had made the same gentle ascent after *King Lear* and *The Cherry Orchard*. I went outside.

It was still snowing. It looked like a blizzard. A cab was stuck in front of the theatre and I remembered then that I had snow tires. This gave me a sense of security and accomplishment that would have disgusted Ozamanides and his naked court; but I seemed not to have exposed my inhibitions but to have hit on some marvelously practical and obdurate part of myself. The wind flung the snow into my face and so, singing and jingling the car keys, I walked to the train.

QUESTIONS

1. What picture of the narrator did you have after reading the first two paragraphs? What was your response to what he says here?
2. How understandable to you was Bertha's enthusiasm for being naked on stage?
3. Has any movie ever captivated you as *The Fourth Alarm* did the narrator? What seems to have been its appeal for him, and why does he remember it during *Ozamanides?*
4. As the narrator describes his reactions in the theater, did you have any different sense of him from what you had at the beginning? Explain.
5. The narrator has "experienced a deep nostalgia for the innocent movie theatres" of his youth. How innocent is the narrator?

Alice Munro (b. 1931)
THE FOUND BOAT

At the end of Bell Street, McKay Street, Mayo Street, there was the Flood. It was the Wawanash River, which every spring overflowed its banks. Some springs, say one in every five, it covered the roads on that side of town and washed over the fields, creating a shallow choppy lake. Light reflected off the water made everything bright and cold, as it is in a lakeside town, and woke or revived in people certain vague hopes of disaster. Mostly during the late afternoon and early evening, there were people straggling out to look at it, and discuss whether it was still rising, and whether this time it might invade the town. In general, those under fifteen and over sixty-five were most certain that it would.

Eva and Carol rode out on their bicycles. They left the road—it was the end of Mayo Street, past any houses—and rode right into a field, over a wire fence entirely flattened by the weight of the winter's snow. They coasted a little way before the long grass stopped them, then left their bicycles lying down and went to the water.

"We have to find a log and ride on it," Eva said.

"Jesus, we'll freeze our legs off."

"Jesus, we'll freeze our legs off!" said one of the boys who were there too at the water's edge. He spoke in a sour whine, the way boys imitated girls although it was nothing like the way girls talked. These boys—there were three of them—were all in the same class as Eva and Carol at school and were known to them by name (their names being Frank, Bud and Clayton), but Eva and Carol, who had seen and recognized them from the road, had not spoken to them or looked at them or, even yet, given any sign of knowing they were there. The boys seemed to be trying to make a raft, from lumber they had salvaged from the water.

Eva and Carol took off their shoes and socks and waded in. The water was so cold it sent pain up their legs, like blue electric sparks shooting through their veins, but they went on, pulling their skirts high, tight behind and bunched so they could hold them in front.

"Look at the fat-assed ducks in wading."

"Fat-assed fucks."

Eva and Carol, of course, gave no sign of hearing this. They laid hold of a log and climbed on, taking a couple of boards floating in the water for paddles. There were always things floating around in the Flood—branches, fence-rails, logs, road signs, old lumber; sometimes boilers, washtubs, pots and pans, or even a car seat or stuffed chair, as if somewhere the Flood had got into a dump.

They paddled away from shore, heading out into the cold lake. The water was perfectly clear, they could see the brown grass swimming along the bottom. Suppose it was the sea, thought Eva. She thought of drowned cities and countries. Atlantis. Suppose they were riding in a Viking boat—Viking boats on the Atlantic were more frail and narrow than this log on the Flood—and they had miles of clear sea beneath them, then a spired city, intact as a jewel irretrievable on the ocean floor.

"This is a Viking boat," she said. "I am the carving on the front." She stuck her chest out and stretched her neck, trying to make a curve, and she made a face, putting out her tongue. Then she turned and for the first time took notice of the boys.

"Hey, you sucks!" she yelled at them. "You'd be scared to come out here, this water is ten feet deep!"

"Liar," they answered without interest, and she was.

They steered the log around a row of trees, avoiding floating barbed wire, and got into a little bay created by a natural hollow of the land. Where the bay was now, there would be a pond full of frogs later in the spring, and by the middle of summer there would be no water visible at all, just a low tangle of reeds and bushes, green, to show that mud was still wet around their roots. Larger bushes, willows, grew around the steep bank of this pond and were still partly out of the water. Eva and Carol let the log ride in. They saw a place where something was caught.

It was a boat, or part of one. An old rowboat with most of one side ripped out, the board that had been the seat just dangling. It was pushed up among the branches, lying on what would have been its side, if it had a side, the prow caught high.

Their idea came to them without consultation, at the same time:

"You guys! Hey, you guys!"

"We found you a boat!"

"Stop building your stupid raft and come and look at the boat!"

What surprised them in the first place was that the boys really did come, scrambling overland, half running, half sliding down the bank, wanting to see.

"Hey, where?"

"Where is it, I don't see no boat."

What surprised them in the second place was that when the boys did actually see what boat was meant, this old flood-smashed wreck held up in the branches, they did not understand that they had been fooled, that a joke had been played on them. They did not show a moment's disappointment, but seemed as pleased at the discovery as if the boat had been whole and new. They were already barefoot, because they had been wading in the water to get lumber, and they waded in here without a stop, surrounding the boat and appraising it, and paying no attention even of an insulting kind to Eva and Carol who bobbed up and down on their log. Eva and Carol had to call to them.

"How do you think you're going to get it off?'

"It won't float anyway."

"What makes you think it will float?"

"It'll sink. Glub-blub-blub, you'll all be drownded."

The boys did not answer, because they were too busy walking around the boat, pulling at it in a testing way to see how it could be got off with the least possible damage. Frank, who was the most literate, talkative and inept of the three, began referring to the boat as *she*, an affectation which Eva and Carol acknowledged with fish-mouths of contempt.

"She's caught two places. You got to be careful not to tear a hole in her bottom. She's heavier than you'd think."

It was Clayton who climbed up and freed the boat, and Bud, a tall fat boy, who got the weight of it on his back to turn it into the water so that they could half float, half carry it to shore. All this took some time. Eva and Carol abandoned their log and waded out of the water. They walked overland to get their shoes and socks and bicycles. They did not need to come back this way but they came. They stood at the top of the hill, leaning on their bicycles. They did not go on home, but they did not sit down and frankly watch, either. They stood more or less facing each other, but glancing down at the water and at the boys struggling with the boat, as if they had just halted for a moment out of curiosity, and staying longer than they intended, to see what came of this unpromising project.

About nine o'clock, or when it was nearly dark—dark to people inside the houses, but not quite dark outside—they all returned to town, going along Mayo Street in a sort of procession. Frank and Bud and Clayton came carrying the boat, upside-down, and Eva and Carol walked behind, wheeling their bicycles. The boys' heads were almost hidden in the darkness of the overturned boat, with its smell of soaked wood, cold swampy water. The girls could look ahead and see the street lights in their tin reflectors, a necklace of lights climbing Mayo Street, reaching all the way up to the standpipe. They turned onto Burns Street heading for Clayton's house, the nearest house belonging to any of them. This was not the way home for Eva or for Carol either, but they followed along. The boys were perhaps too busy carrying the boat to tell them to go away. Some younger children were still out playing, playing hopscotch on the sidewalk though they could hardly see. At this time of year the bare sidewalk was still such a novelty and delight. These children cleared out of the way and watched the boat go by with unwilling respect; they shouted questions after it, wanting to know where it came from and what was going to be done with it. No one answered them. Eva and Carol as well as the boys refused to answer or even look at them.

The five of them entered Clayton's yard. The boys shifted weight, as if they were going to put the boat down.

"You better take it round to the back where nobody can see it," Carol said. That was the first thing any of them had said since they came into town.

The boys said nothing but went on, following a mud path between Clayton's house and a leaning board fence. They let the boat down in the back yard.

"It's a stolen boat, you know," said Eva, mainly for the effect. "It must've belonged to somebody. You stole it."

"You was the ones who stole it then," Bud said, short of breath. "It was you seen it first."

"It was you took it."

"It was all of us then. If one of us gets in trouble then all of us does."

"Are you going to tell anybody on them?" said Carol as she and Eva rode home, along the streets which were dark between the lights now and potholed from winter.

"It's up to you. I won't if you won't."

"I won't if you won't."

They rode in silence, relinquishing something, but not discontented.

The board fence in Clayton's back yard had every so often a post which supported it, or tried to, and it was on these posts that Eva and Carol spent several evenings sitting, jauntily but not very comfortably. Or else they just leaned against the fence while the boys worked on the boat. During the first couple of evenings neighborhood children attracted by the sound of hammering tried to get into the yard to see what was going on, but Eva and Carol blocked their way.

"Who said you could come in here?"

"Just us can come in this yard."

These evenings were getting longer, the air milder. Skipping was starting on the sidewalks. Further along the street there was a row of hard maples that had been tapped. Children drank the sap as fast as it could drip into the buckets. The old man and woman who owned the trees, and who hoped to make syrup, came running out of the house making noises as if they were trying to scare away crows. Finally, every spring, the old man would come out on his porch and fire his shotgun into the air, and then the thieving would stop.

None of those working on the boat bothered about stealing sap, though all had done so last year.

The lumber to repair the boat was picked up here and there, along back lanes. At this time of year things were lying around—old boards and branches, sodden mitts, spoons flung out with the dishwater, lids of pudding pots that had been set in the snow to cool, all the debris that can sift through and survive winter. The tools came from Clayton's cellar—left over, presumably, from the time when his father was alive—and though they had nobody to advise them the boys seemed to figure out more or less the manner in which boats are built, or rebuilt. Frank was the one who showed up with diagrams from books and *Popular Mechanics* magazines. Clayton looked at these diagrams and listened to Frank read the instructions and then went ahead and decided in his own way what was to be done. Bud was best at sawing. Eva and Carol watched everything from the fence and offered criticism and thought up names. The names for the boat that they thought of were: Water Lily, Sea Horse, Flood Queen, and Caro-Eve, after them because they had found it. The boys did not say which, if any, of these names they found satisfactory.

The boat had to be tarred. Clayton heated up a pot of tar on the kitchen stove and brought it out and painted slowly, his thorough way, sitting astride the overturned boat. The other boys were sawing a board to make a new seat. As Clayton worked, the tar cooled and thickened so that finally he could not move the brush any more. He turned to Eva and held out the pot and said, "You can go in and heat this on the stove."

Eva took the pot and went up the back steps. The kitchen seemed black after outside, but it must be light enough to see in, because there was Clayton's mother standing at the ironing board, ironing. She did that for a living, took in wash and ironing.

"Please may I put the tar pot on the stove?" said Eva, who had been brought up to talk politely to parents, even wash-and-iron ladies, and who for some reason especially wanted to make a good impression on Clayton's mother.

"You'll have to poke up the fire then," said Clayton's mother, as if she doubted whether Eva would know how to do that. But Eva could see now, and she picked up the lid with the stove-lifter, and took the poker and poked up a flame. She stirred the tar as it softened. She felt privileged. Then and later. Before she went to sleep a picture of Clayton came to her mind; she saw him sitting astride the boat, tarpainting, with such concentration, delicacy, absorption. She thought of him speaking to her, out of his isolation, in such an ordinary peaceful taking-for-granted voice.

On the twenty-fourth of May, a school holiday in the middle of the week, the boat was carried out of town, a long way now, off the road over fields and fences that had been repaired, to where the river flowed between its normal banks. Eva and Carol, as well as the boys, took turns carrying it. It was launched in the water from a cow-trampled spot between willow bushes that were fresh out in leaf. The boys went first. They yelled with triumph when the boat did float, when it rode amazingly down the river current. The boat was painted black, and green inside, with yellow seats, and a strip of yellow all the way around the outside. There was no name on it, after all. The boys could not imagine that it needed any name to keep it separate from the other boats in the world.

Eva and Carol ran along the bank, carrying bags full of peanut butter-and-jam sandwiches, pickles, bananas, chocolate cake, potato chips, graham crackers stuck together with corn syrup and five bottles of pop to be cooled in the river water. The bottles bumped against their legs. They yelled for a turn.

"If they don't let us they're bastards," Carol said, and they yelled together, "We found it! We found it!"

The boys did not answer, but after a while they brought the boat in, and Carol and Eva came crashing, panting down the bank.

"Does it leak?"

"It don't leak yet."

"We forgot a bailing can," wailed Carol, but nevertheless she got in, with Eva, and Frank pushed them off, crying, "Here's to a Watery Grave!"

And the thing about being in a boat was that it was not solidly bobbing, like a log, but was cupped in the water, so that riding in it was not like being on something in the water, but like being in the water itself. Soon they were all going out in the boat in mixed-up turns, two boys and a girl, two girls and a boy, a girl and a boy, until things were so confused it was impossible to tell whose turn came next, and nobody cared anyway. They went down the river—those who weren't riding, running along the bank to keep up. They passed under two bridges, one iron, one cement. Once they saw a big carp just resting, it seemed to smile at them, in the bridge-shaded water. They did not know how far they had gone on the river, but things had changed—the water had got shallower, and the land flatter. Across an open field they saw a building that looked like a house, abandoned. They dragged the boat up on the bank and tied it and set out across the field.

"That's the old station," Frank said. "That's Pedder Station." The others had heard this name but he was the one who knew, because his father was the station agent in town. He said that this was a station on a branch line that had been torn up, and that there had been a sawmill here, but a long time ago.

Inside the station it was dark, cool. All the windows were broken. Glass lay in shards and in fairly big pieces on the floor. They walked around finding the larger pieces of glass and tramping on them, smashing them, it was like cracking ice on puddles. Some partitions were still in place, you could see where the ticket window had been. There was a bench lying on its side. People had been here, it looked as if people came here all the time, though it was so far from anywhere. Beer bottles and pop bottles were lying around, also cigarette packages, gum and candy wrappers, the paper from a loaf of bread. The walls were covered with dim and fresh pencil and chalk writings and carved with knives.

I LOVE RONNIE COLES

I WANT TO FUCK

KILROY WAS HERE

RONNIE COLES IS AN ASS-HOLE

WHAT ARE YOU DOING HERE?

WAITING FOR A TRAIN

DAWNA MARY-LOU BARBARA JOANNE

It was exciting to be inside this large, dark, empty place, with the loud noise of breaking glass and their voices ringing back from the underside of the roof. They tipped the old beer bottles against their mouths. That reminded them that they were hungry and thirsty and they cleared a place in the middle of the floor and sat down and ate the lunch. They drank the pop just as it was, lukewarm. They ate everything there was and licked the smears of peanut butter and jam off the bread-paper in which the sandwiches had been wrapped.

They played Truth or Dare.

"I dare you to write on the wall, I am a Stupid Ass, and sign your name."

"Tell the truth—what is the worst lie you ever told?"

"Did you ever wet the bed?"

"Did you ever dream you were walking down the street without any clothes on?"

"I dare you to go outside and pee on the railway sign."

It was Frank who had to do that. They could not see him, even his back, but they knew he did it, they heard the hissing sound of his pee. They all sat still, amazed, unable to think of what the next dare would be.

"I dare everybody," said Frank from the doorway, "I dare—Everybody."

"What?"

"Take off all our clothes."

Eva and Carol screamed.

"Anybody who won't do it has to walk—has to *crawl*—around this floor on their hands and knees."

They were all quiet, till Eva said, almost complacently, "What first?"

"Shoes and socks."

"Then we have to go outside, there's too much glass here."

They pulled off their shoes and socks in the doorway, in the sudden blinding sun. The field before them was bright as water. They ran across where the tracks used to go.

"That's enough, that's enough," said Carol. "Watch out for thistles!"

"Tops! Everybody take off their tops!"

"I won't! We won't, will we, Eva?"

But Eva was whirling round and round in the sun where the track used to be. "I don't care, I don't care! Truth or Dare! Truth or Dare!"

She unbuttoned her blouse as she whirled, as if she didn't know what her hand was doing, she flung it off.

Carol took off hers. "I wouldn't have done it, if you hadn't!"

"Bottoms!"

Nobody said a word this time, they all bent and stripped themselves. Eva, naked first, started running across the field, and then all the others ran, all five of them running bare through the knee-high hot grass, running towards the river. Not caring now about being caught but in fact leaping and yelling to call attention to themselves, if there was anybody to hear or see. They felt as if they were going to jump off a cliff and fly. They felt that something was happening to them different from anything that had happened before, and it had to do with the boat, the water, the sunlight, the dark ruined station, and each other. They thought of each other now hardly as names or people, but as echoing shrieks, reflections, all bold and white and loud and scandalous, and as fast as arrows. They went running without a break into the cold water and when it came almost to the tops of their legs they fell on it and swam. It stopped their noise. Silence, amazement, came over them in a rush. They dipped and floated and separated, sleek as mink.

Eva stood up in the water her hair dripping, water running down her face. She was waist deep. She stood on smooth stones, her feet fairly wide apart, water flowing between her legs. About a yard away from her Clayton also stood up, and they were blinking the water out of their eyes, looking at each other. Eva did not turn or try to hide; she was quivering from the cold of the water, but also with pride, shame, boldness, and exhilaration.

Clayton shook his head violently, as if he wanted to bang something out of it, then bent over and took a mouthful of river water. He stood up with his cheeks full and made a tight hole of his mouth and shot the water at her as if it was coming out of a hose, hitting her exactly, first one breast and then the other. Water from his mouth ran down her body. He hooted to see it, a loud self-conscious sound that nobody would have expected, from him. The others looked up from wherever they were in the water and closed in to see.

Eva crouched down and slid into the water, letting her head go right under. She swam, and when she let her head out, downstream, Carol was coming after her and the boys were already on the bank, already running into the grass, showing their skinny backs, their white, flat buttocks. They were laughing and saying things to each other but she couldn't hear, for the water in her ears.

"What did he do?" said Carol.

"Nothing."

They crept in to shore. "Let's stay in the bushes till they go," said Eva. "I hate them anyway. I really do. Don't you hate them?"

"Sure," said Carol, and they waited, not very long, until they heard the boys still noisy and excited coming down to the place a bit upriver where they had left the boat. They heard them jump in and start rowing.

"They've got all the hard part, going back," said Eva, hugging herself and shivering violently. "Who cares? Anyway. It never was our boat."

"What if they tell?" said Carol.

"We'll say it's all a lie."

Eva hadn't thought of this solution until she said it, but as soon as she did she felt almost light-hearted again. The ease and scornfulness of it did make them both giggle, and slapping themselves and splashing out of the water they set about developing one of those fits of laughter in which, as soon as one showed signs of exhaustion, the other would snort and start up again, and they would make helpless—soon genuinely helpless—faces at each other and bend over and grab themselves as if they had the worst pain.

POETRY

Anonymous (c. 1400?)
I SING OF A MAIDEN

I sing of a maiden
  That is makelees:°   *matchless*
King of alle kinges
  To° her sone she chees.°   *for; chose*

He cam also° stille   *as*
  Ther° his moder° was   *where; mother*
As dewe in Aprille
  That falleth on the gras.

He cam also stille
  To his modres bowr   10
As dewe in Aprille
  That falleth on the flowr.

He cam also stille
  Ther his moder lay
As dewe in Aprille
  That falleth on the spray.

Moder and maiden
  Was nevere noon but she:
Wel may swich° a lady   *such*
  Godes moder be.   20

Anonymous (c. 1400?)
ADAM LAY BOUND

Adam lay ybounden, bounden in a bond,
Four thousand winter thoughte he not too long;
And al was for an apple, an apple that he took
As clerkes finden writen, writen in hire book.
Ne hadde° the apple taken been, the apple taken been,   *Had not*
Ne hadde nevere Oure Lady ybeen hevene Queen.
Blessed be the time that apple taken was:
Therfore we mown° singen *Deo Gratias*.   *may*

John Skelton (1460?–1529)

TO MISTRESS MARGARET HUSSEY

Merry Margaret,
  As midsummer flower,
Gentle as falcon
Or hawk of the tower;[1]
With solace and gladness,
Much mirth and no madness,
All good and no badness;
  So joyously,
  So maidenly,
  So womanly   10
  Her demeaning
  In every thing
  Far, far passing
  That I can endite°,   compose
  Or suffice° to write   am able
Of merry Margaret
  As midsummer flower,
Gentle as falcon
Or hawk of the tower.
  As patient and as still   20
  And as full of good will
  As fair Isaphill;[2]
  Colyander,[3]
  Sweet pomander,[4]
  Good Cassander;[5]
Steadfast of thought,
  Well made, well wrought,
  Far may be sought
  Ere that ye can find
  So courteous, so kind   30
As merry Margaret,
  This midsummer flower,
Gentle as falcon
Or hawk of the tower.

---

[1]In falconry, a hawk is said to "tower" before swooping for prey; the female or young of the goshawk is called a falcon-gentle.
[2]Mythic queen of Lemnos, devoted to her father and children.
[3]Or coriander, an aromatic plant with soothing properties.
[4]Ball of fragrant herbs worn to ward off disease.
[5]Princess and prophetess of ancient Troy.

QUESTIONS

1. To which comparisons in the poem do you respond most strongly?
2. What sense do you have of the speaker's relation to Mistress Margaret Hussey?

Christopher Marlowe (1564–1593)

THE PASSIONATE SHEPHERD TO HIS LOVE

Come live with me and be my love,
And we will all the pleasures prove
That valleys, groves, hills, and fields,
Woods, or steepy mountain yields.

And we will sit upon the rocks,
Seeing the shepherds feed their flocks,
By shallow rivers to whose falls
Melodious birds sing madrigals.

And I will make thee beds of roses
And a thousand fragrant posies,   10
A cap of flowers, and a kirtle°   skirt
Embroidered all with leaves of myrtle;

A gown made of the finest wool
Which from our pretty lambs we pull;
Fair lined slippers for the cold,
With buckles of the purest gold;

A belt of straw and ivy buds,
With coral clasps and amber studs:
And if these pleasures may thee move,
Come live with me, and be my love.   20

The shepherds' swains shall dance and sing
For thy delight each May morning:
If these delights thy mind may move,
Then live with me and be my love.

QUESTIONS

1. Does the speaker in the poem sound like a simple man, or a shepherd, to you? Explain.
2. What do the gifts and pleasures promised tell you about the "shepherd" and his love?
3. How do you picture the girl or woman addressed?

Sir Walter Raleigh (1552?–1618)
THE NYMPH'S REPLY TO THE SHEPHERD

If all the world and love were young,
And truth in every shepherd's tongue,
These pretty pleasures might me move
To live with thee and be thy love.

Time drives the flocks from field to fold
When rivers rage and rocks grow cold,
And Philomel° becometh dumb;   the nightingale
The rest complains of cares to come.

The flowers do fade, and wanton fields
To wayward winter reckoning yields;   10
A honey tongue, a heart of gall,
Is fancy's spring, but sorrow's fall.

Thy gowns, thy shoes, thy beds of roses,
Thy cap, thy kirtle, and thy posies
Soon break, soon wither, soon forgotten—
In folly ripe, in reason rotten.

Thy belt of straw and ivy buds,
Thy coral clasps and amber studs,
All these in me no means can move
To come to thee and be thy love.   20

But could youth last and love still breed,
Had joys no date° nor age no need,   end
Then these delights my mind might move
To live with thee and be thy love.

QUESTIONS

1. What sort of voice do you hear speaking and in what tone? Do you imagine a "nymph,"
   or lovely young maiden? Explain.
2. What does this speaker imply about the shepherd of the other poem?
3. What is the effect of the last stanza?

William Blake (1757–1827)
THE LAMB

    Little Lamb, who made thee?
    Dost thou know who made thee?
Gave thee life & bid thee feed,
By the stream & o'er the mead;
Gave thee clothing of delight,
Softest clothing wooly bright;
Gave thee such a tender voice,
Making all the vales rejoice!
    Little Lamb who made thee?
    Dost thou know who made thee?   10

    Little Lamb I'll tell thee,
    Little Lamb I'll tell thee!
He is calléd by thy name,
For he calls himself a Lamb:
He is meek & he is mild,
He became a little child:
I a child & thou a lamb,
We are calléd by his name.
    Little Lamb God bless thee.
    Little Lamb God bless thee.   20

QUESTIONS

1. How does the poem sound to you when you read it aloud?
2. What associations does the image of a lamb have for you?
3. When you consider the details of the poem, which of these associations appear relevant and which may not be?

William Blake [1757–1827]
THE TYGER

Tyger! Tyger! burning bright
In the forests of the night,
What immortal hand or eye
Could frame thy fearful symmetry?

In what distant deeps or skies
Burnt the fire of thine eyes?
On what wings dare he aspire?
What the hand, dare seize the fire?

And what shoulder, & what art,
Could twist the sinews of thy heart?   10
And when thy heart began to beat,
What dread hand? & what dread feet?

What the hammer? what the chain?
In what furnace was thy brain?
What the anvil? what dread grasp
Dare its deadly terrors clasp?

When the stars threw down their spears,
And water'd heaven with their tears,
Did he smile his work to see?
Did he who made the Lamb make thee?   20

Tyger! Tyger! burning bright
In the forests of the night,
What immortal hand or eye
Dare frame thy fearful symmetry?

QUESTIONS

1. How different is the voice in this poem from that in "The Lamb"?
2. What associations does the word "Tyger" (Blake's spelling) have for you?
3. What seems important about the questions asked or the way they are asked?
4. How significant does it seem that this poem, unlike "The Lamb," begins and ends with a question?

William Blake (1757–1827)

THE LITTLE BLACK BOY

My mother bore me in the southern wild,
And I am black, but O! my soul is white;
White as an angel is the English child:
But I am black as if bereav'd of light.

My mother taught me underneath a tree,
And sitting down before the heat of day,

She took me on her lap and kisséd me,
And pointing to the east, began to say:

"Look on the rising sun: there God does live,
And gives his light, and gives his heat away;   10
And flowers and trees and beasts and men receive
Comfort in morning, joy in the noon day.

"And we are put on earth a little space,
That we may learn to bear the beams of love,
And these black bodies and this sun-burnt face
Is but a cloud, and like a shady grove.

"For when our souls have learn'd the heat to bear,
The cloud will vanish; we shall hear his voice,
Saying: 'Come out from the grove, my love & care,
And round my golden tent like lambs rejoice.' "   20

Thus did my mother say, and kisséd me;
And thus I say to little English boy:
When I from black and he from white cloud free,
And round the tent of God like lambs we joy,

I'll shade him from the heat till he can bear
To lean in joy upon our father's knee;
And then I'll stand and stroke his silver hair,
And be like him, and he will then love me.

William Wordsworth (1770–1850)

LINES COMPOSED A FEW MILES ABOVE TINTERN ABBEY ON REVISITING THE BANKS OF THE WYE DURING A TOUR. JULY 13, 1798[1]

Five years have passed; five summers, with the length
Of five long winters! and again I hear
These waters, rolling from their mountain-springs
With a soft inland murmur. Once again
Do I behold these steep and lofty cliffs,
That on a wild secluded scene impress

---

[1]Wordsworth wrote this poem while on a walking tour through the Wye valley with his sister Dorothy.

Thoughts of more deep seclusion; and connect
The landscape with the quiet of the sky.
The day is come when I again repose
Here, under this dark sycamore, and view   10
These plots of cottage ground, these orchard tufts,
Which at this season, with their unripe fruits,
Are clad in one green hue, and lose themselves
'Mid groves and copses. Once again I see
These hedgerows, hardly hedgerows, little lines
Of sportive wood run wild; these pastoral farms,
Green to the very door; and wreaths of smoke
Sent up, in silence, from among the trees!
With some uncertain notice, as might seem
Of vagrant dwellers in the houseless woods,   20
Or of some Hermit's cave, where by his fire
The Hermit sits alone.

                                        These beauteous forms,
Through a long absence, have not been to me
As is a landscape to a blind man's eye;
But oft, in lonely rooms, and 'mid the din
Of towns and cities, I have owed to them
In hours of weariness, sensations sweet,
Felt in the blood, and felt along the heart;
And passing even into my purer mind,
With tranquil restoration—feelings too   30
Of unremembered pleasure; such, perhaps,
As have no slight or trivial influence
On that best portion of a good man's life,
His little, nameless, unremembered, acts
Of kindness and of love. Nor less, I trust,
To them I may have owed another gift,
Of aspect more sublime; that blessed mood,
In which the burthen of the mystery,
In which the heavy and the weary weight
Of all this unintelligible world,   40
Is lightened—that serene and blessed mood,
In which the affections gently lead us on—
Until, the breath of this corporeal frame
And even the motion of our human blood
Almost suspended, we are laid asleep
In body, and become a living soul;
While with an eye made quiet by the power
Of harmony, and the deep power of joy,
We see into the life of things.

                    If this
Be but a vain belief, yet, oh! how oft—   50
In darkness and amid the many shapes
Of joyless daylight; when the fretful stir
Unprofitable, and the fever of the world,
Have hung upon the beatings of my heart—
How oft, in spirit, have I turned to thee,
O sylvan Wye! thou wanderer through the woods,
How often has my spirit turned to thee!

    And now, with gleams of half-extinguished thought
With many recognitions dim and faint,
And somewhat of a sad perplexity,   60
The picture of the mind revives again;
While here I stand, not only with the sense
Of present pleasure, but with pleasing thoughts
That in this moment there is life and food
For future years. And so I dare to hope,
Though changed, no doubt, from what I was when first
I came among these hills; when like a roe
I bounded o'er the mountains, by the sides
Of the deep rivers, and the lonely streams,
Wherever nature led—more like a man   70
Flying from something that he dreads than one
Who sought the thing he loved. For nature then
(The coarser pleasures of my boyish days,
And their glad animal movements all gone by)
To me was all in all.—I cannot paint
What then I was. The sounding cataract
Haunted me like a passion; the tall rock,
The mountain, and the deep and gloomy wood,
Their colors and their forms, were then to me
An appetite; a feeling and a love,   80
That had no need of a remoter charm,
By thought supplied, nor any interest
Unborrowed from the eye.—That time is past,
And all its aching joys are now no more,
And all its dizzy raptures. Not for this
Faint° I, nor mourn nor murmur; other gifts   yearn
Have followed; for such loss, I would believe,
Abundant recompense. For I have learned
To look on nature, not as in the hour
Of thoughtless youth; but hearing oftentimes   90
The still, sad music of humanity,
Nor harsh nor grating, though of ample power

To chasten and subdue. And I have felt
A presence that disturbs me with the joy
Of elevated thoughts; a sense sublime
Of something far more deeply interfused,
Whose dwelling is the light of setting suns,
And the round ocean and the living air,
And the blue sky, and in the mind of man:
A motion and a spirit, that impels   100
All thinking things, all objects of all thought,
And rolls through all things. Therefore am I still
A lover of the meadows and the woods,
And mountains; and of all that we behold
From this green earth; of all the mighty world
Of eye, and ear—both what they half create,
And what perceive; well pleased to recognize
In nature and the language of the sense
The anchor of my purest thoughts, the nurse,
The guide, the guardian of my heart, and soul   110
Of all my moral being.

                    Nor perchance,
If I were not thus taught, should I the more
Suffer my genial spirits to decay:
For thou art with me here upon the banks
Of this fair river; thou my dearest Friend,
My dear, dear Friend; and in thy voice I catch
The language of my former heart, and read
My former pleasures in the shooting lights
Of thy wild eyes. Oh! yet a little while
May I behold in thee what I was once,   120
My dear, dear Sister! and this prayer I make,
Knowing that Nature never did betray
The heart that loved her; 'tis her privilege,
Through all the years of this our life, to lead
From joy to joy: for she can so inform
The mind that is within us, so impress
With quietness and beauty, and so feed
With lofty thoughts, that neither evil tongues,
Rash judgments, nor the sneers of selfish men,
Nor greetings where no kindness is, nor all   130
The dreary intercourse of daily life,
Shall e'er prevail against us, or disturb
Our cheerful faith, that all which we behold
Is full of blessings. Therefore let the moon
Shine on thee in thy solitary walk;
And let the misty mountain winds be free

To blow against thee: and, in after years,
When these wild ecstasies shall be matured
Into a sober pleasure; when thy mind
Shall be a mansion for all lovely forms,   140
Thy memory be as a dwelling place
For all sweet sounds and harmonies; oh! then,
If solitude, or fear, or pain, or grief
Should be thy portion, with what healing thoughts
Of tender joy wilt thou remember me,
And these my exhortations! Nor, perchance—
If I should be where I no more can hear
Thy voice, nor catch from thy wild eyes these gleams
Of past existence—wilt thou then forget
That on the banks of this delightful stream   150
We stood together; and that I, so long
A worshiper of Nature, hither came
Unwearied in that service; rather say
With warmer love—oh! with far deeper zeal
Of holier love. Nor wilt thou then forget,
That after many wanderings, many years
Of absence, these steep woods and lofty cliffs,
And this green pastoral landscape, were to me
More dear, both for themselves and for thy sake!

QUESTIONS

1. Have you had any experience with nature that the poem recalls and that contributes to your understanding of it? Explain.
2. What tone do you hear in the speaker's voice? How much does the tone vary over the course of the poem?
3. What kinds of experience, apart from those of rural nature, does the speaker indicate he has had?
4. What does his sister's presence seem to mean to him?

John Keats (1795–1821)

ON FIRST LOOKING INTO CHAPMAN'S HOMER[1]

Much have I travelled in the realms of gold,
And many goodly states and kingdoms seen:

---

[1]George Chapman, a contemporary of Shakespeare, translated *The Iliad* (1611) and *The Odyssey* (1616) into English.

Round many western islands have I been
Which bards in fealty to Apollo° hold.   god of poetry
Oft of one wide expanse had I been told
That deep-browed Homer ruled as his demesne,°   domain
Yet did I never breathe its pure serene°   air
Till I heard Chapman speak out loud and bold:
Then felt I like some watcher of the skies
When a new planet swims into his ken;   10
Or like stout Cortez[2] when with eagle eyes
He stared at the Pacific—and all his men
Looked at each other with a wild surmise—
    Silent, upon a peak in Darien.

Robert Browning (1812–1889)
MY LAST DUCHESS

FERRARA

That's my last Duchess painted on the wall,
Looking as if she were alive. I call
That piece a wonder, now: Frà Pandolf's[1] hands
Worked busily a day, and there she stands.
Will't please you sit and look at her? I said
"Frà Pandolf" by design, for never read
Strangers like you that pictured countenance,
The depth and passion of its earnest glance,
But to myself they turned (since none puts by
The curtain I have drawn for you, but I)   10
And seemed as they would ask me, if they durst,
How such a glance came there; so, not the first
Are you to turn and ask thus. Sir, 'twas not
Her husband's presence only, called that spot
Of joy into the Duchess' cheek: perhaps
Frà Pandolf chanced to say "Her mantle laps
"Over my lady's wrist too much," or "Paint
"Must never hope to reproduce the faint
"Half-flush that dies along her throat": such stuff

---

[2]Balboa, not Cortez, actually first viewed the Pacific from Darien, in Panama.
My Last Duchess
[1]A fictitious artist, like "Claus of Innsbruck" in the last line.

Was courtesy, she thought, and cause enough   20
For calling up that spot of joy. She had
A heart—how shall I say?—too soon made glad,
Too easily impressed; she liked whate'er
She looked on, and her looks went everywhere.
Sir, 'twas all one! My favor at her breast,
The dropping of the daylight in the West,
The bough of cherries some officious fool
Broke in the orchard for her, the white mule
She rode with round the terrace—all and each
would draw from her alike the approving speech,   30
Or blush, at least. She thanked men—good! but thanked
Somehow—I know not how—as if she ranked
My gift of a nine-hundred-years-old name
With anybody's gift. Who'd stoop to blame
This sort of trifling? Even had you skill
In speech—which I have not—to make your will
Quite clear to such an one, and say, "Just this
"Or that in you disgusts me; here you miss,
"Or there exceed the mark"—and if she let
Herself be lessoned so, nor plainly set
Her wits to yours, forsooth, and made excuse,   40
—E'en then would be some stooping; and I choose
Never to stoop. Oh sir, she smiled, no doubt,
Whene'er I passed her; but who passed without
Much the same smile? This grew; I gave commands;
Then all smiles stopped together. There she stands
As if alive. Will't please you rise? We'll meet
The company below, then. I repeat,
The Count your master's known munificence
Is ample warrant that no just pretense   50
Of mine for dowry will be disallowed;
Though his fair daughter's self, as I avowed
At starting, is my object. Nay, we'll go
Together down, sir. Notice Neptune, though,
Taming a sea-horse, thought a rarity,
Which Claus of Innsbruck cast in bronze for me!

QUESTIONS

1. What picture of the Duchess does your imagination paint as the Duke speaks of her?
2. What emotions, if any, do you hear in the Duke's voice? What do you make of his character?
3. Does the silent presence of another person, along with his reason for being in Ferrara, create any particular effect? Explain.

Walt Whitman (1819–1892)
THERE WAS A CHILD WENT FORTH

There was a child went forth every day,
And the first object he looked upon, that object he became,
And that object became part of him for the day or a certain
    part of the day,
Or for many years or stretching cycles of years.

The early lilacs became part of this child,
And grass and white and red morning-glories, and white
    and red clover, and the song of the phoebe-bird,
And the Third-month lambs and the sow's pink-faint litter,
    and the mare's foal and the cow's calf,
And the noisy brood of the barnyard or by the mire of the
    pond-side,
And the fish suspending themselves so curiously below
    there, and the beautiful curious liquid,
And the water-plants with their graceful flat heads, all
    became part of him.   10

The field-sprouts of Fourth-month and Fifth-month became
    part of him,
Winter-grain sprouts and those of the light-yellow corn,
    and the esculent° roots of the garden,
And the apple-trees covered with blossoms and the fruit
    afterward, and woodberries, and the commonest weeds
    by the road,
And the old drunkard staggering home with the outhouse
    of the tavern whence he had lately risen,
And the schoolmistress that passed on her way to the
    school,
And the friendly boys that passed, and the quarrelsome
    boys,
And the tidy and fresh-cheeked girls, and the barefoot
    negro boy and girl,
And all the changes of city and country wherever he went.

His own parents, he that had fathered him and she that had
    conceived him in her womb and birthed him,
They gave this child more of themselves than that,   20
They gave him afterward every day, they became part of
    him.

The mother at home quietly placing the dishes on the
    supper-table,

The mother with mild words, clean her cap and gown, a
    wholesome odor falling off her person and clothes as she
    walks by,
The father, strong, self-sufficient, manly, mean, angered,
    unjust,
The blow, the quick loud word, the tight bargain, the crafty
    lure,
The family usages, the language, the company, the
    furniture, the yearning and swelling heart,
Affection that will not be gainsayed, the sense of what is
    real, the thought if after all it should prove unreal,
The doubts of day-time and the doubts of night-time, the
    curious whether and how,
Whether that which appears so is so, or is it all flashes and
    specks?
Men and women crowding fast in the streets, if they are
    not flashes and specks what are they?   30
The streets themselves and the façades of houses, and goods
    in the windows,
Vehicles, teams, the heavy-planked wharves, the huge
    crossing at the ferries,
The village on the highland seen from afar at sunset, the
    river between,
Shadows, aureola and mist, the light falling on roofs and
    gables of white or brown two miles off,
The schooner near by sleepily dropping down the tide, the
    little boat slack-towed astern,
The hurrying tumbling waves, quick-broken crests,
    slapping,
The strata of colored clouds, the long bar of maroon-tint
    away solitary by itself, the spread of purity it lies
    motionless in,
The horizon's edge, the flying sea-crow, the fragrance of
    salt marsh and shore mud,
These became part of that child who went forth every day,
    and who now goes, and will always go forth every day.

Thomas Hardy (1840–1928)

THE OXEN

Christmas Eve, and twelve of the clock.
  "Now they are all on their knees,"

An elder said as we sat in a flock
  By the embers in hearthside ease.

We pictured the meek mild creatures where
  They dwelt in their strawy pen,
Nor did it occur to one of us there
  To doubt they were kneeling then.

So fair a fancy few would weave
  In these years! Yet, I feel,
If someone said on Christmas Eve,   10
  "Come; see the oxen kneel,

"In the lonely barton° by yonder coomb°   farmyard; valley
  Our childhood used to know,"
I should go with him in the gloom,
  Hoping it might be so.

Gerard Manley Hopkins (1844–1889)

SPRING

Nothing is so beautiful as spring—
  When weeds, in wheels, shoot long and lovely and lush;
  Thrush's eggs look little low heavens, and thrush
Through the echoing timber does so rinse and wring
The ear, it strikes like lightnings to hear him sing;
  The glassy peartree leaves and blooms, they brush
  The descending blue; that blue is all in a rush
With richness; the racing lambs too have fair their fling.

What is all this juice and all this joy?
  A strain of the earth's sweet being in the beginning   10
In Eden garden.—Have, get, before it cloy,

  Before it cloud, Christ, lord, and sour with sinning,
Innocent mind and Mayday in girl and boy,
  Most, O maid's child, thy choice and worthy the
  winning.

QUESTIONS

1. When you read the poem aloud, do you respond to it primarily by imagining the visible
   beauty of spring? Explain.

2. How often do you find yourself having to stop to consider word choice, grammar, or syntax? If so, does the sense become clearer? Give an example.
3. How does the speaker come to address Christ at the end of the poem?

Gerard Manley Hopkins (1844–1889)
SPRING AND FALL

to a young child

Márgarét, áre you grieving
Over Goldengrove unleaving?°   dropping leaves
Leáves, líke the things of man, you
With your fresh thoughts care for, can you?
Áh! ás the heart grows older
It will come to such sights colder
By and by, nor spare a sigh
Though worlds of wanwood leafmeal lie;[1]
And yet you *will* weep and know why.
Now no matter, child, the name: 10
Sórrow's spríngs áre the same.
Nor mouth had, no nor mind expressed
What heart heard of, ghost° guessed: spirit
It ís the blight man was born for,
It is Margaret you mourn for.

QUESTIONS

1. What do you suppose Goldengrove is?
2. What do you infer about the speaker's attitude towards nature?
3. How does the speaker imagine Margaret in future years?
4. Is he amused by the child's weeping? What is his tone in addressing her?

Robert Frost (1874–1963)
BIRCHES

When I see birches bend to left and right
Across the lines of straighter darker trees,
I like to think some boy's been swinging them.

---

[1]Probably pale woods with leaves fallen and crumbled.

But swinging doesn't bend them down to stay
As ice storms do. Often you must have seen them
Loaded with ice a sunny winter morning
After a rain. They click upon themselves
As the breeze rises, and turn many-colored
As the stir cracks and crazes their enamel.
Soon the sun's warmth makes them shed crystal shells   10
Shattering and avalanching on the snow crust—
Such heaps of broken glass to sweep away
You'd think the inner dome of heaven had fallen.
They are dragged to the withered bracken by the load,
And they seem not to break; though once they are bowed
So low for long, they never right themselves:
You may see their trunks arching in the woods
Years afterwards, trailing their leaves on the ground
Like girls on hands and knees that throw their hair
Before them over their heads to dry in the sun.   20
But I was going to say when Truth broke in
With all her matter of fact about the ice storm,
I should prefer to have some boy bend them
As he went out and in to fetch the cows—
Some boy too far from town to learn baseball,
Whose only play was what he found himself,
Summer or winter, and could play alone.
One by one he subdued his father's trees
By riding them down over and over again
Until he took the stiffness out of them,   30
And not one but hung limp, not one was left
For him to conquer. He learned all there was
To learn about not launching out too soon
And so not carrying the tree away
Clear to the ground. He always kept his poise
To the top branches, climbing carefully
With the same pains you use to fill a cup
Up to the brim, and even above the brim.
Then he flung outward, feet first, with a swish,
Kicking his way down through the air to the ground.   40
So was I once myself a swinger of birches.
And so I dream of going back to be.
It's when I'm weary of considerations,
And life is too much like a pathless wood
Where your face burns and tickles with the cobwebs
Broken across it, and one eye is weeping
From a twig's having lashed across it open.
I'd like to get away from earth awhile

And then come back to it and begin over.
May no fate willfully misunderstand me   50
And half grant what I wish and snatch me away
Not to return. Earth's the right place for love:
I don't know where it's likely to go better.
I'd like to go by climbing a birch tree,
And climb black branches up a snow-white trunk
Toward heaven, till the tree could bear no more,
But dipped its top and set me down again.
That would be good both going and coming back.
One could do worse than be a swinger of birches.

QUESTIONS

1. Does any experience you have had contribute to your response to this poem? Describe it.
2. Who do you suppose is the "you" addressed by the speaker?
3. Is the boy in the poem someone the speaker imagines or remembers? What details suggest who the boy is?
4. How do you picture the speaker? If you picture him as no longer young, does his talk of climbing a birch once again bother you? Explain how you understand what he means.

Robert Frost (1874–1963)

NOTHING GOLD CAN STAY

Nature's first green is gold,
Her hardest hue to hold.
Her early leaf's a flower;
But only so an hour.
Then leaf subsides to leaf.
So Eden sank to grief,
So dawn goes down to day.
Nothing gold can stay.

William Carlos Williams (1883–1963)

RALEIGH WAS RIGHT

We cannot go to the country
for the country will bring us no peace
What can the small violets tell us

that grow on furry stems in
the long grass among lance shaped leaves?

Though you praise us
and call to mind the poets
who sung of our loveliness
it was long ago!
long ago! when country people   10
would plow and sow with
flowering minds and pockets at ease—
if ever this were true.

Not now. Love itself a flower
with roots in a parched ground.
Empty pockets make empty heads.
Cure it if you can but
do not believe that we can live
today in the country
for the country will bring us no peace.   20

T. S. Eliot (1888–1965)
JOURNEY OF THE MAGI[1]

'A cold coming we had of it,
Just the worst time of the year
For a journey, and such a long journey:
The ways deep and the weather sharp,
The very dead of winter.'[2]
And the camels galled, sore-footed, refractory,
Lying down in the melting snow.
There were times we regretted
The summer palaces on slopes, the terraces,
And the silken girls bringing sherbet.   10
Then the camel men cursing and grumbling
And running away, and wanting their liquor and women,

---

[1]The wise men who followed the star to Bethlehem, as told in Matthew 2.
[2]These first five lines adapt words from a 1622 Christmas sermon by the English Bishop
Lancelot Andrewes.

And the night-fires going out, and the lack of shelters,
And the cities hostile and the towns unfriendly
And the villages dirty and charging high prices:
A hard time we had of it.
At the end we preferred to travel all night,
Sleeping in snatches,
With the voices singing in our ears, saying   20
That this was all folly.

   Then at dawn we came down to a temperate valley,
Wet, below the snow line, smelling of vegetation;
With a running stream and a water-mill beating the
   darkness,
And three trees on the low sky,
And an old white horse galloped away in the meadow.
Then we came to a tavern with vine-leaves over the lintel,
Six hands at an open door dicing for pieces of silver,
And feet kicking the empty wine-skins.
But there was no information, and so we continued
And arrived at evening, not a moment too soon   30
Finding the place; it was (you may say) satisfactory.

   All this was a long time ago, I remember,
And I would do it again, but set down
This set down
This: were we led all that way for
Birth or Death? There was a Birth, certainly,
We had evidence and no doubt. I had seen birth and death,
But had thought they were different; this Birth was
Hard and bitter agony for us, like Death, our death.
We returned to our places, these Kingdoms,   40
But no longer at ease here, in the old dispensation,
With an alien people clutching their gods.
I should be glad of another death.

QUESTIONS

1. What do your previous ideas about the journey of the magi, or wise men, to Bethlehem contribute to your response to this poem?
2. What do the images of the middle group of lines (the three trees on the low sky, the hands dicing for silver, the empty wine-skins) suggest to you? How relevant do these suggestions seem to the rest of the poem?
3. What is the speaker's tone, and what effect on him has his experience had?

e. e. cummings (1894–1962)
IN JUST-

in Just-
spring   when the world is mud-
luscious the little
lame balloonman

whistles   far   and wee

and eddieandbill come
running from marbles and
piracies and it's
spring

when the world is puddle-wonderful   10

the queer
old balloonman whistles
far   and   wee
and bettyandisbel come dancing

from hop-scotch and jump-rope and

it's
spring
and
    the

        goat-footed   20

balloonMan   whistles
far
and
wee

Countee Cullen (1903–1946)
FOR A LADY I KNOW

She even thinks that up in heaven
    Her class lies late and snores,

While poor black cherubs rise at seven
  To do celestial chores.

Countee Cullen (1903–1946)

INCIDENT

Once riding in old Baltimore,
  Heart-filled, head-filled with glee,
I saw a Baltimorean
  Keep looking straight at me.

Now I was eight and very small,
  And he was no whit bigger,
And so I smiled, but he poked out
  His tongue, and called me, "Nigger."

I saw the whole of Baltimore
  From May until December;   10
Of all the things that happened there
  That's all that I remember.

Theodore Roethke (1908–1963)

THE MEADOW MOUSE

1

In a shoe box stuffed in an old nylon stocking
Sleeps the baby mouse I found in the meadow,
Where he trembled and shook beneath a stick
Till I caught him up by the tail and brought him in,
Cradled in my hand,
A little quaker, the whole body of him trembling,
His absurd whiskers sticking out like a cartoon-mouse,
His feet like small leaves,
Little lizard-feet,
Whitish and spread wide when he tried to struggle away,   10
Wriggling like a miniscule puppy.

Now he's eaten his three kinds of cheese and drunk from
  his bottle-cap watering-trough—
So much he just lies in one corner,

His tail curled under him, his belly big
As his head; his bat-like ears
Twitching, tilting toward the least sound.

Do I imagine he no longer trembles
When I come close to him?
He seems no longer to tremble.

2

But this morning the shoe-box house on the back porch is
   empty.   20
Where has he gone, my meadow mouse,
My thumb of a child that nuzzled in my palm?—
To run under the hawk's wing,
Under the eye of the great owl watching from the elm-tree,
To live by courtesy of the shrike, the snake, the tom-cat.

I think of the nestling fallen into the deep grass,
The turtle gasping in the dusty rubble of the highway,
The paralytic stunned in the tub, and the water rising,—
All things innocent, hapless, forsaken.

Dylan Thomas (1914–1953)

FERN HILL

Now as I was young and easy under the apple boughs
About the lilting house and happy as the grass was green,
   The night above the dingle° starry,   valley
     Time let me hail and climb
   Golden in the heydays of his eyes,
And honoured among wagons I was prince of the apple towns
And once below a time I lordly had the trees and leaves
     Trail with daisies and barley
   Down the rivers of the windfall light.

And as I was green and carefree, famous among the barns   10
About the happy yard and singing as the farm was home,
   In the sun that is young once only,
     Time let me play and be
   Golden in the mercy of his means,

And green and golden I was huntsman and herdsman, the
        calves
Sang to my horn, the foxes on the hills barked clear and cold,
        And the sabbath rang slowly
    In the pebbles of the holy streams.

All the sun long it was running, it was lovely, the hay
Fields high as the house, the tunes from the chimneys, it
        was air   20
        And playing, lovely and watery
           And fire green as grass.

        And nightly under the simple stars
As I rode to sleep the owls were bearing the farm away,
All the moon long I heard, blessed among stables, the nightjars°
        Flying with the ricks, and the horses
           Flashing into the dark.

And then to awake, and the farm, like a wanderer white
With the dew, come back, the cock on his shoulder: it was all
        Shining, it was Adam and maiden,   30
           The sky gathered again
        And the sun grew round that very day.
So it must have been after the birth of the simple light
In the first, spinning place, the spellbound horses walking
        warm
        Out of the whinnying green stable
           On to the fields of praise.

And honoured among foxes and pheasants by the gay house
Under the new made clouds and happy as the heart was long,
        In the sun born over and over,
           I ran my heedless ways,   40
        My wishes raced through the house high hay
And nothing I cared, at my sky blue trades, that time allows
In all his tuneful turning so few and such morning songs
        Before the children green and golden
           Follow him out of grace,

Nothing I cared, in the lamb white days, that time would
        take me
Up to the swallow thronged loft by the shadow of my hand,
        In the moon that is always rising,
           Nor that riding to sleep
    I should hear him fly with the high fields   50

And wake to the farm forever fled from the childless land.
Oh as I was young and easy in the mercy of his means,
Time held me green and dying
Though I sang in my chains like the sea.   nighthawks

QUESTIONS

1. How difficult did you find the unusual turns of phrase in this poem? What passages seemed especially odd?
2. Does the speaker always seem to be making sense? Give an example of unusual wording that does make sense. Give another of a passage that still troubles you.
3. What associations do the words "green" and "golden" have for you? Do these color images evoke the same responses throughout the poem? Explain.
4. From what the speaker says, how do you imagine Time?

Lawrence Ferlinghetti (b. 1919)
THE PENNYCANDYSTORE BEYOND THE EL

The pennycandystore beyond the El
is where I first
            fell in love
                        with unreality
Jellybeans glowed in the semi-gloom
of that september afternoon
A cat upon the counter moved among
                        the licorice sticks
            and tootsie rolls
      and Oh Boy Gum   10

Outside the leaves were falling as they died

A wind had blown away the sun

A girl ran in
Her hair was rainy
Her breasts were breathless in the little room

Outside the leaves were falling
                  and they cried
            Too soon! too soon!

Maxine Kumin (b. 1925)
THE MAN OF MANY L'S

My whole childhood I feared cripples
and how they got that way: the one-
legged Lavender Man who sold
his sachets by St. Mary's steeple,
the blind who tapped past humming what they knew,
even the hunchback seamstress, a ragdoll
who further sagged to pin my mother's hems,
had once been sturdy, had once been whole.
Something entered people, something chopped,
pressed, punctured, had its way with them   10
and if you looked, bad child, it entered you.

When we found out what the disease would do,
lying, like any council's stalwarts,
all of us swore to play our parts
in the final act as your command.

The first was easy. You gave up your left hand
and the right grew wiser, a juggler for its king.
When the poor dumb leg began to falter
you took up an alpenstock for walking
once flourished Sundays by our dead father.   20
Month by month the battleground grew thinner.
When you could no longer swallow meat
we steamed and mashed your dinner
and bent your straw to chocolate soda treats.

And when you could not talk, still you could write
questions and answers on a magic slate,
then lift the page, like laundry to the wind.
I plucked the memory splinter from your spine
as we played at being normal, who
has eased each other in the cold zoo   30
of childhood. Three months before
you died I wheeled you through the streets
of placid Palo Alto to catch
spring in its flamboyant tracks.
You wrote the name of every idiot flower
I did not know. Yucca rained.
Mimosa shone. The bottlebrush took fire

as you fought to hold your great head on its stem.
Lillac, you wrote, *Magnollia. Lilly.*
And further, *olleander. Dellphinium.*   40

O man of many L's, brother, my wily
resident ghost, may I never spell
these crowfoot dogbane[1] words again
these showy florid words again
except I name them under your spell.

Adrienne Rich (b. 1929)

LIVING IN SIN

She had thought the studio would keep itself;
no dust upon the furniture of love.
Half heresy, to wish the taps less vocal,
the panes relieved of grime. A plate of pears,
a piano with a Persian shawl, a cat
stalking the picturesque amusing mouse
had risen at his urging.
Not that at five each separate stair would writhe
under the milkman's tramp; that morning light
so coldly would delineate the scraps   10
of last night's cheese and three sepulchral bottles;
that on the kitchen shelf among the saucers
a pair of beetle-eyes would fix her own—
envoy from some village in the moldings . . .
Meanwhile, he, with a yawn,
sounded a dozen notes upon the keyboard,
declared it out of tune, shrugged at the mirror,
rubbed at his beard, went out for cigarettes;
while she, jeered by the minor demons,
pulled back the sheets and made the bed and found   20
a towel to dust the table-top,
and let the coffee-pot boil over on the stove.
By evening she was back in love again,
though not so wholly but throughout the night

---

[1]Crowfoot and dogbane are both common wildflowers.

she woke sometimes to feel the daylight coming
like a relentless milkman up the stairs.

Audre Lord (b. 1934)
HANGING FIRE

I am fourteen
and my skin has betrayed me
the boy I cannot live without
still sucks his thumb
in secret
how come my knees are
always so ashy
what if I die
before morning
and momma's in the bedroom   10
with the door closed.

I have to learn how to dance
in time for the next party
my room is too small for me
suppose I die before graduation
they will sing sad melodies
but finally
tell the truth about me
There is nothing I want to do
and too much   20
that has to be done
and momma's in the bedroom
with the door closed.

Nobody even stops to think
about my side of it
I should have been on Math Team
my marks were better than his
why do I have to be
the one
wearing braces   30
I have nothing to wear tomorrow
will I live long enough

to grow up
and momma's in the bedroom
with the door closed.

Seamus Heaney (b. 1939)
BLACKBERRY-PICKING

Late August, given heavy rain and sun
For a full week, the blackberries would ripen.
At first, just one, a glossy purple clot
Among others, red, green, hard as a knot.
You ate that first one and its flesh was sweet
Like thickened wine: summer's blood was in it
Leaving stains upon the tongue and lust for
Picking. Then red ones inked up and that hunger
Sent us out with milk-cans, pea-tins, jam-pots
Where briars scratched and wet grass bleached our boots.   10
Round hayfields, cornfields and potato-drills°   rows
We trekked and picked until the cans were full,
Until the tinkling bottom had been covered
With green ones, and on top big dark blobs burned
Like a plate of eyes. Our hands were peppered
With thorn pricks, our palms sticky as Bluebeard's.

We hoarded the fresh berries in the byre.°   cow barn
But when the bath was filled we found a fur,
A rat-grey fungus, glutting on our cache.
The juice was stinking too. Once off the bush   20
The fruit fermented, the sweet flesh would turn sour.
I always felt like crying. It wasn't fair
That all the lovely canfuls smelt of rot.
Each year I hoped they'd keep, knew they would not.

QUESTIONS

1. What is the first word-choice that foreshadows the unpleasant side of blackberry-picking?
2. What words and images arouse the strongest responses?
3. The speaker indicates that every year the experience was the same. Why do you suppose the berries were picked every year then?
4. As you read the last line, do you suppose the speaker really always knew the berries would not keep? Why didn't this knowledge prevent the hope?

Alice Walker (b. 1944)
STREAKING
(a phenomenon following the sixties)

the students
went out
of their way
to say
they were not
hurting anyone
or damaging
property
as they streaked across the country—
vulnerable
as a rape victim's
character
after ten years
of public
executions
naked
as the decade
they were formed.

DRAMA

Sophocles (496?–406 B.C.)
OEDIPUS REX*

PERSONS REPRESENTED

Oedipus	Messenger
A Priest	Shepherd of Laïos
Creon	Second Messenger
Teiresias	Chorus of Theban Elders
Iocaste	

THE SCENE. *Before the palace of Oedipus, King of Thebes. A central door and two lateral doors open onto a platform which runs the length of the façade. On the platform, right and left, are altars; and three steps lead down into the "orchestra," or chorus-ground. At the beginning of the action these steps are crowded by suppliants who have brought branches and chaplets of olive leaves and who lie in various attitudes of despair. OEDIPUS enters.*

PROLOGUE

Oedipus. My children, generations of the living
　In the line of Kadmos,[1] nursed at his ancient hearth:
　Why have you strewn yourselves before these altars
　In supplication, with your boughs and garlands?
　The breath of incense rises from the city
　With a sound of prayer and lamentation.
　　　　　　　　　　　　　　　　　Children,
　I would not have you speak through messengers,
　And therefore I have come myself to hear you—
　I, Oedipus, who bear the famous name.

　　　　　　　　　　　　　　　　　　　　　　　　　　[To a Priest:　　10

　You, there, since you are eldest in the company,
　Speak for them all, tell me what preys upon you,
　Whether you come in dread, or crave some blessing:
　Tell me, and never doubt that I will help you
　In every way I can; I should be heartless
　Were I not moved to find you suppliant here.

*An English version by Dudley Fitts and Robert Fitzgerald.

---

[1]Legendary founder of Thebes.

116

Priest. Great Oedipus, O powerful King of Thebes!
  You see how all the ages of our people
  Cling to your altar steps: here are boys
  Who can barely stand alone, and here are priests
  By weight of age, as I am a priest of God,   20
  And young men chosen from those yet unmarried;
  As for the others, all that multitude,
  They wait with olive chaplets in the squares,
  At the two shrines of Pallas,[2] and where Apollo[3]
  Speaks in the glowing embers.
                            Your own eyes
  Must tell you: Thebes is tossed on a murdering sea
  And can not lift her head from the death surge.
  A rust consumes the buds and fruits of the earth;
  The herds are sick; children die unborn,
  And labor is vain. The god of plague and pyre   30
  Raids like detestable lightning through the city,
  And all the house of Kadmos is laid waste,
  All emptied, and all darkened: Death alone
  Battens upon the misery of Thebes.

  You are not one of the immortal gods, we know;
  Yet we have come to you to make our prayer
  As to the man surest in mortal ways
  And wisest in the ways of God. You saved us
  From the Sphinx,[4] that flinty singer, and the tribute
  We paid to her so long; yet you were never   40
  Better informed than we, nor could we teach you:
  It was some god breathed in you to set us free.

  Therefore, O mighty King, we turn to you:
  Find us our safety, find us a remedy,
  Whether by counsel of the gods or men.
  A king of wisdom tested in the past
  Can act in a time of troubles, and act well.
  Noblest of men, restore
  Life to your city! Think how all men call you

---

[2]Athenê, goddess of wisdom.
[3]God of the sun and of healing.
[4]A riddling she-monster with a lion's body, wings, and a woman's face, that crouched on the city wall and asked, "What goes on four legs in the morning, two at midday, and three in the evening?" She killed those unable to answer, until Oedipus told her "Man" (who uses a staff in old age), and she threw herself from the wall.

Liberator for your triumph long ago;   50
Ah, when your years of kingship are remembered,
Let them not say *We rose, but later fell*—
Keep the State from going down in the storm!
Once, years ago, with happy augury,
You brought us fortune; be the same again!
No man questions your power to rule the land:
But rule over men, not over a dead city!
Ships are only hulls, citadels are nothing,
When no life moves in the empty passageways.

Oedipus. Poor children! You may be sure I know   60
All that you longed for in your coming here.
I know that you are deathly sick; and yet,
Sick as you are, not one is as sick as I.
Each of you suffers in himself alone
His anguish, not another's; but my spirit
Groans for the city, for myself, for you.

I was not sleeping, you are not waking me.
No, I have been in tears for a long while
And in my restless thought walked many ways.
In all my search, I found one helpful course,   70
And that I have taken: I have sent Creon,
Son of Menoikeus, brother of the Queen,
To Delphi, Apollo's place of revelation,
To learn there, if he can,
What act or pledge of mine may save the city.
I have counted the days, and now, this very day,
I am troubled, for he has overstayed his time.
What is he doing? He has been gone too long.
Yet whenever he comes back, I should do ill
To scant whatever duty God reveals.   80

Priest. It is a timely promise. At this instant
They tell me Creon is here.

Oedipus.   O Lord Apollo!
May his news be fair as his face is radiant!

Priest. It could not be otherwise: he is crowned with bay,
The chaplet is thick with berries.

Oedipus.   We shall soon know;
He is near enough to hear us now.

                                        [*Enter Creon*

                    O Prince:
Brother: son of Menoikeus:
What answer do you bring us from the god?

Creon. A strong one. I can tell you, great afflictions
Will turn out well, if they are taken well.   90

Oedipus. What was the oracle? These vague words
  Leave me still hanging between hope and fear.
Creon. Is it your pleasure to hear me with all these
  Gathered around us? I am prepared to speak,
  But should we not go in?
Oedipus.   Let them all hear it.
  It is for them I suffer, more than for myself.
Creon. Then I will tell you what I heard at Delphi.

  In plain words
  The god commands us to expel from the land of Thebes
  An old defilement we are sheltering.   100
  It is a deathly thing, beyond cure;
  We must not let it feed upon us longer.
Oedipus. What defilement? How shall we rid ourselves of it?
Creon. By exile or death, blood for blood. It was
  Murder that brought the plague-wind on the city.
Oedipus. Murder of whom? Surely the god has named him?
Creon. My lord: long ago Laïos was our king,
  Before you came to govern us.
Oedipus.   I know;
  I learned of him from others; I never saw him.
Creon. He was murdered; and Apollo commands us now   110
  To take revenge upon whoever killed him.
Oedipus. Upon whom? Where are they? Where shall we find a clue
  To solve that crime, after so many years?
Creon. Here in this land, he said.
                         If we make enquiry,
  We may touch things that otherwise escape us.
Oedipus. Tell me: Was Laïos murdered in his house,
  Or in the fields, or in some foreign country?
Creon. He said he planned to make a pilgrimage.
  He did not come home again.
Oedipus.   And was there no one,
  No witness, no companion, to tell what happened?   120
Creon. They were all killed but one, and he got away
  So frightened that he could remember one thing only.
Oedipus. What was that one thing? One may be the key
  To everything, if we resolve to use it.
Creon. He said that a band of highwaymen attacked them,
  Outnumbered them, and overwhelmed the King.
Oedipus. Strange, that a highwayman should be so daring—
  Unless some faction here bribed him to do it.
Creon. We thought of that. But after Laïos' death
  New troubles arose and we had no avenger.   130
Oedipus. What troubles could prevent your hunting down the killers?

Creon. The riddling Sphinx's song
    Made us deaf to all mysteries but her own.
Oedipus. Then once more I must bring what is dark to light.
    It is most fitting that Apollo shows,
    As you do, this compunction for the dead.
    You shall see how I stand by you, as I should,
    To avenge the city and the city's god,
    And not as though it were for some distant friend,
    But for my own sake, to be rid of evil.   140
    Whoever killed King Laïos might—who knows?—
    Decide at any moment to kill me as well.
    By avenging the murdered king I protect myself.

    Come, then, my children: leave the altar steps,
    Lift up your olive boughs!
                One of you go
    And summon the people of Kadmos to gather here.
    I will do all that I can; you may tell them that.

                                   [Exit a Page
    So, with the help of God,
    We shall be saved—or else indeed we are lost.
Priest. Let us rise, children. It was for this we came,   150
    And now the King has promised it himself.
    Phoibos[5] has sent us an oracle; may he descend
    Himself to save us and drive out the plague.
            [Exeunt Oedipus and Creon into the palace by the central door.
            The Priest and the Suppliants disperse R and L. After a short pause
            the Chorus enters the orchestra.

PÁRODOS[6]

Chorus.
    What is God singing in his profound   *[Strophe 1*
    Delphi of gold and shadow?
    What oracle for Thebes, the sunwhipped city?

    Fear unjoints me, the roots of my heart tremble.

    Now I remember, O Healer, your power, and wonder:
    Will you send doom like a sudden cloud, or weave it
    Like nightfall of the past?

---

    [5] Apollo.
    [6] Ode chanted by the Chorus as it enters the theater. A choral ode is divided into alternating
verses, each called a *strophe* or an *antistrophe*. The Chorus here represents the elders of Thebes.

Speak, speak to us, issue of holy sound:
Dearest to our expectancy: be tender!
Let me pray to Athenê, the immortal daughter of Zeus,   [*Antistrophe 1*
And to Artemis her sister   11
Who keeps her famous throne in the market ring,
And to Apollo, bowman at the far butts of heaven—

O gods, descend! Like three streams leap against
The fires of our grief, the fires of darkness;
Be swift to bring us rest!

As in the old time from the brilliant house
Of air you stepped to save us, come again!

Now our afflictions have no end,   [*Strophe 2*
Now all our stricken host lies down   20
And no man fights off death with his mind;

The noble plowland bears no grain,
And groaning mothers can not bear—

See, how our lives like birds take wing,
Like sparks that fly when a fire soars,
To the shore of the god of evening.

The plague burns on, it is pitiless,   [*Antistrophe 2*
Though pallid children laden with death
Lie unwept in the stony ways,

And old gray women by every path   30
Flock to the strand about the altars

There to strike their breasts and cry
Worship of Phoibos in wailing prayers:
Be kind, God's golden child!

There are no swords in this attack by fire,   [*Strophe 3*
No shields, but we are ringed with cries.

Send the besieger plunging from our homes
Into the vast sea-room of the Atlantic
Or into the waves that foam eastward of Thrace—

For the day ravages what the night spares—   40

Destroy our enemy, lord of the thunder!
Let him be riven by lightning from heaven!

Phoibos Apollo, stretch the sun's bowstring,   [*Antistrophe 3*
That golden cord, until it sing for us,
Flashing arrows in heaven!
                         Artemis, Huntress,
Race with flaring lights upon our mountains!

O scarlet god, O golden-banded brow,
O Theban Bacchos[7] in a storm of Maenads,
                                          [*Enter Oedipus, C.*
Whirl upon Death, that all the Undying hate!
Come with blinding torches, come in joy!   50

SCENE I

Oedipus. Is this your prayer? It may be answered. Come,
   Listen to me, act as the crisis demands,
   And you shall have relief from all these evils.

   Until now I was a stranger to this tale,
   As I had been a stranger to the crime.
   Could I track down the murderer without a clue?
   But now, friends,
   As one who became a citizen after the murder,
   I make this proclamation to all Thebans:

   If any man knows by whose hand Laïos, son of Labdakos,   10
   Met his death, I direct that man to tell me everything,
   No matter what he fears for having so long withheld it.
   Let it stand as promised that no further trouble
   Will come to him, but he may leave the land in safety.

   Moreover: If anyone knows the murderer to be foreign,
   Let him not keep silent: he shall have his reward from me.
   However, if he does conceal it; if any man
   Fearing for his friend or for himself disobeys this edict,
   Hear what I propose to do:

   I solemnly forbid the people of this country,   20
   Where power and throne are mine, ever to receive that man
   Or speak to him, no matter who he is, or let him
   Join in sacrifice, lustration, or in prayer.

---

[7]Dionysus, the god of wine, whose female attendants were the Maenads.

I decree that he be driven from every house,
Being, as he is, corruption itself to us: the Delphic
Voice of Zeus has pronounced this revelation.
Thus I associate myself with the oracle
And take the side of the murdered king.

As for the criminal, I pray to God—
Whether it be a lurking thief, or one of a number—   30
I pray that that man's life be consumed in evil and wretchedness.
And as for me, this curse applies no less
If it should turn out that the culprit is my guest here,
Sharing my hearth.
     You have heard the penalty.
I lay it on you now to attend to this
For my sake, for Apollo's, for the sick
Sterile city that heaven has abandoned.
Suppose the oracle had given you no command:
Should this defilement go uncleansed for ever?
You should have found the murderer: your king,   40
A noble king, had been destroyed!
     Now I,
Having the power that he held before me,
Having his bed, begetting children there
Upon his wife, as he would have, had he lived—
Their son would have been my children's brother,
If Laïos had had luck in fatherhood!
(But surely ill luck rushed upon his reign)—
I say I take the son's part, just as though
I were his son, to press the fight for him
And see it won! I'll find the hand that brought   50
Death to Labdakos' and Polydoros' child,
Heir of Kadmos' and Agenor's line.
And as for those who fail me,
May the gods deny them the fruit of the earth,
Fruit of the womb, and may they rot utterly!
Let them be wretched as we are wretched, and worse!

For you, for loyal Thebans, and for all
Who find my actions right, I pray the favor
Of justice, and of all the immortal gods.
Choragos.[8] Since I am under oath, my lord, I swear   60
 I did not do the murder, I can not name

---

[8]The Chorus leader.

The murderer. Might not the oracle
That has ordained the search tell where to find him?
Oedipus. An honest question. But no man in the world
    Can make the gods do more than the gods will.
Choragos. There is one last expedient—
Oedipus.   Tell me what it is.
    Though it seem slight, you must not hold it back.
Choragos. A lord clairvoyant to the lord Apollo,
    As we all know, is the skilled Teiresias.
    One might learn much about this from him, Oedipus.   70
Oedipus. I am not wasting time:
    Creon spoke of this, and I have sent for him—
    Twice, in fact; it is strange that he is not here.
Choragos. The other matter—that old report—seems useless.
Oedipus. Tell me, I am interested in all reports.
Choragos. The King was said to have been killed by highwaymen.
Oedipus. I know. But we have no witnesses to that.
Choragos. If the killer can feel a particle of dread,
    Your curse will bring him out of hiding!
Oedipus.   No.
    The man who dared that act will fear no curse.   80
                    [*Enter the blind seer Teiresias, led by a Page*
Choragos. But there is one man who may detect the criminal.
    This is Teiresias, this is the holy prophet
    In whom, alone of all men, truth was born.
Oedipus. Teiresias: seer: student of mysteries,
    Of all that's taught and all that no man tells,
    Secrets of Heaven and secrets of the earth:
    Blind though you are, you know the city lies
    Sick with plague; and from this plague, my lord,
    We find that you alone can guard or save us.

    Possibly you did not hear the messengers?   90
    Apollo, when we sent to him,
    Sent us back word that this great pestilence
    Would lift, but only if we established clearly
    The identity of those who murdered Laïos.
    They must be killed or exiled.
                        Can you use
    Birdflight or any art of divination
    To purify yourself, and Thebes, and me
    From this contagion? We are in your hands.
    There is no fairer duty
    Than that of helping others in distress.   100

Teiresias. How dreadful knowledge of the truth can be
   When there's no help in truth! I knew this well,
   But made myself forget. I should not have come.
Oedipus. What is troubling you? Why are your eyes so cold?
Teiresias. Let me go home. Bear your own fate, and I'll
   Bear mine. It is better so: trust what I say.
Oedipus. What you say is ungracious and unhelpful
   To your native country. Do not refuse to speak.
Teiresias. When it comes to speech, your own is neither temperate
   Nor opportune. I wish to be more prudent.   110
Oedipus. In God's name, we all beg you—
Teiresias.   You are all ignorant.
   No; I will never tell you what I know.
   Now it is my misery; then, it would be yours.
Oedipus. What! You do know something, and will not tell us?
   You would betray us all and wreck the State?
Teiresias. I do not intend to torture myself, or you.
   Why persist in asking? You will not persuade me.
Oedipus. What a wicked old man you are! You'd try a stone's
   Patience! Out with it! Have you no feeling at all?
Teiresias. You call me unfeeling. If you could only see   120
   The nature of your own feelings . . .
Oedipus.   Why,
   Who would not feel as I do? Who could endure
   Your arrogance toward the city?
Teiresias.   What does it matter!
   Whether I speak or not, it is bound to come.
Oedipus. Then, if "it" is bound to come, you are bound to tell me.
Teiresias. No, I will not go on. Rage as you please.
Oedipus. Rage? Why not!
                       And I'll tell you what I think:
   You planned it, you had it done, you all but
   Killed him with your own hands: if you had eyes,
   I'd say the crime was yours, and yours alone.   130
Teiresias. So? I charge you, then,
   Abide by the proclamation you have made:
   From this day forth
   Never speak again to these men or to me;
   You yourself are the pollution of this country.
Oedipus. You dare say that! Can you possibly think you have
   Some way of going free, after such insolence?
Teiresias. I have gone free. It is the truth sustains me.
Oedipus. Who taught you shamelessness? It was not your craft.
Teiresias. You did. You made me speak. I did not want to.   140

Oedipus. Speak what? Let me hear it again more clearly.
Teiresias. Was it not clear before? Are you tempting me?
Oedipus. I did not understand it. Say it again.
Teiresias. I say that you are the murderer whom you seek.
Oedipus. Now twice you have spat out infamy. You'll pay for it!
Teiresias. Would you care for more? Do you wish to be really angry?
Oedipus. Say what you will. Whatever you say is worthless.
Teiresias. I say you live in hideous shame with those
   Most dear to you. You can not see the evil.
Oedipus. It seems you can go on mouthing like this for ever.   150
Teiresias. I can, if there is power in truth.
Oedipus.   There is:
   But not for you, not for you,
   You sightless, witless, senseless, mad old man!
Teiresias. You are the madman. There is no one here
   Who will not curse you soon, as you curse me.
Oedipus. You child of endless night! You can not hurt me
   Or any other man who sees the sun.
Teiresias. True: it is not from me your fate will come.
   That lies within Apollo's competence,
   As it is his concern.
Oedipus.   Tell me: 160
   Are you speaking for Creon, or for yourself?
Teiresias. Creon is no threat. You weave your own doom.
Oedipus. Wealth, power, craft of statesmanship!
   Kingly position, everywhere admired!
   What savage envy is stored up against these,
   If Creon, whom I trusted, Creon my friend,
   For this great office which the city once
   Put in my hands unsought—if for this power
   Creon desires in secret to destroy me!

   He has bought this decrepit fortune-teller, this   170
   Collector of dirty pennies, this prophet fraud—
   Why, he is no more clairvoyant than I am!
                               Tell us:
   Has your mystic mummery ever approached the truth?
   When that hellcat the Sphinx was performing here,
   What help were you to these people?
   Her magic was not for the first man who came along:
   It demanded a real exorcist. Your birds—
   What good were they? or the gods, for the matter of that?
   But I came by,
   Oedipus, the simple man, who knows nothing—   180
   I thought it out for myself, no birds helped me!

And this is the man you think you can destroy,
That you may be close to Creon when he's king!
Well, you and your friend Creon, it seems to me,
Will suffer most. If you were not an old man,
You would have paid already for your plot.
Choragos. We can not see that his words or yours
Have been spoken except in anger, Oedipus,
And of anger we have no need. How can God's will
Be accomplished best? That is what most concerns us.　　　190
Teiresias. You are a king. But where argument's concerned
I am your man, as much king as you.
I am not your servant, but Apollo's.
I have no need of Creon to speak for me.

Listen to me. You mock my blindness, do you?
But I say that you, with both your eyes, are blind:
You can not see the wretchedness of your life,
Nor in whose house you live, no, nor with whom.
Who are your father and mother? Can you tell me?
You do not even know the blind wrongs　　　200
That you have done them, on earth and in the world below.
But the double lash of your parents' curse will whip you
Out of this land some day, with only night
Upon your precious eyes.
Your cries then—where will they not be heard?
What fastness of Kithairon[9] will not echo them?
And that bridal-descant of yours—you'll know it then,
The song they sang when you came here to Thebes
And found your misguided berthing.
All this, and more, that you can not guess at now,　　　210
Will bring you to yourself among your children.

Be angry, then. Curse Creon. Curse my words.
I tell you, no man that walks upon the earth
Shall be rooted out more horribly than you.
Oedipus. Am I to bear this from him?—Damnation
Take you! Out of this place! Out of my sight!
Teiresias. I would not have come at all if you had not asked me.
Oedipus. Could I have told that you'd talk nonsense, that
You'd come here to make a fool of yourself, and of me?
Teiresias. A fool? Your parents thought me sane enough.　　　220
Oedipus. My parents again!—Wait: who were my parents?

---

[9]Mountain where the infant Oedipus was left to die.

Teiresias. This day will give you a father, and break your heart.
Oedipus. Your infantile riddles! Your damned abracadabra!
Teiresias. You were a great man once at solving riddles.
Oedipus. Mock me with that if you like; you will find it true.
Teiresias. It was true enough. It brought about your ruin.
Oedipus. But if it saved this town?
Teiresias.   [*To the Page:*

                  Boy, give me your hand.
Oedipus. Yes, boy; lead him away.

               —While you are here
  We can do nothing. Go; leave us in peace.
Teiresias. I will go when I have said what I have to say.   230
  How can you hurt me? And I tell you again:
  The man you have been looking for all this time,
  The damned man, the murderer of Laïos,
  That man is in Thebes. To your mind he is foreignborn,
  But it will soon be shown that he is a Theban,
  A revelation that will fail to please.
                            A blind man,
  Who has his eyes now; a penniless man, who is rich now;
  And he will go tapping the strange earth with his staff;
  To the children with whom he lives now he will be
  Brother and father—the very same; to her   240
  Who bore him, son and husband—the very same
  Who came to his father's bed, wet with his father's blood.

  Enough. Go think that over.
  If later you find error in what I have said,
  You may say that I have no skill in prophecy.
        [*Exit Teiresias, led by his page. Oedipus goes into the palace.*

ODE I

Chorus. The Delphic stone of prophecies   [*Strophe 1*
  Remembers ancient regicide
  And a still bloody hand.
  That killer's hour of flight has come.
  He must be stronger than riderless
  Coursers of untiring wind,
  For the son of Zeus[10] armed with his father's thunder
  Leaps in lightning after him;
  And the Furies follow him, the sad Furies.[11]

---

[10]Apollo.
[11]Spirits of divine vengeance.

Holy Parnassos'[12] peak of snow   [*Antistrophe 1*
Flashes and blinds that secret man,   11
That all shall hunt him down:
Though he may roam the forest shade
Like a bull gone wild from pasture
To rage through glooms of stone.
Doom comes down on him; flight will not avail him;
For the world's heart calls him desolate,
And the immortal Furies follow, for ever follow.

But now a wilder thing is heard   [*Strophe 2*
From the old man skilled at hearing Fate in the wingbeat of a bird.   20
Bewildered as a blown bird, my soul hovers and can not find
Foothold in this debate, or any reason or rest of mind.
But no man ever brought—none can bring
Proof of strife between Thebes' royal house,
Labdakos' line, and the son of Polybos;[13]
And never until now has any man brought word
Of Laïos' dark death staining Oedipus the King.

Divine Zeus and Apollo hold   [*Antistrophe 2*
Perfect intelligence alone of all tales ever told;
And well though this diviner works, he works in his own night;   30
No man can judge that rough unknown or trust in second sight,
For wisdom changes hands among the wise.
Shall I believe my great lord criminal
At a raging word that a blind old man let fall?
I saw him, when the carrion woman faced him of old,
Prove his heroic mind! These evil words are lies.

SCENE II

Creon. Men of Thebes:
   I am told that heavy accusations
   Have been brought against me by King Oedipus.

I am not the kind of man to bear this tamely.

If in these present difficulties
He holds me accountable for any harm to him

---

   [12]Mountain sacred to Apollo; at its foot is Delphi, site of the oracle.
   [13]Labdakos was an early king of Thebes; Polybos was king of Corinth and Oedipus's supposed
father.

Through anything I have said or done—why, then,
I do not value life in this dishonor.

It is not as though this rumor touched upon
Some private indiscretion. The matter is grave.   10
The fact is that I am being called disloyal
To the State, to my fellow citizens, to my friends.
Choragos. He may have spoken in anger, not from his mind.
Creon. But did you not hear him say I was the one
   Who seduced the old prophet into lying?
Choragos. The thing was said; I do not know how seriously.
Creon. But you were watching him! Were his eyes steady?
   Did he look like a man in his right mind?
Choragos.   I do not know.
   I can not judge the behavior of great men.
   But here is the King himself.

                                              [*Enter Oedipus*

Oedipus.   So you dared come back.   20
   Why? How brazen of you to come to my house,
   You murderer!
                    Do you think I do not know
   That you plotted to kill me, plotted to steal my throne?
   Tell me, in God's name: am I coward, a fool,
   That you should dream you could accomplish this?
   A fool who could not see your slippery game?
   A coward, not to fight back when I saw it?
   You are the fool, Creon, are you not? hoping
   Without support or friends to get a throne?
   Thrones may be won or bought: you could do neither.   30
Creon. Now listen to me. You have talked; let me talk, too.
   You can not judge unless you know the facts.
Oedipus. You speak well: there is one fact; but I find it hard
   To learn from the deadliest enemy I have.
Creon. That above all I must dispute with you.
Oedipus. That above all I will not hear you deny.
Creon. If you think there is anything good in being stubborn
   Against all reason, then I say you are wrong.
Oedipus. If you think a man can sin against his own kind
   And not be punished for it, I say you are mad.   40
Creon. I agree. But tell me: what have I done to you?
Oedipus. You advised me to send for that wizard, did you not?
Creon. I did. I should do it again.
Oedipus.   Very well. Now tell me:
   How long has it been since Laïos—
Creon.   What of Laïos?

Oedipus. Since he vanished in that onset by the road?
Creon. It was long ago, a long time.
Oedipus.   And this prophet,
   Was he practicing here then?
Creon.   He was; and with honor, as now
Oedipus. Did he speak of me at that time?
Creon.   He never did;
   At least, not when I was present.
Oedipus.   But . . . the enquiry?
   I suppose you held one?
Creon.   We did, but we learned nothing.   50
Oedipus. Why did the prophet not speak against me then?
Creon. I do not know; and I am the kind of man
   Who holds his tongue when he has no facts to go on.
Oedipus. There's one fact that you know, and you could tell it.
Creon. What fact is that? If I know it, you shall have it.
Oedipus. If he were not involved with you, he could not say
   That it was I who murdered Laïos.
Creon. If he says that, you are the one that knows it!—
   But now it is my turn to question you.
Oedipus. Put your questions. I am no murderer.   60
Creon. First, then: You married my sister?
Oedipus.   I married your sister.
Creon. And you rule the kingdom equally with her?
Oedipus. Everything that she wants she has from me.
Creon. And I am the third, equal to both of you?
Oedipus. That is why I call you a bad friend.
Creon. No. Reason it out, as I have done.
   Think of this first: Would any sane man prefer
   Power, with all a king's anxieties,
   To that same power and the grace of sleep?
   Certainly not I.   70
   I have never longed for the king's power—only his rights.
   Would any man differ from me in this?
   As matters stand, I have my way in everything
   With your consent, and no responsibilities.
   If I were king, I should be a slave to policy.

   How could I desire a scepter more
   Than what is now mine—untroubled influence?
   No, I have not gone mad; I need no honors,
   Except those with the perquisites I have now.
   I am welcome everywhere; every man salutes me,   80
   And those who want your favor seek my ear,
   Since I know how to manage what they ask.

Should I exchange this ease for that anxiety?
Besides, no sober mind is treasonable.
I hate anarchy
And never would deal with any man who likes it.

Test what I have said. Go to the priestess
At Delphi, ask if I quoted her correctly.
And as for this other thing: if I am found
Guilty of treason with Teiresias,   90
Then sentence me to death! You have my word
It is a sentence I should cast my vote for—
But not without evidence!
                              You do wrong
When you take good men for bad, bad men for good.
A true friend thrown aside—why, life itself
Is not more precious!
                              In time you will know this well:
For time, and time alone, will show the just man,
Though scoundrels are discovered in a day.
Choragos. This is well said, and a prudent man would ponder it.
    Judgments too quickly formed are dangerous.   100
Oedipus. But is he not quick in his duplicity?
    And shall I not be quick to parry him?
    Would you have me stand still, hold my peace, and let
    This man win everything, through my inaction?
Creon. And you want—what is it, then? To banish me?
Oedipus. No, not exile. It is your death I want,
    So that all the world may see what treason means.
Creon. You will persist, then? You will not believe me?
Oedipus. How can I believe you?
Creon.   Then you are a fool.
Oedipus. To save myself?
Creon.   In justice, think of me.   110
Oedipus. You are evil incarnate.
Creon.   But suppose that you are wrong?
Oedipus. Still I must rule.
Creon.   But not if you rule badly.
Oedipus. O city, city!
Creon.   It is my city, too!
Choragos. Now, my lords, be still. I see the Queen,
    Iocastê, coming from her palace chambers;
    And it is time she came, for the sake of you both.
    This dreadful quarrel can be resolved through her.

                                                            [*Enter Iocaste*

Iocaste. Poor foolish men, what wicked din is this?

With Thebes sick to death, is it not shameful
That you should rake some private quarrel up?   120
                                              [*To Oedipus:*
Come into the house.
                —And you, Creon, go now:
Let us have no more of this tumult over nothing.
Creon. Nothing? No, sister: what your husband plans for me
   Is one of two great evils: exile or death.
Oedipus. He is right.
                     Why, woman I have caught him squarely
   Plotting against my life.
Creon.   No! Let me die
   Accurst if ever I have wished you harm!
Iocaste. Ah, believe it, Oedipus!
   In the name of the gods, respect this oath of his
   For my sake, for the sake of these people here!   130
Choragos.   [*Strophe 1*
   Open your mind to her, my lord. Be ruled by her, I beg you!
Oedipus. What would you have me do?
Choragos. Respect Creon's word. He has never spoken like a fool,
   And now he has sworn an oath.
Oedipus.   You know what you ask?
Choragos.   I do.
Oedipus.   Speak on, then.
Choragos. A friend so sworn should not be baited so,
   In blind malice, and without final proof.
Oedipus. You are aware, I hope, that what you say
   Means death for me, or exile at the least.
Choragos.   [*Strophe 2*
   No, I swear by Helios,[14] first in Heaven!
   May I die friendless and accurst,
   The worst of deaths, if ever I meant that!
      It is the withering fields
         That hurt my sick heart:
      Must we bear all these ills,
         And now your bad blood as well?
Oedipus. Then let him go. And let me die, if I must,
   Or be driven by him in shame from the land of Thebes.
   It is your unhappiness, and not his talk,
   That touches me.
               As for him—
   Wherever he goes, hatred will follow him.   150

___

[14]The sun god, Apollo.

Creon. Ugly in yielding, as you were ugly in rage!
    Natures like yours chiefly torment themselves.
Oedipus. Can you not go? Can you not leave me?
Creon.   I can.
    You do not know me; but the city knows me,
    And in its eyes I am just, if not in yours.

                                             [Exit Creon
Choragos.   *[Antistrophe 1*
    Lady Iocastê, did you not ask the King to go to his chambers?
Iocaste. First tell me what has happened.
Choragos. There was suspicion without evidence; yet it rankled
    As even false charges will.
Iocaste.   On both sides?
Choragos.   On both.
Iocaste.   But what was said?
Choragos. Oh let it rest, let it be done with!   160
    Have we not suffered enough?
Oedipus. You see to what your decency has brought you:
    You have made difficulties where my heart saw none.
Choragos.   *[Antistrophe 2*
    Oedipus, it is not once only I have told you—
      You must know I should count myself unwise
    To the point of madness, should I now forsake you—
        You, under whose hand,
          In the storm of another time,
        Our dear land sailed out free.
        But now stand fast at the helm!   170
Iocaste. In God's name, Oedipus, inform your wife as well:
    Why are you so set in this hard anger?
Oedipus. I will tell you, for none of these men deserves
    My confidence as you do. It is Creon's work,
    His treachery, his plotting against me.
Iocaste. Go on, if you can make this clear to me.
Oedipus. He charges me with the murder of Laïos.
Iocaste. Has he some knowledge? Or does he speak from hearsay?
Oedipus. He would not commit himself to such a charge,
    But he has brought in that damnable soothsayer   180
    To tell his story.
Iocaste.   Set your mind at rest.
    If it is a question of soothsayers, I tell you
    That you will find no man whose craft gives knowledge
    Of the unknowable.
             Here is my proof:

An oracle was reported to Laïos once
(I will not say from Phoibos himself, but from

His appointed ministers, at any rate)
That his doom would be death at the hands of his own son—
His son, born of his flesh and of mine!

Now, you remember the story: Laïos was killed   190
By marauding strangers where three highways meet;
But his child had not been three days in this world
Before the King had pierced the baby's ankles
And left him to die on a lonely mountainside.

Thus, Apollo never caused that child
To kill his father, and it was not Laïos' fate
To die at the hands of his son, as he had feared.
This is what prophets and prophecies are worth!
Have no dread of them.
                                 It is God himself
Who can show us what he wills, in his own way.   200
Oedipus. How strange a shadowy memory crossed my mind,
    Just now while you were speaking; it chilled my heart.
Iocaste. What do you mean? What memory do you speak of?
Oedipus. If I understand you, Laïos was killed
    At a place where three roads meet.
Iocaste.   So it was said;
    We have no later story.
Oedipus.   Where did it happen?
Iocaste. Phokis, it is called: at a place where the Theban Way
    Divides into the roads toward Delphi and Daulia.
Oedipus. When?
Iocaste.   We had the news not long before you came
    And proved the right to your succession here.   210
Oedipus. Ah, what net has God been weaving for me?
Iocaste. Oedipus! Why does this trouble you?
Oedipus.   Do not ask me yet.
    First, tell me how Laïos looked, and tell me
    How old he was.
Iocaste.   He was tall, his hair just touched
    With white; his form was not unlike your own.
Oedipus. I think that I myself may be accurst
    By my own ignorant edict.
Iocaste.   You speak strangely.
    It makes me tremble to look at you, my King.
Oedipus. I am not sure that the blind man can not see.
    But I should know better if you were to tell me—   220
Iocaste. Anything—though I dread to hear you ask it.
Oedipus. Was the King lightly escorted, or did he ride
    With a large company, as a ruler should?

Iocaste. There were five men with him in all: one was a herald,
    And a single chariot, which he was driving.
Oedipus. Alas, that makes it plain enough!
                                   But who—
    Who told you how it happened?
Iocaste.   A household servant,
    The only one to escape.
Oedipus.   And is he still
    A servant of ours?
Iocaste.   No; for when he came back at last
    And found you enthroned in the place of the dead king,   230
    He came to me, touched my hand with his, and begged
    That I would send him away to the frontier district
    Where only the shepherds go—
    As far away from the city as I could send him.
    I granted his prayer; for although the man was a slave,
    He had earned more than this favor at my hands.
Oedipus. Can he be called back quickly?
Iocaste.   Easily.
    But why?
Oedipus.   I have taken too much upon myself
    Without enquiry; therefore I wish to consult him.
Iocaste. Then he shall come.
                       But am I not one also   240
    To whom you might confide these fears of yours?
Oedipus. That is your right; it will not be denied you,
    Now least of all; for I have reached a pitch
    Of wild foreboding. Is there anyone
    To whom I should sooner speak?

    Polybos of Corinth is my father.
    My mother is a Dorian: Meropê.
    I grew up chief among the men of Corinth
    Until a strange thing happened—
    Not worth my passion, it may be, but strange.   250

    At a feast, a drunken man maundering in his cups
    Cries out that I am not my father's son!

    I contained myself that night, though I felt anger
    And a sinking heart. The next day I visited
    My father and mother, and questioned them. They stormed,
    Calling it all the slanderous rant of a fool;
    And this relieved me. Yet the suspicion
    Remained always aching in my mind;

I knew there was talk; I could not rest;
And finally, saying nothing to my parents,   260
I went to the shrine at Delphi.

The god dismissed my question without reply;
He spoke of other things.
                        Some were clear,
Full of wretchedness, dreadful, unbearable:
As, that I should lie with my own mother, breed
Children from whom all men would turn their eyes;
And that I should be my father's murderer.

I heard all this, and fled. And from that day
Corinth to me was only in the stars
Descending in that quarter of the sky,   270
As I wandered farther and farther on my way
To a land where I should never see the evil
Sung by the oracle. And I came to this country
Where, so you say, King Laïos was killed.

I will tell you all that happened there, my lady.

There were three highways
Coming together at a place I passed;
And there a herald came towards me, and a chariot
Drawn by horses, with a man such as you describe
Seated in it. The groom leading the horses   280
Forced me off the road at his lord's command;
But as this charioteer lurched over towards me
I struck him in my rage. The old man saw me
And brought his double goad down upon my head
As I came abreast.
                   He was paid back, and more!
Swinging my club in this right hand I knocked him
Out of his car, and he rolled on the ground.
                                        I killed him.

I killed them all.
Now if that stranger and Laïos were—kin,
Where is a man more miserable than I?   290
More hated by the gods? Citizen and alien alike
Must never shelter me or speak to me—
I must be shunned by all.
                        And I myself
Pronounced this malediction upon myself!

Think of it: I have touched you with these hands,
These hands that killed your husband. What defilement!

Am I all evil, then? It must be so,
Since I must flee from Thebes, yet never again
See my own countrymen, my own country,
For fear of joining my mother in marriage   300
And killing Polybos, my father.
                                        Ah,
If I was created so, born to this fate,
Who could deny the savagery of God?

O holy majesty of heavenly powers!
May I never see that day! Never!
Rather let me vanish from the race of men
Than know the abomination destined me!
Choragos. We too, my lord, have felt dismay at this.
    But there is hope: you have yet to hear the shepherd.
Oedipus. Indeed, I fear no other hope is left me.   310
Iocaste. What do you hope from him when he comes?
Oedipus.   This much:
    If his account of the murder tallies with yours,
    Then I am cleared.
Iocaste.   What was it that I said
    Of such importance?
Oedipus.   Why, "marauders," you said,
    Killed the King, according to this man's story.
    If he maintains that still, if there were several,
    Clearly the guilt is not mine: I was alone.
    But if he says one man, singlehanded, did it,
    Then the evidence all points to me.
Iocaste. You may be sure that he said there were several;   320
    And can he call back that story now? He can not.
    The whole city heard it as plainly as I.
    But suppose he alters some detail of it:
    He can not ever show that Laïos' death
    Fulfilled the oracle: for Apollo said
    My child was doomed to kill him; and my child—
    Poor baby!—it was my child that died first.

    No. From now on, where oracles are concerned,
    I would not waste a second thought on any.
Oedipus. You may be right.
                            But come: let someone go   330
    For the shepherd at once. This matter must be settled.
Iocaste. I will send for him.

I would not wish to cross you in anything,
And surely not in this.—Let us go in.

[*Exeunt into the palace*

ODE II

Chorus: [*Strophe 1*
　　Let me be reverent in the ways of right,
　　Lowly the paths I journey on;
　　Let all my words and actions keep
　　The laws of the pure universe
　　From highest Heaven handed down.
　　For Heaven is their bright nurse,
　　Those generations of the realms of light;
　　Ah, never of mortal kind were they begot,
　　Nor are they slaves of memory, lost in sleep:
　　Their Father is greater than Time, and ages not.   10

　　The tyrant is a child of Pride   [*Antistrophe 1*
　　Who drinks from his great sickening cup
　　Recklessness and vanity,
　　Until from his high crest headlong
　　He plummets to the dust of hope.
　　That strong man is not strong.
　　But let no fair ambition be denied;
　　May God protect the wrestler for the State
　　In government, in comely policy,
　　Who will fear God, and on His ordinance wait.   20

　　Haughtiness and the high hand of disdain   [*Strophe 2*
　　Tempt and outrage God's holy law;
　　And any mortal who dares hold
　　No immortal Power in awe
　　Will be caught up in a net of pain:
　　The price for which his levity is sold.
　　Let each man take due earnings, then,
　　And keep his hands from holy things,
　　And from blasphemy stand apart—
　　Else the crackling blast of heaven   30
　　Blows on his head, and on his desperate heart;
　　Though fools will honor impious men,
　　In their cities no tragic poet sings.

　　Shall we lose faith in Delphi's obscurities,   [*Antistrophe 2*
　　We who have heard the world's core

Discredited, and the sacred wood
Of Zeus at Elis praised no more?
The deeds and the strange prophecies
Must make a pattern yet to be understood.
Zeus, if indeed you are lord of all,   40
Throned in light over night and day,
Mirror this in your endless mind:
Our masters call the oracle
Words on the wind, and the Delphic vision blind!
Their hearts no longer know Apollo,
And reverence for the gods has died away.

SCENE III

[*Enter Iocaste*

Iocaste. Princes of Thebes, it has occurred to me
    To visit the altars of the gods, bearing
    These branches as a suppliant, and this incense.
    Our King is not himself: his noble soul
    I overwrought with fantasies of dread,
    Else he would consider
    The new prophecies in the light of the old.
    He will listen to any voice that speaks disaster,
    And my advice goes for nothing.
                        [*She approaches the Altar, R.*
                    To you, then, Apollo,
    Lycean lord, since you are nearest, I turn in prayer.   10
    Receive these offerings, and grant us deliverance
    From defilement. Our hearts are heavy with fear
    When we see our leader distracted, as helpless sailors
    Are terrified by the confusion of their helmsman.
                        [*Enter Messenger*

Messenger. Friends, no doubt you can direct me:
    Where shall I find the house of Oedipus,
    Or, better still, where is the King himself?
Choragos. It is this very place, stranger; he is inside.
    This is his wife and mother of his children.
Messenger. I wish her happiness in a happy house,   20
    Blest in all the fulfillment of her marriage.
Iocaste. I wish as much for you: your courtesy
    Deserves a like good fortune. But now, tell me:
    Why have you come? What have you to say to us?
Messenger. Good news, my lady, for your house and your husband.
Iocaste. What news? Who sent you here?

Messenger.   I am from Corinth.
  The news I bring ought to mean joy for you,
  Though it may be you will find some grief in it.
Iocaste. What is it? How can it touch us in both ways?
Messenger. The word is that the people of the Isthmus   30
  Intend to call Oedipus to be their king.
Iocaste. But old King Polybos—is he not reigning still?
Messenger. No. Death holds him in his sepulchre.
Iocaste. What are you saying? Polybos is dead?
Messenger. If I am not telling the truth, may I die myself.
Iocaste.   [*To a Maidservant:*
  Go in, go quickly; tell this to your master.

  O riddlers of God's will, where are you now!
  This was the man whom Oedipus, long ago,
  Feared so, fled so, in dread of destroying him—
  But it was another fate by which he died.   40
                              [*Enter Oedipus, C.*
Oedipus. Dearest Iocastê, why have you sent for me?
Iocaste. Listen to what this man says, and then tell me
  What has become of the solemn prophecies.
Oedipus. Who is this man? What is his news for me?
Iocaste. He has come from Corinth to announce your father's death!
Oedipus. Is it true, stranger? Tell me in your own words.
Messenger. I can not say it more clearly: the King is dead.
Oedipus. Was it by treason? Or by an attack of illness?
Messenger. A little thing brings old men to their rest.
Oedipus. It was sickness, then?
Messenger.   Yes, and his many years.   50
Oedipus. Ah!
  Why should a man respect the Pythian hearth,[15] or
  Give heed to the birds that jangle above his head?
  They prophesied that I should kill Polybos,
  Kill my own father; but he is dead and buried,
  And I am here—I never touched him, never,
  Unless he died of grief for my departure,
  And thus, in a sense, through me. No. Polybos
  Has packed the oracles off with him underground.
  They are empty words.
Iocaste.   Had I not told you so?   60
Oedipus. You had; it was my faint heart that betrayed me.
Iocaste. From now on never think of those things again.

———————

[15]The Delphic oracle.

Oedipus. And yet—must I not fear my mother's bed?
Iocaste. Why should anyone in this world be afraid,
    Since Fate rules us and nothing can be foreseen?
    A man should live only for the present day.

    Have no more fear of sleeping with your mother:
    How many men, in dreams, have lain with their mothers!
    No reasonable man is troubled by such things.
Oedipus. That is true; only—   70
    If only my mother were not still alive!
    But she is alive. I can not help my dread.
Iocaste. Yet this news of your father's death is wonderful.
Oedipus. Wonderful. But I fear the living woman.
Messenger. Tell me, who is this woman that you fear?
Oedipus. It is Meropê, man; the wife of King Polybos.
Messenger. Meropê? Why should you be afraid of her?
Oedipus. An oracle of the gods, a dreadful saying.
Messenger. Can you tell me about it or are you sworn to silence?
Oedipus. I can tell you, and I will.   80
    Apollo said through his prophet that I was the man
    Who should marry his own mother, shed his father's blood
    With his own hands. And so, for all these years
    I have kept clear of Corinth, and no harm has come—
    Though it would have been sweet to see my parents again.
Messenger. And is this the fear that drove you out of Corinth?
Oedipus. Would you have me kill my father?
Messenger.   As for that
    You must be reassured by the news I gave you.
Oedipus. If you could reassure me, I would reward you.
Messenger. I had that in mind, I will confess: I thought   90
    I could count on you when you returned to Corinth.
Oedipus. No: I will never go near my parents again.
Messenger. Ah, son, you still do not know what you are doing—
Oedipus. What do you mean? In the name of God tell me!
Messenger. —If these are your reasons for not going home.
Oedipus. I tell you, I fear the oracle may come true.
Messenger. And guilt may come upon you through your parents?
Oedipus. That is the dread that is always in my heart.
Messenger. Can you not see that all your fears are groundless?
Oedipus. How can you say that? They are my parents, surely?   100
Messenger. Polybos was not your father.
Oedipus.   Not my father?
Messenger. No more your father than the man speaking to you.
Oedipus. But you are nothing to me!
Messenger.   Neither was he.
  Oedipus. Then why did he call me son?

Messenger.   I will tell you:
   Long ago he had you from my hands, as a gift.
Oedipus. Then how could he love me so, if I was not his?
Messenger. He had no children, and his heart turned to you.
Oedipus. What of you? Did you buy me? Did you find me by chance?
Messenger. I came upon you in the crooked pass of Kithairon.
Oedipus. And what were you doing there?
Messenger.   Tending my flocks.   110
Oedipus. A wandering shepherd?
Messenger.   But your savior, son, that day.
Oedipus. From what did you save me?
Messenger.   Your ankles should tell you that.
Oedipus. Ah, stranger, why do you speak of that childhood pain?
Messenger. I cut the bonds that tied your ankles together.
Oedipus. I have had the mark as long as I can remember.
Messenger. That was why you were given the name you bear.[16]
Oedipus. God! Was it my father or my mother who did it?
   Tell me!
Messenger. I do not know. The man who gave you to me
   Can tell you better than I.   120
Oedipus. It was not you that found me, but another?
Messenger. It was another shepherd gave you to me.
Oedipus. Who was he? Can you tell me who he was?
Messenger. I think he was said to be one of Laïos' people.
Oedipus. You mean the Laïos who was king here years ago?
Messenger. Yes; King Laïos, and the man was one of his herdsmen.
Oedipus. Is he still alive? Can I see him?
Messenger.   These men here
   Know best about such things.
Oedipus.   Does anyone here
   Know this shepherd that he is talking about?
   Have you seen him in the fields, or in the town?   130
   If you have, tell me. It is time things were made plain.
Choragos. I think the man he means is that same shepherd
   You have already asked to see. Iocastê perhaps
   Could tell you something.
Oedipus.   Do you know anything
   About him, Lady? Is he the man we have summoned?
   Is that the man this shepherd means?
Iocaste.   Why think of him?
   Forget this herdsman. Forget it all.
   This talk is a waste of time.

---

[16]Oedipus means "swollen-foot."

Oedipus.   How can you say that,
   When the clues to my true birth are in my hands?
Iocaste. For God's love, let us have no more questioning!   140
   Is your life nothing to you?
   My own is pain enough for me to bear.
Oedipus. You need not worry. Suppose my mother a slave,
   And born of slaves: no baseness can touch you.
Iocaste. Listen to me, I beg you: do not do this thing!
Oedipus. I will not listen; the truth must be made known.
Iocaste. Everything that I say is for your own good!
Oedipus.   My own good
   Snaps my patience, then; I want none of it.
Iocaste. You are fatally wrong! May you never learn who you are!
Oedipus. Go, one of you, and bring the shepherd here.   150
   Let us leave this woman to brag of her royal name.
Iocaste. Ah, miserable!
   That is the only word I have for you now.
   That is the only word I can ever have.

                                        [*Exit into the palace*

Choragos. Why has she left us, Oedipus? Why has she gone
   In such a passion of sorrow? I fear this silence:
   Something dreadful may come of it.
Oedipus.   Let it come!
   However base my birth, I must know about it.
   The Queen, like a woman, is perhaps ashamed
   To think of my low origin. But I   160
   Am a child of Luck; I can not be dishonored.
   Luck is my mother; the passing months, my brothers,
   Have seen me rich and poor.
                    If this is so,
   How could I wish that I were someone else?
   How could I not be glad to know my birth?

ODE III

Chorus.
   If ever the coming time were known   [*Strophe*
   To my heart's pondering,
   Kithairon, now by Heaven I see the torches
   At the festival of the next full moon,
   And see the dance, and hear the choir sing
   A grace to your gentle shade:
   Mountain where Oedipus was found,
   O mountain guard of a noble race!

May the god who heals us lend his aid,
And let that glory come to pass   10
For our king's cradling-ground.

Of the nymphs that flower beyond the years,   [*Antistrophe*
Who bore you, royal child,
To Pan[17] of the hills or the timberline Apollo,
Cold in delight where the upland clears,
Or Hermês[18] for whom Kyllenê's heights are piled?
Or flushed as evening cloud,
Great Dionysos, roamer of mountains,
He—was it he who found you there,
And caught you up in his own proud   20
Arms from the sweet god-ravisher
Who laughed by the Muses'[19] fountains?

SCENE IV

Oedipus.
   Sirs: though I do not know the man,
   I think I see him coming, this shepherd we want:
   He is old, like our friend here, and the men
   Bringing him seem to be servants of my house.
   But you can tell, if you have ever seen him.
                              [*Enter Shepherd escorted by servants*
Choragos. I know him he was Laïos' man. You can trust him.
Oedipus. Tell me first, you from Corinth: is this the shepherd
   We were discussing?
Messenger.   This is the very man.
Oedipus.   [*To Shepherd*
   Come here. No, look at me. You must answer
   Everything I ask.—You belonged to Laïos?   10
Shepherd. Yes: born his slave, brought up in his house.
Oedipus. Tell me: what kind of work did you do for him?
Shepherd. I was a shepherd of his, most of my life.
Oedipus. Where mainly did you go for pasturage?
Shepherd. Sometimes Kithairon, sometimes the hills near-by.
Oedipus. Do you remember ever seeing this man out there?
Shepherd. What would he be doing there? This man?
Oedipus. This man standing here. Have you ever seen him before?
Shepherd. No. At least, not to my recollection.

---

[17] A rural god.
[18] Messenger of the gods, who was born on Mount Kyllenê.
[19] The nine daughters of Zeus and the nymph Mnemosynê.

Messenger. And that is not strange, my lord. But I'll refresh   20
  His memory: he must remember when we two
  Spent three whole seasons together, March to September,
  On Kithairon or thereabouts. He had two flocks;
  I had one. Each autumn I'd drive mine home
  And he would go back with his to Laïos' sheepfold.—
  Is this not true, just as I have described it?
Shepherd. True, yes; but it was all so long ago.
Messenger. Well, then: do you remember, back in those days,
  That you gave me a baby boy to bring up as my own?
Shepherd. What if I did? What are you trying to say?   30
Messenger. King Oedipus was once that little child.
Shepherd. Damn you, hold your tongue!
Oedipus.   No more of that!
  It is your tongue needs watching, not this man's.
Shepherd. My King, my Master, what is it I have done wrong?
Oedipus. You have not answered his question about the boy.
Shepherd. He does not know . . . He is only making trouble . . .
Oedipus. Come, speak plainly, or it will go hard with you.
Shepherd. In God's name, do not torture an old man!
Oedipus. Come here, one of you; bind his arms behind him.
Shepherd. Unhappy king! What more do you wish to learn?   40
Oedipus. Did you give this man the child he speaks of?
Shepherd.   I did.
  And I would to God I had died that very day.
Oedipus. You will die now unless you speak the truth.
Shepherd. Yet if I speak the truth, I am worse than dead.
Oedipus. Very well; since you insist upon delaying—
Shepherd. No! I have told you already that I gave him the boy.
Oedipus. Where did you get him? From your house? From somewhere
    else?
Shepherd. Not from mine, no. A man gave him to me.
Oedipus. Is that man here? Do you know whose slave he was?
Shepherd. For God's love, my King, do not ask me any more!   50
Oedipus. You are a dead man if I have to ask you again.
Shepherd. Then . . . Then the child was from the palace of Laïos.
Oedipus. A slave child? or a child of his own line?
Shepherd. Ah, I am on the brink of dreadful speech!
Oedipus. And I of dreadful hearing. Yet I must hear.
Shepherd. If you must be told, then . . .
                        They said it was Laïos' child;
  But it is your wife who can tell you about that.
Oedipus. My wife!—Did she give it to you?
Shepherd.   My lord, she did.
Oedipus. Do you know why?
Shepherd.   I was told to get rid of it.

Oedipus. An unspeakable mother!
Shepherd.   There had been prophecies . . .   60
Oedipus. Tell me.
Shepherd.   It was said that the boy would kill his own father.
Oedipus. Then why did you give him over to this old man?
Shepherd. I pitied the baby, my King,
    And I thought that this man would take him far away
    To his own country.
             He saved him—but for what a fate!
    For if you are what this man says you are,
    No man living is more wretched than Oedipus.
Oedipus. Ah God!
    It was true!
        All the prophecies!
              —Now,
    O Light, may I look on you for the last time!   70
    I, Oedipus,
    Oedipus, damned in his birth, in his marriage damned,
    Damned in the blood he shed with his own hand!
                     [*He rushes into the palace*

ODE IV

Chorus.
    Alas for the seed of men.   [*Strophe 1*

    What measure shall I give these generations
    That breathe on the void and are void
    And exist and do not exist?

    Who bears more weight of joy
    Than mass of sunlight shifting in images,
    Or who shall make his thought stay on
    That down time drifts away?

    Your splendor is all fallen.

    O naked brow of wrath and tears,   10
    O change of Oedipus!
    I who saw your days call no man blest—
    Your great days like ghósts góne.

    That mind was a strong bow.   [*Antistrophe 1*

    Deep, how deep you drew it then, hard archer,
    At a dim fearful range,
    And brought dear glory down!

You overcame the stranger—
The virgin with her hooking lion claws—

And though death sang, stood like a tower   20
To make pale Thebes take heart.

Fortress against our sorrow!

True king, giver of laws,
Majestic Oedipus!
No prince in Thebes had ever such renown,
No prince won such grace of power.

And now of all men ever known   [*Strophe 2*
Most pitiful is this man's story:
His fortunes are most changed, his state
Fallen to a low slave's   30
Ground under bitter fate.

O Oedipus, most royal one!
The great door that expelled you to the light
Gave at night—ah, gave night to your glory:
As to the father, to the fathering son.

All understood too late.

How could that queen whom Laïos won,
The garden that he harrowed at his height,
Be silent when that act was done?

But all eyes fail before time's eye,   [*Antistrophe 2*
All actions come to justice there.   41
Though never willed, though far down the deep past,
Your bed, your dread sirings,
Are brought to book at last.

Child by Laïos doomed to die,
Then doomed to lose that fortunate little death,
Would God you never took breath in this air
That with my wailing lips I take to cry:

For I weep the world's outcast.

I was blind, and now I can tell why: 50
Asleep, for you had given ease of breath
To Thebes, while the false years went by.

ÉXODOS

[*Enter, from the palace, Second Messenger*

Second Messenger. Elders of Thebes, most honored in this land,
  What horrors are yours to see and hear, what weight
  Of sorrow to be endured, if, true to your birth,
  You venerate the line of Labdakos!
  I think neither Istros nor Phasis, those great rivers,
  Could purify this place of the corruption
  It shelters now, or soon must bring to light—
  Evil not done unconsciously, but willed.

  The greatest griefs are those we cause ourselves.
Choragos. Surely, friend, we have grief enough already;   10
  What new sorrow do you mean?
Second Messenger.   The Queen is dead.
Choragos. Iocastê? Dead? But at whose hand?
Second Messenger.   Her own.
  The full horror of what happened you can not know,
  For you did not see it; but I, who did, will tell you
  As clearly as I can how she met her death.

  When she had left us,
  In passionate silence, passing through the court,
  She ran to her apartment in the house,
  Her hair clutched by the fingers of both hands.
  She closed the doors behind her; then, by that bed   20
  Where long ago the fatal son was conceived—
  That son who should bring about his father's death—
  We heard her call upon Laïos, dead so many years,
  And heard her wail for the double fruit of her marriage,
  A husband by her husband, children by her child.

  Exactly how she died I do not know:
  For Oedipus burst in moaning and would not let us
  Keep vigil to the end: it was by him
  As he stormed about the room that our eyes were caught.
  From one to another of us he went, begging a sword,   30
  Cursing the wife who was not his wife, the mother
  Whose womb had carried his own children and himself.
  I do not know: it was none of us aided him,
  But surely one of the gods was in control!
  For with a dreadful cry
  He hurled his weight, as though wrenched out of himself,
  At the twin doors: the bolts gave, and he rushed in.
  And there we saw her hanging, her body swaying

From the cruel cord she had noosed about her neck.
A great sob broke from him, heartbreaking to hear,   40
As he loosed the rope and lowered her to the ground.

I would blot out from my mind what happened next!
For the King ripped from her gown the golden brooches
That were her ornament, and raised them, and plunged them down
Straight into his own eyeballs, crying, "No more,
No more shall you look on the misery about me,
The horrors of my own doing! Too long you have known
The faces of those whom I should never have seen,
Too long been blind to those for whom I was searching!
From this hour, go in darkness!" And as he spoke,   50
He struck at his eyes—not once, but many times;
And the blood spattered his beard,
Bursting from his ruined sockets like red hail.

So from the unhappiness of two this evil has sprung,
A curse on the man and woman alike. The old
Happiness of the house of Labdakos
Was happiness enough: where is it today?
It is all wailing and ruin, disgrace, death—all
The misery of mankind that has a name—
And it is wholly and for ever theirs.   60
Choragos. Is he in agony still? Is there no rest for him?
Second Messenger. He is calling for someone to lead him to the gates
  So that all the children of Kadmos may look upon
  His father's murderer, his mother's—no,
  I can not say it!
                    And then he will leave Thebes,
  Self-exiled, in order that the curse
  Which he himself pronounced may depart from the house.
  He is weak, and there is none to lead him,
  So terrible is his suffering.
                    But you will see:
  Look, the doors are opening; in a moment   70
  You will see a thing that would crush a heart of stone.
              [*The central door is opened; Oedipus, blinded, is led in*
Choragos. Dreadful indeed for men to see.
  Never have my own eyes
  Looked on a sight so full of fear.

  Oedipus!
  What madness came upon you, what daemon
  Leaped on your life with heavier

Punishment than a mortal man can bear?
No: I can not even
Look at you, poor ruined one.   80
And I would speak, question, ponder,
If I were able. No.
You make me shudder.
Oedipus. God.   God.
   Is there a sorrow greater?
   Where shall I find harbor in this world?
   My voice is hurled far on a dark wind.
   What has God done to me?
Choragos. Too terrible to think of, or to see.
Oedipus. O cloud of night,   [*Strophe 1*
   Never to be turned away: night coming on,   91
   I can not tell how: night like a shroud!

   My fair winds brought me here.
                           O God. Again
   The pain of the spikes where I had sight,
   The flooding pain
   Of memory, never to be gouged out.
Choragos. This is not strange.
   You suffer it all twice over, remorse in pain,
   Pain in remorse.
Oedipus. Ah dear friend   [*Antistrophe 1*
   Are you faithful even yet, you alone?   101
   Are you still standing near me, will you stay here,
   Patient, to care for the blind?
                           The blind man!
   Yet even blind I know who it is attends me,
   By the voice's tone—
   Though my new darkness hide the comforter.
Choragos. Oh fearful act!
   What god was it drove you to rake black
   Night across your eyes?
Oedipus. Apollo. Apollo. Dear   [*Strophe 2*
   Children, the god was Apollo.   111
   He brought my sick, sick fate upon me.
   But the blinding hand was my own!
   How could I bear to see
   When all my sight was horror everywhere?
Choragos. Everywhere; that is true.
Oedipus. And now what is left?
   Images? Love? A greeting even,
   Sweet to the senses? Is there anything?

Ah, no, friends: lead me away. 120
Lead me away from Thebes.
                    Lead the great wreck
And hell of Oedipus, whom the gods hate.
Choragos. Your fate is clear, you are not blind to that.
    Would God you had never found it out!
Oedipus. Death take the man who unbound   [*Antistrophe 2*
    My feet on that hillside
    And delivered me from death to life! What life?
    If only I had died,
    This weight of monstrous doom
    Could not have dragged me and my darlings down. 130
Choragos. I would have wished the same.
Oedipus. Oh never to have come here
    With my father's blood upon me! Never
    To have been the man they call his mother's husband!
    Oh accurst! Oh child of evil,
    To have entered that wretched bed—
                            the selfsame one!
    More primal than sin itself, this fell to me.
Choragos. I do not know how I can answer you.
    You were better dead than alive and blind.
Oedipus. Do not counsel me any more. This punishment 140
    That I have laid upon myself is just.
    If I had eyes,
    I do not know how I could bear the sight
    Of my father, when I came to the house of Death,
    Or my mother: for I have sinned against them both
    So vilely that I could not make my peace
    By strangling my own life.
                        Or do you think my children,
    Born as they were born, would be sweet to my eyes?
    Ah never, never! Nor this town with its high walls,
    Nor the holy images of the gods.
                            For I, 150
    Thrice miserable!—Oedipus, noblest of all the line
    Of Kadmos, have condemned myself to enjoy
    These things no more, by my own malediction
    Expelling that man whom the gods declared
    To be a defilement in the house of Laïos.
    After exposing the rankness of my own guilt,
    How could I look men frankly in the eyes?
    No, I swear it,
    If I could have stifled my hearing at its source,
    I would have done it and made all this body 160

A tight cell of misery, blank to light and sound:
So I should have been safe in a dark agony
Beyond all recollection.
                              Ah Kithairon!
Why did you shelter me? When I was cast upon you,
Why did I not die? Then I should never
Have shown the world my execrable birth.

Ah Polybos! Corinth, city that I believed
The ancient seat of my ancestors: how fair
I seemed, your child! And all the while this evil
Was cancerous within me!
                              For I am sick   170
In my daily life, sick in my origin.

O three roads, dark ravine, woodland and way
Where three roads met: you, drinking my father's blood,
My own blood, spilled by my own hand: can you remember
The unspeakable things I did there, and the things
I went on from there to do?
                              O marriage, marriage!
The act that engendered me, and again the act
Performed by the son in the same bed—
                              Ah, the net
Of incest, mingling fathers, brothers, sons,
With brides, wives, mothers: the last evil   180
That can be known by men: no tongue can say
How evil!
                 No. For the love of God, conceal me
Somewhere far from Thebes; or kill me; or hurl me
Into the sea, away from men's eyes for ever.

Come, lead me. You need not fear to touch me.
Of all men, I alone can bear this guilt.

                                           [*Enter Creon*

Choragos. We are not the ones to decide; but Creon here
    May fitly judge of what you ask. He only
    Is left to protect the city in your place.
Oedipus. Alas, how can I speak to him? What right have I   190
    To beg his courtesy whom I have deeply wronged?
Creon. I have not come to mock you, Oedipus,
    Or to reproach you, either.

                                           [*To Attendants:*

                 —You, standing there:
If you have lost all respect for man's dignity,
At least respect the flame of Lord Helios:

Do not allow this pollution to show itself
Openly here, an affront to the earth
And Heaven's rain and the light of day. No, take him
Into the house as quickly as you can.
For it is proper   200
That only the close kindred see his grief.
Oedipus. I pray you in God's name, since your courtesy
Ignores my dark expectation, visiting
With mercy this man of all men most execrable:
Give me what I ask—for your good, not for mine.
Creon. And what is it that you would have me do?
Oedipus. Drive me out of this country as quickly as may be
To a place where no human voice can ever greet me.
Creon. I should have done that before now—only,
God's will had not been wholly revealed to me.   210
Oedipus. But his command is plain: the parricide
Must be destroyed. I am that evil man.
Creon. That is the sense of it, yes; but as things are,
We had best discover clearly what is to be done.
Oedipus. You would learn more about a man like me?
Creon. You are ready now to listen to the god.
Oedipus. I will listen. But it is to you
That I must turn for help. I beg you, hear me.

The woman in there—
Give her whatever funeral you think proper: 220
She is your sister.
                        —But let me go, Creon!
Let me purge my father's Thebes of the pollution
Of my living here, and go out to the wild hills,
To Kithairon, that has won such fame with me,
The tomb my mother and father appointed for me,
And let me die there, as they willed I should.
And yet I know
Death will not ever come to me through sickness
Or in any natural way: I have been preserved
For some unthinkable fate. But let that be.   230

As for my sons, you need not care for them.
They are men, they will find some way to live.
But my poor daughters, who have shared my table,
Who never before have been parted from their father—
Take care of them, Creon; do this for me.

And will you let me touch them with my hands
A last time, and let us weep together?
Be kind, my lord,
Great prince, be kind!
         Could I but touch them,
They would be mine again, as when I had my eyes.   240
        [Enter Antigone and Ismene, attended
Ah, God!
Is it my dearest children I hear weeping?
Has Creon pitied me and sent my daughters?
Creon. Yes, Oedipus: I knew that they were dear to you
In the old days, and know you must love them still.
Oedipus. May God bless you for this—and be a friendlier
Guardian to you than he has been to me!

Children, where are you?
Come quickly to my hands: they are your brother's—
Hands that have brought your father's once clear eyes   250
To this way of seeing—
         Ah dearest ones,
I had neither sight nor knowledge then, your father
By the woman who was the source of his own life!
And I weep for you—having no strength to see you—,
I weep for you when I think of the bitterness
That men will visit upon you all your lives.
What homes, what festivals can you attend
Without being forced to depart again in tears?
And when you come to marriageable age,
Where is the man, my daughters, who would dare   260
Risk the bane that lies on all my children?
Is there any evil wanting? Your father killed
His father; sowed the womb of her who bore him;
Engendered you at the fount of his own existence!
That is what they will say of you.
         Then, whom
Can you ever marry? There are no bridegrooms for you,
And your lives must wither away in sterile dreaming.

O Creon, son of Menoikeus!
You are the only father my daughters have,
Since we, their parents, are both of us gone for ever.   270
They are your own blood: you will not let them
Fall into beggary and loneliness;
You will keep them from the miseries that are mine!

Take pity on them; see, they are only children,
Friendless except for you. Promise me this,
Great Prince, and give me your hand in token of it.

                              [Creon clasps his right hand

Children:
I could say much, if you could understand me,
But as it is, I have only this prayer for you:
Live where you can, be as happy as you can—   280
Happier, please God, than God has made your father!
Creon. Enough. You have wept enough. Now go within.
Oedipus. I must; but it is hard.
Creon.   Time eases all things.
Oedipus. But you must promise—
Creon.   Say what you desire.
Oedipus. Send me from Thebes!
Creon.   God grant that I may!
Oedipus. But since God hates me . . .
Creon.   No, he will grant your wish.
Oedipus. You promise?
Creon.   I can not speak beyond my knowledge.
Oedipus. Then lead me in.
Creon.   Come now, and leave your children.
Oedipus. No! Do not take them from me!
Creon.   Think no longer
That you are in command here, but rather think
How, when you were, you served your own destruction.   290
    [Exeunt into the house all but the Chorus; the Choragos
        chants directly to the audience:
Choragos. Men of Thebes: look upon Oedipus.

This is the king who solved the famous riddle
And towered up, most powerful of men.
No mortal eyes but looked on him with envy,
Yet in the end ruin swept over him.

Let every man in mankind's frailty
Consider his last day; and let none
Presume on his good fortune until he find
Life, at his death, a memory without pain.   300

QUESTIONS

1. What prior knowledge of the Oedipus legend, or impressions about it, did you bring
to your reading of the tragedy?

2. What prior ideas about the nature of tragedy have you brought to this drama? How have they influenced your reading?
3. To what degree is Oedipus's character, as you perceive it, responsible for what happens to him?
4. Can Oedipus be called innocent in any sense? Explain.
5. Of what, if anything, is Oedipus guilty? To what extent do your ideas of criminal behavior or of sin apply to him?
6. If you believe in Divine Justice, to what extent does your idea of it accord with Oedipus's experience?
7. What sense of the gods' relations with human beings does this tragedy give you?
8. What thoughts and feelings are evoked by Oedipus's fate?

August Strindberg (1849–1912)
THE STRONGER*

CHARACTERS

Mrs. X., an actress, married
Miss Y., an actress, unmarried
A Waitress

SCENE *The corner of a ladies' café. Two little iron tables, a red velvet sofa, several chairs. Enter Mrs. X., dressed in winter clothes, carrying a Japanese basket on her arm.*

Miss Y. sits with a half-empty beer bottle before her, reading an illustrated paper, which she changes later for another.

Mrs. X. Good afternoon, Amelia. You're sitting here alone on Christmas eve like a poor bachelor!

Miss Y. (*Looks up, nods, and resumes her reading.*)

Mrs. X. Do you know it really hurts me to see you like this, alone, in a café, and on Christmas eve, too. It makes me feel as I did one time when I saw a bridal party in a Paris restaurant, and the bride sat reading a comic paper, while the groom played billiards with the witnesses. Huh, thought I, with such a beginning, what will follow, and what will be the end? He played billiards on his wedding eve! (*Miss Y. starts to speak*) And she read a comic paper, you mean? Well, they are not altogether the same thing.

(*A Waitress enters, places a cup of chocolate before Mrs. X. and goes out.*)

Mrs. X. You know what, Amelia! I believe you would have done better to have kept him! Do you remember, I was the first to say "Forgive him?" Do you remember that? You would be married now and have a home.

*Translated by Edith and Warner Oland.

Remember that Christmas when you went out to visit your fiancé's parents in the country? How you gloried in the happiness of home life and really longed to quit the theater forever? Yes, Amelia dear, home is the best of all—next to the theater—and as for children—well, you don't understand that.

Miss Y. (Looks up scornfully.)

(Mrs. X. sips a few spoonfuls out of the cup, then opens her basket and shows Christmas presents.)

Mrs. X. Now you shall see what I bought for my piggywigs. (*Takes up a doll.*) Look at this! This is for Lisa, ha! Do you see how she can roll her eyes and turn her head, eh? And here is Maja's popgun.

(Loads it and shoots at Miss Y.)

Miss Y. (Makes a startled gesture.)
Mrs. X. Did I frighten you? Do you think I would like to shoot you, eh? On my soul, if I don't think you did! If you wanted to shoot *me* it wouldn't be so surprising, because I stood in your way—and I know you can never forget that—although I was absolutely innocent. You still believe I intrigued and got you out of the Stora theater, but I didn't. I didn't do that, although you think so. Well, it doesn't make any difference what I say to you. You still believe I did it. (*Takes up a pair of embroidered slippers.*) And these are for my better half. I embroidered them myself—I can't bear tulips, but he wants tulips on everything.
Miss Y. (Looks up ironically and curiously.)
Mrs. X. (*putting a hand in each slipper*). See what little feet Bob has! What? And you should see what a splendid stride he has! You've never seen him in slippers! (*Miss Y. laughs aloud.*) Look! (*She makes the slippers walk on the table. Miss Y. laughs loudly.*) And when he is grumpy he stamps like this with his foot. "What! damn those servants who can never learn to make coffee. Oh, now those creatures haven't trimmed the lamp wick properly!" And then there are drafts on the floor and his feet are cold. "Ugh, how cold it is; the stupid idiots can never keep the fire going." (*She rubs the slippers together, one sole over the other.*)
Miss Y. (Shrieks with laughter.)
Mrs. X. And then he comes home and has to hunt for his slippers which Marie has stuck under the chiffonier—oh, but it's sinful to sit here and make fun of one's husband this way when he is kind and a good little man. You ought to have had such a husband, Amelia. What are you laughing at? What? What? And you see he's true to me. Yes, I'm sure of that, because he told me himself—what are you laughing at?—that when I was touring in Norway that brazen Frederika came and wanted to seduce him! Can you fancy anything so infamous? (*pause*) I'd have torn her eyes

out if she had come to see him when I was at home. (*pause*) It was lucky that Bob told me about it himself and that it didn't reach me through gossip. (*pause*) But would you believe it, Frederika wasn't the only one! I don't know why, but the women are crazy about my husband. They must think he has influence about getting them theatrical engagements, because he is connected with the government. Perhaps you were after him yourself. I didn't use to trust you any too much. But now I know he never bothered his head about you, and you always seemed to have a grudge against him someway.

(*Pause. They look at each other in a puzzled way.*)

Mrs. X. Come and see us this evening, Amelia, and show us that you're not put out with us—not put out with me at any rate. I don't know, but I think it would be uncomfortable to have you for an enemy. Perhaps it's because I stood in your way (*more slowly*) or—I really—don't know why—in particular.

(*Pause. Miss Y. stares at Mrs. X. curiously.*)

Mrs. X. (*thoughtfully*). Our acquaintance has been so queer. When I saw you for the first time I was afraid of you, so afraid that I didn't dare let you out of my sight; no matter when or where, I always found myself near you—I didn't dare have you for an enemy, so I became your friend. But there was always discord when you came to our house, because I saw that my husband couldn't endure you, and the whole thing seemed as awry to me as an ill-fitting gown—and I did all I could to make him friendly toward you, but with no success until you became engaged. Then came a violent friendship between you, so that it looked all at once as though you both dared show your real feelings only when you were secure—and then—how was it later? I didn't get jealous—strange to say! And I remember at the christening, when you acted as godmother, I made him kiss you—he did so, and you became so confused—as it were; I didn't notice it then—didn't think about it later, either—have never thought about it until—now! (*Rises suddenly.*) Why are you silent? You haven't said a word this whole time, but you have let me go on talking! You have sat there, and your eyes have reeled out of me all these thoughts which lay like raw silk in its cocoon—thoughts—suspicious thoughts, perhaps. Let me see—why did you break your engagement? Why do you never come to our house any more? Why won't you come to see us tonight?

(*Miss Y. appears as if about to speak.*)

Mrs. X. Hush, you needn't speak—I understand it all! It was because—and because—and because! Yes, yes! Now all the accounts balance. That's it.

Fie, I won't sit at the same table with you. (*Moves her things to another table.*) That's the reason I had to embroider tulips—which I hate—on his slippers, because you are fond of tulips; that's why (*throws slippers on the floor*) we go to Lake Mälarn in the summer, because you don't like salt water; that's why my boy is named Eskil—because it's your father's name; that's why I wear your colors, read your authors, eat your favorite dishes, drink your drinks—chocolate, for instance; that's why—oh—my God—it's terrible, when I think about it; it's terrible. Everything, everything came from you to me, even your passions. Your soul crept into mine, like a worm into an apple, ate and ate, bored and bored, until nothing was left but the rind and a little black dust within. I wanted to get away from you, but I couldn't; you lay like a snake and charmed me with your black eyes; I felt that when I lifted my wings they only dragged me down; I lay in the water with bound feet, and the stronger I strove to keep up the deeper I worked myself down, down, until I sank to the bottom, where you lay like a giant crab to clutch me in your claws—and there I am lying now.

I hate you, hate you, hate you! And you only sit there silent—silent and indifferent; indifferent whether it's new moon or waning moon, Christmas or New Year's, whether others are happy or unhappy; without power to hate or to love; as quiet as a stork by a rat hole—you couldn't scent your prey and capture it, but you could lie in wait for it! You sit here in your corner of the café—did you know it's called "The Rat Trap" for you?—and read the papers to see if misfortune hasn't befallen someone, to see if someone hasn't been given notice at the theater, perhaps; you sit here and calculate about your next victim and reckon on your chances of recompense like a pilot in a shipwreck. Poor Amelia, I pity you, nevertheless, because I know you are unhappy, unhappy like one who has been wounded, and angry because you are wounded. I can't be angry with you, no matter how much I want to be—because you come out the weaker one. Yes, all that with Bob doesn't trouble me. What is that to me, after all? And what difference does it make whether I learned to drink chocolate from you or some one else. (*Sips a spoonful from her cup*) Besides, chocolate is very healthful. And if you taught me how to dress—*tant mieux!*[1]— that has only made me more attractive to my husband; so you lost and I won there. Well, judging by certain signs, I believe you have already lost him; and you certainly intended that I should leave him—do as you did with your fiancé and regret as you now regret; but, you see, I don't do that—we mustn't be too exacting. And why should I take only what no one else wants?

Perhaps, take it all in all, I am at this moment the stronger one. You received nothing from me, but you gave me much. And now I seem like

---

[1]So much the better!

a thief since you have awakened and find I possess what is your loss. How could it be otherwise when everything is worthless and sterile in your hands? You can never keep a man's love with your tulips and your passions—but I can keep it. You can't learn how to live from your authors, as I have learned. You have no little Eskil to cherish, even if your father's name was Eskil. And why are you always silent, silent, silent? I thought that was strength, but perhaps it is because you have nothing to say! Because you never think about anything! (*Rises and picks up slippers.*) Now I'm going home—and take the tulips with me—your tulips! You are unable to learn from another; you can't bend—therefore, you broke like a dry stalk. But I won't break! Thank you, Amelia, for all your good lessons. Thanks for teaching my husband how to love. Now I'm going home to love him. (*Goes*)

QUESTIONS

1. What do you gather about Mrs. X's character and state of mind from her monologue?
2. How believable are her protestations of innocence with respect to Miss Y?
3. What thoughts and feelings do you attribute to Miss Y's silence—and to her laughter at one point?
4. What do the gestures and objects shown onstage during the play reveal about either woman or the conflict between them?
5. What sense do you have of Bob's importance to each?
6. What actually happens over the course of the play?
7. Is Mrs. X the stronger woman? Explain.

ADDITIONAL QUESTIONS

1. In the Biblical story, man's Fall from an original state of innocence resulted in the loss of Eden. That lost lovely place is recalled in the imagery of "Fern Hill" and perhaps the opening scenes of "Big Boy Leaves Home." Considering either of these works, how does the Edenic setting or imagery contribute to its meaning?
2. Curiously like Hawthorne's Goodman Brown, the narrator in Cheever's "The Fourth Alarm" sees his wife in a situation that calls into question his own innocence. How are Goodman and the narrator characterized, and how does each react to his experience?
3. The presence of the Devil in "Young Goodman Brown" introduces the idea of evil as the essential force confronting innocence. In what other works would you say evil is depicted? Choosing one such work, can you explain what idea of evil is found in it?
4. Several works focus upon a child's relationships with adults as a crucial circumstance in the passage from innocence to experience. How important are such relationships to the meaning of "The Fig Tree" or "Winter Night"?
5. Both "I Want to Know Why" and "The Found Boat" are concerned with a first experience of adult sexuality. How do the two stories treat the relation between sexuality and innocence?

6. Several poems in the section associate the world of nature with innocence. In which is this association clearest?
7. Some works emphasize the growth involved in leaving childhood. Consider Wordsworth's "Lines . . . Above Tintern Abbey," Whitman's "There Was a Child Went Forth," and Frost's "Birches." How does such growth appear in each of these?
8. Over two millenia ago, Aristotle used *Oedipus* as his example when he spoke of tragedy as arousing pity and fear in its spectators. What is there in Sophocles's dramatization of the Oedipus story that arouses these emotions?

PART TWO

SELF AND SOCIETY

W. B. Yeats read Henry Thoreau's *Walden* in youth and in the poem "The Lake Isle of Innisfree" imagines a solitary, deliberate life on a small Irish island. Yeats never did go to live there, and solitude in nature is neither possible nor desirable for very long for most people. We may occasionally regard society as at odds with our deeper selves, but mostly we live among others "mid the din/ Of towns and cities" (to borrow Wordsworth's phrase) and endure the stresses of adapting to society's demands.

Solitariness within the social order is still quite possible. Psychological and emotional withdrawal from others is an option that may signal a self-preserving or creative impulse or, at the other extreme, the onset of madness. Moreover, spiritual isolation, loneliness, is a part of the human condition that society never entirely eliminates. J. Alfred Prufrock in T. S. Eliot's poem knows this, as he imagines walking alone on a beach, hearing the human voices in his fearful reverie. In *The Misanthrope* Alceste is happy at least in always having an audience for his anger at humankind. Partly for this reason Molière's play remains a comedy.

Other works in this section offer different perspectives upon the ways people accommodate themselves to their world or fail to do so. Some works suggest how constraining or destructive may be the roles that society imposes upon individuals. Nora Helmer in Ibsen's *A Doll's House* is a striking example of a person who, in rejecting an established role, may begin changing society by changing herself. You will note that the question of female roles in society recurs, in fact, throughout the section. Not every female writer is preoccupied with the question, but some are; and male writers besides Ibsen have given us works in which female experience is central.

Reflect upon that experience when responding to works in this and the other sections. Muriel Rukeyser's little poem about Oedipus's repeat encounter with the Sphinx and his certainty concerning the identity of "man" suggests a blindness that such reflection may help prevent. As you read, you might also ponder how much the gender, race, age, or any distinguishing characteristic of a reader enters into literary experience. You may be a woman and one not usually interested in stories of sailing ships. If you identify to any degree with the unnamed captain in "The Secret Sharer," ask yourself why you do. Is Conrad's use of a first-person narrator mainly responsible? Or does something apart from or beyond the writer's craft speak to you?

Ask the same kinds of questions about reading the works of black writers, if you're not black—or if you are, about reading works from the English literary tradition or by contemporary white authors. Ask also why you should read works about middle-aged or older people, if you are young. Consider whether sexual preference is something you should take into account if you know or infer that a writer's orientation was or is different from yours in this respect.

Ultimately, all such questions involve the larger issue of how literary experience extends personal experience. Sometimes it seems that literature merely extends the struggle among groups in society. But reading is a peculiar activity in which you engage as an individual and on unique terms with the writers and created voices that speak to you. In "Theme for English B" Langston Hughes's speaker suggests that both writer and reader may resist sharing their lives otherwise. He adds that it is "American" to acknowledge that each is part of the other. Be that as it may, in the unlonely solitude of reading you may find that dividing lines of gender, race, or age, as well as distances of place and time, disappear. You may of course close your mind as you close a book. But reading literature enables you to enter other lives and, through these, a larger world.

FICTION

Joseph Conrad (1857–1924)

THE SECRET SHARER

I

On my right hand there were lines of fishing stakes resembling a mysterious system of half-submerged bamboo fences, incomprehensible in its division of the domain of tropical fishes, and crazy of aspect as if abandoned forever by some nomad tribe of fishermen now gone to the other end of the ocean; for there was no sign of human habitation as far as the eye could reach. To the left a group of barren islets, suggesting ruins of stone walls, towers, and blockhouses, had its foundations set in a blue sea that itself looked solid, so still and stable did it lie below my feet; even the track of light from the westering sun shone smoothly, without that animated glitter which tells of an imperceptible ripple. And when I turned my head to take a parting glance at the tug which had just left us anchored outside the bar, I saw the straight line of the flat shore joined to the stable sea, edge to edge, with a perfect and unmarked closeness, in one leveled floor half brown, half blue under the enormous dome of the sky. Corresponding in their insignificance to the islets of the sea, two small clumps of trees, one on each side of the only fault in the impeccable joint, marked the mouth of the river Meinam we had just left on the first preparatory stage of our homeward journey; and, far back on the inland level, a larger and loftier mass, the grove surrounding the great Paknam pagoda, was the only thing on which the eye could rest from the vain task of exploring the monotonous sweep of the horizon. Here and there gleams as of a few scattered pieces of silver marked the windings of the great river; and on the nearest of them, just within the bar, the tug steaming right into the land became lost to my sight, hull and funnel and masts, as though the impassive earth had swallowed her up without an effort, without a tremor. My eye followed the light cloud of her smoke, now here, now there, above the plain, according to the devious curves of the stream, but always fainter and farther away, till I lost it at last behind the miter-shaped hill of the great pagoda. And then I was left alone with my ship, anchored at the head of the Gulf of Siam.

She floated at the starting point of a long journey, very still in an immense stillness, the shadows of her spars flung far to the eastward by the setting sun. At that moment I was alone on her decks. There was not a sound in her—and around us nothing moved, nothing lived, not a canoe on the water, not a bird in the air, not a cloud in the sky. In this breathless pause at the threshold of a long passage we seemed to be measuring our fitness for a long and arduous enterprise, the appointed task of both our existences to be carried out, far from all human eyes, with only sky and sea for spectators and for judges.

There must have been some glare in the air to interfere with one's sight, because it was only just before the sun left us that my roaming eyes made out beyond the highest ridge of the principal islet of the group something which did away with the solemnity of perfect solitude. The tide of darkness flowed on swiftly; and with tropical suddenness a swarm of stars came out above the shadowy earth, while I lingered yet, my hand resting lightly on my ship's rail as if on the shoulder of a trusted friend. But, with all that multitude of celestial bodies staring down at one, the comfort of quiet communion with her was gone for good. And there were also disturbing sounds by this time—voices, footsteps forward; the steward flitted along the main deck, a busily ministering spirit; a hand bell tinkled urgently under the poop deck. . . .

I found my two officers waiting for me near the supper table, in the lighted cuddy. We sat down at once, and as I helped the chief mate, I said:

"Are you aware that there is a ship anchored inside the islands? I saw her mastheads above the ridge as the sun went down."

He raised sharply his simple face, overcharged by a terrible growth of whisker, and emitted his usual ejaculations: "Bless my soul, sir! You don't say so!"

My second mate was a round-cheeked, silent young man, grave beyond his years, I thought; but as our eyes happened to meet I detected a slight quiver on his lips. I looked down at once. It was not my part to encourage sneering on board my ship. It must be said, too, that I knew very little of my officers. In consequence of certain events of no particular significance, except to myself, I had been appointed to the command only a fortnight before. Neither did I know much of the hands forward. All these people had been together for eighteen months or so, and my position was that of the only stranger on board. I mention this because it has some bearing on what is to follow. But what I felt most was my being a stranger to the ship; and if truth must be told, I was somewhat of a stranger to myself. The youngest man on board (barring the second mate), and untried as yet by a position of the fullest responsibility, I was willing to take the adequacy of the others for granted. They had simply to be equal to their tasks: but I wondered how far I should turn out faithful to that ideal conception of one's own personality every man sets up for himself secretly.

Meantime the chief mate, with an almost visible effect of collaboration on the part of his round eyes and frightful whiskers, was trying to evolve a theory of the anchored ship. His dominant trait was to take all things into earnest consideration. He was of a painstaking turn of mind. As he used to say, he "liked to account to himself" for practically everything that came in his way, down to a miserable scorpion he had found in his cabin a week before. The why and the wherefore of that scorpion—how it got on board and came to select his room rather than the pantry (which was a dark place and more what a scorpion would be partial to), and how on earth it managed to drown itself in the inkwell of his writing desk—had exercised him infinitely. The ship within the islands was much more easily accounted for; and just as we were about to rise from the table he made his pronouncement. She was, he doubted not, a ship from home lately arrived. Probably she drew too much water to cross the bar except at the top of spring tides. Therefore she went into that natural harbor to wait for a few days in preference to remaining in an open roadstead.

"That's so," confirmed the second mate, suddenly, in his slightly hoarse voice. "She draws over twenty feet. She's the Liverpool ship *Sephora* with a cargo of coal. Hundred and twenty-three days from Cardiff."

We looked at him in surprise.

"The tugboat skipper told me when he came on board for your letters, sir," explained the young man. "He expects to take her up the river the day after tomorrow."

After thus overwhelming us with the extent of his information he slipped out of the cabin. The mate observed regretfully that he "could not account for that young fellow's whims." What prevented him telling us all about it at once, he wanted to know.

I detained him as he was making a move. For the last two days the crew had had plenty of hard work, and the night before they had very little sleep. I felt painfully that I—a stranger—was doing something unusual when I directed him to let all hands turn in without setting an anchor watch. I proposed to keep on deck myself till one o'clock or thereabouts. I would get the second mate to relieve me at that hour.

"He will turn out the cook and the steward at four," I concluded, "and then give you a call. Of course at the slightest sign of any sort of wind we'll have the hands up and make a start at once."

He concealed his astonishment. "Very well, sir." Outside the cuddy he put his head in the second mate's door to inform him of my unheard-of caprice to take a five hours' anchor watch on myself. I heard the other raise his voice incredulously: "What? The captain himself?" Then a few more murmurs, a door closed, then another. A few moments later I went on deck.

My strangeness, which had made me sleepless, had prompted that unconventional arrangement, as if I had expected in those solitary hours of the night to get on terms with the ship of which I knew nothing, manned by men of whom I knew very little more. Fast alongside a wharf, littered like any ship in port with a tangle of unrelated things, invaded by unrelated shore people, I had hardly seen her yet properly. Now, as she lay cleared for sea, the stretch of her main deck seemed to me very fine under the stars. Very fine, very roomy for her size, and very inviting. I descended the poop and paced the waist, my mind picturing to myself the coming passage through the Malay Archipelago, down the Indian Ocean, and up the Atlantic. All its phases were familiar enough to me, every characteristic, all the alternatives which were likely to face me on the high seas— everything! . . . except the novel responsibility of command. But I took heart from the reasonable thought that the ship was like other ships, the men like other men, and that the sea was not likely to keep any special surprises expressly for my discomfiture.

Arrived at that comforting conclusion, I bethought myself of a cigar and went below to get it. All was still down there. Everybody at the after end of the ship was sleeping profoundly. I came out again on the quarter-deck, agreeably at ease in my sleeping suit on that warm breathless night, barefooted, a glowing cigar in my teeth, and, going forward, I was met by the profound silence of the fore end of the ship. Only as I passed the door of the forecastle I heard a deep, quiet, trustful sigh of some sleeper inside. And suddenly I rejoiced in the great security of the sea as compared with the unrest of the land, in my choice of that untempted life presenting no disquieting problems, invested with an elementary moral beauty by the absolute straightforwardness of its appeal and by the singleness of its purpose.

The riding light in the fore-rigging burned with a clear, untroubled, as if symbolic, flame, confident and bright in the mysterious shades of the night. Passing on my way aft along the other side of the ship, I observed that the rope side ladder, put over, no doubt, for the master of the tug when he came to fetch away our letters, had not been hauled in as it should have been. I became annoyed at this, for exactitude in small matters is the very soul of discipline. Then I reflected that I had myself peremptorily dismissed my officers from duty, and by my own act had prevented the anchor watch being formally set and things properly attended to. I asked myself whether it was wise ever to interfere with the established routine of duties even from the kindest of motives. My action might have made me appear eccentric. Goodness only knew how that absurdly whiskered mate would "account" for my conduct, and what the whole ship thought of that informality of their new captain. I was vexed with myself.

Not from compunction certainly, but, as it were mechanically, I proceeded to get the ladder in myself. Now a side ladder of that sort is a light affair and comes in easily, yet my vigorous tug, which should have brought it flying on board, merely recoiled upon my body in a totally unexpected jerk. What the devil! . . . I was so astounded by the immovableness of that ladder that I remained stock-still, trying to account for it to myself like that imbecile mate of mine. In the end, of course, I put my head over the rail.

The side of the ship made an opaque belt of shadow on the darkling glassy shimmer of the sea. But I saw at once something elongated and pale floating very close to the ladder. Before I could form a guess a faint flash of phosphorescent light, which seemed to issue suddenly from the naked body of a man, flickered in the sleeping water with the elusive, silent play of summer lightning in a night sky. With a gasp I saw revealed to my stare a pair of feet, the long legs, a broad livid back immersed right up to the neck in a greenish cadaverous glow. One hand, awash, clutched the bottom rung of the ladder. He was complete but for the head. A headless corpse! The cigar dropped out of my gaping mouth with a tiny plop and a short hiss quite audible in the absolute stillness of all things under heaven. At that I suppose he raised up his face, a dimly pale oval in the shadow of the ship's side. But even then I could only barely make out down there the shape of his black-haired head. However, it was enough for the horrid, frost-bound sensation which had gripped me about the chest to pass off. The moment of vain exclamations was past, too. I only climbed on the spare spar and leaned over the rail as far as I could, to bring my eyes nearer to that mystery floating alongside.

As he hung by the ladder, like a resting swimmer, the sea lightning played about his limbs at every stir; and he appeared in it ghastly, silvery, fishlike. He remained as mute as a fish, too. He made no motion to get out of the water, either. It was inconceivable that he should not attempt to come on board, and strangely troubling to suspect that perhaps he did not want to. And my first words were prompted by just that troubled incertitude.

"What's the matter?" I asked in my ordinary tone, speaking down to the face upturned exactly under mine.

"Cramp," it answered, no louder. Then slightly anxious, "I say, no need to call anyone."

"I was not going to," I said.

"Are you alone on deck?"

"Yes."

I had somehow the impression that he was on the point of letting go the ladder to swim away beyond my ken—mysterious as he came. But, for the moment, this being appearing as if he had risen from the bottom of the sea (it was certainly the nearest land to the ship) wanted only to know the time. I told him. And he, down there, tentatively:

"I suppose your captain's turned in?"

"I am sure he isn't," I said.

He seemed to struggle with himself, for I heard something like the low, bitter murmur of doubt. "What's the good?" His next words came out with a hesitating effort.

"Look here, my man. Could you call him out quietly?"

I thought the time had come to declare myself.

"*I* am the captain."

I heard a "By Jove!" whispered at the level of the water. The phosphorescence flashed in the swirl of the water all about his limbs, his other hand seized the ladder.

"My name's Leggatt."

The voice was calm and resolute. A good voice. The self-possession of that man had somehow induced a corresponding state in myself. It was very quietly that I remarked:

"You must be a good swimmer."

"Yes. I've been in the water practically since nine o'clock. The question for me now is whether I am to let go this ladder and go on swimming till I sink from exhaustion, or—to come on board here."

I felt this was no mere formula of desperate speech, but a real alternative in the view of a strong soul. I should have gathered from this that he was young; indeed, it is only the young who are ever confronted by such clear issues. But at this time it was pure intuition on my part. A mysterious communication was established already between us two—in the face of that silent darkened tropical sea. I was young, too; young enough to make no comment. The man in the water began suddenly to climb up the ladder, and I hastened away from the rail to fetch some clothes.

Before entering the cabin I stood still, listening in the lobby at the foot of the stairs. A faint snore came through the closed door of the chief mate's room. The second mate's door was on the hook, but the darkness in there was absolutely soundless. He, too, was young and could sleep like a stone. Remained the steward, but he was not likely to wake up before he was called. I got a sleeping suit out of my room and, coming back on deck, saw the naked man from the sea sitting on the main hatch, glimmering white in the darkness, his elbows on his knees and his head in his hands. In a moment he had concealed his damp body in a sleeping suit of the same gray-stripe pattern as the one I was wearing and followed me like my double on the poop. Together we moved right aft, barefooted, silent.

"What is it?" I asked in a deadened voice, taking the lighted lamp out of the binnacle, and raising it to his face.

"An ugly business."

He had rather regular features; a good mouth; light eyes under somewhat heavy, dark eyebrows; a smooth, square forehead; no growth on his cheeks; a small, brown mustache, and a well-shaped, round chin. His expression was concentrated, meditative, under the inspecting light of the lamp I held up to his face; such as a man thinking hard in solitude might wear. My sleeping suit was just right for his size. A well-knit young fellow of twenty-five at most. He caught his lower lip with the edge of white, even teeth.

"Yes," I said, replacing the lamp in the binnacle. The warm, heavy tropical night closed upon his head again.

"There's a ship over there," he murmured.

"Yes, I know. The *Sephora*. Did you know of us?"

"Hadn't the slightest idea. I am the mate of her—" He paused and corrected himself. "I should say I *was*."

"Aha! Something wrong?"

"Yes. Very wrong indeed. I've killed a man."

"What do you mean? Just now?"

"No, on the passage. Weeks ago. Thirty-nine south. When I say a man—"

"Fit of temper," I suggested, confidently.

The shadowy, dark head, like mine, seemed to nod imperceptibly above the ghostly gray of my sleeping suit. It was, in the night, as though I had been faced by my own reflection in the depths of a somber and immense mirror.

"A pretty thing to have to own up to for a Conway boy," murmured my double, distinctly.

"You're a Conway boy?"[1]

"I am," he said, as if startled. Then slowly . . . . "Perhaps you too—"

---

[1] The Conway was a wooden battleship used by the Royal Navy and British merchant service for training young officers.

It was so; but being a couple of years older I had left before he joined. After a quick interchange of dates a silence fell; and I thought suddenly of my absurd mate with his terrific whiskers and the "Bless my soul—you don't say so" type of intellect. My double gave me an inkling of his thoughts by saying:

"My father's a parson in Norfolk. Do you see me before a judge and jury on that charge? For myself I can't see the necessity. There are fellows that an angel from heaven—And I am not that. He was one of those creatures that are just simmering all the time with a silly sort of wickedness. Miserable devils that have no business to live at all. He wouldn't do his duty and wouldn't let anybody else do theirs. But what's the good of talking! You know well enough the sort of ill-conditioned snarling cur—"

He appealed to me as if our experiences had been as identical as our clothes. And I knew well enough the pestiferous danger of such a character where there are no means of legal repression. And I knew well enough also that my double there was no homicidal ruffian. I did not think of asking him for details, and he told me the story roughly in brusque, disconnected sentences. I needed no more. I saw it all going on as though I were myself inside that other sleeping suit.

"It happened while we were setting a reefed foresail, at dusk. Reefed foresail! You understand the sort of weather. The only sail we had left to keep the ship running; so you may guess what it had been like for days. Anxious sort of job, that. He gave me some of his cursed insolence at the sheet. I tell you I was overdone with this terrific weather that seemed to have no end to it. Terrific, I tell you—and a deep ship. I believe the fellow himself was half crazed with funk. It was no time for gentlemanly reproof, so I turned round and felled him like an ox. He up and at me. We closed just as an awful sea made for the ship. All hands saw it coming and took to the rigging, but I had him by the throat, and went on shaking him like a rat, the men above us yelling, 'Look out! Look out!' Then a crash as if the sky had fallen on my head. They say that for over ten minutes hardly anything was to be seen of the ship—just the three masts and a bit of the forecastle head and of the poop all awash driving along in a smother of foam. It was a miracle that they found us, jammed together behind the forebits. It's clear that I meant business, because I was holding him by the throat still when they picked us up. He was black in the face. It was too much for them. It seems they rushed us aft together, gripped as we were, screaming 'Murder!' like a lot of lunatics, and broke into the cuddy. And the ship running for her life, touch and go all the time, any minute her last in a sea fit to turn your hair gray only a-looking at it. I understand that the skipper, too, started raving like the rest of them. The man had been deprived of sleep for more than a week, and to have this sprung on him at the height of a furious gale nearly drove him out of his mind. I wonder they didn't fling me overboard after getting the carcass of their precious shipmate out of my fingers. They had rather a job to separate us, I've been told. A sufficiently fierce story to make an old judge and a respectable jury sit up a bit. The first thing I heard when I came to myself was the maddening howling of that endless gale, and on that the voice of the old man. He was hanging on to my bunk, staring into my face out of his sou'wester.

" 'Mr. Leggatt, you have killed a man. You can act no longer as chief mate of this ship.' "

His care to subdue his voice made it sound monotonous. He rested a hand on the end of the skylight to steady himself with, and all that time did not stir a limb, so far as I could see. "Nice little tale for a quiet tea party," he concluded in the same tone.

One of my hands, too, rested on the end of the skylight; neither did I stir a limb, so far as I knew. We stood less than a foot from each other. It occurred to me that if old "Bless my soul—you don't say so" were to put his head up the companion and catch sight of us, he would think he was seeing double, or imagine himself come upon a scene of weird witchcraft; the strange captain having a quiet confabulation by the wheel with his own gray ghost. I became very much concerned to prevent anything of the sort. I heard the other's soothing undertone.

"My father's a parson in Norfolk," it said. Evidently he had forgotten he had told me this important fact before. Truly a nice little tale.

"You had better slip down into my stateroom now," I said, moving off stealthily. My double followed my movements; our bare feet made no sound; I let him in, closed the door with care, and, after giving a call to the second mate, returned on deck for my relief.

"Not much sign of any wind yet," I remarked when he approached.

"No, sir. Not much," he assented, sleepily, in his hoarse voice, with just enough deference, no more, and barely suppressing a yawn.

"Well, that's all you have to look out for. You have got your orders."

"Yes, sir."

I paced a turn or two on the poop and saw him take up his position face forward with his elbow in the rat-lines of the mizzen-rigging before I went below. The mate's faint snoring was still going on peacefully. The cuddy lamp was burning over the table on which stood a vase with flowers, a polite attention from the ships' provision merchant—the last flowers we should see for the next three months at the very least. Two bunches of bananas hung from the beam symmetrically, one on each side of the rudder casing. Everything was as before in the ship—except that two of her captain's sleeping suits were simultaneously in use, one motionless in the cuddy, the other keeping very still in the captain's stateroom.

It must be explained here that my cabin had the form of the capital letter L, the door being within the angle and opening into the short part of the letter. A couch was to the left, the bed-place to the right; my writing desk and the chronometers' table faced the door. But anyone opening it, unless he stepped right inside, had no view of what I call the long (or vertical) part of the letter. It contained some lockers surmounted by a bookcase; and a few clothes, a thick jacket or two, caps, oilskin coat, and such like, hung on the hooks. There was at the bottom of that part a door opening into my bathroom, which could be entered also directly from the saloon. But that way was never used.

The mysterious arrival had discovered the advantage of this particular shape. Entering my room, lighted strongly by a big bulkhead lamp swung on gimbals above my writing desk, I did not see him anywhere till he stepped out quietly from behind the coats hung in the recessed part.

"I heard somebody moving about, and went in there at once," he whispered.

I, too, spoke under my breath.

"Nobody is likely to come in here without knocking and getting permission."

He nodded. His face was thin and the sunburn faded, as though he had been ill. And no wonder. He had been, I heard presently, kept under arrest in his cabin for nearly seven weeks. But there was nothing sickly in his eyes or in his expression. He was not a bit like me, really; yet as we stood leaning over my bed-place, whispering side by side, with our dark heads together and our backs to the door, anybody bold enough to open it stealthily would have been treated to the uncanny sight of a double captain busy talking in whispers with his other self.

"But all this doesn't tell me how you came to hang on to our side ladder," I inquired, in the hardly audible murmurs we used, after he had told me something more of the proceedings on board the *Sephora* once the bad weather was over.

"When we sighted Java Head I had had time to think all those matters out several times over. I had six weeks of doing nothing else, and with only an hour or so every evening for a tramp on the quarter-deck."

He whispered, his arms folded on the side of my bed-place, staring through the open port. And I could imagine perfectly the manner of this thinking out— a stubborn if not a steadfast operation; something of which I should have been perfectly incapable.

"I reckoned it would be dark before we closed with the land," he continued, so low that I had to strain my hearing, near as we were to each other, shoulder touching shoulder almost. "So I asked to speak to the old man. He always seemed very sick when he came to see me—as if he could not look me in the face. You know, that foresail saved the ship. She was too deep to have run long under bare poles. And it was I that managed to set it for him. Anyway, he came. When I had him in my cabin—he stood by the door looking at me as if I had the halter around my neck already—I asked him right away to leave my cabin door unlocked at night while the ship was going through Sunda Straits. There would be the Java coast within two or three miles, off Angier Point. I wanted nothing more. I've had a prize for swimming my second year in the Conway."

"I can believe it," I breathed out.

"God only knows why they locked me in every night. To see some of their faces you'd have thought they were afraid I'd go about at night strangling people. Am I a murdering brute? Do I look it? By Jove! if I had been he wouldn't have trusted himself like that into my room. You'll say I might have chucked him aside and bolted out, there and then—it was dark already. Well, no. And for the same reason I wouldn't think of trying to smash the door. There would have been a rush to stop me at the noise, and I did not mean to get into a confounded scrimmage. Somebody else might have got killed—for I would not have broken out only to get chucked back, and I did not want any more of that work. He refused, looking more sick than ever. He was afraid of the men, and also of that old second mate of his who had been sailing with him for years—a gray-headed old humbug; and his steward, too, had been with him devil knows how long—seventeen years or more—a dogmatic sort of loafer who hated me like poison, just because I was the chief mate. No chief mate ever made more than one voyage in the *Sephora*, you know. Those two old chaps ran the ship. Devil only knows what the skipper wasn't afraid of (all his nerve went to pieces altogether in that hellish spell of bad weather we had)—of what the law would do to him—of his wife, perhaps. Oh, yes! she's on board. Though I don't think she would have meddled. She would have been only too glad to have me out of the ship in any way. The 'brand of Cain' business, don't you see. That's all right. I was ready enough to go off wandering on the face of the earth—and that was price enough to pay for an Abel of that sort. Anyhow, he wouldn't listen to me. 'This thing must take its course. I represent the law here.' He was shaking like a leaf. 'So you won't?' 'No!' 'Then I hope you will be able to sleep on that,' I said, and turned my back on him. 'I wonder that *you* can,' cries he, and locks the door.

"Well, after that, I couldn't. Not very well. That was three weeks ago. We have had a slow passage through the Java Sea; drifted about Carimata for ten days. When we anchored here they thought, I suppose, it was all right. The nearest land (and that's five miles) is the ship's destination; the consul would soon set about catching me; and there would have been no object in bolting to these islets there. I don't suppose there's a drop of water on them. I don't know how it was, but tonight that steward, after bringing me my supper, went out to let me eat it, and left the door unlocked. And I ate it—all there was, too. After I had finished I strolled out on the quarter-deck. I don't know that I meant to do anything. A breath of fresh air was all I wanted, I believe. Then a sudden temptation came over me. I kicked off my slippers and was in the water before I had made up my mind fairly. Somebody heard the splash and they raised an awful hullabaloo. 'He's gone! Lower the boats! He's committed suicide! No, he's swimming.' Certainly I was swimming. It's not so easy for a swimmer like me to commit suicide by drowning. I landed on the nearest islet before the boat left the ship's side. I heard them pulling about in the dark, hailing, and so on, but after a bit they gave up. Everything quieted down and the anchorage became as still as death. I sat down on a stone and began to think. I felt certain they would start searching for me at daylight. There was no place to hide on those stony things—and if there had been, what would have been the good? But now I was clear of that ship, I was not going back. So after a while I took off all my clothes, tied them up in a bundle with a stone inside, and dropped them in the deep water on the outer side of the islet. That was suicide enough for me. Let them think what they liked, but I didn't mean to drown myself. I meant to swim till I sank—but that's not the same thing. I struck out for another of these little islands, and it was from that one that I first saw your riding light. Something to swim for. I went on easily, and on the way I came upon a flat rock a foot or two above water. In the daytime, I dare say, you might make it out with a glass from your poop. I scrambled up on it and rested myself for a bit. Then I made another start. That last spell must have been over a mile."

His whisper was getting fainter and fainter, and all the time he stared straight out through the porthole, in which there was not even a star to be seen. I had not interrupted him. There was something that made comment impossible in his narrative, or perhaps in himself; a sort of feeling, a quality, which I can't find a name for. And when he ceased, all I found was a futile whisper: "So you swam for our light?"

"Yes—straight for it. It was something to swim for. I couldn't see any stars low down because the coast was in the way, and I couldn't see the land, either. The water was like glass. One might have been swimming in a confounded thousand-feet deep cistern with no place for scrambling out anywhere; but what I didn't like was the notion of swimming round and round like a crazed bullock before I gave out; and as I didn't mean to go back . . . No. Do you see me being hauled back, stark naked, off one of these little islands by the scruff of the neck and fighting like a wild beast? Somebody would have got killed for certain, and I did not want any of that. So I went on. Then your ladder—"

"Why didn't you hail the ship?" I asked, a little louder.

He touched my shoulder lightly. Lazy footsteps came right over our heads and stopped. The second mate had crossed from the other side of the poop and might have been hanging over the rail, for all we knew.

"He couldn't hear us talking—could he?" My double breathed into my very ear, anxiously.

His anxiety was an answer, a sufficient answer, to the question I had put to him. An answer containing all the difficulty of that situation. I closed the porthole quietly, to make sure. A louder word might have been overheard.

"Who's that?" he whispered then.

"My second mate. But I don't know much more of the fellow than you do."

And I told him a little about myself. I had been appointed to take charge while I least expected anything of the sort, not quite a fortnight ago. I didn't know either the ship or the people. Hadn't had the time in port to look about me or size anybody up. And as to the crew, all they knew was that I was appointed to take the ship home. For the rest, I was almost as much of a stranger on board as himself, I said. And at the moment I felt it most acutely. I felt that it would take very little to make me a suspect person in the eyes of the ship's company.

He had turned about meantime; and we, the two strangers in the ship, faced each other in identical attitudes.

"Your ladder—" he murmured, after a silence. "Who'd have thought of finding a ladder hanging over at night in a ship anchored out here! I felt just then a very unpleasant faintness. After the life I've been leading for nine weeks, anybody would have got out of condition. I wasn't capable of swimming round as far as your rudder chains. And, lo and behold! there was a ladder to get hold of. After I gripped it I said to myself, 'What's the good?' When I saw a man's head looking over I thought I could swim away presently and leave him shouting—in whatever language it was. I didn't mind being looked at. I—I liked it. And then you speaking to me so quietly—as if you had expected me—made me hold on a little longer. It had been a confounded lonely time—I don't mean while swimming. I was glad to talk a little to somebody that didn't belong to the *Sephora*. As to asking for the captain, that was a mere impulse. It could have been no use, with all the ship knowing about me and the other people pretty certain to be round here in the morning. I don't know—I wanted to be seen, to talk with somebody, before I went on. I don't know what I would have said. . . . 'Fine night, isn't it?' or something of the sort."

"Do you think they will be round here presently?" I asked with some incredulity.

"Quite likely," he said, faintly.

He looked extremely haggard all of a sudden. His head rolled on his shoulders.

"H'm. We shall see then. Meantime get into that bed," I whispered. "Want help? There."

It was a rather high bed-place with a set of drawers underneath. This amazing swimmer really needed the lift I gave him by seizing his leg. He tumbled in, rolled over on his back, and flung one arm across his eyes. And then, with his face nearly hidden, he must have looked exactly as I used to look in that bed. I gazed upon my other self for a while before drawing across carefully the two green serge curtains which ran on a brass rod. I thought for a moment of pinning them together for greater safety, but I sat down on the couch, and once there I felt unwilling to rise and hunt for a pin. I would do it in a moment. I was extremely tired, in a peculiarly intimate way, by the strain of stealthiness, by the effort of whispering and the general secrecy of this excitement. It was three o'clock by now and I had been on my feet since nine, but I was not sleepy; I could not have gone to sleep. I sat there, fagged out, looking at the curtains, trying to clear my mind of the confused sensation of being in two places at once, and greatly bothered by an exasperating knocking in my head. It was a relief to discover suddenly that it was not in my head at all, but on the outside of the door. Before I could collect myself the words "Come in" were out of my mouth, and the steward entered with a tray, bringing in my morning coffee. I had slept, after all, and I was so frightened that I shouted, "This way! I am here, steward," as though he had been miles away. He put down the tray on the table next to the couch and only then said, very quietly, "I can see you are here, sir." I felt him give me a keen look, but I dared not meet his eyes just then. He must have wondered why I had drawn the curtains of my bed before going to sleep on the couch. He went out, hooking the door open as usual.

I heard the crew washing decks above me. I knew I would have been told at once if there had been any wind. Calm, I thought, and I was doubly vexed. Indeed, I felt dual more than ever. The steward reappeared suddenly in the doorway. I jumped up from the couch so quickly that he gave a start.

"What do you want here?"

"Close your port, sir—they are washing decks."

"It is closed," I said, reddening.

"Very well, sir." But he did not move from the doorway and returned my stare in an extraordinary, equivocal manner for a time. Then his eyes wavered, all his expression changed, and in a voice unusually gentle, almost coaxingly:

"May I come in to take the empty cup away, sir?"

"Of course!" I turned my back on him while he popped in and out. Then I unhooked and closed the door and even pushed the bolt. This sort of thing could not go on very long. The cabin was as hot as an oven, too. I took a peep at my double, and discovered that he had not moved, his arm was still over his eyes; but his chest heaved; his hair was wet; his chin glistened with perspiration. I reached over him and opened the port.

"I must show myself on deck," I reflected.

Of course, theoretically, I could do what I liked, with no one to say nay to me within the whole circle of the horizon; but to lock my cabin door and take the key away I did not dare. Directly I put my head out of the companion I saw the group of my two officers, the second mate barefooted, the chief mate in long india-rubber boots, near the break of the poop, and the steward halfway down the poop ladder talking to them eagerly. He happened to catch sight of me and dived, the second ran down on the main deck shouting some order or other, and the chief mate came to meet me, touching his cap.

There was a sort of curiosity in his eye that I did not like. I don't know whether the steward had told them that I was "queer" only, or downright drunk, but I know the man meant to have a good look at me. I watched him coming with a smile which, as he got into point-blank range, took effect and froze his very whiskers. I did not give him time to open his lips.

"Square the yards by lifts and braces before the hands go to breakfast."

It was the first particular order I had given on board that ship; and I stayed on deck to see it executed, too. I had felt the need of asserting myself without loss of time. That sneering young cub got taken down a peg or two on that occasion, and I also seized the opportunity of having a good look at the face of every foremast man as they filed past me to go to the after braces. At breakfast time, eating nothing myself, I presided with such frigid dignity that the two mates were only too glad to escape from the cabin as soon as decency permitted; and all the time the dual working of my mind distracted me almost to the point of insanity. I was constantly watching myself, my secret self, as dependent on my actions as my own personality, sleeping in that bed, behind that door which faced me as I sat at the head of the table. It was very much like being mad, only it was worse because one was aware of it.

I had to shake him for a solid minute, but when at last he opened his eyes it was in the full possession of his senses, with an inquiring look.

"All's well so far," I whispered. "Now you must vanish into the bathroom."

He did so, as noiseless as a ghost, and I then rang for the steward, and facing him boldly, directed him to tidy up my stateroom while I was having my bath—"and be quick about it." As my tone admitted of no excuses, he said, "Yes, sir," and ran off to fetch his dustpan and brushes. I took a bath and did most of my dressing, splashing, and whistling softly for the steward's edification, while the secret sharer of my life stood drawn up bolt upright in that little space, his face looking very sunken in daylight, his eyelids lowered under the stern, dark line of his eyebrows drawn together by a slight frown.

When I left him there to go back to my room the steward was finished dusting. I sent for the mate and engaged him in some insignificant conversation. It was, as it were, trifling with the terrific character of whiskers; but my object was to give him an opportunity for a good look at my cabin. And then I could at last shut, with a clear conscience, the door of my stateroom and get my double back into the recessed part. There was nothing else for it. He had to sit still on a small folding stool, half smothered by the heavy coats hanging there. We listened to the steward going into the bathroom out of the saloon, filling the water bottles there, scrubbing the bath, setting things to rights, whisk, bang, clatter—out again into the saloon—turn the key—click. Such was my scheme for keeping my second self invisible. Nothing better could be contrived under the circumstances. And there we sat; I at my writing desk ready to appear busy with some papers, he behind me, out of sight of the door. It would not have been prudent to talk in daytime; and I could not have stood the excitement of that queer sense of whispering to myself. Now and then, glancing over my shoulder, I saw him far back there, sitting rigidly on the low stool, his bare feet close together, his arms folded, his head hanging on his breast—and perfectly still. Anybody would have taken him for me.

I was fascinated by it myself. Every moment I had to glance over my shoulder. I was looking at him when a voice outside the door said:

"Beg pardon, sir."

"Well!" . . . I kept my eyes on him, and so, when the voice outside the door announced, "There's a ship's boat coming our way, sir," I saw him give a start—the first movement he had made for hours. But he did not raise his bowed head.

"All right. Get the ladder over."

I hesitated. Should I whisper something to him? But what? His immobility seemed to have been never disturbed. What could I tell him he did not know already? . . . Finally I went on deck.

II

The skipper of the *Sephora* had a thin red whisker all round his face, and the sort of complexion that goes with hair of that color; also the particular, rather smeary shade of blue in the eyes. He was not exactly a showy figure; his shoulders were high, his stature but middling—one leg slightly more bandy than the other. He shook hands, looking vaguely around. A spiritless tenacity was his main characteristic, I judged. I behaved with a politeness which seemed to disconcert him. Perhaps he was shy. He mumbled to me as if he were ashamed of what he was saying; gave his name (it was something like Archbold—but at this distance of years I hardly am sure), his ship's name, and a few other particulars of that sort, in the manner of a criminal making a reluctant and doleful confession. He had had terrible weather on the passage out—terrible—terrible—wife aboard, too.

By this time we were seated in the cabin and the steward brought in a tray with a bottle and glasses. "Thanks! No." Never took liquor. Would have some water, though. He drank two tumblerfuls. Terrible thirsty work. Ever since daylight had been exploring the islands round his ship.

"What was that for—fun?" I asked, with an appearance of polite interest.

"No!" He sighed. "Painful duty."

As he persisted in his mumbling and I wanted my double to hear every word, I hit upon the notion of informing him that I regretted to say I was hard of hearing.

"Such a young man, too!" he nodded keeping his smeary blue, unintelligent eyes fastened upon me. What was the cause of it—some disease? he inquired, without the least sympathy and as if he thought that, if so, I'd got no more than I deserved.

"Yes; disease," I admitted in a cheerful tone which seemed to shock him. But my point was gained, because he had to raise his voice to give me his tale. It is not worth while to record that version. It was just over two months since all this had happened, and he had thought so much about it that he seemed completely muddled as to its bearings, but still immensely impressed.

"What would you think of such a thing happening on board your own ship? I've had the *Sephora* for these fifteen years. I am a well-known shipmaster."

He was densely distressed—and perhaps I should have sympathized with him if I had been able to detach my mental vision from the unsuspected sharer of my cabin as though he were my second self. There he was on the other side of the bulkhead, four or five feet from us, no more, as we sat in the saloon. I looked politely at Captain Archbold (if that was his name), but it was the other I saw, in a gray sleeping suit, seated on a low stool, his bare feet close together, his arms folded, and every word said between us falling into the ears of his dark head bowed on his chest.

"I have been at sea now, man and boy, for seven-and-thirty years, and I've never heard of such a thing happening in an English ship. And that it should be my ship. Wife on board, too."

I was hardly listening to him.

"Don't you think," I said, "that the heavy sea which, you told me, came aboard just then might have killed the man? I have seen the sheer weight of a sea kill a man very neatly, by simply breaking his neck."

"Good God!" he uttered, impressively, fixing his smeary blue eyes on me. "The sea! No man killed by the sea ever looked like that." He seemed positively scandalized at my suggestion. And as I gazed at him, certainly not prepared for anything original on his part, he advanced his head close to mine and thrust his tongue out at me so suddenly that I couldn't help staring back.

After scoring over my calmness in this graphic way he nodded wisely. If I had seen the sight, he assured me, I would never forget it as long as I lived. The weather was too bad to give the corpse a proper sea burial. So next day at dawn they took it up on the poop, covering its face with a bit of bunting; he read a short prayer, and then, just as it was, in its oilskins and long boots, they launched it amongst those mountainous seas that seemed ready every moment to swallow up the ship herself and the terrified lives on board of her.

"That reefed foresail saved you," I threw in.

"Under God—it did," he exclaimed fervently. "It was by a special mercy, I firmly believe, that it stood some of those hurricane squalls."

"It was the setting of that sail which—" I began.

"God's own hand in it," he interrupted me. "Nothing less could have done it. I don't mind telling you that I hardly dared give the order. It seemed impossible that we could touch anything without losing it, and then our last hope would have been gone."

The terror of that gale was on him yet. I let him go on for a bit, then said, casually—as if returning to a minor subject:

"You were very anxious to give up your mate to the shore people, I believe?"

He was. To the law. His obscure tenacity on that point had in it something incomprehensible and a little awful; something, as it were, mystical, quite apart from his anxiety that he should not be suspected of "countenancing any doings of that sort." Seven-and-thirty virtuous years at sea, of which over twenty of immaculate command, and the last fifteen in the *Sephora*, seemed to have laid him under some pitiless obligation.

"And you know," he went on, groping shamefacedly amongst his feelings, "I did not engage that young fellow. His people had some interest with my owners. I was in a way forced to take him on. He looked very smart, very gentlemanly, and all that. But do you know—I never liked him, somehow. I am a plain man. You see, he wasn't exactly the sort for the chief mate of a ship like the *Sephora*."

I had become so connected in thoughts and impressions with the secret sharer of my cabin that I felt as if I, personally, were being given to understand that I, too, was not the sort that would have done for the chief mate of a ship like the *Sephora*. I had no doubt of it in my mind.

"Not at all the style of man. You understand," he insisted, superfluously, looking hard at me.

I smiled urbanely. He seemed at a loss for a while.

"I suppose I must report a suicide."

"Beg pardon?"

"Sui-cide! That's what I'll have to write to my owners directly I get in."

"Unless you manage to recover him before tomorrow," I assented, dispassionately. . . . "I mean, alive."

He mumbled something which I really did not catch, and I turned my ear to him in a puzzled manner. He fairly bawled:

"The land—I say, the mainland is at least seven miles off my anchorage."

"About that."

My lack of excitement, of curiosity, of surprise, of any sort of pronounced interest, began to arouse his distrust. But except for the felicitous pretense of deafness I had not tried to pretend anything. I had felt utterly incapable of playing the part of ignorance properly, and therefore was afraid to try. It is also certain that he had brought some ready-made suspicions with him, and that he viewed my politeness as a strange and unnatural phenomenon. And yet how else could I have received him? Not heartily! That was impossible for psychological reasons,

which I need not state here. My only object was to keep off his inquiries. Surlily?
Yes, but surliness might have provoked a point-blank question. From its novelty
to him and from its nature, punctilious courtesy was the manner best calculated
to restrain the man. But there was the danger of his breaking through my defense
bluntly. I could not, I think, have met him by a direct lie, also for psychological
(not moral) reasons. If he had only known how afraid I was of his putting my
feeling of identity with the other to the test! But, strangely enough—(I thought
of it only afterward)—I believe that he was not a little disconcerted by the reverse
side of that weird situation, by something in me that reminded him of the man
he was seeking—suggested a mysterious similitude to the young fellow he had
distrusted and disliked from the first.

However that might have been, the silence was not very prolonged. He took
another oblique step.

"I reckon I had no more than a two-mile pull to your ship. Not a bit more."

"And quite enough, too, in this awful heat," I said.

Another pause full of mistrust followed. Necessity, they say, is mother of
invention, but fear, too, is not barren of ingenious suggestions. And I was afraid
he would ask me point-blank for news of my other self.

"Nice little saloon, isn't it?" I remarked, as if noticing for the first time the
way his eyes roamed from one closed door to the other. "And very well fitted
out, too. Here, for instance," I continued reaching over the back of my seat
negligently and flinging the door open, "is my bathroom."

He made an eager movement, but hardly gave it a glance. I got up, shut the
door of the bathroom, and invited him to have a look round, as if I were very
proud of my accommodation. He had to rise and be shown round, but he went
through the business without any raptures whatever.

"And now we'll have a look at my stateroom," I declared, in a voice as loud
as I dared to make it, crossing the cabin to the starboard side with purposely
heavy steps.

He followed me in and gazed around. My intelligent double had vanished. I
played my part.

"Very convenient—isn't it?"

"Very nice. Very comf . . ." He didn't finish, and went out brusquely as if
to escape from some unrighteous wiles of mine. But it was not to be. I had been
too frightened not to feel vengeful; I felt I had him on the run, and I meant to
keep him on the run. My polite insistence must have had something menacing in
it, because he gave in suddenly. And I did not let him off a single item; mate's
room, pantry, storerooms, the very sail locker which was also under the poop—
he had to look into them all. When at last I showed him out on the quarter-deck
he drew a long, spiritless sigh, and mumbled dismally that he must really be going
back to his ship now. I desired my mate, who had joined us, to see to the captain's
boat.

The man of whiskers gave a blast on the whistle which he used to wear hanging
round his neck, and yelled, "*Sephora* away!" My double down there in my cabin
must have heard, and certainly could not feel more relieved than I. Four fellows

came running out from somewhere forward and went over the side, while my own men, appearing on deck too, lined the rail. I escorted my visitor to the gangway ceremoniously, and nearly overdid it. He was a tenacious beast. On the very ladder he lingered, and in that unique, guiltily conscientious manner of sticking to the point:

"I say . . . you . . . you don't think that—"

I covered his voice loudly:

"Certainly not. . . . I am delighted. Good-by."

I had an idea of what he meant to say, and just saved myself by the privilege of defective hearing. He was too shaken generally to insist, but my mate, close witness of that parting, looked mystified and his face took on a thoughtful cast. As I did not want to appear as if I wished to avoid all communication with my officers, he had the opportunity to address me.

"Seems a very nice man. His boat's crew told our chaps a very extraordinary story, if what I am told by the steward is true. I suppose you had it from the captain, sir?"

"Yes. I had a story from the captain."

"A very horrible affair—isn't it, sir?"

"It is."

"Beats all these tales we hear about murders in Yankee ships."

"I don't think it beats them. I don't think it resembles them in the least."

"Bless my soul—you don't say so! But of course I've no acquaintance whatever with American ships, not I, so I couldn't go against your knowledge. It's horrible enough for me. . . . But the queerest part is that these fellows seemed to have some idea the man was hidden aboard here. They had really. Did you ever hear of such a thing?"

"Preposterous—isn't it?"

We were walking to and fro athwart the quarter-deck. No one of the crew forward could be seen (the day was Sunday), and the mate pursued:

"There was some little dispute about it. Our chaps took offense. 'As if we would harbor a thing like that,' they said. 'Wouldn't you like to look for him in our coal hole?' Quite a tiff. But they made it up in the end. I suppose he did drown himself. Don't you, sir?"

"I don't suppose anything."

"You have no doubt in the matter, sir?"

"None whatever."

I left him suddenly. I felt I was producing a bad impression, but with my double down there it was most trying to be on deck. And it was almost as trying to be below. Altogether a nerve-trying situation. But on the whole I felt less torn in two when I was with him. There was no one in the whole ship whom I dared take into my confidence. Since the hands had got to know his story, it would have been impossible to pass him off for anyone else, and an accidental discovery was to be dreaded now more than ever. . . .

The steward being engaged in laying the table for dinner, we could talk only with our eyes when I first went down. Later in the afternoon we had a cautious try at whispering. The Sunday quietness of the ship was against us; the stillness of air and water around her was against us; the elements, the men were against us—everything was against us in our secret partnership; time itself—for this could not go on forever. The very trust in Providence was, I suppose, denied to his guilt. Shall I confess that this thought cast me down very much? And as to the chapter of accidents which counts for so much in the book of success, I could only hope that it was closed. For what favorable accident could be expected?

"Did you hear everything?" were my first words as soon as we took up our position side by side, leaning over my bed-place.

He had. And the proof of it was his earnest whisper, "The man told you he hardly dared to give the order."

I understood the reference to be to that saving foresail.

"Yes. He was afraid of it being lost in the setting."

"I assure you he never gave the order. He may think he did, but he never gave it. He stood there with me on the break of the poop after the maintopsail blew away, and whimpered about our last hope—positively whimpered about it and nothing else—and the night coming on! To hear one's skipper go on like that in such weather was enough to drive any fellow out of his mind. It worked me up into a sort of desperation. I just took it into my hands and went away from him, boiling, and—But what's the use telling you? *You* know! . . . Do you think that if I had not been pretty fierce with them I should have got the men to do anything? Not it! The bosun perhaps? Perhaps! It wasn't a heavy sea—it was a sea gone mad! I suppose the end of the world will be something like that; and a man may have the heart to see it coming once and be done with it—but to have to face it day after day—I don't blame anybody. I was precious little better than the rest. Only—I was an officer of that old coal-wagon, anyhow—"

"I quite understand," I conveyed that sincere assurance into his ear. He was out of breath with whispering; I could hear him pant slightly. It was all very simple. The same strung-up force which had given twenty-four men a chance, at least, for their lives, had, in a sort of recoil, crushed an unworthy mutinous existence.

But I had no leisure to weigh the merits of the matter—footsteps in the saloon, a heavy knock. "There's enough wind to get under way with, sir." Here was the call of a new claim upon my thoughts and even upon my feelings.

"Turn the hands up," I cried through the door. "I'll be on deck directly."

I was going out to make the acquaintance of my ship. Before I left the cabin our eyes met—the eyes of the only two strangers on board. I pointed to the recessed part where the little campstool awaited him and laid my finger on my lips. He made a gesture—somewhat vague—a little mysterious, accompanied by a faint smile, as if of regret.

This is not the place to enlarge upon the sensations of a man who feels for the first time a ship move under his feet to his own independent word. In my case they were not unalloyed. I was not wholly alone with my command; for there was that stranger in my cabin. Or rather, I was not completely and wholly with her. Part of me was absent. That mental feeling of being in two places at once affected me physically as if the mood of secrecy had penetrated my very soul. Before an hour had elapsed since the ship had begun to move, having occasion to ask the mate (he stood by my side) to take a compass bearing of the Pagoda, I caught myself reaching up to his ear in whispers. I say I caught myself, but enough had escaped to startle the man. I can't describe it otherwise than by saying that he shied. A grave, preoccupied manner, as though he were in possession of some perplexing intelligence, did not leave him henceforth. A little later I moved away from the rail to look at the compass with such a stealthy gait that the helmsman noticed it—and I could not help noticing the unusual roundness of his eyes. These are trifling instances, though it's to no commander's advantage to be suspected of ludicrous eccentricities. But I was also more seriously affected. There are to a seaman certain words, gestures, that should in given conditions come as naturally, as instinctively as the winking of a menaced eye. A certain order should spring on to his lips without thinking; a certain sign should get itself made, so to speak, without reflection. But all unconscious alertness had abandoned me. I had to make an effort of will to recall myself back (from the cabin) to the conditions of the moment. I felt that I was appearing an irresolute commander to those people who were watching me more or less critically.

And, besides, there were the scares. On the second day out, for instance, coming off the deck in the afternoon (I had straw slippers on my bare feet) I stopped at the open pantry door and spoke to the steward. He was doing something there with his back to me. At the sound of my voice he nearly jumped out of his skin, as the saying is, and incidentally broke a cup.

"What on earth's the matter with you?" I asked, astonished.

He was extremely confused. "Beg your pardon, sir. I made sure you were in your cabin."

"You see I wasn't."

"No, sir. I could have sworn I had heard you moving in there not a moment ago. It's most extraordinary . . . very sorry, sir."

I passed on with an inward shudder. I was so identified with my secret double that I did not even mention the fact in those scanty, fearful whispers we exchanged. I suppose he had made some slight noise of some kind or other. It would have been miraculous if he hadn't at one time or another. And yet, haggard as he appeared, he looked always perfectly self-controlled, more than calm—almost invulnerable. On my suggestion he remained almost entirely in the bathroom, which, upon the whole, was the safest place. There could be really no shadow of an excuse for anyone ever wanting to go in there, once the steward had done with it. It was a very tiny place. Sometimes he reclined on the floor, his legs bent, his head sustained on one elbow. At others I would find him on the campstool, sitting in his gray sleeping suit and with his cropped dark hair like a patient, unmoved convict. At night I would smuggle him into my bed-place, and we would whisper together, with the regular footfalls of the officer of the watch passing and repassing over our heads. It was an infinitely miserable time. It was lucky that some tins of fine preserves were stowed in a locker in my stateroom; hard bread I could always get hold of; and so he lived on stewed chicken, paté de foie

gras, asparagus, cooked oysters, sardines—on all sorts of abominable sham delicacies out of tins. My early morning coffee he always drank; and it was all I
dared do for him in that respect.

Every day there was the horrible maneuvering to go through so that my room
and then the bathroom should be done in the usual way. I came to hate the sight
of the steward, to abhor the voice of that harmless man. I felt that it was he who
would bring on the disaster of discovery. It hung like a sword over our heads.

The fourth day out, I think (we were working down the east side of the Gulf
of Siam, tack for tack, in light winds and smooth water)—the fourth day, I say,
of this miserable juggling with the unavoidable, as we sat at our evening meal,
that man, whose slightest movement I dreaded, after putting down the dishes ran
up on deck busily. This could not be dangerous. Presently he came down again;
and then it appeared that he had remembered a coat of mine which I had thrown
over a rail to dry after having been wetted in a shower which had passed over
the ship in the afternoon. Sitting stolidly at the head of the table I became terrified
at the sight of the garment on his arm. Of course he made for my door. There
was no time to lose.

"Steward," I thundered. My nerves were so shaken that I could not govern
my voice and conceal my agitation. This was the sort of thing that made my
terrifically whiskered mate tap his forehead with his forefinger. I had detected
him using that gesture while talking on deck with a confidential air to the carpenter. It was too far to hear a word, but I had no doubt that this pantomime
could only refer to the strange new captain.

"Yes, sir," the pale-faced steward turned resignedly to me. It was this maddening course of being shouted at, checked without rhyme or reason, arbitrarily
chased out of my cabin, suddenly called into it, sent flying out of his pantry on
incomprehensible errands, that accounted for the growing wretchedness of his
expression.

"Where are you going with that coat?"

"To your room, sir."

"Is there another shower coming?"

"I'm sure I don't know, sir. Shall I go up again and see, sir?"

"No! never mind."

My object was attained, as of course my other self in there would have heard
everything that passed. During this interlude my two officers never raised their
eyes off their respective plates; but the lip of that confounded cub, the second
mate, quivered visibly.

I expected the steward to hook my coat on and come out at once. He was
very slow about it; but I dominated my nervousness sufficiently not to shout after
him. Suddenly I became aware (it could be heard plainly enough) that the fellow
for some reason or other was opening the door of the bathroom. It was the end.
The place was literally not big enough to swing a cat in. My voice died in my
throat and I went stony all over. I expected to hear a yell of surprise and terror,
and made a movement, but had not the strength to get on my legs. Everything
remained still. Had my second self taken the poor wretch by the throat? I don't

know what I would have done next moment if I had not seen the steward come out of my room, close the door, and then stand quietly by the sideboard.

Saved, I thought. But, no! Lost! Gone! He was gone!

I laid my knife and fork down and leaned back in my chair. My head swam. After a while, when sufficiently recovered to speak in a steady voice, I instructed my mate to put the ship round at eight o'clock himself.

"I won't come on deck," I went on. "I think I'll turn in, and unless the wind shifts I don't want to be disturbed before midnight. I feel a bit seedy."

"You did look middling bad a little while ago," the chief mate remarked without showing any great concern.

They both went out, and I stared at the steward clearing the table. There was nothing to be read on that wretched man's face. But why did he avoid my eyes I asked myself. Then I thought I should like to hear the sound of his voice.

"Steward!"

"Sir!" Startled as usual.

"Where did you hang up that coat?"

"In the bathroom, sir." The usual anxious tone. "It's not quite dry yet, sir."

For some time longer I sat in the cuddy. Had my double vanished as he had come? But of his coming there was an explanation, whereas his disappearance would be inexplicable. . . . I went slowly into my dark room, shut the door, lighted the lamp, and for a time dared not turn round. When at last I did I saw him standing bolt upright in the narrow recessed part. It would not be true to say I had a shock, but an irresistible doubt of his bodily existence flitted through my mind. Can it be, I asked myself, that he is not visible to other eyes than mine? It was like being haunted. Motionless, with a grave face, he raised his hands slightly at me in a gesture which meant clearly, "Heavens! what a narrow escape!" Narrow indeed. I think I had come creeping quietly as near insanity as any man who has not actually gone over the border. That gesture restrained me, so to speak.

The mate with the terrific whiskers was now putting the ship on the other tack. In the moment of profound silence which follows upon the hands going to their stations I heard on the poop his raised voice: "Hard alee!" and the distant shout of the order repeated on the maindeck. The sails, in that light breeze, made but a faint fluttering noise. It ceased. The ship was coming round slowly; I held my breath in the renewed stillness of expectation; one wouldn't have thought that there was a single living soul on her decks. A sudden brisk shout, "Mainsail haul!" broke the spell, and in the noisy cries and rush overhead of the men running away with the main brace we two, down in my cabin, came together in our usual position by the bed-place.

He did not wait for my question. "I heard him fumbling here and just managed to squat myself down in the bath," he whispered to me. "The fellow only opened the door and put his arm in to hang the coat up. All the same—"

"I never thought of that," I whispered back, even more appalled than before at the closeness of the shave, and marveling at that something unyielding in his character which was carrying him through so finely. There was no agitation in his whisper. Whoever was being driven distracted, it was not he. He was sane. And the proof of his sanity was continued when he took up the whispering again.

"It would never do for me to come to life again."

It was something that a ghost might have said. But what he was alluding to was his old captain's reluctant admission of the theory of suicide. It would obviously serve his turn—if I had understood at all the view which seemed to govern the unalterable purpose of his action.

"You must maroon me as soon as ever you can get amongst these islands off the Cambodje shore," he went on.

"Maroon you! We are not living in a boy's adventure tale," I protested. His scornful whispering took me up.

"We aren't indeed! There's nothing of a boy's tale in this. But there's nothing else for it. I want no more. You don't suppose I am afraid of what can be done to me? Prison or gallows or whatever they may please. But you don't see me coming back to explain such things to an old fellow in a wig and twelve respectable tradesmen, do you? What can they know whether I am guilty or not—or of *what* I am guilty, either? That's my affair. What does the Bible say? 'Driven off the face of the earth.' Very well. I am off the face of the earth now. As I came at night so I shall go."

"Impossible!" I murmured. "You can't."

"Can't? . . . Not naked like a soul on the Day of Judgment. I shall freeze on to this sleeping suit. The Last Day is not yet—and . . . you have understood thoroughly. Didn't you?"

I felt suddenly ashamed of myself. I may say truly that I understood—and my hesitation in letting that man swim away from my ship's side had been a mere sham sentiment, a sort of cowardice.

"It can't be done now till next night," I breathed out. "The ship is on the offshore tack and the wind may fail us."

"As long as I know that you understand," he whispered. "But of course you do. It's a great satisfaction to have got somebody to understand. You seem to have been there on purpose." And in the same whisper, as if we two whenever we talked had to say things to each other which were not fit for the world to hear, he added, "It's very wonderful."

We remained side by side talking in our secret way—but sometimes silent or just exchanging a whispered word or two at long intervals. And as usual he stared through the port. A breath of wind came now and again into our faces. The ship might have been moored in dock, so gently and on an even keel she slipped through the water, that did not murmur even at our passage, shadowy and silent like a phantom sea.

At midnight I went on deck, and to my mate's surprise put the ship round on the other tack. His terrible whiskers flitted round me in silent criticism. I certainly should not have done it if it had been only a question of getting out of that sleepy gulf as quickly as possible. I believe he told the second mate, who relieved him, that it was a great want of judgment. The other only yawned. That intolerable cub shuffled about so sleepily and lolled against the rails in such a slack, improper fashion that I came down on him sharply.

"Aren't you properly awake yet?"

"Yes, sir! I am awake."

"Well, then, be good enough to hold yourself as if you were. And keep a lookout. If there's any current we'll be closing with some islands before daylight."

The east side of the gulf is fringed with islands, some solitary, others in groups. On the blue background of the high coast they seem to float on silvery patches of calm water, arid and gray, or dark green and rounded like clumps of evergreen bushes, with the larger ones, a mile or two long, showing the outlines of ridges, ribs of gray rock under the dark mantle of matted leafage. Unknown to trade, to travel, almost to geography, the manner of life they harbor is an unsolved secret. There must be villages—settlements of fishermen at least—on the largest of them, and some communication with the world is probably kept up by native craft. But all forenoon, as we headed for them, fanned along by the faintest of breezes, I saw no sign of man or canoe in the field of the telescope I kept on pointing at the scattered group.

At noon I gave no orders for a change of course, and the mate's whiskers became much concerned and seemed to be offering themselves unduly to my notice. At last I said:

"I am going to stand right in. Quite in—as far as I can take her."

The stare of extreme surprise imparted an air of ferocity also to his eyes, and he looked truly terrific for a moment.

"We're not doing well in the middle of the gulf," I continued, casually. "I am going to look for the land breezes tonight."

"Bless my soul! Do you mean, sir, in the dark amongst the lot of all them islands and reefs and shoals?"

"Well—if there are any regular land breezes at all on this coast one must get close inshore to find them, mustn't one?"

"Bless my soul!" he exclaimed again under his breath. All that afternoon he wore a dreamy, contemplative appearance which in him was a mark of perplexity. After dinner I went into my stateroom as if I meant to take some rest. There we two bent our dark heads over a half-unrolled chart lying on my bed.

"There," I said. "It's got to be Koh-ring. I've been looking at it ever since sunrise. It has got two hills and a low point. It must be inhabited. And on the coast opposite there is what looks like the mouth of a biggish river—with some town, no doubt, not far up. It's the best chance for you that I can see."

"Anything. Koh-ring let it be."

He looked thoughtfully at the chart as if surveying chances and distances from a lofty height—and following with his eyes his own figure wandering on the blank land of Cochin China, and then passing off that piece of paper clean out of sight into uncharted regions. And it was as if the ship had two captains to plan her course for her. I had been so worried and restless running up and down that I had not had the patience to dress that day. I had remained in my sleeping suit, with straw slippers and a soft floppy hat. The closeness of the heat in the gulf had been most oppressive, and the crew were used to see me wandering in that airy attire.

"She will clear the south point as she heads now," I whispered into his ear. "Goodness only knows when, though, but certainly after dark. I'll edge her in to half a mile, as far as I may be able to judge in the dark—"

"Be careful," he murmured, warningly—and I realized suddenly that all my future, the only future for which I was fit, would perhaps go irretrievably to pieces in any mishap to my first command.

I could not stop a moment longer in the room. I motioned him to get out of sight and made my way on the poop. That unplayful cub had the watch. I walked up and down for a while thinking things out, then beckoned him over.

"Send a couple of hands to open the two quarter-deck ports," I said, mildly.

He actually had the impudence, or else so forgot himself in his wonder at such an incomprehensible order, as to repeat:

"Open the quarter-deck ports! What for, sir?"

"The only reason you need concern yourself about is because I tell you to do so. Have them open wide and fastened properly."

He reddened and went off, but I believe made some jeering remark to the carpenter as to the sensible practice of ventilating a ship's quarter-deck. I know he popped into the mate's cabin to impart the fact to him because the whiskers came on deck, as it were by chance, and stole glances at me from below—for signs of lunacy or drunkenness, I suppose.

A little before supper, feeling more restless than ever, I rejoined, for a moment, my second self. And to find him sitting so quietly was surprising, like something against nature, inhuman.

I developed my plan in a hurried whisper.

"I shall stand in as close as I dare and then put her round. I shall presently find means to smuggle you out of here into the sail locker, which communicates with the lobby. But there is an opening, a sort of square for hauling the sails out, which gives straight on the quarter-deck and which is never closed in fine weather, so as to give air to the sails. When the ship's way is deadened in stays and all the hands are aft at the main braces you shall have a clear road to slip out and get overboard through the open quarter-deck port. I've had them both fastened up. Use a rope's end to lower yourself into the water so as to avoid a splash—you know. It could be heard and cause some beastly complication."

He kept silent for a while, then whispered, "I understand."

"I won't be there to see you go," I began with an effort. "The rest . . . I only hope I have understood, too."

"You have. From first to last," and for the first time there seemed to be a faltering, something strained in his whisper. He caught hold of my arm, but the ringing of the supper bell made me start. He didn't, though; he only released his grip.

After supper I didn't come below again till well past eight o'clock. The faint, steady breeze was loaded with dew; and the wet, darkened sails held all there was of propelling power in it. The night, clear and starry, sparkled darkly, and the opaque, lightless patches shifting slowly against the low stars were the drifting islets. On the port bow there was a big one more distant and shadowily imposing by the great space of sky it eclipsed.

On opening the door I had a back view of my very own self looking at a chart. He had come out of the recess and was standing near the table.

"Quite dark enough," I whispered.

He stepped back and leaned against my bed with a level, quiet glance. I sat on the couch. We had nothing to say to each other. Over our heads the officer of the watch moved here and there. Then I heard him move quickly. I knew what that meant. He was making for the companion; and presently his voice was outside my door.

"We are drawing in pretty fast, sir. Land looks rather close."

"Very well," I answered. "I am coming on deck directly."

I waited till he was gone out of the cuddy, then rose. My double moved too. The time had come to exchange our last whispers, for neither of us was ever to hear each other's natural voice.

"Look here!" I opened a drawer and took out three sovereigns. "Take this, anyhow. I've got six and I'd give you the lot, only I must keep a little money to buy some fruit and vegetables for the crew from native boats as we go through Sunda Straits."

He shook his head.

"Take it," I urged him, whispering desperately. "No one can tell what—"

He smiled and slapped meaningly the only pocket of the sleeping jacket. It was not safe, certainly. But I produced a large old silk handkerchief of mine, and tying the three pieces of gold in a corner, pressed it on him. He was touched, I suppose, because he took it at last and tied it quickly round his waist under the jacket, on his bare skin.

Our eyes met; several seconds elapsed, till, our glances still mingled, I extended my hand and turned the lamp out. Then I passed through the cuddy, leaving the door of my room wide open. . . . "Steward!"

He was still lingering in the pantry in the greatness of his zeal, giving a rubup to a plated cruet stand the last thing before going to bed. Being careful not to wake up the mate, whose room was opposite, I spoke in an undertone.

He looked round anxiously. "Sir!"

"Can you get me a little hot water from the galley?"

"I am afraid, sir, the galley fire's been out for some time now."

"Go and see."

He fled up the stairs.

"Now," I whispered, loudly, into the saloon—too loudly, perhaps, but I was afraid I couldn't make a sound. He was by my side in an instant—the double captain slipped past the stairs—through the tiny dark passage . . . a sliding door. We were in the sail locker, scrambling on our knees over the sails. A sudden thought struck me. I saw myself wandering barefooted, bareheaded, the sun beating on my dark poll. I snatched off my floppy hat and tried hurriedly in the dark to ram it on my other self. He dodged and fended off silently. I wonder what he thought had come to me before he understood and suddenly desisted. Our hands met gropingly, lingered united in a steady, motionless clasp for a second. . . . No word was breathed by either of us when they separated.

I was standing quietly by the pantry door when the steward returned.

"Sorry, sir. Kettle barely warm. Shall I light the spirit lamp?"

"Never mind."

I came out on deck slowly. It was now a matter of conscience to shave the land as close as possible—for now he must go overboard whenever the ship was put in stays. Must! There could be no going back for him. After a moment I walked over to leeward and my heart flew into my mouth at the nearness of the land on the bow. Under any other circumstances I would not have held on a minute longer. The second mate had followed me anxiously.

I looked on till I felt I could command my voice.

"She will weather," I said then in a quiet tone.

"Are you going to try that, sir?" he stammered out incredulously.

I took no notice of him and raised my tone just enough to be heard by the helmsman.

"Keep her good full."

"Good full, sir."

The wind fanned my cheek, the sail slept, the world was silent. The strain of watching the dark loom of the land grow bigger and denser was too much for me. I had shut my eyes—because the ship must go closer. She must! The stillness was intolerable. Were we standing still?

When I opened my eyes the second view started my heart with a thump. The black southern hill of Koh-ring seemed to hang right over the ship like a towering fragment of the everlasting night. On that enormous mass of blackness there was not a gleam to be seen, not a sound to be heard. It was gliding irresistibly toward us and yet seemed already within reach of the hand. I saw the vague figures of the watch grouped in the waist, gazing in awed silence.

"Are you going on, sir?" inquired an unsteady voice at my elbow.

I ignored it. I had to go on.

"Keep her full. Don't check her way. That won't do now," I said warningly.

"I can't see the sails very well," the helmsman answered me, in strange, quavering tones.

Was she close enough? Already she was, I won't say in the shadow of the land, but in the very blackness of it, already swallowed up as it were, gone too close to be recalled, gone from me altogether.

"Give the mate a call," I said to the young man who stood at my elbow still as death. "And turn all hands up."

My tone had a borrowed loudness reverberated from the height of the land. Several voices cried out together: "We are all on deck, sir."

Then stillness again, with the great shadow gliding closer, towering higher, without a light, without a sound. Such a hush had fallen on the ship that she might have been a bark of the dead floating in slowly under the very gate of Erebus.[2]

"My God! Where are we?"

It was the mate moaning at my elbow. He was thunderstruck, and as it were deprived of the moral support of his whiskers. He clapped his hands and absolutely cried out, "Lost!"

"Be quiet," I said sternly.

He lowered his tone, but I saw the shadowy gesture of his despair. "What are we doing here?"

"Looking for the land wind."

He made as if to tear his hair, and addressed me recklessly.

"She will never get out. You have done it, sir. I knew it'd end in something like this. She will never weather, and you are too close now to stay. She'll drift ashore before she's round. O my God!"

I caught his arm as he was raising it to batter his poor devoted head, and shook it violently.

"She's ashore already," he wailed, trying to tear himself away.

"Is she? . . . Keep good full there!"

"Good full, sir," cried the helmsman in a frightened, thin, childlike voice.

I hadn't let go the mate's arm and went on shaking it. "Ready about, do you hear? You go forward"—shake—"and stop there"—shake—"and hold your noise"—shake—"and see these head sheets properly overhauled"—shake, shake—shake.

And all the time I dared not look toward the land lest my heart should fail me. I released my grip at last and he ran forward as if fleeing for dear life.

I wondered what my double there in the sail locker thought of this commotion. He was able to hear everything—and perhaps he was able to understand why, on my conscience, it had to be thus close—no less. My first order "Hard alee!" re-echoed ominously under the towering shadow of Koh-ring as if I had shouted in a mountain gorge. And then I watched the land intently. In that smooth water and light wind it was impossible to feel the ship coming-to. No! I could not feel her. And my second self was making now ready to slip out and lower himself overboard. Perhaps he was gone already. . . . ?

The great black mass brooding over our very mastheads began to pivot away from the ship's side silently. And now I forgot the secret stranger ready to depart, and remembered only that I was a total stranger to the ship. I did not know her. Would she do it? How was she to be handled?

I swung the mainyard and waited helplessly. She was perhaps stopped, and her very fate hung in the balance, with the black mass of Koh-ring like the gate of the everlasting night towering over her taffrail. What would she do now? Had

---

[2]In Greek mythology, the lightless passageway to the underworld.

she way on her yet? I stepped to the side swiftly, and on the shadowy water I could see nothing except a faint phosphorescent flash revealing the glassy smoothness of the sleeping surface. It was impossible to tell—and I had not learned yet the feel of my ship. Was she moving? What I needed was something easily seen, a piece of paper, which I could throw overboard and watch. I had nothing on me. To run down for it I didn't dare. There was no time. All at once my strained, yearning stare distinguished a white object floating within a yard of the ship's side. White on the black water. A phosphorescent flash passed under it. What was that thing? . . . I recognized my own floppy hat. It must have fallen off his head . . . and he didn't bother. Now I had what I wanted—the saving mark for my eyes. But I hardly thought of my other self, now gone from the ship, to be hidden forever from all friendly faces, to be a fugitive and a vagabond on the earth, with no brand of the curse on his sane forehead to stay a slaying hand . . . too proud to explain.

And I watched the hat—the expression of my sudden pity for his mere flesh. It had been meant to save his homeless head from the dangers of the sun. And now—behold—it was saving the ship, by serving me for a mark to help out the ignorance of my strangeness. Ha! It was drifting forward, warning me just in time that the ship had gathered sternway.

"Shift the helm," I said in a low voice to the seaman standing still like a statue.

The man's eyes glistened wildly in the binnacle light as he jumped round to the other side and spun round the wheel.

I walked to the break of the poop. On the overshadowed deck all hands stood by the forebraces waiting for my order. The stars ahead seemed to be gliding from right to left. And all was so still in the world that I heard the quiet remark "She's round," passed in a tone of intense relief between two seamen.

"Let go and haul."

The foreyards ran round with a great noise, amidst cheery cries. And now the frightful whiskers made themselves heard giving various orders. Already the ship was drawing ahead. And I was alone with her. Nothing! no one in the world should stand now between us, throwing a shadow on the way of silent knowledge and mute affection, the perfect communion of a seaman with his first command.

Walking to the taffrail, I was in time to make out, on the very edge of a darkness thrown by a towering black mass like the very gateway of Erebus—yes, I was in time to catch an evanescent glimpse of my white hat left behind to mark the spot where the secret sharer of my cabin and of my thoughts, as though he were my second self, had lowered himself into the water to take his punishment: a free man, a proud swimmer striking out for a new destiny.

QUESTIONS

1. Before Leggatt appears, what impressions of the captain have you formed?
2. How easy did you find it to form a picture of Leggatt? Explain.
3. Which details of the setting were most important in your response to the story? Have you thought of it primarily as a sea story?

4. The captain describes himself at one point as "distracted almost to the point of insanity." How close to madness would you say he comes?
5. How would you describe his relation to Leggatt?
6. As Leggatt prepares to leave, both he and the captain speak of "understanding" something. What do you understand each man to mean?
7. By the conclusion, how has the captain's relation to his ship and crew changed?

Charlotte Perkins Gilman (1860–1935)

THE YELLOW WALL-PAPER

It is very seldom that mere ordinary people like John and myself secure ancestral halls for the summer.

A colonial mansion, a hereditary estate. I would say a haunted house, and reach the height of romantic felicity—but that would be asking too much of fate!

Still I will proudly declare that there is something queer about it.

Else, why should it be let so cheaply? And why have stood so long untenanted?

John laughs at me, of course, but one expects that in marriage.

John is practical in the extreme. He has no patience with faith, an intense horror of superstition, and he scoffs openly at any talk of things not to be felt and seen and put down in figures.

John is a physician, and *perhaps*—(I would not say it to a living soul, of course, but this is dead paper and a great relief to my mind—) *perhaps* that is one reason I do not get well faster.

You see he does not believe I am sick!

And what can one do?

If a physician of high standing, and one's own husband, assures friends and relatives that there is really nothing the matter with one but temporary nervous depression—a slight hysterical tendency—what is one to do?

My brother is also a physician, and also of high standing, and he says the same thing.

So I take phosphates or phosphites—whichever it is, and tonics, and journeys, and air, and exercise, and am absolutely forbidden to "work" until I am well again.

Personally, I disagree with their ideas.

Personally, I believe that congenial work, with excitement and change, would do me good.

But what is one to do?

I did write for a while in spite of them; but it *does* exhaust me a good deal—having to be so sly about it, or else meet with heavy opposition.

I sometimes fancy that in my condition if I had less opposition and more society and stimulus—but John says the very worst thing I can do is to think about my condition, and I confess it always makes me feel bad.

So I will let it alone and talk about the house.

The most beautiful place! It is quite alone, standing well back from the road, quite three miles from the village. It makes me think of English places that you read about, for there are hedges and walls and gates that lock, and lots of separate little houses for the gardeners and people.

There is a *delicious* garden! I never saw such a garden—large and shady, full of box-bordered paths, and lined with long grape-covered arbors with seats under them.

There were greenhouses, too, but they are all broken now.

There was some legal trouble, I believe, something about the heirs and co-heirs; anyhow, the place has been empty for years.

That spoils my ghostliness, I am afraid, but I don't care—there is something strange about the house—I can feel it.

I even said so to John one moonlight evening, but he said what I felt was a *draught,* and shut the window.

I get unreasonably angry with John sometimes. I'm sure I never used to be so sensitive. I think it is due to this nervous condition.

But John says if I feel so, I shall neglect proper self-control; so I take pains to control myself—before him, at least, and that makes me very tired.

I don't like our room a bit. I wanted one downstairs that opened on the piazza and had roses all over the window, and such pretty old-fashioned chintz hangings! but John would not hear of it.

He said there was only one window and not room for two beds, and no near room for him if he took another.

He is very careful and loving, and hardly lets me stir without special direction.

I have a schedule prescription for each hour in the day; he takes all care from me, and so I feel basely ungrateful not to value it more.

He said we came here solely on my account, that I was to have perfect rest and all the air I could get. "Your exercise depends on your strength, my dear," said he, "and your food somewhat on your appetite; but air you can absorb all the time." So we took the nursery at the top of the house.

It is a big, airy room, the whole floor nearly, with windows that look all ways, and air and sunshine galore. It was nursery first and then playroom and gymnasium, I should judge; for the windows are barred for little children, and there are rings and things in the walls.

The paint and paper look as if a boys' school had used it. It is stripped off—the paper—in great patches all around the head of my bed, about as far as I can reach, and in a great place on the other side of the room low down. I never saw a worse paper in my life.

One of those sprawling flamboyant patterns committing every artistic sin.

It is dull enough to confuse the eye in following, pronounced enough to constantly irritate and provoke study, and when you follow the lame uncertain curves for a little distance they suddenly commit suicide—plunge off at outrageous angles, destroy themselves in unheard of contradictions.

The color is repellent, almost revolting; a smouldering unclean yellow, strangely faded by the slow-turning sunlight.

It is a dull yet lurid orange in some places, a sickly sulphur tint in others.

No wonder the children hated it! I should hate it myself if I had to live in this room long.

There comes John, and I must put this away,—he hates to have me write a word.

We have been here two weeks, and I haven't felt like writing before, since that first day.

I am sitting by the window now, up in this atrocious nursery, and there is nothing to hinder my writing as much as I please, save lack of strength.

John is away all day, and even some nights when his cases are serious.

I am glad my case is not serious!

But these nervous troubles are dreadfully depressing.

John does not know how much I really suffer. He knows there is no *reason* to suffer, and that satisfies him.

Of course it is only nervousness. It does weigh on me so not to do my duty in any way!

I meant to be such a help to John, such a real rest and comfort, and here I am a comparative burden already!

Nobody would believe what an effort it is to do what little I am able—to dress and entertain, and order things.

It is fortunate Mary is so good with the baby. Such a dear baby!

And yet I *cannot* be with him, it makes me so nervous.

I suppose John never was nervous in his life. He laughs at me so about this wall-paper!

At first he meant to repaper the room, but afterwards he said that I was letting it get the better of me, and that nothing was worse for a nervous patient than to give way to such fancies.

He said that after the wall-paper was changed it would be the heavy bedstead, and then the barred windows, and then that gate at the head of the stairs, and so on.

"You know the place is doing you good," he said, "and really, dear, I don't care to renovate the house just for a three months' rental."

"Then do let us go downstairs," I said, "there are such pretty rooms there."

Then he took me in his arms and called me a blessed little goose, and said he would go down cellar, if I wished, and have it whitewashed into the bargain.

But he is right enough about the beds and windows and things.

It is as airy and comfortable a room as any one need wish, and, of course, I would not be so silly as to make him uncomfortable just for a whim.

I'm really getting quite fond of the big room, all but that horrid paper.

Out of one window I can see the garden, those mysterious deep-shaded arbors, the riotous old-fashioned flowers, and bushes and gnarly trees.

Out of another I get a lovely view of the bay and a little private wharf belonging to the estate. There is a beautiful shaded lane that runs down there from the house. I always fancy I see people walking in these numerous paths and arbors, but John has cautioned me not to give way to fancy in the least. He says that with my imaginative power and habit of storymaking, a nervous weakness like mine is sure to lead to all manner of excited fancies, and that I ought to use my will and good sense to check the tendency. So I try.

I think sometimes that if I were only well enough to write a little it would relieve the press of ideas and rest me.

But I find I get pretty tired when I try.

It is so discouraging not to have any advice and companionship about my work. When I get really well, John says we will ask Cousin Henry and Julia down for a long visit; but he says he would as soon put fireworks in my pillow-case as to let me have those stimulating people about now.

I wish I could get well faster.

But I must not think about that. This paper looks to me as if it *knew* what a vicious influence it had!

There is a recurrent spot where the pattern lolls like a broken neck and two bulbous eyes stare at you upside down.

I get positively angry with the impertinence of it and the everlastingness. Up and down and sideways they crawl, and those absurd, unblinking eyes are everywhere. There is one place where two breadths didn't match, and the eyes go all up and down the line, one a little higher than the other.

I never saw so much expression in an inanimate thing before, and we all know how much expression they have! I used to lie awake as a child and get more entertainment and terror out of blank walls and plain furniture than most children could find in a toy-store.

I remember what a kindly wink the knobs of our big, old bureau used to have, and there was one chair that always seemed like a strong friend.

I used to feel that if any of the other things looked too fierce I could always hop into that chair and be safe.

The furniture in this room is no worse than inharmonious, however, for we had to bring it all from downstairs. I suppose when this was used as a playroom they had to take the nursery things out, and no wonder! I never saw such ravages as the children have made here.

The wall-paper, as I said before, is torn off in spots, and it sticketh closer than a brother—they must have had perseverance as well as hatred.

Then the floor is scratched and gouged and splintered, the plaster itself is dug out here and there, and this great heavy bed which is all we found in the room, looks as if it had been through the wars.

But I don't mind it a bit—only the paper.

There comes John's sister. Such a dear girl as she is, and so careful of me! I must not let her find me writing.

She is a perfect and enthusiastic housekeeper, and hopes for no better profession. I verily believe she thinks it is the writing which made me sick!

But I can write when she is out, and see her a long way off from these windows.

There is one that commands the road, a lovely shaded winding road, and one that just looks off over the country. A lovely country, too, full of great elms and velvet meadows.

This wall-paper has a kind of sub-pattern in a different shade, a particularly irritating one, for you can only see it in certain lights, and not clearly then.

But in the places where it isn't faded and where the sun is just so—I can see a strange, provoking, formless sort of figure, that seems to skulk about behind that silly and conspicuous front design.

There's sister on the stairs!

Well, the Fourth of July is over! The people are all gone and I am tired out. John thought it might do me good to see a little company, so we just had mother and Nellie and the children down for a week.

Of course I didn't do a thing. Jennie sees to everything now.

But it tired me all the same.

John says if I don't pick up faster he shall send me to Weir Mitchell[1] in the fall.

But I don't want to go there at all. I had a friend who was in his hands once, and she says he is just like John and my brother, only more so!

Besides, it is such an undertaking to go so far.

I don't feel as if it was worth while to turn my hand over for anything, and I'm getting dreadfully fretful and querulous.

I cry at nothing, and cry most of the time.

Of course I don't when John is here, or anybody else, but when I am alone.

And I am alone a good deal just now. John is kept in town very often by serious cases, and Jennie is good and lets me alone when I want her to.

So I walk a little in the garden or down that lovely lane, sit on the porch under the roses, and lie down up here a good deal.

I'm getting really fond of the room in spite of the wall-paper. Perhaps *because* of the wall-paper.

It dwells in my mind so!

I lie here on this great immovable bed—it is nailed down, I believe—and follow that pattern about by the hour. It is as good as gymnastics, I assure you. I start, we'll say, at the bottom, down in the corner over there where it has not been touched, and I determine for the thousandth time that I *will* follow that pointless pattern to some sort of conclusion.

I know a little of the principle of design, and I know this thing was not arranged on any laws of radiation, or alternation, or repetition, or symmetry, or anything else that I ever heard of.

It is repeated, of course, by the breadths, but not otherwise.

Looked at in one way each breadth stands alone, the bloated curves and flourishes—a kind of "debased Romanesque" with *delirium tremens* go waddling up and down in isolated columns of fatuity.

---

[1]Brilliant American doctor, who treated many patients from among the famous and wealthy of his time. Mitchell (1829–1914) was himself an accomplished novelist.

But, on the other hand, they connect diagonally, and the sprawling outlines run off in great slanting waves of optic horror, like a lot of wallowing seaweeds in full chase.

The whole thing goes horizontally, too, at least it seems so, and I exhaust myself in trying to distinguish the order of its going in that direction.

They have used a horizontal breadth for a frieze, and that adds wonderfully to the confusion.

There is one end of the room where it is almost intact, and there, when the crosslights fade and the low sun shines directly upon it, I can almost fancy radiation after all,—the interminable grotesques seem to form around a common centre and rush off in headlong plunges of equal distraction.

It makes me tired to follow it. I will take a nap I guess.

I don't know why I should write this.

I don't want to.

I don't feel able.

And I know John would think it absurd. But I *must* say what I feel and think in some way—it is such a relief!

But the effort is getting to be greater than the relief.

Half the time now I am awfully lazy, and lie down ever so much.

John says I mustn't lose my strength, and has me take cod liver oil and lots of tonics and things, to say nothing of ale and wine and rare meat.

Dear John! He loves me very dearly, and hates to have me sick. I tried to have a real earnest reasonable talk with him the other day, and tell him how I wish he would let me go and make a visit to Cousin Henry and Julia.

But he said I wasn't able to go, nor able to stand it after I got there; and I did not make out a very good case for myself, for I was crying before I had finished.

It is getting to be a great effort for me to think straight. Just this nervous weakness I suppose.

And dear John gathered me up in his arms, and just carried me upstairs and laid me on the bed, and sat by me and read to me till it tired my head.

He said I was his darling and his comfort and all he had, and that I must take care of myself for his sake, and keep well.

He says no one but myself can help me out of it, that I must use my will and self-control and not let any silly fancies run away with me.

There's one comfort, the baby is well and happy, and does not have to occupy this nursery with the horrid wall-paper.

If we had not used it, the blessed child would have! What a fortunate escape! Why, I wouldn't have a child of mine, an impressionable little thing, live in such a room for worlds.

I never thought of it before, but it is lucky that John kept me here after all, I can stand it so much easier than a baby, you see.

Of course I never mention it to them any more—I am too wise,—but I keep watch of it all the same.

There are things in that paper that nobody knows but me, or ever will.

Behind that outside pattern the dim shapes get clearer every day.

It is always the same shape, only very numerous.

And it is like a woman stooping down and creeping about behind that pattern. I don't like it a bit. I wonder—I begin to think—I wish John would take me away from here!

It is so hard to talk with John about my case, because he is so wise, and because he loves me so.

But I tried it last night.

It was moonlight. The moon shines in all around just as the sun does.

I hate to see it sometimes, it creeps so slowly, and always comes in by one window or another.

John was asleep and I hated to waken him, so I kept still and watched the moonlight on that undulating wall-paper till I felt creepy.

The faint figure behind seemed to shake the pattern, just as if she wanted to get out.

I got up softly and went to feel and see if the paper *did* move, and when I came back John was awake.

"What is it, little girl?" he said. "Don't go walking about like that—you'll get cold."

I thought it was a good time to talk, so I told him that I really was not gaining here, and I wished he would take me away.

"Why, darling!" he said, "our lease will be up in three weeks, and I can't see how to leave before.

"The repairs are not done at home, and I cannot possibly leave town just now. Of course if you were in any danger, I could and would, but you really are better, dear, whether you can see it or not. I am a doctor, dear, and I know. You are gaining flesh and color, your appetite is better, I feel really much easier about you."

"I don't weigh a bit more," said I, "nor as much; and my appetite may be better in the evening when you are here, but it is worse in the morning when you are away!"

"Bless her little heart!" said he with a big hug, "she shall be as sick as she pleases! But now let's improve the shining hours by going to sleep, and talk about it in the morning!"

"And you won't go away?" I asked gloomily.

"Why, how can I, dear? It is only three weeks more and then we will take a nice little trip of a few days while Jennie is getting the house ready. Really dear you are better!"

"Better in body perhaps—" I began, and stopped short, for he sat up straight and looked at me with such a stern, reproachful look that I could not say another word.

"My darling," said he, "I beg of you, for my sake and for our child's sake, as well as for your own, that you will never for one instant let that idea enter your mind! There is nothing so dangerous, so fascinating, to a temperament like yours. It is a false and foolish fancy. Can you not trust me as a physician when I tell you so?"

So of course I said no more on that score, and we went to sleep before long. He thought I was asleep first, but I wasn't, and lay there for hours trying to decide whether that front pattern and the back pattern really did move together or separately.

On a pattern like this, by daylight, there is a lack of sequence, a defiance of law, that is a constant irritant to a normal mind.

The color is hideous enough, and unreliable enough, and infuriating enough, but the pattern is torturing.

You think you have mastered it, but just as you get well underway in following, it turns a back-somersault and there you are. It slaps you in the face, knocks you down, and tramples upon you. It is like a bad dream.

The outside pattern is a florid arabesque, reminding one of a fungus. If you can imagine a toadstool in joints, an interminable string of toadstools, budding and sprouting in endless convolutions—why, that is something like it.

That is, sometimes!

There is one marked peculiarity about this paper, a thing nobody seems to notice but myself, and that is that it changes as the light changes.

When the sun shoots in through the east window—I always watch for that first long, straight ray—it changes so quickly that I never can quite believe it.

That is why I watch it always.

By moonlight—the moon shines in all night when there is a moon—I wouldn't know it was the same paper.

At night in any kind of light, in twilight, candlelight, lamplight, and worst of all by moonlight, it becomes bars! The outside pattern I mean, and the woman behind it is as plain as can be.

I didn't realize for a long time what the thing was that showed behind, that dim sub-pattern, but now I am quite sure it is a woman.

By daylight she is subdued, quiet. I fancy it is the pattern that keeps her so still. It is so puzzling. It keeps me quiet by the hour.

I lie down ever so much now. John says it is good for me, and to sleep all I can.

Indeed he started the habit by making me lie down for an hour after each meal.

It is a very bad habit I am convinced, for you see I don't sleep.

And that cultivates deceit, for I don't tell them I'm awake—O no!

The fact is I am getting a little afraid of John.

He seems very queer sometimes, and even Jennie has an inexplicable look.

It strikes me occasionally, just as a scientific hypothesis,—that perhaps it is the paper!

I have watched John when he did not know I was looking, and come into the room suddenly on the most innocent excuses, and I've caught him several times *looking at the paper!* And Jennie too. I caught Jennie with her hand on it once.

She didn't know I was in the room, and when I asked her in a quiet, a very quiet voice, with the most restrained manner possible, what she was doing with the paper—she turned around as if she had been caught stealing, and looked quite angry—asked me why I should frighten her so!

Then she said that the paper stained everything it touched, that she had found yellow smooches on all my clothes and John's, and she wished we would be more careful!

Did not that sound innocent? But I know she was studying that pattern, and I am determined that nobody shall find it out but myself!

Life is very much more exciting now than it used to be. You see I have something more to expect, to look forward to, to watch. I really do eat better, and am more quiet than I was.

John is so pleased to see me improve! He laughed a little the other day, and said I seemed to be flourishing in spite of my wall-paper.

I turned it off with a laugh. I had no intention of telling him it was *because* of the wall-paper—he would make fun of me. He might even want to take me away.

I don't want to leave now until I have found it out. There is a week more, and I think that will be enough.

I'm feeling ever so much better! I don't sleep much at night, for it is so interesting to watch developments; but I sleep a good deal in the daytime.

In the daytime it is tiresome and perplexing.

There are always new shoots on the fungus, and new shades of yellow all over it. I cannot keep count of them, though I have tried conscientiously.

It is the strangest yellow, that wall-paper! It makes me think of all the yellow things I ever saw—not beautiful ones like buttercups, but old foul, bad yellow things.

But there is something else about that paper—the smell! I noticed it the moment we came into the room, but with so much air and sun it was not bad. Now we have had a week of fog and rain, and whether the windows are open or not, the smell is here.

It creeps all over the house.

I find it hovering in the dining-room, skulking in the parlor, hiding in the hall, lying in wait for me on the stairs.

It gets into my hair.

Even when I go to ride, if I turn my head suddenly and surprise it—there is that smell!

Such a peculiar odor, too! I have spent hours in trying to analyze it, to find what it smelled like.

It is not bad—at first, and very gentle, but quite the subtlest, most enduring odor I ever met.

In this damp weather it is awful. I wake up in the night and find it hanging over me.

It used to disturb me at first. I thought seriously of burning the house—to reach the smell.

But now I am used to it. The only thing I can think of that it is like is the *color* of the paper! A yellow smell.

There is a very funny mark on this wall, low down, near the mopboard. A streak that runs around the room. It goes behind every piece of furniture, except the bed, a long, straight, even *smooch,* as if it had been rubbed over and over.

I wonder how it was done and who did it, and what they did it for. Round and round and round—round and round and round!—it makes me dizzy!

I really have discovered something at last.

Through watching so much at night, when it changes so, I have finally found out.

The front pattern *does* move—and no wonder! The woman behind shakes it!

Sometimes I think there are a great many women behind, and sometimes only one, and she crawls around fast, and her crawling shakes it all over.

Then in the very bright spots she keeps still, and in the very shady spots she just takes hold of the bars and shakes them hard.

And she is all the time trying to climb through. But nobody could climb through that pattern—it strangles so; I think that is why it has so many heads.

They get through, and then the pattern strangles them off and turns them upside down, and makes their eyes white!

If those heads were covered or taken off it would not be half so bad.

I think that woman gets out in the daytime!

And I'll tell you why—privately—I've seen her!

I can see her out of every one of my windows!

It is the same woman, I know, for she is always creeping, and most women do not creep by daylight.

I see her in that long shaded lane, creeping up and down. I see her in those dark grape arbors, creeping all around the garden.

I see her on that long road under the trees, creeping along, and when a carriage comes she hides under the blackberry vines.

I don't blame her a bit. It must be very humiliating to be caught creeping by daylight!

I always lock the door when I creep by daylight. I can't do it at night, for I know John would suspect something at once.

And John is so queer now, that I don't want to irritate him. I wish he would take another room! Besides, I don't want anybody to get that woman out at night but myself.

I often wonder if I could see her out of all the windows at once.

But, turn as fast as I can, I can only see out of one at one time.

And though I always see her, she *may* be able to creep faster than I can turn!

I have watched her sometimes away off in the open country, creeping as fast as a cloud shadow in a high wind.

If only that top pattern could be gotten off from the under one! I mean to try it, little by little.

I have found out another funny thing, but I shan't tell it this time! It does not do to trust people too much.

There are only two more days to get this paper off, and I believe John is beginning to notice. I don't like the look in his eyes.

And I heard him ask Jennie a lot of professional questions about me. She had a very good report to give.

She said I slept a good deal in the daytime.

John knows I don't sleep very well at night, for all I'm so quiet!

He asked me all sorts of questions, too, and pretended to be very loving and kind.

As if I couldn't see through him!

Still, I don't wonder he acts so, sleeping under this paper for three months.

It only interests me, but I feel sure John and Jennie are secretly affected by it.

Hurrah! This is the last day, but it is enough. John is to stay in town over night, and won't be out until this evening.

Jennie wanted to sleep with me—the sly thing! but I told her I should undoubtedly rest better for a night all alone.

That was clever, for really I wasn't alone a bit! As soon as it was moonlight and that poor thing began to crawl and shake the pattern, I got up and ran to help her.

I pulled and she shook, I shook and she pulled, and before morning we had peeled off yards of that paper.

A strip about as high as my head and half around the room.

And then when the sun came and that awful pattern began to laugh at me, I declared I would finish it to-day!

We go away to-morrow, and they are moving all my furniture down again to leave things as they were before.

Jennie looked at the wall in amazement, but I told her merrily that I did it out of pure spite at the vicious thing.

She laughed and said she wouldn't mind doing it herself, but I must not get tired.

How she betrayed herself that time!

But I am here, and no person touches this paper but me,—not *alive!*

She tried to get me out of the room—it was too patent! But I said it was so quiet and empty and clean now that I believed I would lie down again and sleep all I could; and not to wake me even for dinner—I would call when I woke.

So now she is gone, and the servants are gone, and the things are gone, and there is nothing left but that great bedstead nailed down, with the canvas mattress we found on it.

We shall sleep downstairs to-night, and take the boat home to-morrow.

I quite enjoy the room, now it is bare again.

How those children did tear about here!

This bedstead is fairly gnawed!

But I must get to work.

I have locked the door and thrown the key down into the front path.

I don't want to go out, and I don't want to have anybody come in, till John comes.

I want to astonish him.

I've got a rope up here that even Jennie did not find. If that woman does get out, and tries to get away, I can tie her!

But I forgot I could not reach far without anything to stand on!

This bed will *not* move!

I tried to lift and push it until I was lame, and then I got so angry I bit off a little piece at one corner—but it hurt my teeth.

Then I peeled off all the paper I could reach standing on the floor. It sticks horribly and the pattern just enjoys it! All those strangled heads and bulbous eyes and waddling fungus growths just shriek with derision!

I am getting angry enough to do something desperate. To jump out of the window would be admirable exercise, but the bars are too strong even to try.

Besides I wouldn't do it. Of course not. I know well enough that a step like that is improper and might be misconstrued.

I don't like to *look* out of the windows even—there are so many of those creeping women, and they creep so fast.

I wonder if they all come out of that wall-paper as I did?

But I am securely fastened now by my well-hidden rope—you don't get *me* out in the road there!

I suppose I shall have to get back behind the pattern when it comes night, and that is hard!

It is so pleasant to be out in this great room and creep around as I please!

I don't want to go outside. I won't, even if Jennie asks me to.

For outside you have to creep on the ground, and everything is green instead of yellow.

But here I can creep smoothly on the floor, and my shoulder just fits in that long smooch around the wall, so I cannot lose my way.

Why there's John at the door!

It is no use, young man, you can't open it!

How he does call and pound!

Now he's crying for an axe.

It would be a shame to break down that beautiful door!

"John dear!" said I in the gentlest voice, "the key is down by the front steps, under a plaintain leaf!"

That silenced him for a few moments.

Then he said—very quietly indeed, "Open the door, my darling!"

"I can't," said I. "The key is down by the front door under a plaintain leaf!"

And then I said it again, several times, very gently and slowly, and said it so often that he had to go and see, and he got it of course, and came in. He stopped short by the door.

"What is the matter?" he cried. "For God's sake, what are you doing!"

I kept on creeping just the same, but I looked at him over my shoulder.

"I've got out at last," said I, "in spite of you and Jane. And I've pulled off most of the paper, so you can't put me back!"

Now why should that man have fainted? But he did, and right across my path by the wall, so that I had to creep over him every time!

QUESTIONS

1. What sort of relationship does this narrator establish with you as you read?
2. How often did you find yourself processing information given by the narrator in a way different from hers? Give an example.
3. Did any personal experience or prior reading contribute to your response to the story?
4. What importance did the wallpaper and its being yellow assume in your reading?
5. What sense, if any, do you have of the author behind the narrator's voice?
6. What did you make of the story's tone: for example, the almost comic touches at the conclusion?

James Joyce (1882–1941)
COUNTERPARTS

The bell rang furiously and, when Miss Parker went to the tube, a furious voice called out in a piercing North of Ireland accent:

—Send Farrington here!

Miss Parker returned to her machine, saying to a man who was writing at a desk:

—Mr Alleyne wants you upstairs.

The man muttered *Blast him!* under his breath and pushed back his chair to stand up. When he stood up he was tall and of great bulk. He had a hanging face, dark wine-coloured, with fair eyebrows and moustache: his eyes bulged forward slightly and the whites of them were dirty. He lifted up the counter and, passing by the clients, went out of the office with a heavy step.

He went heavily upstairs until he came to the second landing, where a door bore a brass plate with the inscription *Mr Alleyne*. Here he halted, puffing with labour and vexation, and knocked. The shrill voice cried:

—Come in!

The man entered Mr Alleyne's room. Simultaneously Mr Alleyne, a little man wearing gold-rimmed glasses on a clean-shaven face, shot his head up over a pile of documents. The head itself was so pink and hairless that it seemed like a large egg reposing on the papers. Mr Alleyne did not lose a moment:

—Farrington? What is the meaning of this? Why have I always to complain of you? May I ask you why you haven't made a copy of that contract between Bodley and Kirwan? I told you it must be ready by four o'clock.

—But Mr Shelley said, sir—

—*Mr Shelley said, sir.* . . . Kindly attend to what I say and not to what *Mr Shelley says, sir.* You have always some excuse or another for shirking work. Let me tell you that if the contract is not copied before this evening I'll lay the matter before Mr Crosbie. . . . Do you hear me now?

—Yes, sir.

—Do you hear me now? . . . Ay and another little matter! I might as well be talking to the wall as talking to you. Understand once for all that you get a half an hour for your lunch and not an hour and a half. How many courses do you want, I'd like to know. . . . Do you mind me, now?

—Yes, sir.

Mr Alleyne bent his head again upon his pile of papers. The man stared fixedly at the polished skull which directed the affairs of Crosbie & Alleyne, gauging its fragility. A spasm of rage gripped his throat for a few moments and then passed, leaving after it a sharp sensation of thirst. The man recognised the sensation and felt that he must have a good night's drinking. The middle of the month was passed and, if he could get the copy done in time, Mr Alleyne might give him an order on the cashier. He stood still, gazing fixedly at the head upon the pile of papers. Suddenly Mr Alleyne began to upset all the papers, searching for something. Then, as if he had been unaware of the man's presence till that moment, he shot up his head again, saying:

—Eh? Are you going to stand there all day? Upon my word, Farrington, you take things easy!

—I was waiting to see . . .

—Very good, you needn't wait to see. Go downstairs and do your work.

The man walked heavily towards the door and, as he went out of the room, he heard Mr Alleyne cry after him that if the contract was not copied by evening Mr Crosbie would hear of the matter.

He returned to his desk in the lower office and counted the sheets which remained to be copied. He took up his pen and dipped it in the ink but he continued to stare stupidly at the last words he had written: *In no case shall the said Bernard Bodley be* . . . The evening was falling and in a few minutes they would be lighting the gas: then he could write. He felt that he must slake the thirst in his throat. He stood up from his desk and, lifting the counter as before, passed out of the office. As he was passing out the chief clerk looked at him inquiringly.

—It's all right, Mr Shelley, said the man, pointing with his finger to indicate the objective of his journey.

The chief clerk glanced at the hat-rack but, seeing the row complete, offered no remark. As soon as he was on the landing the man pulled a shepherd's plaid cap out of his pocket, put it on his head and ran quickly down the rickety stairs. From the street door he walked on furtively on the inner side of the path towards the corner and all at once dived into a doorway. He was now safe in the dark snug of O'Neill's shop, and, filling up the little window that looked into the bar with his inflamed face, the colour of dark wine or dark meat, he called out:

—Here, Pat, give us a g.p., like a good fellow.

The curate brought him a glass of plain porter. The man drank it at a gulp and asked for a caraway seed. He put his penny on the counter and, leaving the curate to grope for it in the gloom, retreated out of the snug as furtively as he had entered it.

Darkness, accompanied by a thick fog, was gaining upon the dusk of February and the lamps in Eustace Street had been lit. The man went up by the houses until he reached the door of the office, wondering whether he could finish his copy in time. On the stairs a moist pungent odour of perfumes saluted his nose: evidently Miss Delacour had come while he was out in O'Neill's. He crammed his cap back again into his pocket and re-entered the office, assuming an air of absent-mindedness.

—Mr Alleyne has been calling for you, said the chief clerk severely. Where were you?

The man glanced at the two clients who were standing at the counter as if to intimate that their presence prevented him from answering. As the clients were both male the chief clerk allowed himself a laugh.

—I know that game, he said. Five times in one day is a little bit. . . . Well, you better look sharp and get a copy of our correspondence in the Delacour case for Mr Alleyne.

This address in the presence of the public, his run upstairs and the porter he had gulped down so hastily confused the man and, as he sat down at his desk to get what was required, he realised how hopeless was the task of finishing his copy of the contract before half past five. The dark damp night was coming and he longed to spend it in the bars, drinking with his friends amid the glare of gas and the clatter of glasses. He got out the Delacour correspondence and passed out of the office. He hoped Mr Alleyne would not discover that the last two letters were missing.

The moist pungent perfume lay all the way up to Mr Alleyne's room. Miss Delacour was a middle-aged woman of Jewish appearance. Mr Alleyne was said to be sweet on her or on her money. She came to the office often and stayed a long time when she came. She was sitting beside his desk now in an aroma of perfumes, smoothing the handle of her umbrella and nodding the great black feather in her hat. Mr Alleyne had swivelled his chair round to face her and thrown his right foot jauntily upon his left knee. The man put the correspondence on the desk and bowed respectfully but neither Mr Alleyne nor Miss Delacour took any notice of his bow. Mr Alleyne tapped a finger on the correspondence and then flicked it towards him as if to say: *That's all right: you can go.*

The man returned to the lower office and sat down again at his desk. He stared intently at the incomplete phrase: *In no case shall the said Bernard Bodley be* . . . and thought how strange it was that the last three words began with the same letter. The chief clerk began to hurry Miss Parker, saying she would never have the letters typed in time for post. The man listened to the clicking of the machine for a few minutes and then set to work to finish his copy. But his head was not clear and his mind wandered away to the glare and rattle of the public-house. It was a night for hot punches. He struggled on with his copy, but when the clock struck five he had still fourteen pages to write. Blast it! He couldn't finish it in time. He longed to execrate aloud, to bring his fist down on something violently. He was so enraged that he wrote *Bernard Bernard* instead of *Bernard Bodley* and had to begin again on a clean sheet.

He felt strong enough to clear out the whole office single-handed. His body ached to do something, to rush out and revel in violence. All the indignities of his life enraged him. . . . Could he ask the cashier privately for an advance? No, the cashier was no good, no damn good: he wouldn't give an advance. . . . He knew where he would meet the boys: Leonard and O'Halloran and Nosey Flynn. The barometer of his emotional nature was set for a spell of riot.

His imagination had so abstracted him that his name was called twice before he answered. Mr Alleyne and Miss Delacour were standing outside the counter and all the clerks had turned round in anticipation of something. The man got up from his desk. Mr Alleyne began a tirade of abuse, saying that two letters were missing. The man answered that he knew nothing about them, that he had made a faithful copy. The tirade continued: it was so bitter and violent that the man could hardly restrain his fist from descending upon the head of the manikin before him.

—I know nothing about any other two letters, he said stupidly.

—You—know—nothing. Of course you know nothing, said Mr Alleyne. Tell me, he added, glancing first for approval to the lady beside him, do you take me for a fool? Do you think me an utter fool?

The man glanced from the lady's face to the little egg-shaped head and back again; and, almost before he was aware of it, his tongue had found a felicitous moment:

—I don't think, sir, he said, that that's a fair question to put to me.

There was a pause in the very breathing of the clerks. Everyone was astounded (the author of the witticism no less than his neighbours) and Miss Delacour, who was a stout amiable person, began to smile broadly. Mr Alleyne flushed to the hue of a wild rose and his mouth twitched with a dwarf's passion. He shook his fist in the man's face till it seemed to vibrate like the knob of some electric machine:

—You impertinent ruffian! You impertinent ruffian! I'll make short work of you! Wait till you see! You'll apologise to me for your impertinence or you'll quit the office instanter! You'll quit this, I'm telling you, or you'll apologise to me!

He stood in a doorway opposite the office watching to see if the cashier would come out alone. All the clerks passed out and finally the cashier came out with the chief clerk. It was no use trying to say a word to him when he was with the chief clerk. The man felt that his position was bad enough. He had been obliged to offer an abject apology to Mr Alleyne for his impertinence but he knew what a hornet's nest the office would be for him. He could remember the way in which Mr Alleyne had hounded little Peake out of the office in order to make room for his own nephew. He felt savage and thirsty and revengeful, annoyed with himself and with everyone else. Mr Alleyne would never give him an hour's rest; his life would be a hell to him. He had made a proper fool of himself this time. Could he not keep his tongue in his cheek? But they had never pulled together from the first, he and Mr Alleyne, ever since the day Mr Alleyne had overheard him mimicking his North of Ireland accent to amuse Higgins and Miss Parker: that had been the beginning of it. He might have tried Higgins for the money, but sure Higgins never had anything for himself. A man with two establishments to keep up, of course he couldn't. . . .

He felt his great body again aching for the comfort of the public-house. The fog had begun to chill him and he wondered could he touch Pat in O'Neill's. He could not touch him for more than a bob—and a bob was no use. Yet he must get money somewhere or other: he had spent his last penny for the g.p. and soon it would be too late for getting money anywhere. Suddenly, as he was fingering his watch-chain, he thought of Terry Kelly's pawn-office in Fleet Street. That was the dart! Why didn't he think of it sooner?

He went through the narrow alley of Temple Bar quickly, muttering to himself that they could all go to hell because he was going to have a good night of it. The clerk in Terry Kelly's said *A crown!* but the consignor held out for six shillings; and in the end the six shillings was allowed him literally.[1] He came out of the pawn-office joyfully, making a little cylinder of the coins between his thumb and fingers. In Westmoreland Street the footpaths were crowded with young men and women returning from business and ragged urchins ran here and there yelling out the names of the evening editions. The man passed through the crowd, looking on the spectacle generally with proud satisfaction and staring masterfully at the office-girls. His head was full of the noises of tram-gongs and swishing trolleys and his nose already sniffed the curling fumes of punch. As he walked on he preconsidered the terms in which he would narrate the incident to the boys:

—So, I just looked at him—coolly, you know, and looked at her. Then I looked back at him again—taking my time, you know. *I don't think that that's a fair question to put to me,* says I.

Nosey Flynn was sitting up in his usual corner of Davy Byrne's and, when he heard the story, he stood Farrington a half-one, saying it was as smart a thing as ever he heard. Farrington stood a drink in his turn. After a while O'Halloran and Paddy Leonard came in and the story was repeated to them. O'Halloran stood tailors of malt, hot, all round and told the story of the retort he had made to the chief clerk when he was in Callan's of Fownes's Street; but, as the retort was after the manner of the liberal shepherds in the eclogues,[2] he had to admit that it was not so clever as Farrington's retort. At this Farrington told the boys to polish off that and have another.

---

[1] A crown is five shillings; the consignor is Farrington.
[2] Perhaps gross or overly frank. The reference is unclear but recalls a similar allusion in *Hamlet* IV.vii.

Just as they were naming their poisons who should come in but Higgins! Of course he had to join in with the others. The men asked him to give his version of it, and he did so with great vivacity for the sight of five small hot whiskies was very exhilarating. Everyone roared laughing when he showed the way in which Mr Alleyne shook his fist in Farrington's face. Then he imitated Farrington, saying, *And here was my nabs, as cool as you please,* while Farrington looked at the company out of his heavy dirty eyes, smiling and at times drawing forth stray drops of liquor from his moustache with the aid of his lower lip.

When that round was over there was a pause. O'Halloran had money but neither of the other two seemed to have any; so the whole party left the shop somewhat regretfully. At the corner of Duke Street Higgins and Nosey Flynn bevelled off to the left while the other three turned back towards the city. Rain was drizzling down on the cold streets and, when they reached the Ballast Office, Farrington suggested the Scotch House. The bar was full of men and loud with the noise of tongues and glasses. The three men pushed past the whining match-sellers at the door and formed a little party at the corner of the counter. They began to exchange stories. Leonard introduced them to a young fellow named Weathers who was performing at the Tivoli as an acrobat and knockabout *artiste.* Farrington stood a drink all round. Weathers said he would take a small Irish and Apollinaris.[3] Farrington, who had definite notions of what was what, asked the boys would they have an Apollinaris too; but the boys told Tim to make theirs hot. The talk became theatrical. O'Halloran stood a round and then Farrington stood another round, Weathers protesting that the hospitality was too Irish. He promised to get them in behind the scenes and introduce them to some nice girls. O'Halloran said that he and Leonard would go but that Farrington wouldn't go because he was a married man; and Farrington's heavy dirty eyes leered at the company in token that he understood he was being chaffed. Weathers made them all have just one little tincture at his expense and promised to meet them later on at Mulligan's in Poolbeg Street.

When the Scotch House closed they went round to Mulligan's. They went into the parlour at the back and O'Halloran ordered small hot specials all round. They were all beginning to feel mellow. Farrington was just standing another round when Weathers came back. Much to Farrington's relief he drank a glass of bitter this time. Funds were running low but they had enough to keep them going. Presently two young women with big hats and a young man in a check suit came in and sat at a table close by. Weathers saluted them and told the company that they were out of the Tivoli. Farrington's eyes wandered at every moment in the direction of one of the young women. There was something striking in her appearance. An immense scarf of peacock-blue muslin was wound round her hat and knotted in a great bow under her chin; and she wore bright yellow

---

[3]Whiskey with Apollinaris water (a sparkling mineral water).

gloves, reaching to the elbow. Farrington gazed admiringly at the plump arm which she moved very often and with much grace; and when, after a little time, she answered his gaze he admired still more her large dark brown eyes. The oblique staring expression in them fascinated him. She glanced at him once or twice and, when the party was leaving the room, she brushed against his chair and said *O, pardon!* in a London accent. He watched her leave the room in the hope that she would look back at him, but he was disappointed. He cursed his want of money and cursed all the rounds he had stood, particularly all the whiskies and Apollinaris which he had stood to Weathers. If there was one thing that he hated it was a sponge. He was so angry that he lost count of the conversation of his friends.

When Paddy Leonard called him he found that they were talking about feats of strength. Weathers was showing his biceps muscle to the company and boasting so much that the other two had called on Farrington to uphold the national honour. Farrington pulled up his sleeve accordingly and showed his biceps muscle to the company. The two arms were examined and compared and finally it was agreed to have a trial of strength. The table was cleared and the two men rested their elbows on it, clasping hands. When Paddy Leonard said *Go!* each was to try to bring down the other's hand on to the table. Farrington looked very serious and determined.

The trial began. After about thirty seconds Weathers brought his opponent's hand slowly down on to the table. Farrington's dark wine-coloured face flushed darker still with anger and humiliation at having been defeated by such a stripling.

—You're not to put the weight of your body behind it. Play fair, he said.

—Who's not playing fair? said the other.

—Come on again. The two best out of three.

The trial began again. The veins stood out on Farrington's forehead, and the pallor of Weather's complexion changed to peony. Their hands and arms trembled under the stress. After a long struggle Weathers again brought his opponent's hand slowly on to the table. There was a murmur of applause from the spectators. The curate, who was standing beside the table, nodded his red head towards the victor and said with loutish familiarity:

—Ah! that's the knack!

—What the hell do you know about it? said Farrington fiercely, turning on the man. What do you put in your gab for?

—Sh, sh! said O'Halloran, observing the violent expression of Farrington's face. Pony up, boys. We'll have just one little smahan more and then we'll be off.

A very sullen-faced man stood at the corner of O'Connell Bridge waiting for the little Sandymount tram to take him home. He was full of smouldering anger and revengefulness. He felt humiliated and discontented; he did not even feel drunk; and he had only twopence in his pocket. He cursed everything. He had done for himself in the office, pawned his watch, spent all his money; and he had not even got drunk. He began to feel thirsty again and he longed to be back again in the hot reeking public-house. He had lost his reputation as a strong man, having been defeated twice by a mere boy. His heart swelled with fury and, when he thought of the woman in the big hat who had brushed against him and said *Pardon!* his fury nearly choked him.

His tram let him down at Shelbourne Road and he steered his great body along in the shadow of the wall of the barracks. He loathed returning to his home. When he went in by the side-door he found the kitchen empty and the kitchen fire nearly out. He bawled upstairs:

—Ada! Ada!

His wife was a little sharp-faced woman who bullied her husband when he was sober and was bullied by him when he was drunk. They had five children. A little boy came running down the stairs.

—Who is that? said the man, peering through the darkness.

—Me, pa.

—Who are you? Charlie?

—No, pa. Tom.

—Where's your mother?

—She's out at the chapel.

—That's right. . . . Did she think of leaving any dinner for me?

—Yes, pa. I—

—Light the lamp. What do you mean by having the place in darkness? Are the other children in bed?

The man sat down heavily on one of the chairs while the little boy lit the lamp. He began to mimic his son's flat accent, saying half to himself: *At the chapel. At the chapel, if you please!* When the lamp was lit he banged his fist on the table and shouted:

—What's for my dinner?

—I'm going . . . to cook it, pa, said the little boy.

The man jumped up furiously and pointed to the fire.

—On that fire! You let the fire out! By God, I'll teach you to do that again!

He took a step to the door and seized the walking-stick which was standing behind it.

—I'll teach you to let the fire out! he said, rolling up his sleeve in order to give his arm free play.

The little boy cried O, *pa!* and ran whimpering round the table, but the man followed him and caught him by the coat. The little boy looked about him wildly but, seeing no way of escape, fell upon his knees.

—Now, you'll let the fire out the next time! said the man, striking at him viciously with the stick. Take that, you little whelp!

The boy uttered a squeal of pain as the stick cut his thigh. He clasped his hands together in the air and his voice shook with fright.

—O, pa! he cried. Don't beat me, pa! And I'll . . . I'll say a *Hail Mary* for you. . . . I'll say a *Hail Mary* for you, pa, if you don't beat me. . . . I'll say a *Hail Mary. . . .*

James Thurber (1894–1961)
THE GREATEST MAN IN THE WORLD

Looking back on it now, from the vantage point of 1950, one can only marvel that it hadn't happened long before it did. The United States of America had been, ever since Kitty Hawk, blindly constructing the elaborate petard by which, sooner or later, it must be hoist. It was inevitable that some day there would come roaring out of the skies a national hero of insufficient intelligence, background, and character successfully to endure the mounting orgies of glory prepared for aviators who stayed up a long time or flew a great distance. Both Lindbergh and Byrd, fortunately for national decorum and international amity, had been gentlemen; so had our other famous aviators. They wore their laurels gracefully, withstood the awful weather of publicity, married excellent women, usually of fine family, and quietly retired to private life and the enjoyment of their varying fortunes. No untoward incidents, on a worldwide scale, marred the perfection of their conduct on the perilous heights of fame. The exception to the rule was, however, bound to occur and it did, in July, 1937, when Jack ("Pal") Smurch, erstwhile mechanic's helper in a small garage in Westfield, Iowa, flew a second-hand, single-motored Bresthaven Dragon-Fly III monoplane all the way around the world, without stopping.

Never before in the history of aviation had such a flight as Smurch's ever been dreamed of. No one had even taken seriously the weird floating auxiliary gas tanks, invention of the mad New Hampshire professor of astronomy, Dr. Charles Lewis Gresham, upon which Smurch placed full reliance. When the garage worker, a slightly built, surly, unprepossessing young man of twenty-two, appeared at Roosevelt Field in early July, 1937, slowly chewing a great quid of scrap tobacco, and announced, "Nobody ain't seen no flyin' yet," the newspapers touched briefly and satirically upon his projected twenty-five-thousand-mile flight. Aëronautical and automotive experts dismissed the idea curtly, implying that it was a hoax, a publicity stunt. The rusty, battered, second-hand plane wouldn't go. The Gresham auxiliary tanks wouldn't work. It was simply a cheap joke.

Smurch, however, after calling on a girl in Brooklyn who worked in the flap-folding department of a large paper-box factory, a girl whom he later described as his "sweet patootie," climbed nonchalantly into his ridiculous plane at dawn of the memorable seventh of July, 1937, spit a curve of tobacco juice into the still air, and took off, carrying with him only a gallon of bootleg gin and six pounds of salami.

When the garage boy thundered out over the ocean the papers were forced to record, in all seriousness, that a mad, unknown young man—his name was variously misspelled—had actually set out upon a preposterous attempt to span the world in a rickety, one-engined contraption, trusting to the long-distance refuelling device of a crazy schoolmaster. When, nine days later, without having stopped once, the tiny plane appeared above San Francisco Bay, headed for New York, spluttering and choking, to be sure, but still magnificently and miraculously aloft, the headlines, which long since had crowded everything else off the front page—even the shooting of the Governor of Illinois by the Vileti gang—swelled to unprecedented size, and the news stories began to run to twenty-five and thirty columns. It was noticeable, however, that the accounts of the epoch-making flight touched rather lightly upon the aviator himself. This was not because facts about the hero as a man were too meagre, but because they were too complete.

Reporters, who had been rushed out to Iowa when Smurch's plane was first sighted over the little French coast town of Serly-le-Mer, to dig up the story of the great man's life, had promptly discovered that the story of his life could not be printed. His mother, a sullen short-order cook in a shack restaurant on the edge of a tourists' camping ground near Westfield, met all inquiries as to her son with an angry "Ah, the hell with him; I hope he drowns." His father appeared to be in jail somewhere for stealing spotlights and laprobes from tourists' automobiles; his young brother, a weak-minded lad, had but recently escaped from the Preston, Iowa, Reformatory and was already wanted in several Western towns for the theft of money-order blanks from post offices. These alarming discoveries were still piling up at the very time that Pal Smurch, the greatest hero of the twentieth century, blear-eyed, dead for sleep, half-starved, was piloting his crazy junk-heap high above the region in which the lamentable story of his private life was being unearthed, headed for New York and a greater glory than any man of his time had ever known.

The necessity for printing some account in the papers of the young man's career and personality had led to a remarkable predicament. It was of course impossible to reveal the facts, for a tremendous popular feeling in favor of the young hero had sprung up, like a grass fire, when he was halfway across Europe on his flight around the globe. He was, therefore, described as a modest chap, taciturn, blond, popular with his friends, popular with girls. The only available snapshot of Smurch, taken at the wheel of a phony automobile in a cheap photo studio at an amusement park, was touched up so that the little vulgarian looked quite handsome. His twisted leer was smoothed into a pleasant smile. The truth was, in this way, kept from the youth's ecstatic compatriots; they did not dream that the Smurch family was despised and feared by its neighbors in the obscure Iowa town, nor that the hero himself, because of numerous unsavory exploits, had come to be regarded in Westfield as a nuisance and a menace. He had, the reporters discovered, once knifed the principal of his high school—not mortally, to be sure, but he had knifed him; and on another occasion, surprised in the act of stealing an altar-cloth from a church, he had bashed the sacristan over the head with a pot of Easter lilies; for each of these offences he had served a sentence in the reformatory.

Inwardly, the authorities, both in New York and in Washington, prayed that an understanding Providence might, however awful such a thing seemed, bring disaster to the rusty, battered plane and its illustrious pilot, whose unheard-of flight had aroused the civilized world to hosannas of hysterical praise. The authorities were convinced that the character of the renowned aviator was such that the limelight of adulation was bound to reveal him to all the world as a congenital hooligan mentally and morally unequipped to cope with his own prodigious fame. "I trust," said the Secretary of State, at one of many secret Cabinet meetings called to consider the national dilemma, "I trust that his mother's prayer will be answered," by which he referred to Mrs. Emma Smurch's wish that her son might be drowned. It was, however, too late for that—Smurch had leaped the Atlantic and then the Pacific as if they were millponds. At three minutes after two o'clock on the afternoon of July 17, 1937, the garage boy brought his idiotic plane into Roosevelt Field for a perfect three-point landing.

It had, of course, been out of the question to arrange a modest little reception for the greatest flier in the history of the world. He was received at Roosevelt Field with such elaborate and pretentious ceremonies as rocked the world. Fortunately, however, the worn and spent hero promptly swooned, had to be removed bodily from his plane, and was spirited from the field without having opened his mouth once. Thus he did not jeopardize the dignity of this first reception, a reception illumined by the presence of the Secretaries of War and the Navy, Mayor Michael J. Moriarity of New York, the Premier of Canada, Governors Fanniman, Groves, McFeely, and Critchfield, and a brilliant array of European diplomats. Smurch did not, in fact, come to in time to take part in the gigantic hullabaloo arranged at City Hall for the next day. He was rushed to a secluded nursing home and confined to bed. It was nine days before he was able to get up or to be more exact, before he was permitted to get up. Meanwhile the greatest minds in the country, in solemn assembly, had arranged a secret conference of city, state, and government officials, which Smurch was to attend for the purpose of being instructed in the ethics and behavior of heroism.

On the day that the little mechanic was finally allowed to get up and dress and, for the first time in two weeks, took a great chew of tobacco, he was permitted to receive the newspapermen—this by way of testing him out. Smurch did not wait for questions. "Youse guys," he said—and the *Times* man winced—"youse guys can tell the cock-eyed world dat I put it over on Lindbergh, see? Yeh—an' made an ass o' them two frogs." The "two frogs" was a reference to a pair of gallant French fliers who, in attempting a flight only halfway round the world, had, two weeks before, unhappily been lost at sea. The *Times* man was bold enough, at this point, to sketch out for Smurch the accepted formula for interviews in cases of this kind; he explained that there should be no arrogant statements belittling the achievements of other heroes, particularly heroes of foreign nations. "Ah, the hell with that," said Smurch. "I did it, see? I did it, an' I'm talkin' about it." And he did talk about it.

None of this extraordinary interview was, of course, printed. On the contrary, the newspapers, already under the disciplined direction of a secret directorate created for the occasion and composed of statesmen and editors, gave out to a panting and restless world that "Jacky," as he had been arbitrarily nicknamed, would consent to say only that he was very happy and that anyone could have done what he did. "My achievement has been, I fear, slightly exaggerated," the *Times* man's article had him protest, with a modest smile. These newspaper stories were kept from the hero, a restriction which did not serve to abate the rising malevolence of his temper. The situation was, indeed, extremely grave, for Pal Smurch was, as he kept insisting, "rarin' to go." He could not much longer be kept from a nation clamorous to lionize him. It was the most desperate crisis the United States of America had faced since the sinking of the *Lusitania*.

On the afternoon of the twenty-seventh of July, Smurch was spirited away to a conference-room in which were gathered mayors, governors, government officials, behaviorist psychologists, and editors. He gave them each a limp, moist paw and a brief unlovely grin. "Hah ya?" he said. When Smurch was seated, the Mayor of New York arose and, with obvious pessimism, attempted to explain what he must say and how he must act when presented to the world, ending his talk with a high tribute to the hero's courage and integrity. The Mayor was followed by Governor Fanniman of New York, who, after a touching declaration of faith, introduced Cameron Spottiswood, Second Secretary of the American Embassy in Paris, the gentleman selected to coach Smurch in the amenities of public ceremonies. Sitting in a chair, with a soiled yellow tie in his hand and his shirt open at the throat, unshaved, smoking a rolled cigarette, Jack Smurch listened with a leer on his lips. "I get ya, I get ya," he cut in, nastily. "Ya want me to ack like a softy, huh? Ya want me to ack like that —— —— baby-faced Lindbergh, huh? Well, nuts to that, see?" Everyone took in his breath sharply; it was a sigh and a hiss. "Mr. Lindbergh," began a United States Senator, purple with rage, "and Mr. Byrd—" Smurch, who was paring his nails with a jackknife, cut in again. "Byrd!" he exclaimed. "Aw fa God's sake, dat big—" Somebody shut off his blasphemies with a sharp word. A newcomer had entered the room. Everyone stood up, except Smurch, who, still busy with his nails, did not even glance up. "Mr. Smurch," said somebody sternly, "the President of the United States!" It had been thought that the presence of the Chief Executive might have a chastening effect upon the young hero, and the former had been, thanks to the remarkable coöperation of the press, secretly brought to the obscure conference-room.

A great, painful silence fell. Smurch looked up, waved a hand at the President. "How ya comin'?" he asked, and began rolling a fresh cigarette. The silence deepened. Someone coughed in a strained way. "Geez, it's hot, ain't it?" said Smurch. He loosened two more shirt buttons, revealing a hairy chest and the tattooed word "Sadie" enclosed in a stencilled heart. The great and important men in the room, faced by the most serious crisis in recent American history, exchanged worried frowns. Nobody seemed to know how to proceed. "Come awn, come awn," said Smurch. "Let's get the hell out of here! When do I start cuttin' in on de parties, huh? And what's they goin' to be *in* it?" He rubbed a thumb and forefinger together meaningly. "Money!" exclaimed a state senator, shocked, pale. "Yeh, money," said Pal, flipping his cigarette out of a window. "An' big money." He began rolling a fresh cigarette. "Big money," he repeated, frowning over the rice paper. He tilted back in his chair, and leered at each gentleman, separately, the leer of an animal that knows its power, the leer of a leopard loose in a bird-and-dog shop. "Aw fa God's sake, let's get some place where it's cooler," he said. "I been cooped up plenty for three weeks!"

Smurch stood up and walked over to an open window, where he stood staring down into the street, nine floors below. The faint shouting of newsboys floated up to him. He made out his name. "Hot dog!" he cried, grinning, ecstatic. He leaned out over the sill. "You tell 'em, babies!" he shouted down. "Hot diggity dog!" In the tense little knot of men standing behind him, a quick, mad impulse flared up. An unspoken word of appeal, of command, seemed to ring through the room. Yet it was deadly silent. Charles K. L. Brand, secretary to the Mayor of New York City, happened to be standing nearest Smurch; he looked inquiringly at the President of the United States. The President, pale, grim, nodded shortly. Brand, a tall, powerfully built man, once a tackle at Rutgers, stepped forward, seized the greatest man in the world by his left shoulder and the seat of his pants, and pushed him out the window.

"My God, he's fallen out the window!" cried a quick-witted editor.

"Get me out of here!" cried the President. Several men sprang to his side and he was hurriedly escorted out of a door toward a side-entrance of the building. The editor of the Associated Press took charge, being used to such things. Crisply he ordered certain men to leave, others to stay; quickly he outlined a story which all the papers were to agree on, sent two men to the street to handle that end of the tragedy, commanded a Senator to sob and two Congressmen to go to pieces nervously. In a word, he skillfully set the stage for the gigantic task that was to follow, the task of breaking to a grief-stricken world the sad story of the untimely, accidental death of its most illustrious and spectacular figure.

The funeral was, as you know, the most elaborate, the finest, the solemnest, and the saddest ever held in the United States of America. The monument in Arlington Cemetery, with its clean white shaft of marble and the simple device of a tiny plane carved on its base, is a place for pilgrims, in deep reverence, to visit. The nations of the world paid lofty tributes to little Jacky Smurch, America's greatest hero. At a given hour there were two minutes of silence throughout the nation. Even the inhabitants of the small, bewildered town of Westfield, Iowa, observed this touching ceremony; agents of the Department of Justice saw to that. One of them was especially assigned to stand grimly in the doorway of a little shack restaurant on the edge of the tourists' camping ground just outside the town. There, under his stern scrutiny, Mrs. Emma Smurch bowed her head above two hamburger steaks sizzling on her grill—bowed her head and turned away, so that the Secret Service man could not see the twisted, strangely familiar, leer on her lips.

QUESTIONS

1. What tone do you hear in the narrator's voice?
2. How do you respond to the characterization of Jack Smurch?
3. Is the story about the demands upon heroes, the control of the news, both of these things, or something else? Explain.

Ernest Hemingway (1899–1961)

A CLEAN, WELL-LIGHTED PLACE

It was late and every one had left the café except an old man who sat in the shadow the leaves of the tree made against the electric light. In the day time the street was dusty, but at night the dew settled the dust and the old man liked to sit late because he was deaf and now at night it was quiet and he felt the difference. The two waiters inside the café knew that the old man was a little drunk, and while he was a good client they knew that if he became too drunk he would leave without paying, so they kept watch on him.

"Last week he tried to commit suicide," one waiter said.

"Why?"

"He was in despair."

"What about?"

"Nothing."

"How do you know it was nothing?"

"He has plenty of money."

They sat together at a table that was close against the wall near the door of the café and looked at the terrace where the tables were all empty except where the old man sat in the shadow of the leaves of the tree that moved slightly in the wind. A girl and a soldier went by in the street. The street light shone on the brass number on his collar. The girl wore no head covering and hurried beside him.

"The guard will pick him up," one waiter said.

"What does it matter if he gets what he's after?"

"He had better get off the street now. The guard will get him. They went by five minutes ago."

The old man sitting in the shadow rapped on his saucer with his glass. The younger waiter went over to him.

"What do you want?"

The old man looked at him. "Another brandy," he said.

"You'll be drunk," the waiter said. The old man looked at him. The waiter went away.

"He'll stay all night," he said to his colleague. "I'm sleepy now. I never get into bed before three o'clock. He should have killed himself last week."

The waiter took the brandy bottle and another saucer from the counter inside the café and marched out to the old man's table. He put down the saucer and poured the glass full of brandy.

"You should have killed yourself last week," he said to the deaf man. The old man motioned with his finger. "A little more," he said. The waiter poured on into the glass so that the brandy slopped over and ran down the stem into the top saucer of the pile. "Thank you," the old man said. The waiter took the bottle back inside the café. He sat down at the table with his colleague again.

"He's drunk now," he said.

"He's drunk every night."

"What did he want to kill himself for?"

"How should I know?"

"How did he do it?"

"He hung himself with a rope."

"Who cut him down?"

"His niece."

"Why did they do it?"

"Fear for his soul."

"How much money has he got?"

"He's got plenty."

"He must be eighty years old."

"Anyway I should say he was eighty."

"I wish he would go home. I never get to bed before three o'clock. What kind of hour is that to go to bed?"

"He stays up because he likes it."

"He's lonely. I'm not lonely. I have a wife waiting in bed for me."

"He had a wife once too."

"A wife would be no good to him now."

"You can't tell. He might be better with a wife."

"His niece looks after him. You said she cut him down."

"I know."

"I wouldn't want to be that old. An old man is a nasty thing."

"Not always. This old man is clean. He drinks without spilling. Even now, drunk. Look at him."

"I don't want to look at him. I wish he would go home. He has no regard for those who must work."

The old man looked from his glass across the square, then over at the waiters.

"Another brandy," he said, pointing to his glass. The waiter who was in a hurry came over.

"Finished," he said, speaking with that omission of syntax stupid people employ when talking to drunken people or foreigners. "No more tonight. Close now."

"Another," said the old man.

"No. Finished." The waiter wiped the edge of the table with a towel and shook his head.

The old man stood up, slowly counted the saucers, took a leather coin purse from his pocket and paid for the drinks, leaving half a peseta tip.

The waiter watched him go down the street, a very old man walking unsteadily but with dignity.

"Why didn't you let him stay and drink?" the unhurried waiter asked. They were putting up the shutters. "It is not half-past two."

"I want to go home to bed."

"What is an hour?"

"More to me than to him."

"An hour is the same."

"You talk like an old man yourself. He can buy a bottle and drink at home."

"It's not the same."

"No, it is not," agreed the waiter with a wife. He did not wish to be unjust. He was only in a hurry.

"And you? You have no fear of going home before your usual hour?"

"Are you trying to insult me?"

"No, hombre, only to make a joke."

"No," the waiter who was in a hurry said, rising from pulling down the metal shutters. "I have confidence. I am all confidence."

"You have youth, confidence, and a job," the older waiter said. "You have everything."

"And what do you lack?"

"Everything but work."

"You have everything I have."

"No. I have never had confidence and I am not young."

"Come on. Stop talking nonsense and lock up."

"I am of those who like to stay late at the café," the older waiter said. "With all those who do not want to go to bed. With all those who need a light for the night."

"I want to go home and into bed."

"We are of two different kinds," the older waiter said. He was now dressed to go home. "It is not only a question of youth and confidence although those things are very beautiful. Each night I am reluctant to close up because there may be some one who needs the café."

"Hombre, there are bodegas[1] open all night long."

"You do not understand. This is a clean and pleasant café. It is well lighted. The light is very good and also, now, there are shadows of the leaves."

"Good night," said the younger waiter.

"Good night," the other said. Turning off the electric light he continued the conversation with himself. It is the light of course but it is necessary that the place be clean and pleasant. You do not want music. Certainly you do not want music. Nor can you stand before a bar with dignity although that is all that is provided for these hours. What did he fear? It was not fear or dread. It was a nothing that he knew too well. It was all a nothing and a man was nothing too. It was only that and light was all it needed and a certain cleanness and order. Some lived in it and never felt it but he knew it all was nada y pues nada y nada y pues nada.[2] Our nada who art in nada, nada be thy name thy kingdom nada thy will be nada in nada as it is in nada. Give us this nada our daily nada and nada us our nada as we nada our nadas and nada us not into nada but deliver

---

[1]Wineshops.
[2]Nothing and then nothing, and nothing and still nothing.

us from nada; pues nada. Hail nothing full of nothing, nothing is with thee. He smiled and stood before a bar with a shining steam pressure coffee machine.

"What's yours?" asked the barman.

"Nada."

"Otro loco mas,"[3] said the barman and turned away.

"A little cup," said the waiter.

The barman poured it for him.

"The light is very bright and pleasant but the bar is unpolished," the waiter said.

The barman looked at him but did not answer. It was too late at night for conversation.

"You want another copita?" the barman asked.

"No, thank you," said the waiter and went out. He disliked bars and bodegas. A clean, well-lighted café was a very different thing. Now, without thinking further, he would go home to his room. He would lie in the bed and finally, with daylight, he would go to sleep. After all, he said to himself, it is probably only insomnia. Many must have it.

QUESTIONS

1. What do you notice about the way the narrator tells this story?
2. How important do you understand the particular setting, the unnamed café, to be?
3. Is the story about the old man, either or both waiters, or all three of them? Explain.

Joyce Carol Oates (b. 1938)

OUT OF PLACE

I have this memory: I am waiting in line for a movie. The line is long, noisy, restless, mostly kids my age (I seem to be about thirteen). The movie must be . . . a Western, I think. I can almost see the posters and I think I see a man with a cowboy hat. Good. I do see this man and I see a horse on the poster, it is all becoming clear. A Western. I am a kid, thirteen, but not like the thirteen-year-olds who pass by the hospital here on their way home from school—they are older than I was at that age, everyone seems older. I am nineteen now, I think. I will be twenty in a few weeks and my mother talks about how I will be home, then, in time for my birthday. That gives her pleasure and so I like to hear her talk about it. But my memory is more important: the movie house, yes, and the kids, and I am one of them. We are all jostling together, moving forward in surges, a bunch of us from St. Ann's Junior High. Other kids are there from

---

[3]Another crazy.

Clinton, which is a tough school. We are all in line waiting and no one is out of line. I am there, with them. We shuffle up to the ticket window and buy our tickets (50¢) and go inside, running.

There is something pleasant about this memory, but dwelling upon memories is unhealthy. They tell me that. They are afraid I will remember the explosion, and my friend who died, but I have already forgotten these things. There is no secret about it, of course. Everything is open. We were caught in a land mine explosion and some of us were luckier than others, we weren't killed, that's all. I am very lucky to be alive. I am not being sarcastic but quite truthful, because in the end it is only truth you can stand. In camp, and for a while when we fooled around for so long without ever seeing the enemy, then some of the guys were sarcastic—but that went away. Everything falls away except truth and that is what you hang onto.

The truth is that my right leg is gone and that I have some trouble with my "vision." My eyes.

On sunny days we are wheeled outside, so that we can watch the school children playing across the street. The hospital is very clean and white, and there is a kind of patio or terrace or wide walk around the front and sides, where we can sit. Next door, some distance away, is a school that is evidently a grade school. The children play at certain times—ten-fifteen in the morning, at noon, and two in the afternoon. I don't know if they are always the same children. I have trouble with my "vision," it isn't the way it used to be and yet in a way I can't remember what it used to be like. My glasses are heavy and make red marks on my nose, and sometimes my skin is sore around my ears, but that is the only sign that the glasses are new. In a way nothing is new but has always been with me. That is why I am pleased with certain memories, like the memory of the Western movie. Though I do not remember the movie itself, but only waiting in line to get in the theater.

There is a boy named Ed here, a friend of mine. He was hurt at about the same time I was, though in another place. He is about twenty too. His eyes are as good as ever and he can see things I can't; I sometimes ask him to tell me about the playground and the children there. The playground is surrounded by a high wire fence and the children play inside this fence, on their swings and slides and teeter-totters, making a lot of noise. Their voices are very high and shrill. We don't mind the noise, we like it, but sometimes it reminds me of something—I can almost catch the memory but not quite. Cries and screams by themselves are not bad. I mean the sounds are not bad. But if you open your eyes wide you may have latched onto the wrong memory and might see the wrong things—screams that are not happy screams, etc. There was a boy somewhere who was holding onto the hand of his "buddy." ("Buddy" is a word I would not have used before, I don't know where I got it from exactly.) That boy was crying, because the other boy was dead—but I can't quite remember who they were. The memory comes and goes silently. It is nothing to be upset about. The doctor told us all that it is healthier to think about our problems, not to push them back. He is a neat, clean man dressed in white, a very kind man. Sometimes his face looks creased, there are too many wrinkles in it, and he looks like my father—they are about the same age.

I like the way my father calls him *Dr. Pritchard*. You can tell a man's worth by the way my father speaks to him, I know that sounds egotistical but it's true, and my father trusts Dr. Pritchard. It is different when he speaks to someone he doesn't quite trust, oh, for example, certain priests who look too young, too boyish; he hesitates before he calls them *Father*. He hesitates before he says hello to Father Presson, who comes here to see me and hear my confession and all, and then the words "Father Presson" come out a little forced.

"Look at that big kid, by the slide. See?" Ed says nervously.

I think I see him—a short blur of no-color by the slide. "What is he doing?"

"I don't know. I thought he was. . . . No, I don't know," Ed says.

There is hesitation in Ed's voice too. Sometimes he seems not to know what he is saying, whether he should say it. I can hear the distance in his voice, the distance between the school children over there and us up here on the ledge, in the sun. When the children fight we feel nervous and we don't know what to do. Not that they really fight, not exactly. But sometimes the mood of the playground breaks and a new mood comes upon it. It's hard to explain. Ed keeps watching for that though he doesn't want to see it.

Ed has a short, muscular body, and skin that always looks tanned. His hair is black, shaved off close, and his eyebrows of course are black and very thick. He looks hunched up in the wheel chair, about to spring off and run away. His legs just lie there, though, and never move. They are both uninjured. His problem is somewhere else, in his spine—it is a mysterious thing, how a bullet strikes in one place and damages another. We have all learned a lot about the body, here. I think I would like to be a doctor. I think that, to be a doctor like Dr. Pritchard, you must have a great reverence for the body and its springs and wires and tubes, I mean, you must understand how they work together, all together. It is a strange thing. When I tried to talk to my parents about this they acted strange. I told them that Ed and I both would like to be doctors, if things got better.

"Yes," my father said slowly, "the study of medicine is— is—"

"Very beneficial," my mother said.

"Yes, beneficial—"

Then they were silent. I said, "I mean if things get better. I know I couldn't get through medical school, the way I am now."

"I wouldn't be too sure of that," my father said. "You know how they keep discovering all these extraordinary things—"

(My father latches onto special words occasionally. Now it is the word "extraordinary." I don't know where he got it from, from a friend probably. He is a vice-president for a company that makes a certain kind of waxed paper and waxed cardboard.)

"But you will get better," my mother said. "You know that."

I am seized with a feeling of happiness. Not because of what my mother said, maybe it's true and maybe not, I don't know, but because of—the fact of doctors, the fact of the body itself which is such a mystery. I can't explain it. I said, groping for my words, "If this hadn't happened then—then—I guess I'd be just the way I was, I mean, I wouldn't know—what it's like to be like this." But that was a stupid thing to say. Mother began crying again, it was embarrassing. With my glasses off, lying back against the pillow, I could pretend that I didn't notice; so I said, speaking in my new voice which is a little too slow and stumbling, "I mean—there are lots of things that are mysteries—like the way the spine hooks up with things—and the brain—and—and by myself I wouldn't know about these things—"

But it's better to talk about other matters. In my room, away from the other patients, the talk brought to me by my parents and relatives and friends is like a gift from the outside, and it has the quality of the spring days that are here now: sunny and fragrant but very delicate. My visitors' words are like rays of sunlight. It might seem that you could grab hold of them and sit up, but you can't, they're nothing, they don't last—they are gifts, that's all, like the other gifts I have. For instance, my mother says: "Betty is back now. She wants to know when she can see you, but I thought that could wait."

"Oh, is she back?"

"She didn't have a very happy time, you know."

"What's she doing now?"

"Oh, nothing, I don't know. She might go to school."

"Where?"

"A community college, nothing much."

"That's nice."

This conversation is about a cousin of mine who married some jerk and ran away to live in Mexico. But the conversation is not really about her. I don't know what it is about. It is "about" the words themselves. When my mother says, "Betty is back now," that means "Betty-is-back-now" is being talked about, not the girl herself. We hardly know the girl herself. Then we move on to talk about Harold Spender, who is a bachelor friend of my father's. Harold Spender has a funny name and Mother likes him for his name. He is always "spending" too much money. I think he has expensive parties or something, I don't know. But "Harold Spender" is another gift, and I think this gift means: "You see, everything is still the same, your cousin is still a dope and Harold Spender is still with us, spending money. Nothing has changed."

Sometimes when they are here, visiting, and Mother chatters on like that, a terrible door opens in my mind and I can't hear her. It is like waking up at night when you don't know it is night. A door opens and though I know Mother is still talking, I can't hear her. This lasts a few seconds, no more. I go into it and come out of it and no one notices. The door opens by itself, silently, and beyond it everything is black and very quiet, just nothing.

But sometimes I am nervous and feel very sharp. That is a peculiar word, sharp. I mean my body tenses and I seem to be sitting forward and my hands grip the arms of the chair, as if I'm about to throw myself out of it and demand something. Demand something! Ed's voice gets like that too. It gets very thin and demanding and sometimes he begins to cry. It's better to turn away from that, from a boy of twenty crying. I don't know why I get nervous. There is no relationship between what my body feels and what is going on outside, and that is what frightens me.

Dr. Pritchard says there is nothing to be frightened about any longer. Nothing.

He is right, of course. I think it will be nice when I am home again and the regular routine begins. My nervousness will go away and there will not be the strange threat of that door, which opens so silently and invites me in. And Father won't take so much time off from work, and Mother will not chatter so. It will be nice to get back into place and decide what I will do, though there is no hurry about that. When I was in high school I fooled around too much. It wasn't because of basketball either, that was just an excuse, I wasted time and so did the other kids. I wore trousers the color of bone that were pretty short and tight, and I fooled around with my hair, nothing greasy but pretty long in front, flipped down onto my forehead. Mr. Palisano, the physics teacher, was also the basketball coach and he always said: "Hey, Furlong, what's your hurry? Just what's your hurry?" He had a teasing singsong voice he used only on kids he liked. He was a tall, skinny man, a very intelligent man. "Just what's your hurry?" he said when I handed in my physics problems half-finished, or made a fool of myself in basketball practice. He was happy when I told him I was going into physics, but when I failed the first course I didn't want to go back and tell him—the hell with it. So I switched into math because I had to take math anyway. And then what happened? I don't remember. I was just a kid then, I fooled around too much. The kids at the school—it was a middle-sized school run by Holy Cross fathers, who also run Notre Dame—just fooled around too much, some of them flunked out. I don't think I flunked out. It gives me a headache to think about it—

To think about the kids in my calculus class, that gives me a headache. I don't know why. I can remember my notebook, and the rows of desks, and the blackboard (though it was green), and the bell striking the hour from outside (though it was always a little off), and I think of it all like a bubble with the people still inside. All the kids and me among them, still in the same room, still there. I like to think of that.

But they aren't still there in that room. Everything has moved on. They have moved on to other rooms and I am out here, at this particular hospital. I wonder if I will be able to catch up with them. If I can read, if my eyes get better, I don't see why not. Father talks about me returning. It's no problem with a wheelchair these days, he says, and there is the business about the artificial "limb," etc. I think it will be nice to get back to books and reading and regular assignments.

I am thinking about high school, about the halls and the stairways. Mr. Palisano, and physics class, and the afternoon basketball games. I am thinking about the excitement of those games, which was not quite fear, and about the drive back home, in my car or someone else's. I went out a lot. And one night, coming home from a dance, I saw a car parked and a man fooling around by it so I stopped to help him. "Jesus Christ," he kept saying. He had a flat tire and he was very angry. He kept snuffling and wiping his nose on his shoulder, very angry, saying "Jesus Christ" and other things, other words, not the way the kids said them but in a different way—hard to explain. It made me understand that adults had made up those words, not in play but out of hatred. He was not kidding. The way he said those words frightened me. Fear comes up from the earth, the coldness of the earth, flowing up from your feet up your legs and into your bowels, like the clay of the earth itself, and your heart begins to hammer. . . .

I never told anyone about that night, what a fool I was to stop. What if something had happened to me?

I was ashamed of being such a fool. I always did stupid things, always went out of my way and turned out looking like a fool. Then I'd feel shame and not tell anyone. For instance, I am ashamed about something that happened here in the hospital a few days ago. I think it will be nice when I am home again, back in my room, where these things can't happen. There was myself and Ed and another man, out on the terrace by the side entrance, in the sun, and these kids came along. It was funny because they caught my eye when they drove past in a convertible, and they must have turned into the parking lot and got out. They were visiting someone in the hospital. The girl was carrying a grocery bag that probably had fruit in it or something. She had long dark hair and bangs that fell down to her eyebrows, and she wore sunglasses, and bright blue stretch pants of the kind that have stirrups for the feet to keep them stretched down tight. The boy wore sunglasses too, slacks and a sweater, and sandals without socks. He had the critical, unsurprised look of kids from the big university downtown.

They came up the steps, talking. The girl swung her hair back like a horse, a pony—I mean, the motion reminded me of something like that. She looked over at us and stopped talking, and the boy looked too. They were my age. The girl hesitated but the boy kept on walking fast. He frowned. He seemed embarrassed. The girl came toward me, not quite walking directly toward me, and her mouth moved in an awkward smile. She said, "I know you, don't I? Don't I know you?"

I was very excited. I tried to tell her that with her sunglasses on I couldn't see her well. But when I tried to talk the words came out jumbled. She licked her lips nervously. She said, "Were you in the war? Vietnam?"

I nodded.

She stared at me. It was strange that her face showed nothing, unlike the other faces that are turned toward me all the time. The boy, already at the door, said in an irritated sharp voice: "Come on, we're late." The girl took a vague step backward, the way girls swing slowly away from people—you must have seen them often on sidewalks before ice cream parlors or schools? They stare as if fascinated at one person, while beginning the slow inevitable swing toward another who stands behind them. The boy said, opening the door: "Come on! He deserves it!"

They went inside. And then the shame began, an awful shame. I did not understand this though I thought about it a great deal. Someone came out to help me, a nurse. When I cry most people look away in embarrassment but the nurses show nothing, nothing at all. They boss me around a little. Crying makes me think of someone else crying, a soldier holding another soldier's hand, sitting in some rubble. One soldier is alive and the other dead, the one who is alive is holding the other's hand and crying, like a baby. Like a puppy. A kitten, a baby, something small and helpless, when the crying does no good and is not meant for any good.

I think that my name is Jack Furlong. There was another person named Private Furlong, evidently myself. Now I am back home and I am Jack Furlong again. I can imagine many parts of this city without really seeing them, and what is surprising—and very pleasant—is the way these memories come to me, so unexpected. Lying in bed with no thoughts at all I suddenly find myself thinking of a certain dime store where we hung out, by the comic book racks, many years ago; or I think of a certain playground on the edge of a ravine made by a glacier, many thousands of years ago. I don't know what makes these memories come to me but they exert a kind of tug—on my heart, I suppose. It's very strange. My eyes sometimes fill with tears, but a different kind of tears. I was never good at understanding feelings but now, in the hospital, I have a lot of time for thinking. I think that I am a kind of masterpiece. I mean, a miracle. My body and my brain. It is like a little world inside, or a factory, with everything functioning and the dynamo at the very center—my heart—pumping and pumping with no source of energy behind it. I think about that a lot. What keeps it going? And the eyes. Did you know that the eye is strong, very strong? That the muscles are like steel? Yes. Eyes are very strong, I mean the substance of the eyes is strong. It takes a lot to destroy them.

At last they check me out and bring me home—a happy day. It is good to be back home where everything is peaceful and familiar. When I lived in this house before I did not think about "living" in it, or about the house at all. Now, looking out of my window, I can see the front lawn and the street and the other houses facing us, all ranch houses, and I am aware of being very fortunate. A few kids are outside, racing past on bicycles. It is a spring day, very warm. The houses on the block make a kind of design if you look right. I am tired from all the exertion involved getting me here, and so it is difficult to explain what I mean—a design, a setting. Everything in place. It has not changed and won't change. It is a very pleasant neighborhood, and I think I remember hearing Mother once say that our house had cost $45,000. I had "heard" this remark years ago but never paid any attention to it. Now I keep thinking about it, I don't know why. There is something wonderful about that figure: it means something. Is it secret? It is the very opposite of rubble, yes. There are no screams here, no sudden explosions. Yes, I think that is why it pleases me so. I fall asleep thinking of forty-five thousand dollars.

My birthday. It is a few days later. I have been looking through the books in my room, a history textbook, a calculus textbook, and something called *College Rhetoric*. Those were my books and I can recognize my handwriting in the margins, but I have a hard time reading them now. To get away from the reading I look around—or the door in my mind begins to open slowly, scaring me, and so I wheel myself over to the window to look out. Father has just flown back from Boston. Yes, it is my birthday and I am twenty. We have a wheelchair of our own now, not the hospital's chair but our own. There is a wooden ramp from our side door right into the garage, and when they push me out I have a sudden sensation of panic right in my heart—do they know how to handle me? what if they push me too hard? They are sometimes clumsy and a little rough, accidentally. Whenever Father does something wrong I think at once, not meaning to, *They wouldn't do that at the hospital.*

My uncle and my aunt are coming too. We are going out to Skyway for dinner. This is a big restaurant and motel near the airport. There is the usual trouble getting me in and out of the car, but Father is getting used to it. My uncle Floyd keeps saying, "Well, it's great to have you back. I mean it. It's just great, it's just wonderful to have you back." My aunt is wearing a hat with big droopy yellow flowers on it, a pretty hat. But something about the flowers makes me think of giant leaves in the jungle, coated with dust and sweat, and the way the air tasted— it made your throat and lungs ache, the dust in the air. Grit. Things were flying in the air. Someone was screaming, "Don't leave me!" A lot of them were screaming that. But my father said, "We'd better hurry, our reservations are for six."

Six is early to eat, I know. They are hurrying up the evening because I get tired so fast. My uncle opens the door and my father wheels me inside, all of it done easily. My father says to a man, "Furlong, for five—" This restaurant is familiar. On one side there is a stairway going down, carpeted in blue, and down there are rooms for—oh, banquets and meetings and things. Ahead of us is a cocktail lounge, very dark. Off to the left, down a corridor lined with paintings (they are by local artists, for sale) is the restaurant we are going to, the Grotto Room. But the man is looking through his ledger. My mother says to my aunt, "I bought that watercolor here, you know, the one over the piano." The women talk about something but my uncle stares at my father and the manager, silent. Something is wrong. The manager looks through his book and his face is red and troubled. Finally he looks up and says, "Yes, all right. Down this way." He leads us down to the Grotto Room.

We are seated. The table is covered with a white tablecloth, a glaring white. A waitress is already at Father's elbow. She looks at us, her eyes darting around the table and lingering no longer on me than on anyone else. I know that my glasses are thick and that my face is not pleasant to look at, not the same face as before. But still she does not look at me more than a second, maybe two seconds. Father orders drinks. It is my birthday. He glances over to the side and I see that someone at the next table, some men and women, are watching us. A woman in red—I think it is red—does something with her napkin, putting it on the table. Father picks up his menu, which is very large. My mother and aunt chatter about something, my mother hands me a menu. At the next table a man stands. He changes places with the woman, and now her back is to our table. I understand this but pretend to notice nothing, look down at the menu with a pleased, surprised expression, because it is better this way. It is better for everyone.

"What do you think you'll order? Everything looks so tempting," she says.

They were in a hurry and the wounded and the dead were stacked together, brought back together in a truck. But not carried at the end of a nylon cord, from a helicopter, not that. This memory comes to me in a flash, then fades. I was driving the truck, I think. Wasn't I? I was on the truck. I did not hover at the end of a line, in a plastic sack. Those were others—I didn't know them, only saw them from a distance. They screamed: "Don't leave me!"

"Lobster," Father says. He speaks with certainty: he is predicting my choice for dinner. "I bet it's lobster, eh?"

"Lobster."

My mother squeezes my arm, pleased that I have given the right answer. "My choice too," she says. "Always have fish on Fridays . . . the old customs . . . I like the old customs, no matter what people say. The Mass in Latin, and . . . and priests who know what their vocations are . . . . How do you want your lobster, dear? Broiled?"

"Yes."

"Or this way—here—the Skyway Lobster?" She leans over to help me with the menu, pointing at the words. There is a film, a gauzy panel between me and the words, and I keep waiting for it to disappear. The faces around the table, the voices. . . the smiling mouths and eyes . . . I keep glancing up at them, waiting for the veil to be yanked away. *He deserves it. Don't leave me!* In the meantime I think I will have the Skyway Lobster.

"You're sure?"

"Yes."

"My own choice also," my mother says. She looks around the table, in triumph, and the faces smile back at her and at me.

POETRY

Jonathan Swift (1667–1745)
CLEVER TOM CLINCH GOING TO BE HANGED

As Clever Tom Clinch, while the rabble was bawling,
Rode stately through Holborn,[1] to die in his calling;
He stopped at the George for a bottle of sack,
And promised to pay for it when he came back.
His waistcoat and stockings, and breeches were white,
His cap had a new cherry ribbon to tie't.
The maids to the doors and the balconies ran,
And said, lackaday, he's a proper young man.
But, as from the windows the ladies he spied,
Like a beau in the box, he bowed low on each side;   10
And when his last speech the hawkers did cry,
He swore from his cart, it was all a damned lie.
The hangman for pardon fell down on his knee;
Tom gave him a kick in the guts for his fee.
Then said, "I must speak to the people a little,
But I'll see you all damned before I will whittle.[2]
My honest friend Wild,[3] may he long hold his place,
He lengthened my life with a whole year of grace.
Take courage, dear comrades, and be not afraid,
Nor slip this occasion to follow your trade.   20
My conscience is clear, and my spirits are calm,
And thus I go off without prayer-book or psalm."
Then follow the practice of clever Tom Clinch,
Who hung like a hero, and never would flinch.

William Blake (1757–1827)
LONDON

I wander through each chartered[1] street,
Near where the chartered Thames does flow

---

[1]A district of London.
[2]Confess at the gallows.
[3]Jonathan Wild (1682?–1725), a famous thief-catcher, but also head of a thieving business; also hanged eventually.
London
[1]Established and leased by written grants or charters.

And mark in every face I meet
Marks of weakness, marks of woe.

In every cry of every man,
In every infant's cry of fear,
In every voice; in every ban,
The mind-forged manacles I hear:

How the chimney-sweeper's cry
Every blackening church appalls,   10
And the hapless soldier's sigh
Runs in blood down palace-walls.

But most, through midnight streets I hear
How the youthful harlot's curse
Blasts the new-born infant's tear,
And blights with plagues the marriage-hearse.

QUESTIONS

1. How do you imagine the speaker?
2. What effect does the repetition of words and phrases have?
3. Do visual or sound images predominate in the poem?
4. What experience of London does the poem communicate?

Robert Browning (1812–1889)

SOLILOQUY OF THE SPANISH CLOISTER

Gr-r-r—there go, my heart's abhorrence!
    Water your damned flower-pots, do!
If hate killed men, Brother Lawrence,
    God's blood, would not mine kill you!
What? your myrtle-bush wants trimming?
    Oh, that rose has prior claims—
Needs its leaden vase filled brimming?
    Hell dry you up with its flames!

At the meal we sit together;
    Salve tibi!° I must hear   Hail to thee!
Wise talk of the kind of weather,   11
    Sort of season, time of year:

Not a plenteous cork-crop: scarcely
   Dare we hope oak-galls,[1] *I doubt;*
What's the Latin name for "parsley"?
   What's the Greek name for "swine's snout"?

Whew! We'll have our platter burnished,
   Laid with care on our own shelf!
With a fire-new spoon we're furnished,
   And a goblet for ourself,   20
Rinsed like something sacrificial
   Ere 'tis fit to touch our chaps—
Marked with L. for our initial!
   (He-he! There his lily snaps!)

Saint, forsooth! While Brown Dolores
   Squats outside the Convent bank
With Sanchicha, telling stories,
   Steeping tresses in the tank,
Blue-black, lustrous, thick like horsehairs,
   —Can't I see his dead eye glow,   30
Bright as 'twere a Barbary corsair's?
   (That is, if he'd let it show!)

When he finishes refection,
   Knife and fork he never lays
Cross-wise, to my recollection,
   As I do, in Jesu's praise.
I the Trinity illustrate,
   Drinking watered orange-pulp—
In three sips the Arian[2] frustrate;
   While he drains his at one gulp!   40

Oh, those melons! if he's able
   We're to have a feast; so nice!
One goes to the Abbot's table,
   All of us get each a slice.
How go on your flowers? None double?
   Not one fruit-sort can you spy?
Strange!—And I, too, at such trouble,
   Keep them close-nipped on the sly!

---

[1]Used to make ink.
[2]Follower of Arius (c. 260–336 A.D.), a heretic who did not believe in the Trinity.

There's a great text in Galatians,
   Once you trip on it, entails   50
Twenty-nine distinct damnations,
   One sure, if another fails;
If I trip him just a-dying,
   Sure of heaven as sure can be,
Spin him round and send him flying
   Off to hell, a Manichee?[3]

Or, my scrofulous French novel
   On grey paper with blunt type!
Simply glance at it, you grovel
   Hand and foot in Belial's° gripe;   Depravity's
If I double down its pages   61
   At the woeful sixteenth print,
When he gathers his greengages,°   plums
   Ope a sieve and slip it in't?

Or, there's Satan!—one might venture
   Pledge one's soul to him, yet leave
Such a flaw in the indenture
   As he'd miss till, past retrieve,
Blasted lay that rose-acacia
   We're so proud of! *Hy, Zy, Hine. . . .*   70
'St, there's Vespers! *Plena gratia*
   Ave, Virgo![4] Gr-r-r—you swine!

Walt Whitman (1819–1892)

I SAW IN LOUSIANA A LIVE-OAK GROWING

I saw in Lousiana a live-oak growing,
All alone stood it and the moss hung down from the
   branches,
Without any companion it grew there uttering joyous leaves
   of dark green,
And its look, rude, unbending, lusty, made me think of
   myself,

---

[3] Another sort of heretic, who believed in the struggle of good and evil in the world forever.
[4] Hail, Virgin, full of grace!

But I wonder'd how it could utter joyous leaves standing
  alone there without its friend near, for I knew I could
  not,
And I broke off a twig with a certain number of leaves
  upon it, and twined around it a little moss,
And brought it away, and I have placed it in sight in my
  room,
It is not needed to remind me as of my own dear friends,
(For I believe lately I think of little else than of them,)
Yet it remains to me a curious token, it makes me think of
  manly love;   10
For all that, and though the live-oak glistens there in
  Louisiana solitary in a wide flat space,
Uttering joyous leaves all its life without a friend a lover
  near,
I know very well I could not.

Emily Dickinson (1830–1886)
MUCH MADNESS IS DIVINEST SENSE

Much Madness is divinest Sense—
To a discerning Eye—
Much Sense—the starkest Madness—
'Tis the Majority
In this, as All, prevail—
Assent—and you are sane—
Demur—you're straightway dangerous—
And handled with a Chain—

QUESTIONS

1. What is the speaker's tone?
2. Is the poem about madness or nonconformity? Explain.

Emily Dickinson (1830–1886)
THE SOUL SELECTS HER OWN SOCIETY

The Soul selects her own Society—
Then—shuts the Door—

To her divine Majority—
Present no more—

Unmoved—she notes the Chariots—pausing—
At her low Gate—
Unmoved—an Emperor be kneeling
Upon her Mat—

I've known her—from an ample nation—
Choose One—   10
Then—close the Valves of her attention—
Like Stone—

QUESTIONS

1. Do you suppose the speaker is talking about her or his own soul? Why, or why not?
2. How do the figures of speech used make you picture the "Soul"?
3. What word choices make you pause to consider the reason for them?

William Butler Yeats (1865–1939)

THE LAKE ISLE OF INNISFREE[1]

I will arise and go now, and go to Innisfree,
And a small cabin build there, of clay and wattles made:
Nine bean-rows will I have there, a hive for the honeybee,
And live alone in the bee-loud glade.

And I shall have some peace there, for peace comes
    dropping slow,
Dropping from the veils of the morning to where the
    cricket sings;
There midnight's all a glimmer, and noon a purple glow,
And evening full of the linnet's wings.

I will arise and go now, for always night and day
I hear lake water lapping with low sounds by the shore;   10

---

[1]A small island in Lough Gill, County Sligo, Ireland.

While I stand on the roadway, or on the pavements grey,
I hear it in the deep heart's core.

Edwin Arlington Robinson (1869–1935)
RICHARD CORY

Whenever Richard Cory went down town,
We people on the pavement looked at him:
He was a gentleman from sole to crown,
Clean favored, and imperially slim.

And he was always quietly arrayed,
And he was always human when he talked;
But still he fluttered pulses when he said,
"Good-morning," and he glittered when he walked.

And he was rich—yes, richer than a king—
And admirably schooled in every grace: 10
In fine, we thought that he was everything
To make us wish that we were in his place.

So on we worked, and waited for the light,
And went without the meat, and cursed the bread;
And Richard Cory, one calm summer night,
Went home and put a bullet through his head.

Robert Frost (1874–1963)
MENDING WALL

Something there is that doesn't love a wall,
That sends the frozen-ground-swell under it
And spills the upper boulders in the sun,
And makes gaps even two can pass abreast.
The work of hunters is another thing:
I have come after them and made repair
Where they have left not one stone on a stone,
But they would have the rabbit out of hiding,

To please the yelping dogs. The gaps I mean,
No one has seen them made or heard them made,   10
But at spring mending-time we find them there.
I let my neighbor know beyond the hill;
And on a day we meet to walk the line
And set the wall between us once again.
We keep the wall between us as we go.
To each the boulders that have fallen to each.
And some are loaves and some so nearly balls
We have to use a spell to make them balance:
"Stay where you are until our backs are turned!"
We wear our fingers rough with handling them.   20
Oh, just another kind of outdoor game,
One on a side. It comes to little more:
There where it is we do not need the wall:
He is all pine and I am apple orchard.
My apple trees will never get across
And eat the cones under his pines, I tell him.
He only says, "Good fences make good neighbors."
Spring is the mischief in me, and I wonder
If I could put a notion in his head:
"*Why* do they make good neighbors? Isn't it   30
Where there are cows? But here there are no cows.
Before I built a wall I'd ask to know
What I was walling in or walling out,
And to whom I was like to give offense.
Something there is that doesn't love a wall,
That wants it down." I could say "Elves" to him,
But it's not elves exactly, and I'd rather
He said it for himself. I see him there,
Bringing a stone grasped firmly by the top
In each hand, like an old-stone savage armed.   40
He moves in darkness as it seems to me,
Not of woods only and the shade of trees.
He will not go behind his father's saying,
And he likes having thought of it so well
He says again, "Good fences make good neighbors."

QUESTIONS

1. What sense do you have of the speaker? How important is his tone in giving you this sense?
2. What sort of relationship do the speaker and his neighbor appear to have?
3. What does repairing the wall mean to each of them?
4. How just does the speaker's assessment of his neighbor appear to be?

Robert Frost (1874–1963)
THE SILKEN TENT

She is as in a field a silken tent
At midday when a sunny summer breeze
Has dried the dew and all its ropes relent,
So that in guys it gently sways at ease,
And its supporting central cedar pole,
That is its pinnacle to heavenward
And signifies the sureness of the soul,
Seems to owe naught to any single cord,
But strictly held by none, is loosely bound
By countless silken ties of love and thought   10
To everything on earth the compass round,
And only by one's going slightly taut
In the capriciousness of summer air
Is of the slightest bondage made aware.

QUESTIONS

1. Does the comparison between a woman and a tent surprise you?
2. What particular features of this tent make the comparison acceptable or effective?
3. When you read the poem aloud, what sound effects do you notice?
4. What sense of the woman and the speaker's attitude towards her does the image of the tent convey?

T. S. Eliot (1888–1965)
THE LOVE SONG OF J. ALFRED PRUFROCK

S'io credesse che mia risposta fosse
A persona che mai tornasse al mondo,
Questa fiamma staria senza piu scosse.
Ma perciocche giammai di questo fondo
Non torno vivo alcun, s'i'odo il vero,
Senza tema d'infamia ti rispondo.[1]

Let us go then, you and I,
When the evening is spread out against the sky

---

[1]From Dante's *Inferno,* lines from one of the damned, enfolded in flame, who tells his story only because he believes no one returns from Hell: "If I believed my response were to one who might ever return to the world, this flame would quiver no more. But because I understand no one ever escapes from this pit, I'll answer you with no fear of ill fame."

Like a patient etherised upon a table;
Let us go, through certain half-deserted streets,
The muttering retreats
Of restless nights in one-night cheap hotels
And sawdust restaurants with oyster-shells:
Streets that follow like a tedious argument
Of insidious intent
To lead you to an overwhelming question . . .   10
Oh, do not ask, "What is it?"
Let us go and make our visit.

   In the room the women come and go
Talking of Michelangelo.

   The yellow fog that rubs its back upon the window-
     panes,
The yellow smoke that rubs its muzzle on the window-
     panes
Licked its tongue into the corners of the evening,
Lingered upon the pools that stand in drains,
Let fall upon its back the soot that falls from chimneys,
Slipped by the terrace, made a sudden leap,   20
And seeing that it was a soft October night,
Curled once about the house, and fell asleep.

   And indeed there will be time
For the yellow smoke that slides along the street,
Rubbing its back upon the window-panes;
There will be time, there will be time
To prepare a face to meet the faces that you meet;
There will be time to murder and create,
And time for all the works and days of hands
That lift and drop a question on your plate;   30
Time for you and time for me,
And time yet for a hundred indecisions,
And for a hundred visions and revisions,
Before the taking of a toast and tea.

   In the room the women come and go
Talking of Michelangelo.
   And indeed there will be time
To wonder, "Do I dare?" and, "Do I dare?"
Time to turn back and descend the stair,
With a bald spot in the middle of my hair—   40
[They will say: "How his hair is growing thin!"]

My morning coat, my collar mounting firmly to the chin,
My necktie rich and modest, but asserted by a simple pin—
[They will say: "But how his arms and legs are thin!"]
Do I dare
Disturb the universe?
In a minute there is time
For decisions and revisions which a minute will reverse.

For I have known them all already, known them all:—
Have known the evenings, mornings, afternoons,   50
I have measured out my life with coffee spoons;
I know the voices dying with a dying fall
Beneath the music from a farther room.
  So how should I presume?

And I have known the eyes already, known them all—
The eyes that fix you in a formulated phrase,
And when I am formulated, sprawling on a pin,
When I am pinned and wriggling on the wall,
Then how should I begin
To spit out all the butt-ends of my days and ways?   60
  And how should I presume?

And I have known the arms already, known them all—
Arms that are braceleted and white and bare
[But in the lamplight, downed with light brown hair!]
Is it perfume from a dress
That makes me so digress?
Arms that lie along a table, or wrap about a shawl.
  And should I then presume?
  And how should I begin?

          . . . . .

Shall I say, I have gone at dusk through narrow streets   70
And watched the smoke that rises from the pipes
Of lonely men in shirt-sleeves, leaning out
  of windows? . . .

I should have been a pair of ragged claws
Scuttling across the floors of silent seas.

          . . . . .

And the afternoon, the evening, sleeps so peacefully!
Smoothed by long fingers,

Asleep . . . tired . . . or it malingers,
Stretched on the floor, here beside you and me.
Should I, after tea and cakes and ices,
Have the strength to force the moment to its crisis?   80
But though I have wept and fasted, wept and prayed,
Though I have seen my head [grown slightly bald] brought
  in upon a platter,[2]
I am no prophet—and here's no great matter;
I have seen the moment of my greatness flicker,
And I have seen the eternal Footman hold my coat, and
  snicker,
And in short, I was afraid.

And would it have been worth it, after all,
After the cups, the marmalade, the tea,
Among the porcelain, among some talk of you and me,
Would it have been worth while,   90
To have bitten off the matter with a smile,
To have squeezed the universe into a ball[3]
To roll it toward some overwhelming question,
To say: "I am Lazarus,[4] come from the dead,
Come back to tell you all, I shall tell you all"—
If one, settling a pillow by her head,
    Should say: "That is not what I meant at all.
    That is not it, at all."
    And would it have been worth it, after all,   100
Would it have been worth while,
After the sunsets and the dooryards and the sprinkled
  streets,
After the novels, after the teacups, after the skirts that trail
  along the floor—
And this, and so much more?—
It is impossible to say just what I mean!
But as if a magic lantern threw the nerves in patterns on a
  screen:
Would it have been worth while
If one, settling a pillow or throwing off a shawl,
And turning toward the window, should say:

---

[2]Like that of John the Baptist. See Matthew 14.
[3]Echoes Andrew Marvell's "To His Coy Mistress," 11. 41–42.
[4]One Lazarus in the Bible was brought back to life by Jesus; another was a diseased beggar in a parable by Jesus. See John 11 and Luke 16.

"That is not it at all,
That is not what I meant, at all."   110

. . . . .

No! I am not Prince Hamlet, nor was meant to be;
Am an attendant lord, one that will do
To swell a progress°, start a scene or two,   crowd scene
Advise the prince; no doubt, an easy tool,
Deferential, glad to be of use,
Politic, cautious, and meticulous;
Full of high sentence,° but a bit obtuse;   sententiousness
At times, indeed, almost ridiculous—
Almost, at times, the Fool.

   I grow old . . . I grow old . . .   120
I shall wear the bottoms of my trousers rolled.

   Shall I part my hair behind? Do I dare to eat a peach?
I shall wear white flannel trousers, and walk upon the
   beach.
I have heard the mermaids singing, each to each.

   I do not think that they will sing to me.

   I have seen them riding seaward on the waves
Combing the white hair of the waves blown back
When the wind blows the water white and black.

   We have lingered in the chambers of the sea
By sea-girls wreathed with seaweed red and brown   130
Till human voices wake us, and we drown.

QUESTIONS

1. Do you feel that the speaker is addressing you, the reader, throughout the poem? If
   so, why should he? If not, whom is he addressing?
2. What picture do you have of Prufrock and his usual daily life?
3. What does he seem to feel about the place he considers visiting?
4. Why does he not go after all?
5. Is Prufrock a fool, as he suggests he "almost" is "at times"? If he's not entirely a fool,
   what else is he?

Langston Hughes (1902–1967)
THEME FOR ENGLISH B

The instructor said,

> *Go home and write*
> *a page tonight.*
> *And let that page come out of you—*
> *Then, it will be true.*

I wonder if it's that simple?
I am twenty-two, colored, born in Winston-Salem.
I went to school there, then Durham, then here
to this college on the hill above Harlem.
I am the only colored student in my class.   10
The steps from the hill lead down into Harlem,
through a park, then I cross St. Nicholas,
Eighth Avenue, Seventh, and I come to the Y,
the Harlem Branch Y, where I take the elevator
up to my room, sit down, and write this page:

It's not easy to know what is true for you or me
at twenty-two, my age. But I guess I'm what
I feel and see and hear, Harlem, I hear you:
hear you, hear me—we two—you, me, talk on this page.
(I hear New York, too.) Me—who?   20

Well, I like to eat, sleep, drink, and be in love.
I like to work, read, learn, and understand life.
I like a pipe for a Christmas present,
or records—Bessie,[1] bop, or Bach.
I guess being colored doesn't make me *not* like
the same things other folks like who are other races.
So will my page be colored that I write?

Being me, it will not be white.
But it will be
a part of you, instructor.   30
You are white—
yet a part of me, as I am a part of you.

---

[1]Blues singer Bessie Smith (1894?–1937).

That's American.
Sometimes perhaps you don't want to be a part of me.
Nor do I often want to be a part of you.
But we are, that's true!
As I learn from you,
I guess you learn from me—
although you're older—and white—
and somewhat more free.   40

This is my page for English B.

W. H. Auden (1907–1973)
THE UNKNOWN CITIZEN

(To JS/07/M/378
This Marble Monument
Is Erected by the State)

He was found by the Bureau of Statistics to be
One against whom there was no official complaint,
And all the reports on his conduct agree
That, in the modern sense of an old-fashioned word, he
     was a saint,
For in everything he did he served the Greater Community.
Except for the War till the day he retired
He worked in a factory and never got fired,
But satisfied his employers, Fudge Motors Inc.
Yet he wasn't a scab or odd in his views,
For his Union reports that he paid his dues,   10
(Our report on his Union shows it was sound)
And our Social Psychology workers found
That he was popular with his mates and liked a drink.
The Press are convinced that he bought a paper every day
And that his reactions to advertisements were normal in
     every way.
Policies taken out in his name prove that he was fully
     insured,
And his Health-card shows he was once in hospital but left
     it cured.
Both Producers Research and High-Grade Living declare

He was fully sensible to the advantages of the Instalment
   Plan
And had everything necessary to the Modern Man,   20
A phonograph, a radio, a car and a frigidaire.
Our researchers into Public Opinion are content
That he held the proper opinions for the time of year;
When there was peace, he was for peace; when there was
   war, he went.
He was married and added five children to the population,
Which our Eugenist says was the right number for a parent
   of his generation,
And our teachers report that he never interfered with their
   education.
Was he free? Was he happy? The question is absurd:
Had anything been wrong, we should certainly have heard.

QUESTIONS

1. What associations does the poem's title arouse?
2. Whose voice is speaking in the poem?
3. How well do you feel you know the citizen described?
4. Are the questions at the conclusion really absurd? Explain.

W. H. Auden (1907–1973)
WHO'S WHO

A shilling life will give you all the facts:
How Father beat him, how he ran away,
What were the struggles of his youth, what acts
Made him the greatest figure of his day:
Of how he fought, fished, hunted, worked all night,
Though giddy, climbed new mountains; named a sea:
Some of the last researchers even write
Love made him weep his pints like you and me.

With all his honours on, he sighed for one
Who, say astonished critics, lived at home;   10
Did little jobs about the house with skill
And nothing else; could whistle; would sit still
Or potter round the garden; answered some
Of his long marvellous letters but kept none.

Muriel Rukeyser (1913–1980)

MYTH

Long afterward, Oedipus, old and blinded, walked the
roads.   He smelled a familiar smell.   It was
the Sphinx.   Oedipus said, "I want to ask one question.
Why didn't I recognize my mother?"   "You gave the
wrong answer," said the Sphinx.   "But that was what
made everything possible," said Oedipus.   "No," she said.
"When I asked, What walks on four legs in the morning,
two at noon, and three in the evening, you answered,
Man.   You didn't say anything about woman."
"When you say Man," said Oedipus, "you include women   10
too. Everyone knows that."   She said, "That's what
you think."

Gwendolyn Brooks (b. 1917)

WE REAL COOL

The Pool Players.
Seven at the Golden Shovel.

We real cool. We
Left school. We

Lurk late. We
Strike straight. We

Sing sin. We
Thin gin. We

Jazz June. We
Die soon.

QUESTIONS

1. How does this poem sound when read aloud?
2. How is the last line related to what precedes it?

Philip Larkin (1922–1985)
VERS DE SOCIÉTÉ[1]

My wife and I have asked a crowd of craps
To come and waste their time and ours: perhaps
You'd care to join us? In a pig's arse, friend.
Day comes to an end.
The gas fire breathes, the trees are darkly swayed.
And so *Dear Warlock-Williams: I'm afraid—*

Funny how hard it is to be alone.
I could spend half my evenings, if I wanted,
Holding a glass of washing sherry, canted
Over to catch the drivel of some bitch   10
Who's read nothing but *Which;*
Just think of all the spare time that has flown

Straight into nothingness by being filled
With forks and faces, rather than repaid
Under a lamp, hearing the noise of wind,
And looking out to see the moon thinned
To an air-sharpened blade.
A life, and yet how sternly it's instilled

All solitude is selfish. No one now
Believes the hermit with his gown and dish   20
Talking to God (who's gone too); the big wish
Is to have people nice to you, which means
Doing it back somehow.
Virtue is social. Are, then, these routines

Playing at goodness, like going to church?
Something that bores us, something we don't do well
(Asking that ass about his fool research)
But try to feel, because, however crudely,
It shows us what should be?
Too subtle, that. Too decent, too. Oh hell,   30

Only the young can be alone freely.
The time is shorter now for company,

---
[1]Society verse.

And sitting by a lamp more often brings
Not peace, but other things.
Beyond the light stand failure and remorse
Whispering *Dear Warlock-Williams: Why, of course—*

James Dickey (b. 1923)
THE LEAP

The only thing I have of Jane MacNaughton
Is one instant of a dancing-class dance.
She was the fastest runner in the seventh grade,
My scrapbook says, even when boys were beginning
To be as big as the girls,
But I do not have her running in my mind,
Though Frances Lane is there, Agnes Fraser,
Fat Betty Lou Black in the boys-against-girls
Relays we ran at recess: she must have run

Like the other girls, with her skirts tucked up   10
So they would be like bloomers,
But I cannot tell; that part of her is gone.
What I do have is when she came,
With the hem of her skirt where it should be
For a young lady, into the annual dance
Of the dancing class we all hated, and with a light
Grave leap, jumped up and touched the end
Of one of the paper-ring decorations

To see if she could reach it. She could,
And reached me now as well, hanging in my mind   20
From a brown chain of brittle paper, thin
And muscular, wide-mouthed, eager to prove
Whatever it proves when you leap
In a new dress, a new womanhood, among the boys
Whom you easily left in the dust
Of the passionless playground. If I said I saw
In the paper where Jane MacNaughton Hill,

Mother of four, leapt to her death from a window
Of a downtown hotel, and that her body crushed-in
The top of a parked taxi, and that I held   30

Without trembling a picture of her lying cradled
In that papery steel as though lying in the grass,
One shoe idly off, arms folded across her breast,
I would not believe myself. I would say
The convenient thing, that it was a bad dream
Of maturity, to see that eternal process

Most obsessively wrong with the world
Come out of her light, earth-spurning feet
Grown heavy: would say that in the dusty heels
Of the playground some boy who did not depend   40
On speed of foot, caught and betrayed her.
Jane, stay where you are in my first mind:
It was odd in that school, at that dance.
I and the other slow-footed yokels sat in corners
Cutting rings out of drawing paper

Before you leapt in your new dress
And touched the end of something I began,
Above the couples struggling on the floor,
New men and women clutching at each other
And prancing foolishly as bears: hold on   50
To that ring I made for you, Jane—
My feet are nailed to the ground
By dust I swallowed thirty years ago—
While I examine my hands.

QUESTIONS

1. How close do you imagine the speaker was to Jane MacNaughton in school?
2. What is that "first mind" in which the speaker recalls Jane's leap at the dance?
3. What do you know about Jane from reading the poem? About the speaker?

Allen Ginsberg (b. 1926)
MY SAD SELF

Sometimes when my eyes are red
I go up on top of the RCA Building
     and gaze at my world, Manhattan—
          my buildings, streets I've done feats in,
               lofts, beds, coldwater flats

—on Fifth Ave below which I also bear in mind,
    its ant cars, little yellow taxis, men
        walking the size of specks of wool—
Panorama of the bridges, sunrise over Brooklyn machine,
    sun go down over New Jersey where I was born   10
        & Paterson where I played with ants—
my later loves on 15th Street,
    my greater loves of Lower East Side,
        my once fabulous amours in the Bronx
            faraway—
paths crossing in these hidden streets,
    my history summed up, my absences
        and ecstasies in Harlem—
—sun shining down on all I own
    in one eyeblink to the horizon   20
        in my last eternity—
            matter is water.

Sad,
    I take the elevator and go
        down, pondering,
and walk on the pavements staring into all man's
            plateglass, faces,
    questioning after who loves,
and stop, bemused
    in front of an automobile shopwindow   30
standing lost in calm thought,
    traffic moving up & down 5th Avenue blocks
behind me
        waiting for a moment when . . .

Time to go home & cook supper & listen to
    the romantic war news on the radio

        . . . all movement stops
& I walk in the timeless sadness of existence,
    tenderness flowing thru the buildings,
        my fingertips touching reality's face,
my own face streaked with tears in the mirror   40
    of some window—at dusk—
        where I have no desire—
for bonbons—or to own the dresses or Japanese
    lampshades of intellection—

Confused by the spectacle around me,
    Man struggling up the street
        with packages, newspapers,
                ties, beautiful suits
        toward his desire
    Man, woman, streaming over the pavements   50
        red lights clocking hurried watches &
          movements at the curb—
And all these streets leading
    so crosswise, honking, lengthily,
        by avenues
    stalked by high buildings or crusted into slums
        thru such halting traffic
                screaming cars and engines
so painfully to this
    countryside, this graveyard   60
        this stillness
             on deathbed or mountain
    once seen
        never regained or desired
           in the mind to come
where all Manhattan that I've seen must disappear.

Adrienne Rich (b. 1929)
AUNT JENNIFER'S TIGERS

Aunt Jennifer's tigers prance across a screen,
Bright topaz denizens of a world of green.
They do not fear the men beneath the tree;
They pace in sleek chivalric certainty.

Aunt Jennifer's fingers fluttering through her wool
Find even the ivory needle hard to pull.
The massive weight of Uncle's wedding band
Sits heavily upon Aunt Jennifer's hand.

When Aunt is dead, her terrified hands will lie
Still ringed with ordeals she was mastered by.   10
The tigers in the panel that she made
Will go on prancing, proud and unafraid.

QUESTIONS

1. What details tell you most about Aunt Jennifer?
2. Why do you suppose she embroiders those tigers?
3. What can you tell about the speaker's feelings towards Aunt Jennifer?

Linda Pastan (b. 1932)

MARKS

My husband gives me an A
for last night's supper,
an incomplete for my ironing,
a B plus in bed.
My son says I am average,
an average mother, but if
I put my mind to it
I could improve.
My daughter believes
in Pass/Fail and tells me
I pass. Wait 'til they learn
I'm dropping out.

John Updike (b. 1932)

EX-BASKETBALL PLAYER

Pearl Avenue runs past the high-school lot,
Bends with the trolley tracks, and stops, cut off
Before it has a chance to go two blocks,
At Colonel McComsky Plaza. Berth's Garage
Is on the corner facing west, and there,
Most days, you'll find Flick Webb, who helps Berth out.

Flick stands tall among the idiot pumps—
Five on a side, the old bubble-head style,
Their rubber elbows hanging loose and low.
One's nostrils are two S's, and his eyes   10

An E and O.[1] And one is squat, without
A head at all—more of a football type.

Once Flick played for the high-school team, the Wizards.
He was good: in fact, the best. In '46
He bucketed three hundred ninety points,
A county record still. The ball loved Flick.
I saw him rack up thirty-eight or forty
In one home game. His hands were like wild birds.

He never learned a trade, he just sells gas,
Checks oil, and changes flats. Once in a while,   20
As a gag, he dribbles an inner tube,
But most of us remember anyway.
His hands are fine and nervous on the lug wrench.
It makes no difference to the lug wrench, though.

Off work, he hangs around Mae's luncheonette.
Grease-gray and kind of coiled, he plays pinball,
Smokes those thin cigars, nurses lemon phosphates.°   soft drinks
Flick seldom says a word to Mae, just nods
Beyond her face toward bright applauding tiers
Of Necco Wafers, Nibs, and Juju Beads.   30

QUESTIONS

1. What word choices stand out as you read?
2. Who is the speaker?
3. What attitude towards Flick is conveyed by the speaker's tone and the details he records?

Lucille Clifton (b. 1936)

MISS ROSIE

When I watch you
wrapped up like garbage
sitting, surrounded by the smell
of too old potato peels
or
when I watch you

---

[1]Esso, which became Exxon.

in your old man's shoes
with the little toe cut out
sitting, waiting for your mind
like next week's grocery   10
I say
when I watch you
you wet brown bag of a woman
who used to be the best looking gal in Georgia
used to be called the Georgia Rose
I stand up
through your destruction
I stand up

QUESTIONS

1. Who do you suppose the speaker to be?
2. What images create the strongest impression of Miss Rosie and of the speaker's attitude towards her?
3. What is the effect of the repeated phrases in the poem?

Marge Piercy (b. 1936)

TO BE OF USE

The people I love the best
jump into work head first
without dallying in the shallows
and swim off with sure strokes almost out of sight.
They seem to become natives of that element,
the black sleek heads of seals
bouncing like half-submerged balls.

I love people who harness themselves, an ox to a heavy
    cart,
who pull like water buffalo, with massive patience,
who strain in the mud and the muck to move things
    forward,   10
who do what has to be done, again and again.

I want to be with people who submerge
in the task, who go into the fields to harvest
and work in a row and pass the bags along,

who are not parlor generals and field deserters
but move in a common rhythm
when the food must come in or the fire be put out.

The work of the world is common as mud.
Botched, it smears the hands, crumbles to dust.
But the thing worth doing well done   20
has a shape that satisfies, clean and evident.
Greek amphoras for wine or oil,
Hopi vases that held corn, are put in museums
but you know they were made to be used.
The pitcher cries for water to carry
and a person for work that is real.

Marge Piercy (b. 1936)

A WORK OF ARTIFICE

The bonsai tree
in the attractive pot
could have grown eighty feet tall
on the side of a mountain
till split by lightning.
But a gardener
carefully pruned it.
It is nine inches high.
Every day as he
whittles back the branches   10
the gardener croons,
It is your nature
to be small and cozy,
domestic and weak;
how lucky, little tree,
to have a pot to grow in.
With living creatures
one must begin very early
to dwarf their growth:
the bound feet,   20
the crippled brain,
the hair in curlers,

the hands you
love to touch.

Marge Piercy (b. 1936)

THE MORNING HALF-LIFE BLUES

Girls buck the wind in the grooves toward work
in fuzzy coats promised to be warm as fur.
The shop windows snicker
flashing them hurrying over dresses they cannot afford:
you are not pretty enough, not pretty enough.

Blown with yesterday's papers through the boiled coffee
    morning
we dream of the stop on the subway without a name,
the door in the heart of the grove of skyscrapers,
that garden where we nestle to the teats of a furry world,
lie in mounds of peony eating grapes,   10
and need barter ourselves for nothing,
not by the hour, not by the pound, not by the skinful,
that party to which no one will give or sell us the key
though we have all thought briefly we found it
drunk or in bed.

Black girls with thin legs and high necks stalking like
    herons,
plump girls with blue legs and green eyelids and strawberry
    breasts,
swept off to be frozen in fluorescent cubes,
the vacuum of your jobs sucks your brains dry
and fills you with the ooze of melted comics.   20
Living is later. This is your rented death.
You grasp at hard commodities and vague lusts
to make up, to pay for each day
which opens like a can and is empty, and then another,
afternoons like dinosaur eggs stuffed with glue.

Girls of the dirty morning, ticketed and spent,
you will be less at forty than at twenty.

Your living is a waste product of somebody's mill.
I would fix you like buds to a city where people work
to make and do things necessary and good,   30
where work is real as bread and babies and trees in parks
where we would all blossom slowly and ripen to sound
    fruit.

Alfred Corn (b. 1943)

FIFTY-SEVENTH STREET AND FIFTH

Hard-edged buildings; cloudless blue enamel;
Lapidary hours—and that numerous woman,
Put-together, in many a smashing
Suit or dress is somehow what it's, well,
All about. A city designed by *Halston:*
Clean lines, tans, grays, expense; no sentiment.
Off the mirrored boxes the afternoon
Glare fires an instant in her sunglasses
And reflects some of the armored ambition
Controlling deed here; plus the byword   10
That "only the best really counts." Awful
And awe-inspiring. How hard the task,
Keeping up to the mark: opinions, output,
Presentation—strong on every front. So?
Life is strife, the city says, a theory
That tastes of iron and demands assent.

A big lump of iron that's been magnetized.
All the faces I see are—Believers,
Pilgrims immigrated from fifty states   20
To discover, to surrender, themselves.
Success. Money. Fame. Insular dreams all,
Begotten of the dream of Manhattan, island
Of the possessed. When a man's tired of New York,
He's tired of life? Or just of possession?
A whirlpool animates the terrific
Streets, violence of our praise, blockbuster
Miracles down every vista, scored by
Accords and discords intrinsic to this air.
Concerted mind performs as the genius   30
Of place: competition, a trust in facts

And expense. Who loves or works here assumes,
For better or worse, the ground rules. A fate.

QUESTIONS

1. What word choices stand out in this description?
2. What seems to be the speaker's attitude towards New York City? Is this a poem of praise?
3. What do you assume is the "fate" referred to?

Nikki Giovanni (b. 1943)
NIKKI-ROSA

childhood   remembrances are always a drag
if you're Black
you always remember things like living in Woodlawn[1]
with no inside toilet
and if you become famous or something
they never talk about how happy you were to have your
   mother
all to yourself and
how good the water felt when you got your bath from one
   of those
big tubs that folk in chicago barbecue in
and somehow when you talk about home   10
it never gets across how much you
understood their feelings
as the whole family attended meetings about Hollydale
and even though you remember
your biographers never understand
your father's pain as he sells his stock
and another dream goes
and though you're poor it isn't poverty that
concerns you   20
and though they fought a lot
it isn't your father's drinking that makes any difference
but only that everybody is together and you

------

[1] A Cincinnati suburb.

and your sister have happy birthdays and very good
   christmasses
and I really hope no white person ever has cause to write
   about me
because they never understand Black love is Black wealth
   and they'll
probably talk about my hard childhood and never
   understand that
all the while I was quite happy

Alice Walker (b. 1944)
LIGHT BAGGAGE

there is a magic
lingering after people
to whom success is merely personal.
who, when the public prepares a feast
for their belated acceptance parties,
pack it up like light baggage
and disappear into the swamps of Florida
or go looking for newer Gods
in the Oak tree country
of Pennsylvania.   10
Or decide, quite suddenly, to try nursing,
midwifery, anonymous among the sick and the poor.
Stories about such people
tell us little;
and if a hundred photographs survive
each one will show a different face.
someone out of step. alone out there, absorbed;
fishing in the waters of experience
a slouched back against the shoulders
of the world.   20

DRAMA

Moliére (1622–1673)
THE MISANTHROPE*

CHARACTERS

Alceste, in love with Célimène
Philinte, Alceste's friend
Oronte, in love with Célimène
Célimène, Alceste's beloved
Eliante, Célimène's cousin
Arsinoé, a friend of Célimène's

Acaste ⎱ marquesses
Clitandre ⎰
Basque, Célimène's servant
A Guard of the Marshalsea
Dubois, Alceste's valet

The scene throughout is in Celimene's house at Paris.

ACT I
SCENE ONE

PHILINTE, ALCESTE

Philinte. Now, what's got into you?
Alceste, seated.   Kindly leave me alone.
Philinte. Come, come, what is it? This lugubrious tone . . .
Alceste. Leave me, I said; you spoil my solitude.
Philinte. Oh, listen to me, now, and don't be rude.
Alceste. I choose to be rude, Sir, and to be hard of hearing.
Philinte. These ugly moods of yours are not endearing;
    Friends though we are, I really must insist . . .
Alceste, abruptly rising.
    Friends? Friends, you say? Well, cross me off your list.
    I've been your friend till now, as you well know;
    But after what I saw a moment ago   10
    I tell you flatly that our ways must part.
    I wish no place in a dishonest heart.
Philinte. Why, what have I done, Alceste? Is this quite just?
Alceste. My God, you ought to die of self-disgust.
    I call your conduct inexcusable, Sir,
    And every man of honor will concur.
    I see you almost hug a man to death,
    Exclaim for joy until you're out of breath,
    And supplement these loving demonstrations

*Translated by Richard Wilbur.

With endless offers, vows, and protestations;   20
Then when I ask you "Who was that?", I find
That you can barely bring his name to mind!
Once the man's back is turned, you cease to love him,
And speak with absolute indifference of him!
By God, I say it's base and scandalous
To falsify the heart's affections thus;
If I caught myself behaving in such a way,
I'd hang myself for shame, without delay.
Philinte. It hardly seems a hanging matter to me;
  I hope that you will take it graciously   30
  If I extend myself a slight reprieve,
  And live a little longer, by your leave.
Alceste. How dare you joke about a crime so grave?
Philinte. What crime? How else are people to behave?
Alceste. I'd have them be sincere, and never part
  With any word that isn't from the heart.
Philinte. When someone greets us with a show of pleasure,
  It's but polite to give him equal measure,
  Return his love the best that we know how,
  And trade him offer for offer, vow for vow.   40
Alceste. No, no, this formula you'd have me follow,
  However fashionable, is false and hollow,
  And I despise the frenzied operations
  Of all these barterers of protestations,
  These lavishers of meaningless embraces,
  These utterers of obliging commonplaces,
  Who court and flatter everyone on earth
  And praise the fool no less than the man of worth.
  Should you rejoice that someone fondles you,
  Offers his love and service, swears to be true,
  And fills your ears with praises of your name,   50
  When to the first damned fop he'll say the same?
  No, no: no self-respecting heart would dream
  Of prizing so promiscuous an esteem;
  However high the praise, there's nothing worse
  Than sharing honors with the universe.
  Esteem is founded on comparison:
  To honor all men is to honor none.
  Since you embrace this indiscriminate vice,
  Your friendship comes at far too cheap a price;   60
  I spurn the easy tribute of a heart
  Which will not set the worthy man apart:
  I choose, Sir, to be chosen; and in fine,
  The friend of mankind is no friend of mine.

Philinte. But in polite society, custom decrees
   That we show certain outward courtesies. . . .
Alceste. Ah, no! we should condemn with all our force
   Such false and artificial intercourse.
   Let men behave like men; let them display
   Their inmost hearts in everything they say;   70
   Let the heart speak, and let our sentiments
   Not mask themselves in silly compliments.
Philinte. In certain cases it would be uncouth
   And most absurd to speak the naked truth;
   With all respect for your exalted notions,
   It's often best to veil one's true emotions.
   Wouldn't the social fabric come undone
   If we were wholly frank with everyone?
   Suppose you met with someone you couldn't bear;
   Would you inform him of it then and there?   80
Alceste. Yes.
Philinte.   Then you'd tell old Emilie it's pathetic
   The way she daubs her features with cosmetic
   And plays the gay coquette at sixty-four?
Alceste. I would.
Philinte.   And you'd call Dorilas a bore,
   And tell him every ear at court is lame
   From hearing him brag about his noble name?
Alceste. Precisely.
Philinte.   Ah, you're joking.
Alceste.   Au contraire:
   In this regard there's none I'd choose to spare.
   All are corrupt; there's nothing to be seen
   In court or town but aggravates my spleen.   90
   I fall into deep gloom and melancholy
   When I survey the scene of human folly,
   Finding on every hand base flattery,
   Injustice, fraud, self-interest, treachery. . . .
   Ah, it's too much; mankind has grown so base,
   I mean to break with the whole human race.
Philinte. This philosophic rage is a bit extreme;
   You've no idea how comical you seem;
   Indeed, we're like those brothers in the play
   Called *School for Husbands*, one of whom was prey . . .   100
Alceste. Enough, now! None of your stupid similes.
Philinte. Then let's have no more tirades, if you please.
   The world won't change, whatever you say or do;
   And since plain speaking means so much to you,
   I'll tell you plainly that by being frank

You've earned the reputation of a crank,
And that you're thought ridiculous when you rage
And rant against the manners of the age.
Alceste. So much the better; just what I wish to hear.
No news could be more grateful to my ear.   110
All men are so detestable in my eyes,
I should be sorry if they thought me wise.
Philinte. Your hatred's very sweeping, is it not?
Alceste. Quite right: I hate the whole degraded lot.
Philinte. Must all poor human creatures be embraced,
Without distinction, by your vast distaste?
Even in these bad times, there are surely a few . . .
Alceste. No, I include all men in one dim view:
Some men I hate for being rogues; the others
I hate because they treat the rogues like brothers,   120
And, lacking a virtuous scorn for what is vile,
Receive the villain with a complaisant smile.
Notice how tolerant people choose to be
Toward that bold rascal who's at law with me.
His social polish can't conceal his nature;
One sees at once that he's a treacherous creature;
No one could possibly be taken in
By those soft speeches and that sugary grin.
The whole world knows the shady means by which
The low-brow's grown so powerful and rich,   130
And risen to a rank so bright and high
That virtue can but blush, and merit sigh.
Whenever his name comes up in conversation,
None will defend his wretched reputation;
Call him knave, liar, scoundrel, and all the rest,
Each head will nod, and no one will protest.
And yet his smirk is seen in every house,
He's greeted everywhere with smiles and bows,
And when there's any honor that can be got
By pulling strings, he'll get it, like as not.   140
My God! It chills my heart to see the ways
Men come to terms with evil nowadays;
Sometimes, I swear, I'm moved to flee and find
Some desert land unfouled by humankind.
Philinte. Come, let's forget the follies of the times
And pardon mankind for its petty crimes;
Let's have an end of rantings and of railings,
And show some leniency toward human failings.
This world requires a pliant rectitude;

Too stern a virtue makes one stiff and rude;   150
Good sense views all extremes with detestation,
And bids us to be noble in moderation.
The rigid virtues of the ancient days
Are not for us, they jar with all our ways
And ask of us too lofty a perfection.
Wise men accept their times without objection,
And there's no greater folly, if you ask me,
Than trying to reform society.
Like you, I see each day a hundred and one
Unhandsome deeds that might be better done,
But still, for all the faults that meet my view,
I'm never known to storm and rave like you.
I take men as they are, or let them be,
And teach my soul to bear their frailty;
And whether in court or town, whatever the scene,
My phlegm's as philosophic as your spleen.
Alceste. This phlegm which you so eloquently commend,
  Does nothing ever rile it up, my friend?
  Suppose some man you trust should treacherously
  Conspire to rob you of your property,   170
  And do his best to wreck your reputation?
  Wouldn't you feel a certain indignation?
Philinte. Why, no. These faults of which you so complain
  Are part of human nature, I maintain,
  And it's no more a matter for disgust
  That men are knavish, selfish and unjust,
  Than that the vulture dines upon the dead,
  And wolves are furious, and apes ill-bred.
Alceste. Shall I see myself betrayed, robbed, torn to bits,
  And not . . . Oh, let's be still and rest our wits.   180
  Enough of reasoning, now. I've had my fill.
Philinte. Indeed, you would do well, Sir, to be still.
  Rage less at your opponent, and give some thought
  To how you'll win this lawsuit that he's brought.
Alceste. I assure you I'll do nothing of the sort.
Philinte. Then who will plead your case before the court?
Alceste. Reason and right and justice will plead for me.
Philinte. Oh, Lord. What judges do you plan to see?
Alceste. Why, none. The justice of my cause is clear.
Philinte. Of course, man; but there's politics to fear. . . .   190
Alceste. No, I refuse to lift a hand. That's flat.
  I'm either right, or wrong.
Philinte.   Don't count on that.

Alceste. No, I'll do nothing.
Philinte.   Your enemy's influence
 Is great, you know . . .
Alceste.   That makes no difference.
Philinte. It will; you'll see.
Alceste.   Must honor bow to guile?
 If so, I shall be proud to lose the trial.
Philinte. Oh, really . . .
Alceste.   I'll discover by this case
 Whether or not men are sufficiently base
 And impudent and villainous and perverse
 To do me wrong before the universe.   200
Philinte. What a man!
Alceste.   Oh, I could wish, whatever the cost,
 Just for the beauty of it, that my trial were lost.
Philinte. If people heard you talking so, Alceste,
 They'd split their sides. Your name would be a jest.
Alceste. So much the worse for jesters.
Philinte.   May I enquire
 Whether this rectitude you so admire,
 And these hard virtues you're enamored of
 Are qualities of the lady whom you love?
 It much surprises me that you, who seem
 To view mankind with furious disesteem,   210
 Have yet found something to enchant your eyes
 Amidst a species which you so despise.
 And what is more amazing, I'm afraid,
 Is the most curious choice your heart has made.
 The honest Eliante is fond of you,
 Arsinoé, the prude, admires you too;
 And yet your spirit's been perversely led
 To choose the flighty Célimène instead,
 Whose brittle malice and coquettish ways
 So typify the manners of our days.   220
 How is it that the traits you most abhor
 Are bearable in this lady you adore?
 Are you so blind with love that you can't find them?
 Or do you contrive, in her case, not to mind them?
Alceste. My love for that young widow's not the kind
 That can't perceive defects; no, I'm not blind.
 I see her faults, despite my ardent love,
 And all I see I fervently reprove.
 And yet I'm weak; for all her falsity,
 That woman knows the art of pleasing me,   230
 And though I never cease complaining of her,

I swear I cannot manage not to love her.
Her charm outweighs her faults; I can but aim
To cleanse her spirit in my love's pure flame.
Philinte. That's no small task; I wish you all success.
   You think then that she loves you?
Alceste.   Heavens yes!
   I wouldn't love her did she not love me.
Philinte. Well, if her taste for you is plain to see,
   Why do these rivals cause you such despair?
Alceste. True love, Sir, is possessive, and cannot bear   240
   To share with all the world. I'm here today
   To tell her she must send that mob away.
Philinte. If I were you, and had your choice to make,
   Eliante, her cousin, would be the one I'd take;
   That honest heart, which cares for you alone,
   Would harmonize far better with your own.
Alceste. True, true: each day my reason tells me so;
   But reason doesn't rule in love, you know.
Philinte. I fear some bitter sorrow is in store;
   This love . . .

SCENE TWO

ORONTE, ALCESTE, PHILINTE

Oronte, to Alceste. The servants told me at the door
   That Eliante and Célimène were out,
   But when I heard, dear Sir, that you were about,
   I came to say, without exaggeration,
   That I hold you in the vastest admiration,
   And that it's always been my dearest desire
   To be the friend of one I so admire.
   I hope to see my love of merit requited,
   And you and I in friendship's bond united.
   I'm sure you won't refuse—if I may be frank—   10
   A friend of my devotedness—and rank.

*(During this speech of Oronte's, Alceste is abstracted, and seems unaware
that he is being spoken to. He only breaks off his reverie when Oronte
says:)*

It was for you, if you please, that my words were intended.
Alceste. For me, Sir?
Oronte.   Yes, for you. You're not offended?

Alceste. By no means. But this much surprises me. . . .
   The honor comes most unexpectedly. . . .
Oronte. My high regard should not astonish you;
   The whole world feels the same. It is your due.
Alceste. Sir . . .
Oronte.   Why, in all the State there isn't one
   Can match your merits; they shine, Sir, like the sun.
Alceste. Sir . . .
Oronte.   You are higher in my estimation   20
   Than all that's most illustrious in the nation.
Alceste. Sir . . .
Oronte.   If I lie, may heaven strike me dead!
   To show you that I mean what I have said,
   Permit me, Sir, to embrace you most sincerely,
   And swear that I will prize our friendship dearly.
   Give me your hand. And now, Sir, if you choose,
   We'll make our vows.
Alceste.   Sir . . .
Oronte.   What! You refuse?
Alceste. Sir, it's a very great honor you extend:
   But friendship is a sacred thing, my friend;
   It would be profanation to bestow   30
   The name of friend on one you hardly know.
   All parts are better played when well-rehearsed;
   Let's put off friendship, and get acquainted first.
   We may discover it would be unwise
   To try to make our natures harmonize.
Oronte. By heaven! You're sagacious to the core;
   This speech has made me admire you even more.
   Let time, then, bring us closer day by day;
   Meanwhile, I shall be yours in every way.
   If, for example, there should be anything   40
   You wish at court, I'll mention it to the King.
   I have his ear, of course; it's quite well known
   That I am much in favor with the throne.
   In short, I am your servant. And now, dear friend,
   Since you have such fine judgment, I intend
   To please you, if I can, with a small sonnet
   I wrote not long ago. Please comment on it,
   And tell me whether I ought to publish it.
Alceste. You must excuse me, Sir; I'm hardly fit
   To judge such matters.
Oronte.   Why not?
Alceste.   I am, I fear,   50
   Inclined to be unfashionably sincere.

Oronte. Just what I ask; I'd take no satisfaction
   In anything but your sincere reaction.
   I beg you not to dream of being kind.
Alceste. Since you desire it, Sir, I'll speak my mind.
Oronte. Sonnet. It's a sonnet. . . . *Hope* . . . The poem's addressed
   To a lady who wakened hopes within my breast.
   Hope . . . this is not the pompous sort of thing,
   Just modest little verses, with a tender ring.
Alceste. Well, we shall see.
Oronte.   *Hope* . . . I'm anxious to hear   60
   Whether the style seems properly smooth and clear,
   And whether the choice of words is good or bad.
Alceste. We'll see, we'll see.
Oronte.   Perhaps I ought to add
   That it took me only a quarter-hour to write it.
Alceste. The time's irrelevant, Sir: kindly recite it.
Oronte, reading.

Hope comforts us awhile, t'is true,
Lulling our cares with careless laughter,
And yet such joy is full of rue,
My Phyllis, if nothing follows after.

Philinte. I'm charmed by this already; the style's delightful.   70
Alceste, sotto voce, to Philinte.
   How can you say that? Why, the thing is frightful.
Oronte.

Your fair face smiled on me awhile,
But was it kindness so to enchant me?
'Twould have been fairer not to smile,
If hope was all you meant to grant me.

Philinte. What a clever thought! How handsomely you phrase it!
Alceste, sotto voce, to Philinte.
   You know the thing is trash. How dare you praise it?
Oronte.

If it's to be my passion's fate
Thus everlastingly to wait,
Then death will come to set me free: 80
For death is fairer than the fair;
Phyllis, to hope is to despair
When one must hope eternally.

Philinte. The close is exquisite—full of feeling and grace.
Alceste, sotto voce, aside.
    Oh, blast the close; you'd better close your face
    Before you send your lying soul to hell.
Philinte. I can't remember a poem I've liked so well.
Alceste, sotto voce, aside.
    Good Lord!
Oronte, to Philinte.
             I fear you're flattering me a bit.
Philinte. Oh, no!
Alceste, sotto voce, aside.
             What else d'you call it, you hypocrite?
Oronte, to Alceste.
    But you, Sir, keep your promise now: don't shrink   90
    From telling me sincerely what you think.
Alceste. Sir, these are delicate matters; we all desire
    To be told that we've the true poetic fire.
    But once, to one whose name I shall not mention,
    I said, regarding some verse of his invention,
    That gentlemen should rigorously control
    That itch to write which often afflicts the soul;
    That one should curb the heady inclination
    To publicize one's little avocation;
    And that in showing off one's works of art   100
    One often plays a very clownish part.
Oronte. Are you suggesting in a devious way
    That I ought not . . .
Alceste.   Oh, that I do not say.
    Further, I told him that no fault is worse
    Than that of writing frigid, lifeless verse,
    And that the merest whisper of such a shame
    Suffices to destroy a man's good name.
Oronte. D'you mean to say my sonnet's dull and trite?
Alceste. I don't say that. But I went on to cite   110
    Numerous cases of once-respected men
    Who came to grief by taking up the pen.
Oronte. And am I like them? Do I write so poorly?
Alceste. I don't say that. But I told this person, "Surely
    You're under no necessity to compose;
    Why you should wish to publish, heaven knows.
    There's no excuse for printing tedious rot
    Unless one writes for bread, as you do not.
    Resist temptation, then, I beg of you;
    Conceal your pastimes from the public view;   120
    And don't give up, on any provocation,

Your present high and courtly reputation,
To purchase at a greedy printer's shop
The name of silly author and scribbling fop."
These were the points I tried to make him see.
Oronte. I sense that they are also aimed at me;
  But now—about my sonnet—I'd like to be told . . .
Alceste. Frankly, that sonnet should be pigeonholed.
  You've chosen the worst models to imitate.
  The style's unnatural. Let me illustrate: 130

For example, *Your fair face smiled on me awhile,*
Followed by, *'Twould have been fairer not to smile!*
Or this: *such joy is full of rue;*
Or this: *For death is fairer than the fair;*
Or, *Phyllis, to hope is to despair*
    When one must hope eternally!

This artificial style, that's all the fashion,
Has neither taste, nor honesty, nor passion;
It's nothing but a sort of wordy play,
And nature never spoke in such a way.   140
What, in this shallow age, is not debased?
Our fathers, though less refined, had better taste;
I'd barter all that men admire today
For one old love-song I shall try to say:

If the King had given me for my own
Paris, his citadel,
And I for that must leave alone
Her whom I love so well,
I'd say then to the Crown,
Take back your glittering town;   150
My darling is more fair, I swear,
My darling is more fair.

  The rhyme's not rich, the style is rough and old,
  But don't you see that it's the purest gold
  Beside the tinsel nonsense now preferred,
  And that there's passion in its every word?

If the King had given me for my own
Paris, his citadel,
And I for that must leave alone
Her whom I love so well,   160
I'd say then to the Crown,

Take back your glittering town;
My darling is more fair, I swear,
My darling is more fair.

There speaks a loving heart. (*To Philinte*) You're laughing, eh?
Laugh on, my precious wit. Whatever you say,
I hold that song's worth all the bibelots
That people hail today with ah's and oh's.
Oronte. And I maintain my sonnet's very good.
Alceste. It's not at all surprising that you should.   170
   You have your reasons; permit me to have mine
   For thinking that you cannot write a line.
Oronte. Others have praised my sonnet to the skies.
Alceste. I lack their art of telling pleasant lies.
Oronte. You seem to think you've got no end of wit.
Alceste. To praise your verse, I'd need still more of it.
Oronte. I'm not in need of your approval, Sir.
Alceste. That's good; you couldn't have it if you were.
Oronte. Come now, I'll lend you the subject of my sonnet;
   I'd like to see you try to improve upon it.   180
Alceste. I might, by chance, write something just as shoddy;
   But then I wouldn't show it to everybody.
Oronte. You're most opinionated and conceited.
Alceste. Go find your flatterers, and be better treated.
Oronte. Look here, my little fellow, pray watch your tone.
Alceste. My great big fellow, you'd better watch your own.
Philinte, stepping between them.
   Oh, please, please, gentlemen! This will never do.
Oronte. The fault is mine, and I leave the field to you.
   I am your servant, Sir, in every way.
Alceste. And I, Sir, am your most abject valet.   190

SCENE THREE

PHILINTE, ALCESTE

Philinte. Well, as you see, sincerity in excess
   Can get you into a very pretty mess;
   Oronte was hungry for appreciation. . . .
Alceste. Don't speak to me.
Philinte.   What?
Alceste.   No more conversation.
Philinte. Really, now . . .
Alceste.   Leave me alone.

Philinte.   If I . . .
Alceste.   Out of my sight!
Philinte. But what . . .
Alceste.   I won't listen.
Philinte.   But . . .
Alceste.   Silence!
Philinte.   Now, is it polite . . .
Alceste. By heaven, I've had enough. Don't follow me.
Philinte. Ah, you're just joking. I'll keep you company.

ACT II
SCENE ONE

ALCESTE, CELIMENE

Alceste. Shall I speak plainly, Madam? I confess
  Your conduct gives me infinite distress,
  And my resentment's grown too hot to smother.
  Soon, I foresee, we'll break with one another.
  If I said otherwise, I should deceive you;
  Sooner or later, I shall be forced to leave you,
  And if I swore that we shall never part,
  I should misread the omens of my heart.
Celimene. You kindly saw me home, it would appear,
  So as to pour invectives in my ear.   10
Alceste. I've no desire to quarrel. But I deplore
  Your inability to shut the door
  On all these suitors who beset you so.
  There's what annoys me, if you care to know.
Celimene. Is it my fault that all these men pursue me?
  Am I to blame if they're attracted to me?
  And when they gently beg an audience,
  Ought I to take a stick and drive them hence?
Alceste. Madam, there's no necessity for a stick;
  A less responsive heart would do the trick.   20
  Of your attractiveness I don't complain;
  But those your charms attract, you then detain
  By a most melting and receptive manner,
  And so enlist their hearts beneath your banner.
  It's the agreeable hopes which you excite
  That keep these lovers round you day and night;
  Were they less liberally smiled upon,
  That sighing troop would very soon be gone.
  But tell me, Madam, why it is that lately

This man Clitandre interests you so greatly?   30
Because of what high merits do you deem
Him worthy of the honor of your esteem?
Is it that your admiring glances linger
On the splendidly long nail of his little finger?
Or do you share the general deep respect
For the blond wig he chooses to affect?
Are you in love with his embroidered hose?
Do you adore his ribbons and his bows?
Or is it that this paragon bewitches
Your tasteful eye with his vast German breeches?   40
Perhaps his giggle, or his falsetto voice,
Makes him the latest gallant of your choice?
Celimene. You're much mistaken to resent him so.
Why I put up with him you surely know:
My lawsuit's very shortly to be tried,
And I must have his influence on my side.
Alceste. Then lose your lawsuit, Madam, or let it drop;
Don't torture me by humoring such a fop.
Celimene. You're jealous of the whole world, Sir.
Alceste.   That's true,
Since the whole world is well-received by you.   50
Celimene. That my good nature is so unconfined
Should serve to pacify your jealous mind;
Were I to smile on one, and scorn the rest,
Then you might have some cause to be distressed.
Alceste. Well, if I mustn't be jealous, tell me, then,
Just how I'm better treated than other men.
Celimene. You know you have my love. Will that not do?
Alceste. What proof have I that what you say is true?
Celimene. I would expect, Sir, that my having said it
Might give the statement a sufficient credit.   60
Alceste. But how can I be sure that you don't tell
The selfsame thing to other men as well?
Celimene. What a gallant speech! How flattering to me!
What a sweet creature you make me out to be!
Well then, to save you from the pangs of doubt,
All that I've said I hereby cancel out;
Now, none but yourself shall make a monkey of you:
Are you content?
Alceste.   Why, why am I doomed to love you?
I swear that I shall bless the blissful hour
When this poor heart's no longer in your power!   70
I make no secret of it: I've done my best
To exorcise this passion from my breast;

But thus far all in vain; it will not go;
  It's for my sins that I must love you so.
Celimene. Your love for me is matchless, Sir; that's clear.
Alceste. Indeed, in all the world it has no peer;
  Words can't describe the nature of my passion,
  And no man ever loved in such a fashion.
Celimene. Yes, it's a brand-new fashion, I agree:
  You show your love by castigating me,
  And all your speeches are enraged and rude.
  I've never been so furiously wooed.
Alceste. Yet you could calm that fury, if you chose.
  Come, shall we bring our quarrels to a close?
  Let's speak with open hearts, then, and begin . . .

80

SCENE TWO

CELIMENE, ALCESTE, BASQUE

Celimene. What is it?
Basque.   Acaste is here.
Celimene.   Well, send him in.

SCENE THREE

CELIMENE, ALCESTE

Alceste. What! Shall we never be alone at all?
  You're always ready to receive a call,
  And you can't bear, for ten ticks of the clock,
  Not to keep open house for all who knock.
Celimene. I couldn't refuse him: he'd be most put out.
Alceste. Surely that's not worth worrying about.
Celimene. Acaste would never forgive me if he guessed
  That I consider him a dreadful pest.
Alceste. If he's a pest, why bother with him then?
Celimene. Heavens! One can't antagonize such men;
  Why, they're the chartered gossips of the court,
  And have a say in things of every sort.
  One must receive them, and be full of charm;
  They're no great help, but they can do you harm,
  And though your influence be ever so great,
  They're hardly the best people to alienate.
Alceste. I see, dear lady, that you could make a case
  For putting up with the whole human race;
  These friendships that you calculate so nicely . . .

10

SCENE FOUR

ALCESTE, CELIMENE, BASQUE

Basque. Madam, Clitandre is here as well.
Alceste.   Precisely.
Celimene. Where are you going?
Alceste.   Elsewhere.
Celimene.   Stay.
Alceste.   No, no.
Celimene. Stay, Sir.
Alceste.   I can't.
Celimene.   I wish it.
Alceste.   No, I must go.
   I beg you, Madam, not to press the matter;
   You know I have no taste for idle chatter.
Celimene. Stay: I command you.
Alceste.   No, I cannot stay.
Celimene. Very well; you have my leave to go away.

SCENE FIVE

ELIANTE, PHILINTE, ACASTE, CLITANDRE, ALCESTE, CELIMENE, BASQUE

Eliante, to Celimene.
   The Marquesses have kindly come to call.
   Were they announced?
Celimene.   Yes. Basque, bring chairs for all.

   (*Basque provides the chairs, and exits.*)
   (*To Alceste*)

   You haven't gone?
Alceste.   No; and I shan't depart
   Till you decide who's foremost in your heart.
Celimene. Oh, hush.
Alceste.   It's time to choose; take them, or me.
Celimene. You're mad.
Alceste.   I'm not, as you shall shortly see.
Celimene. Oh?
Alceste.   You'll decide.
Celimene.   You're joking now, dear friend.
Alceste. No, no; you'll choose, my patience is at an end.

Clitandre. Madam, I come from court, where poor Cléonte
   Behaved like a perfect fool, as is his wont.   10
   Has he no friend to counsel him, I wonder,
   And teach him less unerringly to blunder?
Celimene. It's true, the man's a most accomplished dunce;
   His gauche behavior charms the eye at once;
   And every time one sees him, on my word,
   His manner's grown a trifle more absurd.
Acaste. Speaking of dunces, I've just now conversed
   With old Damon, who's one of the very worst;
   I stood a lifetime in the broiling sun
   Before his dreary monologue was done.   20
Celimene. Oh, he's a wondrous talker, and has the power
   To tell you nothing hour after hour:
   If, by mistake, he ever came to the point,
   The shock would put his jawbone out of joint.
Eliante, to Philinte.
   The conversation takes it usual turn,
   And all our dear friends' ears will shortly burn.
Clitandre. Timante's a character, Madam.
Celimene.   Isn't he, though?
   A man of mystery from top to toe,
   Who moves about in a romantic mist
   On secret missions which do not exist.
   His talk is full of eyebrows and grimaces;   30
   How tired one gets of his momentous faces;
   He's always whispering something confidential
   Which turns out to be quite inconsequential;
   Nothing's too slight for him to mystify;
   He even whispers when he says "good-by."
Acaste. Tell us about Géralde.
Celimene.   That tiresome ass.
   He mixes only with the titled class,
   And fawns on dukes and princes, and is bored
   With anyone who's not at least a lord.   40
   The man's obsessed with rank, and his discourses
   Are all of hounds and carriages and horses;
   He uses Christian names with all the great,
   And the word Milord, with him, is out of date.
Clitandre. He's very taken with Bélise, I hear.
Celimene. She is the dreariest company, poor dear.
   Whenever she comes to call, I grope about
   To find some topic which will draw her out,
   But, owing to her dry and faint replies,

The conversation wilts, and droops, and dies.   50
In vain one hopes to animate her face
By mentioning the ultimate commonplace;
But sun or shower, even hail or frost
Are matters she can instantly exhaust.
Meanwhile her visit, painful though it is,
Drags on and on through mute eternities,
And though you ask the time, and yawn, and yawn,
She sits there like a stone and won't be gone.

Acaste. Now for Adraste.
Celimene.   Oh, that conceited elf
Has a gigantic passion for himself;   60
He rails against the court, and cannot bear it
That none will recognize his hidden merit;
All honors given to others give offense
To his imaginary excellence.
Clitandre. What about young Cléon? His house, they say,
Is full of the best society, night and day.
Celimene. His cook has made him popular, not he:
It's Cléon's table that people come to see.
Eliante. He gives a splendid dinner, you must admit.
Celimene. But must he serve himself along with it?   70
For my taste, he's a most insipid dish
Whose presence sours the wine and spoils the fish.
Philinte. Damis, his uncle, is admired no end.
What's your opinion, Madam?
Celimene.   Why, he's my friend.
Philinte. He seems a decent fellow, and rather clever.
Celimene. He works too hard at cleverness, however.
I hate to see him sweat and struggle so
To fill his conversation with bons mots.
Since he's decided to become a wit
His taste's so pure that nothing pleases it;   80
He scolds at all the latest books and plays,
Thinking that wit must never stoop to praise,
That finding fault's a sign of intellect,
That all appreciation is abject,
And that by damning everything in sight
One shows oneself in a distinguished light.
He's scornful even of our conversations:
Their trivial nature sorely tries his patience;
He folds his arms, and stands above the battle,
And listens sadly to our childish prattle.   90
Acaste. Wonderful, Madam! You've hit him off precisely.
Clitandre. No one can sketch a character so nicely.

Alceste. How bravely, Sirs, you cut and thrust at all
  These absent fools, till one by one they fall:
  But let one come in sight, and you'll at once
  Embrace the man you lately called a dunce,
  Telling him in a tone sincere and fervent
  How proud you are to be his humble servant.
Clitandre. Why pick on us? Madame's been speaking, Sir,
  And you should quarrel, if you must, with her.   100
Alceste. No, no, by God, the fault is yours, because
  You lead her on with laughter and applause,
  And make her think that she's the more delightful
  The more her talk is scandalous and spiteful.
  Oh, she would stoop to malice far, far less
  If no such claque approved her cleverness.
  It's flatterers like you whose foolish praise
  Nourishes all the vices of these days.
Philinte. But why protest when someone ridicules
  Those you'd condemn, yourself, as knaves or fools?   110
Celimene. Why, Sir? Because he loves to make a fuss.
  You don't expect him to agree with us,
  When there's an opportunity to express
  His heaven-sent spirit of contrariness?
  What other people think, he can't abide;
  Whatever they say, he's on the other side;
  He lives in deadly terror of agreeing;
  'Twould make him seem an ordinary being.
  Indeed, he's so in love with contradiction,
  He'll turn against his most profound conviction   120
  And with a furious eloquence deplore it,
  If only someone else is speaking for it.
Alceste. Go on, dear lady, mock me as you please;
  You have your audience in ecstasies.
Philinte. But what she says is true: you have a way
  Of bridling at whatever people say;
  Whether they praise or blame, your angry spirit
  Is equally unsatisfied to hear it.
Alceste. Men, Sir, are always wrong, and that's the reason
  That righteous anger's never out of season;   130
  All that I hear in all their conversation
  Is flattering praise or reckless condemnation.
Celimene. But . . .
Alceste.   No, no, Madam, I am forced to state
  That you have pleasures which I deprecate,
  And that these others, here, are much to blame
  For nourishing the faults which are your shame.

Clitandre. I shan't defend myself, Sir; but I vow
   I'd thought this lady faultless until now.
Acaste. I see her charms and graces, which are many;
   But as for faults, I've never noticed any.   140
Alceste. I see them, Sir; and rather than ignore them,
   I strenuously criticize her for them.
   The more one loves, the more one should object
   To every blemish, every least defect.
   Were I this lady, I would soon get rid
   Of lovers who approved of all I did,
   And by their slack indulgence and applause
   Endorsed my follies and excused my flaws.
Celimene. If all hearts beat according to your measure,
   The dawn of love would be the end of pleasure;   150
   And love would find its perfect consummation
   In ecstasies of rage and reprobation.
Eliante. Love, as a rule, affects men otherwise,
   And lovers rarely love to criticize.
   They see their lady as a charming blur,
   And find all things commendable in her.
   If she has any blemish, fault, or shame,
   They will redeem it by a pleasing name.
   The pale-faced lady's lily-white, perforce;
   The swarthy one's a sweet brunette, of course;   160
   The spindly lady has a slender grace;
   The fat one has a most majestic pace;
   The plain one, with her dress in disarray,
   They classify as *beauté négligée;*
   The hulking one's a goddess in their eyes,
   The dwarf, a concentrate of Paradise;
   The haughty lady has a noble mind;
   The mean one's witty, and the dull one's kind;
   The chatterbox has liveliness and verve,
   The mute one has a virtuous reserve.   170
   So lovers manage, in their passion's cause,
   To love their ladies even for their flaws.
Alceste. But I still say . . .
Celimene.   I think it would be nice
   To stroll around the gallery once or twice.
   What! You're not going, Sirs?
Clitandre and Acaste   No, Madam, no.
Alceste. You seem to be in terror lest they go.
   Do what you will, Sirs; leave, or linger on,
   But I shan't go till after you are gone.
Acaste. I'm free to linger, unless I should perceive
   Madame is tired, and wishes me to leave.   180

Clitandre. And as for me, I needn't go today
  Until the hour of the King's *coucher.*
Celimene, to Alceste.
  You're joking, surely?
Alceste.   Not in the least; we'll see
  Whether you'd rather part with them, or me.

SCENE SIX

ALCESTE, CELIMENE, ELIANTE, ACASTE, PHILINTE, CLITANDRE, BASQUE

Basque, to Alceste.
  Sir, there's a fellow here who bids me state
  That he must see you, and that it can't wait.
Alceste. Tell him that I have no such pressing affairs.
Basque. It's a long tailcoat that this fellow wears,
  With gold all over.
Celimene, to Alceste.
                       You'd best go down and see.
  Or—have him enter.

SCENE SEVEN

ALCESTE, CELIMENE, ELIANTE, ACASTE, PHILINTE, CLITANDRE, A GUARD
OF THE MARSHALSEA

Alceste, confronting the guard.
                      Well, what do you want with me?
  Come in, Sir.
Guard.   I've a word, Sir, for your ear.
Alceste. Speak it aloud, Sir; I shall strive to hear.
Guard. The Marshals have instructed me to say
  You must report to them without delay.
Alceste. Who? Me, Sir?
Guard.   Yes, Sir; you.
Alceste.   But what do they want?
Philinte, to Alceste.
  To scotch your silly quarrel with Oronte.
Celimene, to Philinte.
  What quarrel?
Philinte.   Oronte and he have fallen out
  Over some verse he spoke his mind about;
  The Marshals wish to arbitrate the matter.
Alceste. Never shall I equivocate or flatter!   10
Philinte. You'd best obey their summons; come, let's go.

Alceste. How can they mend our quarrel, I'd like to know?
    Am I to make a cowardly retraction,
    And praise those jingles to his satisfaction?
    I'll not recant; I've judged that sonnet rightly.
    It's bad.
Philinte.   But you might say so more politely. . . .
Alceste. I'll not back down; his verses make me sick.
Philinte. If only you could be more politic!
    But come, let's go.
Alceste.   I'll go, but I won't unsay
    A single word.
Philinte.   Well, let's be on our way.

20

Alceste. Till I am ordered by my lord the King
    To praise that poem, I shall say the thing
    Is scandalous, by God, and that the poet
    Ought to be hanged for having the nerve to show it.
    (To Clitandre and Acaste, who are laughing)
    By heavens, Sirs, I really didn't know
    That I was being humorous.
Celimene.   Go, Sir, go;
    Settle your business.
Alceste.   I shall, and when I'm through,
    I shall return to settle things with you.

ACT III
SCENE ONE

CLITANDRE, ACASTE

Clitandre. Dear Marquess, how contented you appear;
    All things delight you, nothing mars your cheer.
    Can you, in perfect honesty, declare
    That you've a right to be so debonair?
Acaste. By Jove, when I survey myself, I find
    No cause whatever for distress of mind.
    I'm young and rich; I can in modesty
    Lay claim to an exalted pedigree;
    And owing to my name and my condition
    I shall not want for honors and position.

10

    Then as to courage, that most precious trait,
    I seem to have it, as was proved of late
    Upon the field of honor, where my bearing,
    They say, was very cool and rather daring.
    I've wit, of course; and taste in such perfection

That I can judge without the least reflection,
And at the theater, which is my delight,
Can make or break a play on opening night,
And lead the crowd in hisses or bravos,
And generally be known as one who knows.   20
I'm clever, handsome, gracefully polite;
My waist is small, my teeth are strong and white;
As for my dress, the world's astonished eyes
Assure me that I bear away the prize.
I find myself in favor everywhere,
Honored by men, and worshiped by the fair;
And since these things are so, it seems to me
I'm justified in my complacency.
Clitandre. Well, if so many ladies hold you dear,
Why do you press a hopeless courtship here?   30
Acaste. Hopeless, you say? I'm not the sort of fool
That likes his ladies difficult and cool.
Men who are awkward, shy, and peasantish
May pine for heartless beauties, if they wish,
Grovel before them, bear their cruelties,
Woo them with tears and sighs and bended knees,
And hope by dogged faithfulness to gain
What their poor merits never could obtain.
For men like me, however, it makes no sense
To love on trust, and foot the whole expense.   40
Whatever any lady's merits be,
I think, thank God, that I'm as choice as she;
That if my heart is kind enough to burn
For her, she owes me something in return;
And that in any proper love affair
The partners must invest an equal share.
Clitandre. You think, then, that our hostess favors you?
Acaste. I've reason to believe that that is true.
Clitandre. How did you come to such a mad conclusion?
You're blind, dear fellow. This is sheer delusion.   50
Acaste. All right, then: I'm deluded and I'm blind.
Clitandre. Whatever put the notion in your mind?
Acaste. Delusion.
Clitandre.   What persuades you that you're right?
Acaste. I'm blind.
Clitandre.   But have you any proofs to cite?
Acaste. I tell you I'm deluded.
Clitandre.   Have you, then,
Received some secret pledge from Célimène?
Acaste. Oh, no: she scorns me.

Clitandre.   Tell me the truth, I beg.

Acaste. She just can't bear me.

Clitandre.   Ah, don't pull my leg.
Tell me what hope she's given you, I pray.

Acaste. I'm hopeless, and it's you who win the day.   60
She hates me thoroughly, and I'm so vexed
I mean to hang myself on Tuesday next.

Clitandre. Dear Marquess, let us have an armistice
And make a treaty. What do you say to this?
If ever one of us can plainly prove
That Célimène encourages his love,
The other must abandon hope, and yield,
And leave him in possession of the field.

Acaste. Now, there's a bargain that appeals to me;
With all my heart, dear Marquess, I agree.   70
But hush.

SCENE TWO

CELIMENE, ACASTE, CLITANDRE

Celimene. Still here?

Clitandre.   T'was love that stayed our feet.

Celimene. I think I heard a carriage in the street.
Whose is it? D'you know?

SCENE THREE

CELIMENE, ACASTE, CLITANDRE, BASQUE

Basque.   Arsinoé is here,
Madame.

Celimene.   Arsinoé, you say? Oh, dear.

Basque. Eliante is entertaining her below.

Celimene. What brings the creature here, I'd like to know?

Acaste. They say she's dreadfully prudish, but in fact
I think her piety . . .

Celimene.   It's all an act.
At heart she's worldly, and her poor success
In snaring men explains her prudishness.
It breaks her heart to see the beaux and gallants
Engrossed by other women's charms and talents,
And so she's always in a jealous rage   10
Against the faulty standards of the age.
She lets the world believe that she's a prude

To justify her loveless solitude,
And strives to put a brand of moral shame
On all the graces that she cannot claim.
But still she'd love a lover; and Alceste
Appears to be the one she'd love the best.
His visits here are poison to her pride;
She seems to think I've lured him from her side;
And everywhere, at court or in the town,   20
The spiteful, envious woman runs me down.
In short, she's just as stupid as can be,
Vicious and arrogant in the last degree,
And . . .

SCENE FOUR

ARSINOE, CELIMENE, CLITANDRE, ACASTE

Celimene. Ah! What happy chance has brought you here?
    I've thought about you ever so much, my dear.
Arsinoe. I've come to tell you something you should know.
Celimene. How good of you to think of doing so!

(Clitandre and Acaste go out, laughing.)

SCENE FIVE

ARSINOE, CELIMENE

Arsinoe. It's just as well those gentlemen didn't tarry.
Celimene. Shall we sit down?
Arsinoe.   That won't be necessary.
    Madam, the flame of friendship ought to burn
    Brightest in matters of the most concern,
    And as there's nothing which concerns us more
    Than honor, I have hastened to your door
    To bring you, as your friend, some information
    About the status of your reputation.
    I visited, last night, some virtuous folk,
    And, quite by chance, it was of you they spoke;   10
    There was, I fear, no tendency to praise
    Your light behavior and your dashing ways.
    The quantity of gentlemen you see
    And your by now notorious coquetry
    Were both so vehemently criticized
    By everyone, that I was much surprised.

Of course, I needn't tell you where I stood;
I came to your defense as best I could,
Assured them you were harmless, and declared
Your soul was absolutely unimpaired.   20
But there are some things, you must realize,
One can't excuse, however hard one tries,
And I was forced at last into conceding
That your behavior, Madam, is misleading,
That it makes a bad impression, giving rise
To ugly gossip and obscene surmise,
And that if you were more *overtly* good,
You wouldn't be so much misunderstood.
Not that I think you've been unchaste—no! no!
The saints preserve me from a thought so low!   30
But mere good conscience never did suffice:
One must avoid the outward show of vice.
Madam, you're too intelligent, I'm sure,
To think my motives anything but pure
In offering you this counsel—which I do
Out of a zealous interest in you.
Celimene. Madam, I haven't taken you amiss;
I'm very much obliged to you for this;
And I'll at once discharge the obligation
By telling you about *your* reputation.   40
You've been so friendly as to let me know
What certain people say of me, and so
I mean to follow your benign example
By offering you a somewhat similar sample.
The other day, I went to an affair
And found some most distinguished people there
Discussing piety, both false and true.
The conversation soon came round to you.
Alas! Your prudery and bustling zeal
Appeared to have a very slight appeal.   50
Your affectation of a grave demeanor,
Your endless talk of virtue and of honor,
The aptitude of your suspicious mind
For finding sin where there is none to find,
Your towering self-esteem, that pitying face
With which you contemplate the human race,
Your sermonizings and your sharp aspersions
On people's pure and innocent diversions—
All these were mentioned, Madam, and, in fact,
Were roundly and concertedly attacked.   60
"What good," they said, "are all these outward shows,

When everything belies her pious pose?
She prays incessantly; but then, they say,
She beats her maids and cheats them of their pay;
She shows her zeal in every holy place,
But still she's vain enough to paint her face;
She holds that naked statues are immoral,
But with a naked *man* she'd have no quarrel."
Of course, I said to everybody there
That they were being viciously unfair;   70
But still they were disposed to criticize you,
And all agreed that someone should advise you
To leave the morals of the world alone,
And worry rather more about your own.
They felt that one's self-knowledge should be great
Before one thinks of setting others straight;
That one should learn the art of living well
Before one threatens other men with hell,
And that the Church is best equipped, no doubt,
To guide our souls and root our vices out.   80
Madam, you're too intelligent, I'm sure,
To think my motives anything but pure
In offering you this counsel—which I do
Out of a zealous interest in you.
Arsinoe. I dared not hope for gratitude, but I
    Did not expect so acid a reply;
    I judge, since you've been so extremely tart,
    That my good counsel pierced you to the heart.
Celimene. Far from it, Madam. Indeed, it seems to me
    We ought to trade advice more frequently.   90
    One's vision of oneself is so defective
    That it would be an excellent corrective.
    If you are willing, Madam, let's arrange
    Shortly to have another frank exchange
    In which we'll tell each other, *entre nous,*
    What you've heard tell of me, and I of you.
Arsinoe. Oh, people never censure you, my dear;
    It's me they criticize. Or so I hear.
Celimene. Madam, I think we either blame or praise
    According to our taste and length of days.   100
    There is a time of life for coquetry,
    And there's a season, too, for prudery.
    When all one's charms are gone, it is, I'm sure,
    Good strategy to be devout and pure:
    It makes one seem a little less forsaken.
    Some day, perhaps, I'll take the road you've taken:

Time brings all things. But I have time aplenty,
And see no cause to be a prude at twenty.
Arsinoe. You give your age in such a gloating tone
  That one would think I was an ancient crone;   110
  We're not so far apart, in sober truth,
  That you can mock me with a boast of youth!
  Madam, you baffle me. I wish I knew
  What moves you to provoke me as you do.
Celimene. For my part, Madam, I should like to know
  Why you abuse me everywhere you go.
  Is it my fault, dear lady, that your hand
  Is not, alas, in very great demand?
  If men admire me, if they pay me court
  And daily make me offers of the sort   120
  You'd dearly love to have them make to you,
  How can I help it? What would you have me do?
  If what you want is lovers, please feel free
  To take as many as you can from me.
Arsinoe. Oh, come. D'you think the world is losing sleep
  Over that flock of lovers which you keep,
  Or that we find it difficult to guess
  What price you pay for their devotedness?
  Surely you don't expect us to suppose
  Mere merit could attract so many beaux?   130
  It's not your virtue that they're dazzled by;
  Nor is it virtuous love for which they sigh.
  You're fooling no one, Madam; the world's not blind;
  There's many a lady heaven has designed
  To call men's noblest, tenderest feelings out,
  Who has no lovers dogging her about;
  From which it's plain that lovers nowadays
  Must be acquired in bold and shameless ways,
  And only pay one court for such reward
  As modesty and virtue can't afford.   140
  Then don't be quite so puffed up, if you please,
  About your tawdry little victories;
  Try, if you can, to be a shade less vain,
  And treat the world with somewhat less disdain.
  If one were envious of your amours,
  One soon could have a following like yours;
  Lovers are no great trouble to collect
  If one prefers them to one's self-respect.
Celimene. Collect them then, my dear; I'd love to see
  You demonstrate that charming theory;   150
  Who knows, you might . . .

Arsinoe.   Now, Madam, that will do;
It's time to end this trying interview.
My coach is late in coming to your door,
Or I'd have taken leave of you before.
Celimene. Oh, please don't feel that you must rush away;
    I'd be delighted, Madam, if you'd stay.
    However, lest my conversation bore you,
    Let me provide some better company for you;
    This gentleman, who comes most apropos,
    Will please you more than I could do, I know.   160

SCENE SIX

ALCESTE, CELIMENE, ARSINOE

Celimene. Alceste, I have a little note to write
    Which simply must go out before tonight;
    Please entertain *Madame;* I'm sure that she
    Will overlook my incivility.

SCENE SEVEN

ALCESTE, ARSINOE

Arsinoe. Well, Sir, our hostess graciously contrives
    For us to chat until my coach arrives;
    And I shall be forever in her debt
    For granting me this little tête-à-tête.
    We women very rightly give our hearts
    To men of noble character and parts,
    And your especial merits, dear Alceste,
    Have roused the deepest sympathy in my breast.
    Oh, how I wish they had sufficient sense
    At court, to recognize your excellence!   10
    They wrong you greatly, Sir. How it must hurt you
    Never to be rewarded for your virtue!
Alceste. Why, Madam, what cause have I to feel aggrieved?
    What great and brilliant thing have I achieved?
    What service have I rendered to the King
    That I should look to him for anything?
Arsinoe. Not everyone who's honored by the State
    Has done great services. A man must wait
    Till time and fortune offer him the chance.
    Your merit, Sir, is obvious at a glance,   20
    And . . .
Alceste.   Ah, forget my merit; I'm not neglected.
    The court, I think, can hardly be expected

To mine men's souls for merit, and unearth
Our hidden virtues and our secret worth.
Arsinoe. Some virtues, though, are far too bright to hide;
    Yours are acknowledged, Sir, on every side.
    Indeed, I've heard you warmly praised of late
    By persons of considerable weight.
Alceste. This fawning age has praise for everyone,
    And all distinctions, Madam, are undone.   30
    All things have equal honor nowadays,
    And no one should be gratified by praise.
    To be admired, one only need exist,
    And every lackey's on the honors list.
Arsinoe. I only wish, Sir, that you had your eye
    On some position at court, however high;
    You'd only have to hint at such a notion
    For me to set the proper wheels in motion;
    I've certain friendships I'd be glad to use
    To get you any office you might choose.   40
Alceste. Madam, I fear that any such ambition
    Is wholly foreign to my disposition.
    The soul God gave me isn't of the sort
    That prospers in the weather of a court.
    It's all too obvious that I don't possess
    The virtues necessary for success.
    My one great talent is for speaking plain;
    I've never learned to flatter or to feign;
    And anyone so stupidly sincere
    Had best not seek a courtier's career.   50
    Outside the court, I know, one must dispense
    With honors, privilege, and influence;
    But still one gains the right, foregoing these,
    Not to be tortured by the wish to please.
    One needn't live in dread of snubs and slights,
    Nor praise the verse that every idiot writes,
    Nor humor silly Marquesses, nor bestow
    Politic sighs on Madam So-and-So.
Arsinoe. Forget the court, then; let the matter rest.
    But I've another cause to be distressed   60
    About your present situation, Sir.
    It's to your love affair that I refer.
    She whom you love, and who pretends to love you,
    Is, I regret to say, unworthy of you.
Alceste. Why, Madam! Can you seriously intend
    To make so grave a charge against your friend?
Arsinoe. Alas, I must. I've stood aside too long
    And let that lady do you grievous wrong;

But now my debt to conscience shall be paid:
I tell you that your love has been betrayed. 70
Alceste. I thank you, Madam; you're extremely kind.
Such words are soothing to a lover's mind.
Arsinoe. Yes, though she *is* my friend, I say again
You're very much too good for Célimène.
She's wantonly misled you from the start.
Alceste. You may be right; who knows another's heart?
But ask yourself if it's the part of charity
To shake my soul with doubts of her sincerity.
Arsinoe. Well, if you'd rather be a dupe than doubt her,
That's your affair. I'll say no more about her. 80
Alceste. Madam, you know that doubt and vague suspicion
Are painful to a man in my position;
It's most unkind to worry me this way
Unless you've some real proof of what you say.
Arsinoe. Sir, say no more: all doubt shall be removed,
And all that I've been saying shall be proved.
You've only to escort me home, and there
We'll look into the heart of this affair.
I've ocular evidence which will persuade you
Beyond a doubt, that Célimène's betrayed you. 90
Then, if you're saddened by that revelation,
Perhaps I can provide some consolation.

ACT IV
SCENE ONE

ELIANTE, PHILINTE

Philinte. Madam, he acted like a stubborn child;
I thought they never would be reconciled;
In vain we reasoned, threatened, and appealed;
He stood his ground and simply would not yield.
The Marshals, I feel sure, have never heard
An argument so splendidly absurd.
"No, gentlemen," said he, "I'll not retract.
His verse is bad: extremely bad, in fact.
Surely it does the man no harm to know it.
Does it disgrace him, not to be a poet? 10
A gentleman may be respected still,
Whether he writes a sonnet well or ill.
That I dislike his verse should not offend him;
In all that touches honor, I commend him;
He's noble, brave, and virtuous—but I fear
He can't in truth be called a sonneteer.

I'll gladly praise his wardrobe; I'll endorse
His dancing, or the way he sits a horse;
But, gentlemen, I cannot praise his rhyme.
In fact, it ought to be a capital crime   20
For anyone so sadly unendowed
To write a sonnet, and read the thing aloud."
At length he fell into a gentler mood
And, striking a concessive attitude,
He paid Oronte the following courtesies:
"Sir, I regret that I'm so hard to please,
And I'm profoundly sorry that your lyric
Failed to provoke me to a panegyric."
After these curious words, the two embraced,
And then the hearing was adjourned—in haste.   30

Eliante. His conduct has been very singular lately;
   Still, I confess that I respect him greatly.
   The honesty in which he takes such pride
   Has—to my mind—its noble, heroic side.
   In this false age, such candor seems outrageous;
   But I could wish that it were more contagious.

Philinte. What most intrigues me in our friend Alceste
   Is the grand passion that rages in his breast.
   The sullen humors he's compounded of
   Should not, I think dispose his heart to love;   40
   But since they do, it puzzles me still more
   That he should choose your cousin to adore.

Eliante. It does, indeed, belie the theory
   That love is born of gentle sympathy,
   And that the tender passion must be based
   On sweet accords of temper and of taste.

Philinte. Does she return his love, do you suppose?

Eliante. Ah, that's a difficult question, Sir. Who knows?
   How can we judge the truth of her devotion?
   Her heart's a stranger to its own emotion.   50
   Sometimes it thinks it loves, when no love's there;
   At other times it loves quite unaware.

Philinte. I rather think Alceste is in for more
   Distress and sorrow than he's bargained for;
   Were he of my mind, Madam, his affection
   Would turn in quite a different direction,
   And we would see him more responsive to
   The kind regard which he receives from you.

Eliante. Sir, I believe in frankness, and I'm inclined,
   In matters of the heart, to speak my mind.   60
   I don't oppose his love for her; indeed,
   I hope with all my heart that he'll succeed,

And were it in my power, I'd rejoice
In giving him the lady of his choice.
But if, as happens frequently enough
In love affairs, he meets with a rebuff—
If Célimène should grant some rival's suit—
I'd gladly play the role of substitute;
Nor would his tender speeches please me less
Because they'd once been made without success.   70
Philinte. Well, Madam, as for me, I don't oppose
Your hopes in this affair; and heaven knows
That in my conversations with the man
I plead your cause as often as I can.
But if those two should marry, and so remove
All chance that he will offer you his love,
Then I'll declare my own, and hope to see
Your gracious favor pass from him to me.
In short, should you be cheated of Alceste,
I'd be most happy to be second best.   80
Eliante. Philinte, you're teasing.
Philinte.   Ah, Madam, never fear;
No words of mine were ever so sincere,
And I shall live in fretful expectation
Till I can make a fuller declaration.

SCENE TWO

ALCESTE, ELIANTE, PHILINTE

Alceste. Avenge me, Madam! I must have satisfaction,
Or this great wrong will drive me to distraction!
Eliante. Why, what's the matter? What's upset you so?
Alceste. Madam, I've had a mortal, mortal blow.
If Chaos repossessed the universe,
I swear I'd not be shaken any worse.
I'm ruined. . . . I can say no more. . . . My soul . . .
Eliante. Do try, Sir, to regain your self-control.
Alceste. Just heaven! Why were so much beauty and grace
Bestowed on one so vicious and so base?   10
Eliante. Once more, Sir, tell us. . . .
Alceste.   My world has gone to wrack;
I'm—I'm betrayed; she's stabbed me in the back:
Yes, Célimène (who would have thought it of her?)
Is false to me, and has another lover.
Eliante. Are you quite certain? Can you prove these things?
Philinte. Lovers are prey to wild imaginings
And jealous fancies. No doubt there's some mistake. . . .

Alceste. Mind your own business, Sir, for heaven's sake.
  (*To Eliante*)
  Madam, I have the proof that you demand
  Here in my pocket, penned by her own hand.   20
  Yes, all the shameful evidence one could want
  Lies in this letter written to Oronte—
  Oronte! whom I felt sure she couldn't love,
  And hardly bothered to be jealous of.
Philinte. Still, in a letter, appearances may deceive;
  This may not be so bad as you believe.
Alceste. Once more I beg you, Sir, to let me be;
  Tend to your own affairs; leave mine to me.
Eliante. Compose yourself; this anguish that you feel . . .
Alceste. Is something, Madam, you alone can heal.   30
  My outraged heart, beside itself with grief,
  Appeals to you for comfort and relief.
  Avenge me on your cousin, whose unjust
  And faithless nature has deceived my trust;
  Avenge a crime your pure soul must detest.
Eliante. But how, Sir?
Alceste.   Madam, this heart within my breast
  Is yours; pray take it; redeem my heart from her,
  And so avenge me on my torturer.
  Let her be punished by the fond emotion,
  The ardent love, the bottomless devotion,   40
  The faithful worship which this heart of mine
  Will offer up to yours as to a shrine.
Eliante. You have my sympathy, Sir, in all you suffer;
  Nor do I scorn the noble heart you offer;
  But I suspect you'll soon be mollified,
  And this desire for vengeance will subside.
  When some beloved hand has done us wrong
  We thirst for retribution—but not for long;
  However dark the deed that she's committed,
  A lovely culprit's very soon acquitted.   50
  Nothing's so stormy as an injured lover,
  And yet no storm so quickly passes over.
Alceste. No, Madam, no—this is no lovers' spat;
  I'll not forgive her; it's gone too far for that;
  My mind's made up; I'll kill myself before
  I waste my hopes upon her any more.
  Ah, here she is. My wrath intensifies.
  I shall confront her with her tricks and lies,
  And crush her utterly, and bring you then
  A heart no longer slave to Célimène.   60

SCENE THREE

CELIMENE, ALCESTE

Alceste, aside.
    Sweet heaven, help me to control my passion.
Celimene.
    (*Aside*)
            (*To Alceste*)
    Oh, Lord. Why stand there staring in that fashion?
    And what d'you mean by those dramatic sighs,
    And that malignant glitter in your eyes?
Alceste. I mean that sins which cause the blood to freeze
    Look innocent beside your treacheries;
    That nothing Hell's or Heaven's wrath could do
    Ever produced so bad a thing as you.
Celimene. Your compliments were always sweet and pretty.
Alceste. Madam, it's not the moment to be witty.   10
    No, blush and hang your head; you've ample reason,
    Since I've the fullest evidence of your treason.
    Ah, this is what my sad heart prophesied;
    Now all my anxious fears are verified;
    My dark suspicion and my gloomy doubt
    Divined the truth, and now the truth is out.
    For all your trickery, I was not deceived;
    It was my bitter stars that I believed.
    But don't imagine that you'll go scot-free;
    You shan't misuse me with impunity.   20
    I know that love's irrational and blind;
    I know the heart's not subject to the mind,
    And can't be reasoned into beating faster;
    I know each soul is free to choose its master;
    Therefore had you but spoken from the heart,
    Rejecting my attentions from the start,
    I'd have no grievance, or at any rate
    I could complain of nothing but my fate.
    Ah, but so falsely to encourage me—
    That was a treason and a treachery   30
    For which you cannot suffer too severely,
    And you shall pay for that behavior dearly.
    Yes, now I have no pity, not a shred;
    My temper's out of hand; I've lost my head;
    Shocked by the knowledge of your double-dealings,
    My reason can't restrain my savage feelings;
    A righteous wrath deprives me of my senses,
    And I won't answer for the consequences.

Celimene. What does this outburst mean? Will you please explain?
  Have you, by any chance, gone quite insane? 40
Alceste. Yes, yes, I went insane the day I fell
  A victim to your black and fatal spell,
  Thinking to meet with some sincerity
  Among the treacherous charms that beckoned me.
Celimene. Pooh. Of what treachery can you complain?
Alceste. How sly you are, how cleverly you feign!
  But you'll not victimize me any more.
  Look: here's a document you've seen before.
  This evidence, which I acquired today,
  Leaves you, I think, without a thing to say. 50
Celimene. Is this what sent you into such a fit?
Alceste. You should be blushing at the sight of it.
Celimene. Ought I to blush? I truly don't see why.
Alceste. Ah, now you're being bold as well as sly;
  Since there's no signature, perhaps you'll claim . . .
Celimene. I wrote it, whether or not it bears my name.
Alceste. And you can view with equanimity
  This proof of your disloyalty to me!
Celimene. Oh, don't be so outrageous and extreme.
Alceste. You take this matter lightly, it would seem. 60
  Was it no wrong to me, no shame to you,
  That you should send Oronte this billet-doux?
Celimene. Oronte! Who said it was for him?
Alceste.   Why, those
  Who brought me this example of your prose.
  But what's the difference? If you wrote the letter
  To someone else, it pleases me no better.
  My grievance and your guilt remain the same.
Celimene. But need you rage, and need I blush for shame,
  If this was written to a *woman* friend?
Alceste. Ah! Most ingenious. I'm impressed no end; 70
  And after that incredible evasion
  Your guilt is clear. I need no more persuasion.
  How dare you try so clumsy a deception?
  D'you think I'm wholly wanting in perception?
  Come, come, let's see how brazenly you'll try
  To bolster up so palpable a lie:
  Kindly construe this ardent closing section
  As nothing more than sisterly affection!
  Here, let me read it. Tell me, if you dare to,
  That this is for a woman . . .
Celimene.   I don't care to. 80
  What right have you to badger and berate me,
  And so highhandedly interrogate me?

Alceste. Now, don't be angry; all I ask of you
  Is that you justify a phrase or two . . .
Celimene. No, I shall not. I utterly refuse,
  And you may take those phrases as you choose.
Alceste. Just show me how this letter could be meant
  For a woman's eyes, and I shall be content.
Celimene. No, no, it's for Oronte; you're perfectly right.
  I welcome his attentions with delight,   90
  I prize his character and his intellect,
  And everything is just as you suspect.
  Come, do your worst now; give your rage free rein;
  But kindly cease to bicker and complain.
Alceste, aside.
  Good God! Could anything be more inhuman?
  Was ever a heart so mangled by a woman?
  When I complain of how she has betrayed me,
  She bridles, and commences to upbraid me!
  She tries my tortured patience to the limit;
  She won't deny her guilt; she glories in it!   100
  And yet my heart's too faint and cowardly
  To break these chains of passion, and be free,
  To scorn her as it should, and rise above
  This unrewarded, mad, and bitter love.
  (*To Célimène*)
  Ah, traitress, in how confident a fashion
  You take advantage of my helpless passion,
  And use my weakness for your faithless charms
  To make me once again throw down my arms!
  But do at least deny this black transgression;
  Take back that mocking and perverse confession;   110
  Defend this letter and your innocence,
  And I, poor fool, will aid in your defense.
  Pretend, pretend, that you are just and true,
  And I shall make myself believe in you.
Celimene. Oh, stop it. Don't be such a jealous dunce,
  Or I shall leave off loving you at once.
  Just why should I *pretend?* What could impel me
  To stoop so low as that? And kindly tell me
  Why, if I loved another, I shouldn't merely
  Inform you of it, simply and sincerely!   120
  I've told you where you stand, and that admission
  Should altogether clear me of suspicion;
  After so generous a guarantee,
  What right have you to harbor doubts of me?
  Since women are (from natural reticence)
  Reluctant to declare their sentiments,

And since the honor of our sex requires
That we conceal our amorous desires,
Ought any man for whom such laws are broken
To question what the oracle has spoken?   130
Should he not rather feel an obligation
To trust that most obliging declaration?
Enough, now. Your suspicions quite disgust me;
Why should I love a man who doesn't trust me?
I cannot understand why I continue,
Fool that I am, to take an interest in you.
I ought to choose a man less prone to doubt,
And give you something to be vexed about.

Alceste. Ah, what a poor enchanted fool I am;
These gentle words, no doubt, were all a sham;   140
But destiny requires me to entrust
My happiness to you, and so I must.
I'll love you to the bitter end, and see
How false and treacherous you dare to be.

Celimene. No, you don't really love me as you ought.

Alceste. I love you more than can be said or thought;
Indeed, I wish you were in such distress
That I might show my deep devotedness.
Yes, I could wish that you were wretchedly poor,
Unloved, uncherished, utterly obscure;   150
That fate had set you down upon the earth
Without possessions, rank, or gentle birth;
Then, by the offer of my heart, I might
Repair the great injustice of your plight;
I'd raise you from the dust, and proudly prove
The purity and vastness of my love.

Celimene. This is a strange benevolence indeed!
God grant that I may never be in need. . . .
Ah, here's Monsieur Dubois, in quaint disguise.

SCENE FOUR

CELIMENE, ALCESTE, DUBOIS

Alceste. Well, why this costume? Why those frightened eyes?
What ails you?

Dubois.   Well, Sir, things are most mysterious.

Alceste. What do you mean?

Dubois.   I fear they're very serious.

Alceste. What?

Dubois.   Shall I speak more loudly?

Alceste.   Yes; speak out.
Dubois. Isn't there someone here, Sir?
Alceste.   Speak, you lout!
   Stop wasting time.
Dubois.   Sir, we must slip away.
Alceste. How's that?
Dubois.   We must decamp without delay.
Alceste. Explain yourself.
Dubois.   I tell you we must fly.
Alceste. What for?
Dubois.   We mustn't pause to say good-by.
Alceste. Now what d'you mean by all of this, you clown?   10
Dubois. I mean, Sir, that we've got to leave this town.
Alceste. I'll tear you limb from limb and joint from joint
   If you don't come more quickly to the point.
Dubois. Well, Sir, today a man in a black suit,
   Who wore a black and ugly scowl to boot,
   Left us a document scrawled in such a hand
   As even Satan couldn't understand.
   It bears upon your lawsuit, I don't doubt;
   But all hell's devils couldn't make it out.
Alceste. Well, well, go on. What then? I fail to see   20
   How this event obliges us to flee.
Dubois. Well, Sir: an hour later, hardly more,
   A gentleman who's often called before
   Came looking for you in an anxious way.
   Not finding you, he asked me to convey
   (Knowing I could be trusted with the same)
   The following message. . . . Now, what *was* his name?
Alceste. Forget his name, you idiot. What did he say?
Dubois. Well, it was one of your friends, Sir, anyway.
   He warned you to begone, and he suggested   30
   That if you stay, you may well be arrested.
Alceste. What? Nothing more specific? Think, man, think!
Dubois. No, Sir. He had me bring him pen and ink,
   And dashed you off a letter which, I'm sure,
   Will render things distinctly less obscure.
Alceste. Well—let me have it!
Celimene.   What *is* this all about?
Alceste. God knows; but I have hopes of finding out.
   How long am I to wait, you blitherer?
Dubois, after a protracted search for the letter
   I must have left it on your table, Sir.
Alceste. I ought to . . .
Celimene.   No, no, keep your self-control;   40
   Go find out what's behind his rigmarole.

Alceste. It seems that fate, no matter what I do,
    Has sworn that I may not converse with you;
    But, Madam, pray permit your faithful lover
    To try once more before the day is over.

ACT V
SCENE ONE

ALCESTE, PHILINTE

Alceste. No, it's too much. My mind's made up, I tell you.
Philinte. Why should this blow, however hard, compel you . . .
Alceste. No, no, don't waste your breath in argument;
    Nothing you say will alter my intent;
    This age is vile, and I've made up my mind
    To have no further commerce with mankind.
    Did not truth, honor, decency, and the laws
    Oppose my enemy and approve my cause?
    My claims were justified in all men's sight;
    I put my trust in equity and right;   10
    Yet, to my horror and the world's disgrace,
    Justice is mocked, and I have lost my case!
    A scoundrel whose dishonesty is notorious
    Emerges from another lie victorious!
    Honor and right condone his brazen fraud,
    While rectitude and decency applaud!
    Before his smirking face, the truth stands charmed,
    And virtue conquered, and the law disarmed!
    His crime is sanctioned by a court decree!
    And not content with what he's done to me,   20
    The dog now seeks to ruin me by stating
    That I composed a book now circulating,
    A book so wholly criminal and vicious
    That even to speak its title is seditious!
    Meanwhile Oronte, my rival, lends his credit
    To the same libelous tale, and helps to spread it!
    Oronte! a man of honor and of rank,
    With whom I've been entirely fair and frank;
    Who sought me out and forced me, willy-nilly,
    To judge some verse I found extremely silly;   30
    And who, because I properly refused
    To flatter him, or see the truth abused,
    Abets my enemy in a rotten slander!
    There's the reward of honesty and candor!
    The man will hate me to the end of time

For failing to commend his wretched rhyme!
And not this man alone, but all humanity
Do what they do from interest and vanity;
They prate of honor, truth, and righteousness,
But lie, betray, and swindle nonetheless. 40
Come then: man's villainy is too much to bear;
Let's leave this jungle and this jackal's lair.
Yes! treacherous and savage race of men,
You shall not look upon my face again.
Philinte. Oh, don't rush into exile prematurely;
Things aren't as dreadful as you make them, surely.
It's rather obvious, since you're still at large,
That people don't believe your enemy's charge.
Indeed, his tale's so patently untrue
That it may do more harm to him than you. 50
Alceste. Nothing could do that scoundrel any harm:
His frank corruption is his greatest charm,
And, far from hurting him, a further shame
Would only serve to magnify his name.
Philinte. In any case, his bald prevarication
Has done no injury to your reputation,
And you may feel secure in that regard.
As for your lawsuit, it should not be hard
To have the case reopened, and contest
This judgment . . .
Alceste.   No, no, let the verdict rest. 60
Whatever cruel penalty it may bring,
I wouldn't have it changed for anything.
It shows the times' injustice with such clarity
That I shall pass it down to our posterity
As a great proof and signal demonstration
Of the black wickedness of this generation.
It may cost twenty thousand francs; but I
Shall pay their twenty thousand, and gain thereby
The right to storm and rage at human evil,
And send the race of mankind to the devil. 70
Philinte. Listen to me. . . .
Alceste.   Why? What can you possibly say?
Don't argue, Sir; your labor's thrown away.
Do you propose to offer lame excuses
For men's behavior and the times' abuses?
Philinte. No, all you say I'll readily concede:
This is a low, dishonest age indeed;
Nothing but trickery prospers nowadays,
And people ought to mend their shabby ways.

Yes, man's a beastly creature; but must we then
Abandon the society of men?   80
Here in the world, each human frailty
Provides occasion for philosophy,
And that is virtue's noblest exercise;
If honesty shone forth from all men's eyes,
If every heart were frank and kind and just,
What could our virtues do but gather dust
(Since their employment is to help us bear
The villainies of men without despair)?
A heart well-armed with virtue can endure. . . .
Alceste. Sir, you're a matchless reasoner, to be sure;   90
  Your words are fine and full of cogency;
  But don't waste time and eloquence on me.
  My reason bids me go, for my own good.
  My tongue won't lie and flatter as it should;
  God knows what frankness it might next commit,
  And what I'd suffer on account of it.
  Pray let me wait for Célimène's return
  In peace and quiet. I shall shortly learn,
  By her response to what I have in view,
  Whether her love for me is feigned or true.   100
Philinte. Till then, let's visit Eliante upstairs.
Alceste. No, I am too weighed down with somber cares.
  Go to her, do; and leave me with my gloom
  Here in the darkened corner of this room.
Philinte. Why, that's no sort of company, my friend;
  I'll see if Eliante will not descend.

SCENE TWO

CELIMENE, ORONTE, ALCESTE

Oronte. Yes, Madam, if you wish me to remain
  Your true and ardent lover, you must deign
  To give me some more positive assurance.
  All this suspense is quite beyond endurance.
  If your heart shares the sweet desires of mine,
  Show me as much by some convincing sign;
  And here's the sign I urgently suggest:
  That you no longer tolerate Alceste,
  But sacrifice him to my love, and sever
  All your relations with the man forever.   10
Celimene. Why do you suddenly dislike him so?
  You praised him to the skies not long ago.

Oronte. Madam, that's not the point. I'm here to find
   Which way your tender feelings are inclined.
   Choose, if you please, between Alceste and me,
   And I shall stay or go accordingly.
Alceste, emerging from the corner
   Yes, Madam, choose; this gentleman's demand
   Is wholly just, and I support his stand.
   I too am true and ardent; I too am here
   To ask you that you make your feelings clear.   20
   No more delays, now; no equivocation;
   The time has come to make your declaration.
Oronte. Sir, I've no wish in any way to be
   An obstacle to your felicity.
Alceste. Sir, I've no wish to share her heart with you;
   That may sound jealous, but at least it's true.
Oronte. If, weighing us, she leans in your direction . . .
Alceste. If she regards you with the least affection . . .
Oronte. I swear I'll yield her to you there and then.
Alceste. I swear I'll never see her face again.   30
Oronte. Now, Madam, tell us what we've come to hear.
Alceste. Madam, speak openly and have no fear.
Oronte. Just say which one is to remain your lover.
Alceste. Just name one name, and it will all be over.
Oronte. What! Is it possible that you're undecided?
Alceste. What! Can your feelings possibly be divided?
Celimene. Enough: this inquisition's gone too far:
   How utterly unreasonable you are!
   Not that I couldn't make the choice with ease;
   My heart has no conflicting sympathies;   40
   I know full well which one of you I favor,
   And you'd not see me hesitate or waver.
   But how can you expect me to reveal
   So cruelly and bluntly what I feel?
   I think it altogether too unpleasant
   To choose between two men when both are present;
   One's heart has means more subtle and more kind
   Of letting its affections be divined,
   Nor need one be uncharitably plain
   To let a lover know he loves in vain.   50
Oronte. No, no, speak plainly, I for one can stand it.
   I beg you to be frank.
Alceste.   And I demand it.
   The simple truth is what I wish to know,
   And there's no need for softening the blow.
   You've made an art of pleasing everyone,

But now your days of coquetry are done:
You have no choice now, Madam, but to choose,
For I'll know what to think if you refuse;
I'll take your silence for a clear admission
That I'm entitled to my worst suspicion.   60
Oronte. I thank you for this ultimatum, Sir,
    And I may say I heartily concur.
Celimene. Really, this foolishness is very wearing:
    Must you be so unjust and overbearing?
    Haven't I told you why I must demur?
    Ah, here's Eliante; I'll put the case to her.

SCENE THREE

ELIANTE, PHILINTE, CELIMENE, ORONTE, ALCESTE

Celimene. Cousin, I'm being persecuted here
    By these two persons, who, it would appear,
    Will not be satisfied till I confess
    Which one I love the more, and which the less,
    And tell the latter to his face that he
    Is henceforth banished from my company.
    Tell me, has ever such a thing been done?
Eliante. You'd best not turn to me; I'm not the one
    To back you in a matter of this kind:
    I'm all for those who frankly speak their mind.   10
Oronte. Madam, you'll search in vain for a defender.
Alceste. You're beaten, Madam, and may as well surrender.
Oronte. Speak, speak, you must; and end this awful strain.
Alceste. Or don't, and your position will be plain.
Oronte. A single word will close this painful scene.
Alceste. But if you're silent, I'll know what you mean.

SCENE FOUR

ARSINOE, CELIMENE, ELIANTE, ALCESTE, PHILINTE, ACASTE, CLITANDRE,
ORONTE

Acaste, to Celimene.
    Madam, with all due deference, we two
    Have come to pick a little bone with you.
Clitandre, to Oronte and Alceste.
    I'm glad you're present, Sirs; as you'll soon learn,
    Our business here is also your concern.
Arsinoe, to Celimene.
    Madam, I visit you so soon again

Only because of these two gentlemen,
Who came to me indignant and aggrieved
About a crime too base to be believed.
Knowing your virtue, having such confidence in it,
I couldn't think you guilty for a minute,   10
In spite of all their telling evidence;
And, rising above our little difference,
I've hastened here in friendship's name to see
You clear yourself of this great calumny.
Acaste. Yes, Madam, let us see with what composure
You'll manage to respond to this disclosure.
You lately sent Clitandre this tender note.
Clitandre. And this one, for Acaste, you also wrote.
Acaste, to Oronte and Alceste.
You'll recognize this writing, Sirs, I think;
The lady is so free with pen and ink   20
That you must know it all too well, I fear.
But listen: this is something you should hear.
"How absurd you are to condemn my lightheartedness in society, and to
  accuse me of being happiest in the company of others. Nothing could
  be more unjust; and if you do not come to me instantly and beg pardon
  for saying such a thing, I shall never forgive you as long as I live. Our
  big bumbling friend the Viscount . . ."
What a shame that he's not here.
"Our big bumbling friend the Viscount, whose name stands first in your
  complaint, is hardly a man to my taste; and ever since the day I   30
  watched him spend three-quarters of an hour spitting into a well, so as
  to make circles in the water, I have been unable to think highly of him.
  As for the little Marquess . . ."
In all modesty, gentlemen, that is I.
"As for the little Marquess, who sat squeezing my hand for such a long
  while yesterday, I find him in all respects the most trifling creature alive;
  and the only things of value about him are his cape and his sword.
As for the man with the green ribbons . . ."
(To Alceste)
It's your turn now, Sir.
"As for the man with the green ribbons, he amuses me now and then with 40
  his bluntness and his bearish ill-humor; but there are many times indeed
  when I think him the greatest bore in the world. And as for the sonneteer
  . . ."
(To Oronte)
Here's your helping.
"And as for the sonneteer, who has taken it into his head to be witty, and
  insists on being an author in the teeth of opinion, I simply cannot be
  bothered to listen to him, and his prose wearies me quite as much as
  his poetry. Be assured that I am not always so well-entertained as you

suppose; that I long for your company, more than I dare to say, at all
these entertainments to which people drag me; and that the presence   50
of those one loves is the true and perfect seasoning to all one's
pleasures."

Clitandre. And now for me.

"Clitandre, whom you mention, and who so pesters me with his saccharine
speeches, is the last man on earth for whom I could feel any affection.
He is quite mad to suppose that I love him, and so are you, to doubt
that you are loved. Do come to your senses; exchange your suppositions
for his; and visit me as often as possible, to help me bear the annoyance
of his unwelcome attentions."

It's a sweet character that these letters show,   60
And what to call it, Madam, you well know.
Enough. We're off to make the world acquainted
With this sublime self-portrait that you've painted.

Acaste. Madam, I'll make you no farewell oration;
No, you're not worthy of my indignation.
Far choicer hearts than yours, as you'll discover,
Would like this little Marquess for a lover.

SCENE FIVE

CELIMENE, ELIANTE, ARSINOE, ALCESTE, ORONTE, PHILINTE

Oronte. So! After all those loving letters you wrote,
You turn on me like this, and cut my throat!
And your dissembling, faithless heart, I find,
Has pledged itself by turns to all mankind!
How blind I've been! But now I clearly see;
I thank you, Madam, for enlightening me.
My heart is mine once more, and I'm content;
The loss of it shall be your punishment.
(*To Alceste*)
Sir, she is yours; I'll seek no more to stand
Between your wishes and this lady's hand.   10

SCENE SIX

CELIMENE, ELIANTE, ARSINOE, ALCESTE, PHILINTE

Arsinoe, to Celimene.
Madam, I'm forced to speak. I'm far too stirred
To keep my counsel, after what I've heard.
I'm shocked and staggered by your want of morals.
It's not my way to mix in others' quarrels;
But really, when this fine and noble spirit,

This man of honor and surpassing merit,
Laid down the offering of his heart before you,
How *could* you . . .
Alceste. Madam, permit me, I implore you,
To represent myself in this debate.
Don't bother, please, to be my advocate. 10
My heart, in any case, could not afford
To give your services their due reward;
And if I chose, for consolation's sake,
Some other lady, t'would not be you I'd take.
Arsinoe. What makes you think you could, Sir? And how dare you
Imply that I've been trying to ensnare you?
If you can for a moment entertain
Such flattering fancies, you're extremely vain.
I'm not so interested as you suppose
In Célimène's discarded gigolos. 20
Get rid of that absurd illusion, do.
Women like me are not for such as you.
Stay with this creature, to whom you're so attached;
I've never seen two people better matched.

SCENE SEVEN

CELIMENE, ELIANTE, ALCESTE, PHILINTE

Alceste, to Celimene.
Well, I've been still throughout this exposé,
Till everyone but me has said his say.
Come, have I shown sufficient self-restraint?
And may I now . . .
Celimene. Yes, make your just complaint.
Reproach me freely, call me what you will;
You've every right to say I've used you ill.
I've wronged you, I confess it; and in my shame
I'll make no effort to escape the blame.
The anger of those others I could despise;
My guilt toward you I sadly recognize. 10
Your wrath is wholly justified, I fear;
I know how culpable I must appear,
I know all things bespeak my treachery,
And that, in short, you've grounds for hating me.
Do so; I give you leave.
Alceste. Ah, traitress—how,
How should I cease to love you, even now?
Though mind and will were passionately bent
On hating you, my heart would not consent.

(*To Eliante and Philinte*)
Be witness to my madness, both of you;
See what infatuation drives one to;   20
But wait; my folly's only just begun,
And I shall prove to you before I'm done
How strange the human heart is, and how far
From rational we sorry creatures are.
(*To Celimene*)
Woman, I'm willing to forget your shame,
And clothe your treacheries in a sweeter name;
I'll call them youthful errors, instead of crimes,
And lay the blame on these corrupting times.
My one condition is that you agree
To share my chosen fate, and fly with me   30
To that wild, trackless, solitary place
In which I shall forget the human race.
Only by such a course can you atone
For those atrocious letters; by that alone
Can you remove my present horror of you,
And make it possible for me to love you.
Celimene. What! I renounce the world at my young age,
    And die of boredom in some hermitage?
Alceste. Ah, if you really loved me as you ought,
    You wouldn't give the world a moment's thought;   40
    Must you have me, and all the world beside?
Celimene. Alas, at twenty one is terrified
    Of solitude. I fear I lack the force
    And depth of soul to take so stern a course.
    But if my hand in marriage will content you,
    Why, there's a plan which I might well consent to,
    And . . .
Alceste.   No, I detest you now. I could excuse
    Everything else, but since you thus refuse
    To love me wholly, as a wife should do,
    And see the world in me, as I in you,   50
    Go! I reject your hand, and disenthrall
    My heart from your enchantments, once for all.

SCENE EIGHT

ELIANTE, ALCESTE, PHILINTE

Alceste, to Eliante.
    Madam, your virtuous beauty has no peer;
    Of all this world, you only are sincere;

I've long esteemed you highly, as you know;
Permit me ever to esteem you so,
And if I do not now request your hand,
Forgive me, Madam, and try to understand.
I feel unworthy of it; I sense that fate
Does not intend me for the married state,
That I should do you wrong by offering you
My shattered heart's unhappy residue,   10
And that in short . . .
Eliante.   Your argument's well taken:
Nor need you fear that I shall feel forsaken.
Were I to offer him this hand of mine,
Your friend Philinte, I think, would not decline.
Philinte. Ah, Madam, that's my heart's most cherished goal,
For which I'd gladly give my life and soul.
Alceste, to Eliante and Philinte.
May you be true to all you now profess,
And so deserve unending happiness.
Meanwhile, betrayed and wronged in everything,
I'll flee this bitter world where vice is king,   20
And seek some spot unpeopled and apart
Where I'll be free to have an honest heart.
Philinte. Come, Madam, let's do everything we can
To change the mind of this unhappy man.

Henrik Ibsen (1828–1906)
A DOLL'S HOUSE*

THE CHARACTERS

Torvald Helmer, a lawyer	The Helmers' three small children
Nora, his wife	The children's Nurse, Anne-Marie
Dr. Rank	A Housemaid
Mrs. Linde	A Porter
Krogstad	

THE SCENE: THE HELMERS' LIVING ROOM

ACT I

*A pleasant living room, tastefully but not expensively furnished. A door
on the rear wall, right, leads to the front hall; another door, left, to*

*Translated by Otto Reinert.

HELMER's study. Between the two doors a piano. A third door in the middle of the left wall; further front a window. Near the window a round table and a small couch. Toward the rear of the right wall a fourth door; further front a tile stove with a rocking chair and a couple of armchairs in front of it. Between the stove and the door a small table. Copperplate etchings on the walls. A whatnot with porcelain figurines and other small objects. A small bookcase with de luxe editions. A rug on the floor; fire in the stove. Winter day.

    The doorbell rings, then the sound of the front door opening. NORA, dressed for outdoors, enters, humming cheerfully. She carries several packages, which she puts down on the table, right. She leaves the door to the front hall open; there a PORTER is seen holding a Christmas tree and a basket. He gives them to the MAID, who has let them in.

Nora. Be sure to hide the Christmas tree, Helene. The children mustn't see it till after we've trimmed it tonight. (*Opens her purse; to the PORTER.*) How much?

Porter. Fifty øre.

Nora. Here's a crown. No, keep the change. (*The PORTER thanks her, leaves. NORA closes the door. She keeps laughing quietly to herself as she takes off her coat, etc. She takes a bag of macaroons from her pocket and eats a couple. She walks cautiously over to the door to the study and listens.*) Yes, he's home. (*Resumes her humming, walks over to the table, right.*)

Helmer. (*in his study*) Is that my little lark twittering out there?

Nora. (*opening some of the packages*) That's right.

Helmer. My squirrel bustling about?

Nora. Yes.

Helmer. When did squirrel come home?

Nora. Just now. (*Puts the bag of macaroons back in her pocket, wipes her mouth.*) Come out here, Torvald. I want to show you what I've bought.

Helmer. I'm busy right now! (*After a little while he opens the door and looks in, pen in hand.*) Bought, eh? All that? So little wastrel has been throwing money around again?

Nora. Oh, but Torvald, this Christmas we can be a little extravagant, can't we? It's the first Christmas we haven't had to watch every penny.

Helmer. I don't know about that. We certainly don't have money to throw away.

Nora. Yes, Torvald, we do. A little, anyway. Just a tiny little bit? Now that you're going to get that big salary and all and make lots and lots of money.

Helmer. Starting at New Year's, yes. But payday isn't till the end of the quarter.

Nora. That doesn't matter. We can always borrow.

Helmer. Nora! (*Goes over to her and playfully pulls her ear.*) There you go being irresponsible again. Suppose I borrowed a thousand crowns today and you spent it all for Christmas and on New Year's Eve a tile from the roof laid me out cold?

Nora. (*putting her hand over his mouth*) I won't have you say such horrid things.

Helmer. But suppose it happened. Then what?

Nora. If it did, I wouldn't care whether we owed money or not.

Helmer. But what about the people I had borrowed from?

Nora. Who cares about them! They are strangers!

Helmer. Nora, Nora, you *are* a woman. No, really! You know how I feel about that. No debts! A home in debt isn't a free home, and if it isn't free it isn't beautiful. We've managed nicely so far, you and I, and that's the way we'll go on. It won't be for much longer.

Nora. (*walks over toward the stove*) All right, Torvald. Whatever you say.

Helmer. (*follows her*) Come, come, my little songbird mustn't droop her wings. What's this? Can't have a pouty squirrel in the house, you know. (*Takes out his wallet.*) Nora, what do you think I have here?

Nora. (*turns around quickly*) Money!

Helmer. Here. (*Gives her some bills.*) Don't you think I know Christmas is expensive?

Nora. (*counting*) Ten—twenty—thirty—forty. Thank you, thank you, Torvald. This helps a lot.

Helmer. I certainly hope so.

Nora. It does, it does! But I want to show you what I got. It was cheap, too. Look. New clothes for Ivar. And a sword. And a horse and a trumpet for Bob. And a doll and a little bed for Emmy. It isn't any good, but it wouldn't last, anyway. And here's some dress material and scarves for the maids. I feel bad about old Anne-Marie, though. She really should be getting much more.

Helmer. And what's in here?

Nora. (*cries*) Not till tonight!

Helmer. I see. But now what does my little spendthrift have in mind for herself?

Nora. Oh, nothing. I really don't care.

Helmer. Of course you do. Tell me what you'd like. Within reason.

Nora. Oh, I don't know. Really, I don't. The only thing—

Helmer. Well?

Nora. (*fiddling with his buttons, without looking at him*) If you really want to give me something, you might—you could—

Helmer. All right, let's have it.

Nora. (*quickly*) Some money, Torvald. Just as much as you think you can spare. Then I'll buy myself something one of these days.

Helmer. No, really, Nora—

Nora. Oh yes, please, Torvald. Please? I'll wrap the money in pretty gold paper and hang it on the tree. Won't that be nice?

Helmer. What's the name for little birds that are always spending money?

Nora. Wastrels, I know. But please let's do it my way, Torvald. Then I'll have time to decide what I need most. Now that's sensible, isn't it?

Helmer. (*smiling*). Oh, very sensible. That is, if you really bought yourself something you could use. But it all disappears in the household expenses or you buy things you don't need. And then you come back to me for more.

Nora. Oh, but Torvald—

Helmer. That's the truth, dear little Nora, and you know it. (*Puts his arm around her.*) My wastrel is a little sweetheart, but she *does* go through an awful lot of money awfully fast. You've no idea how expensive it is for a man to keep a wastrel.

Nora. That's not fair, Torvald. I really save all I can.

Helmer. (*laughs*) Oh, I believe that. All you can. Meaning, exactly nothing!

Nora. (*hums, smiles mysteriously*) You don't know all the things we songbirds and squirrels need money for, Torvald.

Helmer. You know, you're funny. Just like your father. You're always looking for ways to get money, but as soon as you do, it runs through your fingers and you can never say what you spent it for. Well, I guess I'll just have to take you the way you are. It's in your blood. Yes, that sort of thing is hereditary, Nora.

Nora. In that case, I wish I had inherited many of Daddy's qualities.

Helmer. And I don't want you any different from just what you are—my own sweet little songbird. Hey!—I think I just noticed something. Aren't you looking—what's the word?—a little—sly—?

Nora. I am?

Helmer. You definitely are. Look at me.

Nora. (*looks at him*) Well?

Helmer. (*wagging a finger*) Little sweet-tooth hasn't by any chance been on a rampage today, has she?

Nora. Of course not. Whatever makes you think that?

Helmer. A little detour by the pastryshop maybe?

Nora. No, I assure you, Torvald—

Helmer. Nibbled a little jam?

Nora. Certainly not!

Helmer. Munched a macaroon or two?

Nora. No, really, Torvald, honestly—

Helmer. All right. Of course I was only joking.

Nora. (*walks toward the table, right*) You know I wouldn't do anything to displease you.

Helmer. I know. And I have your promise. (*Over to her.*) All right, keep your little Christmas secrets to yourself, Nora darling. They'll all come out tonight, I suppose, when we light the tree.

Nora. Did you remember to invite Rank?

Helmer. No, but there's no need to. He knows he'll have dinner with us. Anyway, I'll see him later this morning. I'll ask him then. I did order some good wine. Oh Nora, you've no idea how much I'm looking forward to tonight!

Nora. Me too! And the children, Torvald! They'll have such a good time!

Helmer. You know, it *is* nice to have a good, safe job and a comfortable income. Feels good just thinking about it. Don't you agree?

Nora. Oh, it's wonderful!

Helmer. Remember last Christmas? For three whole weeks you shut yourself up every evening till long after midnight, making ornaments for the Christmas tree and I don't know what else. Some big surprise for all of us, anyway. I'll be damned if I've ever been so bored in my whole life!

Nora. I wasn't bored at all.

Helmer. (*smiling*) But you've got to admit you didn't have much to show for it in the end.

Nora. Oh, don't tease me again about that! Could I help it that the cat got in and tore up everything?

Helmer. Of course you couldn't, my poor little Nora. You just wanted to please the rest of us, and that's the important thing. But I *am* glad the hard times are behind us. Aren't you?

Nora. Oh yes. I think it's just wonderful.

Helmer. This year I won't be bored and lonely. And you won't have to strain your dear eyes and your delicate little hands—

Nora. (*claps her hands*) No I won't, will I, Torvald? Oh, how wonderful, how lovely, to hear you say that! (*Puts her arm under his.*) Let me tell you how I think we should arrange things, Torvald. Soon as Christmas is over—(*The doorbell rings.*) Someone's at the door. (*Straightens things up a bit.*) A caller, I suppose. Bother!

Helmer. Remember, I'm not home.

The Maid. (*in the door to the front hall*) Ma'am, there's a lady here—

Nora. All right. Ask her to come in.

The Maid. (*to* HELMER) And the Doctor just arrived.

Helmer. Is he in the study?

The Maid. Yes, sir.

(HELMER *exits into his study.* THE MAID *shows* MRS. LINDE *in and closes the door behind her as she leaves.* MRS. LINDE *is in travel dress.*)

Mrs. Linde. (*timid and a little hesitant*) Good morning, Nora.

Nora. (*uncertainly*) Good morning.

Mrs. Linde. I don't believe you know who I am.

Nora. No—I'm not sure—Though I know I should—Of course! Kristine! It's you!

Mrs. Linde. Yes, it's me.

Nora. I didn't even recognize you! I had no idea! (*In a lower voice.*) You've changed, Kristine.

Mrs. Linde. I'm sure I have. It's been nine or ten long years.

Nora. Has it really been that long? Yes, you're right. I've been so happy these last eight years. And now you're here. Such a long trip in the middle of winter. How brave!

Mrs. Linde. I got in on the steamer this morning.

Nora. To have some fun over the holidays, of course. That's lovely. For we *are* going to have fun. But take off your coat! You aren't cold, are you? (*Helps her.*) There, now! Let's sit down here by the fire and just relax and talk. No, you sit there. I want the rocking chair. (*Takes her hands.*) And now you've got your old face back. It was just for a minute, right at first—Though you are a little more pale, Kristine. And maybe a little thinner.

Mrs. Linde. And much, much older, Nora.

Nora. Maybe a little older. Just a teeny-weeny bit, not much. (*Interrupts herself, serious.*) Oh, but how thoughtless of me, chatting away like this! Sweet, good Kristine, can you forgive me?

Mrs. Linde. Forgive you what, Nora?

Nora. (*in a low voice*) You poor dear, you lost your husband, didn't you?

Mrs. Linde. Three years ago, yes.

Nora. I know, I saw it in the paper. Oh please believe me, Kristine. I really meant to write you, but I never got around to it. Something was always coming up.

Mrs. Linde. Of course, Nora. I understand.

Nora. No, that wasn't very nice of me. You poor thing, all you must have been through. And he didn't leave you much, either, did he?

Mrs. Linde. No.

Nora. And no children?

Mrs. Linde. No.

Nora. Nothing at all, in other words?

Mrs. Linde. Not so much as a sense of loss—a grief to live on—

Nora. (*incredulous*) But Kristine, how can that *be?*

Mrs. Linde. (*with a sad smile, strokes NORA's hair*) That's the way it sometimes is, Nora.

Nora. All alone. How awful for you. I have three darling children. You can't see them right now, though; they're out with their nurse. But now you must tell me everything—

Mrs. Linde. No, no; I'd rather listen to you.

Nora. No, you begin. Today I won't be selfish. Today I'll think only of you. Except there's one thing I've just got to tell you first. Something marvelous that's happened to us just these last few days. You haven't heard, have you?

Mrs. Linde. No; tell me.

Nora. Just think. My husband's been made manager of the Mutual Bank.

Mrs. Linde. Your husband—! Oh, I'm so glad!

Nora. Yes, isn't that great? You see, private law practice is so uncertain, especially when you won't have anything to do with cases that aren't— you know—quite nice. And of course Torvald won't do that, and I quite agree with him. Oh, you've no idea how delighted we are! He takes over at New Year's, and he'll be getting a big salary and all sorts of extras. From now on we'll be able to live in quite a different way— exactly as we like. Oh, Kristine! I feel so carefree and happy! It's lovely to have lots and lots of money and not have to worry about a thing! Don't you agree?

Mrs. Linde. It would be nice to have enough, at any rate.

Nora. No, I don't mean just enough. I mean lots and lots!

Mrs. Linde. (*smiles*) Nora, Nora, when are you going to be sensible? In school you spent a great deal of money.

Nora. (*quietly laughing*) Yes, and Torvald says I still do. (*Raises her finger at MRS. LINDE.*) But "Nora, Nora" isn't so crazy as you all think. Believe me, we've had nothing to be extravagant with. We've both had to work.

Mrs. Linde. You too?

Nora. Yes. Oh, it's been little things mostly—sewing, crocheting, embroidery—that sort of thing. (*Casually.*) And other things too. You know, of course, that Torvald left government service when we got married? There was no chance of promotion in his department, and of course he had to make more money than he had been making. So for the first few years he worked altogether too hard. He took jobs on the side and worked day and night. It turned out to be too much for him. He became seriously ill. The doctors told him he needed to go south.

Mrs. Linde. That's right; you spent a year in Italy, didn't you?

Nora. Yes, we did. But you won't believe how hard it was to get away. Ivar had just been born. But of course we had to go. Oh, it was a wonderful trip. And it saved Torvald's life. But it took a lot of money, Kristine.

Mrs. Linde. I'm sure it did.

Nora. Twelve hundred dollars of the old money. Four thousand eight hundred crowns. That's a lot.

Mrs. Linde. Yes. So it's lucky you have it when something like that happens.

Nora. Well, actually we got the money from Daddy.

Mrs. Linde. I see. That was about the time your father died, I believe.

Nora. Yes, just about then. And I couldn't even go and take care of him. I was expecting little Ivar any day. And I had poor Torvald to look after, desperately sick and all. My dear, good Daddy! I never saw him again, Kristine. That's the saddest thing that's happened to me since I got married.

Mrs. Linde. I know you were very fond of him. But then you went to Italy?

Nora. Yes, for now we had the money, and the doctors urged us to go. So
  we left about a month later.
Mrs. Linde. And when you came back your husband was well again?
Nora. Healthy as a horse!
Mrs. Linde. But—the doctor?
Nora. What do you mean?
Mrs. Linde. I thought the maid said it was the doctor, that gentleman who
  came the same time I did.
Nora. Oh, that's Doctor Rank. He doesn't come as a doctor. He's our
  closest friend. He looks in at least once every day. No, Torvald hasn't
  been sick once since then. And the children are strong and healthy, too,
  and so am I. (*Jumps up and claps her hands.*) Oh god, Kristine! Isn't it
  wonderful to be alive and happy! Isn't it just lovely!—But now, I'm
  being mean again, talking only about myself and my things. (*Sits down
  on a footstool close to MRS. LINDE and puts her arms on her lap.*)
  Please, don't be angry with me! Tell me, is it really true that you didn't
  care for your husband? Then why did you marry him?
Mrs. Linde. Mother was still alive, but she was bedridden and helpless.
  And I had my two younger brothers to look after. I didn't think I had
  the right to turn him down.
Nora. No, I suppose. So he had money then?
Mrs. Linde. He was quite well off, I think. But it was an uncertain
  business, Nora. When he died, the whole thing collapsed and there was
  nothing left.
Nora. And then—?
Mrs. Linde. Well, I had to manage as best I could. With a little store and a
  little school and anything else I could think of. The last three years have
  been one long work day for me, Nora, without any rest. But now it's
  over. My poor mother doesn't need me any more. She passed away.
  And the boys are on their own too. They've both got jobs and support
  themselves.
Nora. What a relief for you—
Mrs. Linde. No, not relief. Just a great emptiness. Nobody to live for any
  more. (*Gets up, restlessly.*) That's why I couldn't stand it any longer in
  that little hole. It's got to be easier to find something to keep me busy
  and occupy my thoughts here in town. With a little luck I should be
  able to find a good, steady job—something in an office—
Nora. Oh but Kristine, that's exhausting work, and you look worn out
  already. It would be much better if you went to a resort.
Mrs. Linde. (*walks over to the window*) I don't have a Daddy who can
  give me the money, Nora.
Nora. (*getting up*) Oh, don't be angry with me.
Mrs. Linde. (*over to her*) Dear Nora, don't *you* be angry with *me*. That's
  the worst thing about my kind of situation: you become so bitter.
  You've nobody to work for, and yet you have to look out for yourself,
  somehow. You got to keep on living, and so you become selfish. Do

you know—when you told me about your husband's new position I was delighted not so much for your sake as for my own.

Nora. Why was that? Oh, I see. You think maybe Torvald can give you a job?

Mrs. Linde. That's what I had in mind.

Nora. And he will too, Kristine. Just leave it to me. I'll be ever so subtle about it. I'll think of something nice to tell him, something he'll like. I so much want to help you.

Mrs. Linde. That's very good of you, Nora—making an effort like that for me. Especially since you've known so little trouble and hardship in your own life.

Nora. I—have known so little—?

Mrs. Linde. (*smiling*) Oh well, some sewing or whatever it was. You're still a child, Nora.

Nora. (*with a toss of her head, walks away*) You shouldn't sound so superior.

Mrs. Linde. I shouldn't?

Nora. You're just like all the others. None of you think I'm good for anything really serious.

Mrs. Linde. Well, now—

Nora. That I've never been through anything difficult.

Mrs. Linde. But Nora! You just told me all your troubles!

Nora. That's nothing! (*Lowers her voice.*) I haven't told you about *it.*

Mrs. Linde. It? What's that? What do you mean?

Nora. You patronize me, Kristine, and that's not fair. You're proud that you worked so long and so hard for your mother.

Mrs. Linde. I don't think I patronize anyone. But it *is* true that I'm both proud and happy that I could make mother's last years comparatively easy.

Nora. And you're proud of all you did for your brothers.

Mrs. Linde. I think I have the right to be.

Nora. And so do I. But now I want to tell you something, Kristine. I have something to be proud and happy about too.

Mrs. Linde. I don't doubt that for a moment. But what exactly do you mean?

Nora. Not so loud! Torvald mustn't hear—not for anything in the world. Nobody must know about this, Kristine. Nobody but you.

Mrs. Linde. But what is it?

Nora. Come here. (*Pulls her down on the couch beside her.*) You see, I *do* have something to be proud and happy about. I've saved Torvald's life.

Mrs. Linde. Saved—? How do you mean—"saved"?

Nora. I told you about our trip to Italy. Torvald would have died if he hadn't gone.

Mrs. Linde. I understand that. And so your father gave you the money you needed.

Nora. (*smiles*) Yes, that's what Torvald and all the others think. But—

Mrs. Linde. But what?

Nora. Daddy didn't give us a penny. *I* raised that money.

Mrs. Linde. You did? That whole big amount?

Nora. Twelve hundred dollars. Four thousand eight hundred crowns. *Now* what do you say?

Mrs. Linde. But Nora, how could you? Did you win the state lottery?

Nora. (contemptuously) State lottery! *(Snorts.)* What would be so great about that?

Mrs. Linde. Where did it come from then?

Nora. (humming and smiling, enjoying her secret) Hmmm. Tra-la-la-la-la!

Mrs. Linde. You certainly couldn't have borrowed it.

Nora. Oh? And why not?

Mrs. Linde. A wife can't borrow money without her husband's consent.

Nora. (with a toss of her head) Oh, I don't know—take a wife with a little bit of a head for business—a wife who knows how to manage things—

Mrs. Linde. But Nora, I don't understand at all—

Nora. You don't have to. I didn't say I borrowed the money, did I? I could have gotten it some other way. *(Leans back.)* An admirer may have given it to me. When you're as tolerably goodlooking as I am—

Mrs. Linde. Oh, you're crazy.

Nora. I think you're dying from curiosity, Kristine.

Mrs. Linde. I'm beginning to think you've done something very foolish, Nora.

Nora. (sits up) Is it foolish to save your husband's life?

Mrs. Linde. I say it's foolish to act behind his back.

Nora. But don't you see: he couldn't be told! You're missing the whole point, Kristine. We couldn't even let him know how seriously ill he was. The doctors came to *me* and told me his life was in danger, that nothing could save him but a stay in the south. Don't you think I tried to work on him? I told him how lovely it would be if I could go abroad like other young wives. I cried and I begged. I said he'd better remember what condition I was in, that he had to be nice to me and do what I wanted. I even hinted he could borrow the money. But that almost made him angry with me. He told me I was being irresponsible and that it was his duty as my husband not to give in to my whims and moods—I think that's what he called it. All right, I said to myself, you've got to be saved somehow, and so I found a way—

Mrs. Linde. And your husband never learned from your father that the money didn't come from him?

Nora. Never. Daddy died that same week. I thought of telling him all about it and asking him not to say anything. But since he was so sick— It turned out I didn't have to—

Mrs. Linde. And you've never told your husband?

Nora. Of course not! Good heavens, how could I? He, with his strict principles! Besides, you know how men are. Torvald would find it

embarrassing and humiliating to learn that he owed me anything. It
would upset our whole relationship. Our happy, beautiful home would
no longer be what it is.

Mrs. Linde. Aren't you ever going to tell him?

Nora. (reflectively, half smiling) Yes—one day, maybe. Many, many years
from now, when I'm no longer young and pretty. Don't laugh! I mean
when Torvald no longer feels about me the way he does now, when he
no longer thinks it's fun when I dance for him and put on costumes and
recite for him. Then it will be good to have something in reserve—
(Interrupts herself.) Oh, I'm just being silly! That day will never
come.—Well, now, Kristine, what do you say about my great secret?
Don't you think I'm good for something too?—By the way, you
wouldn't believe all the worry I've had because of it. It's been very hard
to meet my obligations on schedule. You see, in business there's
something called quarterly interest and something called installments on
the principal, and those things are terribly hard to come up with. I've
had to save a little here and a little there, whenever I could. I couldn't
use much of the housekeeping money, for Torvald has to eat well. And
I couldn't use what I got for clothes for the children. They have to look
nice, and I didn't think it would be right to spend less than I got—the
sweet little things!

Mrs. Linde. Poor Nora! So you had to take it from your own allowance?

Nora. Yes, of course. After all, it was my affair. Every time Torvald gave
me money for a new dress or what have you, I never used more than
half of it. I always bought the cheapest, simplest things for myself.
Thank god, everything looks good on me, so Torvald never noticed. But
it was hard many times, Kristine, for it's fun to have pretty clothes.
Don't you think?

Mrs. Linde. Certainly.

Nora. Anyway, I had other ways of making money too. Last winter I was
lucky enough to get some copying work. So I locked the door and sat
up writing every night till quite late. God! I often got so tired—! But it
was great fun, too, working and making money. It was almost like
being a man.

Mrs. Linde. But how much have you been able to pay off this way?

Nora. I couldn't tell you exactly. You see, it's very difficult to keep track
of that kind of business. All I know is I have been paying off as much
as I've been able to scrape together. Many times I just didn't know
what to do. *(Smiles.)* Then I used to imagine a rich old gentleman had
fallen in love with me—

Mrs. Linde. What! What old gentleman?

Nora. Phooey! And now he was dead and they were reading his will, and
there it said in big letters, "All my money is to be paid in cash
immediately to the charming Mrs. Nora Helmer."

Mrs. Linde. But dearest Nora—who *was* this old gentleman?

Nora. For heaven's sake, Kristine, don't you see! There *was* no old gentleman. He was just somebody I made up when I couldn't think of any way to raise the money. But never mind him. The old bore can be anyone he likes to for all I care. I have no use for him or his last will, for now I don't have a single worry in the world. (*Jumps up.*) Dear god, what a lovely thought that is! To be able to play and have fun with the children, to have everything nice and pretty in the house, just the way Torvald likes it! Not a care! And soon spring will be here, and the air will be blue and high. Maybe we can travel again. Maybe I'll see the ocean again! Oh, yes, yes!—it's wonderful to be alive and happy!

(*The doorbell rings.*)

Mrs. Linde. (*getting up*) There's the doorbell. Maybe I better be going.
Nora. No, please stay. I'm sure it's just someone for Torvald—
The Maid. (*in the hall door*) Excuse me, ma'am. There's a gentleman here who'd like to see Mr. Helmer.
Nora. You mean the Bank Manager.
The Maid. Sorry, ma'am; the Bank Manager. But I didn't know—since the Doctor is with him—
Nora. Who is the gentleman?
Krogstad. (*appearing in the door*) It's just me, Mrs. Helmer.

(*MRS. LINDE starts, looks, turns away toward the window.*)

Nora. (*takes a step toward him, tense, in a low voice*) You? What do you want? What do you want with my husband?
Krogstad. Bank business—in a way. I have a small job in the Mutual, and I understand your husband is going to be our new boss—
Nora. So it's just—?
Krogstad. Just routine business, ma'am. Nothing else.
Nora. All right. In that case, why don't you go through the door to the office. (*Dismisses him casually as she closes the door. Walks over to the stove and tends the fire.*)
Mrs. Linde. Nora—who was that man?
Nora. His name's Krogstad. He's a lawyer.
Mrs. Linde. So it *was* him.
Nora. Do you know him?
Mrs. Linde. I used to—many years ago. For a while he worked as a clerk in our part of the country.
Nora. Right. He did.
Mrs. Linde. He has changed a great deal.
Nora. I believe he had a very unhappy marriage.
Mrs. Linde. And now he's a widower, isn't he?

Nora. With many children. There now; it's burning nicely again. (*Closes the stove and moves the rocking chair a little to the side.*)

Mrs. Linde. They say he's into all sorts of business.

Nora. Really? Maybe so. I wouldn't know. But let's not talk about business. It's such a bore.

Rank. (*appears in the door to HELMER's study*) No, I don't want to be in the way. I'd rather talk to your wife a bit. (*Closes the door and notices MRS. LINDE.*) Oh, I beg your pardon. I believe I'm in the way here too.

Nora. No, not at all. (*Introduces them.*) Doctor Rank. Mrs. Linde.

Rank. Aha. A name often heard in this house. I believe I passed you on the stairs coming up.

Mrs. Linde. Yes. I'm afraid I climb stairs very slowly. They aren't good for me.

Rank. I see. A slight case of inner decay, perhaps?

Mrs. Linde. Overwork, rather.

Rank. Oh, is that all? And now you've come to town to relax at all the parties?

Mrs. Linde. I have come to look for a job.

Rank. A proven cure for overwork, I take it?

Mrs. Linde. One has to live, Doctor.

Rank. Yes, that seems to be the general opinion.

Nora. Come on, Doctor Rank—you want to live just as much as the rest of us.

Rank. Of course I do. Miserable as I am, I prefer to go on being tortured as long as possible. All my patients feel the same way. And that's true of the moral invalids too. Helmer is talking with a specimen right this minute.

Mrs. Linde. (*in a low voice*) Ah!

Nora. What do you mean?

Rank. Oh, this lawyer, Krogstad. You don't know him. The roots of his character are decayed. But even he began by saying something about having *to live*—as if it were a matter of the highest importance.

Nora. Oh? What did he want with Torvald?

Rank. I don't really know. All I heard was something about the Bank.

Nora. I didn't know that Krog—that this Krogstad had anything to do with the Mutual Bank.

Rank. Yes, he seems to have some kind of job there. (*To MRS. LINDE.*) I don't know if you are familiar in your part of the country with the kind of person who is always running around trying to sniff out cases of moral decrepitude and as soon as he finds one puts the individual under observation in some excellent position or other. All the healthy ones are left out in the cold.

Mrs. Linde. I should think it's the sick who need looking after the most.

Rank. (*shrugs his shoulders*) There we are. That's the attitude that turns society into a hospital.

(*NORA, absorbed in her own thoughts suddenly starts giggling and clapping her hands.*)

Rank. What's so funny about that? Do you even know what society is?
Nora. What do I care about your stupid society! I laughed at something entirely different—something terribly amusing. Tell me, Doctor Rank— all the employees in the Mutual Bank, from now on they'll all be dependent on Torvald, right?
Rank. Is that what you find so enormously amusing?
Nora. (*smiles and hums*) That's my business, that's my business! (*Walks around.*) Yes, I do think it's fun that we—that Torvald is going to have so much influence on so many people's lives. (*Brings out the bag of macaroons.*) Have a macaroon, Doctor Rank.
Rank. Well, well—macaroons. I thought they were banned around here.
Nora. Yes, but these were some that Kristine gave me.
Mrs. Linde. What! I?
Nora. That's all right. Don't look so scared. You couldn't know that Torvald won't let me have macaroons. He's afraid they'll ruin my teeth. But who cares! Just once in a while—! Right, Doctor Rank? Have one! (*Puts a macaroon into his mouth.*) You too, Kristine. And one for me. A very small one. Or at most two. (*Walks around again.*) Yes, I really feel very, very happy. Now there's just one thing I'm dying to do.
Rank. Oh? And what's that?
Nora. Something I want to say so Torvald could hear.
Rank. And why can't you?
Nora. I don't dare to, for it's not nice.
Mrs. Linde. Not nice?
Rank. In that case, I guess you'd better not. But surely to the two of us—? What is it you'd like to say to Helmer?
Nora. I want to say, "goddammit!"
Rank. Are you out of your mind!
Mrs. Linde. For heaven's sake, Nora!
Rank. Say it. Here he comes.
Nora. (*hiding the macaroons*) Shhh!

(*HELMER enters from his study, carrying his hat and overcoat.*)

Nora. (*going to him*) Well, dear, did you get rid of him?
Helmer. Yes, he just left.
Nora. Torvald, I want you to meet Kristine. She's just come to town.
Helmer. Kristine—? I'm sorry; I don't think—
Nora. Mrs. Linde, Torvald dear. Mrs. Kristine Linde.

Helmer. Ah, yes. A childhood friend of my wife's, I suppose.

Mrs. Linde. Yes, we've known each other for a long time.

Nora. Just think; she has come all this way just to see you.

Helmer. I'm not sure I understand—

Mrs. Linde. Well, not really—

Nora. You see, Kristine is an absolutely fantastic secretary, and she would so much like to work for a competent executive and learn more than she knows already—

Helmer. Very sensible, I'm sure, Mrs. Linde.

Nora. So when she heard about your appointment—there was a wire—she came here as fast as she could. How about it, Torvald? Couldn't you do something for Kristine? For my sake? Please?

Helmer. Quite possibly. I take it you're a widow, Mrs. Linde?

Mrs. Linde. Yes.

Helmer. And you've had office experience?

Mrs. Linde. Some—yes.

Helmer. In that case I think it's quite likely that I'll be able to find you a position.

Nora. (*claps her hands*) I knew it! I knew it!

Helmer. You've arrived at a most opportune time, Mrs. Linde.

Mrs. Linde. Oh, how can I ever thank you—

Helmer. Not at all, not at all. (*Puts his coat on.*) But today you'll have to excuse me—

Rank. Wait a minute; I'll come with you. (*Gets his fur coat from the front hall, warms it by the stove.*)

Nora. Don't be long, Torvald.

Helmer. An hour or so, no more.

Nora. Are you leaving, too, Kristine?

Mrs. Linde. (*putting on her things*) Yes, I better go and find a place to stay.

Helmer. Good. Then we'll be going the same way.

Nora. (*helping her*) I'm sorry this place is so small, but I don't think we very well could—

Mrs. Linde. Of course! Don't be silly, Nora. Goodbye, and thank you for everything.

Nora. Goodbye. We'll see you soon. You'll be back this evening, of course. And you too, Doctor Rank; right? If you feel well enough? Of course you will. Just wrap yourself up.

(*General small talk as all exit into the hall. Children's voices are heard on the stairs.*)

Nora. There they are! There they are! (*She runs and opens the door. THE NURSE ANNE-MARIE enters with the children.*) Come in! Come in!

(*Bends over and kisses them.*) Oh, you sweet, sweet darlings! Look at them, Kristine! Aren't they beautiful?

Rank. No standing around in the draft!

Helmer. Come along, Mrs. Linde. This place isn't fit for anyone but mothers right now.

(*DOCTOR RANK, HELMER, and MRS. LINDE go down the stairs. THE NURSE enters the living room with the CHILDREN. NORA follows, closing the door behind her.*)

Nora. My, how nice you all look! Such red cheeks! Like apples and roses. (*The children all talk at the same time.*) You've had so much fun? I *bet* you have. Oh, isn't that nice! You pulled both Emmy and Bob on your sleigh? Both at the same time? That's very good, Ivar. Oh, let me hold her for a minute, Anne-Marie. My sweet little doll baby! (*Takes the smallest of the children from THE NURSE and dances with her.*) Yes, yes, of course; Mama'll dance with you too, Bob. What? You threw snowballs? Oh, I wish I'd been there! No, no; *I* want to take their clothes off, Anne-Marie. Please let me; I think it's so much fun. You go on in. You look frozen. There's hot coffee on the stove.

(*THE NURSE exits in to the room to the left. NORA takes the children's wraps off and throws them all around. They all keep telling her things at the same time.*)

Nora. Oh, really? A big dog ran after you? But it didn't bite you? Of course not. Dogs don't bite sweet little doll babies. Don't peek at the packages, Ivar! What's in them? Wouldn't you like to know! No, no; that's something terrible! Play? You want to play? What do you want to play? Okay, let's play hide-and-seek. Bob hides first. You want *me* to? All right. I'll go first.

(*Laughing and shouting, NORA and the children play in the living room and in the adjacent room, right. Finally, NORA hides herself under the table; the children rush in, look for her, can't find her. They hear her low giggle, run to the table, lift the rug that covers it, see her. General hilarity. She crawls out, pretends to scare them. New delight. In the meantime there has been a knock on the door between the living room and the front hall, but nobody has noticed. Now the door is opened halfway; KROGSTAD appears. He waits a little. The play goes on.*)

Krogstad. Pardon me, Mrs. Helmer—

Nora. (*with a muted cry turns around, jumps up*) Ah! What do you want?

Krogstad. I'm sorry. The front door was open. Somebody must have forgotten to close it—

Nora. (standing up) My husband isn't here, Mr. Krogstad.

Krogstad. I know.

Nora. So what do you want?

Krogstad. I'd like a word with you.

Nora. With—! *(To the children.)* Go in to Anne-Marie. What? No, the strange man won't do anything bad to mama. When he's gone we'll play some more. *(She takes the children into the room to the left and closes the door.)*

Nora. (tense, troubled) You want to speak with me?

Krogstad. Yes I do.

Nora. Today—? It isn't the first of the month yet.

Krogstad. No, it's Christmas Eve. It's up to you what kind of holiday you'll have.

Nora. What do you want? I can't possibly—

Krogstad. Let's not talk about that just yet. There's something else. You do have a few minutes, don't you?

Nora. Yes. Yes, of course. That is,—

Krogstad. Good. I was sitting in Olsen's restaurant when I saw your husband go by.

Nora. Yes—?

Krogstad. —with a lady.

Nora. What of it?

Krogstad. May I be so free as to ask: wasn't that lady Mrs. Linde?

Nora. Yes.

Krogstad. Just arrived in town?

Nora. Yes, today.

Krogstad. She's a good friend of yours, I understand?

Nora. Yes, she is. But I fail to see—

Krogstad. I used to know her myself.

Nora. I know that.

Krogstad. So you know that. I thought as much. In that case, let me ask you a simple question. Is Mrs. Linde going to be employed in the bank?

Nora. What makes you think you have the right to cross examine me like this, Mr. Krogstad—you, one of my husband's employees? But since you ask, I'll tell you. Yes, Mrs. Linde is going to be working in the bank. And it was I who recommended her, Mr. Krogstad. Now you know.

Krogstad. So I was right.

Nora. (walks up and down) After all, one does have a little influence, you know. Just because you're a woman, it doesn't mean that—Really, Mr. Krogstad, people in a subordinate position should be careful not to offend someone who—oh well—

Krogstad. —has influence?

Nora. Exactly.

Krogstad. (*changing his tone*) Mrs. Helmer, I must ask you to be good enough to use your influence on my behalf.

Nora. Oh? What do you mean?

Krogstad. I want you to make sure that I am going to keep my subordinate position in the bank.

Nora. I don't understand. Who is going to take your position away from you?

Krogstad. There's no point in playing ignorant with me, Mrs. Helmer. I can very well appreciate that your friend would find it unpleasant to run into me. So now I know who I can thank for my dismissal.

Nora. But I assure you—

Krogstad. Never mind. I just want to say you still have time. I advise you to use your influence to prevent it.

Nora. But Mr. Krogstad, I don't have any influence—none at all.

Krogstad. No? I thought you just said—

Nora. Of course I didn't mean it that way. I! Whatever makes you think that I have any influence of that kind on my husband?

Krogstad. I went to law school with your husband. I have no reason to think that the Bank Manager is less susceptible than other husbands.

Nora. If you're going to insult my husband, I'll have to ask you to leave.

Krogstad. You're brave, Mrs. Helmer.

Nora. I'm not afraid of you any more. After New Year's I'll be out of this thing with you.

Krogstad. (*more controlled*) Listen, Mrs. Helmer. If necessary, I'll fight as for my life to keep my little job in the bank.

Nora. So it seems.

Krogstad. It isn't just the money; that's really the smallest part of it. There is something else—Well, I guess I might as well tell you. It's like this. I'm sure you know, like everybody else, that some years ago I committed—an impropriety.

Nora. I believe I've heard it mentioned.

Krogstad. The case never came to trial, but from that moment all doors were closed to me. So I took up the kind of business you know about. I had to do something, and I think I can say about myself that I have not been among the worst. But now I want to get out of all that. My sons are growing up. For their sake I must get back as much of my good name as I can. This job in the bank was like the first rung on the ladder. And now your husband wants to kick me down and leave me back in the mud again.

Nora. But I swear to you, Mr. Krogstad; it's not at all in my power to help you.

Krogstad. That's because you don't want to. But I have the means to force you.

Nora. You don't mean you're going to tell my husband I owe you money?

Krogstad. And if I did?

Nora. That would be a mean thing to do. (*Almost crying.*) That secret, which is my joy and my pride—for him to learn about it in such a coarse and ugly way—to learn it from *you*—! It would be terribly unpleasant for me.

Krogstad. Just unpleasant!

Nora. (*heatedly*) But go ahead! Do it! It will be worse for you than for me. When my husband realizes what a bad person you are, you're certainly going to lose your job.

Krogstad. I asked you if it was just domestic unpleasantness you were afraid of?

Nora. When my husband finds out, of course he'll pay off the loan, and then we won't have anything more to do with you.

Krogstad. (*stepping closer*) Listen, Mrs. Helmer—either you have a very bad memory, or you don't know much about business. I think I had better straighten you out on a few things.

Nora. What do you mean?

Krogstad. When your husband was ill, you came to me to borrow twelve hundred dollars.

Nora. I knew nobody else.

Krogstad. I promised to get you the money—

Nora. And you did.

Krogstad. —I promised to get you the money on certain conditions. At the time you were so anxious about your husband's health and so set on getting him away that I doubt very much that you paid much attention to the details of our transaction. That's why I remind you of them now. Anyway, I promised to get you the money if you would sign an I.O.U., which I drafted.

Nora. And which I signed.

Krogstad. Good. But below your signature I added a few lines, making your father security for the loan. Your father was supposed to put his signature to those lines.

Nora. Supposed to—? He did.

Krogstad. I had left the date blank. That is, your father was to date his own signature. You recall that, don't you, Mrs. Helmer?

Nora. I guess so—

Krogstad. I gave the note to you. You were to mail it to your father. Am I correct?

Nora. Yes.

Krogstad. And of course you did so right away, for no more than five or six days later you brought the paper back to me, signed by your father. Then I paid you the money.

Nora. Well? And haven't I been keeping up with the payments?

Krogstad. Fairly well, yes. But to get back to what we were talking about—those were difficult days for you, weren't they, Mrs. Helmer.

Nora. Yes, they were.

Krogstad. Your father was quite ill, I believe.

Nora. He was dying.

Krogstad. And died shortly afterwards?

Nora. That's right.

Krogstad. Tell me, Mrs. Helmer; do you happen to remember the date of your father's death? I mean the exact day of the month?

Nora. Daddy died on September 29.

Krogstad. Quite correct. I have ascertained that fact. That's why there is something peculiar about this (*takes out a piece of paper*), which I can't account for.

Nora. Peculiar? How? I don't understand—

Krogstad. It seems very peculiar, Mrs. Helmer, that your father signed this promissory note three days after his death.

Nora. How so? I don't see what—

Krogstad. Your father died on September 29. Now look. He has dated his signature October 2. Isn't that odd?

(*NORA remains silent*)

Krogstad. Can you explain it?

(*NORA still silent*)

Krogstad. I also find it striking that the date and the month and the year are not in your father's handwriting but in a hand I think I recognize. Well, that might be explained. Your father may have forgotten to date his signature and somebody else may have done it here, guessing at the date before he had learned of your father's death. That's all right. It's only the signature itself that matters. And that is genuine, isn't it, Mrs. Helmer? Your father *did* put his name to this note?

Nora. (*after a brief silence tosses her head back and looks defiantly at him*) No, he didn't. I wrote Daddy's name.

Krogstad. Mrs. Helmer—do you realize what a dangerous admission you just made?

Nora. Why? You'll get your money soon.

Krogstad. Let me ask you something. Why didn't you mail this note to your father?

Nora. Because it was impossible. Daddy was sick—you know that. If I had asked him for his signature I would have had to tell him what the money was for. But I couldn't tell him, as sick as he was, that my husband's life was in danger. That was impossible. Surely you can see that.

Krogstad. Then it would have been better for you if you had given up your trip abroad.

Nora. No, that was impossible! That trip was to save my husband's life. I couldn't give it up.

Krogstad. But didn't you realize that what you did amounted to fraud against me?

Nora. I couldn't let that make any difference. I didn't care about you at all. I hated the way you made all those difficulties for me, even though you knew the danger my husband was in. I thought you were cold and unfeeling.

Krogstad. Mrs. Helmer, obviously you have no clear idea of what you have done. Let me tell you that what I did that time was no more and no worse. And it ruined my name and reputation.

Nora. You! Are you trying to tell me that you did something brave once in order to save your wife's life?

Krogstad. The law doesn't ask about motives.

Nora. Then it's a bad law.

Krogstad. Bad or not—if I produce this note in court you'll be judged according to the law.

Nora. I refuse to believe you. A daughter shouldn't have the right to spare her dying old father worry and anxiety? A wife shouldn't have the right to save her husband's life? I don't know the laws very well, but I'm sure that somewhere they make allowance for cases like that. And you, a lawyer, don't know that? I think you must be a bad lawyer, Mr. Krogstad.

Krogstad. That may be. But business—the kind of business you and I have with one another—don't you think I know something about that? Very well. Do what you like. But let me tell you this: if I'm going to be kicked out again, you'll keep me company. (*He bows and exits through the front hall.*)

Nora. (*pauses thoughtfully; then, with a defiant toss of her head*). Oh, nonsense! Trying to scare me like that! I'm not all that silly. (*Starts picking up the children's clothes; soon stops.*) But—? No! That's impossible! I did it for love!

The Children. (*in the door to the left*) Mama, the strange man just left. We saw him.

Nora. Yes, yes; I know. But don't tell anybody about the strange man. Do you hear? Not even Daddy.

The Children. We won't. But now you'll play with us again, won't you, mama?

Nora. No, not right now.

The Children. Oh, but mama—you promised.

Nora. I know, but I can't just now. Go to your own room. I've so much to do. Be nice now, my little darlings. Do as I say. (*She nudges them gently into the other room and closes the door. She sits down on the couch, picks up a piece of embroidery, makes a few stitches, then stops.*) No! (*Throws the embroidery down, goes to the hall door and calls out:*) Helene! Bring the Christmas tree in here, please! (*Goes to the table, left, opens the drawer, halts.*) No—that's impossible!

The Maid. (*with the Christmas tree*) Where do you want it, ma'am?

Nora. There. The middle of the floor.

The Maid. You want anything else?

Nora. No, thanks. I have everything I need. (*THE MAID goes out. NORA starts trimming the tree.*) I want candles—and flowers—That awful man! Oh, nonsense! There's nothing wrong. This will be a lovely tree. I'll do everything you want me to, Torvald. I'll sing for you—dance for you—

(*HELMER, a bundle of papers under his arm, enters from outside.*)

Nora. Ah—you're back already?

Helmer. Yes. Has anybody been here?

Nora. Here? No.

Helmer. That's funny. I saw Krogstad leaving just now.

Nora. Oh? Oh yes, that's right. Krogstad was here for just a moment.

Helmer. I can tell from your face that he came to ask you to put in a word for him.

Nora. Yes.

Helmer. And it was supposed to be your own idea, wasn't it? You were not to tell me he'd been here. He asked you that too, didn't he?

Nora. Yes, Torvald, but—

Helmer. Nora, Nora, how could you! Talking to a man like that and making him promises! And lying to me about it afterwards—!

Nora. Lying—?

Helmer. Didn't you say nobody had been here? (*Shakes his finger at her.*) My little songbird must never do that again. Songbirds are supposed to have clean beaks to chirp with—no false notes. (*Puts his arm around her waist.*) Isn't that so? Of course it is. (*Lets her go.*) And that's enough about that. (*Sits down in front of the fireplace.*) Ah, it's nice and warm in here. (*Begins to leaf through his papers.*)

Nora. (*busy with the tree. After a brief pause*) Torvald.

Helmer. Yes.

Nora. I'm looking forward so much to the Stenborgs' costume party day after tomorrow.

Helmer. And I can't wait to find out what you're going to surprise me with.

Nora. Oh, that silly idea!

Helmer. Oh?

Nora. I can't think of anything. It all seems so foolish and pointless.

Helmer. Ah, my little Nora admits that?

Nora. (*behind his chair, her arms on the back of the chair*) Are you very busy, Torvald?

Helmer. Well—

Nora. What are all those papers?

Helmer. Bank business.

Nora. Already?

Helmer. I've asked the board to give me the authority to make certain changes in organization and personnel. That's what I'll be doing over the holidays. I want it all settled before New Year's.

Nora. So that's why this poor Krogstad—

Helmer. Hm.

Nora. (*leisurely playing with the hair on his neck*) If you weren't so busy, Torvald, I'd ask you for a great, big favor.

Helmer. Let's hear it, anyway.

Nora. I don't know anyone with better taste than you, and I want so much to look nice at the party. Couldn't you sort of take charge of me, Torvald, and decide what I'll wear—help me with my costume?

Helmer. Aha! Little Lady Obstinate is looking for someone to rescue her?

Nora. Yes, Torvald. I won't get anywhere without your help.

Helmer. All right. I'll think about it. We'll come up with something.

Nora. Oh, you *are* nice! (*Goes back to the Christmas tree. A pause.*) Those red flowers look so pretty.—Tell me, was it really all that bad what this Krogstad fellow did?

Helmer. He forged signatures. Do you have any idea what that means?

Nora. Couldn't it have been because he felt he had to?

Helmer. Yes, or like so many others he may simply have been thoughtless. I'm not so heartless as to condemn a man absolutely because of a single imprudent act.

Nora. Of course not, Torvald!

Helmer. People like him can redeem themselves morally by openly confessing their crime and taking their punishment.

Nora. Punishment—?

Helmer. But that was not the way Krogstad chose. He got out of it with tricks and evasions. That's what has corrupted him.

Nora. So you think that if—?

Helmer. Can't you imagine how a guilty person like that has to lie and fake and dissemble wherever he goes—putting on a mask before everybody he's close to, even his own wife and children? It's this thing with the children that's the worst part of it, Nora.

Nora. Why is that?

Helmer. Because when a man lives inside such a circle of stinking lies he brings infection into his own home and contaminates his whole family. With every breath of air his children inhale the germs of something ugly.

Nora. (*moving closer behind him*) Are you so sure of that?

Helmer. Of course I am. I have seen enough examples of that in my work. Nearly all young criminals have had mothers who lied.

Nora. Why mothers—particularly?

Helmer. Most often mothers. But of course fathers tend to have the same influence. Every lawyer knows that. And yet, for years this Krogstad has been poisoning his own children in an atmosphere of lies and deceit.

That's why I call him a lost soul morally. (*Reaches out for her hands.*) And that's why my sweet little Nora must promise me never to take his side again. Let's shake on that.—What? What's this? Give me your hand! There! Now that's settled. I assure you, I would find it impossible to work in the same room with that man. I feel literally sick when I'm around people like that.

Nora. (*withdraws her hand and goes to the other side of the Christmas tree*) It's so hot in here. And I have so much to do.

Helmer. (*gets up and collects his papers*) Yes, and I really should try to get some of this reading done before dinner. I must think about your costume too. And maybe just possibly I'll have something to wrap in gilt paper and hang on the Christmas tree. (*Puts his hand on her head.*) Oh my adorable little songbird! (*Enters his study and closes the door.*)

Nora. (*after a pause, in a low voice*) It's all a lot of nonsense. It's not that way at all. It's impossible. It has to be impossible.

The Nurse. (*in the door, left*) The little ones are asking ever so nicely if they can't come in and be with their mama.

Nora. No, no, no! Don't let them in here! You stay with them, Anne-Marie.

The Nurse. If you say so, ma'am. (*Closes the door.*)

Nora. (*pale with terror*) Corrupt my little children—! Poison my home—? (*Brief pause; she lifts her head.*) That's not true. Never. Never in a million years.

ACT II

The same room. The Christmas tree is in the corner by the piano, stripped, shabby-looking, with burnt-down candles. NORA's outdoor clothes are on the couch. NORA is alone. She walks around restlessly. She stops by the couch and picks up her coat.

Nora. (*drops the coat again*) There's somebody now! (*Goes to the door, listens.*) No. Nobody. Of course not—not on Christmas. And not tomorrow either.[1]—But perhaps—(*Opens the door and looks.*) No, nothing in the mailbox. All empty. (*Comes forward.*) How silly I am! Of course he isn't serious. Nothing like that could happen. After all, I have three small children.

(THE NURSE enters from the room, left, carrying a big carton.)

The Nurse. Well, at last I found it—the box with your costume.

Nora. Thanks. Just put it on the table.

---

[1] In Norway both December 25 and 26 are legal holidays.

The Nurse. (does so) But it's all a big mess, I'm afraid.

Nora. Oh, I wish I could tear the whole thing to little pieces!

Nurse. Heavens! It's not as bad as all that. It can be fixed all right. All it takes is a little patience.

Nora. I'll go over and get Mrs. Linde to help me.

Nurse. Going out again? In this awful weather? You'll catch a cold.

Nora. That might not be such a bad thing. How are the children?

Nurse. The poor little dears are playing with their presents, but—

Nora. Do they keep asking for me?

Nurse. Well, you know, they're used to being with their mama.

Nora. I know. But Anne-Marie, from now on I can't be with them as much as before.

Nurse. Oh well. Little children get used to everything.

Nora. You think so? Do you think they'll forget their mama if I were gone altogether?

Nurse. Goodness me—gone altogether?

Nora. Listen, Anne-Marie; something I've often wondered about. How could you bring yourself to leave your child with strangers?

Nurse. But I had to, if I were to nurse you.

Nora. Yes, but how could you *want* to?

Nurse. When I could get such a nice place? When something like that happens to a poor young girl, she'd better be grateful for whatever she gets. For *he* didn't do a thing for me—the louse!

Nora. But your daughter has forgotten all about you, hasn't she?

Nurse. Oh no! Not at all! She wrote to me both when she was confirmed and when she got married.

Nora. (putting her arms around her neck) You dear old thing—you were a good mother to me when I was little.

Nurse. Poor little Nora had no one else, you know.

Nora. And if my little ones didn't, I know you'd—oh, I'm being silly! (*Opens the carton.*) Go in to them, please. I really should—. Tomorrow you'll see how pretty I'll be.

Nurse. I know. There won't be anybody at that party half as pretty as you, ma'am. (*Goes out, left.*)

Nora. (begins to take clothes out of the carton. In a moment she throws it all down.) If only I dared to go out. If only I knew nobody would come—that nothing would happen while I was gone.—How silly! Nobody'll come. Just don't think about it. Brush the muff. Beautiful gloves. Beautiful gloves. Forget it. Forget it. One, two, three, four, five, six—(*Cries out.*) There they are! (*Moves toward the door, stops irresolutely.*)

(*MRS. LINDE enters from the hall. She has already taken off her coat.*)

Nora. Oh, it's you, Kristine. There's no one else out there, is there? I'm so glad you're here.

Mrs. Linde. They told me you'd asked for me.

Nora. I just happened to walk by. I need your help with something—badly. Let's sit here on the couch. Look. Torvald and I are going to a costume party tomorrow night—at Consul Stenborg's upstairs—and Torvald wants me to go as a Neapolitan fisher girl and dance the Tarantella. I learned it when we were on Capri, don't you know.

Mrs. Linde. Well, well! So you'll be putting on a whole show?

Nora. Yes. Torvald thinks I should. Look, here's the costume. Torvald had it made for me while we were there. But it's all so torn and everything. I just don't know—

Mrs. Linde. Oh that can be fixed. It's not that much. The trimmings have come loose in a few places. Do you have needle and thread? Ah, here we are. All set.

Nora. I really appreciate it, Kristine.

Mrs. Linde. (*sewing*) So you'll be in disguise tomorrow night, eh? You know—I may come by for just a moment, just to look at you.—Oh dear, I haven't even thanked you for the nice evening last night.

Nora. (*gets up, moves around*) Oh I don't know. I don't think last night was as nice as it usually is.—You should have come to town a little earlier, Kristine.—Yes, Torvald knows how to make it nice and pretty around here.

Mrs. Linde. You too, I should think. After all, you're your father's daughter. By the way, is Dr. Rank always as depressed as he was last night?

Nora. No, last night was unusual. He's a very sick man, you know—very sick. Poor Rank, his spine is rotting away or something. Tuberculosis, I think. You see, his father was a nasty old man with mistresses and all that sort of thing. Rank has been sickly ever since he was a little boy.

Mrs. Linde. (*dropping her sewing to her lap*) But dearest Nora, where have you learned about things like that?

Nora. (*still walking about*) Oh, you know—with three children you sometimes get to talk with—other wives. Some of them know quite a bit about medicine. So you pick up a few things.

Mrs. Linde. (*resumes her sewing. After a brief pause*) Does Dr. Rank come here every day?

Nora. Every single day. He's Torvald's oldest and best friend, after all. And my friend too, for that matter. He's part of the family, almost.

Mrs. Linde. But tell me, is he quite sincere? I mean, isn't he the kind of man who likes to say nice things to people?

Nora. No, not at all. Rather the opposite, in fact. What makes you say that?

Mrs. Linde. When you introduced us yesterday, he told me he'd often heard my name mentioned in this house. But later on it was quite obvious that your husband really had no idea who I was. So how could Dr. Rank—?

Nora. You're right, Kristine, but I can explain that. You see, Torvald loves me so very much that he wants me all to himself. That's what he says. When we were first married he got jealous, almost, when I as much as mentioned anybody from back home that I was fond of. So of course I soon stopped doing that. But with Dr. Rank I often talk about home. You see, he likes to listen to me.

Mrs. Linde. Look here, Nora. In many ways you're still a child. After all, I'm quite a bit older than you and have had more experience. I want to give you a piece of advice. I think you should get out of this thing with Dr. Rank.

Nora. Get out of what thing?

Mrs. Linde. Several things in fact, if you want my opinion. Yesterday you said something about a rich admirer who was going to give you money—

Nora. One who doesn't exist, unfortunately. What of it?

Mrs. Linde. Does Dr. Rank have money?

Nora. Yes he does.

Mrs. Linde. And no dependents?

Nora. No. But—?

Mrs. Linde. And he comes here every day?

Nora. Yes, I told you that already.

Mrs. Linde. But how can that sensitive man be so tactless?

Nora. I haven't the slightest idea what you're talking about.

Mrs. Linde. Don't play games with me, Nora. Don't you think I know who you borrowed the twelve hundred dollars from?

Nora. Are you out of your mind! The very idea—! A friend of both of us who sees us every day—! What a dreadfully uncomfortable position that would be!

Mrs. Linde. So it really isn't Dr. Rank?

Nora. Most certainly not! I would never have dreamed of asking him—not for a moment. Anyway, he didn't have any money then. He inherited it afterwards.

Mrs. Linde. Well, I still think that may have been lucky for you, Nora dear.

Nora. The idea! It would never have occurred to me to ask Dr. Rank—. Though I'm sure that if I *did* ask him—

Mrs. Linde. But of course you won't.

Nora. Of course not. I can't imagine that would ever be necessary. But I am quite sure that if I told Dr. Rank—

Mrs. Linde. Behind your husband's back?

Nora. I must get out of—this other thing. That's also behind his back. I *must* get out of it.

Mrs. Linde. That's what I told you yesterday. But—

Nora. (*walking up and down*) A man manages these things so much better than a woman—

Mrs. Linde. One's husband, yes.

Nora. Silly, silly! (*Stops.*) When you've paid off all you owe, you get your I.O.U. back; right?

Mrs. Linde. Yes, of course.

Nora. And you can tear it into a hundred thousand little pieces and burn it—that dirty, filthy paper!

Mrs. Linde. (*looks hard at her, puts down her sewing, rises slowly*) Nora—you're hiding something from me.

Nora. Can you tell?

Mrs. Linde. Something's happened to you, Nora, since yesterday morning. What is it?

Nora. (*going to her*) Kristine! (*Listens.*) Shhh. Torvald just came back. Listen. Why don't you go in to the children for a while. Torvald can't stand having sewing around. Get Anne-Marie to help you.

Mrs. Linde. (*gathers some of the sewing things together*) All right, but I'm not leaving here till you and I have talked.

(*She goes out left, just as HELMER enters from the front hall.*)

Nora. (*towards him*) I have been waiting and waiting for you, Torvald.

Helmer. Was that the dressmaker?

Nora. No, it was Kristine. She's helping me with my costume. Oh Torvald, just wait till you see how nice I'll look!

Helmer. I told you. Pretty good idea I had, wasn't it?

Nora. Lovely! Marvellous! And wasn't it nice of me to go along with it?

Helmer. (*his hand under her chin*) Nice? To do what your husband tells you? All right, you little rascal; I know you didn't mean it that way. But don't let me interrupt you. I suppose you want to try it on.

Nora. And you'll be working?

Helmer. Yes. (*Shows her a pile of papers.*) Look. I've been down to the bank. (*Is about to enter his study.*)

Nora. Torvald.

Helmer. (*halts*) Yes?

Nora. What if your little squirrel asked you ever so nicely—

Helmer. For what?

Nora. Would you do it?

Helmer. Depends on what it is.

Nora. Squirrel would run around and do all sorts of fun tricks if you'd be nice and agreeable.

Helmer. All right. What is it?

Nora. Lark would chirp and twitter in all the rooms, up and down—

Helmer. So what? Lark does that anyway.

Nora. I'll be your elfmaid and dance for you in the moonlight, Torvald.

Helmer. Nora, don't tell me it's the same thing you mentioned this morning?

Nora. (*closer to him*) Yes, Torvald. I beg you!

Helmer. You really have the nerve to bring that up again?

Nora. Yes. You've just got to do as I say. You *must* let Krogstad keep his job.

Helmer. My dear Nora. It's his job I intend to give to Mrs. Linde.

Nora. I know. And that's ever so nice of you. But can't you just fire somebody else?

Helmer. This is incredible! You just don't give up, do you? Because *you* make some foolish promise, *I* am supposed to—!

Nora. That's not the reason, Torvald. It's for your own sake. That man writes for the worst newspapers. You've said so yourself. There's no telling what he may do to you. I'm scared to death of him.

Helmer. Ah, I understand. You're afraid because of what happened before.

Nora. What do you mean?

Helmer. You're thinking of your father, of course.

Nora. Yes. Yes, you're right. Remember the awful things they wrote about Daddy in the newspapers? I really think they might have forced him to resign if the ministry hadn't sent you to look into the charges and if you hadn't been so helpful and understanding.

Helmer. My dear little Nora, there is a world of difference between your father and me. Your father's official conduct was not above reproach. Mine is, and I intend it to stay that way as long as I hold my position.

Nora. Oh, but you don't know what vicious people like him may think of. Oh Torvald! Now all of us could be so happy together here in our own home, peaceful and carefree. Such a good life, Torvald, for you and me and the children. That's why I implore you—

Helmer. And it's exactly because you plead for him that you make it impossible for me to keep him. It's already common knowledge in the bank that I intend to let Krogstad go. If it gets out that the new manager has changed his mind because of his wife—

Nora. Yes? What then?

Helmer. No, of course, that wouldn't matter at all as long as little Mrs. Pighead here got her way! Do you want me to make myself look ridiculous before my whole staff—make people think I can be pushed around by just anybody—by outsiders? Believe me, I'd soon find out what the consequences would be! Besides, there's another thing that makes it absolutely impossible for Krogstad to stay on in the bank now that I'm in charge.

Nora. What's that?

Helmer. I suppose in a pinch I could overlook his moral shortcomings—

Nora. Yes, you could; couldn't you, Torvald?

Helmer. And I understand he's quite a good worker, too. But we've known each other for a long time. It's one of those imprudent relationships you get into when you're young that embarrass you for the rest of your life. I guess I might as well be frank with you: he and I

are on a first name basis. And that tactless fellow never hides the fact
even when other people are around. Rather, he seems to think it entitles
him to be familiar with me. Every chance he gets he comes out with his
damn "Torvald, Torvald." I'm telling you, I find it most awkward. He
would make my position in the bank intolerable.

Nora. You don't really mean any of this, Torvald.

Helmer. Oh? I don't? And why not?

Nora. No, for it's all so petty.

Helmer. What! Petty? You think I'm being petty?

Nora. No, I *don't* think you are petty, Torvald dear. That's exactly
why I—

Helmer. Never mind. You think my reasons are petty, so it follows that I
must be petty too. Petty! Indeed! By god, I'll put an end to this right
now! (*Opens the door to the front hall and calls out.*) Helene!

Nora. What are you doing?

Helmer. (*searching among his papers*) Making a decision. (*THE MAID
enters.*) Here. Take this letter. Go out with it right away. Find
somebody to deliver it. But quick. The address is on the envelope. Wait.
Here's money.

The Maid. Very good, sir. (*She takes the letter and goes out.*)

Helmer. (*collecting his papers*) There now, little Mrs. Obstinate!

Nora. (*breathless*) Torvald—what was that letter?

Helmer. Krogstad's dismissal.

Nora. Call it back, Torvald! There's still time! Oh Torvald, please—call it
back! For my sake, for your own sake, for the sake of the children!
Listen to me, Torvald! Do it! You don't know what you're doing to all
of us!

Helmer. Too late.

Nora. Yes. Too late.

Helmer. Dear Nora. I forgive you this fear you're in, although it really is
an insult to me. Yes, it is! It's an insult to think that I am scared of a
shabby scrivener's revenge. But I forgive you, for it's such a beautiful
proof how much you love me. (*Takes her in his arms.*) And that's the
way it should be, my sweet darling. Whatever happens, you'll see that
when things get really rough I have both strength and courage. You'll
find out that I am man enough to shoulder the whole burden.

Nora. (*terrified*) What do you mean by that?

Helmer. All of it, I tell you—

Nora. (*composed*) You'll never have to do that.

Helmer. Good. Then we'll share the burden, Nora—like husband and
wife, the way it ought to be. (*Caresses her.*) Now are you satisfied?
There, there, there. Not that look in your eyes—like a frightened little
dove. It's all your own foolish imagination.—Why don't you practise
the Tarantella—and your tambourine, too. I'll be in the inner office.
When I close both doors I won't hear a thing. You may make as much

noise as you like. (*Turning in the doorway.*) And when Rank comes, why don't you tell him where to find me. (*He nods to her, enters his study carrying his papers, and closes the door.*)

Nora. (*transfixed by terror, whispers*) He would do it. He'll do it. He'll do it in spite of the whole world.—No, this mustn't happen. Anything rather than that! There must be a way—! (*The doorbell rings.*) Doctor Rank! Anything rather than that! Anything—anything at all!

(*She passes her hand over her face, pulls herself together, and opens the door to the hall. DR. RANK is out there, hanging up his coat. Darkness begins to fall during the following scene.*)

Nora. Hello there, Dr. Rank. I recognized your ringing. Don't go in to Torvald yet. I think he's busy.
Rank. And you?
Nora. (*as he enters and she closes the door behind him*) You know I always have time for you.
Rank. Thanks. I'll make use of that as long as I can.
Nora. What do you mean by that? "As long as you can"?
Rank. Does that frighten you?
Nora. Well, it's a funny expression. As if something was going to happen.
Rank. Something is going to happen that I've long been expecting. But I admit I hadn't thought it would come quite so soon.
Nora. (*seizes his arm*) What is it you've found out? Dr. Rank—tell me!
Rank. (*sits down by the stove*) I'm going downhill fast. There's nothing to be done about that.
Nora. (*with audible relief*) So it's you—
Rank. Who else? No point in lying to myself. I'm in worse shape than any of my other patients, Mrs. Helmer. These last few days I've been making up my inner status. Bankrupt. Chances are that within a month I'll be rotting up in the cemetery.
Nora. Shame on you! Talking that horrid way!
Rank. The thing itself is horrid—damn horrid. The worst of it, though, is all that other horror that comes first. There is only one more test I need to make. After that I'll have a pretty good idea when I'll start coming apart. There is something I want to say to you. Helmer's refined nature can't stand anything hideous. I don't want him in my sick room.
Nora. Oh but Dr. Rank—
Rank. I don't want him there. Under no circumstance. I'll close my door to him. As soon as I have full certainty that the worst is about to begin I'll give you my card with a black cross on it. Then you'll know the last, horrible destruction has started.
Nora. Today you're really quite impossible. And I had hoped you'd be in a particularly good mood.

Rank. With death on my hands? Paying for someone else's sins? Is there justice in that? And yet there isn't a single family that isn't ruled by that same law of ruthless retribution, in one way or another.

Nora. (*puts her hands over her ears*) Poppycock! Be fun! Be fun!

Rank. Well, yes. You may just as well laugh at the whole thing. My poor, innocent spine is suffering for my father's frolics when he was a young lieutenant.

Nora. (*over by the table, left*) Right. He was addicted to asparagus and goose liver paté, wasn't he?

Rank. And truffles.

Nora. Of course. Truffles. And oysters too, I think.

Rank. And oysters. Obviously.

Nora. And all the port and champagne that go with it. It's really too bad that goodies like that ruin your backbone.

Rank. Particularly an unfortunate backbone that never enjoyed any of it.

Nora. Ah yes, that's the saddest part of it all.

Rank. (*looks searchingly at her*) Hm—

Nora. (*after a brief pause*) Why did you smile just then?

Rank. I didn't. It was you who laughed.

Nora. No, it was you who smiled, Dr. Rank!

Rank. (*gets up*) I see you're more of a mischief-maker than I thought.

Nora. I feel like mischief today.

Rank. So it seems.

Nora. (*with both her hands on his shoulders*) Dear, dear Dr. Rank, don't you go and die and leave Torvald and me.

Rank. Oh, you won't miss me for very long. Those who go away are soon forgotten.

Nora. (*with an anxious look*) Do you believe that?

Rank. You'll make new friends, and then—

Nora. Who'll make new friends?

Rank. Both you and Helmer, once I'm gone. You yourself seem to have made a good start already. What was this Mrs. Linde doing here last night?

Nora. Aha—Don't tell me you're jealous of poor Kristine?

Rank. Yes I am. She'll be my successor in this house. As soon as I have made my excuses, that woman is likely to—

Nora. Shh—not so loud. She's in there.

Rank. Today too? There you are!

Nora. She's mending my costume. My god, you really *are* unreasonable. (*Sits down on the couch.*) Now be nice, Dr. Rank. Tomorrow you'll see how beautifully I'll dance, and then you are to pretend I'm dancing just for you—and for Torvald too, of course. (*Takes several items out of the carton.*) Sit down, Dr. Rank; I want to show you something.

Rank. (*sitting down*) What?

Nora. Look.

Rank. Silk stockings.

Nora. Flesh-colored. Aren't they lovely? Now it's getting dark in here, but tomorrow—No, no. You only get to see the foot. Oh well, you might as well see all of it.

Rank. Hm.

Nora. Why do you look so critical? Don't you think they'll fit?

Rank. That's something I can't possibly have a reasoned opinion about.

Nora. (*looks at him for a moment*) Shame on you. (*Slaps his ear lightly with the stocking.*) That's what you get. (*Puts the things back in the carton.*)

Rank. And what other treasures are you going to show me?

Nora. Nothing at all, because you're naughty. (*She hums a little and rummages in the carton.*)

Rank. (*after a brief silence*) When I sit here like this, talking confidently with you, I can't imagine—I can't possibly imagine what would have become of me if I hadn't had you and Helmer.

Nora. (*smiles*) Well, yes—I do believe you like being with us.

Rank. (*in a lower voice, lost in thought*) And then to have to go away from it all—

Nora. Nonsense. You're not going anywhere.

Rank. (*as before*)—and not leave behind as much as a poor little token of gratitude, hardly a brief memory of someone missed, nothing but a vacant place that anyone can fill.

Nora. And what if I were to ask you—? No—

Rank. Ask me what?

Nora. For a great proof of your friendship—

Rank. Yes, yes—?

Nora. No, I mean—for an enormous favor—

Rank. Would you really for once make me as happy as all that?

Nora. But you don't even know what it is.

Rank. Well, then; tell me.

Nora. Oh, but I can't, Dr. Rank. It's altogether too much to ask—It's advice and help and a favor—

Rank. So much the better. I can't even begin to guess what it is you have in mind. So for heaven's sake tell me! Don't you trust me?

Nora. Yes, I trust you more than anybody I know. You are my best and most faithful friend. I know that. So I will tell you. All right, Dr. Rank. There is something you can help me prevent. You know how much Torvald loves me—beyond all words. Never for a moment would he hesitate to give his life for me.

Rank. (*leaning over her*) Nora—do you really think he's the only one—?

Nora. (*with a slight start*) Who—?

Rank. —who'd gladly give his life for you.

Nora. (*heavily*) I see.

Rank. I have sworn an oath to myself to tell you before I go. I'll never find a better occasion.—All right, Nora; now you know. And now you also know that you can confide in me, more than in anyone else.

Nora. (gets up. In a calm, steady voice) Let me get by.

Rank. (makes room for her but remains seated) Nora—

Nora. (in the door to the front hall). Helene, bring the lamp in here, please. (*Walks over to the stove.*) Oh, dear Dr. Rank. That really wasn't very nice of you.

Rank. (gets up). That I have loved you as much as anybody—was that not nice?

Nora. No, not that. But that you told me. There was no need for that.

Rank. What do you mean? Have you known—?

(*THE MAID enters with the lamp, puts it on the table, and goes out.*)

Rank. Nora—Mrs. Helmer—I'm asking you: did you know?

Nora. Oh, how can I tell what I knew and didn't know! I really can't say—But that you could be so awkward, Dr. Rank! Just when everything was so comfortable.

Rank. Well, anyway, now you know that I'm at your service with my life and soul. And now you must speak.

Nora. (looks at him) After what just happened?

Rank. I beg you—let me know what it is.

Nora. There is nothing I can tell you now.

Rank. Yes, yes. You mustn't punish me this way. Please let me do for you whatever anyone *can* do.

Nora. Now there is nothing you can do. Besides, I don't think I really need any help, anyway. It's probably just my imagination. Of course that's all it is. I'm sure of it! (*Sits down in the rocking chair, looks at him, smiles.*) Well, well, well, Dr. Rank! What a fine gentleman you turned out to be! Aren't you ashamed of yourself, now that we have light?

Rank. No, not really. But perhaps I ought to leave—and not come back?

Nora. Don't be silly; of course not! You'll come here exactly as you have been doing. You know perfectly well that Torvald can't do without you.

Rank. Yes, but what about you?

Nora. Oh, I always think it's perfectly delightful when you come.

Rank. That's the very thing that misled me. You are a riddle to me. It has often seemed to me that you'd just as soon be with me as with Helmer.

Nora. Well, you see, there are people you love, and then there are other people you'd almost rather be with.

Rank. Yes, there is something in that.

Nora. When I lived home with Daddy, of course I loved him most. But I always thought it was so much fun to sneak off down to the maids' room, for they never gave me good advice and they always talked about such fun things.

Rank. Aha! So it's *their* place I have taken.

Nora. (*jumps up and goes over to him*) Oh dear, kind Dr. Rank, you know very well I didn't mean it that way. Can't you see that with Torvald it is the way it used to be with Daddy?

(*THE MAID enters from the front hall.*)

The Maid. Ma'am! (*Whispers to her and gives her a caller's card.*)
Nora. (*glances at the card*). Ah! (*Puts it in her pocket.*)
Rank. Anything wrong?
Nora. No, no; not at all. It's nothing—just my new costume—
Rank. But your costume is lying right there!
Nora. Oh yes, that one. But this is another one. I ordered it. Torvald mustn't know—
Rank. Aha. So that's the great secret.
Nora. That's it. Why don't you go in to him, please. He's in the inner office. And keep him there for a while—
Rank. Don't worry. He won't get away. (*Enters HELMER's study.*)
Nora. (*to the MAID*) You say he's waiting in the kitchen?
The Maid. Yes. He came up the back stairs.
Nora. But didn't you tell him there was somebody with me?
The Maid. Yes, but he wouldn't listen.
Nora. He won't leave?
The Maid. No, not till he's had a word with you, ma'am.
Nora. All right. But try not to make any noise. And, Helene—don't tell anyone he's here. It's supposed to be a surprise for my husband.
The Maid. I understand, ma'am—(*She leaves.*)
Nora. The terrible is happening. It's happening, after all. No, no, no. It can't happen. It won't happen. (*She bolts the study door.*)

(*THE MAID opens the front hall door for KROGSTAD and closes the door behind him. He wears a fur coat for traveling, boots, and a fur hat.*)

Nora. (*toward him*) Keep your voice down. My husband's home.
Krogstad. That's all right.
Nora. What do you want?
Krogstad. To find out something.
Nora. Then hurry. What?
Krogstad. I expect you know I've been fired.
Nora. I couldn't prevent it, Mr. Krogstad. I fought for you as long and as hard as I could, but it didn't do any good.
Krogstad. Your husband doesn't love you any more than that? He knows what I can do to you, and yet he runs the risk—
Nora. Surely you didn't think I'd tell him?
Krogstad. No, I really didn't. It wouldn't be like Torvald Helmer to show that kind of guts—
Nora. Mr. Krogstad, I insist that you show respect for my husband.

Krogstad. By all means. All due respect. But since you're so anxious to keep this a secret, may I assume that you are a little better informed than yesterday about exactly what you have done?

Nora. Better than *you* could ever teach me.

Krogstad. Of course. Such a bad lawyer as I am—

Nora. What do you want of me?

Krogstad. I just wanted to see how you were, Mrs. Helmer. I've been thinking about you all day. You see, even a bill collector, a pen pusher, a—anyway, someone like me—even he has a little of what they call a heart.

Nora. Then show it. Think of my little children.

Krogstad. Have you and your husband thought of mine? Never mind. All I want to tell you is that you don't need to take this business too seriously. I have no intention of bringing charges right away.

Nora. Oh no, you wouldn't; would you? I knew you wouldn't.

Krogstad. The whole thing can be settled quite amicably. Nobody else needs to know anything. It will be between the three of us.

Nora. My husband must never find out about this.

Krogstad. How are you going to prevent it? Maybe you can pay me the balance on the loan?

Nora. No, not right now.

Krogstad. Or do you have some way of raising the money in the next few days?

Nora. None I intend to make use of.

Krogstad. It wouldn't do you any good, anyway. Even if you had the cash in your hand right this minute, I wouldn't give you your note back. It wouldn't make any difference *how* much money you offered me.

Nora. Then you'll have to tell me what you plan to use the note *for*.

Krogstad. Just keep it; that's all. Have it on hand, so to speak. I won't say a word to anybody else. So if you've been thinking about doing something desperate—

Nora. I have.

Krogstad. —like leaving house and home—

Nora. I have!

Krogstad. —or even something worse—

Nora. How did you know?

Krogstad. —then: don't.

Nora. How did you know I was thinking of *that?*

Krogstad. Most of us do, right at first. I did, too, but when it came down to it I didn't have the courage—

Nora. (*tonelessly*) Nor do I.

Krogstad. (*relieved*) See what I mean? I thought so. You don't either.

Nora. I don't. I don't.

Krogstad. Besides, it would be very silly of you. Once that first domestic blow-up is behind you—. Here in my pocket is a letter for your husband.

Nora. Telling him everything?

Krogstad. As delicately as possible.

Nora. (quickly). He mustn't get that letter. Tear it up. I'll get you the money somehow.

Krogstad. Excuse me, Mrs. Helmer. I thought I just told you—

Nora. I'm not talking about the money I owe you. Just let me know how much money you want from my husband, and I'll get it for you.

Krogstad. I want no money from your husband.

Nora. Then what *do* you want?

Krogstad. I'll tell you, Mrs. Helmer. I want to rehabilitate myself; I want to get up in the world; and your husband is going to help me. For a year and a half I haven't done anything disreputable. All that time I have been struggling with the most miserable circumstances. I was content to work my way up step by step. Now I've been kicked out, and I'm no longer satisfied just getting my old job back. I want more than that; I want to get to the top. I'm quite serious. I want the bank to take me back but in a higher position. I want your husband to create a new job for me—

Nora. He'll never do that!

Krogstad. He will. I know him. He won't dare not to. And once I'm back inside and he and I are working together, you'll see! Within a year I'll be the manager's right hand. It will be Nils Krogstad and not Torvald Helmer who'll be running the Mutual Bank.

Nora. You'll never see that happen!

Krogstad. Are you thinking of—?

Nora. Now I *do* have the courage.

Krogstad. You can't scare me. A fine, spoiled lady like you—

Nora. You'll see, you'll see!

Krogstad. Under the ice, perhaps? Down in that cold, black water? Then spring comes, and you float up again—hideous, ugly, unrecognizable, hair all gone—

Nora. You don't frighten me.

Krogstad. Nor you me. One doesn't do that sort of thing, Mrs. Helmer. Besides, what good would it do? He'd still be in my power.

Nora. Afterwards? When I'm no longer—?

Krogstad. Aren't you forgetting that your reputation would be in my hands?

(NORA stares at him, speechless.)

Krogstad. All right; now I've told you what to expect. So don't do anything foolish. When Helmer gets my letter I expect to hear from him. And don't you forget that it's your husband himself who forces me to use such means again. That I'll never forgive him. Goodbye, Mrs. Helmer. *(Goes out through the hall.)*

Nora. (at the door, opens it a little, listens) He's going. And no letter. Of course not! That would be impossible! *(Opens the door more.)* What's he doing? He's still there. Doesn't go down. Having second thoughts—? Will he—?

(The sound of a letter dropping into the mailbox. Then KROGSTAD's steps are heard going down the stairs, gradually dying away.)

Nora. (with a muted cry runs forward to the table by the couch. Brief pause) In the mailbox. *(Tiptoes back to the door to the front hall.)* There it is. Torvald, Torvald—now we're lost!

Mrs. Linde. (enters from the left, carrying NORA's Capri costume) There now. I think it's all fixed. Why don't we try it on you—

Nora. (in a low, hoarse voice). Kristine, come here.

Mrs. Linde. What's wrong with you? You look quite beside yourself.

Nora. Come over here. Do you see that letter? There, look—through the glass in the mailbox.

Mrs. Linde. Yes, yes; I see it.

Nora. That letter is from Krogstad.

Mrs. Linde. Nora—it was Krogstad who lent you the money!

Nora. Yes, and now Torvald will find out about it.

Mrs. Linde. Oh believe me, Nora. That's the best thing for both of you.

Nora. There's more to it than you know. I forged a signature—

Mrs. Linde. Oh my god—!

Nora. I just want to tell you this, Kristine, that you must be my witness.

Mrs. Linde. Witness? How? Witness to what?

Nora. If I lose my mind—and that could very well happen—

Mrs. Linde. Nora!

Nora. —or if something were to happen to me—something that made it impossible for me to be here—

Mrs. Linde. Nora, Nora! You're not yourself!

Nora. —and if someone were to take all the blame, assume the whole responsibility—Do you understand—?

Mrs. Linde. Yes, yes; but how can you think—!

Nora. —then you are to witness that that's not so, Kristine. I am not beside myself. I am perfectly rational, and what I'm telling you is that nobody else has known about this, I've done it all by myself, the whole thing. Just remember that.

Mrs. Linde. I will. But I don't understand any of it.

Nora. Oh, how could you! For it's the wonderful that's about to happen.

Mrs. Linde. The wonderful?

Nora. Yes, the wonderful. But it's so terrible, Kristine. It mustn't happen for anything in the world!

Mrs. Linde. I'm going over to talk to Krogstad right now.

Nora. No, don't. Don't go to him. He'll do something bad to you.

Mrs. Linde. There was a time when he would have done anything for me.

Nora. He!

Mrs. Linde. Where does he live?

Nora. Oh, I don't know—Yes, wait a minute (*reaches into her pocket.*)— here's his card.—But the letter, the letter—!

Helmer. (*in his study, knocks on the door*) Nora!

Nora. (*cries out in fear*) Oh, what is it? What do you want?

Helmer. That's all right. Nothing to be so scared about. We're not coming in. For one thing, we can't. You've bolted the door, you know. Are you trying on your costume?

Nora. Yes—yes, I am. I'm going to be so pretty, Torvald.

Mrs. Linde. (*looking at the card*) He lives just around the corner.

Nora. I know, but it's no use. Nothing can save us now. The letter is in the mailbox.

Mrs. Linde. And your husband has the key?

Nora. Yes. He always keeps it with him.

Mrs. Linde. Krogstad must ask for his letter back, unread. He's got to think up some pretext or other—

Nora. But this is just the time of day when Torvald—

Mrs. Linde. Delay him. Go in to him. I'll be back as soon as I can. (*She hurries out through the hall door.*)

Nora. (*walks over to HELMER's door, opens it, and peeks in*) Torvald!

Helmer. (*still offstage*) Well, well! So now one's allowed in one's own living room again. Come on, Rank. Now we'll see—(*In the doorway.*) But what's this?

Nora. What, Torvald dear?

Helmer. Rank prepared me for a splendid metamorphosis.

Rank. (*in the doorway*) That's how I understood it. Evidently I was mistaken.

Nora. Nobody gets to admire me in my costume before tomorrow.

Helmer. But, dearest Nora—you look all done in. Have you been practising too hard?

Nora. No, I haven't practised at all.

Helmer. But you'll have to, you know.

Nora. I know it, Torvald. I simply must. But I can't do a thing unless you help me. I have forgotten everything.

Helmer. Oh it will all come back. We'll work on it.

Nora. Oh yes, please, Torvald. You just have to help me. Promise? I am so nervous. That big party—. You mustn't do anything else tonight. Not a bit of business. Don't even touch a pen. Will you promise, Torvald?

Helmer. I promise. Tonight I'll be entirely at your service—you helpless little thing.—Just a moment, though. First I want to—(*Goes to the door to the front hall.*)

Nora. What are you doing out there?

Helmer. Just looking to see if there's any mail.

Nora. No, no! Don't, Torvald!

Helmer. Why not?

Nora. Torvald, I beg you. There is no mail.
Helmer. Let me just look, anyway. (*Is about to go out.*)

(*NORA by the piano, plays the first bars of the Tarantella dance.*)

Helmer. (*halts at the door*) Aha!
Nora. I won't be able to dance tomorrow if I don't get to practise with
  you.
Helmer. (*goes to her*) Are you really all that scared, Nora dear?
Nora. Yes, so terribly scared. Let's try it right now. There's still time
  before we eat. Oh please, sit down and play for me, Torvald. Teach me,
  coach me, the way you always do.
Helmer. Of course I will, my darling, if that's what you want. (*Sits down
  at the piano.*)
Nora. (*takes the tambourine out of the carton, as well as a long, many-
  colored shawl. She quickly drapes the shawl around herself. She leaps
  into the middle of the floor and cries*) Play for me! I want to dance!

(*HELMER plays and NORA dances. DOCTOR RANK stands by the
piano behind HELMER and watches.*)

Helmer. (*playing*) Slow down, slow down!
Nora. Can't!
Helmer. Not so violent, Nora!
Nora. It has to be this way.
Helmer. (*stops playing*) No, no. This won't do at all.
Nora. (*laughing, swinging her tambourine*) What did I tell you?
Rank. Why don't you let me play.
Helmer. (*getting up*) Good idea. Then I can direct her better.

(*RANK sits down at the piano and starts playing. NORA dances more
and more wildly. HELMER stands by the stove, repeatedly correcting her.
She doesn't seem to hear. Her hair comes loose and falls down over her
shoulders. She doesn't notice but keeps on dancing. MRS. LINDE enters.*)

Mrs. Linde. (*stops by the door, dumbfounded*) Ah—!
Nora. (*dancing*) We're having such fun, Kristine!
Helmer. My dearest Nora, you're dancing as if it were a matter of life and
  death!
Nora. It is! It is!
Helmer. Rank, stop. This is sheer madness. Stop, I say!

(*RANK stops playing; NORA suddenly stops dancing.*)

Helmer. (*goes over to her*) If I hadn't seen it I wouldn't have believed it.
  You've forgotten every single thing I ever taught you.

Nora. (tosses away the tambourine) See? I told you.

Helmer. Well! You certainly need coaching.

Nora. Didn't I tell you I did? Now you've seen for yourself. I'll need your help till the very minute we're leaving for the party. Will you promise, Torvald?

Helmer. You can count on it.

Nora. You're not to think of anything except me—not tonight and not tomorrow. You're not to read any letters—not to look in the mailbox—

Helmer. Ah, I see. You're still afraid of that man.

Nora. Yes—yes, that too.

Helmer. Nora, I can tell from looking at you. There's a letter from him out there.

Nora. I don't know. I think so. But you're not to read it now. I don't want anything ugly to come between us before it's all over.

Rank. (to HELMER in a low voice) Better not argue with her.

Helmer. (throws his arm around her) The child shall have her way. But tomorrow night, when you've done your dance—

Nora. Then you'll be free.

The Maid. (in the door, right) Dinner can be served any time, ma'am.

Nora. We want champagne, Helene.

The Maid. Very good, ma'am. *(Goes out.)*

Helmer. Aha! Having a party, eh?

Nora. Champagne from now till sunrise! *(Calls out.)* And some macaroons, Helene. Lots!—just this once.

Helmer. (taking her hands) There, there—I don't like this wild—frenzy— Be my own sweet little lark again, the way you always are.

Nora. Oh, I will. But you go on in. You too, Dr. Rank. Kristine, please help me put up my hair.

Rank. (in a low voice to HELMER as they go out) You don't think she is—you know—expecting—?

Helmer. Oh no. Nothing like that. It's just this childish fear I was telling you about. *(They go out, right.)*

Nora. Well?

Mrs. Linde. Left town.

Nora. I saw it in your face.

Mrs. Linde. He'll be back tomorrow night. I left him a note.

Nora. You shouldn't have. I don't want you to try to stop anything. You see, it's a kind of ecstasy, too, this waiting for the wonderful.

Mrs. Linde. But what is it you're waiting *for?*

Nora. You wouldn't understand. Why don't you go in to the others. I'll be there in a minute.

(MRS. LINDE enters the dining room, right.)

Nora. (stands still for a little while, as if collecting herself. She looks at her watch) Five o'clock. Seven hours till midnight. Twenty-four more hours

till next midnight. Then the Tarantella is over. Twenty-four plus
seven—thirty-one more hours to live.

Helmer. (*in the door, right*) What's happening to my little lark?

Nora. (*to him, with open arms*) Here's your lark!

ACT III

*The same room. The table by the couch and the chairs around it have
been moved to the middle of the floor. A lighted lamp is on the table. The
door to the front hall is open. Dance music is heard from upstairs. MRS.
LINDE is seated by the table, idly leafing through the pages of a book.
She tries to read but seems unable to concentrate. Once or twice she turns
her head in the direction of the door, anxiously listening.*

Mrs. Linde. (*Looks at her watch*) Not yet. It's almost too late. If only he
hasn't—(*Listens again.*) Ah! There he is. (*She goes to the hall and opens
the front door carefully. Quiet footsteps on the stairs. She whispers.*)
Come in. There's nobody here.

Krogstad. (*in the door*) I found your note when I got home. What's this all
about?

Mrs. Linde. I've got to talk to you.

Krogstad. Oh? And it has to be here?

Mrs. Linde. It couldn't be at my place. My room doesn't have a separate
entrance. Come in. We're quite alone. The maid is asleep and the
Helmers are at a party upstairs.

Krogstad. (*entering*) Really? The Helmers are dancing tonight, are they?

Mrs. Linde. And why not?

Krogstad. You're right. Why not, indeed.

Mrs. Linde. All right, Krogstad. Let's talk, you and I.

Krogstad. I didn't know we had anything to talk about.

Mrs. Linde. We have much to talk about.

Krogstad. I didn't think so.

Mrs. Linde. No, because you've never really understood me.

Krogstad. What was there to understand? What happened was perfectly
commonplace. A heartless woman jilts a man when she gets a more
attractive offer.

Mrs. Linde. Do you think I'm all that heartless? And do you think it was
easy for me to break with you?

Krogstad. No?

Mrs. Linde. You really thought it was?

Krogstad. If it wasn't, why did you write the way you did that time?

Mrs. Linde. What else could I do? If I had to make a break, I also had the
duty to destroy whatever feelings you had for me.

Krogstad. (*clenching his hands*) So that's the way it was. And you did—
that—just for money!

Mrs. Linde. Don't forget I had a helpless mother and two small brothers.
We couldn't wait for you, Krogstad. You know yourself how uncertain
your prospects were then.

Krogstad. All right. But you still didn't have the right to throw me over
for somebody else.

Mrs. Linde. I don't know. I have asked myself that question many times.
Did I have that right?

Krogstad. (*in a lower voice*) When I lost you I lost my footing. Look at me
now. A shipwrecked man on a raft.

Mrs. Linde. Rescue may be near.

Krogstad. It *was* near. Then you came.

Mrs. Linde. I didn't know that, Krogstad. Only today did I find out it's
your job I'm taking over in the bank.

Krogstad. I believe you when you say so. But now that you *do* know,
aren't you going to step aside?

Mrs. Linde. No, for it wouldn't do you any good.

Krogstad. Whether it would or not—*I* would do it.

Mrs. Linde. I have learned common sense. Life and hard necessity have
taught me that.

Krogstad. And life has taught me not to believe in pretty speeches.

Mrs. Linde. Then life has taught you a very sensible thing. But you do
believe in actions, don't you?

Krogstad. How do you mean?

Mrs. Linde. You referred to yourself just now as a shipwrecked man.

Krogstad. It seems to me I had every reason to do so.

Mrs. Linde. And I am a shipwrecked woman. No one to grieve for, no one
to care for.

Krogstad. You made your choice.

Mrs. Linde. I had no other choice that time.

Krogstad. Let's say you didn't. What then?

Mrs. Linde. Krogstad, how would it be if we two shipwrecked people got
together?

Krogstad. What's this!

Mrs. Linde. Two on one wreck are better off than each on his own.

Krogstad. Kristine!

Mrs. Linde. Why do you think I came to town?

Krogstad. Surely not because of me?

Mrs. Linde. If I'm going to live at all I must work. All my life, for as long
as I can remember, I have worked. That's been my one and only
pleasure. But now that I'm all alone in the world I feel only this terrible
emptiness and desolation. There is no joy in working just for yourself.
Krogstad—give me someone and something to work for.

Krogstad. I don't believe in this. I think you're just another hysterical
female being noble and sacrificing yourself.

Mrs. Linde. Did you ever know me to be hysterical?

Krogstad. You really could do this? Listen—do you know about my past? All of it?

Mrs. Linde. Yes.

Krogstad. Do you also know what people think of me around here?

Mrs. Linde. A little while ago you sounded as if you thought that together with me you might have become a different person.

Krogstad. I'm sure of it.

Mrs. Linde. Couldn't that still be?

Krogstad. Kristine—do you know what you are doing? Yes, I see you do. And you really think you have the courage—?

Mrs. Linde. I need someone to be a mother to, and your children need a mother. You and I need one another. Nils, I believe in you—in the real you. Together with you I dare to do anything.

Krogstad. (*seizes her hands*) Thanks, thanks, Kristine—now I know I'll raise myself in the eyes of others.—Ah, but I forget—!

Mrs. Linde. (*listening*) Shh!—There's the Tarantella. You must go; hurry!

Krogstad. Why? What is it?

Mrs. Linde. Do you hear what they're playing up there? When that dance is over they'll be down.

Krogstad. All right. I'm leaving. The whole thing is pointless, anyway. Of course you don't know what I'm doing to the Helmers.

Mrs. Linde. Yes, Krogstad; I do know.

Krogstad. Still, you're brave enough—?

Mrs. Linde. I very well understand to what extremes despair can drive a man like you.

Krogstad. If only it could be undone!

Mrs. Linde. It could, for your letter is still out there in the mailbox.

Krogstad. Are you sure?

Mrs. Linde. Quite sure. But—

Krogstad. (*looks searchingly at her*) Maybe I'm beginning to understand. You want to save your friend at any cost. Be honest with me. That's it, isn't it?

Mrs. Linde. Krogstad, you may sell yourself once for somebody else's sake, but you don't do it twice.

Krogstad. I'll ask for my letter back.

Mrs. Linde. No, no.

Krogstad. Yes, of course. I'll wait here till Helmer comes down. Then I'll ask him for my letter. I'll tell him it's just about my dismissal—that he shouldn't read it.

Mrs. Linde. No, Krogstad. You are not to do that.

Krogstad. But tell me—wasn't that the real reason you wanted to meet me here?

Mrs. Linde. At first it was, because I was so frightened. But that was yesterday. Since then I have seen the most incredible things going on in this house. Helmer must learn the whole truth. This miserable secret must come out in the open; those two must come to a full understanding. They simple can't continue with all this concealment and evasion.

Krogstad. All right; if you want to take that chance. But there is one thing I *can* do, and I'll do it right now.

Mrs. Linde. (*listening*) But hurry! Go! The dance is over. We aren't safe another minute.

Krogstad. I'll be waiting for you downstairs.

Mrs. Linde. Yes, do. You must see me home.

Krogstad. I've never been so happy in my whole life. (*He leaves through the front door. The door between the living room and the front hall remains open.*)

Mrs. Linde. (*straightens up the room a little and gets her things ready*) What a change! Oh yes!—what a change! People to work for—to live for—a home to bring happiness to. I can't wait to get to work—! If only they'd come soon—(*Listens.*) Ah, there they are. Get my coat on— (*Puts on her coat and hat.*)

(*HELMER's and NORA's voices are heard outside. A key is turned in the lock, and HELMER almost forces NORA into the hall. She is dressed in her Italian costume, with a big, black shawl over her shoulders. He is in evening dress under an open, black cape.*)

Nora. (*in the door, still resisting*) No, no, no! I don't want to! I want to go back upstairs. I don't want to leave so early.

Helmer. But dearest Nora—

Nora. Oh please, Torvald—please! I'm asking you as nicely as I can—just another hour!

Helmer. Not another minute, sweet. You know we agreed. There now. Get inside. You'll catch a cold out here. (*She still resists, but he guides her gently into the room.*)

Mrs. Linde. Good evening.

Nora. Kristine!

Helmer. Ah, Mrs. Linde. Still here?

Mrs. Linde. I know. I really should apologize, but I so much wanted to see Nora in her costume.

Nora. You've been waiting up for me?

Mrs. Linde. Yes, unfortunately I didn't get here in time. You were already upstairs, but I just didn't feel like leaving till I had seen you.

Helmer. (*removing NORA's shawl*) Yes, do take a good look at her, Mrs. Linde. I think I may say she's worth looking at. Isn't she lovely?

Mrs. Linde. She certainly is—

Helmer. Isn't she a miracle of loveliness, though? That was the general opinion at the party, too. But dreadfully obstinate—that she is, the sweet little thing. What can we do about that? Will you believe it—I practically had to use force to get her away.

Nora. Oh Torvald, you're going to be sorry you didn't give me even half an hour more.

Helmer. See what I mean, Mrs. Linde? She dances the Tarantella—she is a tremendous success—quite deservedly so, though perhaps her performance was a little too natural—I mean, more than could be reconciled with the rules of art. But all right! The point is: she's a success, a tremendous success. So should I let her stay, after that? Weaken the effect? Of course not. So I take my lovely little Capri girl— I might say, my capricious little Capri girl—under my arm—a quick turn around the room—a graceful bow in all directions, and—as they say in the novels—the beautiful apparition is gone. A finale should always be done for effect, Mrs. Linde, but there doesn't seem to be any way of getting that into Nora's head. Poooh—! It's hot in here. (*Throws his cape down on a chair and opens the door to his study.*) Why, it's dark! Oh yes—of course. Excuse me—(*Goes inside and lights a couple of candles.*)

Nora. (*in a hurried, breathless whisper*) Well?

Mrs. Linde. (*in a low voice*) I have talked to him.

Nora. And—?

Mrs. Linde. Nora—you've got to tell your husband everything.

Nora. (*no expression in her voice*) I knew it.

Mrs. Linde. You have nothing to fear from Krogstad. But you must speak.

Nora. I'll say nothing.

Mrs. Linde. Then the letter will.

Nora. Thank you, Kristine. Now I know what I have to do. Shh!

Helmer. (*returning*) Well, Mrs. Linde, have you looked your fill?

Mrs. Linde. Yes. And now I'll say goodnight.

Helmer. So soon? Is that your knitting?

Mrs. Linde. (*takes it*) Yes, thank you. I almost forgot.

Helmer. So you knit, do you?

Mrs. Linde. Oh yes.

Helmer. You know—you ought to take up embroidery instead.

Mrs. Linde. Oh? Why?

Helmer. Because it's so much more beautiful. Look. You hold the embroidery so—in your left hand. Then with your right you move the needle—like this—in an easy, elongated arc—you see?

Mrs. Linde. Maybe you're right—

Helmer. Knitting, on the other hand, can never be anything but ugly. Look here: arms pressed close to the sides—the needles going up and down— there's something Chinese about it somehow—. That really was an excellent champagne they served us tonight.

Mrs. Linde. Well; goodnight, Nora. And don't be obstinate any more.

Helmer. Well said, Mrs. Linde!

Mrs. Linde. Goodnight, sir.

Helmer. (*sees her to the front door*) Goodnight, goodnight. I hope you'll get home all right? I'd be very glad to—but of course you don't have far to walk, do you? Goodnight, goodnight. (*She leaves. He closes the door behind her and returns to the living room.*) There! At last we got rid of her. She really is an incredible bore, that woman.

Nora. Aren't you very tired, Torvald?

Helmer. No, not in the least.

Nora. Not sleepy either?

Helmer. Not at all. Quite the opposite. I feel enormously—animated. How about you? Yes, you do look tired and sleepy.

Nora. Yes, I am very tired. Soon I'll be asleep.

Helmer. What did I tell you? I was right, wasn't I? Good thing I didn't let you stay any longer.

Nora. Everything you do is right.

Helmer. (*kissing her forehead*) Now my little lark is talking like a human being. But did you notice what splendid spirits Rank was in tonight?

Nora. Was he? I didn't notice. I didn't get to talk with him.

Helmer. Nor did I—hardly. But I haven't seen him in such a good mood for a long time. (*Looks at her, comes closer to her.*) Ah! It does feel good to be back in our own home again, to be quite alone with you— Oh, how lovely you are!—my exciting young woman!

Nora. Don't look at me like that, Torvald!

Helmer. Am I not to look at my most precious possession? All that loveliness that is mine, nobody's but mine, all of it mine!

Nora. (*walks to the other side of the table*) I won't have you talk to me like that tonight.

Helmer. (*follows her*) The Tarantella is still in your blood. I can tell. That only makes you all the more alluring. Listen! The guests are beginning to leave. (*Softly.*) Nora—darling—soon the whole house will be quiet.

Nora. I hope so.

Helmer. Yes, don't you, my darling? Do you know—when I'm at a party with you, like tonight—do you know why I hardly ever talk to you, why I keep away from you, only look at you once in a while—a few stolen glances—do you know why I do that? It's because I pretend that you are my secret love, my young, secret bride-to-be, and nobody has the slightest suspicion that there is anything between us.

Nora. Yes, I know. All your thoughts are with me.

Helmer. Then when we're leaving and I lay your shawl around your delicate young shoulders—around that wonderful curve of your neck— then I imagine you're my young bride, that we're coming away from the wedding, that I am taking you to my home for the first time—that I am alone with you for the first time—quite alone with you, you young, trembling beauty! I have desired you all evening—all my longing has only been for you. When you were dancing the Tarantella, chasing, inviting—my blood was on fire; I couldn't stand it any longer—that's why I brought you down so early—

Nora. Leave me now, Torvald. Please! I don't want all this.

Helmer. What do you mean? You're only playing your little teasing bird game with me; aren't you, Nora? Don't want to? I'm your husband, aren't I?

(There is a knock on the front door.)

Nora. (with a start) Did you hear that—?
Helmer. (on his way to the hall) Who is it?
Rank. (outside) It's me. May I come in for a moment?
Helmer. (in a low voice, annoyed) Oh, what does he want now? *(Aloud.)* Just a minute. *(Opens the door.)* Well! How good of you not to pass by our door.
Rank. I thought I heard your voice, so I felt like saying hello. *(Looks around.)* Ah yes—this dear, familiar room. What a cozy, comfortable place you have here, you two.
Helmer. Looked to me as if you were quite comfortable upstairs too.
Rank. I certainly was. And why not? Why not enjoy all you can in this world? As much as you can and for as long as you can, anyway. Excellent wine.
Helmer. The champagne, particularly.
Rank. You noticed that too? Incredible how much I managed to put away.
Nora. Torvald drank a lot of champagne tonight, too.
Rank. Did he?
Nora. Yes, he did, and then he's always so much fun afterwards.
Rank. Well, why not have some fun in the evening after a well spent day?
Helmer. Well spent? I'm afraid I can't claim that.
Rank. (slapping him lightly on the shoulder) But you see, I can!
Nora. Dr. Rank, I believe you have been conducting a scientific test today.
Rank. Exactly.
Helmer. What do you know—little Nora talking about scientific experiments!
Nora. May I congratulate you on the result?
Rank. You may indeed.
Nora. It was a good one?
Rank. The best possible for both doctor and patient—certainty.
Nora. (a quick query) Certainty?
Rank. Absolute certainty. So why shouldn't I have myself an enjoyable evening afterwards?
Nora. I quite agree with you, Dr. Rank. You should.
Helmer. And so do I. If only you don't pay for it tomorrow.
Rank. Oh well—you get nothing for nothing in this world.
Nora. Dr. Rank—you are fond of costume parties, aren't you?
Rank. Yes, particularly when there is a reasonable number of amusing disguises.
Nora. Listen—what are the two of us going to be the next time?

Helmer. You frivolous little thing! Already thinking about the next party!

Rank. You and I? That's easy. You'll be Fortune's Child.

Helmer. Yes, but what is a fitting costume for that?

Rank. Let your wife appear just the way she always is.

Helmer. Beautiful. Very good indeed. But how about yourself? Don't you know what you'll go as?

Rank. Yes, my friend. I know precisely what I'll be.

Helmer. Yes?

Rank. At the next masquerade I'll be invisible.

Helmer. That's a funny idea.

Rank. There's a certain black hat—you've heard about the hat that makes you invisible, haven't you? You put that on, and nobody can see you.

Helmer. (*suppressing a smile*) I guess that's right.

Rank. But I'm forgetting what I came for. Helmer, give me a cigar—one of your dark Havanas.

Helmer. With the greatest pleasure. (*Offers him his case.*)

Rank. (*takes one and cuts off the tip*) Thanks.

Nora. (*striking a match*) Let me give you a light.

Rank. Thanks. (*She holds the match; he lights his cigar.*) And now goodbye!

Helmer. Goodbye, goodbye, my friend.

Nora. Sleep well, Dr. Rank.

Rank. I thank you.

Nora. Wish me the same.

Rank. You? Well, if you really want me to—. Sleep well. And thanks for the light. (*He nods to both of them and goes out.*)

Helmer. (*in a low voice*) He had had quite a bit to drink.

Nora. (*absently*) Maybe so.

(*HELMER takes out his keys and goes out into the hall.*)

Nora. Torvald—what are you doing out there?

Helmer. Emptying the mailbox. It is quite full. There wouldn't be room for the newspapers in the morning—

Nora. Are you going to work tonight?

Helmer. You know very well I won't.—Say! What's this? Somebody's been at the lock.

Nora. The lock—?

Helmer. Sure. Why, I wonder. I hate to think that any of the maids—. Here's a broken hairpin. It's one of yours, Nora.

Nora. (*quickly*) Then it must be one of the children.

Helmer. You better make damn sure they stop that. Hm, hm.—There! I got it open, finally. (*Gathers up the mail, calls out to the kitchen:*) Helene?—Oh Helene—turn out the light here in the hall, will you? (*He comes back into the living room and closes the door.*) Look how it's been piling up. (*Shows her the bundle of letters. Starts leafing through it.*) What's this?

Nora. (*by the window*) The letter! Oh no, no, Torvald!

Helmer. Two calling cards—from Rank.

Nora. From Dr. Rank?

Helmer. (*looking at them*) "Doctor of Medicine Rank!" They were on top. He must have put them there when he left just now.

Nora. Anything written on them?

Helmer. A black cross above the name. What a macabre idea. Like announcing his own death.

Nora. That's what it is.

Helmer. Hm? You know about this? Has he said anything to you?

Nora. That card means he's saying goodbye to us. He'll lock himself up to die.

Helmer. My poor friend. I knew of course he wouldn't be with me very long. But so soon—. And this hiding himself away like a wounded animal—

Nora. When it has to be, it's better it happens without words. Don't you think so, Torvald?

Helmer. (*walking up and down*) He'd grown so close to us. I find it hard to think of him as gone. With his suffering and loneliness he was like a clouded background for our happy sunshine. Well, it may be better this way. For him, at any rate. (*Stops.*) And perhaps for us, too, Nora. For now we have nobody but each other. (*Embraces her.*) Oh you—my beloved wife! I feel I just can't hold you close enough. Do you know, Nora—many times I have wished some great danger threatened you, so I could risk my life and blood and everything—everything, for your sake.

Nora. (*frees herself and says in a strong and firm voice*) I think you should go and read your letters now, Torvald.

Helmer. No, no—not tonight. I want to be with you, my darling.

Nora. With the thought of your dying friend—?

Helmer. You are right. This has shaken both of us. Something not beautiful has come between us. Thoughts of death and dissolution. We must try to get over it—out of it. Till then—we'll each go to our own room.

Nora. (*her arms around his neck*) Torvald—goodnight! Goodnight!

Helmer. (*kisses her forehead*) Goodnight, my little songbird. Sleep well, Nora. Now I'll read my letters. (*He goes into his room, carrying the mail. Closes the door.*)

Nora. (*her eyes desperate, her hands groping, finds HELMER's black cloak and throws it around her; she whispers, quickly, brokenly, hoarsely*) Never see him again. Never. Never. Never. (*Puts her shawl over her head.*) And never see the children again, either. Never; never.— The black, icy water—fathomless—this—! If only it was all over.—

Now he has it. Now he's reading it. No, no; not yet. Torvald—
goodbye—you—the children—

(*She is about to hurry through the hall, when HELMER flings open the
door to his room and stands there with an open letter in his hand.*)

Helmer. Nora!
Nora. (*cries out*) Ah—!
Helmer. What is it? You know what's in this letter?
Nora. Yes, I do! Let me go! Let me out!
Helmer. (*holds her back*) Where do you think you're going?
Nora. (*trying to tear herself loose from him*) I won't let you save me,
  Torvald!
Helmer. (*tumbles back*) True! Is it true what he writes? Oh my god! No,
  no—this can't possibly be true.
Nora. It is true. I have loved you more than anything else in the whole
  world.
Helmer. Oh, don't give me any silly excuses.
Nora. (*taking a step towards him*) Torvald—!
Helmer. You wretch! What have you done!
Nora. Let me go. You are not to sacrifice yourself for me. You are not to
  take the blame.
Helmer. No more playacting. (*Locks the door to the front hall.*) You'll
  stay here and answer me. Do you understand what you have done?
  Answer me! Do you understand?
Nora. (*gazes steadily at him with an increasingly frozen expression*) Yes.
  Now I'm beginning to understand.
Helmer. (*walking up and down*) What a dreadful awakening. All these
  years—all these eight years—she, my pride and my joy—a hypocrite, a
  liar—oh worse—worse!—a criminal! Oh, the bottomless ugliness in all
  this! Damn! Damn! Damn!

(*NORA silent, keeps gazing at him.*)

Helmer. (*stops in front of her*) I ought to have guessed that something like
  this would happen. I should have expected it. All your father's loose
  principles—Silence! You have inherited every one of your father's loose
  principles. No religion, no morals, no sense of duty—. Now I am being
  punished for my leniency with him. I did it for your sake, and this is
  how you pay me back.
Nora. Yes. This is how.
Helmer. You have ruined all my happiness. My whole future—you've
  thrown it away. Oh, it's terrible to think about. I am at the mercy of an
  unscrupulous man. He can do with me whatever he likes, demand
  anything of me, command me and dispose of me just as he pleases—I

dare not say a word! To go down so miserably, to be destroyed—all because of an irresponsible woman!

Nora. When I am gone from the world, you'll be free.

Helmer. No noble gestures, please. Your father was always full of such phrases too. What good would it do me if you were gone from the world, as you put it? Not the slightest bit of good at all. He could still make the whole thing public, and if he did I wouldn't be surprised if people thought I'd been your accomplice. They might even think it was my idea—that it was I who urged you to do it! And for all this I have you to thank—you, whom I've borne on my hands through all the years of our marriage. *Now* do you understand what you've done to me?

Nora. (*with cold calm*) Yes.

Helmer. I just can't get it into my head that this is happening; it's all so incredible. But we have to come to terms with it somehow. Take your shawl off. Take it off, I say! I have to satisfy him one way or another. The whole affair must be kept quiet at whatever cost.—And as far as you and I are concerned, nothing must seem to have changed. I'm talking about appearances, of course. You'll go on living here; that goes without saying. But I won't let you bring up the children; I dare not trust you with them.—Oh! Having to say this to one I have loved to much, and whom I still—! But all that has to be past. It's not a question of happiness any more but of hanging on to what can be salvaged—pieces, appearances—(*The doorbell rings. HELMER jumps.*) What's that? So late. Is the worst—? Has he—! Hide, Nora! Say you're sick.

(*NORA doesn't move. HELMER opens the door to the hall.*)

The Maid. (*half dressed, out in the hall*) A letter for your wife, sir.

Helmer. Give it to me. (*Takes the letter and closes the door.*) Yes, it's from him. But I won't let you have it. I'll read it myself.

Nora. Yes—you read it.

Helmer. (*by the lamp*) I hardly dare. Perhaps we're lost, both you and I. No; I've got to know. (*Tears the letter open, glances through it, looks at an enclosure, a cry of joy.*) Nora!

(*NORA looks at him with a question in her eyes.*)

Helmer. Nora!—No, I must read it again.—Yes, yes; it is so! I'm saved! Nora, I'm saved.

Nora. And I?

Helmer. You too, of course; we're both saved, both you and I. Look! He's returning your note. He writes that he's sorry, he regrets, a happy turn in his life—oh, it doesn't matter what he writes. We're saved, Nora!

Nobody can do anything to you now. Oh Nora, Nora—. No, I want to get rid of this disgusting thing first. Let me see—(*Looks at the signature.*) No, I don't want to see it. I don't want it to be more than a bad dream, the whole thing. (*Tears up the note and both letters, throws the pieces in the stove, and watches them burn.*) There! Now it's gone.—He wrote that ever since Christmas Eve—. Good god, Nora, these must have been three terrible days for you.

Nora. I have fought a hard fight these last three days.

Helmer. And been in agony and seen no other way out than—. No, we won't think of all that ugliness. We'll just rejoice and tell ourselves it's over, it's all over! Oh, listen to me, Nora. You don't seem to understand. It's over. What *is* it? Why do you look like that—that frozen expression on your face? Oh my poor little Nora, don't you think I know what it is? You can't make yourself believe that I have forgiven you. But I have, Nora; I swear to you, I have forgiven you for everything. Of course I know that what you did was for love of me.

Nora. That is true.

Helmer. You have loved me the way a wife ought to love her husband. You just didn't have the wisdom to judge the means. But do you think I love you any less because you don't know how to act on your own? Of course not. Just lean on me. I'll advise you; I'll guide you. I wouldn't be a man if I didn't find you twice as attractive because of your womanly helplessness. You mustn't pay any attention to the hard words I said to you right at first. It was just that first shock when I thought everything was collapsing all around me. I have forgiven you, Nora. I swear to you—I really have forgiven you.

Nora. I thank you for your forgiveness. (*She goes out through the door, right.*)

Helmer. No, stay—(*Looks into the room she entered.*) What are you doing in there?

Nora. (*within*) Getting out of my costume.

Helmer. (*by the open door*) Good, good. Try to calm down and compose yourself, my poor little frightened songbird. Rest safely; I have broad wings to cover you with. (*Walks around near the door.*) What a nice and cozy home we have, Nora. Here's shelter for you. Here I'll keep you safe like a hunted dove I have rescued from the hawk's talons. Believe me: I'll know how to quiet your beating heart. It will happen by and by, Nora; you'll see. Why, tomorrow you'll look at all this in quite a different light. And soon everything will be just the way it was before. I won't need to keep reassuring you that I have forgiven you; you'll feel it yourself. Did you really think I could have abandoned you, or even reproached you? Oh, you don't know a real man's heart, Nora. There is something unspeakably sweet and satisfactory for a man to know deep in himself that he has forgiven his wife—forgiven her in all the fullness of his honest heart. You see, that way she becomes his very own all

over again—in a double sense, you might say. He has, so to speak,
given her a second birth; it is as if she had become his wife and his
child, both. From now on that's what you'll be to me, you lost and
helpless creature. Don't worry about a thing, Nora. Only be frank with
me, and I'll be your will and your conscience.—What's this? You're not
in bed? You've changed your dress—!

Nora. (in an everyday dress) Yes, Torvald. I have changed my dress.

Helmer. But why—now—this late—?

Nora. I'm not going to sleep tonight.

Helmer. But my dear Nora—

Nora. (looks at her watch) It isn't all that late. Sit down here with me,
Torvald. You and I have much to talk about. *(Sits down at the table.)*

Helmer. Nora—what is this all about? That rigid face—

Nora. Sit down. This will take a while. I have much to say to you.

Helmer. (sits down, facing her across the table) You worry me, Nora. I
don't understand you.

Nora. No, that's just it. You don't understand me. And I have never
understood you—not till tonight. No, don't interrupt me. Just listen to
what I have to say.—This is a settling of accounts, Torvald.

Helmer. What do you mean by that?

Nora. (after a brief silence) Doesn't one thing strike you, now that we are
sitting together like this?

Helmer. What would that be?

Nora. We have been married for eight years. Doesn't it occur to you that
this is the first time that you and I, husband and wife, are having a
serious talk?

Helmer. Well—serious—. What do you mean by that?

Nora. For eight whole years—longer, in fact—ever since we first met, we
have never talked seriously to each other about a single serious thing.

Helmer. You mean I should forever have been telling you about worries
you couldn't have helped me with anyway?

Nora. I am not talking about worries. I'm saying we have never tried
seriously to get to the bottom of anything together.

Helmer. But dearest Nora, I hardly think that would have been something
you—

Nora. That's the whole point. You have never understood me. Great
wrong has been done to me, Torvald. First by Daddy and then by you.

Helmer. What! by us two? We who have loved you more than anyone
else?

Nora. (shakes her head) You never loved me—neither Daddy nor you.
You only thought it was fun to be in love with me.

Helmer. But, Nora—what an expression to use!

Nora. That's the way it has been, Torvald. When I was home with Daddy,
he told me all his opinions, and so they became my opinions too. If I
disagreed with him I kept it to myself, for he wouldn't have liked that.

He called me his little doll baby, and he played with me the way I
played with my dolls. Then I came to your house—

Helmer. What a way to talk about our marriage!

Nora. (*imperturbably*) I mean that I passed from Daddy's hands into
yours. You arranged everything according to your taste, and so I came
to share it—or I pretended to; I'm not sure which. I think it was a little
of both, now one and now the other. When I look back on it now, it
seems to me I've been living here like a pauper—just a hand-to-mouth
kind of existence. I have earned my keep by doing tricks for you,
Torvald. But that's the way you wanted it. You have great sins against
me to answer for, Daddy and you. It's your fault that nothing has
become of me.

Helmer. Nora, you're being both unreasonable and ungrateful. Haven't
you been happy here?

Nora. No, never. I thought I was, but I wasn't.

Helmer. Not—not happy!

Nora. No; just having fun. And you have always been very good to me.
But our home has never been more than a playroom. I have been your
doll wife here, just the way I used to be Daddy's doll child. And the
children have been my dolls. I thought it was fun when you played with
me, just as they thought it was fun when I played with them. That's
been our marriage, Torvald.

Helmer. There is something in what you are saying—exaggerated and
hysterical though it is. But from now on things will be different.
Playtime is over; it's time for growing up.

Nora. Whose growing up—mine or the children's?

Helmer. Both yours and the children's, Nora darling.

Nora. Oh Torvald, you're not the man to bring me up to be the right kind
of wife for you.

Helmer. How can you say that?

Nora. And I—? What qualifications do I have for bringing up the
children?

Helmer. Nora!

Nora. You said so yourself a minute ago—that you didn't dare to trust me
with them.

Helmer. In the first flush of anger, yes. Surely, you're not going to count
that.

Nora. But you were quite right. I am *not* qualified. Something else has to
come first. Somehow I have to grow up myself. And you are not the
man to help me do that. That's a job I have to do by myself. And that's
why I'm leaving you.

Helmer. (*jumps up*) What did you say!

Nora. I have to be by myself if I am to find out about myself and about all
those other things too. So I can't stay here any longer.

Helmer. Nora, Nora!

Nora. I'm leaving now. I'm sure Kristine will put me up for tonight.

Helmer. You're out of your mind! I won't let you! I forbid you!

Nora. You can't forbid me anything any more; it won't do any good. I'm taking my own things with me. I won't accept anything from you, either now or later.

Helmer. But this is madness!

Nora. Tomorrow I'm going home—I mean back to my old home town. It will be easier for me to find some kind of job there.

Helmer. Oh, you blinded, inexperienced creature—!

Nora. I must see to it that I get experience, Torvald.

Helmer. Leaving your home, your husband, your children! Not a thought of what people will say!

Nora. I can't worry about that. All I know is that I have to leave.

Helmer. Oh, this is shocking! Betraying your most sacred duties like this!

Nora. And what do you consider my most sacred duties?

Helmer. Do I need to tell you that? They are your duties to your husband and your children.

Nora. I have other duties equally sacred.

Helmer. You do not. What duties would they be?

Nora. My duties to myself.

Helmer. You are a wife and a mother before you are anything else.

Nora. I don't believe that any more. I believe I am first of all a human being, just as much as you—or at any rate that I must try to become one. Oh, I know very well that most people agree with you, Torvald, and that it says something like that in all the books. But what people say and what the books say is no longer enough for me. I have to think about these things myself and see if I can't find the answers.

Helmer. You mean to tell me you don't know what your proper place in your own home is? Don't you have a reliable guide in such matters? Don't you have religion?

Nora. Oh but Torvald—I don't really know what religion is.

Helmer. What's this?

Nora. All I know is what the Reverend Hansen told me when he prepared me for confirmation. He said that religion was *this* and it was *that*. When I get by myself, away from here, I'll have to look into that, too. I have to decide if what the Reverend Hansen said was right, or anyway if it is right for *me*.

Helmer. Oh, this is unheard of in a young woman! If religion can't guide you, let me appeal to your conscience. For surely you have moral feelings? Or—answer me—maybe you don't?

Nora. Well, you see, Torvald, I don't really know what to say. I just don't know. I am confused about these things. All I know is that my ideas are quite different from yours. I have just found out that the laws are different from what I thought they were, but in no way can I get it into my head that those laws are right. A woman shouldn't have the right to spare her dying old father or save her husband's life! I just can't believe that.

Helmer. You speak like a child. You don't understand the society you live in.

Nora. No, I don't. But I want to find out about it. I have to make up my mind who is right, society or I.

Helmer. You are sick, Nora; you have a fever. I really don't think you are in your right mind.

Nora. I have never felt so clearheaded and sure of myself as I do tonight.

Helmer. And clearheaded and sure of yourself you're leaving your husband and your children?

Nora. Yes.

Helmer. Then there is only one possible explanation.

Nora. What?

Helmer. You don't love me any more.

Nora. No; that's just it.

Helmer. Nora! How can you say that!

Nora. I am sorry, Torvald, for you have always been so good to me. But I can't help it. I don't love you any more.

Helmer. (*with forced composure*) And this too is a clear and sure conviction?

Nora. Completely clear and sure. That's why I don't want to stay here any more.

Helmer. And are you ready to explain to me how I came to forfeit your love?

Nora. Certainly, I am. It was tonight, when the wonderful didn't happen. That was when I realized you were not the man I thought you were.

Helmer. You have to explain. I don't understand.

Nora. I have waited patiently for eight years, for I wasn't such a fool that I thought the wonderful is something that happens any old day. Then this—thing—came crashing in on me, and then there wasn't a doubt in my mind that now—now comes the wonderful. When Krogstad's letter was in that mailbox, never for a moment did it even occur to me that you would submit to his conditions. I was so absolutely certain that you would say to him: make the whole thing public—tell everybody. And when that had happened—

Helmer. Yes, then what? When I had surrendered my wife to shame and disgrace—!

Nora. When that had happened, I was absolutely certain that you would stand up and take the blame and say, "I am the guilty one."

Helmer. Nora!

Nora. You mean I never would have accepted such a sacrifice from you? Of course not. But what would my protests have counted against yours? *That* was the wonderful I was hoping for in terror. And to prevent that I was going to kill myself.

Helmer. I'd gladly work nights and days for you, Nora—endure sorrow
and want for your sake. But nobody sacrifices his *honor* for his love.

Nora. A hundred thousand women have done so.

Helmer. Oh, you think and talk like a silly child.

Nora. All right. But you don't think and talk like the man I can live with.
When you had gotten over your fright—not because of what threatened
me but because of the risk to *you*—and the whole danger was past,
then you acted as if nothing at all had happened. Once again I was
your little songbird, your doll, just as before, only now you had to
handle her even more carefully, because she was so frail and weak.
(*Rises.*) Torvald—that moment I realized that I had been living here for
eight years with a stranger and had borne him three children—Oh, I
can't stand thinking about it! I feel like tearing myself to pieces!

Helmer. (*heavily*) I see it, I see it. An abyss has opened up between us.—
Oh but Nora—surely it can be filled?

Nora. The way I am now I am no wife for you.

Helmer. I have it in me to change.

Nora. Perhaps—if your doll is taken from you.

Helmer. To part—to part from you! No, no, Nora! I can't grasp that
thought!

Nora. (*goes out, right*) All the more reason why it has to be. (*She returns
with her street clothes and a small bag, which she sets down on the
chair by the table.*)

Helmer. Nora, Nora! Not now! Wait till tomorrow.

Nora. (*putting on her coat*) I can't spend the night in a stranger's rooms.

Helmer. But couldn't we live here together like brother and sister—?

Nora. (*tying on her hat*) You know very well that wouldn't last long—.
(*Wraps her shawl around her.*) Goodbye, Torvald. I don't want to see
the children. I know I leave them in better hands than mine. The way I
am now I can't be anything to them.

Helmer. But some day, Nora—some day—?

Nora. How can I tell? I have no idea what's going to become of me.

Helmer. But you're still my wife, both as you are now and as you will be.

Nora. Listen, Torvald—when a wife leaves her husband's house, the way I
am doing now, I have heard he has no further legal responsibilities for
her. At any rate, I now release you from all responsibility. You are not
to feel yourself obliged to me for anything, and I have no obligations to
you. There has to be full freedom on both sides. Here is your ring back.
Now give me mine.

Helmer. Even this?

Nora. Even this.

Helmer. Here it is.

Nora. There. So now it's over. I'm putting the keys here. The maids know
everything about the house—better than I. Tomorrow, after I'm gone,
Kristine will come over and pack my things from home. I want them
sent after me.

Helmer. Over! It's all over! Nora, will you never think of me?

Nora. I'm sure I'll often think of you and the children and this house.

Helmer. May I write to you, Nora?

Nora. No—never. I won't have that.

Helmer. But send you things—? You must let me—

Nora. Nothing, nothing—

Helmer. —help you, when you need help—

Nora. I told you, no; I won't have it. I'll accept nothing from strangers.

Helmer. Nora—can I never again be more to you than a stranger?

Nora. (*picks up her bag*) Oh Torvald—then the most wonderful of all would have to happen—

Helmer. Tell me what that would be—!

Nora. For that to happen, both you and I would have to change so that— Oh Torvald, I no longer believe in the wonderful.

Helmer. But I *will* believe. Tell me! Change, so that—?

Nora. So that our living together would become a true marriage. Goodbye. (*She goes out through the hall.*)

Helmer. (*sinks down on a chair near the door and covers his face with his hands*) Nora! Nora! (*Looks around him and gets up.*) All empty. She's gone. (*With sudden hope.*) The most wonderful—?!

(*From downstairs comes the sound of a heavy door slamming shut.*)

QUESTIONS

1. How far removed from your own world does this 1879 play by a Norwegian dramatist seem?
2. What details of the particular setting—the Helmers' apartment, the Christmas season— seem important?
3. What are your first impressions of the Helmers' marriage and of Nora and Torvald as individuals?
4. How important is Mrs. Linde to the play? Dr. Rank? Is Krogstad mainly the villain of the piece?
5. As Nora grows more fearful of being exposed by Krogstad, how much do you sympathize with her? Have your first impressions of her been confirmed, or does she appear different now?
6. How surprised are you by her decision to leave Torvald and their children? What do you think about it?
7. How much sympathy do you feel for Torvald?
8. In your view, is the play about women's rights? Explain.

ADDITIONAL QUESTIONS

1. Three stories—"Counterparts," "The Greatest Man in the World," and "A Clean, Well-Lighted Place"—use nonparticipant, third-person narrators; but the narrators in Joyce's and Hemingway's stories enter one character's mind to some extent. How is the point of view of each story related to the sympathy you feel for the characters?

2. Use of a first-person narrator in three stories—"The Secret Sharer," "The Yellow Wall-Paper," and "Out of Place"—draws you into the main character's troubled, secret experience. Consider how the narrative technique of one of these stories contributes to its meaning.

3. What do the images used by Prufrock as speaker in T. S. Eliot's dramatic monologue tell you about how Prufrock sees himself?

4. Several poems present visions of the modern city as experienced by the individual. Consider Blake's "London," Ginsberg's "My Sad Self," Piercy's "Morning Half-Life Blues," and Corn's "Fifty-Seventh Street and Fifth." Compare/contrast the two that seem most interesting when set together.

5. In both Browning's "Soliloquy of the Spanish Cloister" and Larkin's "Vers de Société" you hear an individual raging against others. From what each speaker says, what do you know of his character?

6. Several poems dramatize, in effect, the perception of one person by another or others. Consider "Richard Cory," "Aunt Jennifer's Tigers," "Ex-Basketball Player," "The Leap," and "Miss Rosie." Explain your sense of the relation between the observer(s) and the observed in one or more of these.

7. In *The Misanthrope* Alceste's protests against the hypocrisy and self-seeking behind social behavior contrast with the attitude of his friend Philinte. How important to the play as a whole is Philinte? Consider whether he only contrasts with Alceste as a personality or represents values the latter does not acknowledge.

8. In *A Doll's House*, as Nora prepares to go off by herself, she admits she does not understand society. What useful knowledge about society and the individual's relation to it might she gain by reflecting upon her own life thus far—or upon those of the other characters in the play?

PART THREE

COMPLEXITIES OF LOVE

The works in this section are about different kinds of love, but the majority are about the kind that the word *love* probably suggests first to most of us. Since the Middle Ages, romantic love between the sexes has been a major theme in literature and in Western culture as a whole. Over the centuries, literature has helped readers to define and refine love's often complex emotions.

Love poetry, particularly influential in its definition of feeling, has been written by some of the most skilled poets in English. Two of these, Shakespeare and Donne, are represented here by several poems likely to astonish and delight anyone not totally resistant to poetry. Both poets present you with not only the force of love but also the power of their art. Both confront you also with the old problem of how much writers reveal about their personal lives in their works.

The problem in the case of Shakespeare's sonnets, for instance, has elicited a small library of biographies, literary criticism, and even popular fiction over the years. The story half-glimpsed behind the 154 sonnets is the more tantalizing since what has been documented of Shakespeare's life otherwise does not especially suggest romance. The most respected opinion now is that in writing his sonnets Shakespeare was primarily a creative artist. He may have written the sonnets to display his proficiency. Composing a collection of interrelated sonnets, called a sonnet sequence or cycle, was a vogue during the decade when Shakespeare wrote his. Even the elusive quality of the "story" in them has parallels in sonnets of other poets before and in that time. You can know all this and still fall under the spell cast by Shakespeare's poems, with their varying style, attitudes, and the endlessly fascinating sounds of the voice in them. They are never sentimental and in the best of them emotion is resonant.

Emotion is often devalued or suspect in our world, that so values reason, dispassionate intelligence, and objectivity. As a kind of gentle, easy emotion, sentiment may be indulged, precisely because it may be smiled at and dismissed. Deep emotion is powerful. Like reason, it makes things happen. Poetry (or literature in general) reminds us also that intelligence and emotion are not opposing entities. Writers like Shakespeare and Donne, Marvell and Dickinson combine these in their art.

Literature defines feelings, or causes you to define them, as you respond to works concerned with human beings. Love is the simple word linking all the works in this section, but as you read, notice all its variety. You are far from easy sentiment with a flea or skunk in a love poem and in stories with only one true kiss among them. Literature stimulates us intellectually with its honesty and releases our emotions with its power.

FICTION

Edith Wharton (1862–1937)
ROMAN FEVER

From the table at which they had been lunching two American ladies of ripe but well-cared-for middle age moved across the lofty terrace of the Roman restaurant and, leaning on its parapet, looked first at each other, and then down on the outspread glories of the Palatine and the Forum, with the same expression of vague but benevolent approval.

As they leaned there a girlish voice echoed up gaily from the stairs leading to the court below. "Well, come along, then," it cried, not to them but to an invisible companion, "and let's leave the young things to their knitting"; and a voice as fresh laughed back: "Oh, look here, Babs, not actually *knitting*—" "Well, I mean figuratively," rejoined the first. "After all, we haven't left our poor parents much else to do. . . ." and at that point the turn of the stairs engulfed the dialogue.

The two ladies looked at each other again, this time with a tinge of smiling embarrassment, and the smaller and paler one shook her head and colored slightly.

"Barbara!" she murmured, sending an unheard rebuke after the mocking voice in the stairway.

The other lady, who was fuller, and higher in color, with a small determined nose supported by vigorous black eyebrows, gave a good-humored laugh. "That's what our daughters think of us!"

Her companion replied by a deprecating gesture. "Not of us individually. We must remember that. It's just the collective modern idea of Mothers. And you see—" Half-guiltily she drew from her handsomely mounted black handbag a twist of crimson silk run through by two fine knitting needles. "One never knows," she murmured. "The new system has certainly given us a good deal of time to kill; and sometimes I get tired just looking—even at this." Her gesture was now addressed to the stupendous scene at their feet.

The dark lady laughed again, and they both relapsed upon the view, contemplating it in silence, with a sort of diffused serenity which might have been borrowed from the spring effulgence of the Roman skies. The luncheon hour was long past, and the two had their end of the vast terrace to themselves. At its opposite extremity a few groups, detained by a lingering look at the outspread city, were gathering up guidebooks and fumbling for tips. The last of them scattered, and the two ladies were alone on the air-washed height.

"Well, I don't see why we shouldn't just stay here," said Mrs. Slade, the lady of the high color and energetic brows. Two derelict basket chairs stood near, and

371

she pushed them into the angle of the parapet, and settled herself in one, her gaze upon the Palatine. "After all, it's still the most beautiful view in the world."

"It always will be, to me," assented her friend Mrs. Ansley, with so slight a stress on the "me" that Mrs. Slade, though she noticed it, wondered if it were not merely accidental, like the random underlinings of old-fashioned letter writers.

"Grace Ansley was always old-fashioned," she thought; and added aloud, with a retrospective smile: "It's a view we've both been familiar with for a good many years. When we first met here we were younger than our girls are now. You remember?"

"Oh, yes, I remember," murmured Mrs. Ansley, with the same undefinable stress. "There's that headwaiter wondering," she interpolated. She was evidently far less sure than her companion of herself and of her rights in the world.

"I'll cure him of wondering," said Mrs. Slade, stretching her hand toward a bag as discreetly opulent-looking as Mrs. Ansley's. Signing to the headwaiter, she explained that she and her friend were old lovers of Rome, and would like to spend the end of the afternoon looking down on the view—that is, if it did not disturb the service? The headwaiter, bowing over her gratuity, assured her that the ladies were most welcome, and would be still more so if they would condescend to remain for dinner. A full-moon night, they would remember. . . .

Mrs. Slade's black brows drew together, as though references to the moon were out of place and even unwelcome. But she smiled away her frown as the headwaiter retreated. "Well, why not? We might do worse. There's no knowing, I suppose, when the girls will be back. Do you even know back from *where?* I don't!"

Mrs. Ansley again colored slightly. "I think those young Italian aviators we met at the Embassy invited them to fly to Tarquinia for tea. I suppose they'll want to wait and fly back by moonlight."

"Moonlight—moonlight! What a part it still plays. Do you suppose they're as sentimental as we were?"

"I've come to the conclusion that I don't in the least know what they are," said Mrs. Ansley. "And perhaps we didn't know much more about each other."

"No; perhaps we didn't."

Her friend gave her a shy glance. "I never should have supposed you were sentimental, Alida."

"Well, perhaps I wasn't." Mrs. Slade drew her lids together in retrospect; and for a few moments the two ladies, who had been intimate since childhood, reflected how little they knew each other. Each one, of course, had a label ready to attach to the other's name; Mrs. Delphin Slade, for instance, would have told herself, or anyone who asked her, that Mrs. Horace Ansley, twenty-five years ago, had been exquisitely lovely—no, you wouldn't believe it, would you? . . . though, of course, still charming, distinguished. . . . Well, as a girl she had been exquisite; far more beautiful than her daughter Barbara, though certainly Babs, according to the new standards at any rate, was more effective—had more *edge*, as they say. Funny where she got it, with those two nullities as parents. Yes; Horace

Ansley was—well, just the duplicate of his wife. Museum specimens of old New York. Good-looking, irreproachable, exemplary. Mrs. Slade and Mrs. Ansley had lived opposite each other—actually as well as figuratively—for years. When the drawing-room curtains in No. 20 East 73rd Street were renewed, No. 23, across the way, was always aware of it. And of all the movings, buyings, travels, anniversaries, illnesses—the tame chronicle of an estimable pair. Little of it escaped Mrs. Slade. But she had grown bored with it by the time her husband made his big *coup* in Wall Street, and when they bought in upper Park Avenue had already begun to think: "I'd rather live opposite a speakeasy for a change; at least one might see it raided." The idea of seeing Grace raided was so amusing that (before the move) she launched it at a woman's lunch. It made a hit, and went the rounds— she sometimes wondered if it had crossed the street, and reached Mrs. Ansley. She hoped not, but didn't much mind. Those were the days when respectability was at a discount, and it did the irreproachable no harm to laugh at them a little.

A few years later, and not many months apart, both ladies lost their husbands. There was an appropriate exchange of wreaths and condolences, and a brief renewal of intimacy in the half-shadow of their mourning; and now, after another interval, they had run across each other in Rome, at the same hotel, each of them the modest appendage of a salient daughter. The similarity of their lot had again drawn them together, lending itself to mild jokes, and the mutual confession that, if in old days it must have been tiring to "keep up" with daughters, it was now, at times, a little dull not to.

No doubt, Mrs. Slade reflected, she felt her unemployment more than poor Grace ever would. It was a big drop from being the wife of Delphin Slade to being his widow. She had always regarded herself (with a certain conjugal pride) as his equal in social gifts, as contributing her full share to the making of the exceptional couple they were: but the difference after his death was irremediable. As the wife of the famous corporation lawyer, always with an international case or two on hand, every day brought its exciting and unexpected obligation: the impromptu entertaining of eminent colleagues from abroad, the hurried dashes on legal business to London, Paris or Rome, where the entertaining was so handsomely reciprocated; the amusement of hearing in her wake: "What, that handsome woman with the good clothes and the eyes is Mrs. Slade—*the* Slade's wife? Really? Generally the wives of celebrities are such frumps."

Yes; being *the* Slade's widow was a dullish business after that. In living up to such a husband all her faculties had been engaged; now she had only her daughter to live up to, for the son who seemed to have inherited his father's gifts had died suddenly in boyhood. She had fought through that agony because her husband was there, to be helped and to help; now, after the father's death, the thought of the boy had become unbearable. There was nothing left but to mother her daughter; and dear Jenny was such a perfect daughter that she needed no excessive mothering. "Now with Babs Ansley I don't know that I *should* be so quiet," Mrs. Slade sometimes half-enviously reflected; but Jenny, who was younger than her brilliant friend, was that rare accident, an extremely pretty girl who somehow made youth and prettiness seem as safe as their absence. It was all perplexing—

and to Mrs. Slade a little boring. She wished that Jenny would fall in love—with the wrong man, even; that she might have to be watched, out-maneuvered, rescued. And instead, it was Jenny who watched her mother, kept her out of drafts, made sure that she had taken her tonic. . . .

Mrs. Ansley was much less articulate than her friend, and her mental portrait of Mrs. Slade was slighter, and drawn with fainter touches. "Alida Slade's awfully brilliant; but not as brilliant as she thinks," would have summed it up; though she would have added, for the enlightenment of strangers, that Mrs. Slade had been an extremely dashing girl; much more so than her daughter, who was pretty, of course, and clever in a way, but had none of her mother's—well, "vividness," someone had once called it. Mrs. Ansley would take up current words like this, and cite them in quotation marks, as unheard-of audacities. No; Jenny was not like her mother. Sometimes Mrs. Ansley thought Alida Slade was disappointed; on the whole she had had a sad life. Full of failures and mistakes; Mrs. Ansley had always been rather sorry for her. . . .

So these two ladies visualized each other, each through the wrong end of her little telescope.

II

For a long time they continued to sit side by side without speaking. It seemed as though, to both, there was a relief in laying down their somewhat futile activities in the presence of the vast Memento Mori which faced them. Mrs. Slade sat quite still, her eyes fixed on the golden slope of the Palace of the Caesars, and after a while Mrs. Ansley ceased to fidget with her bag, and she too sank into meditation. Like many intimate friends, the two ladies had never before had occasion to be silent together, and Mrs. Ansley was slightly embarrassed by what seemed, after so many years, a new stage in their intimacy, and one with which she did not yet know how to deal.

Suddenly the air was full of that deep clangor of bells which periodically covers Rome with a roof of silver. Mrs. Slade glanced at her wristwatch. "Five o'clock already," she said, as though surprised.

Mrs. Ansley suggested interrogatively: "There's bridge at the Embassy at five." For a long time Mrs. Slade did not answer. She appeared to be lost in contemplation, and Mrs. Ansley thought the remark had escaped her. But after a while she said, as if speaking out of a dream: "Bridge, did you say? Not unless you want to. . . . But I don't think I will, you know."

"Oh, no," Mrs. Ansley hastened to assure her. "I don't care to at all. It's so lovely here; and so full of old memories, as you say." She settled herself in her chair, and almost furtively drew forth her knitting. Mrs. Slade took sideway note of this activity, but her own beautifully cared-for hands remained motionless on her knee.

"I was just thinking," she said slowly, "what different things Rome stands for to each generation of travelers. To our grandmothers, Roman fever; to our mothers, sentimental dangers—how we used to be guarded!—to our daughters, no more dangers than the middle of Main Street. They don't know it—but how much they're missing!"

The long golden light was beginning to pale, and Mrs. Ansley lifted her knitting a little closer to her eyes. "Yes; how we were guarded!"

"I always used to think," Mrs. Slade continued, "that our mothers had a much more difficult job than our grandmothers. When Roman fever stalked the streets it must have been comparatively easy to gather in the girls at the danger hour; but when you and I were young, with such beauty calling us, and the spice of disobedience thrown in, and no worse risk than catching cold during the cool hour after sunset, the mothers used to be put to it to keep us in—didn't they?"

She turned again toward Mrs. Ansley, but the latter had reached a delicate point in her knitting. "One, two, three—slip two; yes, they must have been," she assented, without looking up.

Mrs. Slade's eyes rested on her with a deepened attention. "She can knit—in the face of *this!* How like her. . . ."

Mrs. Slade leaned back, brooding, her eyes ranging from the ruins which faced her to the long green hollow of the Forum, the fading glow of the church fronts beyond it, and the outlying immensity of the Colosseum. Suddenly she thought: "It's all very well to say that our girls have done away with sentiment and moonlight. But if Babs Ansley isn't out to catch that young aviator—the one who's a Marchese—then I don't know anything. And Jenny has no chance beside her. I know that too. I wonder if that's why Grace Ansley likes the two girls to go everywhere together? My poor Jenny as a foil—!" Mrs. Slade gave a hardly audible laugh, and at the sound Mrs. Ansley dropped her knitting.

"Yes—?"

"I—oh, nothing. I was only thinking how your Babs carries everything before her. That Campolieri boy is one of the best matches in Rome. Don't look so innocent, my dear—you know he is. And I was wondering, ever so respectfully, you understand . . . wondering how two such exemplary characters as you and Horace had managed to produce anything quite so dynamic." Mrs. Slade laughed again, with a touch of asperity.

Mrs. Ansley's hands lay inert across her needles. She looked straight out at the great accumulated wreckage of passion and splendor at her feet. But her small profile was almost expressionless. At length she said: "I think you overrate Babs, my dear."

Mrs. Slade's tone grew easier. "No; I don't. I appreciate her. And perhaps envy you. Oh, my girl's perfect; if I were a chronic invalid I'd—well, I think I'd rather be in Jenny's hands. There must be times . . . but there! I always wanted a brilliant daughter . . . and never quite understood why I got an angel instead."

Mrs. Ansley echoed her laugh in a faint murmur. "Babs is an angel too."

"Of course—of course! But she's got rainbow wings. Well, they're wandering by the sea with their young men; and here we sit . . . and it all brings back the past a little too acutely."

Mrs. Ansley had resumed her knitting. One might almost have imagined (if one had known her less well, Mrs. Slade reflected) that, for her also, too many memories rose from the lengthening shadows of those august ruins. But no; she was simply absorbed in her work. What was there for her to worry about? She knew that Babs would almost certainly come back engaged to the extremely eligible Campolieri. "And she'll sell the New York house, and settle down near them in Rome, and never be in their way . . . she's much too tactful. But she'll have an excellent cook, and just the right people in for bridge and cocktails . . . and a perfectly peaceful old age among her grandchildren."

Mrs. Slade broke off this prophetic flight with a recoil of self-disgust. There was no one of whom she had less right to think unkindly than of Grace Ansley. Would she never cure herself of envying her? Perhaps she had begun too long ago.

She stood up and leaned against the parapet, filling her troubled eyes with the tranquilizing magic of the hour. But instead of tranquilizing her the sight seemed to increase her exasperation. Her gaze turned toward the Colosseum. Already its golden flank was drowned in purple shadow, and above it the sky curved crystal clear, without light or color. It was the moment when afternoon and evening hang balanced in midheaven.

Mrs. Slade turned back and laid her hand on her friend's arm. The gesture was so abrupt that Mrs. Ansley looked up, startled.

"The sun's set. You're not afraid, my dear?"

"Afraid—?"

"Of Roman fever or pneumonia? I remember how ill you were that winter. As a girl you had a very delicate throat, hadn't you?"

"Oh, we're all right up here. Down below, in the Forum, it does get deathly cold, all of a sudden . . . but not here."

"Ah, of course you know because you had to be so careful." Mrs. Slade turned back to the parapet. She thought: "I must make one more effort not to hate her." Aloud she said: "Whenever I look at the Forum from up here, I remember that story about a great-aunt of yours, wasn't she? A dreadfully wicked great-aunt?"

"Oh, yes; great-aunt Harriet. The one who was supposed to have sent her young sister out to the Forum after sunset to gather a night-blooming flower for her album. All our great-aunts and grandmothers used to have albums of dried flowers."

Mrs. Slade nodded. "But she really sent her because they were in love with the same man—"

"Well, that was the family tradition. They said Aunt Harriet confessed it years afterward. At any rate, the poor little sister caught the fever and died. Mother used to frighten us with the story when we were children."

"And you frightened *me* with it, that winter when you and I were here as girls. The winter I was engaged to Delphin."

Mrs. Ansley gave a faint laugh. 'Oh, did I? Really frightened you? I don't believe you're easily frightened."

"Not often; but I was then. I was easily frightened because I was too happy. I wonder if you know what that means?"

"I—yes . . ." Mrs. Ansley faltered.

"Well, I suppose that was why the story of your wicked aunt made such an impression on me. And I thought: 'There's no more Roman fever, but the Forum is deathly cold after sunset—especially after a hot day. And the Colosseum's even colder and damper.' "

"The Colosseum—?"

"Yes. It wasn't easy to get in, after the gates were locked for the night. Far from easy. Still, in those days it could be managed; it *was* managed, often. Lovers met there who couldn't meet elsewhere. You knew that?"

"I—I dare say. I don't remember."

"You don't remember? You don't remember going to visit some ruins or other one evening, just after dark, and catching a bad chill? You were supposed to have gone to see the moon rise. People always said that expedition was what caused your illness."

There was a moment's silence; then Mrs. Ansley rejoined: "Did they? It was all so long ago."

"Yes. And you got well again—so it didn't matter. But I suppose it struck your friends—the reason given for your illness, I mean—because everybody knew you were so prudent on account of your throat, and your mother took such care of you. . . . You *had* been out late sight-seeing, hadn't you, that night?"

"Perhaps I had. The most prudent girls aren't always prudent. What made you think of it now?"

Mrs. Slade seemed to have no answer ready. But after a moment she broke out: "Because I simply can't bear it any longer—!"

Mrs. Ansley lifted her head quickly. Her eyes were wide and very pale. "Can't bear what?"

"Why—your not knowing that I've always known why you went."

"Why I went—?"

"Yes. You think I'm bluffing, don't you? Well, you went to meet the man I was engaged to— and I can repeat every word of the letter that took you there."

While Mrs. Slade spoke Mrs. Ansley had risen unsteadily to her feet. Her bag, her knitting and gloves, slid in a panic-stricken heap to the ground. She looked at Mrs. Slade as though she were looking at a ghost.

"No, no—don't," she faltered out.

"Why not? Listen, if you don't believe me. 'My one darling, things can't go on like this. I must see you alone. Come to the Colosseum immediately after dark tomorrow. There will be somebody to let you in. No one whom you need fear will suspect'—but perhaps you've forgotten what the letter said?"

Mrs. Ansley met the challenge with an unexpected composure. Steadying herself against the chair she looked at her friend, and replied: "No; I know it by heart too."

"And the signature? 'Only *your* D.S.' Was that it? I'm right, am I? That was the letter that took you out that evening after dark?"

Mrs. Ansley was still looking at her. It seemed to Mrs. Slade that a slow struggle was going on behind the voluntarily controlled mask of her small quiet face. "I shouldn't have thought she had herself so well in hand," Mrs. Slade reflected, almost resentfully. But at this moment Mrs. Ansley spoke. "I don't know how you knew. I burnt that letter at once."

"Yes; you would, naturally—you're so prudent!" The sneer was open now. "And if you burnt the letter you're wondering how on earth I know what was in it. That's it, isn't it?"

Mrs. Slade waited, but Mrs. Ansley did not speak.

"Well, my dear, I know what was in that letter because I wrote it!"

"You wrote it?"

"Yes."

The two women stood for a minute staring at each other in the last golden light. Then Mrs. Ansley dropped back into her chair. "Oh," she murmured, and covered her face with her hands.

Mrs. Slade waited nervously for another word or movement. None came, and at length she broke out: "I horrify you."

Mrs. Ansley's hands dropped to her knee. The face they uncovered was streaked with tears. "I wasn't thinking of you. I was thinking—it was the only letter I ever had from him!"

"And I wrote it. Yes; I wrote it! But I was the girl he was engaged to. Did you happen to remember that?"

Mrs. Ansley's head drooped again. "I'm not trying to excuse myself . . . I remembered. . . ."

"And still you went?"

"Still I went."

Mrs. Slade stood looking down on the small bowed figure at her side. The flame of her wrath had already sunk, and she wondered why she had ever thought there would be any satisfaction in inflicting so purposeless a wound on her friend. But she had to justify herself.

"You do understand? I'd found out—and I hated you, hated you. I knew you were in love with Delphin—and I was afraid; afraid of you, of your quiet ways, your sweetness . . . your . . . well, I wanted you out of the way, that's all. Just for a few weeks; just till I was sure of him. So in a blind fury I wrote that letter. . . . I don't know why I'm telling you now."

"I suppose," said Mrs. Ansley slowly, "it's because you've always gone on hating me."

"Perhaps. Or because I wanted to get the whole thing off my mind." She paused. "I'm glad you destroyed the letter. Of course I never thought you'd die."

Mrs. Ansley relapsed into silence, and Mrs. Slade, leaning above her, was conscious of a strange sense of isolation, of being cut off from the warm current of human communion. "You think me a monster!"

"I don't know. . . . It was the only letter I had, and you say he didn't write it?"

"Ah, how you care for him still!"

"I cared for that memory," said Mrs. Ansley.

Mrs. Slade continued to look down on her. She seemed physically reduced by the blow—as if, when she got up, the wind might scatter her like a puff of dust.

Mrs. Slade's jealously suddenly leapt up again at the sight. All these years the woman had been living on that letter. How she must have loved him, to treasure the mere memory of its ashes! The letter of the man her friend was engaged to. Wasn't it she who was the monster?

"You tried your best to get him away from me, didn't you? But you failed; and I kept him. That's all."

"Yes. that's all."

"I wish now I hadn't told you. I'd no idea you'd feel about it as you do; I thought you'd be amused. It all happened so long ago, as you say; and you must do me the justice to remember that I had no reason to think you'd ever taken it seriously. How could I, when you were married to Horace Ansley two months afterward? As soon as you could get out of bed your mother rushed you off to Florence and married you. People were rather surprised—they wondered at its being done so quickly; but I thought I knew. I had an idea you did it out of *pique*—to be able to say you'd got ahead of Delphin and me. Girls have such silly reasons for doing the most serious things. And your marrying so soon convinced me that you'd never really cared."

"Yes. I suppose it would," Mrs. Ansley assented.

The clear heaven overhead was emptied of all its gold. Dusk spread over it, abruptly darkening the Seven Hills. Here and there lights began to twinkle through the foliage at their feet. Steps were coming and going on the deserted terrace—waiters looking out of the doorway at the head of the stairs, then reappearing with trays and napkins and flasks of wine. Tables were moved, chairs straightened. A feeble string of electric lights flickered out. Some vases of faded flowers were carried away, and brought back replenished. A stout lady in a dust coat suddenly appeared, asking in broken Italian if anyone had seen the elastic band which held together her tattered Baedeker. She poked with her stick under the table at which she had lunched, the waiters assisting.

The corner where Mrs. Slade and Mrs. Ansley sat was still shadowy and deserted. For a long time neither of them spoke. At length Mrs. Slade began again: "I suppose I did it as a sort of joke—"

"A joke?"

"Well, girls are ferocious sometimes, you know. Girls in love especially. And I remember laughing to myself all that evening at the idea that you were waiting around there in the dark, dodging out of sight, listening for every sound, trying to get in—Of course I was upset when I heard you were so ill afterward."

Mrs. Ansley had not moved for a long time. But now she turned slowly toward her companion. "But I didn't wait. He'd arranged everything. He was there. We were let in at once," she said.

Mrs. Slade sprang up from her leaning position. "Delphin there? They let you in?—Ah, now you're lying!" she burst out with violence.

Mrs. Ansley's voice grew clearer, and full of surprise. "But of course he was there. Naturally he came—"

"Came? How did he know he'd find you there? You must be raving!"

Mrs. Ansley hesitated, as though reflecting. "But I answered the letter. I told him I'd be there. So he came."

Mrs. Slade flung her hands up to her face. "Oh, God—you answered! I never thought of your answering. . . ."

"It's odd you never thought of it, if you wrote the letter."

"Yes. I was blind with rage."

Mrs. Ansley rose, and drew her fur scarf about her. "It is cold here. We'd better go. . . I'm sorry for you," she said, as she clasped the fur about her throat.

The unexpected words sent a pang through Mrs. Slade. "Yes; we'd better go." She gathered up her bag and cloak. "I don't know why you should be sorry for me," she muttered.

Mrs. Ansley stood looking away from her toward the dusky secret mass of the Colosseum. "Well—because I didn't have to wait that night."

Mrs. Slade gave an unquiet laugh. "Yes; I was beaten there. But I oughtn't to begrudge it to you, I suppose. At the end of all these years. After all, I had everything; I had him for twenty-five years. And you had nothing but that one letter that he didn't write."

Mrs. Ansley was again silent. At length she turned toward the door of the terrace. She took a step, and turned back, facing her companion.

"I had Barbara," she said, and began to move ahead of Mrs. Slade toward the stairway.

D. H. Lawrence (1885–1930)

THE HORSE DEALER'S DAUGHTER

"Well, Mabel, and what are you going to do with yourself?" asked Joe, with foolish flippancy. He felt quite safe himself. Without listening for an answer, he turned aside, worked a grain of tobacco to the tip of his tongue, and spat it out. He did not care about anything, since he felt safe himself.

The three brothers and the sister sat round the desolate breakfast table, attempting some sort of desultory consultation. The morning's post had given the final tap to the family fortune, and all was over. The dreary dining-room itself, with its heavy mahogany furniture, looked as if it were waiting to be done away with.

But the consultation amounted to nothing. There was a strange air of ineffectuality about the three men, as they sprawled at table, smoking and reflecting vaguely on their own condition. The girl was alone, a rather short, sullen-looking young woman of twenty-seven. She did not share the same life as her brothers. She would have been good-looking, save for the impassive fixity of her face, "bull-dog," as her brothers called it.

There was a confused tramping of horses' feet outside. The three men all sprawled round in their chairs to watch. Beyond the dark hollybushes that separated the strip of lawn from the high-road, they could see a cavalcade of shire horses swinging out of their own yard, being taken for exercise. This was the last time. These were the last horses that would go through their hands. The young men watched with critical, callous look. They were all frightened at the collapse of their lives, and the sense of disaster in which they were involved left them no inner freedom.

Yet they were three fine, well-set fellows enough. Joe, the eldest, was a man of thirty-three, broad and handsome in a hot, flushed way. His face was red, he twisted his black moustache over a thick finger, his eyes were shallow and restless. He had a sensual way of uncovering his teeth when he laughed, and his bearing was stupid. Now he watched the horses with a glazed look of helplessness in his eyes, a certain stupor of downfall.

The great draught-horses swung past. They were tied head to tail, four of them, and they heaved along to where a lane branched off from the highroad, planting their great hoofs floutingly in the fine black mud, swinging their great rounded haunches sumptuously, and trotting a few sudden steps as they were led into the lane, round the corner. Every movement showed a massive, slumbrous strength, and a stupidity which held them in subjection. The groom at the head looked back, jerking the leading rope. And the cavalcade moved out of sight up the lane, the tail of the last horse bobbed up tight and stiff, held out taut from the swinging great haunches as they rocked behind the hedges in a motion like sleep.

Joe watched with glazed hopeless eyes. The horses were almost like his own body to him. He felt he was done for now. Luckily he was engaged to a woman as old as himself, and therefore her father, who was steward of a neighbouring estate, would provide him with a job. He would marry and go into harness. His life was over, he would be a subject animal now.

He turned uneasily aside, the retreating steps of the horses echoing in his ears. Then, with foolish restlessness, he reached for the scraps of bacon-rind from the plates, and making a faint whistling sound, flung them to the terrier that lay against the fender. He watched the dog swallow them, and waited till the creature looked into his eyes. Then a faint grin came on his face, and in a high, foolish voice he said:

"You won't get much more bacon, shall you, you little bitch?"

The dog faintly and dismally wagged its tail, then lowered its haunches, circled round, and lay down again.

There was another helpless silence at the table. Joe sprawled uneasily in his seat, not willing to go till the family conclave was dissolved. Fred Henry, the second brother, was erect, clean-limbed, alert. He had watched the passing of the horses with more sangfroid. If he was an animal, like Joe, he was an animal which controls, not one which is controlled. He was master of any horse, and he carried himself with a well-tempered air of mastery. But he was not master of the situations of life. He pushed his coarse brown moustache upwards, off his lip, and glanced irritably at his sister, who sat impassive and inscrutable.

"You'll go and stop with Lucy for a bit, shan't you?" he asked. The girl did not answer.

"I don't see what else you can do," persisted Fred Henry.

"Go as a skivvy," Joe interpolated laconically.

The girl did not move a muscle.

"If I was her, I should go in for training for a nurse," said Malcolm, the youngest of them all. He was the baby of the family, a young man of twenty-two, with a fresh, jaunty *museau*.[1]

But Mabel did not take any notice of him. They had talked at her and round her for so many years, that she hardly heard them at all.

The marble clock on the mantelpiece softly chimed the half-hour, the dog rose uneasily from the hearthrug and looked at the party at the breakfast table. But still they sat on in ineffectual conclave.

"Oh, all right," sad Joe suddenly, apropos of nothing. "I'll get a move on."

He pushed back his chair, straddled his knees with a downward jerk, to get them free, in horsey fashion, and went to the fire. Still he did not go out of the room; he was curious to know what the others would do or say. He began to charge his pipe, looking down at the dog and saying, in a high, affected voice:

"Going wi' me? Going wi' me are ter? Tha'rt going further than tha counts on just now, dost hear?"

The dog faintly wagged its tail, the man stuck out his jaw and covered his pipe with his hands, and puffed intently, losing himself in the tobacco, looking down all the while at the dog with an absent brown eye. The dog looked up at him in mournful distrust. Joe stood with his knees stuck out, in real horsey fashion.

"Have you had a letter from Lucy?" Fred Henry asked of his sister.

"Last week," came the neutral reply.

"And what does she say?"

There was no answer.

"Does she *ask* you to go and stop there?" persisted Fred Henry.

"She says I can if I like."

"Well, then, you'd better. Tell her you'll come on Monday."

This was received in silence.

"That's what you'll do then, is it?" said Fred Henry, in some exasperation.

But she made no answer. There was a silence of futility and irritation in the room. Malcolm grinned fatuously.

"You'll have to make up your mind between now and next Wednesday," said Joe loudly, "or else find yourself lodgings on the kerbstone."

The face of the young woman darkened, but she sat on immutable.

"Here's Jack Fergusson!" exclaimed Malcolm, who was looking aimlessly out of the window.

"Where?" exclaimed Joe, loudly.

"Just gone past."

"Coming in?"

---

[1]Face, or literally, muzzle.

Malcolm craned his neck to see the gate.

"Yes," he said.

There was a silence. Mabel sat on like one condemned, at the head of the table. Then a whistle was heard from the kitchen. The dog got up and barked sharply. Joe opened the door and shouted:

"Come on."

After a moment a young man entered. He was muffled up in overcoat and a purple woollen scarf, and his tweed cap, which he did not remove, was pulled down on his head. He was of medium height, his face was rather long and pale, his eyes looked tired.

"Hello, Jack! Well, Jack!" exclaimed Malcolm and Joe. Fred Henry merely said, "Jack."

"What's doing?" asked the newcomer, evidently addressing Fred Henry.

"Same. We've got to be out by Wednesday. Got a cold?"

"I have—got it bad, too."

"Why don't you stop in?"

"*Me* stop in? When I can't stand on my legs, perhaps I shall have a chance." The young man spoke huskily. He had a slight Scotch accent.

"It's a knock-out, isn't it?" said Joe, boisterously, "if a doctor goes round croaking with a cold. Looks bad for the patients, doesn't it?"

The young doctor looked at him slowly.

"Anything the matter with *you*, then?" he asked sarcastically.

"Not as I know of. Damn your eyes, I hope not. Why?"

"I thought you were very concerned about the patients, wondered if you might be one yourself."

"Damn it, no. I've never been patient to no flaming doctor, and hope I never shall be," returned Joe.

At this point Mabel rose from the table, and they all seemed to become aware of her existence. She began putting the dishes together. The young doctor looked at her, but did not address her. He had not greeted her. She went out of the room with the tray, her face impassive and unchanged.

"When are you off then, all of you?" asked the doctor.

"I'm catching the eleven-forty," replied Malcolm. "Are you goin' down wi' th' trap, Joe?"

"Yes, I've told you I am going down wi' th' trap, haven't I?"

"We'd better be getting her in then. So long, Jack, if I don't see you before I go," said Malcolm, shaking hands.

He went out, followed by Joe, who seemed to have his tail between his legs.

"Well, this is the devil's own," exclaimed the doctor, when he was left alone with Fred Henry. "Going before Wednesday, are you."

"That's the orders," replied the other.

"Where, to Northampton?"

"That's it."

"The devil!" exclaimed Fergusson, with quiet chagrin.

And there was silence between the two.

"All settled up, are you?" asked Fergusson.

"About."

There was another pause.

"Well, I shall miss yer, Freddy, boy," said the young doctor.

"And I shall miss thee, Jack," returned the other.

"Miss you like hell," mused the doctor.

Fred Henry turned aside. There was nothing to say. Mabel came in again, to finish clearing the table.

"What are *you* going to do, then, Miss Pervin?" asked Fergusson. "Going to your sister's, are you?"

Mabel looked at him with her steady, dangerous eyes, that always made him uncomfortable, unsettling his superficial ease.

"No," she said.

"Well, what in the name of fortune are *you* going to do? Say what you mean to do," cried Fred Henry, with futile intensity.

But she only averted her head, and continued her work. She folded the white table-cloth, and put on the chenille cloth.

"The sulkiest bitch that ever trod!" muttered her brother.

But she finished her task with perfectly impassive face, the young doctor watching her interestedly all the while. Then she went out.

Fred Henry stared after her, clenching his lips, his blue eyes fixing in sharp antagonism, as he made a grimace of sour exasperation.

"You could bray her into bits, and that's all you'd get out of her," he said in a small narrowed tone.

The doctor smiled faintly.

"What's she *going* to do, then?" he asked.

"Strike me if I know!" returned the other.

There was a pause. Then the doctor stirred.

"I'll be seeing you to-night, shall I?" he said to his friend.

"Ay—where's it to be? Are we going over to Jessdale?"

"I don't know. I've got such a cold on me. I'll come round to the Moon and Stars, anyway."

"Let Lizzie and May miss their night for once, eh?"

"That's it—if I feel as I do now."

"All's one—"

The two young men went through the passage and down to the back door together. The house was large, but it was servantless now, and desolate. At the back was a small bricked house-yard, and beyond that a big square, gravelled fine and red, and having stables on two sides. Sloping, dank, winter-dark fields stretched away on the open sides.

But the stables were empty. Joseph Pervin, the father of the family, had been a man of no education, who had become a fairly large horse dealer. The stables had been full of horses, there was a great turmoil and come-and-go of horses and of dealers and grooms. Then the kitchen was full of servants. But of late things had declined. The old man had married a second time, to retrieve his fortunes.

Now he was dead and everything was gone to the dogs, there was nothing but debt and threatening.

For months, Mabel had been servantless in the big house, keeping the home together in penury for her ineffectual brothers. She had kept house for ten years. But previously it was with unstinted means. Then, however brutal and coarse everything was, the sense of money had kept her proud, confident. The men might be foul-mouthed, the women in the kitchen might have bad reputations, her brothers might have illegitimate children. But so long as there was money, the girl felt herself established and brutally proud, reserved.

No company came to the house, save dealers and coarse men. Mabel had no associates of her own sex, after her sister went away. But she did not mind. She went regularly to church, she attended to her father. And she lived in the memory of her mother, who had died when she was fourteen, and whom she had loved. She had loved her father, too, in a different way, depending upon him, and feeling secure in him, until at the age of fifty-four he married again. And then she had set hard against him. Now he had died and left them all hopelessly in debt.

She had suffered badly during the period of poverty. Nothing, however, could shake the curious sullen, animal pride that dominated each member of the family. Now, for Mabel, the end had come. Still she would not cast about her. She would follow her own way just the same. She would always hold the keys of her own situation. Mindless and persistent, she endured from day to day. What should she think? Why should she answer anybody? It was enough that this was the end and there was no way out. She need not pass any more darkly along the main street of the small town, avoiding every eye. She need not demean herself any more, going into the shops and buying the cheapest food. This was at an end. She thought of nobody, not even of herself. Mindless and persistent, she seemed in a sort of ecstasy to be coming nearer to her fulfillment, her own glorification, approaching her dead mother, who was glorified.

In the afternoon she took a little bag, with shears and sponge and a small scrubbing brush, and went out. It was a grey, wintry day, with saddened, dark green fields and an atmosphere blackened by the smoke of foundries not far off. She went quickly, darkly along the causeway, heeding nobody, through the town to the churchyard.

There she always felt secure, as if no one could see her, although as a matter of fact she was exposed to the stare of every one who passed along under the churchyard wall. Nevertheless, once under the shadow of the great looming church, among the graves, she felt immune from the world, reserved within the thick churchyard wall as in another country.

Carefully she clipped the grass from the grave, and arranged the pinky white, small chrysanthemums in the tin cross. When this was done, she took an empty jar from the neighbouring grave, brought water, and carefully, most scrupulously sponged the marble head-stone and the coping-stone.

It gave her sincere satisfaction to do this. She felt in immediate contact with the world of her mother. She took minute pains, went through the park in a state bordering on pure happiness, as if in performing this task she came into a subtle, intimate connection with her mother. For the life she followed here in the world was far less real than the world of death she inherited from her mother.

The doctor's house was just by the church. Fergusson, being a mere hired assistant, was slave to the country-side. As he hurried now to attend to the outpatients in the surgery, glancing across the graveyard with his quick eye, he saw the girl at her task at the grave. She seemed so intent and remote, it was like looking into another world. Some mystical element was touched in him. He slowed down as he walked, watching her as if spell-bound.

She lifted her eyes, feeling him looking. Their eyes met. And each looked away again at once, each feeling, in some way, found out by the other. He lifted his cap and passed on down the road. There remained distinct in his consciousness, like a vision, the memory of her face, lifted from the tombstone in the churchyard, and looking at him with slow, large, portentous eyes. It *was* portentous, her face. It seemed to mesmerize him. There was a heavy power in her eyes which laid hold of his whole being, as if he had drunk some powerful drug. He had been feeling weak and done before. Now the life came back into him, he felt delivered from his own fretted, daily self.

He finished his duties at the surgery as quickly as might be, hastily filling up the bottles of the waiting people with cheap drugs. Then, in perpetual haste, he set off again to visit several cases in another part of his round, before tea-time. At all times he preferred to walk if he could, but particularly when he was not well. He fancied the motion restored him.

The afternoon was falling. It was grey, deadened, and wintry, with a slow, moist, heavy coldness sinking in and deadening all the faculties. But why should he think or notice? He hastily climbed the hill and turned across the dark green fields, following the black cinder-track. In the distance, across a shallow dip in the country, the small town was clustered like smouldering ash, a tower, a spire, a heap of low, raw extinct houses. And on the nearest fringe of the town, sloping into the dip, was Oldmeadow, the Pervins' house. He could see the stables and the outbuildings distinctly, as they lay towards him on the slope. Well, he would not go there many more times! Another resource would be lost to him, another place gone: the only company he cared for in the alien, ugly little town he was losing. Nothing but work, drudgery, constant hastening from dwelling to dwelling among the colliers and the ironworkers. It wore him out, but at the same time he had a craving for it. It was a stimulant to him to be in the homes of the working people, moving as it were through the innermost body of their life. His nerves were excited and gratified. He could come so near, into the very lives of the rough, inarticulate, powerfully emotional men and women. He grumbled, he said he hated the hellish hole. But as a matter of fact it excited him, the contact with the rough, strongly feeling people was a stimulant applied direct to his nerves.

Below Oldmeadow, in the green, shallow, soddened hollow of fields lay a square, deep pond. Roving across the landscape, the doctor's quick eye detected a figure in black passing through the gate of the field, down towards the pond.

He looked again. It would be Mabel Pervin. His mind suddenly became alive and attentive.

Why was she going down there? He pulled up on the path on the slope above, and stood staring. He could just make sure of the small black figure moving in the hollow of the failing day. He seemed to see her in the midst of such obscurity, that he was like a clairvoyant, seeing rather with the mind's eye than with ordinary sight. Yet he could see her positively enough, whilst he kept his eye attentive. He felt, if he looked away from her, in the thick, ugly falling dusk, he would lose her altogether.

He followed her minutely as she moved, direct and intent, like something transmitted rather than stirring in voluntary activity, straight down the field towards the pond. There she stood on the bank for a moment. She never raised her head. Then she waded slowly into the water.

He stood motionless as the small black figure walked slowly and deliberately towards the centre of the pond, very slowly, gradually moving deeper into the motionless water, and still moving forward as the water got up to her breast. Then he could see her no more in the dusk of the dead afternoon.

"There!" he exclaimed. "Would you believe it?"

And he hastened straight down, running over the wet, soddened fields, pushing through the hedges, down into the depression of callous wintry obscurity. It took him several minutes to come to the pond. He stood on the bank, breathing heavily. He could see nothing. His eyes seemed to penetrate the dead water. Yes, perhaps that was the dark shadow of her black clothing beneath the surface of the water.

He slowly ventured into the pond. The bottom was deep, soft clay, he sank in, and water clasped dead cold round his legs. As he stirred he could smell the cold, rotten clay that fouled up into the water. It was objectionable in his lungs. Still, repelled and yet not heeding, he moved deeper into the pond. The cold water rose over his thighs, over his loins, upon his abdomen. The lower part of his body was all sunk in the hideous cold element. And the bottom was so deeply soft and uncertain, he was afraid of pitching with his mouth underneath. He could not swim, and was afraid.

He crouched a little, spreading his hands under the water and moving them round, trying to feel for her. The dead cold pond swayed upon his chest. He moved again, a little deeper, and again with his hands underneath, he felt all around the water. And he touched her clothing. But it evaded his fingers. He made a desperate effort to grasp it.

And so doing he lost his balance and went under, horribly, suffocating in the foul earthy water, struggling madly for a few moments. At last, after what seemed an eternity, he got his footing, rose again into the air and looked around. He gasped, and knew he was in the world. Then he looked at the water. She had risen near him. He grasped her clothing, and drawing her nearer, turned to take his way to land again.

He went very slowly, carefully, absorbed in the slow progress. He rose higher, climbing out of the pond. The water was now only about his legs; he was thankful, full of relief to be out of the clutches of the pond. He lifted her and staggered on to the bank, out of the horror of wet, grey clay.

He laid her down on the bank. She was quite unconscious and running with water. He made the water come from her mouth, he worked to restore her. He did not have to work very long before he could feel the breathing begin again in her; she was breathing naturally. He worked a little longer. He could feel her live beneath his hands; she was coming back. He wiped her face, wrapped her in his overcoat, looked round into the dim, dark grey world, then lifted her and staggered down the bank and across the fields.

It seemed an unthinkably long way, and his burden so heavy he felt he would never get to the house. But at last he was in the stable-yard, and then in the house-yard. He opened the door and went into the house. In the kitchen he laid her down on the hearth-rug, and called. The house was empty. But the fire was burning in the grate.

Then again he kneeled to attend to her. She was breathing regularly, her eyes were wide open and as if conscious, but there seemed something missing in her look. She was conscious in herself, but unconscious of her surroundings.

He ran upstairs, took blankets from a bed, and put them before the fire to warm. Then he removed her saturated, earthy-smelling clothing, rubbed her dry with a towel, and wrapped her naked in the blankets. Then he went into the dining-room, to look for spirits. There was a little whisky. He drank a gulp himself, and put some into her mouth.

The effect was instantaneous. She looked full into his face, as if she had been seeing him for some time, and yet had only just become conscious of him.

"Dr. Fergusson?" she said.

"What?" he answered.

He was divesting himself of his coat, intending to find some dry clothing upstairs. He could not bear the smell of the dead, clayey water, and he was mortally afraid for his own health.

"What did I do?" she asked.

"Walked into the pond," he replied. He had begun to shudder like one sick, and could hardly attend to her. Her eyes remained full on him, he seemed to be going dark in his mind, looking back at her helplessly. The shuddering became quieter in him, his life came back in him, dark and unknowing, but strong again.

"Was I out of my mind?" she asked, while her eyes were fixed on him all the time.

"Maybe, for the moment," he replied. He felt quiet, because his strength had come back. The strange fretful strain had left him.

"Am I out of my mind now?" she asked.

"Are you?" he reflected a moment. "No," he answered truthfully. "I don't see that you are." He turned his face aside. He was afraid now, because he felt dazed, and felt dimly that her power was stronger than his, in this issue. And she continued to look at him fixedly all the time. "Can you tell me where I shall find some dry things to put on?" he asked.

"Did you dive into the pond for me?" she asked.

"No," he answered. "I walked in. But I went in overhead as well."

There was silence for a moment. He hesitated. He very much wanted to go upstairs to get into dry clothing. But there was another desire in him. And she seemed to hold him. His will seemed to have gone to sleep, and left him, standing there slack before her. But he felt warm inside himself. He did not shudder at all, though his clothes were sodden on him.

"Why did you?" she asked.

"Because I didn't want you to do such a foolish thing," he said.

"It wasn't foolish," she said, still gazing at him as she lay on the floor, with a sofa cushion under her head. "It was the right thing to do. *I* knew best, then."

"I'll go and shift these wet things," he said. But still he had not the power to move out of her presence, until she sent him. It was as if she had the life of his body in her hands, and he could not extricate himself. Or perhaps he did not want to.

Suddenly she sat up. Then she became aware of her own immediate condition. She felt the blankets about her, she knew her own limbs. For a moment it seemed as if her reason were going. She looked round, with wild eye, as if seeking something. He stood still with fear. She saw her clothing lying scattered.

"Who undressed me?" she asked, her eyes resting full and inevitable on his face.

"I did," he replied, "to bring you round."

For some moments she sat and gazed at him awfully, her lips parted.

"Do you love me, then?" she asked.

He only stood and stared at her, fascinated. His soul seemed to melt.

She shuffled forward on her knees, and put her arms around him, round his legs, as he stood there, pressing her breasts against his knees and thighs, clutching him with strange, convulsive certainty, pressing his thighs against her, drawing him to her face, her throat, as she looked up at him with flaring, humble eyes of transfiguration, triumphant in first possession.

"You love me," she murmured, in strange transport, yearning and triumphant and confident. "You love me. I know you love me, I know."

And she was passionately kissing his knees, through the wet clothing, passionately and indiscriminately kissing his knees, his legs, as if unaware of everything.

He looked down at the tangled wet hair, the wild, bare, animal shoulders. He was amazed, bewildered, and afraid. He had never thought of loving her. He had never wanted to love her. When he rescued her and restored her, he was a doctor, and she was a patient. He had had no single personal thought of her. Nay, this introduction of the personal element was very distasteful to him, a violation of his professional honour. It was horrible to have her there embracing his knees. It was horrible. He revolted from it, violently. And yet—and yet—he had not the power to break away.

She looked at him again, with the same supplication of powerful love, and that same transcendent, frightening light of triumph. In view of the delicate flame which seemed to come from her face like a light, he was powerless. And yet he had never intended to love her. He had never intended. And something stubborn in him could not give way.

"You love me," she repeated, in a murmur of deep rhapsodic assurance. "You love me."

Her hands were drawing him, drawing him down to her. He was afraid, even a little horrified. For he had, really, no intention of loving her. Yet her hands were drawing him towards her. He put out his hand quickly to steady himself, and grasped her bare shoulder. A flame seemed to burn the hand that grasped her soft shoulder. He had no intention of loving her: his whole will was against his yielding. It was horrible. And yet wonderful was the touch of her shoulders, beautiful the shining of her face. Was she perhaps mad? He had a horror of yielding to her. Yet something in him ached also.

He had been staring away at the door, away from her. But his hand remained on her shoulder. She had gone suddenly very still. He looked down at her. Her eyes were now wide with fear, with doubt, the light was dying from her face, a shadow of terrible greyness was returning. He could not bear the touch of her eyes' question upon him, and the look of death behind the question.

With an inward groan he gave way, and let his heart yield towards her. A sudden gentle smile came on his face. And her eyes, which never left his face, slowly, slowly filled with tears. He watched the strange water rise in her eyes, like some slow fountain coming up. And his heart seemed to burn and melt away in his breast.

He could not bear to look at her any more. He dropped on his knees and caught her head with his arms and pressed her face against his throat. She was very still. His heart, which seemed to have broken, was burning with a kind of agony in his breast. And he felt her slow, hot tears wetting his throat. But he could not move.

He felt the hot tears wet his neck and the hollows of his neck, and he remained motionless, suspended through one of man's eternities. Only now it had become indispensable to him to have her face pressed close to him; he could never let her go again. He could never let her head go away from the close clutch of his arm. He wanted to remain like that for ever, with his heart hurting him in a pain that was also life to him. Without knowing, he was looking down on her damp, soft brown hair.

Then, as it were suddenly, he smelt the horrid stagnant smell of that water. And at the same moment she drew away from him and looked at him. Her eyes were wistful and unfathomable. He was afraid of them, and he fell to kissing her, not knowing what he was doing. He wanted her eyes not to have that terrible, wistful, unfathomable look.

When she turned her face to him again, a faint delicate flush was glowing, and there was again dawning that terrible shining of joy in her eyes, which really terrified him, and yet which he now wanted to see, because he feared the look of doubt still more.

"You love me?" she said, rather faltering.

"Yes." The word cost him a painful effort. Not because it wasn't true. But because it was too newly true, the *saying* seemed to tear open again his newly torn heart. And he hardly wanted it to be true, even now.

She lifted her face to him, and he bent forward and kissed her on the mouth, gently, with the one kiss that is an eternal pledge. And as he kissed her his heart strained again in his breast. He never intended to love her. But now it was over. He had crossed over the gulf to her, and all that he had left behind had shrivelled and become void.

After the kiss, her eyes again slowly filled with tears. She sat still, away from him, with her face drooped aside, and her hands folded in her lap. The tears fell very slowly. There was complete silence. He too sat there motionless and silent on the hearthrug. The strange pain of his heart that was broken seemed to consume him. That he should love her? That this was love! That he should be ripped open in this way! Him, a doctor! How they would all jeer if they knew! It was agony to him to think they might know.

In the curious naked pain of the thought he looked again to her. She was sitting there drooped into a muse. He saw a tear fall, and his heart flared hot. He saw for the first time that one of her shoulders was quite uncovered, one arm bare, he could see one of her small breasts; dimly, because it had become almost dark in the room.

"Why are you crying?" he asked, in an altered voice.

She looked up at him, and behind her tears the consciousness of her situation for the first time brought a dark look of shame to her eyes.

"I'm not crying, really," she said, watching him half frightened.

He reached his hand, and softly closed it on her bare arm.

"I love you! I love you!" he said in a soft, low vibrating voice, unlike himself.

She shrank, and dropped her head. The soft, penetrating grip of his hand on her arm distressed her. She looked up at him.

"I want to go," she said. "I want to go and get you some dry things."

"Why?" he said. "I'm all right."

"But I want to go," she said. "And I want you to change your things."

He released her arm, and she wrapped herself in the blanket, looking at him rather frightened. And still she did not rise.

"Kiss me," she said wistfully.

He kissed her, but briefly, half in anger.

Then, after a second, she rose nervously, all mixed up in the blanket. He watched her in her confusion, as she tried to extricate herself and wrap herself up so that she could walk. He watched her relentlessly, as she knew. And as she went, the blanket trailing, and as he saw a glimpse of her feet and her white leg, he tried to remember her as she was when he had wrapped her in the blanket. But then he didn't want to remember, because she had been nothing to him then, and his nature revolted from remembering her as she was when she was nothing to him.

A tumbling, muffled noise from within the dark house startled him. Then he heard her voice:—"There are clothes." He rose and went to the foot of the stairs, and gathered up the garments she had thrown down. Then he came back to the fire, to rub himself down and dress. He grinned at his own appearance when he had finished.

The fire was sinking, so he put on coal. The house was now quite dark, save for the light of a street-lamp that shone in faintly from beyond the holly trees. He lit the gas with matches he found on the mantelpiece. Then he emptied the pockets of his own clothes, and threw all his wet things in a heap into the scullery. After which he gathered up her sodden clothes, gently, and put them in a separate heap on the copper-top in the scullery.

It was six o'clock on the clock. His own watch had stopped. He ought to go back to the surgery. He waited, and still she did not come down. So he went to the foot of the stairs and called:

"I shall have to go."

Almost immediately he heard her coming down. She had on her best dress of black voile, and her hair was tidy, but still damp. She looked at him—and in spite of herself, smiled.

"I don't like you in those clothes," she said.

"Do I look a sight?" he answered.

They were shy of one another.

"I'll make you some tea," she said.

"No, I must go."

"Must you?" And she looked at him again with the wide, strained, doubtful eyes. And again, from the pain of his breast, he knew how he loved her. He went and bent to kiss her, gently, passionately, with his heart's painful kiss.

"And my hair smells so horrible," she murmured in distraction. "And I'm so awful, I'm so awful! Oh, no, I'm too awful." And she broke into bitter, heart-broken sobbing. "You can't want to love me, I'm horrible."

"Don't be silly, don't be silly," he said, trying to comfort her, kissing her, holding her in his arms. "I want you, I want to marry you, we're going to be married, quickly, quickly—tomorrow if I can."

But she only sobbed terribly, and cried:

"I feel awful. I feel awful. I feel I'm horrible to you."

"No, I want you, I want you," was all he answered, blindly, with that terrible intonation which frightened her almost more than her horror lest he should *not* want her.

QUESTIONS

1. Could you identify the broader setting—the time and region—of this story?
2. What details of the particular settings of house and stables, graveyard, fields and pond, evoke strong responses?
3. At the beginning of the story, how much sympathy with the Pervins do you feel?
4. What thoughts or feelings do you imagine to be behind Mabel's long silence at the start? Do the narrator's subsequent comments contradict any of your impressions?

5. What do you suppose is the basis of Fergusson's friendship with Fred Henry?
6. What picture does the story give of male/female relations generally?
7. At the conclusion, in what way does Mabel love Fergusson?

Bernard Malamud (b. 1914)
THE MAGIC BARREL

Not long ago there lived in uptown New York, in a small, almost meager room, though crowded with books, Leo Finkle, a rabbinical student in the Yeshivah University. Finkle, after six years of study, was to be ordained in June and had been advised by an acquaintance that he might find it easier to win himself a congregation if he were married. Since he had no present prospects of marriage, after two tormented days of turning it over in his mind, he called in Pinye Salzman, a marriage broker whose two-line advertisement he had read in the *Forward.*

The matchmaker appeared one night out of the dark fourth-floor hallway of the graystone rooming house where Finkle lived, grasping a black, strapped portfolio that had been worn thin with use. Salzman, who had been long in the business, was of slight but dignified build, wearing an old hat, and an overcoat too short and tight for him. He smelled frankly of fish, which he loved to eat, and although he was missing a few teeth, his presence was not displeasing, because of an amiable manner curiously contrasted with mournful eyes. His voice, his lips, his wisp of beard, his bony fingers were animated, but give him a moment of repose and his mild blue eyes revealed a depth of sadness, a characteristic that put Leo a little at ease although the situation, for him, was inherently tense.

He at once informed Salzman why he had asked him to come, explaining that his home was in Cleveland, and that but for his parents, who had married comparatively late in life, he was alone in the world. He had for six years devoted himself almost entirely to his studies, as a result of which, understandably, he had found himself without time for a social life and the company of young women. Therefore he thought it the better part of trial and error—of embarrassing fumbling—to call in an experienced person to advise him on these matters. He remarked in passing that the function of the marriage broker was ancient and honorable, highly approved in the Jewish community, because it made practical the necessary without hindering joy. Moreover, his own parents had been brought together by a matchmaker. They had made, if not a financially profitable marriage—since neither had possessed any worldly goods to speak of—at least a successful one in the sense of their everlasting devotion to each other. Salzman listened in embarrassed surprise, sensing a sort of apology. Later, however, he experienced a glow of pride in his work, an emotion that had left him years ago, and he heartily approved of Finkle.

The two went to their business. Leo had led Salzman to the only clear place in the room, a table near a window that overlooked the lamp-lit city. He seated himself at the matchmaker's side but facing him, attempting by an act of will to suppress the unpleasant tickle in his throat. Salzman eagerly unstrapped his portfolio and removed a loose rubber band from a thin packet of much-handled cards. As he flipped through them, a gesture and sound that physically hurt Leo, the student pretended not to see and gazed steadfastly out the window. Although it was still February, winter was on its last legs, signs of which he had for the first time in years begun to notice. He now observed the round white moon, moving high in the sky through a cloud menagerie, and watched with half-open mouth as it penetrated a huge hen, and dropped out of her like an egg laying itself. Salzman, though pretending through eyeglasses he had just slipped on, to be engaged in scanning the writing on the cards, stole occasional glances at the young man's distinguished face, noting with pleasure the long, severe scholar's nose, brown eyes heavy with learning, sensitive yet ascetic lips, and a certain, almost hollow quality of the dark cheeks. He gazed around at shelves upon shelves of books and let out a soft, contented sigh.

When Leo's eyes fell upon the cards, he counted six spread out in Salzman's hand.

"So few?" he asked in disappointment.

"You wouldn't believe me how much cards I got in my office," Salzman replied. "The drawers are already filled to the top, so I keep them now in a barrel, but is every girl good for a new rabbi?"

Leo blushed at this, regretting all he had revealed of himself in a curriculum vitae he had sent to Salzman. He had thought it best to acquaint him with his strict standards and specifications, but in having done so, felt he had told the marriage broker more than was absolutely necessary.

He hesitantly inquired, "Do you keep photographs of your clients on file?"

"First comes family, amount of dowry, also what kind promises," Salzman replied, unbuttoning his tight coat and settling himself in the chair. "After comes pictures, rabbi."

"Call me Mr. Finkle. I'm not yet a rabbi."

Salzman said he would, but instead called him doctor, which he changed to rabbi when Leo was not listening too attentively.

Salzman adjusted his horn-rimmed spectacles, gently cleared his throat and read in an eager voice the contents of the top card:

"Sophie P. Twenty four years. Widow one year. No children. Educated high school and two years college. Father promises eight thousand dollars. Has wonderful wholesale business. Also real estate. On the mother's side comes teachers, also one actor. Well known on Second Avenue."

Leo gazed up in surprise. "Did you say a widow?"

"A widow don't mean spoiled, rabbi. She lived with her husband maybe four months. He was a sick boy she made a mistake to marry him."

"Marrying a widow has never entered my mind."

"This is because you have no experience. A widow, especially if she is young and healthy like this girl, is a wonderful person to marry. She will be thankful to you the rest of her life. Believe me, if I was looking now for a bride, I would marry a widow."

Leo reflected, then shook his head.

Salzman hunched his shoulders in an almost imperceptible gesture of disappointment. He placed the card down on the wooden table and began to read another:

"Lily H. High school teacher. Regular. Not a substitute. Has savings and new Dodge car. Lived in Paris one year. Father is successful dentist thirty-five years. Interested in professional man. Well Americanized family. Wonderful opportunity."

"I knew her personally," said Salzman. "I wish you could see this girl. She is a doll. Also very intelligent. All day you could talk to her about books and theater and what not. She also knows current events."

"I don't believe you mentioned her age?"

"Her age?" Salzman said, raising his brows. "Her age is thirty-two years."

Leo said after a while, "I'm afraid that seems a little too old."

Salzman let out a laugh. "So how old are you, rabbi?"

"Twenty-seven."

"So what is the difference, tell me, between twenty-seven and thirty-two? My own wife is seven years older than me. So what did I suffer?—Nothing. If Rothschild's daughter wants to marry you, would you say on account her age, no?"

"Yes," Leo said dryly.

Salzman shook off the no in the yes. "Five years don't mean a thing. I give you my word that when you will live with her for one week you will forget her age. What does it mean five years—that she lived more and knows more than somebody who is younger? On this girl, God bless her, years are not wasted. Each one that it comes makes better the bargain."

"What subject does she teach in high school?"

"Languages. If you heard the way she speaks French, you will think it is music. I am in the business twenty-five years, and I recommend her with my whole heart. Believe me, I know what I'm talking, rabbi."

"What's on the next card?" Leo said abruptly.

Salzman reluctantly turned up the third card:

"Ruth K. Nineteen years. Honor student. Father offers thirteen thousand cash to the right bridegroom. He is a medical doctor. Stomach specialist with marvelous practice. Brother in law owns own garment business. Particular people."

Salzman looked as if he had read his trump card.

"Did you say nineteen?" Leo asked with interest.

"On the dot."

"Is she attractive?" He blushed. "Pretty?"

Salzman kissed his finger tips. "A little doll. On this I give you my word. Let me call the father tonight and you will see what means pretty."

But Leo was troubled. "You're sure she's that young?"

"This I am positive. The father will show you the birth certificate."

"Are you positive there isn't something wrong with her?" Leo insisted.

"Who says there is wrong?"

"I don't understand why an American girl her age should go to a marriage broker."

A smile spread over Salzman's face.

"So for the same reason you went, she comes."

Leo flushed. "I am pressed for time."

Salzman, realizing he had been tactless, quickly explained. "The father came, not her. He wants she should have the best, so he looks around himself. When we will locate the right boy he will introduce him and encourage. This makes a better marriage than if a young girl without experience takes for herself. I don't have to tell you this."

"But don't you think this young girl believes in love?" Leo spoke uneasily.

Salzman was about to guffaw but caught himself and said soberly, "Love comes with the right person, not before."

Leo parted dry lips but did not speak. Noticing that Salzman had snatched a glance at the next card, he cleverly asked, "How is her health?"

"Perfect," Salzman said, breathing with difficulty. "Of course, she is a little lame on her right foot from an auto accident that it happened to her when she was twelve years, but nobody notices on account she is so brilliant and also beautiful."

Leo got up heavily and went to the window. He felt curiously bitter and upbraided himself for having called in the marriage broker. Finally he shook his head.

"Why not?" Salzman persisted, the pitch of his voice rising.

"Because I detest stomach specialists."

"So what do you care what is his business? After you marry her do you need him? Who says he must come every Friday night in your house?"

Ashamed of the way the talk was going, Leo dismissed Salzman, who went home with heavy, melancholy eyes.

Though he had felt only relief at the marriage broker's departure, Leo was in low spirits the next day. He explained it as arising from Salzman's failure to produce a suitable bride for him. He did not care for his type of clientele. But when Leo found himself hesitating whether to seek out another matchmaker, one more polished than Pinye, he wondered if it could be—his protestations to the contrary, and although he honored his father and mother—that he did not, in essence, care for the matchmaking institution? This thought he quickly put out of mind yet found himself still upset. All day he ran around in the woods—missed an important appointment, forgot to give out his laundry, walked out of a Broadway cafeteria without paying and had to run back with the ticket in his hand; had even not recognized his landlady in the street when she passed with a friend and courteously called out, "A good evening to you, Doctor Finkle." By nightfall, however, he had regained sufficient calm to sink his nose into a book and there found peace from his thoughts.

Almost at once there came a knock on the door. Before Leo could say enter, Salzman, commercial cupid, was standing in the room. His face was gray and meager, his expression hungry, and he looked as if he would expire on his feet.

Yet the marriage broker managed, by some trick of the muscles, to display a broad smile.

"So good evening. I am invited?"

Leo nodded, disturbed to see him again, yet unwilling to ask the man to leave.

Beaming still, Salzman laid his portfolio on the table. "Rabbi, I got for you tonight good news."

"I've asked you not to call me rabbi. I'm still a student."

"Your worries are finished. I have for you a first-class bride."

"Leave me in peace concerning this subject." Leo pretended lack of interest.

"The world will dance at your wedding."

"Please, Mr. Salzman, no more."

"But first must come back my strength," Salzman said weakly. He fumbled with the portfolio straps and took out of the leather case an oily paper bag, from which he extracted a hard, seeded roll and a small, smoked white fish. With a quick motion of his hand he stripped the fish out of its skin and began ravenously to chew. "All day in a rush," he muttered.

Leo watched him eat.

"A sliced tomato you have maybe?" Salzman hesitantly inquired.

"No."

The marriage broker shut his eyes and ate. When he had finished he carefully cleaned up the crumbs and rolled up the remains of the fish, in the paper bag. His spectacled eyes roamed the room until he discovered, amid some piles of books, a one-burner gas stove. Lifting his hat he humbly asked, "A glass tea you got, rabbi?"

Conscience-stricken, Leo rose and brewed the tea. He served it with a chunk of lemon and two cubes of lump sugar, delighting Salzman.

After he had drunk his tea, Salzman's strength and good spirits were restored.

"So tell me, rabbi," he said amiably, "you considered some more the three clients I mentioned yesterday?"

"There was no need to consider."

"Why not?"

"None of them suits me."

"What then suits you?"

Leo let it pass because he could give only a confused answer.

Without waiting for a rely, Salzman asked, "You remember this girl I talked to you—the high school teacher?"

"Age thirty-two?"

But, surprisingly, Salzman's face lit in a smile. "Age twenty-nine."

Leo shot him a look. "Reduced from thirty-two?"

"A mistake," Salzman avowed. "I talked today with the dentist. He took me to his safety deposit box and showed me the birth certificate. She was twenty-nine years last August. They made her a party in the mountains where she went for her vacation. When her father spoke to me the first time I forgot to write the age and I told you thirty-two, but now I remember this was a different client, a widow."

"The same one you told me about? I thought she was twenty-four?"

"A different. Am I responsible that the world is filled with widows?"

"No, but I'm not interested in them, nor for that matter, in school teachers."

Salzman pulled his clasped hands to his breast. Looking at the ceiling he devoutly exclaimed, "Yiddishe kinder, what can I say to somebody that he is not interested in high school teachers? So what then you are interested?"

Leo flushed but controlled himself.

"In what else will you be interested," Salzman went on, "if you not interested in this fine girl that she speaks four languages and has personally in the bank ten thousand dollars? Also her father guarantees further twelve thousand. Also she has a new car, wonderful clothes, talks on all subjects, and she will give you a first-class home and children. How near do we come in our life to paradise?"

"If she's so wonderful, why wasn't she married ten years ago?"

"Why?" said Salzman with a heavy laugh. "—Why? Because she is *partikiler*. This is why. She wants the *best*."

Leo was silent, amused at how he had entangled himself. But Salzman had aroused his interest in Lily H., and he began seriously to consider calling on her. When the marriage broker observed how intently Leo's mind was at work on the facts he had supplied, he felt certain they would soon come to an agreement.

Late Saturday afternoon, conscious of Salzman, Leo Finkle walked with Lily Hirschorn along Riverside Drive. He walked briskly and erectly, wearing with distinction the black fedora he had that morning taken with trepidation out of the dusty hat box on his closet shelf, and the heavy black Saturday coat he had thoroughly whisked clean. Leo also owned a walking stick, a present from a distant relative, but quickly put temptation aside and did not use it. Lily, petite and not unpretty, had on something signifying the approach of spring. She was au courant, animatedly, with all sorts of subjects, and he weighed her words and found her surprisingly sound—score another for Salzman, whom he uneasily sensed to be somewhere around, hiding perhaps high in a tree along the street, flashing the lady signals with a pocket mirror; or perhaps a cloven-hoofed Pan, piping nuptial ditties as he danced his invisible way before them, strewing wild buds on the walk and purple grapes in their path, symbolizing fruit of a union, though there was of course still none.

Lily startled Leo by remarking, "I was thinking of Mr. Salzman, a curious figure, wouldn't you say?"

Not certain what to answer, he nodded.

She bravely went on, blushing, "I for one am grateful for his introducing us. Aren't you?"

He courteously replied, "I am."

"I mean," she said with a little laugh—and it was all in good taste, or at least gave the effect of being not in bad—"do you mind that we came together so?"

He was not displeased with her honesty, recognizing that she meant to set the relationship aright, and understanding that it took a certain amount of experience in life, and courage, to want to do it quite that way. One had to have some sort of past to make that kind of beginning.

He said that he did not mind. Salzman's function was traditional and honorable—valuable for what it might achieve, which, he pointed out, was frequently nothing.

Lily agreed with a sigh. They walked on for a while and she said after a long silence, again with a nervous laugh, "Would you mind if I asked you something a little bit personal? Frankly, I find the subject fascinating." Although Leo shrugged, she went on half embarrassedly, "How was it that you came to your calling? I mean was it a sudden passionate inspiration?"

Leo, after a time, slowly replied, "I was always interested in the Law."

"You saw revealed in it the presence of the Highest?"

He nodded and changed the subject. "I understand that you spent a little time in Paris, Miss Hirschorn?"

"Oh, did Mr. Salzman tell you, Rabbi Finkle?" Leo winced but she went on, "It was ages ago and almost forgotten. I remember I had to return for my sister's wedding."

And Lily would not be put off. "When," she asked in a trembly voice, "did you become enamored of God?"

He stared at her. Then it came to him that she was talking not about Leo Finkle, but of a total stranger, some mystical figure, perhaps even passionate prophet that Salzman had dreamed up for her—no relation to the living or dead. Leo trembled with rage and weakness. The trickster had obviously sold her a bill of goods, just as he had him, who'd expected to become acquainted with a young lady of twenty-nine, only to behold, the moment he laid eyes upon her strained and anxious face, a woman past thirty-five and aging rapidly. Only his self control had kept him this long in per presence.

"I am not," he said gravely, "a talented religious person," and in seeking words to go on, found himself possessed by shame and fear. "I think," he said in a strained manner, "that I came to God not because I loved Him, but because I did not."

This confession he spoke harshly because its unexpectedness shook him.

Lily wilted. Leo saw a profusion of loaves of bread go flying like ducks high over his head, not unlike the winged loaves by which he counted himself to sleep last night. Mercifully, then, it snowed, which he would not put past Salzman's machinations.

He was infuriated with the marriage broker and swore he would throw him out of the room the minute he reappeared. But Salzman did not come that night, and when Leo's anger had subsided, an unaccountable despair grew in its place. At first he thought this was caused by his disappointment in Lily, but before long it became evident that he had involved himself with Salzman without a true knowledge of his own intent. He gradually realized—with an emptiness that seized him with six hands—that he had called in the broker to find him a bride because he was incapable of doing it himself. This terrifying insight he had derived as a result of his meeting and conversation with Lily Hirschorn. Her probing questions had somehow irriated him into revealing—to himself more than her—the true nature of his relationship to God, and from that it had come upon him, with shocking force, that apart from his parents, he had never loved anyone. Or perhaps it went the other way, that he did not love God so well as he might, because he had not loved man. It seemed to Leo that his whole life stood starkly revealed and he saw himself for the first time as he truly was—unloved and loveless. This bitter but somehow not fully unexpected revelation brought him to a point of panic, controlled only by extraordinary effort. He covered his face with his hands and cried.

The week that followed was the worst of his life. He did not eat and lost weight. His beard darkened and grew ragged. He stopped attending seminars and almost never opened a book. He seriously considered leaving the Yeshivah, although he was deeply troubled at the thought of the loss of all his years of study—saw them like pages torn from a book, strewn over the city—and at the devastating effect of this decision upon his parents. But he had lived without knowledge of himself, and never in the Five Books and all the Commentaries—mea culpa—had the truth been revealed to him. He did not know where to turn, and in all this desolating loneliness there was no *to whom*, although he often thought of Lily but not once could bring himself to go downstairs and make the call. He became touchy and irritable, especially with his landlady, who asked him all manner of personal questions; on the other hand, sensing his own disagreeableness, he waylaid her on the stairs and apologized abjectly, until mortified, she ran from him. Out of this, however, he drew the consolation that he was a Jew and that a Jew suffered. But gradually, as the long and terrible week drew to a close, he regained his composure and some idea of purpose in life: to go on as planned. Although he was imperfect, the ideal was not. As for his question of a bride, the thought of continuing afflicted him with anxiety and heartburn, yet perhaps with this new knowledge of himself he would be more successful than in the past. Perhaps love would now come to him and a bride to that love. And for this sanctified seeking who needed a Salzman?

The marriage broker, a skeleton with haunted eyes, returned that very night. He looked, withal, the picture of frustrated expectancy—as if he had steadfastly waited the week at Miss Lily Hirschorn's side for a telephone call that never came.

Casually coughing, Salzman came immediately to the point: "So how did you like her?"

Leo's anger rose and he could not refrain from chiding the matchmaker: "Why did you lie to me, Salzman?"

Salzman's pale face went dead white, the world had snowed on him.

"Did you not state that she was twenty-nine?" Leo insisted.

"I give you my word—"

"She was thirty-five, if a day. *At least* thirty-five."

"Of this don't be too sure. Her father told me—"

"Never mind. The worst of it was that you lied to her."

"How did I lie to her, tell me?"

"You told her things about me that weren't true. You made me out to be more, consequently less than I am. She had in mind a totally different person, a sort of semimystical Wonder Rabbi."

"All I said, you was a religious man."

"I can imagine."

Salzman sighed. "This is my weakness that I have," he confessed. "My wife says to me I shouldn't be a salesman, but when I have two fine people that they would be wonderful to be married, I am so happy that I talk too much." He smiled wanly. "This is why Salzman is a poor man."

Leo's anger left him. "Well, Salzman, I'm afraid that's all."

The marriage broker fastened hungry eyes on him.

"You don't want any more a bride?"

"I do," said Leo, "but I have decided to seek her in a different way. I am no longer interested in an arranged marriage. To be frank, I now admit the necessity of premarital love. That is, I want to be in love with the one I marry."

"Love?" said Salzman, astounded. After a moment he remarked, "For us, our love is our life, not for the ladies. In the ghetto they—"

"I know, I know," said Leo. "I've thought of it often. Love, I have said to myself, should be a by-product of living and worship rather than its own end. Yet for myself I find it necessary to establish the level of my need and fulfill it."

Salzman shrugged but answered, "Listen, rabbit, if you want love, this I can find for you also. I have such beautiful clients that you will love them the minute your eyes will see them."

Leo smiled unhappily. "I'm afraid you don't understand."

But Salzman hastily unstrapped his portfolio and withdrew a manila packet from it.

"Pictures," he said, quickly laying the envelope on the table.

Leo called after him to take the pictures away, but as if on the wings of the wind, Salzman had disappeared.

March came. Leo had returned to his regular routine. Although he felt not quite himself yet—lacked energy—he was making plans for a more active social life. Of course it would cost something, but he was an expert in cutting corners; and when there were no corners left he would make circles rounder. All the while Salzman's pictures had lain on the table, gathering dust. Occasionally as Leo sat studying, or enjoying a cup of tea, his eyes fell on the manila envelope, but he never opened it.

The days went by and no social life to speak of developed with a member of the opposite sex—it was difficult, given the circumstances of his situation. One morning Leo toiled up the stairs to his room and stared out the window at the city. Although the day was bright his view of it was dark. For some time he watched the people in the street below hurrying along and then turned with a heavy heart to his little room. On the table was the packet. With a sudden relentless gesture he tore it open. For a half-hour he stood by the table in a state of excitement, examining the photographs of the ladies Salzman had included. Finally, with a deep sigh he put them down. There were six, of varying degrees of attractiveness, but look at them long enough and they all became Lily Hirschorn: all past their prime, all starved behind bright smiles, not a true personality in the lot. Life, despite their frantic yoohooings, had passed them by; they were pictures in a brief case that stank of fish. After a while, however, as Leo attempted to return the photographs into the envelope, he found in it another, a snapshot of the type taken by a machine for a quarter. He gazed at it a moment and let out a cry.

Her face deeply moved him. Why, he could at first not say. It gave him the impression of youth—spring flowers, yet age—a sense of having been used to the bone, wasted; this came from the eyes, which were hauntingly familiar, yet absolutely strange. He had a vivid impression that he had met her before, but try as he might he could not place her although he could almost recall her name, as if he had read it in her own handwriting. No, this couldn't be; he would have remembered her. It was not, he affirmed, that she had an extraordinary beauty—no, though her face was attractive enough; it was that *something* about her moved him. Feature for feature, even some of the ladies of the photographs could do better; but she leaped forth to his heart—had *lived*, or wanted to—more than just wanted, perhaps regretted how she had lived—had somehow deeply suffered: it could be seen in the depths of those reluctant eyes, and from the way the light enclosed and shone from her, and within her, opening realms of possibility: this was her own. Her he desired. His head ached and eyes narrowed with the intensity of his gazing, then as if an obscure fog had blown up in the mind, he experienced fear of her and was aware that he had received an impression, somehow, of evil. He shuddered, saying softly, it is thus with us all. Leo brewed some tea in a small pot and sat sipping it without sugar, to calm himself. But before he had finished drinking, again with excitement he examined the face and found it good: good for Leo Finkle. Only such a one could understand him and help him seek whatever he was seeking. She might, perhaps, love him. How she had happened to be among the discards in Salzman's barrel he could never guess, but he knew he must urgently go find her.

Leo rushed downstairs, grabbed up the Bronx telephone book, and searched for Salzman's home address. He was not listed, nor was his office. Neither was he in the Manhattan book. But Leo remembered having written down the address on a slip of paper after he had read Salzman's advertisement in the "personals" column of the *Forward*. He ran up to his room and tore through his papers, without luck. It was exasperating. Just when he needed the matchmaker he was nowhere to be found. Fortunately Leo remembered to look in his wallet. There on a card he found his name written and a Bronx address. No phone number was listed, the reason—Leo now recalled—he had originally communicated with Salzman by letter. He got on his coat, put a hat on over his skull cap and hurried to the subway station. All the way to the far end of the Bronx he sat on the edge of his seat. He was more than once tempted to take out the picture and see if the girl's face was as he remembered it, but he refrained, allowing the snapshot to remain in his inside coat pocket, content to have her so close. When the train pulled into the station he was waiting at the door and bolted out. He quickly located the street Salzman had advertised.

The building he sought was less than a block from the subway, but it was not an office building, nor even a loft, nor a store in which one could rent office space. It was a very old tenement house. Leo found Salzman's name in pencil on a soiled tag under the bell and climbed three dark flights to his apartment. When he knocked, the door was opened by a thin asthmatic, gray-haired woman, in felt slippers.

"Yes?" she said, expecting nothing. She listened without listening. He could have sworn he had seen her, too, before but knew it was an illusion.

"Salzman—does he live here? Pinye Salzman," he said, "the matchmaker?"

She stared at him a long minute. "Of course."

He felt embarrassed. "Is he in?"

"No." Her mouth, though left open, offered nothing more.

"The matter is urgent. Can you tell me where his office is?"

"In the air." She pointed upward.

"You mean he has no office?" Leo asked.

"In his socks."

He peered into the apartment. It was sunless and dingy, one large room divided by a half-open curtain, beyond which he could see a sagging metal bed. The near side of the room was crowded with rickety chairs, old bureaus, a three-legged table, racks of cooking utensils, and all the apparatus of a kitchen. But there was no sign of Salzman or his magic barrel, probably also a figment of the imagination. An odor of frying fish made Leo weak to the knees.

"Where is he?" he insisted. "I've got to see your husband."

At length she answered, "So who knows where he is? Every time he thinks a new thought he runs to a different place. Go home, he will find you."

"Tell him Leo Finkle."

She gave no sign she had heard.

He walked downstairs, depressed.

But Salzman, breathless, stood waiting at his door.

Leo was astounded and overjoyed. "How did you get here before me?"

"I rushed."

"Come inside."

They entered. Leo fixed tea, and a sardine sandwich for Salzman. As they were drinking he reached behind him for the packet of pictures and handed them to the marriage broker.

Salzman put down his glass and said expectantly, "You found somebody you like?"

"Not among these."

The marriage broker turned away.

"Here is the one I want." Leo held forth the snapshot.

Salzman slipped on his glasses and took the picture into his trembling hand. He turned ghastly and let out a groan.

"What's the matter?" cried Leo.

"Excuse me. Was an accident this picture. She isn't for you."

Salzman frantically shoved the manila packet into his portfolio. He thrust the snapshot into his pocket and fled down the stairs.

Leo, after momentary paralysis, gave chase and cornered the marriage broker in the vestibule. The landlady made hysterical outcries but neither of them listened.

"Give me back the picture, Salzman."

"No." The pain in his eyes was terrible.

"Tell me who she is then."

"This I can't tell you. Excuse me."

He made to depart, but Leo, forgetting himself, seized the matchmaker by his tight coat and shook him frenziedly.

"Please," signed Salzman. *"Please."*

Leo ashamedly let him go. "Tell me who she is," he begged. "It's very important for me to know."

"She is not for you. She is a wild one—wild, without shame. This is not a bride for a rabbi."

"What do you mean wild?"

"Like an animal. Like a dog. For her to be poor was a sin. This is why to me she is dead now."

"In God's name, what do you mean?"

"Her I can't introduce to you," Salzman cried.

"Why are you so excited?"

"Why, he asks," Salzman said, bursting into tears. "This is my baby, my Stella, she should burn in hell."

Leo hurried up to bed and hid under the covers. Under the covers he thought his life through. Although he soon fell asleep he could not sleep her out of his mind. He woke, beating his breast. Though he prayed to be rid of her, his prayers went unanswered. Through days of torment he endlessly struggled not to love her; fearing success, he escaped it. He then concluded to convert her to goodness, himself to God. The idea alternately nauseated and exalted him.

He perhaps did not know that he had come to a final decision until he encountered Salzman in a Broadway cafeteria. He was sitting alone at a rear table, sucking the bony remains of a fish. The marriage broker appeared haggard, and transparent to the point of vanishing.

Salzman looked up at first without recognizing him. Leo had grown a pointed beard and his eyes were weighted with wisdom.

"Salzman," he said, "love has at last come to my heart."

"Who can love from a picture?" mocked the marriage broker.

"It is not impossible."

"If you can love her, then you can love anybody. Let me show you some new clients that they just sent me their photographs. One is a little doll."

"Just her I want," Leo murmured.

"Don't be a fool, doctor. Don't bother with her."

"Put me in touch with her, Salzman," Leo said humbly."Perhaps I can be of service."

Salzman had stopped eating and Leo understood with emotion that it was now arranged.

Leaving the cafeteria, he was, however, afflicted by a tormenting suspicion that Salzman had planned it all to happen this way.

Leo was informed by letter that she would meet him on a certain corner, and she was there one spring night, waiting under a street lamp. He appeared, carrying a small bouquet of violets and rosebuds. Stella stood by the lamp post, smoking. She wore white with red shoes, which fitted his expectations, although in a troubled moment he had imagined the dress red, and only the shoes white. She waited uneasily and shyly. From afar he saw that her eyes—clearly her father's—were filled with desperate innocence. He pictured, in her, his own redemption. Violins and lit candles revolved in the sky. Leo ran forward with flowers outthrust.

Around the corner, Salzman, leaning against a wall, chanted prayers for the dead.

QUESTIONS

1. Is Leo what you would expect a young rabbi to be? Explain.
2. What can you tell about Salzman's attitude towards Leo?
3. Is Salzman a "trickster," as Leo thinks at one point? Explain.
4. How does Salzman seem to understand "love"? How does Leo?
5. Is Leo deluding himself about Stella? What do you suppose will happen to them?

Carson McCullers (1917–1967)
A TREE. A ROCK. A CLOUD.

It was raining that morning, and still very dark. When the boy reached the streetcar café he had almost finished his route and he went in for a cup of coffee. The place was an all-night café owned by a bitter and stingy man called Leo. After the raw, empty street the café seemed friendly and bright: along the counter there were a couple of soldiers, three spinners from the cotton mill, and in a corner a man who sat hunched over with his nose and half his face down in a beer mug. The boy wore a helmet such as aviators wear. When he went into the café he unbuckled the chin strap and raised the right flap up over his pink little ear; often as he drank his coffee someone would speak to him in a friendly way. But this morning Leo did not look into his face and none of the men were talking. He paid and was leaving the café when a voice called out to him:

'Son! Hey Son!'

He turned back and the man in the corner was crooking his finger and nodding to him. He had brought his face out of the beer mug and he seemed suddenly very happy. The man was long and pale, with a big nose and faded orange hair.

'Hey Son!'

The boy went toward him. He was an undersized boy of about twelve, with one shoulder drawn higher than the other because of the weight of the paper sack. His face was shallow, freckled, and his eyes were round child eyes.

'Yeah Mister?'

The man laid one hand on the paper boy's shoulders, then grasped the boy's chin and turned his face slowly from one side to the other. The boy shrank back uneasily.

'Say! What's the big idea?'

The boy's voice was shrill; inside the café it was suddenly very quiet.

The man said slowly: 'I love you.'

All along the counter the men laughed. The boy, who had scowled and sidled away, did not know what to do. He looked over the counter at Leo, and Leo watched him with a weary, brittle jeer. The boy tried to laugh also. But the man was serious and sad.

'I did not mean to tease you, Son,' he said. 'Sit down and have a beer with me. There is something I have to explain.'

Cautiously, out of the corner of his eye, the paper boy questioned the men along the counter to see what he should do. But they had gone back to their beer or their breakfast and did not notice him. Leo put a cup of coffee on the counter and a little jug of cream.

'He is a minor,' Leo said.

The paper boy slid himself up onto the stool. His ear beneath the upturned flap of the helmet was very small and red. The man was nodding at him soberly. 'It is important,' he said. Then he reached in his hip pocket and brought out something which he held up in the palm of his hand for the boy to see.

'Look very carefully,' he said.

The boy stared, but there was nothing to look at very carefully. The man held in his big, grimy palm a photograph. It was the face of a woman, but blurred, so that only the hat and the dress she was wearing stood out clearly.

'See?' the man asked.

The boy nodded and the man placed another picture in his palm. The woman was standing on a beach in a bathing suit. The suit made her stomach very big, and that was the main thing you noticed.

'Got a good look?' He leaned over closer and finally asked: 'You ever seen her before?'

The boy sat motionless, staring slantwise at the man. 'Not so I know of.'

'Very well.' The man blew on the photographs and put them back into his pocket. 'That was my wife.'

'Dead?' the boy asked.

Slowly the man shook his head. He pursed his lips as though about to whistle and answered in a long-drawn way: 'Nuuu—' he said. 'I will explain.'

The beer on the counter before the man was in a large brown mug. He did not pick it up to drink. Instead he bent down and, putting his face over the rim, he rested there for a moment. Then with both hands he tilted the mug and sipped.

'Some night you'll go to sleep with your big nose in a mug and drown,' said Leo. 'Prominent transient drowns in beer. That would be a cute death.'

The paper boy tried to signal to Leo. While the man was not looking he screwed up his face and worked his mouth to question soundlessly: 'Drunk?' But Leo only raised his eyebrows and turned away to put some pink strips of bacon on the grill. The man pushed the mug away from him, straightened himself, and folded his loose crooked hands on the counter. His face was sad as he looked at the paper boy. He did not blink, but from time to time the lids closed down with delicate gravity over his pale green eyes. It was nearing dawn and the boy shifted the weight of the paper sack.

'I am talking about love,' the man said. 'With me it is a science.'

The boy half slid down from the stool. But the man raised his forefinger, and there was something about him that held the boy and would not let him go away.

"Twelve years ago I married the woman in the photograph. She was my wife for one year, nine months, three days, and two nights. I loved her. Yes . . .' He tightened his blurred, rambling voice and said again: 'I loved her. I thought also that she loved me. I was a railroad engineer. She had all home comforts and luxuries. It never crept into my brain that she was not satisfied. But do you know what happened?'

'Mgneeow!' said Leo.

The man did not take his eyes from the boy's face. 'She left me. I came in one night and the house was empty and she was gone. She left me.'

'With a fellow?' the boy asked.

Gently the man placed his palm down on the counter. 'Why naturally, Son. A woman does not run off like that alone.'

The café was quiet, the soft rain black and endless in the street outside. Leo pressed down the frying bacon with the prongs of his long fork. 'So you have been chasing the floozie for eleven years. You frazzled old rascal!'

For the first time the man glanced at Leo. 'Please don't be vulgar. Besides, I was not speaking to you.' He turned back to the boy and said in a trusting and secretive undertone: 'Let's not pay any attention to him. O.K.?'

The paper boy nodded doubtfully.

'It was like this,' the man continued. 'I am a person who feels many things. All my life one thing after another has impressed me. Moonlight. The leg of a pretty girl. One thing after another. But the point is that when I had enjoyed anything there was a peculiar sensation as though it was laying around loose in me. Nothing seemed to finish itself up or fit in with the other things. Women? I had my portion of them. The same. Afterwards laying around loose in me. I was a man who had never loved.'

Very slowly he closed his eyelids, and the gesture was like a curtain drawn at the end of a scene in a play. When he spoke again his voice was excited and the words came fast—the lobes of his large, loose ears seemed to tremble.

'Then I met this woman. I was fifty-one years old and she always said she was thirty. I met her at a filling station and we were married within three days. And do you know what it was like? I just can't tell you. All I had ever felt was gathered together around this woman. Nothing lay around loose in me any more but was finished up by her.'

The man stopped suddenly and stroked his long nose. His voice sank down to a steady and reproachful undertone: 'I'm not explaining this right. What happened was this. There were these beautiful feelings and loose little pleasures inside me. And this woman was something like an assembly line for my soul. I run these little pieces of myself through her and I come out complete. Now do you follow me?'

'What was her name?' the boy asked.

'Oh,' he said. 'I called her Dodo. But that is immaterial.'

'Did you try to make her come back?'

The man did not seem to hear. 'Under the circumstances you can imagine how I felt when she left me.'

Leo took the bacon from the grill and folded two strips of it between a bun. He had a gray face, with slitted eyes, and a pinched nose saddled by faint blue shadows. One of the mill workers signaled for more coffee and Leo poured it. He did not give refills on coffee free. The spinner ate breakfast there every morning, but the better Leo knew his customers the stingier he treated them. He nibbled his own bun as though he grudged it to himself.

'And you never got hold of her again?'

The boy did not know what to think of the man, and his child's face was uncertain with mingled curiosity and doubt. He was new on the paper route; it was still strange to him to be out in the town in the black, queer early morning.

'Yes,' the man said. 'I took a number of steps to get her back. I went around trying to locate her. I went to Tulsa where she had folks. And to Mobile. I went to every town she had ever mentioned to me, and I hunted down every man she had formerly been connected with. Tulsa, Atlanta, Chicago, Cheehaw, Memphis. . . . For the better part of two years I chased around the country trying to lay hold of her.'

'But the pair of them had vanished from the face of the earth!' said Leo.

'Don't listen to him,' the man said confidentially. 'And also just forget those two years. They are not important. What matters is that around the third year a curious thing begun to happen to me.'

'What?' the boy asked.

The man leaned down and tilted his mug to take a sip of beer. But as he hovered over the mug his nostrils fluttered slightly; he sniffed the staleness of the

beer and did not drink. 'Love is a curious thing to begin with. At first I thought
only of getting her back. It was a kind of mania. But then as time went on I tried
to remember her. But do you know what happened?'

'No,' the boy said.

'When I laid myself down on a bed and tried to think about her my mind
became a blank. I couldn't see her. I would take out her pictures and look. No
good. Nothing doing. A blank. Can you imagine it?'

'Say Mac!' Leo called down the counter. 'Can you imagine this bozo's mind
a blank!'

Slowly, as though fanning away flies, the man waved his hand. His green eyes
were concentrated and fixed on the shallow little face of the paper boy.

'But a sudden piece of glass on a sidewalk. Or a nickel tune in a music box.
A shadow on a wall at night. And I would remember. It might happen in a street
and I would cry or bang my head against a lamppost. You follow me?'

'A piece of glass . . .' the boy said.

'Anything. I would walk around and I had no power of how and when to
remember her. You think you can put up a kind of shield. But remembering don't
come to a man face forward—it corners around sideways. I was at the mercy of
everything I saw and heard. Suddenly instead of me combing the countryside to
find her she begun to chase me around in my very soul. *She* chasing *me*, mind
you! And in my soul.'

The boy asked finally: 'What part of the country were you in then?'

'Ooh,' the man groaned. 'I was a sick mortal. It was like smallpox. I confess,
Son, that I boozed. I fornicated. I committed any sin that suddenly appealed to
me. I am loath to confess it but I will do so. When I recall that period it is all
curdled in my mind, it was so terrible.'

The man leaned his head down and tapped his forehead on the counter. For
a few seconds he stayed bowed over in this position, the back of his stringy neck
covered with orange furze, his hands with their long warped fingers held palm
to palm in an attitude of prayer. Then the man straightened himself; he was
smiling and suddenly his face was bright and tremulous and old.

'It was in the fifth year that it happened,' he said. 'And with it I started my
science.'

Leo's mouth jerked with a pale, quick grin. 'Well none of we boys are getting
any younger,' he said. Then with sudden anger he balled up a dishcloth he was
holding and threw it down hard on the floor. 'You draggle-tailed old Romeo!'

'What happened?' the boy asked.

The old man's voice was high and clear: 'Peace,' he answered.

'Huh?'

'It is hard to explain scientifically, Son,' he said. 'I guess the logical explanation
is that she and I had fleed around from each other for so long that finally we
just got tangled up together and lay down and quit. Peace. A queer and beautiful
blankness. It was spring in Portland and the rain came every afternoon. All evening
I just stayed there on my bed in the dark. And that is how the science come
to me.'

The windows in the streetcar were pale blue with light. The two soldiers paid for their beers and opened the door—one of the soldiers combed his hair and wiped off his muddy puttees before they went outside. The three mill workers bent silently over their breakfasts. Leo's clock was ticking on the wall.

'It is this. And listen carefully. I meditated on love and reasoned it out. I realized what is wrong with us. Men fall in love for the first time. And what do they fall in love with?'

The boy's soft mouth was partly open and he did not answer.

'A woman,' the old man said. 'Without science, with nothing to go by, they undertake the most dangerous and sacred experience in God's earth. They fall in love with a woman. Is that correct, Son?'

'Yeah,' the boy said faintly.

'They start at the wrong end of love. They begin at the climax. Can you wonder it is so miserable? Do you know how men should love?'

The old man reached over and grasped the boy by the collar of his leather jacket. He gave him a gentle little shake and his green eyes gazed down unblinking and grave.

'Son, do you know how love should be begun?'

The boy sat small and listening and still. Slowly he shook his head. The old man leaned closer and whispered:

'A tree. A rock. A cloud.'

It was still raining outside in the street: a mild, gray, endless rain. The mill whistle blew for the six o'clock shift and the three spinners paid and went away. There was no one in the café but Leo, the old man, and the little paper boy.

'The weather was like this in Portland,' he said. 'At the time my science was begun. I meditated and I started very cautious. I would pick up something from the street and take it home with me. I bought a goldfish and I concentrated on the goldfish and I loved it. I graduated from one thing to another. Day by day I was getting this technique. On the road from Portland to San Diego—'

'Aw shut up!' screamed Leo suddenly. 'Shut up! Shut up!'

The old man still held the collar of the boy's jacket; he was trembling and his face was earnest and bright and wild. 'For six years now I have gone around by myself and built up my science. And now I am a master. Son. I can love anything. No longer do I have to think about it even. I see a street full of people and a beautiful light comes in me. I watch a bird in the sky. Or I meet a traveler on the road. Everything, Son. And anybody. All strangers and all loved! Do you realize what a science like mine can mean?'

The boy held himself stiffly, his hands curled tight around the counter edge. Finally he asked: 'Did you ever really find that lady?'

'What? What say, Son?'

'I mean,' the boy asked timidly. 'Have you fallen in love with a woman again?'

The old man loosened his grasp on the boy's collar. He turned away and for the first time his green eyes had a vague and scattered look. He lifted the mug from the counter, drank down the yellow beer. His head was shaking slowly from side to side. Then finally he answered: 'No, Son. You see that is the last step in my science. I go cautious. And I am not quite ready yet.'

'Well!' said Leo. 'Well well well!'

The old man stood in the open doorway. 'Remember,' he said. Framed there in the gray damp light of the early morning he looked shrunken and seedy and frail. But his smile was bright. 'Remember I love you,' he said with a last nod. And the door closed quietly behind him.

The boy did not speak for a long time. He pulled down the bangs on his forehead and slid his grimy little forefinger around the rim of his empty cup. Then without looking at Leo he finally asked:

'Was he drunk?'

'No,' said Leo shortly.

The boy raised his clear voice higher. 'Then was he a dope fiend?'

'No.'

The boy looked up at Leo, and his flat little face was desperate, his voice urgent and shrill. 'Was he crazy? Do you think he was a lunatic?' The paper boy's voice dropped suddenly with doubt. 'Leo? Or not?'

But Leo would not answer him. Leo had run a night café for fourteen years, and he held himself to be a critic of craziness. There were the town characters and also the transients who roamed in from the night. He knew the manias of all of them. But he did not want to satisfy the questions of the waiting child. He tightened his pale face and was silent.

So the boy pulled down the right flap of his helmet and as he turned to leave he made the only comment that seemed safe to him, the only remark that could not be laughed down and despised:

'He sure has done a lot of traveling.'

QUESTIONS

1. Apart from the man in the corner, what is the atmosphere in this cafe?
2. How important is the boy's point of view in your response to the story?
3. What do you imagine is going on inside Leo as the man talks?
4. Why won't Leo answer the boy's last question? Would you have answered it? How?

John Updike (b. 1932)
SEPARATING

The day was fair. Brilliant. All that June the weather had mocked the Maples' internal misery with solid sunlight—golden shafts and cascades of green in which their conversations had wormed unseeing, their sad murmuring selves the only stain in Nature. Usually by this time of the year they had acquired tans; but when they met their elder daughter's plane on her return from a year in England they were almost as pale as she, though Judith was too dazzled by the sunny opulent jumble of her native land to notice. They did not spoil her homecoming by telling her immediately. Wait a few days, let her recover from jet lag, had been one of their formulations, in that string of gray dialogues—over coffee, over cocktails, over Cointreau—that had shaped the strategy of their dissolution, while the earth performed its annual stunt of renewal unnoticed beyond their closed windows. Richard had thought to leave at Easter; Joan had insisted they wait until the four children were at last assembled, with all exams passed and ceremonies attended, and the bauble of summer to console them. So he had drudged away, in love, in dread, repairing screens, getting the mowers sharpened, rolling and patching their new tennis court.

The court, clay, had come through its first winter pitted and windswept bare of redcoat. Years ago the Maples had observed how often, among their friends, divorce followed a dramatic home improvement, as if the marriage were making one last effort to live; their own worst crisis had come amid the plaster dust and exposed plumbing of a kitchen renovation. Yet, a summer ago, as canary-yellow bulldozers gaily churned a grassy, daisy-dotted knoll into a muddy plateau, and a crew of pigtailed young men raked and tamped clay into a plane, this transformation did not strike them as ominous, but festive in its impudence; their marriage could rend the earth for fun. The next spring, waking each day at dawn to a sliding sensation as if the bed were being tipped, Richard found the barren tennis court—its nets and tapes still rolled in the barn—an environment congruous with his mood of purposeful desolation, and the crumbling of handfuls of clay into cracks and holes (dogs had frolicked on the court in a thaw; rivulets had eroded trenches) an activity suitably elemental and interminable. In his sealed heart he hoped the day would never come.

Now it was here. A Friday. Judith was re-acclimated; all four children were assembled, before jobs and camps and visits again scattered them. Joan thought they should be told one by one. Richard was for making an announcement at the table. She said, "I think just making an announcement is a cop-out. They'll start quarrelling and playing to each other instead of focusing. They're each individuals, you know, not just some corporate obstacle to your freedom."

"O.K., O.K. I agree." Joan's plan was exact. That evening, they were giving Judith a belated welcome-home dinner, of lobster and champagne. Then, the party over, they, the two of them, who nineteen years before would push her in a baby carriage along Fifth Avenue to Washington Square, were to walk her out of the house, to the bridge across the salt creek, and tell her, swearing her to secrecy. Then Richard Jr., who was going directly from work to a rock concert in Boston, would be told, either late when he returned on the train or early Saturday morning before he went off to his job; he was seventeen and employed as one of a golf-course maintenance crew. Then the two younger children, John and Margaret, could, as the morning wore on, be informed.

"Mopped up, as it were," Richard said.

"Do you have any better plan? That leaves you the rest of Saturday to answer any questions, pack, and make your wonderful departure."

"No," he said, meaning he had no better plan, and agreed to hers, though to him it showed an edge of false order, a hidden plea for control, like Joan's long chore lists and financial accountings and, in the days when he first knew her, her too-copious lecture notes. Her plan turned one hurdle for him into four—four knife-sharp walls, each with a sheer blind drop on the other side.

All spring he had moved through a world of insides and outsides, of barriers and partitions. He and Joan stood as a thin barrier between the children and the truth. Each moment was a partition, with the past on one side and the future on the other, a future containing this unthinkable *now*. Beyond four knifelike walls a new life for him waited vaguely. His skull cupped a secret, a white face, a face both frightened and soothing, both strange and known, that he wanted to shield from tears, which he felt all about him, solid as the sunlight. So haunted, he had become obsessed with battening down the house against his absence, replacing screens and sash cords, hinges and latches—a Houdini making things snug before his escape.

The lock. He had still to replace a lock on one of the doors of the screened porch. The task, like most such, proved more difficult than he had imagined. The old lock, aluminum frozen by corrosion, had been deliberately rendered obsolete by manufacturers. Three hardware stores had nothing that even approximately matched the mortised hole its removal (surprisingly easy) left. Another hole had to be gouged, with bits too small and saws too big, and the old hole fitted with a block of wood—the chisels dull, the saw rusty, his fingers thick with lack of sleep. The sun poured down, beyond the porch, on a world of neglect. The bushes already needed pruning, the windward side of the house was shedding flakes of paint, rain would get in when he was gone, insects, rot, death. His family, all those he would lose, filtered through the edges of his awareness as he struggled with screw holes, splinters, opaque instructions, minutiae of metal.

Judith sat on the porch, a princess returned from exile. She regaled them with stories of fuel shortages, of bomb scares in the Underground, of Pakistani workmen loudly lusting after her as she walked past on her way to dance school. Joan came and went, in and out of the house, calmer than she should have been, praising his struggles with the lock as if this were one more and not the last of their long succession of shared chores. The younger of his sons for a few minutes held the rickety screen door while his father clumsily hammered and chiseled, each blow a kind of sob in Richard's ears. His younger daughter, having been at a slumber party, slept on the porch hammock through all the noise—heavy and pink, trusting and forsaken. Time, like the sunlight, continued relentlessly; the sunlight slowly slanted. Today was one of the longest days. The lock clicked, worked. He was through. He had a drink; he drank it on the porch, listening to his daughter. "It was so sweet," she was saying, "during the worst of it, how all the butchers and bakery shops kept open by candlelight. They're all so plucky and cute. From the papers, things sounded so much worse here—people shooting people in gas lines, and everybody freezing."

Richard asked her, "Do you still want to live in England forever?" *Forever:* the concept, now a reality upon him, pressed and scratched at the back of his throat.

"No," Judith confessed, turning her oval face to him, its eyes still childishly far apart, but the lips set as over something succulent and satisfactory. "I was anxious to come home. I'm an American." She was a woman. They had raised her; he and Joan had endured together to raise her, alone of the four. The others had still some raising left in them. Yet it was the thought of telling Judith—the image of her, their first baby, walking between them arm in arm to the bridge—that broke him. The partition between his face and the tears broke. Richard sat down to the celebratory meal with the back of his throat aching; the champagne, the lobster seemed phases of sunshine; he saw them and tasted them through tears. He blinked, swallowed, croakily joked about hay fever. The tears would not stop leaking through; they came not through a hole that could be plugged but through a permeable spot in a membrane, steadily, purely, endlessly, fruitfully. They became, his tears, a shield for himself against these others—their faces, the fact of their assembly, a last time as innocents, at a table where he sat the last time as head. Tears dropped from his nose as he broke the lobster's back; salt flavored his champagne as he sipped it; the raw clench at the back of his throat was delicious. He could not help himself.

His children tried to ignore his tears. Judith, on his right, lit a cigarette, gazed upward in the direction of her too energetic, too sophisticated exhalation; on her other side, John earnestly bent his face to the extraction of the last morsels—legs, tail segments—from the scarlet corpse. Joan, at the opposite end of the table, glanced at him surprised, her reproach displaced by a quick grimace, of forgiveness, or of salute to his superior gift of strategy. Between them, Margaret, no longer called Bean, thirteen and large for her age, gazed from the other side of his pane of tears as if into a shopwindow at something she coveted—at her father, a crystalline heap of splinters and memories. It was not she, however, but John who, in the kitchen, as they cleared the plates and carapaces away, asked Joan the question: *"Why is Daddy crying?"*

Richard heard the question but not the murmured answer. Then he heard Bean cry, "Oh, no-oh!"—the faintly dramatized exclamation of one who had long expected it.

John returned to the table carrying a bowl of salad. He nodded tersely at his father and his lips shaped the conspiratorial words "She told."

"Told what?" Richard asked aloud, insanely.

The boy sat down as if to rebuke his father's distraction with the example of his own good manners. He said quietly, "The separation."

Joan and Margaret returned; the child, in Richard's twisted vision, seemed diminished in size, and relieved, relieved to have had the bogieman at last proved real. He called out to her—the distances at the table had grown immense—"You knew, you always knew," but the clenching at the back of his throat prevented him from making sense of it. From afar he heard Joan talking, levelly, sensibly, reciting what they had prepared: it was a separation for the summer, an experiment. She and Daddy both agreed it would be good for them; they needed space and time to think; they liked each other but did not make each other happy enough, somehow.

Judith, imitating her mother's factual tone, but in her youth off-key, too cool, said, "I think it's silly. You should either live together or get divorced."

Richard's crying, like a wave that has crested and crashed, had become tumultuous; but it was overtopped by another tumult, for John, who had been so reserved, now grew larger and larger at the table. Perhaps his younger sister's being credited with knowing set him off. "Why didn't you *tell* us?" he asked, in a large round voice quite unlike his own. "You should have *told* us you weren't getting along."

Richard was startled into attempting to force words through his tears. "We *do* get along, that's the trouble, so it doesn't show even to us—" *That we do not love each other* was the rest of the sentence; he couldn't finish it.

Joan finished for him, in her style. "And we've always, *especially*, loved our children."

John was not mollified. "What do you care about *us*?" he boomed. "We're just little things you *had*." His sisters' laughing forced a laugh from him, which he turned hard and parodistic: "Ha, ha *ha*." Richard and Joan realized simultaneously that the child was drunk, on Judith's homecoming champagne. Feeling bound to keep the center of the stage, John took a cigarette from Judith's pack, poked it into his mouth, let it hang from his lower lip, and squinted like a gangster.

"You're not little things we had," Richard called to him. "You're the whole point. But you're grown. Or almost."

The boy was lighting matches. Instead of holding them to his cigarette (for they had never seen him smoke; being "good" had been his way of setting himself apart), he held them to his mother's face, closer and closer, for her to blow out. Then he lit the whole folder—a hiss and then a torch, held against his mother's face. Prismed by tears, the flame filled Richard's vision; he didn't know how it was extinguished. He heard Margaret say, "Oh stop showing off," and saw John, in response, break the cigarette in two and put the halves entirely into his mouth and chew, sticking out his tongue to display the shreds to his sister.

Joan talked to him, reasoning—a fountain of reason, unintelligible. "Talked about it for years . . . our children must help us . . . Daddy and I both want . . ." As the boy listened, he carefully wadded a paper napkin into the leaves of his salad, fashioned a ball of paper and lettuce, and popped it into his mouth, looking around the table for the expected laughter. None came. Judith said, "Be mature," and dismissed a plume of smoke.

Richard got up from this stifling table and led the boy outside. Though the house was in twilight, the outdoors still brimmed with light, the lovely waste light of high summer. Both laughing, he supervised John's spitting out the lettuce and paper and tobacco into the pachysandra. He took him by the hand—a square gritty hand, but for its softness a man's. Yet, it held on. They ran together up into the field, past the tennis court. The raw banking left by the bulldozers was dotted with daisies. Past the court and a flat stretch where they used to play family baseball stood a soft green rise glorious in the sun, each weed and species of grass distinct as illumination on parchment. "I'm sorry, so sorry," Richard cried. "You were the only one who ever tried to help me with all the goddam jobs around this place."

Sobbing, safe within his tears and the champagne, John explained, "It's not just the separation, it's the whole crummy year, I *hate* that school, you can't make any friends, the history teacher's a scud."

They sat on the crest of the rise, shaking and warm from their tears but easier in their voices, and Richard tried to focus on the child's sad year—the weekdays long with homework, the weekends spent in his room with model airplanes, while his parents murmured down below, nursing their separation. How selfish, how blind, Richard thought; his eyes felt scoured. He told his son, "We'll think about getting you transferred. Life's too short to be miserable."

They had said what they could, but did not want the moment to heal, and talked on, about the school, about the tennis court, whether it would ever again be as good as it had been that first summer. They walked to inspect it and pressed a few more tapes more firmly down. A little stiltedly, perhaps trying now to make too much of the moment, Richard led the boy to the spot in the field where the view was best, of the metallic blue river, the emerald marsh, the scattered islands velvety with shadow in the low light, the white bits of beach far away. "See," he said. "It goes on being beautiful. It'll be here tomorrow."

"I know," John answered, impatiently. The moment had closed.

Back in the house, the others had opened some white wine, the champagne being drunk, and still sat at the table, the three females, gossiping. Where Joan sat had become the head. She turned, showing him a tearless face, and asked, "All right?"

"We're fine," he said, resenting it, though relieved, that the party went on without him.

In bed she explained, "I couldn't cry I guess because I cried so much all spring. It really wasn't fair. It's your idea, and you made it look as though I was kicking you out."

"I'm sorry," he said. "I couldn't stop. I wanted to but couldn't."

"You *didn't* want to. You loved it. You were having your way, making a general announcement."

"I love having it over," he admitted. "God, those kids were great. So brave and funny." John, returned to the house, had settled to a model airplane in his room, and kept shouting down to them, "I'm O.K. No sweat." "And the way," Richard went on, cozy in his relief, "they never questioned the reasons we gave. No thought of a third person. Not even Judith."

"That *was* touching," Joan said.

He gave her a hug. "You were great too. Very reassuring to everybody. Thank you." Guiltily, he realized he did not feel separated.

"You still have Dickie to do," she told him. These words set before him a black mountain in the darkness; its cold breath, its near weight affected his chest. Of the four children, his elder son was most nearly his conscience. Joan did not need to add, "That's one piece of your dirty work I won't do for you."

"I know. I'll do it. You go to sleep."

Within minutes, her breathing slowed, became oblivious and deep. It was quarter to midnight. Dickie's train from the concert would come in at one-fourteen. Richard set the alarm for one. He had slept atrociously for weeks. But whenever he closed his lids some glimpse of the last hours scorched them—Judith exhaling toward the ceiling in a kind of aversion, Bean's mute staring, the sun-struck growth in the field where he and John had rested. The mountain before him moved closer, moved within him; he was huge, momentous. The ache at the back of his throat felt stale. His wife slept as if slain beside him. When, exasperated by his hot lids, his crowded heart, he rose from bed and dressed, she awoke enough to turn over. He told her then, "Joan, if I could undo it all, I would."

"Where would you begin?" she asked. There was no place. Giving him courage, she was always giving him courage. He put on shoes without socks in the dark. The children were breathing in their rooms, the downstairs was hollow. In their confusion they had left lights burning. He turned off all but one, the kitchen overhead. The car started. He had hoped it wouldn't. He met only moonlight on the road; it seemed a diaphanous companion, flickering in the leaves along the roadside, haunting his rearview mirror like a pursuer, melting under his head-lights. The center of town, not quite deserted, was eerie at this hour. A young cop in uniform kept company with a gang of T-shirted kids on the steps of the bank. Across from the railroad station, several bars kept open. Customers, mostly young, passed in and out of the warm night, savoring summer's novelty. Voices shouted from cars as they passed; an immense conversation seemed in progress. Richard parked and in his weariness put his head on the passenger seat, out of the commotion and wheeling lights. It was as when, in the movies, an assassin grimly carries his mission through the jostle of a carnival—except the movies cannot show the precipitous, palpable slope you cling to within. You cannot climb back down; you can only fall. The synthetic fabric of the car seat, warmed by his cheek, confided to him an ancient, distant scent of vanilla.

A train whistle caused him to lift his head. It was on time; he had hoped it would be late. The slender drawgates descended. The bell of approach tingled happily. The great metal body, horizontally fluted, rocked to a stop, and sleepy teen-agers disembarked, his son among them. Dickie did not show surprise that his father was meeting him at this terrible hour. He sauntered to the car with two friends, both taller than he. He said "Hi" to his father and took the passenger's seat with an exhausted promptness that expressed gratitude. The friends got in the back, and Richard was grateful; a few more minutes' postponement would be won by driving them home.

He asked, "How was the concert?"

"Groovy," one boy said from the back seat.

"It bit," the other said.

"It was O.K.," Dickie said, moderate by nature, so reasonable that in his childhood the unreason of the world had given him headaches, stomach aches, nausea. When the second friend had been dropped off at his dark house, the boy blurted, "Dad, my eyes are killing me with hay fever! I'm out there cutting that mothering grass all day!"

"Do we still have those drops?"

"They didn't do any good last summer."

"They might this." Richard swung a U-turn on the empty street. The drive home took a few minutes. The mountain was here, in his throat. "Richard," he said, and felt the boy, slumped and rubbing his eyes, go tense at his tone, "I didn't come to meet you just to make your life easier. I came because your mother and I have some news for you, and you're a hard man to get ahold of these days. It's sad news."

"That's O.K." The reassurance came out soft, but quick, as if released from the tip of a spring.

Richard had feared that his tears would return and choke him, but the boy's manliness set an example, and his voice issued forth steady and dry. "It's sad news, but it needn't be tragic news, at least for you. It should have no practical effect on your life, though it's bound to have an emotional effect. You'll work at your job, and go back to school in September. Your mother and I are really proud of what you're making of your life; we don't want that to change at all."

"Yeah," the boy said lightly, on the intake of his breath, holding himself up. They turned the corner; the church they went to loomed like a gutted fort. The home of the woman Richard hoped to marry stood across the green. Her bedroom light burned.

"Your mother and I," he said, "have decided to separate. For the summer. Nothing legal, no divorce yet. We want to see how it feels. For some years now, we haven't been doing enough for each other, making each other as happy as we should be. Have you sensed that?"

"No," the boy said. It was an honest, unemotional answer: true or false in a quiz.

Glad for the factual basis, Richard pursued, even garrulously, the details. His apartment across town, his utter accessibility, the split vacation arrangements, the advantages to the children, the added mobility and variety of the summer. Dickie listened, absorbing. "Do the others know?"

"Yes."

"How did they take it?"

"The girls pretty calmly. John flipped out; he shouted and ate a cigarette and made a salad out of his napkin and told us how much he hated school."

His brother chuckled. "He did?"

"Yeah. The school issue was more upsetting for him than Mom and me. He seemed to feel better for having exploded."

"He did?" The repetition was the first sign that he was stunned.

"Yes. Dickie, I want to tell you something. This last hour, waiting for your train to get in, has been about the worst of my life. I hate this. *Hate* it. My father would have died before doing it to me." He felt immensely lighter, saying this. He had dumped the mountain on the boy. They were home. Moving swiftly as a shadow, Dickie was out of the car, through the bright kitchen. Richard called after him, "Want a glass of milk or anything?"

"No thanks."

"Want us to call the course tomorrow and say you're too sick to work?"

"No, that's all right." The answer was faint, delivered at the door to his room; Richard listened for the slam that went with a tantrum. The door closed normally, gently. The sound was sickening.

Joan had sunk into that first deep trough of sleep and was slow to awake. Richard had to repeat, "I told him."

"What did he say?"

"Nothing much. Could you go say goodnight to him? Please."

She left their room, without putting on a bathrobe. He sluggishly changed back into his pajamas and walked down the hall. Dickie was already in bed, Joan was sitting beside him, and the boy's bedside clock radio was murmuring music. When she stood, an inexplicable light—the moon?—outlined her body through the nightie. Richard sat on the warm place she had indented on the child's narrow mattress. He asked him, "Do you want the radio on like that?"

"It always is."

"Doesn't it keep you awake? It would me."

"No."

"Are you sleepy?"

"Yeah."

"Good. Sure you want to get up and go to work? You've had a big night."

"I want to."

Away at school this winter he had learned for the first time that you can go short of sleep and live. As an infant he had slept with an immobile, sweating intensity that had alarmed his babysitters. In adolescence he had often been the first of the four children to go to bed. Even now, he would go slack in the middle of a television show, his sprawled legs hairy and brown. "O.K. Good boy. Dickie, listen. I love you so much, I never knew how much until now. No matter how this works out, I'll always be with you. Really."

Richard bent to kiss an averted face but his son, sinewy, turned and with wet cheeks embraced him and gave him a kiss, on the lips, passionate as a woman's. In his father's ear he moaned one word, the crucial, intelligent word: *"Why?"*

Why. It was a whistle of wind in a crack, a knife thrust, a window thrown open on emptiness. The white face was gone, the darkness was featureless. Richard had forgotten why.

Jayne Anne Phillips (b. 1952)
SOUVENIR

Kate always sent her mother a card on Valentine's Day. She timed the mails from wherever she was so that the cards arrived on February 14th. Her parents had celebrated the day in some small fashion, and since her father's death six years before, Kate made a gesture of compensatory remembrance. At first, she made the cards herself: collage and pressed grasses on construction paper sewn in fabric. Now she settled for art reproductions, glossy cards with blank insides. Kate wrote in them with colored inks, "You have always been my Valentine," or simply "Hey, take care of yourself." She might enclose a present as well, something small enough to fit into an envelope; a sachet, a perfumed soap, a funny tintype of a prune-faced man in a bowler hat.

This time, she forgot. Despite the garish displays of paper cupids and heart-shaped boxes in drugstore windows, she let the day nearly approach before remembering. It was too late to send anything in the mail. She called her mother long-distance at night when the rates were low.

"Mom? How are you?"

"It's you! How are *you?*" Her mother's voice grew suddenly brighter; Kate recognized a tone reserved for welcome company. Sometimes it took a while to warm up.

"I'm fine," answered Kate. "What have you been doing?"

"Well, actually I was trying to sleep."

"Sleep? You should be out setting the old hometown on fire."

"The old hometown can burn up without me tonight."

"Really? What's going on?"

"I'm running in-service training sessions for the primary teachers." Kate's mother was a school superintendent. "They're driving me batty. You'd think their brains were rubber."

"They are," Kate said. "Or you wouldn't have to train them. Think of them as a salvation, they create a need for your job."

"Some salvation. Besides, your logic is ridiculous. Just because someone needs training doesn't mean they're stupid."

"I'm just kidding. But *I'm* stupid. I forgot to send you a Valentine's card."

"You did? That's bad. I'm trained to receive one. They bring me luck."

"You're receiving a phone call instead," Kate said. "Won't that do?"

"Of course," said her mother, "but this is costing you money. Tell me quick, how are you?"

"Oh, you know. Doctoral pursuits. Doing my student trip, grooving with the professors."

"The professors? You'd better watch yourself."

"It's a joke, Mom, a joke. But what about you? Any men on the horizon?"

"No, not really. A married salesman or two asking me to dinner when they come through the office. Thank heavens I never let those things get started."

"You should do what you want to," Kate said.

"Sure," said her mother. "And where would I be then?"

"I don't know. Maybe Venezuela."

"They don't even have plumbing in Venezuela."

"Yes, but their sunsets are perfect, and the villages are full of dark passionate men in blousy shirts."

"That's your department, not mine."

"Ha," Kate said, "I wish it were my department. Sounds a lot more exciting than teaching undergraduates."

Her mother laughed. "Be careful," she said. "You'll get what you want. End up sweeping a dirt floor with a squawling baby around your neck."

"A dark baby," Kate said, "to stir up the family blood."

"Nothing would surprise me," her mother said as the line went fuzzy. Her voice was submerged in static, then surfaced. "Listen," she was saying. "Write to me. You seem so far away."

They hung up and Kate sat watching the windows of the neighboring house. The curtains were transparent and flowered and none of them matched. Silhouettes of the window frames spread across them like single dark bars. Her mother's curtains were all the same, white cotton hemmed with a ruffle, tiebacks blousing the cloth into identical shapes. From the street it looked as if the house was always in order.

Kate made a cup of strong Chinese tea, turned the lights off, and sat holding the warm cup in the dark. Her mother kept no real tea in the house, just packets of instant diabetic mixture which tasted of chemical sweetener and had a bitter aftertaste. The packets sat on the shelf next to her mother's miniature scales. The scales were white. Kate saw clearly the face of the metal dial on the front, its markings and trembling needle. Her mother weighed portions of food for meals: frozen broccoli, slices of plastic-wrapped Kraft cheese, careful chunks of roast beef. A dog-eared copy of *The Diabetic Diet* had remained propped against the salt shaker for the last two years.

Kate rubbed her forehead. Often at night she had headaches. Sometimes she wondered if there were an agent in her body, a secret in her blood making ready to work against her.

The phone blared repeatedly, careening into her sleep. Kate scrambled out of bed, naked and cold, stumbling, before she recognized the striped wallpaper of her bedroom and realized the phone was right there on the bedside table, as always. She picked up the receiver.

"Kate?" said her brother's voice. "It's Robert. Mom is in the hospital. They don't know what's wrong but she's in for tests."

"Tests? What's happened? I just talked to her last night."

"I'm not sure. She called the neighbors and they took her to the emergency room around dawn." Robert's voice still had that slight twang Kate knew was disappearing from her own. He would be calling from his insurance office, nine o'clock their time, in his thick glasses and wide, perfectly knotted tie. He was a member of the million-dollar club and his picture, tiny, the size of a postage stamp, appeared in the Mutual of Omaha magazine. His voice seemed small too over the distance. Kate felt heavy and dulled. She would never make much money, and recently she had begun wearing make-up again, waking in smeared mascara as she had in high school.

"Is Mom all right?" she managed now. "How serious is it?"

"They're not sure," Robert said. "Her doctor thinks it could have been any of several things, but they're doing X rays."

"Her doctor *thinks*? Doesn't he know? Get her to someone else. There aren't any doctors in that one-horse town."

"I don't know about that," Robert said defensively. "Anyway, I can't force her. You know how she is about money."

"Money? She could have a stroke and drop dead while her doctor wonders what's wrong."

"Doesn't matter. You know you can't tell her what to do."

"Could I call her somehow?"

"No, not yet. And don't get her all worried. She's been scared enough as it is. I'll tell her what you said about getting another opinion, and I'll call you back in a few hours when I have some news. Meanwhile, she's all right, do you hear?"

The line went dead with a click and Kate walked to the bathroom to wash her face. She splashed her eyes and felt guilty about the Valentine's card. Slogans danced in her head like reprimands. *For A Special One. Dearest Mother. My Best Friend.* Despite Robert, after breakfast she would call the hospital.

She sat a long time with her coffee, waiting for minutes to pass, considering how many meals she and her mother ate alone. Similar times of day, hundreds of miles apart. Women by themselves. The last person Kate had eaten breakfast with had been someone she'd met in a bar. He was passing through town. He liked his fried eggs gelatinized in the center, only slightly runny, and Kate had studiously looked away as he ate. The night before he'd looked down from above her as he finished and she still moved under him. "You're still wanting," he'd said. "That's nice." Mornings now, Kate saw her own face in the mirror and was glad she'd forgotten his name. When she looked at her reflection from the side, she saw a faint etching of lines beside her mouth. She hadn't slept with anyone for five weeks, and the skin beneath her eyes had taken on a creamy darkness.

She reached for the phone but drew back. It seemed bad luck to ask for news, to push toward whatever was coming as though she had no respect for it.

Standing in the kitchen last summer, her mother had stirred gravy and argued with her.

"I'm thinking of your own good, not mine," she'd said. "Think of what you put yourself through. And how can you feel right about it? You were born here, I don't care what you say." Her voice broke and she looked, perplexed, at the broth in the pan.

"But, hypothetically," Kate continued, her own voice unaccountably shaking, "if I'm willing to endure whatever I have to, do you have a right to object? You're my mother. You're supposed to defend my choices."

"You'll have enough trouble without choosing more for yourself. Using birth control that'll ruin your insides, moving from one place to another. I can't defend your choices. I can't even defend myself against you." She wiped her eyes on a napkin.

"Why do you have to make me feel so guilty?" Kate said, fighting tears of frustration. "I'm not attacking you."

"You're not? Then who are you talking to?"

"Oh Mom, give me a break."

"I've tried to give you more than that," her mother said. "I know what your choices are saying to me." She set the steaming gravy off the stove. "You may feel very differently later on. It's just a shame I won't be around to see it."

"Oh? Where will you be?"

"Floating around on a fleecy cloud."

Kate got up to set the table before she realized her mother had already done it.

The days went by. They'd gone shopping before Kate left. Standing at the cash register in an antique shop on Main Street, they bought each other pewter candle holders. "A souvenir," her mother said. "A reminder to always be nice to yourself. If you live alone you should eat by candlelight."

"Listen," Kate said, "I eat in a heart-shaped tub with bubbles to my chin. I sleep on satin sheets and my mattress has a built-in massage engine. My overnight guests are impressed. You don't have to tell me about the solitary pleasures."

They laughed and touched hands.

"Well," her mother said. "If you like yourself, I must have done something right."

Robert didn't phone until evening. His voice was fatigued and thin. "I've moved her to the university hospital," he said. "They can't deal with it at home."

Kate waited, saying nothing. She concentrated on the toes of her shoes. They needed shining. *You never take care of anything,* her mother would say.

"She has a tumor in her head." He said it firmly, as though Kate might challenge him.

"I'll take a plane tomorrow morning," Kate answered, "I'll be there by noon."

Robert exhaled. "Look," he said, "don't even come back here unless you can keep your mouth shut and do it my way."

"Get to the point."

"The point is they believe she has a malignancy and we're not going to tell her. I almost didn't tell you." His voice faltered. "They're going to operate but if they find what they're expecting, they don't think they can stop it."

For a moment there was no sound except an oceanic vibration of distance on the wire. Even that sound grew still. Robert breathed. Kate could almost see him, in a booth at the hospital, staring straight ahead at the plastic instructions screwed to the narrow rectangular body of the telephone. It seemed to her that she was hurtling toward him.

"I'll do it your way," she said.

The hospital cafeteria was a large room full of orange Formica tables. Its southern wall was glass. Across the highway, Kate saw a small park modestly dotted with amusement rides and bordered by a narrow band of river. How odd, to build a children's park across from a medical center. The sight was pleasant in a cruel way. The rolling lawn of the little park was perfectly, relentlessly green.

Robert sat down. Their mother was to have surgery in two days.

"After it's over," he said, "they're not certain what will happen. The tumor is in a bad place. There may be some paralysis."

"What kind of paralysis?" Kate said. She watched him twist the green-edged coffee cup around and around on its saucer.

"Facial. And maybe worse."

"You've told her this?"

He didn't answer.

"Robert, what is she going to think if she wakes up and—"

He leaned forward, grasping the cup and speaking through clenched teeth. "Don't you think I thought of that?" He gripped the sides of the table and the cup rolled onto the carpeted floor with a dull thud. He seemed ready to throw the table after it, then grabbed Kate's wrists and squeezed them hard.

"You didn't drive her here," he said. "She was so scared she couldn't talk. How much do you want to hand her at once?"

Kate watched the cup sitting solidly on the nubby carpet.

"We've told her it's benign," Robert said, "that the surgery will cause complications, but she can learn back whatever is lost."

Kate looked at him. "Is that true?"

"They hope so."

"We're lying to her, all of us, more and more." Kate pulled her hands away and Robert touched her shoulder.

"What do *you* want to tell her, Kate? 'You're fifty-five and you're done for'?"

She stiffened. "Why put her through the operation at all?"

He sat back and dropped his arms, lowering his head. "Because without it she'd be in bad pain. Soon." They were silent, then he looked up. "And anyway," he said softly, "we don't *know*, do we? She may have a better chance than they think."

Kate put her hands on her face. Behind her closed eyes she saw a succession of blocks tumbling over.

They took the elevator up to the hospital room. They were alone and they stood close together. Above the door red numerals lit up, flashing. Behind the illuminated shapes droned an impersonal hum of machinery.

Then the doors opened with a sucking sound. Three nurses stood waiting with a lunch cart, identical covered trays stacked in tiers. There was a hot bland smell, like warm cardboard. One of the women caught the thick steel door with her arm and smiled. Kate looked quickly at their rubber-soled shoes. White polish, the kind that rubs off. And their legs seemed only white shapes, boneless and two-dimensional, stepping silently into the metal cage.

She looked smaller in the white bed. The chrome side rails were pulled up and she seemed powerless behind them, her dark hair pushed back from her face and her forearms delicate in the baggy hospital gown. Her eyes were different in some nearly imperceptible way; she held them wider, they were shiny with a veiled wetness. For a moment the room seemed empty of all else; there were only her eyes and the dark blossoms of the flowers on the table beside her. Red roses with pine. Everyone had sent the same thing.

Robert walked close to the bed with his hands clasped behind his back, as though afraid to touch. "Where did all the flowers come from?" he asked.

"From school, and the neighbors. And Katie." She smiled.

"FTD," Kate said. "Before I left home. I felt so bad for not being here all along."

"That's silly," said their mother. "You can hardly sit at home and wait for some problem to arise."

"Speaking of problems," Robert said, "the doctor tells me you're not eating. Do I have to urge you a little?" He sat down on the edge of the bed and shook the silverware from its paper sleeve.

Kate touched the plastic tray. "Jell-O and canned cream of chicken soup. Looks great. We should have brought you something."

"They don't *want* us to bring her anything," Robert said. "This is a hospital. And I'm sure your comments make her lunch seem even more appetizing."

"I'll eat it!" said their mother in mock dismay. "Admit they sent you in here to stage a battle until I gave in."

"I'm sorry," Kate said. "He's right."

Robert grinned. "Did you hear that? She says I'm right. I don't believe it." He pushed the tray closer to his mother's chest and made a show of tucking a napkin under her chin.

"Of course you're right, dear." She smiled and gave Kate an obvious wink.

"Yeah," Robert said, "I know you two. But seriously, you eat this. I have to go make some business calls from the motel room."

Their mother frowned. "That motel must be costing you a fortune."

"No, it's reasonable," he said. "Kate can stay for a week or two and I'll drive back and forth from home. If you think this food is bad, you should see the meals in that motel restaurant." He got up to go, flashing Kate a glance of collusion. "I'll be back after supper."

His footsteps echoed down the hallway. Kate and her mother looked wordlessly at each other, relieved. Kate looked away guiltily. Then her mother spoke, apologetic. "He's so tired," she said. "He's been with me since yesterday."

She looked at Kate, then into the air of the room. "I'm in a fix," she said. "Except for when the pain comes, it's all a show that goes on without me. I'm like an invalid, or a lunatic."

Kate moved close and touched her mother's arms. "That's all right, we're going to get you through it. Someone's covering for you at work?"

"I had to take a leave of absence. It's going to take a while afterward—"

"I know. But it's the last thing to worry about, it can't be helped."

"Like spilt milk. Isn't that what they say?"

"I don't' know what they say. But why didn't you tell me? Didn't you know something was wrong?"

"Yes . . . bad headaches. Migraines, I thought, or the diabetes getting worse. I was afraid they'd start me on insulin." She tightened the corner of her mouth. "Little did I know . . ."

They heard the shuffle of slippers. An old woman stood at the open door of the room, looking in confusedly. She seemed about to speak, then moved on.

"Oh," said Kate's mother in exasperation, "shut that door, please? They let these old women wander around like refugees." She sat up, reaching for a robe. "And let's get me out of this bed."

They sat near the window while she finished eating. Bars of moted yellow banded the floor of the room. The light held a tinge of spring which seemed painful because it might vanish. They heard the rattle of the meal cart outside the closed door, and the clunk-slide of patients with aluminum walkers. Kate's mother sighed and pushed away the half-empty soup bowl.

"They'll be here after me any minute. More tests. I just want to stay with you." Her face was warm and smooth in the slanted light, lines in her skin delicate, unreal; as though a face behind her face was now apparent after many years. She sat looking at Kate and smiled.

"One day when you were about four you were dragging a broom around the kitchen. I asked what you were doing and you told me that when you got old you were going to be an angel and sweep the rotten rain off the clouds."

"What did you say to that?"

"I said that when you were old I was sure God would see to it." Her mother laughed. "I'm glad you weren't such a smart aleck then," she said. "You would have told me my view of God was paternalistic."

"Ah yes," sighed Kate. "God, that famous dude. Here I am, getting old, facing unemployment, alone, and where is He?"

"You're not alone," her mother said, "I'm right here."

Kate didn't answer. She sat motionless and felt her heart begin to open like a box with a hinged lid. The fullness had no edges.

Her mother stood. She rubbed her hands slowly, twisting her wedding rings. "My hands are so dry in the winter," she said softly, "I brought some hand cream with me but I can't find it anywhere, my suitcase is so jumbled. Thank heavens spring is early this year. . . . They told me that little park over there doesn't usually open till the end of March . . ."

She's helping me, thought Kate, I'm not supposed to let her down.

". . . but they're already running it on weekends. Even past dusk. We'll see the lights tonight. You can't see the shapes this far away, just the motion . . ."

A nurse came in with a wheelchair. Kate's mother pulled a wry face. "This wheelchair is a bit much," she said.

"We don't want to tire you out," said the nurse.

The chair took her weight quietly. At the door she put out her hand to stop, turned, and said anxiously, "Kate, see if you can find that hand cream?"

It was the blue suitcase from years ago, still almost new. She'd brought things she never used for everyday; a cashmere sweater, lace slips, silk underpants wrapped in tissue. Folded beneath was a stack of postmarked envelopes, slightly ragged, tied with twine. Kate opened one and realized that all the cards were there, beginning with the first of the marriage. There were a few photographs of her and Robert, baby pictures almost indistinguishable from each other, and then Kate's homemade Valentines, fastened together with rubber bands. Kate stared. *What will I do with these things?* She wanted air; she needed to breathe. She walked to the window and put the bundled papers on the sill. She'd raised the glass and pushed back the screen when suddenly, her mother's clock radio went off with a flat buzz. Kate moved to switch it off and brushed the cards with her arm. Envelopes shifted and slid, scattering on the floor of the room. A few snapshots wafted silently out the window. They dipped and turned, twirling. Kate didn't try to reach them. They seemed only scraps, buoyant and yellowed, blown away, the faces small as pennies. Somewhere far-off there were sirens, almost musical, drawn out and carefully approaching.

The nurse came in with evening medication. Kate's mother lay in bed. "I hope this is strong enough," she said. "Last night I couldn't sleep at all. So many sounds in a hospital . . ."

"You'll sleep tonight," the nurse assured her.

Kate winked at her mother. "That's right," she said, "I'll help you out if I have to."

They stayed up for an hour, watching the moving lights outside and the stationary glows of houses across the distant river. The halls grew darker, were lit with night lights, and the hospital dimmed. Kate waited. Her mother's eyes fluttered and finally she slept. Her breathing was low and regular.

Kate didn't move. Robert had said he'd be back; where was he? She felt a sunken anger and shook her head. She'd been on the point of telling her mother everything. The secrets were a travesty. What if there were things her mother wanted done, people she needed to see? Kate wanted to wake her before these hours passed in the dark and confess that she had lied. Between them, through the tension, there had always been a trusted clarity. Now it was twisted. Kate sat leaning forward, nearly touching the hospital bed.

Suddenly her mother sat bolt upright, her eyes open and her face transfixed. She looked blindly toward Kate but seemed to see nothing. "Who are you?" she whispered. Kate stood, at first unable to move. The woman in the bed opened and closed her mouth several times, as though she were gasping. Then she said loudly, "Stop moving the table. Stop it this instant!" Her eyes were wide with fright and her body was vibrating.

Kate reached her. "Mama, wake up, you're dreaming." Her mother jerked, flinging her arms out. Kate held her tightly.

"I can hear the wheels," she moaned.

"No, no," Kate said. "You're here with me."

"It's not so?"

"No," Kate said. "It's not so."

She went limp. Kate felt for her pulse and found it rapid, then regular. She sat rocking her mother. In a few minutes she lay her back on the pillows and smoothed the damp hair at her temples, smoothed the sheets of the bed. Later she slept fitfully in a chair, waking repeatedly to assure herself that her mother was breathing.

Near dawn she got up, exhausted, and left the room to walk in the corridor. In front of the window at the end of the hallway she saw a man slumped on a couch; the man slowly stood and wavered before her like a specter. It was Robert.

"Kate?" he said.

Years ago he had flunked out of a small junior college and their mother sat in her bedroom rocker, crying hard for over an hour while Kate tried in vain to comfort her. Kate went to the university the next fall, so anxious that she studied frantically, outlining whole textbooks in yellow ink. She sat in the front rows of large classrooms to take voluminous notes, writing quickly in her thick notebook. Robert had gone home, held a job in a plant that manufactured business forms and worked his way through the hometown college. By that time their father was dead, and Robert became, always and forever, the man of the house.

"Robert," Kate said, "I'll stay. Go home."

After breakfast they sat waiting for Robert, who had called and said he'd arrive soon. Kate's fatigue had given way to an intense awareness of every sound, every gesture. How would they get through the day? Her mother had awakened from the drugged sleep still groggy, unable to eat. The meal was sent away untouched and she watched the window as though she feared the walls of the room.

"I'm glad your father isn't here to see this," she said. There was a silence and Kate opened her mouth to speak. "I mean," said her mother quickly, "I'm going to look horrible for a few weeks, with my head all shaved." She pulled an afghan up around her lap and straightened the magazines on the table beside her chair.

"Mom," Kate said, "your hair will grow back."

Her mother pulled the afghan closer. "I've been thinking of your father," she said. "It's not that I'd have wanted him to suffer. But if he had to die, sometimes I wish he'd done it more gently. That heart attack, so finished; never a warning. I wish I'd had some time to nurse him. In a way, it's a chance to settle things."

"Did things need settling?"

"They always do, don't they?" She sat looking out the window, then said softly, "I wonder where I'm headed."

"You're not headed anywhere," Kate said. "I want you right here to see me settle down into normal American womanhood."

Her mother smiled reassuringly. "Where are my grandchildren?" she said. "That's what I'd like to know."

"You stick around," said Kate, "and I promise to start working on it." She moved her chair closer, so that their knees were touching and they could both see out the window. Below them cars moved on the highway and the Ferris wheel in the little park was turning.

"I remember when you were one of the little girls in the parade at the county fair. You weren't even in school yet; you were beautiful in that white organdy dress and pinafore. You wore those shiny black patent shoes and crown of real apple blossoms. Do you remember?"

"Yes," Kate said. "That long parade. They told me not to move and I sat so still my legs went to sleep. When they lifted me off the float I couldn't stand up. They put me under a tree to wait for you, and you came, in a full white skirt and white sandals, your hair tied back in a red scarf. I can see you yet."

Her mother laughed. "Sounds like a pretty exaggerated picture."

Kate nodded. "I was little. You were big."

"You loved the county fair. You were wild about the carnivals." They looked down at the little park. "Magic, isn't it?" her mother said.

"Maybe we could go see it," said Kate. "I'll ask the doctor."

They walked across a pedestrian footbridge spanning the highway. Kate had bundled her mother into a winter coat and gloves despite the sunny weather. The day was sharp, nearly still, holding its bright air like illusion. Kate tasted the brittle water of her breath, felt for the cool handrail and thin steel of the webbed fencing. Cars moved steadily under the bridge. Beyond a muted roar of motors the park spread green and wooded, its limits clearly visible.

Kate's mother had combed her hair and put on lipstick. Her mouth was defined and brilliant; she linked arms with Kate like an escort. "I was afraid they'd tell us no," she said. "I was ready to run away!"

"I promised I wouldn't let you. And we only have ten minutes, long enough for the Ferris wheel." Kate grinned.

"I haven't ridden one in years. I wonder if I still know how."

"Of course you do. Ferris wheels are genetic knowledge."

"All right, whatever you say." She smiled. "We'll just hold on."

They drew closer and walked quickly through the sounds of the highway. When they reached the grass it was ankle-high and thick, longer and more ragged than it appeared from a distance. The Ferris wheel sat squarely near a grove of swaying elms, squat and laboring, taller than trees. Its neon lights still burned, pale in the sun, spiraling from inside like an imagined bloom. The naked elms surrounded it, their topmost branches tapping. Steel ribs of the machine were graceful and slightly rusted, squeaking faintly above a tinkling music. Only a few people were riding.

"Looks a little rickety," Kate said.

"Oh, don't worry," said her mother.

Kate tried to buy tickets but the ride was free. The old man running the motor wore an engineer's cap and patched overalls. He stopped the wheel and led them on a short ramp to an open car. It dipped gently, padded with black cushions. An orderly and his children rode in the car above. Kate saw their dangling feet, the girls' dusty sandals and gray socks beside their father's shoes and the hem of his white pants. The youngest one swung her feet absently, so it seemed the breeze blew her legs like fabric hung on a line.

Kate looked at her mother. "Are you ready for the big sky?" They laughed. Beyond them the river moved lazily. Houses on the opposite bank seemed empty, but a few rowboats bobbed at the docks. The surface of the water lapped and reflected clouds, and as Kate watched, searching for a definition of line, the Ferris wheel jerked into motion. The car rocked. They looked into the distance and Kate caught her mother's hand as they ascended.

Far away the hospital rose up white and glistening, its windows catching the glint of the sun. Directly below, the park was nearly deserted. There were a few cars in the parking lot and several dogs chasing each other across the grass. Two or three lone women held children on the teeter-totters and a wind was coming up. The forlorn swings moved on their chains. Kate had a vision of the park at night, totally empty, wind weaving heavily through the trees and children's playthings like a great black fish about to surface. She felt a chill on her arms. The light had gone darker, quietly, like a minor chord.

"Mom," Kate said, "it's going to storm." Her own voice seemed distant, the sound strained through layers of screen or gauze.

"No," said her mother, "it's going to pass over." She moved her hand to Kate's knee and touched the cloth of her daughter's skirt.

Kate gripped the metal bar at their waists and looked straight ahead. They were rising again and she felt she would scream. She tried to breathe rhythmically, steadily. She felt the immense weight of the air as they moved through it.

They came almost to the top and stopped. The little car swayed back and forth.

"You're sick, aren't you," her mother said.

Kate shook her head. Below them the grass seemed to glitter coldly, like a sea. Kate sat wordless, feeling the touch of her mother's hand. The hand moved away and Kate felt the absence of the warmth.

They looked at each other levelly.

"I know all about it," her mother said, "I know what you haven't told me."

The sky circled around them, a sure gray movement. Kate swallowed calmly and let their gaze grow endless. She saw herself in her mother's wide brown eyes and felt she was falling slowly into them.

QUESTIONS

1. How alike are Kate and her mother?
2. What has being "the man of the house" meant for Robert?
3. Does this seem to be a close family? Explain.
4. At the end of the story, what does the mother mean in saying she knows "all about it"?
5. What, if anything, has been resolved by the conclusion?

POETRY

Anonymous (c. 1400?)
WESTERN WIND

Westron° wind, when will thou blow?   western
The small rain down can rain.
Christ, that my love were in my arms,
And I in my bed again.

Sir Thomas Wyatt (1503–1542)
THEY FLEE FROM ME

They flee from me, that sometime did me seek,
With naked foot stalking in my chamber.
I have seen them, gentle, tame, and meek,
That now are wild, and do not remember
That sometime they put themselves in danger
To take bread at my hand; and now they range,
Busily seeking with a continual change.

Thankéd be fortune it hath been otherwise.
Twenty times better; but once in special,
In thin array, after a pleasant guise,   10
When her loose gown from her shoulders did fall,
And she me caught in her arms long and small,°   slender
Therewithall sweetly did me kiss
And softly said, "Dear heart, how like you this?"

It was no dream, I lay broad waking.
But all is turned, thorough° my gentleness,   through
Into a strange fashion of forsaking;
And I have leave to go, of her goodness,
And she also to use newfangleness.
But since that I so kindely am servéd,   20
I fain would know what she hath deservéd.

431

QUESTIONS

1. How much does the speaker reveal about his relations with women?
2. How much variation in the speaker's tone do you hear?
3. What word choices and metaphors create the strongest effects?

Michael Drayton (1563–1631)

SINCE THERE'S NO HELP

Since there's no help, come, let us kiss and part.
Nay, I have done, you get no more of me,
And I am glad, yea glad with all my heart
That thus so cleanly I myself can free;
Shake hands forever, cancel all our vows,
And when we meet at any time again
Be it not seen in either of our brows
That we one jot of former love retain.
Now at the last gasp of Love's latest breath,
When, his pulse failing, Passion speechless lies,   10
When Faith is kneeling by his bed of death
And Innocence is closing up his eyes,
    Now if thou would'st, when all have given him over,
    From death to life thou might'st him yet recover.

QUESTIONS

1. What is the effect of the personification in lines 9–14?
2. Do you hear a difference in tone between the first eight lines and the last six? If so, how would you describe the tone in each part?

William Shakespeare (1564–1616)

SONNET 18

Shall I compare thee to a summer's day?
Thou art more lovely and more temperate:
Rough winds do shake the darling buds of May,

And summer's lease hath all too short a date;
Sometime too hot the eye of heaven shines,
And often is his gold complexion dimmed;
And every fair from fair sometime declines,
By chance or nature's changing course untrimmed:
But thy eternal summer shall not fade,   9
Nor lose possession of that fair thou ow'st,°   ownest
Nor shall death brag thou wand'rest in his shade,
When in eternal lines to time thou grow'st.
   So long as men can breathe or eyes can see,
   So long lives this, and this gives life to thee.

QUESTIONS

1. What picture of a summer's day is presented?
2. While you read, do you respond at all to the rejected idea of a summer's day? Explain.
3. What is your relation, as reader, to the speaker, the person he addresses, and the poem?

William Shakespeare (1564–1616)
SONNET 73

That time of year thou mayst in me behold,
When yellow leaves, or none, or few, do hang
Upon those boughs which shake against the cold,
Bare ruined choirs, where late the sweet birds sang.
In me thou seest the twilight of such day,
As after sunset fadeth in the west,
Which by and by black night doth take away,
Death's second self, that seals up all in rest.
In me thou seest the glowing of such fire,
That on the ashes of his youth doth lie,   10
As the death-bed whereon it must expire,
Consumed with that which it was nourished by.
   This thou perceiv'st, which makes thy love more strong,
   To love that well which thou must leave ere long.

QUESTIONS

1. Whom is the speaker addressing?
2. What does the figurative language in each quatrain add to what is being said?

3. How much progression in thought occurs in the three quatrains?
4. Is there a difference in tone in the concluding couplet from what you hear in the speaker's voice earlier? If so, describe the difference.
5. Is the poem more about dying or love? Explain.

William Shakespeare (1564–1616)
SONNET 98

From you have I been absent in the spring,
When proud-pied° April, dressed in all his trim,   *proudly colored*
Hath put a spirit of youth in everything,
That heavy Saturn° laughed and leapt with him.   *god of melancholy*
Yet nor the lays of birds, nor the sweet smell
Of different flow'rs in odor and in hue,
Could make me any summer's story tell,
Or from their proud lap pluck them where they grew.
Nor did I wonder at the lily's white,
Nor praise the deep vermilion in the rose;   10
They were but sweet, but figures of delight,
Drawn after you, you pattern of all those.
 Yet seemed it winter still, and, you away,
 As with your shadow I with these did play.

William Shakespeare (1564–1616)
SONNET 130

My mistress' eyes are nothing like the sun,
Coral is far more red, than her lips red,
If snow be white, why then her breasts are dun:
If hairs be wires, black wires grow on her head:
I have seen roses damasked,° red and white,   *variegated*
But no such roses see I in her cheeks,
And in some perfumes is there more delight,
Then in the breath that from my mistress reeks.
I love to hear her speak; yet well I know,
That music hath a far more pleasing sound: 10
I grant I never saw a goddess go,
My mistress when she walks treads on the ground.
 And yet by heaven I think my love as rare,
 As any she belied with false compare.°   *comparison*

William Shakespeare (1564–1616)
SONNET 138

When my love swears that she is made of truth,
I do believe her, though I know she lies,
That she might think me some untutored youth,
Unlearnèd in the world's false subtleties.
Thus vainly thinking that she thinks me young,
Although she knows my days are past the best,
Simply I credit her false-speaking tongue;
On both sides thus is simple truth supprest.
But wherefore says she not she is unjust?°   untrue
And wherefore say not I that I am old?   10
Oh, love's best habit is in seeming trust,
And age in love loves not to have years told:
Therefore I lie with her and she with me,
And in our faults by lies we flattered be.

QUESTIONS

1. How do you picture the speaker and the lady of this poem?
2. How would you characterize the speaker's attitude towards love?

William Shakespeare (1564–1616)
SONNET 144

Two loves I have of comfort and despair,
Which like two spirits do suggest me still:°   tempt me
                                                               constantly
The better angel is a man right fair,
The worser spirit a woman, colored ill.°   dark
To win me soon to hell, my female evil
Tempteth my better angel from my side,
And would corrupt my saint to be a devil,
Wooing his purity with her foul pride.
And whether that my angel be turned fiend
Suspect I may, yet not directly tell;   10
But being both from° me, both to each friend,   apart from
I guess one angel in another's hell.
Yet this shall I ne'er know, but live in doubt,
Till my bad angel fire my good one out.

John Donne (1572–1631)

THE CANONIZATION

For God's sake, hold your tongue, and let me love!
    Or chide my palsy or my gout,
My five gray hairs or ruined fortune flout;
With wealth your state, your mind with arts improve,
    Take you a course, get you a place,
      Observe His Honor or His Grace,
Or the king's real or his stamped° face   *on a coin*
    Contemplate; what you will, approve,
      So you will let me love.

Alas, alas, who's injured by my love?   10
    What merchant ships have my sighs drowned?
Who says my tears have overflowed his ground?
When did my colds a forward° spring remove?   *early*
    When did the heats which my veins fill
      Add one more to the plaguy bill?[1]
Soldiers find wars, and lawyers find out still
    Litigious men which quarrels move,
      Though she and I do love.

Call us what you will, we are made such by love.
    Call her one, me another fly;   20
We are tapers too, and at our own cost die;
And we in us find the eagle and the dove;[2]
    The phoenix[3] riddle hath more wit°   *meaning*
    By us; we two, being one, are it.
So to one neutral thing both sexes fit.
    We die and rise the same, and prove
      Mysterious by this love.

We can die by it, if not live by love,
    And if unfit for tombs and hearse
Our legend be, it will be fit for verse;   30
And if no piece of chronicle we prove,
    We'll build in sonnets pretty rooms:
    As well a well-wrought urn becomes

---

[1] The list of hot-weather plague victims.
[2] Symbols of strength and purity.
[3] A mythological bird, symbolizing immortality through regeneration.

The greatest ashes as half-acre tombs,
   And by these hymns all shall approve
     Us canonized for love,

And thus invoke us: "You whom reverend love
   Made one another's hermitage,
You to whom love was peace, that now is rage,
Who did the whole world's soul contract, and drove   40
   Into the glasses of your eyes
    (So made into such mirrors and such spies°   *spyglasses*
That they did all to you epitomize)
   Countries, towns, courts: beg from above
    A pattern of your love!"[4]

John Donne (1572–1631)

THE FLEA

Mark but this flea, and mark in this
How little that which thou deny'st me is;
It sucked me first, and now sucks thee,
And in this flea our two bloods mingled be;
Thou know'st that this cannot be said
A sin, nor shame, nor loss of maidenhead;
   Yet this enjoys before it woo,
   And pampered swells with one blood made of two,
   And this, alas, is more than we would do.

Oh stay, three lives in one flea spare,   10
Where we almost, yea more than married are,
This flea is you and I, and this
Our marriage bed and marriage temple is;
Though parents grudge, and you, we are met
And cloistered in these living walls of jet.
   Though use° make you apt to kill me,   *custom*
   Let not to that, self-murder added be,

And sacrilege, three sins in killing three.
Cruel and sudden, hast thou since

---

[4]That is, so that others may follow these lovers' example.

Purpled thy nail in blood of innocence?   20
Wherein could this flea guilty be,
Except in that drop which it sucked from thee?
Yet thou triumph'st and say'st that thou
Find'st not thyself, nor me, the weaker now.
　　'Tis true. Then learn how false fears be:
　　Just so much honor, when thou yield'st to me,
　　Will waste, as this flea's death took life from thee.

QUESTIONS

1. What picture do you have of the speaker and the woman addressed? Do you have any sense of the latter's mood?
2. How would you describe the speaker's tone?
3. What words and images evoke a strong response?
4. Do you suppose your response and the woman's would be about the same? Explain.

John Donne (1572–1631)

A VALEDICTION: FORBIDDING MOURNING

As virtuous men pass mildly away,
　　And whisper to their souls to go,
Whilst some of their sad friends do say
　　The breath goes now, and some say, No;

So let us melt, and make no noise,
　　No tear-floods, nor sigh-tempests move,
'Twere profanation of our joys
　　To tell the laity our love.

Moving of th' earth brings harms and fears,
　　Men reckon what it did and meant;   10
But trepidation of the spheres,
　　Though greater far, is innocent.[1]

Dull sublunary[2] lovers' love
　　(Whose soul is sense) cannot admit
Absence, because it doth remove
　　Those things which elemented° it.   composed

---

[1]Movement of the heavenly spheres goes unnoticed.
[2]Earthly: literally, beneath the moon.

But we by a love so much refined
    That our selves know not what it is,
Inter-assuréd of the mind,
    Care less, eyes, lips, and hands to miss.   20

Our two souls therefore, which are one,
    Though I must go, endure not yet
A breach, but an expansion,
    Like gold to airy thinness beat.

If they be two, they are two so
    As stiff twin compasses are two;
Thy soul, the fixed foot, makes no show
    To move, but doth, if th' other do.

And though it in the center sit,
    Yet when the other far doth roam,
It leans and harkens after it,
    And grows erect, as that comes home.

Such wilt thou be to me, who must
    Like th' other foot, obliquely run;
Thy firmness makes my circle just,
    And makes me end where I begun.

QUESTIONS

1. What sense do you have, from the title and details within the poem, of the occasion which prompted it?
2. What details indicate the speaker's feelings at parting? How would you describe his tone?
3. Do you find the images of the poem surprising? Do they seem appropriate, given the subject of the poem? How effective are they?

John Donne (1572–1631)

BATTER MY HEART, THREE-PERSONED GOD

Batter my heart, three-personed God; for you
As yet but knock, breathe, shine, and seek to mend;
That I may rise and stand, o'erthrow me, and bend
Your force to break, blow, burn, and make me new.
I, like an usurped town, to another due,
Labor to admit you, but oh, to no end;

Reason, your viceroy in me, me should defend,
But is captived, and proves weak or untrue.
Yet dearly I love you and would be lovèd fain,°   gladly
But am betrothed unto your enemy;   10
Divorce me, untie or break that knot again,
Take me to you, imprison me, for I,
Except you enthrall me, never shall be free,
Nor ever chaste, except you ravish me.

QUESTIONS

1. What does the figurative language in the poem tell you about the way the speaker
   regards God, himself, and their relationship? Do you find the speaker's manner of
   speaking to God shocking?
2. Why does the speaker use paradoxes in addressing God? How much sense do the
   various paradoxes make?

Robert Herrick (1591–1674)

CORINNA'S GOING A-MAYING

Get up! get up for shame! the blooming morn
Upon her wings presents the god unshorn.°   the sun
    See how Aurora[1] throws her fair
    Fresh-quilted colors through the air:
    Get up, sweet slug-a-bed, and see
    The dew bespangling herb and tree.
Each flower has wept and bowed toward the east
Above an hour since, yet you not dressed;
    Nay, not so much as out of bed?
    When all the birds have matins said,
    And sung their thankful hymns, 'tis sin,   10
    Nay, profanation to keep in,
Whenas a thousand virgins on this day
Spring, sooner than the lark, to fetch in May.

Rise, and put on your foliage, and be seen
To come forth, like the springtime, fresh and green,
    And sweet as Flora.[2] Take no care
    For jewels for your gown or hair;

---

[1]Goddess of the dawn.
[2]Goddess of flowers.

Fear not; the leaves will strew
    Gems in abundance upon you;   20
Besides, the childhood of the day has kept,
Against you come, some orient pearls unwept;
    Come and receive them while the light
    Hangs on the dew-locks of the night,
    And Titan° on the eastern hill   the sun
    Retires himself, or else stands still
Till you come forth. Wash, dress, be brief in praying:
Few beads° are best when once we go a-Maying.   prayers

Come, my Corinna, come; and, coming mark
How each field turns a street, each street a park   30
    Made green and trimmed with trees; see how
    Devotion gives each house a bough
    Or branch: each porch, each door ere this,
    An ark, a tabernacle is,
Made up of whitethorn neatly interwove,
As if here were those cooler shades of love.
    Can such delights be in the street
    And open fields, and we not see 't?
    Come, we'll abroad; and let's obey
    The proclamation made for May,   40
And sin no more, as we have done, by staying;
But, my Corinna, come, let's go a-Maying.

There's not a budding boy or girl this day
But is got up and gone to bring in May;
    A deal of youth, ere this, is come
    Back, and with whitethorn laden home.
    Some have dispatched their cakes and cream
    Before that we have left to dream;
And some have wept, and wooed, and plighted troth,
And chose their priest, ere we can cast off sloth.   50
    Many a green-gown[3] has been given,
    Many a kiss, both odd and even,
    Many a glance, too, has been sent
    From out the eye, love's firmament;
Many a jest told of the keys betraying
This night, and locks picked; yet we're not a-Maying.

---

[3]That is, colored by the grass.

Come, let us go while we are in our prime,
And take the harmless folly of the time.
    We shall grow old apace, and die
    Before we know our liberty.   60
    Our life is short, and our days run
    As fast away as does the sun;
And, as a vapor or a drop of rain
Once lost, can ne'er be found again;
    So when or you or I are made
    A fable, song, or fleeting shade,
    All love, all liking, all delight
    Lies drowned with us in endless night.
Then while time serves, and we are but decaying,
Come, my Corinna, come, let's go a-Maying.   70

George Herbert (1593–1663)
BITTER-SWEET

Ah, my dear angry Lord,
Since Thou dost love, yet strike;
Cast down, yet help afford;
Sure I will do the like.

I will complain, yet praise;
I will bewail, approve:
And all my sour-sweet days
I will lament, and love.

George Herbert (1593–1633)
LOVE

Love bade me welcome; yet my soul drew back,
    Guilty of dust and sin.
But quick-eyed Love, observing me grow slack
    From my first entrance in,
Drew nearer to me, sweetly questioning
    If I lacked anything.

"A guest," I answered, "worthy to be here";
    Love said, "You shall be he."
"I, the unkind, ungrateful? Ah, my dear,
    I cannot look on Thee." 10
Love took my hand, and smiling did reply,
    "Who made the eyes but I?"

"Truth, Lord, but I have marred them; let my shame
    Go where it doth deserve."
"And know you not," says Love, "who bore the blame?"
    "My dear, then I will serve."
"You must sit down," says Love, "and taste My meat."
    So I did sit and eat.

QUESTIONS

1. Do you suppose a specific incident prompted this poem?
2. What is the effect of the personification of Love?
3. What relations between God and the speaker does the poem indicate?

Andrew Marvell (1621–1678)
TO HIS COY MISTRESS

Had we but world enough, and time,
This coyness, Lady, were° no crime.   *would be*
We would sit down, and think which way
To walk, and pass our long love's day.
Thou by the Indian Ganges' side
Shouldst rubies find; I by the tide
Of Humber[1] would complain. I would
Love you ten years before the Flood;
And you should, if you please, refuse
Till the conversion of the Jews. 10
My vegetable° love should grow   *vegetative*
Vaster than empires, and more slow.

---

[1]Estuary in eastern England. Marvell was born near Hull, a seaport on the Humber.

An hundred years should go to praise
Thine eyes, and on thy forehead gaze;
Two hundred to adore each breast;
But thirty thousand to the rest:
An age, at least, to every part,
And the last age should show your heart.
For, Lady, you deserve this state,
Nor would I love at lower rate.   20
   But, at my back, I always hear
Time's wingèd chariot hurrying near:
And yonder, all before us lie
Deserts of vast eternity.
Thy beauty shall no more be found;
Nor, in thy marble vault, shall sound
My echoing song. Then worms shall try
That long preserved virginity:
And your quaint honour turn to dust;
And into ashes all my lust.   30
The grave's a fine and private place,
But none, I think, do there embrace.
   Now, therefore, while the youthful hue
Sits on thy skin like morning dew,
And while thy willing soul transpires
At every pore with instant fires,
Now let us sport us while we may;
And now, like amorous birds of prey,
Rather at once our time devour,
Than languish in his slow-chapt° power.   slow-jawed
Let us roll all our strength, and all   41
Our sweetness, up into one ball;
And tear our pleasures, with rough strife,
Thorough° the iron gates of life.   through
   Thus, though we cannot make our sun
Stand still, yet we will make him run.

QUESTIONS

1. How serious in his declarations of love does the speaker seem in the first group of lines (to 1. 20)?
2. How does his strategy in wooing change in the second part (to 1. 32)?
3. Has the speaker proved something in the first two sections, as his "therefore" in 1. 33 implies?
4. What images in the poem evoke the strongest responses?
5. What sense do you have of the lady, apart from her being "coy"? How do you suppose she might react to the speaker's argument?

Robert Burns (1759–1796)
A RED, RED ROSE

O My Luve's like a red, red rose,
   That's newly sprung in June;
O My Luve's like a melodie
   That's sweetly played in tune.

As fair art thou, my bonnie lass;
   So deep in luve am I;
And I will luve thee still, my dear,
   Till a' the seas gang dry.

Till a' the seas gang dry, my dear,
   And the rocks melt wi' the sun: 10
O I will love thee still, my dear,
   While the sands o' life shall run.

And fare thee weel, my only luve,
   And fare thee weel awhile!
And I will come again, my luve,
   Though it were ten thousand mile.

Robert Browning (1812–1889)
PORPHYRIA'S LOVER

The rain set early in to-night,
   The sullen wind was soon awake,
It tore the elm-tops down for spite,
   And did its worst to vex the lake:
   I listened with heart fit to break.
When glided in Porphyria; straight
   She shut the cold out and the storm,
And kneeled and made the cheerless grate
   Blaze up, and all the cottage warm;
   Which done, she rose, and from her form   10
Withdrew the dripping cloak and shawl,
   And laid her soiled gloves by, untied
Her hat and let the damp hair fall,
   And, last, she sat down by my side
   And called me. When no voice replied,

She put my arm about her waist,
  And made her smooth white shoulder bare,
And all her yellow hair displaced,
  And, stooping, made my cheek lie there,
  And spread, o'er all, her yellow hair,   20
Murmuring how she loved me—she
  Too weak, for all her heart's endeavour,
To set its struggling passion free
  From pride, and vainer ties dissever,°   sever
  And give herself to me for ever.
But passion sometimes would prevail,
  Nor could to-night's gay feast restrain
A sudden thought of one so pale
  For love of her, and all in vain:
  So, she was come through wind and rain.   30
Be sure I looked up at her eyes
  Happy and proud; at last I knew
Porphyria worshipped me; surprise
  Made my heart swell, and still it grew
  While I debated what to do.
That moment she was mine, mine, fair,
  Perfectly pure and good: I found
A thing to do, and all her hair
  In one long yellow string I wound
  Three times her little throat around,   40
And strangled her. No pain felt she;
  I am quite sure she felt no pain.
As a shut bud that holds a bee,
  I warily oped her lids: again
  Laughed the blue eyes without a stain.
And I untightened next the tress
  About her neck; her cheek once more
Blushed bright beneath my burning kiss:
  I propped her head up as before,
  Only, this time my shoulder bore   50
Her head, which droops upon it still:
  The smiling rosy little head,
So glad it has its utmost will,
  That all it scorned at once is fled,
  And I, its love, am gained instead!
Porphyria's love: she guessed not how
  Her darling one wish would be heard.
And thus we sit together now,
  And all night long we have not stirred,
  And yet God has not said a word!   60

Emily Dickinson (1830–1886)
WILD NIGHTS—WILD NIGHTS!

Wild Nights—Wild Nights!
Were I with thee
Wild Nights should be
Our luxury!

Futile—the Winds—
To a Heart in port—
Done with the Compass—
Done with the Chart!

Rowing in Eden—
Ah, the Sea!
Might I but moor—Tonight—
In Thee!

QUESTIONS

1. What does the phrase "Wild Nights" suggest?
2. What do you suppose the "Compass" and "Chart" to be?
3. Are the speaker's apparent longings for "Wild Nights," "luxury," and for a "Heart in port" contradictory? Explain.

Thomas Hardy (1840–1928)
NEUTRAL TONES

We stood by a pond that winter day,
And the sun was white, as though chidden of God,
And a few leaves lay on the starving sod;
    —They had fallen from an ash, and were gray.

Your eyes on me were as eyes that rove
Over tedious riddles of years ago;
And some words played between us to and fro
    On which lost the more by our love.

The smile on your mouth was the deadest thing
Alive enough to have strength to die;

And a grin of bitterness swept thereby
    Like an ominous bird a-wing. . . .

Since then, keen lessons that love deceives,
And wrings with wrong, have shaped to me
Your face, and the God-curst sun, and a tree,
    And a pond edged with grayish leaves.

Robert Frost (1874–1963)

TO EARTHWARD

Love at the lips was touch
As sweet as I could bear;
And once that seemed too much;
I lived on air

That crossed me from sweet things,
The flow of—was it musk
From hidden grapevine springs
Downhill at dusk?

I had the swirl and ache
From sprays of honeysuckle
That when they're gathered shake
Dew on the knuckle.   10

I craved strong sweets, but those
Seemed strong when I was young;
The petal of the rose
It was that stung.

Now no joy but lacks salt,
That is not dashed with pain
And weariness and fault;
I crave the stain   20

Of tears, the aftermark
Of almost too much love,
The sweet of bitter bark
And burning clove.

When stiff and sore and scarred
I take away my hand

From leaning on it hard
In grass and sand,

The hurt is not enough:
I long for weight and strength   30
To feel the earth as rough
To all my length.

Ezra Pound (1885–1972)

THE RIVER-MERCHANT'S WIFE: A LETTER

WHILE my hair was still cut straight across my forehead
I played about the front gate, pulling flowers.
You came by on bamboo stilts, playing horse,
You walked about my seat, playing with blue plums.
And we went on living in the village of Chōkan:
Two small people, without dislike or suspicion.

At fourteen I married My Lord you.
I never laughed, being bashful.
Lowering my head, I looked at the wall.
Called to, a thousand times, I never looked back.   10

At fifteen I stopped scowling,
I desired my dust to be mingled with yours
Forever and forever and forever.
Why should I climb the look out?

At sixteen you departed,
You went into far Ku-tō-en, by the river of swirling eddies,
And you have been gone five months.
The monkeys make sorrowful noise overhead.

You dragged your feet when you went out.
By the gate now, the moss is grown, the different mosses,   20
Too deep to clear them away!
The leaves fall early this autumn, in wind.
The paired butterflies are already yellow with August
Over the grass in the West garden;
They hurt me.   I grow older.
If you are coming down through the narrows of the river
    Kiang,

Please let me know beforehand,
And I will come out to meet you
            As far as Chō-fū-Sa.
                    By Rihaku (Li T'ai Po)[1]

QUESTIONS

1. What picture do you have of the speaker?
2. Why does she repeatedly refer to her age?
3. Is she reproaching her husband for his absence?
4. How can moss grow too deep to clear away, and how can butterflies hurt anyone?
5. Does not knowing Cho-fu-Sa's distance weaken the conclusion of the poem for you?

Edna St. Vincent Millay (1892–1950)

WELL, I HAVE LOST YOU; AND I LOST YOU FAIRLY

Well, I have lost you; and I lost you fairly;
In my own way, and with my full consent.
Say what you will, kings in a tumbrel rarely
Went to their deaths more proud than this one went.
Some nights of apprehension and hot weeping
I will confess; but that's permitted me;
Day dried my eyes; I was not one for keeping
Rubbed in a cage a wing that would be free.
If I had loved you less or played you slyly
I might have held you for a summer more,   10
But at the cost of words I value highly,
And no such summer as the one before.
Should I outlive this anguish--and men do--
I shall have only good to say of you.

QUESTIONS

1. Is the speaker a man or a woman?
2. In what way did the speaker "lose" the other person?
3. What "cost," other than that of words, was involved?
4. When you read the poem aloud, how does the last line sound?

---

[1]The poem is an adaptation of one written by the Chinese poet Li Po (in Japanese called Rihaku) in the eighth century A.D.

e. e. cummings (1894–1962)

SINCE FEELING IS FIRST

since feeling is first
who pays any attention
to the syntax of things
will never wholly kiss you;

wholly to be a fool
while Spring is in the world

my blood approves,
and kisses are a better fate
than wisdom
lady i swear by all flowers. Don't cry   10
—the best gesture of my brain is less than
your eyelids' flutter which says

we are for each other: then
laugh, leaning back in my arms
for life's not a paragraph

And death i think is no parenthesis

QUESTIONS

1. What purpose, if any, is served by the arrangement of the lines of this poem?
2. Do you have any sense of the speaker's usual occupation?
3. Whose "better fate" (1. 8) is at issue?
4. How trustworthy would you consider an oath "by all the flowers" to be?
5. To whom is the last line addressed, and what is the effect of "i think"?

Theodore Roethke (1908–1963)

I KNEW A WOMAN

I knew a woman, lovely in her bones,
When small birds sighed, she would sigh back at them;
Ah, when she moved, she moved more ways than one:
The shapes a bright container can contain!
Of her choice virtues only gods should speak,
Or English poets who grew up on Greek
(I'd have them sing in chorus, cheek to cheek).

How well her wishes went! She stroked my chin,
She taught me Turn, and Counter-turn, and Stand;[1]
She taught me Touch, that undulant white skin;   10
I nibbled meekly from her proffered hand;
She was the sickle; I, poor I, the rake,
Coming behind her for her pretty sake
(But what prodigious mowing we did make).

Love likes a gander, and adores a goose:
Her full lips pursed, the errant note to seize;
She played it quick, she played it light and loose;
My eyes, they dazzled at her flowing knees;
Her several parts could keep a pure repose,
Or one hip quiver with a mobile nose   20
(She moved in circles, and those circles moved).

Let seed be grass, and grass turn into hay:
I'm martyr to a motion not my own;
What's freedom for? To know eternity.
I swear she cast a shadow white as stone.
But who would count eternity in days?
These old bones live to learn her wanton ways:
(I measure time by how a body sways).

QUESTIONS

1. What is the speaker's tone generally?
2. What sense do you have of the relationship between the speaker and the woman described?
3. What do you make of the verb tenses throughout the poem?
4. What details especially convey the speaker's feeling?

Robert Hayden (1913–1980)

THOSE WINTER SUNDAYS

Sundays too my father got up early
and put his clothes on in the blueblack cold,
then with cracked hands that ached
from labor in the weekday weather made
banked fires blaze. No one ever thanked him.

---

[1]The terms recall the parts of a classical Greek ode.

I'd wake and hear the cold splintering, breaking.
When the rooms were warm, he'd call,
and slowly I would rise and dress,
fearing the chronic angers of that house,

Speaking indifferently to him,   10
who had driven out the cold
and polished my good shoes as well.
What did I know, what did I know
of love's austere and lonely offices?

Philip Larkin (1922–1985)

TALKING IN BED

Talking in bed ought to be easiest,
Lying together there goes back so far,
An emblem of two people being honest.

Yet more and more time passes silently.
Outside, the wind's incomplete unrest
Builds and disperses clouds about the sky,

And dark towns heap up on the horizon.
None of this cares for us. Nothing shows why
At this unique distance from isolation

It becomes still more difficult to find   10
Words at once true and kind,
Or not untrue and not unkind.

Sylvia Plath (1932–1963)

DADDY

You do not do, you do not do
Any more, black shoe
In which I have lived like a foot
For thirty years, poor and white,
Barely daring to breathe or Achoo.

Daddy, I have had to kill you.
You died before I had time—
Marble-heavy, a bag full of God,
Ghastly statue with one grey toe
Big as a Frisco seal   10

And a head in the freakish Atlantic
Where it pours bean green over blue
In the waters off beautiful Nauset.[1]
I used to pray to recover you.
Ach, du.[2]

In the German tongue, in the Polish town
Scraped flat by the roller
Of wars, wars, wars.
But the name of the town is common.
My Polack friend   20

Says there are a dozen or two.
So I never could tell where you
Put your foot, your root,
I never could talk to you.
The tongue stuck in my jaw.

It stuck in a barb wire snare.
Ich, ich, ich, ich,[3]
I could hardly speak.
I thought every German was you.
And the language obscene   30

An engine, an engine
Chuffing me off like a Jew.
A Jew to Dachau, Auschwitz, Belsen.
I began to talk like a Jew.
I think I may well be a Jew.

The snows of the Tyrol, the clear beer of Vienna
Are not very pure or true.
With my gypsy ancestress and my weird luck
And my Taroc pack[4] and my Taroc pack
I may be a bit of a Jew.   40

---

[1]The outer elbow of Cape Cod, in Massachusetts.
[2]German for 'O you.'
[3]German for 'I.'
[4]Or Tarot: fortune-telling cards used for centuries by gypsies.

I have always been scared of *you*,
With your Luftwaffe,[5] your gobbledygoo.
And your neat moustache
And your Aryan eye, bright blue.
Panzer-man,[6] panzer-man, O You—

Not God but a swastika
So black no sky could squeak through.
Every woman adores a Fascist,
The boot in the face, the brute
Brute heart of a brute like you.

        50

You stand at the blackboard, daddy,[7]
In the picture I have of you,
A cleft in your chin instead of your foot
But no less a devil for that, no not
Any less the black man who

Bit my pretty red heart in two.
I was ten when they buried you.
At twenty I tried to die
And get back, back, back to you.
I thought even the bones would do.

        60

But they pulled me out of the sack,
And they stuck me together with glue.
And then I knew what to do.
I made a model of you,
A man in black with a Meinkampf look

And a love of the rack and the screw.
And I said I do, I do.
So daddy, I'm finally through.
The black telephone's off at the root,
The voices just can't worm through.

        70

If I've killed one man, I've killed two—
The vampire who said he was you
And drank my blood for a year,
Seven years, if you want to know.
Daddy, you can lie back now.

---

[5]The Nazi air force in World War II.
[6]Literally, armored; German tank divisions in World War II were called *panzer* divisions.
[7]Plath's father was a professor of entomology at Boston University.

There's a stake in your fat black heart
And the villagers never liked you.
They are dancing and stamping on you.
They always *knew* it was you.
Daddy, daddy, you bastard, I'm through.   80

QUESTIONS

1. How do you imagine the speaker?
2. Why is the speaker trying to kill someone who died many years earlier?
3. What pictures of her father does the speaker convey? What details suggest she has mixed feelings about him?
4. How do you respond to the references to Nazi Germany and the speaker's suggestion that she "may well be a Jew"? Do you suppose her to be speaking literally?
5. Do you suppose the speaker really is "through" with her father? Explain.

Bob Kaufman (b. 1935)

BLUES NOTE

*For Ray Charles's birthday
N.Y.C./1961*

Ray Charles is the black wind of Kilimanjaro,
Screaming up-and-down blues,
Moaning happy on all the elevators of my time.

Smiling into the camera, with an African symphony
Hidden in his throat, and (*I Got a Woman*) wails, too.

He burst from Bessie's[1] crushed black skull
One cold night outside of Nashville, shouting,
And grows bluer from memory, glowing bluer, still.

At certain times you can see the moon
Balanced on his head.   10

---

[1]Bessie Smith, "Empress of the Blues" (1894?–1937) died after an automobile accident in Clarksdale, Mississippi, on September 26, 1937. In classical mythology, Athene sprang from the head of Zeus.

From his mouth he hurls chunks of raw soul.
He separated the sea of polluted sounds
And led the blues into the Promised Land.

Ray Charles is a dangerous man ('way cross town),
And I love him.

Marge Piercy (b. 1936)

TO HAVE WITHOUT HOLDING

Learning to love differently is hard,
love with the hands wide open, love
with the doors banging on their hinges,
the cupboard unlocked, the wind
roaring and whimpering in the rooms
rustling the sheets and snapping the blinds
that thwack like rubber bands
in an open palm.

It hurts to love wide open
stretching the muscles that feel   10
as if they are made of wet plaster,
then of blunt knives, then
of sharp knives.

It hurts to thwart the reflexes
of grab, of clutch; to love and let
go again and again. It pesters to remember
the lover who is not in the bed,
to hold back what is owed to the work
that gutters like a candle in a cave
without air, to love consciously,   20
conscientiously, concretely, constructively.

I can't do it, you say it's killing
me, but you thrive, you glow
on the street like a neon raspberry,
You float and sail, a helium balloon
bright bachelor's button blue and bobbing
on the cold and hot winds of our breath,
as we make and unmake in passionate

diastole and systole the rhythm
of our unbound bonding, to have   30
and not to hold, to love
with minimized malice, hunger
and anger moment by moment balanced.

Margaret Atwood (b. 1939)

VARIATION ON THE WORD *SLEEP*

I would like to watch you sleeping,
which may not happen.
I would like to watch you,
sleeping. I would like to sleep
with you, to enter
your sleep as its smooth dark wave
slides over my head

and walk with you through that lucent
wavering forest of bluegreen leaves
with its watery sun & three moons   10
towards the cave where you must descend,
towards your worst fear

I would like to give you the silver
branch, the small white flower, the one
word that will protect you
from the grief at the center
of your dream, from the grief
at the center. I would like to follow
you up the long stairway
again & become   20
the boat that would row you back
carefully, a flame
in two cupped hands
to where your body lies
beside me, and you enter
it as easily as breathing in

I would like to be the air
that inhabits you for a moment
only. I would like to be that unnoticed   30
& that necessary.

Seamus Heaney (b. 1939)

THE SKUNK

Up, black, striped and damasked like the chasuble
At a funeral mass, the skunk's tail
Paraded the skunk. Night after night
I expected her like a visitor.

The refrigerator whinnied into silence.
My desk light softened beyond the verandah.
Small oranges loomed in the orange tree.
I began to be tense as a voyeur.

After eleven years I was composing
Love-letters again, broaching the word 'wife'   10
Like a stored cask, as if its slender vowel
Had mutated into the night earth and air

Of California. The beautiful, useless
Tang of eucalyptus spelt your absence.
The aftermath of a mouthful of wine
Was like inhaling you off a cold pillow.

And there she was, the intent and glamorous,
Ordinary, mysterious skunk,
Mythologized, demythologized,
Snuffing the boards five feet beyond me.   20

It all came back to me last night, stirred
By the sootfall of your things at bedtime,
Your head-down, tail-up hunt in a bottom drawer
For the black plunge-line nightdress.

QUESTIONS

1. Is the speaker comparing his wife to a skunk here? If not, what connection between
   the two is he making?
2. What are the most effective images that accompany the memory of the skunk?
3. How much variation in the speaker's tone do you hear?
4. Is the poem about the skunk, the wife, or perhaps something else?

Sharon Olds (b. 1942)
SEX WITHOUT LOVE

How do they do it, the ones who make love
without love? Beautiful as dancers,
gliding over each other like ice-skaters
over the ice, fingers hooked
inside each other's bodies, faces
red as steak, wine, wet as the
children at birth whose mothers are going to
give them away. How do they come to the
come to the   come to the   God   come to the
still waters, and not love   10
the one who came there with them, light
rising slowly as steam off their joined
skin? These are the true religious,
the purists, the pros, the ones who will not
accept a false Messiah, love the
priest instead of the God. They do not
mistake the lover for their own pleasure,
they are like great runners: they know they are alone
with the road surface, the cold, the wind,
the fit of their shoes, their over-all cardio-   20
vascular health—just factors, like the partner
in the bed, and not the truth, which is the
single body alone in the universe
against its own best time.

QUESTIONS

1. What images evoke the strongest responses?
2. What is the speaker's tone?
3. How much does she admire those "who make love/without love"?

DRAMA

William Shakespeare (1564–1616)
THE TAMING OF THE SHREW

DRAMATIS PERSONAE

Baptista Minola, of Padua, father of Kate and Bianca
Kate, the shrew
Bianca
Petruchio, of Verona, suitor of Kate
Lucentio (Cambio) ⎤
Gremio, a pantaloon ⎬ suitors of Bianca
Hortensio (Litio) ⎦
Vincentio, of Pisa, father of Lucentio
A Pedant (impersonating Vincentio)
Tranio (later impersonating ⎤
   Lucentio) ⎬ servants of Lucentio
Biondello ⎦
Grumio ⎤
Curtis ⎟
Nathaniel, Nicholas ⎬ servants of Petruchio
Joseph, Philip, Peter ⎦
A Tailor
A Haberdasher
A Widow
Servants of Baptista and Lucentio

SCENE: **Padua; the country near Verona.**

[ACT 1
SCENE I. *Padua. A street.*]

Flourish.° Enter Lucentio and his man° Tranio.

Lucentio. Tranio, since for the great desire I had
  To see fair Padua,° nursery of arts,
  I am arrived for fruitful Lombardy,
  The pleasant garden of great Italy,
  And by my father's love and leave am armed   5

I.i.s.d. **Flourish** fanfare of trumpets   s.d. **man** servant   2 **Padua** (noted for its university)

461

With his good will and thy good company,
My trusty servant well approved° in all,
Here let us breathe and haply institute
A course of learning and ingenious° studies.
Pisa, renownèd for grave citizens,   10
Gave me my being and my father first,°
A merchant of great traffic° through the world,
Vincentio, come of the Bentivolii.
Vincentio's son, brought up in Florence,
It shall become to serve° all hopes conceived,   15
To deck his fortune with his virtuous deeds;
And therefore, Tranio, for the time I study,
Virtue and that part of philosophy
Will I apply° that treats of happiness
By virtue specially to be achieved.   20
Tell me thy mind, for I have Pisa left
And am to Padua come, as he that leaves
A shallow plash° to plunge him in the deep
And with satiety seeks to quench his thirst.
Tranio. Mi perdonato,° gentle master mine,   25
  I am in all affected° as yourself,
  Glad that you thus continue your resolve
  To suck the sweets of sweet philosophy.
  Only, good master, while we do admire
  This virtue and this moral discipline,   30
  Let's be no stoics nor no stocks,° I pray,
  Or so devote° to Aristotle's checks°
  As° Ovid° be an outcast quite abjured.
  Balk logic° with acquaintance that you have
  And practice rhetoric in your common talk.   35
  Music and poesy use to quicken° you.
  The mathematics and the metaphysics,
  Fall to them as you find your stomach° serves you.
  No profit grows where is no pleasure ta'en.
  In brief, sir, study what you most affect.°   40
Lucentio. Gramercies,° Tranio, well dost thou advise.
  If, Biondello, thou wert come ashore,
  We could at once put us in readiness
  And take a lodging fit to entertain

---

7 **approved** proved, found reliable   9 **ingenious** mind-training   11 **first** i.e., before that   12 **traffic** business   15 **serve** work for   19 **apply** apply myself to   23 **plash** pool   25 **Mi perdonato** pardon me   26 **affected** inclined   31 **stocks** sticks (with pun on Stoics)   32 **devote** devoted   32 **checks** restraints   33 **As** so that   33 **Ovid** Roman love poet   34 **Balk logic** engage in arguments   36 **quicken** make alive   38 **stomach** taste, preference   40 **affect** like   41 **Gramercies** many thanks

Such friends as time in Padua shall beget. 45
But stay awhile, what company is this?
Tranio. Master, some show to welcome us to town.

Enter Baptista with his two daughters, Kate and Bianca; Gremio, a pan-taloon;° [and] Hortensio, suitor to Bianca. Lucentio [and] Tranio stand by.°

Baptista. Gentlemen, importune me no farther,
For how I firmly am resolved you know,
That is, not to bestow my youngest daughter 50
Before I have a husband for the elder.
If either of you both love Katherina,
Because I know you well and love you well,
Leave shall you have to court her at your pleasure.
Gremio. To cart° her rather. She's too rough for me. 55
There, there, Hortensio, will you any wife?
Kate. I pray you, sir, is it your will
To make a stale° of me amongst these mates?°
Hortensio. Mates, maid? How mean you that? No mates for you
Unless you were of gentler, milder mold. 60
Kate. I' faith, sir, you shall never need to fear:
Iwis° it° is not halfway to her° heart.
But if it were, doubt not her care should be
To comb your noddle with a three-legged stool
And paint° your face and use you like a fool. 65
Hortensio. From all such devils, good Lord deliver us!
Gremio. And me too, good Lord!
Tranio. [*Aside*] Husht, master, here's some good pastime toward.°
That wench is stark mad or wonderful froward.°
Lucentio. [*Aside*] But on the other's silence do I see 70
Maid's mild behavior and sobriety.
Peace, Tranio.
Tranio. [*Aside*] Well said, master. Mum, and gaze your fill.
Baptista. Gentlemen, that I may soon make good
What I have said: Bianca, get you in, 75
And let it not displease thee, good Bianca,
For I will love thee ne'er the less, my girl.

47s.d. **pantaloon** laughable old man (a stock character with baggy pants, in Italian Renaissance comedy) 47s.d. **by** nearby 55 **cart** drive around in an open cart (a punishment for prostitutes) 58 **stale** (1) laughingstock (2) prostitute 58 **mates** low fellows (with pun on *stalemate* and leading to pun on *mate* = husband) 62 **Iwis** certainly 62 **it** i.e., getting a mate 62 **her** Kate's 65 **paint** i.e., red with blood 68 **toward** coming up 69 **froward** willful

Kate. A pretty peat!° It is best
    Put finger in the eye,° and° she knew why.
Bianca. Sister, content you in my discontent.   80
    Sir, to your pleasure humbly I subscribe.
    My books and instruments shall be my company,
    On them to look and practice by myself.
Lucentio [*Aside*]. Hark, Tranio, thou mayst hear Minerva° speak.
Hortensio. Signior Baptista, will you be so strange?°   85
    Sorry am I that our good will effects
    Bianca's grief.
Gremio.   Why will you mew° her up,
    Signior Baptista, for this fiend of hell
    And make her bear the penance of her tongue?
Baptista. Gentlemen, content ye. I am resolved.   90
    Go in, Bianca.   [*Exit Bianca.*]
    And for° I know she taketh most delight
    In music, instruments, and poetry,
    Schoolmasters will I keep within my house,
    Fit to instruct her youth. If you, Hortensio,   95
    Or Signior Gremio, you, know any such,
    Prefer° them hither; for to cunning° men
    I will be very kind, and liberal
    To mine own children in good bringing up.
    And so, farewell. Katherina, you may stay,   100
    For I have more to commune with° Bianca.   *Exit.*
Kate. Why, and I trust I may go too, may I not?
    What, shall I be appointed hours, as though, belike,°
    I knew not what to take and what to leave? Ha!   *Exit.*
Gremio. You may go to the devil's dam;° your gifts are so good, here's none 105
will hold you. Their love is not so great,° Hortensio, but we may blow
our nails together° and fast it fairly out. Our cake's dough on both sides.°
Farewell. Yet for the love I bear my sweet Bianca, if I can by any means
light on a fit man to teach her that wherein she delights, I will wish° him
to her father.   110
Hortensio. So will I, Signior Gremio. But a word, I pray. Though the nature
of our quarrel yet never brooked parle,° know now, upon advice,° it touch-
eth° us both—that we may yet again have access to our fair mistress and
be happy rivals in Bianca's love—to labor and effect one thing specially.

---

    78 **peat** pet (cf. "teacher's pet")   79 **Put finger in the eye** cry   79 **and** if   84 **Minerva** goddess
of wisdom   85 **strange** rigid   87 **mew** cage (falconry term)   92 **for** because   97 **Prefer**
recommend   97 **cunning** talented   101 **commune with** communicate to   103 **belike** it seems
likely   105 **dam** mother (used of animals)   106 **great** important   106–07 **blow our nails together**
i.e., wait patiently   107 **Our cake's dough on both sides** we've both failed (proverbial)   109 **wish**
commend   112 **brooked parle** allowed negotiation   112 **advice** consideration   112–13 **toucheth**
concerns

Gremio. What's that, I pray? 115
Hortensio. Marry, sir, to get a husband for her sister.
Gremio. A husband! A devil.
Hortensio. I say, a husband.
Gremio. I say, a devil. Think'st thou, Hortensio, though her father be very
    rich, any man is so very° a fool to° be married to hell? 120
Hortensio. Tush, Gremio, though it pass your patience and mind to endure
    her loud alarums,° why, man, there be good fellows in the world, and° a
    man could light on them, would take her with all faults, and money enough.
Gremio. I cannot tell, but I had as lief° take her dowry with this condition,
    to be whipped at the high cross° every morning. 125
Hortensio. Faith, as you say, there's small choice in rotten apples. But come,
    since this bar in law° makes us friends, it shall be so far forth° friendly
    maintained, till by helping Baptista's eldest daughter to a husband, we set
    his youngest free for a husband, and then have to't° afresh. Sweet Bianca!
    Happy man be his dole!° He that runs fastest gets the ring. How say you, 130
    Signior Gremio?
Gremio. I am agreed, and would I had given him the best horse in Padua to
    begin his wooing, that° would thoroughly woo her, wed her, and bed her
    and rid the house of her. Come on.

    Exeunt ambo.° Manet° Tranio and Lucentio. 135

Tranio. I pray, sir, tell me, is it possible
    That love should of a sudden take such hold?
Lucentio. O Tranio, till I found it to be true
    I never thought it possible or likely.
    But see, while idly I stood looking on, 140
    I found the effect of love-in-idleness°
    And now in plainness do confess to thee,
    That art to me as secret° and as dear
    As Anna° to the Queen of Carthage was,
    Tranio, I burn, I pine, I perish, Tranio, 145
    If I achieve not this young modest girl.
    Counsel me, Tranio, for I know thou canst.
    Assist me, Tranio, for I know thou wilt.

---

120 **very** thorough   120 **to** as to   122 **alarums** outcries   122 **and** if   124 **had as lief** would as
willingly   125 **high cross** market cross (prominent spot)   127 **bar in law** legal action of preventive
sort   127 **so far forth** so long   129 **have to't** renew our competition   130 **Happy man be his dole**
let being a happy man be his (the winner's) destiny   133 **that** (antecedent is *his*)   135s.d. **ambo**
both   135s.d. **Manet** remain (though the Latin plural is properly *manent*, the singular with a
plural subject is common in Elizabethan texts)   141 **love-in-idleness** popular name for pansy
(believed to have mysterious power in love   143 **to me as secret** as much in my confidence   144
Anna sister and confidante of Queen Dido

Tranio. Master, it is no time to chide you now.
   Affection is not rated° from the heart. 150
   If love have touched you, naught remains but so,°
   "Redime te captum, quam queas minimo."°
Lucentio. Gramercies,° lad, go forward. This contents.
   The rest will comfort, for thy counsel's sound.
Tranio. Master, you looked so longly° on the maid, 155
   Perhaps you marked not what's the pith of all.°
Lucentio. O yes, I saw sweet beauty in her face,
   Such as the daughter of Agenor° had,
   That made great Jove to humble him to her hand
   When with his knees he kissed the Cretan strond.° 160
Tranio. Saw you no more? Marked you not how her sister
   Began to scold and raise up such a storm
   That mortal ears might hardly endure the din?
Lucentio. Tranio, I saw her coral lips to move
   And with her breath she did perfume the air. 165
   Sacred and sweet was all I saw in her.
Tranio. Nay, then, 'tis time to stir him from his trance.
   I pray, awake, sir. If you love the maid,
   Bend thoughts and wits to achieve her. Thus it stands:
   Her elder sister is so curst and shrewd° 170
   That till the father rid his hands of her,
   Master, your love must live a maid at home;
   And therefore has he closely mewed° her up,
   Because° she will not be annoyed with suitors.
Lucentio. Ah, Tranio, what a cruel father's he! 175
   But art thou not advised° he took some care
   To get her cunning° schoolmasters to instruct her?
Tranio. Ay, marry, am I, sir—and now 'tis plotted!°
Lucentio. I have it, Tranio!
Tranio.   Master, for° my hand,
   Both our inventions° meet and jump in one.° 180
Lucentio. Tell me thine first.
Tranio.   You will be schoolmaster
   And undertake the teaching of the maid.
   That's your device.

---

150 **rated** scolded   151 **so** to act thus   152 **Redime . . . minimo** ransom yourself, a captive, at the smallest possible price (from Terence's play *The Eunuch*, as quoted inaccurately in Lilly's *Latin Grammar*)   153 **Gramercies** many thanks   155 **longly** (1) longingly (2) interminably   156 **pith of all** heart of the matter   158 **daughter of Agenor** Europa, loved by Jupiter, who, in the form of a bull, carried her to Crete   160 **strond** strand, shore   170 **curst and shrewd** sharp-tempered and shrewish   173 **mewed** caged   174 **Because** so that   176 **advised** informed   177 **cunning** knowing   178 **'tis plotted** I've a scheme   179 **for** I bet   180 **inventions** schemes   180 **jump in one** are identical

Lucentio. It is. May it be done?
Tranio. Not possible, for who shall bear° your part
  And be in Padua here Vincentio's son? 185
  Keep house and ply his book, welcome his friends,
  Visit his countryman and banquet them?
Lucentio. Basta,° content thee, for I have it full.°
  We have not yet been seen in any house,
  Nor can we be distinguished by our faces 190
  For man or master. Then it follows thus:
  Thou shalt be master, Tranio, in my stead,
  Keep house and port° and servants as I should.
  I will some other be—some Florentine,
  Some Neapolitan, or meaner° man of Pisa. 195
  'Tis hatched and shall be so. Tranio, at once
  Uncase° thee, take my colored° hat and cloak.
  When Biondello comes he waits on thee,
  But I will charm° him first to keep his tongue.
Tranio. So had you need. 200
  In brief, sir, sith° it your pleasure is
  And I am tied° to be obedient—
  For so your father charged me at our parting;
  "Be serviceable to my son," quoth he,
  Although I think 'twas in another sense— 205
  I am content to be Lucentio
  Because so well I love Lucentio.
Lucentio. Tranio, be so, because Lucentio loves,
  And let me be a slave, t'achieve that maid
  Whose sudden sight hath thralled° my wounded eye. 210

Enter Biondello

Here comes the rogue. Sirrah, where have you been?
Biondello. Where have I been? Nay, how now, where are you?
  Master, has my fellow Tranio stol'n your clothes,
  Or you stol'n his, or both? Pray, what's the news?
Lucentio. Sirrah, come hither. 'Tis no time to jest, 215
  And therefore frame your manners to the time.°
  Your fellow Tranio, here, to save my life,
  Puts my apparel and my count'nance° on,
  And I for my escape have put on his,

---

184 **bear** act   188 **Basta** enough (Italian)   188 **full** fully (worked out)   193 **port** style   195 **meaner** of lower rank   197 **Uncase** undress   197 **colored** (masters dressed colorfully; servants wore dark blue)   199 **charm** exercise power over   201 **sith** since   202 **tied** obligated   210 **thralled** enslaved   216 **frame your manners to the time** adjust your conduct to the situation

For in a quarrel since I came ashore   220
I killed a man and fear I was descried.°
Wait you on him, I charge you, as becomes,
While I make way from hence to save my life.
You understand me?
Biondello.   I, sir? Ne'er a whit.
Lucentio. And not a jot of Tranio in your mouth.   225
  Tranio is changed into Lucentio.
Biondello. The better for him. Would I were so too.
Tranio. So could I, faith, boy, to have the next wish after,
  That Lucentio indeed had Baptista's youngest daughter.
  But, sirrah, not for my sake but your master's, I advise   230
  You use your manners discreetly in all kind of companies.
  When I am alone, why, then I am Tranio,
  But in all places else your master, Lucentio.
Lucentio. Tranio, let's go.
  One thing more rests,° that thyself execute°—   235
  To make one among these wooers. If thou ask me why,
  Sufficeth my reasons are both good and weighty.

                                                   Exeunt.

[SCENE II. *Padua. The street in front of Hortensio's house.*]

  Enter Petruchio° and his man Grumio.

Petruchio. Verona, for a while I take my leave
  To see my friends in Padua, but of all
  My best belovèd and approvèd friend,
  Hortensio, and I trow° this is his house.
  Here, sirrah Grumio, knock, I say.   5
Grumio. Knock, sir? Whom should I knock? Is there
  any man has rebused° your worship?
Petruchio. Villain, I say, knock me here° soundly.
Grumio. Knock you here, sir? Why, sir, what am I,
  sir, that I should knock you here, sir?   10
Petruchio. Villain, I say, knock me at this gate°
  And rap me well or I'll knock your knave's pate.°
Grumio. My master is grown quarrelsome. I should knock you first,
  And then I know after who comes by the worst.

---

218 **count'nance** demeanor   221 **descried** seen, recognized   235 **rests** remains   235 **execute** are to perform   I.ii.s.d. **Petruchio** (correct form *Petrucio*, with *c* pronounced *tch*)   4 **trow** think   7 **rebused** (Grumio means *abused*)   8 **knock me here** knock here for me (Grumio plays game of misunderstanding, taking "me here" as "my ear")   11 **gate** door   12 **pate** head

Petruchio. Will it not be? 15
    Faith, sirrah, and° you'll not knock, I'll ring° it;
    I'll try how you can *sol, fa,*° and sing it.

He wrings him by the ears.

Grumio. Help, masters, help! My master is mad.
Petruchio. Now, knock when I bid you, sirrah villain.

Enter Hortensio.

Hortensio. How now, what's the matter? My old friend Grumio, and my 20
    good friend Petruchio! How do you all at Verona?
Petruchio. Signior Hortensio, come you to part the fray?
    Con tutto il cuore ben trovato,° may I say.
Hortensio. Alla nostra casa ben venuto, molto honorato signior mio Petru-
    chio.°
    Rise, Grumio, rise. We will compound° this quarrel. 25
Grumio. Nay, 'tis no matter, sir, what he 'leges° in Latin.° If this be not a
    lawful cause for me to leave his service—look you, sir, he bid me knock
    him and rap him soundly, sir. Well, was it fit for a servant to use his
    master so, being perhaps, for aught I see, two-and-thirty, a peep out?°
    Whom would to God I had well knocked at first, 30
    Then had not Grumio come by the worst.
Petruchio. A senseless villain! Good Hortensio,
    I bade the rascal knock upon your gate
    And could not get him for my heart° to do it.
Grumio. Knock at the gate? O heavens! Spake you not these words plain, 35
    "Sirrah, knock me here, rap me here, knock me well, and knock me
    soundly"? And come you now with "knocking at the gate"?
Petruchio. Sirrah, be gone or talk not, I advise you.
Hortensio. Petruchio, patience, I am Grumio's pledge.
    Why, this's a heavy chance° 'twixt him and you, 40
    Your ancient, trusty, pleasant servant Grumio.
    And tell me now, sweet friend, what happy gale
    Blows you to Padua here from old Verona?
Petruchio. Such wind as scatters young men through the world
    To seek their fortunes farther than at home, 45

---

    16 **and** if   16 **ring** (pun on *wring*)   17 **sol, fa** go up and down the scales (possibly with puns on meanings now lost)   23 **Con . . . trovato** with all [my] heart well found (i.e., welcome)   24 **Alla . . . Petruchio** welcome to our house, my much honored Signior Petruchio   25 **compound** settle   26 **'leges** alleges   26 **Latin** (as if he were English, Grumio does not recognize Italian)   29 **two-and-thirty, a peep out** (1) an implication that Petruchio is aged (2) a term from cards, slang for "drunk" (*peep* is an old form of *pip,* a marking on a card)   34 **heart** life   40 **heavy chance** sad happening

Where small experience grows. But in a few,°
Signior Hortensio, thus it stands with me:
Antonio my father is deceased,
And I have thrust myself into this maze,°
Happily° to wive and thrive as best I may.   50
Crowns in my purse I have and goods at home
And so am come abroad to see the world.

Hortensio. Petruchio, shall I then come roundly° to thee
And wish thee to a shrewd ill-favored° wife?
Thou'ldst thank me but a little for my counsel—   55
And yet I'll promise thee she shall be rich,
And very rich—but thou'rt too much my friend,
And I'll not wish thee to her.

Petruchio. Signior Hortensio, 'twixt such friends as we
Few words suffice; and therefore if thou know   60
One rich enough to be Petruchio's wife—
As wealth is burthen° of my wooing dance—
Be she as foul° as was Florentius'° love,
As old as Sibyl,° and as curst and shrewd
As Socrates' Xanthippe° or a worse,   65
She moves me not, or not removes, at least,
Affection's edge in me, were she as rough
As are the swelling Adriatic seas.
I come to wive it wealthily in Padua;
If wealthily, then happily in Padua.   70

Grumio. Nay, look you, sir, he tells you flatly what his mind is. Why, give
him gold enough and marry him to a puppet or an aglet-baby° or an old
trot° with ne'er a tooth in her head, though she have as many diseases as
two-and-fifty horses. Why, nothing comes amiss so money comes withal.°

Hortensio. Petruchio, since we are stepped thus far in,   75
I will continue that° I broached in jest.
I can, Petruchio, help thee to a wife
With wealth enough and young and beauteous,
Brought up as best becomes a gentlewoman.
Her only fault—and that is faults enough—   80
Is that she is intolerable curst°
And shrewd and froward,° so beyond all measure

---

46 **few** i.e., words   49 **maze** traveling; uncertain course   50 **Happily** haply, perchance   53
come roundly talk frankly   54 **shrewd ill-favored** shrewish, poorly qualified   62 **burthen** burden
(musical accompaniment)   63 **foul** homely   63 **Florentius** knight in Gower's *Confessio Amantis*
(cf. Chaucer's Wife of Bath's Tale; knight marries hag who turns into beautiful girl)   64 **Sibyl**
prophetess in Greek and Roman myth   65 **Xanthippe** Socrates' wife, legendarily shrewish   72
aglet-baby small female figure forming metal tip of cord or lace (French *aiguillette*, point)   73 **trot**
hag   74 **withal** with it   73 **that** what   81 **intolerable curst** intolerably sharp-tempered   82
froward willful

That were my state° far worser than it is,
I would not wed her for a mine of gold.
Petruchio. Hortensio, peace. Thou know'st not gold's effect.   85
Tell me her father's name, and 'tis enough,
For I will board° her though she chide as loud
As thunder when the clouds in autumn crack.°
Hortensio. Her father is Baptista Minola,
An affable and courteous gentleman.   90
Her name is Katherina Minola,
Renowned in Padua for her scolding tongue.
Petruchio. I know her father though I know not her,
And he knew my deceasèd father well.
I will not sleep, Hortensio, till I see her,   95
And therefore let me be thus bold with you,
To give you over° at this first encounter
Unless you will accompany me thither.
Grumio. I pray you, sir, let him go while the humor° lasts. A° my word, and°
she knew him as well as I do, she would think scolding would do little   100
good° upon him. She may perhaps call him half a score knaves or so—
why, that's nothing. And he begin once, he'll rail in his rope-tricks.° I'll
tell you what, sir, and she stand° him but a little, he will throw a figure
in her face and so disfigure her with it that she shall have no more eyes
to see withal than a cat. You know him not, sir.   105
Hortensio. Tarry, Petruchio, I must go with thee,
For in Baptista's keep° my treasure is.
He hath the jewel of my life in hold,°
His youngest daughter, beautiful Bianca,
And her withholds from me and other more,   110
Suitors to her and rivals in my love,
Supposing it a thing impossible,
For° those defects I have before rehearsed,
That ever Katherina will be wooed.
Therefore this order° hath Baptista ta'en,   115
That none shall have access unto Bianca
Till Katherine the curst have got a husband.
Grumio. Katherine the curst!
A title for a maid of all titles the worst.

---

83 **state** estate, revenue   87 **board** naval term, with double sense: (1) accost (2) go on board
88 **crack** make explosive roars   97 **give you over** leave you   99 **humor** mood   99 **A** on   99 **and
if**   101 **do little good** have little effect   102 **rope-tricks** (1) Grumio's version of *rhetoric*, going
with *figure* just below (2) rascally conduct, deserving hanging (3) possible sexual innuendo, as in
following lines   103 **stand** withstand   107 **keep** heavily fortified inner tower of castle   108 **hold**
stronghold   113 **For** because of   115 **order** step

Hortensio. Now shall my friend Petruchio do me grace°   120
  And offer° me, disguised in sober robes,
  To old Baptista as a schoolmaster
  Well seen° in music, to instruct Bianca,
  That so I may, by this device, at least
  Have leave and leisure to make love to her   125
  And unsuspected court her by herself.

Enter Gremio, and Lucentio disguised [as a schoolmaster, Cambio].

Grumio. Here's no knavery! See, to beguile the old folks, how the young
  folks lay their heads together! Master, master, look about you. Who goes
  there, ha?
Hortensio. Peace, Grumio. It is the rival of my love.   130
  Petruchio, stand by awhile.   *[They eavesdrop.]*
Grumio. A proper stripling,° and an amorous!
Gremio. O, very well, I have perused the note.°
  Hark you, sir, I'll have them very fairly bound—
  All books of love, see that at any hand,°   135
  And see you read no other lectures° to her.
  You understand me. Over and beside
  Signior Baptista's liberality,
  I'll mend it with a largess.° Take your paper° too
  And let me have them° very well perfumed,   140
  For she is sweeter than perfume itself
  To whom they go to. What will you read to her?
Lucentio. Whate'er I read to her, I'll plead for you
  As for my patron, stand you so assured,
  As firmly as° yourself were still in place°—   145
  Yea, and perhaps with more successful words
  Than you unless you were a scholar, sir.
Gremio. O this learning, what a thing it is!
Grumio. *[Aside]* O this woodcock,° what an ass it is!
Petruchio. Peace, sirrah!   150
Hortensio. Grumio, mum! *[Coming forward]* God save you, Signior
  Gremio.
Gremio. And you are well met, Signior Hortensio.
  Trow° you whither I am going? To Baptista Minola.

---

120 **grace** a favor   121 **offer** present, introduce   123 **seen** trained   132 **proper stripling**
handsome youth (sarcastic comment on Gremio)   133 **note** memorandum (reading list for
Bianca)   135 **at any hand** in any case   136 **read no other lectures** assign no other readings   139
mend it with a largess add a gift of money to it   139 **paper** note (line 144)   140 **them** i.e., the
books   145 **as** as if you   145 **in place** present   149 **woodcock** bird easily trapped, so considered
silly   153 **Trow** know

I promised to inquire carefully
About a schoolmaster for the fair Bianca,   155
And, by good fortune, I have lighted well
On this young man—for° learning and behavior
Fit for her turn,° well read in poetry
And other books, good ones I warrant ye.
Hortensio. 'Tis well. And I have met a gentleman   160
 Hath promised me to help me to° another,
 A fine musician to instruct our mistress.
 So shall I no whit be behind in duty
 To fair Bianca, so beloved of me.
Gremio. Beloved of me, and that my deeds shall prove.   165
Grumio. [*Aside*] And that his bags° shall prove.
Hortensio. Gremio, 'tis now no time to vent° our love.
 Listen to me, and if you speak me fair,
 I'll tell you news indifferent° good for either.
 Here is a gentleman whom by chance I met,   170
 Upon agreement from us to his liking,°
 Will undertake° to woo curst Katherine,
 Yea, and to marry her if her dowry please.
Gremio. So said, so done, is well.
 Hortensio, have you told him all her faults?   175
Petruchio. I know she is an irksome, brawling scold;
 If that be all, masters, I hear no harm.
Gremio. No, say'st me so, friend? What countryman?
Petruchio. Born in Verona, old Antonio's son.
 My father dead, my fortune lives for me,   180
 And I do hope good days and long to see.
Gremio. O, sir, such a life with such a wife were strange.
 But if you have a stomach,° to't a° God's name;
 You shall have me assisting you in all.
 But will you woo this wildcat?
Petruchio.   Will I live?   185
Grumio. [*Aside*] Will he woo her? Ay, or I'll hang her.
Petruchio. Why came I hither but to that intent?
 Think you a little din can daunt mine ears?
 Have I not in my time heard lions roar?
 Have I not heard the sea, puffed up with winds,   190
 Rage like an anger boar chafèd with sweat?
 Have I not heard great ordnance° in the field

---

156 **for** in   157 **turn** situation (with unconscious bawdy pun on the sense of
"copulation")   161 **help me to** (1) find (2) become (Hortensio's jest)   166 **bags** i.e., of money
167 **vent** express   169 **indifferent** equally   171 **Upon . . . liking** if we agree to his terms (paying
costs)   172 **undertake** promise   183 **stomach** inclination   183 **a** in   192 **ordnance** cannon

And heaven's artillery thunder in the skies?
Have I not in a pitchèd battle heard
Loud 'larums,° neighing steeds, and trumpets' clang?   195
And do you tell me of a woman's tongue,
That gives not half so great a blow to hear
As will a chestnut in a farmer's fire?
Tush, tush, fear° boys with bugs.°
Grumio. [*Aside*]   For he fears none.
Gremio. Hortensio, hark.   200
  This gentleman is happily arrived,
My mind presumes, for his own good and ours.
Hortensio. I promised we would be contributors
  And bear his charge of° wooing, whatsoe'er.
Gremio. And so we will, provided that he win her.   205
Grumio. [*Aside*] I would I were as sure of a good dinner.

  Enter Tranio brave° [*as Lucentio*] *and Biondello.*

Tranio. Gentlemen, God save you. If I may be bold,
  Tell me, I beseech you, which is the readiest way
  To the house of Signior Baptista Minola?
Biondello. He that has the two fair daughters? Is't he you mean?   210
Tranio. Even he, Biondello.
Gremio. Hark you, sir. You mean not her to—
Tranio. Perhaps, him and her, sir. What have you to do?°
Petruchio. Not her that chides, sir, at any hand,° I pray.
Tranio. I love no chiders, sir. Biondello, let's away.   215
Lucentio. [*Aside*] Well begun, Tranio.
Hortensio.   Sir, a word ere you go.
  Are you a suitor to the maid you talk of, yea or no?
Tranio. And if I be, sir, is it any offense?
Gremio. No, if without more words you will get you hence.
Tranio. Why, sir, I pray, are not the streets as free   220
  For me as for you?
Gremio.   But so is not she.
Tranio. For what reason, I beseech you?
Gremio. For this reason, if you'll know,
  That she's the choice° love of Signior Gremio.
Hortensio. That she's the chosen of Signior Hortensio.   225
Tranio. Softly, my masters! If you be gentlemen,
  Do me this right; hear me with patience.

_____

195 **'larums** calls to arms, sudden attacks 199 **fear** frighten 199 **bugs** bugbears 204 **his charge of** the cost of his 206s.d. **brave** elegantly attired 213 **to do** i.e., to do with this 214 **at any hand** in any case 224 **choice** chosen

Baptista is a noble gentleman
To whom my father is not all unknown,
And were his daughter fairer than she is, 230
She may more suitors have, and me for one.
Fair Leda's daughter° had a thousand wooers;
Then well one more may fair Bianca have.
And so she shall. Lucentio shall make one,
Though Paris° came° in hope to speed° alone. 235
Gremio. What, this gentleman will out-talk us all.
Lucentio. Sir, give him head. I know he'll prove a jade.°
Petruchio. Hortensio, to what end are all these words?
Hortensio. Sir, let me be so bold as ask you,
Did you yet ever see Baptista's daughter? 240
Tranio. No, sir, but hear I do that he hath two,
The one as famous for a scolding tongue
As is the other for beauteous modesty.
Petruchio. Sir, sir, the first's for me; let her go by.
Gremio. Yea, leave that labor to great Hercules, 245
And let it be more than Alcides'° twelve.
Petruchio. Sir, understand you this of me in sooth:°
The youngest daughter, whom you hearken° for,
Her father keeps from all access of suitors
And will not promise her to any man 250
Until the elder sister first be wed.
The younger then is free, and not before.
Tranio. If it be so, sir, that you are the man
Must stead° us all, and me amongst the rest,
And if you break the ice and do this feat, 255
Achieve° the elder, set the younger free
For our access, whose hap° shall be to have her
Will not so graceless be to be ingrate.°
Hortensio. Sir, you say well, and well you do conceive,°
And since you do profess to be a suitor, 260
You must, as we do, gratify° this gentleman
To whom we all rest° generally beholding.°
Tranio. Sir, I shall not be slack, in sign whereof,
Please ye we may contrive° this afternoon
And quaff carouses° to our mistress' health 265

---

232 **Leda's daughter** Helen of Troy   235 **Paris** lover who took Helen to Troy (legendary cause of Trojan War)   235 **came** should come   235 **speed** succeed   237 **prove a jade** soon tire (cf. "jaded")   246 **Alcides** Hercules (after Alcaeus, a family ancestor)   247 **sooth** truth   248 **hearken** long   254 **stead** aid   256 **Achieve** succeed with   257 **whose hap** the man whose luck   258 **to be ingrate** as to be ungrateful   259 **conceive** put the case   261 **gratify** compensate   262 **rest** remain   262 **beholding** indebted   264 **contrive** pass   265 **quaff carouses** empty our cups

And do as adversaries° do in law,
Strive mightily but eat and drink as friends.
Grumio, Biondello. O excellent motion! Fellows, let's be gone.
Hortensio. The motion's good indeed, and be it so.
Petruchio, I shall be your *ben venuto*°.   *Exeunt.* 270

[ACT II
SCENE I. *In Baptista's house.*]

    Enter Kate and Bianca [with her hands tied].

Bianca. Good sister, wrong me not nor wrong yourself
    To make a bondmaid and a slave of me.
    That I disdain. But for these other gawds,°
    Unbind my hands, I'll pull them off myself,
    Yea, all my raiment, to my petticoat,   5
    Or what you will command me will I do,
    So well I know my duty to my elders.
Kate. Of all thy suitors, here I charge thee, tell
    Whom thou lov'st best. See thou dissemble not.
Bianca. Believe me, sister, of all the men alive   10
    I never yet beheld that special face
    Which I could fancy more than any other.
Kate. Minion,° thou liest. Is't not Hortensio?
Bianca. If you affect° him, sister, here I swear
    I'll plead for you myself but you shall have him.   15
Kate. O then, belike,° you fancy riches more:
    You will have Gremio to keep you fair.°
Bianca. Is it for him you do envy° me so?
    Nay, then you jest, and now I well perceive
    You have but jested with me all this while.   20
    I prithee, sister Kate, untie my hands.
Kate. If that be jest then all the rest was so.   *Strikes her.*

    Enter Baptista.

Baptista. Why, how now, dame, whence grows this insolence?
    Bianca, stand aside. Poor girl, she weeps.
    Go ply thy needle; meddle not with her.   25
    For shame, thou hilding° of a devilish spirit,

---

    266 **adversaries** attorneys   270 **ben venuto** welcome (i.e., host)   II.i.3 **gawds** adornments
13 **Minion** impudent creature   14 **affect** like   16 **belike** probably   17 **fair** in fine clothes   18
envy hate   26 **hilding** base wretch

Why dost thou wrong her that did ne'er wrong thee?
When did she cross thee with a bitter word?
Kate. Her silence flouts me and I'll be revenged.   *Flies after Bianca.*
Baptista. What, in my sight? Bianca, get thee in.   *Exit [Bianca].*   30
Kate. What, will you not suffer° me? Nay, now I see
  She is your treasure, she must have a husband;
  I must dance barefoot on her wedding day,°
  And, for your love to her, lead apes in hell.°
  Talk not to me; I will go sit and weep   35
  Till I can find occasion of revenge.   *[Exit.]*
Baptista. Was ever gentleman thus grieved as I?
  But who comes here?

*Enter Gremio, Lucentio in the habit of a mean° man [Cambio], Petruchio,
with [Hortensio as a music teacher, Litio, and] Tranio [as Lucentio], with
his boy [Biondello] bearing a lute and books.*

Gremio. Good morrow, neighbor Baptista.
Baptista. Good morrow, neighbor Gremio. God save you, gentlemen.   40
Petruchio. And you, good sir. Pray, have you not a daughter
  Called Katherina, fair and virtuous?
Baptista. I have a daughter, sir, called Katherina.
Gremio. [*Aside*] You are too blunt; go to it orderly.°
Petruchio. [*Aside*] You wrong me, Signior Gremio, give me leave.   45
  [*To Baptista*] I am a gentleman of Verona, sir,
  That, hearing of her beauty and her wit,
  Her affability and bashful modesty,
  Her wondrous qualities and mild behavior,
  Am bold to show myself a forward° guest   50
  Within your house, to make mine eye the witness
  Of that report which I so oft have heard.
  And, for an entrance to° my entertainment,°
  I do present you with a man of mine,   *[presenting Hortensio]*
  Cunning in music and the mathematics,   55
  To instruct her fully in those sciences,
  Whereof I know she is not ignorant.
  Accept of him, or else you do me wrong.
  His name is Litio, born in Mantua.

---

  31 **suffer** permit (i.e., to deal with you)   33 **dance . . . day** (expected of older maiden
sisters)   34 **lead apes in hell** (proverbial occupation of old maids)   38s.d. **mean** lower class   44
orderly gradually   50 **forward** eager   53 **entrance to** price of admission for   53 **entertainment**
reception

Baptista. Y'are welcome, sir, and he for your good sake.   60
   But for my daughter Katherine, this I know,
   She is not for your turn,° the more my grief.
Petruchio. I see you do not mean to part with her,
   Or else you like not of my company.
Baptista. Mistake me not; I speak but as I find.   65
   Whence are you, sir? What may I call your name?
Petruchio. Petruchio is my name, Antonio's son,
   A man well known throughout all Italy.
Baptista. I know him well. You are welcome for his sake.
Gremio. Saving° your tale, Petruchio, I pray,   70
   Let us, that are poor petitioners, speak too.
   Backare,° you are marvelous° forward.
Petruchio. O pardon me, Signior Gremio, I would fain° be doing.°
Gremio. I doubt it not, sir, but you will curse your wooing.
   Neighbor, this is a gift very grateful,° I am sure of it. To express the like   75
   kindness myself, that° have been more kindly beholding to you than any,
   freely give unto you this young scholar [*presenting Lucentio*] that hath
   been long studying at Rheims—as cunning in Greek, Latin, and other
   languages, as the other in music and mathematics. His name is Cambio.°
   Pray accept his service.   80
Baptista. A thousand thanks, Signior Gremio. Welcome, good Cambio. [*To
   Tranio*] But, gentle sir, methinks you walk like° a stranger. May I be so
   bold to know the cause of your coming?
Tranio. Pardon me, sir, the boldness is mine own,
   That,° being a stranger in this city here,   85
   Do make myself a suitor to your daughter,
   Unto Bianca, fair and virtuous.
   Nor is your firm resolve unknown to me
   In the preferment of° the eldest sister.
   This liberty is all that I request,   90
   That, upon knowledge of my parentage,
   I may have welcome 'mongst the rest that woo
   And free access and favor° as the rest.
   And, toward the education of your daughters
   I here bestow a simple instrument,°   95
   And this small packet of Greek and Latin books.
   If you accept them, then their worth is great.

---

   62 **turn** purpose (again, with bawdy pun)   70 **Saving** with all respect for   72 **Backare** back
(proverbial quasi-Latin)   72 **marvelous** very   73 **would fain** am eager to   73 **doing** (with a sexual
jest)   75 **grateful** worthy of gratitude   76 **myself, that** I myself, who   79 **Cambio** (Italian for
"exchange")   82 **walk like** have the bearing of   85 **That** who   89 **preferment of** giving priority
to   93 **favor** countenance, acceptance   95 **instrument** i.e., the lute

Baptista. [*Looking at books*] Lucentio is your name. Of whence, I pray?
Tranio. Of Pisa, sir, son to Vincentio.
Baptista. A mighty man of Pisa; by report   100
   I know him° well. You are very welcome, sir.
   [*To Hortensio*] Take you the lute, [*to Lucentio*] and you the set of books;
   You shall go see your pupils presently.°
   Holla, within!

Enter a Servant.

                    Sirrah, lead these gentlemen
To my daughters and tell them both   105
These are their tutors; bid them use them well.

   [*Exit Servant, with Lucentio, Hortensio, and Biondello following.*]

   We will go walk a little in the orchard°
   And then to dinner. You are passing° welcome,
   And so I pray you all to think yourselves.
Petruchio. Signior Baptista, my business asketh haste,   110
   And every day I cannot come to woo.
   You knew my father well, and in him me,
   Left solely heir to all his lands and goods,
   Which I have bettered rather than decreased.
   Then tell me, if I get your daughter's love   115
   What dowry shall I have with her to wife?
Baptista. After my death the one half of my lands,
   And in possession° twenty thousand crowns.
Petruchio. And, for that dowry, I'll assure her of
   Her widowhood,° be it that she survive me,   120
   In all my lands and leases whatsoever.
   Let specialties° be therefore drawn between us
   That covenants may be kept on either hand.
Baptista. Ay, when the special thing is well obtained,
   That is, her love, for that is all in all.   125
Petruchio. Why, that is nothing, for I tell you, father,
   I am as peremptory° as she proud-minded.
   And where two raging fires meet together
   They do consume the thing that feeds their fury.
   Though little fire grows great with little wind,   130
   Yet extreme gusts will blow out fire and all.

---

   101 **him** his name   102 **presently** at once   106 **orchard** garden   107 **passing** very   118
possession i.e., at the time of marriage   120 **widowhood** estate settled on a widow (Johnson)
122 **specialties** special contracts   127 **peremptory** resolved

So I to her, and so she yields to me,
For I am rough and woo not like a babe.
Baptista. Well mayst thou woo, and happy be thy speed!°
But be thou armed for some unhappy words.   135
Petruchio. Ay, to the proof,° as mountains are for winds
That shakes not, though they blow perpetually.

Enter Hortensio with his head broke.

Baptista. How now, my friend, why dost thou look so pale?
Hortensio. For fear, I promise you, if I look pale.
Baptista. What, will my daughter prove a good musician?   140
Hortensio. I think she'll sooner prove a soldier.
Iron may hold with her,° but never lutes.
Baptista. Why, then thou canst not break° her to the lute?
Hortensio. Why, no, for she hath broke the lute to me.
I did but tell her she mistook her frets°   145
And bowed° her hand to teach her fingering,
When, with a most impatient devilish spirit,
"Frets, call you these?" quoth she; "I'll fume with them."
And with that word she stroke° me on the head,
And through the instrument my pate made way.   150
And there I stood amazèd for a while
As on a pillory,° looking through the lute,
While she did call me rascal, fiddler,
And twangling Jack,° with twenty such vile terms
As° had she studied° to misuse me so.   155
Petruchio. Now, by the world, it is a lusty° wench!
I love her ten times more than e'er I did.
O how I long to have some chat with her!
Baptista. [*To Hortensio*] Well, go with me, and be not so discomfited.
Proceed in practice° with my younger daughter;   160
She's apt° to learn and thankful for good turns.
Signior Petruchio, will you go with us
Or shall I send my daughter Kate to you?

Exit [Baptista, with Gremio, Tranio, and Hortensio]. Manet Petruchio.°

Petruchio. I pray you do. I'll attend° her here
And woo her with some spirit when she comes.   165

---

134 **speed** progress   136 **to the proof** in tested steel armor   142 **hold with her** stand her
treatment   143 **break** train   145 **frets** ridges where strings are pressed   146 **bowed** bent   149
stroke stuck   152 **pillory** i.e., with a wooden collar (old structure for public punishment)   154
Jack (term of contempt)   155 **As** as if   155 **studied** prepared   156 **lusty** spirited   160 **practice**
instruction   161 **apt** disposed   163s.d. (is in the F position, which need not be changed; Petruchio
speaks to the departing Baptista)   164 **attend** wait for

Say that she rail,° why then I'll tell her plain
She sings as sweetly as a nightingale.
Say that she frown, I'll say she looks as clear
As morning roses newly washed with dew.   170
Say she be mute and will not speak a word,
Then I'll commend her volubility
And say she uttereth piercing eloquence.
If she do bid me pack,° I'll give her thanks
As though she bid me stay by her a week.   175
If she deny° to wed, I'll crave the day
When I shall ask the banns° and when be marrièd.
But here she comes, and now, Petruchio, speak.

Enter Kate.

Good morrow, Kate, for that's your name, I hear.
Kate. Well have you heard,° but something hard of hearing.   180
They call me Katherine that do talk of me.
Petruchio. You lie, in faith, for you are called plain Kate.
And bonny° Kate, and sometimes Kate the curst.
But, Kate, the prettiest Kate in Christendom,
Kate of Kate Hall,° my super-dainty Kate,   185
For dainties° are all Kates,° and therefore, Kate,
Take this of me, Kate of my consolation.
Hearing thy mildness praised in every town,
Thy virtues spoke of, and thy beauty sounded°—
Yet not so deeply as to thee belongs—   190
Myself am moved to woo thee for my wife.
Kate. Moved! In good time,° let him that moved you hither
Remove you hence. I knew you at the first
You were a movable.°
Petruchio.   Why, what's a movable?
Kate. A joint stool.°
Petruchio.   Thou hast hit it; come sit on me.   195
Kate. Asses are made to bear° and so are you.
Petruchio. Women are made to bear° and so are you.
Kate. No such jade° as you, if me you mean.

---

166 **rail** scold, scoff   174 **pack** go away   176 **deny** refuse   177 **banns** public announcement
in church of intent to marry   180 **heard** (pun: pronounced like *hard*)   183 **bonny** big, fine
(perhaps with pun on *bony*, the F spelling)   185 **Kate Hall** (possible topical reference; several
places have been proposed)   186 **dainties** delicacies   186 **Kates** i.e., *cates*, delicacies   189
sounded (1) measured (effect of *deeply*) (2) spoken of (pun)   192 **In good time** indeed   194
movable article of furniture (with pun)   195 **joint stool** stool made by a joiner (standard term of
disparagement)   196 **bear** carry   197 **bear** i.e., bear children (with second sexual meaning in
Petruchio's "I will not burden thee")   198 **jade** worn-out horse (Kate has now called him both
"ass" and "sorry horse")

Petruchio. Alas, good Kate, I will not burden thee,
    For, knowing thee to be but young and light—   200
Kate. Too light for such a swain° as you to catch
    And yet as heavy as my weight should be.
Petruchio. Should be!° Should—buzz!
Kate.   Well ta'en, and like a buzzard.°
Petruchio. O slow-winged turtle,° shall a buzzard take° thee?
Kate. Ay, for a turtle, as he takes a buzzard.°   205
Petruchio. Come, come, you wasp, i' faith you are too angry.
Kate. If I be waspish, best beware my sting.
Petruchio. My remedy is then to pluck it out.
Kate. Ay, if the fool could find it where it lies.
Petruchio. Who knows not where a wasp does wear his sting?   210
    In his tail.
Kate.   In his tongue.
Petruchio.   Whose tongue?
Kate. Yours, if you talk of tales,° and so farewell.
Petruchio. What, with my tongue in your tail? Nay, come again.
    Good Kate, I am a gentleman—
Kate.   That I'll try.

                                        She strikes him.
Petruchio. I swear I'll cuff you if you strike again.   215
Kate. So may you lose your arms:°
    If you strike me you are no gentleman,
    And if no gentleman, why then no arms.
Petruchio. A herald,° Kate? O, put me in thy books.°
Kate. What is your crest?° A coxcomb?°   220
Petruchio. A combless° cock, so° Kate will be my hen.
Kate. No cock of mine; you crow too like a craven.°
Petruchio. Nay, come, Kate, come, you must not look so sour.
Kate. It is my fashion when I see a crab.°
Petruchio. Why, here's no crab, and therefore look not sour.   225
Kate. There is, there is.
Petruchio. Then show it me.
Kate.   Had I a glass° I would.

---

    201 **swain** country boy   203 **be** (pun on *bee*; hence *buzz*, scandal, i.e., about "light"
woman)   203 **buzzard** hawk unteachable in falconry (hence idiot)   204 **turtle** turtledove, noted
for affectionateness   204 **take** capture (with pun, "mistake for," in next line)   205 **buzzard**
buzzing insect (hence "wasp")   212 **of tales** idle tales (leading to bawdy pun on *tail* = pudend)
216 **arms** (pun on "coat of arms")   219 **herald** one skilled in heraldry   219 **books** registers of
heraldry (with pun on "in your good books")   220 **crest** heraldic device   220 **coxcomb**
identifying feature of court Fool's cap; the cap itself   221 **combless** i.e., unwarlike   221 **so** if
222 **craven** defeated cock   224 **crab** crab apple   227 **glass** mirror

Petruchio. What, you mean my face?
Kate.   Well aimed of° such a young one.
Petruchio. Now, by Saint George, I am too young for you.
Kate. Yet you are withered.
Petruchio.   'Tis with cares.
Kate.   I care not.   230
Petruchio. Nay, hear you, Kate, in sooth° you scape° not so.
Kate. I chafe° you if I tarry. Let me go.
Petruchio. No, not a whit. I find you passing gentle.
   'Twas told me you were rough and coy° and sullen,
   And now I find report a very liar,   235
   For thou art pleasant, gamesome, passing courteous,
   But slow in speech, yet sweet as springtime flowers.
   Thou canst not frown, thou canst not look askance,
   Nor bite the lip as angry wenches will,
   Nor hast thou pleasure to be cross in talk,   240
   But thou with mildness entertain'st thy wooers,
   With gentle conference,° soft and affable.
   Why does the world report that Kate doth limp?
   O sland'rous world! Kate like the hazel-twig
   Is straight and slender, and as brown in hue   245
   As hazelnuts and sweeter than the kernels.
   O, let me see thee walk. Thou dost not halt.°
Kate. Go, fool, and whom thou keep'st° command.
Petruchio. Did ever Dian° so become a grove
   As Kate this chamber with her princely gait?   250
   O, be thou Dian and let her be Kate,
   And then let Kate be chaste and Dian sportful!°
Kate. Where did you study all this goodly speech?
Petruchio. It is extempore, from my mother-wit.°
Kate. A witty mother! Witless else° her son.   255
Petruchio. Am I not wise?
Kate.   Yes,° keep you warm.
Petruchio. Marry, so I mean, sweet Katherine, in thy bed.
   And therefore, setting all this chat aside,
   Thus in plain terms: your father hath consented
   That you shall be my wife, your dowry 'greed on,   260
   And will you, nill° you, I will marry you.
   Now, Kate, I am a husband for your turn,°

---

   228 **well aimed of** a good shot (in the dark)   231 **sooth** truth   231 **scape** escape   232 **chafe**
(1) annoy (2) warm up   234 **coy** offish   242 **conference** conversation   247 **halt** limp   248 **whom
thou keep'st** i.e., your servants   249 **Dian** Diana, goddess of hunting and virginity   252 **sportful**
(i.e., in the game of love)   254 **mother-wit** natural intelligence   255 **else** otherwise would be
256 **Yes** yes, just enough to (refers to a proverbial saying)   261 **nill** won't

For, by this light, whereby I see thy beauty—
Thy beauty that doth make me like thee well—
Thou must be married to no man but me.   265

Enter Baptista, Gremio, Tranio.

For I am he am born to tame you, Kate,
And bring you from a wild Kate° to a Kate
Conformable° as other household Kates.
Here comes your father. Never make denial;
I must and will have Katherine to my wife.   270
Baptista. Now, Signior Petruchio, how speed° you with my daughter?
Petruchio. How but well, sir? How but well?
It were impossible I should speed amiss.
Baptista. Why, how now, daughter Katherine, in your dumps?°
Kate. Call you me daughter? Now, I promise° you   275
You have showed a tender fatherly regard
To wish me wed to one half lunatic,
A madcap ruffian and a swearing Jack
That thinks with oaths to face° the matter out.
Petruchio. Father, 'tis thus: yourself and all the world   280
That talked of her have talked amiss of her.
If she be curst it is for policy,°
For she's not froward but modest as the dove.
She is not hot° but temperate as the morn;
For patience she will prove a second Grissel°   285
And Roman Lucrece° for her chastity.
And to conclude, we have 'greed so well together
That upon Sunday is the wedding day.
Kate. I'll see thee hanged on Sunday first.
Gremio. Hark, Petruchio, she says she'll see thee hanged first. 290
Tranio. Is this your speeding?° Nay, then good night our part!
Petruchio. Be patient, gentlemen, I choose her for myself.
If she and I be pleased, what's that to you?
'Tis bargained 'twixt us twain, being alone,
That she shall still be curst in company.   295
I tell you, 'tis incredible to believe
How much she loves me. O, the kindest Kate,
She hung about my neck, and kiss on kiss

---

262 **turn** advantage (with bawdy second meaning)   267 **wild Kate** (pun on "wildcat")   268 **Conformable** submissive   271 **speed** get on   274 **dumps** low spirits   275 **promise** tell   279 **face** brazen   282 **policy** tactics   284 **hot** intemperate   285 **Grissel** Griselda (patient wife in Chaucer's Clerk's Tale)   286 **Lucrece** (killed herself after Tarquin raped her)   291 **speeding** success

She vied° so fast, protesting oath on oath,
That in a twink° she won me to her love. 300
O, you are novices. 'Tis a world° to see
How tame, when men and women are alone,
A meacock° wretch can make the curstest shrew.
Give me thy hand, Kate. I will unto Venice
To buy apparel 'gainst° the wedding day. 305
Provide the feast, father, and bid the guests;
I will be sure my Katherine shall be fine.°
Baptista. I know not what to say, but give me your hands.
God send you joy, Petruchio! 'Tis a match.
Gremio, Tranio. Amen, say we. We will be witnesses. 310
Petruchio. Father, and wife, and gentlemen, adieu.
I will to Venice; Sunday comes apace.
We will have rings and things and fine array,
And, kiss me, Kate, "We will be married a Sunday."°
                              Exit Petruchio and Kate.
Gremio. Was ever match clapped° up so suddenly? 315
Baptista. Faith, gentlemen, now I play a merchant's part
And venture madly on a desperate mart.°
Tranio. 'Twas a commodity° lay fretting° by you;
'Twill bring you gain or perish on the seas.
Baptista. The gain I seek is quiet in the match. 320
Gremio. No doubt but he hath got a quiet catch.
But now, Baptista, to your younger daughter;
Now is the day we long have looked for.
I am your neighbor and was suitor first.
Tranio. And I am one that love Bianca more 325
Than words can witness or your thoughts can guess.
Gremio. Youngling, thou canst not love so dear as I.
Tranio. Graybeard, thy love doth freeze.
Gremio.   But thine doth fry.
Skipper,° stand back, 'tis age that nourisheth.
Tranio. But youth in ladies' eyes that flourisheth. 330
Baptista. Content you, gentlemen; I will compound° this strife.
'Tis deeds must win the prize, and he of both°
That can assure my daughter greatest dower°
Shall have my Bianca's love.
Say, Signior Gremio, what can you assure her? 335

---

299 **vied** made higher bids (card-playing terms), i.e., kissed more frequently 300 **twink** twinkling 301 **world** wonder 303 **meacock** timid 305 **'gainst** in preparation for 307 **fine** well dressed 314 **"We . . . Sunday"** (line from a ballad) 315 **clapped** fixed 317 **mart** "deal" 318 **commodity** (here a coarse term for women; see Partridge, *Shakespeare's Bawdy*) 318 **fretting** decaying in storage (with pun) 329 **Skipper** skipping (irresponsible) fellow 331 **compound** settle 332 **he of both** the one of you two 333 **dower** man's gift to bride

Gremio. First, as you know, my house within the city
  Is richly furnishèd with plate and gold,
  Basins and ewers to lave° her dainty hands;
  My hangings all of Tyrian° tapestry;
  In ivory coffers I have stuffed my crowns,   340
  In cypress chests my arras counterpoints,°
  Costly apparel, tents,° and canopies,
  Fine linen, Turkey cushions bossed° with pearl,
  Valance° of Venice gold in needlework,
  Pewter and brass, and all things that belongs   345
  To house or housekeeping. Then, at my farm
  I have a hundred milch-kine to the pail,°
  Six score fat oxen standing in my stalls
  And all things answerable to this portion.°
  Myself am struck° in years, I must confess,   350
  And if I die tomorrow, this is hers,
  If whilst I live she will be only mine.
Tranio. That "only" came well in. Sir, list to me.
  I am my father's heir and only son.
  If I may have your daughter to my wife,   355
  I'll leave her houses three or four as good,
  Within rich Pisa walls, as any one
  Old Signior Gremio has in Padua,
  Besides two thousands ducats° by the year
  Of° fruitful land, all which shall be her jointure.°   360
  What, have I pinched° you, Signior Gremio?
Gremio. [*Aside*] Two thousand ducats by the year of land!
  My land amounts not to so much in all.
  [*To others*] That she shall have besides an argosy°
  That now is lying in Marcellus' road.°   365
  What, have I choked you with an argosy?
Tranio. Gremio, 'tis known my father hath no less
  Than three great argosies, besides two galliasses°
  And twelve tight° galleys. These I will assure her
  And twice as much, whate'er thou off'rest next.   370
Gremio. Nay, I have off'red all, I have no more,
  And she can have no more than all I have.
  If you like me, she shall have me and mine.

---

338 **lave** wash   339 **Tyrian** purple   341 **arras counterpoints** counterpanes woven in Arras
342 **tents** bed tester (hanging cover)   343 **bossed** embroidered   344 **Valance** bed fringes and
drapes   347 **milch-kine to the pail** cows producing milk for human use   349 **answerable to this
portion** corresponding to this settlement (?)   350 **struck** advanced   359 **ducats** Venetian gold
coins   360 **Of** from   360 **jointure** settlement   361 **pinched** put the screws on   364 **argosy** largest
type of merchant ship   365 **Marcellus' road** Marseilles' harbor   368 **galliasses** large galleys   369
tight watertight

Tranio. Why, then the maid is mine from all the world
    By your firm promise. Gremio is outvied.°   375
Baptista. I must confess your offer is the best,
    And let your father make her the assurance,°
    She is your own; else you must pardon me.
    If you should die before him, where's her dower?
Tranio. That's but a cavil.° He is old, I young.   380
Gremio. And may not young men die as well as old?
Baptista. Well, gentlemen,
    I am thus resolved. On Sunday next, you know,
    My daughter Katherine is to be married.
    Now on the Sunday following shall Bianca   385
    Be bride to you if you make this assurance;
    If not, to Signior Gremio.
    And so I take my leave and thank you both.   *Exit.*
Gremio. Adieu, good neighbor. Now I fear thee not.
    Sirrah° young gamester,° your father were° a fool   390
    To give thee all and in his waning age
    Set foot under thy table.° Tut, a toy!°
    An old Italian fox is not so kind, my boy.   *Exit.*
Tranio. A vengeance on your crafty withered hide!
    Yet I have faced it with a card of ten.°   395
    'Tis in my head to do my master good.
    I see no reason but supposed Lucentio
    Must get° a father, called "supposed Vincentio,"
    And that's a wonder. Fathers commonly
    Do get their children, but in this case of wooing   400
    A child shall get a sire if I fail not of my cunning.   *Exit.*

[ACT III
SCENE I. *Padua. In Baptista's house.*]

    Enter Lucentio [as Cambio], Hortensio [as Litio], and Bianca.

Lucentio. Fiddler, forbear. You grow too forward, sir.
    Have you so soon forgot the entertainment°
    Her sister Katherine welcomed you withal?
Hortensio. But, wrangling pedant, this is
    The patroness of heavenly harmony.   5

---

   375 **outvied** outbid   377 **assurance** guarantee   380 **cavil** small point   390 **Sirrah** (used contemptuously)   390 **gamester** gambler   390 **were** would be   392 **Set foot under thy table** be dependent on you   392 **a toy** a joke   393 **faced it with a card of ten** bluffed with a ten-spot   398 **get** beget   III.i.2 **entertainment** i.e., "pillorying" him with the lute

Then give me leave to have prerogative,°
And when in music we have spent an hour,
Your lecture° shall have leisure for as much.

Lucentio. Preposterous° ass, that never read so far
   To know the cause why music was ordained!   10
   Was it not to refresh the mind of man
   After his studies or his usual pain?°
   Then give me leave to read° philosophy,
   And while I pause, serve in your harmony.

Hortensio. Sirrah, I will not bear these braves° of thine.   15

Bianca. Why, gentlemen, you do me double wrong
   To strive for that which resteth in my choice.
   I am no breeching° scholar° in the schools.
   I'll not be tied to hours nor 'pointed times,
   But learn my lessons as I please myself.   20
   And, to cut off all strife, here sit we down.
   [*To Hortensio*] Take you your instrument, play you the whiles;°
   His lecture will be done ere you have tuned.

Hortensio. You'll leave his lecture when I am in tune?

Lucentio. That will be never. Tune your instrument.   25

Bianca. Where left we last?

Lucentio. Here, madam:
   Hic ibat Simois, hic est Sigeia tellus,
     Hic steterat Priami regia celsa senis.°

Bianca. Conster° them.   30

Lucentio. *Hic ibat,* as I told you before, *Simois,* I am Lucentio, *hic est,* son
   unto Vincentio of Pisa, *Sigeia tellus,* disguised thus to get your love, *Hic*
   steterat, and that Lucentio that comes a wooing, *Priami,* is my man Tranio,
   regia, bearing my port,° *celsa senis,* that we might beguile the old pantaloon.°

Hortensio. [*Breaks in*] Madam, my instrument's in tune.   35

Bianca. Let's hear. O fie, the treble jars.°

Lucentio. Spit in the hole, man, and tune again.

Bianca. Now let me see if I can conster it. *Hic ibat Simois,* I know you not,
   hic est Sigeia tellus, I trust you not, *Hic steterat Priami,* take heed he hear
   us not, *regia,* presume not, *celsa senis,* despair not.   40

Hortensio. [*Breaks in again*] Madam, 'tis now in tune.

Lucentio.   All but the bass.

---

   6 **prerogative** priority   8 **lecture** instruction   9 **Preposterous** putting later things (*post-*) first
(*pre-*)   12 **pain** labor   13 **read** give a lesson in   15 **braves** defiances   18 **breeching** (1) in breeches
(young) (2) whippable   18 **scholar** schoolboy   22 **the whiles** meanwhile   28–29 **Hic . . . senis**
here flowed the Simois, here is the Sigeian (Trojan) land, here had stood old Priam's high palace
(Ovid)   30 **Conster** construe   34 **bearing my port** taking on my style   34 **pantaloon** Gremio   36
treble jars highest tone is off

Hortensio. The bass is right; 'tis the base knave that jars.
　[*Aside*] How fiery and forward our pedant is!
　Now, for my life, the knave doth court my love.
　Pedascule,° I'll watch you better yet.　　　　　　　45
Bianca. In time I may believe, yet I mistrust.
Lucentio. Mistrust it not, for sure Aeacides
　Was Ajax,° called so from his grandfather.
Bianca. I must believe my master; else, I promise you,
　I should be arguing still upon that doubt.　　　　　50
　But let it rest. Now, Litio, to you.
　Good master, take it not unkindly, pray,
　That I have been thus pleasant° with you both.
Hortensio. [*To Lucentio*] You may go walk and give me leave° a while.
　My lessons make no music in three parts.°　　　　55
Lucentio. Are you so formal, sir? [*Aside*] Well, I must wait
　And watch withal,° for but° I be deceived,
　Our fine musician groweth amorous.
Hortensio. Madam, before you touch the instrument,
　To learn the order of my fingering,　　　　　　60
　I must begin with rudiments of art
　To teach you gamut° in a briefer sort,
　More pleasant, pithy, and effectual,
　Than hath been taught by any of my trade;
　And there it is in writing, fairly drawn.　　　　65
Bianca. Why, I am past my gamut long ago.
Hortensio. Yet read the gamut of Hortensio.
Bianca. [*Reads*]
　Gamut I am, the ground° of all accord.°
　　A re, to plead Hortensio's passion:
　B mi, Bianca, take him for thy lord,　　　　　70
　　C fa ut, that loves with all affection;
　D sol re, one clef, two notes have I:
　　E la mi, show pity or I die.

Call you this gamut? Tut, I like it not.
Old fashions please me best; I am not so nice°　　75
To change true rules for odd inventions.

Enter a Messenger.

---

45 **Pedascule** little pedant (disparaging quasi-Latin)　47–48 **Aeacides/Was Ajax** Ajax, Greek warrior at Troy, was grandson of Aeacus (Lucentio comments on next passage in Ovid)　53 **pleasant** merry　54 **give me leave** leave me alone　55 **in three parts** for three voices　57 **withal** besides　57 **but** unless　62 **gamut** the scale　68 **ground** beginning, first note　68 **accord** harmony　75 **nice** whimsical

Messenger. Mistress, your father prays you leave your books
    And help to dress your sister's chamber up.
    You know tomorrow is the wedding day.
Bianca. Farewell, sweet masters both, I must be gone.   80
                    [Exeunt Bianca and Messenger.]
Lucentio. Faith, mistress, then I have no cause to stay.
                                [Exit.]
Hortensio. But I have cause to pry into this pedant.
    Methinks he looks as though he were in love.
    Yet if thy thoughts, Bianca, be so humble
    To cast thy wand'ring eyes on every stale,°   85
    Seize thee that list.° If once I find thee ranging,°
    Hortensio will be quit with thee by changing.°   *Exit.*

[**SCENE II.** *Padua. The street in front of Baptista's house.*]

Enter Baptista, Gremio, Tranio [as Lucentio], Kate, Bianca, [Lucentio as Cambio] and others, Attendants.

Baptista. [*To Tranio*] Signior Lucentio, this is the 'pointed day
    That Katherine and Petruchio should be marrièd,
    And yet we hear not of our son-in-law.
    What will be said? What mockery will it be
    To want° the bridegroom when the priest attends   5
    To speak the ceremonial rites of marriage!
    What says Lucentio to this shame of ours?
Kate. No shame but mine. I must, forsooth, be forced
    To give my hand opposed against my heart
    Unto a mad-brain rudesby,° full of spleen,°   10
    Who wooed in haste and means to wed at leisure.
    I told you, I, he was a frantic fool,
    Hiding his bitter jests in blunt behavior.
    And to be noted for° a merry man,
    He'll woo a thousand, 'point the day of marriage,   15
    Make friends, invite,° and proclaim the banns,
    Yet never means to wed where he hath wooed.
    Now must the world point at poor Katherine
    And say, "Lo, there is mad Petruchio's wife,
    If it would please him come and marry her."   20

---

85 **stale** lure (as in hunting) 86 **Seize thee that list** let him who likes capture you 86 **ranging** going astray 87 **changing** i.e., sweethearts III.ii.5 **want** be without 10 **rudesby** uncouth fellow 10 **spleen** caprice 14 **noted for** reputed 16 **Make friends, invite** (some editors emend to "Make feast, invite friends")

Tranio. Patience, good Katherine, and Baptista too.
  Upon my life, Petruchio means but well,
  Whatever fortune stays° him from his word.
  Though he be blunt, I know him passing° wise;
  Though he be merry, yet withal he's honest.   25
Kate. Would Katherine had never seen him though!
                    Exit weeping [followed by Bianca and others].
Baptista. Go, girl, I cannot blame thee now to weep.
  For such an injury would vex a very saint,
  Much more a shrew of thy impatient humor.°

Enter Biondello.

Biondello. Master, Master, news! And such old° news as you never heard of!   30
Baptista. Is it new and old too? How may that be?
Biondello. Why, is it not news to hear of Petruchio's coming?
Baptista. Is he come?
Biondello. Why, no, sir.
Baptista. What then?   35
Biondello. He is coming.
Baptista. When will he be here?
Biondello. When he stands where I am and sees you there.
Tranio. But, say, what to thine old news?
Biondello. Why, Petruchio is coming in a new hat and an old jerkin;° a pair   40
  of old breeches thrice turned;° a pair of boots that have been candle-cases,°
  one buckled, another laced; an old rusty sword ta'en out of the town
  armory, with a broken hilt and chapeless;° with two broken points;° hish-
  orse hipped° (with an old mothy saddle and stirrups of no kindred),°
  besides, possessed with the glanders° and like to mose in the chine;° trou- 45
  bled with the lampass,° infected with the fashions,° full of windgalls,° sped
  with spavins,° rayed° with the yellows,° past cure of the fives,° stark spoiled
  with the staggers,° begnawn with the bots,° swayed° in the back, and
  shoulder-shotten;° near-legged before,° and with a half-cheeked° bit and

---

23 **stays** keeps   24 **passing** very   29 **humor** temper   30 **old** strange   40 **jerkin** short outer
coat   41 **turned** i.e., inside out (to conceal wear and tear)   41 **candle-cases** worn-out boots used
to keep candle ends in   43 **chapeless** lacking the metal mounting at end of scabbard   43 **points**
laces to fasten hose to garment above   44 **hipped** with dislocated hip   44 **of no kindred** not
matching   46 **glanders** bacterial disease affecting mouth and nose   46 **mose in the chine** (1)
glanders (2) nasal discharge   46 **lampass** swollen mouth   46 **fashions** tumors (related to
glanders)   46 **windgalls** swellings on lower leg   47 **spavins** swellings on upper hind leg   47 **rayed**
soiled   47 **yellows** jaundice   47 **fives** vives: swelling of submaxillary glands   48 **staggers** nervous
disorder causing loss of balance   48 **begnawn with the bots** gnawed by parasitic worms (larvae of
the botfly)   48 **swayed** sagging   49 **shoulder-shotten** with dislocated shoulder   49 **near-legged
before** with forefeet knocking together   49 **half-cheeked** wrongly adjusted to bridle and affording
less control

a head-stall° of sheep's leather,° which, being restrained° to keep him from   50
stumbling, hath been often burst and now repaired with knots; one girth°
six times pieced,° and a woman's crupper° of velure,° which hath two
letters for her name fairly set down in studs,° and here and there pieced
with packthread.°
Baptista. Who comes with him?   55
Biondello. O sir, his lackey, for all the world caparisoned° like the horse:
with a linen stock° on one leg and a kersey boot-hose° on the other, gart'red
with a red and blue list;° an old hat, and the humor of forty fancies°
pricked° in't for a feather—a monster, a very monster in apparel, and not
like a Christian footboy° or a gentleman's lackey.   60
Tranio. 'Tis some odd humor° pricks° him to this fashion,
    Yet oftentimes he goes but mean-appareled.
Baptista. I am glad he's come, howsoe'er he comes.
Biondello. Why, sir, he comes not.
Baptista. Didst thou not say he comes?   65
Biondello. Who? That Petruchio came?
Baptista. Ay, that Petruchio came.
Biondello. No, sir, I say his horse comes, with him on his back.
Baptista. Why, that's all one.°
Biondello. [Sings]

            Nay, by Saint Jamy,   70
            I hold° you a penny,
            A horse and a man
            Is more than one
            And yet not many.

    Enter Petruchio and Grumio.

Petruchio. Come, where be these gallants?° Who's at home?   75
Baptista. You are welcome, sir.
Petruchio.   And yet I come not well.
Baptista. And yet you halt° not.

---

    50 **head-stall** part of bridle which surrounds head   50 **sheep's leather** (weaker than pigskin)
50 **restrained** pulled back   51 **girth** saddle strap under belly   52 **pieced** patched   52 **crupper**
leather loop under horse's tail to help steady saddle   52 **velure** velvet   53 **studs** largeheaded nails
of brass or silver   53–54 **pieced with packthread** tied together with coarse thread   56
caparisoned outfitted   57 **stock** stocking   57 **kersey boot-hose** coarse stocking worn with riding
boot   58 **list** strip of discarded border-cloth   58 **humor of forty fancies** fanciful decoration (in
place of feather)   59 **pricked** pinned   60 **footboy** page in livery   61 **humor** mood, fancy   62
pricks incites   69 **all one** the same thing   71 **hold** bet   75 **gallants** men of fashion   77 **halt** limp
(pun on *come* meaning "walk")

Tranio.   Not so well appareled
As I wish you were.
Petruchio. Were it better,° I should rush in thus.
But where is Kate? Where is my lovely bride?   80
How does my father? Gentles,° methinks you frown.
And wherefore gaze this goodly company
As if they saw some wondrous monument,°
Some comet or unusual prodigy?°
Baptista. Why, sir, you know this is your wedding day.   85
First were we sad, fearing you would not come,
Now sadder that you come so unprovided.°
Fie, doff this habit,° shame to your estate,°
An eyesore to our solemn festival.
Tranio. And tell us what occasion of import°   90
Hath all so long detained you from your wife
And sent you hither so unlike yourself.
Petruchio. Tedious it were to tell and harsh to hear.
Sufficeth, I am come to keep my word
Though in some part enforcèd to digress,°   95
Which, at more leisure, I will so excuse
As you shall well be satisfied with all.
But where is Kate? I stay too long from her.
The morning wears, 'tis time we were at church.
Tranio. See not your bride in these unreverent robes.   100
Go to my chamber; put on clothes of mine.
Petruchio. Not I, believe me; thus I'll visit her.
Baptista. But thus, I trust, you will not marry her.
Petruchio. Good sooth,° even thus; therefore ha' done with words.
To me she's married, not unto my clothes.   105
Could I repair what she will wear° in me
As I can change these poor accoutrements,
'Twere well for Kate and better for myself.
But what a fool am I to chat with you
When I should bid good morrow to my bride   110
And seal the title° with a lovely° kiss.   *Exit [with Grumio].*
Tranio. He hath some meaning in his mad attire.
We will persuade him, be it possible,
To put on better ere he go to church.
Baptista. I'll after him and see the event° of this.   115
                          Exit [with Gremio and Attendants].

---

79 **Were it better** even if I were better   81 **Gentles** sirs   83 **monument** warning sign   84 **prodigy** marvel   87 **unprovided** ill–outfitted   88 **habit** costume   88 **estate** status   90 **of import** important   95 **enforcèd to digress** forced to depart (perhaps from his plan to "buy apparel 'gainst the wedding day"   104 **Good sooth** yes indeed   106 **wear** wear out   111 **title** i.e., as of ownership   111 **lovely** loving   115 **event** upshot, outcome

Tranio. But to her love concerneth us to add
  Her father's liking, which to bring to pass,
  As I before imparted to your worship,
  I am to get a man—whate'er he be
  It skills° not much, we'll fit him to our turn°— 120
  And he shall be Vincentio of Pisa,
  And make assurance° here in Padua
  Of greater sums than I have promisèd.
  So shall you quietly enjoy your hope
  And marry sweet Bianca with consent. 125
Lucentio. Were it not that my fellow schoolmaster
  Doth watch Bianca's steps so narrowly,
  'Twere good, methinks, to steal our marriage,°
  Which once performed, let all the world say no,
  I'll keep mine own despite of all the world. 130
Tranio. That by degrees we mean to look into
  And watch our vantage° in this business.
  We'll overreach° the graybeard, Gremio,
  The narrow-prying father, Minola,
  The quaint° musician, amorous Litio— 135
  All for my master's sake, Lucentio.

  Enter Gremio.

  Signior Gremio, came you from the church?
Gremio. As willingly as e'er I came from school.
Tranio. And is the bride and bridegroom coming home?
Gremio. A bridegroom say you? 'Tis a groom° indeed, 140
  A grumbling groom, and that the girl shall find.
Tranio. Curster than she? Why, 'tis impossible.
Gremio. Why, he's a devil, a devil, a very fiend.
Tranio. Why, she's a devil, a devil, the devil's dam.°
Gremio. Tut, she's a lamb, a dove, a fool to° him. 145
  I'll tell you, Sir Lucentio, when the priest
  Should ask, if Katherine should be his wife,
  "Ay, by goggs woones!"° quoth he and swore so loud
  That, all amazed, the priest let fall the book,
  And as he stooped again to take it up, 150
  This mad-brained bridegroom took° him such a cuff

---

120 **skills** matters   120 **turn** purpose   122 **assurance** guarantee   128 **steal our marriage** elope   132 **vantage** advantage   133 **overreach** get the better of   135 **quaint** artful   140 **groom** menial (i.e., coarse fellow)   144 **dam** mother   145 **fool to** harmless person compared with   148 **goggs woones** by God's wounds (a common oath)   151 **took** gave

That down fell priest and book and book and priest.
"Now, take them up," quoth he, "if any list."°
Tranio. What said the wench when he rose again?
Gremio. Trembled and shook, for why° he stamped and swore   155
  As if the vicar meant to cozen° him.
  But after many ceremonies done
  He calls for wine. "A health!" quoth he as if
  He had been aboard, carousing° to his mates
  After a storm; quaffed off the muscadel°   160
  And threw the sops° all in the sexton's face,
  Having no other reason
  But that his beard grew thin and hungerly,°
  And seemed to ask him sops as he was drinking.
  This done, he took the bride about the neck   165
  And kissed her lips with such a clamorous smack
  That at the parting all the church did echo,
  And I, seeing this, came thence for very shame.
  And after me, I know, the rout° is coming.
  Such a mad marriage never was before.   170
  Hark, hark, I hear the minstrels play.   *Music plays.*

Enter Petruchio, Kate, Bianca, Hortensio [as Litio], Baptista [with Grumio and others].

Petruchio. Gentlemen and friends, I thank you for your pains.
  I know you think to dine with me today
  And have prepared great store of wedding cheer,°
  But so it is, my haste doth call me hence   175
  And therefore here I mean to take my leave.
Baptista. Is't possible you will away tonight?
Petruchio. I must away today, before night come.
  Make it no wonder;° if you knew my business,
  You would entreat me rather go than stay.   180
  And, honest company, I thank you all
  That have beheld me give away myself
  To this most patient, sweet, and virtuous wife.
  Dine with my father, drink a health to me,
  For I must hence, and farewell to you all.   185
Tranio. Let us entreat you stay till after dinner.

---

153 **list** pleases to   155 **for why** because   151 **cozen** cheat   159 **carousing** calling "Bottoms up"   160 **muscadel** sweet wine, conventionally drunk after marriage service   161 **sops** pieces of cake soaked in wine; dregs   163 **hungerly** as if poorly nourished   169 **rout** crowd   174 **cheer** food and drink   179 **Make it no wonder** don't be surprised

Petruchio. It may not be.
Gremio.   Let me entreat you.
Petruchio. It cannot be.
Kate.   Let me entreat you.
Petruchio. I am content.
Kate.   Are you content to stay?
Petruchio. I am content you shall entreat me stay,   190
    But yet not stay, entreat me how you can.
Kate. Now if you love me, stay.
Petruchio.   Grumio, my horse!°
Grumio. Ay, sir, they be ready; the oats have eaten the horses.°
Kate. Nay then,
    Do what thou canst, I will not go today,   195
    No, nor tomorrow, not till I please myself.
    The door is open, sir, there lies your way.
    You may be jogging whiles your boots are green;°
    For me, I'll not be gone till I please myself.
    'Tis like you'll prove a jolly° surly groom,   200
    That take it on you° at the first so roundly.°
Petruchio. O Kate, content thee; prithee,° be not angry.
Kate. I will be angry. What hast thou to do?°
    Father, be quiet; he shall stay my leisure.°
Gremio. Ay, marry, sir, now it begins to work.   205
Kate. Gentlemen, forward to the bridal dinner.
    I see a woman may be made a fool
    If she had not a spirit to resist.
Petruchio. They shall go forward, Kate, at thy command.
    Obey the bride, you that attend on her.   210
    Go to the feast, revel and domineer,°
    Carouse full measure to her maidenhead,
    Be mad and merry, or go hang yourselves.
    But for my bonny Kate, she must with me.
    Nay, look not big,° nor stamp, nor stare,° nor fret;   215
    I will be master of what is mine own.
    She is my goods, my chattels; she is my house,
    My household stuff, my field, my barn,
    My horse, my ox, my ass, my anything,°
    And here she stands. Touch her whoever dare,   220

---

192 **horse** horses   193 **oats have eaten the horses** (1) a slip of the tongue or (2) an ironic jest   198 **You . . . green** (proverbial way of suggesting departure to a guest, *green* = new, cleaned)   200 **jolly** domineering   201 **take it on you** do as you please   201 **roundly** roughly   202 **prithee** I pray thee   203 **What hast thou to do** what do you have to do with it   204 **stay my leisure** await my willingness   211 **domineer** cut up in a lordly fashion   215 **big** challenging   215 **stare** swagger   219 **My horse . . . anything** (echoing Tenth Commandment)

I'll bring mine action° on the proudest he
That stops my way in Padua. Grumio,
Draw forth thy weapon, we are beset with thieves.
Rescue thy mistress, if thou be a man.
Fear not, sweet wench; they shall not touch thee, Kate. 225
I'll buckler° thee against a million.

Exeunt Petruchio, Kate [and Grumio].

Baptista. Nay, let them go, a couple of quiet ones.
Gremio. Went they not quickly, I should die with laughing.
Tranio. Of all mad matches never was the like.
Lucentio. Mistress, what's your opinion of your sister? 230
Bianca. That being mad herself, she's madly mated.
Gremio. I warrant him, Petruchio is Kated.
Baptista. Neighbors and friends, though bride and bridegroom wants°
For to supply the places at the table,
You know there wants no junkets° at the feast. 235
[*To Tranio*] Lucentio, you shall supply the bridegroom's place,
And let Bianca take her sister's room.
Tranio. Shall sweet Bianca practice how to bride it?
Baptista. She shall, Lucentio. Come, gentlemen, let's go. *Exeunt.*

[ACT IV
SCENE I. *Petruchio's country house.*]

Enter Grumio.

Grumio. Fie, fie, on all tired jades,° on all mad masters, and all foul ways!°
Was ever man so beaten? Was ever man so rayed?° Was ever man so
weary? I am sent before to make a fire, and they are coming after to warm
them. Now were not I a little pot and soon hot,° my very lips might freeze
to my teeth, my tongue to the roof of my mouth, my heart in my belly, 5
ere I should come by a fire to thaw me. But I with blowing the fire shall
warm myself, for considering the weather, a taller° man than I will take
cold. Holla, ho, Curtis!

Enter Curtis [a Servant].

Curtis. Who is that calls so coldly?
Grumio. A piece of ice. If thou doubt it, thou mayst slide from my shoulder
to my heel with no greater a run° but my head and my neck. A fire, good 10
Curtis.

---

221 **action** lawsuit   226 **buckler** shield   233 **wants** are lacking   235 **junkets** sweetmeats,
confections   IV.i.1 **jades** worthless horses   1 **foul ways** bad roads   2 **rayed** befouled   4 **little pot
and soon hot** (proverbial for small person of short temper)   7 **taller** sturdier (with allusion to
"little pot")   10 **run** running start

Curtis. Is my master and his wife coming, Grumio?

Grumio. O ay, Curtis, ay, and therefore fire, fire; cast on no water.°

Curtis. Is she so hot a shrew as she's reported?

Grumio. She was, good Curtis, before this frost, but thou know'st winter
tames man, woman, and beast; for it hath tamed my old master, and my   15
new mistress, and myself, fellow Curtis.

Curtis. Away, you three-inch° fool! I am no beast.

Grumio. Am I but three inches? Why, thy horn° is a foot, and so long am I
at the least. But wilt thou make a fire, or shall I complain on thee to our
mistress, whose hand—she being now at hand—thou shalt soon feel, to   20
thy cold comfort, for being slow in thy hot office?°

Curtis. I prithee, good Grumio, tell me, how goes the world?

Grumio. A cold world, Curtis, in every office but thine, and therefore, fire.
Do thy duty and have thy duty,° for my master and mistress are almost
frozen to death.

Curtis. There's fire ready, and therefore, good Grumio, the news.   25

Grumio. Why, "Jack boy, ho boy!"° and as much news as wilt thou.

Curtis. Come, you are so full of cony-catching.°

Grumio. Why therefore fire, for I have caught extreme cold. Where's the
cook? Is supper ready, the house trimmed, rushes strewed,° cobwebs swept,
the servingmen in their new fustian,° the white stockings, and every officer°   30
his wedding garment on? Be the jacks° fair within, the jills° fair without,
the carpets° laid and everything in order?

Curtis. All ready, and therefore, I pray thee, news.

Grumio. First, know my horse is tired, my master and mistress fall'n out.

Curtis. How?

Grumio. Out of their saddles into the dirt—and thereby hangs a tale.   35

Curtis. Let's ha't, good Grumio.

Grumio. Lend thine ear.

Curtis. Here.

Grumio. There.   [*Strikes him.*]

Curtis. This 'tis to feel a tale, not to hear a tale.   40

Grumio. And therefore 'tis called a sensible° tale, and this cuff was but to
knock at your ear and beseech list'ning. Now I begin. *Imprimis,*° we came
down a foul° hill, my master riding behind my mistress—

---

12 **cast on no water** (alters "Cast on more water" in a well-known round)   17 **three-inch** (1)
another allusion to Grumio's small stature (2) a phallic jest, the first of several   18 **horn** (symbol
of cuckold)   21 **hot office** job of making a fire   24 **thy duty** what is due thee   26 **"Jack boy, ho
boy!"** (from another round or catch)   27 **cony-catching** rabbit-catching (i.e., tricking simpletons;
with pun on *catch*, the song)   29 **strewed** i.e., on floor (for special occasion)   30 **fustian** coarse
cloth (cotton and flax)   30 **officer** servant   31 **jacks** (1) menservants (2) half-pint leather drinking
cups   31 **jills** (1) maids (2) gill-size metal drinking cups   32 **carpets** table covers   41 **sensible** (1)
rational (2) "feel"-able   42 **Imprimis** first   43 **foul** muddy

Curtis. Both of° one horse?

Grumio. What's that to thee? 45

Curits. Why, a horse.

Grumio. Tell thou the tale. But hadst thou not crossed° me thou shouldst have heard how her horse fell and she under her horse. Thou shouldst have heard in how miry a place, how she was bemoiled,° how he left her with the horse upon her, how he beat me because her horse stumbled, 50 how she waded through the dirt to pluck him off me; how he swore, how she prayed that never prayed before; how I cried, how the horses ran away, how her bridle was burst, how I lost my crupper, with many things of worthy memory which now shall die in oblivion, and thou return unexperienced° to thy grave.

Curtis. By this reck'ning° he is more shrew than she. 55

Grumio. Ay, and that thou and the proudest of you all shall find when he comes home. But what° talk I of this? Call forth Nathaniel, Joseph, Nicholas, Philip, Walter, Sugarsop, and the rest. Let their heads be slickly° combed, their blue° coats brushed, and their garters of an indifferent° knit. Let them curtsy with their left legs and not presume to touch a hair of my 60 master's horsetail till they kiss their hands. Are they all ready?

Curtis. They are.

Grumio. Call them forth.

Curtis. Do you hear, ho? You must meet my master to countenance° my mistress.

Grumio. Why, she hath a face of her own. 65

Curtis. Who knows not that?

Grumio. Thou, it seems, that calls for company to countenance her.

Curtis. I call them forth to credit° her.

Grumio. Why, she comes to borrow nothing of them.

Enter four or five Servingmen.

Nathaniel. Welcome home, Grumio! 70

Philip. How now, Grumio?

Joseph. What, Grumio!

Nicholas. Fellow Grumio!

Nathaniel. How now, old lad!

Grumio. Welcome, you; how now, you; what, you; fellow, you; and thus 75 much for greeting. Now, my spruce companions, is all ready and all things neat?

Nathaniel. All things is ready. How near is our master?

---

44 **of** on 47 **crossed** interrupted 49 **bemoiled** muddied 54 **unexperienced** uninformed 55 **reck'ning** account 57 **what** why 58 **slickly** smoothly 59 **blue** (usual color of servants' clothing) 59 **indifferent** matching (?) appropriate (?) 64 **countenance** show respect to (with puns following) 68 **credit** honor

Grumio. E'en at hand, alighted by this,° and therefore be not—Cock's°
   passion, silence! I hear my master.

Enter Petruchio and Kate.

Petruchio. Where be these knaves? What, no man at door
   To hold my stirrup nor to take my horse?   80
   Where is Nathaniel, Gregory, Philip?
All Servingmen. Here, here, sir, here, sir.
Petruchio. Here, sir, here, sir, here, sir, here, sir!
   You loggerheaded° and unpolished grooms!
   What, no attendance? No regard? No duty?   85
   Where is the foolish knave I sent before?
Grumio. Here, sir, as foolish as I was before.
Petruchio. You peasant swain!° You whoreson° malt-horse drudge!°
   Did I not bid thee meet me in the park°
   And bring along these rascal knaves with thee?   90
Grumio. Nathaniel's coat, sir, was not fully made
   And Gabrel's pumps were all unpinked° i'th' heel.
   There was no link° to color Peter's hat,
   And Walter's dagger was not come from sheathing.°
   There were none fine but Adam, Rafe, and Gregory;   95
   The rest were ragged, old, and beggarly.
   Yet, as they are, here are they come to meet you.
Petruchio. Go, rascals, go, and fetch my supper in.   *Exeunt Servants.*
   [*Sings*] "Where is the life that late I led?"°
   Where are those°—Sit down, Kate, and welcome.   100
   Soud,° soud, soud, soud!

Enter Servants with supper.

   Why, when,° I say?—Nay, good sweet Kate, be merry.—
   Off with my boots, you rogues, you villains! When?
   [*Sings*] "It was the friar of orders gray,
   As he forth walkèd on his way"°—   105
   Out, you rogue, you pluck my foot awry!
   Take that, and mend° the plucking of the other.   [*Strikes him.*]
   Be merry, Kate. Some water here! What ho!

---

78 **this** now   78 **Cock's** God's (i.e., Christ's)   84 **loggerheaded** blockheaded   88 **swain**
bumpkin   88 **whoreson** bastardly   88 **malt-horse drudge** slow horse on brewery treadmill   89
park country-house grounds   92 **unpinked** lacking embellishment made by pinking (making small
holes in leather)   93 **link** torch, providing blacking   94 **sheathing** repairing scabbard   99 "Where
. . . led?" (from an old ballad)   100 **those** servants   101 **Soud** (exclamation variously explained;
some editors emend to *Food*)   102 **when** (exclamation of annoyance, as in next line)   104–105
"It was . . . his way" (from another old song)   107 **mend** improve

Enter one with water.

Where's my spaniel Troilus? Sirrah, get you hence
And bid my cousin Ferdinand come hither—   *[Exit Servant.]*   110
One, Kate, that you must kiss and be acquainted with.
Where are my slippers? Shall I have some water?
Come, Kate, and wash, and welcome heartily.
You whoreson villain, will you let it fall?   *[Strikes him.]*
Kate. Patience, I pray you. 'Twas a fault unwilling.   115
Petruchio. A whoreson, beetle-headed,° flap-eared knave!
  Come, Kate, sit down; I know you have a stomach.°
  Will you give thanks,° sweet Kate, or else shall I?
  What's this? Mutton?
First Servingman.   Ay.
Petruchio.   Who brought it?
Peter.   I.
Petruchio. 'Tis burnt, and so is all the meat.   120
  What dogs are these! Where is the rascal cook?
  How durst you, villains, bring it from the dresser,°
  And serve it thus to me that love it not?
  There, take it to you, trenchers,° cups, and all,
                  [Throws food and dishes at them.]
  You heedless joltheads° and unmannered slaves!   125
  What, do you grumble? I'll be with° you straight.°
Kate. I pray you, husband, be not so disquiet.
  The meat was well if you were so contented.°
Petruchio. I tell thee, Kate, 'twas burnt and dried away,
  And I expressly am forbid to touch it,   130
  For it engenders choler,° planteth anger,
  And better 'twere that both of us did fast—
  Since of ourselves, ourselves are choleric°—
  Than feed it° with such overroasted flesh.
  Be patient. Tomorrow't shall be mended,°   135
  And for this night we'll fast for company.°
  Come, I will bring thee to thy bridal chamber.   *Exeunt.*

Enter Servants severally.

---

116 **beetle-headed** mallet-headed   117 **stomach** (1) hunger (2) irascibility   118 **give thanks** say grace   122 **dresser** sideboard   124 **trenchers** wooden platters   125 **joltheads** boneheads (*jolt* is related to *jaw* or *jowl*)   126 **with** even with   126 **straight** directly   128 **so contented** willing to see it as it was   131 **choler** bile, the "humor" (fluid) supposed to produce anger   133 **choleric** bilious, i.e., hot-tempered   134 **it** i.e., their choler   135 **'t shall be mended** things will be better 136 **for company** together

Nathaniel. Peter, didst ever see the like?
Peter. He kills her in her own humor.°

   Enter Curtis, a Servant.

Grumio. Where is he?   140
Curtis. In her chamber, making a sermon of continency to her,
   And rails and swears and rates,° that she, poor soul,
   Knows not which way to stand, to look, to speak,
   And sits as one new-risen from a dream.
   Away, away, for he is coming hither.   [*Exeunt.*] 145

   Enter Petruchio.

Petruchio. Thus have I politicly° begun my reign,
   And 'tis my hope to end successfully.
   My falcon° now is sharp° and passing empty,
   And till she stoop° she must not be full gorged,°
   For then she never looks upon her lure.°   150
   Another way I have to man° my haggard,°
   To make her come and know her keeper's call,
   That is, to watch° her as we watch these kites°
   That bate and beat° and will not be obedient.
   She eat° no meat today, nor none shall eat.   155
   Last night she slept not, nor tonight she shall not.
   As with the meat, some undeservèd fault
   I'll find about the making of the bed,
   And here I'll fling the pillow, there the bolster,°
   This way the coverlet, another way the sheets.   160
   Ay, and amid this hurly° I intend°
   That all is done in reverent care of her,
   And in conclusion she shall watch° all night.
   And if she chance to nod I'll rail and brawl
   And with the clamor keep her still awake.   165
   This is a way to kill a wife with kindness,°

---

139 **kills her in her own humor** conquers her by using her own disposition   142 **rates** scolds
146 **politicly** with a calculated plan   148 **falcon** hawk trained for hunting (falconry figures
continue for seven lines)   148 **sharp** pinched with hunger   149 **stoop** (1) obey (2) swoop to the
lure   149 **full gorged** fully fed   150 **lure** device used in training a hawk to return from flight
151 **man** (1) tame (2) be a man to   151 **haggard** hawk captured after reaching maturity   153
watch keep from sleep   153 **kites** type of small hawk   154 **bate and beat** flap and flutter (i.e., in
jittery resistance to training)   155 **eat** ate (pronounced *et*, as still in Britain)   159 **bolster** cushion
extending width of bed as under-support for pillows   161 **hurly** disturbance   161 **intend**
profess   163 **watch** stay awake   166 **kill a wife with kindness** (ironic allusion to proverb on
ruining a wife by pampering)

And thus I'll curb her mad and headstrong humor.
He that knows better how to tame a shrew,°
Now let him speak—'tis charity to show.   *Exit.*

[**Scene II.** *Padua. The street in front of Baptista's house.*]

Enter Tranio [as Lucentio] and Hortensio [as Litio].

Tranio. Is't possible, friend Litio, that Mistress Bianca
　　Doth fancy° any other but Lucentio?
　　I tell you, sir, she bears me fair in hand.°
Hortensio. Sir, to satisfy you in what I have said,
　　Stand by and mark the manner of his teaching.   [*They eavesdrop.*]   5

Enter Bianca [and Lucentio as Cambio].

Lucentio. Now mistress, profit you in what you read?
Bianca. What, master, read you? First resolve° me that.
Lucentio. I read that° I profess,° the Art to Love.°
Bianca. And may you prove, sir, master of your art.
Lucentio. While you, sweet dear, prove mistress of my heart. [*They court.*]   10
Hortensio. Quick proceeders,° marry!° Now, tell me, I pray,
　　You that durst swear that your mistress Bianca
　　Loved none in the world so well as Lucentio.
Tranio. O despiteful° love! Unconstant womankind!
　　I tell thee, Litio, this is wonderful.°   15
Hortensio. Mistake no more. I am not Litio,
　　Nor a musician, as I seem to be,
　　But one that scorn to live in this disguise,
　　For such a one as leaves a gentleman
　　And makes a god of such a cullion.°   20
　　Know, sir, that I am called Hortensio.
Tranio. Signior Hortensio, I have often heard
　　Of your entire affection to Bianca,
　　And since mine eyes are witness of her lightness,°
　　I will with you, if you be so contented,   25
　　Forswear° Bianca and her love forever.
Hortensio. See, how they kiss and court! Signior Lucentio,
　　Here is my hand and here I firmly vow

---

168 **shrew** (rhymes with "show")   IV.ii.2 **fancy** like   3 **bears me fair in hand** leads me on   7
resolve answer   8 **that** what   8 **profess** avow, practice   8 **Art to Love** (i.e., Ovid's *Ars Amandi*)
11 **proceeders** (pun on idiom "proceed Master of Arts")   11 **marry** by Mary (mild exclamation)
14 **despiteful** spiteful   15 **wonderful** causing wonder   20 **cullion** low fellow (literally, testicle)   24
lightness (cf. "light woman")   26 **Forswear** "swear off"

Never to woo her more, but do forswear her,
As one unworthy all the former favors°   30
That I have fondly° flattered her withal.
Tranio. And here I take the like unfeignèd oath,
Never to marry with her though she would entreat.
Fie on her! See how beastly° she doth court him.
Hortensio. Would all the world but he had quite forsworn.°   35
For me, that I may surely keep mine oath,
I will be married to a wealthy widow
Ere three days pass, which° hath as long loved me
As I have loved this proud disdainful haggard.
And so farewell, Signior Lucentio.   40
Kindness in women, not their beauteous looks,
Shall win my love, and so I take my leave
In resolution as I swore before.   [*Exit.*]
Tranio. Mistress Bianca, bless you with such grace
As 'longeth to a lover's blessèd case.   45
Nay, I have ta'en you napping,° gentle love,
And have forsworn you with Hortensio.
Bianca. Tranio, you jest. But have you both forsworn me?
Tranio. Mistress, we have.
Lucentio.   Then we are rid of Litio.
Tranio. I' faith, he'll have a lusty° widow now,   50
That shall be wooed and wedded in a day.
Bianca. God give him joy!
Tranio. Ay, and he'll tame her.
Bianca.   He says so, Tranio.
Tranio. Faith, he is gone unto the taming school.
Bianca. The taming school! What, is there such a place?   55
Tranio. Ay, mistress, and Petruchio is the master,
That teacheth tricks eleven and twenty long°
To tame a shrew and charm her chattering tongue.

Enter Biondello.

Biondello. O master, master, I have watched so long
That I am dog-weary, but at last I spied   60
An ancient angel° coming down the hill
Will serve the turn.°

---

30 **favors** marks of esteem   31 **fondly** foolishly   34 **beastly** unashamedly   35 **Would . . .
forsworn** i.e., would she had only one lover   38 **which** who   46 **ta'en you napping** seen you "kiss
and court" (line 27)   50 **lusty** lively   57 **tricks eleven and twenty long** (1) many tricks (2)
possibly an allusion to card game "thirty-one"   60 **ancient angel** man of good old stamp (*angel* =
coin; cf. "gentleman of the old school")   61 **Will serve the turn** who will do for our purposes

Tranio.   What° is he, Biondello?
Biondello. Master, a mercantante° or a pendant,°
  I know not what, but formal in apparel,
  In gait and countenance° surely like a father.   65
Lucentio. And what of him, Tranio?
Tranio. If he be credulous and trust my tale,
  I'll make him glad to seem Vincentio,
  And give assurance to Baptista Minola
  As if he were the right Vincentio.   70
  Take in your love and then let me alone.

                    [*Exeunt Lucentio and Bianca.*]

Enter a Pedant.

Pedant. God save you, sir.
Tranio.   And you, sir. You are welcome.
  Travel you far on, or are you at the farthest?
Pedant. Sir, at the farthest for a week or two,
  But then up farther and as far as Rome,   75
  And so to Tripoli if God lend me life.
Tranio. What countryman,° I pray?
Pedant.   Of Mantua.
Tranio. Of Mantua, sir? Marry, God forbid!
  And come to Padua, careless of your life?
Pedant. My life, sir? How, I pray? For that goes hard.°   80
Tranio. 'Tis death for anyone in Mantua
  To come to Padua. Know you not the cause?
  Your ships are stayed° at Venice and the Duke,
  For private quarrel 'twixt your duke and him,
  Hath published and proclaimed it openly.   85
  'Tis marvel, but that you are but newly come,
  You might have heard it else proclaimed about.
Pedant. Alas, sir, it is worse for me than so,°
  For I have bills for money by exchange
  From Florence and must here deliver them.   90
Tranio. Well, sir, to do you courtesy,
  This will I do and this I will advise° you.
  First tell me, have you ever been at Pisa?
Pedant. Ay, sir, in Pisa have I often been—
  Pisa, renownèd for grave citizens.   95

———

62 **What** what kind of man   63 **mercantante** merchant   63 **pedant** schoolmaster   65 **gait and countenance** bearing and style   77 **What countryman** a man of what country   80 **goes hard** (cf. "is rough")   83 **stayed** held   88 **than so** than it appears so far   92 **advise** explain to

Tranio. Among them, know you one Vincentio?
Pedant. I know him not but I have heard of him—
  A merchant of incomparable wealth.
Tranio. He is my father, sir, and, sooth to say,
  In count'nance somewhat doth resemble you.   100
Biondello. [*Aside*] As much as an apple doth an oyster, and all one.°
Tranio. To save your life in this extremity,
  This favor will I do you for his sake,
  And think it not the worst of all your fortunes
  That you are like to Sir Vincentio.   105
  His name and credit° shall you undertake,°
  And in my house you shall be friendly lodged.
  Look that you take upon you° as you should.
  You understand me, sir? So shall you stay
  Till you have done your business in the city.   110
  If this be court'sy, sir, accept of it.
Pedant. O sir, I do, and will repute° you ever
  The patron of my life and liberty.
Tranio. Then go with me to make the matter good.
  This, by the way,° I let you understand: 115
  My father is here looked for every day
  To pass assurance° of a dower in marriage
  'Twixt me and one Baptista's daughter here.
  In all these circumstances I'll instruct you.
  Go with me to clothe you as becomes you.   *Exeunt.*   120

[**SCENE III.** *In Petruchio's house.*]

  Enter Kate and Grumio.

Grumio. No, no, forsooth, I dare not for my life.
Kate. The more my wrong,° the more his spite appears.
  What, did he marry me to famish me?
  Beggars that come unto my father's door,
  Upon entreaty have a present° alms;   5
  If not, elsewhere they meet with charity.
  But I, who never knew how to entreat
  Nor never needed that I should entreat,
  Am starved for meat,° giddy for lack of sleep,
  With oaths kept waking and with brawling fed.   10

_____

  101 **all one** no difference 106 **credit** standing 106 **undertake** adopt 108 **take upon you**
assume your role 112 **repute** esteem 115 **by the way** as we walk along 117 **pass assurance**
give a guarantee IV.iii.2 **The more my wrong** the greater the wrong done me 5 **present**
prompt 9 **meat** food

And that which spites me more than all these wants,
He does it under name of perfect love,
As who should say,° if I should sleep or eat
'Twere deadly sickness or else present death.
I prithee go and get me some repast,   15
I care not what, so° it be wholesome food.
Grumio. What say you to a neat's° foot?
Kate. 'Tis passing good; I prithee let me have it.
Grumio. I fear it is too choleric° a meat.
　How say you to a fat tripe finely broiled?   20
Kate. I like it well. Good Grumio, fetch it me.
Grumio. I cannot tell, I fear 'tis choleric.
　What say you to a piece of beef and mustard?
Kate. A dish that I do love to feed upon.
Grumio. Ay, but the mustard is too hot a little.   25
Kate. Why then, the beef, and let the mustard rest.
Grumio. Nay then, I will not. You shall have the mustard
　Or else you get no beef of Grumio.
Kate. Then both or one, or anything thou wilt.
Grumio. Why then, the mustard without the beef.   30
Kate. Go, get thee gone, thou false deluding slave.

　　　　　　　　　　　　　　　　　　　　　　　　　　Beats him.

That feed'st me with the very name° of meat.
Sorrow on thee and all the pack of you
That triumph thus upon my misery.
Go, get thee gone, I say.   35

Enter Petruchio and Hortensio with meat.

Petruchio. How fares my Kate? What, sweeting, all amort?°
Hortensio. Mistress, what cheer?°
Kate.　　　　　　　　　　　Faith, as cold° as can be.
Petruchio. Pluck up thy spirits; look cheerfully upon me.
　Here, love, thou seest how diligent I am
　To dress thy meat° myself and bring it thee.   40
　I am sure, sweet Kate, this kindness merits thanks.
　What, not a word? Nay then, thou lov'st it not,
　And all my pains is sorted to no proof.°
　Here, take away this dish.

---

　　13 **As who should say** as if to say   16 **so** as long as   17 **neat's** ox's or calf's   19 **choleric** temper-producing   32 **very name** name only   36 **all amort** depressed, lifeless (cf. "mortified")   37 **what cheer** how are things   37 **cold** (cf. "not so hot"; "cold comfort")   40 **To dress thy meat** in fixing your food   43 **sorted to no proof** have come to nothing

Kate.   I pray you, let it stand.
Petruchio. The poorest service is repaid with thanks,   45
  And so shall mine before you touch the meat.
Kate. I thank you, sir.
Hortensio. Signior Petruchio, fie, you are to blame.
  Come, Mistress Kate, I'll bear you company.
Petruchio. [*Aside*] Eat it up all, Hortensio, if thou lovest me;   50
  Much good do it unto thy gentle heart.
  Kate, eat apace. And now, my honey love,
  Will we return unto thy father's house
  And revel it as bravely° as the best,
  With silken coats and caps and golden rings,   55
  With ruffs° and cuffs and fardingales° and things,
  With scarfs and fans and double change of brav'ry,°
  With amber bracelets, beads, and all this knav'ry.°
  What, hath thou dined? The tailor stays thy leisure°
  To deck thy body with his ruffling° treasure.   60

Enter Tailor.

Come, tailor, let us see these ornaments.

Enter Haberdasher.

Lay forth the gown. What news with you, sir?
Haberdasher. Here is the cap your Worship did bespeak.°
Petruchio. Why, this was molded on a porringer°—
  A velvet dish. Fie, fie, 'tis lewd° and filthy.   65
  Why, 'tis a cockle° or a walnut shell,
  A knack,° a toy, a trick,° a baby's cap.
  Away with it! Come, let me have a bigger.
Kate. I'll have no bigger. This doth fit the time,°
  And gentlewomen wear such caps as these.   70
Petruchio. When you are gentle you shall have one too,
  And not till then.
Hortensio. [*Aside*] That will not be in haste.
Kate. Why, sir, I trust I may have leave to speak,
  And speak I will. I am no child, no babe.   75
  Your betters have endured me say my mind,

---

54 **bravely** handsomely dressed   56 **ruffs** stiffly starched, wheelshaped collars   56 **fardingales** farthingales, hooped skirts of petticoats   57 **brav'ry** handsome clothes   58 **knav'ry** girlish things   59 **stays thy leisure** awaits your permission   60 **ruffling** gaily ruffled   63 **bespeak** order   64 **porringer** soup bowl   65 **lewd** vile   66 **cockle** shell of a mollusk   67 **knack** knickknack   67 **trick** plaything   69 **doth fit the time** is in fashion

And if you cannot, best you stop your ears.
My tongue will tell the anger of my heart,
Or else my heart, concealing it, will break,
And rather than it shall I will be free   80
Even to the uttermost, as I please, in words.
Petruchio. Why, thou sayst true. It is a paltry cap,
   A custard-coffin° a bauble, a silken pie.°
   I love thee well in that thou lik'st it not.
Kate. Love me or love me not, I like the cap,   85
   And it I will have or I will have none.   [*Exit Haberdasher.*]
Petruchio. Thy gown? Why, ay. Come, tailor, let us see't.
   O mercy, God! What masquing° stuff is here?
   What's this? A sleeve? 'Tis like a demi-cannon.°
   What, up and down,° carved like an apple tart?   90
   Here's snip and nip and cut and slish and slash,
   Like to a censer° in a barber's shop.
   Why, what, a° devil's name, tailor, call'st thou this?
Hortensio. [*Aside*] I see she's like to have neither cap nor gown.
Tailor. You bid me make it orderly and well,   95
   According to the fashion and the time.
Petruchio. Marry, and did, but if you be rememb'red,
   I did not bid you mar it to the time.°
   Go, hop me over every kennel° home,
   For you shall hop without my custom, sir.   100
   I'll none of it. Hence, make your best of it.
Kate. I never saw a better-fashioned gown,
   More quaint,° more pleasing, nor more commendable.
   Belike° you mean to make a puppet of me.
Petruchio. Why, true, he means to make a puppet of thee.   105
Tailor. She says your worship means to make a puppet of her.
Petruchio. O monstrous arrogance!
   Thou liest, thou thread, thou thimble,
   Thou yard, three-quarters, half-yard, quarter, nail!°
   Thou flea, thou nit,° thou winter cricket thou!   110
   Braved° in mine own house with° a skein of thread!
   Away, thou rag, thou quantity,° thou remnant,
   Or I shall so bemete° thee with thy yard

---

83 **custard-coffin** custard crust 83 **pie** meat pie 88 **masquing** for masquerades or actors' costumes 89 **demi-cannon** big cannon 90 **up and down** entirely 92 **censer** incense burned with perforated top 93 **a** in the 98 **to the time** for all time (cf. line 96, in which "the time" is "the contemporary style") 99 **kennel** gutter (canal) 103 **quaint** skillfully made 104 **Belike** no doubt 109 **nail** 1/16 of a yard 110 **nit** louse's egg 111 **Braved** defied 111 **with** by 112 **quantity** fragment 113 **bemete** (1) measure (2) beat

As thou shalt think on prating° whilst thou liv'st.
I tell thee, I, that thou hast marred her gown.   115
Tailor. Your worship is deceived. The gown is made
  Just as my master had direction.°
  Grumio gave order how it should be done.
Grumio. I gave him no order; I gave him the stuff.
Tailor. But how did you desire it should be made?   120
Grumio. Marry, sir, with needle and thread.
Tailor. But did you not request to have it cut?
Grumio. Thou hast faced° many things.
Tailor. I have.
Grumio. Face° not me. Thou hast braved° many men; brave° not me. I will   125
  neither be faced nor braved. I say unto thee, I bid thy master cut out the
  gown, but I did not bid him cut it to pieces. *Ergo,*° thou liest.
Tailor. Why, here is the note° of the fashion to testify.
Petruchio. Read it.
Grumio. The note lies in's throat° if he° say I said so.   130
Tailor. "*Imprimis,*° a loose-bodied gown."°
Grumio. Master, if ever I said loose-bodied gown, sew me in the skirts of it
  and beat me to death with a bottom° of brown thread. I said, a gown.
Petruchio. Proceed.
Tailor. "With a small compassed° capé."   135
Grumio. I confess the cape.
Tailor. "With a trunk° sleeve."
Grumio. I confess two sleeves.
Tailor. "The sleeves curiously° cut."
Petruchio. Ay, there's the villainy.   140
Grumio. Error i' th' bill,° sir, error i' th' bill. I commanded the sleeves should
  be cut out and sewed up again, and that I'll prove upon° thee, though thy
  little finger be armed in a thimble.
Tailor. This is true that I say. And° I had thee in place where,° thou shouldst
  know it.
Grumio. I am for° thee straight.° Take thou the bill,° and give thy mete-yard,° 145
  and spare not me.
Hortensio. God-a-mercy, Grumio, then he shall have no odds.
Petruchio. Well, sir, in brief, the gown is not for me.
Grumio. You are i' th' right, sir; 'tis for my mistress.

---

114 **think on prating** remember your silly talk   117 **had direction** received orders   123 **faced** trimmed   125 **Face** challenge   125 **braved** equipped with finery   125 **brave** defy   127 **Ergo** therefore   128 **note** written notation   130 **in's throat** from the heart, with premeditation   130 **he** it   131 **Imprimis** first   131 **loose-bodied gown** (worn by prostitutes, with *loose* in pun)   133 **bottom** spool   135 **compassed** with circular edge   137 **trunk** full   140 **curiously** painstakingly   141 **bill** i.e., the "note"   142 **prove upon** test by dueling with   143 **And if**   143 **place where** the right place   145 **for** ready for   145 **straight** right now   145 **bill** (1) written order (2) long-handled weapon   145 **mete-yard** yardstick

Petruchio. Go, take it up unto° thy master's use.°
Grumio. Villain, not for thy life! Take up my mistress' gown for thy master's 150
  use!
Petruchio. Why sir, what's your conceit° in that?
Grumio. O sir, the conceit is deeper than you think for.
  Take up my mistress' gown to his master's use!
  O, fie, fie, fie!
Petruchio. [*Aside*] Hortensio, say thou wilt see the tailor paid. 155
  [*To Tailor*] Go take it hence; be gone and say no more.
Hortensio. Tailor, I'll pay thee for thy gown tomorrow;
  Take no unkindness of his hasty words.
  Away, I say, commend me to thy master. *Exit Tailor.*
Petruchio. Well, come, my Kate, we will unto your father's, 160
  Even in these honest mean habiliments.°
  Our purses shall be proud, our garments poor,
  For 'tis the mind that makes the body rich,
  And as the sun breaks through the darkest clouds
  So honor peereth° in the meanest habit.° 165
  What, is the jay more precious than the lark
  Because his feathers are more beautiful?
  Or is the adder better than the eel
  Because his painted skin contents the eye?
  O no, good Kate, neither art thou the worse 170
  For this poor furniture° and mean array.
  If thou account'st it shame, lay° it on me,
  And therefore frolic. We will hence forthwith
  To feast and sport us at thy father's house.
  [*To Grumio*] Go call my men, and let us straight to him; 175
  And bring our horses unto Long-lane end.
  There will we mount, and thither walk on foot.
  Let's see, I think 'tis now some seven o'clock,
  And well we may come there by dinnertime.°
Kate. I dare assure you, sir, 'tis almost two, 180
  And 'twill be suppertime ere you come there.
Petruchio. It shall be seven ere I go to horse.
  Look what° I speak or do or think to do,
  You are still crossing° it. Sirs, let't alone:
  I will not go today, and ere I do, 185
  It shall be what o'clock I say it is.
Hortensio. [*Aside*] Why, so this gallant will command the sun. [*Exeunt.*]

---

149 **up unto** away for   149 **use** i.e., in whatever way he can; Grumio uses these words for a
sex joke   151 **conceit** idea   161 **habiliments** clothes   165 **peereth** is recognized   165 **habit**
clothes   171 **furniture** outfit   172 **lay** blame   179 **dinnertime** midday   183 **Look what**
whatever   184 **crossing** obstructing, going counter to

[SCENE IV. *Padua. The street in front of Baptista's house.*]

Enter Tranio [as Lucentio] and the Pedant dressed like Vincentio.

Tranio. Sir, this is the house. Please it you that I call?
Pedant. Ay, what else? And but° I be deceived,
  Signior Baptista may remember me
  Near twenty years ago in Genoa,
  Where we were lodgers at the Pegasus.°   5
Tranio. 'Tis well, and hold your own° in any case
  With such austerity as 'longeth to a father.
Pedant. I warrant° you. But sir, here comes your boy;
  'Twere good he were schooled.°

Enter Biondello.

Tranio. Fear you not him. Sirrah Biondello,   10
  Now do your duty throughly,° I advise you.
  Imagine 'twere the right Vincentio.
Biondello. Tut, fear not me.
Tranio. But hast thou done thy errand to Baptista?
Biondello. I told him that your father was at Venice   15
  And that you looked for him this day in Padua.
Tranio. Th'art a tall° fellow. Hold thee that° to drink.
  Here comes Baptista. Set your countenance, sir.

Enter Baptista and Lucentio [as Cambio]. Pedant booted and bareheaded.°

  Signior Baptista, you are happily met.
  [*To the Pedant*] Sir, this is the gentleman I told you of.   20
  I pray you, stand good father to me now,
  Give me Bianca for my patrimony.
Pedant. Soft,° son.
  Sir, by your leave. Having come to Padua
  To gather in some debts, my son Lucentio   25
  Made me acquainted with a weighty cause°
  Of love between your daughter and himself.
  And—for the good report I hear of you,

IV.iv.2 **but** unless   3–5 **Signior Baptista . . . Pegasus** (the Pedant is practicing as Vincentio)
5 **Pegasus** common English inn name (after mythical winged horse symbolizing poetic
inspiration)   6 **hold your own** act your role   8 **warrant** guarantee   9 **schooled** informed (about
his role)   11 **throughly** thoroughly   17 **tall** excellent   17 **Hold thee that** i.e., take this tip   18 s.d.
booted and bareheaded i.e., arriving from a journey and courteously greeting Baptista   23 **Soft**
take it easy   26 **weighty cause** important matter

And for the love he beareth to your daughter,
And she to him—to stay° him not too long,   30
I am content, in a good father's care,
To have him matched. And if you please to like°
No worse than I, upon some agreement
Me shall you find ready and willing
With one consent to have her so bestowed,   35
For curious° I cannot be with you,
Signior Baptista, of whom I hear so well.
Baptista. Sir, pardon me in what I have to say.
  Your plainness and your shortness° please me well.
  Right true it is, your son Lucentio here   40
  Doth love my daughter and she loveth him—
  Or both dissemble deeply their affections—
  And therefore, if you say no more than this,
  That like a father you will deal with him
  And pass° my daughter a sufficient dower,   45
  The match is made, and all is done.
  Your son shall have my daughter with consent.
Tranio. I thank you, sir. Where, then, do you know° best
  We be affied° and such assurance ta'en
  As shall with either part's° agreement stand?   50
Baptista. Not in my house, Lucentio, for you know
  Pitchers have ears, and I have many servants.
  Besides, old Gremio is heark'ning still,°
  And happily° we might be interrupted.
Tranio. Then at my lodging and it like° you.   55
  There doth my father lie,° and there this night
  We'll pass° the business privately and well.
  Send for your daughter by your servant here;
  My boy shall fetch the scrivener° presently.
  The worst is this, that at so slender warning°   60
  You are like to have a thin and slender pittance.°
Baptista. It likes° me well. Cambio, hie you home
  And bid Bianca make her ready straight,
  And, if you will, tell what hath happenèd:
  Lucentio's father is arrived in Padua,   65
  And how she's like to be Lucentio's wife.   [*Exit Lucentio.*]
Biondello. I pray the gods she may with all my heart!   *Exit.*

---

  30 **stay** delay   32 **like** i.e., the match   36 **curious** overinsistent on fine points   39 **shortness**
conciseness   45 **pass** legally settle upon   48 **know** think   49 **affied** formally engaged   50 **part's**
party's   53 **heark'ning still** listening constantly   54 **happily** perchance   55 **and it like** if it
please   56 **lie** stay   57 **pass** settle   59 **scrivener** notary   60 **slender warning** short notice   61
pittance meal   62 **likes** pleases

Tranio. Dally not with the gods, but get thee gone.
  Signior Baptista, shall I lead the way?
  Welcome, one mess° is like to be your cheer.°   70
  Come, sir, we will better it in Pisa.
Baptista. I follow you.   *Exeunt.*

  Enter Lucentio [as Cambio] and Biondello.

Biondello. Cambio!
Lucentio. What sayst thou, Biondello?
Biondello. You saw my master° wink and laugh upon you?   75
Lucentio. Biondello, what of that?
Biondello. Faith, nothing, but has° left me here behind to expound the
  meaning or moral of his signs and tokens.
Lucentio. I pray thee, moralize° them.
Biondello. Then thus. Baptista is safe, talking with the deceiving father of a   80
  deceitful son.
Lucentio. And what of him?
Biondello. His daughter is to be brought by you to the supper.
Lucentio. And then?
Biondello. The old priest at Saint Luke's church is at your command at all
  hours.
Lucentio. And what of all this?   85
Biondello. I cannot tell, except they are busied about a counterfeit assurance.°
  Take you assurance° of her, *"cum previlegio ad impremendum solem."*°
  To th' church! Take the priest, clerk, and some sufficient honest witnesses.
  If this be not that you look for, I have no more to say,
  But bid Bianca farewell forever and a day.   90
Lucentio. Hear'st thou, Biondello?
Biondello. I cannot tarry. I knew a wench married in an afternoon as she
  went to the garden for parsley to stuff a rabbit. And so may you, sir. And
  so adieu, sir. My master hath appointed me to go to Saint Luke's, to bid
  the priest be ready to come against you come° with your appendix.°   95
                                                          Exit.
Lucentio. I may, and will, if she be so contented.
  She will be pleased; then wherefore should I doubt?
  Hap what hap may, I'll roundly° go about° her.
  It shall go hard if Cambio go without her.   *Exit.*

---

  70 **mess** dish   70 **cheer** entertainment   75 **my master** i.e., Tranio   77 **has** he has   79 **moralize**
"expound"   86 **assurance** betrothal document   87 **Take you assurance** make sure   87 **cum . . .
solem** (Biondello's version of *cum previlegio ad imprimendum solum,* "with right of sole printing,"
a licensing phrase, with sexual pun in *imprimendum,* literally "pressing upon")   95 **against you
come** in preparing for your coming   95 **appendix** (1) servant (2) wife (another metaphor from
printing)   98 **roundly** directly   98 **about** after

[SCENE V. *The road to Padua.*]

Enter Petruchio, Kate, Hortensio [with Servants.]

Petruchio. Come on, a° God's name, once more toward our father's.
    Good Lord, how bright and goodly shines the moon.
Kate. The moon? The sun. It is not moonlight now.
Petruchio. I say it is the moon that shines so bright.
Kate. I know it is the sun that shines so bright.   5
Petruchio. Now, by my mother's son, and that's myself,
    It shall be moon or star or what I list,°
    Or ere° I journey to your father's house.
    [*To Servants*] Go on and fetch our horses back again.
    Evermore crossed and crossed, nothing but crossed!°   10
Hortensio. [*To Kate*] Say as he says or we shall never go.
Kate. Forward, I pray, since we have come so far,
    And be it moon or sun or what you please.
    And if you please to call it a rush-candle,°
    Henceforth I vow it shall be so for me.   15
Petruchio. I say it is the moon.
Kate.   I know it is the moon.
Petruchio. Nay, then you lie. It is the blessèd sun.
Kate. Then God be blessed, it is the blessèd sun.
    But sun it is not when you say it is not,
    And the moon changes even as your mind.   20
    What you will have it named, even that it is,
    And so it shall be so for Katherine.
Hortensio. [*Aside*] Petruchio, go thy ways. The field is won.
Petruchio. Well, forward, forward! Thus the bowl° should run
    And not unluckily against the bias.°   25
    But soft,° company° is coming here.

Enter Vincentio.

[*To Vincentio*] Good morrow, gentle mistress; where away?
    Tell me, sweet Kate, and tell me truly too,
    Hast thou beheld a fresher° gentlewoman?
    Such war of white and red within her cheeks!   30
    What stars do spangle heaven with such beauty
    As those two eyes become that heavenly face?

    IV.v.1 **a** in   7 **list** please   8 **Or ere** before   10 **crossed** opposed, challenged   14 **rush-candle** rush dipped in grease and used as candle   24 **bowl** bowling ball   25 **against the bias** not in the planned curving route, made possible by a lead insertion (bias) weighting one side of the ball   26 **soft** hush   26 **company** someone   29 **fresher** more radiant

Fair lovely maid, once more good day to thee.
Sweet Kate, embrace her for her beauty's sake.
Hortensio. [*Aside*] 'A° will make the man mad, to make a woman of him. 35
Kate. Young budding virgin, fair and fresh and sweet,
Whither away, or where is thy abode?
Happy the parents of so fair a child!
Happier the man whom favorable stars
Allots thee for his lovely bedfellow! 40
Petruchio. Why, how now, Kate, I hope thou are not mad.
This is a man, old, wrinkled, faded, withered,
And not a maiden, as thou sayst he is.
Kate. Pardon; old father, my mistaking eyes
That have been so bedazzled with the sun 45
That everything I look on seemeth green.°
Now I perceive thou art a reverend father;
Pardon, I pray thee, for my mad mistaking.
Petruchio. Do, good old grandsire, and withal make known
Which way thou travelest. If along with us, 50
We shall be joyful of thy company.
Vincentio. Fair sir, and you my merry mistress,
That with your strange encounter° much amazed me,
My name is called Vincentio, my dwelling Pisa,
And bound I am to Padua, there to visit 55
A son of mine which long I have not seen.
Petruchio. What is his name?
Vincentio.   Lucentio, gentle sir.
Petruchio. Happily met, the happier for thy son.
And now by law as well as reverend age,
I may entitle thee my loving father. 60
The sister to my wife, this gentlewoman,
Thy son by this° hath married. Wonder not
Nor be not grieved. She is of good esteem,
Her dowry wealthy, and of worthy birth;
Beside, so qualified° as may beseem° 65
The spouse of any noble gentleman.
Let me embrace with old Vincentio
And wander we to see thy honest son,
Who will of thy arrival be full joyous.
Vincentio. But is this true, or is it else your pleasure, 70
Like pleasant° travelers, to break a jest
Upon the company you overtake?

---

35 'A he   46 green young   53 encounter mode of address   62 this now   65 so qualified
having qualities   65 beseem befit   71 pleasant addicted to pleasantries

Hortensio. I do assure thee, father, so it is.
Petruchio. Come, go along, and see the truth hereof,
  For our first merriment hath made thee jealous.° 75

                    Exeunt [all but Hortensio].
Hortensio. Well, Petruchio, this has put me in heart.
  Have to° my widow, and if she be froward,°
  Then hast thou taught Hortensio to be untoward.°   *Exit.*

[ACT V
SCENE I. *Padua. The street in front of Lucentio's house.]*

Enter Biondello, Lucentio [as Cambio], and Bianca; Gremio is out before.°

Biondello. Softly and swiftly, sir, for the priest is ready.
Lucentio. I fly, Biondello. But they may chance to need thee at home; therefore
  leave us.   *Exit [with Bianca].*
Biondello. Nay, faith, I'll see the church a your back,° and then come back
  to my master's as soon as I can.   *[Exit]*
Gremio. I marvel Cambio comes not all this while.   5

Enter Petruchio, Kate, Vincentio, [and] Grumio, with Attendants.

Petruchio. Sir, here's the door, this is Lucentio's house.
  My father's bears° more toward the marketplace;
  Thither must I, and here I leave you, sir.
Vincentio. You shall not choose but drink before you go.
  I think I shall command your welcome here,   10
  And by all likelihood some cheer is toward.°   *Knock.*
Gremio. They're busy within. You were best knock louder.

Pedant [as Vincentio] looks out of the window [above].

Pedant. What's° he that knocks as he would beat down the gate?
Vincentio. Is Signior Lucentio within, sir?
Pedant. He's within, sir, but not to be spoken withal.°   15
Vincentio. What if a man bring him a hundred pound or two, to make merry
  withal?
Pedant. Keep your hundred pounds to yourself; he shall need none so long
  as I live.

---

75 **jealous** suspicious   77 **Have to** on to   77 **froward** fractious   78 **untoward** difficult
V.i.s.d. **out before** precedes, and does not see, the others   3 **a your back** on your back (see you
enter the church? or, married?)   7 **bears** lies   11 **toward** at hand   13 **What's** who is   15 **withal**
with

Petruchio. Nay, I told you your son was well beloved in Padua. Do you hear,
    sir? To leave frivolous circumstances,° I pray you tell Signior Lucentio that
    his father is come from Pisa and is here at the door to speak with him.   20
Pedant. Thou liest. His father is come from Padua° and here looking out at
    the window.
Vincentio. Art thou his father?
Pedant. Ay sir, so his mother says, if I may believe her.
Petruchio. [*To Vincentio*] Why how now, gentleman?
    Why this is flat° knavery, to take upon you another man's name.   25
Pedant. Lay hands on the villain. I believe 'a° means to cozen° somebody
    in this city under my countenance.°

Enter Biondello.

Biondello. I have seen them in the church together;
    God send 'em good shipping!° But who is here?
    Mine old master, Vincentio! Now we are undone°   30
    and brought to nothing.°
Vincentio. Come hither, crack-hemp.°
Biondello. I hope I may choose,° sir.
Vincentio. Come hither, you rogue. What, have you forgot me?
Biondello. Forgot you? No, sir. I could not forget you, for I never saw you   35
    before in all my life.
Vincentio. What, you notorious° villain, didst thou never see thy master's
    father, Vincentio?
Biondello. What, my old worshipful old master? Yes, marry, sir, see where
    he looks out of the window.
Vincentio. Is't so, indeed?   *He beats Biondello.*
Biondello. Help, help, help! Here's a madman will murder me.   [*Exit.*]   40
Pedant. Help, son! Help, Signior Baptista!

                                [*Exit from above.*]
Petruchio. Prithee, Kate, let's stand aside and see the end of this
    controversy.

                                [*They stand aside.*]

Enter Pedant [below] with Servants, Baptista, [and] Tranio [as Lucentio].

Tranio. Sir, what are you that offer° to beat my servant?

---

    19 **frivolous circumstances** trivial matters   21 **Padua** (perhaps Shakespeare's slip of the pen for
Pisa, home of the real Vincentio, or *Mantua,* where the Pedant comes from; cf. IV.ii.77)   25 **flat**
unvarnished   26 **'a** he   26 **cozen** defraud   27 **countenance** identity   29 **shipping** journey   30
undone defeated   31 **brought to nothing** (cf. "annihilated")   32 **crack-hemp** rope-stretcher (i.e.,
subject for hanging)   33 **choose** have some choice (in the matter)   36 **notorious** extraordinary
43 **offer** attempt

Vincentio. What am I, sir? Nay, what are you, sir? O immortal gods! O fine°
villain! A silken doublet, a velvet hose, a scarlet cloak, and a copatain° 45
hat! O, I am undone, I am undone! While I play the good husband° at
home, my son and my servant spend all at the university.
Tranio. How now, what's the matter?
Baptista. What, is the man lunatic?
Tranio. Sir, you seem a sober ancient gentleman by your habit,° but your 50
words show you a madman. Why sir, what 'cerns° it you if I wear pearl
and gold? I thank my good father, I am able to maintain it.
Vincentio. Thy father! O villain, he is a sailmaker in Bergamo.
Baptista. You mistake, sir, you mistake, sir. Pray, what do you think is his
name?
Vincentio. His name! As if I knew not his name! I have brought him up ever 55
since he was three years old, and his name is Tranio.
Pedant. Away, away, mad ass! His name is Lucentio, and he is mine only
son and heir to the lands of me, Signior Vincentio.
Vincentio. Lucentio! O he hath murd'red his master. Lay hold on him, I
charge you in the Duke's name. O my son, my son! Tell me, thou villain, 60
where is my son Lucentio?
Tranio. Call forth an officer.

[*Enter an Officer.*]

Carry this mad knave to the jail. Father Baptista, I charge you see that he
be forthcoming.°
Vincentio. Carry me to the jail!
Gremio. Stay, officer. He shall not go to prison. 65
Baptista. Talk not, Signior Gremio. I say he shall go to prison.
Gremio. Take heed, Signior Baptista, lest you be cony-catched° in this busi-
ness. I dare swear this is the right Vincentio.
Pedant. Swear, if thou dar'st.
Gremio. Nay, I dare not swear it. 70
Tranio. Then thou wert best° say that I am not Lucentio.
Gremio. Yes, I know thee to be Signior Lucentio.
Baptista. Away with the dotard,° to the jail with him!
Vincentio. Thus strangers may be haled° and abused.
  O monstrous villain! 75

Enter Biondello, Lucentio, and Bianca.

---

44 **fine** well dressed   45 **copatain** high conical   46 **husband** manager   50 **habit** manner   51
'cerns concerns   63 **forthcoming** available (for trial)   67 **cony-catched** fooled   71 **thou wert best**
maybe you'll dare   73 **dotard** old fool   74 **haled** pulled about

Biondello. O we are spoiled°—and yonder he is. Deny him, forswear him,
  or else we are all undone.

Exit Biondello, Tranio, and Pedant as fast as may be.

Lucentio. Pardon, sweet father. *Kneel.*
Vincentio.   Lives my sweet son?
Bianca. Pardon, dear father.
Baptista.   How hast thou offended?
  Where is Lucentio?
Lucentio.   Here's Lucentio, 80
  Right son to the right Vincentio,
  That have by marriage made thy daughter mine
  While counterfeit supposes° bleared thine eyne.°
Gremio. Here's packing,° with a witness,° to deceive us all!
Vincentio. Where is that damnèd villain Tranio 85
  That faced and braved° me in this matter so?
Baptista. Why, tell me, is not this my Cambio?
Bianca. Cambio is changed into Lucentio.
Lucentio. Love wrought these miracles. Bianca's love
  Made me exchange my state with Tranio 90
  While he did bear my countenance° in the town,
  And happily I have arrived at the last
  Unto the wishèd haven of my bliss.
  What Tranio did, myself enforced him to.
  Then pardon him, sweet father, for my sake. 95
Vincentio. I'll slit the villain's nose that would have sent me to the jail.
Baptista. [*To Lucentio*] But do you hear, sir? Have you married my
  daughter without asking my good will?
Vincentio. Fear not, Baptista; we will content you, go to.°
  But I will in, to be revenged for this villainy. 100

Exit.

Baptista. And I, to sound the depth° of this knavery.

Exit.

Lucentio. Look not pale, Bianca. Thy father will not frown.

Exeunt [*Lucentio and Bianca*].

Gremio. My cake is dough,° but I'll in among the rest
  Out of hope of all but my share of the feast. [*Exit.*]
Kate. Husband, let's follow, to see the end of this ado. 105
Petruchio. First kiss me, Kate, and we will.

---

76 **spoiled** ruined   83 **supposes** pretendings (evidently an allusion to Gascoigne's play
Supposes, one of Shakespeare's sources)   83 **eyne** eyes   84 **packing** plotting   84 **with a witness**
outright, unabashed   86 **faced and braved** impudently challenged and defied   91 **bear my**
countenance take on my identity   99 **go to** (mild remonstrance; cf. "go on," "come, come,"
"don't worry")   101 **sound the depth** get to the bottom of   103 **cake is dough** project hasn't
worked out

Kate. What, in the midst of the street?
Petruchio. What, art thou ashamed of me?
Kate. No sir, God forbid, but ashamed to kiss.
Petruchio. Why, then let's home again. [*To Grumio*]   110
   Come sirrah, let's away.
Kate. Nay, I will give thee a kiss. Now pray thee, love, stay.
Petruchio. Is not this well? Come, my sweet Kate.
   Better once° than never, for never too late.°   *Exeunt.*

[**SCENE II.** *Padua. In Lucentio's house.*]

   Enter Baptista, Vincentio, Gremio, the Pedant, Lucentio, and Bianca [Pe-
   truchio, Kate, Hortensio,] Tranio, Biondello, Grumio, and Widow; the
   Servingmen with Tranio bringing in a banquet.°

Lucentio. At last, though long,° our jarring notes agree,
   And time it is, when raging war is done,
   To smile at 'scapes and perils overblown.°
   My fair Bianca, bid my father welcome
   While I with self-same kindness welcome thine.   5
   Brother Petruchio, sister Katherina,
   And thou, Hortensio, with thy loving widow,
   Feast with the best and welcome to my house.
   My banquet is to close our stomachs° up
   After our great good cheer.° Pray you, sit down,   10
   For now we sit to chat as well as eat.
Petruchio. Nothing but sit and sit, and eat and eat.
Baptista. Padua affords this kindness, son Petruchio.
Petruchio. Padua affords nothing but what is kind.
Hortensio. For both our sakes I would that word were true.   15
Petruchio. Now, for my life, Hortensio fears° his widow.
Widow. Then never trust me if I be afeard.°
Petruchio. You are very sensible and yet you miss my sense:
   I mean Hortensio is afeard of you.
Widow. He that is giddy thinks the world turns round.   20
Petruchio. Roundly° replied.
Kate.   Mistress, how mean you that?

---

   114 **once** at some time   114 **Better . . . late** better late than never   V.ii.s.d. **banquet** dessert
1 **At last, though long** at long last   3 **overblown** that have blown over   9 **stomachs** (with pun on
"irascibility"   10 **cheer** (reception at Baptista's)   16 **fears** is afraid of (the Widow puns on the
meaning "frightens")   17 **afeard** (1) frightened (2) suspected   21 **Roundly** outspokenly

Widow. Thus I conceive by° him.

Petruchio. Conceives by° me! How likes Hortensio that?

Hortensio. My widow says, thus she conceives her tale.°

Petruchio. Very well mended. Kiss him for that, good widow.   25

Kate. "He that is giddy thinks the world turns round."
    I pray you, tell me what you meant by that.

Widow. Your husband, being troubled with a shrew,
    Measures° my husband's sorrow by his° woe,
    And now you know my meaning.   30

Kate. A very mean° meaning.

Widow.   Right, I mean you.

Kate. And I am mean° indeed, respecting you.

Petruchio. To her, Kate!

Hortensio. To her, widow!

Petruchio. A hundred marks, my Kate does put her down.°   35

Hortensio. That's my office.°

Petruchio. Spoke like an officer. Ha'° to thee, lad.   *Drinks to Hortensio.*

Baptista. How likes Gremio these quick-witted folks?

Gremio. Believe me, sir, they butt° together well.

Bianca. Head and butt!° An hasty-witted body   40
    Would say your head and butt were head and horn.°

Vincentio. Ay, mistress bride, hath that awakened you?

Bianca. Ay, but not frighted me; therefore I'll sleep again.

Petruchio. Nay, that you shall not. Since you have begun,
    Have at you° for a bitter° jest or two.   45

Bianca. Am I your bird?° I mean to shift my bush,
    And then pursue me as you draw your bow.
    You are welcome all.   *Exit Bianca [with Kate and Widow].*

Petruchio. She hath prevented me.° Here, Signior Tranio,
    This bird you aimed at, though you hit her not;   50
    Therefore a health to all that shot and missed.

Tranio. O sir, Lucentio slipped° me, like his greyhound,
    Which runs himself and catches for his master.

Petruchio. A good swift° simile but something currish.

Tranio. 'Tis well, sir, that you hunted for yourself;   55
    'Tis thought your deer° does hold you at a bay.°

Baptista. O, O, Petruchio, Tranio hits you now.

---

22 **conceive by** understand   23 **Conceives by** is made pregnant by   24 **conceives her tale** understands her statement (with another pun)   29 **Measures** estimates   29 **his** his own   31 **mean** paltry   32 **am mean** (1) am moderate (2) have a low opinion   35 **put her down** defeat her (with sexual pun by Hortensio)   36 **office** job   37 **Ha'** here's, hail   39 **butt** (perhaps also "but," i.e., argue or differ)   40 **butt** (with pun on "bottom")   41 **horn** (1) butting instrument (2) symbol of cuckoldry (3) phallus   45 **Have at you** let's have   45 **bitter** biting (but good-natured)   46 **bird** prey   49 **prevented me** beaten me to it   52 **slipped** unleashed   54 **swift** quick-witted   56 **deer** (1) doe (2) dear   56 **at a bay** at bay (i.e., backed up at a safe distance)

Lucentio. I thank thee for that gird,° good Tranio.
Hortensio. Confess, confess, hath he not hit you here?
Petruchio. 'A has a little galled° me, I confess, 60
  And as the jest did glance away from me,
  'Tis ten to one it maimed you two outright.
Baptista. Now, in good sadness,° son Petruchio,
  I think thou hast the veriest° shrew of all.
Petruchio. Well, I say no. And therefore, for assurance,° 65
  Let's each one send unto his wife,
  And he whose wife is most obedient
  To come at first when he doth send for her
  Shall win the wager which we will propose.
Hortensio. Content. What's the wager?
Lucentio.   Twenty crowns. 70
Petruchio. Twenty crowns!
  I'll venture so much of° my hawk or hound,
  But twenty times so much upon my wife.
Lucentio. A hundred then.
Hortensio.   Content.°
Petruchio.   A match,° tis done.
Hortensio. Who shall begin?
Lucentio.   That will I. 75
  Go Biondello, bid your mistress come to me.
Biondello. I go.   *Exit.*
Baptista. Son, I'll be your half,° Bianca comes.
Lucentio. I'll have no halves; I'll bear it all myself.

  Enter Biondello.

  How now,° what news?
Biondello.   Sir, my mistress sends you word 80
  That she is busy and she cannot come.
Petruchio. How?° She's busy and she cannot come?
  Is that an answer?
Gremio.   Ay, and a kind one too.
  Pray God, sir, your wife send you not a worse.
Petruichio. I hope, better. 85
Hortensio. Sirrah Biondello, go and entreat my wife
  To come to me forthwith.°
                                Exit Biondello.

---

58 **gird** gibe   60 **galled** chafed   63 **sadness** seriousness   64 **veriest** most genuine   65 **assurance** proof   72 **of** on   74 **Content** agreed   74 **A match** (it's) a bet   78 **be your half** assume half your bet   80 **How now** (mild exclamation; cf. "well")   82 **How** what   87 **forthwith** right away

Petruchio.   O ho, entreat her!
    Nay, then she must needs come.
Hortensio.   I am afraid, sir,
    Do what you can, yours will not be entreated.

    Enter Biondello.

    Now where's my wife?   90
Biondello. She says you have some goodly jest in hand.
    She will not come. She bids you come to her.
Petruchio. Worse and worse. She will not come. O vile,
    Intolerable, not to be endured!
    Sirrah Grumio, go to your mistress; say   95
    I command her come to me.   *Exit* [*Grumio*].
Hortensio. I know her answer.
Petruchio.   What?
Hortensio.   She will not.
Petruchio. The fouler fortune mine, and there an end.

    Enter Kate.

Baptista. Now, by my holidame,° here comes Katherina.
Kate. What is your will, sir, that you send for me?   100
Petruchio. Where is your sister and Hortensio's wife?
Kate. They sit conferring by the parlor fire.
Petruchio. Go fetch them hither. If they deny° to come,
    Swinge° me them soundly° forth unto their husbands.
    Away, I say, and bring them hither straight.   105
                                            [*Exit Kate.*]
Lucentio. Here is a wonder, if you talk of a wonder.
Hortensio. And so it is. I wonder with it bodes.
Petruchio. Marry, peace it bodes, and love, and quiet life,
    An awful° rule and right supremacy;
    And, to be short, what not° that's sweet and happy.   110
Baptista. Now fair befall° thee, good Petruchio.
    The wager thou hast won, and I will add
    Unto their losses twenty thousand crowns,
    Another dowry to another daughter,
    For she is changed as she had never been.   115

---

99 **holidame** holy dame (some editors emend to *halidom*, sacred place or relic)   102 **conferring** conversing   103 **deny** refuse   104 **Swinge** thrash   104 **soundly** throughly (cf. "sound beating" 109 **awful** inspiring respect   110 **what not** i.e., everything   111 **fair befall** good luck to

Petruchio. Nay, I will win my wager better yet
  And show more sign of her obedience,
  Her new-built virtue and obedience.

Enter Kate, Bianca, and Widow.

  See where she comes and brings your froward° wives
  As prisoners to her womanly persuasion.   120
  Katherine, that cap of yours becomes you not.
  Off with that bauble, throw it under foot.   [*She throws it.*]
Widow. Lord, let me never have a cause to sigh
  Till I be brought to such a silly pass.°
Bianca. Fie, what a foolish—duty call you this?   125
Lucentio. I would your duty were as foolish too.
  The wisdom of your duty, fair Bianca,
  Hath cost me five hundred° crowns since suppertime.
Bianca. The more fool you for laying° on my duty.
Petruchio. Katherine, I charge thee, tell these headstrong women   130
  What duty they do owe their lords and husbands.
Widow. Come, come, you're mocking. We will have no telling.
Petruchio. Come on, I say, and first begin with her.
Widow. She shall not.
Petruchio. I say she shall—and first begin with her.   135
Kate. Fie, fie, unknit that threatening unkind° brow
  And dart not scornful glances from those eyes
  To wound thy lord, thy king, thy governor.
  It blots thy beauty as frosts do bite the meads,
  Confounds thy fame° as whirlwinds shake° fair buds,   140
  And in no sense is meet or amiable.
  A woman moved° is like a fountain troubled,
  Muddy, ill-seeming, thick, bereft of beauty,
  And while it is so, none so dry or thirsty
  Will deign to sip or touch one drop of it.   145
  Thy husband is thy lord, thy life, thy keeper,
  Thy head, they sovereign—one that cares for thee,
  And for thy maintenance commits his body
  To painful labor both by sea and land,
  To watch° the night in storms, the day in cold,   150

---

  119 **froward** uncooperative   124 **pass** situation   128 **five hundred** (1) Lucentio makes it look
worse than it is, or (2) he made several bets, or (3) the text errs (some editors emend to "a
hundred," assuming that the manuscript's "a" was misread as the roman numeral v)   129 **laying**
betting   136 **unkind** hostile   140 **Confounds thy fame** spoils people's opinion of you   140 **shake**
shake off   142 **moved** i.e., by ill temper   150 **watch** stay awake, be alert during

Whilst thou li'st warm at home, secure and safe;
And craves no other tribute at thy hands
But love, fair looks, and true obedience:
Too little payment for so great a debt.
Such duty as the subject owes the prince,   155
Each such a woman oweth to her husband,
And when she is froward, peevish, sullen, sour,
And not obedient to his honest° will,
What is she but a foul contending rebel
And graceless traitor to her loving lord?   160
I am ashamed that women are so simple°
To offer war where they should kneel for peace,
Or seek for rule, supremacy, and sway,
When they are bound to serve, love, and obey.
Why are our bodies soft and weak and smooth,   165
Unapt to° toil and trouble in the world,
But that our soft conditions° and our hearts
Should well agree with our external parts?
Come, come, you froward and unable worms,°
My mind hath been as big° as one of yours,   170
My heart as great, my reason haply more,
To bandy word for word and frown for frown.
But now I see our lances are but straws,
Our strength as weak, our weakness past compare,
That seeming to be most which we indeed least are.   175
Then vail your stomachs,° for it is no boot,°
And place your hands below your husband's foot,
In token of which duty, if he please,
My hand is ready, may it° do him ease.
Petruchio. Why, there's a wench! Come on and kiss me, Kate.   180
Lucentio. Well, go thy ways, old lad, for thou shalt ha't.
Vincentio. 'Tis a good hearing° when children are toward.°
Lucentio. But a harsh hearing when women are froward.
Petruchio. Come, Kate, we'll to bed.
We three are married, but you two are sped.°   185
'Twas I won the wager, [*to Lucentio*] though you hit the white,°
And, being a winner, God give you good night.
                              Exit Petruchio [with Kate].

---

158 **honest** honorable   161 **simple** silly   166 **Unapt to** unfitted for   167 **conditions**
qualities   169 **unable worms** weak, lowly creatures   170 **big** inflated (cf. "think big")   176 **vail
your stomachs** fell your pride   176 **no boot** useless, profitless   179 **may it** (1) I hope it may (2) if
it may   182 **hearing** thing to hear; report   182 **toward** tractable   185 **sped** done for   186 **white**
(1) bull's eye (2) *Bianca* means white

Hortensio. Now, go thy ways; thou hast tamed a curst shrow.
Lucentio. 'Tis a wonder, by your leave, she will be tamèd so.   [*Exeunt.*]

FINIS

QUESTIONS

1. What are your first impressions of Kate and her situation from Act I?
2. How difficult do you find sorting out Bianca's various suitors? Which of them do you find most interesting or promising?
3. To what extent do you suppose Petruchio's courtship of Kate is prompted by his need for money?
4. How loving and responsible a father does Baptista Minola appear to be?
5. What meaning do you attribute to Petruchio's "mad attire" and reported behavior as a bridegroom?
6. While Kate says little in Act III, what do you imagine she is thinking and feeling?
7. How do you respond to Petruchio's methods for taming Kate?
8. Are you surprised by what seems a change in Bianca in Act V? Can you explain it?
9. At the conclusion of the play, do you suppose Kate's spirit has been broken? If so, how amusing do you find this comedy?

Tennessee Williams (1911–1983)
CAT ON A HOT TIN ROOF
CHARACTERS OF THE PLAY

Margaret
Brick
Mae, sometimes called Sister Woman
Big Mama
Dixie, a little girl
Big Daddy
Reverend Tooker
Gooper, sometimes called Brother Man
Doctor Baugh, pronounced "Baw"
Lacey, a Negro servant
Sookey, another
Another little girl and two small boys

(The playing script of Act III also includes Trixie, another little girl, also Daisy, Brightie and Small, servants.)
    The bathroom door, showing only pale-blue tile and silver towel racks, is in one side wall; the hall door in the opposite wall. Two articles of furniture need mention: a big double bed which staging should make a functional part of the

set as often as suitable, the surface of which should be slightly raked to make figures on it seen more easily; and against the wall space between the two huge double doors upstage: a monumental monstrosity peculiar to our times, a *huge* console combination of radio-phonograph (Hi-Fi with three speakers) TV set *and* liquor cabinet, bearing and containing many glasses and bottles, all in one piece, which is a composition of muted silver tones, and the opalescent tones of reflecting glass, a chromatic link, this thing, between the sepia (tawny gold) tones of the interior and the cool (white and blue) tones of the gallery and sky. This piece of furniture (?!), this monument, is a very complete and compact little shrine to virtually all the comforts and illusions behind which we hide from such things as the characters in the play are faced with. . . .

The set should be far less realistic than I have so far implied in this description of it. I think the walls below the ceiling should dissolve mysteriously into air; the set should be roofed by the sky; stars and moon suggested by traces of milky pallor, as if they were observed through a telescope lens out of focus.

Anything else I can think of? Oh, yes, fanlights (transoms shaped like an open glass fan) above all the doors in the set, with panes of blue and amber, and above all, the designer should take as many pains to give the actors room to move about freely (to show their restlessness, their passion for breaking out) as if it were a set for a ballet.

An evening in summer. The action is continuous, with two intermissions.

ACT ONE

At the rise of the curtain someone is taking a shower in the bathroom, the door of which is half open. A pretty young woman, with anxious lines in her face, enters the bedroom and crosses to the bathroom door.

Margaret [*shouting above roar of water*]. One of those no-neck monsters hit me with a hot buttered biscuit so I have t' change!

[*Margaret's voice is both rapid and drawling. In her long speeches she has the vocal tricks of a priest delivering a liturgical chant, the lines are almost sung, always continuing a little beyond her breath so she has to gasp for another. Sometimes she intersperses the lines with a little wordless singing, such as "Da-da-daaaa!"*]
[*Water turns off and Brick calls out to her, but is still unseen. A tone of politely feigned interest, masking indifference, or worse, is characteristic of his speech with Margaret.*]

Brick. Wha'd you say, Maggie? Water was on s' loud I couldn't hearya. . . .
Margaret. Well, I!—just remarked that!—one of th' no-neck monsters messed up m' lovely lace dress so I got t'—cha-a-ange. . . .

[She opens and kicks shut drawers of the dresser.]

Brick. Why d'ya call Gooper's kiddies no-neck monsters?
Margaret. Because they've got no necks! Isn't that a good enough reason?
Brick. Don't they have any necks?
Margaret. None visible. Their fat little heads are set on their fat little bodies
 without a bit of connection.
Brick. That's too bad.
Margaret. Yes, it's too bad because you can't wring their necks if they've got
 no necks to wring! Isn't that right, honey?

[She steps out of her dress, stands in a slip of ivory satin and lace.]

Yep, they're no-neck monsters, all no-neck people are monsters . . .

[Children shriek downstairs.]

Hear them? Hear them screaming? I don't know where their voice-
boxes are located since they don't have necks. I tell you I got so
nervous at that table tonight I thought I would throw back my head
and utter a scream you could hear across the Arkansas border an' parts
of Louisiana an' Tennessee. I said to your charming sister-in-law, Mae,
honey, couldn't you feed those precious little things at a separate table
with an oilcloth cover? They make such a mess an' the lace cloth looks
so pretty! She made enormous eyes at me and said, "Ohhh, noooooo!
On Big Daddy's birthday? Why, he would never forgive me!" Well, I
want you to know, Big Daddy hadn't been at the table two minutes
with those five no-neck monsters slobbering and drooling over their
food before he threw down his fork an' shouted, "Fo' God's sake,
Gooper, why don't you put them pigs at a trough in th' kitchen?"—
Well, I swear, I simply could have di-ieed!
Think of it, Brick, they've got five of them and number six is coming.
They've brought the whole bunch down here like animals to display at
a county fair. Why, they have those children doin' tricks all the time!
"Junior, show Big Daddy how you do this, show Big Daddy how you
do that, say your little piece fo' Big Daddy, Sister. Show your dimples,
Sugar. Brother, show Big Daddy how you stand on your head!"—It
goes on all the time, along with constant little remarks and innuendos
about the fact that you and I have not produced any children, are
totally childless and therefore totally useless!—Of course it's comical
but it's also disgusting since it's so obvious what they're up to!
Brick *[without interest]*. What are they up to, Maggie?
Margaret. Why, you know what they're up to!
Brick *[appearing]*. No, I don't know what they're up to.

[*He stands there in the bathroom doorway drying his hair with a a towel and hanging onto the towel rack because one ankle is broken, plastered and bound. He is still slim and firm as a boy. His liquor hasn't started tearing him down outside. He has the additional charm of that cool air of detachment that people have who have given up the struggle. But now and then, when disturbed, something flashes behind it, like lightning in a fair sky, which shows that at some deeper level he is far from peaceful. Perhaps in a stronger light he would show some signs of deliquescence, but the fading, still warm, light from the gallery treats him gently.*]

Margaret. I'll tell you what they're up to, boy of mine!—They're up to cutting you out of your father's estate, and—

[*She freezes momentarily before her next remark. Her voice drops as if it were somehow a personally embarrassing admission.*]

—Now we know that Big Daddy's dying of—*cancer.* . . .

[*There are voices on the lawn below: long-drawn calls across distance. Margaret raises her lovely bare arms and powders her armpits with a light sigh.*
[*She adjusts the angle of a magnifying mirror to straighten an eyelash, then rises fretfully saying:*]

There's so much light in the room it—
Brick [*softly but sharply*]. Do we?
Margaret. Do we what?
Brick. Know Big Daddy's dyin' of cancer?
Margaret. Got the report today.
Brick. Oh . . .
Margaret [*letting down bamboo blinds which cast long, gold-fretted shadows over the room*]. Yep, got th' report just now . . . it didn't surprise me, Baby. . . .

[*Her voice has range, and music; sometimes it drops low as a boy's and you have a sudden image of her playing boy's games as a child.*]

I recognized the symptoms soon's we got here last spring and I'm willin' to bet you that Brother Man and his wife were pretty sure of it, too. That more than likely explains why their usual summer migration to the coolness of the Great Smokies was passed up this summer in favor of—hustlin' down here ev'ry whipstitch with their whole screamin' tribe! And why so many allusions have been made to Rainbow Hill lately. You know what Rainbow Hill is? Place that's famous for treatin' alcoholics an' dope fiends in the movies!

Brick. I'm not in the movies.

Margaret. No, and you don't take dope. Otherwise you're a perfect candidate
for Rainbow Hill, Baby, and that's where they aim to ship you—over my
dead body! Yep, over my dead body they'll ship you there, but nothing
would please them better. Then Brother Man could get a-hold of the purse
strings and dole out remittances to us, maybe get power-of-attorney and
sign checks for us and cut off our credit wherever, whenever he wanted!
Son-of-a-bitch!—How'd you like that, Baby?—Well, you've been doin'
just about ev'rything in your power to bring it about, you've just been
doin' ev'rything you can think of to aid and abet them in this scheme of
theirs! Quittin' work, devoting yourself to the occupation of drinkin'!—
Breaking' your ankle last night on the high school athletic field: doin'
what? Jumpin' hurdles? At two or three in the morning? Just fantastic!
Got in the paper. *Clarksdale Register* carried a nice little item about it,
human interest story about a well-known former athlete stagin' a one-man
track meet on the Glorious Hill High School athletic field last night, but
was slightly out of condition and didn't clear the first hurdle! Brother Man
Gooper claims he exercised his influence t' keep it from goin' out over AP
or UP or every goddam "P."
But, Brick? You still have one big advantage!

[*During the above swift flood of words, Brick has reclined with contra-*
puntal leisure on the snowy surface of the bed and has rolled over carefully
on his side or belly.]

Brick [*wryly*]. Did you *say* something, Maggie?

Margaret. Big Daddy dotes on you, honey. And he can't stand Brother Man
and Brother Man's wife, that monster of fertility, Mae; she's downright
odious to him! Know how I know? By little expressions that flicker over
his face when that woman is holding fo'th on one of her choice topics
such as—how she refused twilight sleep!—when the twins were delivered!
Because she feels motherhood's an experience that a woman ought to
experience fully!—in order to fully appreciate the wonder and beauty of
it! HAH!

[*This loud "HAH!" is accompanied by a violent action such as slamming*
a drawer shut.]

—and how she made Brother Man come in an' stand beside her in the
delivery room so he would not miss out on the "wonder and beauty" of
it either!—producin' those no-neck monsters. . . .

[*A speech of this kind would be antipathetic from almost anybody but*
Margaret; she makes it oddly funny, because her eyes constantly twinkle
and her voice shakes with laughter which is basically indulgent.]

—Big Daddy shares my attitude toward those two! As for me, well—I
give him a laugh now and than and he tolerates me. In fact!—I sometimes
suspect that Big Daddy harbors a little unconscious "lech" fo' me. . . .
Brick. What makes you think that Big Daddy has a lech for you, Maggie?
Margaret: Way he always drops his eyes down my body when I'm talkin' to
    him, drops his eyes to my boobs an' licks his old chops! Ha ha!
Brick. That kind of talk is disgusting.
Margaret. Did anyone ever tell you that you're an ass-aching Puritan, Brick?
    I think it's mighty fine that that ole fellow, on the doorstep of death, still
    takes in my shape with what I think is deserved appreciation!
    And you wanta know something else? Big Daddy didn't know how many
    little Maes and Goopers had been produced! "How many kids have you
    got?" he asked at the table, just like Brother Man and his wife were new
    acquaintances to him! Big Mama said he was jokin', but that ole boy
    wasn't jokin', Lord, no!
    And when they infawmed him that they had five already and were turning
    out number six!—the news seemed to come as a sort of unpleasant surprise
    . . .

[*Children yell below.*]

Scream, monsters!

[*Turns to Brick with a sudden, gay, charming smile which fades as she
notices that he is not looking at her but into fading gold space with a
troubled expression.*
[*It is constant rejection that makes her humor "bitchy."*]

Yes, you should of been at that supper-table, Baby.

[*Whenever she calls him "baby" the word is a soft caress.*]

Y'know, Big Daddy, bless his ole sweet soul, he's the dearest ole thing in
the world, but he does hunch over his food as if he preferred not to notice
anything else. Well, Mae an' Gooper were side by side at the table, direckly
across from Big Daddy, watchin' his face like hawks while they jawed an'
jabbered about the cuteness an' brilliance of th' no-neck monsters!

[*She giggles with a hand fluttering at her throat and her breast and her
long throat arched.*
[*She comes downstage and recreates the scene with voice and gesture.*]

And the no-neck monsters were ranged around the table, some in high
chairs and some on th' *Books of Knowledge,* all in fancy little paper caps
in honor of Big Daddy's birthday, and all through dinner, well, I want

you to know that Brother Man an' his partner never once, for one moment, stopped exchanging pokes an' pinches an' kicks an' signs an' signals!— Why, they were like a couple of cardsharps fleecing a sucker.—Even Big Mama, bless her ole sweet soul, she isn't th' quickest an' brightest thing in the world, she finally noticed, at last, an' said to Gooper, "Gooper, what are you an Mae makin' all these signs at each other about?"—I swear t' goodness, I nearly choked on my chicken!

[Margaret, back at the dressing-table, still doesn't see Brick. He is watching her with a look that is not quite definable.—Amused? shocked? contemptuous?—part of those and part of something else.]

Y'know—your brother Gooper still cherishes the illusion he took a giant step up on the social ladder when he married Miss Mae Flynn of the Memphis Flynns.

[Margaret moves about the room as she talks, stops before the mirror, moves on.]

But I have a piece of Spanish news for Gooper. The Flynns never had a thing in this world but money and they lost that, they were nothing at all but fairly successful climbers. Of course, Mae Flynn came out in Memphis eights years before I made my debut in Nashville, but I had friends at Ward-Belmont who came from Memphis and they used to come to see me and I used to go to see them for Christmas and spring vacations, and so I know who rates an' who doesn't rate in Memphis society. Why, y'know ole Papa Flynn, he barely escaped doing time in the Federal pen for shady manipulations on th' stock market when his chain stores crashed, and as for Mae having been a cotton carnival queen, as they remind us so often, lest we forget, well, that's one honor that I don't envy her for!—Sit on a brass throne on a tacky float an' ride down Main Street, smilin', bowin', and blowin' kisses to all the trash on the street—

[She picks out a pair of jeweled sandals and rushes to the dressing-table.]

Why, year before last, when Susan McPheeters was singled out fo' that honor, y' know what happened to her? Y'know what happened to poor little Susie McPheeters?
Brick [*absently*]. No. What happened to little Susie McPheeters?
Margaret. Somebody spit tobacco juice in her face.
Brick [*dreamily*]. Somebody spit tobacco juice in her face?
Margaret. That's right, some old drunk leaned out of a window in the Hotel Gayoso and yelled, "Hey, Queen, hey, hey, there, Queenie!" Poor Susie looked up and flashed him a radiant smile and he shot out a squirt of tobacco juice right in poor Susie's face.

Brick. Well, what d'you know about that.
Margaret [*gaily*]. What do I know about it? I was there, I saw it!
Brick [*absently*]. Must have been kind of funny.
Margaret. Susie didn't think so. Had hysterics. Screamed like a banshee.
They had to stop th' parade an' remove her from her throne an' go on
with—

[*She catches sight of him in the mirror, gasps slightly, wheels about to
face him. Count ten.*]

—Why are you looking at me like that?
Brick [*whistling softly, now*]. Like what, Maggie?
Margaret [*intensely, fearfully*]. The way y' were lookin' at me just now, befo'
I caught your eye in the mirror and you started t' whistle! I don't know
how t' describe it but it froze my blood!—I've caught you lookin' at me
like that so often lately. What are you thinkin' of when you look at me
like that?
Brick. I wasn't conscious of lookin' at you, Maggie.
Margaret. Well, I was conscious of it! What were you thinkin'?
Brick. I don't remember thinking of anything, Maggie.
Margaret. Don't you think I know that—? Don't you—?—Think I know
that—?
Brick [*coolly*]. Know *what*, Maggie?
Margaret [*struggling for expression*]. That I've gone through this—*hideous!*—
transformation, become—*hard! Frantic!*

[*Then she adds, almost tenderly.*]

—*cruel!!*
That's what you've been observing in me lately. How could y' help but
observe it? That's all right. I'm not—*thin-skinned any more*, can't afford
t' be thin-skinned any more.

[*She is now recovering her power.*]

—But Brick? Brick?
Brick. Did you say something?
Margaret. I was goin' t' say something: that I get—lonely. Very!
Brick. Ev'rybody gets that . . .
Margaret. Living with someone you love can be lonelier—than living entirely
alone!—if the one that y' love doesn't love you. . . .

[*There is a pause. Brick hobbles downstage and asks, without looking at
her:*]

Brick. Would you like to live alone, Maggie?

[*Another pause: then—after she has caught a quick, hurt breath:*]

Margaret. No!—God!—I wouldn't!

[*Another gasping breath. She forcibly controls what must have been an impulse to cry out. We see her deliberately, very forcibly, going all the way back to the world in which you can talk about ordinary matters.*]

Did you have a nice shower?
Brick. Uh-huh.
Margaret. Was the water cool?
Brick. No.
Margaret. But it made y' feel fresh, huh?
Brick. Fresher. . . .
Margaret. I know something would make y' feel *much* fresher!
Brick. What?
Margaret. An alcohol rub. Or cologne, a rub with cologne!
Brick. That's good after a workout but I haven't been workin' out, Maggie.
Margaret. You've kept in good shape, though.
Brick [*indifferently*]. You think so, Maggie?
Margaret. I always thought drinkin' men lost their looks, but I was plainly mistaken.
Brick [*wryly*]. Why, thanks, Maggie.
Margaret. You're the only drinkin' man I know that it never seems t' put fat on.
Brick. I'm gettin' softer, Maggie.
Margaret. Well, sooner or later it's bound to soften you up. It was just beginning to soften up Skipper when—

[*She stops short.*]

I'm sorry. I never could keep my finger off a sore—I wish you *would* lose your looks. If you did it would make the martyrdom of Saint Maggie a little more bearable. But no such goddam luck. I actually believe you've gotten better looking since you've gone on the bottle. Yeah, a person who didn't know you would think you'd never had a tense nerve in your body or a strained muscle.

[*There are sounds of croquet on the lawn below: the click of mallets, light voices, near and distant.*]

Of course, you always had that detached quality as if you were playing a game without much concern over whether you won or lost, and now that you've lost the game, not lost but just quit playing, you have that rare sort of charm that usually only happens in very old or hopelessly sick people, the charm of the defeated.—You look so cool, so cool, so enviably cool.

[*Music is heard.*]

They're playing croquet. The moon has appeared and it's white, just beginning to turn a little bit yellow. . . .
You were a wonderful lover. . . .
Such a wonderful person to go to bed with, and I think mostly because
you were really indifferent to it. Isn't that right? Never had any anxiety
about it, did it naturally, easily, slowly, with absolute confidence and
perfect calm, more like opening a door for a lady or seating her at a table
than giving expression to any longing for her. Your indifference made you
wonderful at lovemaking—*strange?*—but true. . . .
You know, if I thought you would never, never, *never* make love to me
again—I would go downstairs to the kitchen and pick out the longest and
sharpest knife I could find and stick it straight into my heart, I swear that
I would!
But one thing I don't have is the charm of the defeated, my hat is still in
the ring, and I am determined to win!

[*There is the sound of croquet mallets hitting croquet balls.*]

—What is the victory of a cat on a hot tin roof?—I wish I knew. . . .
Just staying on it, I guess, as long as she can. . . .

[*More croquet sounds.*]

Later tonight I'm going to tell you I love you an' maybe by that time you'll
be drunk enough to believe me. Yes, they're playing croquet. . . .
Big Daddy is dying of cancer. . . .
What were you thinking of when I caught you looking at me like that?
Were you thinking of Skipper?

[*Brick takes up his crutch, rises.*]

Oh, excuse me, forgive me, but laws of silence don't work! No, laws of
silence don't work. . . .

[*Brick crosses to the bar, takes a quick drink, and rubs his head with a
towel.*]

Laws of silence don't work. . . .
When something is festering in your memory or your imagination, laws
of silence don't work, it's just like shutting a door and locking it on a
house on fire in hope of forgetting that the house is burning. But not facing
a fire doesn't put it out. Silence about a thing just magnifies it. It grows
and festers in silence, becomes malignant. . . .
Get dressed, Brick.

[*He drops his crutch.*]

Brick. I've dropped my crutch.

[*He has stopped rubbing his hair dry but still stands hanging onto the towel rack in a white towel-cloth robe.*]

Margaret. Lean on me.
Brick. No, just give me my crutch.
Margaret. Lean on my shoulder.
Brick. I don't want to lean on your shoulder, I want my crutch!

[*This is spoken like sudden lightning.*]

Are you going to give me my crutch or do I have to get down on my knees on the floor and—
Margaret. Here, here, take it, take it!

[*She has thrust the crutch at him.*]

Brick [*hobbling out*]. Thanks . . .
Margaret. We mustn't scream at each other, the walls in this house have ears. . . .

[*He hobbles directly to liquor cabinet to get a new drink.*]

—but that's the first time I've heard you raise your voice in a long time, Brick. A crack in the wall?—Of composure?
—I think that's a good sign. . . .
A sign of nerves in a player on the defensive!

[*Brick turns and smiles at her coolly over his fresh drink.*]

Brick. It just hasn't happened yet, Maggie.
Margaret. What?
Brick. The click I get in my head when I've had enough of this stuff to make me peaceful. . . .
Will you do me a favor?
Margaret. Maybe I will. What favor?
Brick. Just, just keep your voice down!
Margaret [*in a hoarse whisper*]. I'll do you that favor, I'll speak in a whisper, if not shut up completely, if *you* will do *me* a favor and make that drink your last one till after the party.
Brick. What party?
Margaret. Big Daddy's birthday party.
Brick. Is this Big Daddy's birthday?

Margaret. You know this is Big Daddy's birthday!
Brick. No, I don't, I forgot it.
Margaret. Well, I remembered it for you. . . .

[*They are both speaking as breathlessly as a pair of kids after a fight, drawing deep exhausted breaths and looking at each other with faraway eyes, shaking and panting together as if they had broken apart from a violent struggle.*]

Brick. Good for you, Maggie.
Margaret. You just have to scribble a few lines on this card.
Brick. You scribble something, Maggie.
Margaret. It's got to be your handwriting; it's your present, I've given him my present; it's got to be your handwriting!

[*The tension between them is building again, the voices becoming shrill once more.*]

Brick. I didn't get him a present.
Margaret. I got one for you.
Brick. All right. You write the card, then.
Margaret. And have him know you didn't remember his birthday?
Brick. I didn't remember his birthday.
Margaret. You don't have to prove you didn't!
Brick. I don't want to fool him about it.
Margaret. Just write "Love, Brick!" for God's—
Brick. No.
Margaret. You've *got* to!
Brick. I don't have to do anything I don't want to do. You keep forgetting the conditions on which I agreed to stay on living with you.
Margaret [*out before she knows it*]. I'm not living with you. We occupy the same cage.
Brick. You've got to remember the conditions agreed on.
Margaret. They're impossible conditions!
Brick. Then why don't you—?
Margaret. HUSH! Who is out there? Is somebody at the door?

[*There are footsteps in hall.*]

Mae [*outside*]. May I enter a moment?
Margaret. Oh, *you!* Sure. Come in, Mae.

[*Mae enters bearing aloft the bow of a young lady's archery set.*]

Mae. Brick, is this thing yours?

Margaret. Why, Sister Woman—that's my Diana Trophy. Won it at the intercollegiate archery contest on the Ole Miss campus.

Mae. It's a mighty dangerous thing to leave exposed round a house full of nawmal rid-blooded children attracted t'weapons.

Margaret. 'Nawmal rid-blooded children attracted t'weapons" ought t'be taught to keep their hands off things that don't belong to them.

Mae. Maggie, honey, if you had children of your own you'd know how funny that is. Will you please lock this up and put the key out of reach?

Margaret. Sister Woman, nobody is plotting the destruction of your kiddies. —Brick and I still have our special archers' license. We're goin' deer-huntin' on Moon Lake as soon as the season starts. I love to run with dogs through chilly woods, run, run leap over obstructions—

[*She goes into the closet carrying the bow.*]

Mae. How's the injured ankle, Brick?

Brick. Doesn't hurt. Just itches.

Mae. Oh, my! Brick—Brick, you should've been downstairs after supper! Kiddies put on a show. Polly played the piano, Buster an' Sonny drums, an' then they turned out the lights an' Dixie an' Trixie puhfawmed a toe dance in fairy costume with *spahkluhs!* Big Daddy just beamed! He just beamed!

Margaret [*from the closet with a sharp laugh*]. Oh, I bet. It breaks my heart that we missed it!

[*She reenters.*]

But Mae? Why did y'give dawgs' names to all your kiddies?

Mae. Dogs' names?

[*Margaret has made this observation as she goes to raise the bamboo blinds, since the sunset glare has diminished. In crossing she winks at Brick.*]

Margaret [*sweetly*]. Dixie, Trixie, Buster, Sonny, Polly!—Sounds like four dogs and a parrot . . . animal act in a circus!

Mae. Maggie?

[*Margaret turns with a smile.*]

Why are you so catty?

Margaret. Cause I'm a cat! But why can't *you* take a joke, Sister Woman?

Mae. Nothin' pleases me more than a joke that's funny. You know the real names of our kiddies. Buster's real name is Robert. Sonny's real name is Saunders. Trixie's real name is Marlene and Dixie's—

[*Someone downstairs calls for her. "Hey, Mae!"—She rushes to door, saying:*]

Intermission is over!

Margaret [*as Mae closes door*]. I wonder what Dixie's real name is?

Brick. Maggie, being catty doesn't help things any . . .

Margaret. I know! *WHY!*—Am I so catty?—Cause I'm consumed with envy an' eaten up with longing?—Brick, I've laid out your beautiful Shantung silk suit from Rome and one of your monogrammed silk shirts. I'll put your cuff-links in it, those lovely star sapphires I get you to wear so rarely. . . .

Brick. I can't get trousers on over this plaster cast.

Margaret. Yes, you can, I'll help you.

Brick. I'm not going to get dressed, Maggie.

Margaret. Will you just put on a pair of white silk pajamas?

Brick. Yes, I'll do that, Maggie.

Margaret. Thank you, thank you *so much!*

Brick. Don't mention it.

Margaret. Oh, Brick! How long does it have t' go on? This punishment? Haven't I done time enough, haven't I served my term, can't I apply for a—pardon?

Brick. Maggie, you're spoiling my liquor. Lately your voice always sounds like you'd been running upstairs to warn somebody that the house was on fire!

Margaret. Well, no wonder, no wonder. Y'know what I feel like, Brick?

[*Children's and grownups' voices are blended, below, in a loud but uncertain rendition of "My Wild Irish Rose."*]

I feel all the time like a cat on a hot tin roof!

Brick. Then jump off the roof, jump off it, cats can jump off roofs and land on their four feet uninjured!

Margaret. Oh, yes!

Brick. Do it!—fo' God's sake, do it . . .

Margaret. Do what?

Brick. Take a lover!

Margaret. I can't see a man but you! Even with my eyes closed, I just see you! Why don't you get ugly, Brick, why don't you please get fat or ugly or something so I could stand it?

[*She rushes to hall door, opens it, listens.*]

The concert is still going on! Bravo, no-necks, bravo!

[*She slams and locks door fiercely.*]

Brick. What did you lock the door for?
Margaret. To give us a little privacy for a while.
Brick. You know better, Maggie.
Margaret. No, I don't know better. . . .

[*She rushes to gallery doors, draws the rose-silk drapes across them.*]

Brick. Don't make a fool of yourself.
Margaret. I don't mind makin' a fool of myself over you!
Brick. I mind, Maggie. I feel embarrassed for you.
Margaret. Feel embarrassed! But don't continue my torture. I can't live on
  and on under these circumstances.
Brick. You agreed to—
Margaret. I know but—
Brick. —Accept that condition!
Margaret. I CAN'T! CAN'T! CAN'T!

[*She seizes his shoulder.*]

Brick. Let go!

[*He breaks away from her and seizes the small boudoir chair and raises
it like a lion-tamer facing a big circus cat.*
[*Count five. She stares at him with her fist pressed to her mouth, then
bursts into shrill, almost hysterical laughter. He remains grave for a moment, then grins and puts the chair down.*
[*Big Mama calls through closed door.*]

Big Mama. Son? Son? Son?
Brick. What is it, Big Mama?
Big Mama [*outside*]. Oh, son! We got the most wonderful news about Big
  Daddy. I just had t' run up an' tell you right this—

[*She rattles the knob.*]

—What's this door doin', locked, faw? You all think there's robbers in
  the house?
Margaret. Big Mama, Brick is dressin', he's not dressed yet.
Big Mama. That's all right, it won't be the first time I've seen Brick not
  dressed. Come on, open this door!

[*Margaret, with a grimace, goes to unlock and open the hall door, as Brick
hobbles rapidly to the bathroom and kicks the door shut. Big Mama has
disappeared from the hall.*]

Margaret. Big Mama?

[*Big Mama appears through the opposite gallery doors behind Margaret, huffing and puffing like an old bulldog. She is a short, stout woman; her sixty years and 170 pounds have left her somewhat breathless most of the time; she's always tensed like a boxer, or rather, a Japanese wrestler. Her "family" was maybe a little superior to Big Daddy's, but not much. She wears a black or silver lace dress and at least half a million in flashy gems. She is very sincere.*]

Big Mama [*loudly, startling Margaret*]. Here—I come through Gooper's and Mae's gall'ry door. Where's Brick? *Brick*—Hurry on out of there, son, I just have a second and want to give you the news about Big Daddy.—I hate locked doors in a house. . . .

Margaret [*with affected lightness*]. I've noticed you do, Big Mama, but people have got to have *some* moments of privacy, don't they?

Big Mama. No, ma'am, not in *my* house. [*Without pause*] Whacha took off you' dress faw? I thought that little lace dress was so sweet on yuh, honey.

Margaret. I thought it looked sweet on me, too, but one of m' cute little table-partners used it for a napkin so—!

Big Mama [*picking up stockings on floor*]. What?

Margaret. You know, Big Mama, Mae and Gooper's so touchy about those children—thanks, Big Mama . . .

[*Big Mama has thrust the picked-up stockings in Margaret's hand with a grunt.*]

—that you just don't dare to suggest there's any room for improvement in their—

Big Mama. Brick, hurry out!—Shoot, Maggie, you just don't like children.

Margaret. I do SO like children! Adore them!—well brought up!

Big Mama [*gentle—loving*]. Well, why don't you have some and bring them up well, then, instead of all the time pickin' on Gooper's an' Mae's?

Gooper [*shouting up the stairs*]. Hey, hey, Big Mama, Betsy an' Hugh got to go, waitin' t' tell yuh g'by!

Big Mama. Tell 'em to hold their hawses, I'll be right down in a jiffy!

[*She turns to the bathroom door and calls out.*]

Son? Can you hear me in there?

[*There is a muffled answer.*]

We just got the full report from the laboratory at the Ochsner Clinic, completely negative, son, ev'rything negative, right on down the line!

Nothin' a-tall's wrong with him but some little functional thing called a spastic colon. Can you hear me, son?

Margaret. He can hear you, Big Mama.

Big Mama. Then why don't he say something? God Almighty, a piece of news like that should make him shout. It makes *me* shout, I can tell you. I shouted and sobbed and fell right down on my knees!—Look!

[*She pulls up her skirt.*]

See the bruises where I hit my kneecaps? Took both doctors to haul me back on my feet!

[*She laughs—she always laughs like hell at herself.*]

Big Daddy was furious with me! But ain't that wonderful news?

[*Facing bathroom again, she continues:*]

After all the anxiety we been through to git a report like that on Big Daddy's birthday? Big Daddy tried to hide how much of a load that news took off his mind, but didn't fool *me.* He was mighty close to crying about it *himself!*

[*Goodbyes are shouted downstairs, and she rushes to door.*]

Hold those people down there, don't let them go!—Now, git dressed, we're all comin' up to this room fo' Big Daddy's birthday party because of your ankle.—How's his ankle, Maggie?

Margaret. Well, he broke it, Big Mama.

Big Mama. I know he broke it.

[*A phone is ringing in hall. A Negro voice answers: "Mistuh Polly's res'd-ence."*]

I mean does it hurt him much still.

Margaret. I'm afraid I can't give you that information, Big Mama. You'll have to ask Brick if it hurts much still or not.

Sookey [*in the hall*]. It's Memphis, Mizz Polly, it's Miss Sally in Memphis.

Big Mama. Awright, Sookey.

[*Big Mama rushes into the hall and is heard shouting on the phone:*]

Hello, Miss Sally. How are you, Miss Sally?—Yes, well, I was just gonna call you about it. *Shoot!*—

[*She raises her voice to a bellow.*]

Miss Sally? Don't ever call me from the Gayoso Lobby, too much talk goes on in that hotel lobby, no wonder you can't hear me! Now listen, Miss Sally. They's nothin' serious wrong with Big Daddy. We got the report just now, they's nothin' wrong but a thing called a—spastic! *SPAS-TIC!*—colon. . . .

[*She appears at the hall door and calls to Margaret.*]

—Maggie, come out here and talk to that fool on the phone. I'm shouted breathless!

Margaret [*goes out and is heard sweetly at phone*]. Miss Sally? This is Brick's wife, Maggie. So nice to hear your voice. Can you hear *mine*? Well, *good!*— Big Mama just wanted you to know that they've got the report from the Ochsner Clinic and what Big Daddy has is a spastic colon. Yes. Spastic colon, Miss Sally. That's right, spastic colon. *G'bye, Miss Sally, hope I'll see you real soon!*

[*Hangs up a little before Miss Sally was probably ready to terminate the talk. She returns through the hall door.*]

She heard me perfectly. I've discovered with deaf people the thing to do is not shout at them but just enunciate clearly. My rich old Aunt Cornelia was deaf as the dead but I could make her hear me just by sayin' each word slowly, distinctly, close to her ear. I read her the *Commercial Appeal* ev'ry night, read her the classified ads in it, even, she never missed a word of it. But was she a mean ole thing! Know what I got when she died? Her unexpired subscriptions to five magazines and the Book-of-the-Month Club and a LIBRARY full of ev'ry dull book ever written! All else went to her hellcat of a sister . . . meaner than she was, even!

[*Big Mama has been straightening things up in the room during this speech.*]

Big Mama [*closing closet door on discarded clothes*]. Miss Sally sure is a case! Big Daddy says she's always got her hand out fo' something. He's not mistaken. That poor ole thing always has her hand out fo' somethin'. I don't think Big Daddy gives her as much as he should.

[*Somebody shouts for her downstairs and she shouts:*]

I'm comin'!

[*She starts out. At the hall door, turns and jerks a forefinger, first toward the bathroom door, then toward the liquor cabinet, meaning: "Has Brick been drinking?" Margaret pretends not to understand, cocks her head and*]

raises her brows as if the pantomimic performance was completely mys-
tifying to her.
[*Big Mama rushes back to Margaret:*]

Shoot! Stop playin' so dumb!—I mean has he been drinkin' that stuff much
   yet?
Margaret [*with a little laugh*]. Oh! I think he had a highball after supper.
Big Mama. Don't laugh about it!—Some single men stop drinkin' when they
   git married and others start! Brick never touched liquor before he—!
Margaret [*crying out*]. *THAT'S NOT FAIR!*
Big Mama. Fair or not fair I want to ask you a question, one question: D'you
   make Brick happy in bed?
Margaret. Why don't you ask if he makes *me* happy in bed?
Big Mama. Because I know that—
Margaret. It works both ways!
Big Mama. Something's not right! You're childless and my son drinks!

[*Someone has called her downstairs and she has rushed to the door on
the line above. She turns at the door and points at the bed.*]

—When a marriage goes on the rocks, the rocks are *there*, right *there!*
Margaret. That's—

[*Big Mama has swept out of the room and slammed the door.*]

—not—*fair . . .*

[*Margaret is alone, completely alone, and she feels it. She draws in, hunches
her shoulders, raises her arms with fists clenched, shuts her eyes tight as
a child about to be stabbed with a vaccination needle. When she opens
her eyes again, what she sees is the long oval mirror and she rushes straight
to it, stares into it with a grimace and says: "Who are you?"—Then she
crouches a little and answers herself in a different voice which is high,
thin, mocking: "I am Maggie the Cat!"—Straightens quickly as bathroom
door opens a little and Bricks calls out to her.*]

Brick. Has Big Mama gone?
Margaret. She's gone.

[*He opens the bathroom door and hobbles out, with his liquor glass now
empty, straight to the liquor cabinet. He is whistling softly. Margaret's
head pivots on her long, slender throat to watch him.*
[*She raises a hand uncertainly to the base of her throat, as if it was difficult
for her to swallow, before she speaks:*]

You know, our sex life didn't just peter out in the usual way, it was cut off short, long before the natural time for it to, and it's going to revive again, just as sudden as that. I'm confident of it. That's what I'm keeping myself attractive for. For the time when you'll see me again like other men see me. Yes, like other men see me. They still see me, Brick, and they like what they see. Uh-huh. Some of them would give their—
Look, Brick!

[*She stands before the long oval mirror, touches her breast and then her hips with her two hands.*]

How high my body stays on me!—Nothing has fallen on me—not a fraction. . . .

[*Her voice is soft and trembling: a pleading child's. At this moment as he turns to glance at her—a look which is like a player passing a ball to another player, third down and goal to go—she has to capture the audience in a grip so tight that she can hold it till the first intermission without any lapse of attention.*]

Other men still want me. My face looks strained, sometimes, but I've kept my figure as well as you've kept yours, and men admire it. I still turn heads on the street. Why, last week in Memphis everywhere that I went men's eyes burned holes in my clothes, at the country club and in restaurants and department stores, there wasn't a man I met or walked by that didn't just eat me up with his eyes and turn around when I passed him and look back at me. Why, at Alice's party for her New York cousins, the best lookin' man in the crowd—followed me upstairs and tried to force his way in the powder room with me, followed me to the door and tried to force his way in!
Brick. Why didn't you let him, Maggie?
Margaret. Because I'm not that common, for one thing. Not that I wasn't almost tempted to. You like to know who it was? It was Sonny Boy Maxwell, that's who!
Brick. Oh, yeah, Sonny Boy Maxwell, he was a good end-runner but had a little injury to his back and had to quit.
Margaret. He has no injury now and has no wife and still has a lech for me!
Brick. I see no reason to lock him out of a powder room in that case.
Margaret. And have someone catch me at it? I'm not that stupid. Oh, I might sometime cheat on you with someone, since you're so insultingly eager to have me do it!—But if I do, you can be damned sure it will be in a place and a time where no one but me and the man could possibly know. Because I'm not going to give you any excuse to divorce me for being unfaithful or anything else. . . .

Brick. Maggie, I wouldn't divorce you for being unfaithful or anything else. Don't you know that? Hell. I'd be relieved to know that you'd found yourself a lover.

Margaret. Well, I'm taking no chances. No, I'd rather stay on this hot tin roof.

Brick. A hot tin roof's 'n uncomfo'table place t' stay on. . . .

[*He starts to whistle softly.*]

Margaret [*through his whistle*]. Yeah, but I can stay on it just as long as I have to.

Brick. You could leave me, Maggie.

[*He resumes whistle. She wheels about to glare at him.*]

Margaret. Don't want to and will not! Besides if I did, you don't have a cent to pay for it but what you get from Big Daddy and he's dying of cancer!

[*For the first time a realization of Big Daddy's doom seems to penetrate to Brick's consciousness, visibly, and he looks at Margaret.*]

Brick. Big Mama just said he *wasn't,* that the report was okay.

Margaret. That's what she thinks because she got the same story that they gave Big Daddy. And was just as taken in by it as he was, poor ole things. . . .

But tonight they're going to tell her the truth about it. When Big Daddy goes to bed, they're going to tell her that he is dying of cancer.

[*She slams the dresser drawer.*]

—It's malignant and it's terminal.

Brick. Does Big Daddy know it?

Margaret. Hell, do they *ever* know it? Nobody says, "You're dying." You have to fool them. They have to fool *themselves.*

Brick. Why?

Margaret. Why? Because human beings dream of life everlasting, that's the reason! But most of them want it on earth and not in heaven.

[*He gives a short, hard laugh at her touch of humor.*]

Well. . . . [*She touches up her mascara.*] That's how it is, anyhow. . . . [*She looks about.*] Where did I put down my cigarette? Don't want to burn up the home-place, at least not with Mae and Gooper and their five monsters in it!

[*She has found it and sucks at it greedily. Blows out smoke and continues:*]

So this is Big Daddy's last birthday. And Mae and Gooper, they know it, oh, *they* know it, all right. They got the first information from the Ochsner Clinic. That's why they rushed down here with their no-neck monsters. Because. Do you know something? Big Daddy's made no will? Big Daddy's never made out any will in his life, and so this campaign's afoot to impress him, forcibly as possible, with the fact that you drink and I've borne no children!

[*He continues to stare at her a moment, then mutters something sharp but not audible and hobbles rather rapidly out onto the long gallery in the fading, much faded, gold light.*]

Margaret [*continuing her liturgical chant*]. Y'know, I'm *fond* of Big Daddy, I am genuinely fond of that old man, I really *am*, you know. . . .
Brick [*faintly, vaguely*]. Yes, I know you are. . . .
Margaret. I've always sort of admired him in spite of his coarseness, his four-letter words and so forth. Because Big Daddy *is* what he *is,* and he makes no bones about it. He hasn't turned gentleman farmer, he's still a Mississippi red neck, as much of a red neck as he must have been when he was just overseer here on the old Jack Straw and Peter Ochello place. But he got hold of it an' built it into th' biggest an' finest plantation in the Delta.— I've always *liked* Big Daddy. . . .

[*She crosses to the proscenium.*]

Well, this is Big Daddy's last birthday. I'm sorry about it. But I'm facing the facts. It takes money to take care of a drinker and that's the office that I've been elected to lately.
Brick. You don't have to take care of me.
Margaret. Yes, I do. Two people in the same boat have got to take care of each other. At least you want money to buy more Echo Spring when this supply is exhausted, or will you be satisfied with a ten-cent beer?
Mae an' Gooper are plannin' to freeze us out of Big Daddy's estate because you drink and I'm childless. But we can defeat that plan. We're *going* to defeat that plan!
Brick, *y'know, I've been so God damn disgustingly poor all my life!*— That's the *truth*, Brick!
Brick. I'm not sayin' it isn't.
Margaret. Always had to suck up to people I couldn't stand because they had money and I was poor as Job's turkey. You don't know what that's like. Well, I'll tell you, it's like you would feel a thousand miles away from Echo Spring!—And had to get back to it on that broken ankle . . . without a crutch!

That's how it feels to be as poor as Job's turkey and have to suck up to relatives that you hated because they had money and all you had was a bunch of hand-me-down clothes and a few old moldy three per cent government bonds. My daddy loved his liquor, he fell in love with his liquor the way you've fallen in love with Echo Spring!—And my poor Mama, having to maintain some semblance of social position, to keep appearances up, on an income of one hundred and fifty dollars a month on those old government bonds!

When I came out, the year that I made by debut, I had just two evening dresses! One Mother made me from a pattern in *Vogue*, the other a hand-me-down from a snotty rich cousin I hated!

—The dress that I married you in was my grandmother's weddin' gown . . .

So that's why I'm like a cat on a hot tin roof!

[*Brick is still on the gallery. Someone below calls up to him in a warm Negro voice, "Hiya, Mistuh Brick, how yuh feelin'?" Brick raises his liquor glass as if that answered the question.*]

Margaret. You can be young without money but you can't be old without it. You've got to be old *with* money because to be old without it is just too awful, you've got to be one or the other, either *young* or *with money*, you can't be old and *without* it. —That's the *truth*, Brick. . . .

[*Brick whistles softly, vaguely.*]

Well, now I'm dressed, I'm all dressed, there's nothing else for me to do.

[*Forlornly, almost fearfully.*]

I'm dressed, all dressed, nothing else for me to do. . . .

[*She moves about restlessly, aimlessly, and speaks, as if to herself.*]

I know when I made my mistake.—What am I—? Oh!—my bracelets. . . .

[*She starts working a collection of bracelets over her hands onto her wrists, about six on each, as she talks.*]

I've thought a whole lot about it and now I know when I made my mistake. Yes, I made my mistake when I told you the truth about that thing with Skipper. Never should have confessed it, a fatal error, tellin' you about that thing with Skipper.

Brick. Maggie, shut up about Skipper. I mean it, Maggie; you got to shut up about Skipper.

Margaret. You ought to understand that Skipper and I—

Brick. You don't think I'm serious Maggie? You're fooled by the fact that I am saying this quiet? Look, Maggie. What you're doing is a dangerous thing to do. You're—you're—you're—foolin' with something that—nobody ought to fool with.

Margaret. This time I'm going to finish what I have to say to you. Skipper and I made love, if love you could call it, because it made both of us feel a little bit closer to you. You see, you son of a bitch, you asked too much of people, of me, of him, of all the unlucky poor damned sons of bitches that happen to love you, and there was a whole pack of them, yes, there was a pack of them besides me and Skipper, you asked too goddam much of people that loved you, you—superior creature!—you godlike being!— And so we made love to each other to dream it was you, both of us! Yes, yes, yes! Truth, truth! What's so awful about it? I like it, I think the truth is—yeah! I shouldn't have told you. . . .

Brick [*holding his head unnaturally still and uptilted a bit*]. It was Skipper that told me about it. Not you, Maggie.

Margaret. I told you!

Brick. After he told me!

Margaret. What does it matter who—?

[*Brick turns suddenly out upon the gallery and calls:*]

Brick. Little girl! Hey, little girl!

Little Girl [*at a distance*]. What, Uncle Brick?

Brick. Tell the folks to come up!—Bring everybody upstairs!

Margaret. I can't stop myself! I'd go on telling you this in front of them all, if I had to!

Brick. Little girl! Go on, go on, will you? Do what I told you, call them!

Margaret. Because it's got to be told and you, you!—you never let me!

[*She sobs, then controls herself, and continues almost calmly.*]

It was one of those beautiful, ideal things they tell about in the Greek legends, it couldn't be anything else, you being you, and that's what made it so sad, that's what made it so awful, because it was love that never could be carried through to anything satisfying or even talked about plainly. Brick, I tell you, you got to believe me, Brick, I *do* understand all about it! I—I think it was—*noble!* Can't you tell I'm sincere when I say I respect it? My only point, the only point that I'm making, is life has got to be allowed to continue even after the *dream* of life is—all—over. . . .

[*Brick is without his crutch. Leaning on furniture, he crosses to pick it up as she continues as if possessed by a will outside herself:*]

Why I remember when we double-dated at college, Gladys Fitzgerald and I and you and Skipper, it was more like a date between you and Skipper. Gladys and I were just sort of tagging along as if it was necessary to chaperone you!—to make a good public impression—

Brick [*turns to face her, half lifting his crutch*]. Maggie, you want me to hit you with this crutch? Don't you know I could kill you with this crutch?

Margaret. Good Lord, man, d' you think I'd care if you did?

Brick. A man has one great good true thing in his life. One great good thing which is true!—I had friendship with Skipper.—You are naming it dirty!

Margaret. I'm not naming it dirty! I am naming it clean.

Brick. Not love with you, Maggie, but friendship with Skipper was that one great true thing, and you are naming it dirty!

Margaret. Then you haven't been listenin', not understood what I'm saying! I'm naming it so damn clean that it killed poor Skipper!—You two had something that had to be kept on ice, yes, incorruptible, yes!—and death was the only icebox where you could keep it. . . .

Brick. I married you, Maggie. Why would I marry you, Maggie, if I was—?

Margaret. Brick, don't brain me yet, let me finish!—I know, believe me I know, that it was only Skipper that harbored even any *unconscious* desire for anything not perfectly pure between you two!—Now let me skip a little. You married me early that summer we graduated out of Ole Miss, and we were happy, weren't we, we were blissful, yes, hit heaven together ev'ry time that we loved! But that fall you an' Skipper turned down wonderful offers of jobs in order to keep on bein' football heroes—pro-football heroes. You organized the Dixie Stars that fall, so you could keep on bein' team-mates forever! But somethin' was not right with it!—*Me included!*—between you. Skipper began hittin' the bottle . . . you got a spinal injury— couldn't play the Thanksgivin' game in Chicago, watched it on TV from a traction bed in Toledo. I joined Skipper. The Dixie Stars lost because poor Skipper was drunk. We drank together that night all night in the bar of the Blackstone and when cold day was comin' up over the Lake an' we were comin' out drunk to take a dizzy look at it, I said, "SKIPPER! STOP LOVIN' MY HUSBAND OR TELL HIM HE'S GOT TO LET YOU ADMIT IT TO HIM!"—one way or another!

HE SLAPPED ME HARD ON THE MOUTH!—then turned and ran without stopping once, I am sure, all the way back into his room at the Blackstone. . . .

—When I came to his room that night, with a little scratch like a shy little mouse at his door, he made that pitiful, ineffectual little attempt to prove that what I had said wasn't true. . . .

[*Brick strikes at her with crutch, a blow that shatters the gemlike lamp on the table.*]

—In this way, I destroyed him, by telling him truth that he and his world which he was born and raised in, yours and his world, had told him could not be told?
—From then on Skipper was nothing at all but a receptacle for liquor and drugs. . . .
—*Who shot cock-robin? I with my*—

[*She throws back her head with tight shut eyes.*]

—merciful arrow!

[*Brick strikes at her; misses.*]

Missed me!—Sorry,—I'm not tryin' to whitewash my behavior, Christ, no! Brick, I'm not good. I don't know why people have to pretend to be good, nobody's good. The rich or the well-to-do can afford to respect moral patterns, conventional moral patterns, but I could never afford to, yeah, but—I'm honest! Give me credit for just that, will you *please?*— Born poor, raised poor, expect to die poor unless I manage to get us something out of what Big Daddy leaves when he dies of cancer! But Brick?!—*Skipper is dead! I'm alive!* Maggie the cat is—

[*Brick hops awkwardly forward and strikes at her again with his crutch.*]

—alive! I am alive, alive! I am . . .

[*He hurls the crutch at her, across the bed she took refuge behind, and pitches forward on the floor as she completes her speech.*]

—alive!

[*A little girl, Dixie, bursts into the room, wearing an Indian war bonnet and firing a cap pistol at Margaret and shouting: "Bang, bang, bang!"* [*Laughter downstairs floats through the open hall door. Margaret had crouched gasping to bed at child's entrance. She now rises and says with cool fury:*]

Little girl, your mother or someone should teach you— [*Gasping*]—to knock at a door before you come into a room. Otherwise people might think that you—lack—good breeding. . . .
Dixie. Yanh, yanh, yanh, what is Uncle Brick doin' on th' floor?
Brick. I tried to kill your Aunt Maggie, but I failed—and I fell. Little girl, give me my crutch so I can get up off th' floor.

Margaret. Yes, give your uncle his crutch, he's a cripple, honey, he broke his ankle last night jumping hurdles on the high school athletic field!

Dixie. What were you jumping hurdles for, Uncle Brick?

Brick. Because I used to jump them, and people like to do what they used to do, even after they've stopped being able to do it. . . .

Margaret. That's right, that's your answer, now go away, little girl.

[*Dixie fires cap pistol at Margaret three times.*]

Stop, you stop that, monster! You little no-neck monster!

[*She seizes the cap pistol and hurls it through gallery doors.*]

Dixie [*with a precocious instinct for the cruelest thing*]. You're *jealous!*— You're just jealous because you can't have babies!

[*She sticks out her tongue at Margaret as she sashays past her with her stomach stuck out, to the gallery. Margaret slams the gallery doors and leans panting against them. There is a pause. Brick has replaced his spilt drink and sits, faraway, on the great four-poster bed.*]

Margaret. You see?—they gloat over us being childless, even in front of their five little no-neck monsters!

[*Pause. Voices approach on the stairs.*]

Brick?—I've been to a doctor in Memphis, a—a gynecologist. . . .
I've been completely examined, and there is no reason why we can't have a child whenever we want one. And this is my time by the calendar to conceive. Are you listening to me? Are you? Are you LISTENING TO ME!

Brick. Yes. I hear you, Maggie.

[*His attention returns to her inflamed face.*]

—But how in hell on earth do you imagine—that you're going to have a child by a man that can't stand you?

Margaret. That's a problem that I will have to work out.

[*She wheels about to face the hall door.*]

Here they come!

[*The lights dim.*]

CURTAIN

ACT TWO

There is no lapse of time. Margaret and Brick are in the same positions they held at the end of Act I.

Margaret [*at door*]. Here they come!

[*Big Daddy appears first, a tall man with a fierce, anxious look, moving carefully not to betray his weakness even, or especially, to himself.*]

Big Daddy. Well, Brick.
Brick. Hello, Big Daddy.—Congratulations!
Big Daddy. —Crap. . . .

[*Some of the people are approaching through the hall, others along the gallery: voices from both directions Gooper and Reverend Tooker become visible outside gallery doors, and their voices come in clearly.*
[*They pause outside as Gooper lights a cigar.*]

Reverend Tooker [*vivaciously*]. Oh, but St. Paul's in Grenada has three memorial windows, and the latest one is a Tiffany stained-glass window that cost twenty-five hundred dollars, a picture of Christ the Good Shepherd with a Lamb in His arms.
Gooper. Who give that window, Preach?
Reverend Tooker. Clyde Fletcher's widow. Also presented St. Paul's with a baptismal font.
Gooper. Y'know what somebody ought t' give your church is a *coolin'* system, Preach.
Reverend Tooker. Yes, siree, Bob! And y'know what Gus Hamma's family gave in his memory to the church at Two Rivers? A complete new stone parish-house with a basketball court in the basement and a—
Big Daddy [*uttering a loud barking laugh which is far from truly mirthful*]. Hey, Preach! What's all this talk about memorials, Preach? Y' think somebody's about t' kick off around here? 'S that it?

[*Startled by this interjection, Reverend Tooker decides to laugh at the question almost as loud as he can.*
[*How he would answer the question we'll never know, as he's spared that embarrassment by the voice of Gooper's wife, Mae, rising high and clear as she appears with "Doc" Baugh, the family doctor, through the hall door.*]

Mae [*almost religiously*]. —Let's see now, they've had their *tyyy*-phoid shots, and their tetanus shots, their diphtheria shots and their hepatitis shots and their polio shots, they got *those* shots every month from May through

September, and—Gooper? Hey! Gooper!—What all have the kiddies been shot faw?

Margaret [*overlapping a bit*]. Turn on the Hi-Fi, Brick! Let's have some music t' start off th' party with!

[*The talk becomes so general that the room sounds like a great aviary of chattering birds. Only Brick remains unengaged, leaning upon the liquor cabinet with his faraway smile, an ice cube in a paper napkin with which he now and then rubs his forehead. He doesn't respond to Margaret's command. She bounds forward and stoops over the instrument panel of the console.*]

Gooper. We gave 'em that thing for a third anniversary present, got three speakers in it.

[*The room is suddenly blasted by the climax of a Wagnerian opera or a Beethoven symphony.*]

Big Daddy. Turn that dam thing off!

[*Almost instant silence, almost instantly broken by the shouting charge of Big Mama, entering through hall door like a charging rhino.*]

Big Mama. Wha's my Brick, wha's mah precious baby!!
Big Daddy. Sorry! Turn it back on!

[*Everyone laughs very loud. Big Daddy is famous for his jokes at Big Mama's expense, and nobody laughs louder at these jokes than Big Mama herself, though sometimes they're pretty cruel and Big Mama has to pick up or fuss with something to cover the hurt that the loud laugh doesn't quite cover.*
[*On this occasion, a happy occasion because the dread in her heart has also been lifted by the false report on Big Daddy's condition, she giggles, grotesquely, coyly, in Big Daddy's direction and bears down upon Brick, all very quick and alive.*]

Big Mama. Here he is, here's my precious baby! What's that you've got in your hand? You put that liquor down, son, your hand was made fo' holdin' somethin' better than that!
Gooper. Look at Brick put it down!

[*Brick has obeyed Big Mama by draining the glass and handing it to her. Again everyone laughs, some high, some low.*]

Big Mama. Oh, you bad boy, you, you're my bad little boy. Give Big Mama a kiss, you bad boy, you!—Look at him shy away, will you? Brick never liked bein' kissed or made a fuss over, I guess because he's always had too much of it!
Son, you turn that thing off!

[*Brick has switched on the TV set.*]

I can't stand TV, radio was bad enough but TV has gone it one better, I mean—[*Plops wheezing in chair*]—one worse, ha ha! Now what'm I sittin' down here faw? I want t' sit next to my sweetheart on the sofa, hold hands with him and love him up a little!

[*Big Mama has on a black and white figured chiffon. The large irregular patterns, like the markings of some massive animal, the luster of her great diamonds and many pearls, the brilliants set in the silver frames of her glasses, her riotous voice, booming laugh, have dominated the room since she entered. Big Daddy has been regarding her with a steady grimace of chronic annoyance.*]

Big Mama [*still louder*]. Preacher, Preacher, hey, Preach! Give me you' hand an' help me up from this chair!
Reverend Tooker. None of your tricks, Big Mama!
Big Mama. What tricks? You give me you' hand so I can get up an'—

[*Reverend Tooker extends her his hand. She grabs it and pulls him into her lap with a shrill laugh that spans an octave in two notes.*]

Ever seen a preacher in a fat lady's lap? Hey, hey, folks! Ever seen a preacher in a fat lady's lap?

[*Big Mama is notorious throughout the Delta for this sort of inelegant horseplay. Margaret looks on with indulgent humor, sipping Dubonnet "on the rocks" and watching Brick, but Mae and Gooper exchange signs of humorless anxiety over these antics, the sort of behavior which Mae thinks may account for their failure to quite get in with the smartest young married set in Memphis, despite all. One of the Negroes, Lacy or Sookey, peeks in, cackling. They are waiting for a sign to bring in the cake and champagne. But Big Daddy's not amused. He doesn't understand why, in spite of the infinite mental relief he's received from the doctor's report, he still has these same old fox teeth in his guts. "This spastic thing sure is something," he says to himself, but aloud he roars at Big Mama:*]

Big Daddy. BIG MAMA, WILL YOU QUIT HORSIN'?—You're too old an' too fat fo' that sort of crazy kid stuff an' besides a woman with your blood-pressure—she had two hundred last spring!—is riskin' a stroke when you mess around like that. . . .

Big Mama. Here comes Big Daddy's birthday!

[*Negroes in white jackets enter with an enormous birthday cake ablaze with candles and carrying buckets of champagne with satin ribbons about the bottle necks.*
[*Mae and Gooper strike up song, and everybody, including the Negroes and Children, joins in. Only Brick remains aloof.*]

Everyone. Happy birthday to you.
Happy birthday to you.
Happy birthday, Big Daddy—

[*Some sing: "Dear, Big Daddy!"*]

Happy birthday to you.

[*Some sing: "How old are you?"*]
[*Mae has come down center and is organizing her children like a chorus. She gives them a barely audible: "One, two, three!" and they are off in the new tune.*]

Children. Skinamarinka—dinka—dink
Skinamarinka—do
We love you.
Skinamarinka—dinka—dink
Skinamarinka—do

[*All together, they turn to Big Daddy.*]

Big Daddy, you!

[*They turn back front, like a musical comedy chorus.*]

We love you in the morning;
We love you in the night.
We love you when we're with you,
And we love you out of sight.
Skinamarinka—dinka—dink
Skinamarinka—do.

[*Mae turns to Big Mama.*]

Big Mama, too!

[*Big Mama bursts into tears. The Negroes leave.*]

Big Daddy. Now Ida, what the hell is the matter with you?
Mae. She's just so happy.
Big Mama. I'm just so happy, Big Daddy, I have to cry or something.

[*Sudden and loud in the hush:*]

Brick, do you know the wonderful news that Doc Baugh got from the
clinic about Big Daddy? Big Daddy's one hundred per cent!
Margaret. Isn't that wonderful?
Big Mama. He's just one hundred per cent. Passed the examination with
flying colors. Now that we know there's nothing wrong with Big Daddy
but a spastic colon, I can tell you something. I was worried sick, half out
of my mind, for fear that Big Daddy might have a thing like—

[*Margaret cuts through this speech, jumping up and exclaiming shrilly:*]

Margaret. Brick, honey, aren't you going to give Big Daddy his birthday
present?

[*Passing by him, she snatches his liquor glass from him.*
[*She picks up a fancily wrapped package.*]

Here it is, Big Daddy, this is from Brick!
Big Mama. This is the biggest birthday Big Daddy's ever had, a hundred
presents and bushels of telegrams from—
Mae [*at same time*]. What is it, Brick?
Gooper. I bet 500 to 50 that Brick don't *know* what it is.
Big Mama. The fun of presents is not knowing what they are till you open
the package. Open your present, Big Daddy.
Big Daddy. Open it you'self. I want to ask Brick somethin! Come here, Brick.
Margaret. Big Daddy's callin' you, Brick.

[*She is opening the package.*]

Brick. Tell Big Daddy I'm crippled.
Big Daddy. I see you're crippled. I want to know how you got crippled.
Margaret [*making diversionary tactics*]. Oh, look, oh, look, why, it's a cash-
mere robe!

[*She holds the robe up for all to see.*]

Mae. You sound surprised, Maggie.
Margaret. I never saw one before.

Mae. That's funny.—*Hah!*

Margaret [*turning on her fiercely, with a brilliant smile*]. Why is it funny? All my family ever had was family—and luxuries such as cashmere robes still surprise me!

Big Daddy [*ominously*]. Quiet!

Mae [*heedless in her fury*]. I don't see how you could be so surprised when you bought it yourself at Loewenstein's in Memphis last Saturday. You know how I know?

Big Daddy. I said, Quiet!

Mae. —I know because the salesgirl that sold it to you waited on me and said, Oh, Mrs. Pollitt, your sister-in-law just bought a cashmere robe for your husband's father!

Margaret. Sister Woman! Your talents are wasted as a housewife and mother, you really ought to be with the FBI or—

Big Daddy. QUIET!

[*Reverend Tooker's reflexes are slower than the others'. He finishes a sentence after the bellow.*]

Reverend Tooker [*to Doc Baugh*]. —the Stork and the Reaper are running neck and neck!

[*He starts to laugh gaily when he notices the silence and Big Daddy's glare. His laugh dies falsely.*]

Big Daddy. Preacher, I hope I'm not butting in on more talk about memorial stained-glass windows, am I, Preacher?

[*Reverend Tooker laughs feebly, then coughs dryly in the embarrassed silence.*]

Preacher?

Big Mama. Now, Big Daddy, don't you pick on Preacher!

Big Daddy [*raising his voice*]. You ever hear that expression all hawk and no spit? You bring that expression to mind with that little dry cough of yours, all hawk an' no spit. . . .

[*The pause is broken only by a short startled laugh from Margaret, the only one there who is conscious of and amused by the grotesque.*]

Mae [*raising her arms and jangling her bracelets*]. I wonder if the mosquitoes are active tonight?

Big Daddy. What's that, Little Mama? Did you make some remark?

Mae. Yes, I said I wondered if the mosquitoes would eat us alive if we went out on the gallery for a while.

Big Daddy. Well, if they do, I'll have your bones pulverized for fertilizer!

Big Mama [*quickly*]. Last week we had an airplane spraying the place and I think it done some good, at least I haven't had a—

Big Daddy [*cutting her speech*]. Brick, they tell me, if what they tell me is true, that you done some jumping last night on the high school athletic field?

Big Mama. Brick, Big Daddy is talking to you, son.

Brick [*smiling vaguely over his drink*]. What was that, Big Daddy?

Big Daddy. They said you done some jumping on the high school track field last night.

Brick. That's what they told me, too.

Big Daddy. Was it jumping or humping that you were doing out there? What were doing out there at three A.M., layin' a woman on that cinder track?

Big Mama. Big Daddy, you are off the sick-list, now, and I'm not going to excuse you for talkin' so—

Big Daddy. Quiet!

Big Mama. —*nasty* in front of Preacher and—

Big Daddy. QUIET!—I ast you, Brick, if you was cuttin' you'self a piece o' poon-tang last night on that cinder track? I thought maybe you were chasin' poon-tang on that track an' tripped over something in the heat of the chase—'sthat it?

[*Gooper laughs, loud and false, others nervously following suit. Big Mama stamps her foot, and purses her lips, crossing to Mae and whispering something to her as Brick meets his father's hard, intent, grinning stare with a slow, vague smile that he offers all situations from behind the screen of his liquor.*]

Brick. No, sir, I don't think so. . . .

Mae [*at the same time, sweetly*]. Reverend Tooker, let's you and I take a stroll on the widow's walk.

[*She and the preacher go out on the gallery as Big Daddy says:*]

Big Daddy. Then what the hell were you doing out there at three o'clock in the morning?

Brick. Jumping the hurdles, Big Daddy, runnin' and jumpin' the hurdles, but those high hurdles have gotten too high for me, now.

Big Daddy. Cause you was drunk?

Brick [*his vague smile fading a little*]. Sober I wouldn't have tried to jump the *low* ones. . . .

Big Mama [*quickly*]. Big Daddy, blow out the candles on your birthday cake!

Margaret [*at the same time*]. I want to propose a toast to Big Daddy Pollitt on his sixty-fifth birthday, the biggest cotton-planter in—

Big Daddy [*bellowing with fury and disgust*]. I told you to stop it, now stop it, quit this—!

Big Mama [*coming in front of Big Daddy with the cake*]. Big Daddy, I will
   not allow you to talk that way, now even on your birthday, I—
Big Daddy. I'll talk like I want to on my birthday, Ida, or any other goddam
   day of the year and anybody here that don't like it knows what they can
   do!
Big Mama. You don't mean that!
Big Daddy. What makes you think I don't mean it?

[*Meanwhile various discreet signals have been exchanged and Gooper has
also gone out on the gallery.*]

Big Mama. I just know you don't mean it.
Big Daddy. You don't know a goddam thing and you never did!
Big Mama. Big Daddy, you don't mean that.
Big Daddy. Oh, yes, I do, oh, yes, I do, I mean it! I put up with a whole lot
   of crap around here because I thought I was dying. And you thought I
   was dying and you started taking over, well, you can stop taking over
   now, Ida, because I'm not gonna die, you can just stop now this business
   of taking over because you're not taking over because I'm not dying, I
   went through the laboratory and the goddam exploratory operation and
   there's nothing wrong with me but a spastic colon. And I'm not dying of
   cancer which you thought I was dying of. Ain't that so? Didn't you think
   that I was dying of cancer, Ida?

[*Almost everybody is out on the gallery but the two old people glaring at
each other across the blazing cake.*
[*Big Mama's chest heaves and she presses a fat fist to her mouth.*
[*Big Daddy continues, hoarsely:*]

Ain't that so, Ida? Didn't you have an idea I was dying of cancer and now
   you could take control of this place and everything on it? I got that
   impression, I seemed to get that impression. Your loud voice everywhere,
   you fat old body butting in here and there!
Big Mama. Hush! The Preacher!
Big Daddy. Rut the goddam preacher!

[*Big Mama gasps loudly and sits down on the sofa which is almost too
small for her.*]

Did you hear what I said? I said rut the goddam preacher!

[*Somebody closes the gallery doors from outside just as there is a burst
of fireworks and excited cries from the children.*]

Big Mama. I never seen you act like this before and I can't think what's got
   in you!

Big Daddy. I went through all that laboratory and operation and all just so I would know if you or me was boss here! Well, now it turns out that I am and you ain't—and that's my birthday present—and my cake and champagne!—because for three years now you been gradually taking over. Bossing. Talking. Sashaying your fat old body around the place I made! I made this place! I was overseer on it! I was the overseer on the old Straw and Ochello plantation. I quit school at ten! I quit school at ten years old and went to work like a nigger in the fields. And I rose to be overseer of the Straw and Ochello plantation. And old Straw died and I was Ochello's partner and the place got bigger and bigger and bigger and bigger and bigger! I did all that myself with no goddam help from you, and now you think you're just about to take over. Well, I am just about to tell you that you are not just about to take over, you are not just about to take over a God damn thing. Is that clear to you, Ida? Is that very plain to you, now? Is that understood completely? I been through the laboratory from A to Z. I've had the goddam exploratory operation, and nothing is wrong with me but a spastic colon—made spastic, I guess, by *disgust!* By all the goddam lies and liars that I have had to put up with, and all the goddam hypocrisy that I lived with all these forty years that we been livin' together! Hey! Ida!! Blow out the candles on the birthday cake! Purse up your lips and draw a deep breath and blow out the goddam candles on the cake!
Big Mama. Oh, Big Daddy, oh, oh, oh, Big Daddy!
Big Daddy. What's the matter with you?
Big Mama. In all these years you never believed that I loved you??
Big Daddy. Huh?
Big Mama. And I did, I did so much, I did love you!—I even loved your hate and your hardness, Big Daddy!

[*She sobs and rushes awkwardly out onto the gallery.*]

Big Daddy [*to himself*]. *Wouldn't it be funny if that was true. . . .*

[*A pause is followed by a burst of light in the sky from the fireworks.*]

BRICK! HEY, BRICK!

[*He stands over his blazing birthday cake.*
[*After some moments, Brick hobbles in on his crutch, holding his glass.*
[*Margaret follows him with a bright, anxious smile.*]

I didn't call you, Maggie. I called Brick.
Margaret. I'm just delivering him to you.

[*She kisses Brick on the mouth which he immediately wipes with the back of his hand. She flies girlishly back out. Brick and his father are alone.*]

Big Daddy. Why did you do that?

Brick. Do what, Big Daddy?

Big Daddy. Wipe her kiss off your mouth like she'd spit on you.

Brick. I don't know. I wasn't conscious of it.

Big Daddy. That woman of yours has a better shape on her than Gooper's but somehow or other they got the same look about them.

Brick. What sort of look is that, Big Daddy?

Big Daddy. I don't know how to describe it but it's the same look.

Brick. They don't look peaceful, do they?

Big Daddy. No, they sure in hell don't.

Brick. They look nervous as cats?

Big Daddy. That's right, they look nervous as cats.

Brick. Nervous as a couple of cats on a hot tin roof?

Big Daddy. That's right, boy, they look like a couple of cats on a hot tin roof. It's funny that you and Gooper being so different would pick out the same type of woman.

Brick. Both of us married into society, Big Daddy.

Big Daddy. Crap . . . I wonder what gives them both that look?

Brick. Well. They're sittin' in the middle of a big piece of land, Big Daddy, twenty-eight thousand acres is a pretty big piece of land and so they're squaring off on it, each determined to knock off a bigger piece of it than the other whenever you let it go.

Big Daddy. I got a surprise for those women. I'm not gonna let it go for a long time yet if that's what they're waiting for.

Brick. That's right, Big Daddy. You just sit tight and let them scratch each other's eyes out. . . .

Big Daddy. You bet your life I'm going to sit tight on it and let those sons of bitches scratch their eyes out, ha ha ha. . . .

But Gooper's wife's a good breeder, you got to admit she's fertile. Hell, at supper tonight she had them all at the table and they had to put a couple of extra leafs in the table to make room for them, she's got five head of them, now, and another one's comin'.

Brick. Yep, number six is comin'. . . .

Big Daddy. Brick, you know, I swear to God, I don't know the way it happens?

Brick. The way what happens, Big Daddy?

Big Daddy. You git you a piece of land, by hook or crook, an' things start growin' on it, things accumulate on it, and the first thing you know it's completely out of hand, completely out of hand!

Brick. Well, they say nature hates a vacuum, Big Daddy.

Big Daddy. That's what they say, but sometimes I think that a vacuum is a hell of a lot better than some of the stuff that nature replaces it with.

Is someone out there by that door?

Brick. Yep.

Big Daddy. Who?

[*He has lowered his voice.*]

Brick. Someone int'rested in what we say to each other.
Big Daddy. Gooper?——GOOPER!

[*After a discreet pause, Mae appears in the gallery door.*]

Mae. Did you call Gooper, Big Daddy?
Big Daddy. Aw, it was you.
Mae. Do you want Gooper, Big Daddy?
Big Daddy. No, and I don't want you. I want some privacy here, while I'm
   having a confidential talk with my son Brick. Now it's too hot in here to
   close them doors, but if I have to close those rutten doors in order to have
   a private talk with my son Brick, just let me know and I'll close 'em.
   Because I hate eavesdroppers, I don't like any kind of sneakin' an' spyin'.
Mae. Why, Big Daddy—
Big Daddy. You stood on the wrong side of the moon, it threw your shadow!
Mae. I was just—
Big Daddy. You was just nothing but *spyin'* an' you *know* it!
Mae [*begins to sniff and sob*]. Oh, Big Daddy, you're so unkind for some
   reason to those that really love you!
Big Daddy. Shut up, shut up, shut up! I'm going to move you and Gooper
   out of that room next to this! It's none of your goddam business what
   goes on in here at night between Brick an' Maggie. You listen at night
   like a couple of rutten peek-hole spies and go and give a report on what
   you hear to Big Mama an' she comes to me and says they say such and
   such and so and so about what they heard goin' on between Brick an'
   Maggie, and Jesus, it makes me sick. I'm goin' to move you an' Gooper
   out of that room, I can't stand sneakin' an' spyin', it makes me sick. . . .

[*Mae throws back her head and rolls her eyes heavenward and extends
her arms as if invoking God's pity for this unjust martyrdom; then she
presses a handkerchief to her nose and flies from the room with a loud
swish of skirts.*]

Brick [*now at the liquor cabinet*]. They listen, do they?
Big Daddy. Yeah. They listen and give reports to Big Mama on what goes
   on in here between you and Maggie. They say that—

[*He stops as if embarrassed.*]

—You won't sleep with her, that you sleep on the sofa. Is that true or not
   true? If you don't like Maggie, get rid of Maggie!—What are you doin'
   there now?
Brick. Fresh'nin' up my drink.

Big Daddy. Son, you know you got a real liquor problem?

Brick. Yes, sir, yes, I know.

Big Daddy. Is that why you quit sports-announcing, because of this liquor problem?

Brick. Yes, sir, yes, sir, I guess so.

[*He smiles vaguely and amiably at his father across his replenished drink.*]

Big Daddy. Son, don't guess about it, it's too important.

Brick [*vaguely*]. Yes, sir.

Big Daddy. And listen to me, don't look at the damn chandelier. . . .

[*Pause. Big Daddy's voice is husky.*]

—Somethin' else we picked up at th' big fire sale in Europe.

[*Another pause.*]

Life is important. There's nothing else to hold onto. A man that drinks is throwing his life away. Don't do it, hold onto your life. There's nothing else to hold onto. . . .

Sit down over here so we don't have to raise our voices, the walls have ears in this place.

Brick [*hobbling over to sit on the sofa beside him*]. All right, Big Daddy.

Big Daddy. Quit!—how'd that come about? Some disappointment?

Brick. I don't know. Do you?

Big Daddy. I'm askin' you, God damn it! How in hell would I know if you don't?

Brick I just got out there and found that I had a mouth full of cotton. I was always two or three beats behind what was goin' on on the field and so I—

Big Daddy. Quit!

Brick [*amiably*]. Yes, quit.

Big Daddy. Son?

Brick. Huh?

Big Daddy [*inhales loudly and deeply from his cigar; then bends suddenly a little forward, exhaling loudly and raising a hand to his forehead*]. —Whew!—ha ha!—I took in too much smoke, it made me a little light-headed. . . .

[*The mantel clock chimes.*]

Why is it so damn hard for people to talk?

Brick. Yeah. . . .

[*The clock goes on sweetly chiming till it has completed the stroke of ten.*]

—Nice peaceful-soundin' clock, I like to hear it all night. . . .

[*He slides low and comfortable on the sofa; Big Daddy sits up straight and rigid with some unspoken anxiety. All his gestures are tense and jerky as he talks. He wheezes and pants and sniffs through his nervous speech, glancing quickly, shyly, from time to time, at his son.*]

Big Daddy. We got that clock the summer we wint to Europe, me an' Big Mama on that damn Cook's Tour, never had such an awful time in my life, I'm tellin' you, son, those gooks over there, they gouge your eyeballs out in their grand hotels. And Big Mama bought more stuff than you could haul in a couple of boxcars, that's no crap. Everywhere she wint on this whirlwind tour, she bought, bought, bought. Why, half that stuff she bought is still crated up in the cellar, under water last spring!

[*He laughs.*]

That Europe is nothin' on earth but a great big auction, that's all it is, that bunch of old worn-out places, it's just a big firesale, the whole rutten thing, an' Big Mama wint wild in it, why, you couldn't hold that woman with a mule's harness! Bought, bought, bought!—lucky I'm a rich man, yes siree, Bob, an' half that stuff is mildewin' in th' basement. It's lucky I'm a rich man, it sure is lucky, well, I'm a rich man, Brick, yep, I'm a mighty rich man.

[*His eyes light up for a moment.*]

Y'know how much I'm worth? Guess, Brick! Guess how much I'm worth!

[*Brick smiles vaguely over his drink.*]

Close on ten million in cash an' blue chip stocks, outside, mind you, of twenty-eight thousand acres of the richest land this side of the valley Nile!

[*A puff and crackle and the night sky blooms with an eerie greenish glow. Children shriek on the gallery.*]

But a man can't buy his life with it, he can't buy back his life with it when his life has been spent, that's one thing not offered in the Europe fire-sale or in the American markets or any markets on earth, a man can't buy his life with it, he can't buy back his life when his life is finished. . . .
That's a sobering thought, a very sobering thought, and that's a thought that I was turning over in my head, over and over and over—until to-day. . . .

I'm wiser and sadder, Brick, for this experience which I just gone through.
They's one thing else that I remember in Europe.

Brick. What is that, Big Daddy?

Big Daddy. The hills around Barcelona in the country of Spain and the
children running over those bare hills in their bare skins beggin' like starvin'
dogs with howls and screeches, and how fat the priests are on the streets
of Barcelona, so many of them and so fat and so pleasant, ha ha!—Y'know
I could feed that country? I got money enough to feed that goddam country,
but the human animal is a selfish beast and I don't reckon the money I
passed out there to those howling children in the hills around Barcelona
would more than upholster one of the chairs in this room, I mean pay to
put a new cover on this chair!

Hell, I threw them money like you'd scatter feed corn for chickens, I threw
money at them just to get rid of them long enough to climb back into th'
car and—drive away. . . .

And then in Morocco, them Arabs, why, prostitution begins at four or
five, that's no exaggeration, why, I remember one day in Marrakech, that
old walled Arab city, I set on a brokendown wall to have a cigar, it was
fearful hot there and this Arab woman stood in the road and looked at
me till I was embarrassed, she stood stock still in the dusty hot road and
looked at me till I was embarrassed. But listen to this. She had a naked
child with her, a little naked girl with her, barely able to toddle, and after
a while she set this child on the ground and give her a push and whispered
something to her.

This child come toward me, barely able t' walk, come toddling up to me
and—

Jesus, it makes you sick t' remember a thing like this!

It stuck out its hand and tried to unbutton my trousers!

That child was not yet five! Can you believe me? Or do you think that I
am making this up? I wint back to the hotel and said to Big Mama, Git
packed! We're clearing out of this country. . . .

Brick. Big Daddy, you're on a talkin' jag tonight.

Big Daddy [*ignoring this remark*]. Yes, sir, that's how it is, the human animal
is a beast that dies but the fact that he's dying don't given him pity for
others, no, sir, it—

—Did you say something?

Brick. Yes.

Big Daddy. What?

Brick. Hand me over that crutch so I can get up.

Big Daddy. Where you goin'?

Brick. I'm takin' a little short trip to Echo Spring.

Big Daddy. To where?

Brick. Liquor cabinet. . . .

Big Daddy. Yes, sir, boy—

[*He hands Brick the crutch.*]

—the human animal is a beast that dies and if he's got money he buys and buys and buys and I think the reason he buys everything he can buy is that in the back of his mind he has the crazy hope that one of his purchases will be life everlasting!—Which it never can be. . . . The human animal is a beast that—

Brick [*at the liquor cabinet*]. Big Daddy, you sure are shootin' th' breeze here tonight.

[*There is a pause and voices are heard outside.*]

Big Daddy. I been quiet here lately, spoke not a word, just sat and stared into space. I had something heavy weighing on my mind but tonight that load was took off me. That's why I'm talking.—The sky looks diff'rent to me. . . .

Brick. You know what I like to hear most?

Big Daddy. What?

Brick. Solid quiet. Perfect unbroken quiet.

Big Daddy. Why?

Brick. Because it's more peaceful.

Big Daddy. Man, you'll hear a lot of that in the grave.

[*He chuckles agreeably.*]

Brick. Are you through talkin' to me?

Big Daddy. Why are you so anxious to shut me up?

Brick. Well, sir, ever so often you say to me, Brick, I want to have a talk with you, but when we talk, it never materializes. Nothing is said. You sit in a chair and gas about this and that and I look like I listen. I try to look like I listen, but I don't listen, not much. Communication is—awful hard between people an'—somehow between you and me, it just don't—

Big Daddy. Have you ever been scared? I mean have you ever felt downright terror of something?

[*He gets up.*]

Just one moment. I'm going to close these doors. . . .

[*He closes doors on gallery as if he were going to tell an important secret.*]

Brick. What?

Big Daddy. Brick?

Brick. Huh?

Big Daddy. Son, I thought I had it!

Brick. Had what? Had what, Big Daddy?

Big Daddy. Cancer!

Brick. Oh . . .

Big Daddy. I thought the old man made out of bones had laid his cold and heavy hand on my shoulder!

Brick. Well, Big Daddy, you kept a tight mouth about it.

Big Daddy. A pig squeals. A man keeps a tight mouth about it, in spite of a man not having a pig's advantage.

Brick. What advantage is that?

Big Daddy. Ignorance—of mortality—is a comfort. A man don't have that comfort, he's the only living thing that conceives of death, that knows what it is. The others go without knowing which is the way that anything living should go, go without knowing, without any knowledge of it, and yet a pig squeals, but a man sometimes, he can keep a tight mouth about it. Sometimes he—

[*There is a deep, smoldering ferocity in the old man.*]

—can keep a tight mouth about it. I wonder if—

Brick. What, Big Daddy?

Big Daddy. A whiskey highball would injure this spastic condition?

Brick. No, sir, it might do it good.

Big Daddy [*grins suddenly, wolfishly*]. Jesus, I can't tell you! *The sky is open! Christ, it's open again! It's open, boy, it's open!*

[*Brick looks down at his drink.*]

Brick. You feel better, Big Daddy?

Big Daddy. Better? Hell! I can breathe!—All of my life I been like a doubled up fist. . . .

[*He pours a drink.*]

—Poundin', smashin', drivin'!—now I'm going to loosen these doubled up hands and touch things *easy* with them. . . .

[*He spreads his hands as if caressing the air.*]

You know what I'm contemplating?

Brick [*vaguely*]. No, sir. what are you contemplating?

Big Daddy. Ha ha!—*Pleasure!*—pleasure with *women!*

[*Brick's smile fades a little but lingers.*]

Brick, this stuff burns me!—

—Yes, boy. I'll tell you something that you might not guess. I still have desire for women and this is my sixty-fifth birthday.

Brick. I think that's mighty remarkable, Big Daddy.

Big Daddy. Remarkable?

Brick. Admirable, Big Daddy.

Big Daddy. You're damn right it is, remarkable and admirable both. I realize now that I never had me enough. I let many chances slip by because of scruples about it, scruples, convention—crap. . . . All that stuff is bull, bull, bull!—It took the shadow of death to make me see it. Now that shadow's lifted, I'm going to cut loose and have, what is it they call it, have me a—ball!

Brick. A ball, huh?

Big Daddy. That's right, a ball, a ball! Hell!—I slept with Big Mama till, let's see, five years ago, till I was sixty and she was fifty-eight, and never even liked her, never did!

[*The phone has been ringing down the hall. Big Mama enters, exclaiming:*]

Big Mama. Don't you men hear that phone ring? I heard it way out on the gall'ry.

Big Daddy. There's five rooms off this front gall'ry that you could go through. Why do you go through this one?

[*Big Mama makes a playful face as she bustles out the hall door.*]

Hunh!—Why, when Big Mama goes out of a room, I can't remember what that woman looks like, but when Big Mama comes back into the room, boy, then I see what she looks like, and I wish I didn't!

[*Bends over laughing at this joke till it hurts his guts and he straightens with a grimace. The laugh subsides to a chuckle as he puts the liquor glass a little distrustfully down on the table.*
[*Brick has risen and hobbled to the gallery doors.*]

Hey! Where you goin'?

Brick. Out for a breather.

Big Daddy. Not yet you ain't. Stay here till this talk is finished, young fellow.

Brick. I thought it was finished, Big Daddy.

Big Daddy. It ain't even begun.

Brick. My mistake. Excuse me. I just wanted to feel that river breeze.

Big Daddy. Turn on the ceiling fan and set back down in that chair.

[*Big Mama's voice rises, carrying down the hall.*]

Big Mama. Miss Sally, you're a case! You're a caution, Miss Sally. Why didn't you give me a chance to explain it to you?

Big Daddy. Jesus, she's talking to my old maid sister again.

Big Mama. Well, goodbye, now, Miss Sally. You come down real soon, Big Daddy's dying to see you! Yaisss, goodbye, Miss Sally. . . .

[*She hangs up and bellows with mirth. Big Daddy groans and covers his ears as she approaches.*

[*Bursting in:*]

Big Daddy, that was Miss Sally callin' from Memphis again! You know what she done, Big Daddy? She called her doctor in Memphis to git him to tell her what that spastic thing is! Ha-*HAAAA!*—And called back to tell me how relieved she was that—Hey! Let me in!

[*Big Daddy has been holding the door half closed against her.*]

Big Daddy. Naw I ain't. I told you not to come and go through this room. You just back out and go through those five other rooms.
Big Mama. Big Daddy? Big Daddy? Oh, big Daddy!—You didn't mean those things you said to me, did you?

[*He shuts door firmly against her but she still calls.*]

Sweetheart? Sweetheart? Big Daddy? You didn't mean those awful things you said to me?—I know you didn't. I know you didn't mean those things in your heart. . . .

[*The childlike voice fades with a sob and heavy footsteps retreat down the hall. Brick has risen once more on his crutches and starts for the gallery again.*]

Big Daddy. All I ask of that woman is that she leave me alone. But she can't admit to herself that she makes me sick. That comes of having slept with her too many years. Should of quit much sooner but that old woman she never got enough of it—and I was good in bed . . . I never should of wasted so much of it on her. . . . They say you got just so many and each one is numbered. Well, I got a few left in me, a few, and I'm going to pick me a good one to spend 'em on! I'm going to pick me a choice one, I don't care how much she costs, I'll smother her in—minks! Ha ha! I'll strip her naked and smother her in minks and choke her with diamonds! Ha ha! I'll strip her naked and choke her with diamonds and smother her with minks and hump her from hell to breakfast. *Ha aha ha ha ha!*
Mae [*gaily at door*]. Who's that laughin' in there?
Gooper. Is Big Daddy laughin' in there?
Big Daddy. Crap!—them two—*drips.* . . .

[*He goes over and touches Brick's shoulder.*]

Yes, son. Brick, boy.—I'm—*happy!* I'm happy, son, I'm happy!

[*He chokes a little and bites his under lip, pressing his head quickly, shyly against his son's head and then, coughing with embarrassment, goes uncertainly back to the table where he set down the glass. He drinks and makes a grimace as it burns his guts. Brick sighs and rises with effort.*]

What makes you so restless? Have you got ants in your britches?
Brick. Yes, sir . . .
Big Daddy. Why?
Brick. —Something—hasn't—happened. . . .
Big Daddy. Yeah? What is that!
Brick [*sadly*]. —the click. . . .
Big Daddy. Did you say click?
Brick. Yes, click.
Big Daddy. What click?
Brick. A click that I get in my head that makes me peaceful.
Big Daddy. I sure in hell don't know what you're talking about, but it disturbs me.
Brick. It's just a mechanical thing.
Big Daddy. What is a mechanical thing?
Brick. This click that I get in my head that makes me peaceful. I got to drink till I get it. It's just a mechanical thing, something like a—like a—like a—
Big Daddy. Like a—
Brick. Switch clicking off in my head, turning the hot light off and the cool night on and—

[*He looks up, smiling sadly.*]

—all of a sudden there's—peace!
Big Daddy [*whistles long and soft with astonishment; he goes back to Brick and clasps his son's two shoulders*]: Jesus! I didn't know it had gotten that bad with you. Why, boy, you're—*alcoholic!*
Brick. That's the truth, Big Daddy. I'm alcoholic.
Big Daddy. This shows how I—let things go!
Brick. I have to hear that little click in my head that makes me peaceful. Usually I hear it sooner than this, sometimes as early as—noon, but—
—Today it's—dilatory. . . .
—I just haven't got the right level of alcohol in my bloodstream yet!

[*This last statement is made with energy as he freshens his drink.*]

Big Daddy. Uh—huh. Expecting death made me blind. I didn't have no idea that a son of mine was turning into a drunkard under my nose.
Brick [*gentle*]. Well, now you do, Big Daddy, the news has penetrated.
Big Daddy. UH-huh, yes, now I do, the news has—penetrated. . . .
Brick. And so if you'll excuse me—

Big Daddy. No, I won't excuse you.

Brick. —I'd better sit by myself till I hear that click in my head, it's just a mechanical thing but it don't happen except when I'm alone or talking to no one. . . .

Big Daddy. You got a long, long time to sit still, boy, and talk to no one, but now you're talkin' to me. At least I'm talking to you. And you set there and listen until I tell you the conversation is over!

Brick. But this talk is like all the others we've ever had together in our lives! It's nowhere, nowhere!—it's—it's *painful,* Big Daddy. . . .

Big Daddy. All right, then let it be painful, but don't you move from that chair!—I'm going to remove that crutch. . . .

[*He seizes the crutch and tosses it across room.*]

Brick. I can hop on one foot, and if I fall, I can crawl!

Big Daddy. If you ain't careful you're gonna crawl off this plantation and then, by Jesus, you'll have to hustle your drinks along Skid Row!

Brick. That'll come, Big Daddy.

Big Daddy. Naw, it won't. You're my son and I'm going to straighten you out; now that *I'm* straightened out, I'm going to straighten out you!

Brick. Yeah?

Big Daddy. Today the report come in from Ochsner Clinic. Y'know what they told me?

[*His face glows with triumph.*]

The only thing that they could detect with all the instruments of science in that great hospital is a little spastic condition of the colon! And nerves torn to pieces by all that worry about it.

[*A little girl bursts into room with a sparkler clutched in each fist, hops and shrieks like a monkey gone mad and rushes back out again as Big Daddy strikes at her.*
[*Silence. The two men stare at each other. A woman laughs gaily outside.*]

I want you to know I breathed a sigh of relief almost as powerful as the Vicksburg tornado!

Brick. You weren't ready to go?

Big Daddy. GO WHERE?—crap. . . .

—When you are gone from here, boy, you are long gone and no where! The human machine is not no different from the animal machine or the fish machine or the bird machine or the reptile machine or the insect machine! It's just a whole God damn lot more complicated and consequently more trouble to keep together. Yep. I thought I had it. The earth shook under my foot, the sky come down like the black lid of a kettle and I couldn't breathe!—Today!!—that lid was lifted, I drew my first free breath in—how many years?—*God!—three.* . . .

[*There is laughter outside, running footsteps, the soft, plushy sound and light of exploding rockets.*

[*Brick stares at him soberly for a long moment; then makes a sort of startled sound in his nostrils and springs up on one foot and hops across the room to grab his crutch, swinging on the furniture for support. He gets the crutch and flees as if in horror for the gallery. His father seizes him by the sleeve of his white silk pajamas.*]

Stay here, you son of a bitch—till I say go!
Brick. I can't.
Big Daddy. You sure in hell will, God damn it.
Brick. No, I can't. We talk, you talk, in—circles! We get no where, no where! It's always the same, you say you want to talk to me and don't have a ruttin' thing to say to me!
Big Daddy. Nothin' to say when I'm tellin' you I'm going to live when I thought I was dying?!
Brick. Oh—*that!*—Is that what you have to say to me?
Big Daddy. Why, you son of a bitch! Ain't that, ain't that—*important?!*
Brick. Well, you said that, that's said, and now I—
Big Daddy. Now you set back down.
Brick. You're all balled up, you—
Big Daddy. I ain't balled up!
Brick. You are, you're all balled up!
Big Daddy. Don't tell me what I am, you drunken whelp! I'm going to tear this coat sleeve off if you don't set down!
Brick. Big Daddy—
Big Daddy. Do what I tell you! I'm the boss here, now! I want you to know I'm back in the driver's seat now!

[*Big Mama rushes in, clutching her great heaving bosom.*]

What in hell do you want in here, Big Mama?
Big Mama. Oh, Big Daddy! Why are you shouting like that? I just cain't stainnnnnnnd—it. . . .
Big Daddy [*raising the back of his hand above his head*]. GIT!—outa here.

[*She rushes back out, sobbing.*]

Brick [*softly, sadly*]. Christ. . . .
Big Daddy [*fiercely*]. Yeah! Christ!—is right . . .

[*Brick breaks loose and hobbles toward the gallery.*
[*Big Daddy jerks his crutch from under Brick so he steps with the injured ankle. He utters a hissing cry of anguish, clutches a chair and pulls it over on top of him on the floor.*]

Son of a—tub of—hog fat. . . .
Brick. Big Daddy! Give me my crutch.

[*Big Daddy throws the crutch out of reach.*]

Give me that crutch, Big Daddy.
Big Daddy. Why do you drink?
Brick. Don't know, give me my crutch!
Big Daddy. You better think why you drink or give up drinking!
Brick. Will you please give me my crutch so I can get up off this floor?
Big Daddy. First you answer my question. Why do you drink? Why are you throwing your life away, boy, like somethin' disgusting you picked up on the street?
Brick [*getting onto his knees*]. Big Daddy, I'm in pain, I stepped on that foot.
Big Daddy. Good! I'm glad you're not too numb with the liquor in you to feel some pain!
Brick. You—spilled my—drink . . .
Big Daddy. I'll make a bargain with you. You tell me why you drink and I'll hand you one. I'll pour you the liquor myself and hand it to you.
Brick. Why do I drink?
Big Daddy. Yea! Why?
Brick. Give me a drink and I'll tell you.
Big Daddy. Tell me first!
Brick. I'll tell you in one word.
Big Daddy. What word?
Brick. DISGUST!

[*The clock chimes softly, sweetly. Big Daddy gives it a short, outraged glance.*]

Now how about that drink?
Big Daddy. What are you disgusted with? You got to tell me that, first. Otherwise being disgusted don't make no sense!
Brick. Give me my crutch.
Big Daddy. You heard me, you got to tell me what I asked you first.
Brick. I told you, I said to kill my disgust!
Big Daddy. DISGUST WITH WHAT!
Brick. You strike a hard bargain.
Big Daddy. What are you disgusted with?—an' I'll pass you the liquor.

Brick. I can hop on one foot, and if I fall, I can crawl.
Big Daddy. You want liquor that bad?
Brick [*dragging himself up, clinging to bedstead*]. Yeah, I want it that bad.
Big Daddy. If I give you a drink, will you tell me what it is you're disgusted with, Brick?
Brick. Yes, sir, I will try to.

[*The old man pours him a drink and solemnly passes it to him.*
[*There is silence as Brick drinks.*]

Have you ever heard the word "mendacity"?
Big Daddy. Sure. Mendacity is one of them five dollar words that cheap politicians throw back and forth at each other.
Brick. You know what it means?
Big Daddy. Don't it mean lying and liars?
Brick. Yes, sir, lying and liars.
Big Daddy. Has someone been lying to you?
Children [*chanting in chorus offstage*]. We want Big Dad-dee!
We want Big Dad-dee!

[*Gooper appears in the gallery door.*]

Gooper. Big Daddy, the kiddies are shouting for you out there.
Big Daddy [*fiercely*]. Keep out, Gooper!
Gooper: 'Scuse *me!*

[*Big Daddy slams the doors after Gooper.*]

Big Daddy. Who's been lying to you, has Margaret been lying to you, has your wife been lying to you about something, Brick?
Brick. Not her. That wouldn't matter.
Big Daddy. Then who's been lying to you, and what about?
Brick. No one single person and no one lie. . . .
Big Daddy. Then what, what then, for Christ's sake?
Brick. —The whole, the whole—thing. . . .
Big Daddy. Why are you rubbing your head? You got a headache?
Brick. No, I'm tryin' to—
Big Daddy. —Concentrate, but you can't because your brain's all soaked with liquor, is that the trouble? Wet brain!

[*He snatches the glass from Brick's hand.*]

What do you know about this mendacity thing? Hell! I could write a book on it! Don't you know that? I could write a book on it and still not cover the subject? Well, I could, I could write a goddam book on it and still not cover the subject anywhere near enough!!—Think of all the lies I got to put up with!—Pretenses! Ain't that mendacity? Having to protend stuff you don't think or feel or have any idea of? Having for instance to act like I care for Big Mama!—I haven't been able to stand the sight, sound, or smell of that woman for forty years now!—even when I *laid* her!— regular as a piston. . . .

Pretend to love that son of a bitch of a Gooper and his wife Mae and those five same screechers out there like parrots in a jungle? Jesus! Can't stand to look at 'em!

Church!—it bores the Bejesus out of me but I go!—I go an' sit there and listen to the fool preacher!

Clubs!—Elks! Masons! Rotary!—*crap!*

[*A spasm of pain makes him clutch his belly. He sinks into a chair and his voice is softer and hoarser.*]

You I *do* like for some reason, did always have some kind of real feeling for—affection—respect—yes, always. . . .

You and being a success as a planter is all I ever had any devotion to in my whole life!—and that's the truth. . . .

I don't know why, but it is!

I've lived with mendacity!—Why can't *you* live with it? Hell, you *got* to live with it, there's nothing *else* to *live* with except mendacity, is there?

Brick. Yes, sir. Yes, sir there is something else that you can live with!

Big Daddy. What?

Brick [*lifting his glass*]. This!—Liquor. . . .

Big Daddy. That's not living, that's dodging away from life.

Brick. I want to dodge away from it.

Big Daddy. Then why don't you kill yourself, man?

Brick. I like to drink. . . .

Big Daddy. Oh, God, I can't talk to you. . . .

Brick. I'm sorry, Big Daddy.

Big Daddy. Not as sorry as I am. I'll tell you something. A little while back when I thought my number was up—

[*This speech should have torrential pace and fury.*]

—before I found out it was just this—spastic—colon. I thought about you. Should I or should I not, if the jig was up, give you this place when I go— since I hate Gooper an' Mae an' know that they hate me, and since all five same monkeys are little Maes an' Goopers.—And I thought, No!— Then I thought, Yes!—I couldn't make up my mind. I hate Gooper and his five same monkeys and that bitch Mae! Why should I turn over twenty-eight thousand acres of the richest land this side of the valley Nile to not my kind?—But why in hell, on the other hand, Brick—should I subsidize

a goddam fool on the bottle?—Liked or not liked, well, maybe even—
loved!—Why should I do that?—Subsidize worthless behavior? Rot? Corruption?

Brick [*smiling*]. I understand.

Big Daddy. Well, if you do, you're smarter than I am, God damn it, because
I don't understand. And this I will tell you frankly. I didn't make up my
mind at all on that question and still to this day I ain't made out no will!—
Well, now I don't *have* to. The pressure is gone. I can just wait and see
if you pull yourself together or if you don't.

Brick. That's right, Big Daddy.

Big Daddy. You sound like you thought I was kidding.

Brick [*rising*]. No, sir, I know you're not kidding.

Big Daddy. But you don't care—?

Brick [*hobbling toward the gallery door*]. No, sir, I don't care. . . .
Now how about taking a look at your birthday fireworks and getting some
of that cool breeze off the river?

[*He stands in the gallery doorway as the night sky turns pink and green
and gold with successive flashes of light.*]

Big Daddy. WAIT!—Brick. . . .

[*His voice drops. Suddenly there is something shy, almost tender, in his
restraining gesture.*]

Don't let's—leave it like this, like them other talks we've had, we've always—talked around things, we've—just talked around things for some
rutten reason, I don't know what, it's always like something was left not
spoken, something avoided because neither of us was honest enough with
the—other. . . .

Brick. I never lied to you, Big Daddy.

Big Daddy. Did I ever to *you?*

Brick. No, sir. . . .

Big Daddy. Then there is at least two people that never lied to each other.

Brick. But we've never *talked* to each other.

Big Daddy. We can *now.*

Brick. Big Daddy, there don't seem to be anything much to say.

Big Daddy. You say that you drink to kill your disgust with lying.

Brick. You said to give you a reason.

Big Daddy. Is liquor the only thing that'll kill this disgust?

Brick. Now. Yes.

Big Daddy. But not once, huh?

Brick. Not when I was still young an' believing. A drinking man's someone
who wants to forget he isn't still young an' believing.

Big Daddy. Believing what?

Brick. Believing. . . .
Big Daddy. Believing *what?*
Brick [*stubbornly evasive*]. Believing. . . .
Big Daddy. I don't know what the hell you mean by believing and I don't
think you know what you mean by believing, but if you still got sports in
your blood, go back to sports announcing and—
Brick. Sit in a glass box watching games I can't play? Describing what I can't
do while players do it? Sweating out their disgust and confusion in contests
I'm not fit for? Drinkin' a coke, half bourbon, so I can stand it? That's
no goddam good any more, no help—time just outran me, Big Daddy—
got there first . . .
Big Daddy. I think you're passing the buck.
Brick. You know many drinkin' men?
Big Daddy [*with a slight, charming smile*]. I have known a fair number of
that species.
Brick. Could any of them tell you why he drank?
Big Daddy. Yep, you're passin' the buck to things like time and disgust with
"mendacity" and—crap!—if you got to use that kind of language about
a thing, it's ninety-proof bull, and I'm not buying any.
Brick. I had to give you a reason to get a drink!
Big Daddy. You started drinkin' when your friend Skipper died.

[*Silence for five beats. Then Brick makes a startled movement, reaching
for his crutch.*]

Brick. What are you suggesting?
Big Daddy. I'm suggesting nothing.

[*The shuffle and clop of Brick's rapid hobble away from his father's steady,
grave attention.*]

—But Gooper an' Mae suggested that there was something not right exactly
in your—
Brick [*stopping short downstage as if backed to a wall*]. "Not right"?
Big Daddy. Not, well, exactly *normal* in your friendship with—
Brick. They suggested that, too? I thought that was Maggie's suggestion.

[*Brick's detachment is at last broken through. His heart is accelerated; his
forehead sweat-beaded; his breath becomes more rapid and his voice
hoarse. The thing they're discussing, timidly and painfully on the side of
Big Daddy, fiercely, violently on Brick's side, is the inadmissible thing that
Skipper died to disavow between them. The fact that if it existed it had
to be disavowed to "keep face" in the world they lived in, may be at the
heart of the "mendacity" that Brick drinks to kill his disgust with. It may
be the root of his collapse. Or maybe it is only a single manifestation of*

it, not even the most important. The bird that I hope to catch in the net of this play is not the solution of one man's psychological problem. I'm trying to catch the true quality of experience in a group of people, that cloudy, flickering, evanescent—fiercely charged!—interplay of live human beings in the thundercloud of a common crisis. Some mystery should be left in the revelation of character in a play, just as a great deal of mystery is always left in the revelation of character in life, even in one's own character to himself. This does not absolve the playwright of his duty to observe and probe as clearly and deeply as he legitimately *can: but it should steer him away from "pat" conclusions, facile definitions which make a play just a play, not a snare for the truth of human experience.*

[The following scene should be played with great concentration, with most of the power leashed but palpable in what is left unspoken.]

Who else's suggestion is it, is it *yours?* How many others thought that Skipper and I were—

Big Daddy [*gently*]. Now, hold on, hold on a minute, son.—I knocked around in my time.

Brick. What's that got to do with—

Big Daddy. I said 'Hold on!'—I bummed, I bummed this country till I was—

Brick. Whose suggestion, who else's suggestion is it?

Big Daddy. Slept in hobo jungles and railroad Y's and flophouses in all cities before I—

Brick. Oh, *you* think so, too, you call me your son and a queer. Oh! Maybe that's why you put Maggie and me in this room that was Jack Straw's and Peter Ochello's, in which that pair of old sisters slept in a double bed where both of 'em died!

Big Daddy. Now just don't go throwing rocks at—

[Suddenly Reverend Tooker appears in the gallery doors, his head slightly, playfully, fatuously cocked, with a practised clergyman's smile, sincere as a bird-call blown on a hunter's whistle, the living embodiment of the pious, conventional lie.

[Big Daddy gasps a little at this perfectly timed, but incongruous, apparition.]

—What're you lookin' for, Preacher?

Reverend Tooker. The gentleman's lavatory, ha ha!—heh, heh . . .

Big Daddy [*with strained courtesy*]. —Go back out and walk down to the other end of the gallery, Reverend Tooker, and use the bathroom connected with my bedroom, and if you can't find it, ask them where it is!

Reverend Tooker. Ah, thanks.

[He goes out with a deprecatory chuckle.]

Big Daddy. It's hard to talk in this place . . .
Brick. Son of a—!
Big Daddy [*leaving a lot unspoken*]. —I seen all things and understood a lot
of them, till 1910. Christ, the year that—I had worn my shoes through,
hocked my—I hopped off a yellow dog freight car half a mile down the
road, slept in a wagon of cotton outside the gin—Jack Straw an' Peter
Ochello took me in. Hired me to manage this place which grew into this
one.—When Jack Straw died—why, old Peter Ochello quit eatin' like a
dog does when its master's dead, and died, too!
Brick. Christ!
Big Daddy. I'm just saying I understand such—
Brick [*violently*]. Skipper is dead. I have not quit eating!
Big Daddy. No, but you started drinking.

[*Brick wheels on his crutch and hurls his glass across the room shouting.*]

Brick. YOU THINK SO, TOO?
Big Daddy. Shhh!

[*Footsteps run on the gallery. There are women's calls.*
[*Big Daddy goes toward the door.*]

Go way!—Just broke a glass. . . .

[*Brick is transformed, as if a quiet mountain blew suddenly up in volcanic
flame.*]

Brick. You think so, too? You think so, too? You think me an' Skipper did,
did, did!—*sodomy!*—together?
Big Daddy. Hold—!
Brick. That what you—
Big Daddy. —ON—a minute!
Brick. You think we did dirty things between us, Skipper an'—
Big Daddy. Why are you shouting like that? Why are you—
Brick. —Me, is that what you think of Skipper, is that—
Big Daddy. —so excited? I don't think nothing. I don't know nothing. I'm
simply telling you what—
Brick. You think that Skipper and me were a pair of dirty old men?
Big Daddy. Now that's—
Brick. Straw? Ochello? A couple of—
Big Daddy. Now just—
Brick. —ducking sissies? Queers? Is that what you—
Big Daddy. Shhh.
Brick. —think?

[*He loses his balance and pitches to his knees without noticing the pain. He grabs the bed and drags himself up.*]

Big Daddy. Jesus!—Whew. . . . Grab my hand!
Brick. Naw, I don't want your hand. . . .
Big Daddy. Well, I want yours. Git up!

[*He draws him up, keeps an arm about him with concern and affection.*]

You broken out in a sweat! You're panting like you'd run a race with—
Brick [*freeing himself from his father's hold*]. Big Daddy, you shock me, Big Daddy, you, you—*shock* me! Talking' so—

[*He turns away from his father*]

—casually!—about a—thing like that . . .
—Don't you know how people *feel* about things like that? How, how *disgusted* they are by things like that? Why, at Ole Miss when it was discovered a pledge to our fraternity, Skipper's and mine, did a, *attempted* to do a, unnatural thing with—
We not only dropped him like a hot rock!—We told him to git off the campus, and he did, he got!—All the way to—

[*He halts, breathless.*]

Big Daddy. —Where?
Brick. —North Africa, last I heard!
Big Daddy. Well, I have come back from further away than that, I have just now returned from the other side of the moon, death's country, son, and I'm not easy to shock by anything here.

[*He comes downstage and faces out.*]

Always, anyhow, lived with too much space around me to be infected by ideas of other people. One thing you can grow on a big place more important than cotton!—is *tolerance!*—I grown it.

[*He returns toward Brick.*]

Brick. Why can't exceptional friendship, *real, real, deep, deep friendship!* between two men be respected as something clean and decent without being thought of as—
Big Daddy. It can, it is, for God's sake.
Brick. —Fairies. . . .

[*In his utterance of this word, we gauge the wide and profound reach of the conventional mores he got from the world that crowned him with early laurel.*]

Big Daddy. I told Mae an' Gooper—

Brick. Frig Mae and Gooper, frig all dirty lies and liars!—Skipper and me had a clean, true thing between us!—had a clean friendship, practically all our lives, till Maggie got the idea you're talking about. Normal? No!—It was too rare to be normal, any true thing between two people is too rare to be normal. Oh, once in a while he put his hand on my shoulder or I'd put mine on his, oh, maybe even, when we were touring the country in pro-football an' shared hotel-rooms we'd reach across the space between the two beds and shake hands to say goodnight, yeah, one or two times we—

Big Daddy. Brick, nobody thinks that that's not normal!

Brick. Well, they're mistaken, it was! It was a pure an' true thing an' that's not normal.

[*They both stare straight at each other for a long moment. The tension breaks and both turn away as if tired.*]

Big Daddy. Yeah, it's—hard t'—talk. . . .

Brick. All right, then, let's—let it go. . . .

Big Daddy. Why did Skipper crack up? Why have you?

[*Brick looks back at his father again. He has already decided, without knowing that he has made this decision, that he is going to tell his father that he is dying of cancer. Only this could even the score between them: one inadmissible thing in return for another.*]

Brick [*ominously*]. All right. You're asking for it, Big Daddy. We're finally going to have that real true talk you wanted. It's too late to stop it, now, we got to carry it through and cover every subject.

[*He hobbles back to the liquor cabinet.*]

Uh-huh.

[*He opens the ice bucket and picks up the silver tongs with slow admiration of their frosty brightness.*]

Maggie declares that Skipper and I went into pro-football after we left "Ole Miss" because we were scared to grow up . . .

[*He moves downstage with the shuffle and clop of a cripple on a crutch. As Margaret did when her speech became "recitative," he looks out into the house, commanding its attention by his direct, concentrated gaze—a broken, "tragically elegant" figure telling simply as much as he knows of "the Truth":*]

—Wanted to—keep on tossing—those long, long!—high, high!—passes that—couldn't be intercepted except by time, the aerial attack that made us famous! And so we did, we did, we kept it up for one season, that aerial attack, we held it high!—Yeah, but—
—that summer, Maggie, she laid the law down to me, said, Now or never, and so I married Maggie. . . .
Big Daddy. How was Maggie in bed?
Brick [*wryly*]. Great! the greatest!

[*Big Daddy nods as if he thought so.*]

She went on the road that fall with the Dixie Stars. Oh, she made a great show of being the world's best sport. She wore a—wore a—tall bearskin cap! A shako, they call it, a dyed moleskin coat, a moleskin coat dyed red!—Cut up crazy! Rented hotel ballrooms for victory celebrations, wouldn't cancel them when it—turned out—defeat. . . .
MAGGIE THE CAT! Ha ha!

[*Big Daddy nods.*]

—But Skipper, he had some fever which came back on him which doctors couldn't explain and I got that injury—turned out to be just a shadow on the X-ray plate—and a touch of bursitis. . . .
I lay in a hospital bed, watched our games on TV, saw Maggie on the bench next to Skipper when he was hauled out of a game for stumbles, fumbles!—Burned me up the way she hung on his arm!—Y'know, I think that Maggie had always felt sort of left out because she and me never got any closer together than two people just get in bed, which is not much closer than two cats on a—fence humping. . . .
So! She took this time to work on poor dumb Skipper. He was a less than average student at Ole Miss, you know that, don't you?!—Poured in his mind the dirty, false idea that what we were, him and me, was a frustrated case of that ole pair of sisters that lived in this room, Jack Straw and Peter Ochello!—He, poor Skipper, went to bed with Maggie to prove it wasn't true, and when it didn't work out, he thought it *was* true!—Skipper broke in two like a rotten stick—nobody ever turned so fast to a lush—or died of it so quick. . . .
—Now are you satisfied?

[*Big Daddy has listened to this story, dividing the grain from the chaff. Now he looks at his son.*]

Big Daddy. Are *you* satisfied?
Brick. With what?
Big Daddy. That half-ass story!
Brick. What's half-ass about it?
Big Daddy. Something's left out of that story. What did you leave out?

[*The phone has started ringing in the hall. As if it reminded him of something, Brick glances suddenly toward the sound and says:*]

Brick. Yes!—I left out a long-distance call which I had from Skipper, in which he made a drunken confession to me and on which I hung up!—last time we spoke to each other in our lives. . . .

[*Muted ring stops as someone answers phone in a soft, indistinct voice in hall.*]

Big Daddy. You hung up?
Brick. Hung up. Jesus! Well—
Big Daddy. Anyhow now!—we have tracked down the lie with which you're disgusted and which you are drinking to kill your disgust with, Brick. You been passing the buck. This disgust with mendacity is disgust with yourself. You!—dug the grave of your friend and kicked him in it!—before you'd face truth with him!
Brick. *His* truth, not *mine!*
Big Daddy. His truth, okay! But you wouldn't face it with him!
Brick. Who *can* face truth? Can *you?*
Big Daddy. Now don't start passin' the rotten buck again, boy!
Brick. How about these birthday congratulations, these many, many happy returns of the day, when ev'rybody but you knows there won't be any!

[*Whoever has answered the hall phone lets out a high, shrill laugh; the voice becomes audible saying: "no, no, you got it all wrong! Upside down! Are you crazy?"*
[*Brick suddenly catches his breath as he realized that he has made a shocking disclosure. He hobbles a few paces, then freezes, and without looking at his father's shocked face, says:*]

Let's, let's—go out, now, and—

[*Big Daddy moves suddenly forward and grabs hold of the boy's crutch like it was a weapon for which they were fighting for possession.*]

Big Daddy. Oh, no, no! No one's going out! What did you start to say?

Brick. I don't remember.

Big Daddy. "Many happy returns when they know there won't be any"?

Brick. Aw, hell, Big Daddy, forget it. Come on out on the gallery and look at the fireworks they're shooting off for your birthday. . . .

Big Daddy. First you finish that remark you were makin' before you cut off. "Many happy returns when they know there won't be any"?—Ain't that what you just said?

Brick. Look, now. I can get around without that crutch if I have to but it would be a lot easier on the furniture an' glassware if I didn' have to go swinging along like Tarzan of th'—

Big Daddy. FINISH! WHAT YOU WAS SAYIN'!

[*An eerie green glow shows in sky behind him.*]

Brick [*sucking the ice in his glass, speech becoming thick*]. Leave th' place to Gooper and Mae an' their five little same little monkeys. All I want is—

Big Daddy. "LEAVE TH' PLACE," did you say?

Brick [*vaguely*]. All twenty-eight thousand acres of the richest land this side of the valley Nile.

Big Daddy. Who said I was "leaving the place" to Gooper or anybody? This is my sixty-fifth birthday! I got fifteen years or twenty years left in me! I'll outlive *you!* I'll bury you an' have to pay for your coffin!

Brick. Sure. Many happy returns. Now let's go watch the fireworks, come on, let's—

Big Daddy. Lying, have they been lying? About the report from th'—clinic? Did they, did they—find something?—*Cancer.* Maybe?

Brick. Mendacity is a system that we live in. Liquor is one way out an' death's the other. . . .

[*He takes the crutch from Big Daddy's loose grip and swings out on the gallery leaving the doors open.*
[*A song, "Pick a Bale of Cotton," is heard.*]

Mae [*appearing in door*]. Oh, Big Daddy, the field-hands are singin' fo' you!

Big Daddy [*shouting hoarsely*]. BRICK! BRICK!

Mae. He's outside drinkin', Big Daddy.

Big Daddy. BRICK!

[*Mae retreats, awed by the passion of his voice. Children call Brick in tones mocking Big Daddy. His face crumbles like broken yellow plaster about to fall into dust.*
[*There is a glow in the sky. Brick swings back through the doors, slowly, gravely, quite soberly.*]

Brick. I'm sorry, Big Daddy. My head don't work any more and it's hard for me to understand how anybody could care if he lived or died or was dying or cared about anything but whether or not there was liquor left in the bottle and so I said what I said without thinking. In some ways I'm no better than the others, in some ways worse because I'm less alive. Maybe it's being alive that makes them lie, and being almost *not* alive makes me sort of accidentally truthful—I don't know but—anyway—we've been friends . . .
—And being friends is telling each other the truth. . . .

[*There is a pause.*]

You told *me!* I told *you!*

[*A child rushes into the room and grabs a fistful of firecrackers and runs out again.*]

Child [*screaming*]. Bang, bang, bang, bang, bang, bang, bang, bang, bang!
Big Daddy [*slowly and passionately*]. CHRIST—DAMN—ALL—LYING SONS OF—LYING BITCHES!

[*He straightens at last and crosses to the inside door. At the door he turns and looks back as if he had some desperate question he couldn't put into words. Then he nods reflectively and says in a hoarse voice:*]

Yes, all liars, all liars, all lying dying liars!

[*This is said slowly, slowly, with a fierce revulsion. He goes on out.*]

—Lying! Dying! Liars!

[*His voice dies out. There is the sound of a child being slapped. It rushes, hideously bawling, through room and out the hall door.*
[*Brick remains motionless as the lights dim out and the curtain falls.*]

CURTAIN

ACT THREE

> *There is no lapse of time.*
> *Mae enters with Reverend Tooker.*

Mae. Where is Big Daddy! Big Daddy!

Big Mama [*entering*]. Too much smell of burnt fireworks makes me feel a little bit sick at my stomach.—Where is Big Daddy?

Mae. That's what I want to know, where has Big Daddy gone?

Big Mama. He must have turned in, I reckon he went to baid. . . .

> [*Gooper enters.*]

Gooper. Where is Big Daddy?

Mae. We don't know where he is!

Big Mama. I reckon he's gone to baid.

Gooper. Well, then, now we can talk.

Big Mama. What *is* this talk, *what* talk?

> [*Margaret appears on gallery, talking to Dr. Baugh.*]

Margaret [*musically*]. My family freed their slaves ten years before abolition, my great-great grandfather gave his slaves their freedom five years before the war between the States started!

Mae. Oh, for God's sake! Maggie's climbed back up in her family tree!

Margaret [*sweetly*]. What, Mae?—Oh, where's Big Daddy?!

> [*The pace must be very quick. Great Southern animation.*]

Big Mama [*addressing them all*]. I think Big Daddy was just worn out. He loves his family, he loves to have them around him, but it's a strain on his nerves. He wasn't himself tonight, Big Daddy wasn't himself, I could tell he was all worked up.

Reverend Tooker. I think he's remarkable.

Big Mama. Yaisss! Just remarkable. Did you all notice the food he ate at that table? Did you all notice the supper he put away? Why, he ate like a hawss!

Gooper. I hope he doesn't regret it.

Big Mama. Why, that man—ate a huge piece of cawn-bread with molasses on it! Helped himself twice to hoppin' john.

Margaret. Big Daddy loves hoppin' john.—We had a real country dinner.

Big Mama [*overlapping Margaret*]. Yais, he simply adores it! An' candied yams? That man put away enough food at that table to stuff a nigger *field*-hand!

Gooper [*with grim relish*]. I hope he don't have to pay for it later on. . . .
Big Mama [*fiercely*]. What's *that*, Gooper?
Mae. Gooper says he hopes Big Daddy doesn't suffer tonight.
Big Mama. Oh, shoot, Gooper says, Gooper says! Why should Big Daddy
　　suffer for satisfying a normal appetite? There's nothin' wrong with that
　　man but nerves, he's sound as a dollar! And now he knows he
　　is an' that's why he ate such a supper. He had a big load off his mind,
　　knowin' he wasn't doomed t'—what he thought he was doomed to. . . .
Margaret [*sadly and sweetly*]. Bless his old sweet soul. . . .
Big Mama [*vaguely*]. Yais, bless his heart, wher's Brick?
Mae. Outside.
Gooper. —Drinkin' . . .
Big Mama. I know he's drinkin. You all don't have to keep tellin' *me* Brick
　　is drinkin'. Cain't I see he's drinkin' without you continually tellin' me
　　that boy's drinkin'?
Margaret. Good for you, Big Mama!

[*She applauds.*]

Big Mama. Other people *drink* and *have* drunk an' will *drink,* as long as
　　they make that stuff an' put it in bottles.
Margaret. That's the truth. I never trusted a man that didn't drink.
Mae. Gooper never drinks. Don't you trust Gooper?
Margaret. Why, Gooper don't you drink? If I'd known you didn't drink, I
　　wouldn't of made that remark—
Big Mama. Brick?
Margaret. —at least not in your presence.

[*She laughs sweetly.*]

Big Mama. Brick!
Margaret. He's still on the gall'ry. I'll go bring him in so we can talk.
Big Mama [*worriedly*]. I don't know what this mysterious family conference
　　is about.

[*Awkward silence. Big Mama looks from face to face, then belches slightly
and mutters, "Excuse me. . . ." She opens an ornamental fan suspended
about her throat, a black lace fan to go with her black lace gown and fans
her wilting corsage, sniffing nervously and looking from face to face in
the uncomfortable silence as Margaret calls "Brick?" and Brick sings to
the moon on the gallery.*]

I don't know what's wrong here, you all have such long faces! Open that
door on the hall and let some air circulate through here, will you please,
Gooper?

Mae. I think we'd better leave that door closed, Big Mama, till after the talk.

Big Mama. Reveren' Tooker, will *you* please open that door?!

Reverend Tooker. I sure will, Big Mama.

Mae. I just didn't think we ought t' take any chance of Big Daddy hearin' a word of this discussion.

Big Mama. I *swan!* Nothing's going to be said in Big Daddy's house that he cain't hear if he wants to!

Gooper. Well, Big Mama, it's—

[*Mae gives him a quick, hard poke to shut him up. He glares at her fiercely as she circles before him like a burlesque ballerina, raising her skinny bare arms over her head, jangling her bracelets, exclaiming.*]

Mae. A breeze! A breeze!

Reverend Tooker. I think this house is the coolest house in the Delta.—Did you all know that Halsey Banks' widow put air-conditioning units in the church and rectory at Friar's Point in memory of Halsey?

[*General conversation has resumed; everybody is chatting so that the stage sounds like a big bird-cage.*]

Gooper. Too bad nobody cools your church off for you. I bet you sweat in that pulpit these hot Sundays, Reverend Tooker.

Reverend Tooker. Yes, my vestments are drenched.

Mae [*at the same time to Dr. Baugh*]. You think those vitamin B_{12} injections are what they're cracked up t' be, Doc Baugh?

Doctor Baugh. Well, if you want to be stuck with something I guess they're as good to be stuck with as anything else.

Big Mama [*at gallery door*]. Maggie, Maggie, aren't you comin' with Brick?

Mae [*suddenly and loudly, creating a silence*]. I have a strange feeling, I have a peculiar feeling!

Big Mama [*turning from gallery*]. What feeling?

Mae. That Brick said somethin' he shouldn't of said t' Big Daddy.

Big Mama. Now what on earth could Brick of said t' Big Daddy that he shouldn't say?

Gooper. Big Mama, there's somethin'—

Mae. NOW, WAIT!

[*She rushes up to Big Mama and gives her a quick hug and kiss. Big Mama pushes her impatiently off as the Reverend Tooker's voice rises serenely in a little pocket of silence.*]

Reverend Tooker. Yes, last Sunday the gold in my chasuble faded into th' purple. . . .

Gooper. Reveren' you must of been preachin' hell's fire last Sunday!

[*He guffaws at this witticism but the Reverend is not sincerely amused. At the same time Big Mama has crossed over to Dr. Baugh and is saying to him.*]

Big Mama [*her breathless voice rising high-pitched above the others*]. In my day they had what they call the Keeley cure for heavy drinkers. But now I understand they just take some kind of tablets, they call them "Annie Bust" tablets. But *Brick* don't need to take *nothin'*.

[*Brick appears in gallery doors with Margaret behind him.*]

Big Mama [*unaware of his presence behind her*]. That boy is just broken up over Skipper's death. You know how poor Skipper died. They gave him a big, big dose of that sodium amytal stuff at his home and then they called the ambulance and give him another big, big dose of it at the hospital and that and all of the alcohol in his system fo' months an' months an' months just proved too much for his heart. . . . I'm scared of needles! I'm more scared of a needle than the knife. . . . I think more people have been needled out of this world than—

[*She stops short and wheels about.*]

OH!—here's Brick! My precious baby—

[*She turns upon Brick with short, fat arms extended, at the same time uttering a loud, short sob, which is both comic and touching.*
[*Brick smiles and bows slightly, making a burlesque gesture of gallantry for Maggie to pass before him into the room. Then he hobbles on his crutch directly to the liquor cabinet and there is absolute silence, with everybody looking at Brick as everybody has always looked at Brick when he spoke or moved or appeared. One by one he drops ice cubes in his glass, then suddenly, but not quickly, looks back over his shoulder with a wry, charming smile, and says.*]

Brick. I'm sorry! Anyone else?
Big Mama [*sadly*]. No, son. I *wish* you wouldn't!
Brick. I wish I didn't have to, Big Mama, but I'm still waiting for that click in my head which makes it all smooth out!
Big Mama. Aw, Brick, you—BREAK MY HEART!
Margaret [*at the same time*]. Brick, go sit with Big Mama!
Big Mama. I just cain't *staiiiiiiiii-nnnnd*—it. . . .

[*She sobs.*]

Mae. Now that we're all assembled—
Gooper. We kin talk. . . .

Big Mama. Breaks my heart. . . .
Margaret. Sit with big Mama, Brick, and hold her hand.

[*Big Mama sniffs very loudly three times, almost like three drum beats in the pocket of silence.*]

Brick. You do that, Maggie. I'm a restless cripple. I got to stay on my crutch.

[*Brick hobbles to the gallery door; leans there as if waiting.*
[*Mae sits beside Big Mama, while Gooper moves in front and sits on the end of the couch, facing her. Reverend Tooker moves nervously into the space between them; on the other side, Dr. Baugh stands looking at nothing in particular and lights a cigar. Margaret turns away.*]

Big Mama. Why're you all *surroundin'* me—like this? Why're you all starin' at me like this an' makin' signs at each other?

[*Reverend Tooker steps back startled.*]

Mae. Calm youself, Big Mama.
Big Mama. Calm you'self, *you'self*, Sister Woman. How could I calm myself with everyone starin' at me as if big drops of blood had broken out on m'face? What's this all about, Annh! What?

[*Gooper coughs and takes a center position.*]

Gooper. Now, Doc Baugh.
Mae. Doc Baugh?
Brick [*suddenly*]. SHHH!—

[*Then he grins and chuckles and shakes his head regretfully.*]

—Naw!—that wasn't th' click.
Gooper. Brick, shut up or stay out there on the gallery with your liquor! We got to talk about a serious matter. Big Mama wants to know the complete truth about the report we got today from Ochsner Clinic.
Mae [*eagerly*]. —on Big Daddy's condition!
Gooper. Yais, on Big Daddy's condition, we got to face it.
Doctor Baugh. Well. . . .
Big Mama [*terrified, rising*]. Is there? Something? Something that I? Don't— Know?

[*In these few words, this startled, very soft, question, Big Mama reviews the history of her forty-five years with Big Daddy, her great, almost em-*

barrassingly true-hearted and simple-minded devotion to Big Daddy, who must have had something Brick has, who made himself loved so much by the "simple expedient" of not loving enough to disturb his charming detachment, also once coupled, like Brick's, with virile beauty.
[*Big Mama has a dignity at this moment: she almost stops being fat.*]

Doctor Baugh [*after a pause, uncomfortably*]. Yes?—Well—
Big Mama. I!!!—want to—knowwwwwww. . . .

[*Immediately she thrusts her fist to her mouth as if to deny that statement.* [*Then, for some curious reason, she snatches the withered corsage from her breast and hurls it on the floor and steps on it with her short, fat feet.*]

—*Somebody must be lyin'!—I want to know!*
Mae. Sit down, Big Mama, sit down on this sofa.
Margaret [*quickly*]. Brick, go sit with Big Mama.
Big Mama. What is it, what is it?
Doctor Baugh. I never have seen a more thorough examination than Big Daddy Pollitt was given in all my experience with the Ochsner Clinic.
Gooper. It's one of the best in the country.
Mae. It's THE best in the country—*bar none!*

[*For some reason she gives Gooper a violent poke as she goes past him. He slaps at her hand without removing his eyes from his mother's face.*]

Doctor Baugh. Of course they were ninety-nine and nine-tenths percent sure before they even started.
Big Mama. Sure of what, sure of what, sure of—*what?—what!*

[*She catches her breath in a startled sob. Mae kisses her quickly. She thrusts Mae fiercely away from her, staring at the doctor.*]

Mae. Mommy, be a brave girl!
Brick [*in the doorway, softly*]. "By the light, by the light,
  Of the sil-ve-ry mo-ooo-n . . ."
Gooper. Shut up!—Brick.
Brick. —Sorry. . . .

[*He wanders out on the gallery.*]

Doctor Baugh. But now, you see, Big Mama, they cut a piece off this growth, a specimen of the tissue and—
Big Mama. Growth? You told Big Daddy—
Doctor Baugh. Now wait.

Big Mama [*fiercely*]. You told me and Big Daddy there wasn't a thing wrong
   with him but—
Mae. Big Mama, they always—
Gooper. Let Doc Baugh talk, will yuh?
Big Mama. —little spastic condition of—

[*Her breath gives out in a sob.*]

Doctor Baugh. Yes, that's what we told Big Daddy. But we had this bit of
   tissue run through the laboratory and I'm sorry to say the test was positive
   on it. It's—well—malignant. . . .

[*Pause*]

Big Mama. —Cancer?! Cancer?!

[*Dr. Baugh nods gravely.*
[*Big Mama gives a long gasping cry.*]

Mae and Gooper. Now, now, now, Big Mama, you had to know. . . .
Big Mama. WHY DIDN'T THEY CUT IT OUT OF HIM? HANH? HANH?
Doctor Baugh. Involved too much, Big Mama, too many organs affected.
Mae. Big Mama, the liver's affected and so's the kidneys, both! It's gone way
   past what they call a—
Gooper. A surgical risk.
Mae. —Uh-huh. . . .

[*Big Mama draws a breath like a dying gasp.*]

Reverend Tooker. Tch, tch, tch, tch, tch!
Doctor Baugh. Yes, it's gone past the knife.
Mae. That's why he's turned yellow, Mommy!
Big Mama. Git away from me, git away from me, Mae!

[*She rises abruptly.*]

   I want Brick! Where's Brick? Where is my only son?
Mae. Mama! Did she say "*only* son"?
Gooper. What does that make *me*?
Mae. A sober responsible man with five precious children!—*Six!*
Big Mama. I want Brick to tell me! Brick! Brick!
Margaret [*rising from her reflections in a corner*]. Brick was so upset he went
   back out.
Big Mama. Brick!
Margaret. Mama, let *me* tell you!

Big Mama. No, no, leave me alone, you're not my blood!
Gooper. Mama, I'm your son! Listen to *me!*
Mae. Gooper's your son, Mama, he's your first-born!
Big Mama. Gooper never liked Daddy.
Mae [*as if terribly shocked*]. *That's not TRUE!*

[*There is a pause. The minister coughs and rises.*]

Reverend Tooker [*to Mae*]. I think I'd better slip away at this point.
Mae [*sweetly and sadly*]. Yes, Doctor Tooker, you go.
Reverend Tooker [*discreetly*]. Goodnight, goodnight, everybody, and God
   bless you all . . . on this place. . . .

[*He slips out.*]

Doctor Baugh. That man is a good man but lacking in tact. Talking about
   people giving memorial windows—if he mentioned one memorial window,
   he must have spoke of a dozen, and saying how awful it was when somebody died intestate, the legal wrangles, and so forth.

[*Mae coughs, and points at Big Mama.*]

Doctor Baugh. Well, Big Mama. . . .

[*He sighs.*]

Big Mama. It's all a mistake, I know it's just a bad dream.
Doctor Baugh. We're gonna keep Big Daddy as comfortable as we can.
Big Mama. Yes, it's just a bad dream, that's all it is, it's just an awful dream.
Gooper. In my opinion Big Daddy is having some pain but won't admit that
   he has it.
Big Mama. Just a dream, a bad dream.
Doctor Baugh. That's what lots of them do, they think if they don't admit
   they're having the pain they can sort of escape the fact of it.
Gooper [*with relish*]. Yes, they get sly about it, they get real sly about it.
Mae. Gooper and I think—
Gooper. Shut up, Mae!—Big Daddy ought to be started on morphine.
Big Mama. Nobody's going to give Big Daddy morphine.
Doctor Baugh. Now, Big Mama, when that pain strikes it's going to strike
   mighty hard and Big Daddy's going to need the needle to bear it.
Big Mama. I tell you, nobody's going to give him morphine.
Mae. Big Mama, you don't want to see Big Daddy suffer, you know you—

[*Gooper standing beside her gives her a savage poke.*]

Doctor Baugh [*placing a package on the table*]. I'm leaving this stuff here, so if there's a sudden attack you all won't have to send out for it.
Mae. I know how to give a hypo.
Gooper. Mae took a course in nursing during the war.
Margaret. Somehow I don't think Big Daddy would want Mae to give him a hypo.
Mae. You think he'd want *you* to do it?

[*Dr. Baugh rises.*]

Gooper. Doctor Baugh is goin'.
Doctor Baugh. Yes, I got to be goin'. Well, keep your chin up, Big Mama.
Gooper [*with jocularity*]. She's gonna keep *both* chins up, aren't you Big Mama?

[*Big Mama sobs.*]

Now stop that, Big Mama.
Mae. Sit down with me, Big Mama.
Gooper [*at door with Dr. Baugh*]. Well, Doc, we sure do appreciate all you done. I'm telling you, we're surely obligated to you for—

[*Dr. Baugh has gone out without a glance at him.*]

Gooper. —I guess that doctor has got a lot on his mind but it wouldn't hurt him to act a little more human. . . .

[*Big Mama sobs.*]

Now be a brave girl, Mommy.
Big Mama. It's not true, I know that it's just not true!
Gooper. Mama, those tests are infallible!
Big Mama. Why are you so determined to see your father daid?
Mae. Big Mama!
Margaret [*gently*]. I know what Big Mama means.
Mae [*fiercely*]. Oh, do you?
Margaret [*quietly and very sadly*]. Yes, I think I do.
Mae. For a newcomer in the family you sure do show a lot of understanding.
Margaret. Understanding is needed on this place.
Mae. I guess you must have needed a lot of it in your family, Maggie, with your father's liquor problem and now you've got Brick with his!
Margaret. Brick does not have a liquor problem at all. Brick is devoted to Big Daddy. This thing is a terrible strain on him.
Big Mama. Brick is Big Daddy's boy, but he drinks too much and it worries me and Big Daddy, and, Margaret, you've got to cooperate with us, you've

got to cooperate with Big Daddy and me in getting Brick straightened out.
Because it will break Big Daddy's heart if Brick don't pull himself together
and take hold of things.

Mae. Take hold of *what* things, Big Mama?

Big Mama. The place.

[*There is a quick violent look between Mae and Gooper.*]

Gooper. Big Mama, you've had a shock.

Mae. Yais, we've all had a shock, but . . .

Gooper. Let's be realistic—

Mae. —Big Daddy would never, would *never*, be foolish enough to—

Gooper. —put this place in irresponsible hands!

Big Mama. Big Daddy ain't going to leave the place in anybody's hands; Big
Daddy is *not* going to die. I want you to get that in your heads, all of
you!

Mae. Mommy, Mommy, Big Mama, we're just as hopeful an' optimistic as
you are about Big Daddy's prospects, we have faith in *prayer*—but nevertheless there are certain matters that have to be discussed an' dealt with,
because otherwise—

Gooper. Eventualities have to be considered and now's the time. . . . Mae,
will you please get my briefcase out of our room?

Mae. Yes, honey.

[*She rises and goes out through the hall door.*]

Gooper [*standing over Big Mama*]. Now Big Mom. What you said just now
was not at all true and you know it. I've always loved Big Daddy in my
own quiet way. I never made a show of it, and I know that Big Daddy
has always been fond of me in a quiet way, too, and he never made a
show of it neither.

[*Mae returns with Gooper's briefcase.*]

Mae. Here's your briefcase, Gooper, honey.

Gooper [*handing the briefcase back to her*]. Thank you. . . . Of ca'use, my
relationship with Big Daddy is different from Brick's.

Mae. You're eight years older'n Brick an' always had t'carry a bigger load
of th' responsibilities than Brick ever had t'carry. He never carried a thing
in his life but a football or a highball.

Gooper. Mae, will y' let me talk, please?

Mae. Yes, honey.

Gooper. Now, a twenty-eight thousand acre plantation's a mighty big thing
t'run.

Mae. Almost singlehanded.

[*Margaret has gone out onto the gallery, and can he heard calling softly to Brick.*]

Big Mama. You never had to run this place! What are you talking about? As if Big Daddy was dead and in his grave, you had to run it? Why, you just helped him out with a few business details and had your law practice at the same time in Memphis!

Mae. Oh, Mommy, Mommy, Big Mommy! Let's be fair! Why, Gooper has given himself body and soul to keeping this place up for the past five years since Big Daddy's health started failing. Gooper won't say it, Gooper never thought of it as a duty, he just did it. And what did Brick do? Brick kept living in his past glory at college! Still a football player at twenty-seven!

Margaret [*returning alone*]. Who are you talking about, now? Brick? A football player? He isn't a football player and you know it. Brick is a sport's announcer on TV and one of the best-known ones in the country!

Mae. I'm talking about what he was.

Margaret. Well, I wish you would just stop talking about my husband.

Gooper. I've got a right to discuss my brother with other members of MY OWN family which don't include *you.* Why don't you go out there and drink with Brick?

Margaret. I've never seen such malice toward a brother.

Gooper. How about his for me? Why, he can't stand to be in the same room with me!

Margaret. This is a deliberate campaign of vilification for the most disgusting and sordid reason on earth, and I know what it is! It's *avarice, avarice, greed, greed!*

Big Mama. Oh, I'll scream! I will scream in a moment unless this stops!

[*Gooper has stalked up to Margaret with clenched fists at his sides as if he would strike her. Mae distorts her face again into a hideous grimace behind Margaret's back.*]

Margaret. We only remain on the place because of Big Mom and Big Daddy. If it is true what they say about Big Daddy we are going to leave here just as soon as it's over. Not a moment later.

Big Mama [*sobs*]. Margaret. Child. Come here. Sit next to Big Mama.

Margaret. Precious Mommy. I'm sorry, I'm so sorry, I—!

[*She bends her long graceful neck to press her forehead to Big Mama's bulging shoulder under its black chiffon.*]

Gooper. How beautiful, how touching, this display of devotion!

Mae. Do you know why she's childless? She's childless because that big beautiful athlete husband of hers won't go to bed with her!

Gooper. You jest won't let me do this in a nice way, will yah? Aw right—
Mae and I have five kids with another one coming! I don't give a goddam
if Big Daddy likes me or don't like me or did or never did or will or will
never! I'm just appealing to a sense of common decency and fair play. I'll
tell you the truth. I've resented Big Daddy's partiality to Brick ever since
Brick was born, and the way I've been treated like I was just barely good
enough to spit on and sometimes not even good enough for that. Big
Daddy is dying of cancer, and it's spread all through him and it's attacked
all his vital organs including the kidneys and right now he is sinking into
uremia, and you all know what uremia is, it's poisoning of the whole
system due to the failure of the body to eliminate its poisons.

Margaret [*to herself, downstage, hissingly*]. Poisons, poisons! *Venomous*
thoughts and words! In hearts and minds!—That's poisons!

Gooper [*overlapping her*]. I am asking for a square deal, and I expect to get
one. But if I don't get one, if there's any peculiar shenanigans going on
around here behind my back, or before me, well, I'm not a corporation
lawyer for nothing, I know how to protect my own interests.—*OH! A*
late arrival!

[*Brick enters from the gallery with a tranquil, blurred smile, carrying an*
empty glass with him.]

Mae. Behold the conquering hero comes!

Gooper. The fabulous Brick Pollitt! Remember him?—Who could forget him!

Mae. He looks like he's been injured in a game!

Gooper. Yep, I'm afraid you'll have to warm the bench at the Sugar Bowl
this year, Brick!

[*Mae laughs shrilly.*]

Or was it the Rose Bowl that he made that famous run in?

Mae. The punch bowl, honey. It was in the punch bowl, the cutglass punch
bowl!

Gooper. Oh, that's right, I'm getting the bowls mixed up!

Margaret. Why don't you stop venting your malice and envy on a sick boy?

Big Mama. Now you two hush, I mean it, hush, all of you, hush!

Gooper. All right, Big Mama. A family crisis brings out the best and the
worst in every member of it.

Mae. That's the truth.

Margaret. Amen!

Big Mama. I said, hush! I won't tolerate any more catty talk in my house.

[*Mae gives Gooper a sign indicating briefcase.*
[*Brick's smile has grown both brighter and vaguer. As he prepares a drink,*
he sings softly]

Brick. Show me the way to go home,
   I'm tired and I wanta go to bed,
   I had a little drink about an hour ago—
Gooper [*at the same time*]. Big Mama, you know it's necessary for me t'go
   back to Memphis in th' mornin' t'represent the Parker estate in a lawsuit.

[*Mae sits on the bed and arranges papers she has taken from the briefcase.*]

Brick [*continuing the song*]. *Wherever I may roam,*
   On land or sea or foam.
Big Mama. Is it, Gooper?
Mae. Yaiss.
Gooper. That's why I'm forced to—to bring up a problem that—
Mae. Somethin' that's too import t' be put off!
Gooper. If Brick was sober, he ought to be in on this.
Margaret. Brick is present; we're here.
Gooper. Well, good. I will now give you this outline my partner, Tom Bullitt,
   an' me have drawn up—a sort of dummy—trusteeship.
Margaret. Oh, that's it! You'll be in charge an' dole out remittances, will
   you?
Gooper. This we did as soon as we got the report on Big Daddy from th'
   Ochsner Laboratories. We did this thing, I mean we drew up this dummy
   outline with the advice and assistance of the Chairman of the Boa'd of
   Directors of th' Southern Plantahs Bank and Trust Company in Memphis,
   C. C. Bellowes, a man who handles estates for all th' prominent fam'lies
   in West Tennessee and th' Delta.
Big Mama. Gooper?
Gooper [*crouching in front of Big Mama*]. Now this is not—not final, or
   anything like it. This is just a preliminary outline. But it does provide a
   basis—a design—a—possible, feasible—*plan!*
Margaret. Yes, I'll bet.
Mae. It's a plan to protect the biggest estate in the Delta from irresponsibility
   an'—
Big Mama. Now you listen to me, all of you, you listen here! They's not
   goin' to be any more catty talk in my house! And Gooper, you put that
   away before I grab it out of our hand and tear it right up! I don't know
   what the hell's in it, and I don't want to know what the hell's in it. I'm
   talkin' in Big Daddy's language now; I'm his *wife,* not his *widow,* I'm still
   his *wife!* And I'm talkin' to you in his language an'—
Gooper. Big Mama, what I have here is—
Mae. Gooper explained that it's just a plan. . . .
Big Mama. I don't care what you got there. Just put it back where it came
   from, an' don't let me see it again, not even the outside of the envelope
   of it! Is that understood? Basis! Plan! Preliminary! Design! I say—what is
   it Big Daddy always says when he's disgusted?

Brick [from the bar]. Big Daddy says "crap" when he's disgusted.

Big Mama [rising]. That's right—CRAP! I say CRAP too, like Big Daddy!

Mae. Coarse language doesn't seem called for in this—

Gooper. Somethin' in me is *deeply outraged* by hearin' you talk like this.

Big Mama. Nobody's goin' to take nothin'!—till Big Daddy lets go of it, and maybe, just possibly, not—not even then! No, not even then!

Brick. You can always hear me singin' this song,
   Show me the way to go home.

Big Mama. Tonight Brick looks like he used to look when he was a little boy, just like he did when he played wild games and used to come home all sweaty and pink-cheeked and sleepy, with his—red curls shining. . . .

[*She comes over to him and runs her fat shaky hand through his hair. He draws aside as he does from all physical contact and continues the song in a whisper, opening the ice bucket and dropping in the ice cubes one by one as if he were mixing some important chemical formula.*]

Big Mama [continuing]. Time goes by so fast. Nothin' can outrun it. Death commences too early—almost before you're half-acquainted with life— you meet with the other. . . .
   Oh, you know we just got to love each other an' stay together, all of us, just as close as we can, especially now that such a *black* thing has come and moved into this place without invitation.

[*Awkwardly embracing Brick, she presses her head to his shoulder.*
[*Gooper has been returning papers to Mae who has restored them to briefcase with an air of severely tried patience.*]

Gooper. Big Mama? Big Mama?

[*He stands behind her, tense with sibling envy.*]

Big Mama [oblivious of Gooper]. Brick, you hear me, don't you?

Margaret. Brick hears you, Big Mama, he understands what you're saying.

Big Mama. Oh, Brick, son of Big Daddy! Big Daddy does so love you! Y'know what would be his fondest dream come true? If before he passed on, if Big Daddy has to pass on, you gave him a child of yours, a grandson as much like his son as his son is like Big Daddy!

Mae [zipping briefcase shut: an incongruous sound]. Such a pity that Maggie an' Brick can't oblige!

Margaret [suddenly and quietly but forcefully]. Everybody listen.

[*She crosses to the center of the room, holding her hands rigidly together.*]

Mae. Listen to what, Maggie?

Margaret. I have an announcement to make.

Gooper. A sports announcement, Maggie?

Margaret. Brick and I are going to—*have a child!*

[*Big Mama catches her breath in a loud gasp.*]
[*Pause. Big Mama rises.*]

Big Mama. Maggie! Brick! This is too good to believe!

Mae. That's right, too good to believe.

Big Mama. Oh, my, my! This is Big Daddy's dream, his dream come true! I'm going to tell him right now before he—

Margaret. We'll tell him in the morning. Don't disturb him now.

Big Mama. I want to tell him before he goes to sleep, I'm going to tell him his dream's come true this minute! And Brick! A child will make you pull yourself together and quit this drinking!

[*She seizes the glass from his hand.*]

The responsibilities of a father will—

[*Her face contorts and she makes an excited gesture; bursting into sobs, she rushes out, crying.*]

I'm going to tell Big Daddy right this minute!

[*Her voice fades out down the hall.*
[*Brick shrugs slightly and drops an ice cube into another glass. Margaret crosses quickly to his side, saying something under her breath, and she pours the liquor for him, staring up almost fiercely into his face.*]

Brick [*coolly*]. Thank you, Maggie, that's a nice big shot.

[*Mae has joined Gooper and she gives him a fierce poke, making a low hissing sound and a grimace of fury.*]

Gooper [*pushing her aside*]. Brick, could you possibly spare me one small shot of that liquor?

Brick. Why, help yourself, Gooper boy.

Gooper. I will.

Mae [*shrilly*]. Of course we know that this is—

Gooper. Be still, Mae!

Mae. I won't be still! I know she's made this up!

Gooper. God damn it, I said to shut up!

Margaret. Gracious! I didn't know that my little announcement was going to provoke such a storm!

Mae. *That* woman isn't *pregnant!*

Gooper. Who said she was?
Mae. *She* did.
Gooper. The doctor didn't. Doc Baugh didn't.
Margaret. I haven't gone to Doc Baugh.
Gooper. Then who'd you go to, Maggie?
Margaret. One of the best gynecologists in the South.
Gooper. Uh huh, uh huh!—I see. . . .

[*He takes out pencil and notebook.*]

—May we have his name, please?
Margaret. No, you may not, Mister Prosecuting Attorney!
Mae. He doesn't have any name, he doesn't exist!
Margaret. Oh, he exists all right, and so does my child, Brick's baby!
Mae. You can't conceive a child by a man that won't sleep with you unless
you think you're—

[*Brick has turned on the phonograph. A scat song cuts Mae's speech.*]

Gooper. Turn that off!
Mae. We know it's a lie because we hear you in here; he won't sleep with
you, we hear you! So don't imagine you're going to put a trick over on
us, to fool a dying man with a—

[*A long drawn cry of agony and rage fills the house. Margaret turns
phonograph down to a whisper.*
[*The cry is repeated.*]

Mae [*awed*]. Did you hear that, Gooper, did you hear that?
Gooper. Sounds like the pain has struck.
Mae. Go see, Gooper!
Gooper. Come along and leave these love birds together in their nest!

[*He goes out first. Mae follows but turns at the door, contorting her face
and hissing at Margaret.*]

Mae. Liar!

[*She slams the door.*
[*Margaret exhales with relief and moves a little unsteadily to catch hold
of Brick's arm.*]

Margaret. Thank you for—keeping still . . .
Brick. OK, Maggie.

Margaret. It was gallant of you to save my face!

Brick. —It hasn't happened yet.

Margaret. What?

Brick. The click. . . .

Margaret. —the click in your head that makes you peaceful, honey?

Brick. Uh-huh. It hasn't happened. . . . I've got to make it happen before I can sleep. . . .

Margaret. —I—know what you—mean. . . .

Brick. Give me that pillow in the big chair, Maggie.

Margaret. I'll put it on the bed for you.

Brick. No, put it on the sofa, where I sleep.

Margaret. Not tonight, Brick.

Brick. I want it on the sofa. That's where I sleep.

[*He has hobbled to the liquor cabinet. He now pours down three shots in quick succession and stands waiting, silent. All at once he turns with a smile and says:*]

There!

Margaret. What?

Brick. The *click.* . . .

[*His gratitude seems almost infinite as he hobbles out on the gallery with a drink. We hear his crutch as he swings out of sight. Then, at some distance, he begins singing to himself a peaceful song.*
[*Margaret holds the big pillow forlornly as if it were her only companion, for a few moments, then throws it on the bed. She rushes to the liquor cabinet, gathers all the bottles in her arms, turns about undecidedly, then runs out of the room with them, leaving the door ajar on the dim yellow hall. Brick is heard hobbling back along the gallery, singing his peaceful song. He comes back in, sees the pillow on the bed, laughs lightly, sadly, picks it up. He has it under his arm as Margaret returns to the room. Margaret softly shuts the door and leans against it, smiling softly at Brick.*]

Margaret. Brick, I used to think that you were stronger than me and I didn't want to be overpowered by you. But now, since you've taken to liquor— you know what?—I guess it's bad, but now I'm stronger than you and I can love you more truly!

Don't move that pillow. I'll move it right back if you do!
—Brick?

[*She turns out all the lamps but a single rose-silk-shaded one by the bed.*]

I really have been to a doctor and I know what to do and—Brick?—this is my time by the calendar to conceive!

Brick. Yes, I understand, Maggie. But how are you going to conceive a child by a man in love with his liquor?

Margaret. By locking his liquor up and making him satisfy my desire before I unlock it!

Brick. Is that what you've done, Maggie?

Margaret. Look and see. That cabinet's mighty empty compared to before!

Brick. Well, I'll be a son of a—

[*He reaches for his crutch but she beats him to it and rushes out on the gallery, hurls the crutch over the rail and comes back in, panting.*
[*There are running footsteps. Big Mama bursts into the room, her face all awry, gasping, stammering.*]

Big Mama. Oh, my God, oh, my God, oh, my God, where is it?

Margaret. Is this what you want, Big Mama?

[*Margaret hands her the package left by the doctor.*]

Big Mama. I can't bear it, oh, God! Oh, Brick! Brick, baby!

[*She rushes at him. He averts his face from her sobbing kisses. Margaret watches with a tight smile.*]

My son, Big Daddy's boy! Little Father!

[*The groaning cry is heard again. She runs out, sobbing.*]

Margaret. And so tonight we're going to make the lie true, and when that's done, I'll bring the liquor back here and we'll get drunk together, here, tonight, in this place that death has come into. . . .
—What do you say?

Brick. I don't say anything. I guess there's nothing to say.

Margaret. Oh, you weak people, you weak, beautiful people!—who give up.—What you want is someone to—

[*She turns out the rose-silk lamp.*]

—take hold of you.—Gently, gently, with love! And—

[*The curtain begins to fall slowly.*]

I *do* love you, Brick, I *do!*

Brick [*smiling with charming sadness*]. Wouldn't it be funny if that was true?

THE CURTAIN COMES DOWN
THE END

QUESTIONS

1. Which character in the play arouses most sympathy or interest in you?
2. How important are Big Daddy and the fact that he is dying of cancer?
3. What feelings and thoughts do you suppose lie behind Brick's cool, drunken facade? How much is he suffering?
4. Why do you suppose people love Brick? How capable of love does he seem to be?
5. How troublesome do you find the question of homosexual love to be here? With so much truth-telling in the play, how clear is the truth about Brick and Skipper?
6. What is Maggie's most important characteristic? What motivates her lie at the conclusion?
7. Besides this lie and the painful truth-telling that occurs over the course of the play, what, if anything, happens?

ADDITIONAL QUESTIONS

1. The conclusions of both *The Taming of the Shrew* and *Cat on a Hot Tin Roof* have troubled modern readers and playgoers. Choose one of these plays, and consider what changes you might make in its last scenes, if you were free to rewrite them at will.
2. In both Shakespeare's and Williams's plays, a struggle between the two main characters for dominance goes beyond the trite phrase about the battle of the sexes. Choosing one of the plays, explain how dominance is achieved by either Maggie or Brick, Petruchio or Kate—if you think it is.
3. Compare Marvell's "To His Coy Mistress" and Robert Herrick's "Corinna's Going A-Maying." In both *carpe diem* poems, a speaker attempts to persuade a young woman to enjoy youth and love while she can. (Herrick's title suggests his speaker is successful.) Considered as an example of persuasion, which poem do you think uses the more effective technique?
4. Shakespeare's "Sonnet 130" pokes fun at conventional imagery overused in love sonnets of his period and substitutes other, startling images while doing so. Consider another love poem or two that achieve their effects at least partly through use of surprising images.
5. Compare/contrast Donne's "Batter My Heart" and George Herbert's "Love" as poems about the love between a person and God.
6. John Updike's "Separating" and Jayne Anne Phillips's "Souvenir" are both about love between parents and children. The central character in each story experiences strong tensions, however, in his or her family. Choose one of the stories, and consider how the love and the tension are related.
7. The transforming power of love is suggested by "The Horse Dealer's Daughter," and "The Magic Barrel." But each story also suggests how vulnerable a person is made by love. In which story is the power of love shown more vividly?
8. "Roman Fever" and "A Tree. A Rock. A Cloud." are alike in focusing upon two characters in a carefully detailed setting. Consider how the setting, in terms of place and time of day, contributes to each story.

PART FOUR

SUSTAINING VISIONS

A reader's ability to see in the imagination what a writer's words evoke is part of the creative process. To see means here both to visualize and to find meaning in what another mind has conveyed by a text. The exact way a reader does either is unknown. So is the way the process begins with the writer. The question of the origins of creativity leaves us with the sense of a greater mystery.

A few writers have been actual visionaries, "seeing things" (as we say) before their eyes while in a trancelike state. William Blake, who once saw angels in his back yard, was such a writer. A very different sort of poet from Blake, William Wordsworth evidently had comparable experiences. In his "Lines . . . above Tintern Abbey," he speaks of a "gift," a "serene and blessed mood" whereby "with an eye made quiet by the power/Of harmony, and the deep power of joy,/ We see into the life of things." Notice that Wordsworth speaks as though this gift were common.

Perhaps we have all had moments when suddenly we experience what Sylvia Plath calls "that rare, random descent" of "the angel" that can light up with radiance even a black rook on a rainy day. Plath's choice of words suggests religious grace—not a frequent subject in her poems. But it is in Gerard Manley Hopkins's, where what is seen—dawn, a hovering bird, the furrows of a field— may be invested with light that the speaker knows comes from God. Similarly, in at least two stories in this section, religious grace appears to explain what a suffering character sees in the midst of deep misery.

Most of the poems and short stories here are not about grace, nor are they religious. Nevertheless, the understanding a character may achieve by seeing something intensely often occurs as if by a miracle. James Joyce called moments of such intense inward seeing "epiphanies." Used without any particular religious intent, the word has become a critical term, applied especially to fiction. Usually the emphasis in fiction that focuses on these moments is on the progress towards

607

understanding. The moment is the culmination of glimpses into a truth not fully discerned before.

In any literary work something becomes a symbol when seen by a character or speaker as being meaningful. Whatever you see in a work so that the thing remains itself but is irradiated with meaning is a symbol as well. The act of perception is still apt to be more remarkable than the thing seen. Thus in Raymond Carver's story the drawing of the cathedral is far less important than the narrator's insight, achieved appropriately with his eyes closed. In John Keats's "Ode on a Grecian Urn" the speaker gazes at the urn, reflects upon what he sees there, and, equally important, recognizes the limitations of his vision. He is, nevertheless, sustained by his experience.

Whether seen by the eye or inwardly, visions sustain by lifting the spirit and conferring strengthened belief and courage. The focus in some works is upon the moral strength resulting from inward vision, as the two dramas in this section illustrate. In Sophocles's *Antigone*, people stand around Antigone, witnesses to her act and to her confrontations with Creon and death. Seeing her life from a perspective of years, they can place her story in a context of myth. Yet she stands out from all others, because she alone sees the gods' will in her scattered handful of dust. In Lorraine Hansberry's modern play, the Youngers all have different dreams of what they want from life. Seeing in a small house of their own an affirmation of their worth as a family gives them the courage to move forward.

FICTION

Sarah Orne Jewett (1849–1909)

A WHITE HERON

I

The woods were already filled with shadows one June evening, just before eight o'clock, though a bright sunset still glimmered faintly among the trunks of the trees. A little girl was driving home her cow, a plodding, dilatory, provoking creature in her behavior, but a valued companion for all that. They were going away from the western light, and striking deep into the dark woods, but their feet were familiar with the path, and it was no matter whether their eyes could see it or not.

There was hardly a night the summer through when the old cow could be found waiting at the pasture bars; on the contrary, it was her greatest pleasure to hide herself away among the high huckleberry bushes, and though she wore a loud bell she had made the discovery that if one stood perfectly still it would not ring. So Sylvia had to hunt for her until she found her, and call Co'! Co'! with never an answering Moo, until her childish patience was quite spent. If the creature had not given good milk and plenty of it, the case would have seemed very different to her owners. Besides, Sylvia had all the time there was, and very little use to make of it. Sometimes in pleasant weather it was a consolation to look upon the cow's pranks as an intelligent attempt to play hide and seek, and as the child had no playmates she lent herself to this amusement with a good deal of zest. Though this chase had been so long that the wary animal herself had given an unusual signal of her whereabouts, Sylvia had only laughed when she came upon Mistress Moolly at the swamp side, and urged her affectionately homeward with a twig of birch leaves. The old cow was not inclined to wander farther, she even turned in the right direction for once as they left the pasture, and stepped along the road at a good pace. She was quite ready to be milked now, and seldom stopped to browse.

Sylvia wondered what her grandmother would say because they were so late. It was a great while since she had left home at half past five o'clock, but everybody knew the difficulty of making this errand a short one. Mrs. Tilley had chased the hornéd torment too many summer evenings herself to blame any one else for lingering, and was only thankful as she waited that she had Sylvia, nowadays, to give such valuable assistance. The good woman suspected that Sylvia loitered occasionally on her own account; there never was such a child for straying about out of doors since the world was made! Everybody said that it was a good change for a little maid who had tried to grow for eight years in a crowded manufacturing town, but, as for Sylvia herself, it seemed as if she never had been alive at all before she came to live at the farm. She thought often with wistful compassion of a wretched dry geranium that belonged to a town neighbor.

"'Afraid of folks,'" old Mrs. Tilley said to herself, with a smile, after she had made the unlikely choice of Sylvia from her daughter's houseful of children, and was returning to the farm. "'Afraid of folks,' they said! I guess she won't be troubled no great with 'em up to the old place!" When they reached the door of the lonely house and stopped to unlock it, and the cat came to purr loudly, and rub against them, a deserted pussy, indeed, but fat with young robins, Sylvia whispered that this was a beautiful place to live in, and she never should wish to go home.

The companions followed the shady woodroad, the cow taking slow steps, and the child very fast ones. The cow stopped long at the brook to drink, as if the pasture were not half a swamp, and Sylvia stood still and waited, letting her bare feet cool themselves in the shoal water, while the great twilight moths struck softly against her. She waded on through the brook as the cow moved away, and listened to the thrushes with a heart that beat fast with pleasure. There was a stirring in the great boughs overhead. They were full of little birds and beasts that seemed to be wide-awake, and going about their world, or else saying good-night to each other in sleepy twitters. Sylvia herself felt sleepy as she walked along. However it was not much farther to the house, and the air was soft and sweet. She was not often in the woods so late as this, and it made her feel as if she were a part of the gray shadows and the moving leaves. She was just thinking how long it seemed since she first came to the farm a year ago, and wondering if everything went on in the noisy town just the same as when she was there; the thought of the great red-faced boy who used to chase and frighten her made her hurry along the path to escape from the shadow of the trees.

Suddenly this little woods girl is horror stricken to hear a clear whistle not very far away. Not a bird's whistle, which would have a sort of friendliness, but a boy's whistle, determined, and somewhat aggressive. Sylvia left the cow to whatever sad fate might await her, and stepped discreetly aside into the bushes, but she was just too late. The enemy had discovered her, and called out in a very cheerful and persuasive tone, "Halloa, little girl, how far is it to the road?" and trembling Sylvia answered almost inaudibly, "A good ways."

She did not dare to look boldly at the tall young man, who carried a gun over his shoulder, but she came out of her bush and again followed the cow, while he walked alongside.

"I have been hunting for some birds," the stranger said kindly, "and I have lost my way, and need a friend very much. Don't be afraid," he added gallantly. "Speak up and tell me what your name is, and whether you think I can spend the night at your house, and go out gunning early in the morning."

Sylvia was more alarmed than before. Would not her grandmother consider her much to blame? But who could have foreseen such an accident as this? It did not appear to be her fault, and she hung her head as if the stem of it were broken, but managed to answer "Sylvy," with much effort when her companion again asked her name.

Mrs. Tilley was standing in the doorway when the trio came into view. The cow gave a loud moo by way of explanation.

"Yes, you'd better speak up for yourself, you old trial! Where'd she tuck herself away this time, Sylvy?" Sylvia kept an awed silence; she knew by instinct that her grandmother did not comprehend the gravity of the situation. She must be mistaking the stranger for one of the farmer lads of the region.

The young man stood his gun beside the door, and dropped a heavy game-bag beside it; then he bade Mrs. Tilley good-evening, and repeated his wayfarer's story, and asked if he could have a night's lodging.

"Put me anywhere you like," he said. "I must be off early in the morning, before day; but I am very hungry, indeed. You can give me some milk at any rate, that's plain."

"Dear sakes, yes," responded the hostess, whose long slumbering hospitality seemed to be easily awakened. "You might fare better if you went out on the main road a mile or so, but you're welcome to what we've got. I'll milk right off, and you make yourself at home. You can sleep on husks or feathers," she proffered graciously. "I raised them all myself. There's good pasturing for geese just below here towards the ma'sh. Now step round and set a plate for the gentleman, Sylvy!" And Sylvia promptly stepped. She was glad to have something to do, and she was hungry herself.

It was a surprise to find so clean and comfortable a little dwelling in this New England wilderness. The young man had known the horrors of its most primitive housekeeping, and the dreary squalor of that level of society which does not rebel at the companionship of hens. This was the best thrift of an old-fashioned farm-stead, though on such a small scale that it seemed like a hermitage. He listened eagerly to the old woman's quaint talk, he watched Sylvia's pale face and shining gray eyes with ever growing enthusiasm, and insisted that this was the best supper he had eaten for a month; then, afterward, the new-made friends sat down in the doorway together while the moon came up.

Soon it would be berry time, and Sylvia was a great help at picking. The cow was a good milker, though a plaguy thing to keep track of, the hostess gossiped frankly, adding presently that she had buried four children, so that Sylvia's mother, and a son (who might be dead) in California were all the children she had left. "Dan, my boy, was a great hand to go gunning," she explained sadly. "I never wanted for pa'tridges or gray squer'ls while he was to home. He's been a great wand'rer, I expect, and he's no hand to write letters. There, I don't blame him, I'd ha' seen the world myself if it had been so I could.

"Sylvia takes after him," the grandmother continued affectionately, after a minute's pause. "There ain't a foot o' ground she don't know her way over, and the wild creatur's counts her one o' themselves. Squer'ls she'll tame to come an' feed right out o' her hands, and all sorts o' birds. Last winter she got the jay birds to bangeing[1] here, and I believe she'd 'a' scanted herself of her own meals to have plenty to throw out amongst 'em, if I hadn't kep' watch. Anything but crows, I tell her, I'm willin' to help support,—though Dan he went an' tamed

---

[1]Staying about: New England dialect.

one o' them that did seem to have reason same as folks. It was round here a good spell after he went away. Dan an' his father they didn't hitch,—but he never held up his head ag'in after Dan had dared him an' gone off.''

The guest did not notice this hint of family sorrows in his eager interest in something else.

"So Sylvy knows all about birds, does she?" he exclaimed, as he looked round at the little girl who sat, very demure but increasingly sleepy, in the moonlight. "I am making a collection of birds myself. I have been at it ever since I was a boy." (Mrs. Tilley smiled.) "There are two or three very rare ones I have been hunting for these five years. I mean to get them on my own ground if they can be found."

"Do you cage 'em up?" asked Mrs. Tilley doubtfully, in response to this enthusiastic announcement.

"Oh, no, they're stuffed and preserved, dozens and dozens of them," said the ornithologist, "and I have shot or snared every one myself. I caught a glimpse of a white heron three miles from here on Saturday, and I have followed it in this direction. They have never been found in this district at all. The little white heron, it is," and he turned again to look at Sylvia with the hope of discovering that the rare bird was one of her acquaintances.

But Sylvia was watching a hop toad in the narrow footpath.

"You would know the heron if you saw it," the stranger continued eagerly. "A queer tall white bird with soft feathers and long thin legs. And it would have a nest perhaps in the top of a high tree, made of sticks, something like a hawk's nest."

Sylvia's heart gave a wild beat; she knew that strange white bird, and had once stolen softly near where it stood in some bright green swamp grass, away over at the other side of the woods. There was an open place where the sunshine always seemed strangely yellow and hot, where tall, nodding rushes grew, and her grandmother had warned her that she might sink in the soft black mud underneath and never be heard of more. Not far beyond were the salt marshes and beyond those was the sea, the sea which Sylvia wondered and dreamed about, but never had looked upon, though its great voice could often be heard above the noise of the woods on stormy nights.

"I can't think of anything I should like so much as to find that heron's nest," the handsome stranger was saying. "I would give ten dollars to anybody who could show it to me," he added desperately, "and I mean to spend my whole vacation hunting for it if need be. Perhaps it was only migrating, or had been chased out of its own region by some bird of prey."

Mrs. Tilley gave amazed attention to all this, but Sylvia still watched the toad, not divining, as she might have done at some calmer time, that the creature wished to get to its hole under the doorstep, and was much hindered by the unusual spectators at that hour of the evening. No amount of thought, that night, could decide how many wished-for treasures the ten dollars, so lightly spoken of, would buy.

The next day the young sportsman hovered about the woods, and Sylvia kept him company, having lost her first fear of the friendly lad, who proved to be most kind and sympathetic. He told her many things about the birds and what they knew and where they lived and what they did with themselves. And he gave her a jackknife, which she thought as great a treasure as if she were a desert islander. All day long he did not once make her troubled or afraid except when he brought down some unsuspecting singing creature from its bough. Sylvia would have liked him vastly better without his gun; she could not understand why he killed the very birds he seemed to like so much. But as the day waned, Sylvia watched the young man with loving admiration. She had never seen anybody so charming and delightful; the woman's heart, asleep in the child, was vaguely thrilled by a dream of love. Some premonition of that great power stirred and swayed these young foresters who traversed the solemn woodlands with soft-footed silent care. They stopped to listen to a bird's song; they pressed forward again eagerly, parting the branches,—speaking to each other rarely and in whispers; the young man going first and Sylvia following, fascinated, a few steps behind, with her gray eyes dark with excitement.

She grieved because the longed-for white heron was elusive, but she did not lead the guest, she only followed, and there was no such thing as speaking first. The sound of her own unquestioned voice would have terrified her,—it was hard enough to answer yes or no when there was need of that. At last evening began to fall, and they drove the cow together, and Sylvia smiled with pleasure when they came to the place where she heard the whistle and was afraid only the night before.

II

Half a mile from home, at the farther edge of the woods, where the land was highest, a great pine tree stood, the last of its generation. Whether it was left for a boundary mark, or for what reason, no one could say; the woodchoppers who had felled its mates were dead and gone long ago, and a whole forest of sturdy trees, pines and oaks and maples, had grown again. But the stately head of this old pine towered above them all and made a landmark for sea and shore miles and miles away. Sylvia knew it well. She had always believed that whoever climbed to the top of it could see the ocean; and the little girl had often laid her hand on the great rough trunk and looked wistfully at those dark boughs that the wind always stirred, no matter how hot and still the air might be below. Now she thought of the tree with a new excitement, for why, if one climbed it at break of day, could not one see all the world, and easily discover whence the white heron flew, and mark the place, and find the hidden nest?

What a spirit of adventure, what wild ambition! What fancied triumph and delight and glory for the later morning when she could make known the secret! It was almost too real and too great for the childish heart to bear.

All night the door of the little house stood open, and the whippoorwills came and sang upon the very step. The young sportsman and his old hostess were sound asleep, but Sylvia's great design kept her broad awake and watching. She forgot to think of sleep. The short summer night seemed as long as the winter darkness, and at last when the whippoorwills ceased, and she was afraid the morning would after all come too soon, she stole out of the house and followed the pasture path through the woods, hastening toward the open ground beyond, listening with a sense of comfort and companionship to the drowsy twitter of a half-awakened bird, whose perch she had jarred in passing. Alas, if the great wave of human interest which flooded for the first time this dull little life should sweep away the satisfactions of an existence heart to heart with nature and the dumb life of the forest!

There was the huge tree asleep yet in the paling moonlight, and small and hopeful Sylvia began with utmost bravery to mount to the top of it, with tingling, eager blood coursing the channels of her whole frame, with her bare feet and fingers, that pinched and held like bird's claws to the monstrous ladder reaching up, up, almost to the sky itself. First she must mount the white oak tree that grew alongside, where she was almost lost among the dark branches and the green leaves heavy and wet with dew; a bird fluttered off its nest, and a red squirrel ran to and fro and scolded pettishly at the harmless house breaker. Sylvia felt her way easily. She had often climbed there, and knew that higher still one of the oak's upper branches chafed against the pine trunk, just where its lower boughs were set close together. There, when she made the dangerous pass from one tree to the other, the great enterprise would really begin.

She crept out along the swaying oak limb at last, and took the daring step across into the old pine tree. The way was harder than she thought; she must reach far and hold fast, the sharp dry twigs caught and held her and scratched her like angry talons, the pitch made her thin little fingers clumsy and stiff as she went round and round the tree's great stem, higher and higher upward. The sparrows and robins in the woods below were beginning to wake and twitter to the dawn, yet it seemed much lighter there aloft in the pine tree, and the child knew that she must hurry if her project were to be of any use.

The tree seemed to lengthen itself out as she went up, and to reach farther and farther upward. It was like a great mainmast to the voyaging earth; it must truly have been amazed that morning through all its ponderous frame as it felt this determined spark of human spirit creeping and climbing from higher branch to branch. Who knows how steadily the least twigs held themselves to advantage this light, weak creature on her way! The old pine must have loved his new dependent. More than all the hawks, and bats, and moths, and even the sweet-voiced thrushes, was the brave, beating heart of the solitary gray-eyed child. And the tree stood still and held away the winds that June morning while the dawn grew bright in the east.

Sylvia's face was like a pale star, if one had seen it from the ground, when the last thorny bough was past, and she stood trembling and tired but wholly triumphant, high in the treetop. Yes, there was the sea with the dawning sun making a golden dazzle over it, and toward that glorious east flew two hawks with slow-moving pinions. How low they looked in the air from that height when before one had only seen them far up, and dark against the blue sky. Their gray feathers were as soft as moths; they seemed only a little way from the tree, and Sylvia felt as if she too could go flying away among the clouds. Westward, the woodlands and farms reached miles and miles into the distance; here and there were church steeples, and white villages; truly it was a vast and awesome world.

The birds sang louder and louder. At last the sun came up bewilderingly bright. Sylvia could see the white sails of ships out at sea, and the clouds that were purple and rose-colored and yellow at first began to fade away. Where was the white heron's nest in the sea of green branches, and was this wonderful sight and pageant of the world the only reward for having climbed to such a giddy height? Now look down again, Sylvia, where the green marsh is set among the shining birches and dark hemlocks; there where you saw the white heron once you will see him again; look, look! a white spot of him like a single floating feather comes up from the dead hemlock and grows larger, and rises, and comes close at last, and goes by the landmark pine with steady sweep of wing and outstretched slender neck and crested head. And wait! wait! do not move a foot or a finger, little girl, do not send an arrow of light and consciousness from your two eager eyes, for the heron has perched on a pine bough not far beyond yours, and cries back to his mate on the nest, and plumes his feathers for the new day!

The child gives a long sigh a minute later when a company of shouting catbirds comes also to the tree, and vexed by their fluttering and lawlessness the solemn heron goes away. She knows his secret now, the wild, light slender bird that floats and wavers, and goes back like an arrow presently to his home in the green world beneath. Then Sylvia, well satisfied, makes her perilous way down again, not daring to look far below the branch she stands on, ready to cry sometimes because her fingers ache and her lamed feet slip. Wondering over and over again what the stranger would say to her, and what he would think when she told him how to find his way straight to the heron's nest.

"Sylvy, Sylvy!" called the busy old grandmother again and again, but nobody answered, and the small husk bed was empty, and Sylvia had disappeared.

The guest waked from a dream, and remembering his day's pleasure hurried to dress himself that it might sooner begin. He was sure from the way the shy little girl looked once or twice yesterday that she had at least seen the white heron, and now she must really be persuaded to tell. Here she comes now, paler than ever, and her worn old frock is torn and tattered, and smeared with pine pitch. The grandmother and the sportsman stand in the door together and question her, and the splendid moment has come to speak of the dead hemlock tree by the green marsh.

But Sylvia does not speak after all, though the old grandmother fretfully rebukes her, and the young man's kind appealing eyes are looking straight in her own. He can make them rich with money; he has promised it, and they are poor now. He is so well worth making happy, and he waits to hear the story she can tell.

No, she must keep silence! What is it that suddenly forbids her and makes her dumb? Has she been nine years growing, and now, when the great world for the first time puts out a hand to her, must she thrust it aside for a bird's sake? The murmur of the pine's green branches is in her ears, she remembers how the white heron came flying through the golden air and how they watched the sea and the morning together, and Sylvia cannot speak; she cannot tell the heron's secret and give its life away.

Dear loyalty, that suffered a sharp pang as the guest went away disappointed later in the day, that could have served and followed him and loved him as a dog loves! Many a night Sylvia heard the echo of his whistle haunting the pasture path as she came home with the loitering cow. She forgot even her sorrow at the sharp report of his gun and the piteous sight of thrushes and sparrows dropping silent to the ground, their songs hushed and their pretty feathers stained and wet with blood. Were the birds better friends than their hunter might have been,— who can tell? Whatever treasures were lost to her, woodlands and summer time, remember! Bring your gifts and graces and tell your secrets to this lonely country child!

QUESTIONS

1. What attitude, if any, does the narrator express towards "this New England wilderness" and its inhabitants?
2. How is the young man characterized? How does his relation to nature differ from Sylvy's?
3. What is the effect of the detailed description of Sylvy's climb up the tree?
4. Why does Sylvy remain silent about the heron? How important in her life do you suppose her decision will be?

Langston Hughes (1902–1967)

ON THE ROAD

He was not interested in the snow. When he got off the freight, one early evening during the depression, Sargeant never even noticed the snow. But he must have felt it seeping down his neck, cold, wet, sopping in his shoes. But if you had asked him, he wouldn't have known it was snowing. Sargeant didn't see the snow, not even under the bright lights of the main street, falling white and flaky against the night. He was too hungry, too sleepy, too tired.

The Reverend Mr. Dorset, however, saw the snow when he switched on his porch light, opened the front door of his parsonage, and found standing there before him a big black man with snow on his face, a human piece of night with snow on his face—obviously unemployed.

Said the Reverend Mr. Dorset before Sargeant even realized he'd opened his mouth: "I'm sorry. No! Go right on down this street four blocks and turn to your left, walk up seven and you'll see the Relief Shelter. I'm sorry. No!" He shut the door.

Sargeant wanted to tell the holy man that he had already been to the Relief Shelter, been to hundreds of relief shelters during the depression years, the beds were always gone and supper was over, the place was full, and they drew the color line anyhow. But the minister said, "No," and shut the door. Evidently he didn't want to hear about it. And he *had* a door to shut.

The big black man turned away. And even yet he didn't see the snow, walking right into it. Maybe he sensed it, cold, wet, sticking to his jaws, wet on his black hands, sopping in his shoes. He stopped and stood on the sidewalk hunched over—hungry, sleepy, cold—looking up and down. Then he looked right where he was—in front of a church. Of course! A church! Sure, right next to a parsonage, certainly a church.

It had *two* doors.

Broad white steps in the night all snowy white. Two high arched doors with slender stone pillars on either side. And way up, a round lacy window with a stone crucifix in the middle and Christ on the crucifix in stone. All this was pale in the street lights, solid and stony pale in the snow.

Sargeant blinked. When he looked up the snow fell into his eyes. For the first time that night he *saw* the snow. He shook his head. He shook the snow from his coat sleeves, felt hungry, felt lost, felt not lost, felt cold. He walked up the steps of the church. He knocked at the door. No answer. He tried the handle. Locked. He put his shoulder against the door and his long black body slanted like a ramrod. He pushed. With loud rhythmic grunts, like the grunts in a chain-gang song, he pushed against the door.

"I'm tired . . . Huh! . . . Hongry . . . Uh! . . . I'm sleepy . . . Huh! I'm cold . . . I got to sleep somewheres," Sargeant said. "This here is a church, ain't it? Well, uh!"

He pushed against the door.

Suddenly, with an undue cracking and screaking, the door began to give way to the tall black Negro who pushed ferociously against the door.

By now two or three white people had stopped in the street, and Sargeant was vaguely aware of some of them yelling at him concerning the door. Three or four more came running, yelling at him.

"Hey!" they said. "Hey!"

"Un-huh," answered the big tall Negro, "I know it's a white folks' church, but I got to sleep somewhere." He gave another lunge at the door. "Huh!"

And the door broke open.

But just when the door gave way, two white cops arrived in a car, ran up the steps with their clubs and grabbed Sargeant. But Sargeant for once had no intention of being pulled or pushed away from the door.

Sargeant grabbed, but not for anything so weak as a broken door. He grabbed for one of the tall stone pillars beside the door, grabbed at it and caught it. And held it. The cops pulled and Sargeant pulled. Most of the people in the street got behind the cops and helped them pull.

"A big black unemployed Negro holding onto our church!" thought the people. "The idea!"

The cops began to beat Sargeant over the head, and nobody protested. But he held on.

And then the church fell down.

Gradually, the big stone front of the church fell down, the walls and the rafters, the crucifix and the Christ. Then the whole thing fell down, covering the cops and the people with bricks and stones and debris. The whole church fell down in the snow.

Sargeant got out from under the church and went walking on up the street with the stone pillar on his shoulder. He was under the impression that he had buried the parsonage and the Reverend Mr. Dorset who said, "No!" So he laughed, and threw the pillar six blocks up the street and went on.

Sargeant thought he was alone, but listening to the crunch, crunch, crunch on the snow of his own footsteps, he heard other footsteps, too, doubling his own. He looked around and there was Christ walking along beside him, the same Christ that had been on the cross on the church—still stone with a rough stone surface, walking along beside him just like he was broken off the cross when the church fell down.

"Well, I'll be dogged," said Sargeant. "This here's the first time I ever seed you off the cross."

"Yes," said Christ, crunching his feet in the snow. "You had to pull the church down to get me off the cross."

"You glad?" said Sargeant.

"I sure am," said Christ.

They both laughed.

"I'm a hell of a fellow, ain't I?" said Sargeant. "Done pulled the church down!"

"You did a good job," said Christ. "They have kept me nailed on a cross for nearly two thousand years."

"Whee-ee-e!" said Sargeant. "I know you are glad to get off."

"I sure am," said Christ.

They walked on in the snow. Sargeant looked at the man of stone.

"And you been up there two thousand years?"

"I sure have," Christ said.

"Well, if I had a little cash," said Sargeant, "I'd show you around a bit."

"I been around," said Christ.

"Yeah, but that was a long time ago."

"All the same," said Christ, "I've been around."

They walked on in the snow until they came to the railroad yards. Sargeant was tired, sweating and tired.

"Where you goin'?" Sargeant said, stopping by the tracks. He looked at Christ. Sargeant said, "I'm just a bum on the road. How about you? Where you goin'?"

"God knows," Christ said, "but I'm leavin' here."

They saw the red and green lights of the railroad yard half veiled by the snow that fell out of the night. Away down the track they saw a fire in a hobo jungle.

"I can go there and sleep," Sargeant said.

"You can?"

"Sure," said Sargeant. "That place ain't got no doors."

Outside the town, along the tracks, there were barren trees and bushes below the embankment, snow-gray in the dark. And down among the trees and bushes there were makeshift houses made out of boxes and tin and old pieces of wood and canvas. You couldn't see them in the dark, but you knew they were there if you'd ever been on the road, if you had ever lived with the homeless and hungry in a depression.

"I'm side-tracking," Sargeant said. "I'm tired."

"I'm gonna make it on to Kansas City," said Christ.

"O.K.," Sargeant said. "So long!"

He went down into the hobo jungle and found himself a place to sleep. He never did see Christ no more. About six A.M. a freight came by. Sargeant scrambled out of the jungle with a dozen or so more hoboes and ran along the track, grabbing at the freight. It was dawn, early dawn, cold and gray.

"Wonder where Christ is by now?" Sargeant thought. "He must-a gone on way on down the road. He didn't sleep in this jungle."

Sargeant grabbed the train and started to pull himself up into a moving coal car, over the edge of a wheeling coal car. But strangely enough, the car was full of cops. The nearest cop rapped Sargeant soundly across the knuckles with his night stick. Wham! Rapped his big black hands for clinging to the top of the car. Wham! But Sargeant did not turn loose. He clung on and tried to pull himself into the car. He hollered at the top of his voice, "Damn it, lemme in this car!"

"Shut up," barked the cop. "You crazy coon!" He rapped Sargeant across the knuckles and punched him in the stomach. "You ain't out in no jungle now. This ain't no train. You in jail."

Wham! across his bare black fingers clinging to the bars of his cell. Wham! between the steel bars low down against his shins.

Suddenly Sargeant realized that he really was in jail. He wasn't on no train. The blood of the night before had dried on his face, his head hurt terribly, and a cop outside in the corridor was hitting him across the knuckles for holding onto the door, yelling and shaking the cell door.

"They must-a took me to jail for breaking down the door last night," Sargeant thought, "that church door."

Sargeant went over and sat on a wooden bench against the cold stone wall. He was emptier than ever. His clothes were wet, clammy cold wet, and shoes sloppy with snow water. It was just about dawn. There he was, locked up behind a cell door, nursing his bruised fingers.

The bruised fingers were his, but not the *door*.

Not the *club*, but the fingers.

"You wait," mumbled Sargeant, black against the jail wall. "I'm gonna break down this door, too."

"Shut up—or I'll paste you one," said the cop.

"I'm gonna break down this door," yelled Sargeant as he stood up in his cell.

Then he must have been talking to himself because he said, "I wonder where Christ's gone? I wonder if he's gone to Kansas City?"

James Baldwin (1924–1987)
SONNY'S BLUES

I read about it in the the paper, in the subway, on my way to work. I read it, and I couldn't believe it, and I read it again. Then perhaps I just stared at it, at the newsprint spelling out his name, spelling out the story. I stared at it in the swinging lights of the subway car, and in the faces and bodies of the people, and in my own face, trapped in the darkness which roared outside.

It was not to be believed and I kept telling myself that, as I walked from the subway station to the high school. And at the same time I couldn't doubt it. I was scared, scared for Sonny. He became real to me again. A great block of ice got settled in my belly and kept melting there slowly all day long, while I taught my classes algebra. It was a special kind of ice. It kept melting, sending trickles of ice water all up and down my veins, but it never got less. Sometimes it hardened and seemed to expand until I felt my guts were going to come spilling out or that I was going to choke or scream. This would always be at a moment when I was remembering some specific thing Sonny had once said or done.

When he was about as old as the boys in my classes his face had been bright and open, there was a lot of copper in it; and he'd had wonderfully direct brown eyes, and great gentleness and privacy. I wondered what he looked like now. He had been picked up, the evening before, in a raid on an apartment downtown, for peddling and using heroin.

I couldn't believe it: but what I mean by that is that I couldn't find any room for it anywhere inside me. I had kept it outside me for a long time. I hadn't wanted to know. I had had suspicions, but I didn't name them, I kept putting them away. I told myself that Sonny was wild, but he wasn't crazy. And he'd always been a good boy, he hadn't ever turned hard or evil or disrespectful, the way kids can, so quick, so quick, especially in Harlem. I didn't want to believe that I'd ever see my brother going down, coming to nothing, all that light in his face gone out, in the condition I'd already seen so many others. Yet it had happened and here I was, talking about algebra to a lot of boys who might, every one of them for all I knew, be popping off needles every time they went to the head. Maybe it did more for them than algebra could.

I was sure that the first time Sonny had ever had horse,[1] he couldn't have been much older than these boys were now. These boys, now, were living as we'd been living then, they were growing up with a rush and their heads bumped abruptly against the low ceiling of their actual possibilities. They were filled with rage. All they really knew were two darknesses, the darkness of their lives, which was now closing in on them, and the darkness of the movies, which had blinded them to that other darkness, and in which they now, vindictively, dreamed, at once more together than they were at any other time, and more alone.

---

[1]Heroin.

When the last bell rang, the last class ended, I let out my breath. It seemed I'd been holding it for all that time. My clothes were wet—I may have looked as though I'd been sitting in a steam bath, all dressed up, all afternoon. I sat alone in the classroom a long time. I listened to the boys outside, downstairs, shouting and cursing and laughing. Their laughter struck me for perhaps the first time. It was not the joyous laughter which—God knows why—one associates with children. It was mocking and insular, its intent was to denigrate. It was disenchanted, and in this, also, lay the authority of their curses. Perhaps I was listening to them because I was thinking about my brother and in them I heard my brother. And myself.

One boy was whistling a tune, at once very complicated and very simple, it seemed to be pouring out of him as though he were a bird, and it sounded very cool and moving through all that harsh, bright air, only just holding its own through all those other sounds.

I stood up and walked over to the window and looked down into the courtyard. It was the beginning of the spring and the sap was rising in the boys. A teacher passed through them every now and again, quickly, as though he or she couldn't wait to get out of that courtyard, to get those boys out of their sight and off their minds. I started collecting my stuff. I thought I'd better get home and talk to Isabel.

The courtyard was almost deserted by the time I got downstairs. I saw this boy standing in the shadow of a doorway, looking just like Sonny. I almost called his name. Then I saw that it wasn't Sonny, but somebody we used to know, a boy from around our block. He'd been Sonny's friend. He'd never been mine, having been too young for me, and, anyway, I'd never liked him. And now, even though he was a grown-up man, he still hung around that block, still spent hours on the street corners, was always high and raggy. I used to run into him from time to time and he'd often work around to asking me for a quarter or fifty cents. He always had some real good excuse, too, and I always gave it to him, I don't know why.

But now, abruptly, I hated him. I couldn't stand the way he looked at me, partly like a dog, partly like a cunning child. I wanted to ask him what the hell he was doing in the school courtyard.

He sort of shuffled over to me, and he said, "I see you got the papers. So you already know about it."

"You mean about Sonny? Yes, I already know about it. How come they didn't get you?"

He grinned. It made him repulsive and it also brought to mind what he'd looked like as a kid. "I wasn't there. I stay away from them people."

"Good for you." I offered him a cigarette and I watched him through the smoke. "You come all the way down here just to tell me about Sonny?"

"That's right." He was sort of shaking his head and his eyes looked strange, as though they were about to cross. The bright sun deadened his damp dark brown skin and it made his eyes look yellow and showed up the dirt in his kinked hair. He smelled funky. I moved a little away from him and I said, "Well, thanks. But I already know about it and I got to get home."

"I'll walk you a little ways," he said. We started walking. There were a couple of kids still loitering in the courtyard and one of them said goodnight to me and looked strangely at the boy beside me.

"What're you going to do?" he asked me. "I mean, about Sonny?"

"Look. I haven't seen Sonny for over a year, I'm not sure I'm going to do anything. Anyway, what the hell *can* I do?"

"That's right," he said quickly, "ain't nothing you can do. Can't much help old Sonny no more, I guess."

It was what I was thinking and so it seemed to me he had no right to say it.

"I'm surprised at Sonny, though," he went on—he had a funny way of talking, he looked straight ahead as though he were talking to himself—"I thought Sonny was a smart boy, I thought he was too smart to get hung."

"I guess he thought so too," I said sharply, "and that's how he got hung. And how about you? You're pretty goddamn smart, I bet."

Then he looked directly at me, just for a minute. "I ain't smart," he said. "If I was smart, I'd have reached for a pistol a long time ago."

"Look. Don't tell *me* your sad story, if it was up to me, I'd give you one." Then I felt guilty—guilty, probably, for never having supposed that the poor bastard *had* a story of his own, much less a sad one, and I asked, quickly, "What's going to happen to him now?"

He didn't answer this. He was off by himself some place. "Funny thing," he said, and from his tone we might have been discussing the quickest way to get to Brooklyn, "when I saw the papers this morning, the first thing I asked myself was if I had anything to do with it. I felt sort of responsible."

I began to listen more carefully. The subway station was on the corner, just before us, and I stopped. He stopped, too. We were in front of a bar and he ducked slightly, peering in, but whoever he was looking for didn't seem to be there. The juke box was blasting away with something black and bouncy and I half watched the barmaid as she danced her way from the juke box to her place behind the bar. And I watched her face as she laughingly responded to something someone said to her, still keeping time to the music. When she smiled one saw the little girl, one sensed the doomed, still-struggling woman beneath the battered face of the semi-whore.

"I never *give* Sonny nothing," the boy said finally, "but a long time ago I come to school high and Sonny asked me how it felt." He paused, I couldn't bear to watch him, I watched the barmaid, and I listened to the music which seemed to be causing the pavement to shake. "I told him it felt great." The music stopped, the barmaid paused and watched the juke box until the music began again. "It did."

All this was carrying me some place I didn't want to go. I certainly didn't want to know how it felt. It filled everything, the people, the houses, the music, the dark, quicksilver barmaid, with menace; and this menace was their reality.

"What's going to happen to him now?" I asked again.

"They'll send him away some place and they'll try to cure him." He shook his head. "Maybe he'll even think he's kicked the habit. Then they'll let him loose"—he gestured, throwing his cigarette into the gutter. "That's all."

"What do you mean, that's *all*?"

But I knew what he meant.

"I *mean*, that's *all*." He turned his head and looked at me, pulling down the corners of his mouth. "Don't you know what I mean?" he asked, softly.

"How the hell *would* I know what you mean?" I almost whispered it, I don't know why.

"That's right," he said to the air, "how would *he* know what I mean?" He turned toward me again, patient and calm, and yet I somehow felt him shaking, shaking as though he were going to fall apart. I felt that ice in my guts again, the dread I'd felt all afternoon; and again I watched the barmaid, moving about the bar, washing glasses, and singing. "Listen. They'll let him out and then it'll just start all over again. That's what I mean."

"You mean—they'll let him out. And then he'll just start working his way back in again. You mean he'll never kick the habit. Is that what you mean?"

"That's right," he said, cheerfully. "*You* see what I mean."

"Tell me," I said at last, "why does he want to die? He must want to die, he's killing himself, why does he want to die?"

He looked at me in surprise. He licked his lips. "He don't want to die. He wants to live. Don't nobody want to die, ever."

Then I wanted to ask him—too many things. He could not have answered, or if he had, I could not have borne the answers. I started walking. "Well, I guess it's none of my business."

"It's going to be rough on old Sonny," he said. We reached the subway station. "This is your station?" he asked. I nodded. I took one step down. "Damn!" he said, suddenly. I looked up at him. He grinned again. "Damn it if I didn't leave all my money home. You ain't got a dollar on you, have you? Just for a couple of days, is all."

All at once something inside gave and threatened to come pouring out of me. I didn't hate him any more. I felt that in another moment I'd start crying like a child.

"Sure," I said. "Don't sweat." I looked in my wallet and didn't have a dollar, I only had a five. "Here," I said. "That hold you?"

He didn't look at it—he didn't want to look at it. A terrible, closed look came over his face, as though he were keeping the number on the bill a secret from him and me. "Thanks," he said, and now he was dying to see me go. "Don't worry about Sonny. Maybe I'll write him or something."

"Sure," I said. "You do that. So long."

"Be seeing you," he said. I went on down the steps.

And I didn't write Sonny or send him anything for a long time. When I finally did, it was just after my little girl died, he wrote me back a letter which made me feel like a bastard.

Here's what he said:

Dear brother,

You don't know how much I needed to hear from you. I wanted to write you many a time but I dug how much I must have hurt you and so I didn't write. But now I feel like a man who's been trying to climb up out of some deep, real deep and funky hole and just saw the sun up there, outside. I got to get outside.

I can't tell you much about how I got here. I mean I don't know how to tell you. I guess I was afraid of something or I was trying to escape from something and you know I have never been very strong in the head (smile). I'm glad Mama and Daddy are dead and can't see what's happened to their son and I swear if I'd known what I was doing I would never have hurt you so, you and a lot of other fine people who were nice to me and who believed in me.

I don't want you to think it had anything to do with me being a musician. It's more than that. Or maybe less than that. I can't get anything straight in my head down here and I try not to think about what's going to happen to me when I get outside again. Sometime I think I'm going to flip and *never* get outside and sometime I think I'll come straight back. I tell you one thing, though, I'd rather blow my brains out than go through this again. But that's what they all say, so they tell me. If I tell you when I'm coming to New York and if you could meet me, I sure would appreciate it. Give my love to Isabel and the kids and I was sure sorry to hear about little Gracie. I wish I could be like Mama and say the Lord's will be done, but I don't know it seems to me that trouble is the one thing that never does get stopped and I don't know what good it does to blame it on the Lord. But maybe it does some good if you believe it.

> Your brother,
> Sonny

Then I kept in constant touch with him and I sent him whatever I could and I went to meet him when he came back to New York. When I saw him many things I thought I had forgotten came flooding back to me. This was because I had begun, finally, to wonder about Sonny, about the life that Sonny lived inside. This life, whatever it was, had made him older and thinner and it had deepened the distant stillness in which he had always moved. He looked very unlike my baby brother. Yet, when he smiled, when we shook hands, the baby brother I'd never known looked out from the depths of his private life, like an animal waiting to be coaxed into the light.

"How you been keeping?" he asked me.

"All right. And you?"

"Just fine." He was smiling all over his face. "It's good to see you again."

"It's good to see you."

The seven years' difference in our ages lay between us like a chasm: I wondered if these years would ever operate between us as a bridge. I was remembering, and it made it hard to catch my breath, that I had been there when he was born; and I had heard the first words he had ever spoken. When he started to walk, he walked from our mother straight to me. I caught him just before he fell when he took the first steps he ever took in this world.

"How's Isabel?"

"Just fine. She's dying to see you."

"And the boys?"

"They're fine, too. They're anxious to see their uncle."

"Oh, come on. You know they don't remember me."

"Are you kidding? Of course they remember you."

He grinned again. We got into a taxi. We had a lot to say to each other, far too much to know how to begin.

As the taxi began to move, I asked, "You still want to go to India?"

He laughed. "You still remember that. Hell, no. This place is Indian enough for me."

"It used to belong to them," I said.

And he laughed again. "They damn sure knew what they were doing when they got rid of it."

Years ago, when he was around fourteen, he'd been all hipped on the idea of going to India. He read books about people sitting on rocks, naked, in all kinds of weather, but mostly bad, naturally, and walking barefoot through hot coals and arriving at wisdom. I used to say that it sounded to me as though they were getting away from wisdom as fast as they could. I think he sort of looked down on me for that.

"Do you mind," he asked, "if we have the driver drive alongside the park? On the west side—I haven't seen the city in so long."

"Of course not," I said. I was afraid that I might sound as though I were humoring him, but I hoped he wouldn't take it that way.

So we drove along, between the green of the park and the stony, lifeless elegance of hotels and apartment buildings, toward the vivid, killing streets of our childhood. These streets hadn't changed, though housing projects jutted up out of them now like rocks in the middle of a boiling sea. Most of the houses in which we had grown up had vanished, as had the stores from which we had stolen, the basements in which we had first tried sex, the rooftops from which we had hurled tin cans and bricks. But houses exactly like the houses of our past yet dominated the landscape, boys exactly like the boys we once had been found themselves smothering in these houses, came down into the streets for light and air and found themselves encircled by disaster. Some escaped the trap, most didn't. Those who got out always left something of themselves behind, as some animals amputate a leg and leave it in the trap. It might be said, perhaps, that I had escaped, after all, I was a school teacher; or that Sonny had, he hadn't lived in Harlem for years. Yet, as the cab moved uptown through streets which seemed, with a rush, to darken with dark people, and as I covertly studied Sonny's face, it came to me that what we both were seeking through our separate cab windows was that part of ourselves which had been left behind. It's always at the hour of trouble and confrontation that the missing member aches.

We hit 110th Street and started rolling up Lenox Avenue. And I'd known this avenue all my life, but it seemed to me again, as it had seemed on the day I'd first heard about Sonny's trouble, filled with a hidden menace which was its very breath of life.

"We almost there," said Sonny.

"Almost." We were both too nervous to say anything more.

We live in a housing project. It hasn't been up long. A few days after it was up it seemed uninhabitably new, now, of course, it's already rundown. It looks like a parody of the good, clean, faceless life—God knows the people who live in it do their best to make it a parody. The beat-looking grass lying around isn't enough to make their lives green, the hedges will never hold out the streets, and they know it. The big windows fool no one, they aren't big enough to make space out of no space. They don't bother with the windows, they watch the TV screen instead. The playground is most popular with the children who don't play at jacks, or skip rope, or roller skate, or swing, and they can be found in it after dark. We moved in partly because it's not too far from where I teach, and partly for the kids; but it's really just like the houses in which Sonny and I grew up. The same things happen, they'll have the same things to remember. The moment Sonny and I started into the house I had the feeling that I was simply bringing him back into the danger he had almost died trying to escape.

Sonny has never been talkative. So I don't know why I was sure he'd be dying to talk to me when supper was over the first night. Everything went fine, the oldest boy remembered him, and the youngest boy liked him, and Sonny had remembered to bring something for each of them; and Isabel, who is really much nicer than I am, more open and giving, had gone to a lot of trouble about dinner and was genuinely glad to see him. And she's always been able to tease Sonny in a way that I haven't. It was nice to see her face so vivid again and to hear her laugh and watch her make Sonny laugh. She wasn't, or, anyway, she didn't seem to be, at all uneasy or embarrassed. She chatted as though there were no subject which had to be avoided and she got Sonny past his first, faint stiffness. And thank God she was there, for I was filled with that icy dread again. Everything I did seemed awkward to me, and everything I said sounded freighted with hidden meaning. I was trying to remember everything I'd heard about dope addiction and I couldn't help watching Sonny for signs. I wasn't doing it out of malice. I was trying to find out something about my brother. I was dying to hear him tell me he was safe.

"Safe!" my father grunted, whenever Mama suggested trying to move to a neighborhood which might be safer for children. "Safe, hell! Ain't no place safe for kids, nor nobody."

He always went on like this, but he wasn't, ever, really as bad as he sounded, not even on weekends, when he got drunk. As a matter of fact, he was always on the lookout for "something a little better," but he died before he found it. He died suddenly, during a drunken weekend in the middle of the war, when Sonny was fifteen. He and Sonny hadn't ever got on too well. And this was partly because Sonny was the apple of his father's eye. It was because he loved Sonny so much and was frightened for him, that he always fighting with him. It doesn't do any good to fight with Sonny. Sonny just moves back, inside himself, where he can't be reached. But the principal reason that they never hit it off is that they were so much alike. Daddy was big and rough and loud-talking, just the opposite of Sonny, but they both had—that same privacy.

Mama tried to tell me something about this, just after Daddy died. I was home on leave from the army.

This was the last time I ever saw my mother alive. Just the same, this picture gets all mixed up in my mind with pictures I had of her when she was younger. The way I always see her is the way she used to be on a Sunday afternoon, say, when the old folks were talking after the big Sunday dinner. I always see her wearing pale blue. She'd be sitting on the sofa. And my father would be sitting in the easy chair, not far from her. And the living room would be full of church folks and relatives. There they sit, in chairs all around the living room, and the night is creeping up outside, but nobody knows it yet. You can see the darkness growing against the windowpanes and you hear the street noises every now and again, or maybe the jangling beat of a tambourine from one of the churches close by, but it's real quiet in the room. For a moment nobody's talking, but every face looks darkening, like the sky outside. And my mother rocks a little from the waist, and my father's eyes are closed. Everyone is looking at something a child can't see. For a minute they've forgotten the children. Maybe a kid is lying on the rug half asleep. Maybe somebody's got a kid in his lap and is absent-mindedly stroking the kid's head. Maybe there's a kid, quiet and big-eyed, curled up in a big chair in the corner. The silence, the darkness coming, and the darkness in the faces frightens the child obscurely. He hopes that the hand which strokes his forehead will never stop—will never die. He hopes that there will never come a time when the old folks won't be sitting around the living room, talking about where they've come from, and what they've seen, and what's happened to them and their kinfolk.

But something deep and watchful in the child knows that this is bound to end, is already ending. In a moment someone will get up and turn on the light. Then the old folks will remember the children and they won't talk any more that day. And when light fills the room, the child is filled with darkness. He knows that every time this happens he's moved just a little closer to that darkness outside. The darkness outside is what the old folks have been talking about. It's what they've come from. It's what they endure. The child knows that they won't talk any more because if he knows too much about what's happened to *them,* he'll know too much too soon, about what's going to happen to *him.*

The last time I talked to my mother, I remember I was restless. I wanted to get out and see Isabel. We weren't married then and we had a lot to straighten out between us.

There Mama sat, in black, by the window. She was humming an old church song, *Lord, you brought me from a long ways off.* Sonny was out somewhere. Mama kept watching the streets.

"I don't know," she said, "if I'll ever see you again, after you go off from here. But I hope you'll remember the things I tried to teach you."

"Don't talk like that," I said, and smiled. "You'll be here a long time yet."

She smiled, too, but she said nothing. She was quiet for a long time. And I said, "Mama, don't you worry about nothing. I'll be writing all the time, and you be getting the checks. . . ."

"I want to talk to you about your brother," she said, suddenly. "If anything happens to me he ain't going to have nobody to look out for him."

"Mama," I said, "ain't nothing going to happen to you *or* Sonny. Sonny's all right. He's a good boy and he's got good sense."

"It ain't a question of his being a good boy," Mama said, "nor of his having good sense. It ain't only the bad ones, nor yet the dumb ones that gets sucked under." She stopped, looking at me. "Your Daddy once had a brother," she said, and she smiled in a way that made me feel she was in pain. "You didn't never know that, did you?"

"No," I said, "I never knew that," and I watched her face.

"Oh, yes," she said, "your Daddy had a brother." She looked out of the window again. "I know you never saw your Daddy cry. But *I* did—many a time, through all these years."

I asked her, "What happened to his brother? How come nobody's ever talked about him?"

This was the first time I ever saw my mother look old.

"His brother got killed," she said, "when he was just a little younger than you are now. I knew him. He was a fine boy. He was maybe a little full of the devil, but he didn't mean nobody no harm."

Then she stopped and the room was silent, exactly as it had sometimes been on those Sunday afternoons. Mama kept looking out into the streets.

"He used to have a job in the mill," she said, "and, like all young folks, he just liked to perform on Saturday nights. Saturday nights, him and your father would drift around to different place, go to dances and things like that, or just sit around with people they knew, and your father's brother would sing, he had a fine voice, and play along with himself on his guitar. Well, this particular Saturday night, him and your father was coming home from some place, and they were both a little drunk and there was a moon that night, it was bright like day. Your father's brother was feeling kind of good, and he was whistling to himself, and he had his guitar slung over his shoulder. They were coming down a hill and beneath them was a road that turned off from the highway. Well, your father's brother, being always kind of frisky, decided to run down this hill, and he did, with that guitar banging and clanging behind him, and he ran across the road, and he was making water behind a tree. And your father was sort of amused at him and he was still coming down the hill, kind of slow. Then he heard a car motor and that same minute his brother stepped from behind the tree, into the road, in the moonlight. And he started to cross the road. And your father started to run down the hill, he says he don't know why. This car was full of white men. They was all drunk, and when they seen your father's brother they let out a great whoop and holler and they aimed the car straight at him. They was having fun, they just wanted to scare him, the way they do sometimes, you know. But they was drunk. And I guess the boy, being drunk, too, and scared, kind of lost his head. By the time he jumped it was too late. Your father says he heard his brother scream when the car rolled over him, and he heard the wood of the guitar when it give, and he heard them strings go flying, and he heard them white men shouting, and the car kept on a-going and it ain't stopped till this day. And, time your father got down the hill, his brother weren't nothing but blood and pulp."

Tears were gleaming on my mother's face. There wasn't anything I could say.

"He never mentioned it," she said, "because I never let him mention it before you children. Your Daddy was like a crazy man that night and for many a night thereafter. He says he never in his life seen anything as dark as that road after the lights of that car had gone away. Weren't nothing, weren't nobody on that road, just your Daddy and his brother and that busted guitar. Oh, yes. Your Daddy never did really get right again. Till the day he died he weren't sure but that every white man he saw was the man that killed his brother."

She stopped and took out her handkerchief and dried her eyes and looked at me.

"I ain't telling you all this," she said, "to make you scared or bitter or to make you hate nobody. I'm telling you this because you got a brother. And the world ain't changed."

I guess I didn't want to believe this. I guess she saw this in my face. She turned away from me, toward the window again, searching those streets.

"But I praise my Redeemer," she said at last, "that He called your Daddy home before me. I ain't saying it to throw no flowers at myself, but, I declare, it keeps me from feeling too cast down to know I helped your father get safely through this world. Your father always acted like he was the roughest, strongest man on earth. And everybody took him to be like that. But if he hadn't had *me* there—to see his tears!"

She was crying again. Still, I couldn't move. I said, "Lord, Lord, Mama, I didn't know it was like that."

"Oh, honey," she said, "there's a lot that you don't know. But you are going to find out." She stood up from the window and came over to me. "You got to hold on to your brother," she said, "and don't let him fall, no matter what it looks like is happening to him and no matter how evil you gets with him. You going to be evil with him many a time. But don't you forget what I told you, you hear?"

"I won't forget," I said, "Don't you worry, I won't forget. I won't let nothing happen to Sonny."

My mother smiled as though she were amused at something she saw in my face. Then, "You may not be able to stop nothing from happening. But you got to let him know you's *there*."

Two days later I was married, and then I was gone. And I had a lot of things on my mind and I pretty well forgot my promise to Mama until I got shipped home on a special furlough for her funeral.

And, after the funeral, with just Sonny and me alone in the empty kitchen, I tried to find out something about him.

"What do you want to do?" I asked him.

"I'm going to be a musician," he said.

For he had graduated, in the time I had been away, from dancing to the juke box to finding out who was playing what, and what they were doing with it, and he had bought himself a set of drums.

"You mean, you want to be a drummer?" I somehow had the feeling that being a drummer might be all right for other people but not for my brother Sonny.

"I don't think," he said, looking at me very gravely, "that I'll ever be a good drummer. But I think I can play a piano."

I frowned. I'd never played the role of the older brother quite so seriously before, had scarcely ever, in fact, *asked* Sonny a damn thing. I sensed myself in the presence of something I didn't really know how to handle, didn't understand. So I made my frown a little deeper as I asked: "What kind of musician do you want to be?"

He grinned. "How many kinds do you think there are?"

"Be *serious*," I said.

He laughed, throwing his head back, and then looked at me. "I *am* serious."

"Well, then, for Christ's sake, stop kidding around and answer a serious question. I mean, do you want to be a concert pianist, you want to play classical music and all that, or—or what?" Long before I finished he was laughing again. "For Christ's *sake*, Sonny!"

He sobered, but with difficulty. "I'm sorry. But you sound so—*scared!*" and he was off again.

"Well, you may think it's funny now, baby, but it's not going to be so funny when you have to make your living at it, let me tell you *that*." I was furious because I knew he was laughing at me and I didn't know why.

"No," he said, very sober now, and afraid, perhaps, that he'd hurt me, "I don't want to be a classical pianist. That isn't what interests me. I mean"—he paused, looking hard at me, as though his eyes would help me to understand, and then gestured helplessly, as though perhaps his hand would help—"I mean, I'll have a lot of studying to do, and I'll have to study *everything*, but, I mean, I want to play *with*—jazz musicians." He stopped. "I want to play jazz," he said.

Well, the word had never before sounded as heavy, as real, as it sounded that afternoon in Sonny's mouth. I just looked at him and I was probably frowning a real frown by this time. I simply couldn't see why on earth he'd want to spend his time hanging around nightclubs, clowning around on bandstands, while people pushed each other around a dance floor. It seemed—beneath him, somehow. I had never thought about it before, had never been forced to, but I suppose I had always put jazz musicians in a class with what Daddy called "good-time people."

"Are you *serious?*"

"Hell, *yes*, I'm serious."

He looked more helpless than ever, and annoyed, and deeply hurt.

I suggested, helpfully: "You mean—like Louis Armstrong?"

His face closed as though I'd struck him. "No. I'm not talking about none of that old-time, down home crap."

"Well, look, Sonny, I'm sorry, don't get mad. I just don't altogether get it, that's all. Name somebody—you know, a jazz musician you admire."

"Bird."

"Who?"

"Bird! Charlie Parker! Don't they teach you nothing in the goddamn army?"

I lit a cigarette. I was surprised and then a little amused to discover that I was trembling. "I've been out of touch," I said. "You'll have to be patient with me. Now. Who's this Parker character?"

"He's just one of the greatest jazz musicians alive," said Sonny, sullenly, his hands in his pockets, his back to me. "Maybe *the* greatest," he added, bitterly, "that's probably why *you* never heard of him."

"All right," I said, "I'm ignorant. I'm sorry. I'll go out and buy all the cat's records right away, all right?"

"It don't," said Sonny, with dignity, "make any difference to me. I don't care what you listen to. Don't do me no favors."

I was beginning to realize that I'd never seen him so upset before. With another part of my mind I was thinking that this would probably turn out to be one of those things kids go through and that I shouldn't make it seem important by pushing it too hard. Still, I didn't think it would do any harm to ask: "Doesn't all this take a lot of time? Can you make a living at it?"

He turned back to me and half leaned, half sat, on the kitchen table. "Everything takes time," he said, "and—well, yes, sure, I can make a living at it. But what I don't seem to be able to make you understand is that it's the only thing I want to do."

"Well, Sonny," I said, gently, "you know people can't always do exactly what they *want* to do—"

"*No,* I don't know that," said Sonny, surprising me. "I think people *ought* to do what they want to do, what else are they alive for?"

"You getting to be a big boy," I said desperately, "it's time you started thinking about your future."

"I'm thinking about my future," said Sonny, grimly. "I think about it all the time."

I gave up. I decided, if he didn't change his mind, that we could always talk about it later. "In the meantime," I said, "you got to finish school." We had already decided that he'd have to move in with Isabel and her folks. I knew this wasn't the ideal arrangement because Isabel's folks are inclined to be dicty and they hadn't especially wanted Isabel to marry me. But I didn't know what else to do. "And we have to get you fixed up at Isabel's."

There was a long silence. He moved from the kitchen table to the window. "That's a terrible idea. You know it yourself."

"Do you have a *better* idea?"

He just walked up and down the kitchen for a minute. He was as tall as I was. He had started to shave. I suddenly had the feeling that I didn't know him at all.

He stopped at the kitchen table and picked up my cigarettes. Looking at me with a kind of mocking, amused defiance, he put one between his lips. "You mind?"

"You smoking already?"

He lit the cigarette and nodded, watching me through the smoke. "I just wanted to see if I'd have the courage to smoke in front of you." He grinned and blew a great cloud of smoke to the ceiling. "It was easy." He looked at my face. "Come on, now. I bet you was smoking at my age, tell the truth."

I didn't say anything but the truth was on my face, and he laughed. But now there was something very strained in his laugh. "Sure. And I bet that ain't all you was doing."

He was frightening me a little. "Cut the crap," I said. "We already decided that you was going to go and live at Isabel's. Now what's got into you all of a sudden?"

"*You* decided it," he pointed out. "*I* didn't decide nothing." He stopped in front me, leaning against the stove, arms loosely folded. "Look, brother. I don't want to stay in Harlem no more, I really don't." He was very earnest. He looked at me, then over toward the kitchen window. There was something in his eyes I'd never seen before, some thoughtfulness, some worry all his own. He rubbed the muscle of one arm. "It's time I was getting out of here."

"Where do you want to *go*, Sonny?"

"I want to join the army. Or the navy, I don't care. If I say I'm old enough, they'll believe me."

Then I got mad. It was because I was so scared. "You must be crazy. You goddamn fool, what the hell do you want to go and join the *army* for?"

"I just told you. To get out of Harlem."

"Sonny, you haven't even finished *school*. And if you really want to be a musician, how do you expect to study if you're in the *army*?"

He looked at me, trapped, and in anguish. "There's ways. I might be able to work out some kind of deal. Anyway, I'll have the G.I. Bill when I come out."

"*If* you come out." We stared at each other. "Sonny, please. Be reasonable. I know the setup is far from perfect. But we got to do the best we can."

"I ain't learning nothing in school," he said. "Even when I go." He turned away from me and opened the window and threw his cigarette out into the narrow alley. I watched his back. "At least, I ain't learning nothing you'd want me to learn." He slammed the window so hard I thought the glass would fly out, and turned back to me. "And I'm sick of the stink of these garbage cans!"

"Sonny," I said, "I know how you feel. But if you don't finish school now, you're going to be sorry later that you didn't." I grabbed him by the shoulders. "And you only got another year. It ain't so bad. And I'll come back and I swear I'll help you do *whatever* you want to do. Just try to put up with it till I come back. Will you please do that? For me?"

He didn't answer and he wouldn't look at me.

"Sonny. You hear me?"

He pulled away. "I hear you. But you never hear anything *I* say."

I didn't know what to say to that. He looked out of the window and then back at me. "OK," he said, and sighed. "I'll try."

Then I said, trying to cheer him up a little, "They got a piano at Isabel's. You can practice on it."

And as a matter of fact, it did cheer him up for a minute. "That's right," he said to himself. "I forgot that." His face relaxed a little. But the worry, the thoughtfulness, played on it still, the way shadows play on a face which is staring into the fire.

But I thought I'd never hear the end of that piano. At first, Isabel would write me, saying how nice it was that Sonny was so serious about his music and how, as soon as he came in from school, or wherever he had been when he was supposed to be at school, he went straight to that piano and stayed there until suppertime. And, after supper, he went back to that piano and stayed there until everybody went to bed. He was at the piano all day Saturday and all day Sunday. Then he bought a record player and started playing records. He'd play one record over and over again, all day long sometimes, and he'd improvise along with it on the piano. Or he'd play one section of the record, one chord, one change, one progression, then he'd do it on the piano. Then back to the record. Then back to the piano.

Well, I really don't know how they stood it. Isabel finally confessed that it wasn't like living with a person at all, it was like living with sound. And the sound didn't make any sense to her, didn't make any sense to any of them—naturally. They began, in a way, to be afflicted by this presence that was living in their home. It was as though Sonny were some sort of god, or monster. He moved in an atmosphere which wasn't like theirs at all. They fed him and he ate, he washed himself, he walked in and out of their door; he certainly wasn't nasty or unpleasant or rude, Sonny isn't any those things; but it was as though he were all wrapped up in some cloud, some fire, some vision all his own; and there wasn't any way to reach him.

At the same time, he wasn't really a man yet, he was still a child, and they had to watch out for him in all kinds of ways. They certainly couldn't throw him out. Neither did they dare to make a great scene about that piano because even they dimly sensed, as I sensed, from so many thousands of miles away, that Sonny was at that piano playing for his life.

But he hadn't been going to school. One day a letter came from the school board and Isabel's mother got it—there had, apparently, been other letters but Sonny had torn them up. This day, when Sonny came in, Isabel's mother showed him the letter and asked where he'd been spending his time. And she finally got it out of him that he'd been down in Greenwich Village, with musicians and other characters, in a white girl's apartment. And this scared her and she started to scream at him and what came up, once she began—though she denies it to this day—was what sacrifices they were making to give Sonny a decent home and how little he appreciated it.

Sonny didn't play the piano that day. By evening, Isabel's mother had calmed down but then there was the old man to deal with, and Isabel herself. Isabel says she did her best to be calm but she broke down and started crying. She says she just watched Sonny's face. She could tell, by watching him, what was happening with him. And what was happening was that they penetrated his cloud, they had reached him. Even if their fingers had been a thousand times more gentle than human fingers ever are, he could hardly help feeling that they had stripped him naked and were spitting on that nakedness. For he also had to see that his presence, that music, which was life or death to him, had been torture for them and that they had endured it, not at all for his sake, but only for mine. And Sonny couldn't take that. He can take it a little better today than he could then but he's still not very good at it and, frankly, I don't know anybody who is.

The silence of the next few days must have been louder than the sound of all the music ever played since time began. One morning, before she went to work, Isabel was in his room for something and she suddenly realized that all of his records were gone. And she knew for certain that he was gone. And he was. He went as far as the navy would carry him. He finally sent me a postcard from some place in Greece and that was the first I knew that Sonny was still alive. I didn't see him any more until we were both back in New York and the war had long been over.

He was a man by then, of course, but I wasn't willing to see it. He came by the house from time to time, but we fought almost every time we met. I didn't like the way he carried himself, loose and dreamlike all the time, and I didn't like his friends, and his music seemed to be merely an excuse for the life he led. It sounded just that weird and disordered.

Then we had a fight, a pretty awful fight, and I didn't see him for months. By and by I looked him up, where he was living, in a furnished room in the Village, and I tried to make it up. But there were lots of other people in the room and Sonny just lay on his bed, and he wouldn't come downstairs with me, and he treated these other people as though they were his family and I weren't. So I got mad and then he got mad, and then I told him that he might just as well be dead as live the way he was living. Then he stood up and he told me not to worry about him any more in life, that he *was* dead as far as I was concerned. Then he pushed me to the door and the other people looked on as though nothing were happening, and he slammed the door behind me. I stood in the hallway, staring at the door. I heard somebody laugh in the room and then the tears came to my eyes. I started down the steps, whistling to keep from crying. I kept whistling to myself, *You going to need me, baby, one of these cold, rainy days.*

I read about Sonny's trouble in the spring. Little Grace died in the fall. She was a beautiful little girl. But she only lived a little over two years. She died of polio and she suffered. She had a slight fever for a couple of days, but it didn't seem like anything and we just kept her in bed. And we would certainly have called the doctor, but the fever dropped, she seemed to be all right. So we thought it had just been a cold. Then, one day, she was up, playing, Isabel was in the kitchen fixing lunch for the two boys when they'd come in from school, and she heard Grace fall down in the living room. When you have a lot of children you don't always start running when one of them falls, unless they start screaming or something. And, this time, Grace was quiet. Yet, Isabel says that when she heard that *thump* and then that silence, something happened in her to make her afraid. And she ran to the living room and there was little Grace on the floor, all twisted up, and the reason she hadn't screamed was that she couldn't get her breath. And when she did scream, it was the worst sound, Isabel says, that she'd ever heard in all her life, and she still hears it sometimes in her dreams. Isabel will sometimes wake me up with a low, moaning, strangled sound and I have to be quick to awaken her and hold her to me and where Isabel is weeping against me seems a mortal wound.

I think I may have written Sonny the very day that little Grace was buried. I was sitting in the living room in the dark, by myself, and I suddenly thought of Sonny. My trouble made his real.

One Saturday afternoon, when Sonny had been living with us, or, anyway, been in our house, for nearly two weeks, I found myself wandering aimlessly about the living room, drinking from a can of beer, and trying to work up the courage to search Sonny's room. He was out, he was usually out whenever I was home, and Isabel had taken the children to see their grandparents. Suddenly I was standing still in front of the living room window, watching Seventh Avenue. The idea of searching Sonny's room made me still. I scarcely dared to admit to myself what I'd be searching for. I didn't know what I'd do if I found it. Or if I didn't.

On the sidewalk across from me, near the entrance to a barbecue joint, some people were holding an old-fashioned revival meeting. The barbecue cook, wearing a dirty white apron, his conked hair reddish and metallic in the pale sun and a cigarette between his lips, stood in the doorway, watching them. Kids and older people paused in their errands and stood there, along with some older men and a couple of very tough-looking women who watched everything that happened on the avenue, as though they owned it, or were maybe owned by it. Well, they were watching this, too. The revival was being carried on by three sisters in black, and a brother. All they had were their voices and their Bibles and a tambourine. The brother was testifying and while he testified two of the sisters stood together, seeming to say, amen, and the third sister walked around with the tambourine outstretched and a couple of people dropped coins into it. Then the brother's testimony ended and the sister who had been taking up the collection dumped the coins into her palm and transferred them to the pocket of her long black robe. Then she raised both hands, striking the tambourine against the air, and then against one hand, and she started to sing. And the two other sisters and the brother joined in.

It was strange, suddenly, to watch, though I had been seeing these street meetings all my life. So, of course, had everybody else down there. Yet, they paused and watched and listened and I stood still at the window. *"Tis the old ship of Zion,"* they sang, and the sister with the tambourine kept a steady, jangling beat, *"it has rescued many a thousand!"* Not a soul under the sound of their voices was hearing this song for the first time, not one of them had been rescued. Nor had they seen much in the way of rescue work being done around them.

Neither did they especially believe in the holiness of the three sisters and the brother, they knew too much about them, knew where they lived, and how. The woman with the tambourine, whose voice dominated the air, whose face was bright with joy, was divided by very little from the woman who stood watching her, a cigarette between her heavy, chapped lips, her hair a cuckoo's nest, her face scarred and swollen from many beatings, and her black eyes glittering like coal. Perhaps they both knew this, which was why, when, as rarely, they addressed each other, they addressed each other as Sister. As the singing filled the air the watching, listening faces underwent a change, the eyes focusing on something within; the music seemed to soothe a poison out of them; and time seemed, nearly, to fall away from the sullen, belligerent, battered faces, as though they were fleeing back to their first condition, while dreaming of their last. The barbecue cook half shook his head and smiled, and dropped his cigarette and disappeared into his joint. A man fumbled in his pockets for change and stood holding it in his hand impatiently, as though he had just remembered a pressing appointment further up the avenue. He looked furious. Then I saw Sonny, standing on the edge of the crowd. He was carrying a wide, flat notebook with a green cover, and it made him look, from where I was standing, almost like a schoolboy. The coppery sun brought out the copper in his skin, he was very faintly smiling, standing very still. Then the singing stopped, the tambourine turned into a collection plate again. The furious man dropped in his coins and vanished, so did a couple of the women, and Sonny dropped some change in the plate, looking directly at the woman with a little smile. He started across the avenue, toward the house. He has a slow, loping walk, something like the way Harlem hipsters walk, only he's imposed on this his own half-beat. I had never really noticed it before.

I stayed at the window, both relieved and apprehensive. As Sonny disappeared from my sight, they began singing again. And they were still singing when his key turned in the lock.

"Hey," he said.

"Hey, yourself. You want some beer?"

"No. Well, maybe." But he came up to the window and stood beside me, looking out. "What a warm voice," he said.

They were singing *If I could only hear my mother pray again!*

"Yes," I said, "and she can sure beat that tambourine."

"But what a terrible song," he said, and laughed. He dropped his notebook on the sofa and disappeared into the kitchen. "Where's Isabel and the kids?"

"I think they went to see their grandparents. You hungry?"

"No." He came back into the living room with his can of beer. "You want to come some place with me tonight?"

I sensed, I don't know how, that I couldn't possibly say no. "Sure. Where?"

He sat down on the sofa and picked up his notebook and started leafing through it. "I'm going to sit in with some fellows in a joint in the Village."

"You mean, you're going to play, tonight?"

"That's right." He took a swallow of his beer and moved back to the window. He gave me a sidelong look. "If you can stand it."

"I'll try," I said.

He smiled to himself and we both watched as the meeting across the way broke up. The three sisters and the brother, heads bowed, were singing *God be with you till we meet again*. The faces around them were very quiet. Then the song ended. The small crowd dispersed. We watched the three women and the lone man walk slowly up the avenue.

"When she was singing before," said Sonny, abruptly, "her voice reminded me for a minute of what heroin feels like sometimes—when it's in your veins. It makes you feel sort of warm and cool at the same time. And distant. And—and sure." He sipped his beer, very deliberately not looking at me. I watched his face. "It makes you feel—in control. Sometimes you've got to have that feeling."

"Do you?" I sat down slowly in the easy chair.

"Sometimes." He went to the sofa and picked up his notebook again. "Some people do."

"In order," I asked, "to play?" And my voice was very ugly, full of contempt and anger.

"Well"—he looked at me with great, troubled eyes, as though, in fact, he hoped his eyes would tell me things he could never otherwise say—"they *think* so. And *if* they think so—!"

"And what do *you* think?" I asked.

He sat on the sofa and put his can of beer on the floor. "I don't know," he said, and I couldn't be sure if he were answering my question or pursuing his thoughts. His face didn't tell me. "It's not so much to *play*. It's to *stand* it, to be able to make it at all. On any level." He frowned and smiled: "In order to keep from shaking to pieces."

"But these friends of yours," I said, "they seem to shake themselves to pieces pretty goddamn fast."

"Maybe." He played with the notebook. And something told me that I should curb my tongue, that Sonny was doing his best to talk, that I should listen. "But of course you only know the ones that've gone to pieces. Some don't—or at least they haven't *yet* and that's just about all *any* of us can say." He paused. "And then there are some who just live, really, in hell, and they know it and they see what's happening and they go right on. I don't know." He sighed, dropped the notebook, folded his arms. "Some guys, you can tell from the way they play, they on something *all* the time. And you can see that, well, it makes something real for them. But of course," he picked up his beer from the floor and sipped it and put the can down again, "they *want* to, too, you've got to see that. Even some of them that say they don't—*some*, not all."

"And what about you?" I asked—I couldn't help it. "What about you? Do *you* want to?"

He stood up and walked to the window and remained silent for a long time. Then he sighed. "Me," he said. Then: "While I was downstairs before, on my way here, listening to that woman sing, it struck me all of a sudden how much suffering she must have had to go through—to sing like that. It's *repulsive* to think you have to suffer that much."

I said: "But there's no way not to suffer—is there, Sonny?"

"I believe not," he said and smiled, "but that's never stopped anyone from trying." He looked at me. "Has it?" I realized, with this mocking look, that there stood between us, forever, beyond the power of time or forgiveness, the fact that I had held silence—so long!—when he had needed human speech to help him. He turned back to the window. "No, there's no way not to suffer. But you try all kinds of ways to keep from drowning in it, to keep on top of it, and to make it seem—well, like *you*. Like you did something, all right, and now you're suffering for it. You know?" I said nothing. "Well you know," he said, impatiently, "why *do* people suffer? Maybe it's better to do something to give it a reason, *any* reason."

"But we just agreed," I said, "that there's no way not to suffer. Isn't it better, then, just to—take it?"

"But nobody just takes it," Sonny cried, "that's what I'm telling you! *Everybody* tries not to. You're just hung up on the *way* some people try—it's not *your* way!"

The hair on my face began to itch, my face felt wet. "That's not true," I said, "that's not true. I don't give a damn what other people do, I don't even care how they suffer. I just care how *you* suffer." And he looked at me. "Please believe me," I said, "I don't want to see you—die—trying not to suffer."

"I won't," he said, flatly, "die trying not to suffer. At least, not any faster than anybody else."

"But there's no need," I said, trying to laugh, "is there? in killing yourself."

I wanted to say more, but I couldn't. I wanted to talk about will power and how life could be—well, beautiful. I wanted to say that it was all within; but was it? or, rather, wasn't that exactly the trouble? And I wanted to promise that I would never fail him again. But it would all have sounded—empty words and lies.

So I made the promise to myself and prayed that I would keep it.

"It's terrible sometimes, inside," he said, "that's what's the trouble. You walk these streets, black and funky and cold, and there's not really a living ass to talk to, and there's nothing shaking, and there's no way of getting it out—that storm inside. You can't talk it and you can't make love with it, and when you finally try to get with it and play it, you realize *nobody's* listening. So *you've* got to listen. You got to find a way to listen."

And then he walked away from the window and sat on the sofa again, as though all the wind had suddenly been knocked out of him. "Sometimes you'll do *anything* to play, even cut your mother's throat." He laughed and looked at me. "Or your brother's." Then he sobered. "Or your own." Then: "Don't worry. I'm all right now and I think I'll *be* all right. But I can't forget—where I've been. I don't mean just the physical place I've been, I mean where I've *been*. And *what* I've been."

"What have you been, Sonny?" I asked.

He smiled—but sat sideways on the sofa, his elbow resting on the back, his fingers playing with his mouth and chin, not looking at me. "I've been something I didn't recognize, didn't know I could be. Didn't know anybody could be." He stopped, looking inward, looking helplessly young, looking old. "I'm not talking about it now because I feel *guilty* or anything like that—maybe it would be better if I did, I don't know. Anyway, I can't really talk about it. Not to you, not to anybody," and now he turned and faced me. "Sometimes, you know, and it was actually when I was most *out* of the world, I felt that I was in it, that I was *with* it, really, and I could play or I didn't really have to *play,* it just came out of me, it was there. And I don't know how I played, thinking about it now, but I know I did awful things, those times, sometimes, to people. Or it wasn't that I *did* anything to them—it was that they weren't real." He picked up the beer can; it was empty; he rolled it between his palms: "And other times—well, I needed a fix, I needed to find a place to lean, I needed to clear a space to *listen*—and I couldn't find it, and I—went crazy, I did terrible things to *me,* I was terrible *for* me." He began pressing the beer can between his hands, I watched the metal begin to give. It glittered, as he played with it, like a knife, and I was afraid he would cut himself, but I said nothing. "Oh well. I can never tell you. I was all by myself at the bottom of something, stinking and sweating and crying and shaking, and I smelled it, you know? *my* stink, and I thought I'd die if I couldn't get away from it and yet, all the same, I knew that everything I was doing was just locking me in with it. And I didn't know," he paused, still flattening the beer can, "I didn't know, I still *don't* know, something kept telling me that maybe it was good to smell your own stink, but I didn't think that *that* was what I'd been trying to do—and—who can stand it?" and he abruptly dropped the ruined beer can, looking at me with a small, still smile, and then rose, walking to the window as though it were the lodestone rock. I watched his face, he watched the avenue. "I couldn't tell you when Mama died—but the reason I wanted to leave Harlem so bad was to get away from drugs. And then, when I ran away, that's what I was running from—really. When I came back, nothing had changed, *I* hadn't changed, I was just—older." And he stopped, drumming with his fingers on the windowpane. The sun had vanished, soon darkness would fall. I watched his face. "It can come again," he said, almost as though speaking to himself. Then he turned to me. "It can come again," he repeated. "I just want you to know that."

"All right," I said, at last. "So it can come again, All right."

He smiled, but the smile was sorrowful. "I had to try to tell you," he said.

"Yes," I said. "I understand that."

"You're my brother," he said, looking straight at me, and not smiling at all.

"Yes," I repeated, "yes. I understand that."

He turned back to the window, looking out. "All that hatred down there," he said, "all that hatred and misery and love. It's a wonder it doesn't blow the avenue apart."

We went to the only nightclub on a short, dark street, downtown. We squeezed through the narrow, chattering, jampacked bar to the entrance of the big room, where the bandstand was. And we stood there for a moment, for the lights were very dim in this room and we couldn't see. Then, "Hello, boy," said a voice and an enormous black man, much older than Sonny or myself, erupted out of all that atmospheric lighting and put an arm around Sonny's shoulder. "I been sitting right here," he said, "waiting for you."

He had a big voice, too, and heads in the darkness turned toward us.

Sonny grinned and pulled a little away, and said, "Creole, this is my brother. I told you about him."

Creole shook my hand. "I'm glad to meet you, son," he said, and it was clear that he was glad to meet me *there,* for Sonny's sake. And he smiled, "You got a real musician in *your* family," and he took his arm from Sonny's shoulder and slapped him, lightly, affectionately, with the back of his hand.

"Well. Now I've heard it all," said a voice behind us. This was another musician, and a friend of Sonny's a coal-black, cheerful-looking man, built close to the ground. He immediately began confiding to me, at the top of his lungs, the most terrible things about Sonny, his teeth gleaming like a lighthouse and his laugh coming up out of him like the beginning of an earthquake. And it turned out that everyone at the bar knew Sonny, or almost everyone; some were musicians, working there, or nearby, or not working, some were simply hangers-on, and some were there to hear Sonny play. I was introduced to all of them and they were all very polite to me. Yet, it was clear that, for them, I was only Sonny's brother. Here, I was in Sonny's world. Or, rather: his kingdom. Here, it was not even a question that his veins bore royal blood.

They were going to play soon and Creole installed me, by myself, at a table in a dark corner. Then I watched them, Creole, and the little black man, and Sonny, and the others, while they horsed around, standing just below the bandstand. The light from the bandstand spilled just a little short of them and, watching them laughing and gesturing and moving about I had the feeling that they, nevertheless, were being most careful not to step into that circle of light too suddenly: that if they moved into the light too suddenly, without thinking, they would perish in flame. Then, while I watched, one of them, the small, black man, moved into the light and crossed the bandstand and started fooling around with his drums. Then—being funny and being, also, extremely ceremonious—Creole took Sonny by the arm and led him to the piano. A woman's voice called Sonny's name and a few hands started clapping. And Sonny, also being funny and being ceremonious, and so touched, I think, that he could have cried, but neither hiding it nor showing it, riding it like a man, grinned, and put both hands to his heart and bowed from the waist.

Creole then went to the bass fiddle and a lean, very bright-skinned brown man jumped up on the bandstand and picked up his horn. So there they were, and the atmosphere on the bandstand and in the room began to change and tighten. Someone stepped up to the microphone and announced them. Then there were all kinds of murmurs. Some people at the bar shushed others. The waitress ran around, frantically getting in the last orders, guys and chicks got closer to each other, and the lights on the bandstand, on the quartet, turned to a kind of indigo. Then they all looked different there. Creole looked about him for the last time, as though he were making certain that all his chickens were in the coop, and then he—jumped and struck the fiddle. And there they were.

All I know about music is that not many people ever really hear it. And even then, on the rare occasions when something opens within, and the music enters, what we mainly hear, or hear corroborated, are personal, private, vanishing evocations. But the man who creates the music is hearing something else, is dealing with the roar rising from the void and imposing order on it as it hits the air. What is evoked in him, then, is of another order, more terrible because it has no words, and triumphant, too, for that same reason. And his triumph, when he triumphs, is ours. I just watched Sonny's face. His face was troubled, he was working hard, but he wasn't with it. And I had the feeling that, in a way, everyone on the bandstand was waiting for him, both waiting for him and pushing him along. But as I began to watch Creole, I realized that it was Creole who held them all back. He had them on a short rein. Up there, keeping the beat with his whole body, wailing on the fiddle, with his eyes half closed, he was listening to everything, but he was listening to Sonny. He was having a dialogue with Sonny. He wanted Sonny to leave the shoreline and strike out for the deep water. He was Sonny's witness that deep water and drowning were not the same thing— he had been there, and he knew. And he wanted Sonny to know. He was waiting for Sonny to do the things on the keys which would let Creole know that Sonny was in the water.

And, while Creole listened, Sonny moved, deep within, exactly like someone in torment. I had never before thought of how awful the relationship must be between the musician and his instrument. He has to fill it, this instrument, with the breath of life, his own. He has to make it do what he wants it to do. And a piano is just a piano. It's made out of so much wood and wires and little hammers and big ones, and ivory. While there's only so much you can do with it, the only way to find this out is to try; to try and make it do everything.

And Sonny hadn't been near a piano for over a year. And he wasn't on much better terms with his life, not the life that stretched before him now. He and the piano stammered, started one way, got scared, stopped; started another way, panicked, marked time, started again; then seemed to have found a direction, panicked again, got stuck. And the face I saw on Sonny I'd never seen before. Everything had been burned out of it, and, at the same time, things usually hidden were being burned in, by the fire and fury of the battle which was occurring in him up there.

Yet, watching Creole's face as they neared the end of the first set, I had the feeling that something had happened, something I hadn't heard. Then they finished, there was scattered applause, and then, without an instant's warning, Creole started into something else, it was almost sardonic, it was *Am I Blue*. And, as though he commanded, Sonny began to play. Something began to happen. And Creole let out the reins. The dry, low, black man said something awful on the drums, Creole answered, and the drums talked back. Then the horn insisted, sweet and high, slightly detached perhaps, and Creole listened, commenting now and then, dry, and driving, beautiful and calm and old. Then they all came together again, and Sonny was part of the family again. I could tell this from his face. He seemed to have found, right there beneath his fingers, a damn brand-new piano. It seemed that he couldn't get over it. Then, for awhile, just being happy with

Sonny, they seemed to be agreeing with him that brand-new pianos certainly were a gas.

Then Creole stepped forward to remind them that what they were playing was the blues. He hit something in all of them, he hit something in me, myself, and the music tightened and deepened, apprehension began to beat the air. Creole began to tell us what the blues were all about. They were not about anything very new. He and his boys up there were keeping it new, at the risk of ruin, destruction, madness, and death, in order to find new ways to make us listen. For, while the tale of how we suffer, and how we are delighted, and how we may triumph is never new, it always must be heard. There isn't any other tale to tell, it's the only light we've got in all this darkness.

And this tale, according to that face, that body, those strong hands on those strings, has another aspect in every country, and a new depth in every generation. Listen, Creole seemed to be saying, listen. Now these are Sonny's blues. He made the little black man on the drums know it, and the bright, brown man on the horn. Creole wasn't trying any longer to get Sonny in the water. He was wishing him Godspeed. Then he stepped back, very slowly, filling the air with the immense suggestion that Sonny speak for himself.

Then they all gathered around Sonny and Sonny played. Every now and again one of them seemed to say, amen. Sonny's fingers filled the air with life, his life. But that life contained so many others. And Sonny went all the way back, he really began with the spare, flat statement of the opening phrase of the song. Then he began to make it his. It was very beautiful because it wasn't hurried and it was no longer a lament. I seemed to hear with what burning he had made it his, with what burning we had yet to make it ours, how we could cease lamenting. Freedom lurked around us and I understood, at last, that he could help us to be free if we would listen, that he would never be free until we did. Yet, there was no battle in his face now. I heard what he had gone through, and would continue to go through until he came to rest in earth. He had made it his: that long line, of which we knew only Mama and Daddy. And he was giving it back, as everything must be given back, so that, passing through death, it can live forever. I saw my mother's face again, and felt, for the first time, how the stones of the road she had walked on must have bruised her feet. I saw the moonlit road where my father's brother died. And it brought something else back to me, and carried me past it, I saw my little girl again and felt Isabel's tears again, and I felt my own tears begin to rise. And I was yet aware that this was only a moment, that the world waited outside, as hungry as a tiger, and that trouble stretched above us, longer than the sky.

Then it was over. Creole and Sonny let out their breath, both soaking wet, and grinning. There was a lot of applause and some of it was real. In the dark, the girl came by and I asked her to take drinks to the bandstand. There was a long pause, while they talked up there in the indigo light and after awhile I saw the girl put a Scotch and milk on top of the piano for Sonny. He didn't seem to notice it, but just before they started playing again, he sipped from it and looked toward me, and nodded. Then he put it back on top of the piano. For me, then, as they began to play again, it glowed and shook above my brother's head like the very cup of trembling.

QUESTIONS

1. Why do you think the narrator dwells so much on his own limitations of sympathy and understanding?
2. What is the source of the fear that the narrator admits early in the story and that Sonny has seen in him?
3. Who is the stronger person—Sonny or the narrator? Explain.
4. What statement, if any, does the story make about drug use?
5. From what you see of Sonny, how likely is it that he will eventually destroy himself?

Flannery O'Connor (1925–1964)
THE ARTIFICIAL NIGGER

Mr. Head awakened to discover that the room was full of moonlight. He sat up and stared at the floor boards—the color of silver—and then at the ticking on his pillow, which might have been brocade, and after a second, he saw half of the moon five feet away in his shaving mirror, paused as if it were waiting for his permission to enter. It rolled forward and cast a dignifying light on everything. The straight chair against the wall looked stiff and attentive as if it were awaiting an order and Mr. Head's trousers, hanging to the back of it, had an almost noble air, like the garment some great man had just flung to his servant; but the face on the moon was a grave one. It gazed across the room and out the window where it floated over the horse stall and appeared to contemplate itself with the look of a young man who sees his old age before him.

Mr. Head could have said to it that age was a choice blessing and that only with years does a man enter into that calm understanding of life that makes him a suitable guide for the young. This, at least, had been his own experience.

He sat up and grasped the iron posts at the foot of his bed and raised himself until he could see the face on the alarm clock which sat on an overturned bucket beside the chair. The hour was two in the morning. The alarm on the clock did not work but he was not dependent on any mechanical means to awaken him. Sixty years had not dulled his responses; his physical reactions, like his moral ones, were guided by his will and strong character, and these could be seen plainly in his features. He had a long tube-like face with a long rounded open jaw and a long depressed nose. His eyes were alert but quiet, and in the miraculous moonlight they had a look of composure and of ancient wisdom as if they belonged to one of the great guides of men. He might have been Vergil summoned in the middle of the night to go to Dante, or better, Raphael, awakened by a blast of

God's light to fly to the side of Tobias. The only dark spot in the room was Nelson's pallet, underneath the shadow of the window.

Nelson was hunched over on his side, his knees under his chin and his heels under his bottom. His new suit and hat were in the boxes that they had been sent in and these were on the floor at the foot of the pallet where he could get his hands on them as soon as he woke up. The slop jar, out of the shadow and made snow-white in the moonlight, appeared to stand guard over him like a small personal angel. Mr. Head lay back down, feeling entirely confident that he could carry out the moral mission of the coming day. He meant to be up before Nelson and to have the breakfast cooking by the time he awakened. The boy was always irked when Mr. Head was the first up. They would have to leave the house at four to get to the railroad junction by five-thirty. The train was to stop for them at five forty-five and they had to be there on time for this train was stopping merely to accommodate them.

This would be the boy's first trip to the city though he claimed it would be his second because he had been born there. Mr. Head had tried to point out to him that when he was born he didn't have the intelligence to determine his whereabouts but this had made no impression on the child at all and he continued to insist that this was to be his second trip. It would be Mr. Head's third trip. Nelson had said, "I will've already been there twict and I ain't but ten."

Mr. Head had contradicted him.

"If you ain't been there in fifteen years, how you know you'll be able to find your way about?" Nelson had asked. "How you know it hasn't changed some?"

"Have you ever," Mr. Head had asked, "seen me lost?"

Nelson certainly had not but he was a child who was never satisfied until he had given an impudent answer and he replied, "It's nowhere around here to get lost at."

"The day is going to come," Mr. Head prophesied, "when you'll find you ain't as smart as you think you are." He had been thinking about this trip for several months but it was for the most part in moral terms that he conceived it. It was to be a lesson that the boy would never forget. He was to find out from it that he had no cause for pride merely because he had been born in a city. He was to find out that the city is not a great place. Mr. Head meant him to see everything there is to see in a city so that he would be content to stay at home for the rest of his life. He fell asleep thinking how the boy would at last find out that he was not as smart as he thought he was.

He was awakened at three-thirty by the smell of fatback frying and he leaped off his cot. The pallet was empty and the clothes boxes had been thrown open. He put on his trousers and ran into the other room. The boy had a corn pone on cooking and had fried the meat. He was sitting in the half-dark at the table, drinking cold coffee out of a can. He had on his new suit and his new gray hat pulled low over his eyes. It was too big for him but they had ordered it a size large because they expected his head to grow. He didn't say anything but his entire figure suggested satisfaction at having arisen before Mr. Head.

Mr. Head went to the stove and brought the meat to the table in the skillet. "It's no hurry," he said. "You'll get there soon enough and it's no guarantee you'll like it when you do neither," and he sat down across from the boy whose hat teetered back slowly to reveal a fiercely expressionless face, very much the same shape as the old man's. They were grandfather and grandson but they looked enough alike to be brothers and brothers not too far apart in age, for Mr. Head had a youthful expression by daylight, while the boy's look was ancient, as if he knew everything already and would be pleased to forget it.

Mr. Head had once had a wife and daughter and when the wife died, the daughter ran away and returned after an interval with Nelson. Then one morning, without getting out of bed, she died and left Mr. Head with sole care of the year-old child. He had made the mistake of telling Nelson that he had been born in Atlanta. If he hadn't told him that, Nelson couldn't have insisted that this was going to be his second trip.

"You may not like it a bit," Mr. Head continued. "It'll be full of niggers."

The boy made a face as if he could handle a nigger.

"All right," Mr. Head said. "You ain't ever seen a nigger."

"You wasn't up very early," Nelson said.

"You ain't ever seen a nigger," Mr. Head repeated. "There hasn't been a nigger in this county since we run that one out twelve years ago and that was before you were born." He looked at the boy as if he were daring him to say he had ever seen a Negro.

"How you know I never saw a nigger when I lived there before?" Nelson asked. "I probably saw a lot of niggers."

"If you seen one you didn't know what he was," Mr. Head said, completely exasperated. "A six-month-old child don't know a nigger from anybody else."

"I reckon I'll know a nigger if I see one," the boy said and got up and straightened his slick sharply creased gray hat and went outside to the privy.

They reached the junction some time before the train was due to arrive and stood about two feet from the first set of tracks. Mr. Head carried a paper sack with some biscuits and a can of sardines in it for their lunch. A coarse-looking orange-colored sun coming up behind the east range of mountains was making the sky a dull red behind them, but in front of them it was still gray and they faced a gray transparent moon, hardly stronger than a thumbprint and completely without light. A small tin switch box and a black fuel tank were all there was to mark the place as a junction; the tracks were double and did not converge again until they were hidden behind the bends at either end of the clearing. Trains passing appeared to emerge from a tunnel of trees and, hit for a second by the cold sky, vanish terrified into the woods again. Mr. Head had had to make special arrangements with the ticket agent to have this train stop and he was secretly afraid it would not, in which case, he knew Nelson would say, "I never thought no train was going to stop for you." Under the useless morning moon the tracks looked white and fragile. Both the old man and the child stared ahead as if they were awaiting an apparition.

Then suddenly, before Mr. Head could make up his mind to turn back, there was a deep warning bleat and the train appeared, gliding very slowly, almost silently around the bend of trees about two hundred yards down the track, with one yellow front light shining. Mr. Head was still not certain it would stop and he felt it would make an even bigger idiot of him if it went by slowly. Both he and Nelson, however, were prepared to ignore the train if it passed them.

The engine charged by, filling their noses with the smell of hot metal and then the second coach came to a stop exactly where they were standing. A conductor with the face of an ancient bloated bulldog was on the step as if he expected them, though he did not look as if it mattered one way or the other to him if they got on or not. "To the right," he said.

Their entry took only a fraction of a second and the train was already speeding on as they entered the quiet car. Most of the travelers were still sleeping, some with their heads hanging off the chair arms, some stretched across two seats, and some sprawled out with their feet in the aisle. Mr. Head saw two unoccupied seats and pushed Nelson toward them. "Get in there by the winder," he said in his normal voice which was very loud at this hour of the morning. "Nobody cares if you sit there because it's nobody in it. Sit right there."

"I heard you," the boy muttered. "It's no use in you yelling," and he sat down and turned his head to the glass. There he saw a pale ghost-like face scowling at him beneath the brim of a pale ghost-like hat. His grandfather, looking quickly too, saw a different ghost, pale but grinning, under a black hat.

Mr. Head sat down and settled himself and took out his ticket and started reading aloud everything that was printed on it. People began to stir. Several woke up and stared at him. "Take off your hat," he said to Nelson and took off his own and put it on his knee. He had a small amount of white hair that had turned tobacco-colored over the years and this lay flat across the back of his head. The front of his head was bald and creased. Nelson took off his hat and put it on his knee and they waited for the conductor to come ask for their tickets.

The man across the aisle from them was spread out over two seats, his feet propped on the window and his head jutting into the aisle. He had on a light blue suit and a yellow shirt unbuttoned at the neck. His eyes had just opened and Mr. Head was ready to introduce himself when the conductor came up from behind and growled, "Tickets."

When the conductor had gone, Mr. Head gave Nelson the return half of his ticket and said, "Now put that in your pocket and don't lose it or you'll have to stay in the city."

"Maybe I will," Nelson said as if this were a reasonable suggestion.

Mr. Head ignored him. "First time this boy has ever been on a train," he explained to the man across the aisle, who was sitting up now on the edge of his seat with both feet on the floor.

Nelson jerked his hat on again and turned angrily to the window.

"He's never seen anything before," Mr. Head continued. "Ignorant as the day he was born, but I mean for him to get his fill once and for all."

The boy leaned forward, across his grandfather and toward the stranger. "I was born in the city," he said. "I was born there. This is my second trip." He said it in a high positive voice but the man across the aisle didn't look as if he understood. There were heavy purple circles under his eyes.

Mr. Head reached across the aisle and tapped him on the arm. "The thing to do with a boy," he said sagely, "is to show him all it is to show. Don't hold nothing back."

"Yeah," the man said. He gazed down at his swollen feet and lifted the left one about ten inches from the floor. After a minute he put it down and lifted the other. All through the car people began to get up and move about and yawn and stretch. Separate voices could be heard here and there and then a general hum. Suddenly Mr. Head's serene expression changed. His mouth almost closed and a light, fierce and cautious both, came into his eyes. He was looking down the length of the car. Without turning, he caught Nelson by the arm and pulled him forward. "Look," he said.

A huge coffee-colored man was coming slowly forward. He had on a light suit and a yellow satin tie with a ruby pin in it. One of his hands rested on his stomach which rode majestically under his buttoned coat, and in the other he held the head of a black walking stick that he picked up and set down with a deliberate outward motion each time he took a step. He was proceeding very slowly, his large brown eyes gazing over the heads of the passengers. He had a small white mustache and white crinkly hair. Behind him there were two young women, with coffee-colored, one in a yellow dress and one in a green. Their progress was kept at the rate of his and they chatted in low throaty voices as they followed him.

Mr. Head's grip was tightening insistently on Nelson's arm. As the procession passed them, the light from a sapphire ring on the brown hand that picked up the cane reflected in Mr. Head's eye, but he did not look up nor did the tremendous man look at him. The group proceeded up the rest of the aisle and out of the car. Mr. Head's grip on Nelson's arm loosened. "What was that?" he asked.

"A man," the boy said and gave him an indignant look as if he were tired of having his intelligence insulted.

"What kind of a man?" Mr. Head persisted, his voice expressionless.

"A fat man," Nelson said. He was beginning to feel that he had better be cautious.

"You don't know what kind?" Mr. Head said in a final tone.

"An old man," the boy said and had a sudden foreboding that he was not going to enjoy the day.

"That was a nigger," Mr. Head said and sat back.

Nelson jumped up on the seat and stood looking backward to the end of the car but the Negro had gone.

"I'd of thought you'd know a nigger since you seen so many when you was in the city on your first visit," Mr. Head continued. "That's his first nigger," he said to the man across the aisle.

The boy slid down into the seat. "You said they were black," he said in an angry voice. "You never said they were tan. How do you expect me to know anything when you don't tell me right?"

"You're just ignorant is all," Mr. Head said and he got up and moved over in the vacant seat by the man across the aisle.

Nelson turned backward again and looked where the Negro had disappeared. He felt that the Negro had deliberately walked down the aisle in order to make a fool of him and he hated him with a fierce raw fresh hate; and also, he understood now why his grandfather disliked them. He looked toward the window and the face there seemed to suggest that he might be inadequate to the day's exactions. He wondered if he would even recognize the city when they came to it.

After he had told several stories, Mr. Head realized that the man he was talking to was asleep and he got up and suggested to Nelson that they walk over the train and see the parts of it. He particularly wanted the boy to see the toilet so they went first to the men's room and examined the plumbing. Mr. Head demonstrated the ice-water cooler as if he had invented it and showed Nelson the bowl with the single spigot where the travelers brushed their teeth. They went through several cars and came to the diner.

This was the most elegant car in the train. It was painted a rich egg-yellow and had a wine-colored carpet on the floor. There were wide windows over the tables and great spaces of the rolling view were caught in miniature in the sides of the coffee pots and in the glasses. Three very black Negroes in white suits and aprons were running up and down the aisle, swinging trays and bowing and bending over the travelers eating breakfast. One of them rushed up to Mr. Head and Nelson and said, holding up two fingers, "Space for two!" but Mr. Head replied in a loud voice, "We eaten before we left!"

The waiter wore large brown spectacles that increased the size of his eye whites. "Stan' aside then please," he said with an airy wave of the arm as if he were brushing aside flies.

Neither Nelson nor Mr. Head moved a fraction of an inch. "Look," Mr. Head said.

The near corner of the diner, containing two tables, was set off from the rest by a saffron-colored curtain. One table was set but empty but at the other, facing them, his back to the drape, sat the tremendous Negro. He was speaking in a soft voice to the two women while he buttered a muffin. He had a heavy sad face and his neck bulged over his white collar on either side. "They rope them off," Mr. Head explained. Then he said, "Let's go see the kitchen," and they walked the length of the diner but the black waiter was coming fast behind them.

"Passengers are not allowed in the kitchen!" he said in a haughty voice. "Passengers are NOT allowed in the kitchen!"

Mr. Head stopped where he was and turned. "And there's good reason for that," he shouted into the Negro's chest, "because the cockroaches would run the passengers out!"

All the travelers laughed and Mr. Head and Nelson walked out, grinning. Mr. Head was known at home for his quick wit and Nelson felt a sudden keen pride in him. He realized the old man would be his only support in the strange place they were approaching. He would be entirely alone in the world if he were ever lost from his grandfather. A terrible excitement shook him and he wanted to take hold of Mr. Head's coat and hold on like a child.

As they went back to their seats they could see through the passing windows that the countryside was becoming speckled with small houses and shacks and that a highway ran alongside the train. Cars sped by on it, very small and fast. Nelson felt that there was less breath in the air than there had been thirty minutes ago. The man across the aisle had left and there was no one near for Mr. Head to hold a conversation with so he looked out the window, through his own reflection, and read aloud the names of the buildings they were passing. "The Dixie Chemical Corp!" he announced. "Southern Maid Flour! Dixie Doors! Southern Belle Cotton Products! Patty's Peanut Butter! Southern Mammy Cane Syrup!"

"Hush up!" Nelson hissed.

All over the car people were beginning to get up and take their luggage off the overhead racks. Women were putting on their coats and hats. The conductor stuck his head in the car and snarled, "Firstoppppppmry," and Nelson lunged out of his sitting position, trembling. Mr. Head pushed him down by the shoulder.

"Keep your seat," he said in dignified tones. "The first stop is on the edge of town. The second stop is at the main railroad station." He had come by this knowledge on his first trip when he had got off at the first stop and had had to pay a man fifteen cents to take him into the heart of town. Nelson sat back down, very pale. For the first time in his life, he understood that his grandfather was indispensable to him.

The train stopped and let off a few passengers and glided on as if it had never ceased moving. Outside, behind rows of brown rickety houses, a line of blue buildings stood up, and beyond them a pale rose-gray sky faded away to nothing. The train moved into the railroad yard. Looking down, Nelson saw lines and lines of silver tracks multiplying and criss-crossing. Then before he could start counting them, the face in the window started out at him, gray but distinct, and he looked the other way. The train was in the station. Both he and Mr. Head jumped up and ran to the door. Neither noticed that they had left the paper sack with the lunch in it on the seat.

They walked stiffly through the small station and came out of a heavy door into the squall of traffic. Crowds were hurrying to work. Nelson didn't know where to look. Mr. Head leaned against the side of the building and glared in front of him.

Finally Nelson said, "Well, how do you see what all it is to see?"

Mr. Head didn't answer. Then as if the sight of people passing had given him the clue, he said, "You walk," and started off down the street. Nelson followed, steadying his hat. So many sights and sounds were flooding in on him that for the first block he hardly knew what he was seeing. At the second corner, Mr. Head turned and looked behind him at the station they had left, a putty-colored terminal with a concrete dome on top. He thought that if he could keep the dome always in sight, he would be able to get back in the afternoon to catch the train again.

As they walked along, Nelson began to distinguish details and take note of the store windows, jammed with every kind of equipment—hardware, drygoods, chicken feed, liquor. They passed one that Mr. Head called his particular attention to where you walked in and sat on a chair with your feet upon two rests and let a Negro polish your shoes. They walked slowly and stopped and stood at the entrances so he could see what went on in each place but they did not go into any of them. Mr. Head was determined not to go into any city store because on his first trip here, he had got lost in a large one and had found his way out only after many people had insulted him.

They came in the middle of the next block to a store that had a weighing machine in front of it and they both in turn stepped up on it and put in a penny and received a ticket. Mr. Head's ticket said, "You weigh 120 pounds. You are upright and brave and all your friends admire you." He put the ticket in his pocket, surprised that the machine should have got his character correct but his weight wrong, for he had weighed on a grain scale not long before and knew he weighed 110. Nelson's ticket said, "You weigh 98 pounds. You have a great destiny ahead of you but beware of dark women." Nelson did not know any women and he weighed only 68 pounds but Mr. Head pointed out that the machine had probably printed the number upsidedown, meaning the 9 for a 6.

They walked on and at the end of five blocks the dome of the terminal sank out of sight and Mr. Head turned to the left. Nelson could have stood in front of every store window for an hour if there had not been another more interesting one next to it. Suddenly he said, "I was born here!" Mr. Head turned and looked at him with horror. There was a sweaty brightness about his face. "This is where I come from!" he said.

Mr. Head was appalled. He saw the moment had come for drastic action. "Lemme show you one thing you ain't seen yet," he said and took him to the corner where there was a sewer entrance. "Squat down," he said, "and stick you head in there," and he held the back of the boy's coat while he got down and put his head in the sewer. He drew it back quickly, hearing a gurgling in the depths under the sidewalk. Then Mr. Head explained the sewer system, how the entire city was underlined with it, how it contained all the drainage and was full of rats and how a man could slide into it and be sucked along down endless pitchblack tunnels. At any minute any man in the city might be sucked into the sewer and never heard from again. He described it so well that Nelson was for some seconds shaken. He connected the sewer passages with the entrance to hell and understood for the first time how the world was put together in its lower parts. He drew away from the curb.

Then he said, "Yes, but you can stay away from the holes," and his face took on that stubborn look that was so exasperating to his grandfather. "This is where I come from!" he said.

Mr. Head was dismayed but he only muttered, "You'll get your fill," and they walked on. At the end of two more blocks he turned to the left, feeling that he was circling the dome; and he was correct for in a half-hour they passed in front of the railroad station again. At first Nelson did not notice that he was seeing the same stores twice but when they passed the one where you put your feet on the rests while the Negro polished your shoes, he perceived that they were walking in a circle.

"We done been here!" he shouted. "I don't believe you know where you're at!"

"The direction just slipped my mind for a minute," Mr. Head said and they turned down a different street. He still did not intend to let the dome get too far away and after two blocks in their new direction, he turned to the left. This street contained two- and three-story wooden dwellings. Anyone passing on the sidewalk could see into the rooms and Mr. Head, glancing through one window, saw a woman lying on an iron bed, looking out, with a sheet pulled over her. Her knowing expression shook him. A fierce-looking boy on a bicycle came driving down out of nowhere and he had to jump to the side to keep from being hit. "It's nothing to them if they knock you down," he said. "You better keep closer to me."

They walked on for some time on streets like this before he remembered to turn again. The houses they were passing now were all unpainted and the wood in them looked rotten; the street between was narrower. Nelson saw a colored man. Then another. Then another. "Niggers live in these houses," he observed.

"Well come on and we'll go somewheres else," Mr. Head said. "We didn't come to look at niggers," and they turned down another street but they continued to see Negroes everywhere. Nelson's skin began to prickle and they stepped along at a faster pace in order to leave the neighborhood as soon as possible. There were colored men in their undershirts standing in the doors and colored women rocking on sagging porches. Colored children played in the gutters and stopped what they were doing to look at them. Before long they began to pass rows of stores with colored customers in them but they didn't pause at the entrances of these. Black eyes in black faces were watching them from every direction. "Yes," Mr. Head said, "this is where you were born—right here with all these niggers."

Nelson scowled. "I think you done got us lost," he said.

Mr. Head swung around sharply and looked for the dome. It was nowhere in sight. "I ain't got us lost either," he said. "You're just tired of walking."

"I ain't tired, I'm hungry," Nelson said. "Give me a biscuit."

They discovered then that they had lost the lunch.

"You were the one holding the sack," Nelson said. "I would have kepaholt of it."

"If you want to direct this trip, I'll go on by myself and leave you right here," Mr. Head said and was pleased to see the boy turn white. However, he realized they were lost and drifting farther every minute from the station. He was hungry himself and beginning to be thirsty and since they had been in the colored neighborhood, they had both begun to sweat. Nelson had on his shoes and he was unaccustomed to them. The concrete sidewalks were very hard. They both wanted to find a place to sit down but this was impossible and they kept on walking, the boy muttering under his breath, "First you lost the sack and then you lost the way," and Mr. Head growling from time to time, "Anybody wants to be from this nigger heaven can be from it!"

By now the sun was well forward in the sky. The odor of dinners cooking drifted out to them. The Negroes were all at their doors to see them pass. "Whyn't you ast one of these niggers the way?" Nelson said. "You got us lost."

"This is where you were born," Mr. Head said. "You can ast one yourself if you want to."

Nelson was afraid of the colored men and he didn't want to be laughed at by the colored children. Up ahead he saw a large colored woman leaning in a doorway that opened onto the sidewalk. Her hair stood straight out from her head for about four inches all around and she was resting on bare brown feet that turned pink at the sides. She had on a pink dress that showed her exact shape. As they came abreast of her, she lazily lifted one hand to her head and her fingers disappeared into her hair.

Nelson stopped. He felt his breath drawn up by the woman's dark eyes. "How do you get back to town?" he said in a voice that did not sound like his own.

After a minute she said, "You in town now," in a rich low tone that made Nelson feel as if a cool spray had been turned on him.

"How do you get back to the train?" he said in the same reed-like voice.

"You can catch you a car," she said.

He understood she was making fun of him but he was too paralyzed even to scowl. He stood drinking in every detail of her. His eyes traveled up from her great knees to her forehead and then made a triangular path from the glistening sweat on her neck down and across her tremendous bosom and over her bare arm back to where her fingers lay hidden in her hair. He suddenly wanted her to reach down and pick him up and draw him against her and then he wanted to feel her breath on his face. He wanted to look down and down into her eyes while she held him tighter and tighter. He had never had such a feeling before. He felt as if he were reeling down through a pitchblack tunnel.

"You can go a block down yonder and catch you a car take you to the railroad station, Sugarpie," she said.

Nelson would have collapsed at her feet if Mr. Head had not pulled him roughly away. "You act like you don't have any sense!" the old man growled.

They hurried down the street and Nelson did not look back at the woman. He pushed his hat sharply forward over his face which was already burning with shame. The sneering ghost he had seen in the train window and all the foreboding feelings he had on the way returned to him and he remembered that his ticket from the scale had said to beware of dark women and that his grandfather's had said he was upright and brave. He took hold of the old man's hand, a sign of dependence that he seldom showed.

They headed down the street toward the car tracks where a long yellow rattling trolley was coming. Mr. Head had never boarded a streetcar and he let that one pass. Nelson was silent. From time to time his mouth trembled slightly but his grandfather, occupied with his own problems, paid him no attention. They stood on the corner and neither looked at the Negroes who were passing, going about their business just as if they had been white, except that most of them stopped and eyed Mr. Head and Nelson. It occurred to Mr. Head that since the streetcar ran on tracks, they could simply follow the tracks. He gave Nelson a slight push and explained that they would follow the tracks on into the railroad station, walking, and they set off.

Presently to their great relief they began to see white people again and Nelson sat down on the sidewalk against the wall of a building. "I got to rest myself some," he said. "You lost the sack and the direction. You can just wait on me to rest myself."

"There's the tracks in front of us," Mr. Head said. "All we got to do is keep them in sight and you could have remembered the sack as good as me. This is where you were born. This is your old home town. This is your second trip. You ought to know how to do," and he squatted down and continued in this vein but the boy, easing his burning feet out of his shoes, did not answer.

"And standing there grinning like a chim-pan-zee while a nigger woman gives you directions. Great Gawd!" Mr. Head said.

"I never said I was nothing but born here," the boy said in a shaky voice. "I never said I would or wouldn't like it. I never said I wanted to come. I only said I was born here and I never had nothing to do with that. I want to go home. I never wanted to come in the first place. It was all your big idea. How you know you ain't following the tracks in the wrong direction?"

This last had occurred to Mr. Head too. "All these people are white," he said.

"We ain't passed here before," Nelson said. This was a neighborhood of brick buildings that might have been lived in or might not. A few empty automobiles were parked along the curb and there was an occasional passerby. The heat of the pavement came up through Nelson's thin suit. His eyelids began to droop, and after a few minutes his head tilted forward. His shoulders twitched once or twice and then he fell over on his side and lay sprawled in an exhausted fit of sleep.

Mr. Head watched him silently. He was very tired himself but they could not both sleep at the same time and he could not have slept anyway because he did not know where he was. In a few minutes Nelson would wake up, refreshed by his sleep and very cocky, and would begin complaining that he had lost the sack and the way. You'd have a mighty sorry time if I wasn't here, Mr. Head thought; and then another idea occurred to him. He looked at the sprawled figure for several minutes; presently he stood up. He justified what he was going to do on the grounds that it is sometimes necessary to teach a child a lesson he won't forget, particularly when the child is always reasserting his position with some new impudence. He walked without a sound to the corner about twenty feet away and sat down on a covered garbage can in the alley where he could look out and watch Nelson wake up alone.

The boy was dozing fitfully, half conscious of vague noises and black forms moving up from some dark part of him into the light. His face worked in his sleep and he had pulled his knees up under his chin. The sun shed a dull dry light on the narrow street; everything looked like exactly what it was. After a while

Mr. Head, hunched like an old monkey on the garbage can lid, decided that if Nelson didn't wake up soon, he would make a loud noise by bamming his foot against the can. He looked at his watch and discovered that it was two o'clock. Their train left at six and the possibility of missing it was too awful for him to think of. He kicked his foot backwards on the can and a hollow boom reverberated in the alley.

Nelson shot up onto his feet with a shout. He looked where his grandfather should have been and stared. He seemed to whirl several times and then, picking up his feet and throwing his head back, he dashed down the street like a wild maddened pony. Mr. Head jumped off the can and galloped after but the child was almost out of sight. He saw a streak of gray disappearing diagonally a block ahead. He ran as fast as he could, looking both ways down every intersection, but without sight of him again. Then as he passed the third intersection, completely winded, he saw about half a block down the street a scene that stopped him altogether. He crouched behind a trash box to watch and get his bearings.

Nelson was sitting with both legs spread out and by his side lay an elderly woman, screaming. Groceries were scattered about the sidewalk. A crowd of women had already gathered to see justice done and Mr. Head distinctly heard the old woman on the pavement shout, "You've broken my ankle and your daddy'll pay for it! Every nickel! Police! Police!" Several of the women were plucking at Nelson's shoulder but the boy seemed too dazed to get up.

Something forced Mr. Head from behind the trash box and forward, but only at a creeping pace. He had never in his life been accosted by a policeman. The women were milling around Nelson as if they might suddenly all dive on him at once and tear him to pieces, and the old woman continued to scream that her ankle was broken and to call for an officer. Mr. Head came on so slowly that he could have been taking a backward step after each forward one, but when he was about ten feet away, Nelson saw him and sprang. The child caught him around the hips and clung panting against him.

The women all turned on Mr. Head. The injured one sat up and shouted, "You sir! You'll pay every penny of my doctor's bill that your boy has caused. He's a juve-nile delinquent! Where is an officer? Somebody take this man's name and address!"

Mr. Head was trying to detach Nelson's fingers from the flesh in the back of his legs. The old man's head had lowered itself into his collar like a turtle's; his eyes were glazed with fear and caution.

"Your boy has broken my ankle!" the old woman shouted. "Police!"

Mr. Head sensed the approach of the policeman from behind. He stared straight ahead at the women who were massed in their fury like a solid wall to block his escape. "This is not my boy," he said. "I never seen him before."

He felt Nelson's fingers fall out of his flesh.

The women dropped back, staring at him with horror, as if they were so repulsed by a man who would deny his own image and likeness that they could not bear to lay hands on him. Mr. Head walked on, through a space they silently cleared, and left Nelson behind. Ahead of him he saw nothing but a hollow tunnel that had once been the street.

The boy remained standing where he was, his neck craned forward and his hands hanging by his sides. His hat was jammed on his head so that there were no longer any creases in it. The injured woman got up and shook her fist at him and the others gave him pitying looks, but he didn't notice any of them. There was no policeman in sight.

In a minute he began to move mechanically, making no effort to catch up with his grandfather but merely following at about twenty paces. They walked on for five blocks in this way. Mr. Head's shoulders were sagging and his neck hung forward at such an angle that it was not visible from behind. He was afraid to turn his head. Finally he cut a short hopeful glance over his shoulder. Twenty feet behind him, he saw two small eyes piercing into his back like pitchfork prongs.

The boy was not of a forgiving nature but this was the first time he had ever had anything to forgive. Mr. Head had never disgraced himself before. After two more blocks, he turned and called over his shoulder in a high desperately gay voice, "Let's us go get us a Co' Cola somewhere!"

Nelson, with a dignity he had never shown before, turned and stood with his back to his grandfather.

Mr. Head began to feel the depth of his denial. His face as they walked on became all hollows and bare ridges. He saw nothing they were passing but he perceived that they had lost the car tracks. There was no dome to be seen anywhere and the afternoon was advancing. He knew that if dark overtook them in the city, they would be beaten and robbed. The speed of God's justice was only what he expected for himself, but he could not stand to think that his sins would be visited upon Nelson and that even now, he was leading the boy to his doom.

They continued to walk on block after block through an endless section of small brick houses until Mr. Head almost fell over a water spigot sticking up about six inches off the edge of a grass plot. He had not had a drink of water since early morning but he felt he did not deserve it now. Then he thought that Nelson would be thirsty and they would both drink and be brought together. He squatted down and put his mouth to the nozzle and turned a cold stream of water into his throat. Then he called out in the high desperate voice, "Come on and getcher some water!"

This time the child stared through him for nearly sixty seconds. Mr. Head got up and walked on as if he had drunk poison. Nelson, though he had not had water since some he had drunk out of a paper cup on the train, passed by the spigot, disdaining to drink where his grandfather had. When Mr. Head realized this, he lost all hope. His face in the waning afternoon light looked ravaged and abandoned. He could feel the boy's steady hate, traveling at an even pace behind him and he knew that (if by some miracle they escaped being murdered in the city) it would continue just that way for the rest of his life. He knew that now he was wandering into a black strange place where nothing was like it had ever been before, a long old age without respect and an end that would be welcome because it would be the end.

As for Nelson, his mind had frozen around his grandfather's treachery as if he were trying to preserve it intact to present at the final judgment. He walked without looking to one side or the other, but every now and then his mouth would twitch and this was when he felt, from some remote place inside himself, a black mysterious form reach up as if it would melt his frozen vision in one hot grasp.

The sun dropped down behind a row of houses and hardly noticing, they passed into an elegant suburban section where mansions were set back from the road by lawns with birdbaths on them. Here everything was entirely deserted. For blocks they didn't pass even a dog. The big white houses were like partially submerged icebergs in the distance. There were no sidewalks, only drives, and these wound around and around in endless ridiculous circles. Nelson made no move to come nearer to Mr. Head. The old man felt that if he saw a sewer entrance he would drop down into it and let himself be carried away; and he could imagine the boy standing by, watching with only a slight interest, while he disappeared.

A loud bark jarred him to attention and he looked up to see a fat man approaching with two bulldogs. He waved both arms like someone shipwrecked on a desert island. "I'm lost!" he called. "I'm lost and can't find my way and me and this boy have got to catch this train and I can't find the station. Oh Gawd I'm lost! Oh hep me Gawd I'm lost!"

The man, who was bald-headed and had on golf knickers, asked him what train he was trying to catch and Mr. Head began to get out his tickets, trembling so violently he could hardly hold them. Nelson had come up to within fifteen feet and stood watching.

"Well," the fat man said, giving him back the tickets, "you won't have time to get back to town to make this but you can catch it at the suburb stop. That's three blocks from here," and he began explaining how to get there.

Mr. Head stared as if he were slowly returning from the dead and when the man had finished and gone off with the dogs jumping at his heels, he turned to Nelson and said breathlessly, "We're going to get home!"

The child was standing about ten feet away, his face bloodless under the gray hat. His eyes were triumphantly cold. There was no light in them, no feeling, no interest. He was merely there, a small figure, waiting. Home was nothing to him.

Mr. Head turned slowly. He felt he knew now what time would be like without seasons and what heat would be like without light and what man would be like without salvation. He didn't care if he never made the train and if it had not been for what suddenly caught his attention, like a cry out of the gathering dusk, he might have forgotten there was a station to go to.

He had not walked five hundred yards down the road when he saw, within reach of him, the plaster figure of a Negro sitting bent over on a low yellow brick fence that curved around a wide lawn. The Negro was about Nelson's size and he was pitched forward at an unsteady angle because the putty that held him to the wall had cracked. One of his eyes was entirely white and he held a piece of brown watermelon.

Mr. Head stood looking at him silently until Nelson stopped at a little distance. Then as the two of them stood there, Mr. Head breathed, "An artificial nigger!"

It was not possible to tell if the artificial Negro were meant to be young or old; he looked too miserable to be either. He was meant to look happy because his mouth was stretched up at the corners but the chipped eye and the angle he was cocked at gave him a wild look of misery instead.

"An artificial nigger!" Nelson repeated in Mr. Head's exact tone.

The two of them stood there with their necks forward at almost the same angle and their shoulders curved in almost exactly the same way and their hands trembling identically in their pockets. Mr. Head looked like an ancient child and Nelson like a miniature old man. They stood gazing at the artificial Negro as if they were faced with some great mystery, some monument to another's victory that brought them together in their common defeat. They could both feel it dissolving their differences like an action of mercy. Mr. Head had never known before what mercy felt like because he had been too good to deserve any, but he felt he knew now. He looked at Nelson and understood that he must say something to the child to show that he was still wise and in the look the boy returned he saw a hungry need for that assurance. Nelson's eyes seemed to implore him to explain once and for all the mystery of existence.

Mr. Head opened his lips to make a lofty statement and heard himself say, "They ain't got enough real ones here. They got to have an artificial one."

After a second, the boy nodded with a strange shivering about his mouth, and said, "Let's go home before we get ourselves lost again."

Their train glided into the suburb stop just as they reached the station and they boarded it together, and ten minutes before it was due to arrive at the junction, they went to the door and stood ready to jump off if it did not stop; but it did, just as the moon, restored to its full splendor, sprang from a cloud and flooded the clearing with light. As they stepped off, the sage grass was shivering gently in shades of silver and the clinkers under their feet glittered with a fresh black light. The treetops, fencing the junction like the protecting walls of a garden, were darker than the sky which was hung with gigantic white clouds illuminated like lanterns.

Mr. Head stood very still and felt the action of mercy touch him again but this time he knew that there were no words in the world that could name it. He understood that it grew out of agony, which is not denied to any man and which is given in strange ways to children. He understood it was all a man could carry into death to give his Maker and he suddenly burned with shame that he had so little of it to take with him. He stood appalled, judging himself with the thoroughness of God, while the action of mercy covered his pride like a flame and consumed it. He had never thought himself a great sinner before but he saw now that his true depravity had been hidden from him lest it cause him despair. He realized that he was forgiven for sins from the beginning of time, when he had conceived in his own heart the sin of Adam, until the present, when he had denied poor Nelson. He saw that no sin was too monstrous for him to claim as his own, and since God loved in proportion as He forgave, he felt ready at that instant to enter Paradise.

Nelson, composing his expression under the shadow of his hat brim, watched him with a mixture of fatigue and suspicion, but as the train glided past them and disappeared like a frightened serpent into the woods, even his face lightened and he muttered, "I'm glad I've went once, but I'll never go back again!"

QUESTIONS

1. How early in the story are you aware of the narrator's tone?
2. What has made Mr. Head devise this moral lesson for his grandson? What place do Negroes occupy in Mr. Head's morality?
3. Why does Mr. Head feel as he does about the city?
4. Do you feel sympathy for Mr. Head at any point? For Nelson? Explain.
5. What do Mr. Head and Nelson see in the artificial Negro?

Raymond Carver (1939–1988)

CATHEDRAL

This blind man, an old friend of my wife's, he was on his way to spend the night. His wife had died. So he was visiting the dead wife's relatives in Connecticut. He called my wife from his in-laws'. Arrangements were made. He would come by train, a five-hour trip, and my wife would meet him at the station. She hadn't seen him since she worked for him one summer in Seattle ten years ago. But she and the blind man had kept in touch. They made tapes and mailed them back and forth. I wasn't enthusiastic about his visit. He was no one I knew. And his being blind bothered me. My idea of blindness came from the movies. In the movies, the blind moved slowly and never laughed. Sometimes they were led by seeing-eye dogs. A blind man in my house was not something I looked forward to.

That summer in Seattle she had needed a job. She didn't have any money. The man she was going to marry at the end of the summer was in officers' training school. He didn't have any money, either. But she was in love with the guy, and he was in love with her, etc. She'd seen something in the paper: HELP WANTED— *Reading to Blind Man,* and a telephone number. She phoned and went over, was hired on the spot. She'd worked with this blind man all summer. She read stuff to him, case studies, reports, that sort of thing. She helped him organize his little office in the county social-service department. They'd become good friends, my wife and the blind man. How do I know these things? She told me. And she told me something else. On her last day in the office, the blind man asked if he could touch her face. She agreed to this. She told me he touched his fingers to every part of her face, her nose—even her neck! She never forgot it. She even tried to write a poem about it. She was always trying to write a poem. She wrote a poem or two every year, usually after something really important had happened to her.

When we first started going out together, she showed me the poem. In the poem, she recalled his fingers and the way they had moved around over her face.

In the poem, she talked about what she had felt at the time, about what went through her mind when the blind man touched her nose and lips. I can remember I didn't think much of the poem. Of course, I didn't tell her that. Maybe I just don't understand poetry. I admit it's not the first thing I reach for when I pick up something to read.

Anyway, this man who'd first enjoyed her favors, the officer-to-be, he'd been her childhood sweetheart. So okay. I'm saying that at the end of the summer she let the blind man run his hands over her face, said goodbye to him, married her childhood etc., who was now a commissioned officer, and she moved away from Seattle. But they'd kept in touch, she and the blind man. She made the first contact after a year or so. She called him up one night from an Air Force base in Alabama. She wanted to talk. They talked. He asked her to send him a tape and tell him about her life. She did this. She sent the tape. On the tape, she told the blind man about her husband and about their life together in the military. She told the blind man she loved her husband but she didn't like it where they lived and she didn't like it that he was a part of the military-industrial thing. She told the blind man she'd written a poem and he was in it. She told him that she was writing a poem about what it was like to be an Air Force officer's wife. The poem wasn't finished yet. She was still writing it. The blind man made a tape. He sent her the tape. She made a tape. This went on for years. My wife's officer was posted to one base and then another. She sent tapes from Moody AFB, McGuire, Mc-Connell, and finally Travis, near Sacramento, where one night she got to feeling lonely and cut off from people she kept losing in that moving-around life. She got to feeling she couldn't go it another step. She went in and swallowed all the pills and capsules in the medicine chest and washed them down with a bottle of gin. Then she got into a hot bath and passed out.

But instead of dying, she got sick. She threw up. Her officer—why should he have a name? he was the childhood sweetheart, and what more does he want?—came home from somewhere, found her, and called the ambulance. In time, she put it all on a tape and sent the tape to the blind man. Over the years, she put all kinds of stuff on tapes and sent the tapes off lickety-split. Next to writing a poem every year, I think it was her chief means of recreation. On one tape, she told the blind man she'd decided to live away from her officer for a time. On another tape, she told him about her divorce. She and I began going out, and of course she told her blind man about it. She told him everything, or so it seemed to me. Once she asked me if I'd like to hear the latest tape from the blind man. This was a year ago. I was on the tape, she said. So I said okay, I'd listen to it. I got us drinks and we settled down in the living room. We made ready to listen. First she inserted the tape into the player and adjusted a couple of dials. Then she pushed a lever. The tape squeaked and someone began to talk in this loud voice. She lowered the volume. After a few minutes of harmless chitchat, I heard my own name in the mouth of this stranger, this blind man I didn't even know! And then this: "From all you've said about him, I can only conclude—" But we were interrupted, a knock at the door, something, and we didn't ever get back to the tape. Maybe it was just as well. I'd heard all I wanted to.

Now this same blind man was coming to sleep in my house.

"Maybe I could take him bowling," I said to my wife. She was at the draining board doing scalloped potatoes. She put down the knife she was using and turned around.

"If you love me," she said, "you can do this for me. If you don't love me, okay. But if you had a friend, any friend, and the friend came to visit, I'd make him feel comfortable." She wiped her hands with the dish towel.

"I don't have any blind friends," I said.

"You don't have *any* friends," she said. "Period. Besides," she said, "goddamn it, his wife's just died! Don't you understand that? The man's lost his wife!"

I didn't answer. She'd told me a little about the blind man's wife. Her name was Beulah. Beulah! That's a name for a colored woman.

"Was his wife a Negro?" I asked.

"Are you crazy?" my wife said. "Have you just flipped or something?" She picked up a potato. I saw it hit the floor, then roll under the stove. "What's wrong with you?" she said. "Are you drunk?"

"I'm just asking," I said.

Right then my wife filled me in with more detail than I cared to know. I made a drink and sat at the kitchen table to listen. Pieces of the story began to fall into place.

Beulah had gone to work for the blind man the summer after my wife had stopped working for him. Pretty soon Beulah and the blind man had themselves a church wedding. It was a little wedding—who'd want to go to such a wedding in the first place?—just the two of them, plus the minister and the minister's wife. But it was a church wedding just the same. It was what Beulah had wanted, he'd said. But even then Beulah must have been carrying the cancer in her glands. After they had been inseparable for eight years—my wife's word, *inseparable*—Beulah's health went into a rapid decline. She died in a Seattle hospital room, the blind man sitting beside the bed and holding on to her hand. They'd married, lived and worked together, slept together—had sex, sure—and then the blind man had to bury her. All this without his having ever seen what the goddamned woman looked like. It was beyond my understanding. Hearing this, I felt sorry for the blind man for a little bit. And then I found myself thinking what a pitiful life this woman must have led. Imagine a woman who could never see herself as she was seen in the eyes of her loved one. A woman who could go on day after day and never receive the smallest compliment from her beloved. A woman whose husband could never read the expression on her face, be it misery or something better. Someone who could wear makeup or not—what difference to him? She could, if she wanted, wear green eye-shadow around one eye, a straight pin in her nostril, yellow slacks and purple shoes, no matter. And then to slip off into death, the blind man's hand on her hand, his blind eyes streaming tears—I'm imagining now—her last thought maybe this: that he never even knew what she looked like, and she on an express to the grave. Robert was left with a small insurance policy and half of a twenty-peso Mexican coin. The other half of the coin went into the box with her. Pathetic.

So when the time rolled around, my wife went to the depot to pick him up. With nothing to do but wait—sure, I blamed him for that—I was having a drink and watching the TV when I heard the car pull into the drive. I got up from the sofa with my drink and went to the window to have a look.

I saw my wife laughing as she parked the car. I saw her get out of the car and shut the door. She was still wearing a smile. Just amazing. She went around to the other side of the car to where the blind man was already starting to get out. This blind man, feature this, he was wearing a full beard! A beard on a blind man! Too much, I say. The blind man reached into the back seat and dragged out a suitcase. My wife took his arm, shut the car door, and, talking all the way, moved him down the drive and then up the steps to the front porch. I turned off the TV. I finished my drink, rinsed the glass, dried my hands. Then I went to the door.

My wife said, "I want you to meet Robert. Robert, this is my husband. I've told you all about him." She was beaming. She had this blind man by his coat sleeve.

The blind man let go of his suitcase and up came his hand.

I took it. He squeezed hard, held my hand, and then he let it go.

"I feel like we've already met," he boomed.

"Likewise," I said. I didn't know what else to say. Then I said, "Welcome. I've heard a lot about you." We began to move then, a little group, from the porch into the living room, my wife guiding him by the arm. The blind man was carrying his suitcase in his other hand. My wife said things like, "To your left here, Robert. That's right. Now watch it, there's a chair. That's it. Sit down right here. This is the sofa. We just bought this sofa two weeks ago."

I started to say something about the old sofa. I'd liked that old sofa. But I didn't say anything. Then I wanted to say something else, small-talk, about the scenic ride along the Hudson. How going *to* New York, you should sit on the righthand side of the train, and coming *from* New York, the left-hand side.

"Did you have a good train ride?" I said. "Which side of the train did you sit on, by the way?"

"What a question, which side!" my wife said. "What's it matter which side?" she said.

"I just asked," I said.

"Right side," the blind man said. "I hadn't been on a train in nearly forty years. Not since I was a kid. With my folks. That's been a long time. I'd nearly forgotten the sensation. I have winter in my beard now," he said. "So I've been told, anyway. Do I look distinguished, my dear?" the blind man said to my wife.

"You look distinguished, Robert," she said. "Robert," she said. "Robert, it's just so good to see you."

My wife finally took her eyes off the blind man and looked at me. I had the feeling she didn't like what she saw. I shrugged.

I've never met, or personally known, anyone who was blind. This blind man was late forties, a heavy-set, balding man with stooped shoulders, as if he carried a great weight there. He wore brown slacks, brown shoes, a light-brown shirt, a tie, a sports coat. Spiffy. He also had this full beard. But he didn't use a cane and he didn't wear dark glasses. I'd always thought dark glasses were a must for the blind. Fact was, I wished he had a pair. At first glance, his eyes looked like anyone else's eyes. But if you looked close, there was something different about them. Too much white in the iris, for one thing, and the pupils seemed to move around in the sockets without his knowing it or being able to stop it. Creepy. As I stared at his face, I saw the left pupil turn in toward his nose while the other made an effort to keep in one place. But it was only an effort, for that eye was on the roam without his knowing it or wanting it to be.

I said, "Let me get you a drink. What's your pleasure? We have a little of everything. It's one of our pastimes."

"Bub, I'm a Scotch man myself," he said fast enough in this big voice.

"Right," I said. Bub! "Sure you are. I knew it."

He let his fingers touch his suitcase, which was sitting alongside the sofa. He was taking his bearings. I didn't blame him for that.

"I'll move that up to your room," my wife said.

"No, that's fine," the blind man said loudly. "It can go up when I go up."

"A little water with the Scotch?" I said.

"Very little," he said.

"I knew it," I said.

He said, "Just a tad. The Irish actor, Barry Fitzgerald? I'm like that fellow. When I drink water, Fitzgerald said, I drink water. When I drink whiskey, I drink whiskey." My wife laughed. The blind man brought his hand up under his beard. He lifted his beard slowly and let it drop.

I did the drinks, three big glasses of Scotch with a splash of water in each. Then we made ourselves comfortable and talked about Robert's travels. First the long flight from the West Coast to Connecticut, we covered that. Then from Connecticut up here by train. We had another drink concerning that leg of the trip.

I remembered having read somewhere that the blind didn't smoke because, as speculation had it, they couldn't see the smoke they exhaled. I thought I knew that much and that much only about blind people. But this blind man smoked his cigarette down to the nubbin and then lit another one. This blind man filled his ashtray and my wife emptied it.

When we sat down at the table for dinner, we had another drink. My wife heaped Robert's plate with cube steak, scalloped potatoes, green beans. I buttered him up two slices of bread. I said, "Here's bread and butter for you." I swallowed some of my drink. "Now let us pray," I said, and the blind man lowered his head. My wife looked at me, her mouth agape. "Pray the phone won't ring and the food doesn't get cold," I said.

We dug in. We ate everything there was to eat on the table. We ate like there was no tomorrow. We didn't talk. We ate. We scarfed. We grazed that table. We were into serious eating. The blind man had right away located his foods, he knew just where everything was on his plate. I watched with admiration as he used his knife and fork on the meat. He'd cut two pieces of meat, fork the meat into his mouth, and then go all out for the scalloped potatoes, the beans next, and then he'd tear off a hunk of buttered bread and eat that. He'd follow this up with a big drink of milk. It didn't seem to bother him to use his fingers once in a while, either.

We finished everything, including half a strawberry pie. For a few moments, we sat as if stunned. Sweat beaded on our faces. Finally, we got up from the table and left the dirty plates. We didn't look back. We took ourselves into the living room and sank into our places again. Robert and my wife sat on the sofa. I took the big chair. We had us two or three more drinks while they talked about the major things that had come to pass for them in the past ten years. For the most part, I just listened. Now and then I joined in. I didn't want him to think I'd left the room, and I didn't want her to think I was feeling left out. They talked of things that had happened to them—to them!—these past ten years. I waited in vain to hear my name on my wife's sweet lips: "And then my dear husband came into my life"—something like that. But I heard nothing of the sort. More talk of Robert. Robert had done a little of everything, it seemed, a regular blind jack-of-all-trades. But most recently he and his wife had had an Amway distributorship, from which, I gathered, they'd earned their living, such as it was. The blind man was also a ham radio operator. He talked in his loud voice about conversations he'd had with fellow operators in Guam, in the Philippines, in Alaska, and even in Tahiti. He said he'd have a lot of friends there if he ever wanted to go visit those places. From time to time, he'd turn his blind face toward me, put his hand under his beard, ask me something. How long had I been in my present position? (Three years.) Did I like my work? (I didn't.) Was I going to stay with it? (What were the options?) Finally, when I thought he was beginning to run down, I got up and turned on the TV.

My wife looked at me with irritation. She was heading toward a boil. Then she looked at the blind man and said, "Robert, do you have a TV?"

The blind man said, "My dear, I have two TVs. I have a color set and a black-and-white thing, an old relic. It's funny, but if I turn the TV on, and I'm always turning it on, I turn on the color set. It's funny, don't you think?"

I didn't know what to say to that. I had absolutely nothing to say to that. No opinion. So I watched the news program and tried to listen to what the announcer was saying.

"This is a color TV," the blind man said. "Don't ask me how, but I can tell."

"We traded up a while ago," I said.

The blind man had another taste of his drink. He lifted his beard, sniffed it, and let it fall. He leaned forward on the sofa. He positioned his ashtray on the coffee table, then put the lighter to his cigarette. He leaned back on the sofa and crossed his legs at the ankles.

My wife covered her mouth, and then she yawned. She stretched. She said, "I think I'll go upstairs and put on my robe. I think I'll change into something else. Robert, you make yourself comfortable," she said.

"I'm comfortable," the blind man said.

"I want you to feel comfortable in this house," she said.

"I am comfortable," the blind man said.

After she'd left the room, he and I listened to the weather report and then to the sports roundup. By that time, she'd been gone so long I didn't know if she was going to come back. I thought she might have gone to bed. I wished she'd come back downstairs. I didn't want to be left alone with a blind man. I asked him if he wanted another drink, and he said sure. Then I asked if he wanted to smoke some dope with me. I said I'd just rolled a number. I hadn't, but I planned to do so in about two shakes.

"I'll try some with you," he said.

"Damn right," I said. "That's the stuff."

I got our drinks and sat down on the sofa with him. Then I rolled us two fat numbers. I lit one and passed it. I brought it to his fingers. He took it and inhaled.

"Hold it as long as you can," I said. I could tell he didn't know the first thing.

My wife came back downstairs wearing her pink robe and her pink slippers.

"What do I smell?" she said.

"We thought we'd have us some cannabis," I said.

My wife gave me a savage look. Then she looked at the blind man and said, "Robert, I didn't know you smoked."

He said, "I do now, my dear. There's a first time for everything. But I don't feel anything yet."

"This stuff is pretty mellow," I said. "This stuff is mild. It's dope you can reason with," I said. "It doesn't mess you up."

"Not much it doesn't, bub," he said, and laughed.

My wife sat on the sofa between the blind man and me. I passed her the number. She took it and toked and then passed it back to me. "Which way is this going?" she said. Then she said, "I shouldn't be smoking this. I can hardly keep my eyes open as it is. That dinner did me in. I shouldn't have eaten so much."

"It was the strawberry pie," the blind man said. "That's what did it," he said, and he laughed his big laugh. Then he shook his head.

"There's more strawberry pie," I said.

"Do you want some more, Robert?" my wife said.

"Maybe in a little while," he said.

We gave our attention to the TV. My wife yawned again. She said, "Your bed is made up when you feel like going to bed, Robert. I know you must have had a long day. When you're ready to go to bed, say so." She pulled his arm. "Robert?"

He came to and said, "I've had a real nice time. This beats tapes, doesn't it?"

I said, "Coming at you," and I put the number between his fingers. He inhaled, held the smoke, and then let it go. It was like he'd been doing it since he was nine years old.

"Thanks, bub," he said. "But I think this is all for me. I think I'm beginning to feel it," he said. He held the burning roach out for my wife.

"Same here," she said. "Ditto. Me, too." She took the roach and passed it to me. "I may just sit here for a while between you two guys with my eyes closed.

But don't let me bother you, okay? Either one of you. If it bothers you, say so. Otherwise, I may just sit here with my eyes closed until you're ready to go to bed," she said. "Your bed's made up, Robert, when you're ready. It's right next to our room at the top of the stairs. We'll show you up when you're ready. You wake me up now, you guys, if I fall asleep." She said that and then she closed her eyes and went to sleep.

The news program ended. I got up and changed the channel. I sat back down on the sofa. I wished my wife hadn't pooped out. Her head lay across the back of the sofa, her mouth open. She'd turned so that her robe had slipped away from her legs, exposing a juicy thigh. I reached to draw her robe back over her, and it was then that I glanced at the blind man. What the hell! I flipped the robe open again.

"You say when you want some strawberry pie," I said.

"I will," he said.

I said, "Are you tired? Do you want me to take you up to your bed? Are you ready to hit the hay?"

"Not yet," he said. "No, I'll stay up with you, bub. If that's all right. I'll stay up until you're ready to turn in. We haven't had a chance to talk. Know what I mean? I feel like me and her monopolized the evening." He lifted his beard and he let it fall. He picked up his cigarettes and his lighter.

"That's all right," I said. Then I said, "I'm glad for the company."

And I guess I was. Every night I smoked dope and stayed up as long as I could before I fell asleep. My wife and I hardly ever went to bed at the same time. When I did go to sleep, I had these dreams. Sometimes I'd wake up from one of them, my heart going crazy.

Something about the church and the Middle Ages was on the TV. Not your run-of-the-mill TV fare. I wanted to watch something else. I turned to the other channels. But there was nothing on them, either. So I turned back to the first channel and apologized.

"Bub, it's all right," the blind man said. "It's fine with me. Whatever you want to watch is okay. I'm always learning something. Learning never ends. It won't hurt me to learn something tonight. I got ears," he said.

We didn't say anything for a time. He was leaning forward with his head turned at me, his right ear aimed in the direction of the set. Very disconcerting. Now and then his eyelids drooped and then they snapped open again. Now and then he put his fingers into his beard and tugged, like he was thinking about something he was hearing on the television.

On the screen, a group of men wearing cowls was being set upon and tormented by men dressed in skeleton costumes and men dressed as devils. The men dressed as devils wore devil masks, horns, and long tails. This pageant was part of a procession. The Englishman who was narrating the thing said it took place in Spain once a year. I tried to explain to the blind man what was happening.

"Skeletons," he said. "I know about skeletons," he said, and he nodded.

The TV showed this one cathedral. Then there was a long, slow look at another one. Finally, the picture switched to the famous one in Paris, with its flying buttresses and its spires reaching up to the clouds. The camera pulled away to show the whole of the cathedral rising above the skyline.

There were times when the Englishman who was telling the thing would shut up, would simply let the camera move around over the cathedrals. Or else the camera would tour the countryside, men in fields walking behind oxen. I waited as long as I could. Then I felt I had to say something. I said, "They're showing the outside of this cathedral now. Gargoyles. Little statues carved to look like monsters. Now I guess they're in Italy. Yeah, they're in Italy. There's paintings on the walls of this one church."

"Are those fresco paintings, bub?" he asked, and he sipped from his drink.

I reached for my glass. But it was empty. I tried to remember what I could remember. "You're asking me are those frescoes?" I said. "That's a good question. I don't know."

The camera moved to a cathedral outside Lisbon. The differences in the Portuguese cathedral compared with the French and Italian were not that great. But they were there. Mostly the interior stuff. Then something occurred to me, and I said, "Something has occurred to me. Do you have any idea what a cathedral is? What they look like, that is? Do you follow me? If somebody says cathedral to you, do you have any notion what they're talking about? Do you know the difference between that and a Baptist church, say?"

He let the smoke dribble from his mouth. "I know they took hundreds of workers fifty or a hundred years to build," he said. "I just heard the man say that, of course. I know generations of the same families worked on a cathedral. I heard him say that, too. The men who began their life's work on them, they never lived to see the completion of their work. In that wise, bub, they're no different from the rest of us, right?" He laughed. Then his eyelids drooped again. His head nodded. He seemed to be snoozing. Maybe he was imagining himself in Portugal. The TV was showing another cathedral now. This one was in Germany. The Englishman's voice droned on. "Cathedrals," the blind man said. He sat up and rolled his head back and forth. "If you want the truth, bub, that's about all I know. What I just said. What I heard him say. But maybe you could describe one to me? I wish you'd do it. I'd like that. If you want to know, I really don't have a good idea."

I stared hard at the shot of the cathedral on the TV. How could I even begin to describe it? But say my life depended on it. Say my life was being threatened by an insane guy who said I had to do it or else.

I stared some more at the cathedral before the picture flipped off into the countryside. There was no use. I turned to the blind man and said, "To begin with, they're very tall." I was looking around the room for clues. "They reach way up. Up and up. Toward the sky. They're so big, some of them, they have to have these supports. To help hold them up, so to speak. These supports are called buttresses. They remind me of viaducts, for some reason. But maybe you don't know viaducts, either? Sometimes the cathedrals have devils and such carved into the front. Sometimes lords and ladies. Don't ask me why this is," I said.

He was nodding. The whole upper part of his body seemed to be moving back and forth.

"I'm not doing so good, am I?" I said.

He stopped nodding and leaned forward on the edge of the sofa. As he listened to me, he was running his fingers thorough his beard. I wasn't getting through to him, I could see that. But he waited for me to go on just the same. He nodded, like he was trying to encourage me. I tried to think what else to say. "They're really big," I said. "They're massive. They're built of stone. Marble, too, sometimes. In those olden days, when they built cathedrals, men wanted to be close to God. In those olden days, God was an important part of everyone's life. You could tell this from their cathedral-building. I'm sorry," I said, "but it looks like that's the best I can do for you. I'm just no good at it."

"That's all right, bub," the blind man said. "Hey, listen. I hope you don't mind my asking you. Can I ask you something? Let me ask you a simple question, yes or no. I'm just curious and there's no offense. You're my host. But let me ask if you are in any way religious? You don't mind my asking?"

I shook my head. He couldn't see that, though. A wink is the same as a nod to a blind man. "I guess I don't believe in it. In anything. Sometimes it's hard. You know what I'm saying?"

"Sure, I do," he said.

"Right," I said.

The Englishman was still holding forth. My wife sighed in her sleep. She drew a long breath and went on with her sleeping.

"You'll have to forgive me" I said. "But I can't tell you what a cathedral looks like. It just isn't in me to do it. I can't do any more than I've done."

The blind man sat very still, his head down, as he listened to me.

I said, "The truth is, cathedrals don't mean anything special to me. Nothing. Cathedrals. They're something to look at on late-night TV. That's all they are."

It was then that the blind man cleared his throat. He brought something up. He took a handkerchief from his back pocket. Then he said, "I get it, bub. It's okay. It happens. Don't worry about it," he said. "Hey, listen to me. Will you do me a favor? I got an idea. Why don't you find us some heavy paper? And a pen. We'll do something. We'll draw one together. Get us a pen and some heavy paper. Go on, bub, get the stuff," he said.

So I went upstairs. My legs felt like they didn't have any strength in them. They felt like they did after I'd done some running. In my wife's room, I looked around. I found some ballpoints in a little basket on her table. And then I tried to think where to look for the kind of paper he was talking about.

Downstairs, in the kitchen, I found a shopping bag with onion skins in the bottom of the bag. I emptied the bag and shook it. I brought it into the living room and sat down with it near his legs. I moved some things, smoothed the wrinkles from the bag, spread it out on the coffee table.

The blind man got down from the sofa and sat next to me on the carpet.

He ran his fingers over the paper. He went up and down the sides of the paper. The edges, even the edges. He fingered the corners.

"All right," he said. "All right, let's do her."

He found my hand, the hand with the pen. He closed his hand over my hand. "Go ahead, bub, draw," he said. "Draw. You'll see. I'll follow along with you. It'll be okay. Just begin now like I'm telling you. You'll see. Draw," the blind man said.

So I began. First I drew a box that looked like a house. It could have been the house I lived in. Then I put a roof on it. At either end of the roof, I drew spires. Crazy.

"Swell," he said. "Terrific. You're doing fine," he said. "Never thought anything like this could happen in your lifetime, did you, bub? Well, it's a strange life, we all know that. Go on now. Keep it up."

I put in windows with arches. I drew flying buttresses. I hung great doors. I couldn't stop. The TV station went off the air. I put down the pen and closed and opened my fingers. The blind man felt around over the paper. He moved the tips of his fingers over the paper, all over what I had drawn, and he nodded.

"Doing fine," the blind man said.

I took up the pen again, and he found my hand. I kept at it. I'm no artist. But I kept drawing just the same.

My wife opened up her eyes and gazed at us. She sat up on the sofa, her robe hanging open. She said, "What are you doing? Tell me, I want to know."

I didn't answer her.

The blind man said, "We're drawing a cathedral. Me and him are working on it. Press hard," he said to me. "That's right. That's good," he said. "Sure. You got it, bub. I can tell. You didn't think you could. But you can, can't you? You're cooking with gas now. You know what I'm saying? We're going to really have us something here in a minute. How's the old arm?" he said. "Put some people in there now. What's a cathedral without people?"

My wife said, "What's going on? Robert, what are you doing? What's going on?"

"It's all right," he said to her. "Close your eyes now," the blind man said to me.

I did it. I closed them just like he said.

"Are they closed?" he said. "Don't fudge."

"They're closed," I said.

"Keep them that way," he said. He said, "Don't stop now. Draw."

So we kept on with it. His fingers rode my fingers as my hand went over the paper. It was like nothing else in my life up to now.

Then he said, "I think that's it. I think you got it," he said. "Take a look. What do you think?"

But I had my eyes closed. I thought I'd keep them that way for a little longer. I thought it was something I ought to do.

"Well?" he said. "Are you looking?"

My eyes were still closed. I was in my house. I knew that. But I didn't feel like I was inside anything.

"It's really something," I said.

Alice Walker (b. 1944)
EVERYDAY USE

for your grandmama

I will wait for her in the yard that Maggie and I made so clean and wavy yesterday afternoon. A yard like this is more comfortable than most people know. It is not just a yard. It is like an extended living room. When the hard clay is swept clean as a floor and the fine sand around the edges lined with tiny, irregular grooves, anyone can come and sit and look up into the elm tree and wait for the breezes that never come inside the house.

Maggie will be nervous until after her sister goes: she will stand hopelessly in corners, homely and ashamed of the burn scars down her arms and legs, eying her sister with a mixture of envy and awe. She thinks her sister has held life always in the palm of one hand, that "no" is a word the world never learned to say to her.

You've no doubt seen those TV shows where the child who has "made it" is confronted, as a surprise, by her own mother and father, tottering in weakly from backstage. (A pleasant surprise, of course: What would they do if parent and child came on the show only to curse out and insult each other?) On TV mother and child embrace and smile into each other's faces. Sometimes the mother and father weep, the child wraps them in her arms and leans across the table to tell how she would not have made it without their help. I have seen these programs.

Sometimes I dream a dream in which Dee and I are suddenly brought together on a TV program of this sort. Out of a dark and soft-seated limousine I am ushered into a bright room filled with many people. There I meet a smiling, gray, sporty man like Johnny Carson who shakes my hand and tells me what a fine girl I have. Then we are on the stage and Dee is embracing me with tears in her eyes. She pins on my dress a large orchid, even though she has told me once that she thinks orchids are tacky flowers.

In real life I am a large, big-boned woman with rough, man-working hands. In the winter I wear flannel nightgowns to bed and overalls during the day. I can kill and clean a hog as mercilessly as a man. My fat keeps me hot in zero weather. I can work outside all day, breaking ice to get water for washing; I can eat pork liver cooked over the open fire minutes after it comes steaming from the hog. One winter I knocked a bull calf straight in the brain between the eyes with a sledge hammer and had the meat hung up to chill before nightfall. But of course all this does not show on television. I am the way my daughter would want me to be: a hundred pounds lighter, my skin like an uncooked barley pancake. My hair glistens in the hot bright lights. Johnny Carson has much to do to keep up with my quick and witty tongue.

But that is a mistake. I know even before I wake up. Who ever knew a Johnson with a quick tongue? Who can even imagine me looking a strange white man in the eye? It seems to me I have talked to them always with one foot raised in flight, with my head turned in whichever way is farthest from them. Dee, though. She would always look anyone in the eye. Hesitation was no part of her nature.

"How do I look, Mama?" Maggie says, showing just enough of her thin body enveloped in pink skirt and red blouse for me to know she's there, almost hidden by the door.

"Come out into the yard," I say.

Have you ever seen a lame animal, perhaps a dog run over by some careless person rich enough to own a car, sidle up to someone who is ignorant enough to be kind to him? That is the way my Maggie walks. She has been like this, chin on chest, eyes on ground, feet in shuffle, ever since the fire that burned the other house to the ground.

Dee is lighter than Maggie, with nicer hair and a fuller figure. She's a woman now, though sometimes I forget. How long ago was it that the other house burned? Ten, twelve years? Sometimes I can still hear the flames and feel Maggie's arms sticking to me, her hair smoking and her dress falling off her in little black papery flakes. Her eyes seemed stretched open, blazed open by the flames reflected in them. And Dee. I see her standing off under the sweet gum tree she used to dig gum out of; a look of concentration on her face as she watched the last dingy gray board of the house fall in toward the red-hot brick chimney. Why don't you do a dance around the ashes? I'd wanted to ask her. She had hated the house that much.

I used to think she hated Maggie, too. But that was before we raised the money, the church and me, to send her to Augusta to school. She used to read to us without pity; forcing words, lies, other folks' habits, whole lives upon us two, sitting trapped and ignorant underneath her voice. She washed us in a river of make-be-lieve, burned us with a lot of knowledge we didn't necessarily need to know. Pressed us to her with the serious way she read, to shove us away at just the moment, like dimwits, we seemed about to understand.

Dee wanted nice things. A yellow organdy dress to wear to her graduation from high school; black pumps to match a green suit she'd made from an old suit somebody gave me. She was determined to stare down any disaster in her efforts. Her eyelids would not flicker for minutes at a time. Often I fought off the temptation to shake her. At sixteen she had a style of her own: and knew what style was.

I never had an education myself. After second grade the school was closed down. Don't ask my why: in 1927 colored asked fewer questions than they do now. Sometimes Maggie reads to me. She stumbles along good-naturedly but can't see well. She knows she is not bright. Like good looks and money, quickness passed her by. She will marry John Thomas (who has mossy teeth in an earnest face) and then I'll be free to sit here and I guess just sing church songs to myself. Although I never was a good singer. Never could carry a tune. I was always better at a man's job. I used to love to milk till I was hooked in the side in '49. Cows are soothing and slow and don't bother you, unless you try to milk them the wrong way.

I have deliberately turned my back on the house. It is three rooms, just like the one that burned, except the roof is tin; they don't make shingle roofs any more. There are no real windows, just some holes cut in the sides, like the portholes in a ship, but not round and not square, with rawhide holding the shutters up on the outside. This house is in a pasture, too, like the other one. No doubt when Dee sees it she will want to tear it down. She wrote me once that no matter where we "choose" to live, she will manage to come see us. But she will never bring her friends. Maggie and I thought about this and Maggie asked me, "Mama, when did Dee ever *have* any friends?"

She had a few. Furtive boys in pink shirts hanging about on washday after school. Nervous girls who never laughed. Impressed with her they worshiped the well-turned phrase, the cute shape, the scalding humor that erupted like bubbles in lye. She read to them.

When she was courting Jimmy T she didn't have much time to pay to us, but turned all her faultfinding power on him. He *flew* to marry a cheap city girl from a family of ignorant flashy people. She hardly had time to recompose herself.

When she comes I will meet—but there they are!

Maggie attempts to make a dash for the house, in her shuffling way, but I stay her with my hand. "Come back here," I say. And she stops and tries to dig a well in the sand with her toe.

It is hard to see them clearly through the strong sun. But even the first glimpse of leg out of the car tells me it is Dee. Her feet were always neat-looking, as if God himself had shaped them with a certain style. From the other side of the car comes a short, stocky man. Hair is all over his head a foot long and hanging from his chin like a kinky mule tail. I hear Maggie suck in her breath. "Uhnnnh," is what it sounds like. Like when you see the wriggling end of a snake just in front of your foot on the road. "Uhnnnh."

Dee next. A dress down to the ground, in this hot weather. A dress so loud it hurts my eyes. There are yellows and oranges enough to throw back the light of the sun. I feel my whole face warming from the heat waves it throws out. Earrings gold, too, and hanging down to her shoulders. Bracelets dangling and making noises when she moves her arm up to shake the folds of the dress out of her armpits. The dress is loose and flows, and as she walks closer, I like it. I hear Maggie go "Uhnnnh" again. It is her sister's hair. It stands straight up like the wool on a sheep. It is black as night and around the edges are two long pigtails that rope about like small lizards disappearing behind her ears.

"Wa-su-zo-Tean-o!" she says, coming on in that gliding way the dress makes her move. The short stocky fellow with the hair to his navel is all grinning and he follows up with "Asalamalakim, my mother and sister!" He moves to hug Maggie but she falls back, right up against the back of my chair. I feel her trembling there and when I look up I see the perspiration falling off her chin.

"Don't get up," says Dee. Since I am stout it takes something of a push. You can see me trying to move a second or two before I make it. She turns, showing white heels through her sandals, and goes back to the car. Out she peeks next with a Polaroid. She stoops down quickly and lines up picture after picture of me sitting there in front of the house with Maggie cowering behind me. She never takes a shot without making sure the house is included. When a cow comes nibbling around the edge of the yard she snaps it and me and Maggie *and* the house. Then she puts the Polaroid in the back seat of the car, and comes up and kisses me on the forehead.

Meanwhile Asalamalakim is going through motions with Maggie's hand. Maggie's hand is as limp as a fish, and probably as cold, despite the sweat, and she keeps trying to pull it back. It looks like Asalamalakim wants to shake hands but wants to do it fancy. Or maybe he don't know how people shake hands. Anyhow, he soon gives up on Maggie.

"Well," I say. "Dee."

"No, Mama," she says. "Not 'Dee,' Wangero Leewanika Kemanjo!"

"What happened to 'Dee'?" I wanted to know.

"She's dead," Wangero said. "I couldn't bear it any longer, being named after the people who oppress me."

"You know as well as me you was named after your aunt Dicie," I said. Dicie is my sister. She named Dee. We called her "Big Dee" after Dee was born.

"But who was *she* named after?" asked Wangero.

"I guess after Grandma Dee," I said.

"And who was she named after?" asked Wangero.

"Her mother," I said, and saw Wangero was getting tired. "That's about as far back as I can trace it," I said. Though, in fact, I probably could have carried it back beyond the Civil War through the branches.

"Well," said Asalamalakim, "there you are."

"Uhnnnh," I heard Maggie say.

"There I was not," I said, "before 'Dicie' cropped up in our family, so why should I try to trace it that far back?"

He just stood there grinning, looking down on me like somebody inspecting a Model A car. Every once in a while he and Wangero sent eye signals over my head.

"How do you pronounce this name?" I asked.

"You don't have to call me by it if you don't want to," said Wangero.

"Why shouldn't I?" I asked. "If that's what you want us to call you, we'll call you."

"I know it might sound awkward at first," said Wangero.

"I'll get used to it," I said. "Ream it out again."

Well, soon we got the name out of the way. Asalamalakim had a name twice as long and three times as hard. After I tripped over it two or three times he told me to just call him Hakim-a-barber. I wanted to ask him was he a barber, but I didn't really think he was, so I didn't ask.

"You must belong to those beef-cattle peoples down the road," I said. They said "Asalamalakim" when they met you, too, but they didn't shake hands. Always too busy: feeding the cattle, fixing the fences, putting up salt-lick shelters, throwing down hay. When the white folks poisoned some of the herd the men stayed up all night with rifles in their hands. I walked a mile and a half just to see the sight.

Hakim-a-barber said, "I accept some of their doctrines, but farming and raising cattle is not my style." (They didn't tell me, and I didn't ask, whether Wangero (Dee) had really gone and married him.)

We sat down to eat and right away he said he didn't eat collards and pork was unclean. Wangero, though, went on through the chitlins and corn bread, the greens and everything else. She talked a blue streak over the sweet potatoes. Everything delighted her. Even the fact that we still used the benches her daddy made for the table when we couldn't afford to buy chairs.

"Oh, Mama!" she cried. Then turned to Hakim-a-barber. "I never knew how lovely these benches are. You can feel the rump prints," she said, running her hands underneath her and along the bench. Then she gave a sigh and her hand closed over Grandma Dee's butter dish. "That's it!" she said. "I knew there was something I wanted to ask you if I could have." She jumped up from the table and went over in the corner where the churn stood, the milk in it clabber by now. She looked at the churn and looked at it.

"This churn top is what I need," she said. "Didn't Uncle Buddy whittle it out of a tree you all used to have?"

"Yes," I said.

"Uh huh," she said happily. "And I want the dasher, too."

"Uncle Buddy whittle that, too?" asked the barber.

Dee (Wangero) looked up at me.

"Aunt Dee's first husband whittled the dash," said Maggie so low you almost couldn't hear her. "His name was Henry, but they called him Stash."

"Maggie's brain is like an elephant's," Wangero said, laughing. "I can use the churn top as a centerpiece for the alcove table," she said, sliding a plate over the churn, "and I'll think of something artistic to do with the dasher."

When she finished wrapping the dasher the handle stuck out. I took it for a moment in my hands. You didn't even have to look close to see where hands pushing the dasher up and down to make butter had left a kind of sink in the wood. In fact, there were a lot of small sinks; you could see where thumbs and fingers had sunk into the word. It was beautiful light yellow wood, from a tree that grew in the yard where Big Dee and Stash had lived.

After dinner Dee (Wangero) went to the trunk at the foot of my bed and started rifling through it. Maggie hung back in the kitchen over the dishpan. Out came Wangero with two quilts. They had been pieced by Grandma Dee and then Big Dee and me had hung then on the quilt frames on the front porch and quilted them. One was in the Lone Star pattern. The other was Walk Around the Mountain. In both of them were scraps of dresses Grandma Dee had worn fifty and more years ago. Bits and pieces of Grandpa Jarrell's Paisley shirts. And one teeny faded blue piece, about the size of a penny matchbox, that was from Great Grandpa Ezra's uniform that he wore in the Civil War.

"Mama," Wangero said sweet as a bird. "Can I have these old quilts?"

I heard something fall in the kitchen, and a minute later the kitchen door slammed.

"Why don't you take one or two of the others?" I asked. "These old things was just done by me and Big Dee from some tops your grandma pieced before she died."

"No," said Wangero. "I don't want those. They are stitched around the borders by machine."

"That'll make them last better," I said.

"That's not the point," said Wangero. "These are all pieces of dresses Grandma used to wear. She did all this stitching by hand. Imagine!" She held the quilts securely in her arms, stroking them.

"Some of the pieces, like those lavender ones, come from old clothes her mother handed down to her," I said, moving up to touch the quilts. Dee (Wangero) moved back just enough so that I couldn't reach the quilts. They already belonged to her.

"Imagine!" she breathed again, clutching them closely to her bosom.

"The truth is," I said, "I promised to give them quilts to Maggie, for when she marries John Thomas."

She gasped like a bee had stung her.

"Maggie can't appreciate these quilts!" she said. "She'd probably be backward enough to put them to everyday use."

"I reckon she would," I said. "God knows I been saving 'em for long enough with nobody using 'em. I hope she will!" I didn't want to bring up how I had offered Dee (Wangero) a quilt when she went away to college. Then she had told me they were old-fashioned, out of style.

"But they're *priceless!*" she was saying now, furiously; for she has a temper. "Maggie would put them on the bed and in five years they'd be in rags. Less than that!"

"She can always make some more," I said. "Maggie knows how to quilt."

Dee (Wangero) looked at me with hatred. "You just will not understand. The point is these quilts, *these* quilts!"

"Well," I said, stumped. "What would *you* do with them?"

"Hang them," she said. As if that was the only thing you *could* do with quilts.

Maggie by now was standing in the door. I could almost hear the sound her feet made as they scraped over each other.

"She can have them, Mama," she said, like somebody used to never winning anything, or having anything reserved for her. "I can 'member Grandma Dee without the quilts."

I looked at her hard. She had filled her bottom lip with checkerberry snuff and it gave her face a kind of dopey, hangdog look. It was Grandma Dee and Big Dee who taught her how to quilt herself. She stood there with her scarred hands hidden in the folds of her skirt. She looked at her sister with something like fear but she wasn't mad at her. This was Maggie's portion. This was the way she knew God to work.

When I looked at her like that something hit me in the top of my head and ran down to the soles of my feet. Just like when I'm in church and the spirit of God touches me and I get happy and shout. I did something I never had done before: hugged Maggie to me, then dragged her on into the room, snatched the quilts out of Miss Wangero's hands and dumped them into Maggie's lap. Maggie just sat there on my bed with her mouth open.

"Take one or two of the others," I said to Dee.

But she turned without a word and went out to Hakim-a-barber.

"You just don't understand," she said, as Maggie and I came out to the car.

"What don't I understand?" I wanted to know.

"Your heritage," she said. And then she turned to Maggie, kissed her, and said, "You ought to try to make something of yourself, too, Maggie. It's really a new day for us. But from the way you and Mama still live you'd never know it."

She put on some sunglasses that hid everything above the tip of her nose and her chin.

Maggie smiled; maybe at the sunglasses. But a real smile, not scared. After we watched the car dust settle I asked Maggie to bring me a dip of snuff. And then the two of us sat there just enjoying, until it was time to go in the house and go to bed.

QUESTIONS

1. What details in the story help you place it in a particular time?
2. Why does the narrator present herself as she does at the beginning? What are the most important details in her self-portrait?
3. What does Dee's change in name represent? A real change in herself?
4. How much do you sympathize with Dee's wish for the quilt and other items?
5. What has happened to the narrator and Maggie as the result of Dee's visit?

William Shakespeare (1564–1616)
SONNET 43

When most I wink, then do my eyes best see,
For all the day they view things unrespected,
But when I sleep, in dreams they look on thee,
And darkly bright, are bright in dark directed.
Then thou, whose shadow shadows doth make bright—
How would thy shadow's form form happy show
To the clear day with thy much clearer light,
When to unseeing eyes thy shade shines so!
How would, I say, mine eyes be blessèd made,
By looking on thee in the living day,   10
When in dead night thy fair imperfect shade
Through heavy sleep on sightless eyes doth stay!
   All days are nights to see till I see thee,
   And nights bright days when dreams do show thee me.

Robert Herrick (1591–1674)
DELIGHT IN DISORDER

A sweet disorder in the dress
Kindles in clothes a wantonness.
A lawn[1] about the shoulders thrown
Into a fine distractiön;
An erring lace, which here and there
Enthralls the crimson stomacher;[2]
A cuff neglectful, and thereby
Ribbons to flow confusedly;
A winning wave, deserving note,

Delight in Disorder
  [1]Fine linen scarf.
  [2]A decorative, triangular garment formerly worn by women. It covered the chest and stomach and was held in place by the laces of a bodice or outer vest.

In the tempestuous petticoat; 10
A careless shoestring, in whose tie
I see a wild civility;
Do more bewitch me than when art
Is too precise in every part.

QUESTIONS

1. What word choices stand out? What responses do they evoke?
2. What sounds are effective when you listen to the poem?
3. Can you imagine details of contemporary dress in place of those in the poem? Do you share the speaker's sentiments?
4. Is the poem about style in dress, a woman, women generally, or something else?

Robert Herrick (1591–1674)

UPON JULIA'S CLOTHES

Whenas in silks my Julia goes,
Then, then, methinks, how sweetly flows
That liquefaction of her clothes.

Next, when I cast mine eyes and see
That brave vibration each way free;
O, how that glittering taketh me!

John Milton (1608–1674)

ON HIS BLINDNESS

When I consider how my light is spent
Ere half my days in this dark world and wide,
And that one talent[1] which is death to hide
Lodged with me useless, though my soul more bent
To serve therewith my Maker, and present

On His Blindness
   [1]A pun, since Milton also recalls Jesus' parable of the talents (measures of money) in Matthew 25.

My true account, lest He returning chide,
"Doth God exact day-labor, light denied?"
I fondly° ask. But Patience, to prevent   foolishly
That murmur, soon replies, "God doth not need
Either man's work or his own gifts. Who best   10
Bear His mild yoke, they serve Him best. His state
Is kingly: thousands at His bidding speed,
And post o'er land and ocean without rest;
They also serve who only stand and wait."

William Wordsworth (1770–1850)

I WANDERED LONELY AS A CLOUD

I wandered lonely as a cloud
That floats on high o'er vales and hills,
When all at once I saw a crowd,
A host, of golden daffodils;
Beside the lake, beneath the trees,
Fluttering and dancing in the breeze.

Continuous as the stars that shine
And twinkle on the milky way,
They stretched in never-ending line
Along the margin of a bay: 10
Ten thousand saw I at a glance,
Tossing their heads in sprightly dance.

The waves beside them danced; but they
Outdid the sparkling waves in glee;
A poet could not but be gay,
In such a jocund company;
I gazed—and gazed—but little thought
What wealth the show to me had brought:

For oft, when on my couch I lie
In vacant or in pensive mood,   20
They flash upon that inward eye
Which is the bliss of solitude;
And then my heart with pleasure fills,
And dances with the daffodils.

John Keats (1795–1821)

ODE ON A GRECIAN URN

Thou still unravished bride of quietness,
  Thou foster-child of silence and slow time,
Sylvan historian, who canst thus express
  A flowery tale more sweetly than our rhyme:
What leaf-fringed legend haunts about thy shape
  Of deities or mortals, or of both,
    In Tempe[1] or the dales of Arcady?
What men or gods are these? What maidens loth?°   reluctant
What mad pursuit? What struggle to escape?
  What pipes and timbrels? What wild ecstasy?   10

Heard melodies are sweet, but those unheard
  Are sweeter; therefore, ye soft pipes, play on;
Not to the sensual ear, but, more endeared,
  Pipe to the spirit ditties of no tone:
Fair youth, beneath the trees, thou canst not leave
  Thy song, nor ever can those trees be bare;
    Bold lover, never, never canst thou kiss,
Though winning near the goal—yet, do not grieve;
  She cannot fade, though thou hast not thy bliss,
For ever wilt thou love, and she be fair!   20

Ah, happy, happy boughs! that cannot shed
  Your leaves, nor ever bid the spring adieu;
And, happy melodist, unwearièd,
  For ever piping songs for ever new;
More happy love! more happy, happy love!
  For ever warm and still to be enjoyed,
    For ever panting and for ever young;
All breathing human passion far above,
  That leaves a heart high-sorrowful and cloyed,
    A burning forehead, and a parching tongue.   30

Ode on a Grecian Urn
   [1]Tempe was the name of a Greek valley sacred to Apollo in ancient times; Arcady was an
ancient Greek state, famed for the ideal beauty of its valleys.

Who are these coming to the sacrifice?
  To what green altar, O mysterious priest,
Lead'st thou that heifer lowing at the skies,
  And all her silken flanks with garlands drest?
What little town by river or sea shore,
  Or mountain-built with peaceful citadel,
    Is emptied of its folk, this pious morn?
And, little town, thy streets for evermore
  Will silent be; and not a soul to tell
    Why thou art desolate, can e'er return.   40

O Attic² shape! Fair attitude! with brede°   design
  Of marble men and maidens overwrought,
With forest branches and the trodden weed;
  Thou, silent form, dost tease us out of thought
As doth eternity: Cold Pastoral!
  When old age shall this generation waste,
    Thou shalt remain, in midst of other woe
Than ours, a friend to man, to whom thou say'st,
Beauty is truth, truth beauty,—that is all
  Ye know on earth, and all ye need to know.   50

QUESTIONS

1. How clearly can you imagine the urn described?
2. What responses do the images on the urn arouse in the speaker? What details suggest his feelings?
3. What conclusion, if any, does he reach as the result of contemplating the urn?
4. Do you respond more strongly to the image of the urn or to the speaker's voice?
5. Is the poem about anything besides the urn? Explain.

Walt Whitman (1819–1892)

WHEN I HEARD THE LEARN'D ASTRONOMER

When I heard the learn'd astronomer,
When the proofs, the figures, were ranged in columns
  before me,

---

²Of Attica, the region of Greece in which Athens is located.

When I was shown the charts and diagrams, to add, divide,
　and measure them,
When I sitting heard the astronomer where he lectured with
　much applause in the lecture-room,
How soon unaccountable I became tired and sick,
Till rising and gliding out I wander'd off by myself,
In the mystical moist night-air, and from time to time,
Look'd up in perfect silence at the stars.

Emily Dickinson (1830–1886)
WE GROW ACCUSTOMED TO THE DARK

We grow accustomed to the Dark—
When Light is put away—
As when the Neighbor holds the Lamp
To witness her Goodbye—

A Moment—We uncertain step
For newness of the night—
Then—fit our Vision to the Dark—
And meet the Road—erect—

And so of larger—Darknesses—
Those Evenings of the Brain—　　　　　　　　　10
When not a Moon disclose a sign—
Or Star—come out—within—

The Bravest—grope a little—
And sometimes hit a Tree
Directly in the Forehead—
But as they learn to see—

Either the Darkness alters—
Or something in the sight
Adjusts itself to Midnight—
And Life steps almost straight.　　　　　　　　　20

QUESTIONS

1. What does reading the poem aloud contribute to your experience of it?
2. How do you respond to what happens sometimes to the "Bravest"?
3. Why does Life step "almost straight" rather than "erect," from the earlier line?

Gerard Manley Hopkins (1844–1889)

GOD'S GRANDEUR

The world is charged with the grandeur of God.
　It will flame out, like shining from shook foil;
　It gathers to a greatness, like the ooze of oil
Crushed. Why do men then now not reck his rod?
Generations have trod, have trod, have trod;
　And all is seared with trade; bleared, smeared with toil;
　And wears man's smudge and shares man's smell: the soil
Is bare now, nor can foot feel, being shod.

And for all this, nature is never spent;
　There lives the dearest freshness deep down things;　　　　　　10
And though the last lights off the black West went
　Oh, morning, at the brown brink eastward, springs—
Because the Holy Ghost over the bent
　World broods with warm breast and with ah! bright wings.

Gerard Manley Hopkins (1844–1889)

PIED BEAUTY

Glory be to God for dappled things—
　For skies of couple-colour as a brinded° cow;　　　　　　spotted
　　For rose-moles all in stipple upon trout that swim;
Fresh-firecoal chestnut-falls; finches' wings;
　Landscape plotted and pieced—fold, fallow, and plow;
　　And all trades, their gear and tackle and trim.

All things counter, original, spare strange;
   Whatever is fickle, freckled (who knows how?)
     With swift, slow; sweet, sour; adazzle, dim;
His fathers-forth whose beauty is past change: 10
     Praise him.

Gerard Manley Hopkins (1844–1889)

THE WINDHOVER[1]
To Christ Our Lord

I caught this morning morning's minion,° king-   *favorite*
   dom of daylight's dauphin,° dapple-dawn-drawn Falcon, in his riding *heir*
   Of the rolling level underneath him steady air, and striding
High there, how he rung upon the rein of a wimpling° wing   *rippling*
In his ecstasy! then off, off forth on swing,
   As a skate's heel sweeps smooth on a bow-bend: the hurl and gliding
   Rebuffed the big wind. My heart in hiding
Stirred for a bird,—the achieve of, the mastery of the thing!

Brute beauty and valor and act, oh, air, pride, plume, here
   Buckle! AND the fire that breaks from thee then, a billion   10
Times told lovelier, more dangerous, O my chevalier!°   *champion*

   No wonder of it: sheer plod makes plough down sillion°   *furrow*
Shine, and blue-bleak embers, ah my dear,
   Fall, gall themselves, and gash gold-vermilion.

QUESTIONS

1. In what way has the speaker "caught" the windhover?
2. What details convey the speaker's reaction to the sight?
3. Have you ever had an experience comparable to the speaker's?
4. Is the speaker addressing the windhover as "O my chevalier" and "ah my dear"? If not, whom is he addressing?
5. What do the sounds of the poem and its diction contribute to your experience of it?

The Windhover
[1]A small hawk that hovers in the wind.

William Butler Yeats (1865–1939)

THE WILD SWANS AT COOLE[1]

The trees are in their autumn beauty,
The woodland paths are dry,
Under the October twilight the water
Mirrors a still sky;
Upon the brimming water among the stones
Are nine-and-fifty swans.

The nineteenth autumn has come upon me
Since I first made my count;
I saw, before I had well finished,
All suddenly mount   10
And scatter wheeling in great broken rings
Upon their clamorous wings.

I have looked upon those brilliant creatures,
And now my heart is sore.
All's changed since I, hearing at twilight,
The first time on this shore,
The bell-beat of their wings above my head,
Trod with a lighter tread.

Unwearied still, lover by lover,
They paddle in the cold   20
Companionable streams or climb the air;
Their hearts have not grown old;
Passion or conquest, wander where they will,
Attend upon them still.

But now they drift on the still water,
Mysterious, beautiful;
Among what rushes will they build,
By what lake's edge or pool
Delight men's eyes when I awake some day
To find they have flown away?   30

The Wild Swans at Coole
[1]Coole Park, an estate in County Galway, Ireland, where Yeats often visited.

QUESTIONS

1. What is the speaker's tone as he describes the scene before him and recalls his first sight of the swans?
2. What difference does he suggest exists between himself and them?
3. What is the "some day" the speaker imagines in the last stanza?
4. Is the poem about the swans or the speaker?

William Butler Yeats (1865–1939)

SAILING TO BYZANTIUM

I

That is no country for old men. The young
In one another's arms, birds in the trees
—Those dying generations—at their song,
The salmon-falls, the mackerel-crowded seas,
Fish, flesh, or fowl, commend all summer long
Whatever is begotten, born, and dies.
Caught in that sensual music all neglect
Monuments of unageing intellect.

II

An aged man is but a paltry thing,
A tattered coat upon a stick, unless   10
Soul clap its hands and sing, and louder sing
For every tatter in its mortal dress,
Nor is there singing school but studying
Monuments of its own magnificence;
And therefore I have sailed the seas and come
To the holy city of Byzantium.[1]

III

O sages[2] standing in God's holy fire
As in the gold mosaic of a wall,
Come from the holy fire, perne in a gyre,[3]

Sailing to Byzantium
  [1]Yeats idealized this eastern capital of the Roman Empire and of ancient Christendom as a "holy" city because of its reverence for art, represented by its splendid mosaics.
  [2]Figures on a mosaic frieze.
  [3]Whirl down in a spiraling movement. Yeats imagined all of time as moving in great gyres, or spirals.

And be the singing-masters of my soul.   20
Consume my heart away; sick with desire
And fastened to a dying animal
It knows not what it is; and gather me
Into the artifice of eternity.

IV

Once out of nature I shall never take
My bodily form from any natural thing,
But such a form as Grecian goldsmiths make
Of hammered gold and gold enamelling
To keep a drowsy Emperor awake;
Or set upon a golden bough to sing   30
To lords and ladies of Byzantium
Of what is past, or passing, or to come.

QUESTIONS

1. What country does the speaker first refer to, and what seems to be his relation to it?
2. Besides age, what seems to trouble the speaker most?
3. Is the speaker content to be a "paltry thing" as an "aged man"?
4. What does he hope to become?

Edward Arlington Robinson (1869–1935)
UNCLE ANANIAS[1]

His words were magic and his heart was true,
    And everywhere he wandered he was blessed.
Out of all ancient men my childhood knew
    I choose him and I mark him for the best.
Of all authoritative liars, too,
    I crown him loveliest.

How fondly I remember the delight
    That always glorified him in the spring;

Uncle Ananias
[1]Ananias in Acts 5 of the *New Testament* was struck dead for lying to God.

The joyous courage and the benedight°   blessed
  Profusion of his faith in everything!   10
He was a good old man, and it was right
  That he should have his fling.

And often, underneath the apple-trees,
  When we surprised him in the summer time,
With what superb magnificence and ease
  He sinned enough to make the day sublime!
And if he liked us there about his knees,
  Truly it was no crime.

All summer long we loved him for the same
  Perennial inspiration of his lies;   20
And when the russet wealth of autumn came,
  There flew but fairer visions to our eyes—
Multiple, tropical, winged with a feathery flame,
  Like birds of paradise.

So to the sheltered end of many a year
  He charmed the seasons out with pageantry
Wearing upon his forehead, with no fear,
  The laurel of approved iniquity.
And every child who knew him, far or near,
  Did love him faithfully.   30

D. H. Lawrence (1885–1930)

SNAKE

A snake came to my water-trough
On a hot, hot day, and I in pyjamas for the heat,
To drink there.

In the deep, strange-scented shade of the great dark carob-
    tree
I came down the steps with my pitcher
And must wait, must stand and wait, for there he was at
  the trough before me.

He reached down from a fissure in the earth-wall in the
    gloom
And trailed his yellow-brown slackness soft-bellied down,
    over the edge of the stone trough
And rested his throat upon the stone bottom,
And where the water had dripped from the tap, in a small
    clearness,   10
He sipped with his straight mouth,
Softly drank through his straight gums, into his slack long
    body,
Silently.

Someone was before me at my water-trough,
And I, like a second comer, waiting.

He lifted his head from his drinking, as cattle do,
And looked at me vaguely, as drinking cattle do,
And flickered his two-forked tongue from his lips, and
    mused a moment,
And stooped and drank a little more,
Being earth-brown, earth-golden from the burning bowels
    of the earth   20
On the day of Sicilian July, with Etna smoking.

The voice of my education said to me
He must be killed,
For in Sicily the black, black snakes are innocent, the gold
    are venomous.

And voices in me said, If you were a man
You would take a stick and break him now, and finish
    him off.

But must I confess how I liked him,
How glad I was he had come like a guest in quiet, to drink
    at my water-trough
And depart peaceful, pacified, and thankless,
Into the burning bowels of this earth?   30

Was it cowardice, that I dared not kill him?
Was it perversity, that I longed to talk to him?
Was it humility, to feel so honoured?
I felt so honoured.

And yet those voices:
If you were not afraid, you would kill him!

And truly I was afraid, I was most afraid,
But even so, honoured still more
That he should seek my hospitality
From out the dark door of the secret earth.   40

He drank enough
And lifted his head, dreamily, as one who has drunken,
And flickered his tongue like a forked night on the air, so
    black,
Seeming to lick his lips,
And looked around like a god, unseeing, into the air,
And slowly turned his head,
And slowly, very slowly, as if thrice adream,
Proceeded to draw his slow length curving round
And climb again the broken bank of my wall-face.

And as he put his head into that dreadful hole,   50
And as he slowly drew up, snake-easing his shoulders, and
    entered farther,
A sort of horror, a sort of protest against his withdrawing
    into that horrid black hole,
Deliberately going into the blackness, and slowly drawing
    himself after,
Overcame me now his back was turned.

I looked around, I put down my pitcher,
I picked up a clumsy log
And threw it at the water-trough with a clatter.

I think it did not hit him,
But suddenly that part of him that was left behind
    convulsed in undignified haste,
Writhed like lightning, and was gone   60
Into the black hole, the earth-lipped fissure in the wall-
    front,
At which, in the intense still noon, I stared with fascination.

And immediately I regretted it.
I thought how paltry, how vulgar, what a mean act!
I despised myself and the voices of my accursed human
    education.

And I thought of the albatross,
And I wished he would come back, my snake.

For he seemed to me again like a king,
Like a king in exile, uncrowned in the underworld,
Now due to be crowned again.   70

And so, I missed my chance with one of the lords
Of life.
And I have something to expiate;
A pettiness.

QUESTIONS

1. What associations have snakes for you?
2. What response does the description of this snake evoke?
3. What does the reference to the albatross mean to you?
4. How does the speaker come to speak of "my snake" (l. 67)?
5. What is it about the snake that causes the speaker to despise his "accursed human education" and believe he must "expiate" his own "pettiness"?

Ezra Pound (1885–1972)

IN A STATION OF THE METRO[1]

The apparition of these faces in the crowd;
Petals on a wet, black bough.

Robinson Jeffers (1887–1962)

CARMEL POINT

The extraordinary patience of things!
This beautiful place defaced with a crop of suburban
    houses—

In a Station of the Metro
[1]The Paris subway.

How beautiful when we first beheld it,
Unbroken field of poppy and lupin walled with clean cliffs;
No intrusion but two or three horses pasturing,
Or a few milch cows rubbing their flanks on the outcrop
    rockheads—
Now the spoiler has come: does it care?
Not faintly. It has all time. It knows the people are a tide
That swells and in time will ebb, and all
Their works dissolve. Meanwhile the image of the pristine
    beauty   10
Lives in the very grain of the granite,
Safe as the endless ocean that climbs our cliff.—As for us:
We must uncenter our minds from ourselves;
We must unhumanize our views a little, and become
    confident
As the rock and ocean that we were made from.

Langston Hughes (1902–1967)

DREAM VARIATIONS

To fling my arms wide
In some place of the sun,
To whirl and to dance
Till the white day is done.
Then rest at cool evening
Beneath a tall tree
While night comes on gently,
    Dark like me—
That is my dream!

To fling my arms wide
In the face of the sun,
Dance! Whirl! Whirl!
Till the quick day is done.
Rest at pale evening . . .
A tall, slim tree . . .
Night coming tenderly
    Black like me.

Langston Hughes (1902–1967)

HOPE

Sometimes when I'm lonely,
Don't know why,
Keep thinkin' I won't be lonely
By and by.

Langston Hughes (1902–1967)

THE NEGRO SPEAKS OF RIVERS

I've known rivers;
I've known rivers ancient as the world and older than the
    flow of human blood in human veins.

My soul has grown deep like the rivers.   10

I bathed in the Euphrates when dawns were young.
I built my hut near the Congo and it lulled me to sleep.
I looked upon the Nile and raised the pyramids above it.
I heard the singing of the Mississippi when Abe Lincoln
    went down to New Orleans, and I've seen its muddy
    bosom turn all golden in the sunset.

I've known rivers:
Ancient, dusky rivers.

My soul has grown deep like the rivers.

Robert Penn Warren (b. 1905)

GOLD GLADE

Wandering, in autumn, the woods of boyhood,
Where cedar, black, thick, rode the ridge,
Heart aimless as rifle, boy-blankness of mood,
I came where ridge broke, and the great ledge,
Limestone, set the toe high as treetop by dark edge

Of a gorge, and water hid, grudging and grumbling,
And I saw, in mind's eye, foam white on
Wet stone, stone wet-black, white water tumbling,
And so went down, and with some fright on
Slick boulders, crossed over. The gorge-depth drew
   night on,   10

But high over high rock and leaf-lacing, sky
Showed yet bright, and declivity wooed
My foot by the quietening stream, and so I
Went on, in quiet, through the beech wood:
There, in gold light, where the glade gave, it stood.

The glade was geometric, circular, gold,
No brush or weed breaking that bright gold of leaf-fall.
In the center it stood, absolute and bold
Beyond any heart-hurt, or eye's grief-fall.
Gold-massy in air, it stood in gold light-fall,   20

No breathing of air, no leaf now gold-falling,
No tooth-stitch of squirrel, or any far fox bark,
No woodpecker coding, or late jay calling.
Silence: gray-shagged, the great shagbark
Gave forth gold light. There could be no dark.

But of course dark came, and I can't recall
What county it was, for the life of me.
Montgomery, Todd, Christian—I know them all.
Was it even Kentucky or Tennessee?
Perhaps just an image that keeps haunting me.   30

No, no! in no mansion under earth,
Nor imagination's domain of bright air,
But solid in soil that gave it its birth,
It stands, wherever it is, but somewhere.
I shall set my foot, and go there.

QUESTIONS

1. When you read the poem aloud, what variations in style or tone do you notice?
2. What does the speaker mean in saying (l. 25), "There could be no dark"?
3. How can the speaker be so uncertain as to the great shagbark's location and propose to go there?
4. What exactly does the speaker wish to see again?

Elizabeth Bishop (1911–1979)
FILLING STATION

Oh, but it is dirty!
—this little filling station,
oil-soaked, oil-permeated
to a disturbing, over-all
black translucency.
Be careful with that match!

Father wears a dirty,
oil-soaked monkey suit
that cuts him under the arms,
and several quick and saucy   10
and greasy sons assist him
(it's a family filling station),
all quite thoroughly dirty.

Do they live in the station?
It has a cement porch
behind the pumps, and on it
a set of crushed and grease-
impregnated wickerwork;
on the wicker sofa
a dirty dog, quite comfy.   20

Some comic books provide
the only note of color—
of certain color. They lie
upon a big dim doily
draping a taboret
(part of the set), beside
a big hirsute begonia.

Why the extraneous plant?
Why the taboret?
Why, oh why, the doily?   30
(Embroidered in daisy stitch
with marguerites, I think,
and heavy with gray crochet.)

Somebody embroidered the doily.
Somebody waters the plant,

or oils it, maybe. Somebody
arranges the rows of cans
so that they softly say:
ESSO—SO—SO—SO
to high-strung automobiles.   40
Somebody loves us all.

QUESTIONS

1. How do you imagine the speaker?
2. How does the speaker see the filling station? What prompts her questions?
3. Who is the "somebody" the speaker envisions? What is the tone of the last line?

Robert Hayden (1913–1980)

FREDERICK DOUGLASS[1]

When it is finally ours, this freedom, this liberty, this beautiful
and terrible thing, needful to man as air,
usable as earth; when it belongs at last to all,
when it is truly instinct, brain matter, diastole, systole,
reflex action; when it is finally won; when it is more
than the gaudy mumbo jumbo of politicians:
this man, this Douglass, this former slave, this Negro
beaten to his knees, exiled, visioning a world
where none is lonely, none hunted, alien,
this man, superb in love and logic, this man   10
shall be remembered. Oh, not with statues' rhetoric,
not with legends and poems and wreaths of bronze alone,
but with the lives grown out of his life, the lives
fleshing his dream of the beautiful, needful thing.

Frederick Douglass
   [1]American orator, leader, statesman. As publisher of the abolitionist newspaper *North Star* for
seventeen years, Douglass (1817–1895) fought for education for black people, women's suffrage,
and the use of black troops in the Civil War.

Henry Reed (b. 1914)
NAMING OF PARTS

Today we have naming of parts. Yesterday,
We had daily cleaning. And tomorrow morning
We shall have what to do after firing. But today,
Today we have naming of parts. Japonica
Glistens like coral in all of the neighboring gardens,
   And today we have naming of parts.

This is the lower sling swivel. And this
Is the upper sling swivel, whose use you will see,
When you are given your slings. And this is the piling swivel,
Which in your case you have not got. The branches   10
Hold in the gardens their silent, eloquent gestures,
   Which in our case we have not got.

This is the safety-catch, which is always released
With an easy flick of the thumb. And please do not let me
See anyone using his finger. You can do it quite easy
If you have any strength in your thumb. The blossoms
Are fragile and motionless, never letting anyone see
   Any of them using their finger.

And this you can see is the bolt. The purpose of this
Is to open the breech, as you see. We can slide it   20
Rapidly backwards and forwards: we call this
Easing the spring. And rapidly backwards and forwards
The early bees are assaulting and fumbling the flowers:
   They call it easing the Spring.

They call it easing the Spring: it is perfectly easy
If you have any strength in your thumb: like the bolt,
And the breech, and the cocking-piece, and the point of
   balance,
Which in our case we have not got; and the almond-
   blossom
Silent in all of the gardens and the bees going backwards
   and forwards,
   For today we have naming of parts.   30

QUESTIONS

1. What scene do you imagine in reading this poem?
2. Who is speaking?
3. What tone or tones do you hear in each stanza?
4. Are any word choices particularly striking?
5. Does the last stanza contain a conclusion or resolution of some sort?

Robert Lowell (1917–1977)

FOR THE UNION DEAD

"Relinquunt Omnia Servare Rem Publicam."[1]

The old South Boston Aquarium stands
in a Sahara of snow now. Its broken windows are boarded.
The bronze weathervane cod has lost half its scales.
The airy tanks are dry.

Once my nose crawled like a snail on the glass;
my hand tingled
to burst the bubbles
drifting from the noses of the cowed, compliant fish.

My hand draws back. I often sigh still
for the dark downward and vegetating kingdom   10
of the fish and reptile. One morning last March,
I pressed against the new barbed and galvanized

fence on the Boston Common. Behind their cage,
yellow dinosaur steamshovels were grunting
as they cropped up tons of mush and grass
to gouge their underworld garage.

Parking spaces luxuriate like civic
sandpiles in the heart of Boston.
A girdle of orange, Puritan-pumpkin colored girders
braces the tingling Statehouse,   20

shaking over the excavations, as it faces Colonel Shaw[2]
and his bell-cheeked Negro infantry

For the Union Dead
   [1]They gave up everything to serve the republic.
   [2]Robert Gould Shaw (1837–1863) led the 54th Massachusetts, a black regiment, in the Civil War.

on St. Gaudens'[3] shaking Civil War relief,
propped by a plank splint against the garage's earthquake.

Two months after marching through Boston,
half the regiment was dead;
at the dedication,
William James[4] could almost hear the bronze Negroes
    breathe.

Their monument sticks like a fishbone
in the city's throat.   30
Its Colonel is as lean
as a compass-needle.

He has an angry wrenlike vigilance,
a greyhound's gentle tautness;
he seems to wince at pleasure,
and suffocate for privacy.

He is out of bounds now. He rejoices in man's lovely,
peculiar power to choose life and die—
when he leads his black soldiers to death,
he cannot bend his back.   40

On a thousand small town New England greens,
the old white churches hold their air
of sparse, sincere rebellion; frayed flags
quilt the graveyards of the Grand Army of the Republic.

The stone statues of the abstract Union Soldier
grow slimmer and younger each year—
wasp-waisted, they doze over muskets
and muse through their sideburns . . .

Shaw's father wanted no monument
except the ditch,   50
where his son's body was thrown
and lost with his "niggers."

---

[3] Augustus St. Gaudens (1848–1907), American sculptor.
[4] William James (1842–1910), philosopher and professor at Harvard University.

The ditch is nearer.
There are no statues for the last war here;
on Boylston Street, a commercial photograph
shows Hiroshima boiling

over a Mosler Safe, the "Rock of Ages"
that survived the blast. Space is nearer.
When I crouch to my television set,
the drained faces of Negro school-children rise like
    balloons.   60

Colonel Shaw
is riding on his bubble,
he waits
for the blessèd break.

The Aquarium is gone. Everywhere,
giant finned cars nose forward like fish;
a savage servility
slides by on grease.

QUESTIONS

1. What seem to be the speaker's feelings towards the present-day scene he observes?
2. What does he see in the Shaw memorial?
3. What images suggest the connections he makes between the memorialized past and the present?
4. Do any details in the poem help you to date it and explain its tone?

Denise Levertov (b. 1923)

STEPPING WESTWARD

What is green in me
darkens, muscadine.[1]

If woman is inconstant,
good, I am faithful to

Stepping Westward
[1] A purple wine-grape.

ebb and flow, I fall
in season and now

is a time of ripening.
If her part

is to be true,
a north star,   10

good, I hold steady
in the black sky

and vanish by day,
yet burn there

in blue or above
quilts of cloud.

There is no savor
more sweet, more salt

than to be glad to be
what, woman,   20

and who, myself,
I am, a shadow

that grows longer as the sun
moves, drawn out

on a thread of wonder.
If I bear burdens

they begin to be remembered
as gifts, goods, a basket

of bread that hurts
my shoulders but closes me   30

in fragrance. I can
eat as I go.

QUESTIONS

1. Where is the speaker actually going?
2. What do you usually associate with the words "inconstant" and "true"? Does the speaker seem to recognize their usual associations?
3. What do you suppose are the "burdens" referred to in l. 26?
4. Could you describe in your own terms how the speaker sees herself? What does her language convey that your terms do not?

Ted Hughes (b. 1930)
HAWK ROOSTING

I sit in the top of the wood, my eyes closed.
Inaction, no falsifying dream
Between my hooked head and hooked feet:
Or in sleep rehearse perfect kills and eat.

The convenience of the high trees!
The air's buoyancy and the sun's ray
Are of advantage to me;
And the earth's face upward for my inspection.

My feet are locked upon the rough bark.
It took the whole of Creation   10
To produce my foot, my each feather:
Now I hold Creation in my foot

Or fly up, and revolve it all slowly—
I kill where I please because it is all mine.
There is no sophistry in my body:
My manners are tearing off heads—

The allotment of death.
For the one path of my flight is direct
Through the bones of the living.
No arguments assert my right: 20

The sun is behind me.
Nothing has changed since I began.
My eye has permitted no change.
I am going to keep things like this.

QUESTIONS

1. How do you get past the absurdity of having a hawk as speaker? Do you assume, in reading, that a hawk thinks like this?
2. Do you recognize any characteristics of the hawk as especially true to life or frightening?
3. How do you react to the hawk's vision of things?

Sylvia Plath (1932–1963)

BLACK ROOK IN RAINY WEATHER

On the stiff twig up there
Hunches a wet black rook
Arranging and rearranging its feathers in the rain.
I do not expect a miracle
Or an accident

To set the sight on fire
In my eye, nor seek
Any more in the desultory weather some design,
But let spotted leaves fall as they fall,
Without ceremony, or portent.   10

Although, I admit, I desire,
Occasionally, some backtalk
From the mute sky, I can't honestly complain:
A certain minor light may still
Leap incandescent

Out of kitchen table or chair
As if a celestial burning took
Possession of the most obtuse objects now and then—
Thus hallowing an interval
Otherwise inconsequent   20

By bestowing largesse, honor,
One might say love. At any rate, I now walk
Wary (for it could happen
Even in this dull, ruinous landscape); sceptical,
Yet politic; ignorant

Of whatever angel may choose to flare
Suddenly at my elbow. I only know that a rook

Ordering its black feathers can so shine
As to seize my senses, haul
My eyelids up, and grant   30

A brief respite from fear
Of total neutrality. With luck,
Trekking stubborn through this season
Of fatigue, I shall
Patch together a content

Of sorts. Miracles occur,
If you care to call those spasmodic
Tricks of radiance miracles. The wait's begun again,
The long wait for the angel,
For that rare, random descent.   40

Nikki Giovanni (b. 1943)
ALABAMA POEM

if trees could talk
    wonder what they'd say
met an old man
    on the road late afternoon
    hat pulled over to shade
    his eyes
    jacket slumped over his
    shoulders
    told me "girl! my hands seen
    more than all   10
    them books they got
    at tuskegee[1]"
    smiled at me
    half waved his hand
    walked on down the dusty road
met an old woman
    with a corncob pipe

Alabama Poem
  [1]Tuskegee Institute in Alabama.

      sitting and rocking
      on a spring evening
      "sista" she called to me   20
      "let me tell you—my feet
      seen more than yo eyes
      ever gonna read"
      smiled at her and kept
      on moving
      gave it a thought and went
      back to the porch
      "i say gal" she called down
      "you a student at the institute?
      better come here and study   30
      these feet
      i'm gonna cut a bunion off
      soons i gets up"
      i looked at her
      she laughed at me
if trees would talk
      wonder what they'd tell me

Gary Soto (b. 1952)

BLACK HAIR

At eight I was brilliant with my body.
In July, that ring of heat
We all jumped through, I sat in the bleachers
Of Romain Playground, in the lengthening
Shade that rose from our dirty feet.
The game before us was more than baseball.
It was a figure—Hector Moreno
Quick and hard with turned muscles,
His crouch the one I assumed before an altar
Of worn baseball cards, in my room.   10

I came here because I was Mexican, a stick
Of brown light in love with those
Who could do it—the triple and hard slide,
The gloves eating balls into double plays.
What could I do with 50 pounds, my shyness,

My black torch of hair, about to go out?
Father was dead, his face no longer
Hanging over the table or our sleep,
And mother was the terror of mouths
Twisting hurt by butter knives.   20

In the bleachers I was brilliant with my body,
Waving players in and stomping my feet,
Growing sweaty in the presence of white shirts.
I chewed sunflower seeds. I drank water
And bit my arm through the late innings.
When Hector lined balls into deep
Center, in my mind I rounded the bases
With him, my face flared, my hair lifting
Beautifully, because we were coming home
To the arms of brown people.   30

DRAMA

Sophocles (496?–406 B.C.)
ANTIGONE*

PERSONS REPRESENTED

Antigone	Teiresias
Ismene	A Sentry
Eurydice	A Messenger
Creon	Chorus
Haimon	

SCENE: *Before the palace of Creon, King of Thebes. A central double door, and two lateral doors. A platform extends the length of the façade, and from this platform three steps lead down into the "orchestra," or chorus-ground.* TIME: *dawn of the day after the repulse of the Argive army from the assault on Thebes.*

PROLOGUE

ANTIGONE and ISMENE enter from the central door of the Palace.

Antigone. Ismenê, dear sister,
　　You would think that we had already suffered enough
　　For the curse on Oedipus:[1]
　　I cannot imagine any grief
　　That you and I have not gone through. And now—
　　Have they told you of the new decree of our King Creon?
Ismene. I have heard nothing: I know
　　That two sisters lost two brothers, a double death
　　In a single hour; and I know that the Argive army
　　Fled in the night; but beyond this, nothing.　　　　　　　　10
Antigone. I thought so. And that is why I wanted you
　　To come out here with me. There is something we must do.

*An English version by Dudley Fitts and Robert Fitzgerald.

---

[1]Oedipus, formerly King of Thebes and the father of Antigonê and Ismenê, unknowingly killed his father and married his own mother, with whom he also had two sons, Polyneicês and Eteoclês. On discovering what he had done, he blinded himself and left Thebes. His sons quarreled, and Polyneicês was driven out, but returned with an army to assault Thebes. The brothers killed each other in battle; Creon become king and decreed that Polyneicês' body be left to rot unburied as punishment for treason.

706

Ismene. Why do you speak so strangely?.
Antigone. Listen, Ismenê:
  Creon buried our brother Eteoclês
  With military honors, gave him a soldier's funeral,
  And it was right that he should; but Polyneicês,
  Who fought as bravely and died as miserably,—
  They say that Creon has sworn
  No one shall bury him, no one mourn for him,   20
  But his body must lie in the fields, a sweet treasure
  For carrion birds to find as they search for food.
  That is what they say, and our good Creon is coming here
  To announce it publicly; and the penalty—
  Stoning to death in the public square!
                          There it is,
  And now you can prove what you are:
  A true sister, or a traitor to your family.
Ismene. Antigonê, you are mad! What could I possibly do?
Antigone. You must decide whether you will help me or not.
Ismene. I do not understand you. Help you in what?   30
Antigone. Ismenê, I am going to bury him. Will you come?
Ismene. Bury him! You have just said the new law forbids it.
Antigone. He is my brother. And he is your brother, too.
Ismene. But think of the danger! Think what Creon will do!
Antigone. Creon is not strong enough to stand in my way.
Ismene. Ah sister!
  Oedipus died, everyone hating him
  For what his own search brought to light, his eyes
  Ripped out by his own hand; and Iocastê died,
  His mother and wife at once: she twisted the cords   40
  That strangled her life; and our two brothers died,
  Each killed by the other's sword. And we are left:
  But oh, Antigonê,
  Think how much more terrible than these
  Our own death would be if we should go against Creon
  And do what he has forbidden! We are only women,
  We cannot fight with men, Antigonê!
  The law is strong, we must give in to the law
  In this thing, and in worse. I beg the Dead
  To forgive me, but I am helpless: I must yield   50
  To those in authority. And I think it is dangerous business
  To be always meddling.
Antigone.   If that is what you think,
  I should not want you, even if you asked to come.
  You have made your choice, you can be what you want to be.
  But I will bury him; and if I must die,

I say that this crime is holy: I shall lie down
With him in death, and I shall be as dear
To him as he to me.
               It is the dead,
Not the living, who make the longest demands:
We die for ever . . .
                       You may do as you like,   60
Since apparently the laws of the gods mean nothing to you.
Ismene. They mean a great deal to me; but I have no strength
    To break laws that were made for the public good.
Antigone. That must be your excuse, I suppose. But as for me,
    I will bury the brother I love.
Ismene.   Antigonê,
    I am so afraid for you!
Antigone.   You need not be:
    You have yourself to consider, after all.
Ismene. But no one must hear of this, you must tell no one!
    I will keep it a secret, I promise!
Antigone.   Oh tell it! Tell everyone!
    Think how they'll hate you when it all comes out   70
    If they learn that you knew about it all the time!
Ismene. So fiery! You should be cold with fear.
Antigone. Perhaps. But I am doing only what I must.
Ismene. But can you do it? I say that you cannot.
Antigone. Very well: when my strength gives out, I shall do no more.
Ismene. Impossible things should not be tried at all.
Antigone. Go away, Ismenê:
    I shall be hating you soon, and the dead will too,
    For your words are hateful. Leave me my foolish plan:
    I am not afraid of the danger; if it means death,   80
    It will not be the worst of deaths—death without honor.
Ismene. Go then, if you feel that you must.
    You are unwise,
    But a loyal friend indeed to those who love you.
             [*Exit into the Palace.* ANTIGONE *goes off, L. Enter the*
               CHORUS.

PÁRODOS[2]

Chorus. Now the long blade of the sun, lying   [STROPHE 1
    Level east to west, touches with glory

---

[2]Ode chanted by the Chorus as it enters the theater. A choral ode is divided into alternating verses, each called a *strophe* or an *antistrophe,* and is sometimes concluded by an *epode,* as in Scene IV. The Chorus here represents the elders of Thebes.

Thebes of the Seven Gates. Open, unlidded
Eye of golden day! O marching light
Across the eddy and rush of Dircê's stream,³
Striking the white shields of the enemy
Thrown headlong backward from the blaze of morning!
*Choragos.*⁴ Polyneicês their commander
 Roused them with windy phrases,
 He the wild eagle screaming   10
 Insults above our land,
 His wings their shields of snow,
 His crest their marshalled helms.
Chorus. Against our seven gates in a yawning ring [ANTISTROPHE 1
 The famished spears came onward in the night;
 But before his jaws were sated with our blood,
 Or pinefire took the garland of our towers,
 He was thrown back; and as he turned, great Thebes—
 No tender victim for his noisy power—
 Rose like a dragon behind him, shouting war.   20
Choragos. For God hates utterly
 The bray of bragging tongues;
 And when he beheld their smiling,
 Their swagger of golden helms,
 The frown of his thunder blasted
 Their first man from our walls.
Chorus. We heard his shout of triumph high in the air [STROPHE 2
 Turn to a scream; far out in a flaming arc
 He fell with his windy torch, and the earth struck him.
 And others storming in fury no less than his   30
 Found shock of death in the dusty joy of battle.
Choragos. Seven captains at seven gates
 Yielded their clanging arms to the god
 That bends the battle-line and breaks it.
 These two only, brothers in blood,
 Face to face in matchless rage,
 Mirroring each the other's death,
 Clashed in long combat.
Chorus. But now in the beautiful morning of victory [ANTISTROPHE 2
 Let Thebes of the many chariots sing for joy!   40
 With hearts for dancing we'll take leave of war:
 Our temples shall be sweet with hymns of praise,
 And the long night shall echo with our chorus.

³Located near Thebes.
⁴The Chorus leader.

SCENE I

Choragos. But now at last our new King is coming:
Creon of Thebes, Menoikeus' son.
In this auspicious dawn of his reign
What are the new complexities
That shifting Fate has woven for him?
What is his counsel? Why has he summoned
The old men to hear him?

> [*Enter* CREON *from the Palace, C. He addresses the* CHORUS
> *from the top step*

Creon. Gentlemen: I have the honor to inform you that our Ship of State,
which recent storms have threatened to destroy, has come safely to harbor
at last, guided by the merciful wisdom of Heaven. I have summoned you   10
here this morning because I know that I can depend upon you: your
devotion to King Laïos was absolute; you never hesitated in your duty to
our late ruler Oedipus; and when Oedipus died, your loyalty was transferred to his children. Unfortunately, as you know, his two sons, the princes
Eteoclês and Polyneicês, have killed each other in battle; and I, as the next
in blood, have succeeded to the full power of the throne.

I am aware, of course, that no ruler can expect complete loyalty from his
subjects until he has been tested in office. Nevertheless, I say to you at the
very outset that I have nothing but contempt for the kind of Governor
who is afraid, for whatever reason, to follow the course that he knows is   20
best for the State; and as for the man who sets private friendship above
the public welfare,—I have no use for him, either. I call God to witness
that if I saw my country headed for ruin, I should not be afraid to speak
out plainly; and I need hardly remind you that I would never have any
dealings with an enemy of the people. No one values friendship more
highly than I; but we must remember that friends made at the risk of
wrecking our Ship are not real friends at all.

These are my principles, at any rate, and that is why I have made the following
decision concerning the sons of Oedipus: Eteoclês, who died as a man
should die, fighting for his country, is to be buried with full military honors,   30
with all the ceremony that is usual when the greatest heroes die; but his
brother Polyneicês, who broke his exile to come back with fire and sword
against his native city and the shrines of his fathers' gods, whose one idea
was to spill the blood of his blood and sell his own people into slavery—
Polyneicês, I say, is to have no burial: no man is to touch him or say the
least prayer for him; he shall lie on the plain, unburied; and the birds and
the scavenging dogs can do with him whatever they like.

This is my command, and you can see the wisdom behind it. As long as I
am King, no traitor is going to be honored with the loyal man. But whoever
shows by word and deed that he is on the side of the State,—he shall have   40
my respect while he is living, and my reverence when he is dead.

Choragos. If that is your will, Creon son of Menoikeus,
   You have the right to enforce it: we are yours.
Creon. That is my will. Take care that you do your part.
Choragos. We are old men: let the younger ones carry it out.
Creon. I do not mean that: the sentries have been appointed.
Choragos. Then what is it that you would have us do?
Creon. You will give no support to whoever breaks this law.
Choragos. Only a crazy man is in love with death!
Creon. And death it is; yet money talks, and the wisest   50
   Have sometimes been known to count a few coins too many.
                                    [*Enter* SENTRY *from L.*
Sentry. I'll not say that I'm out of breath from running, King, because every
   time I stopped to think about what I have to tell you, I felt like going
   back. And all the time a voice kept saying, "You fool, don't you know
   you're walking straight into trouble?"; and then another voice: "Yes, but
   if you let somebody else get the news to Creon first, it will be even worse
   than that for you!" But good sense won out, at least I hope it was good
   sense, and here I am with a story that makes no sense at all; but I'll tell
   it anyhow, because, as they say, what's going to happen's going to happen,
   and—   60
Creon. Come to the point. What have you to say?
Sentry. I did not do it. I did not see who did it. You must not punish me
   for what someone else has done.
Creon. A comprehensive defense! More effective, perhaps,
   If I knew its purpose. Come: what is it?
Sentry. A dreadful thing . . . I don't know how to put it—
Creon. Out with it!
Sentry.   Well, then;
   The dead man
             Polyneicês

[*Pause. The* SENTRY *is overcome, fumbles for words.* CREON *waits
impassively.*

                 out there—
                          someone,—
   New dust on the slimy flesh!
                                    [*Pause. No sign from* CREON
   Someone has given it burial that way, and   70
   Gone . . .
   [*Long pause.* CREON *finally speaks with deadly control:*

Creon. And the man who dared do this?
Sentry.   I swear I
   Do not know! You must believe me!
                          Listen:

The ground was dry, not a sign of digging, no,
Not a wheeltrack in the dust, no trace of anyone.
It was when they relieved us this morning: and one of them,
The corporal, pointed to it.
                     There it was,
The strangest—
            Look:
The body, just mounded over with light dust: you see?
Not buried really, but as if they'd covered it   80
Just enough for the ghost's peace. And no sign
Of dogs or any wild animal that had been there.
And then what a scene there was! Every man of us
Accusing the other: we all proved the other man did it,
We all had proof that we could not have done it.
We were ready to take hot iron in our hands,
Walk through fire, swear by all the gods,
It was not I!
I do not know who it was, but it was not I!

[CREON'S *rage has been mounting steadily, but the* SENTRY *is too intent
upon his story to notice it*
And then, when this came to nothing, someone said   90
A thing that silenced us and made us stare
Down at the ground: you had to be told the news,
And one of us had to do it! We threw the dice,
And the bad luck fell to me. So here I am,
No happier to be here than you are to have me:
Nobody likes the man who brings bad news.
Choragos. I have been wondering, King: can it be that the gods have done
    this?
Creon.   *[Furiously*
Stop!
Must you doddering wrecks
Go out of your heads entirely? "The gods!"   100
Intolerable!
The gods favor this corpse? Why? How had he served them?
Tried to loot their temples, burn their images,
Yes, and the whole State, and its laws with it!
Is it your senile opinion that the gods love to honor bad men?
A pious thought!—
                No, from the very beginning
There have been those who have whispered together,
Stiff-necked anarchists, putting their heads together,
Scheming against me in alleys. These are the men,
And they have bribed my own guard to do this thing.   110
Money!   *[Sententiously*

There's nothing in the world so demoralizing as money.
Down go your cities,
Homes gone, men gone, honest hearts corrupted,
Crookedness of all kinds, and all for money!

[*To* SENTRY

But you—!
I swear by God and by the throne of God,
The man who has done this thing shall pay for it!
Find that man, bring him here to me, or your death
Will be the least of your problems: I'll string you up
Alive, and there will be certain ways to make you   120
Discover your employer before you die;
And the process may teach you a lesson you seem to have missed:
The dearest profit is sometimes all too dear:
That depends on the source. Do you understand me?
A fortune won is often misfortune.
Sentry. King, may I speak?
Creon.   Your very voice distresses me.
Sentry. Are you sure that it is my voice, and not your conscience?
Creon. By God, he wants to analyze me now!
Sentry. It is not what I say, but what has been done, that hurts you.
Creon. You talk too much.
Sentry.   Maybe; but I've done nothing.   130
Creon. Sold your soul for some silver: that's all you've done.
Sentry. How dreadful it is when the right judge judges wrong!
Creon. Your figures of speech
May entertain you now; but unless you bring me the man,
You will get little profit from them in the end.

[*Exit* CREON *into the Palace.*

Sentry. "Bring me the man"—!
I'd like nothing better than bringing him the man!
But bring him or not, you have seen the last of me here.
At any rate, I am safe!

[*Exit* SENTRY

ODE I

Chorus.   [STROPHE 1
Numberless are the world's wonders, but none
More wonderful than man; the stormgray sea
Yields to his prows, the huge crests bear him high;
Earth, holy and inexhaustible, is graven
With shining furrows where his plows have gone
Year after year, the timeless labor of stallions.

[ANTISTROPHE 1

The lightboned birds and beasts that cling to cover,
The lithe fish lighting their reaches of dim water,
All are taken, tamed in the net of his mind;
The lion on the hill, the wild horse windy-maned,   10
Resign to him; and his blunt yoke has broken
The sultry shoulders of the mountain bull.

                                                    [STROPHE 2

Words also, and thought as rapid as air,
He fashions to his good use; statecraft is his,
And his the skill that deflects the arrows of snow,
The spears of winter rain: from every wind
He has made himself secure—from all but one:
In the late wind of death he cannot stand.

                                                  [ANTISTROPHE 2

O clear intelligence, force beyond all measure!
O fate of man, working both good and evil!   20
When the laws are kept, how proudly his city stands!
When the laws are broken, what of his city then?
Never may the anárchic man find rest at my hearth,
Never be it said that my thoughts are his thoughts.

SCENE II

                            [*Re-enter* SENTRY *leading* ANTIGONE.
Choragos. What does this mean? Surely this captive woman
    Is the Princess, Antigonê. Why should she be taken?
Sentry. Here is the one who did it! We caught her
    In the very act of burying him.—Where is Creon?
Choragos. Just coming from the house.

                                                    [*Enter* CREON, C.

Creon.   What has happened?
    Why have you come back so soon?
Sentry.   O King,   [*Expansively*
    A man should never be too sure of anything:
    I would have sworn
    That you'd not see me here again: your anger
    Frightened me so, and the things you threatened me with;   10
    But how could I tell then
    That I'd be able to solve the case so soon?
    No dice-throwing this time: I was only too glad to come!
    Here is this woman. She is the guilty one:
    We found her trying to bury him.
    Take her, then; question her; judge her as you will.
    I am through with the whole thing now, and glad of it.
Creon. But this is Antigonê! Why have you brought her here?

Sentry. She was burying him, I tell you!
Creon.   [*Severely*
                          Is this the truth?
Sentry. I saw her with my own eyes. Can I say more?   20
Creon. The details: come, tell me quickly!
Sentry.   It was like this:
   After those terrible threats of yours, King,
   We went back and brushed the dust away from the body.
   The flesh was soft by now, and stinking,
   So we sat on a hill to windward and kept guard.
   No napping this time! We kept each other awake.
   But nothing happened until the white round sun
   Whirled in the center of the round sky over us:
   Then, suddenly,
   A storm of dust roared up from the earth, and the sky   30
   Went out, the plain vanished with all its trees
   In the stinging dark. We closed our eyes and endured it.
   The whirlwind lasted a long time, but it passed;
   And then we looked, and there was Antigonê!
   I have seen
   A mother bird come back to a stripped nest, heard
   Her crying bitterly a broken note or two
   For the young ones stolen. Just so, when this girl
   Found the bare corpse, and all her love's work wasted,
   She wept, and cried on heaven to damn the hands   40
   That had done this thing.
                          And then she brought more dust
   And sprinkled wine three times for her brother's ghost.
   We ran and took her at once. She was not afraid,
   Not even when we charged her with what she had done.
   She denied nothing.
                          And this was a comfort to me,
   And some uneasiness: for it is a good thing
   To escape from death, but it is no great pleasure
   To bring death to a friend.
                          Yet I always say
   There is nothing so comfortable as your own safe skin!
Creon.   [*Slowly, dangerously*
   And you, Antigonê,   50
   You with your head hanging,—do you confess this thing?
Antigone. I do, I deny nothing.
Creon.   [*To* SENTRY.
                 You may go.
                                         [*Exit* SENTRY
                                         [*To* ANTIGONE.

Tell me, tell me briefly:
Had you heard my proclamation touching this matter?
Antigone. It was public. Could I help hearing it?
Creon. And yet you dared defy the law.
Antigone.   I dared.
  It was not God's proclamation. That final Justice
  That rules the world below makes no such laws.

  Your edict, King, was strong,
  But all your strength is weakness itself against   60
  The immortal unrecorded laws of God.
  They are not merely now: they were, and shall be,
  Operative for ever, beyond man utterly.

  I knew I must die, even without your decree:
  I am only mortal. And if I must die
  Now, before it is my time to die,
  Surely this is no hardship: can anyone
  Living, as I live, with evil all about me,
  Think Death less than a friend? This death of mine
  Is of no importance; but if I had left my brother   70
  Lying in death unburied, I should have suffered.
  Now I do not.
                   You smile at me. Ah Creon,
  Think me a fool, if you like; but it may well be
  That a fool convicts me of folly.
Choragos. Like father, like daughter: both headstrong, deaf to reason!
  She has never learned to yield.
Creon.   She has much to learn.
  The inflexible heart breaks first, the toughest iron
  Cracks first, and the wildest horses bend their necks
  At the pull of the smallest curb.
                              Pride? In a slave?
  This girl is guilty of a double insolence,   80
  Breaking the given laws and boasting of it.
  Who is the man here,
  She or I, if this crime goes unpunished?
  Sister's child, or more than sister's child,
  Or closer yet in blood—she and her sister
  Win bitter death for this!

                                                        [*To servants:*
                   Go, some of you,
  Arrest Ismenê. I accuse her equally.
  Bring her: you will find her sniffling in the house there.

  Her mind's a traitor: crimes kept in the dark

Cry for light, and the guardian brain shudders;   90
But how much worse than this
Is brazen boasting of barefaced anarchy!
Antigone. Creon, what more do you want than my death?
Creon.   Nothing.
   That gives me everything.
Antigone.   Then I beg you: kill me.
   This talking is a great weariness: your words
   Are distasteful to me, and I am sure that mine
   Seem so to you. And yet they should not seem so:
   I should have praise and honor for what I have done.
   All these men here would praise me
   Were their lips not frozen shut with fear of you.   100

                                                          [*Bitterly*
   Ah the good fortune of kings,
   Licensed to say and do whatever they please!
Creon. You are alone here in that opinion.
Antigone. No, they are with me. But they keep their tongues in leash.
Creon. Maybe. But you are guilty, and they are not.
Antigone. There is no guilt in reverence for the dead.
Creon. But Eteoclês—was he not your brother too?
Antigone. My brother too.
Creon.   And you insult his memory?
Antigone.   [*Softly*
   The dead man would not say that I insult it.
Creon. He would: for you honor a traitor as much as him.   110
Antigone. His own brother, traitor or not, and equal in blood.
Creon. He made war on his country. Eteoclês defended it.
Antigone. Nevertheless, there are honors due all the dead.
Creon. But not the same for the wicked as for the just.
Antigone. Ah Creon, Creon,
   Which of us can say what the gods hold wicked?
Creon. An enemy is an enemy, even dead.
Antigone. It is my nature to join in love, not hate.
Creon.   [*Finally losing patience*
   Go join them, then; if you must have your love,
   Find it in hell!   120
Choragos. But see, Ismenê comes:

                                          [*Enter* ISMENE, *guarded*
   Those tears are sisterly, the cloud
   That shadows her eyes rains down gentle sorrow.
Creon. You too, Ismenê,
   Snake in my ordered house, sucking my blood
   Stealthily—and all the time I never knew
   That these two sisters were aiming at my throne!
                                          Ismenê,

Do you confess your share in this crime, or deny it?
Answer me.
Ismene. Yes, if she will let me say so. I am guilty.   130
Antigone.   [*Coldly*
No, Ismenê. You have no right to say so.
You would not help me, and I will not have you help me.
Ismene. But now I know what you meant; and I am here
To join you, to take my share of punishment.
Antigone. The dead man and the gods who rule the dead
Know whose act this was. Words are not friends.
Ismene. Do you refuse me, Antigonê? I want to die with you:
I too have a duty that I must discharge to the dead.
Antigone. You shall not lessen my death by sharing it.
Ismene. What do I care for life when you are dead?   140
Antigone. Ask Creon. You're always hanging on his opinions.
Ismene. You are laughing at me. Why, Antigonê?
Antigone. It's a joyless laughter, Ismenê.
Ismene.   But can I do nothing?
Antigone. Yes. Save yourself. I shall not envy you.
There are those who will praise you; I shall have honor, too.
Ismene. But we are equally guilty!
Antigone.   No more, Ismenê.
You are alive, but I belong to Death.
Creon.   [*To the* CHORUS.
Gentlemen, I beg you to observe these girls:
One has just now lost her mind; the other,
It seems, has never had a mind at all.   150
Ismene. Grief teaches the steadiest minds to waver, King.
Creon. Yours certainly did, when you assumed guilt with the guilty!
Ismene. But how could I go on living without her?
Creon.   You are.
She is already dead.
Ismene.   But your own son's bride!
Creon. There are places enough for him to push his plow.
I want no wicked women for my sons!
Ismene. O dearest Haimon, how your father wrongs you!
Creon. I've had enough of your childish talk of marriage!
Choragos. Do you really intend to steal this girl from your son?
Creon. No; Death will do that for me.
Choragos.   Then she must die?   160
Creon.   [*Ironically*
You dazzle me.
          —But enough of this talk!
                                              [*To* GUARDS.
You, there, take them away and guard them well:

For they are but women, and even brave men run
When they see Death coming.

[*Exeunt* ISMENE, ANTIGONE, *and* GUARDS

ODE II

Chorus.   [STROPHE 1
Fortunate is the man who has never tasted God's vengeance!
Where once the anger of heaven has struck, that house is shaken
For ever: damnation rises behind each child
Like a wave cresting out of the black northeast,
When the long darkness under sea roars up
And bursts drumming death upon the windwhipped sand.

[ANTISTROPHE 1
I have seen this gathering sorrow from time long past
Loom upon Oedipus' children: generation from generation
Takes the compulsive rage of the enemy god.
So lately this last flower of Oedipus' line   10
Drank the sunlight! but now a passionate word
And a handful of dust have closed up all its beauty.

[STROPHE 2
   What mortal arrogance
   Transcends the wrath of Zeus?
Sleep cannot lull him, nor the effortless long months
Of the timeless gods: but he is young for ever,
And his house is the shining day of high Olympos.
     All that is and shall be,
     And all the past, is his.
No pride on earth is free of the curse of heaven.   20

[ANTISTROPHE 2
   The straying dreams of men
   May bring them ghosts of joy:
But as they drowse, the waking embers burn them;
Or they walk with fíxed éyes, as blind men walk.
But the ancient wisdom speaks for our own time:
   Fate works most for woe
   With Folly's fairest show.
Man's little pleasure is the spring of sorrow.

SCENE III

Choragos. But here is Haimon, King, the last of all your sons.
   Is it grief for Antigonê that brings him here,
   And bitterness at being robbed of his bride?

[*Enter* HAIMON

Creon. We shall soon see, and no need of diviners.
                                        —Son,
    You have heard my final judgment on that girl:
    Have you come here hating me, or have you come
    With deference and with love, whatever I do?
Haimon. I am your son, father. You are my guide.
    You make things clear for me, and I obey you.
    No marriage means more to me than your continuing wisdom.   10
Creon. Good. That is the way to behave: subordinate
    Everything else, my son, to your father's will.
    This is what a man prays for, that he may get
    Sons attentive and dutiful in his house,
    Each one hating his father's enemies,
    Honoring his father's friends. But if his sons
    Fail him, if they turn out unprofitably,
    What has he fathered but trouble for himself
    And amusement for the malicious?
                     So you are right
Not to lose your head over this woman.   20
Your pleasure with her would soon grow cold, Haimon,
And then you'd have a hellcat in bed and elsewhere.
Let her find her husband in Hell!
Of all the people in this city, only she
Has had contempt for my law and broken it.

Do you want me to show myself weak before the people?
Or to break my sworn word? No, and I will not.
The woman dies.
I suppose she'll plead "family ties." Well, let her.
If I permit my own family to rebel,   30
How shall I earn the world's obedience?
Show me the man who keeps his house in hand,
He's fit for public authority.
                  I'll have no dealings
With law-breakers, critics of the government:
Whoever is chosen to govern should be obeyed—
Must be obeyed, in all things, great and small,
Just and unjust! O Haimon,
The man who knows how to obey, and that man only,
Knows how to give commands when the time comes.
You can depend on him, no matter how fast   40
The spears come: he's a good soldier, he'll stick it out.

Anarchy, anarchy! Show me a greater evil!
This is why cities tumble and the great houses rain down,
This is what scatters armies!

No, no: good lives are made so by discipline.
We keep the laws then, and the lawmakers,
And no woman shall seduce us. If we must lose,
Let's lose to a man, at least! Is a woman stronger than we?
Choragos. Unless time has rusted my wits,
    What you say, King, is said with point and dignity.   50
Haimon.   *[Boyishly earnest*
    Father:
Reason is God's crowning gift to man, and you are right
To warn me against losing mine. I cannot say—
I hope that I shall never want to say!—that you
Have reasoned badly. Yet there are other men
Who can reason, too; and their opinions might be helpful.
You are not in a position to know everything
That people say or do, or what they feel:
Your temper terrifies them—everyone
Will tell you only what you like to hear.   60
But I, at any rate, can listen; and I have heard them
Muttering and whispering in the dark about this girl.
They say no woman has ever, so unreasonably,
Died so shameful a death for a generous act:
"She covered her brother's body. Is this indecent?
She kept him from dogs and vultures. Is this a crime?
Death?—She should have all the honor that we can give her!"

This is the way they talk out there in the city.

You must believe me:
Nothing is closer to me than your happiness.   70
What could be closer? Must not any son
Value his father's fortune as his father does his?
I beg you, do not be unchangeable:
Do not believe that you alone can be right.
The man who thinks that,
The man who maintains that only he has the power
To reason correctly, the gift to speak, the soul—
A man like that, when you know him, turns out empty.

It is not reason never to yield to reason!

In flood time you can see how some trees bend,   80
And because they bend, even their twigs are safe,
While stubborn trees are torn up, roots and all.
And the same thing happens in sailing:
Make your sheet fast, never slacken,—and over you go,
Head over heels and under: and there's your voyage.

Forget you are angry! Let yourself be moved!
I know I am young; but please let me say this:
The ideal condition
Would be, I admit, that men should be right by instinct;
But since we are all too likely to go astray,   90
The reasonable thing is to learn from those who can teach.
Choragos. You will do well to listen to him, King,
If what he says is sensible. And you, Haimon,
Must listen to your father.—Both speak well.
Creon. You consider it right for a man of my years and experience
To go to school to a boy?
Haimon.   It is not right
If I am wrong. But if I am young, and right,
What does my age matter?
Creon. You think it right to stand up for an anarchist?
Haimon. Not at all. I pay no respect to criminals.   100
Creon. Then she is not a criminal?
Haimon. The City would deny it, to a man.
Creon. And the City proposes to teach me how to rule?
Haimon. Ah. Who is it that's talking like a boy now?
Creon. My voice is the one voice giving orders in this City!
Haimon. It is no city if it takes orders from one voice.
Creon. The State is the King!
Haimon.   Yes, if the State is a desert.

                                                    [*Pause*

Creon. This boy, it seems, has sold out to a woman.
Haimon. If you are a woman: my concern is only for you.
Creon. So? Your "concern"! In a public brawl with your father!   110
Haimon. How about you, in a public brawl with justice?
Creon. With justice, when all that I do is within my rights?
Haimon. You have no right to trample on God's right.
Creon.   [*Completely out of control*
Fool, adolescent fool! Taken in by a woman!
Haimon. You'll never see me taken in by anything vile.
Creon. Every word you say is for her!
Haimon.   [*Quietly, darkly*
                    And for you.
And for me. And for the gods under the earth.
Creon. You'll never marry her while she lives.
Haimon. Then she must die.—But her death will cause another.
Creon. Another?   120
Have you lost your senses? Is this an open threat?
Haimon. There is no threat in speaking to emptiness.
Creon. I swear you'll regret this superior tone of yours!
You are the empty one!

Haimon.   If you were not my father,
    I'd say you were perverse.
Creon. You girlstruck fool, don't play at words with me!
Haimon. I am sorry. You prefer silence.
Creon.   Now, by God—!
    I swear, by all the gods in heaven above us,
    You'll watch it, I swear you shall!
                                        [*To the* SERVANTS.
                            Bring her out!
    Bring the woman out! Let her die before his eyes!   130
    Here, this instant, with her bridegroom beside her!
Haimon. Not here, no; she will not die here, King.
    And you will never see my face again.
    Go on raving as long as you've a friend to endure you.
                                        [*Exit* HAIMON
Choragos. Gone, gone.
    Creon, a young man in a rage is dangerous!
Creon. Let him do, or dream to do, more than a man can.
    He shall not save these girls from death.
Choragos.   These girls?
    You have sentenced them both?
Creon.   No, you are right.
    I will not kill the one whose hands are clean.   140
Choragos. But Antigonê?
Creon.   [*Somberly*
                        I will carry her far away
    Out there in the wilderness, and lock her
    Living in a vault of stone. She shall have food,
    As the custom is, to absolve the State of her death.
    And there let her pray to the gods of hell:
    They are her only gods:
    Perhaps they will show her an escape from death,
    Or she may learn,
                    though late,
    That piety shown the dead is pity in vain.
                                        [*Exit* CREON

ODE III

Chorus.   [STROPHE
    Love, unconquerable
    Waster of rich men, keeper
    Of warm lights and all-night vigil
    In the soft face of a girl:
    Sea-wanderer, forest-visitor!

Even the pure Immortals cannot escape you,
And mortal man, in his one day's dusk,
Trembles before your glory.

[ANTISTROPHE

Surely you swerve upon ruin
The just man's consenting heart,   10
As here you have made bright anger
Strike between father and son—
And none has conquered but Love!
A girl's glánce wórking the will of heaven:
Pleasure to her alone who mocks us,
Merciless Aphroditê.[5]

SCENE IV

Choragos.   [As ANTIGONE *enters guarded*
    But I can no longer stand in awe of this,
    Nor, seeing what I see, keep back my tears.
    Here is Antigonê, passing to that chamber
    Where all find sleep at last.
Antigone. Look upon me, friends, and pity me   [STROPHE 1
    Turning back at the night's edge to say
    Good-by to the sun that shines for me no longer;
    Now sleepy Death
    Summons me down to Acheron,[6] that cold shore:
    There is no bridesong there, nor any music.   10
Chorus. Yet not unpraised, not without a kind of honor,
    You walk at last into the underworld;
    Untouched by sickness, broken by no sword.
    What woman has ever found your way to death?
Antigone.   [ANTISTROPHE 1
    How often I have heard the story of Niobê,[7]
    Tantalos' wretched daughter, how the stone
    Clung fast about her, ivy-close: and they say
    The rain falls endlessly
    And sifting soft snow; her tears are never done.
    I feel the loneliness of her death in mine.   20
Chorus. But she was born of heaven, and you
    Are woman, woman-born. If her death is yours,

---

[5]Goddess of love
[6]River of the underworld.
[7]Transformed to a rock on Mount Sipylos, whose streams are her tears for her fourteen children. They were killed by Apollo and Artemis, because Niobê boasted that her children were superior to the gods.

A mortal woman's, is this not for you
Glory in our world and in the world beyond?
Antigone. You laugh at me. Ah, friends, friends,   [STROPHE 2
  Can you not wait until I am dead? O Thebes,
  O men many-charioted, in love with Fortune,
  Dear springs of Dircê, sacred Theban grove,
  Be witnesses for me, denied all pity,
  Unjustly judged! and think a word of love   30
  For her whose path turns
  Under dark earth, where there are no more tears.
Chorus. You have passed beyond human daring and come at last
  Into a place of stone where Justice sits.
  I cannot tell
  What shape of your father's guilt appears in this.
Antigone.   [ANTISTROPHE 2
  You have touched it at last: that bridal bed
  Unspeakable, horror of son and mother mingling:
  Their crime, infection of all our family!
  O Oedipus, father and brother!   40
  Your marriage strikes from the grave to murder mine.
  I have been a stranger here in my own land:
  All my life
  The blasphemy of my birth has followed me
Chorus. Reverence is a virtue, but strength
  Lives in established law: that must prevail.
  You have made your choice,
  Your death is the doing of your conscious hand.
Antigone.   [EPODE
  Then let me go, since all your words are bitter,
  And the very light of the sun is cold to me.   50
  Lead me to my vigil, where I must have
  Neither love nor lamentation; no song, but silence.
              [CREON *interrupts impatiently*
Creon. If dirges and planned lamentations could put off death,
  Men would be singing for ever.   [*To the* SERVANTS.
            Take her, go!
  You know your orders: take her to the vault
  And leave her alone there. And if she lives or dies,
  That's her affair, not ours: our hands are clean.
Antigone. O tomb, vaulted bride-bed in eternal rock,
  Soon I shall be with my own again
  Where Persephonê[8] welcomes the thin ghosts underground: 60

---

[8]Queen of the underworld.

And I shall see my father again, and you, mother,
And dearest Polyneicês—
                            dearest indeed
To me, since it was my hand
That washed him clean and poured the ritual wine:
And my reward is death before my time!

And yet, as men's hearts know, I have done no wrong,
I have not sinned before God. Or if I have,
I shall know the truth in death. But if the guilt
Lies upon Creon who judged me, then, I pray,
May his punishment equal my own.
Choragos.   O passionate heart,   70
    Unyielding, tormented still by the same winds!
Creon. Her guards shall have good cause to regret their delaying.
Antigone. Ah! That voice is like the voice of death!
Creon. I can give you no reason to think you are mistaken.
Antigone. Thebes, and you my fathers' gods,
    And rulers of Thebes, you see me now, the last
    Unhappy daughter of a line of kings,
    Your kings, led away to death. You will remember
    What things I suffer, and at what men's hands,
    Because I would not transgress the laws of heaven.   80

                            [*To the* GUARDS, *simply:*

Come: let us wait no longer.

                            [*Exit* ANTIGONE, *L., guarded*

ODE IV

Chorus. All Danaê's[9] beauty was locked away   [STROPHE 1
    In a brazen cell where the sunlight could not come:
    A small room, still as any grave, enclosed her.
    Yet she was a princess too,
    And Zeus in a rain of gold poured love upon her.
    O child, child,
    No power in wealth or war
    Or tough sea-blackened ships
    Can prevail against untiring Destiny!

                            [ANTISTROPHE 1

And Dryas' son[10] also, that furious king,
    Bore the god's prisoning anger for his pride: 11

---

[9]Her father imprisoned her, but Zeus' visit, in a shower of gold, caused her to conceive the hero Perseus.
[10]Lycurgus, King of Thrace, imprisoned and driven mad by the god Dionysus.

Sealed up by Dionysos in deaf stone,
His madness died among echoes.
So at the last he learned what dreadful power
His tongue had mocked:
For he had profaned the revels,
And fired the wrath of the nine
Implacable Sisters[11] that love the sound of the flute.

[STROPHE 2

And old men tell a half-remembered tale
Of horror done where a dark ledge splits the sea   20
And a double surf beats on the gráy shóres:
How a king's new woman,[12] sick
With hatred for the queen he had imprisoned,
Ripped out his two sons' eyes with her bloody hands
While grinning Arês[13] watched the shuttle plunge
Four times: four blind wounds crying for revenge,

[ANTISTROPHE 2

Crying, tears and blood mingled.—Piteously born,
Those sons whose mother was of heavenly birth!
Her father was the god of the North Wind
And she was cradled by gales,   30
She raced with young colts on the glittering hills
And walked untrammeled in the open light:
But in her marriage deathless Fate found means
To build a tomb like yours for all her joy.

SCENE V.

> [*Enter blind* TEIRESIAS, *led by a boy. The opening speeches
> of* TEIRESIAS *should be in singsong contrast to the
> realistic lines of* CREON

Teiresias. This is the way the blind man comes, Princes, Princes,
    Lock-step, two heads lit by the eyes of one.
Creon. What new thing have you to tell us, old Teiresias?
Teiresias. I have much to tell you: listen to the prophet, Creon.
Creon. I am not aware that I have ever failed to listen.
Teiresias. Then you have done wisely, King, and ruled well.
Creon. I admit my debt to you. But what have you to say?

---

[11]The Muses, nine daughters of Zeus.
[12]Eidothea, second wife of King Phineus of Salmydessus, blinded her stepsons. Neither their imprisoned mother's high birth nor their father's kingly ancestry could prevent their suffering.
[13]God of war.

Teiresias. This, Creon: you stand once more on the edge of fate.
Creon. What do you mean? Your words are a kind of dread.
Teiresias. Listen, Creon: 10
    I was sitting in my chair of augury, at the place
    Where the birds gather about me. They were all a-chatter,
    As is their habit, when suddenly I heard
    A strange note in their jangling, a scream, a
    Whirring fury; I knew that they were fighting,
    Tearing each other, dying
    In a whirlwind of wings clashing. And I was afraid.
    I began the rites of burnt-offering at the altar,
    But Hephaistos[14] failed me: instead of bright flame,
    There was only the sputtering slime of the fat thigh-flesh   20
    Melting: the entrails dissolved in gray smoke,
    The bare bone burst from the welter. And no blaze!

    This was a sign from heaven. My boy described it,
    Seeing for me as I see for others.

    I tell you, Creon, you yourself have brought
    This new calamity upon us. Our hearths and altars
    Are stained with the corruption of dogs and carrion birds
    That glut themselves on the corpse of Oedipus' son.
    The gods are deaf when we pray to them, their fire
    Recoils from our offering, their birds of omen   30
    Have no cry of comfort, for they are gorged
    With the thick blood of the dead.
                 O my son,
    These are no trifles! Think: all men make mistakes,
    But a good man yields when he knows his course is wrong,
    And repairs the evil. The only crime is pride.
    Give in to the dead man, then: do not fight with a corpse—
    What glory is it to kill a man who is dead?
    Think, I beg you:
    It is for your own good that I speak as I do.
    You should be able to yield for your own good.   40
Creon. It seems that prophets have made me their especial province.
    All my life long
    I have been a kind of butt for the dull arrows
    Of doddering fortune-tellers!
              No, Teiresias:
    If your birds—if the great eagles of God himself

---

[14]God of fire.

Should carry him stinking bit by bit to heaven,
I would not yield. I am not afraid of pollution:
No man can defile the gods.

                      Do what you will,
Go into business, make money, speculate
In India gold or that synthetic gold from Sardis,   50
Get rich otherwise than by my consent to bury him.
Teiresias, it is a sorry thing when a wise man
Sells his wisdom, lets out his words for hire!
Teiresias. Ah Creon! Is there no man left in the world—
Creon. To do what?—Come, let's have the aphorism!
Teiresias. No man who knows that wisdom outweighs any wealth?
Creon. As surely as bribes are baser than any baseness.
Teiresias. You are sick, Creon! You are deathly sick!
Creon. As you say: it is not my place to challenge a prophet.
Teiresias. Yet you have said my prophecy is for sale.   60
Creon. The generation of prophets has always loved gold.
Teiresias. The generation of kings has always loved brass.
Creon. You forget yourself! You are speaking to your King.
Teiresias. I know it. You are a king because of me.
Creon. You have a certain skill; but you have sold out.
Teiresias. King, you will drive me to words that—
Creon.   Say them, say them!
Only remember: I will not pay you for them.
Teiresias. No, you will find them too costly.
Creon.   No doubt. Speak:
Whatever you say, you will not change my will.
Teiresias. Then take this, and take it to heart!   70
The time is not far off when you shall pay back
Corpse for corpse, flesh of your own flesh.
You have thrust the child of this world into living night,
You have kept from the gods below the child that is theirs:
The one in a grave before her death, the other,
Dead, denied the grave. This is your crime:
And the Furies and the dark gods of Hell
Are swift with terrible punishment for you.

Do you want to buy me now, Creon?
                         Not many days,   80
And your house will be full of men and women weeping,
And curses will be hurled at you from far
Cities grieving for sons unburied, left to rot
Before the walls of Thebes.

These are my arrows, Creon: they are all for you.

But come, child: lead me home.   [*To* BOY:
Let him waste his fine anger upon younger men.
Maybe he will learn at last
To control a wiser tongue in a better head.

                                     [*Exit* TEIRESIAS

Choragos. The old man has gone, King, but his words
    Remain to plague us. I am old, too,   90
    But I cannot remember that he was ever false.
Creon. That is true. . . . It troubles me.
    Oh it is hard to give in! but it is worse
    To risk everything for stubborn pride.
Choragos.
    Creon: take my advice.
Creon.   What shall I do?
Choragos.
    Go quickly: free Antigonê from her vault
    And build a tomb for the body of Polyneicês.
Creon. You would have me do this?
Choragos.   Creon, yes!
    And it must be done at once: God moves
    Swiftly to cancel the folly of stubborn men.   100
Creon. It is hard to deny the heart! But I
    Will do it: I will not fight with destiny.
Choragos.
    You must go yourself, you cannot leave it to others.
Creon. I will go.
            —Bring axes, servants:
    Come with me to the tomb. I buried her, I
    Will set her free.
                  Oh quickly!
    My mind misgives—
    The laws of the gods are mighty, and a man must serve them
    To the last day of his life!

                                     [*Exit* CREON

PÆAN[15]

Choragos. God of many names   [STROPHE 1
Chorus.   O Iacchos
                            son
    of Kadmeian Sémelê

---

[15]A hymn, dedicated here to Dionysos, also called Iacchos. Sémelê, his mother, was daughter of Kadmos, founder of Thebes, and his father was Zeus. Female followers of Dionysos were the Maenads, whose cry was *Evohé, evohé.*

O born of the Thunder!
Guardian of the West
        Regent
of Eleusis' plain
        O Prince of maenad Thebes
and the Dragon Field by rippling Ismenos:[16]

Choragos. God of many names   [ANTISTROPHE 1
Chorus.   the flame of torches
flares on our hills
        the nymphs of Iacchos
dance at the spring of Castalia:[17]

from the vine-close mountain
                come ah come in ivy:
Evohé evohé! sings through the streets of Thebes   10

Choragos. God of many names   [STROPHE 2
Chorus.   Iacchos of Thebes
heavenly Child
        of Sémelê bride of the Thunderer!
The shadow of plague is upon us:
                come
with clement feet
        oh come from Parnasos
down the long slopes
        across the lamenting water

Choragos.   [ANTISTROPHE 2
Iô Fire! Chorister of the throbbing stars!
O purest among the voices of the night!
Thou son of God, blaze for us!

Chorus. Come with choric rapture of circling Maenads
Who cry *Iô Iacche!*
        God of many names!   20

EXODOS   [*Enter* MESSENGER, *L.*

Messenger. Men of the line of Kadmos, you who live
    Near Amphion's[18] citadel:
                I cannot say
Of any condition of human life "This is fixed,
This is clearly good, or bad". Fate raises up,

---

[16]A river of Thebes. The ancestors of Theban nobility sprang from dragon's teeth shown by Kadmos near the river.
[17]Spring on Mount Parnassos.
[18]He built the wall around Thebes by charming the stones with music from his lyre.

And Fate casts down the happy and unhappy alike:
No man can foretell his Fate.
                            Take the case of Creon:
Creon was happy once, as I count happiness:
Victorious in battle, sole governor of the land,
Fortunate father of children nobly born.
And now it has all gone from him! Who can say   10
That a man is still alive when his life's joy fails?
He is a walking dead man. Grant him rich,
Let him live like a king in his great house:
If his pleasure is gone, I would not give
So much as the shadow of smoke for all he owns.
Choragos. Your words hint at sorrow: what is your news for us?
Messenger. They are dead. The living are guilty of their death.
Choragos. Who is guilty? Who is dead? Speak!
Messenger.   Haimon.
    Haimon is dead; and the hand that killed him
    Is his own hand.
Choragos.   His father's? or his own?   20
Messenger. His own, driven mad by the murder his father had done.
Choragos. Teiresias, Teiresias, how clearly you saw it all!
Messenger. This is my news: you must draw what conclusions you can
        from it.
Choragos. But look: Eurydicê, our Queen:
    Has she overheard us?
                            [*Enter* EURYDICE *from the Palace, C.*
Eurydice. I have heard something, friends:
    As I was unlocking the gate of Pallas'[19] shrine,
    For I needed her help today, I heard a voice
    Telling of some new sorrow. And I fainted
    There at the temple with all my maidens about me.   30
    But speak again: whatever it is, I can bear it:
    Grief and I are no strangers.
Messenger.   Dearest Lady,
    I will tell you plainly all that I have seen.
    I shall not try to comfort you: what is the use,
    Since comfort could lie only in what is not true?
    The truth is always best.
                            I went with Creon
    To the outer plain where Polyneicês was lying,
    No friend to pity him, his body shredded by dogs.
    We made our prayers in that place to Hecatê
    And Pluto,[20] that they would be merciful. And we bathed   40

---

[19]Athene, goddess of wisdom.
[20]Hecatê and Pluto are both deities of the underworld.

The corpse with holy water, and we brought
Fresh-broken branches to burn what was left of it,
And upon the urn we heaped up a towering barrow
Of the earth of his own land.
                              When we were done, we ran
To the vault where Antigonê lay on her couch of stone.
One of the servants had gone ahead,
And while he was yet far off he heard a voice
Grieving within the chamber, and he came back
And told Creon. And as the King went closer,
The air was full of wailing, the words lost,   50
And he begged us to make all haste. "Am I a prophet?"
He said, weeping, "And must I walk this road,
The saddest of all that I have gone before?
My son's voice calls me on. Oh quickly, quickly!
Look through the crevice there, and tell me
If it is Haimon, or some deception of the gods!"

We obeyed; and in the cavern's farthest corner
We saw her lying:
She had made a noose of her fine linen veil
And hanged herself. Haimon lay beside her,   60
His arms about her waist, lamenting her,
His love lost under ground, crying out
That his father had stolen her away from him.

When Creon saw him the tears rushed to his eyes
And he called to him: "What have you done, child? Speak to me.
What are you thinking that makes your eyes so strange?
O my son, my son, I come to you on my knees!"
But Haimon spat in his face. He said not a word,
Staring—
        And suddenly drew his sword
And lunged. Creon shrank back, the blade missed; and the boy,   70
Desperate against himself, drove it half its length
Into his own side, and fell. And as he died
He gathered Antigonê close in his arms again,
Choking, his blood bright red on her white cheek.
And now he lies dead with the dead, and she is his
At last, his bride in the houses of the dead.
                              [*Exit* EURYDICE *into the Palace*
Choragos. She has left us without a word. What can this mean?
Messenger. It troubles me, too; yet she knows what is best,
    Her grief is too great for public lamentation,
    And doubtless she has gone to her chamber to weep   80
    For her dead son, leading her maidens in his dirge.

Choragos. It may be so: but I fear this deep silence

[*Pause*

Messenger. I will see what she is doing. I will go in.

[*Exit* MESSENGER *into the Palace*

[*Enter* CREON *with attendants, bearing* HAIMON'S *body*

Choragos. But here is the King himself: oh look at him,
 Bearing his own damnation in his arms.
Creon. Nothing you say can touch me any more.
 My own blind heart has brought me
 From darkness to final darkness. Here you see
 The father murdering, the murdered son—
 And all my civic wisdom!   90

 Haimon my son, so young, so young to die,
 I was the fool, not you; and you died for me.
Choragos. That is the truth; but you were late in learning it.
Creon. This truth is hard to bear. Surely a god
 Has crushed me beneath the hugest weight of heaven
 And driven me headlong a barbaric way
 To trample out the thing I held most dear.

 The pains that men will take to come to pain!

[*Enter* MESSENGER *from the Palace*

Messenger. The burden you carry in your hands is heavy,
 But it is not all: you will find more in your house.   100
Creon. What burden worse than this shall I find there?
Messenger. The Queen is dead.
Creon. O port of death, deaf world,
 Is there no pity for me? And you, Angel of evil,
 I was dead, and your words are death again.
 Is it true, boy? Can it be true?
 Is my wife dead? Has death bred death?
Messenger. You can see for yourself.

[*The doors are opened, and the body of* EURYDICE *is
disclosed within.*

Creon. Oh pity!
 All true, all true, and more than I can bear!   110
 O my wife, my son!
Messenger. She stood before the altar, and her heart
 Welcomed the knife her own hand guided,
 And a great cry burst from her lips for Megareus[21] dead,

---

[21]Eurydicê's and Creon's other son, killed in the attack on Thebes.

And for Haimon dead, her sons; and her last breath
Was a curse for their father, the murderer of her sons.
And she fell, and the dark flowed in through her closing eyes
Creon. O God, I am sick with fear.
Are there no swords here? Has no one a blow for me?
Messenger. Her curse is upon you for the deaths of both.   120
Creon. It is right that it should be. I alone am guilty.
I know it, and I say it. Lead me in,
Quickly, friends.
I have neither life nor substance. Lead me in.
Choragos. You are right, if there can be right in so much wrong.
The briefest way is best in a world of sorrow.
Creon. Let it come,
Let death come quickly, and be kind to me.
I would not ever see the sun again.
Choragos. All that will come when it will; but we, meanwhile,   130
Have much to do. Leave the future to itself.
Creon. All my heart was in that prayer!
Choragos. Then do not pray any more: the sky is deaf.
Creon. Lead me away. I have been rash and foolish.
I have killed my son and my wife.
I look for comfort; my comfort lies here dead.
Whatever my hands have touched has come to nothing.
Fate has brought all my pride to a thought of dust.

[*As* CREON *is being led into the house, the* CHORAGOS *advances and speaks directly to the audience*
Choragos. There is no happiness where there is no wisdom;
No wisdom but in submission to the gods.   140
Big words are always punished,
And proud men in old age learn to be wise.

QUESTIONS

1. What do you imagine the atmosphere in Thebes to be in the immediate wake of the battle?
2. Does the idea of a body left unburied, as Polyneicês' is, strike any particular responses in you?
3. What considerations motivate Antigonê's action and serve to characterize her?
4. Can you understand the reasoning and, perhaps, the feelings behind Creon's decree? What do you see as his strongest motivation?
5. Is Antigonê clearly right, and Creon as clearly wrong?
6. How much insight into the significance of events does the Chorus appear to have?
7. What feelings does Antigonê's fate arouse?
8. How much sympathy with Creon do you feel at the conclusion?

Lorraine Hansberry (1930–1965)

A RAISIN IN THE SUN

To Mama:
in gratitude for the dream

CHARACTERS

Ruth Younger	Joseph Asagai
Travis Younger	George Murchison
Walter Lee Younger (Brother)	Karl Lindner
Beneatha Younger	Bobo
Lena Younger (Mama)	Moving Men

The action of the play is set in Chicago's Southside, sometime between World War II and the present.

ACT ONE
  SCENE 1. Friday morning.
  SCENE 2. The following morning.

ACT TWO
  SCENE 1. Later, the same day.
  SCENE 2. Friday night, a few weeks later.
  SCENE 3. Moving day, one week later.

ACT THREE
  An hour later.

What happens to a dream deferred?
Does it dry up
Like a raisin in the sun?
Or fester like a sore—
And then run?
Does it stink like rotten meat?
Or crust and sugar over—
Like a syrupy sweet?

Maybe it just sags
Like a heavy load.

Or does it explode?

—Langston Hughes[1]

---

[1]"Dream Deferred." Copyright 1951 by Langston Hughes. Reprinted from *The Panther and the Lash* by Langston Hughes, by permission of Alfred A. Knopf, Inc.

ACT ONE
SCENE I

The YOUNGER *living room would be a comfortable and well-ordered room if it were not for a number of indestructible contradictions to this state of being. Its furnishings are typical and undistinguished and their primary feature now is that they have clearly had to accommodate the living of too many people for too many years—and they are tired. Still, we can see that at some time, a time probably no longer remembered by the family (except perhaps for* MAMA*), the furnishings of this room were actually selected with care and love and even hope—and brought to this apartment and arranged with taste and pride.*

That was a long time ago. Now the once loved pattern of the couch upholstery has to fight to show itself from under acres of crocheted doilies and couch covers which have themselves finally come to be more important than the upholstery. And here a table or a chair has been moved to disguise the worn places in the carpet; but the carpet has fought back by showing its weariness, with depressing uniformity, elsewhere on its surface.

Weariness has, in fact, won in this room. Everything has been polished, washed, sat on, used, scrubbed too often. All pretenses but living itself have long since vanished from the very atmosphere of this room.

Moreover, a section of this room, for it is not really a room unto itself, though the landlord's lease would make it seem so, slopes backward to provide a small kitchen area, where the family prepares the meals that are eaten in the living room proper, which must also serve as dining room. The single window that has been provided for these "two" rooms is located in this kitchen area. The sole natural light the family may enjoy in the course of a day is only that which fights its way through this little window. At left, a door leads to a bedroom which is shared by MAMA *and her daughter,* BENEATHA. *At right, opposite, is a second room (which in the beginning of the life of this apartment was probably a breakfast room) which serves as a bedroom for* WALTER *and his wife,* RUTH.

Time: Sometime between World War II and the present.

Place: Chicago's Southside.

At Rise: It is morning dark in the living room. TRAVIS *is asleep on the make-down bed at center. An alarm clock sounds from within the bedroom at right, and presently* RUTH *enters from that room and closes the door behind her. She crosses sleepily toward the window. As she passes her sleeping son she reaches down and shakes him a little. At the window she raises the shade and a dusky Southside morning light comes in feebly. She fills a pot with water and puts it on to boil. She calls to the boy, between yawns, in a slightly muffled voice.*

RUTH *is about thirty. We can see that she was a pretty girl, even exceptionally so, but now it is apparent that life has been little that she expected, and disappointment has already begun to hang in her face. In a few years,*

before thirty-five even, she will be known among her people as a "settled woman."
She crosses to her son and gives him a good, final, rousing shake.

Ruth. Come on now, boy, it's seven thirty! (*Her son sits up at last, in a stupor of sleepiness*) I say hurry up, Travis! You ain't the only person in the world got to use a bathroom!

(*The child, a sturdy, handsome little boy of ten or eleven, drags himself out of the bed and almost blindly takes his towels and "today's clothes" from drawers and a closet and goes out to the bathroom, which is in an outside hall and which is shared by another family or families on the same floor.* RUTH *crosses to the bedroom door at right and opens it and calls in to her husband*)

Walter Lee! . . . It's after seven thirty! Lemme see you do some waking up in there now! (*She waits*) You better get up from there, man! It's after seven thirty I tell you. (*She waits again*) All right, you just go ahead and lay there and next thing you know Travis be finished and Mr. Johnson'll be in there and you'll be fussing and cussing round here like a mad man! And be late too! (*She waits, at the end of patience*) Walter Lee—it's time for you to get up!

(*She waits another second and then starts to go into the bedroom, but is apparently satisfied that her husband has begun to get up. She stops, pulls the door to, and returns to the kitchen area. She wipes her face with a moist cloth and runs her fingers through her sleep-disheveled hair in a vain effort and ties an apron around her housecoat. The bedroom door at right opens and her husband stands in the doorway in his pajamas, which are rumpled and mismated. He is a lean, intense young man in his middle thirties, inclined to quick nervous movements and erratic speech habits— and always in his voice there is a quality of indictment*)

Walter. Is he out yet?
Ruth. What you mean *out*? He ain't hardly got in there good yet.
Walter (*Wandering in, still more oriented to sleep than to a new day*). Well, what was you doing all that yelling for if I can't even get in there yet? (*Stopping and thinking*) Check coming today?
Ruth. They *said* Saturday and this is just Friday and I hopes to God you ain't going to get up here first thing this morning and start talking to me 'bout no money—'cause I 'bout don't want to hear it.
Walter. Something the matter with you this morning?
Ruth. No—I'm just sleepy as the devil. What kind of eggs you want?
Walter. Not scrambled. (*Ruth starts to scramble eggs*) Paper come? (*Ruth points impatiently to the rolled up* Tribune *on the table, and he gets it*

and spreads it out and vaguely reads the front page) Set off another bomb yesterday.

Ruth (Maximum indifference). Did they?

Walter (Looking up). What's the matter with you?

Ruth. Ain't nothing the matter with me. And don't keep asking me that this morning.

Walter. Ain't nobody bothering you. *(Reading the news of the day absently again)* Say Colonel McCormick is sick.

Ruth (Affecting tea-party interest). Is he now? Poor thing.

Walter (Sighing and looking at his watch). Oh, me. *(He waits)* Now what is that boy doing in that bathroom all this time? He just going to have to start getting up earlier. I can't be being late to work on account of him fooling around in there.

Ruth (Turning on him). Oh, no he ain't going to be getting up no earlier no such thing! It ain't his fault that he can't get to bed no earlier nights 'cause he got a bunch of crazy good-for-nothing clowns sitting up running their mouths in what is supposed to be his bedroom after ten o'clock at night . . .

Walter. That's what you mad about, ain't it? The things I want to talk about with my friends just couldn't be important in your mind, could they?

(He rises and finds a cigarette in her handbag on the table and crosses to the little window and looks out, smoking and deeply enjoying this first one)

Ruth (Almost matter of factly, a complaint too automatic to deserve emphasis). Why you always got to smoke before you eat in the morning?

Walter (At the window). Just look at 'em down there . . . Running and racing to work . . . *(He turns and faces his wife and watches her a moment at the stove, and then, suddenly)* You look young this morning, baby.

Ruth (Indifferently). Yeah?

Walter. Just for a second—stirring them eggs. It's gone now—just for a second it was—you looked real young again. *(Then, drily)* It's gone now—you look like yourself again.

Ruth. Man, if you don't shut up and leave me alone.

Walter (Looking out to the street again). First thing a man ought to learn in life is not to make love to no colored woman first thing in the morning. You all some evil people at eight o'clock in the morning.

(TRAVIS appears in the hall doorway, almost fully dressed and quite wide awake now, his towels and pajamas across his shoulders. He opens the door and signals for his father to make the bathroom in a hurry)

Travis (Watching the bathroom). Daddy, come on!

(WALTER gets his bathroom utensils and flies out to the bathroom)

Ruth. Sit down and have your breakfast, Travis.

Travis. Mama, this is Friday. *(Gleefully)* Check coming tomorrow, huh?

Ruth. You get your mind off money and eat your breakfast.

Travis (Eating). This is the morning we supposed to bring the fifty cents to school.

Ruth. Well, I ain't got no fifty cents this morning.

Travis. Teacher say we have to.

Ruth. I don't care what teacher say. I ain't got it. Eat your breakfast, Travis.

Travis. I *am* eating.

Ruth. Hush up now and just eat!

(The boy gives her an exasperated look for her lack of understanding, and eats grudgingly)

Travis. You think Grandmama would have it?

Ruth. No! And I want you to stop asking your grandmother for money, you hear me?

Travis (Outraged). Gaaaleee! I don't ask her, she just gimme it sometimes!

Ruth. Travis Willard Younger—I got too much on me this morning to be—

Travis. Maybe Daddy—

Ruth. Travis!

(The boy hushes abruptly. They are both quiet and tense for several seconds)

Travis (Presently). Could I maybe go carry some groceries in front of the supermarket for a little while after school then?

Ruth. Just hush, I said. *(Travis jabs his spoon into his cereal bowl viciously, and rests his head in anger upon his fists)* If you through eating, you can get over there and make up your bed.

(The boy obeys stiffly and crosses the room, almost mechanically, to the bed and more or less carefully folds the covering. He carries the bedding into his mother's room and returns with his books and cap)

Travis (Sulking and standing apart from her unnaturally). I'm gone.

Ruth (Looking up from the stove to inspect him automatically) Come here. *(He crosses to her and she studies his head)* If you don't take this comb and fix this here head, you better! (TRAVIS *puts down his books with a great sigh of oppression, and crosses to the mirror. His mother mutters under her breath about his "slubbornness")* 'Bout to march out of here with that head looking just like chickens slept in it! I just don't know where you get your slubborn ways . . . And get your jacket, too. Looks chilly out this morning.

Travis (With conspicuously brushed hair and jacket). I'm gone.

Ruth. Get carfare and milk money—(*Waving one finger*)—and not a single penny for no caps, you hear me?

Travis (With sullen politeness). Yes'm.

(*He turns in outrage to leave. His mother watches after him as in his frustration he approaches the door almost comically. When she speaks to him, her voice has become a very gentle tease*)

Ruth (Mocking; as she thinks he would say it). Oh, Mama makes me so mad sometimes, I don't know what to do! (*She waits and continues to his back as he stands stock-still in front of the door*) I wouldn't kiss that woman good-bye for nothing in this world this morning! (*The boy finally turns around and rolls his eyes at her, knowing the mood has changed and he is vindicated; he does not, however, move toward her yet*) Not for nothing in this world! (*She finally laughs aloud at him and holds out her arms to him and we see that it is a way between them, very old and practiced. He crosses to her and allows her to embrace him warmly but keeps his face fixed with masculine rigidity. She holds him back from her presently and looks at him and runs her fingers over the features of his face. With utter gentleness—*) Now—whose little old angry man are you?

Travis (The masculinity and gruffness start to fade at last). Aw gaalee— Mama . . .

Ruth (Mimicking). Aw—gaaaaalleeeee, Mama! (*She pushes him, with rough playfulness and finality, toward the door*) Get on out of here or you going to be late.

Travis (In the face of love, new aggressiveness). Mama, could I *please* go carry groceries?

Ruth. Honey, it's starting to get so cold evenings.

Walter (Coming in from the bathroom and drawing a make-believe gun from a make-believe holster and shooting at his son). What is it he wants to do?

Ruth. Go carry groceries after school at the supermarket.

Walter. Well, let him go . . .

Travis (Quickly, to the ally). I have to—she won't gimme the fifty cents . . .

Walter (To his wife only). Why not?

Ruth (Simply, and with flavor). 'Cause we don't have it.

Walter (To RUTH only). What you tell the boy things like that for? (*Reaching down into his pants with a rather important gesture*) Here, son—

(*He hands the boy the coin, but his eyes are directed to his wife's.* TRAVIS *takes the money happily*)

Travis. Thanks, Daddy.

(He starts out. RUTH *watches both of them with murder in her eyes.* WALTER *stands and stares back at her with defiance, and suddenly reaches into his pocket again on an afterthought)*

Walter (Without even looking at his son, still staring hard at his wife). In fact, here's another fifty cents . . . Buy yourself some fruit today—or take a taxi cab to school or something!
Travis. Whoopee—

(He leaps up and clasps his father around the middle with his legs, and they face each other in mutual appreciation; slowly WALTER LEE *peeks around the boy to catch the violent rays from his wife's eyes and draws his head back as if shot)*

Walter. You better get down now—and get to school, man.
Travis (At the door). O.K. Good-bye.

(He exits)

Walter (After him, pointing with pride). That's *my* boy. *(She looks at him in disgust and turns back to her work).* You know what I was thinking 'bout in the bathroom this morning?
Ruth. No.
Walter. How come you always try to be so pleasant!
Ruth. What is there to be pleasant 'bout!
Walter. You want to know what I was thinking 'bout in the bathroom or not!
Ruth. I know what you was thinking 'bout.
Walter (Ignoring her). 'Bout what me and Willy Harris was talking about last night.
Ruth (Immediately—a refrain). Willy Harris is a good-for-nothing loud mouth.
Walter. Anybody who talks to me has got to be a good-for-nothing loud mouth, ain't he? And what you know about who is just a good-for-nothing loud mouth? Charlie Atkins was just a "good-for-nothing loud mouth" too, wasn't he! When he wanted me to go in the dry-cleaning business with him. And now—he's grossing a hundred thousand a year. A hundred thousand dollars a year! You still call *him* a loud mouth!
Ruth (Bitterly). Oh, Walter Lee . . .

(She folds her head on her arms over on the table)

Walter (Rising and coming to her and standing over her). You tired, ain't you? Tired of everything. Me, the boy, the way we live—this beat-up hole—everything. Ain't you? *(She doesn't look up, doesn't answer)* So tired—moaning and groaning all the time, but you wouldn't do nothing to help, would you? You couldn't be on my side that long for nothing, could you?

Ruth. Walter, please leave me alone.

Walter. A man needs for a woman to back him up . . .

Ruth. Walter—

Walter. Mama would listen to you. You know she listen to you more than she do me and Bennie. She think more of you. All you have to do is just sit down with her when you drinking your coffee one morning and talking 'bout things like you do and—*(He sits down beside her and demonstrates graphically what he thinks her methods and tone should be)*—you just sip your coffee, see, and say easy like that you been thinking 'bout that deal Walter Lee is so interested in, 'bout the store and all, and sip some more coffee, like what you saying ain't really that important to you— And the next thing you know, she be listening good and asking you questions and when I come home—I can tell her the details. This ain't no fly-by-night proposition, baby. I mean we figured it out, me and Willy and Bobo.

Ruth (With a frown). Bobo?

Walter. Yeah. You see, this little liquor store we got in mind cost seventy-five thousand and we figured the initial investment on the place be 'bout thirty thousand, see. That be ten thousand each. Course, there's a couple of hundred you got to pay so's you don't spend your life just waiting for them clowns to let your license get approved—

Ruth. You mean graft?

Walter (Frowning impatiently). Don't call it that. See there, that just goes to show you what women understand about the world. Baby, don't *nothing* happen for you in this world 'less you pay *somebody* off!

Ruth. Walter, leave me alone! *(She raises her head and stares at him vigorously—then says, more quietly)* Eat your eggs, they gonna be cold.

Walter (Straightening up from her and looking off). That's it. There you are. Man say to his woman: I got me a dream. His woman say: Eat your eggs. *(Sadly, but gaining in power)* Man say: I got to take hold of this here world, baby! And a woman will say: Eat your eggs and go to work. *(Passionately now)* Man say: I got to change my life, I'm choking to death, baby! And his woman say—*(In utter anguish as he bring his fists down on his thighs)*—Your eggs is getting cold!

Ruth (Softly). Walter, that ain't none of our money.

Walter (Not listening at all or even looking at her). This morning, I was lookin' in the mirror and thinking about it . . . I'm thirty-five years old; I been married eleven years and I got a boy who sleeps in the living room— *(Very, very quietly)*—and all I got to give him is stories about how rich white people live . . .

Ruth. Eat your eggs, Walter.

Walter. Damn my eggs . . . *damn all the eggs that ever was!*

Ruth. Then go to work.

Walter (Looking up at her). See—I'm trying to talk to you 'bout myself— *(Shaking his head with the repetition)*—and all you can say is eat them eggs and go to work.

Ruth (Wearily). Honey, you never say nothing new. I listen to you every day, every night and every morning, and you never say nothing new. *(Shrugging)* So you would rather *be* Mr. Arnold than be his chauffeur. So—I would *rather* be living in Buckingham Palace.

Walter. That is just what is wrong with the colored woman in this world . . . . Don't understand about building their men up and making 'em feel like they somebody. Like they can do something.

Ruth (Drily, but to hurt). There *are* colored men who do things.

Walter. No thanks to the colored woman.

Ruth. Well, being a colored woman, I guess I can't help myself none.

(She rises and gets the ironing board and sets it up and attacks a huge pile of rough-dried clothes, sprinkling them in preparation for the ironing and then rolling them into tight fat balls)

Walter (Mumbling). We one group of men tied to a race of women with small minds.

(His sister BENEATHA *enters. She is about twenty, as slim and intense as her brother. She is not as pretty as her sister-in-law, but her lean, almost intellectual face has a handsomeness of its own. She wears a bright-red flannel nightie, and her thick hair stands wildly about her head. Her speech is a mixture of many things; it is different from the rest of the family's insofar as education has permeated her sense of English—and perhaps the Midwest rather than the South has finally—at last—won out in her inflection; but not altogether, because over all of it is a soft slurring and transformed use of vowels which is the decided influence of the Southside. She passes through the room without looking at either* RUTH *or* WALTER *and goes to the outside door and looks, a little blindly, out to the bathroom. She sees that it has been lost to the Johnsons. She closes the door with a sleepy vengeance and crosses to the table and sits down a little defeated)*

Beneatha. I am going to start timing those people.

Walter. You should get up earlier.

Beneatha (Her face in her hands. She is still fighting the urge to go back to bed). Really—would you suggest dawn? Where's the paper?

Walter (Pushing the paper across the table to her as he studies her almost clinically, as though he has never seen her before). You a horrible-looking chick at this hour.

Beneatha (Drily). Good morning, everybody.

Walter (Senselessly). How is school coming?

Beneatha (In the same spirit). Lovely. Lovely. And you know, biology is the greatest. *(Looking up at him)* I dissected something that looked just like you yesterday.

Walter. I just wondered if you've made up your mind and everything.

Beneatha (Gaining in sharpness and impatience). And what did I answer yesterday morning—and the day before that?

Ruth (From the ironing board, like someone disinterested and old). Don't be so nasty, Bennie.

Beneatha (Still to her brother). And the day before that and the day before that!

Walter (Defensively). I'm interested in you. Something wrong with that? Ain't many girls who decide—

Walter and Beneatha (In unison). —"to be a doctor." *(Silence)*

Walter. Have we figured out yet just exactly how much medical school is going to cost?

Ruth. Walter Lee, why don't you leave that girl alone and get out of here to work?

Beneatha (Exits to the bathroom and bangs on the door). Come on out of there, please!

(She comes back into the room)

Walter (Looking at his sister intently). You know the check is coming tomorrow.

Beneatha (Turning on him with a sharpness all her own). That money belongs to Mama, Walter, and it's for her to decide how she wants to use it. I don't care if she wants to buy a house or a rocket ship or just nail it up somewhere and look at it. It's hers. Not ours—*hers*.

Walter (Bitterly). Now ain't that fine! You just got your mother's interest at heart, ain't you, girl? You such a nice girl—but if Mama got that money she can always take a few thousand and help you through school too—can't she?

Beneatha. I have never asked anyone around here to do anything for me!

Walter. No! And the line between asking and just accepting when the time comes is big and wide—ain't it!

Beneatha (With fury). What do you want from me, Brother—that I quit school or just drop dead, which!

Walter. I don't want nothing but for you to stop acting holy 'round here. Me and Ruth done made some sacrifices for you—why can't you do something for the family?

Ruth. Walter, don't be dragging me in it.

Walter. You are in it— Don't you get up and go work in somebody's kitchen for the last three years to help put clothes on her back?

Ruth. Oh, Walter—that's not fair . . .

Walter. It ain't that nobody expects you to get on your knees and say thank you, Brother; thank you, Ruth; thank you, Mama—and thank you Travis, for wearing the same pair of shoes for two semesters—

Beneatha (Dropping to her knees). Well—I *do*—all right?—thank everybody . . . and forgive me for ever wanting to be anything at all . . . forgive me, forgive me!

Ruth. Please stop it! Your mama'll hear you.

Walter. Who the hell told you you had to be a doctor? If you so crazy 'bout messing 'round with sick people—then go be a nurse like other women— or just get married and be quiet . . .

Beneatha. Well—you finally got it said . . . It took you three years but you finally got it said. Walter, give up; leave me alone—it's Mama's money.

Walter. He was my father, too!

Beneatha. So what? He was mine, too—and Travis' grandfather—but the insurance money belongs to Mama. Picking on me is not going to make her give it to you to invest in any liquor stores—*(Underbreath, dropping into a chair)*—and I for one say, God bless Mama for that!

Walter (To RUTH*).* See—did you hear? Did you hear!

Ruth. Honey, please go to work.

Walter. Nobody in this house is ever going to understand me.

Beneatha. Because you're a nut.

Walter. Who's a nut?

Beneatha. You—you are a nut. Thee is mad, boy.

Walter (Looking at his wife and his sister from the door, very sadly). The world's most backward race of people, and that's a fact.

Beneatha (Turning slowly in her chair). And then there are all those prophets who would lead us out of the wilderness—*(*WALTER *slams out of the house)*—into the swamps!

Ruth. Bennie, why you always gotta be pickin' on your brother? Can't you be a little sweeter sometimes? *(Door opens.* WALTER *walks in)*

Walter (To RUTH*).* I need some money for carfare.

Ruth. (Looks at him, then warms; teasing, but tenderly). Fifty cents? *(She goes to her bag and gets money).* Here, take a taxi.

*(*WALTER *exits,* MAMA *enters. She is a woman in her early sixties, full-bodied and strong. She is one of those women of a certain grace and beauty who wear it so unobstrusively that it takes a while to notice. Her dark-brown face is surrounded by the total whiteness of her hair, and, being a woman who has adjusted to many things in life and overcome many more, her face is full of strength. She has, we can see, wit and faith of a kind that keep her eyes lit and full of interest and expectancy. She is, in a word, a beautiful woman. Her bearing is perhaps most like the noble bearing of the women of the Hereros of Southwest Africa—rather as if she imagines that as she walks she still bears a basket or a vessel upon her head. Her speech, on the other hand, is as careless as her carriage is precise—she is*

inclined to slur everything—but her voice is perhaps not so much quiet as simply soft)

Mama. Who that 'round here slamming doors at this hour?

(She crosses through the room, goes to the window, opens it, and brings in a feeble little plant growing doggedly in a small pot on the window sill. She feels the dirt and puts it back out)

Ruth. That was Walter Lee. He and Bennie was at it again.

Mama. My children and they tempers. Lord, if this little old plant don't get more sun than it's been getting it ain't never going to see spring again. *(She turns from the window)* What's the matter with you this morning, Ruth? You looks right peaked. You aiming to iron all them things? Leave some for me. I'll get to 'em this afternoon. Bennie honey, it's too drafty for you to be sitting 'round half dressed. Where's your robe?

Beneatha. In the cleaners.

Mama. Well, go get mine and put it on.

Beneatha. I'm not cold, Mama, honest.

Mama. I know—but you so thin . . .

Beneatha. (Irritably). Mama, I'm not cold.

Mama. (Seeing the make-down bed as TRAVIS *has left it).* Lord have mercy, look at that poor bed. Bless his heart—he tries, don't he?

(She moves to the bed TRAVIS *has sloppily made up)*

Ruth. No—he don't half try at all 'cause he knows you going to come along behind him and fix everything. That's just how come he don't know how to do nothing right now—you done spoiled that boy so.

Mama. Well—he's a little boy. Ain't supposed to know 'bout housekeeping. My baby, that's what he is. What you fix for his breakfast this morning?

Ruth (Angrily). I feed my son, Lena!

Mama. I ain't meddling—*(Underbreath; busy-bodyish)* I just noticed all last week he had cold cereal, and when it starts getting this chilly in the fall a child ought to have some hot grits or something when he goes out in the cold—

Ruth (Furious). I gave him hot oats—is that all right!

Mama. I ain't meddling. *(Pause)* Put a lot of nice butter on it? *(*RUTH *shoots her an angry look and does not reply)* He likes lots of butter.

Ruth (Exasperated). Lena—

Mama (To BENEATHA. MAMA *is inclined to wander conversationally sometimes).* What was you and your brother fussing 'bout this morning?

Beneatha. It's not important, Mama.

(She gets up and goes to look out at the bathroom, which is apparently free, and she picks up her towels and rushes out)

Mama. What was they fighting about?

Ruth. Now you know as well as I do.

Mama (Shaking her head). Brother still worrying hisself sick about that money?

Ruth. You know he is.

Mama. You had breakfast?

Ruth. Some coffee.

Mama. Girl, you better start eating and looking after yourself better. You almost thin as Travis.

Ruth. Lena—

Mama. Uh-hunh?

Ruth. What are you going to do with it?

Mama. Now don't you start, child. It's too early in the morning to be talking about money. It ain't Christian.

Ruth. It's just that he got his heart set on that store—

Mama. You mean that liquor store that Willy Harris want him to invest in?

Ruth. Yes—

Mama. We ain't no business people, Ruth. We just plain working folks.

Ruth. Ain't nobody business people till they go into business. Walter Lee say colored people ain't never going to start getting ahead till they start gambling on some different kinds of things in the world—investments and things.

Mama. What done got into you girl? Walter Lee done finally sold you on investing.

Ruth. No. Mama, something is happening between Walter and me. I don't know what it is—but he needs something—something I can't give him any more. He needs this chance, Lena.

Mama (Frowning deeply). But liquor, honey—

Ruth. Well—like Walter say—I spec people going to always be drinking themselves some liquor.

Mama. Well—whether they drinks it or not ain't none of my business. But whether I go into business selling it to 'em *is,* and I don't want that on my ledger this late in life. *(Stopping suddenly and studying her daughter-in-law)* Ruth Younger, what's the matter with you today? You look like you could fall over right there.

Ruth. I'm tired.

Mama. Then you better stay home from work today.

Ruth. I can't stay home. She'd be calling up the agency and screaming at them, "My girl didn't come in today—send me somebody! My girl didn't come in!" Oh, she just have a fit . . .

Mama. Well, let her have it. I'll just call her up and say you got the flu—

Ruth (Laughing). Why the flu?

Mama. 'Cause it sounds respectable to 'em. Something white people get, too. They know 'bout the flu. Otherwise they think you been cut up or something when you tell 'em you sick.

Ruth. I got to go in. We need the money.

Mama. Somebody would of thought my children done all but starved to death the way they talk about money here late. Child, we got a great big old check coming tomorrow.

Ruth (Sincerely, but also self-righteously). Now that's your money. It ain't got nothing to do with me. We all feel like that—Walter and Bennie and me—even Travis.

Mama (Thoughtfully, and suddenly very far away). Ten thousand dollars—

Ruth. Sure is wonderful.

Mama. Ten thousand dollars.

Ruth. You know what you should do, Miss Lena? You should take yourself a trip somewhere. To Europe or South America or someplace—

Mama (Throwing up her hands at the thought). Oh, child!

Ruth. I'm serious. Just pack up and leave! Go on away and enjoy yourself some. Forget about the family and have yourself a ball for once in your life—

Mama (Drily). You sound like I'm just about ready to die. Who'd go with me? What I look like wandering 'round Europe by myself?

Ruth. Shoot—these here rich white women do it all the time. They don't think nothing of packing up they suitcases and piling on one of them big steamships and—swoosh!—they gone, child.

Mama. Something always told me I wasn't no rich white woman.

Ruth. Well—what are you going to do with it then?

Mama. I ain't rightly decided. *(Thinking. She speaks now with emphasis).* Some of it got to be put away for Beneatha and her schoolin'—and ain't nothing going to touch that part of it. Nothing. *(She waits several seconds, trying to make up her mind about something, and looks at* RUTH *a little tentatively before going on)* Been thinking that we maybe could meet the notes on a little old two-story somewhere, with a yard where Travis could play in the summertime, if we use part of the insurance for a down payment and everybody kind of pitch in. I could maybe take on a little day work again, few days a week—

Ruth (Studying her mother-in-law furtively and concentrating on her ironing, anxious to encourage without seeming to). Well, Lord knows, we've put enough rent into this here rat trap to pay for four houses by now . . .

Mama (Looking up at the words "rat trap" and then looking around and leaning back and sighing—in a suddenly reflective mood—). "Rat trap"— yes, that's all it is. *(Smiling)* I remember just as well the day me and Big Walter moved in here. Hadn't been married but two weeks and wasn't planning on living here no more than a year. *(She shakes her head at the dissolved dream)* We was going to set away, little by little, don't you know, and buy a little place out in Morgan Park. We had even picked out the house. *(Chuckling a little)* Looks right dumpy today. But Lord, child, you should know all the dreams I had 'bout buying that house and fixing it

up and making me a little garden in the back— *(She waits and stops
smiling)* And didn't none of it happen.

(Dropping her hands in a futile gesture)

Ruth (Keeps her head down, ironing). Yes, life can be a barrel of disappoint-
ments, sometimes.

Mama. Honey, Big Walter would come in here some nights back then and
slump down on that couch there and just look at the rug, and look at me
and look at the rug and then back at me—and I'd know he was down
then . . . really down. *(After a second very long and thoughtful pause;
she is seeing back to times that only she can see)* And then, Lord, when I
lost that baby—little Claude—I almost thought I was going to lose Big
Walter too. Oh, that man grieved hisself! He was one man to love his
children.

Ruth. Ain't nothin' can tear at you like losin' your baby.

Mama. I guess that's how come that man finally worked hisself to death like
he done. Like he was fighting his own war with this here world that took
his baby from him.

Ruth. He sure was a fine man, all right. I always liked Mr. Younger.

Mama. Crazy 'bout his children! God knows there was plenty wrong with
Walter Younger—hard-headed, mean, kind of wild with women—plenty
wrong with him. But he sure loved his children. Always wanted them to
have something—be something. That's where Brother gets all these notions, I reckon. Big Walter used to say, he'd get right wet in the eyes
sometimes, lean his head back with the water standing in his eyes and say,
"Seem like God didn't see fit to give the black man nothing but dreams—
but He did give us children to make them dreams seem worth while." *(She
smiles)* He could talk like that, don't you know.

Ruth. Yes, he sure could. He was a good man, Mr. Younger.

Mama. Yes, a fine man—just couldn't never catch up with his dreams, that's
all.

*(BENEATHA comes in, brushing her hair and looking up to the ceiling,
where the sound of a vacuum cleaner has started up)*

Beneatha. What could be so dirty on that woman's rugs that she has to
vacuum them every single day?

Ruth. I wish certain young women 'round here who I could name would
take inspiration about certain rugs in a certain apartment I could also
mention.

Beneatha (Shrugging). How much cleaning can a house need, for Christ's
sakes.

Mama (Not liking the Lord's name used thus). Bennie!

Ruth. Just listen to her—just listen!

Beneatha. Oh, God!

Mama. If you use the Lord's name just one more time—

Beneatha (A bit of a whine). Oh, Mama—

Ruth. Fresh—just fresh as salt, this girl!

Beneatha (Drily). Well—if the salt loses its savor—

Mama. Now that will do. I just ain't going to have you 'round here reciting the scriptures in vain—you hear me?

Beneatha. How did I manage to get on everybody's wrong side by just walking into a room?

Ruth. If you weren't so fresh—

Beneatha. Ruth, I'm twenty years old.

Mama. What time you be home from school today?

Beneatha. Kind of late. *(With enthusiasm)* Madeline is going to start my guitar lessons today.

(MAMA *and* RUTH *look up with the same expression)*

Mama. Your *what* kind of lessons?

Beneatha. Guitar.

Ruth. Oh, Father!

Mama. How come you done taken it in your mind to learn to play the guitar?

Beneatha. I just want to, that's all.

Mama (Smiling). Lord, child, don't you know what to do with yourself? How long it going to be before you get tired of this now—like you got tired of that little play-acting group you joined last year? *(Looking at Ruth)* And what was it the year before that?

Ruth. The horseback-riding club for which she bought that fifty-five-dollar riding habit that's been hanging in the closet ever since!

Mama (To BENEATHA*).* Why you got to flit so from one thing to another, baby?

Beneatha (Sharply). I just want to learn to play the guitar. Is there anything wrong with that?

Mama. Ain't nobody trying to stop you. I just wonders sometimes why you has to flit so from one thing to another all the time. You ain't never done nothing with all that camera equipment you brought home—

Beneatha. I don't flit! I—I experiment with different forms of expression—

Ruth. Like riding a horse?

Beneatha. —People have to express themselves one way or another.

Mama. What is it you want to express?

Beneatha (Angrily) Me! (MAMA *and* RUTH *look at each other and burst into raucous laughter)* Don't worry—I don't expect you to understand.

Mama (To change the subject). Who you going out with tomorrow night?

Beneatha (With displeasure). George Murchison again.

Mama (Pleased). Oh—you getting a little sweet on him?

Ruth. You ask me, this child ain't sweet on nobody but herself —*(Under-breath)* Express herself!

(They laugh)

Beneatha. Oh—I like George all right, Mama. I mean I like him enough to go out with him and stuff, but—

Ruth (For devilment). What does *and stuff* mean?

Beneatha. Mind your own business.

Mama. Stop picking at her now, Ruth. *(A thoughtful pause, and then a suspicious sudden look at her daughter as she turns in her chair for emphasis)* What *does* it mean?

Beneatha (Wearily). Oh, I just mean I couldn't ever really be serious about George. He's—he's so shallow.

Ruth. Shallow—what do you mean he's shallow? He's *Rich!*

Mama. Hush, Ruth.

Beneatha. I know he's rich. He knows he's rich, too.

Ruth. Well—what other qualities a man got to have to satisfy you, little girl?

Beneatha. You wouldn't even begin to understand. Anybody who married Walter could not possibly understand.

Mama (Outraged). What kind of way is that to talk about your brother?

Beneatha. Brother is a flip—let's face it.

Mama (To RUTH, *helplessly).* What's a flip?

Ruth (Glad to add kindling). She's saying he's crazy.

Beneatha. Not crazy. Brother isn't really crazy yet—he—he's an elaborate neurotic.

Mama. Hush your mouth!

Beneatha. As for George. Well. George looks good—he's got a beautiful car and he takes me to nice places and, as my sister-in-law says, he is probably the richest boy I will ever get to know and I even like him sometimes— but if the Youngers are sitting around waiting to see if their little Bennie is going to tie up the family with the Murchisons, they are wasting their time.

Ruth. You mean you wouldn't marry George Murchison if he asked you someday? That pretty, rich thing? Honey, I knew you was odd—

Beneatha. No I would not marry him if all I felt for him was what I feel now. Besides, George's family wouldn't really like it.

Mama. Why not?

Beneatha. Oh, Mama—the Murchisons are honest-to-God-real-*live*-rich colored people, and the only people in the world who are more snobbish than rich white people are rich colored people. I thought everybody knew that. I've met Mrs. Murchison. She's a scene!

Mama. You must not dislike people 'cause they well off, honey.

Beneatha. Why not? It makes just as much sense as disliking people 'cause they are poor, and lots of people do that.

Ruth (A wisdom-of-the-ages manner. To MAMA*).* Well, she'll get over some of this—

Beneatha. Get over it? What are you talking about, Ruth? Listen, I'm going to be a doctor. I'm not worried about who I'm going to marry yet—if I ever get married.

Mama and Ruth. If!

Mama. Now, Bennie—

Beneatha. Oh, I probably will . . . but first I'm going to be a doctor, and George, for one, still thinks that's pretty funny. I couldn't be bothered with that. I am going to be a doctor and everybody around here better understand that!

Mama (Kindly). 'Course you going to be a doctor, honey, God willing.

Beneatha (Drily). God hasn't got a thing to do with it.

Mama. Beneatha—that just wasn't necessary.

Beneatha. Well—neither is God. I get sick of hearing about God.

Mama. Beneatha!

Beneatha. I mean it! I'm just tired of hearing about God all the time. What has he got to do with anything? Does he pay tuition?

Mama. You 'bout to get your fresh little jaw slapped!

Ruth. That's just what she needs, all right!

Beneatha. Why? Why can't I say what I want to around here, like everybody else?

Mama. It don't sound nice for a young girl to say things like that—you wasn't brought up that way. Me and your father went to trouble to get you and Brother to church every Sunday.

Beneatha. Mama, you don't understand. It's all a matter of ideas, and God is just one idea I don't accept. It's not important. I am not going out and be immoral or commit crimes because I don't believe in God. I don't even think about it. It's just that I get tired of Him getting credit for all the things the human race achieves through its own stubborn effort. There simply is no blasted God—there is only man and it is he who makes miracles!

(MAMA *absorbs this speech, studies her daughter and rises slowly and crosses to* BENEATHA *and slaps her powerfully across the face. After, there is only silence and the daughter drops her eyes from her mother's face, and* MAMA *is very tall before her)*

Mama. Now—you say after me, in my mother's house there is still God. *(There is a long pause and* BENEATHA *stares at the floor wordlessly.* MAMA *repeats the phrase with precision and cool emotion)* In my mother's house there is still God.

Beneatha. In my mother's house there is still God.

(A long pause)

Mama (Walking away from BENEATHA, *too disturbed for triumphant posture. Stopping and turning back to her daughter).* There are some ideas we ain't going to have in this house. Not long as I am at the head of this family.
Beneatha. Yes, ma'am.

(MAMA *walks out of the room)*

Ruth (Almost gently, with profound understanding). You think you a woman, Bennie—but you still a little girl. What you did was childish—so you got treated like a child.
Beneatha. I see. *(Quietly).* I also see that everybody thinks it's all right for Mama to be a tyrant. But all the tyranny in the world will never put a God in the heavens!

(She picks up her books and goes out)

Ruth (Goes to MAMA's *door).* She said she was sorry.
Mama (Coming out, going to her plant). They frightens me, Ruth. My children.
Ruth. You got good children, Lena. They just a little off sometimes—but they're good.
Mama. No—there's something come down between me and them that don't let us understand each other and I don't know what it is. One done almost lost his mind thinking 'bout money all the time and the other done commence to talk about things I can't seem to understand in no form or fashion. What is it that's changing, Ruth?
Ruth (Soothingly, older than her years). Now . . . you taking it all too seriously. You just got strong-willed children and it takes a strong woman like you to keep 'em in hand.
Mama (Looking at her plant and sprinkling a little water on it). They spirited all right, my children. Got to admit they got spirit—Bennie and Walter. Like this little old plant that ain't never had enough sunshine or nothing— and look at it . . .

(She has her back to RUTH, *who has had to stop ironing and lean against something and put the back of her hand to her forehead)*

Ruth (Trying to keep MAMA *from noticing).* You . . . sure . . . loves that little old thing, don't you? . . .
Mama. Well, I always wanted me a garden like I used to see sometimes at the back of the houses down home. This plant is close as I ever got to having one. *(She looks out of the window as she replaces the plant)* Lord, ain't nothing as dreary as the view from this window on a dreary day, is

there? Why ain't you singing this morning, Ruth? Sing that "No Ways
Tired." That song always lifts me up so—*(She turns at last to see that*
RUTH *has slipped quietly into a chair, in a state of semiconsciousness)*
Ruth! Ruth! honey—what's the matter with you . . . Ruth!

Curtain

SCENE 2

*It is the following morning; a Saturday morning, and house cleaning is in
progress at the* YOUNGERS. *Furniture has been shoved hither and yon and*
MAMA *is giving the kitchen-area walls a washing down.* BENEATHA, *in
dungarees, with a handkerchief tied around her face, is spraying insecticide
into the cracks in the walls. As they work, the radio is on and a Southside
disk-jockey program is inappropriately filling the house with a rather exotic
saxophone blues.* TRAVIS, *the sole idle one, is leaning on his arms, looking
out of the window.*

Travis. Grandmama, that stuff Bennie is using smells awful. Can I go downstairs, please?

Mama. Did you get all them chores done already? I ain't seen you doing
much.

Travis. Yes'm—finished early. Where did Mama go this morning?

Mama (Looking at BENEATHA*).* She had to go on a little errand.

Travis. Where?

Mama. To tend to her business.

Travis. Can I go outside then?

Mama. Oh, I guess so. You better stay right in front of the house, though
. . . and keep a good lookout for the postman.

Travis. Yes'm. *(He starts out and decides to give his* AUNT BENEATHA *a good
swat on the legs as he passes her)* Leave them poor little old cockroaches
alone, they ain't bothering you none.

(He runs as she swings the spray gun at him both viciously and playfully.
WALTER *enters from the bedroom and goes to the phone)*

Mama. Look out there, girl, before you be spilling some of that stuff on that
child!

Travis (Teasing). That's right—look out now!

(He exits)

Beneatha (Drily). I can't imagine that it would hurt him—it has never hurt
the roaches.

Mama. Well, little boys' hides ain't as tough as Southside roaches.

Walter (Into phone). Hello—Let me talk to Willy Harris.

Mama. You better get over there behind the bureau. I seen one marching out of there like Napoleon yesterday.

Walter. Hello, Willy? It ain't come yet. It'll be here in a few minutes. Did the lawyer give you the papers?

Beneatha. There's really only one way to get rid of them, Mama—

Mama. How?

Beneatha. Set fire to this building.

Walter. Good. Good. I'll be right over.

Beneatha. Where did Ruth go, Walter?

Walter. I don't know.

(He exits abruptly)

Beneatha. Mama, where did Ruth go?

Mama (Looking at her with meaning). To the doctor, I think.

Beneatha The doctor? What's the matter? *(They exchange glances)* You don't think—

Mama (With her sense of drama). Now I ain't saying what I think. But I ain't never been wrong 'bout a woman either.

(The phone rings)

Beneatha (At the phone). Hay-lo . . . *(Pause, and a moment of recognition).* Well—when did you get back! . . . And how was it? . . . Of course I've missed you—in my way . . . This morning? No . . . house cleaning and all that and Mama hates it if I let people come over when the house is like this . . . You *have?* Well, that's different . . . What is it— Oh, what the hell, come on over . . . Right, see you then.

(She hangs up)

Mama (Who has listened vigorously, as is her habit). Who is that you inviting over here with this house looking like this? You ain't got the pride you was born with!

Beneatha. Asagai doesn't care how houses look, Mama—he's an intellectual.

Mama. Who?

Beneatha. Asagai—Joseph Asagai. He's an African boy I met on campus. He's been studying in Canada all summer.

Mama. What's his name?

Beneatha. Asagai, Joseph. As-sah-guy . . . He's from Nigeria.

Mama. Oh, that's the little country that was founded by slaves way back . . .

Beneatha. No, Mama—that's Liberia.

Mama. I don't think I never met no African before.

Beneatha. Well, do me a favor and don't ask him a whole lot of ignorant questions about Africans. I mean, do they wear clothes and all that—

Mama. Well, now, I guess if you think we so ignorant 'round here maybe you shouldn't bring your friends here—

Beneatha. It's just that people ask such crazy things. All anyone seems to know about when it comes to Africa is Tarzan—

Mama (Indignantly). Why should I know anything about Africa?

Beneatha. Why do you give money at church for the missionary work?

Mama. Well, that's to help save people.

Beneatha. You mean save them from *heathenism*—

Mama (Innocently). Yes.

Beneatha. I'm afraid they need more salvation from the British and the French.

(RUTH *comes in forlornly and pulls off her coat with dejection. They both turn to look at her*)

Ruth (Dispiritedly). Well, I guess from all the happy faces—everybody knows.

Beneatha. You pregnant?

Mama. Lord have mercy, I sure hope it's a little old girl. Travis ought to have a sister.

(BENEATHA *and* RUTH *give her a hopeless look for this grandmotherly enthusiasm*)

Beneatha. How far along are you?

Ruth. Two months.

Beneatha. Did you mean to? I mean did you plan it or was it an accident?

Mama. What do you know about planning or not planning?

Beneatha. Oh, Mama.

Ruth (Wearily). She's twenty years old, Lena.

Beneatha. Did you plan it, Ruth?

Ruth. Mind your own business.

Beneatha. It is my business—where is he going to live, on the *roof*? (*There is silence following the remark as the three women react to the sense of it*) Gee—I didn't mean that, Ruth honest. Gee, I don't feel like that at all. I—I think it is wonderful.

Ruth (Dully). Wonderful.

Beneatha. Yes—really.

Mama (Looking at RUTH, *worried*). Doctor say everything going to be all right?

Ruth (Far away). Yes—she says everything is going to be fine . . .

Mama (Immediately suspicious). "She"—What doctor you went to?

(RUTH *folds over, near hysteria*)

Mama (Worriedly hovering over RUTH). Ruth honey—what's the matter with you—you sick?

(RUTH *has her fists clenched on her thighs and is fighting hard to suppress a scream that seems to be rising in her*)

Beneatha. What's the matter with her, Mama?
Mama (*Working her fingers in* RUTH'S *shoulder to relax her*). She be all right. Women gets right depressed sometimes when they get her way. (*Speaking softly, expertly, rapidly*) Now you just relax. That's right . . . just lean back, don't think 'bout nothing at all . . . nothing at all—
Ruth. I'm all right . . .

(*The glassy-eyed look melts and then she collapses into a fit of heavy sobbing. The bell rings*)

Beneatha. Oh, my god—that must be Asagai.
Mama (*To* RUTH). Come on now, honey. You need to lie down and rest awhile . . . then have some nice hot food.

(*They exit,* RUTH'S *weight on her mother-in-law.* BENEATHA, *herself profoundly disturbed, opens the door to admit a rather dramatic-looking young man with a large package*)

Asagai. Hello, Alaiyo—
Beneatha (*Holding the door open and regarding him with pleasure*). Hello . . . (*Long pause*) Well—come in. And please excuse everything. My mother was very upset about my letting anyone come here with the place like this.
Asagai (*Coming into the room*). You look disturbed too . . . Is something wrong?
Beneatha (*Still at the door, absently*). Yes . . . we've all got acute ghetto-itis. (*She smiles and comes toward him, finding a cigarette and sitting*) So—sit down! How was Canada?
Asagai (*A sophisticate*). Canadian.
Beneatha (*Looking at him*). I'm very glad you are back.
Asagai (*Looking back at her in turn*). Are you really?
Beneatha. Yes—very.
Asagai. Why—you were quite glad when I went away. What happened?
Beneatha. You went away.
Asagai. Ahhhhhhhh.
Beneatha. Before—you wanted to be so serious before there was time.
Asagai. How much time must there be before one knows what one feels?
Beneatha (*Stalling this particular conversation. Her hands pressed together, in a deliberately childish gesture*). What did you bring me?
Asagai (*Handing her the package*). Open it and see.
Beneatha (*Eagerly opening the package and drawing out some records and the colorful robes of a Nigerian woman*). Oh, Asagai! . . . You got them

for me! . . . How beautiful . . . and the records too! *(She lifts out the robes and runs to the mirror with them and holds the drapery up in front of herself)*

Asagai (Coming to her at the mirror). I shall have to teach you how to drape it properly. *(He flings the material about her for the moment and stands back to look at her)* Ah—Oh-pay-gay-day, oh-gbah-mu-shay. *(A Yoruba exclamation for admiration)* You wear it well. . . . very well. . . . mutilated hair and all.

Beneatha (Turning suddenly). My hair—what's wrong with my hair?

Asagai (Shrugging). Were you born with it like that?

Beneatha (Reaching up to touch it). No . . . of course not.

(She looks back to the mirror, disturbed)

Asagai (Smiling) How then?

Beneatha. You know perfectly well how . . . as crinkly as yours . . . that's how.

Asagai. And it is ugly to you that way?

Beneatha (Quickly). Oh, no—not ugly . . . *(More slowly, apologetically)* But it's so hard to manage when it's, well—raw.

Asagai. And so to accommodate that—you mutilate it every week?

Beneatha. It's not mutilation!

Asagai (Laughing aloud at her seriousness). Oh . . . please! I am only teasing you because you are so very serious about these things. *(He stands back from her and folds his arms across his chest as he watches her pulling at her hair and frowning in the mirror)* Do you remember the first time you met me at school? . . . *(He laughs)* You came up to me and you said— and I thought you were the most serious little thing I had ever seen—you said: *(He imitates her)* "Mr. Asagai—I want very much to talk with you. About Africa. You see, Mr. Asagai, I am looking for my *identity!*"

(He laughs)

Beneatha (Turning to him, not laughing). Yes—

(Her face is quizzical, profoundly disturbed)

Asagai (Still teasing and reaching out and taking her face in his hands and turning her profile to him). Well . . . it is true that this is not so much a profile of a Hollywood queen as perhaps a queen of the Nile—*(A mock dismissal of the importance of the question)* But what does it matter? Assimilationism is so popular in your country.

Beneatha (Wheeling, passionately, sharply) I am not an assimilationist!

Asagai (The protest hangs in the room for a moment and ASAGAI *studies her, his laughter fading)* Such a serious one. *(There is a pause)* So—you like the robes? You must take excellent care of them—they are from my sister's personal wardrobe.

Beneatha (With incredulity) You—you sent all the way home—for me?

Asagai (With charm) For you—I would do much more . . . Well, that is what I came for. I must go.

Beneatha. Will you call me Monday?

Asagai. Yes . . . We have a great deal to talk about. I mean about identity and time and all that.

Beneatha. Time?

Asagai. Yes. About how much time one needs to know what one feels.

Beneatha. You never understood that there is more than one kind of feeling which can exist between a man and a woman—or, at least, there should be.

Asagai (Shaking his head negatively but gently). No. Between a man and a woman there need be only one kind of feeling. I have that for you . . . Now even . . . right this moment . . .

Beneatha. I know—and by itself—it won't do. I can find that anywhere.

Asagai. For a woman it should be enough.

Beneatha. I know—because that's what it says in all the novels that men write. But it isn't. Go ahead and laugh—but I'm not interested in being someone's little episode in America or—*(With feminine vengeance)*—one of them! (ASAGAI *has burst into laughter again)* That's funny as hell, huh!

Asagai. It's just that every American girl I have known has said that to me. White—black—in this you are all the same. And the same speech, too!

Beneatha (Angrily) Yuk, yuk, yuk!

Asagai. It's how you can be sure that the world's most liberated women are not liberated at all. You all talk about it too much!

(MAMA enters and is immediately all social charm because of the presence of a guest)

Beneatha. Oh—Mama—this is Mr. Asagai.

Mama. How do you do?

Asagai (Total politeness to an elder). How do you do, Mrs. Younger. Please forgive me for coming at such an outrageous hour on a Saturday.

Mama. Well, you are quite welcome. I just hope you understand that our house don't always look like this. *(Chatterish)* You must come again. I would love to hear all about—*(Not sure of the name)*—your country. I think it's so sad the way our American Negroes don't know nothing about Africa 'cept Tarzan and all that. And all that money they pour into these churches when they ought to be helping you people over there drive out them French and Englishmen done taken away your land.

(The mother flashes a slightly superior look at her daughter upon completion of the recitation)

Asagai (Taken aback by this sudden and acutely unrelated expression of sympathy). Yes . . . yes . . .

Mama (Smiling at him suddenly and relaxing and looking him over). How many miles is it from here to where you come from?

Asagai. Many thousands.

Mama (looking at him as she would WALTER*).* I bet you don't half look after yourself, being away from your mama either. I spec you better come 'round here from time to time and get yourself some decent home-cooked meals . . .

Asagai (Moved) Thank you. Thank you very much. *(They are all quiet, then—)* Well . . . I must go. I will call you Monday, Alaiyo.

Mama. What's that he call you?

Asagai. Oh—"Alaiyo." I hope you don't mind. It is what you would call a nickname, I think. It is a Yoruba word. I am a Yoruba.

Mama (Looking at BENEATHA*).* I—I thought he was from—

Asagai (Understanding). Nigeria is my country. Yoruba is my tribal origin—

Beneatha. You didn't tell us what Alaiyo means . . . for all I know, you might be calling me Little Idiot or something . . .

Asagai. Well . . . let me see . . . I do not know how just to explain it . . . The sense of a thing can be so different when it changes languages.

Beneatha. You're evading.

Asagai. No—really it is difficult . . . *(Thinking)* It means . . . it means One for Whom Bread—Food—Is Not Enough. *(He looks at her)* Is that all right?

Beneatha (Understanding, softly). Thank you.

Mama (Looking from one to the other and not understanding any of it) Well . . . that's nice . . . You must come see us again—Mr.—

Asagai. Ah-sah-guy . . .

Mama. Yes . . . Do come again.

Asagai. Good-bye.

(He exits)

Mama (After him). Lord, that's a pretty thing just went out here! *(Insinuatingly, to her daughter)* Yes, I guess I see why we done commence to get so interested in Africa 'round here. Missionaries my aunt Jenny!

(She exits)

Beneatha. Oh, Mama! . . .

(She picks up the Nigerian dress and holds it up to her in front of the mirror again. She sets the headdress on haphazardly and then notices her hair again and clutches at it and then replaces the headdress and frowns at herself. Then she starts to wriggle in front of the mirror as she thinks a Nigerian woman might. TRAVIS *enters and regards her)*

Travis. You cracking up?
Beneatha. Shut up.

> *(She pulls the headdress off and looks at herself in the mirror and clutches at her hair again and squinches her eyes as if trying to imagine something. Then, suddenly, she gets her raincoat and kerchief and hurriedly prepares for going out)*

Mama (Coming back into the room). She's resting now. Travis, baby, run next door and ask Miss Johnson to please let me have a little kitchen cleanser. This here can is empty as Jacob's kettle.
Travis. I just came in.
Mama. Do as you told. *(He exits and she looks at her daughter)* Where you going?
Beneatha (Halting at the door). To become a queen of the Nile!

> *(She exits in a breathless blaze of glory.* RUTH *appears in the bedroom doorway)*

Mama. Who told you to get up?
Ruth. Ain't nothing wrong with me to be lying in no bed for. Where did Bennie go?
Mama (Drumming her fingers). Far as I could make out—to Egypt. *(*RUTH *just looks at her)* What time is it getting to?
Ruth. Ten twenty. And the mailman going to ring that bell this morning just like he done every morning for the last umpteen years.

> *(*TRAVIS *comes in with the cleanser can)*

Travis. She say to tell you that she don't have much.
Mama (Angrily). Lord, some people I could name sure is tight-fisted! *(Directing her grandson)* Mark two cans of cleanser down on the list there. If she that hard up for kitchen cleanser, I sure don't want to forget to get her none!
Ruth. Lena—maybe the woman is just short on cleanser—
Mama (Not listening). —Much baking powder as she done borrowed from me all these years, she could of done gone into the baking business!

> *(The bell sounds suddenly and sharply and all three are stunned—serious and silent—mid-speech. In spite of all the other conversations and distractions of the morning, this is what they have been waiting for, even* TRAVIS, *who looks helplessly from his mother to his grandmother.* RUTH *is the first to come to life again)*

Ruth (To TRAVIS*). Get down them steps, boy!*

(TRAVIS *snaps to life and flies out to get the mail*)

Mama (Her eyes wide, her hand to her breast). You mean it done really come?

Ruth (Excited). Oh, Miss Lena!

Mama (Collecting herself). Well . . . I don't know what we all so excited about 'round here for. We known it was coming for months.

Ruth. That's a whole lot different from having it come and being able to hold it in your hands . . . a piece of paper worth ten thousand dollars . . . (TRAVIS *bursts back into the room. He holds the envelope high above his head, like a little dancer, his face is radiant and he is breathless. He moves to his grandmother with sudden slow ceremony and puts the envelope into her hands. She accepts it, and then merely holds it and looks at it*). Come on! Open it . . . Lord have mercy, I wish Walter Lee was here!

Travis. Open it, Grandmama!

Mama (Staring at it). Now you all be quiet. It's just a check.

Ruth. Open it . . .

Mama (Still staring at it). Now don't act silly . . . We ain't never been no people to act silly 'bout no money—

Ruth (Swiftly). We ain't never had none before—*open it!*

(MAMA *finally makes a good strong tear and pulls out the thin blue slice of paper and inspects it closely. The boy and his mother study it raptly over* MAMA'S *shoulders*)

Mama. Travis! *(She is counting off with doubt)* Is that the right number of zeros?

Travis. Yes'm . . . ten thousand dollars. Gaaalee, Grandmama, you rich.

Mama (She holds the check away from her, still looking at it. Slowly her face sobers into a mask of unhappiness). Ten thousand dollars. *(She hands it to* RUTH*)* Put it away somewhere, Ruth. *(She does not look at* RUTH; *her eyes seem to be seeing something somewhere very far off)* Ten thousand dollars they give you. Ten thousand dollars.

Travis (To his mother, sincerely). What's the matter with Grandmama— don't she want to be rich?

Ruth (Distractedly). You go on out and play now, baby. (TRAVIS *exits.* MAMA *starts wiping dishes absently, humming intently to herself.* RUTH *turns to her, with kind exasperation)* You've gone and got yourself upset.

Mama (Not looking at her). I spec if it wasn't for you all . . . I would just put that money away or give it to the church or something.

Ruth. Now what kind of talk is that. Mr. Younger would just be plain mad if he could hear you talking foolish like that.

Mama (Stopping and staring off). Yes . . . he sure would. *(Sighing)* We got enough to do with that money, all right. *(She halts then, and turns and looks at her daughter-in-law hard;* RUTH *avoids her eyes and* MAMA *wipes her hands with finality and starts to speak firmly to* RUTH) Where did you go today, girl?

Ruth. To the doctor.

Mama (Impatiently). Now, Ruth . . . you know better than that. Old Doctor Jones is strange enough in his way but there ain't nothing 'bout him make somebody slip and call him "she"—like you done this morning.

Ruth. Well, that's what happened—my tongue slipped.

Mama. You went to see that woman, didn't you?

Ruth (Defensively, giving herself away). What woman you talking about?

Mama (Angrily). That woman who—

(WALTER *enters in great excitement*)

Walter. Did it come?

Mama (Quietly). Can't you give people a Christian greeting before you start asking about money?

Walter (to RUTH). Did it come? (RUTH *unfolds the check and lays it quietly before him, watching him intently with thoughts of her own.* WALTER *sits down and grasps it close and counts off the zeros*) Ten thousand dollars— *(He turns suddenly, frantically to his mother and draws some papers out of his breast pocket)* Mama—look. Old Willy Harris put everything on paper—

Mama. Son—I think you ought to talk to your wife . . . I'll go on out and leave you alone if you want—

Walter. I can talk to her later—Mama, look—

Mama. Son—

Walter. WILL SOMEBODY PLEASE LISTEN TO ME TODAY!

Mama (Quietly). I don't 'low no yellin' in this house, Walter Lee, and you know it—(WALTER *stares at them in frustration and starts to speak several times*) And there ain't going to be no investing in no liquor stores. I don't aim to have to speak on that again.

(A long pause)

Walter. Oh—so you don't aim to have to speak on that again? So *you* have decided . . . *(Crumpling his papers)* Well, *you* tell that to my boy tonight when you put him to sleep on the living-room couch . . . *(Turning to* MAMA *and speaking directly to her)* Yeah—and tell it to my wife, Mama, tomorrow when she has to go out of here to look after somebody else's kids. And tell it to *me*, Mama, every time we need a new pair of curtains and I have to watch *you* go out and work in somebody's kitchen. Yeah, you tell me then!

(WALTER *starts out*)

Ruth. Where you going?

Walter. I'm going out!

Ruth. Where?

Walter. Just out of this house somewhere—

Ruth (Getting her coat). I'll come too.

Walter. I don't want you to come!

Ruth. I got something to talk to you about, Walter.

Walter. That's too bad.

Mama (Still quietly). Walter Lee—*(She waits and he finally turns and looks at her)* Sit down.

Walter. I'm a grown man, Mama.

Mama. Ain't nobody said you wasn't grown. But you still in my house and my presence. And as long as you are—you'll talk to your wife civil. Now sit down.

Ruth (Suddenly). Oh, let him go on out and drink himself to death! He makes me sick to my stomach! *(She flings her coat against him)*

Walter (Violently). And you turn mine too, baby! *(RUTH goes into their bedroom and slams the door behind her)* That was my greatest mistake—

Mama (Still quietly). Walter, what is the matter with you?

Walter. Matter with me? Ain't nothing the matter with *me*!

Mama. Yes there is. Something eating you up like a crazy man. Something more than me not giving you this money. The past few years I been watching it happen to you. You get all nervous acting and kind of wild in the eyes—*(WALTER jumps up impatiently at her words)* I said sit there now, I'm talking to you!

Walter. Mama—I don't need no nagging at me today.

Mama. Seem like you getting to a place where you always tied up in some kind of knot about something. But if anybody ask you 'bout it you just yell at 'em and bust out the house and go out and drink somewheres. Walter Lee, people can't live with that. Ruth's a good, patient girl in her way—but you getting to be too much. Boy, don't make the mistake of driving that girl away from you.

Walter. Why—what she do for me?

Mama. She loves you.

Walter. Mama—I'm going out. I want to go off somewhere and be by myself for a while.

Mama. I'm sorry 'bout your liquor store, son. It just wasn't the thing for us to do. That's what I want to tell you about—

Walter. I got to go out, Mama—

(He rises)

Mama. It's dangerous, son.

Walter. What's dangerous?

Mama. When a man goes outside his home to look for peace.

Walter (Beseechingly). Then why can't there never be no peace in this house then?

Mama. You done found it in some other house?

Walter. No—there ain't no woman! Why do women always think there's a woman somewhere when a man gets restless. *(Coming to her)* Mama—Mama—I want so many things . . .

Mama. Yes, son—

Walter. I want so many things that they are driving me kind of crazy . . . Mama—look at me.

Mama. I'm looking at you. You a good-looking boy. You got a job, a nice wife, a fine boy and—

Walter. A job *(looks at her)*. Mama, a job? I open and close car doors all day long. I drive a man around in his limousine and I say, "Yes, sir; no, sir; very good, sir; shall I take the Drive, sir?" Mama, that ain't no kind of job . . . that ain't nothing at all. *(Very quietly)* Mama, I don't know if I can make you understand.

Mama. Understand what, baby?

Walter (Quietly) Sometimes it's like I can see the future stretched out in front of me—just plain as day. The future, Mama. Hanging over there at the edge of my days. Just waiting for me—a big, looming blank space—full of *nothing*. Just waiting for *me*. *(Pause)* Mama—sometimes when I'm downtown and I pass them cool, quiet-looking restaurants where them white boys are sitting back and talking 'bout things . . . sitting there turning deals worth millions of dollars . . . sometimes I see guys don't look much older than me—

Mama. Son—how come you talk so much 'bout money?

Walter (With immense passion). Because it is life, Mama!

Mama (Quietly). Oh—*(Very quietly)* So now it's life. Money is life. Once upon a time freedom used to be life—now it's money. I guess the world really do change . . .

Walter. No—it was always money, Mama. We just didn't know about it.

Mama. No . . . something has changed. *(She looks at him)* You something new, boy. In my time we was worried about not being lynched and getting to the North if we could and how to stay alive and still have a pinch of dignity too . . . Now here come you and Beneatha—talking 'bout things we ain't never even thought about hardly, me and your daddy. You ain't satisfied or proud of nothing we done. I mean that you had a home; that we kept you out of trouble till you was grown; that you don't have to ride to work on the back of nobody's streetcar— You my children—but how different we done become.

Walter. You just don't understand, Mama, you just don't understand.

Mama. Son—do you know your wife is expecting another baby? *(*WALTER *stands, stunned, and absorbs what his mother has said)* That's what she wanted to talk to you about. *(*WALTER *sinks down into a chair)* This ain't for me to be telling—but you ought to know. *(She waits)* I think Ruth is thinking 'bout getting rid of that child.

Walter (Slowly understanding). No—no—Ruth wouldn't do that.

Mama. When the world gets ugly enough—a woman will do anything for her family. *The part that's already living.*

Walter. You don't know Ruth, Mama, if you think she would do that.

(RUTH *opens the bedroom door and stands there a little limp.*)

Ruth (Beaten). Yes I would too, Walter. *(Pause)* I gave her a five-dollar down payment.

(There is total silence as the man stares at his wife and the mother stares at her son)

Mama (Presently). Well—*(Tightly)* Well—son, I'm waiting to hear you say something . . . I'm waiting to hear how you be your father's son. Be the man he was . . . *(Pause)* Your wife say she going to destroy your child. And I'm waiting to hear you talk like him and say we a people who give children life, not who destroys them—*(She rises)* I'm waiting to see you stand up and look like your daddy and say we done give up one baby to poverty and that we ain't going to give up nary another one . . . I'm waiting.

Walter. Ruth—

Mama. If you a son of mine, tell her! *(WALTER turns, looks at her and can say nothing. She continues, bitterly)* You . . . you are a disgrace to your father's memory. Somebody get me my hat.

Curtain

ACT TWO
SCENE I

Time: Later the same day.

At rise: RUTH *is ironing again. She has the radio going. Presently* BE-NEATHA'S *bedroom door opens and* RUTH'S *mouth falls and she puts down the iron in fascination.*

Ruth. What have we got on tonight!

Beneatha (Emerging grandly from the doorway so that we can see her thoroughly robed in the costume Asagai brought). You are looking at what a well-dressed Nigerian woman wears—*(She parades for* RUTH, *her hair completely hidden by the headdress; she is coquettishly fanning herself with an ornate oriental fan, mistakenly more like Butterfly[2] than any Nigerian that ever was)* Isn't it beautiful? *(She promenades to the radio and, with an arrogant flourish, turns off the good loud blues that is playing)* Enough of this assimilationist junk! *(RUTH follows her with her eyes as she goes to the phonograph and puts on a record and turns and waits ceremoniously for the music to come up. Then, with a shout—)* OCOM-OGOSIAY!

(RUTH jumps. The music comes up, a lovely Nigerian melody. BENEATHA *listens, enraptured, her eyes far away—"back to the past." She begins to dance.* RUTH *is dumfounded)*

Ruth. What kind of dance is that?
Beneatha. A folk dance.
Ruth (Pearl Bailey). What kind of folks do that, honey?
Beneatha. It's from Nigeria. It's a dance of welcome.
Ruth. Who you welcoming?
Beneatha. The men back to the village.
Ruth. Where they been?
Beneatha. How should I know—out hunting or something. Anyway, they are coming back now . . .
Ruth. Well, that's good.
Beneatha (With the record)
   Alundi, alundi
   Alundi alunya
   Jop pu a jeepua
   Ang gu soooooooooo

   Ai yai yae . . .
   Ayehaye—alundi . . .

(WALTER comes in during this performance; he has obviously been drinking. He leans against the door heavily and watches his sister, at first with distaste. Then his eyes look off—"back to the past"—as he lifts both his fists to the roof, screaming)

Walter. YEAH . . . AND ETHIOPIA STRETCH FORTH HER HANDS AGAIN! . . .
Ruth (Drily, looking at him). Yes—and Africa sure is claiming her own tonight. *(She gives them both up and starts ironing again)*
Walter (All in a drunken, dramatic shout). Shut up! . . . I'm digging them drums . . . them drums move me! . . . *(He makes his weaving way to*

---

[2]Heroine of 1904 opera *Madame Butterfly* by Giacomo Puccini.

his wife's face and leans in close to her) In my *heart of hearts—(He thumps his chest)*—I am much warrior!

Ruth (Without even looking up). In your heart of hearts you are much drunkard.

Walter (Coming away from her and starting to wander around the room, shouting). Me and Jomo . . . *(Intently, in his sister's face. She has stopped dancing to watch him in this unknown mood)* That's my man, Kenyatta.[3] *(Shouting and thumping his chest)* FLAMING SPEAR! HOT DAMN! *(He is suddenly in possession of an imaginary spear and actively spearing enemies all over the room)* OCOMOGOSIAY . . THE LION IS WALKING . . . OWIMOWEH! *(He pulls his shirt open and leaps up on a table and gestures with his spear. The bell rings.* RUTH *goes to answer)*

Beneatha (To encourage WALTER, *thoroughly caught up with this side of him).* OCOMOGOSIAY, FLAMING SPEAR!

Walter (On the table, very far gone, his eyes pure glass sheets. He sees what we cannot, that he is a leader of his people, a great chief, a descendant of Chaka, and that the hour to march has come). Listen, my black brothers—

Beneatha. OCOMOGOSIAY!

Walter —Do you hear the waters rushing against the shores of the coast-lands—

Beneatha. OCOMOGOSIAY!

Walter. Do you hear the screeching of the cocks in yonder hills beyond where the chiefs meet in council for the coming of the mighty war—

Beneatha. OCOMOGOSIAY!

Walter. —Do you hear the beating of the wings of the birds flying low over the mountains and the low places of our land—

*(*RUTH *opens the door.* GEORGE MURCHISON *enters)*

Beneatha. OCOMOGOSIAY!

Walter. —Do you hear the singing of the women, singing the war songs of our fathers to the babies in the great houses . . . singing the sweet war songs? OH, DO YOU HEAR, MY BLACK BROTHERS!

Beneatha (Completely gone). We hear you, Flaming Spear—

Walter. Telling us to prepare for the greatness of the time— *(To* GEORGE*)* Black Brother!

(He extends his hand for the fraternal clasp)

George. Black Brother, hell!

---

[3]Jomo Kenyatta (1893–1978), African nationalist leader from Kenya.

Ruth (Having had enough, and embarrassed for the family). Beneatha, you got company—what's the matter with you? Walter Lee Younger, get down off that table and stop acting like a fool . . .

(WALTER *comes down off the table suddenly and makes a quick exit to the bathroom*)

Ruth. He's had a little to drink . . . I don't know what her excuse is.

George (To BENEATHA). Look honey, we're going *to* the theatre—we're not going to be *in* it . . . so go change, huh?

Ruth. You expect this boy to go out with you looking like that?

Beneatha (Looking at GEORGE). That's up to George. If he's ashamed of his heritage—

George. Oh, don't be so proud of yourself, Bennie—just because you look eccentric.

Beneatha. How can something that's natural be eccentric?

George. That's what being eccentric means—being natural. Get dressed.

Beneatha. I don't like that, George.

Ruth. Why must you and your brother make an argument out of everything people say?

Beneatha. Because I hate assimilationist Negroes!

Ruth. Will somebody please tell me what assimila-whoever means!

George. Oh, it's just a college girl's way of calling people Uncle Toms—but that isn't what it means at all.

Ruth. Well, what does it mean?

Beneatha. (Cutting GEORGE *off and staring at him as she replies to* RUTH). It means someone who is willing to give up his own culture and submerge himself completely in the dominant, and in this case, *oppressive* culture!

George. Oh, dear, dear, dear! Here we go! A lecture on the African past! On our Great West African Heritage! In one second we will hear all about the great Ashanti empires; the great Songhay civilizations; and the great sculpture of Bénin—and then some poetry in the Bantu—and the whole monologue will end with the word *heritage! (Nastily)* Let's face it, baby, your heritage is nothing but a bunch of raggedy-assed spirituals and some grass huts!

Beneatha. Grass huts! (RUTH *crosses to her and forcibly pushes her toward the bedroom*) See there . . . you are standing there in your splendid ignorance talking about people who were the first to smelt iron on the face of the earth! (RUTH *is pushing her through the door*) The Ashanti were performing surgical operations when the English—(RUTH *pulls the door to, with* BENEATHA *on the other side, and smiles graciously at* GEORGE. BENEATHA *opens the door and shouts the end of the sentence defiantly at* GEORGE)—were still tatooing themselves with blue dragons . . . *(She goes back inside)*

Ruth. Have a seat, George. *(They both sit.* RUTH *folds her hands rather primly on her lap, determined to demonstrate the civilization of the family)* Warm, ain't it? I mean for September. *(Pause)* Just like they always say about Chicago weather: If it's too hot or cold for you, just wait a minute and it'll change. *(She smiles happily at this cliché of clichés)* Everybody say it's got to do with them bombs and things they keep setting off. *(Pause)* Would you like a nice cold beer?

George. No thank you. I don't care for beer. *(He looks at his watch)* I hope she hurries up.

Ruth. What time is the show?

George. It's an eight-thirty curtain. That's just Chicago though. In New York standard curtain time is eight forty.

(He is rather proud of this knowledge)

Ruth (Properly appreciating it). You get to New York a lot?

George (Offhand). Few times a year.

Ruth. Oh—that's nice. I've never been to New York.

*(*WALTER *enters. We feel he has relieved himself, but the edge of unreality is still with him)*

Walter. New York ain't got nothing Chicago ain't. Just a bunch of hustling people all squeezed up together—being "Eastern."

(He turns his face into a screw of displeasure)

George. Oh—you've been?

Walter. Plenty of times.

Ruth (Shocked at the lie). Walter Lee Younger!

Walter (Staring her down). Plenty! *(Pause)* What we got to drink in this house? Why don't you offer this man some refreshment. *(To* GEORGE*)* They don't know how to entertain people in his house, man.

George. Thank you—I don't really care for anything.

Walter (Feeling his head; sobriety coming). Where's Mama?

Ruth. She ain't come back yet.

Walter (Looking MURCHISON *over from head to toe, scrutinizing his carefully casual tweed sports jacket over cashmere V-neck sweater over soft eyelet shirt and tie, and soft slacks, finished off with white buckskin shoes)* Why all you college boys wear them fairyish-looking white shoes?

Ruth. Walter Lee!

*(*GEORGE MURCHISON *ignores the remark)*

Walter (To RUTH*).* Well, they look crazy as hell—white shoes, cold as it is.

Ruth (Crushed). You have to excuse him—

Walter. No he don't! Excuse me for what? What you always excusing me for! I'll excuse myself when I needs to be excused! *(A pause)* They look as funny as them black knee socks Beneatha wears out of here all the time.

Ruth. It's the college *style,* Walter.

Walter. Style, hell. She looks like she got burnt legs or something!

Ruth. Oh, Walter—

Walter (An irritable mimic). Oh, Walter! Oh, Walter! *(To* MURCHISON*)* How's your old man making out? I understand you all going to buy that big hotel on the Drive? *(He finds a beer in the refrigerator, wanders over to* MUR-CHISON*, sipping and wiping his lips with the back of his hand, and straddling a chair backwards to talk to the other man)* Shrewd move. Your old man is all right, man. *(Tapping his head and half winking for emphasis)* I mean he knows how to operate. I mean he things *big,* you know what I mean, I mean for a *home,* you know? But I think he's kind of running out of ideas now. I'd like to talk to him. Listen, man, I got some plans that could turn this city upside down. I mean I think like he does. *Big.* Invest big, gamble big, hell, lose *big* if you have to, you know what I mean. It's hard to find a man on this whole Southside who understands my kind of thinking—you dig? *(He scrutinizes* MURCHISON *again, drinks his beer, squints his eyes and leans in close, confidential, man to man)* Me and you ought to sit down and talk sometimes, man. Man, I got me some ideas . . .

Murchison (With boredom). Yeah—sometimes we'll have to do that, Walter.

Walter (Understanding the indifference, and offended). Yeah—well, when you get the time, man. I know you a busy little boy.

Ruth. Walter, please—

Walter (Bitterly, hurt). I know ain't nothing in this world as busy as you colored college boys with your fraternity pins and white shoes . . .

Ruth (Covering her face with humiliation). Oh, Walter Lee—

Walter. I see you all all the time—with the books tucked under your arms— going to your *(British A—a mimic)* "clahsses." And for what! What the hell you learning over there? Filling up your heads—*(Counting off on his fingers)*—with the sociology and the psychology—but they teaching you how to be a man? How to take over and run the world? They teaching you how to run a rubber plantation or a steel mill? Naw—just to talk proper and read books and wear white shoes . . .

George (Looking at him with distaste, a little above it all). You're all wacked up with bitterness, man.

Walter (Intently, almost quietly, between the teeth, glaring at the boy). And you—ain't you bitter, man? Ain't you just about had it yet? Don't you see no stars gleaming that you can't reach out and grab? You happy?— you contented son-of-a-bitch—you happy? You got it made? Bitter? Man,

I'm a volcano. Bitter? Here I am a giant—surrounded by ants! Ants who can't even understand what it is the giant is talking about.

Ruth (Passionately and suddenly). Oh, Walter—ain't you with nobody!

Walter (Violently). No! 'Cause ain't nobody with me! Not even my own mother!

Ruth. Walter, that's a terrible thing to say!

(BENEATHA *enters, dressed for the evening in a cocktail dress and earrings*)

George. Well—hey, you look great.

Beneatha. Let's go, George. See you all later.

Ruth. Have a nice time.

George. Thanks. Good night. *(To* WALTER, *sarcastically)* Good night, Prometheus.

(BENEATHA *and* GEORGE *exit*)

Walter (To RUTH*).* Who is Prometheus?

Ruth. I don't know. Don't worry about it.

Walter (In fury, pointing after GEORGE*).* See there—they get to a point where they can't insult you man to man—they got to go talk about something ain't nobody never heard of!

Ruth. How you know it was an insult? *(To humor him)* Maybe Prometheus is a nice fellow.

Walter. Prometheus! I bet there ain't even no such thing! I bet that simpleminded clown—

Ruth. Walter—

(She stops what she is doing and looks at him)

Walter (Yelling). Don't start!

Ruth. Start what?

Walter. Your nagging! Where was I? Who was I with? How much money did I spend?

Ruth (Plaintively). Walter Lee—why don't we just try to talk about it . . .

Walter (Not listening). I been out talking with people who understand me. People who care about the things I got on my mind.

Ruth (Wearily). I guess that means people like Willy Harris.

Walter. Yes, people like Willy Harris.

Ruth (With a sudden flash of impatience). Why don't you all just hurry up and go into the banking business and stop talking about it!

Walter. Why? You want to know why? 'Cause we all tied up in a race of people that don't know how to do nothing but moan, pray and have babies!

(The line is too bitter even for him and he looks at her and sits down)

Ruth. Oh, Walter . . . *(Softly)* Honey, why can't you stop fighting me?
Walter (Without thinking). Who's fighting you? Who even cares about you?

(This line begins the retardation of his mood)

Ruth. Well—*(She waits a long time, and then with resignation starts to put away her things)* I guess I might as well go on to bed . . . *(More or less to herself)* I don't know where we lost it . . . but we have . . . *(Then, to him)* I—I'm sorry about this new baby, Walter. I guess maybe I better go on and do what I started . . . I guess I just didn't realize how bad things was with us . . . I guess I just didn't really realize—*(She starts out to the bedroom and stops)* You want some hot milk?
Walter. Hot milk?
Ruth. Yes—hot milk.
Walter. Why hot milk?
Ruth. 'Cause after all that liquor you come home with you ought to have something hot in your stomach.
Walter. I don't want no milk.
Ruth. You want some coffee then?
Walter. No. I don't want no coffee. I don't want nothing hot to drink. *(Almost plaintively)* Why you always trying to give me something to eat?
Ruth (Standing and looking at him helplessly). What else can I give you, Walter Lee Younger?

(She stands and looks at him and presently turns to go out again. He lifts his head and watches her going away from him in a new mood which began to emerge when he asked her "Who cares about you?")

Walter. It's been rough, ain't it, baby? *(She hears and stops but does not turn around and he continues to her back)* I guess between two people there ain't never as much understood as folks generally thinks there is. I mean like between me and you—*(She turns to face him)* How we gets to the place where we scared to talk softness to each other. *(He waits, thinking hard himself)* Why you think it got to be like that? *(He is thoughtful, almost as a child would be)* Ruth, what is it gets into people ought to be close?
Ruth. I don't know, honey. I think about it a lot.
Walter. On account of you and me, you mean? The way things are with us. The way something done come down between us.
Ruth. There ain't so much between us, Walter . . . Not when you come to me and try to talk to me. Try to be with me . . . a little even.
Walter (Total honesty). Sometimes . . . sometimes . . . I don't even know how to try.

Ruth. Walter—
Walter. Yes

Ruth (Coming to him, gently and with misgiving, but coming to him). Honey
. . . life don't have to be like this. I mean sometimes people can do things
so that things are better . . . You remember how we used to talk when
Travis was born . . . about the way we were going to live . . . the kind
of house . . . *(She is stroking his head)* Well, it's all starting to slip away
from us . . .

(MAMA enters, and WALTER jumps up and shout at her)

Walter. Mama, where have you been?
Mama. My—them steps is longer than they used to be. Whew! *(She sits down
and ignores him)* How you feeling this evening, Ruth?

*(RUTH shrugs, disturbed some at having been prematurely interrupted and
watching her husband knowingly)*

Walter. Mama, where have you been all day?
*Mama (Still ignoring him and leaning on the table and changing to more
comfortable shoes).* Where's Travis?
Ruth. I let him go out earlier and he ain't come back yet. Boy, is he gong to
get it!
Walter. Mama!
Mama (As if she has heard him for the first time). Yes, son?
Walter. Where did you go this afternoon?
Mama. I went down town to tend to some business that I had to tend to.
Walter. What kind of business?
Mama. You know better than to question me like a child, Brother.
Walter (Rising and bending over the table). Where were you, Mama? *(Bring-
ing his fists down and shouting)* Mama, you didn't go do something with
that insurance money, something crazy?

*(The front door opens slowly, interrupting him, and TRAVIS peeks his head
in, less than hopefully)*

Travis (To his mother). Mama, I—
Ruth. "Mama I" nothing! You're going to get it, boy! Get on in that bedroom
and get yourself ready!
Travis. But I—
Mama. Why don't you all never let the child explain hisself.
Ruth. Keep out of it now, Lena.

*(MAMA clamps her lips together, and RUTH advances toward her son men-
acingly)*

Ruth. A thousand times I have told you not to go off like that—

Mama (Holding out her arms to her grandson). Well—at least let me tell him something. I want him to be the first one to hear . . . Come here, Travis. *(The boy obeys, gladly)* Travis—*(She takes him by the shoulders and looks into his face)*—you know that money we got in the mail this morning?

Travis. Yes'm—

Mama. Well—what you think your grandmama gone and done with that money?

Travis. —I don't know, Grandmama.

Mama (Putting her finger on his nose for emphasis). She went out and she bought you a house! *(The explosion comes from* WALTER *at the end of the revelation and he jumps up and turns away from all of them in a fury.* MAMA *continues, to* TRAVIS*)* You glad about the house? It's going to be yours when you get to be a man.

Travis. Yeah—I always wanted to live in a house.

Mama. All right, gimme some sugar then—*(*TRAVIS *puts his arms around her neck as she watches her son over the boy's shoulder. Then, to* TRAVIS*, after the embrace)* Now when you say your prayers tonight, you thank God and your grandfather—'cause it was him who give you the house—in his way.

Ruth (Taking the boy from MAMA *and pushing him toward the bedroom).* Now you get out of here and get ready for your beating.

Travis. Aw, Mama—

Ruth. Get on in there—*(Closing the door behind him and turning radiantly to her mother-in-law)* So you went and did it!

Mama (Quietly, looking at her son with pain). Yes, I did.

Ruth (Raising both arms classically) Praise God! (Looks at WALTER *a moment, who says nothing. She crosses rapidly to her husband)* Please, honey—let me be glad . . . you be glad too. *(She has laid her hands on his shoulder, but he shakes himself free of her roughly, without turning to face her)* Oh, Walter . . . a home . . . a home. *(She comes back to* MAMA*)* Well—where is it? How big is it? How much it going to cost?

Mama. Well—

Ruth. When we moving?

Mama (Smiling at her). First of the month.

Ruth (Throwing back her head with jubilance) Praise God!

Mama (Tentatively, still looking at her son's back turned against her and RUTH*).* It's—it's a nice house too . . . *(She cannot help speaking directly to him. An imploring quality in her voice, her manner, makes her almost like a girl now)* Three bedrooms—nice big one for you and Ruth. . . . Me and Beneatha still have to share our room, but Travis have one of his own—and—*(With difficulty)* I figures if the—new baby—is a boy, we could get one of them double-decker outfits . . . And there's a yard with a little patch of dirt where I could maybe get to grow me a few flowers . . . And a nice big basement . . .

Ruth. Walter honey, be glad—

Mama (Still to his back, fingering things on the table). 'Course I don't want to make it sound fancier than it is . . . It's just a plain little old house— but it's made good and solid—and it will be *ours*. Walter Lee—it makes a difference in a man when he can walk on floors that belong to *him* . . .

Ruth. Where is it?

Mama (Frightened at this telling). Well—well—it's out there in Clybourne Park—

(RUTH'S *radiance fades abruptly, and* WALTER *finally turns slowly to face his mother with incredulity and hostility*)

Ruth. Where?

Mama (Matter-of-factly). Four o six Clybourne Street, Clybourne Park.

Ruth. Clybourne Park? Mama, there ain't no colored people living in Clybourne Park.

Mama (Almost idiotically). Well, I guess there's going to be some now.

Walter (Bitterly). So that's the peace and comfort you went out and bought for us today!

Mama (Raising her eyes to meet his finally). Son—I just tried to find the nicest place for the least amount of money for my family.

Ruth (Trying to recover from the shock). Well—well—'course I ain't one never been 'fraid of no crackers, mind you—but—well, wasn't there no other houses nowhere?

Mama. Them houses they put up for colored in them areas way out all seem to cost twice as much as other houses. I did the best I could.

Ruth (Struck senseless with the news, in its various degrees of goodness and trouble, she sits a moment, her fists propping her chin in thought, and then she starts to rise, bringing her fists down with vigor, the radiance spreading from cheek to cheek again). Well—well!—All I can say is—if this is my time in life—*my time*—to say good-bye—*(And she builds with momentum as she starts to circle the room with an exuberant, almost tearfully, happy release)*—to these God-damned cracking walls!—*(She pounds the walls)*—and these marching roaches!—*(She wipes at an imaginary army of marching roaches)*—and this cramped little closet which ain't now or never was no kitchen! . . . then I say it loud and good, *Hallelujah! and good-bye misery . . . I don't never want to see your ugly face again! (She laughs joyously, having practically destroyed the apartment, and flings her arms up and lets them come down happily, slowly, reflectively, over her abdomen, aware for the first time perhaps that the life therein pulses with happiness and not despair)* Lena?

Mama (Moved, watching her happiness). Yes, honey?

Ruth (Looking off). Is there—is there a whole lot of sunlight?

Mama (Understanding). Yes, child, there's a whole lot of sunlight.

(Long pause)

Ruth (Collecting herself and going to the door of the room TRAVIS *is in).* Well—I guess I better see 'bout Travis. *(To* MAMA*)* Lord, I sure don't feel like whipping nobody today!

(She exits)

Mama (The mother and son are left alone now and the mother waits a long time, considering deeply, before she speaks). Son—you—you understand what I done, don't you? *(*WALTER *is silent and sullen)* I—I just seen my family falling apart today . . . just falling to pieces in front of my eyes . . . We couldn't of gone on like we was today. We was going backwards 'stead of forwards—talking 'bout killing babies and wishing each other was dead . . . When it get like that in life—you just got to do something different, push on out and do something bigger . . . *(She waits)* I wish you say something, son . . . I wish you'd say how deep inside you you think I done the right thing—
Walter (Crossing slowly to his bedroom door and finally turning there and speaking measuredly). What you need me to say you done right for? *You* the head of this family. You run our lives like you want to. It was your money and you did what you wanted with it. So what you need for me to say it was all right for? *(Bitterly, to hurt her as deeply as he knows is possible)* So you butchered up a dream of mine—you—who always talking 'bout your children's dreams . . .
Mama. Walter Lee—

(He just closes the door behind him. MAMA *sits alone, thinking heavily)*

Curtain

SCENE 2

Time: Friday night. A few weeks later.
At rise: Packing crates mark the intention of the family to move. BENEATHA *and* GEORGE *come in, presumably from an evening out again.*

George. O.K. . . . O.K., whatever you say . . . *(They both sit on the couch. He tries to kiss her. She moves away)* Look we've had a nice evening; let's not spoil it, huh? . . .

(He again turns her head and tries to nuzzle in and she turns away from him, not with distaste but with momentary lack of interest; in a mood to pursue what they were talking about)

Beneatha. I'm *trying* to talk to you.

George. We always talk.

Beneatha. Yes—and I love to talk.

George (Exasperated; rising). I know it and I don't mind it sometimes . . . I want you to cut it out, see— The moody stuff, I mean. I don't like it. You're a nice-looking girl . . . all over. That's all you need, honey, forget the atmosphere. Guys aren't going to go for the atmosphere—they're going to go for what they see. Be glad for that. Drop the Garbo routine. It doesn't go with you. As for myself, I want a nice—*(Groping)*—simple—*(Thoughtfully)*—sophisticated girl . . . not a poet—O.K.?

(She rebuffs him again and he starts to leave)

Beneatha. Why are you angry?

George. Because this is stupid! I don't go out with you to discuss the nature of "quiet desperation" or to hear all about your thoughts—because the world will go on thinking what it thinks regardless—

Beneatha. Then why read books? Why go to school?

George (With artificial patience, counting on his fingers). It's simple. You read books—to learn facts—to get grades—to pass the course—to get a degree. That's all—it has nothing to do with thoughts.

(A long pause)

Beneatha. I see. *(A longer pause as she looks at him)* Good night, George.

(GEORGE looks at her a little oddly, and starts to exit. He meets MAMA coming in)

George. Oh—hello, Mrs. Younger.

Mama. Hello, George, how you feeling?

George. Fine—fine, how are you?

Mama. Oh, a little tired. You know them steps can get you after a day's work. You all have a nice time tonight?

George. Yes—a fine time. Well, good night.

Mama. Good night. *(He exits. MAMA closes the door behind her)* Hello, honey. What you sitting like that for?

Beneatha. I'm just sitting.

Mama. Didn't you have a nice time?

Beneatha. No.

Mama. No? What's the matter?

Beneatha. Mama, George is a fool—honest. *(She rises)*

Mama (Hustling around unloading the packages she has entered with. She stops). Is he, baby?

Beneatha. Yes.

(BENEATHA *makes up* TRAVIS' *bed as she talks*)

Mama. You sure?
Beneatha. Yes.
Mama. Well—I guess you better not waste your time with no fools.

(BENEATHA *looks up at her mother, watching her put groceries in the refrigerator. Finally she gathers up her things and starts into the bedroom. At the door she stops and looks back at her mother*)

Beneatha. Mama—
Mama. Yes, baby—
Beneatha. Thank you.
Mama. For what?
Beneatha. For understanding me this time.

(*She exits quickly and the mother stands, smiling a little, looking at the place where* BENEATHA *just stood.* RUTH *enters*)

Ruth. Now don't you fool with any of this stuff, Lena—
Mama. Oh, I just thought I'd sort a few things out.

(*The phone rings.* RUTH *answers*)

Ruth (At the phone). Hello—Just a minute. (*Goes to door*) Walter, it's Mrs. Arnold. (*Waits. Goes back to the phone. Tense*) Hello. Yes, this is his wife speaking . . . He's lying down now. Yes . . . well, he'll be in tomorrow. He's been very sick. Yes—I know we should have called, but we were so sure he'd be able to come in today. Yes—yes, I'm very sorry. Yes . . . Thank you very much. (*She hangs up.* WALTER *is standing in the doorway of the bedroom behind her*) That was Mrs. Arnold.
Walter (Indifferently). Was it?
Ruth. She said if you don't come in tomorrow that they are getting a new man . . .
Walter. Ain't that sad—ain't that crying sad.
Ruth. She said Mr. Arnold has had to take a cab for three days . . . Walter, you ain't been to work for three days! (*This is a revelation to her*) Where you been, Walter Lee Younger? (WALTER *looks at her and starts to laugh*) You're going to lose your job.
Walter. That's right . . .
Ruth. Oh, Walter, and with your mother working like a dog every day—
Walter. That's sad too—Everything is sad.
Mama. What you been doing for these three days, son?
Walter. Mama—you don't know all the things a man what got leisure can find to do in this city . . . What's this—Friday night? Well—Wednesday

I borrowed Willy Harris' car and I went for a drive . . . just me and myself and I drove and drove . . . Way out . . . way past South Chicago, and I parked the car and I sat and looked at the steel mills all day long. I just sat in the car and looked at them big black chimneys for hours. Then I drove back and I went to the Green Hat. *(Pause)* And Thursday—Thursday I borrowed the car again and I got in it and I pointed it the other way and I drove the other way—for hours—way, way up to Wisconsin, and I looked at the farms. I just drove and looked at the farms. Then I drove back and I went to the Green Hat. *(Pause)* And today—today I didn't get the car. Today I just walked. All over the Southside. And I looked at the Negroes and they looked at me and finally I just sat down on the curb at Thirty-ninth and South Parkway and I just sat there and watched the Negroes go by. And then I went to the Green Hat. You all sad? You all depressed? And you know where I am going right now—

(RUTH goes out quietly)

Mama. Oh, Big Walter, is this the harvest of our days?

Walter. You know what I like about the Green Hat? *(He turns the radio on and a steamy, deep blues pours into the room)* I like this little cat they got there who blows a sax . . . He blows. He talks to me. He ain't but 'bout five feet tall and he's got a conked head and his eyes is always closed and he's all music—

Mama (Rising and getting some papers out of her handbag). Walter—

Walter. And there's this other guy who plays the piano . . . and they got a sound. I mean they can work on some music . . . They got the best little combo in the world in the Green Hat . . . You can just sit there and drink and listen to them three men play and you realize that don't nothing matter worth a damn, but just being there—

Mama. I've helped do it to you, haven't I, son? Walter, I been wrong.

Walter. Naw—you ain't never been wrong about nothing, Mama.

Mama. Listen to me, now. I say I been wrong, son. That I been doing to you what the rest of the world been doing to you. *(She stops and he looks up slowly at her and she meets his eyes pleadingly)* Walter—what you ain't never understood is that I ain't got nothing, don't own nothing, ain't never really wanted nothing that wasn't for you. There ain't nothing as precious to me . . . There ain't nothing worth holding on to, money, dreams, nothing else—if it means—if it means it's going to destroy my boy. *(She puts her papers in front of him and he watches her without speaking or moving)* I paid the man thirty-five hundred dollars down on the house. That leaves sixty-five hundred dollars. Monday morning I want you to take this money and take three thousand dollars and put it in a savings account for Beneatha's medical schooling. The rest you put in a checking account—with your name on it. And from now on any penny that come out of it or that go in it is for you to look after. For you to decide. *(She drops her hands a little helplessly)* It ain't much, but it's all I got in the world and I'm putting in your hands. I'm telling you to be the head of this family from now on like you supposed to be.

Walter (Stares at the money). You trust me like that, Mama?

Mama. I ain't never stop trusting you. Like I ain't never stop loving you.

(She goes out, and WALTER *sits looking at the money on the table as the music continues in its idiom, pulsing in the room. Finally, in a decisive gesture, he gets up, and, in mingled joy and desperation, picks up the money. At the same moment,* TRAVIS *enters for bed)*

Travis. What's the matter, Daddy? You drunk?

Walter (Sweetly, more sweetly than we have ever known him). No, Daddy ain't drunk. Daddy ain't going to never be drunk again. . . .

Travis. Well, good night, Daddy.

(The FATHER *has come from behind the couch and leans over, embracing his son)*

Walter. Son, I feel like talking to you tonight.

Travis. About what?

Walter. Oh, about a lot of things. About you and what kind of man you going to be when you grow up. . . . Son—son, what do you want to be when you grow up?

Travis. A bus driver.

Walter (Laughing a little). A what? Man, that ain't nothing to want to be!

Travis. Why not?

Walter. 'Cause, man—it ain't big enough—you know what I mean.

Travis. I don't know then. I can't make up my mind. Sometimes Mama asks me that too. And sometimes when I tell her I just want to be like you— she says she don't want me to be like that and sometimes she says she does. . . .

Walter (Gathering him up in his arms). You know what, Travis? In seven years you going to be seventeen years old. And things is going to be very different with us in seven years, Travis. . . . One day when you are seventeen I'll come home—home from my office downtown somewhere—

Travis. You don't work in no office, Daddy.

Walter. No—but after tonight. After what your daddy gonna do tonight, there's going to be offices—a whole lot of offices. . . .

Travis. What you gonna do tonight, Daddy?

Walter. You wouldn't understand yet, son, but your daddy's gonna make a transaction . . . a business transaction that's going to change our lives. . . . That's how come one day when you 'bout seventeen years old I'll come home and I'll be pretty tired, you know what I mean, after a day of conferences and secretaries getting things wrong the way they do . . .

'cause an executive's life is hell, man—*(The more he talks the farther away he gets)* And I'll pull the car up on the driveway . . . just a plain black Chrysler, I think, with white walls—no—black tires. More elegant. Rich people don't have to be flashy . . . though I'll have to get something a little sportier for Ruth—maybe a Cadillac convertible to do her shopping in. . . . And I'll come up the steps to the house and the gardener will be clipping away at the hedges and he'll say, "Good evening, Mr. Younger." And I'll say, "Hello, Jefferson, how are you this evening?" And I'll go inside and Ruth will come downstairs and meet me at the door and we'll kiss each other and she'll take my arm and we'll go up to your room to see you sitting on the floor with the catalogues of all the great schools in America around you. . . . All the great schools in the world! And—and I'll say, all right son—it's your seventeenth birthday, what is it you've decided? . . . Just tell me where you want to go to school and you'll *go.* Just tell me, what it is you want to be—and you'll *be* it. . . . Whatever you want to be—Yessir! *(He holds his arms open for* TRAVIS*)* You just name it, son . . . *(*TRAVIS *leaps into them)* and I hand you the world!

*(*WALTER*'s voice has risen in pitch and hysterical promise and on the last line he lifts* TRAVIS *high)*

(Blackout)

SCENE 3

Time: Saturday, moving day, one week later.
Before the curtain rises, RUTH*'s voice, a strident, dramatic church alto, cuts through the silence.*
It is, in the darkness, a triumphant surge, a penetrating statement of expectation: "Oh, Lord, I don't feel no ways tired! Children, oh, glory hallelujah!"
As the curtain rises we see that RUTH *is alone in the living room, finishing up the family's packing. It is moving day. She is nailing crates and tying cartons.* BENEATHA *enters, carrying a guitar case, and watches her exuberant sister-in-law.*

Ruth. Hey!
Beneatha (Putting away the case). Hi.
Ruth (Pointing at a package). Honey—look in that package there and see what I found on sale this morning at the South Center. *(*RUTH *gets up and moves to the package and draws out some curtains)* Lookahere—hand-turned hems!
Beneatha. How do you know the window size out there?
Ruth (Who hadn't thought of that). Oh— Well, they bound to fit something in the whole house. Anyhow, they was too good a bargain to pass up. *(*RUTH *slaps her head, suddenly remembering something)* Oh, Bennie—I

meant to put a special note on that carton over there. That's your mama's good china and she wants 'em to be very careful with it.

Beneatha. I'll do it.

(BENEATHA *finds a piece of paper and starts to draw large letters on it*)

Ruth. You know what I'm going to do soon as I get in that new house?

Beneatha. What?

Ruth. Honey—I'm going to run me a tub of water up to here . . . *(With her fingers practically up to her nostrils)* And I'm going to get in it—and I am going to sit . . . and sit . . . and sit in that hot water and the first person who knocks to tell *me* to hurry up and come out—

Beneatha. Gets shot at sunrise.

Ruth (Laughing happily). You said it, sister! *(Noticing how large* BENEATHA *is absent-mindedly making the note)* Honey, they ain't going to read that from no airplane.

Beneatha (Laughing herself). I guess I always think things have more emphasis if they are big, somehow.

Ruth (Looking up at her and smiling). You and your brother seem to have that as a philosophy of life. Lord, that man—done changed so 'round here. You know—you know what we did last night? Me and Walter Lee?

Beneatha. What?

Ruth (Smiling to herself). We went to the movies. *(Looking at* BENEATHA *to see if she understands)* We went to the movies. You know the last time me and Walter went to the movies together?

Beneatha. No.

Ruth. Me neither. That's how long it been. *(Smiling again)* But we went last night. The picture wasn't much good, but that didn't seem to matter. We went—and we held hands.

Beneatha. Oh, Lord!

Ruth. We held hands—and you know what?

Beneatha. What?

Ruth. When we come out of the show it was late and dark and all the stores and things was closed up . . . and it was kind of chilly and there wasn't many people on the streets . . . and we was still holding hands, me and Walter.

Beneatha. You're killing me.

(WALTER *enters with a large package. His happiness is deep in him; he cannot keep still with his new-found exuberance. He is singing and wiggling and snapping his fingers. He puts his package in a corner and puts a phonograph record, which he has brought in with him, on the record player. As the music comes up he dances over to* RUTH *and tries to get her to dance with him. She gives in at last to his raunchiness and in a fit of giggling allows herself to be drawn into his mood and together they deliberately burlesque an old social dance of their youth)*

Beneatha (Regarding them a long time as they dance, then drawing in her breath for a deeply exaggerated comment which she does not particularly mean) Talk about—oldddddddddd-fasionedddddddd—Negroes!

Walter (Stopping momentarily). What kind of Negroes?

(He says this in fun. He is not angry with her today, nor with anyone. He starts to dance with his wife again)

Beneatha. Old-fashioned.

Walter (As he dances with RUTH). You know, when these *New Negroes* have their convention—*(Pointing at his sister)*—that is going to be the chairman of the Committee on Unending Agitation. *(He goes on dancing, then stops)* Race, race, race! . . . Girl, I do believe you are the first person in the history of the entire human race to successfully brainwash yourself. *(BE-NEATHA breaks up and he goes on dancing. He stops again, enjoying his tease)* Damn, even the N double A C P takes a holiday sometimes! *(BE-NEATHA and* RUTH *laugh. He dances with* RUTH *some more and starts to laugh and stops and pantomimes someone over an operating table)* I can just seen that chick someday looking down at some poor cat on an operating table before she starts to slice him, saying . . . *(Pulling his sleeves back maliciously)* "By the way, what are your views on civil rights down there? . . ."

(He laughs at her again and starts to dance happily. The bell sounds)

Beneatha. Sticks and stones may break my bones but . . . words will never hurt me!

(BENEATHA goes to the door and opens it as WALTER *and* RUTH *go on with the clowning.* BENEATHA *is somewhat surprised to see a quiet-looking middle-aged white man in a business suit holding his hat and a briefcase in his hand and consulting a small piece of paper)*

Man. Uh—how do you do, miss. I am looking for a Mrs.—*(He looks at the slip of paper)* Mrs. Lena Younger?

Beneatha (Smoothing her hair with slight embarrassment). Oh—yes, that's my mother. Excuse me. *(She closes the door and turns to quiet the other two)* Ruth! Brother! Somebody's here. *(Then she opens the door. The man casts a curious quick glance at all of them)* Uh—come in please.

Man (Coming in). Thank you.

Beneatha. My mother isn't here just now. Is it business?

Man. Yes . . . well, of a sort.

Walter (Freely, the Man of the House). Have a seat. I'm Mrs. Younger's son. I look after most of her business matters.

(RUTH *and* BENEATHA *exchange amused glances)*

Man (Regarding WALTER, *and sitting).* Well— My name is Karl Lindner . . .

Walter (Stretching out his hand). Walter Younger. This is my wife—(RUTH *nods politely)*—and my sister.

Lindner. How do you do.

Walter (Amiably, as he sits himself easily on a chair, learning with interest forward on his knees and looking expectantly into the newcomer's face). What can we do for you, Mr. Lindner!

Lindner (Some minor shuffling of the hat and briefcase on his knees). Well— I am a representative of the Clybourne Park Improvement Association—

Walter (Pointing). Why don't you sit your things on the floor?

Lindner. Oh—yes. Thank you. *(He slides the briefcase and hat under the chair).* And as I was saying—I am from the Clybourne Park Improvement Association and we have had it brought to our attention at the last meeting that you people—or at least your mother—has bought a piece of residential property at—*(He digs for the slip of paper again)*—four o six Clybourne Street . . .

Walter. That's right. Care for something to drink? Ruth, get Mr. Lindner a beer.

Lindner (Upset for some reason). Oh—no, really. I mean thank you very much, but no thank you.

Ruth (Innocently). Some coffee?

Lindner. Thank you, nothing at all.

(BENEATHA *is watching the man carefully)*

Lindner. Well, I don't know how much you folks know about our organization. *(He is a gentle man; thoughtful and somewhat labored in his manner)* It is one of these community organizations set up to look after— oh, you know, things like block upkeep and special projects and we also have what we call our New Neighbors Orientation Committee . . .

Beneatha (Drily). Yes—and what do they do?

Lindner (Turning a little to her and then returning the main force to WALTER*).* Well—it's what you might call a sort of welcoming committee, I guess. I mean they, we, I'm the chairman of the committee—go around and see the new people who move into the neighborhood and sort of give them the lowdown on the way we do things out in Clybourne Park.

Beneatha (With appreciation of the two meanings, which escape RUTH *and* WALTER*).* Un-huh.

Lindner. And we also have the category of what the association calls—*(He looks elsewhere)*—uh—special community problems . . .

Beneatha. Yes—and what are some of those?

Walter. Girl, let the man talk.

Lindner (With understated relief). Thank you. I would sort of like to explain this thing in my own way. I mean I want to explain to you in a certain way.

Walter. Go ahead.

Lindner. Yes. Well. I'm going to try to get right to the point. I'm sure we'll all appreciate that in the long run.

Beneatha. Yes.

Walter. Be still now!

Lindner. Well—

Ruth (Still innocently). Would you like another chair—you don't look comfortable.

Lindner (More frustrated than annoyed). No, thank you very much. Please. Well—to get right to the point I—*(A great breath, and he is off at last)* I am sure you people must be aware of some of the incidents which have happened in various parts of the city when colored people have moved into certain areas—*(BENEATHA exhales heavily and starts tossing a piece of fruit up and down in the air)* Well—because we have what I think is going to be a unique type of organization in American community life— not only do we deplore that kind of thing—but we are trying to do something about it. *(BENEATHA stops tossing and turns with a new and quizzical interest to the man)* We feel—*(gaining confidence in his mission because of the interest in the faces of the people he is talking to)*—we feel that most of the trouble in this world, when you come right down to it—*(He hits his knee for emphasis)*—most of the trouble exists because people just don't sit down and talk to each other.

Ruth (Nodding as she might in church, pleased with the remark). You can say that again, mister.

Lindner (More encouraged by such affirmation). That we don't try hard enough in this world to understand the other fellow's problem. The other guy's point of view.

Ruth. Now that's right.

(BENEATHA and WALTER merely watch and listen with genuine interest)

Lindner. Yes—that's the way we feel out in Clybourne Park. And that's why I was elected to come here this afternoon and talk to you people. Friendly like, you know, the way people should talk to each other and see if we couldn't find some way to work this thing out. As I say, the whole business is a matter of *caring* about the other fellow. Anybody can see that you are a nice family of folks, hard working and honest I'm sure. *(BENEATHA frowns slightly, quizzically, her head tilted regarding him)* Today everybody knows what it means to be on the outside of *something*. And of course, there is always somebody who is out to take the advantage of people who don't always understand.

Walter. What do you mean?

Lindner. Well—you see our community is made up of people who've worked hard as the dickens for years to build up that little community. They're not rich and fancy people; just hard-working, honest people who don't really have much but those little homes and a dream of the kind of community they want to raise their children in. Now, I don't say we are perfect and there is a lot wrong in some of the things they want. But you've got to admit that a man, right or wrong, has the right to want to have the neighborhood he lives in a certain kind of way. And at the moment the overwhelming majority of our people out there feel that people get along better, take more of a common interest in the life of the community, when they share a common background. I want you to believe me when I tell you that race prejudice simply doesn't enter into it. It is a matter of the people of Clybourne Park believing, rightly or wrongly, as I say, that for the happiness of all concerned that our Negro families are happier when they live in their *own* communities.

Beneatha (With a grand a bitter gesture). This, friends, is the Welcoming Committee!

Walter (Dumfounded, looking at LINDNER*).* Is this what you came marching all the way over here to tell us?

Lindner. Well, now we've been having a fine conversation. I hope you'll hear me all the way through.

Walter (Tightly). Go ahead, man.

Lindner. You see—in the face of all things I have said, we are prepared to make your family a very generous offer . . .

Beneatha. Thirty pieces and not a coin less!

Walter. Yeah?

Lindner (Putting on his glasses and drawing a form out of the briefcase). Our association is prepared, through the collective effort of our people, to buy the house from you at a financial gain to your family.

Ruth. Lord have mercy, ain't this the living gall!

Walter. All right, you through?

Lindner. Well, I want to give you the exact terms of the financial arrangement—

Walter. We don't want to hear no exact terms of no arrangements. I want to know if you got any more to tell us 'bout getting together?

Lindner (Taking off his glasses). Well—I don't suppose that you feel . . .

Walter. Never mind how I feel—you got any more to say 'bout how people ought to sit down and talk to each other? . . . Get out of my house, man.

(*He turns his back and walks to the door*)

Lindner (Looking around at the hostile faces and reaching and assembling his hat and briefcase). Well—I don't understand why you people are reacting this way. What do you think you are going to gain by moving into a neighborhood where you just aren't wanted and where some elements—well—people can get awful worked up when they feel that their whole way of life and everything they've ever worked for is threatened.

Walter. Get out.

Lindner (At the door, holding a small card). Well—I'm sorry it went like this.

Walter. Get out.

Lindner (Almost sadly regarding WALTER*).* You just can't force people to change their hearts, son.

(He turns and puts his card on a table and exits. WALTER *pushes the door to with stinging hatred, and stands looking at it.* RUTH *just sits and* BENEATHA *just stands. They say nothing.* MAMA *and* TRAVIS *enter)*

Mama. Well—this all the packing got done since I left out of here this morning. I testify before God that my children got all the energy of the dead. What time the moving men due?

Beneatha. Four o'clock. You had a caller. Mama.

(She is smiling, teasingly)

Mama. Sure enough—who?

Beneatha (Her arms folded saucily). The Welcoming Committee.

*(*WALTER *and* RUTH *giggle)*

Mama (Innocently). Who?

Beneatha. The Welcoming Committee. They said they're sure going to be glad to see you when you get there.

Walter (Devilishly). Yeah, they said they can't hardly wait to see your face.

(Laughter)

Mama (Sensing their facetiousness). What's the matter with you all?

Walter. Ain't nothing the matter with us. We just telling you 'bout the gentleman who came to see you this afternoon. From the Clybourne Park Improvement Association.

Mama. What he want?

Ruth (In the same mood as BENEATHA *and* WALTER*).* To welcome you, honey.

Walter. He said they can't hardly wait. He said the one thing they don't have, that they just *dying* to have out there is a fine family of colored people! *(To* RUTH *and* BENEATHA*)* Ain't that right!

Ruth and Beneatha (Mockingly). Yeah! He left his card in case—

(They indicate the card, and MAMA *picks it up and throws it on the floor— understanding and looking off as she draws her chair up to the table on which she has put her plant and some sticks and some cord)*

Mama. Father, give us strength. *(Knowingly—and without fun)* Did he threaten us?
Beneatha. Oh—Mama—they don't do it like that any more. He talked Brotherhood. He said everybody ought learn how to sit down and hate each other with good Christian fellowship.

(She and WALTER *shake hands to ridicule the remark)*

Mama *(Sadly)*. Lord, protect us . . .
Ruth. You should hear the money those folks raised to buy the house from us. All we paid and then some.
Beneatha. What they think we going to do—eat 'em?
Ruth. No, honey, marry 'em.
Mama *(Shaking her head)*. Lord, Lord, Lord . . .
Ruth. Well—that's the way the crackers crumble. Joke.
Beneatha *(Laughingly noticing what her mother is doing)*. Mama, what are you doing?
Mama. Fixing my plant so it won't get hurt none on the way . . .
Beneatha. Mama, you going to take *that* to the new house?
Mama. Un-huh—
Beneatha. That raggedy-looking old thing?
Mama *(Stopping and looking at her)*. It expresses *me*.
Ruth *(With delight, to* BENEATHA*)*. So there, Miss Thing!

*(*WALTER *comes to* MAMA *suddenly and bends down behind her and squeezes her in his arms with all his strength. She is overwhelmed by the suddenness of it and, though delighted, her manner is like that of* RUTH *with* TRAVIS*)*

Mama. Look out now, boy! You make me mess up my thing here!
Walter *(His face lit, he slips down on his knees beside her, his arms still about her)*. Mama . . . you know what it means to climb up in the chariot?
Mama *(Gruffly, very happy)*. Get on away from me now . . .
Ruth *(Near the gift-wrapped package, trying to catch* WALTER'S *eye)*. Psst—
Walter. What the old song say, Mama . . .
Ruth. Walter— Now?

(She is pointing at the package)

Walter *(Speaking the lines, sweetly, playfully, in his mother's face)*
I got wings . . . you got wings . . .
All God's children got wings . . .

Mama. Boy—get out of my face and do some work . . .
Walter.
  When I get to heaven gonna put on my wings,
  Gonna fly all over God's heaven . . .
Beneatha (Teasingly, from across the room). Everybody talking 'bout heaven ain't going there!
Walter (To RUTH, *who is carrying the box across to them).* I don't know, you think we ought to give her that . . . Seems to me she ain't been very appreciative around here.
Mama (Eying the box, which is obviously a gift). What is that?
Walter (Taking it from RUTH *and putting it on the table in front of* MAMA). Well—what you all think. Should we give it to her?
Ruth. Oh—she was pretty good today.
Mama. I'll good you—

(She turns her eyes to the box again)

Beneatha. Open it, Mama.

(She stands up, looks at it, turns and looks at all of them, and then presses her hands together and does not open the package)

Walter (Sweetly). Open it, Mama. It's for you. (MAMA *looks in his eyes. It is the first present in her life without its being Christmas. Slowly she opens her package and lifts out, one by one, a brand-new sparkling set of gardening tools.* WALTER *continues, prodding)* Ruth made up the note—read it . . .
Mama (Picking up the card and adjusting her glasses). "To our own Mrs. Miniver[4]—Love from Brother, Ruth, and Beneatha." Ain't that lovely . . .
Travis (Tugging at his father's sleeve). Daddy, can I give her mine now?
Walter. All right, son. (TRAVIS *flies to get his gift)* Travis didn't want to go in with the rest of us, Mama. He got his own. *(Somewhat amused)* We don't know what it is . . .
Travis (Racing back in the room with a large hatbox and putting it in front of his grandmother). Here!
Mama. Lord have mercy, baby. You done gone and bought your grandmother a hat?
Travis (Very proud). Open it!

(She does and lifts out an elaborate, but very elaborate, wide gardening hat, and all the adults break up at the sight of it)

---

[4]Heroine of a movie based on a 1940 best-seller by Jan Struther. Mrs. Miniver is a middle-class Englishwoman in the early years of World War II.

Ruth. Travis, honey, what is that?

Travis (Who thinks it is beautiful and appropriate). It's a gardening hat! Like the ladies always have on in the magazines when they work in their gardens.

Beneatha (Giggling fiercely). Travis—we were trying to make Mama Mrs. Miniver—not Scarlett O'Hara!

Mama (Indignantly). What's the matter with you all! This here is a beautiful hat! *(Absurdly)* I always wanted me one just like it!

(She pops it on her head to prove it to her grandson, and the hat is ludicrous and considerably oversized)

Ruth. Hot dog! Go, Mama!

Walter (Doubled over with laughter). I'm sorry, Mama—but you look like you ready to go out and chop you some cotton sure enough!

(They all laugh except MAMA, out of deference to TRAVIS' feelings)

Mama (Gathering the boy up to her). Bless your heart—this is the prettiest hat I ever owned— *(WALTER, RUTH and BENEATHA chime in—noisily, festively and insincerely congratulating TRAVIS on his gift)* What are we all standing around here for? We ain't finished packin' yet. Bennie, you ain't packed one book.

(The bell rings)

Beneatha. That couldn't be the movers . . . it's not hardly two good yet—

(BENEATHA goes into her room. MAMA starts for door)

Walter (Turning, stiffening). Wait—wait—I'll get it.

(He stands and looks at the door)

Mama. You expecting company, son?

Walter (Just looking at the door). Yeah—yeah . . .

(MAMA looks at RUTH, and they exchange innocent and unfrightened glances)

Mama (Not understanding). Well, let them in, son.

Beneatha. (From her room). We need some more string.

Mama. Travis—you run to the hardware and get me some string cord.

(MAMA goes out and WALTER turns and looks at RUTH. TRAVIS goes to a dish for money)

Ruth. Why don't you answer the door, man?

Walter (Suddenly bounding across the floor to her). 'Cause sometimes it hard to let the future begin! *(Stooping down in her face)*

I got wings? You got wings?
All God's children got wings!

(He crosses to the door and throws it open. Standing there is a very slight little man in a not too prosperous business suit and with haunted frightened eyes and a hat pulled down tightly, brim up, around his forehead. TRAVIS *passes between the men and exits.* WALTER *leans deep in the man's face, still in his jubilance)*

When I get to heaven gonna put on my wings,
Gonna fly all over God's heaven . . .

(The little man just stares at him)

Heaven—
(Suddenly he stops and looks past the little man into the empty hallway)
Where's Willy, man?

Bobo. He ain't with me.

Walter (Not disturbed). Oh—come on in. You know my wife.

Bobo (Dumbly, taking off his hat). Yes—h'you, Miss Ruth.

Ruth (Quietly, a mood apart from her husband already, seeing BOBO*).* Hello, Bobo.

Walter. You right on time today . . . Right on time. That's the way! *(He slaps* BOBO *on his back)* Sit down . . . lemme hear.

*(*RUTH *stands stiffly and quietly in back of them, as though somehow she senses death, her eyes fixed on her husband)*

Bobo (His frightened eyes on the floor, his hat in his hands) Could I please get a drink a water, before I tell you about it, Walter Lee?

*(*WALTER *does not take his eyes off the man.* RUTH *goes blindly to the tap and gets a glass of water and brings it to* BOBO*)*

Walter. There ain't nothing wrong, is there?

Bobo. Lemme tell you—

Walter. Man—didn't nothing go wrong?

Bobo. Lemme tell you—Walter Lee. *(Looking at* RUTH *and talking to her more than to* WALTER*)* You know how it was. I got to tell you how it was.

I mean first I got to tell you how it was all the way . . . I mean about
the money I put in, Walter Lee . . .

Walter (With taut agitation now). What about the money you put in?

Bobo. Well—It wasn't much as we told you—me and Willy—*(He stops)* I'm
sorry, Walter. I got a bad feeling about it. I got a real bad feeling about
it . . .

Walter. Man, what you telling me about all this for? . . . Tell me what
happened in Springfield . . .

Bobo. Springfield.

Ruth (Like a dead woman). What was supposed to happen in Springfield?

Bobo (To her). This deal that me and Walter went into with Willy— Me
and Willy was going to go down to Springfield and spread some money
'round so's we wouldn't have to wait so long for the liquor license . . .
That's what we were going to do. Everybody said that was the way you
had to do, you understand, Miss Ruth?

Walter. Man—what happened down there?

Bobo (A pitiful man, near tears). I'm trying to tell you, Walter.

Walter (Screaming at him suddenly). THEN TELL ME, GODDAMNIT . . .
WHAT'S THE MATTER WITH YOU?

Bobo. Man . . . I didn't go to no Springfield, yesterday.

Walter (Halted, life hanging in the moment). Why not?

Bobo (The long way, the hard way to tell). 'Cause I didn't have no reasons
to . . .

Walter. Man, what are you talking about!

Bobo. I'm talking about the fact that when I got to the train station yesterday
morning—eight o'clock like we planned . . . Man—*Willy didn't never
show up.*

Walter. Why . . . where was he . . . where is he?

Bobo. That's what I'm trying to tell you . . . I don't know . . . I waited six
hours . . . I called his house . . . and I waited . . . six hours . . . I
waited in that train station six hours . . . *(Breaking into tears)* That was
all the extra money I had in the world . . . *(Looking up at* WALTER *with
the tears running down his face)* Man, *Willy is gone.*

Walter. Gone, what you mean Willy is gone? Gone where? You mean he
went by himself. You mean he went off to Springfield by himself—to take
care of getting the license—*(Turns and looks anxiously at* RUTH*)* You
mean maybe he didn't want too many people in on the business down
there? *(Looks to* RUTH *again, as before)* You know Willy got his own
ways. *(Looks back to* BOBO*)* Maybe you was late yesterday and he just
went on down there without you. Maybe—maybe—he's been callin' you
at home tryin' to tell you what happened or something. Maybe—maybe—
he just got sick. He's somewhere—he's got to be somewhere. We just got
to find him—me and you got to find him. *(Grabs* BOBO *senselessly by the
collar and starts to shake him)* We got to!

Bobo (In sudden angry, frightened agony). What's the matter with you, Walter! *When a cat take off with your money he don't leave you no maps!*
Walter (Turning madly, as though he is looking for WILLY *in the very room).* Willy! . . . Willy . . . don't do it . . . Please don't do it . . . Man, not with that money . . . Man, please, not with that money . . . Oh, God . . . Don't let it be true . . . *(He is wandering around, crying out for Willy and looking for him or perhaps for help from God)* Man . . . I trusted you . . . Man, I put my life in your hands . . . *(He starts to crumple down on the floor as* RUTH *just covers her face in horror.* MAMA *opens the door and comes into the room, with* BENEATHA *behind her)* Man . . . *(He starts to pound the floor with his fists, sobbing wildly)* That money is made out of my father's flesh . . .
Bobo (Standing over him helplessly). I'm sorry, Walter . . . *(Only* WALTER'S *sobs reply.* BOBO *puts on his hat)* I had my life staked on this deal, too . . .

(He exits)

Mama (To WALTER*).* Son—*(She goes to him, bends down to him, talks to his bent head)* Son . . . Is it gone? Son, I gave you sixty-five hundred dollars. Is it gone? All of it? Beneatha's money too?
Walter (Lifting his head slowly). Mama . . . I never . . . went to the bank at all . . .
Mama (Not wanting to believe him). You mean . . . your sister's school money . . . you used that too . . . Walter? . . .
Walter. Yesss! . . . All of it . . . It's all gone . . .

(There is total silence. RUTH *stands with her face covered with her hands;* BENEATHA *leans forlornly against a wall, fingering a piece of red ribbon from the mother's gift.* MAMA *stops and looks at her son without recognition and then, quite without thinking about it, starts to beat him senselessly in the face.* BENEATHA *goes to them and stops it)*

Beneatha. Mama!

*(*MAMA *stops and looks at both of her children and rises slowly and wanders vaguely, aimlessly away from them)*

Mama. I seen . . . him . . . night after night . . . come in . . . and look at that rug . . . and then look at me . . . the red showing in his eyes . . . the veins moving in his head . . . I seen him grow thin and old before he was forty . . . working and working and working like somebody's old horse . . . killing himself . . . and you—you give it all away in a day . . .

Beneatha. Mama—

Mama. Oh, God . . . *(She looks up to Him)* Look down here—and show me the strength.

Beneatha. Mama—

Mama (Folding over). Strength . . .

Beneatha (Plaintively). Mama . . .

Mama. Strength!

Curtain

ACT THREE

An hour later.

At curtain, there is a sullen light of gloom in the living room, gray light not unlike that which began the first scene of Act One. At left we can see WALTER *within his room, alone with himself. He is stretched out on the bed, his shirt out and open, his arms under his head. He does not smoke, he does not cry out, he merely lies there, looking up at the ceiling, much as if he were alone in the world.*

In the living room BENEATHA *sits at the table, still surrounded by the now almost ominous packing crates. She sits looking off. We feel that this is a mood struck perhaps an hour before, and it lingers now, full of the empty sound of profound disappointment. We see on a line from her brother's bedroom the sameness of their attitudes. Presently the bell rings and* BE-NEATHA *rises without ambition or interest in answering. It is* ASAGAI, *smiling broadly, striding into the room with energy and happy expectation and conversation.*

Asagai. I came over . . . I had some free time. I thought I might help with the packing. Ah, I like the look of packing crates! A household in preparation for a journey! It depresses some people . . . but for me . . . it is another feeling. Something full of the flow of life, do you understand? Movement, progress . . . It makes me think of Africa.

Beneatha. Africa!

Asagia. What kind of a mood is this? Have I told you how deeply you move me?

Beneatha. He gave away the money, Asagai . . .

Asagai. Who gave away what money?

Beneatha. The insurance money. My brother gave it away.

Asagai. Gave it away?

Beneatha. He made an investment! With a man even Travis wouldn't have trusted.

Asagai. And it's gone?

Beneatha. Gone!

Asagai. I'm very sorry . . . And you, now?

Beneatha. Me? . . . Me? . . . Me I'm nothing . . . Me. When I was very small . . . we used to take our sleds out in the wintertime and the only hills we had were the ice-covered stone steps of some houses down the street. And we used to fill them in with snow and make them smooth and slide down them all day . . . and it was very dangerous you know . . . far too steep . . . and sure enough one day a kid named Rufus came down too fast and hit the sidewalk . . . and we saw his face just split open right there in front of us . . . And I remember standing there looking at his bloody open face thinking that was the end of Rufus. But the ambulance came and they took him to the hospital and they fixed the broken bones and they sewed it all up . . . and the next time I saw Rufus he just had a little line down the middle of his face . . . I never got over that . . .

Asagai. What?

Beneatha. That that was what one person could do for another, fix him up—sew up the problem, make him all right again. That was the most marvelous thing in the world . . . I wanted to do that. I always thought it was the one concrete thing in the world that a human being could do. Fix up the sick, you know—and make them whole again. This was truly being God. . . .

Asagai. You wanted to be God?

Beneatha. No—I wanted to cure. It used to be so important to me. I wanted to cure. It used to matter. I used to care. I mean about people and how their bodies hurt . . .

Asagai. And you've stopped caring?

Beneatha. Yes—I think so.

Asagai. Why?

(WALTER *rises, goes to the door of his room and is about to open it, then stops and stands listening, leaning on the door jamb*)

Beneatha. Because it doesn't seem deep enough, close enough to what ails mankind—I mean this thing of sewing up bodies or administering drugs. Don't you understand? It was a child's reaction to the world. I thought that doctors had the secret to all the hurts. . . . That's the way a child see things—or an idealist.

Asagai. Children see things very well sometimes—and idealists even better.

Beneatha. I know that's what you think. Because you are still where I left off—you still care. This is what you see for the world, for Africa. You with the dreams of the future will patch up all Africa—you are going to cure the Great Sore of colonialism with Independence—

Asagai. Yes!

Beneatha. Yes—and you think that one word is the penicillin of the human spirit: "Independence!" But then what?

Asagai. That will be the problem for another time. First we must get there.

Beneatha. And where does it end?

Asagai. End? Who even spoke of an end? To life? To living?

Beneatha. An end to misery!

Asagai (Smiling). You sound like a French intellectual.

Beneatha. No! I sound like a human being who just had her future taken right out of her hands! While I was sleeping in my bed in there, things were happening in this world that directly concerned me—and nobody asked me, consulted me—they just went out and did things—and changed my life. Don't you see there isn't any real progress, Asagai, there is only one large circle that we march in, around and around, each of us with our own little picture—in front of us—our own little mirage that we think is the future.

Asagai. That is the mistake.

Beneatha. What?

Asagai. What you just said—about the circle. It isn't a circle—it is simply a long line—as in geometry, you know, one that reaches into infinity. And because we cannot see the end—we also cannot see how it changes. And it is very odd but those who see the changes are called "idealists"—and those who cannot, or refuse to think, they are the "realists." It is very strange, and amusing too, I think.

Beneatha. You—you are almost religious.

Asagai. Yes . . . I think I have the religion of doing what is necessary in the world—and of worshipping man—because he is so marvelous, you see.

Beneatha. Man is foul! And the human race deserves its misery!

Asagai. You see: *you* have become the religious one in the old sense. Already, and after such a small defeat, you are worshipping despair.

Beneatha. From now on, I worship the truth—and the truth is that people are puny, small and selfish. . . .

Asagai. Truth? Why is it that you despairing ones always think that only you have the truth? I never thought to see *you* like that. Your brother made a stupid, childish mistake—and you are grateful to him. So that now you can give up the ailing human race on account of it. You talk about what good is struggle; what good is anything? Where are we all going? And why are we bothering?

Beneatha. And you cannot answer it! All your talk and dreams about Africa and Independence. Independence and then what? What about all the crooks and petty thieves and just plain idiots who will come into power to steal and plunder the same as before—only now they will be black and do it in the name of the new Independence— You cannot answer that.

Asagai (Shouting over her). I live the answer! (Pause) In my village at home it is the exceptional man who can even read a newspaper . . . or who ever *sees* a book at all. I will go home and much of what I will have to say will seem strange to the people of my village . . . But I will teach and work and things will happen, slowly and swiftly. At times it will seem that nothing changes at all . . . and then again . . . the sudden dramatic events which make history leap into the future. And then quiet again. Retrogression even. Guns, murder, revolution. And I even will have moments when I wonder if the quiet was not better than all that death and hatred. But I will look about my village at the illiteracy and disease and ignorance and I will not wonder long. And perhaps . . . perhaps I will be a great man . . . I mean perhaps I will hold on to the substance of truth and find my way always with the right course . . . and perhaps for it I will be butchered in my bed some night by the servants of empire . . .

Beneatha. The martyr!

Asagai. . . . or perhaps I shall live to be a very old man respected and esteemed in my new nation . . . And perhaps I shall hold office and this is what I'm trying to tell you, Alaiyo; perhaps the things I believe now for my country will be wrong and outmoded, and I will not understand and do terrible things to have things my way or merely to keep my power. Don't you see that there will be young men and women, not British soldiers then, but my own black countrymen . . . to step out of the shadows some evening and slit my then useless throat? Don't you see they have always been there . . . that they always will be. And that such a thing as my own death will be an advance? They who might kill me even . . . actually replenish me!

Beneatha. Oh, Asagai, I know all that.

Asagai. Good! Then stop moaning and groaning and tell me what you plan to do.

Beneatha. Do?

Asagai. I have a bit of a suggestion.

Beneatha. What?

Asagai (Rather quietly for him). That when it is all over—that you come home with me—

Beneatha (Slapping herself on the forehead with exasperation born of misunderstanding). Oh—Asagai—at this moment you decide to be romantic!

Asagai (Quickly understanding the misunderstanding). My dear, young creature of the New World—I do not mean across the city—I mean across the ocean; home—to Africa.

Beneatha (Slowly understanding and turning to him with murmured amazement). To—to Nigeria?

Asagai. Yes! . . . *(Smiling and lifting his arms playfully)* Three hundred years later the African Prince rose up out of the seas and swept the maiden back across the middle passage over which her ancestors had come—

Beneatha (Unable to play). Nigeria?

Asagai. Nigeria. Home. *(Coming to her with genuine romantic flippancy)* I will show you our mountains and our stars; and give you cool drinks from gourds and teach you the old songs and the ways of our people—and, in time, we will pretend that—*(Very softly)*—you have only been away for a day—

(She turns her back to him, thinking. He swings her around and takes her full in his arms in a long embrace which proceeds to passion)

Beneatha *(Pulling away)*. You're getting me all mixed up—
Asagai. Why?
Beneatha. Too many things—too many things have happened today. I must sit down and think. I don't know what I feel about anything right this minute.

(She promptly sits down and props her chin on her fist)

Asagai *(Charmed)*. All right, I shall leave you. No—don't get up. *(Touching her, gently, sweetly)* Just sit awhile and think . . . Never be afraid to sit awhile and think. *(He goes to door and looks at her)* How often I have looked at you and said, "Ah—so this is what the New World hath finally wrought . . ."

(He exits. BENEATHA *sits on alone. Presently* WALTER *enters from his room and starts to rummage through things, feverishly looking for something. She look up and turns in her seat)*

Beneatha *(Hissingly)*. Yes—just look at what the New World hath wrought! . . . Just look! *(She gestures with bitter disgust)* There he is! *Monsieur le petit bourgeois noir*—himself! There he is—Symbol of a Rising Class! Entrepreneur! Titan of the system! *(*WALTER *ignores her completely and continues frantically and destructively looking for something and hurling things to floor and tearing things out of their place in his search.* BENEATHA *ignores the eccentricity of his actions and goes on with the monologue of insult)* Did you dream of yachts on Lake Michigan, Brother? Did you see yourself on that Great Day sitting down at the Conference Table, surrounded by all the mighty bald-headed men in America? All halted, waiting, breathless, waiting for your pronouncements on industry? Waiting for you—Chairman of the Board? *(*WALTER *finds what he is looking for—a small piece of white paper—and pushes it in his pocket and puts on his coat and rushes out without ever having looked at her. She shouts after him)* I look at you and I see the final triumph of stupidity in the world!

(The door slams and she returns to just sitting again. RUTH *comes quickly out of* MAMA'S *room)*

Ruth. Who was that?
Beneatha. Your husband.
Ruth. Where did he go?
Beneatha. Who knows—maybe he has an appointment at U.S. Steel.
Ruth *(Anxiously, with frightened eyes)*. You didn't say nothing bad to him, did you?

Beneatha. Bad? Say anything bad to him? No—I told him he was a sweet boy and full of dreams and everything is strictly peachy keen, as the ofay[5] kids say!

(MAMA *enters from her bedroom. She is lost, vague, trying to catch hold, to make some sense of her former command of the world, but it still eludes her. A sense of waste overwhelms her gait; a measure of apology rides on her shoulders. She goes to her plant, which has remained on the table, looks at it, picks it up and takes it to the window sill and sits it outside, and she stands and looks at it a long moment. Then she closes the window, straightens her body with effort and turns around to her children*)

Mama. Well—ain't it a mess in here, though? (*A false cheerfulness, a beginning of something*) I guess we all better stop moping around and get some work done. All this unpacking and everything we got to do. (RUTH *raises her head slowly in response to the sense of the line; and* BENEATHA *in similar manner turns very slowly to look at her mother*) One of you all better call the moving people and tell 'em not to come.
Ruth. Tell 'em not to come?
Mama. Of course, baby. Ain't no need in 'em coming all the way here and having to go back. They charges for that too. (*She sits down, fingers to her brow, thinking*) Lord, ever since I was a little girl, I always remembers people saying, "Lena—Lena Eggleston, you aims too high all the time. You needs to slow down and see life a little more like it is. Just slow down some." That's what they always used to say down home—"Lord, that Lena Eggleston is a high-minded thing. She'll get her due one day!"
Ruth. No, Lena . . .
Mama. Me and Big Walter just didn't never learn right.
Ruth. Lena, no! We gotta go. Bennie—tell her . . . (*She rises and crosses to* BENEATHA *with her arms outstretched,* BENEATHA *doesn't respond*) Tell her we can still move . . . the notes ain't but a hundred and twenty five a month. We got four grown people in this house—we can work . . .
Mama (To herself). Just aimed too high all the time—
Ruth (Turning and going to MAMA *fast—the words pouring out with urgency and desperation*). Lena—I'll work . . . I'll work twenty hours a day in all the kitchens in Chicago . . . I'll strap my baby on my back if I have to and scrub all the floors in America and wash all the sheets in America if I have to—but we got to move . . . We got to get out of here . . .

(MAMA *reaches out absently and pats* RUTH'S *hand*)

Mama. No—I sees things differently now. Been thinking 'bout some of the things we could do to fix this place up some. I seen a second-hand bureau

---

[5]White.

over on Maxwell Street just the other day that could fit right there. *(She points to where the new furniture might go.* RUTH *wanders away from her)* Would need some new handles on it and then a little varnish and then it look like something brand-new. And—we can put up them new curtains in the kitchen . . . Why this place be looking fine. Cheer us all up so that we forget trouble ever came . . . *(To* RUTH*)* And you could get some nice screens to put up in your room round the baby's basinet . . . *(She looks at both of them, pleadingly)* Sometimes you just got to know when to give up some things . . . and hold on to what you got.

*(*WALTER *enters from the outside, looking spent and leaning again the door, his coat hanging from him)*

Mama. Where you been, son?
Walter (Breathing hard). Made a call.
Mama. To who, son?
Walter. To The Man.
Mama. What man, baby?
Walter. The Man, Mama. Don't you know who The Man is?
Ruth. Walter Lee?
Walter. The Man. Like the guys in the streets say—The Man. Captain Boss— Mistuh Charley . . . Old Captain Please Mr. Bossman . . .
Beneatha (Suddenly). Lindner!
Walter. That's right! That's good. I told him to come right over.
Beneatha (Fiercely, understanding). For what? What do you want to see him for!
Walter (Looking at his sister). We going to do business with him.
Mama. What you talking 'bout, son?
Walter. Talking 'bout life, Mama. You all always telling me to see life like it is. Well—I laid in there on my back today . . . and I figured it out. Life just like it is. Who gets and who don't get. *(He sits down with his coat on and laughs)* Mama, you know it's all divided up. Life is. Sure enough. Between the takers and the "tooken." *(He laughs)* I've figured it out finally. *(He looks around at them)* Yeah. Some of us always getting "tooken." *(He laughs)* People like Willy Harris, they don't never get "tooken." And you know why the rest of us do? 'Cause we all mixed up. Mixed up bad. We get to looking 'round for the right and the wrong; and we worry about it and cry about it and stay up nights trying to figure out 'bout the wrong and the right of things all the time . . . And all the time, man, them takers is out there operating, just taking and taking. Willy Harris? Shoot—Willy Harris don't even count. He don't even count in the big scheme of things. But I'll say one thing for old Willy Harris . . . he's taught me something. He's taught me to keep my eye on what counts in this world. Yeah— *(Shouting out a little)* Thanks, Willy!
Ruth. What did you call that man for, Walter Lee?

Walter. Called him to tell him to come on over to the show. Gonna put on a show for the man. Just what he wants to see. You see, Mama, the man came here today and he told us that them people out there where you want us to move—well they so upset they willing to pay us not to move out there. *(He laughs again)* And—and oh, Mama—you would of been proud of the way me and Ruth and Bennie acted. We told him to get out . . . Lord have mercy! We told the man to get out. Oh, we was some proud folks this afternoon, yeah. *(He lights a cigarette)* We were still full of that old-time stuff . . .

Ruth (Coming toward him slowly). You talking 'bout taking them people's money to keep us from moving in that house?

Walter. I ain't just talking 'bout it, baby—I'm telling you that's what's going to happen.

Beneatha. Oh, God! Where is the bottom! Where is the real honest-to-God bottom so he can't go any farther!

Walter. See—that's the old stuff. You and that boy that was here today. You all want everybody to carry a flag and a spear and sing some marching songs, huh? You wanna spend your life looking into things and trying to find the right and the wrong part, huh? Yeah. You know what's going to happen to that boy someday—he'll find himself sitting in a dungeon, locked in forever—and the takers will have the key! Forget it, baby! There ain't no causes—there ain't nothing but taking in this world, and he who takes most is smartest—and it don't make a damn bit of difference *how*.

Mama. You making something inside me cry, son. Some awful pain inside me.

Walter. Don't cry, Mama. Understand. That white man is going to walk in that door able to write checks for more money than we ever had. It's important to him and I'm going to help him . . . I'm going to put on the show, Mama.

Mama. Son—I come from five generations of people who was slaves and sharecroppers—but ain't nobody in my family never let nobody pay 'em no money that was a way of telling us we wasn't fit to walk the earth. We ain't never been that poor. *(Raising her eyes and looking at him)* We ain't never been that dead inside.

Beneatha. Well—we are dead now. All the talk about dreams and sunlight that goes on in this house. All dead.

Walter. What's the matter with you all! I didn't make this world! It was give to me this way! Hell, yes, I want me some yachts someday! Yes, I want to hang some real pearls 'round my wife's neck. Ain't she supposed to wear no pearls? Somebody tell me—tell me, who decides which women is suppose to wear pearls in this world. I tell you I am a *man*—and I think my wife should wear some pearls in this world!

(This last line hangs a good while and WALTER *begins to move about the room. The world "Man" has penetrated his consciousness; he mumbles it to himself repeatedly between strange agitated pauses as he moves about)*

Mama. Baby, how you going to feel on the inside?

Walter. Fine! . . . Going to feel fine . . . a man . . .

Mama. You won't have nothing left then, Walter Lee.

Walter (Coming to her). I'm going to feel fine, Mama. I'm going to look that son-of-a-bitch in the eyes and say—*(He falters)*—and say, "All right, Mr. Lindner—*(He falters even more)*—that's your neighborhood out there. You got the right to keep it like you want. You got the right to have it like you want. Just write the check and—the house is yours." And, and I am going to say—*(His voice almost breaks)* And you—you people just put the money in my hand and you won't have to live next to this bunch of stinking niggers! . . . *(He straightens up and moves away from his mother, walking around the room)* Maybe—maybe I'll just get down on my black knees . . . *(He does so;* RUTH *and* BENNIE *and* MAMA *watch him in frozen horror)* Captain, Mistuh, Bossman. *(He starts crying)* A-hee-hee-hee! *(Wringing his hands in profoundly anguished imitation)* Yasssssuh! Great White Father, just gi' ussen de money, fo' God's sake, and we's ain't gwine come out deh and dirty up yo' white folks neighborhood . . .

(He breaks down completely, then gets up and goes into the bedroom)

Beneatha. That is not a man. That is nothing but a toothless rat.

Mama. Yes—death done come in this here house. *(She is nodding, slowly, reflectively)* Done come walking in my house. On the lips of my children. You what supposed to be my beginning again. You—what supposed to be my harvest. *(To* BENEATHA*)* You—you mourning your brother?

Beneatha. He's no brother of mine.

Mama. What you say?

Beneatha. I said that that individual in that room is no brother of mine.

Mama. That's what I thought you said. You feeling like you better than he is today? *(*BENEATHA *does not answer)* Yes? What you tell him a minute ago? That he wasn't a man? Yes? You give him up for me? You done write his epitaph too—like the rest of the world? Well, who give you the privilege?

Beneatha. Be on my side for once! You saw what he just did, Mama! You saw him—down on his knees. Wasn't it you who taught me—to despise any man who would do that. Do what he's going to do.

Mama. Yes—I taught you that. Me and your daddy. But I thought I taught you something else too . . . . I thought I taught you to love him.

Beneatha. Love him? There is nothing left to love.

Mama. There is always something left to love. And if you ain't learned that, you ain't learned nothing. *(Looking at her)* Have you cried for that boy today? I don't mean for yourself and for the family 'cause we lost the money. I mean for him; what he been through and what it done to him. Child, when do you think is the time to love somebody the most; when they done good and made things easy for everybody? Well then, you ain't through learning—because that ain't the time at all. It's when he's at his lowest and can't believe in hisself 'cause the world done whipped him so. When you starts measuring somebody, measure him right, child, measure him right. Make sure you done taken into account what hills and valleys he come through before he got to wherever he is.

(TRAVIS *bursts into the room at the end of the speech, leaving the door open)*

Travis. Grandmama—the moving men are downstairs! The truck just pulled up.

Mama (Turning and looking at him). Are they, baby? They downstairs?

(She sighs and sits. Lindner appears in the doorway. He peers in and knocks lightly, to gain attention, and comes in. All turn to look at him)

Lindner (Hat and briefcase in hand). Uh—hello . . .

(RUTH *crosses mechanically to the bedroom door and opens it and lets it swing open freely and slowly as the lights come up on* WALTER *within, still in his coat, sitting at the far corner of the room. He looks up and out through the room to* LINDNER)

Ruth. He's here.

(A long minute passes and WALTER *slowly gets up)*

Lindner (Coming to the table with efficiency, putting his briefcase on the table and starting to unfold papers and unscrew fountain pens). Well, I certainly was glad to hear from you people. (WALTER *has begun the trek out of the room, slowly and awkwardly, rather like a small boy, passing the back of his sleeve across his mouth from time to time)* Life can really be so much simpler than people let it be most of the time. Well—with whom do I negotiate? You, Mrs. Younger, or your son here? (MAMA *sits with her hands folded on her lap and her eyes closed as* WALTER *advances.* TRAVIS *goes close to* LINDNER *and looks at the papers curiously)* Just some official papers, sonny.

Ruth. Travis, you go downstairs.

Mama (Opening her eyes and looking into WALTER'S). No, Travis, you stay right here. And you make him understand what you doing, Walter Lee. You teach him good. Like Willy Harris taught you. You show where our five generations done come to. Go ahead, son—

Walter (Looks down into his boy's eyes. TRAVIS *grins at him merrily and* WALTER *draws him beside him with his arm lightly around his shoulder).* Well, Mr. Lindner. (BENEATHA *turns away)* We called you—(*There is a*

profound, simple groping quality in his speech)*—because, well, me and
my family *(He looks around and shifts from one foot to the other)* Well—
we are very plain people . . .

Lindner. Yes—

Walter. I mean—I have worked as a chauffeur most of my life—and my wife
here, she does domestic work in people's kitchens. So does my mother. I
mean—we are plain people . . .

Lindner. Yes, Mr. Younger—

*Walter (Really like a small boy, looking down at his shoes and then up at
the man).* And—uh—well, my father, well, he was a laborer most of his
life.

Lindner (Absolutely confused). Uh, yes—

Walter (Looking down at his toes once again). My father almost beat a man
to death once because this man called him a bad name or something, you
know what I mean?

Lindner. No, I'm afraid I don't.

Walter (Finally straightening up). Well, what I mean is that we come from
people who had a lot of pride. I mean—we are very proud people. And
that's my sister over there and she's going to be a doctor—and we are
very proud—

Lindner. Well—I am sure that is very nice, but—

Walter (Starting to cry and facing the man eye to eye). What I am telling you
is that we called you over here to tell you that we are very proud and that
this is—this is my son, who makes the sixth generation of our family in
this country, and that we have all thought about your offer and we have
decided to move into our house because my father—my father—he earned
it. *(MAMA has her eyes closed and is rocking back and forth as though she
were in church, with her head nodding the amen yes)* We don't want to
make no trouble for nobody or fight no causes—but we will try to be
good neighbors. That's all we got to say. *(He looks the man absolutely in
the eyes)* We don't want your money.

(He turns and walks away from the man)

Lindner (Looking around at all of them). I take it then that you have decided
to occupy.

Beneatha. That's what the man said.

Lindner (To MAMA in her reverie). Then I would like to appeal to you, Mrs.
Younger. You are older and wiser and understand things better I am sure
. . .

Mama (Rising). I am afraid you don't understand. My son said we was going
to move and there ain't nothing left for me to say. *(Shaking her head with
double meaning)* You know how these young folks is nowadays, mister.
Can't do a thing with 'em. Good-bye.

Lindner (Folding up his materials). Well—if you are that final about it . . . There is nothing left for me to say. *(He finishes. He is almost ignored by the family, who are concentrating on* WALTER LEE. *At the door* LIND-NER *halts and looks around)* I sure hope you people know what you're doing.

(He shakes his head and exits)

Ruth (Looking around and coming to life). Well, for God's sake—if the moving men are here—LET'S GET THE HELL OUT OF HERE!
Mama (Into action). Ain't it the truth! Look at all this here mess. Ruth put Travis' good jacket on him . . . Walter Lee, fix your tie and tuck your shirt in, you look just like somebody's hoodlum. Lord have mercy, where is my plant? *(She flies to get it amid the general bustling of the family, who are deliberately trying to ignore the nobility of the past moment)* You all start on down . . . Travis child, don't go empty-handed . . . Ruth, where did I put that box with my skillets in it? I want to be in charge of it myself . . . I'm going to make us the biggest dinner we ever ate tonight . . . Beneatha, what's the matter with them stockings? Pull them things up, girl . . .

(The family starts to file out as two moving men appear and begin to carry out the heavier pieces of furniture, bumping into the family as they move about)

Beneatha. Mama, Asagai—asked me to marry him today and go to Africa—
Mama (In the middle of her getting-ready activity). He did? You ain't old enough to marry nobody—*(Seeing the moving men lifting one of her chairs precariously)* Darling, that ain't no bale of cotton, please handle it so we can sit in it again. I had the chair twenty-five years . . .

(The movers sigh with exasperation and go on with their work)

Beneatha (Girlishly and unreasonably trying to pursue the conversation). To go to Africa, mama—be a doctor in Africa . . .
Mama (Distracted). Yes, baby—
Walter. Africa! What he want you to go to Africa for?
Beneatha. To practice there . . .
Walter. Girl, if you don't get all them silly ideas out your head! You better marry yourself a man with some loot . . .
Beneatha (Angrily, precisely as in the first scene of the play). What have you got to do with who I marry!
Walter. Plenty. Now I think George Murchison—

(He and BENEATHA *go out yelling at each other vigorously;* BENEATHA *is heard saying that she would not marry* GEORGE MURCHISON *if he were Adam and she were Eve, etc. The anger is loud and real till their voices diminish.* RUTH *stands at the door and turns to* MAMA *and smiles knowingly)*

Mama (Fixing her hat at last). Yeah—they something all right, my children . . .

Ruth. Yeah—they're something. Let's go, Lena.

Mama (Stalling, starting to look around at the house). Yes—I'm coming. Ruth—

Ruth. Yes?

Mama (Quietly, woman to woman). He finally come into his manhood today, didn't he? Kind of like a rainbow after the rain . . .

Ruth (Biting her lip lest her own pride explode in front of MAMA). Yes, Lena.

*(*WALTER'S *voice calls for them raucously)*

Mama (Waving RUTH *out vaguely)*. All right, honey—go on down. I be down directly.

*(*RUTH *hesitates, then exits.* MAMA *stands, at last alone in the living room, her plant on the table before her as the lights start to come down. She looks around at all the walls and ceilings and suddenly, despite herself, while the children call below, a great heaving thing rises in her and she puts her fist to her mouth, takes a final desperate look, pulls her coat about her, pats her hat and goes out. The lights dim down. The door opens and she comes back in, grabs her plant, and goes out for the last time)*

Curtain

QUESTIONS

1. This play was first produced in 1959. Did you identify its period while reading it? If so, how?
2. How does the Younger family compare with pictures of black home life you may bring to your reading?
3. What is the atmosphere of the room where the action occurs?
4. Which character evokes the strongest response from you? Is that character the central figure of the play?
5. How important are the supporting characters who enter the Youngers' apartment at various points?
6. Can you identify a major conflict in this drama? How is it resolved, if you think it is?
7. At the conclusion, what has changed and what remains the same as the Youngers move on?

ADDITIONAL QUESTIONS

1. Throughout *A Raisin in the Sun,* the characters reveal their different dreams, but at the conclusion they seem to share a vision as they move to the new house. What is this vision? What are the forces within and from outside the family that have threatened the vision and then cause it to be shared?
2. The conclusion of *Antigone* is full of death, including the living death Creon now faces, with his family gone. Can Antigone be said to have done more than caused such disaster by her adherence to her principles?
3. In both "A White Heron" and "Everyday Use" the central character makes a decision because of something she sees differently than before. Choose either story, and explain exactly what is seen, how it relates to the decision made, and what the consequences of the decision are likely to be.
4. In both "Sonny's Blues" and "Cathedral" the narrator sees more deeply than before with the help of another person. Choose either story, and analyze the narrator's progress towards understanding. Explain what is seen at the story's conclusion.
5. The central characters in both Langston Hughes's "On the Road" and Flannery O'-Connor's "The Artificial Nigger" journey through a hostile world. What they see sustains them, although they see very different things. Choose either story, and explain the meaning of the vision experienced. Is there anything ironic or contradictory in it?
6. Choose a poem, or perhaps two, wherein seeing is associated with religious grace. Explain the importance of specific details and word choices in conveying the meaning.
7. A kind of double vision occurs in several poems, including "Naming of Parts," "For the Union Dead," and "Sailing to Byzantium." The speaker's attention seems divided by two things seen, and with different feelings. Choose one of these poems, and analyze what is seen and with what feelings. Does one vision or feeling predominate in the poem?
8. A reader can often infer much about a speaker from the vision expressed in a poem. Choose one or more poems in which the character of the speaker is emphasized. Explain what specific details tell you about the speaker(s).

PART FIVE

LIFE'S CONCLUSIONS

At the ends of the first two stories of this section, a man reflects upon the meaning of a death that has touched him. In both cases, an outflowing of sympathy marks the moment in a life otherwise engaged in the activities of a busy career. The narrator in Melville's story and Gabriel Conroy in Joyce's are like most of us in being preoccupied by day-to-day concerns. Dwelling upon death, except when we must, seems morbid. But we know also that understanding the full value and meaning of life requires some reflection upon its end.

The works that follow suggest some of the ways that creative writers have thought about death. For the religious, for instance, death may mean the passage to an eternal life. In their different ways the two poems by John Donne express the faith that death is merely the "soul's delivery": beyond death, the promise of Christ's Redemption awaits fulfillment for the person who trusts in it. Emily Dickinson's two poems also look with hope beyond this world to another, unknown one. For believers, to move towards that "next world" is to move from a kind of sleep to being at last awake. While not overtly religious, Robert Frost's "After Apple-Picking" and Theodore Roethke's "The Waking" echo this ancient faith.

The world of nature often brings comfort and holds out its own promise that relieves fear and grief. In Walt Whitman's great elegy the return of spring, the flowering of lilacs, and the song of a bird in the deep night all help to free the mourning soul from its harsh trouble. Here, as in other works, phenomena of nature become symbols, read gratefully. In several works the cold of winter is a familiar symbol for death, but in both Percy Bysshe Shelley's "Ode to the West Wind" and John Keats's "To Autumn," even winter's precursor has a beauty, full of wildness or calm poise, that provides hope. Similarly, in Thomas Hardy's poem the aged thrush singing his joyous evensong defeats despair. Elsewhere, the piping of a flock of small birds, the flowering of a daffodil, or the lifting of a glass in salute make of the cold only a condition through which life endures.

810

Not all the works included here express such certitude. Several voice confusion or anger over the death of the young. Wilfred Owen's two poems about death in war are perhaps the bitterest, but in A. E. Housman's and W. H. Auden's poems even the way life goes on appears bleak or indifferent. In this respect they contrast Dylan Thomas's poem, written as his father neared death. The speaker in Thomas's poem views life as light to be caught and held. The approaching darkness prompts the rage that demands his father not "go gentle" into that "good night"—a fierce pun.

The human spirit may be fiercely brave when confronting the end of all that a person has valued in life. Like the echoes of battle, courage rings in the voice of Alfred, Lord Tennyson's aged Ulysses, determined to "drink life to the lees." Lesser heroes, Dorothy Parker's little old lady and Langston Hughes's Sylvester still are a fine pair. They smile and provoke smiles, as their happily misspent lives draw to their close. Megan Terry's two wicked old women, vying over Mr. Birdsong, are like them. They also refuse to succumb quietly to old age. To the last moment of life they enjoy the old song-and-dance.

All these stories, poems, and plays are in some way about dying—but are also about living. Hamlet broods over whether it is better to be or not to be when he feels, by his own description, robbed of the delight he has once known. It could be argued, however, that the man who in a "tow'ring passion" attacks Laertes, jokes with Horatio over a ridiculous messenger, and relies on the "special providence in the fall of a sparrow" has moved beyond his earlier apathy. The concluding scenes of *Hamlet* would not move us as they do if Hamlet chose suicide over life or ended in death a story with no meaning.

Literature has little to do with meaninglessness. Writers shape language to satisfy those who listen or read. Through literature we explore the meaning of experience and come to understand how we share in humanity. The process of finding meaning extends our lives beyond the limits of mere existence.

FICTION

Herman Melville (1819–1891)
BARTLEBY THE SCRIVENER
A Story of Wall Street

I am a rather elderly man. The nature of my avocations, for the last thirty years, has brought me into more than ordinary contact with what would seem an interesting and somewhat singular set of men, of whom, as yet, nothing, that I know of, has ever been written—I mean, the law-copyists, or scriveners. I have known very many of them, professionally and privately, and, if I pleased, could relate divers histories, at which good-natured gentlemen might smile, and sentimental souls might weep. But I waive the biographies of all other scriveners, for a few passages in the life of Bartleby, who was a scrivener, the strangest I ever saw, or heard of. While, of other law-copyists, I might write the complete life, of Bartleby nothing of that sort can be done. I believe that no materials exist for a full and satisfactory biography of this man. It is an irreparable loss to literature. Bartleby was one of those beings of whom nothing is ascertainable, except from the original sources, and, in his case, those are very small. What my own astonished eyes saw of Bartleby, *that* is all I know of him, except, indeed, one vague report, which will appear in the sequel.

Ere introducing the scrivener, as he first appeared to me, it is fit I make some mention of myself, my employees, my business, my chambers, and general surroundings; because some such description is indispensable to an adequate understanding of the chief character about to be presented. Imprimis:[1] I am a man who, from his youth upwards, has been filled with a profound conviction that the easiest way of life is the best. Hence, though I belong to a profession proverbially energetic and nervous, even to turbulence, at times, yet nothing of that sort have I ever suffered to invade my peace. I am one of those unambitious lawyers who never addresses a jury, or in any way draws down public applause; but, in the cool tranquillity of a snug retreat, do a snug business among rich men's bonds, and mortgages, and title-deeds. All who know me, consider me an eminently *safe* man. The late John Jacob Astor,[2] a personage little given to poetic enthusiasm, had no hesitation in pronouncing my first grand point to be prudence; my next, method. I do not speak it in vanity, but simply record the fact, that I was not unemployed in my profession by the late John Jacob Astor; a name which, I admit, I love to repeat; for it hath a rounded and orbicular sound to it, and rings

---

[1]First.
[2]John Jacob Astor (1763–1848), German-born American business tycoon.

Herman Melville 813

like unto bullion. I will freely add, that I was not insensible to the late John Jacob Astor's good opinion.

Some time prior to the period at which this little history begins, my avocations had been largely increased. The good old office, now extinct in the State of New York, of a Master in Chancery,[3] had been conferred upon me. It was not a very arduous office, but very pleasantly remunerative. I seldom lose my temper; much more seldom indulge in dangerous indignation at wrongs and outrages; but, I must be permitted to be rash here, and declare that I consider the sudden and violent abrogation of the office of Master in Chancery, by the new Constitution, as a—premature act; inasmuch as I had counted upon a life-lease of the profits, whereas I only received those of a few short years. But this is by the way.

My chambers were up stairs, at No.——Wall Street. At one end, they looked upon the white wall of the interior of a spacious sky-light shaft, penetrating the building from top to bottom.

This view might have been considered rather tame than otherwise, deficient in what landscape painters call "life." But, if so, the view from the other end of my chambers offered, at least, a contrast, if nothing more. In that direction, my windows commanded an unobstructed view of a lofty brick wall, black by age and everlasting shade; which wall required no spyglass to bring out its lurking beauties, but, for the benefit of all near-sighted spectators, was pushed up to within ten feet of my window panes. Owing to the great height of the surrounding buildings, and my chambers being on the second floor, the interval between this wall and mine not a little resembled a huge square cistern.

At the period just preceding the advent of Bartleby, I had two persons as copyists in my employment, and a promising lad as an office-boy. First, Turkey; second, Nippers; third, Ginger Nut. These may seem names, the like of which are not usually found in the Directory. In truth, they were nicknames, mutually conferred upon each other by my three clerks, and were deemed expressive of their respective persons or characters. Turkey was a short, pursy Englishman, of about my own age—that is, somewhere not far from sixty. In the morning, one might say, his face was of a fine florid hue, but after twelve o'clock, meridian— his dinner hour—it blazed like a grate full of Christmas coals; and continued blazing—but, as it were, with a gradual wane—till six o'clock P.M., or there-abouts; after which, I saw no more of the proprietor of the face, which, gaining its meridian with the sun, seemed to set with it, to rise, culminate, and decline the following day, with the like regularity and undiminished glory. There are many singular coincidences I have known in the course of my life, not the least among which was the fact, that, exactly when Turkey displayed his fullest beams from his red and radiant countenance, just then, too, at that critical moment, began the daily period when I considered his business capacities as seriously disturbed for the remainder of the twenty-four hours. Not that he was absolutely

[3]A Court of Chancery was an equity court that handled business disputes. A Master was a court officer who assisted the judge, as by hearing evidence.

idle, or averse to business, then; far from it. The difficulty was, he was apt to be altogether too energetic. There was a strange, inflamed, flurried, flighty reckless-ness of activity about him. He would be incautious in dipping his pen into his inkstand. All his blots upon my documents were dropped there after twelve o'clock meridian. Indeed, not only would he be reckless, and sadly given to making blots in the afternoon, but, some days, he went further, and was rather noisy. At such times, too, his face flamed with augmented blazonry, as if cannel coal had been heaped on anthracite. He made an unpleasant racket with his chair; spilled his sand-box; in mending his pens, impatiently split them all to pieces, and threw them on the floor in a sudden passion; stood up, and leaned over his table, boxing his papers about in a most indecorous manner, very sad to behold in an elderly man like him. Nevertheless, as he was in many ways a most valuable person to me, and all the time before twelve o'clock meridian, was the quickest, steadiest creature, too, accomplishing a great deal of work in a style not easily to be matched—for these reasons, I was willing to overlook his eccentricities, though, indeed, occasionally, I remonstrated with him. I did this very gently, however, because, though the civilest, nay, the blandest and most reverential of men in the morning, yet, in the afternoon, he was disposed, upon provocation, to be slightly rash with his tongue—in fact, insolent. Now, valuing his morning services as I did, and resolved not to lose them—yet, at the same time, made uncomfortable by his inflamed ways after twelve o'clock—and being a man of peace, unwilling by my admonitions to call forth unseemly retorts from him, I took upon me, one Saturday noon (he was always worse on Saturdays) to hint to him, very kindly, that, perhaps, now that he was growing old, it might be well to abridge his labors; in short, he need not come to my chambers after twelve o'clock, but, dinner over, had best go home to his lodgings, and rest himself till tea-time. But no; he insisted upon his afternoon devotions. His countenance became intolerably fervid, as he oratorically assured me—gesticulating with a long ruler at the other end of the room—that if his services in the morning were useful, how indispensable, then, in the afternoon?

"With submission, sir," said Turkey, on this occasion, "I consider myself your right-hand man. In the morning I but marshal and deploy my columns; but in the afternoon I put myself at their head, and gallantly charge the foe, thus"—and he made a violent thrust with the ruler.

"But the blots, Turkey," intimated I.

"True; but, with submission, sir, behold these hairs! I am getting old. Surely, sir, a blot or two of a warm afternoon is not to be severely urged against gray hairs. Old age—even if it blot the page—is honorable. With submission, sir, we *both* are getting old."

This appeal to my fellow-feeling was hardly to be resisted. At all events, I saw that go he would not. So, I made up my mind to let him stay, resolving, never-theless, to see to it that, during the afternoon, he had to do with my less important papers.

Nippers, the second on my list, was a whiskered, sallow, and upon the whole, rather piratical-looking young man, of about five and twenty. I always deemed him the victim of two evil powers—ambition and indigestion. The ambition was evinced by a certain impatience of the duties of a mere copyist, an unwarrantable usurpation of strictly professional affairs, such as the original drawing up of legal documents. The indigestion seemed betokened in an occasional nervous testiness and grinning irritability, causing the teeth to audibly grind together over mistakes committed in copying; unnecessary maledictions, hissed, rather than spoken, in the heat of business; and especially by a continual discontent with the height of the table where he worked. Though of a very ingenious, mechanical turn, Nippers could never get this table to suit him. He put chips under it, blocks of various sorts, bits of pasteboard, and at last went so far as to attempt an exquisite adjustment, by final pieces of folded blotting-paper. But no invention would answer. If, for the sake of easing his back, he brought the table lid at a sharp angle well up towards his chin, and wrote there like a man using the steep roof of a Dutch house for his desk, then he declared that it stopped the circulation in his arms. If now he lowered the table to his waistbands, and stooped over it in writing, then there was a sore aching in his back. In short, the truth of the matter was, Nippers knew not what he wanted. Or, if he wanted anything, it was to be rid of a scrivener's table altogether. Among the manifestations of his diseased ambition was a fondness he had for receiving visits from certain ambiguous-looking fellows in seedy coats, whom he called his clients. Indeed, I was aware that not only was he, at times, considerable of a ward-politician, but he occasionally did a little business at the Justices' courts, and was not unknown on the steps of the Tombs.[4] I have good reason to believe, however, that one individual who called upon him at my chambers, and who, with a grand air, he insisted was his client, was no other than a dun, and the alleged title-deed, a bill. But, with all his failings, and the annoyances he caused me, Nippers, like his compatriot Turkey, was a very useful man to me; wrote a neat, swift hand; and, when he chose, was not deficient in a gentlemanly sort of deportment. Added to this, he always dressed in a gentlemanly sort of way; and so, incidentally, reflected credit upon my chambers. Whereas, with respect to Turkey, I had much ado to keep him from being a reproach to me. His clothes were apt to look oily, and smell of eating-houses. He wore his pantaloons very loose and baggy in summer. His coats were execrable; his hat not to be handled. But while the hat was a thing of indifference to me, inasmuch as his natural civility and deference, as a dependent Englishman, always led him to doff it the moment he entered the room, yet his coat was another matter. Concerning his coats, I reasoned with him; but with no effect. The truth was, I suppose, that a man with so small an income could not afford to sport such a lustrous face and a lustrous coat at one and the same time. As Nippers once observed, Turkey's money went chiefly for red ink. One winter day, I presented Turkey with a highly respectable-looking coat of my own—a padded gray coat, of a most comfortable warmth, and which buttoned straight up from the knee to the neck. I thought Turkey would appreciate the

---

[4]New York City prison.

favor, and abate his rashness and obstreperousness of afternoons. But no; I verily believe that buttoning himself up in so downy and blanket-like a coat had a pernicious effect upon him—upon the same principle that too much oats are bad for horses. In fact, precisely as a rash, restive horse is said to feel his oats, so Turkey felt his coat. It made him insolent. He was a man whom prosperity harmed.

Though, concerning the self-indulgent habits of Turkey, I had my own private surmises, yet, touching Nippers, I was well persuaded that, whatever might be his faults in other respects, he was, at least, a temperate young man. But, indeed, nature herself seemed to have been his vintner, and, at his birth, charged him so thoroughly with an irritable, brandy-like disposition, that all subsequent potations were needless. When I consider how, amid the stillness of my chambers, Nippers would sometimes impatiently rise from his seat, and stopping over his table, spread his arms wide apart, seize the whole desk, and move it, and jerk it, with a grim, grinding motion on the floor, as if the table were a perverse voluntary agent and vexing him, I plainly perceive that, for Nippers, brandy-and-water were altogether superfluous.

It was fortunate for me that, owing to its peculiar cause—indigestion—the irritability and consequent nervousness of Nippers were mainly observable in the morning, while in the afternoon he was comparatively mild. So that, Turkey's paroxysms only coming on about twelve o'clock, I never had to do with their eccentricities at one time. Their fits relieved each other, like guards. When Nipper's was on, Turkey's was off; and *vice versa*. This was a good natural arrangement, under the circumstances.

Ginger Nut, the third on my list, was a lad, some twelve years old. His father was a car-man, ambitious of seeing his son on the bench instead of a cart, before he died. So he sent him to my office, as student at law, errand-boy, cleaner and sweeper, at the rate of one dollar a week. He had a little desk to himself; but he did not use it much. Upon inspection, the drawer exhibited a great array of shells of various sorts of nuts. Indeed, to this quick-witted youth, the whole noble science of the law was contained in a nutshell. Not the least among the employments of Ginger Nut, as well as one which he discharged with the most alacrity, was his duty as cake and apple purveyor for Turkey and Nippers. Copying law-papers being proverbially a dry, husky sort of business, my two scriveners were fain to moisten their mouths very often with Spitzenbergs,[5] to be had at the numerous stalls nigh the Custom House and Post Office. Also, they sent Ginger Nut very frequently for that peculiar cake—small, flat, round, and very spicy—after which he had been named by them. Of a cold morning, when business was but dull, Turkey would gobble up scores of these cakes, as if they were mere wafers—indeed, they sell them at the rate of six or eight for a penny—the scrape of his pen blending with the crunching of the crisp particles in his mouth. Rashest of all the fiery afternoon blunders and flurried rashnesses of Turkey, was his once moistening a ginger-cake between his lips, and clapping it on to a mortgage, for

---

[5]Variety of apple native to New York State.

a seal. I came within an ace of dismissing him then. But he mollified me by making an oriental bow, and saying—

"With submission, sir, it was generous of me to find you in stationery on my own account."

Now my original business—that of a conveyancer and title hunter, and drawer-up of recondite documents of all sorts—was considerably increased by receiving the master's office. There was now great work for scriveners. Not only must I push the clerks already with me, but I must have additional help.

In answer to my advertisement, a motionless young man one morning stood upon my office threshold, the door being open, for it was summer. I can see that figure now—pallidly neat, pitiably respectable, incurably forlorn! It was Bartleby.

After a few words touching his qualifications, I engaged him, glad to have among my corps of copyists a man of so singularly sedate an aspect, which I thought might operate beneficially upon the flighty temper of Turkey, and the fiery one of Nippers.

I should have stated before that ground glass folding-doors divided my premises into two parts, one of which was occupied by my scriveners, the other by myself. According to my humor, I threw open these doors, or closed them. I resolved to assign Bartleby a corner by the folding-doors, but on my side of them, so as to have this quiet man within easy call, in case any trifling thing was to be done. I placed his desk close up to a small side-window in that part of the room, a window which originally had afforded a lateral view of certain grimy backyards and bricks, but which, owing to subsequent erections, commanded at present no view at all, though it gave some light. Within three feet of the panes was a wall, and the light came down from far above, between two lofty buildings, as from a very small opening in a dome. Still further to a satisfactory arrangement, I procured a high green folding screen, which might entirely isolate Bartleby from my sight, though not remove him from my voice. And thus, in a manner, privacy and society were conjoined.

At first, Bartleby did an extraordinary quantity of writing. As if long famishing for something to copy, he seemed to gorge himself on my documents. There was no pause for digestion. He ran a day and night line, copying by sun-light and by candle-light. I should have been quite delighted with his application, had he been cheerfully industrious. But he wrote on silently, palely, mechanically.

It is, of course, an indispensable part of a scrivener's business to verify the accuracy of his copy, word by word. Where there are two or more scriveners in an office, they assist each other in this examination, one reading from the copy, the other holding the original. It is a very dull, wearisome, and lethargic affair. I can readily imagine that, to some sanguine temperaments, it would be altogether intolerable. For example, I cannot credit that the mettlesome poet, Byron, would have contentedly sat down with Bartleby to examine a law document of, say five hundred pages, closely written in a crimpy hand.

Now and then, in the haste of business, it has been my habit to assist in comparing some brief document myself, calling Turkey or Nippers for this purpose. One object I had, in placing Bartleby so handy to me behind the screen, was to avail myself of his services on such trivial occasions. It was on the third day, I think, of his being with me, and before any necessity had arisen for having his own writing examined, that, being much hurried to complete a small affair I had in hand, I abruptly called to Bartleby. In my haste and natural expectancy of instant compliance, I sat with my head bent over the original on my desk, and my right hand sideways, and somewhat nervously extended with the copy, so that immediately upon emerging from his retreat, Bartley might snatch it and proceed to business without the least delay.

In this very attitude did I sit when I called to him, rapidly stating what it was I wanted him to do—namely, to examine a small paper with me. Imagine my surprise, nay, my consternation, when, without moving from his privacy, Bartleby, in a singularly mild, firm voice, replied, "I would prefer not to."

I sat awhile in perfect silence, rallying my stunned faculties. Immediately it occurred to me that my ears had deceived me, or Bartleby had entirely misunderstood my meaning. I repeated my request in the clearest tone I could assume; but in quite as clear a one came the previous reply, "I would prefer not to."

"Prefer not to," echoed I, rising in high excitement, and crossing the room with a stride. "What do you mean? Are you moon-struck? I want you to help me compare this sheet here—take it," and I thrust it towards him.

"I would prefer not to," said he.

I looked at him steadfastly. His face was leanly composed; his gray eye dimly calm. Not a wrinkle of agitation rippled him. Had there been the least uneasiness, anger, impatience, or impertinence in his manner; in other words, had there been any thing ordinarily human about him, doubtless I should have violently dismissed him from the premises. But as it was, I should have as soon thought of turning my pale plaster-of-paris bust of Cicero out of doors. I stood gazing at him awhile, as he went on with his own writing, and then reseated myself at my desk. This is very strange, thought I. What had one best do? But my business hurried me. I concluded to forget the matter for the present, reserving it for my future leisure. So calling Nippers from the other room, the paper was speedily examined.

A few days after this, Bartleby concluded four lengthy documents, being quadruplicates of a week's testimony taken before me in my High Court of Chancery. It became necessary to examine them. It was an important suit, and great accuracy was imperative. Having all things arranged, I called Turkey, Nippers, and Ginger Nut from the next room, meaning to place the four copies in the hands of my four clerks, while I should read from the original. Accordingly, Turkey, Nippers, and Ginger Nut had taken their seats in a row, each with his document in his hand, when I called to Bartleby to join this interesting group.

"Bartleby! quick, I am waiting."

I heard a slow scrape of his chair legs on the uncarpeted floor, and soon he appeared standing at the entrance of his hermitage.

"What is wanted?" said he, mildly.

"The copies, the copies," said I, hurriedly. "We are going to examine them. There—" and I held towards him the fourth quadruplicate.

"I would prefer not to," he said, and gently disappeared behind the screen.

For a few moments I was turned into a pillar of salt, standing at the head of my seated column of clerks.

Recovering myself, I advanced towards the screen, and demanded the reason for such extraordinary conduct.

"*Why* do you refuse?"

"I would prefer not to."

With any other man I should have flown outright into a dreadful passion, scorned all further words, and thrust him ignominiously from my presence. But there was something about Bartleby that not only strangely disarmed me, but in a wonderful manner, touched and disconcerted me. I began to reason with him.

"These are your own copies we are about to examine. It is labor saving to you, because one examination will answer for your four papers. It is common usage. Every copyist is bound to help examine his copy. Is it not so? Will you not speak? Answer!"

"I prefer not to," he replied in a flutelike tone. It seemed to me that, while I had been addressing him, he carefully revolved every statement that I made; fully comprehended the meaning; could not gainsay the irresistible conclusion; but, at the same time, some paramount consideration prevailed with him to reply as he did.

"You are decided, then, not to comply with my request—a request made according to common usage and common sense?"

He briefly gave me to understand, that on that point my judgment was sound. Yes: his decision was irreversible.

It is not seldom the case that, when a man is browbeaten in some unprecedented and violently unreasonable way, he begins to stagger in his own plainest faith. He begins, as it were, vaguely to surmise that, wonderful as it may be, all the justice and all the reason is on the other side. Accordingly, if any disinterested persons are present, he turns to them for some reinforcement of his own faltering mind.

"Turkey," said I, "what do you think of this? Am I not right?"

"With submission, sir," said Turkey, in his blandest tone, "I think that you are."

"Nippers," said I, "what do *you* think of it?"

"I think I should kick him out of the office."

(The reader, of nice perceptions, will here perceive that, it being morning, Turkey's answer is couched in polite and tranquil terms, but Nipper's replies in ill-tempered ones. Or, to repeat a previous sentence, Nippers's ugly mood was on duty, and Turkey's off.)

"Ginger Nut," said I, willing to enlist the smallest suffrage in my behalf, "what do *you* think of it?"

"I think, sir, he's a little *luny,*" replied Ginger Nut, with a grin.

"You hear what they say," said I, turning towards the screen, "come forth and do your duty."

But he vouchsafed no reply. I pondered a moment in sore perplexity. But once more business hurried me. I determined again to postpone the consideration of this dilemma to my future leisure. With a little trouble we made out to examine the papers without Bartleby, though at every page or two Turkey deferentially dropped his opinion, that this proceeding was quite out of the common; while Nippers, twitching in his chair with a dyspeptic nervousness, ground out, between his set teeth, occasional hissing maledictions against the stubborn oaf behind the screen. And for his (Nippers's) part, this was the first and the last time he would do another man's business without pay.

Meanwhile Bartleby sat in his hermitage, oblivious to everything but his own peculiar business there.

Some days passed, the scrivener being employed upon another lengthy work. His late remarkable conduct led me to regard his ways narrowly. I observed that he never went to dinner; indeed, that he never went anywhere. As yet I had never, of my personal knowledge, known him to be outside of my office. He was a perpetual sentry in the corner. At about eleven o'clock though, in the morning, I noticed that Ginger Nut would advance toward the opening in Bartleby's screen, as if silently beckoned thither by a gesture invisible to me where I sat. The boy would then leave the office, jingling a few pence, and reappear with a handful of ginger-nuts, which he delivered in the hermitage, receiving two of the cakes for his trouble.

He lives, then, on ginger-nuts, thought I; never eats a dinner, properly speaking; he must be a vegetarian, then; but no; he never eats even vegetables; he eats nothing but ginger-nuts. My mind then ran on in reveries concerning the probable effects upon the human constitution of living entirely on ginger-nuts. Ginger-nuts are so called, because they contain ginger as one of their peculiar constituents, and the final flavoring one. Now, what was ginger? A hot, spicy thing. Was Bartleby hot and spicy? Not at all. Ginger, then, had no effect upon Bartleby. Probably he preferred it should have none.

Nothing so aggravates an earnest person as a passive resistance. If the individual so resisted be of a not inhuman temper, and the resisting one perfectly harmless in his passivity, then, in the better moods of the former, he will endeavor charitably to construe to his imagination what proves impossible to be solved by his judgement. Even so, for the most part, I regarded Bartleby and his ways. Poor fellow! thought I, he means no mischief; it is plain he intends no insolence; his aspect sufficiently evinces that his eccentricities are involuntary. He is useful to me. I can get along with him. If I turn him away, the chances are he will fall in with some less-indulgent employer, and then he will be rudely treated, and perhaps driven forth miserably to starve. Yes. Here I can cheaply purchase a delicious self-approval. To befriend Bartleby; to humor him in his strange willfulness, will cost me little or nothing, while I lay up in my soul what will eventually prove a sweet morsel for my conscience. But this mood was not invariable with me. The passiveness of Bartleby sometimes irritated me. I felt strangely goaded on to encounter him in new opposition—to elicit some angry spark from him answerable to my own. But, indeed, I might as well have essayed to strike fire with my knuckles against a bit of Windsor soap. But one afternoon the evil impulse in me mastered me, and the following little scene ensued:

"Bartleby," said I, "when those papers are all copied, I will compare them with you."

"I would prefer not to."

"How? Surely you do not mean to persist in that mulish vagary?"

No answer.

I threw open the folding-doors near by, and, turning upon Turkey and Nippers, exclaimed:

"Bartleby a second time says, he won't examine his papers. What do you think of it, Turkey?"

It was afternoon, be it remembered. Turkey sat glowing like a brass boiler; his bald head steaming; his hands reeling among his blotted papers.

"Think of it?" roared Turkey; "I think I'll just step behind his screen, and black his eyes for him!"

So saying, Turkey rose to his feet and threw his arms into a pugilistic position. He was hurrying away to make good his promise, when I detained him, alarmed at the effect of incautiously rousing Turkey's combativeness after dinner.

"Sit down, Turkey," said I, "and hear what Nippers has to say. What do you think of it, Nippers? Would I not be justified in immediately dismissing Bartleby?"

"Excuse me, that is for you to decide, sir. I think his conduct quite unusual, and, indeed, unjust, as regards Turkey and myself. But it may only be a passing whim."

"Ah," exclaimed I, "you have strangely changed your mind, then—you speak very gently of him now."

"All beer," cried Turkey; "gentleness is effects of beer—Nippers and I dined together to-day. You see how gentle *I* am, sir. Shall I go and black his eyes?"

"You refer to Bartleby, I suppose. No, not to-day, Turkey," I replied; "pray, put up your fists."

I closed the doors, and again advanced towards Bartleby. I felt additional incentives tempting me to my fate. I burned to be rebelled against again. I remembered that Bartleby never left the office.

"Bartleby," said I, "Ginger Nut is away; just step around to the Post Office, won't you? (it was but a three minutes' walk), and see if there is anything for me."

"I would prefer not to."

"You *will* not?"

"I *prefer* not."

I staggered to my desk, and sat there in a deep study. My blind inveteracy returned. Was there any other thing in which I could procure myself to be ig-nominiously repulsed by this lean, penniless wight?—my hired clerk? What added thing is there, perfectly reasonable, that he will be sure to refuse to do? "Bartleby!"

No answer.

"Bartleby," in a louder tone.

No answer.

"Bartleby," I roared.

Like a very ghost, agreeably to the laws of magical invocation, at the third summons, he appeared at the entrance of his hermitage.

"Go to the next room, and tell Nippers to come to me."

"I prefer not to," he respectfully and slowly said and mildly disappeared.

"Very good, Bartleby," said I, in a quiet sort of serenely-severe, self-possessed tone, intimating the unalterable purpose of some terrible retribution very close at hand. At the moment I half intended something of the kind. But upon the whole, as it was drawing towards my dinner-hour, I thought it best to put on my hat and walk home for the day, suffering much from perplexity and distress of mind.

Shall I acknowledge it? The conclusion of this whole business was, that it soon became a fixed fact of my chambers, that a pale young scrivener, by the name of Bartleby, had a desk there; that he copied for me at the usual rate of four cents a folio (one hundred words); but he was permanently exempt from examining the work done by him, that duty being transferred to Turkey and Nippers, out of compliment, doubtless, to their superior acuteness; moreover, said Bartleby was never, on any account, to be dispatched on the most trivial errand of any sort; and that even if entreated to take upon him such a matter, it was generally understood that he would "prefer not to"—in other words, he would refuse point blank.

As days passed on, I became considerably reconciled to Bartleby. His steadiness, his freedom from all dissipation, his incessant industry (except when he chose to throw himself into a standing revery behind his screen), his great stillness, his unalterableness of demeanor under all circumstances, made him a valuable acquisition. One prime thing was this—*he was always there*—first in the morning, continually through the day, and the last at night. I had a singular confidence in his honesty. I felt my most precious papers perfectly safe in his hands. Sometimes, to be sure, I could not, for the very soul of me, avoid falling into sudden spasmodic passions with him. For it was exceeding difficult to bear in mind all the time those strange peculiarities, privileges, and unheard of exemptions, forming the tacit stipulations on Bartleby's part under which he remained in my office. Now and then, in the eagerness of dispatching pressing business, I would inadvertently summon Bartleby, in a short, rapid tone, to put his finger, say, on the incipient tie of a bit of red tape with which I was about compressing some papers. Of course, from behind the screen the usual answer, "I prefer not to," was sure to come; and then, how could a human creature, with the common infirmities of our nature, refrain from bitterly exclaiming upon such perverseness—such unreasonableness. However, every added repulse of this sort which I received only tended to lessen the probability of my repeating the inadvertence.

Here it must be said, that according to the custom of most legal gentlemen occupying chambers in densely-populated law buildings, there were several keys to my door. One was kept by a woman residing in the attic, which person weekly scrubbed and daily swept and dusted my apartments. Another was kept by Turkey for convenience sake. The third I sometimes carried in my own pocket. The fourth I knew not who had.

Now, one Sunday morning I happened to go to Trinity Church, to hear a celebrated preacher, and finding myself rather early on the ground I thought I would walk around to my chambers for a while. Luckily I had my key with me; but upon applying it to the lock, I found it resisted by something inserted from the inside. Quite surprised, I called out; when to my consternation a key was turned from within; and thrusting his lean visage at me, and holding the door ajar, the apparition of Bartleby appeared, in his shirt sleeves, and otherwise in a strangely tattered *déshabillé,* saying quietly that he was sorry, but he was deeply engaged just then, and—preferred not admitting me at present. In a brief word or two, he moreover added, that perhaps I had better walk around the block two or three times, and by that time he would probably have concluded his affairs.

Now, the utterly unsurmised appearance of Bartleby, tenanting my law-chambers of a Sunday morning, with his cadaverously gentlemanly *nonchalance,* yet withal firm and self-possessed, had such a strange effect upon me, that incontinently I slunk away from my own door, and did as desired. But not without sundry twinges of impotent rebellion against the mild effrontery of this unaccountable scrivener. Indeed, it was his wonderful mildness chiefly, which not only disarmed me, but unmanned me as it were. For I consider that one, for the time, is somehow unmanned when he tranquilly permits his hired clerk to dictate to him, and order him away from his own premises. Furthermore, I was full of uneasiness as to what Bartleby could possibly be doing in my office in his shirt sleeves, and in an otherwise dismantled condition of a Sunday morning. Was anything amiss going on? Nay, that was out of the question. It was not to be thought of for a moment that Bartleby was an immoral person. But what could he be doing there?—copying? Nay again, whatever might be his eccentricities, Bartleby was an eminently decorous person. He would be the last man to sit down to his desk in any state approaching to nudity. Besides, it was Sunday; and there was something about Bartleby that forbade the supposition that he would by any secular occupation violate the proprieties of the day.

Nevertheless, my mind was not pacified; and full of a restless curiosity, at last I returned to the door. Without hindrance I inserted my key, opened it, and entered. Bartleby was not to be seen. I looked around anxiously, peeped behind his screen; but it was very plain that he was gone. Upon more closely examining the place, I surmised that for an indefinite period Bartleby must have eaten, dressed, and slept in my office, and that, too, without plate, mirror, or bed. The cushioned seat of a rickety old sofa in one corner bore the faint impress of a lean, reclining form. Rolled away under his desk, I found a blanket; under the empty grate, a blacking box and brush; on a chair, a tin basin, with soap and a ragged towel; in a newspaper a few crumbs of ginger-nuts and a morsel of cheese. Yes, thought I, it is evident enough that Bartleby has been making his home here, keeping bachelor's hall all by himself. Immediately then the thought came sweeping across me, what miserable friendlessness and loneliness are here revealed! His poverty is great; but his solitude, how horrible! Think of it. Of a Sunday, Wall Street is deserted as Petra[6], and every night of every day it is an emptiness. This building, too, which of week-days hums with industry and life, at nightfall echoes with sheer vacancy, and all through Sunday is forlorn. And here Bartleby makes his home; sole spectator of a solitude which he has seen all populous—a sort of innocent and transformed Marius[7] brooding among the ruins of Carthage!

For the first time in my life a feeling of over-powering stinging melancholy seized me. Before, I had never experienced aught but a not unpleasing sadness. The bond of a common humanity now drew me irresistibly to gloom. A fraternal melancholy! for both I and Bartleby were sons of Adam. I remembered the bright silks and sparkling faces I had seen that day, in gala trim, swan-like sailing down the Mississippi of Broadway; and I contrasted them with the pallid copyist, and thought to myself, Ah, happiness courts the light, so we deem the world is gay; but misery hides aloof, so we deem that misery there is none. These sad fancyings—chimeras, doubtless, of a sick and silly brain—led on to other and more special thoughts, concerning the eccentricities of Bartleby. Presentiments of strange discoveries hovered round me. The scrivener's pale form appeared to me laid out, among uncaring strangers, in its shivering winding sheet.

Suddenly I was attracted by Bartleby's closed desk, the key in open sight left in the lock.

I mean no mischief, seek the gratification of no heartless curiosity, thought I; besides, the desk is mine, and its contents, too, so I will make bold to look within. Everything was methodically arranged, the papers smoothly placed. The pigeon holes were deep, and removing the files of documents, I groped into their recesses. Presently I felt something there, and dragged it out. It was an old bandanna handkerchief, heavy and knotted. I opened it, and saw it was a savings bank.

I now recalled all the quiet mysteries which I had noted in the man. I remembered that he never spoke but to answer; that, though at intervals he had considerable time to himself, yet I had never seen him reading—no, not even a newspaper; that for long periods he would stand looking out, at his pale window behind the screen, upon the dead brick wall; I was quite sure he never visited any refectory or eating house; while his pale face clearly indicated that he never drank beer like Turkey, or tea and coffee even, like other men; that he never went anywhere in particular that I could learn; never went out for a walk, unless, indeed, that was the case at present; that he had declined telling who he was, or whence he came, or whether he had any relatives in the world; that though so thin and pale, he never complained of ill health. And more than all, I remembered a certain unconscious air of pallid—how shall I call it?—of pallid haughtiness, say, or rather an austere reserve about him, which had positively awed me into

---

[6]Ruined ancient city in Jordan.
[7]Gaius Marius (155?–86 B.C.), Roman general and consul driven from Rome during a civil war, who fled to Africa. *Carthage* was a North African city destroyed by Rome in 146 B.C.

my tame compliance with his eccentricities, when I had feared to ask him to do the slightest incidental thing for me, even though I might know, from his long-continued motionlessness, that behind his screen he must be standing in one of those dead-wall reveries of his.

Revolving all these things, and coupling them with the recently discovered fact, that he made my office his constant abiding place and home, and not forgetful of his morbid moodiness; revolving all these things, a prudential feeling began to steal over me. My first emotions had been those of pure melancholy and sincerest pity; but just in proportion as the forlornness of Bartleby grew and grew to my imagination, did that same melancholy merge into fear, that pity into repulsion. So true it is, and so terrible, too, that up to a certain point the thought or sight of misery enlists our best affections; but, in certain special cases, beyond that point it does not. They err who would assert that invariably this is owing to the inherent selfishness of the human heart. It rather proceeds from a certain hopelessness of remedying excessive and organic ill. To a sensitive being, pity is not seldom pain. And when at last it is perceived that such pity cannot lead to effectual succor, common sense bids the soul be rid of it. What I saw that morning persuaded me that the scrivener was the victim of innate and incurable disorder. I might give alms to his body; but his body did not pain him; it was his soul that suffered, and his soul I could not reach.

I did not accomplish the purpose of going to Trinity Church that morning. Somehow, the things I had seen disqualified me for the time from churchgoing. I walked homeward, thinking what I would do with Bartleby. Finally, I resolved upon this—I would put certain calm questions to him the next morning, touching his history, etc., and if he declined to answer them openly and unreservedly (and I supposed he would prefer not), then to give him a twenty dollar bill over and above whatever I might owe him, and tell him his services were no longer required; but that if in any other way I could assist him, I would be happy to do so, especially if he desired to return to his native place, wherever that might be, I would willingly help to defray the expenses. Moreover, if, after reaching home, he found himself at any time in want of aid, a letter from him would be sure of a reply.

The next morning came.

"Bartleby," said I, gently calling to him behind his screen.

No reply.

"Bartleby," said I, in a still gentler tone, "come here; I am not going to ask you to do anything you would prefer not to do—I simply wish to speak to you."

Upon this he noiselessly slid into view.

"Will you tell me, Bartleby, where you were born?"

"I would prefer not to."

"Will you tell me *anything* about yourself?"

"I would prefer not to."

"But what reasonable objection can you have to speak to me? I feel friendly towards you."

He did not look at me while I spoke, but kept his glance fixed upon my bust of Cicero, which, as I then sat, was directly behind me, some six inches above my head.

"What is your answer, Bartleby," said I, after waiting a considerable time for a reply, during which his countenance remained immovable, only there was the faintest conceivable tremor of the white attenuated mouth.

"At present I prefer to give no answer," he said, and retired into his hermitage. It was rather weak in me I confess, but his manner, on this occasion, nettled me. Not only did there seem to lurk in it a certain calm disdain, but his perverseness seemed ungrateful, considering the undeniable good usage and indulgence he had received from me.

Again I sat ruminating what I should do. Mortified as I was at his behavior, and resolved as I had been to dismiss him when I entered my office, nevertheless I strangely felt something superstitious knocking at my heart, and forbidding me to carry out my purpose, and denouncing me for a villain if I dared to breathe one bitter word against this forlornest of mankind. At last, familiarly drawing my chair behind his screen, I sat down and said: "Bartleby, never mind, then, about revealing your history; but let me entreat you, as a friend, to comply as far as may be with the usages of this office. Say now, you will help to examine papers to-morrow or next day: in short, say now, that in a day or two you will begin to be a little reasonable:—say so, Bartleby."

"At present I would prefer not to be a little reasonable," was his mildly cadaverous reply.

Just then the folding-doors opened, and Nippers approached. He seemed suffering from an unusually bad night's rest, induced by severer indigestion than common. He overheard those final words of Bartleby.

"*Prefer not*, eh?" gritted Nippers—"I'd *prefer* him, if I were you, sir," addressing me—"I'd *prefer* him; I'd give him preferences, the stubborn mule! What is it, sir, pray, that he *prefers* not to do now?"

Bartleby moved not a limb.

"Mr. Nippers," said I, "I'd prefer that you would withdraw for the present."

Somehow, of late, I had got into the way of involuntarily using this word "prefer" upon all sorts of not exactly suitable occasions. And I trembled to think that my contact with the scrivener had already and seriously affected me in a mental way. And what further and deeper aberration might it not yet produce? This apprehension had not been without efficacy in determining me to summary measures.

As Nippers, looking very sour and sulky, was departing, Turkey blandly and deferentially approached.

"With submission, sir," said he, "yesterday I was thinking about Bartleby here, and I think that if he would but prefer to take a quart of good ale every day, it would do much towards mending him, and enabling him to assist in examining his papers."

"So you have got the word, too," said I, slightly excited.

"With submission, what word, sir," asked Turkey, respectfully crowding himself into the contracted space behind the screen, and by so doing, making me jostle the scrivener. "What word, sir?"

"I would prefer to be left alone here," said Bartleby, as if offended at being mobbed in his privacy.

"*That's* the word, Turkey," said I—"*that's* it."

"Oh, *prefer?* oh yes—queer word. I never use it myself. But, sir, as I was saying, if he would but prefer—"

"Turkey," interrupted I, "you will please withdraw."

"Oh certainly, sir, if you prefer that I should."

As he opened the folding-door to retire, Nippers at his desk caught a glimpse of me, and asked whether I would prefer to have a certain paper copied on blue paper or white. He did not in the least roguishly accent the word prefer. It was plain that it involuntarily rolled from his tongue. I thought to myself, surely I must get rid of a demented man, who already has in some degree turned the tongues, if not the heads of myself and clerks. But I thought it prudent not to break the dismission at once.

The next day I noticed that Bartleby did nothing but stand at his window in his dead-wall revery. Upon asking him why he did not write, he said that he had decided upon doing no more writing."

"Why, how now? What next?" exclaimed I, "do no more writing?"

"No more."

"And what is the reason?"

"Do you not see the reason for yourself," he indifferently replied.

I looked steadfastly at him, and perceived that his eyes looked dull and glazed. Instantly it occurred to me, that his unexampled diligence in copying by his dim window for the first few weeks of his stay with me might have temporarily impaired his vision.

I was touched. I said something in condolence with him. I hinted that of course he did wisely in abstaining from writing for a while; and urged him to embrace that opportunity of taking wholesome exercise in the open air. This, however, he did not do. A few days after this, my other clerks being absent, and being in a great hurry to dispatch certain letters by the mail, I thought that, having nothing else earthly to do, Bartleby would surely be less inflexible than usual, and carry these letters to the post-office. But he blankly declined. So, much to my inconvenience, I went myself.

Still added days went by. Whether Bartleby's eyes improved or not, I could not say. To all appearance I thought they did. But when I asked him if they did, he vouchsafed no answer. At all events, he would do no copying. At last, in reply to my urgings, he informed me that he had permanently given up copying.

"What!" exclaimed I; "suppose your eyes should get entirely well—better than ever before—would you not copy then?"

"I have given up copying," he answered, and slid aside.

He remained as ever, a fixture in my chamber. Nay—if that were possible— he became still more of a fixture than before. What was to be done? He would do nothing in the office; why should he stay there? In plain fact, he had now become a millstone to me, not only useless as a necklace, but afflictive to bear. Yet I was sorry for him. I speak less than truth when I say that, on his own account, he occasioned me uneasiness. If he would but have named a single relative or friend, I would instantly have written, and urged their taking the poor fellow away to some convenient retreat. But he seemed alone, absolutely alone in the universe. A bit of wreck in the mid-Atlantic. At length, necessities connected with my business tyrannized over all other considerations. Decently as I could, I told Bartleby that in six days time he must unconditionally leave the office. I warned him to take measures, in the interval, for procuring some other abode. I offered to assist him in his endeavor, if he himself would but take the first step towards a removal. "And when you finally quit me, Bartleby," added I, "I shall see that you go not away entirely unprovided. Six days from this hour, remember."

At the expiration of that period, I peeped behind the screen, and lo! Bartleby was there.

I buttoned up my coat, balanced myself; advanced slowly towards him, touched his shoulder, and said, "The time has come; you must quit this place; I am sorry for you; here is money; but you must go."

"I would prefer not" he replied, with his back still towards me.

"You *must*."

He remained silent.

Now I had an unbounded confidence in this man's common honesty. He had frequently restored to me sixpences and shillings carelessly dropped upon the floor, for I am apt to be very reckless in such shirt-button affairs. The proceeding, then, which followed will not be deemed extraordinary.

"Bartleby," said I, "I owe you twelve dollars on account; here are thirty-two; the odd twenty are yours—Will you take it?" and I handed the bills towards him.

But he made no motion.

"I will leave them here, then," putting them under a weight on the table. Then taking my hat and cane and going to the door, I tranquilly turned and added— "After you have removed your things from these offices, Bartleby, you will of course lock the door—since every one is now gone for the day but you—and if you please, slip your key underneath the mat, so that I may have it in the morning. I shall not see you again; so good-by to you. If, hereafter, in your new place of abode, I can be of any service to you, do not fail to advise me by letter. Good-by, Bartleby, and fare you well.

But he answered not a word; like the last column of some ruined temple, he remained standing mute and solitary in the middle of the otherwise deserted room.

As I walked home in a pensive mood, my vanity got the better of my pity. I could not but highly plume myself on my masterly management in getting rid of Bartleby. Masterly I call it, and such it must appear to any dispassionate thinker. The beauty of my procedure seemed to consist in its perfect quietness. There was no vulgar bullying, no bravado of any sort, no choleric hectoring, and striding to and fro across the apartment, jerking out vehement commands for Bartleby to bundle himself off with his beggarly traps. Nothing of the kind. Without loudly bidding Bartleby depart—as an inferior genius might have done—I *assumed* the ground that depart he must; and upon that assumption built all I had to say. The more I thought over my procedure, the more I was charmed with it. Nevertheless, next morning, upon awakening, I had my doubts—I had somehow slept off the fumes of vanity. One of the coolest and wisest hours a man has, is just after he awakes in the morning. My procedure seemed as sagacious as ever—but only in theory. How it would prove in practice—there was the rub. It was truly a beautiful thought to have assumed Bartleby's departure; but, after all, that assumption was simply my own, and none of Bartleby's. The great point was, not whether I had assumed that he would quit me, but whether he would prefer so to do. He was more a man of preferences than assumptions.

After breakfast, I walked down town, arguing the probabilities *pro* and *con*. One moment I thought it would prove a miserable failure, and Bartleby would be found all alive at my office as usual; the next moment it seemed certain that I should find his chair empty. And so I kept veering about. At the corner of Broadway and Canal Street, I saw quite an excited group of people standing in earnest conversation.

"I'll take odds he doesn't," said a voice as I passed.

"Doesn't go?—done!" said I; "put up your money."

I was instinctively putting my hand in my pocket to produce my own, when I remembered that this was an election day. The words I had overheard bore no reference to Bartleby, but to the success or non-success of some candidate for the mayoralty. In my intent frame of mind, I had, as it were, imagined that all Broadway shared in my excitement, and were debating the same question with me. I passed on, very thankful that the uproar of the street screened my momentary absent-mindedness.

As I had intended, I was earlier than usual at my office door. I stood listening for a moment. All was still. He must be gone. I tried the knob. The door was locked. Yes, my procedure had worked to a charm; he indeed must be vanished. Yet a certain melancholy mixed with this: I was almost sorry for my brilliant success. I was fumbling under the door mat for the key, which Bartleby was to have left there for me, when accidentally my knee knocked against a panel, producing a summoning sound, and in response a voice came to me from within—"Not yet; I am occupied."

It was Bartleby.

I was thunderstruck. For an instant I stood like the man who, pipe in mouth, was killed one cloudless afternoon long ago in Virginia, by summer lightning; at his own warm open window he was killed, and remained leaning out there upon the dreamy afternoon, till some one touched him, when he fell.

"Not gone!" I murmured at last. But again obeying that wondrous ascendancy which the inscrutable scrivener had over me, and from which ascendancy, for all my chafing, I could not completely escape, I slowly went down stairs and out into the street, and while walking round the block, considered what I should next do in this unheard-of perplexity. Turn the man out by an actual thrusting I could not; to drive him away by calling him hard names would not do; calling in the police was an unpleasant idea; and yet, permit him to enjoy his cadaverous triumph over me—this, too, I could not think of. What was to be done? or, if nothing could be done, was there anything further that I could *assume* in the matter? Yes, as before I had prospectively assumed that Bartleby would depart, so now I might retrospectively assume that departed he was. In the legitimate carrying out of this assumption, I might enter my office in a great hurry, and pretending not to see Bartleby at all, walk straight against him as if he were air. Such a proceeding would in a singular degree have the appearance of a homethrust. It was hardly possible that Bartleby could withstand such an application of the doctrine of assumptions. But upon second thoughts the success of the plan seemed rather dubious. I resolved to argue the matter over with him again.

"Bartleby," said I, entering the office, with a quietly severe expression, "I am seriously displeased. I am pained, Bartleby. I had thought better of you. I had imagined you of such a gentlemanly organization, that in any delicate dilemma a slight hint would suffice—in short, an assumption. But it appears I am deceived. Why," I added, unaffectedly starting, "you have not even touched that money yet," pointing to it, just where I had left it the evening previous.

He answered nothing.

"Will you, or will you not, quit me?" I now demanded in a sudden passion, advancing close to him.

"I would prefer *not* to quit you," he replied, gently emphasizing the *not*.

"What earthly right have you to stay here? Do you pay any rent? Do you pay my taxes? Or is this property yours?"

He answered nothing.

"Are you ready to go on and write now? Are your eyes recovered? Could you copy a small paper for me this morning? or help examine a few lines? or step round to the post-office? In a word, will you do anything at all, to give a coloring to your refusal to depart the premises?"

He silently retired into his hermitage.

I was now in such a state of nervous resentment that I thought it but prudent to check myself at present from further demonstrations. Bartleby and I were alone. I remembered the tragedy of the unfortunate Adams and the still more unfortunate Colt in the solitary office of the latter; and how poor Colt, being dreadfully incensed by Adams, and imprudently permitting himself to get wildly excited, was at unawares hurried into his fatal act—an act which certainly no man could possibly deplore more than the actor himself.[8] Often it had occurred to me in my ponderings upon the subject, that had that altercation taken place in the public street, or at a private residence, it would not have terminated as it did. It was the circumstance of being alone in a solitary office, up stairs, of a building entirely unhallowed by humanizing domestic associations—an uncarpeted office, doubtless, of a dusty, haggard sort of appearance—this it must have

---

[8]Sensational murder case of 1842, John Colt having killed Samuel Adams in a fit of passion.

been, which greatly helped to enhance the irritable desperation of the hapless Colt.

But when this old Adam of resentment rose in me and tempted me concerning Bartleby, I grappled him and threw him. How? Why, simply by recalling the divine injunction: "A new commandment give I unto you, that ye love one another." Yes, this it was that saved me. Aside from higher considerations, charity often operates as a vastly wise and prudent principle—a great safeguard to its possessor. Men have committed murder for jealousy's sake, and anger's sake, and hatred's sake, and selfishness' sake, and spiritual pride's sake; but no man that ever I heard of, ever committed a diabolical murder for sweet charity's sake. Mere self-interest, then, if no better motive can be enlisted, should, especially with high-tempered men, prompt all beings to charity and philanthropy. At any rate, upon the occasion in question, I strove to drown my exasperated feelings towards the scrivener by benevolently construing his conduct. Poor fellow, poor fellow! thought I, he don't mean anything; and besides, he has seen hard times, and ought to be indulged.

I endeavored, also, immediately to occupy myself, and at the same time to comfort my despondency. I tried to fancy, that in the course of the morning, at such time as might prove agreeable to him, Bartleby, of his own free accord, would emerge from his hermitage and take up some decided line of march in the direction of the door. But no. Half-past twelve o'clock came; Turkey began to glow in the face, overturn his inkstand, and become generally obstreperous; Nippers abated down into quietude and courtesy; Ginger Nut munched his noon apple; and Bartleby remained standing at his window in one of his profoundest dead-wall reveries. Will it be credited? Ought I to acknowledge it? That afternoon I left the office without saying one further word to him.

Some days now passed, during which, at leisure intervals I looked a little into "Edwards on the Will," and "Priestley on Necessity."[9] Under the circumstances, those books induced a salutary feeling. Gradually I slid into the persuasion that these troubles of mine, touching the scrivener, had been all predestinated from eternity, and Bartleby was billeted upon me for some mysterious purpose of an all-wise Providence, which it was not for a mere mortal like me to fathom. Yes, Bartleby, stay there behind your screen, thought I; I shall persecute you no more; you are harmless and noiseless as any of these old chairs; in short, I never feel so private as when I know you are here. At last I see it, I feel it; I penetrate to the predestinated purpose of my life. I am content. Others may have loftier parts to enact; but my mission in this world, Bartleby, is to furnish you with office-room for such period as you may see fit to remain.

I believe that this wise and blessed frame of mind would have continued with me, had it not been for the unsolicited and uncharitable remarks obtruded upon

---

[9]Jonathan Edwards (1703–1758), American theologian and author of *Freedom of the Will;* Joseph Priestley (1733–1804), English clergyman and chemist. Both believed that events are predetermined.

me by my professional friends who visited the rooms. But thus it often is, that the constant friction of illiberal minds wears out at last the best resolves of the more generous. Though to be sure, when I reflected upon it, it was not strange that people entering my office should be struck by the peculiar aspect of the unaccountable Bartleby, and so be tempted to throw out some sinister observations concerning him. Sometimes an attorney, having business with me, and calling at my office, and finding no one but the scrivener there, would undertake to obtain some sort of precise information from him touching my whereabouts; but without heeding his idle talk, Bartleby would remain standing immovable in the middle of the room. So after contemplating him in that position for a time, the attorney would depart, no wiser than he came.

Also, when a reference was going on, and the room full of lawyers and witnesses, and business driving fast, some deeply-occupied legal gentleman present, seeing Bartleby wholly unemployed, would request him to run round to his (the legal gentleman's) office and fetch some papers for him. Thereupon, Bartleby would tranquilly decline, and yet remain idle as before. Then the lawyer would give a great stare, and turn to me. And what could I say? At last I was made aware that all through the circle of my professional acquaintance, a whisper of wonder was running round, having reference to the strange creature I kept at my office. This worried me very much. And as the idea came upon me of his possibly turning out a long-lived man, and keep occupying my chambers, and denying my authority; and perplexing my visitors; and scandalizing my professional reputation; and casting a general gloom over the premises; keeping soul and body together to the last upon his savings (for doubtless he spent but half a dime a day), and in the end perhaps outlive me, and claim possession of my office by right of his perpetual occupancy: as all these dark anticipations crowded upon me more and more, and my friends continually intruded their relentless remarks upon the apparition in my room; a great change was wrought in me. I resolved to gather all my faculties together, and forever rid me of this intolerable incubus.

Ere revolving any complicated project, however, adapted to this end, I first simply suggested to Bartleby the propriety of his permanent departure. In a calm and serious tone, I commended the idea to his careful and mature consideration. But, having taken three days to meditate upon it, he apprised me, that his original determination remained the same; in short, that he still preferred to abide with me.

What shall I do? I now said to myself, buttoning up my coat to the last button. What shall I do? what ought I to do? what does conscience say I *should* do with this man, or, rather, ghost. Rid myself of him, I must; go, he shall. But how? You will not thrust him, the poor, pale, passive mortal—you will not thrust such a helpless creature out of your door? you will not dishonor yourself by such cruelty? No, I will not, I cannot do that. Rather would I let him live and die here, and then mason up his remains in the wall. What, then, will you do? For all your coaxing, he will not budge. Bribes he leaves under your own paper-weight on your table; in short, it is quite plain that he prefers to cling to you.

Then something severe, something unusual must be done, What! surely you will not have him collared by a constable, and commit his innocent pallor to the common jail? And upon what ground could you procure such a thing to be done?—a vagrant, is he? What! he a vagrant, a wanderer, who refuses to budge? It is because he will *not* be a vagrant, then, that you seek to count him *as* a vagrant. This is too absurd. No visible means of support: there I have him. Wrong again: for indubitably he *does* support himself, and that is the only unanswerable proof that any man can show of his possessing the means so to do. No more, then. Since he will not quit me, I must quit him. I will change my offices; I will move elsewhere, and give him fair notice, that if I find him on my new premises I will then proceed against him as a common trespasser.

Acting accordingly, next day I thus addressed him: "I find these chambers too far from the City Hall; the air is unwholesome. In a word, I propose to remove my offices next week, and shall no longer require your services. I tell you this now, in order that you may seek another place."

He made no reply; and nothing more was said.

On the appointed day I engaged carts and men, proceeded to my chambers, and, having but little furniture, everything was removed in a few hours. Throughout, the scrivener remained standing behind the screen, which I directed to be removed the last thing. It was withdrawn; and being folded up like a huge folio, left him the motionless occupant of a naked room. I stood in the entry watching him a moment, while something from within me upbraided me.

I re-entered, with my hand in my pocket—and—and my heart in my mouth.

"Good-by, Bartleby; I am going—good-by, and God some way bless you; and that," slipping something in his hand. But it dropped upon the floor, and then—strange to say—I tore myself from him whom I had so longed to be rid of.

Established in my new quarters, for a day or two I kept the door locked, and started at every footfall in the passages. When I returned to my rooms, after any little absence, I would pause at the threshold for an instant, and attentively listen, ere applying my key. But these fears were needless. Bartleby never came nigh me.

I thought all was going well, when a perturbed-looking stranger visited me, inquiring whether I was the person who had recently occupied rooms at No.——Wall Street.

Full of forebodings, I replied that I was.

"Then, sir," said the stranger, who proved a lawyer, "you are responsible for the man you left there. He refuses to do any copying; he refuses to do anything; he says he prefers not to; and he refuses to quit the premises."

"I am very sorry, sir," said I, with assumed tranquillity, but an inward tremor, "but, really, the man you allude to is nothing to me—he is no relation or apprentice of mine, that you should hold me responsible for him."

"In mercy's name, who is he?"

"I certainly cannot inform you. I know nothing about him. Formerly I employed him as a copyist; but he has done nothing for me now for some time past."

"I shall settle him, then—good morning, sir."

Several days passed, and I heard nothing more; and, though I often felt a charitable prompting to call at the place and see poor Bartleby, yet a certain squeamishness, of I know not what, withheld me.

All is over with him, by this time, thought I, at last, when, through another week, no further intelligence reached me. But, coming to my room the day after, I found several persons waiting at my door in a high state of nervous excitement.

"That's the man—here he comes," cried the foremost one, whom I recognized as the lawyer who had previously called upon me alone.

"You must take him away, sir, at once," cried a portly person among them, advancing upon me, and whom I knew to be the landlord of No.——Wall Street. "These gentlemen, my tenants, cannot stand it any longer; Mr. B—," pointing to the lawyer, "has turned him out of his room, and he now persists in haunting the building generally, sitting upon the banisters of the stairs by day, and sleeping in the entry by night. Everybody is concerned; clients are leaving the offices; some fears are entertained of a mob; something you must do, and that without delay."

Aghast at this torrent, I fell back before it, and would fain have locked myself in my new quarters. In vain I persisted that Bartleby was nothing to me—no more than to any one else. In vain—I was the last person known to have anything to do with him, and they held me to the terrible account. Fearful, then, of being exposed in the papers (as one person present obscurely threatened), I considered the matter, and, at length, said, that if the lawyer would give me a confidential interview with the scrivener, in his (the lawyer's) own room, I would, that afternoon, strive my best to rid them of the nuisance they complained of.

Going up stairs to my old haunt, there was Bartleby silently sitting upon the banister at the landing.

"What are you doing here, Bartleby?" said I.

"Sitting upon the banister," he mildly replied.

I motioned him into the lawyer's room, who then left us.

"Bartleby," said I, "are you aware that you are the cause of great tribulation to me, by persisting in occupying the entry after being dismissed from the office?"

No answer.

"Now one of two things must take place. Either you must do something, or something must be done to you. Now what sort of business would you like to engage in? Would you like to re-engage in copying for some one?"

"No; I would prefer not to make any change."

"Would you like a clerkship in a dry-goods store?"

"There is too much confinement about that. No, I would not like a clerkship; but I am not particular."

"Too much confinement," I cried, "why you keep yourself confined all the time!"

"I would prefer not to take a clerkship," he rejoined, as if to settle that little item at once.

"How would a bar-tender's business suit you? There is no trying of the eyesight in that."

"I would not like it at all; though, as I said before, I am not particular."

His unwonted wordiness inspirited me. I returned to the charge.

"Well, then, would you like to travel through the country collecting bills for the merchants? That would improve your health."

"No, I would prefer to be doing something else."

"How, then, would going as a companion to Europe, to entertain some young gentleman with your conversation—how would that suit you?"

"Not at all. It does not strike me that there is anything definite about that. I like to be stationary. But I am not particular."

"Stationary you shall be, then," I cried, now losing all patience, and, for the first time in all my exasperating connection with him, fairly flying into a passion. "If you do not go away from these premises before night, I shall feel bound—indeed, I *am* bound—to—to—to quit the premises myself!" I rather absurdly concluded, knowing not with what possible threat to try to frighten his immobility into compliance. Despairing of all further efforts, I was precipitately leaving him, when a final thought occurred to me—one which had not been wholly unindulged before.

"Bartleby," said I, in the kindest tone I could assume under such exciting circumstances, "will you go home with me now—not to my office, but my dwelling—and remain there till we can conclude upon some convenient arrangement for you at our leisure? Come, let us start now, right away."

"No: at present I would prefer not to make any change at all."

I answered nothing; but, effectually dodging every one by the suddenness and rapidity of my flight, rushed from the building, ran up Wall Street towards Broadway, and, jumping into the first omnibus, was soon removed from pursuit. As soon as tranquillity returned, I distinctly perceived that I had now done all that I possibly could, both in respect to the demands of the landlord and his tenants, and with regard to my own desire and sense of duty, to benefit Bartleby, and shield him from rude persecution. I now strove to be entirely care-free and quiescent; and my conscience justified me in the attempt; though, indeed, it was not so successful as I could have wished. So fearful was I of being again hunted out by the incensed landlord and his exasperated tenants, that, surrendering my business to Nippers, for a few days, I drove about the upper part of the town and through the suburbs, in my rockaway,[10] crossed over to Jersey City and Hoboken, and paid fugitive visits to Manhattanville and Astoria. In fact, I almost lived in my rockaway for the time.

When again I entered my office, lo, a note from the landlord lay upon the desk. I opened it with trembling hands. It informed me that the writer had sent to the police, and had Bartleby removed to the Tombs as a vagrant. Moreover, since I knew more about him than any one else, he wished me to appear at that place, and make a suitable statement of the facts. These tidings had a conflicting effect upon me. At first I was indignant; but, at last, almost approved. The

[10]A light, four-wheeled carriage.

landlord's energetic, summary disposition, had led him to adopt a procedure which I not think I would have decided upon myself; and yet, as a last resort, under such peculiar circumstances, it seemed the only plan.

As I afterwards learned, the poor scrivener, when told that he must be conducted to the Tombs, offered not the slightest obstacle, but, in his pale, unmoving way, silently acquiesced.

Some of the compassionate and curious bystanders joined the party; and headed by one of the constables arm in arm with Bartleby, the silent procession filed its way through all the noise, and heat, and joy of the roaring thoroughfares at noon.

The same day I received the note, I went to the Tombs, or, to speak more properly, the Halls of Justice. Seeking the right officer, I stated the purpose of my call, and was informed that the individual I described was, indeed, within. I then assured the functionary that Bartleby was a perfectly honest man, and greatly to be compassionated, however unaccountably eccentric. I narrated all I knew, and closed by suggesting the idea of letting him remain in as indulgent confinement as possible, till something less harsh might be done—though, indeed, I hardly knew what. At all events, if nothing else could be decided upon, the alms-house must receive him. I then begged to have an interview.

Being under no disgraceful charge, and quite serene and harmless in all his ways, they had permitted him freely to wander about the prison, and, especially, in the inclosed grass-platted yards thereof. And so I found him there, standing all alone in the quietest of the yards, his face towards a high wall, while all around, from the narrow slits of the jail windows, I thought I saw peering out upon him the eyes of murderers and thieves.

"Bartleby!"

"I know you," he said, without looking round—"and I want nothing to say to you."

"It was not I that brought you here, Bartleby," said I, keenly pained at his implied suspicion. "And to you, this should not be so vile a place. Nothing reproachful attaches to you by being here. And see, it is not so sad a place as one might think. Look, there is the sky, and here is the grass."

"I know where I am" he replied, but would say nothing more, and so I left him.

As I entered the corridor again, a broad meat-like man, in an apron, accosted me, and, jerking his thumb over his shoulder, said—"Is that your friend?"

"Yes."

"Does he want to starve? If he does, let him live on the prison fare, that's all."

"Who are you?" asked I, not knowing what to make of such an unofficially speaking person in such a place.

"I am the grub-man. Such gentlemen as have friends here, hire me to provide them with something good to eat."

"Is this so?" said I, turning to the turnkey.

He said it was.

"Well, then," said I, slipping some silver into the grub-man's hands (for so they called him), "I want you to give particular attention to my friend there; let him have the best dinner you can get. And you must be as polite to him as possible."

"Introduce me, will you?" said the grub-man, looking at me with an expression which seemed to say he was all impatience for an opportunity to give a specimen of his breeding.

Thinking it would prove of benefit to the scrivener, I acquiesced; and, asking the grub-man his name, went up with him to Bartleby.

"Bartleby, this is a friend; you will find him very useful to you."

"Your sarvant, sir, your sarvant," said the grub-man, making a low salutation behind his apron. "Hope you find it pleasant here, sir; nice grounds—cool apartments—hope you'll stay with us sometime—try to make it agreeable. What will you have for dinner to-day?"

"I prefer not to dine to-day," said Bartleby, turning away. "It would disagree with me; I am unused to dinners." So saying, he slowly moved to the other side of the inclosure, and took up a position fronting the dead-wall.

"How's this?" said the grub-man, addressing me with a stare of astonishment. "He's odd, ain't he?"

"I think he is a little deranged," said I, sadly.

"Deranged? deranged is it? Well, now, upon my word, I thought that friend of yourn was a gentleman forger; they are always pale and genteel-like, them forgers. I can't help pity 'em—can't help it, sir. Did you know Monroe Edwards?" he added, touchingly, and paused. Then, laying his hand piteously on my shoulder, sighed, "he died of consumption at Sing-Sing. So you weren't acquainted with Monroe?"

"No, I was never socially acquainted with any forgers. But I cannot stop longer. Look to my friend yonder. You will not lose by it. I will see you again."

Some few days after this, I again obtained admission to the Tombs, and went through the corridors in quest of Bartleby; but without finding him.

"I saw him coming from his cell not long ago," said a turnkey, "may be he's gone to loiter in the yards."

So I went in that direction.

"Are you looking for the silent man?" said another turnkey, passing me. "Yonder he lies—sleeping in the yard there. 'Tis not twenty minutes since I saw him lie down."

The yard was entirely quiet. It was not accessible to the common prisoners. The surrounding walls of amazing thickness, kept off all sounds behind them. The Egyptian character of the masonry weighed upon me with its gloom. But a soft imprisoned turf grew under foot. The heart of the eternal pyramids, it seemed, wherein, by some strange magic, through the clefts, grass-seed, dropped by birds, had sprung.

Strangely huddled at the base of the wall, his knees drawn up, and lying on his side, his head touching the cold stones, I saw the wasted Bartleby. But nothing stirred. I paused; then went close up to him; stooped over, and saw that his dim eyes were open; otherwise he seemed profoundly sleeping. Something prompted me to touch him. I felt his hand, when a tingling shiver ran up my arm and down my spine to my feet.

The round face of the grub-man peered upon me now. "His dinner is ready. Won't he dine to-day, either? Or does he live without dining?"

"Lives without dining," said I, and closed the eyes.

"Eh!—He's asleep, ain't he?"

"With kings and counselors," murmured I.

There would seem little need for proceeding further in this history. Imagination will readily supply the meagre recital of poor Bartleby's interment. But, ere parting with the reader, let me say, that if this little narrative has sufficiently interested him, to awaken curiosity as to who Bartleby was, and what manner of life he led prior to the present narrator's making his acquaintance, I can only reply, that in such curiosity I fully share, but am wholly unable to gratify it. Yet here I hardly know whether I should divulge one little item of rumor, which came to my ear a few months after the scrivener's decease. Upon what basis it rested, I could never ascertain; and hence, how true it is I cannot now tell. But, inasmuch as this vague report has not been without a certain suggestive interest to me, however said, it may prove the same with some others; and so I will briefly mention it. The report was this: that Bartleby had been a subordinate clerk in the Dead Letter Office at Washington, from which he had been suddenly removed by a change in the administration. When I think over this rumor, hardly can I express the emotions which seize me. Dead letters! does it not sound like dead men? Conceive a man by nature and misfortune prone to a pallid hopelessness, can any business seem more fitted to heighten it than that of continually handling these dead letters, and assorting them for the flames? For by the cart-load they are annually burned. Some times from out the folded paper the pale clerk takes a ring—the finger it was meant for, perhaps, moulders in the grave; a bank-note sent in swiftest charity—he whom it would relieve, nor eats nor hungers any more; pardon for those who died despairing; hope for those who died unhoping; good tidings for those who died stifled by unrelieved calamities. On errands of life, these letters speed to death.

Ah, Bartleby! Ah, humanity!

QUESTIONS

1. How would you characterize the narrator, taking his self-description into account?
2. Do you suppose the narrator gives you a generally accurate picture of the other characters? How reliable does he seem to be throughout the account?
3. What details of the setting evoke the strongest responses from you? How similar is your view of the office and the work done here to what the narrator's appears to be?
4. What thoughts and feelings do you attribute to Bartleby's silence, apart from what the narrator suggests?

5. How strongly do you sympathize with Bartleby? With the narrator?
6. Are you amused by the story at any point, and if so, what is the nature of the humor?
7. How alike do you suppose your values and the narrator's are? Yours and Bartleby's?
8. Is the story Bartleby's or the narrator's ultimately? Explain.

James Joyce (1882–1941)
THE DEAD

Lily, the caretaker's daughter, was literally run off her feet. Hardly had she brought one gentleman into the little pantry behind the office on the ground floor and helped him off with his overcoat than the wheezy hall-door bell clanged again and she had to scamper along the bare hallway to let in another guest. It was well for her she had not to attend to the ladies also. But Miss Kate and Miss Julia had thought of that and had converted the bathroom upstairs into a ladies' dressing-room. Miss Kate and Miss Julia were there, gossiping and laughing and fussing, walking after each other to the head of the stairs, peering down over the banisters and calling down to Lily to ask her who had come.

It was always a great affair, the Misses Morkan's annual dance. Everybody who knew them came to it, members of the family, old friends of the family, the members of Julia's choir, any of Kate's pupils that were grown up enough and even some of Mary Jane's pupils too. Never once had it fallen flat. For years and years it had gone off in splendid style as long as anyone could remember; ever since Kate and Julia, after the death of their brother Pat, had left the house in Stoney Batter and taken Mary Jane, their only niece, to live with them in the dark gaunt house on Usher's Island, the upper part of which they had rented from Mr Fulham, the corn-factor on the ground floor.[1] That was a good thirty years ago if it was a day. Mary Jane, who was then a little girl in short clothes, was now the main prop of the household for she had the organ in Haddington Road. She had been through the Academy and gave a pupils' concert every year in the upper room of the Antient Concert Rooms. Many of her pupils belonged to better-class families on the Kingstown and Dalkey line. Old as they were, her aunts also did their share. Julia, though she was quite grey, was still the leading soprano in Adam and Eve's, and Kate, being too feeble to go about much, gave music lessons to beginners on the old square piano in the back room. Lily, the caretaker's daughter, did housemaid's work for them. Though their life was modest they believed in eating well; the best of everything: diamond-bone sirloins, three-shilling tea and the best bottled stout. But Lily seldom made a mistake in

---

[1] Most places named in the story are located in or near the city of Dublin, Ireland.

the orders so that she got on well with her three mistresses. They were fussy, that was all. But the only thing they would not stand was back answers.

Of course they had good reason to be fussy on such a night. And then it was long after ten o'clock and yet there was no sign of Gabriel and his wife. Besides they were dreadfully afraid that Freddy Malins might turn up screwed. They would not wish for worlds that any of Mary Jane's pupils should see him under the influence; and when he was like that it was sometimes very hard to manage him. Freddy Malins always came late but they wondered what could be keeping Gabriel: and that was what brought them every two minutes to the banisters to ask Lily had Gabriel or Freddy come.

—O, Mr Conroy, said Lily to Gabriel when she opened the door for him, Miss Kate and Miss Julia thought you were never coming. Good-night, Mrs Conroy.

—I'll engage they did, said Gabriel, but they forget that my wife here takes three mortal hours to dress herself.

He stood on the mat, scraping the snow from his goloshes, while Lily led his wife to the foot of the stairs and called out:

—Miss Kate, here's Mrs Conroy.

Kate and Julia came toddling down the dark stairs at once. Both of them kissed Gabriel's wife, said she must be perished alive and asked was Gabriel with her.

—Here I am as right as the mail, Aunt Kate! Go on up. I'll follow, called out Gabriel from the dark.

He continued scraping his feet vigorously while the three women went upstairs, laughing, to the ladies' dressing-room. A light fringe of snow lay like a cape on the shoulders of his overcoat and like toecaps on the toes of his goloshes; and, as the buttons of his overcoat slipped with a squeaking noise through the snow-stiffened frieze, a cold fragrant air from out-of-doors escaped from crevices and folds.

—Is it snowing again, Mr Conroy? asked Lily.

She had preceded him into the pantry to help him off with his overcoat. Gabriel smiled at the three syllables she had given his surname and glanced at her. She was a slim, growing girl, pale in complexion and with hay-coloured hair. The gas in the pantry made her look still paler. Gabriel had known her when she was a child and used to sit on the lowest step nursing a rag doll.

—Yes, Lily, he answered, and I think we're in for a night of it.

He looked up at the pantry ceiling, which was shaking with the stamping and shuffling of feet on the floor above, listened for a moment to the piano and then glanced at the girl, who was folding his overcoat carefully at the end of a shelf.

—Tell me, Lily, he said in a friendly tone, do you still go to school?

—O no, sir, she answered. I'm done schooling this year and more.

—O, then, said Gabriel gaily, I suppose we'll be going to your wedding one of these fine days with your young man, eh?

The girl glanced back at him over her shoulder and said with great bitterness:

—The men that is now is only all palaver and what they can get out of you.

Gabriel coloured as if he felt he had made a mistake and, without looking at her, kicked off his goloshes and flicked actively with his muffler at his patent-leather shoes.

He was a stout tallish young man. The high colour of his cheeks pushed upwards even to his forehead where it scattered itself in a few formless patches of pale red; and on his hairless face there scintillated restlessly the polished lenses and the bright gilt rims of the glasses which screened his delicate and restless eyes. His glossy black hair was parted in the middle and brushed in a long curve behind his ears where it curled slightly beneath the groove left by his hat.

When he had flicked lustre into his shoes he stood up and pulled his waistcoat down more tightly on his plump body. Then he took a coin rapidly from his pocket.

—O Lily, he said, thrusting it into her hands, it's Christmastime, isn't it? Just . . . here's a little. . . .

He walked rapidly towards the door.

—O no, sir! cried the girl, following him. Really, sir, I wouldn't take it.

—Christmas-time! Christmas-time! said Gabriel, almost trotting to the stairs and waving his hand to her in deprecation.

The girl, seeing that he had gained the stairs, called out after him:

—Well, thank you, sir.

He waited outside the drawing-room door until the waltz should finish, listening to the skirts that swept against it and to the shuffling of feet. He was still discomposed by the girl's bitter and sudden retort. It had cast a gloom over him which he tried to dispel by arranging his cuffs and the bows of his tie. Then he took from his waistcoat pocket a little paper and glanced at the headings he had made for his speech. He was undecided about the lines from Robert Browning for he feared they would be above the heads of his hearers. Some quotation that they could recognise from Shakespeare or from the Melodies[2] would be better. The indelicate clacking of the men's heels and the shuffling of their soles reminded him that their grade of culture differed from his. He would only make himself ridiculous by quoting poetry to them which they could not understand. They would think that he was airing his superior education. He would fail with them just as he had failed with the girl in the pantry. He had taken up a wrong tone. His whole speech was a mistake from first to last, an utter failure.

Just then his aunts and his wife came out of the ladies' dressing-room. His aunts were two small plainly dressed old women. Aunt Julia was an inch or so the taller. Her hair, drawn low over the tops of her ears, was grey; and grey also, with darker shadows, was her large flaccid face. Though she was stout in build and stood erect her slow eyes and parted lips gave her the appearance of a woman who did not know where she was or where she was going. Aunt Kate was more vivacious. Her face, healthier than her sister's, was all puckers and creases, like

---

[2]*Irish Melodies*, favorite songs by the poet Thomas Moore (1779–1852).

a shrivelled red apple, and her hair, braided in the same old-fashioned way, had not lost its ripe nut colour.

They both kissed Gabriel frankly. He was their favourite nephew, the son of their dead elder sister, Ellen, who had married T. J. Conroy of the Port and Docks.

—Gretta tells me you're not going to take a cab back to Monkstown to-night, Gabriel, said Aunt Kate.

—No, said Gabriel, turning to his wife, we had quite enough of that last year, hadn't we? Don't you remember, Aunt Kate, what a cold Gretta got out of it? Cab windows rattling all the way, and the east wind blowing in after we passed Merrion. Very jolly it was. Gretta caught a dreadful cold.

Aunt Kate frowned severely and nodded her head at every word.

—Quite right, Gabriel, quite right, she said. You can't be too careful.

—But as for Gretta there, said Gabriel, she'd walk home in the snow if she were let.

Mrs Conroy laughed.

—Don't mind him, Aunt Kate, she said. He's really an awful bother, what with green shades for Tom's eyes at night and making him do the dumb-bells, and forcing Eva to eat the stirabout. The poor child! And she simply hates the sight of it! . . . O, but you'll never guess what he makes me wear now!

She broke out into a peal of laughter and glanced at her husband, whose admiring and happy eyes had been wandering from her dress to her face and hair. The two aunts laughed heartily too, for Gabriel's solicitude was a standing joke with them.

—Goloshes! said Mrs Conroy. That's the latest. Whenever it's wet underfoot I must put on my goloshes. To-night even he wanted me to put them on, but I wouldn't. The next thing he'll buy me will be a diving suit.

Gabriel laughed nervously and patted his tie reassuringly while Aunt Kate nearly doubled herself, so heartily did she enjoy the joke. The smile soon faded from Aunt Julia's face and her mirthless eyes were directed towards her nephew's face. After a pause she asked:

—And what are goloshes, Gabriel?

—Goloshes, Julia! exclaimed her sister. Goodness me, don't you know what goloshes are? You wear them over your . . . over your boots, Gretta, isn't it?

—Yes, said Mrs Conroy. Guttapercha[3] things. We both have a pair now. Gabriel says everyone wears them on the continent.

—O, on the continent, murmured Aunt Julia, nodding her head slowly.

Gabriel knitted his brows and said, as if he were slightly angered:

—It's nothing very wonderful but Gretta thinks it very funny because she says the word reminds her of Christy Minstrels.[4]

—But tell me, Gabriel, said Aunt Kate, with brisk tact. Of course, you've seen about the room. Gretta was saying . . .

---

[3] A rubberlike material.
[4] A troupe of minstrels organized in New York c. 1842 by Edwin P. Christy.

—O, the room is all right, replied Gabriel. I've taken one in the Gresham.

—To be sure, said Aunt Kate, by far the best thing to do. And the children, Gretta, you're not anxious about them?

—O, for one night, said Mrs Conroy. Besides, Bessie will look after them.

—To be sure, said Aunt Kate again. What a comfort it is to have a girl like that, one you can depend on! There's that Lily, I'm sure I don't know what has come over her lately. She's not the girl she was at all.

Gabriel was about to ask his aunt some questions on this point but she broke off suddenly to gaze after her sister who had wandered down the stairs and was craning her neck over the banisters.

—Now, I ask you, she said, almost testily, where is Julia going? Julia! Julia! Where are you going?

Julia, who had gone halfway down one flight, came back and announced blandly:

—Here's Freddy.

At the same moment a clapping of hands and a final flourish of the pianist told that the waltz had ended. The drawing-room door was opened from within and some couples came out. Aunt Kate drew Gabriel aside hurriedly and whispered into his ear:

—Slip down, Gabriel, like a good fellow and see if he's all right, and don't let him up if he's screwed. I'm sure he's screwed. I'm sure he is.

Gabriel went to the stairs and listened over the banisters. He could hear two persons talking in the pantry. Then he recognised Freddy Malins' laugh. He went down the stairs noisily.

—It's such a relief, said Aunt Kate to Mrs Conroy, that Gabriel is here. I always feel easier in my mind when he's here. . . . Julia, there's Miss Daly and Miss Power will take some refreshment. Thanks for your beautiful waltz, Miss Daly. It made lovely time.

A tall wizen-faced man, with a stiff grizzled moustache and swarthy skin, who was passing out with his partner said:

—And may we have some refreshment, too, Miss Morkan?

—Julia, said Aunt Kate summarily, and here's Mr Browne and Miss Furlong. Take them in, Julia, with Miss Daly and Miss Power.

—I'm the man for the ladies, said Mr Browne, pursing his lips until his moustache bristled and smiling in all his wrinkles. You know, Miss Morkan, the reason they are so fond of me is—

He did not finish his sentence, but, seeing that Aunt Kate was out of earshot, at once led the three young ladies into the back room. The middle of the room was occupied by two square tables placed end to end, and on these Aunt Julia and the caretaker were straightening and smoothing a large cloth. On the sideboard were arrayed dishes and plates, and glasses and bundles of knives and forks and spoons. The top of the closed square piano served also as a sideboard for viands and sweets. At a smaller sideboard in one corner two young men were standing, drinking hop-bitters.

Mr Browne led his charges thither and invited them all, in jest, to some ladies' punch, hot, strong and sweet. As they said they never took anything strong he opened three bottles of lemonade for them. Then he asked one of the young men to move aside, and, taking hold of the decanter, filled out for himself a goodly measure of whisky. The young men eyed him respectfully while he took a trial sip.

—God help me, he said, smiling, it's the doctor's orders.

His wizened face broke into a broader smile, and the three young ladies laughed in musical echo to his pleasantry, swaying their bodies to and fro, with nervous jerks of their shoulders. The boldest said:

—O, now, Mr Browne, I'm sure the doctor never ordered anything of the kind.

Mr Browne took another sip of his whisky and said, with sidling mimicry:

—Well, you see, I'm like the famous Mrs Cassidy, who is reported to have said: *Now, Mary Grimes, if I don't take it, make me take it, for I feel I want it.*

His hot face had leaned forward a little too confidentially and he had assumed a very low Dublin accent so that the young ladies, with one instinct, received his speech in silence. Miss Furlong, who was one of Mary Jane's pupils, asked Miss Daly what was the name of the pretty waltz she had played; and Mr Browne, seeing that he was ignored, turned promptly to the two young men who were more appreciative.

A red-faced young woman, dressed in pansy, came into the room, excitedly clapping her hands and crying:

—Quadrilles! Quadrilles![5]

Close on her heels came Aunt Kate, crying:

—Two gentlemen and three ladies, Mary Jane!

—O, here's Mr Bergin and Mr Kerrigan, said Mary Jane.

Mr. Kerrigan, will you take Miss Power? Miss Furlong, may I get you a partner, Mr Bergin. O, that'll just do now.

—Three ladies, Mary Jane, said Aunt Kate.

The two young gentlemen asked the ladies if they might have the pleasure, and Mary Jane turned to Miss Daly.

—O, Miss Daly, you're really awfully good, after playing for the last two dances, but really we're so short of ladies to-night.

—I don't mind in the least, Miss Morkan.

—But I've a nice partner for you, Mr Bartell D'Arcy, the tenor. I'll get him to sing later on. All Dublin is raving about him.

—Lovely voice, lovely voice! said Aunt Kate.

As the piano had twice begun the prelude to the first figure Mary Jane led her recruits quickly from the room. They had hardly gone when Aunt Julia wandered slowly into the room, looking behind her at something.

—What is the matter, Julia? asked Aunt Kate anxiously. Who is it?

---

[5]A square dance, originally French, for four couples.

Julia, who was carrying in a column of table-napkins, turned to her sister and said, simply, as if the question had surprised her:

—It's only Freddy, Kate, and Gabriel with him.

In fact right behind her Gabriel could be seen piloting Freddy Malins across the landing. The latter, a young man of about forty, was of Gabriel's size and build, with very round shoulders. His face was fleshy and pallid, touched with colour only at the thick hanging lobes of his ears and at the wide wings of his nose. He had coarse features, a blunt nose, a convex and receding brow, tumid and protruded lips. His heavy-lidded eyes and the disorder of his scanty hair made him look sleepy. He was laughing heartily in a high key at a story which he had been telling Gabriel on the stairs and at the same time rubbing the knuckles of his left fist backwards and forwards into his left eye.

—Good-evening, Freddy, said Aunt Julia.

Freddy Malins bade the Misses Morkan good-evening in what seemed an offhand fashion by reason of the habitual catch in his voice and then, seeing that Mr Browne was grinning at him from the sideboard, crossed the room on rather shaky legs and began to repeat in an undertone the story he had just told to Gabriel.

—He's not so bad, is he? said Aunt Kate to Gabriel.

Gabriel's brows were dark but he raised them quickly and answered:

—O no, hardly noticeable.

—Now, isn't he a terrible fellow! she said. And his poor mother made him take the pledge on New Year's Eve. But come on, Gabriel, into the drawing-room.

Before leaving the room with Gabriel she signalled to Mr Browne by frowning and shaking her forefinger in warning to and fro. Mr Browne nodded in answer and, when she had gone, said to Freddy Malins:

—Now, then, Freddy, I'm going to fill you out a good glass of lemonade just to buck you up.

Freddy Malins, who was nearing the climax of his story, waved the offer aside impatiently but Mr Browne, having first called Freddy Malins' attention to a disarray in his dress, filled out and handed him a full glass of lemonade. Freddy Malins' left hand accepted the glass mechanically, his right hand being engaged in the mechanical readjustment of his dress. Mr Browne, whose face was once more wrinkling with mirth, poured out for himself a glass of whisky while Freddy Malins exploded, before he had well reached the climax of his story, in a kink of high-pitched bronchitic laughter and, setting down his untasted and overflowing glass, began to rub the knuckles of his left fist backwards and forwards into his left eye, repeating words of his last phrase as well as his fit of laughter would allow him.

Gabriel could not listen while Mary Jane was playing her Academy piece, full of runs and difficult passages, to the hushed drawing-room. He liked music but the piece she was playing had no melody for him and he doubted whether it had any melody for the other listeners, though they had begged Mary Jane to play something. Four young men, who had come from the refreshment-room to stand in the doorway at the sound of the piano, had gone away quietly in couples after a few minutes. The only persons who seemed to follow the music were Mary Jane herself, her hands racing along the key-board or lifted from it at the pauses like those of a priestess in momentary imprecation, and Aunt Kate standing at her elbow to turn the page.

Gabriel's eyes, irritated by the floor, which glittered with beeswax under the heavy chandelier, wandered to the wall above the piano. A picture of the balcony scene in *Romeo and Juliet* hung there and beside it was a picture of the two murdered princes in the Tower which Aunt Julia had worked in red, blue and brown wools when she was a girl. Probably in the school they had gone to as girls that kind of work had been taught, for one year his mother had worked for him as a birthday present a waistcoat of purple tabinet, with little foxes' heads upon it, lined with brown satin and having round mulberry buttons. It was strange that his mother had had no musical talent though Aunt Kate used to call her the brains carrier of the Morkan family. Both she and Julia had always seemed a little proud of their serious and matronly sister. Her photograph stood before the pierglass. She held an open book on her knees and was pointing out something in it to Constantine who, dressed in a man-o'-war suit, lay at her feet. It was she who had chosen the names for her sons for she was very sensible of the dignity of family life. Thanks to her, Constantine was now senior curate in Balbriggan and, thanks to her, Gabriel himself had taken his degree in the Royal University. A shadow passed over his face as he remembered her sullen opposition to his marriage. Some slighting phrases she had used still rankled in his memory; she had once spoken of Gretta as being country cute and that was not true of Gretta at all. It was Gretta who had nursed her during all her last long illness in their house at Monkstown.

He knew that Mary Jane must be near the end of her piece for she was playing again the opening melody with runs of scales after every bar and while he waited for the end the resentment died down in his heart. The piece ended with a trill of octaves in the treble and a final deep octave in the bass. Great applause greeted Mary Jane as, blushing and rolling up her music nervously, she escaped from the room. The most vigorous clapping came from the four young men in the doorway who had gone away to the refreshment-room at the beginning of the piece but had come back when the piano had stopped.

Lancers[6] were arranged. Gabriel found himself partnered with Miss Ivors. She was a frank-mannered talkative young lady, with a freckled face and prominent brown eyes. She did not wear a low-cut bodice and the large brooch which was fixed in the front of her collar bore on it an Irish device.

When they had taken their places she said abruptly:

—I have a crow to pluck with you.

—With me? said Gabriel.

---

[6]A nineteenth-century square dance.

She nodded her head gravely.

—What is it? asked Gabriel, smiling at her solemn manner.

—Who is G. C.? answered Miss Ivors, turning her eyes upon him.

Gabriel coloured and was about to knit his brows, as if he did not understand, when she said bluntly:

—O, innocent Amy! I have found out that you write for *The Daily Express.* Now, aren't you ashamed of yourself?

—Why should I be ashamed of myself? asked Gabriel, blinking his eyes and trying to smile.

—Well, I'm ashamed of you, said Miss Ivors frankly. To say you'd write for a rag like that. I didn't think you were a West Briton.[7]

A look of perplexity appeared on Gabriel's face. It was true that he wrote a literary column every Wednesday in *The Daily Express,* for which he was paid fifteen shillings. But that did not make him a West Briton surely. The books he received for review were almost more welcome than the paltry cheque. He loved to feel the covers and turn over the pages of newly printed books. Nearly every day when his teaching in the college was ended he used to wander down the quays to the second-hand booksellers, to Hickey's on Bachelor's Walk, to Webb's or Massey's on Aston's Quay, or to O'Clohissey's in the by-street. He did not know how to meet her charge. He wanted to say that literature was above politics. But they were friends of many years' standing and their careers had been parallel, first at the University and then as teachers: he could not risk a grandiose phrase with her. He continued blinking his eyes and trying to smile and murmured lamely that he saw nothing political in writing reviews of books.

When their turn to cross had come he was still perplexed and inattentive. Miss Ivors promptly took his hand in a warm grasp and said in a soft friendly tone:

—Of course, I was only joking. Come, we cross now.

When they were together again she spoke of the University question and Gabriel felt more at ease. A friend of hers had shown her his review of Browning's poems. That was how she had found out the secret: but she liked the review immensely. Then she said suddenly:

—O, Mr Conroy, will you come for an excursion to the Aran Isles this summer? We're going to stay there a whole month. It will be splendid out in the Atlantic. You ought to come. Mr Clancy is coming, and Mr Kilkelly and Kathleen Kearney. It would be splendid for Gretta too if she'd come. She's from Connacht,[8] isn't she?

—Her people are, said Gabriel shortly.

—But you will come, won't you? said Miss Ivors, laying her warm hand eagerly on his arm.

—The fact is, said Gabriel, I have already arranged to go—

—Go where? asked Miss Ivors.

[7]Similar to Anglophile. Someone more interested in things English than in Ireland.
[8]Region on the west coast of Ireland.

—Well, you know, every year I go for a cycling tour with some fellows and so—

—But where? asked Miss Ivors.

—Well, we usually go to France or Belgium or perhaps Germany, said Gabriel awkwardly.

—And why do you go to France and Belgium, said Miss Ivors, instead of visiting your own land?

—Well, said Gabriel, it's partly to keep in touch with the languages and partly for a change.

—And haven't you your own language to keep in touch with—Irish? asked Miss Ivors.

—Well, said Gabriel, if it comes to that, you know, Irish is not my language.

Their neighbours had turned to listen to the cross-examination. Gabriel glanced right and left nervously and tried to keep his good humour under the ordeal which was making a blush invade his forehead.

—And haven't you your own land to visit, continued Miss Ivors, that you know nothing of, your own people, and your own country?

—O, to tell you the truth, retorted Gabriel suddenly, I'm sick of my own country, sick of it!

—Why? asked Miss Ivors.

Gabriel did not answer for his retort had heated him.

—Why? repeated Miss Ivors.

They had to go visiting together[9] and, as he had not answered her, Miss Ivors said warmly:

—Of course, you've no answer.

Gabriel tried to cover his agitation by taking part in the dance with great energy. He avoided her eyes for he had seen a sour expression on her face. But when they met in the long chain he was surprised to feel his hand firmly pressed. She looked at him from under her brows for a moment quizzically until he smiled. Then, just as the chain was about to start again, she stood on tiptoe and whispered into his ear:

—West Briton!

When the lancers were over Gabriel went away to a remote corner of the room where Freddy Malins' mother was sitting. She was a stout feeble old woman with white hair. Her voice had a catch in it like her son's and she stuttered slightly. She had been told that Freddy had come and that he was nearly all right. Gabriel asked her whether she had had a good crossing. She lived with her married daughter in Glasgow and came to Dublin on a visit once a year. She answered placidly that she had had a beautiful crossing and that the captain had been most attentive to her. She spoke also of the beautiful house her daughter kept in Glasgow, and of all the nice friends they had there. While her tongue rambled

---

[9]That is, cross over together in the dance.

on Gabriel tried to banish from his mind all memory of the unpleasant incident with Miss Ivors. Of course the girl or woman, or whatever she was, was an enthusiast but there was a time for all things. Perhaps he ought not to have answered her like that. But she had no right to call him a West Briton before people, even in joke. She had tried to make him ridiculous before people, heckling him and staring at him with her rabbit's eyes.

He saw his wife making her way towards him through the waltzing couples. When she reached him she said into his ear:

—Gabriel, Aunt Kate wants to know won't you carve the goose as usual. Miss Daly will carve the ham and I'll do the pudding.

—All right, said Gabriel.

—She's sending in the younger ones first as soon as this waltz is over so that we'll have the table to ourselves.

—Were you dancing? asked Gabriel.

—Of course I was. Didn't you see me? What words had you with Molly Ivors?

—No words. Why? Did she say so?

—Something like that. I'm trying to get that Mr D'Arcy to sing. He's full of conceit, I think.

—There were no words, said Gabriel moodily, only she wanted me to go for a trip to the west of Ireland and I said I wouldn't.

His wife clasped her hands excitedly and gave a little jump.

—O, do go, Gabriel, she cried. I'd love to see Galway again.

—You can go if you like, said Gabriel coldly.

She looked at him for a moment, then turned to Mrs Malins and said:

—There's a nice husband for you, Mrs Malins.

While she was threading her way back across the room Mrs Malins, without adverting to the interruption, went on to tell Gabriel what beautiful places there were in Scotland and beautiful scenery. Her son-in-law brought them every year to the lakes and they used to go fishing. Her son-in-law was a splendid fisher. One day he caught a fish, a beautiful big big fish, and the man in the hotel boiled it for their dinner.

Gabriel hardly heard what she said. Now that supper was coming near he began to think again about his speech and about the quotation. When he saw Freddy Malins coming across the room to visit his mother Gabriel left the chair free for him and retired into the embrasure of the window. The room had already cleared and from the back room came the clatter of plates and knives. Those who still remained in the drawing-room seemed tired of dancing and were conversing quietly in little groups. Gabriel's warm trembling fingers tapped the cold pane of the window. How cool it must be outside! How pleasant it would be to walk out alone, first along by the river and then through the park! The snow would be lying on the branches of the trees and forming a bright cap on the top of the Wellington Monument. How much more pleasant it would be there than at the supper-table!

He ran over the headings of his speech: Irish hospitality, sad memories, the Three Graces, Paris, the quotation from Browning. He repeated to himself a phrase he had written in his review: *One feels that one is listening to a thought-tormented music.* Miss Ivors had praised the review. Was she sincere? Had she really any life of her own behind all her propagandism? There had never been any ill-feeling between them until that night. It unnerved him to think that she would be at the supper-table, looking up at him while he spoke with her critical quizzing eyes. Perhaps she would not be sorry to see him fail in his speech. An idea came into his mind and gave him courage. He would say, alluding to Aunt Kate and Aunt Julia: *Ladies and Gentlemen, the generation which is now on the wane among us may have had its faults but for my part I think it had certain qualities of hospitality, of humour, of humanity, which the new and very serious and hypereducated generation that is growing up around us seems to me to lack.* Very good: that was one for Miss Ivors. What did he care that his aunts were only two ignorant old women?

A murmur in the room attracted his attention. Mr Browne was advancing from the door, gallantly escorting Aunt Julia, who leaned upon his arm, smiling and hanging her head. An irregular musketry of applause escorted her also as far as the piano and then, as Mary Jane seated herself on the stool, and Aunt Julia, no longer smiling, half turned so as to pitch her voice fairly into the room, gradually ceased. Gabriel recognised the prelude. It was that of an old song of Aunt Julia's—*Arrayed for the Bridal.* Her voice, strong and clear in tone, attacked with great spirit the runs which embellish the air and though she sang very rapidly she did not miss even the smallest of the grace notes. To follow the voice, without looking at the singer's face, was to feel and share the excitement of swift and secure flight. Gabriel applauded loudly with all the others at the close of the song and loud applause was borne in from the invisible supper-table. It sounded so genuine that a little colour struggled into Aunt Julia's face as she bent to replace in the music-stand the old leather-bound song-book that had her initials on the cover. Freddy Malins, who had listened with his head perched sideways to hear her better, was still applauding when everyone else had ceased and talking animatedly to his mother who nodded her head gravely and slowly in acquiescence. At last, when he could clap no more, he stood up suddenly and hurried across the room to Aunt Julia whose hand he seized and held in both his hands, shaking it when words failed him or the catch in his voice proved too much for him.

—I was just telling my mother, he said, I never heard you sing so well, never. No, I never heard your voice so good as it is to-night. Now! Would you believe that now? That's the truth. Upon my word and honour that's the truth. I never heard your voice sound so fresh and so . . . so clear and fresh, never.

Aunt Julia smiled broadly and murmured something about compliments as she released her hand from his grasp. Mr Browne extended his open hand towards her and said to those who were near him in the manner of a showman introducing a prodigy to an audience:

—Miss Julia Morkan, my latest discovery!

He was laughing very heartily at this himself when Freddy Malins turned to him and said:

—Well, Browne, if you're serious you might make a worse discovery. All I can say is I never heard her sing half so well as long as I am coming here. And that's the honest truth.

—Neither did I, said Mr Browne. I think her voice has greatly improved.

Aunt Julia shrugged her shoulders and said with meek pride:

—Thirty years ago I hadn't a bad voice as voices go.

—I often told Julia, said Aunt Kate emphatically, that she was simply thrown away in that choir. But she never would be said by me.

She turned as if to appeal to the good sense of the others against a refractory child while Aunt Julia gazed in front of her, a vague smile of reminiscence playing on her face.

—No, continued Aunt Kate, she wouldn't be said or led by anyone, slaving there in that choir night and day, night and day. Six o'clock on Christmas morning! And all for what?

—Well, isn't it for the honour of God, Aunt Kate? asked Mary Jane, twisting round on the piano-stool and smiling.

Aunt Kate turned fiercely on her niece and said:

—I know all about the honour of God, Mary Jane, but I think it's not at all honourable for the pope to turn out the women out of the choirs that have slaved there all their lives and put little whipper-snappers of boys over their heads. I suppose it is for the good of the Church if the pope does it. But it's not just, Mary Jane, and it's not right.

She had worked herself into a passion and would have continued in defence of her sister for it was a sore subject with her but Mary Jane, seeing that all the dancers had come back, intervened pacifically:

—Now, Aunt Kate, you're giving scandal to Mr Browne who is of the other persuasion.

Aunt Kate turned to Mr Browne, who was grinning at this allusion to his religion, and said hastily:

—O, I don't question the pope's being right. I'm only a stupid old woman and I wouldn't presume to do such a thing. But there's such a thing as common everyday politeness and gratitude. And if I were in Julia's place I'd tell that Father Healy straight up to his face . . .

—And besides, Aunt Kate, said Mary Jane, we really are all hungry and when we are hungry we are all very quarrelsome.

—And when we are thirsty we are also quarrelsome, added Mr Browne.

—So that we had better go to supper, said Mary Jane, and finish the discussion afterwards.

On the landing outside the drawing-room Gabriel found his wife and Mary Jane trying to persuade Miss Ivors to stay for supper. But Miss Ivors, who had put on her hat and was buttoning her cloak, would not stay. She did not feel in the least hungry and she had already overstayed her time.

—But only for ten minutes, Molly, said Mrs Conroy. That won't delay you.

—To take a pick itself, said Mary Jane, after all your dancing.

—I really couldn't, said Miss Ivors.

—I am afraid you didn't enjoy yourself at all, said Mary Jane hopelessly.

—Ever so much, I assure you, said Miss Ivors, but you really must let me run off now.

—But how can you get home? asked Mrs Conroy.

—O, it's only two steps up the quay.

Gabriel hesitated a moment and said:

—If you will allow me, Miss Ivors, I'll see you home if you really are obliged to go.

But Miss Ivors broke away from them.

—I won't hear of it, she cried. For goodness sake go in to your suppers and don't mind me. I'm quite well able to take care of myself.

—Well, you're the comical girl, Molly, said Mrs Conroy frankly.

—*Beannacht libh*,[10] cried Miss Ivors, with a laugh, as she ran down the staircase.

Mary Jane gazed after her, a moody puzzled expression on her face, while Mrs Conroy leaned over the banisters to listen for the hall-door. Gabriel asked himself was he the cause of her abrupt departure. But she did not seem to be in ill humour: she had gone away laughing. He stared blankly down the staircase.

At that moment Aunt Kate came toddling out of the supper-room, almost wringing her hands in despair.

—Where is Gabriel? she cried. Where on earth is Gabriel? There's everyone waiting in there, stage to let, and nobody to carve the goose!

—Here I am, Aunt Kate! cried Gabriel, with sudden animation, ready to carve a flock of geese, if necessary.

A fat brown goose lay at one end of the table and at the other end, on a bed of creased paper strewn with sprigs of parsley, lay a great ham, stripped of its outer skin and peppered over with crust crumbs, a neat paper frill round its shin and beside this was a round of spiced beef. Between these rival ends ran parallel lines of side-dishes: two little minsters of jelly, red and yellow; a shallow dish full of blocks of blancmange and red jam, a large green leaf-shaped dish with a stalk-shaped handle, on which lay bunches of purple raisins and peeled almonds, a companion dish on which lay a solid rectangle of Smyrna figs, a dish of custard topped with grated nutmeg, a small bowl full of chocolates and sweets wrapped in gold and silver papers and a glass vase in which stood some tall celery stalks. In the centre of the table there stood, as sentries to a fruit-stand which upheld a pyramid of oranges and American apples, two squat old-fashioned decanters of cut glass, one containing port and the other dark sherry. On the closed square piano a pudding in a huge yellow dish lay in waiting and behind it were three squads of bottles of stout and ale and minerals, drawn up according to the colours of their uniforms, the first two black, with brown and red labels, the third and smallest squad white, with transverse green sashes.

---

[10]'Farewell' in Gaelic, used as a blessing.

Gabriel took his seat boldly at the head of the table and, having looked to the edge of the carver, plunged his fork firmly into the goose. He felt quite at ease now for he was an expert carver and liked nothing better than to find himself at the head of a well-laden table.

—Miss Furlong, what shall I send you? he asked. A wing or a slice of the breast?

—Just a small slice of the breast.

—Miss Higgins, what for you?

—O, anything at all, Mr Conroy.

While Gabriel and Miss Daly exchanged plates of goose and plates of ham and spiced beef Lily went from guest to guest with a dish of hot floury potatoes wrapped in a white napkin. This was Mary Jane's idea and she had also suggested apple sauce for the goose but Aunt Kate had said that plain roast goose without apple sauce had always been good enough for her and she hoped she might never eat worse. Mary Jane waited on her pupils and saw that they got the best slices and Aunt Kate and Aunt Julia opened and carried across from the piano bottles of stout and ale for the gentlemen and bottles of minerals for the ladies. There was a great deal of confusion and laughter and noise, the noise of orders and counter-orders, of knives and forks, of corks and glass-stoppers. Gabriel began to carve second helpings as soon as he had finished the first round without serving himself. Everyone protested loudly so that he compromised by taking a long draught of stout for he had found the carving hot work. Mary Jane settled down quietly to her supper but Aunt Kate and Aunt Julia were still toddling round the table, walking on each other's heels, getting in each other's way and giving each other unheeded orders. Mr Browne begged of them to sit down and eat their suppers and so did Gabriel but they said there was time enough so that, at last, Freddy Malins stood up and, capturing Aunt Kate, plumped her down on her chair amid general laughter.

When everyone had been well served Gabriel said, smiling:

—Now, if anyone wants a little more of what vulgar people call stuffing let him or her speak.

A chorus of voices invited him to begin his own supper and Lily came forward with three potatoes which she had reserved for him.

—Very well, said Gabriel amiably, as he took another preparatory draught, kindly forget my existence, ladies and gentlemen, for a few minutes.

He set to his supper and took no part in the conversation with which the table covered Lily's removal of the plates. The subject of talk was the opera company which was then at the Theatre Royal. Mr Bartell D'Arcy, the tenor, a dark-complexioned young man with a smart moustache, praised very highly the leading contralto of the company but Miss Furlong thought she had a rather vulgar style of production. Freddy Malins said there was a negro chieftain singing in the second part of the Gaiety pantomime who had one of the finest tenor voices he had ever heard.

—Have you heard him? he asked Mr Bartell D'Arcy across the table.

—No, answered Mr Bartell D'Arcy carelessly.

—Because, Freddy Malins explained, now I'd be curious to hear your opinion of him. I think he has a grand voice.

—It takes Freddy to find out the really good things, said Mr Browne familiarly to the table.

—And why couldn't he have a voice too? asked Freddy Malins sharply. Is it because he's only a black?

Nobody answered this question and Mary Jane led the table back to the legitimate opera. One of her pupils had given her a pass for *Mignon.* Of course it was very fine, she said, but it made her think of poor Georgina Burns. Mr Browne could go back farther still, to the old Italian companies that used to come to Dublin—Tietjens, Ilma de Murzka, Campanini, the great Trebelli, Giuglini, Ravelli, Aramburo. Those were the days, he said, when there was something like singing to be heard in Dublin. He told too of how the top gallery of the old Royal used to be packed night after night, of how one night an Italian tenor had sung five encores to *Let Me Like a Soldier Fall,* introducing a high C every time, and of how the gallery boys would sometimes in their enthusiasm unyoke the horses from the carriage of some great *prima donna* and pull her themselves through the streets to her hotel. Why did they never play the grand old operas now, he asked, *Dinorah, Lucrezia Borgia?* Because they could not get the voices to sing them: that was why.

—O, well, said Mr Bartell D'Arcy, I presume there are as good singers to-day as there were then.

—Where are they? asked Mr Browne defiantly.

—In London, Paris, Milan, said Mr Bartell D'Arcy warmly. I suppose Caruso, for example, is quite as good, if not better than any of the men you have mentioned.

—Maybe so, said Mr Browne. But I may tell you I doubt it strongly.

—O, I'd give anything to hear Caruso sing, said Mary Jane.

—For me, said Aunt Kate, who had been picking a bone, there was only one tenor. To please me, I mean. But I suppose none of you ever heard of him.

—Who was he, Miss Morkan? asked Mr Bartell D'Arcy politely.

—His name, said Aunt Kate, was Parkinson. I heard him when he was in his prime and I think he had then the purest tenor voice that was ever put into a man's throat.

—Strange, said Mr Bartell D'Arcy. I never even heard of him.

—Yes, yes, Miss Morkan is right, said Mr Browne. I remember hearing of old Parkinson but he's too far back for me.

—A beautiful pure sweet mellow English tenor, said Aunt Kate with enthusiasm.

Gabriel having finished, the huge pudding was transferred to the table. The clatter of forks and spoons began again. Gabriel's wife served out spoonfuls of the pudding and passed the plates down the table. Midway down they were held up by Mary Jane, who replenished them with raspberry or orange jelly or with blancmange and jam. The pudding was of Aunt Julia's making and she received praises for it from all quarters. She herself said that it was not quite brown enough.

—Well, I hope, Miss Morkan, said Mr Browne, that I'm brown enough for you because, you know, I'm all brown.

All the gentlemen, except Gabriel, ate some of the pudding out of compliment to Aunt Julia. As Gabriel never ate sweets the celery had been left for him. Freddy Malins also took a stalk of celery and ate it with his pudding. He had been told that celery was a capital thing for the blood and he was just then under doctor's care. Mrs Malins, who had been silent all through the supper, said that her son was going down to Mount Melleray in a week or so. The table then spoke of Mount Melleray, how bracing the air was down there, how hospitable the monks were and how they never asked for a penny-piece from their guests.

—And do you mean to say, asked Mr Browne incredulously, that a chap can go down there and put up there as if it were a hotel and live on the fat of the land and then come away without paying a farthing?

—O, most people give some donation to the monastery when they leave, said Mary Jane.

—I wish we had an institution like that in our Church, said Mr Browne candidly.

He was astonished to hear that the monks never spoke, got up at two in the morning and slept in their coffins. He asked what they did it for.

—That's the rule of the order, said Aunt Kate firmly.

—Yes, but why? asked Mr Browne.

Aunt Kate repeated that it was the rule, that was all. Mr Browne still seemed not to understand. Freddy Malins explained to him, as best he could, that the monks were trying to make up for the sins committed by all the sinners in the outside world. The explanation was not very clear for Mr Browne grinned and said:

—I like that idea very much but wouldn't a comfortable spring bed do them as well as a coffin?

—The coffin, said Mary Jane, is to remind them of their last end.

As the subject had grown lugubrious it was buried in a silence of the table during which Mrs Malins could be heard saying to her neighbour in an indistinct undertone:

—They are very good men, the monks, very pious men.

The raisins and almonds and figs and apples and oranges and chocolates and sweets were now passed about the table and Aunt Julia invited all the guests to have either port or sherry. At first Mr Bartell D'Arcy refused to take either but one of his neighbours nudged him and whispered something to him upon which he allowed his glass to be filled. Gradually as the last glasses were being filled the conversation ceased. A pause followed, broken only by the noise of the wine and by unsettlings of chairs. The Misses Morkan, all three, looked down at the tablecloth. Someone coughed once or twice and then a few gentlemen patted the table gently as a signal for silence. The silence came and Gabriel pushed back his chair and stood up.

The patting at once grew louder in encouragement and then ceased altogether. Gabriel leaned his ten trembling fingers on the tablecloth and smiled nervously at the company. Meeting a row of upturned faces he raised his eyes to the chandelier. The piano was playing a waltz tune and he could hear the skirts sweeping against the drawing-room door. People, perhaps, were standing in the snow on the quay outside, gazing up at the lighted windows and listening to the waltz music. The air was pure there. In the distance lay the park where the trees were weighted with snow. The Wellington Monument wore a gleaming cap of snow that flashed westward over the white field of Fifteen Acres.

He began:

—Ladies and Gentlemen.

—It has fallen to my lot this evening, as in years past, to perform a very pleasing task but a task for which I am afraid my poor powers as a speaker are all too inadequate.

—No, no! said Mr Browne.

—But, however that may be, I can only ask you to-night to take the will for the deed and to lend me your attention for a few moments while I endeavour to express to you in words what my feelings are on this occasion.

—Ladies and Gentlemen. It is not the first time that we have gathered together under this hospitable roof, around this hospitable board. It is not the first time that we have been the recipients—or perhaps, I had better say, the victims—of the hospitality of certain good ladies.

He made a circle in the air with his arm and paused. Everyone laughed or smiled at Aunt Kate and Aunt Julia and Mary Jane who all turned crimson with pleasure. Gabriel went on more boldly:

—I feel more strongly with every recurring year that our country has no tradition which does it so much honour and which it should guard so jealously as that of its hospitality. It is a tradition that is unique as far as my experience goes (and I have visited not a few places abroad) among the modern nations. Some would say, perhaps, that with us it is rather a failing than anything to be boasted of. But granted even that, it is, to my mind, a princely failing, and one that I trust will long be cultivated among us. Of one thing, at least, I am sure. As long as this one roof shelters the good ladies aforesaid—and I wish from my heart it may do so for many and many a long year to come—the tradition of genuine warm-hearted courteous Irish hospitality, which our forefathers have handed down to us and which we in turn must hand down to our descendants, is still alive among us.

A hearty murmur of assent ran round the table. It shot through Gabriel's mind that Miss Ivors was not there and that she had gone away discourteously: and he said with confidence in himself:

—Ladies and Gentlemen.

—A new generation is growing up in our midst, a generation actuated by new ideas and new principles. It is serious and enthusiastic for these new ideas and its enthusiasm, even when it is misdirected, is, I believe, in the main sincere. But we are living in a sceptical and, if I may use the phrase, a thought-tormented age: and sometimes I fear that this new generation, educated or hypereducated as it is, will lack those qualities of humanity, of hospitality, of kindly humour which belonged to an older day. Listening to-night to the names of all those great singers of the past it seemed to me, I must confess, that we were living in a less spacious age. Those days might, without exaggeration, be called spacious days: and if they are gone beyond recall let us hope, at least, that in gatherings such as this we shall still speak of them with pride and affection, still cherish in our hearts the memory of those dead and gone great ones whose fame the world will not willingly let die.

—Hear, hear! said Mr Browne loudly.

—But yet, continued Gabriel, his voice falling into a softer inflection, there are always in gatherings such as this sadder thoughts that will recur to our minds: thoughts of the past, of youth, of changes, of absent faces that we miss here tonight. Our path through life is strewn with many such sad memories: and were we to brood upon them always we could not find the heart to go on bravely with our work among the living. We have all of us living duties and living affections which claim, and rightly claim, our strenuous endeavours.

—Therefore, I will not linger on the past. I will not let any gloomy moralising intrude upon us here to-night. Here we are gathered together for a brief moment from the bustle and rush of our everyday routine. We are met here as friends, in the spirit of good-fellowship, as colleagues, also to a certain extent, in the true spirit of *camaraderie,* and as the guests of—what shall I call them?—The Three Graces[11] of the Dublin musical world.

The table burst into applause and laughter at this sally. Aunt Julia vainly asked each of her neighbours in turn to tell her what Gabriel had said.

—He says we are the Three Graces, Aunt Julia, said Mary Jane.

Aunt Julia did not understand but she looked up, smiling, at Gabriel, who continued in the same vein:

—Ladies and Gentlemen.

—I will not attempt to play to-night the part that Paris[12] played on another occasion. I will not attempt to choose between them. The task would be an invidious one and one beyond my poor powers. For when I view them in turn, whether it be our chief hostess herself, whose good heart, whose too good heart, has become a byword with all who know her, or her sister, who seems to be gifted with perennial youth and whose singing must have been a surprise and a revelation to us all to-night, or, last but not least, when I consider our youngest hostess, talented, cheerful, hard-working and the best of nieces, I confess, Ladies and Gentlemen, that I do not know to which of them I should award the prize.

Gabriel glanced down at his aunts and, seeing the large smile on Aunt Julia's face and the tears which had risen to Aunt Kate's eyes, hastened to his close. He raised his glass of port gallantly, while every member of the company fingered a glass expectantly, and said loudly:

---

[11]In Greek myth, three sister goddesses who embodied and dispensed beauty, charm, and grace.
[12]The Greek prince who judged the beauty of the three goddesses Hera, Athena, and Aphrodite, before he eloped with Helen of Troy.

—Let us toast them all three together. Let us drink to their health, wealth, long life, happiness and prosperity and may they long continue to hold the proud and self-won position which they hold in their profession and the position of honour and affection which they hold in our hearts.

All the guests stood up, glass in hand, and, turning towards the three seated ladies, sang in unison, with Mr Browne as leader:

> *For they are jolly gay fellows,*
> *For they are jolly gay fellows,*
> *For they are jolly gay fellows,*
> *Which nobody can deny.*

Aunt Kate was making frank use of her handkerchief and even Aunt Julia seemed moved. Freddy Malins beat time with his pudding-fork and the singers turned towards one another, as if in melodious conference, while they sang, with emphasis:

> *Unless he tells a lie,*
> *Unless he tells a lie.*

Then, turning once more towards their hostesses, they sang:

> *For they are jolly gay fellows,*
> *For they are jolly gay fellows,*
> *For they are jolly gay fellows,*
> *Which nobody can deny.*

The acclamation which followed was taken up beyond the door of the supper-room by many of the other guests and renewed time after time, Freddy Malins acting as officer with his fork on high.

The piercing morning air came into the hall where they were standing so that Aunt Kate said:

—Close the door, somebody. Mrs Malins will get her death of cold.

—Browne is out there, Aunt Kate, said Mary Jane.

—Browne is everywhere, said Aunt Kate, lowering her voice. Mary Jane laughed at her tone.

—Really, she said archly, he is very attentive.

—He has been laid on here like the gas, said Aunt Kate in the same tone, all during the Christmas.

She laughed herself this time good-humouredly and then added quickly:

—But tell him to come in, Mary Jane, and close the door. I hope to goodness he didn't hear me.

At that moment the hall-door was opened and Mr Browne came in from the doorstep, laughing as if his heart would break. He was dressed in a long green overcoat with mock astrakhan cuffs and collar and wore on his head an oval fur cap. He pointed down the snow-covered quay from where the sound of shrill prolonged whistling was borne in.

—Freddy will have all the cabs in Dublin out, he said.

Gabriel advanced from the little pantry behind the office, struggling into his overcoat and, looking round the hall, said:

—Gretta not down yet?

—She's getting on her things, Gabriel, said Aunt Kate.

—Who's playing up there? asked Gabriel.

—Nobody. They're all gone.

—O no, Aunt Kate, said Mary Jane. Bartell D'Arcy and Miss O'Callaghan aren't gone yet.

—Someone is strumming at the piano, anyhow, said Gabriel.

Mary Jane glanced at Gabriel and Mr Browne and said with a shiver:

—It makes me feel cold to look at you two gentlemen muffled up like that. I wouldn't like to face your journey home at this hour.

—I'd like nothing better this minute, said Mr Browne stoutly, than a rattling fine walk in the country or a fast drive with a good spanking goer between the shafts.

We used to have a very good horse and trap at home, said Aunt Julia sadly.

—The never-to-be-forgotten Johnny, said Mary Jane, laughing.

Aunt Kate and Gabriel laughed too.

—Why, what was wonderful about Johnny? asked Mr Browne.

—The late lamented Patrick Morkan, our grandfather, that is, explained Gabriel, commonly known in his later years as the old gentleman, was a glue-boiler.

—O, now, Gabriel, said Aunt Kate, laughing, he had a starch mill.

—Well, glue or starch, said Gabriel, the old gentleman had a horse by the name of Johnny. And Johnny used to work in the old gentleman's mill, walking round and round in order to drive the mill. That was all very well; but now comes the tragic part about Johnny. One fine day the old gentleman thought he'd like to drive out with the quality to a military review in the park.

—The Lord have mercy on his soul, said Aunt Kate compassionately.

—Amen, said Gabriel. So the old Gentleman, as I said, harnessed Johnny and put on his very best tall hat and his very best stock collar and drove out in grand style from his ancestral mansion somewhere near Back Lane, I think.

Everyone laughed, even Mrs Malins, at Gabriel's manner and Aunt Kate said:

—O now, Gabriel, he didn't live in Back Lane, really. Only the mill was there.

—Out from the mansion of his forefathers, continued Gabriel, he drove with Johnny. And everything went on beautifully until Johnny came in sight of King Billy's statue: and whether he fell in love with the horse King Billy sits on or whether he thought he was back again in the mill, anyhow he began to walk round the statue.

Gabriel paced in a circle round the hall in his goloshes amid the laughter of the others.

—Round and round he went, said Gabriel, and the old gentleman, who was a very pompous old gentleman, was highly indignant. *Go on, sir! What do you mean, sir? Johnny! Johnny! Most extraordinary conduct! Can't understand the horse!*

The peals of laughter which followed Gabriel's imitation of the incident were interrupted by a resounding knock at the hall-door. Mary Jane ran to open it and let in Freddy Malins. Freddy Malins, with his hat well back on his head and his shoulders humped with cold, was puffing and steaming after his exertions.

—I could only get one cab, he said.

—O, we'll find another along the quay, said Gabriel.

—Yes, said Aunt Kate. Better not keep Mrs Malins standing in the draught.

Mrs Malins was helped down the front steps by her son and Mr Browne and, after many manœuvres, hoisted into the cab. Freddy Malins clambered in after her and spent a long time settling her on the seat, Mr Browne helping him with advice. At last she was settled comfortably and Freddy Malins invited Mr Browne into the cab. There was a good deal of confused talk, and then Mr Browne got into the cab. The cabman settled his rug over his knees, and bent down for the address. The confusion grew greater and the cabman was directed differently by Freddy Malins and Mr Browne, each of whom had his head out through a window of the cab. The difficulty was to know where to drop Mr Browne along the route and Aunt Kate, Aunt Julia and Mary Jane helped the discussion from the doorstep with cross-directions and contradictions and abundance of laughter. As for Freddy Malins he was speechless with laughter. He popped his head in and out of the window every moment, to the great danger of his hat, and told his mother how the discussion was progressing till at last Mr Browne shouted to the bewildered cabman above the din of everybody's laughter:

—Do you know Trinity College?

—Yes, sir, said the cabman.

—Well, drive bang up against Trinity College gates, said Mr Browne, and then we'll tell you where to go. You understand now?

—Yes, sir, said the cabman.

—Make like a bird for Trinity College.

—Right, sir, cried the cabman.

The horse was whipped up and the cab rattled off along the quay amid a chorus of laughter and adieus.

Gabriel had not gone to the door with the others. He was in a dark part of the hall gazing up the staircase. A woman was standing near the top of the first flight, in the shadow also. He could not see her face but he could see the terracotta and salmonpink panels of her skirt which the shadow made appear black and white. It was his wife. She was leaning on the banisters, listening to something. Gabriel was surprised at her stillness and strained his ear to listen also. But he could hear little save the noise of laughter and dispute on the front steps, a few chords struck on the piano and a few notes of a man's voice singing.

He stood still in the gloom of the hall, trying to catch the air that the voice was singing and gazing up at his wife. There was grace and mystery in her attitude as if she were a symbol of something. He asked himself what is a woman standing on the stairs in the shadow, listening to distant music, a symbol of. If he were a painter he would paint her in that attitude. Her blue felt hat would show off the bronze of her hair against the darkness and the dark panels of her shirt would show off the light ones. *Distant Music* he would call the picture if he were a painter.

The hall-door was closed; and Aunt Kate, Aunt Julia and Mary Jane came down the hall, still laughing.

—Well, isn't Freddy terrible? said Mary Jane. He's really terrible.

Gabriel said nothing but pointed up the stairs towards where his wife was standing. Now that the hall-door was closed the voice and the piano could be heard more clearly. Gabriel held up his hand for them to be silent. The song seemed to be in the old Irish tonality and the singer seemed uncertain both of his words and of his voice. The voice, made plaintive by distance and by the singer's hoarseness, faintly illuminated the cadence of the air with words expressing grief:

> O, the rain falls on my heavy locks
> And the dew wets my skin,
> My babe lies cold . . .

—O, exclaimed Mary Jane. It's Bartell D'Arcy singing and he wouldn't sing all the night. O, I'll get him to sing a song before he goes.

—O do, Mary Jane, said Aunt Kate.

Mary Jane brushed past the others and ran to the staircase but before she reached it the singing stopped and the piano was closed abruptly.

—O, what a pity! she cried. Is he coming down, Gretta?

Gabriel heard his wife answer yes and saw her come down towards them. A few steps behind her were Mr Bartell D'Arcy and Miss O'Callaghan.

—O, Mr D'Arcy, cried Mary Jane, it's downright mean of you to break off like that when we were all in raptures listening to you.

—I have been at him all the evening, said Miss O'Callaghan, and Mrs Conroy too and he told us he had a dreadful cold and couldn't sing.

—O, Mr D'Arcy, said Aunt Kate, now that was a great fib to tell.

—Can't you see that I'm as hoarse as a crow? said Mr D'Arcy roughly.

He went into the pantry hastily and put on his overcoat. The others, taken aback by his rude speech, could find nothing to say. Aunt Kate wrinkled her brows and made signs to the others to drop the subject. Mr D'Arcy stood swathing his neck carefully and frowning.

—It's the weather, said Aunt Julia, after a pause.

—Yes, everybody has colds, said Aunt Kate readily, everybody.

—They say, said Mary Jane, we haven't had snow like it for thirty years; and I read this morning in the newspapers that the snow is general all over Ireland.

—I love the look of snow, said Aunt Julia sadly.

—So do I, said Miss O'Callaghan. I think Christmas is never really Christmas unless we have the snow on the ground.

—But poor Mr D'Arcy doesn't like the snow, said Aunt Kate, smiling.

Mr D'Arcy came from the pantry, fully swathed and buttoned, and in a repentant tone told them the history of his cold. Everyone gave him advice and said it was a great pity and urged him to be very careful of his throat in the night air. Gabriel watched his wife who did not join in the conversation. She was standing right under the dusty fanlight and the flame of the gas lit up the rich bronze of her hair which he had seen her drying at the fire a few days before. She was in the same attitude and seemed unaware of the talk about her. At last she turned towards them and Gabriel saw that there was colour on her cheeks and that her eyes were shining. A sudden tide of joy went leaping out of his heart.

—Mr D'Arcy, she said, what is the name of that song you were singing?

—It's called *The Lass of Aughrim,* said Mr D'Arcy, but I couldn't remember it properly. Why? Do you know it?

—*The Lass of Aughrim,* she repeated. I couldn't think of the name.

—It's a very nice air, said Mary Jane. I'm sorry you were not in voice to-night.

—Now, Mary Jane, said Aunt Kate, don't annoy Mr D'Arcy. I won't have him annoyed.

Seeing that all were ready to start she shepherded them to the door where good-night was said:

—Well, good-night, Aunt Kate, and thanks for the pleasant evening.

—Good-night, Gabriel. Good-night, Gretta!

—Good-night, Aunt Kate, and thanks ever so much. Good-night, Aunt Julia.

—O, good-night, Gretta, I didn't see you.

—Good-night, Mr D'Arcy. Good-night, Miss O'Callaghan.

—Good-night, Miss Morkan.

—Good-night, again.

—Good-night, all. Safe home.

—Good-night. Good-night.

The morning was still dark. A dull yellow light brooded over the houses and the river; and the sky seemed to be descending. It was slushy underfoot; and only streaks and patches of snow lay on the roofs, on the parapets of the quay and on the area railings. The lamps were still burning redly in the murky air and, across the river, the palace of the Four Courts stood out menacingly against the heavy sky.

She was walking on before him with Mr Bartell D'Arcy, her shoes in a brown parcel tucked under one arm and her hands holding her skirt up from the slush. She had no longer any grace of attitude but Gabriel's eyes were still bright with happiness. The blood went bounding along his veins; and the thoughts went rioting through his brain, proud, joyful, tender, valorous.

She was walking on before him so lightly and so erect that he longed to run after her noiselessly, catch her by the shoulders and say something foolish and affectionate into her ear. She seemed to him so frail that he longed to defend her against something and then to be alone with her. Moments of their secret life together burst like stars upon his memory. A heliotrope envelope was lying beside his breakfast-cup and he was caressing it with his hand. Birds were twittering in the ivy and the sunny web of the curtain was shimmering along the floor: he could not eat for happiness. They were standing on the crowded platform and he was placing a ticket inside the warm palm of her glove. He was standing with her in the cold, looking in through a grated window at a man making bottles in a roaring furnace. It was very cold. Her face, fragrant in the cold air, was quite close to his; and suddenly she called out to the man at the furnace:

—Is the fire hot, sir?

But the man could not hear her with the noise of the furnace. It was just as well. He might have answered rudely.

A wave of yet more tender joy escaped from his heart and went coursing in warm flood along his arteries. Like the tender fires of stars moments of their life together, that no one knew of or would ever know of, broke upon and illumined his memory. He longed to recall to her those moments, to make her forget the years of their dull existence together and remember only their moments of ecstasy. For the years, he felt, had not quenched his soul or hers. Their children, his writing, her household cares had not quenched all their souls' tender fire. In one letter that he had written to her then he had said: *Why is it that words like these seem to me so dull and cold? Is it because there is no word tender enough to be your name?*

Like distant music these words that he had written years before were borne towards him from the past. He longed to be alone with her. When the others had gone away, when he and she were in their room in the hotel, then they would be alone together. He would call her softly:

—Gretta!

Perhaps she would not hear at once: she would be undressing. Then something in his voice would strike her. She would turn and look at him. . . .

At the corner of Winetavern Street they met a cab. He was glad of its rattling noise as it saved him from conversation. She was looking out of the window and seemed tired. The others spoke only a few words, pointing out some building or street. The horse galloped along wearily under the murky morning sky, dragging his old rattling box after his heels, and Gabriel was again in a cab with her, galloping to catch the boat, galloping to their honeymoon.

As the cab drove across O'Connell Bridge Miss O'Callaghan said:

—They say you never cross O'Connell Bridge without seeing a white horse.

—I see a white man this time, said Gabriel.

—Where? asked Mr Bartell D'Arcy.

Gabriel pointed to the statue, on which lay patches of snow. Then he nodded familiarly to it and waved his hand.

—Good-night, Dan, he said gaily.

When the cab drew up before the hotel Gabriel jumped out and, in spite of Mr Bartell D'Arcy's protest, paid the driver. He gave the man a shilling over his fare. The man saluted and said:

—A prosperous New Year to you, sir.

—The same to you, said Gabriel cordially.

She leaned for a moment on his arm in getting out of the cab and while standing at the curbstone, bidding the others good-night. She leaned lightly on his arm, as lightly as when she had danced with him a few hours before. He had felt proud and happy then, happy that she was his, proud of her grace and wifely carriage. But now, after the kindling again of so many memories, the first touch of her body, musical and strange and perfumed, sent through him a keen pang of lust. Under cover of her silence he pressed her arm closely to his side; and, as they stood at the hotel door, he felt that they had escaped from their lives and duties, escaped from home and friends and run away together with wild and radiant hearts to a new adventure.

An old man was dozing in a great hooded chair in the hall. He lit a candle in the office and went before them to the stairs. They followed him in silence, their feet falling in soft thuds on the thickly carpeted stairs. She mounted the stairs behind the porter, her head bowed in the ascent, her frail shoulders curved as with a burden, her skirt girt tightly about her. He could have flung his arms about her hips and held her still for his arms were trembling with desire to seize her and only the stress of his nails against the palms of his hands held the wild impulse of his body in check. The porter halted on the stairs to settle his guttering candle. They halted too on the steps below him. In the silence Gabriel could hear the falling of the molten wax into the tray and the thumping of his own heart against his ribs.

The porter led them along a corridor and opened a door. Then he set his unstable candle down on a toilet-table and asked at what hour they were to be called in the morning.

—Eight, said Gabriel.

The porter pointed to the tap of the electric-light and began a muttered apology but Gabriel cut him short.

—We don't want any light. We have light enough from the street. And I say, he added, pointing to the candle, you might remove that handsome article, like a good man.

The porter took up his candle again, but slowly for he was surprised by such a novel idea. Then he mumbled good-night and went out. Gabriel shot the lock to.

A ghostly light from the street lamp lay in a long shaft from one window to the door. Gabriel threw his overcoat and hat on a couch and crossed the room towards the window. He looked down into the street in order that his emotion might calm a little. Then he turned and leaned against a chest of drawers with his back to the light. She had taken off her hat and cloak and was standing before a large swinging mirror, unhooking her waist. Gabriel paused for a few moments, watching her, and then said:

—Gretta!

She turned away from the mirror slowly and walked along the shaft of light towards him. Her face looked so serious and weary that the words would not pass Gabriel's lips. No, it was not the moment yet.

—You looked tired, he said.

—I am a little, she answered.

—You don't feel ill or weak?

—No, tired: that's all.

She went on to the window and stood there, looking out. Gabriel waited again and then, fearing that diffidence was about to conquer him, he said abruptly:

—By the way, Gretta!

—What is it?

—You know that poor fellow Malins? he said quickly.

—Yes. What about him?

—Well, poor fellow, he's a decent sort of chap after all, continued Gabriel in a false voice. He gave me back that sovereign I lent him and I didn't expect it really. It's a pity he wouldn't keep away from that Browne, because he's not a bad fellow at heart.

He was trembling now with annoyance. Why did she seem so abstracted? He did not know how he could begin. Was she annoyed, too, about something? If she would only turn to him or come to him of her own accord! To take her as she was would be brutal. No, he must see some ardour in her eyes first. He longed to be master of her strange mood.

—When did you lend him the pound? she asked, after a pause.

Gabriel strove to restrain himself from breaking out into brutal language about the sottish Malins and his pound. He longed to cry to her from his soul, to crush her body against his, to overmaster her. But he said:

—O, at Christmas, when he opened that little Christmas-card shop in Henry Street.

He was in such a fever of rage and desire that he did not hear her come from the window. She stood before him for an instant, looking at him strangely. Then, suddenly raising herself on tiptoe and resting her hands lightly on his shoulders, she kissed him.

—You are a very generous person, Gabriel, she said.

Gabriel, trembling with delight at her sudden kiss and at the quaintness of her phrase, put his hands on her hair and began smoothing it back, scarcely touching it with his fingers. The washing had made it fine and brilliant. His heart was brimming over with happiness. Just when he was wishing for it she had come to him of her own accord. Perhaps her thoughts had been running with his. Perhaps she had felt the impetuous desire that was in him and then the yielding mood had come upon her. Now that she had fallen to him so easily he wondered why he had been so diffident.

He stood, holding her head between his hands. Then, slipping one arm swiftly about her body and drawing her towards him, he said softly:

—Gretta dear, what are you thinking about?

She did not answer nor yield wholly to his arm. He said again, softly:

—Tell me what it is, Gretta. I think I know what is the matter. Do I know?

She did not answer at once. Then she said in an outburst of tears:

—O, I am thinking about that song. *The Lass of Aughrim.*

She broke loose from him and ran to the bed and, throwing her arms across the bed-rail, hid her face. Gabriel stood stockstill for a moment in astonishment and then followed her. As he passed in the way of the cheval-glass he caught sight of himself in full length, his broad, well-filled shirt-front, the face whose expression always puzzled him when he saw it in a mirror and his glimmering gilt-rimmed eyeglasses. He halted a few paces from her and said:

—What about the song? Why does that make you cry?

She raised her head from her arms and dried her eyes with the back of her hand like a child. A kinder note than he had intended went into his voice.

—Why, Gretta? he asked.

—I am thinking about a person long ago who used to sing that song.

—And who was the person long ago? asked Gabriel, smiling.

—It was a person I used to know in Galway when I was living with my grandmother, she said.

The smile passed away from Gabriel's face. A dull anger began to gather again at the back of his mind and the dull fires of his lust began to glow angrily in his veins.

—Someone you were in love with? he asked ironically.

—It was a young boy I used to know, she answered, named Michael Furey. He used to sing that song, *The Lass of Aughrim*. He was very delicate.

Gabriel was silent. He did not wish her to think that he was interested in this delicate boy.

—I can see him so plainly, she said after a moment. Such eyes as he had: big dark eyes! And such an expression in them—an expression!

—O then, you were in love with him? said Gabriel.

—I used to go out walking with him, she said, when I was in Galway.

A thought flew across Gabriel's mind.

—Perhaps that was why you wanted to go to Galway with that Ivors girl? he said coldly.

She looked at him and asked in surprise:

—What for?

Her eyes made Gabriel feel awkward. He shrugged his shoulders and said:

—How do I know? To see him perhaps.

She looked away from him along the shaft of light towards the window in silence.

—He is dead, she said at length. He died when he was only seventeen. Isn't it a terrible thing to die so young as that?

—What was he? asked Gabriel, still ironically.

—He was in the gasworks, she said.

Gabriel felt humiliated by the failure of his irony and by the evocation of this figure from the dead, a boy in the gasworks. While he had been full of memories of their secret life together, full of tenderness and joy and desire, she had been comparing him in her mind with another. A shameful consciousness of his own person assailed him. He saw himself as a ludicrous figure, acting as a pennyboy for his aunts, a nervous well-meaning sentimentalist, orating to vulgarians and idealising his own clownish lusts, the pitiable fatuous fellow he had caught a glimpse of in the mirror. Instinctively he turned his back more to the light lest she might see the shame that burned upon his forehead.

He tried to keep up his tone of cold interrogation but his voice when he spoke was humble and indifferent.

—I suppose you were in love with this Michael Furey, Gretta, he said.

—I was great with him at that time, she said.

Her voice was veiled and sad. Gabriel, feeling now how vain it would be to try to lead her whither he had purposed, caressed one of her hands and said, also sadly:

—And what did he die of so young, Gretta? Consumption, was it?

—I think he died for me, she answered.

A vague terror seized Gabriel at this answer as if, at that hour when he had hoped to triumph, some impalpable and vindictive being was coming against him, gathering forces against him in its vague world. But he shook himself free of it with an effort of reason and continued to caress her hand. He did not question her again for he felt that she would tell him of herself. Her hand was warm and moist: it did not respond to his touch but he continued to caress it just as he had caressed her first letter to him that spring morning.

—It was in the winter, she said, about the beginning of the winter when I was going to leave my grandmother's and come up here to the convent. And he was ill at the time in his lodgings in Galway and wouldn't be let out and his people in Oughterard were written to. He was in decline, they said, or something like that. I never knew rightly.

She paused for a moment and sighed.

—Poor fellow, she said. He was very fond of me and he was such a gentle boy. We used to go out together, walking, you know, Gabriel, like the way they do in the country. He was going to study singing only for his health. He had a very good voice, poor Michael Furey.

—Well; and then? asked Gabriel.

—And then when it came to the time for me to leave Galway and come up to the convent he was much worse and I wouldn't be let see him so I wrote a letter saying I was going up to Dublin and would be back in the summer and hoping he would be better then.

She paused for a moment to get her voice under control and then went on:

—Then the night before I left I was in my grandmother's house in Nuns' Island, packing up, and I heard gravel thrown up against my window. The window was so wet I couldn't see so I ran downstairs as I was and slipped out the back into the garden and there was the poor fellow at the end of the garden, shivering.

—And did you not tell him to go back? asked Gabriel.

I implored of him to go home at once and told him he would get his death in the rain. But he said he did not want to live. I can see his eyes as well as well! He was standing at the end of the wall where there was a tree.

—And did he go home? asked Gabriel.

—Yes, he went home. And when I was only a week in the convent he died and he was buried in Oughterard where his people came from. O, the day I heard that, that he was dead!

She stopped, choking with sobs, and, overcome by emotion, flung herself face downward on the bed, sobbing in the quilt. Gabriel held her hand for a moment longer, irresolutely, and then, shy of intruding on her grief, let it fall gently and walked quietly to the window.

She was fast asleep.

Gabriel, leaning on his elbow, looked for a few moments unresentfully on her tangled hair and half-open mouth, listening to her deep-drawn breath. So she had had that romance in her life: a man had died for her sake. It hardly pained him now to think how poor a part he, her husband, had played in her life. He watched her while she slept as though he and she had never lived together as man and wife. His curious eyes rested long upon her face and on her hair: and, as he thought of what she must have been then, in that time of her first girlish beauty, a strange friendly pity for her entered his soul. He did not like to say even to himself that her face was no longer beautiful but he knew that it was no longer the face for which Michael Furey had braved death.

Perhaps she had not told him all the story. His eyes moved to the chair over which she had thrown some of her clothes. A petticoat string dangled to the floor. One boot stood upright, its limp upper fallen down: the fellow of it lay upon its side. He wondered at his riot of emotions of an hour before. From what had it proceeded? From his aunt's supper, from his own foolish speech, from the wine and dancing, the merrymaking when saying good-night in the hall, the pleasure of the walk along the river in the snow. Poor Aunt Julia! She, too, would soon be a shade with the shade of Patrick Morkan and his horse. He had caught that haggard look upon her face for a moment when she was singing *Arrayed for the Bridal*. Soon, perhaps, he would be sitting in that same drawing-room, dressed in black, his silk hat on his knees. The blinds would be drawn down and Aunt Kate would be sitting beside him, crying and blowing her nose and telling him how Julia had died. He would cast about in his mind for some words that might console her, and would find only lame and useless ones. Yes, yes: that would happen very soon.

The air of the room chilled his shoulders. He stretched himself cautiously along under the sheets and lay down beside his wife. One by one they were all becoming shades. Better pass boldly into that other world, in the full glory of some passion, than fade and wither dismally with age. He thought of how she who lay beside him had locked in her heart for so many years that image of her lover's eyes when he had told her that he did not wish to live.

Generous tears filled Gabriel's eyes. He had never felt like that himself towards any woman but he knew that such a feeling must be love. The tears gathered more thickly in his eyes and in the partial darkness he imagined he saw the form of a young man standing under a dripping tree. Other forms were near. His soul had approached that region where dwell the vast hosts of the dead. He was conscious of, but could not apprehend, their wayward and flickering existence. His own identity was fading out into a grey impalpable world: the solid world itself which these dead had one time reared and lived in was dissolving and dwindling.

A few light taps upon the pane made him turn to the window. It had begun to snow again. He watched sleepily the flakes, silver and dark, falling obliquely against the lamplight. The time had come for him to set out on his journey westward. Yes, the newspapers were right: snow was general all over Ireland. It was falling on every part of the dark central plain, on the treeless hills, falling softly upon the Bog of Allen and, farther westward, softly falling into the dark mutinous Shannon waves. It was falling, too, upon every part of the lonely churchyard on the hill where Michael Furey lay buried. It lay thickly drifted on the crooked crosses and headstones, on the spears of the little gate, on the barren thorns. His soul swooned slowly as he heard the snow falling faintly through the universe and faintly falling, like the descent of their last end, upon all the living and the dead.

QUESTIONS

1. What do you sense is the atmosphere of the Misses Morkan's annual dance? What details of the setting evoke the strongest responses?
2. How does the narrative focus upon Gabriel Conroy influence your sense of the "great affair"?
3. What sense do you have of Gabriel, from his thoughts, conversation, and behavior at the party?
4. As you read the final scenes between Gabriel and Gretta, did you recall details from earlier in the story?
5. In those final scenes after the party, what more do you learn about Gabriel? Do you respond differently to him now than earlier?
6. What is the most important thing that happens in the story?

William Faulkner (1897–1962)

BARN BURNING

The store in which the Justice of the Peace's court was sitting smelled of cheese. The boy, crouched on his nail keg at the back of the crowded room, knew he smelled cheese, and more: from where he sat he could see the ranked shelves close-packed with the solid, squat, dynamic shapes of tin cans whose labels his stomach read, not from the lettering which meant nothing to his mind but from the scarlet devils and the silver curve of fish—this, the cheese which he knew he smelled and the hermetic meat which his intestines believed he smelled coming in intermittent gusts momentary and brief between the other constant one, the smell and sense just a little of fear because mostly of despair and grief, the old fierce pull of blood. He could not see the table where the Justice sat and before which his father and his father's enemy (*our enemy* he thought in that despair;

ourn! mine and hisn both! He's my father!) stood, but he could hear them, the two of them that is, because his father had said no word yet:

"But what proof have you, Mr. Harris?"

"I told you. The hog got into my corn. I caught it up and sent it back to him. He had no fence that would hold it. I told him so, warned him. The next time I put the hog in my pen. When he came to get it I gave him enough wire to patch up his pen. The next time I put the hog up and kept it. I rode down to his house and saw the wire I gave him still rolled on to the spool in his yard. I told him he could have the hog when he paid me a dollar pound fee. That evening a nigger came with the dollar and got the hog. He was a strange nigger. He said, 'He say to tell you wood and hay kin burn.' I said, 'What?' 'That whut he say to tell you,' the nigger said. 'Wood and hay kin burn.' That night my barn burned. I got the stock out but I lost the barn."

"Where is the nigger? Have you got him?"

"He was a strange nigger, I tell you. I don't know what became of him."

"But that's not proof. Don't you see that's not proof?"

"Get that boy up here. He knows." For a moment the boy thought too that the man meant his older brother until Harris said, "Not him. The little one. The boy," and, crouching, small for his age, small and wiry like his father, in patched and faded jeans even too small for him, with straight, uncombed, brown hair and eyes gray and wild as storm scud, he saw the men between himself and the table part and become a lane of grim faces, at the end of which he saw the Justice, a shabby, collarless, graying man in spectacles, beckoning him. He felt no floor under his bare feet; he seemed to walk beneath the palpable weight of the grim turning faces. His father, stiff in his black Sunday coat donned not for the trial but for the moving, did not even look at him. *He aims for me to lie,* he thought, again with that frantic grief and despair. *And I will have to do hit.*

"What's your name, boy?" the Justice said.

"Colonel Sartoris Snopes," the boy whispered.

"Hey?" the Justice said. "Talk louder. Colonel Sartoris? I reckon anybody named for Colonel Sartoris in this country can't help but tell the truth, can they?" The boy said nothing. *Enemy! Enemy!* he thought; for a moment he could not even see, could not see that the Justice's face was kindly nor discern that his voice was troubled when he spoke to the man named Harris: "Do you want me to question this boy?" But he could hear, and during those subsequent long seconds while there was absolutely no sound in the crowded little room save that of quiet and intent breathing it was as if he had swung outward at the end of a grape vine, over a ravine, and at the top of the swing had been caught in a prolonged instant of mesmerized gravity, weightless in time.

"No!" Harris said violently, explosively. "Damnation! Send him out of here!" Now time, the fluid world, rushed beneath him again, the voices coming to him again through the smell of cheese and sealed meat, the fear and despair and the old grief of blood:

"This case is closed. I can't find against you, Snopes, but I can give you advice. Leave this country and don't come back to it."

His father spoke for the first time, his voice cold and harsh, level, without emphasis: "I aim to. I don't figure to stay in a country among people who . . ." he said something unprintable and vile, addressed to no one.

"That'll do," the Justice said. "Take your wagon and get out of this country before dark. Case dismissed."

His father turned, and he followed the stiff black coat, the wiry figure walking a little stiffly from where a Confederate provost's man's musket ball had taken him in the heel on a stolen horse thirty years ago, followed the two backs now, since his older brother had appeared from somewhere in the crowd, no taller than the father but thicker, chewing tobacco steadily, between the two lines of grim-faced men and out of the store and across the worn gallery and down the sagging steps and among the dogs and half-grown boys in the mild May dust, where as he passed a voice hissed:

"Barn burner!"

Again he could not see, whirling; there was a face in a red haze, moonlike, bigger than the full moon, the owner of it half again his size, he leaping in the red haze toward the face, feeling no blow, feeling no shock when his head struck the earth, scrabbling up and leaping again, feeling no blow this time either and tasting no blood, scrabbling up to see the other boy in full flight and himself already leaping into pursuit as his father's hand jerked him back, the harsh, cold voice speaking above him: "Go get in the wagon."

It stood in a grove of locusts and mulberries across the road. His two hulking sisters in their Sunday dresses and his mother and her sister in calico and sun-bonnets were already in it, sitting on and among the sorry residue of the dozen and more movings which even the boy could remember—the battered stove, the broken beds and chairs, the clock inlaid with mother-of-pearl, which would not run, stopped at some fourteen minutes past two o'clock of a dead and forgotten day and time, which had been his mother's dowry. She was crying, though when she saw him she drew her sleeve across her face and began to descend from the wagon. "Get back," the father said.

"He's hurt. I got to get some water and wash his . . ."

"Get back in the wagon," his father said. He got in too, over the tail-gate. His father mounted to the seat where the older brother already sat and struck the gaunt mules two savage blows with the peeled willow, but without heat. It was not even sadistic; it was exactly that same quality which in later years would cause his descendants to over-run the engine before putting a motor car into motion, striking and reining back in the same movement. The wagon went on, the store with its quiet crowd of grimly watching men dropped behind; a curve in the road hid it. *Forever* he thought. *Maybe he's done satisfied now, now that he has . . .* stopping himself, not to say it aloud even to himself. His mother's hand touched his shoulder.

"Does hit hurt?" she said.

"Naw," he said. "Hit don't hurt. Lemme be."

"Can't you wipe some of the blood off before hit dries?"

"I'll wash to-night," he said. "Lemme be, I tell you."

The wagon went on. He did not know where they were going. None of them ever did or ever asked, because it was always somewhere, always a house of sorts waiting for them a day or two days or even three days away. Likely his father had already arranged to make a crop on another farm before he . . . Again he had to stop himself. He (the father) always did. There was something about his wolflike independence and even courage when the advantage was at least neutral which impressed strangers, as if they got from his latent ravening ferocity not so much a sense of dependability as a feeling that his ferocious conviction in the rightness of his own actions would be of advantage to all whose interest lay with his.

That night they camped, in a grove of oaks and beeches where a spring ran. The nights were still cool and they had a fire against it, of a rail lifted from a nearby fence and cut into lengths—a small fire, neat, niggard almost, a shrewd fire; such fires were his father's habit and custom always, even in freezing weather. Older, the boy might have remarked this and wondered why not a big one; why should not a man who had not only seen the waste and extravagance of war, but who had in his blood an inherent voracious prodigality with material not his own, have burned everything in sight? Then he might have gone a step farther and thought that that was the reason: that niggard blaze was the living fruit of nights passed during those four years in the woods hiding from all men, blue or gray, with his strings of horses (captured horses, he called them). And older still, he might have divined the true reason: that the element of fire spoke to some deep mainspring of his father's being, as the element of steel or of powder spoke to other men, as the one weapon for the preservation of integrity, else breath were not worth the breathing, and hence to be regarded with respect and used with discretion.

But he did not think this now and he had seen those same niggard blazes all his life. He merely ate his supper beside it and was already half asleep over his iron plate when his father called him, and once more he followed the stiff back, the stiff and ruthless limp, up the slope and on to the starlit road where, turning, he could see his father against the stars but without face or depth—a shape black, flat, and bloodless as though cut from tin in the iron folds of the frockcoat which had not been made for him, the voice harsh like tin and without heat like tin:

"You were fixing to tell them. You would have told him." He didn't answer. His father struck him with the flat of his hand on the side of the head, hard but without heat, exactly as he had struck the two mules at the store, exactly as he would strike either of them with any stick in order to kill a horse fly, his voice still without heat or anger: "You're getting to be a man. You got to learn. You got to learn to stick to your own blood or you ain't going to have any blood to stick to you. Do you think either of them, any man there this morning, would? Don't you know all they wanted was a chance to get at me because they knew I had them beat? Eh?" Later, twenty years later, he was to tell himself, "If I had said they wanted only truth, justice, he would have hit me again." But now he said nothing. He was not crying. He just stood there. "Answer me," his father said.

"Yes," he whispered. His father turned.

"Get on to bed. We'll be there tomorrow."

To-morrow they were there. In the early afternoon the wagon stopped before a paintless two-room house identical almost with the dozen others it had stopped before even in the boy's ten years, and again, as on the other dozen occasions, his mother and aunt got down and began to unload the wagon, although his two sisters and his father and brother had not moved.

"Likely hit ain't fitten for hawgs," one of the sisters said.

"Nevertheless, fit it will and you'll hog it and like it," his father said. "Get out of them chairs and help your Ma unload."

The two sisters got down, big, bovine, in a flutter of cheap ribbons; one of them drew from the jumbled wagon bed a battered lantern, the other a worn broom. His father handed the reins to the older son and began to climb stiffly over the wheel. "When they get unloaded, take the team to the barn and feed them." Then he said, and at first the boy thought he was still speaking to his brother: "Come with me."

"Me?" he said.

"Yes," his father said. "You."

"Abner," his mother said. His father paused and looked back—the harsh level stare beneath the shaggy, graying, irascible brows.

"I reckon I'll have a word with the man that aims to begin to-morrow owning me body and soul for the next eight months."

They went back up the road. A week ago—or before last night that is—he would have asked where they were going, but not now. His father had struck him before last night but never before had he paused afterward to explain why; it was as if the blow and the following calm, outrageous voice still rang, repercussed, divulging nothing to him save the terrible handicap of being young, the light weight of his few years, just heavy enough to prevent his soaring free of the world as it seemed to be ordered but not heavy enough to keep him footed solid in it, to resist it and try to change the course of its events.

Presently he could see the grove of oaks and cedars and the other flowering trees and shrubs where the house would be, though not the house yet. They walked beside a fence massed with honeysuckle and Cherokee roses and came to a gate swinging open between two brick pillars, and now, beyond a sweep of drive, he saw the house for the first time and at that instant he forgot his father and the terror and despair both, and even when he remembered his father again (who had not stopped) the terror and despair did not return. Because, for all the twelve movings, they had sojourned until now in a poor country, a land of small farms and fields and houses, and he had never seen a house like this before. *Hit's big as a courthouse* he thought quietly, with a surge of peace and joy whose reason he could not have thought into words, being too young for that: *They are safe from him. People whose lives are a part of this peace and dignity are beyond his touch, he no more to them than a buzzing wasp: capable of stinging for a little moment but that's all; the spell of this peace and dignity rendering even the barns and stable and cribs which belong to it impervious to the puny flames he might contrive* . . . this, the peace and joy, ebbing for an instant as he looked again at the stiff black back, the stiff and implacable limp of the figure which was not dwarfed by the house, for the reason that it had never looked big anywhere and which now, against the serene columned backdrop, had more than ever that impervious quality of something cut ruthlessly from tin, depthless, as though, sidewise to the sun, it would cast no shadow. Watching him, the boy remarked the absolutely undeviating course which his father held and saw the stiff foot come squarely down in a pile of fresh droppings where a horse had stood in the drive and which his father could have avoided by a simple change of stride. But it ebbed only for a moment, though he could not have thought this into words either, walking on in the spell of the house, which he could even want but without envy, without sorrow, certainly never with that ravening and jealous rage which unknown to him walked in the ironlike black coat before him: *Maybe he will feel it too. Maybe it will even change him now from what maybe he couldn't help but be.*

They crossed the portico. Now he could hear his father's stiff foot as it came down on the boards with clocklike finality, a sound out of all proportion to the displacement of the body it bore and which was not dwarfed either by the white door before it, as though it had attained to a sort of vicious and ravening minimum not to be dwarfed by anything—the flat, wide, black hat, the formal coat of broadcloth which had once been black but which had now that friction-glazed greenish cast of the bodies of old house flies, the lifted sleeve which was too large, the lifted hand like a curled claw. The door opened so promptly that the boy knew the Negro must have been watching them all the time, an old man with neat grizzled hair, in a linen jacket, who stood barring the door with his body, saying, "Wipe yo foots, white man, fo you come in here. Major ain't home nohow."

"Get out of my way, nigger," his father said, without heat too, flinging the door back and the Negro also and entering, his hat still on his head. And now the boy saw the prints of the stiff foot on the doorjamb and saw them appear on the pale rug behind the machinelike deliberation of the foot which seemed to bear (or transmit) twice the weight which the body compassed. The Negro was shouting "Miss Lula! Miss Lula!" somewhere behind them, then the boy, deluged as though by a warm wave by a suave turn of carpeted stair and a pendant glitter of chandeliers and a mute gleam of gold frames, heard the swift feet and saw her too, a lady—perhaps he had never seen her like before either—in a gray, smooth gown with lace at the throat and an apron tied at the waist and the sleeves turned back, wiping cake or biscuit dough from her hands with a towel as she came up the hall, looking not at his father at all but at the tracks on the blond rug with an expression of incredulous amazement.

"I tried," the Negro cried. "I tole him to . . ."

"Will you please go away?" she said in a shaking voice. "Major de Spain is not at home. Will you please go away?"

His father had not spoken again. He did not speak again. He did not even look at her. He just stood stiff in the center of the rug, in his hat, the shaggy iron-gray brows twitching slightly above the pebble-colored eyes as he appeared to examine the house with brief deliberation. Then with the same deliberation he turned; the boy watched him pivot on the good leg and saw the stiff foot drag round the arc of the turning, leaving a final long and fading smear. His father never looked at it, he never once looked down at the rug. The Negro held the door. It closed behind them, upon the hysteric and indistinguishable woman-wail. His father stopped at the top of the steps and scraped his boot clean on the edge of it. At the gate he stopped again. He stood for a moment, planted stiffly on the stiff foot, looking back at the house. "Pretty and white, ain't it?" he said. "That's sweat. Nigger sweat. Maybe it ain't white enough yet to suit him. Maybe he wants to mix some white sweat with it."

Two hours later the boy was chopping wood behind the house within which his mother and aunt and the two sisters (the mother and aunt, not the two girls, he knew that; even at this distance and muffled by walls the flat loud voices of the two girls emanated an incorrigible idle inertia) were setting up the stove to prepare a meal, when he heard the hooves and saw the linen-clad man on a fine sorrel mare, whom he recognized even before he saw the rolled rug in front of the Negro youth following on a fat bay carriage horse—a suffused, angry face vanishing, still at full gallop, beyond the corner of the house where his father and brother were sitting in the two tilted chairs; and a moment later, almost before he could have put the axe down, he heard the hooves again and watched the sorrel mare go back out of the yard, already galloping again. Then his father began to shout one of the sisters' names, who presently emerged backward from the kitchen door dragging the rolled rug along the ground by one end while the other sister walked behind it.

"If you ain't going to tote, go on and set up the wash pot," the first said.

"You, Sarty!" the second shouted. "Set up the wash pot!" His father appeared at the door, framed against that shabbiness, as he had been against that other bland perfection, impervious to either, the mother's anxious face at his shoulder.

"Go on," the father said. "Pick it up." The two sisters stooped, broad, lethargic; stooping, they presented an incredible expanse of pale cloth and a flutter of tawdry ribbons.

"If I thought enough of a rug to have to git hit all the way from France I wouldn't keep hit where folks coming in would have to tromp on hit," the first said. They raised the rug.

"Abner," the mother said. "Let me do it."

"You go back and git dinner," his father said. "I'll tend to this."

From the woodpile through the rest of the afternoon the boy watched them, the rug spread flat in the dust beside the bubbling wash-pot, the two sisters stooping over it with that profound and lethargic reluctance, while the father stood over them in turn, implacable and grim, driving them though never raising his voice again. He could smell the harsh homemade lye they were using; he saw his mother come to the door once and look toward them with an expression not anxious now but very like despair; he saw his father turn, and he fell to with the axe and saw from the corner of his eye his father raise from the ground a flattish fragment of field stone and examine it and return to the pot, and this time his mother actually spoke: "Abner. Abner. Please don't. Please, Abner."

Then he was done too. It was dusk; the whippoorwills had already begun. He could smell coffee from the room where they would presently eat the cold food remaining from the mid-afternoon meal, though when he entered the house he realized they were having coffee again probably because there was a fire on the hearth, before which the rug now lay spread over the backs of the two chairs. The tracks of his father's foot were gone. Where they had been were now long, water-cloudy scoriations resembling the sporadic course of a lilliputian mowing machine.

It still hung there while they ate the cold food and then went to bed, scattered without order or claim up and down the two rooms, his mother in one bed, where his father would later lie, the older brother in the other, himself, the aunt, and the two sisters on pallets on the floor. But his father was not in bed yet. The last thing the boy remembered was the depthless, harsh silhouette of the hat and coat bending over the rug and it seemed to him that he had not even closed his eyes when the silhouette was standing over him, the fire almost dead behind it, the stiff foot prodding him awake. "Catch up the mule," his father said.

When he returned with the mule his father was standing in the black door, the rolled rug over his shoulder. "Ain't you going to ride?" he said.

"No. Give me your foot."

He bent his knee into his father's hand, the wiry, surprising power flowed smoothly, rising, he rising with it, on to the mule's bare back (they had owned a saddle once; the boy could remember it though not when or where) and with the same effortlessness his father swung the rug up in front of him. Now in the starlight they retraced the afternoon's path, up the dusty road rife with honeysuckle, through the gate and up the black tunnel of the drive to the lightless house, where he sat on the mule and felt the rough warp of the rug drag across his thighs and vanish.

"Don't you want me to help?" he whispered. His father did not answer and now he heard again that stiff foot striking the hollow portico with that wooden and clocklike deliberation, that outrageous overstatement of the weight it carried. The rug, hunched, not flung (the boy could tell that even in the darkness) from his father's shoulder struck the angle of wall and floor with a sound unbelievably loud, thunderous, then the foot again, unhurried and enormous; a light came on in the house and the boy sat, tense, breathing steadily and quietly and just a little fast, though the foot itself did not increase its beat at all, descending the steps now; now the boy could see him.

"Don't you want to ride now?" he whispered. "We kin both rid now," the light within the house altering now, flaring up and sinking. *He's coming down the stairs now,* he thought. He had already ridden the mule up beside the horse block; presently his father was up behind him and he doubled the reins over and slashed the mule across the neck, but before the animal could begin to trot the hard, thin arm came round him, the hard, knotted hand jerking the mule back to a walk.

In the first red rays of the sun they were in the lot, putting plow gear on the mules. This time the sorrel mare was in the lot before he heard it at all, the rider collarless and even bareheaded, trembling, speaking in a shaking voice as the woman in the house had done, his father merely looking up once before stooping again to the hame he was buckling, so that the man on the mare spoke to his stooping back:

"You must realize you have ruined that rug. Wasn't there anybody here, any of your women . . ." he ceased, shaking, the boy watching him, the older brother leaning now in the stable door, chewing, blinking slowly and steadily at nothing apparently. "It cost a hundred dollars. But you never had a hundred dollars. You never will. So I'm going to charge you twenty bushels of corn against your crop. I'll add it in your contract and when you come to the commissary you can sign it. That won't keep Mrs. de Spain quiet but maybe it will teach you to wipe your feet off before you enter her house again."

Then he was gone. The boy looked at his father, who still had not spoken or even looked up again, who was now adjusting the logger-head in the hame.

"Pap," he said. His father looked at him—the inscrutable face, the shaggy brows beneath which the gray eyes glinted coldly. Suddenly the boy went toward him, fast, stopping as suddenly. "You done the best you could!" he cried. "If he wanted hit done different why didn't he wait and tell you how? He won't git no twenty bushels! He won't git none! We'll gether hit and hide hit! I kin watch . . ."

"Did you put the cutter back in that straight stock like I told you?"

"No, sir," he said.

"Then go do it."

That was Wednesday. During the rest of that week he worked steadily, at what was within his scope and some which was beyond it, with an industry that did not need to be driven nor even commanded twice; he had this from his mother, with the difference that some at least of what he did he liked to do, such as splitting wood with the half-size axe which his mother and aunt had earned, or saved money somehow, to present him with at Christmas. In company with the two older women (and on one afternoon, even one of the sisters), he built pens for the shoat and the cow which were a part of his father's contract with the landlord, and one afternoon, his father being absent, gone somewhere on one of the mules, he went to the field.

They were running a middle buster now, his brother holding the plow straight while he handled the reins, and walking beside the straining mule, the rich black soil shearing cool and damp against his bare ankles, he thought *Maybe this is the end of it. Maybe even that twenty bushels that seems hard to have to pay for just a rug will be a cheap price for him to stop forever and always from being what he used to be*; thinking, dreaming now, so that his brother had to speak sharply to him to mind the mule: *Maybe he even won't collect the twenty bushels. Maybe it will all add up and balance and vanish—corn, rug, fire; the terror and grief, the being pulled two ways like between two teams of horses—gone, done with for ever and ever.*

Then it was Saturday; he looked up from beneath the mule he was harnessing and saw his father in the black coat and hat. "Not that," his father said. "The wagon gear." And then, two hours later, sitting in the wagon bed behind his father and brother on the seat, the wagon accomplished a final curve, and he saw the weathered paintless store with its tattered tobacco- and patent-medicine posters and the tethered wagons and saddle animals below the gallery. He mounted the gnawed steps behind his father and brother, and there again was the lane of quiet, watching faces for the three of them to walk through. He saw the man in spectacles sitting at the plank table and he did not need to be told this was a Justice of the Peace; he sent one glare of fierce, exultant, partisan defiance at the man in collar and cravat now, whom he had seen but twice before in his life, and that on a galloping horse, who now wore on his face an expression not of rage but of amazed unbelief which the boy could not have known was at the incredible circumstance of being sued by one of his own tenants, and came and stood against his father and cried at the Justice: "He ain't done it! He ain't burnt . . ."

"Go back to the wagon," his father said.

"Burnt?" the Justice said. "Do I understand this rug was burned too?"

"Does anybody here claim it was?" his father said. "Go back to the wagon." But he did not, he merely retreated to the rear of the room, crowded as that other had been, but not to sit down this time, instead, to stand pressing among the motionless bodies, listening to the voices:

"And you claim twenty bushels of corn is too high for the damage you did to the rug?"

"He brought the rug to me and said he wanted the tracks washed out of it. I washed the tracks out and took the rug back to him."

"But you didn't carry the rug back to him in the same condition it was in before you made the tracks on it."

His father did not answer, and now for perhaps half a minute there was no sound at all save that of breathing, the faint, steady suspiration of complete and intent listening.

"You decline to answer that, Mr. Snopes?" Again his father did not answer. "I'm going to find against you, Mr. Snopes. I'm going to find that you were responsible for the injury to Major de Spain's rug and hold you liable for it. But twenty bushels of corn seems a little high for a man in your circumstances to have to pay. Major de Spain claims it cost a hundred dollars. October corn will be worth about fifty cents. I figure that if Major de Spain can stand a ninety-five dollar loss on something he paid cash for, you can stand a five-dollar loss you haven't earned yet. I hold you in damages to Major de Spain to the amount of ten bushels of corn over and above your contract with him, to be paid to him out of your crop at gathering time. Court adjourned."

It had taken no time hardly, the morning was but half begun. He thought they would return home and perhaps back to the field, since they were late, far behind all other farmers. But instead his father passed on behind the wagon, merely indicating with his hand for the older brother to follow with it, and crossed the road toward the blacksmith shop opposite, pressing on after his father, overtaking him, speaking, whispering up at the harsh, calm face beneath the weathered hat: "He won't git no ten bushels neither. He won't git one. We'll . . ." until his father glanced for an instant down at him, the face absolutely calm, the grizzled eyebrows tangled above the cold eyes, the voice almost pleasant, almost gentle: "You think so? Well, we'll wait till October anyway."

The matter of the wagon—the setting of a spoke or two and the tightening of the tires—did not take long either, the business of the tires accomplished by driving the wagon into the spring branch behind the shop and letting it stand there, the mules nuzzling into the water from time to time, and the boy on the seat with the idle reins, looking up the slope and through the sooty tunnel of the shed where the slow hammer rang and where his father sat on an upended cypress bolt, easily, either talking or listening, still sitting there when the boy brought the dripping wagon up out of the branch and halted it before the door.

"Take them on to the shade and hitch," his father said. He did so and returned. His father and the smith and a third man squatting on his heels inside the door were talking, about crops and animals; the boy, squatting too in the ammoniac dust and hoof-parings and scales of rust, heard his father tell a long and unhurried story out of the time before the birth of the older brother even when he had been a professional horsetrader. And then his father came up beside him where he stood before a tattered last year's circus poster on the other side of the store, gazing rapt and quiet at the scarlet horses, the incredible poisings and convolutions of tulle and tights and the painted leers of comedians, and said, "It's time to eat."

But not at home. Squatting beside his brother against the front wall, he watched his father emerge from the store and produce from a paper sack a segment of cheese and divide it carefully and deliberately into three with his pocket knife and produce crackers from the same sack. They all three squatted on the gallery and ate, slowly, without talking; then in the store again, they drank from a tin dipper tepid water smelling of the cedar bucket and of living beech trees. And still they did not go home. It was a horse lot this time, a tall rail fence upon and along which men stood and sat and out of which one by one horses were led, to be walked and trotted and then cantered back and forth along the road while the slow swapping and buying went on and the sun began to slant westward, they—the three of them—watching and listening, the older brother with his muddy eyes and his steady, inevitable tobacco, the father commenting now and then on certain of the animals, to no one in particular.

It was after sundown when they reached home. They ate supper by lamplight, then, sitting on the doorstep, the boy watched the night fully accomplish, listening to the whippoorwills and the frogs, when he heard his mother's voice: "Abner! No! No! Oh, God. Oh, God. Abner!" and he rose, whirled, and saw the altered light through he door where a candle stub now burned in a bottle neck on the table and his father, still in the hat and coat, at once formal and burlesque as though dressed carefully for some shabby and ceremonial violence, emptying the reservoir of the lamp back into the five-gallon kerosene can from which it had been filled, while the mother tugged at his arm until he shifted the lamp to the other hand and flung her back, not savagely or viciously, just hard, into the wall, her hands flung out against the wall for balance, her mouth open and in her face the same quality of hopeless despair as had been in her voice. Then his father saw him standing in the door.

"Go to the barn and get that can of oil we were oiling the wagon with," he said. The boy did not move. Then he could speak.

"What . . ." he cried. "What are you . . ."

"Go get that oil," his father said. "Go."

Then he was moving, running, outside the house, toward the stable: this the old habit, the old blood which he had not been permitted to choose for himself, which had been bequeathed him willy nilly and which had run for so long (and who knew where, battening on what of outrage and savagery and lust) before it came to him. *I could keep on,* he thought. *I could run on and on and never look back, never need to see his face again. Only I can't. I can't,* the rusted can in his hand now, the liquid sploshing in it as he ran back to the house and into it, into the sound of his mother's weeping in the next room, and handed the can to his father.

"Ain't you going to even send a nigger?" he cried. "At least you sent a nigger before!"

This time his father didn't strike him. The hand came even faster than the blow had, the same hand which had set the can on the table with almost excruciating care flashing from the can toward him too quick for him to follow it, gripping him by the back of his shirt and on to tiptoe before he had seen it quit the can, the face stooping at him in breathless and frozen ferocity, the cold, dead voice speaking over him to the older brother who leaned against the table, chewing with the steady, curious, sidewise motion of cows:

"Empty the can into the big one and go on. I'll catch up with you."

"Better tie him up to the bedpost," the brother said.

"Do like I told you," the father said. Then the boy was moving, his bunched shirt and the hard, bony hand between his shoulder-blades, his toes just touching the floor, across the room and into the other one, past the sisters sitting with spread heavy thighs in the two chairs over the cold hearth, and to where his mother and aunt sat side by side on the bed, the aunt's arms about his mother's shoulders.

"Hold him," the father said. The aunt made a startled movement. "Not you," the father said. "Lennie. Take hold of him. I want to see you do it." His mother took him by the wrist. "You'll hold him better than that. If he gets loose don't you know what he is going to do? He will go up yonder." He jerked his head toward the road. "Maybe I'd better tie him."

"I'll hold him," his mother whispered.

"See you do then." Then his father was gone, the stiff foot heavy and measured upon the boards, ceasing at last.

Then he began to struggle. His mother caught him in both arms, he jerking and wrenching at them. He would be stronger in the end, he knew that. But he had no time to wait for it. "Lemme go!" he cried. " I don't want to have to hit you!"

"Let him go!" the aunt said. "If he don't go, before God, I am going up there myself!"

"Don't you see I can't?" his mother cried. "Sarty! Sarty! No! No! Help me, Lizzie!"

Then he was free. His aunt grasped at him but it was too late. He whirled, running, his mother stumbled forward on to her knees behind him, crying to the nearer sister: "Catch him, Net! Catch him!" But that was too late too, the sister (the sisters were twins, born at the same time, yet either of them now gave the impression of being, encompassing as much living meat and volume and weight as any other two of the family) not yet having begun to rise from the chair, her head, face, alone merely turned, presenting to him in the flying instant an astonishing expanse of young female features untroubled by any surprise even, wearing only an expression of bovine interest. Then he was out of the room, out of the house, in the mild dust of the starlit road and the heavy rifeness of honeysuckle, the pale ribbon unspooling with terrific slowness under his running feet, reaching the gate at last and turning in, running, his heart and lungs drumming, on up the drive toward the lighted house, the lighted door. He did not knock, he burst in, sobbing for breath, incapable for the moment of speech; he saw the astonished face of the Negro in the linen jacket without knowing when the Negro had appeared.

"De Spain!" he cried, panted. "Where's . . ." then he saw the white man too emerging from a white door down the hall. "Barn!" he cried. "Barn!"

"What?" the white man said. "Barn?"

"Yes!" the boy cried. "Barn!"

"Catch him!" the white man shouted.

But it was too late this time too. The Negro grasped his shirt, but the entire sleeve, rotten with washing, carried away, and he was out that door too and in the drive again, and had actually never ceased to run even while he was screaming into the white man's face.

Behind him the white man was shouting, "My horse! Fetch my horse!" and he thought for an instant of cutting across the park and climbing the fence into the road, but he did not know the park nor how high the vine-massed fence might be and he dared not risk it. So he ran on down the drive, blood and breath roaring; presently he was in the road again though he could not see it. He could not hear either: the galloping mare was almost upon him before he heard her, and even then he held his course, as if the very urgency of his wild grief and need must in a moment more find him wings, waiting until the ultimate instant to hurl himself aside and into the weed-choked roadside ditch as the horse thundered past and on, for an instant in furious silhouette against the stars, the tranquil early summer night sky which, even before the shape of the horse and rider vanished, stained abruptly and violently upward: a long, swirling roar incredible and soundless, blotting the stars, and he springing up and into the road again, running again, knowing it was too late yet still running even after he heard the shot and, an instant later, two shots, pausing now without knowing he had ceased to run, crying "Pap! Pap!", running again before he knew he had begun to run, stumbling, tripping over something and scrabbling up again without ceasing to run, looking backward over his shoulder at the glare as he got up, running on among the invisible trees, panting, sobbing, "Father! Father!"

At midnight he was sitting on the crest of a hill. He did not know it was midnight and he did not know how far he had come. But there was no glare behind him now and he sat now, his back toward what he had called home for four days anyhow, his face toward the dark woods which he would enter when breath was strong again, small, shaking steadily in the chill darkness, hugging himself into the remainder of his thin, rotten shirt, the grief and despair now no longer terror and fear but just grief and despair. *Father. My father,* he thought. "He was brave!" he cried suddenly, aloud but not loud, no more than a whisper: "He was! He was in the war! He was in Colonel Sartoris' cav'ry!" not knowing that his father had gone to that war a private in the fine old European sense, wearing no uniform, admitting the authority of and giving fidelity to no man or army or flag, going to war as Malbrouck[1] himself did: for booty—it meant nothing and less than nothing to him if it were enemy booty or his own.

The slow constellations wheeled on. It would be dawn and then sun-up after a while and he would be hungry. But that would be to-morrow and now he was only cold, and walking would cure that. His breathing was easier now and he decided to get up and go on, and then he found that he had been asleep because he knew it was almost dawn, the night almost over. He could tell that from the whippoorwills. They were everywhere now among the dark trees below him, constant and inflectioned and ceaseless, so that, as the instant for giving over to the day birds drew nearer and nearer, there was no interval at all between them. He got up. He was a little stiff, but walking would cure that too as it would the cold, and soon there would be the sun. He went on down the hill, toward the dark woods within which the liquid silver voices of the birds called unceasing—the rapid and urgent beating of the urgent and quiring heart of the late spring night. He did not look back.

QUESTIONS

1. How does the narrator's style influence your response to what he recounts?
2. What seems to be the narrator's relation to the events recounted? To Sarty?
3. How much do you understand about Sarty's feelings towards his father?
4. Why isn't the boy questioned at the first trial?
5. Were you surprised by Sarty's action in running to warn Major de Spain? How did you respond to his doing so?
6. What details at the conclusion indicate what his action will mean for Sarty?

---

[1]Hero of an old French song, in which his wife awaits his return from war, not knowing he has been killed.

Flannery O'Connor (1925–1964)

A GOOD MAN IS HARD TO FIND

The grandmother didn't want to go to Florida. She wanted to visit some of her connections in east Tennessee and she was seizing at every chance to change Bailey's mind. Bailey was the son she lived with, her only boy. He was sitting on the edge of his chair at the table, bent over the orange sports section of the *Journal*. "Now look here, Bailey," she said, "see here, read this," and she stood with one hand on her thin hip and the other rattling the newspaper at his bald head. "Here this fellow that calls himself The Misfit is aloose from the Federal Pen and headed toward Florida and you read here what it says he did to these people. Just you read it. I wouldn't take my children in any direction with a criminal like that aloose in it. I couldn't answer to my conscience if I did."

Bailey didn't look up from his reading so she wheeled around then and faced the children's mother, a young woman in slacks, whose face was as broad and innocent as a cabbage and was tied around with a green head-kerchief that had two points on the top like rabbit's ears. She was sitting on the sofa, feeding the baby his apricots out of a jar. "The children have been to Florida before," the old lady said. "You all ought to take them somewhere else for a change so they would see different parts of the world and be broad. They never have been to east Tennessee."

The children's mother didn't seem to hear her but the eight-year-old boy, John Wesley, a stocky child with glasses, said, "If you don't want to go to Florida, why dontcha stay at home?" He and the little girl, June Star, were reading the funny papers on the floor.

"She wouldn't stay at home to be queen for a day," June Star said without raising her yellow head.

"Yes and what would you do if this fellow, The Misfit, caught you?" the grandmother asked.

"I'd smack his face," John Wesley said.

"She wouldn't stay at home for a million bucks," June Star said. "Afraid she'd miss something. She has to go everywhere we go."

"All right, Miss," the grandmother said. "Just remember that the next time you want me to curl your hair."

June Star said her hair was naturally curly.

The next morning the grandmother was the first one in the car, ready to go. She had her big black valise that looked like the head of a hippopotamus in one corner, and underneath it she was hiding a basket with Pitty Sing, the cat, in it. She didn't intend for the cat to be left alone in the house for three days because he would miss her too much and she was afraid he might brush against one of the gas burners and accidentally asphyxiate himself. Her son, Bailey, didn't like to arrive at a motel with a cat.

She sat in the middle of the back seat with John Wesley and June Star on either side of her. Bailey and the children's mother and the baby sat in front and they left Atlanta at eight forty-five with the mileage on the car at 55890. The grandmother wrote this down because she thought it would be interesting to say how many miles they had been when they got back. It took them twenty minutes to reach the outskirts of the city.

The old lady settled herself comfortably, removing her white cotton gloves and putting them up with her purse on the shelf in front of the back window. The children's mother still had on slacks and still had her head tied up in a green kerchief, but the grandmother had on a navy blue straw sailor hat with a bunch of white violets on the brim and a navy blue dress with a small white dot in the print. Her collars and cuffs were white organdy trimmed with lace and at her neckline she had pinned a purple spray of cloth violets containing a sachet. In case of an accident, anyone seeing her dead on the highway would know at once that she was a lady.

She said she thought it was going to be a good day for driving, neither too hot nor too cold, and she cautioned Bailey that the speed limit was fifty-five miles an hour and that the patrolmen hid themselves behind billboards and small clumps of trees and sped out after you before you had a chance to slow down. She pointed out interesting details of the scenery: Stone Mountain; the blue granite that in some places came up to both sides of the highway; the brilliant red clay banks slightly streaked with purple; and the various crops that made rows of green lace-work on the ground. The trees were full of silver-white sunlight and the meanest of them sparkled. The children were reading comic magazines and their mother had gone back to sleep.

"Let's go through Georgia fast so we won't have to look at it much," John Wesley said.

"If I were a little boy," said the grandmother, " I wouldn't talk about my native state that way. Tennessee has the mountains and Georgia has the hills."

"Tennessee is just a hillbilly dumping ground," John Wesley said, "and Georgia is a lousy state too."

"You said it," June Star said.

"In my time," said the grandmother, folding her thin veined fingers, "children were more respectful of their native states and their parents and everything else. People did right then. Oh look at the cute little pickaninny!" she said and pointed to a Negro child standing in the door of a shack. "Wouldn't that make a picture, now?" she asked and they all turned and looked at the little Negro out of the back window. He waved.

"He didn't have any britches on," June Star said.

"He probably didn't have any," the grandmother explained. "Little niggers in the country don't have things like we do. If I could paint, I'd paint that picture," she said.

The children exchanged comic books.

The grandmother offered to hold the baby and the children's mother passed him over the front seat to her. She set him on her knee and bounced him and told him about the things they were passing. She rolled her eyes and screwed up her mouth and stuck her leathery thin face into his smooth bland one. Occasionally he gave her a faraway smile. They passed a large cotton field with five or six graves fenced in the middle of it, like a small island. "Look at the graveyard!" the grandmother said, pointing it out. "That was the old family burying ground. That belonged to the plantation."

"Where's the plantation?" John Wesley asked.

"Gone With the Wind," said the grandmother. "Ha. Ha."

When the children finished all the comic books they had brought, they opened the lunch and ate it. The grandmother ate a peanut butter sandwich and an olive and would not let the children throw the box and the paper napkins out the window. When there was nothing else to do they played a game by choosing a cloud and making the other two guess what shape it suggested. John Wesley took one the shape of a cow and June Star guessed a cow and John Wesley said, no, an automobile, and June Star said he didn't play fair, and they began to slap each other over the grandmother.

The grandmother said she would tell them a story if they would keep quiet. When she told a story, she rolled her eyes and waved her head and was very dramatic. She said once when she was a maiden lady she had been courted by a Mr. Edgar Atkins Teagarden from Jasper, Georgia. She said he was a very good-looking man and a gentleman and that he brought her a watermelon every Saturday afternoon with his initials cut in it, E. A. T. Well, one Saturday, she said, Mr. Teagarden brought the watermelon and there was nobody at home and he left it on the front porch and returned in his buggy to Jasper, but she never got the watermelon, she said, because a nigger boy ate it when he saw the initials, E. A. T.! This story tickled John Wesley's funny bone and he giggled and giggled but June Star didn't think it was any good. She said she wouldn't marry a man that just brought her a watermelon on Saturday. The grandmother said she would have done well to marry Mr. Teagarden because he was a gentleman and had bought Coca-Cola stock when it first came out and that he had died only a few years ago, a very wealthy man.

They stopped at The Tower for barbecued sandwiches. The Tower was a part stucco and part wood filling station and dance hall set in a clearing outside of Timothy. A fat man named Red Sammy Butts ran it and there were signs stuck here and there on the building and for miles up and down the highway saying, TRY RED SAMMY'S FAMOUS BARBECUE. NONE LIKE FAMOUS RED SAMMY'S! RED SAM! THE FAT BOY WITH THE HAPPY LAUGH. A VETERAN! RED SAMMY'S YOUR MAN!

Red Sammy was lying on the bare ground outside The Tower with his head under a truck while a gray monkey about a foot high, chained to a small chinaberry tree, chattered nearby. The monkey sprang back into the tree and got on the highest limb as soon as he saw the children jump out of the car and run toward him.

Inside, The Tower was a long dark room with a counter at one end and tables at the other and dancing space in the middle. They all sat down at a board table next to the nickelodeon and Red Sam's wife, a tall burnt-brown woman with hair and eyes lighter than her skin, came and took their order. The children's mother put a dime in the machine and played "The Tennessee Waltz," and the grandmother said that tune always made her want to dance. She asked Bailey if he would like to dance but he only glared at her. He didn't have a naturally sunny disposition like she did and trips made him nervous. The grandmother's brown eyes were very bright. She swayed her head from side to side and pretended she was dancing in her chair. June Star said play something she could tap to so the children's mother put in another dime and played a fast number and June Star stepped out onto the dance floor and did her tap routine.

"Ain't she cute?" Red Sam's wife said, leaning over the counter. "Would you like to come be my little girl?"

"No I certainly wouldn't," June Star said. "I wouldn't live in a broken-down place like this for a million bucks!" and she ran back to the table.

"Ain't she cute?" the woman repeated, stretching her mouth politely.

"Aren't you ashamed?" hissed the grandmother.

Red Sam came in and told his wife to quit lounging on the counter and hurry up with these people's order. His khaki trousers reached just to his hip bones and his stomach hung over them like a sack of meal swaying under his shirt. He came over and sat down at a table nearby and let out a combination sigh and yodel. "You can't win," he said. "You can't win," and he wiped his sweating red face off with a gray handkerchief. "These days you don't know who to trust," he said. "Ain't that the truth?"

"People are certainly not nice like they used to be," said the grandmother.

"Two fellers come in here last week," Red Sammy said, "driving a Chrysler. It was a old beat-up car but it was a good one and these boys looked all right to me. Said they worked at the mill and you know I let them fellers charge the gas they bought? Now why did I do that?"

"Because you're a good man!" the grandmother said at once.

"Yes'm, I suppose so," Red Sam said as if he were struck with this answer.

His wife brought the orders, carrying the five plates all at once without a tray, two in each hand and one balanced on her arm. "It isn't a soul in this green world of God's that you can trust," she said. "And I don't count nobody out of that, not nobody," she repeated, looking at Red Sammy.

"Did you read about that criminal, The Misfit, that's escaped?" asked the grandmother.

"I wouldn't be a bit surprised if he didn't attact this place right here," said the woman. "If he hears about it being here, I wouldn't be none surprised to see him. If he hears it's two cent in the cash register, I wouldn't be a tall surprised if he . . ."

"That'll do," Red Sam said. "Go bring these people their Co'-Colas," and the woman went off to get the rest of the order.

"A good man is hard to find," Red Sammy said. "Everything is getting terrible. I remember the day you could go off and leave your screen door unlatched. Not no more."

He and the grandmother discussed better times. The old lady said that in her opinion Europe was entirely to blame for the way things were now. She said the way Europe acted you would think we were made of money and Red Sam said it was no use talking about it, she was exactly right. The children ran outside into the white sunlight and looked at the monkey in the lacy chinaberry tree. He was busy catching fleas on himself and biting each one carefully between his teeth as if it were a delicacy.

They drove off again into the hot afternoon. The grandmother took cat naps and woke up every few minutes with her own snoring. Outside of Toombsboro she woke up and recalled an old plantation that she had visited in this neighborhood once when she was a young lady. She said the house had six white columns across the front and that there was an avenue of oaks leading up to it and two little wooden trellis arbors on either side in front where you sat down with your suitor after a stroll in the garden. She recalled exactly which road to turn off to get to it. She knew that Bailey would not be willing to lose any time looking at an old house, but the more she talked about, the more she wanted to see it once again and find out if the little twin arbors were still standing. "There was a secret panel in this house," she said craftily, not telling the truth but wishing that she were, "and the story went that all the family silver was hidden in it when Sherman came through but it was never found . . ."

"Hey!" John Wesley said. "Let's go see it! We'll find it! We'll poke all the woodwork and find it! Who lives there? Where do you turn off at? Hey Pop, can't we turn off there?"

"We never have seen a house with a secret panel!" June Star shrieked. "Let's go to the house with the secret panel! Hey Pop, can't we go see the house with the secret panel!"

"It's not far from here, I know," the grandmother said. "It wouldn't take over twenty minutes."

Bailey was looking straight ahead. His jaw was as rigid as a horseshoe. "No," he said.

The children began to yell and scream that they wanted to see the house with the secret panel. John Wesley kicked the back of the front seat and June Star hung over her mother's shoulder and whined desperately into her ear that they never had any fun even on their vacation, that they could never do what THEY wanted to do. The baby began to scream and John Wesley kicked the back of the seat so hard that his father could feel the blows in his kidney.

"All right!" he shouted and drew the car to a stop at the side of the road. "Will you all shut up? Will you all just shut up for one second? If you don't shut up, we won't go anywhere."

"It would be very educational for them," the grandmother murmured.

"All right," Bailey said, "but get this: this is the only time we're going to stop for anything like this. This is the one and only time."

"The dirt road that you have to turn down is about a mile back," the grandmother directed. "I marked it when we passed."

"A dirt road," Bailey groaned.

After they had turned around and were headed toward the dirt road, the grandmother recalled other points about the house, the beautiful glass over the front doorway and the candle-lamp in the hall. John Wesley said that the secret panel was probably in the fireplace.

"You can't go inside this house," Bailey said. "You don't know who lives there."

"While you all talk to the people in front, I'll run around behind and get in a window," John Wesley suggested.

"We'll all stay in the car," his mother said.

They turned onto the dirt road and the car raced roughly along in a swirl of pink dust. The grandmother recalled the times when there were no paved roads and thirty miles was a day's journey. The dirt road was hilly and there were sudden washes in it and sharp curves on dangerous embankments. All at once they would be on a hill, looking down over the blue tops of trees for miles around, then the next minute, they would be in a red depression with the dust-coated trees looking down on them.

"This place had better turn up in a minute," Bailey said, "or I'm going to turn around."

The road looked as if no one had traveled on it in months.

"It's not much farther," the grandmother said and just as she said it, a horrible thought came to her. The thought was so embarrassing that she turned red in the face and her eyes dilated and her feet jumped up, upsetting her valise in the corner. The instant the valise moved, the newspaper top she had over the basket under it rose with a snarl and Pitty Sing, the cat, sprang onto Bailey's shoulder.

The children were thrown to the floor and their mother, clutching the baby, was thrown out the door onto the ground; the old lady was thrown into the front seat. The car turned over once and landed right-side-up in a gulch off the side of the road. Bailey remained in the driver's seat with the cat—gray-striped with a broad white face and an orange nose—clinging to his neck like a caterpillar.

As soon as the children saw they could move their arms and legs, they scrambled out of the car, shouting, "We've had an ACCIDENT!" The grandmother was curled up under the dashboard, hoping she was injured so that Bailey's wrath would not come down on her all at once. The horrible thought she had had before the accident was that the house she had remembered so vividly was not in Georgia but in Tennessee.

Bailey removed the cat from his neck with both hands and flung it out the window against the side of a pine tree. Then he got out of the car and started looking for the children's mother. She was sitting against the side of the red gutted ditch, holding the screaming baby, but she only had a cut down her face and a broken shoulder. "We've had an ACCIDENT!" the children screamed in a frenzy of delight.

"But nobody's killed," June Star said with disappointment as the grandmother limped out of the car, her hat still pinned to her head but the broken front brim standing up at a jaunty angle and the violet spray hanging off the side. They all sat down in the ditch, except the children, to recover from the shock. They were all shaking.

"Maybe a car will come along," said the children's mother hoarsely.

"I believe I have injured an organ," said the grandmother, pressing her side, but no one answered her. Bailey's teeth were clattering. He had on a yellow sport shirt with bright blue parrots designed in it and his face was as yellow as the shirt. The grandmother decided that she would not mention that the house was in Tennessee.

The road was about ten feet above and they could see only the tops of the trees on the other side of it. Behind the ditch they were sitting in there were more woods, tall and dark and deep. In a few minutes they saw a car some distance away on top of a hill, coming slowly as if the occupants were watching them. The grandmother stood up and waved both arms dramatically to attract their attention. The car continued to come on slowly, disappeared around a bend and appeared again, moving even slower, on top of the hill they had gone over. It was a big black battered hearse-like automobile. There were three men in it.

It came to a stop just over them and for some minutes, the driver looked down with a steady expressionless gaze to where they were sitting, and didn't speak. Then he turned his head and muttered something to the other two and they got out. One was a fat boy in black trousers and a red sweat shirt with a silver stallion embossed on the front of it. He moved around on the right side of them and stood staring, his mouth partly open in a kind of loose grin. The other had on khaki pants and a blue striped coat and a gray hat pulled down very low, hiding most of his face. He came around slowly on the left side. Neither spoke.

The driver got out of the car and stood by the side of it, looking down at them. He was an older man than the other two. His hair was just beginning to gray and he wore silver-rimmed spectacles that gave him a scholarly look. He had a long creased face and didn't have on any shirt or undershirt. He had on blue jeans that were too tight for him and was holding a black hat and a gun. The two boys also had guns.

"We've had an ACCIDENT!" the children screamed.

The grandmother had the peculiar feeling that the bespectacled man was someone she knew. His face was as familiar to her as if she had known him all her life but she could not recall who he was. He moved away from the car and began to come down the embankment, placing his feet carefully so that he wouldn't slip. He had on tan and white shoes and no socks, and his ankles were red and thin. "Good afternoon," he said. "I see you all had you a little spill."

"We turned over twice!" said the grandmother.

"Oncet," he corrected. "We seen it happen. Try their car and see will it run, Hiram," he said quietly to the boy with the gray hat.

"What you got that gun for?" John Wesley asked. "Whatcha gonna do with that gun?"

"Lady," the man said to the children's mother, "would you mind calling them children to sit down by you? Children make me nervous. I want all you all to sit down right together there where you're at."

"What are you telling US what to do for?" June Star asked.

Behind them the line of woods gaped like a dark open mouth. "Come here," said their mother.

"Look here now," Bailey began suddenly, "we're in a predicament! We're in . . ."

The grandmother shrieked. She scrambled to her feet and stood staring. "You're The Misfit!" she said. "I recognized you at once!"

Yes'm," the man said, smiling slightly as if he were pleased in spite of himself to be known, "but it would have been better for all of you, lady, if you hadn't of reckernized me."

Bailey turned his head sharply and said something to his mother that shocked even the children. The old lady began to cry and The Misfit reddened.

"Lady," he said, "don't you get upset. Sometimes a man says things he don't mean. I don't reckon he meant to talk to you thataway."

"You wouldn't shoot a lady, would you?" the grandmother said and removed a clean handkerchief from her cuff and began to slap at her eyes with it.

The Misfit pointed the toe of his shoe into the ground and made a little hole and then covered it up again. "I would hate to have to," he said.

"Listen," the grandmother almost screamed, "I know you're a good man. You don't look a bit like you have common blood. I know you must come from nice people!"

"Yes mam," he said, "finest people in the world." When he smiled he showed a row of strong white teeth. "God never made a finer woman than my mother and my daddy's heart was pure gold," he said. The boy with the red sweat shirt had come around behind them and was standing with his gun at his hip. The Misfit squatted down on the ground. "Watch them children, Bobby Lee," he said. "You know they make me nervous." He looked at the six of them huddled together in front of him and he seemed to be embarrassed as if he couldn't think of anything to say. "Ain't a cloud in the sky," he remarked, looking up at it. "Don't see no sun but don't see no cloud neither."

"Yes, it's a beautiful day," said the grandmother. "Listen," she said, "you shouldn't call yourself The Misfit because I know you're a good man at heart. I can just look at you and tell."

"Hush!" Bailey yelled. "Hush! Everybody shut up and let me handle this!" He was squatting in the position of a runner about to sprint forward but he didn't move.

"I pre-chate that, lady," The Misfit said and drew a little circle in the ground with the butt of his gun.

"It'll take a half a hour to fix this here car," Hiram called, looking over the raised hood of it.

"Well, first you and Bobby Lee get him and that little boy to step over yonder with you," The Misfit said, pointing to Bailey and John Wesley. "The boys want to ast you something," he said to Bailey. "Would you mind stepping back in them woods there with them?"

"Listen," Bailey began, "we're in a terrible predicament! Nobody realizes what this is," and his voice cracked. His eyes were as blue and intense as the parrots in his shirt and he remained perfectly still.

The grandmother reached up to adjust her hat brim as if she were going to the woods with him but it came off in her hand. She stood staring at it and after a second she let it fall on the ground. Hiram pulled Bailey up by the arm as if he were assisting an old man. John Wesley caught hold of his father's hand and Bobby Lee followed. They went off toward the woods and just as they reached the dark edge, Bailey turned and supporting himself against a gray naked pine trunk, he shouted, "I'll be back in a minute, Mamma, wait on me!"

"Come back this instant!" his mother shrilled but they all disappeared into the woods.

"Bailey Boy!" the grandmother called in a tragic voice but she found she was looking at The Misfit squatting on the ground in front of her. "I just know you're a good man," she said desperately. "You're not a bit common!"

"Nome, I ain't a good man," The Misfit said after a second as if he had considered her statement carefully, "but I ain't the worst in the world neither. My daddy said I was a different breed of dog from my brothers and sisters. 'You know,' Daddy said, 'it's some that can live their whole life out without asking about it and it's others has to know why it is, and this boy is one of the latters. He's going to be into everything!'" He put on his black hat and looked up suddenly and then away deep into the woods as if he were embarrassed again. "I'm sorry I don't have on a shirt before you ladies," he said, hunching his shoulders slightly. "We buried our clothes that we had on when we escaped and we're just making do until we can get better. We borrowed these from some folks we met," he explained.

"That's perfectly all right," the grandmother said. "Maybe Bailey has an extra shirt in his suitcase."

"I'll look and see terrectly," The Misfit said.

"Where are they taking him?" the children's mother screamed.

"Daddy was a card himself," The Misfit said. "You couldn't put anything over on him. He never got in trouble with the Authorities though. Just had the knack of handling them."

"You could be honest too if you'd only try," said the grandmother. "Think how wonderful it would be to settle down and live a comfortable life and not have to think about somebody chasing you all the time."

The Misfit kept scratching in the ground with the butt of his gun as if he were thinking about it. "Yes'm, somebody is always after you," he murmured.

The grandmother noticed how thin his shoulder blades were just behind his hat because she was standing up looking down on him. "Do you ever pray?" she asked.

He shook his head. All she saw was the black hat wiggle between his shoulder blades. "Nome," he said.

There was a pistol shot from the woods, followed closely by another. Then silence. The old lady's head jerked around. She could hear the wind move through the tree tops like a long satisfied insuck of breath. "Bailey Boy!" she called.

"I was a gospel singer for a while," the Misfit said. "I been most everything. Been in the arm service, both land and sea, at home and abroad, been twict married, been an undertaker, been with the railroads, plowed Mother Earth, been in a tornado, seen a man burnt alive oncet," and he looked up at the children's mother and the little girl who were sitting close together, their faces white and their eyes glassy; "I even seen a woman flogged," he said.

"Pray, pray," the grandmother began, "pray, pray . . ."

"I never was a bad boy that I remember of," The Misfit said in an almost dreamy voice, "but somewheres along the line I done something wrong and got sent to the penitentiary. I was buried alive," and he looked up and held her attention to him by a steady stare.

"That's when you should have started to pray," she said. "What did you do to get sent to the penitentiary that first time?"

"Turn to the right, it was a wall," The Misfit said, looking up again at the cloudless sky. "Turn to the left, it was a wall. Look up it was a ceiling, look down it was a floor. I forget what I done, lady. I set there and set there, trying to remember what it was I done and I ain't recalled it to this day. Oncet in a while, I would think it was coming to me, but it never come."

"Maybe they put you in by mistake," the old lady said vaguely.

"Nome," he said. "It wasn't no mistake. They had the papers on me."

"You must have stolen something," she said.

The Misfit sneered slightly. "Nobody had nothing I wanted," he said. "It was a head-doctor at the penitentiary said what I had done was kill my daddy but I known that for a lie. My daddy died in nineteen ought nineteen of the epidemic flu and I never had a thing to do with it. He was buried in the Mount Hopewell Baptist churchyard and you can go there and see for yourself."

"If you would pray," the old lady said, "Jesus would help you."

"That's right," The Misfit said.

"Well then, why don't you pray?" she asked trembling with delight suddenly.

"I don't want no hep," he said. "I'm doing all right by myself."

Bobby Lee and Hiram came ambling back from the woods. Bobby Lee was dragging a yellow shirt with bright blue parrots in it.

"Throw me that shirt, Bobby Lee," the Misfit said. The shirt came flying at him and landed on his shoulder and he put it on. The grandmother couldn't name what the shirt reminded her of. "No, lady," The Misfit said while he was buttoning it up, "I found out the crime don't matter. You can do one thing or you can do another, kill a man or take a tire off his car, because sooner or later you're going to forget what it was you done and just be punished for it."

The children's mother had begun to make heaving noises as if she couldn't get her breath. "Lady," he asked, "would you and that little girl like to step off yonder with Bobby Lee and Hiram and join your husband?"

"Yes, thank you," the mother said faintly. Her left arm dangled helplessly and she was holding the baby, who had gone to sleep, in the other. "Hep that lady up, Hiram," The Misfit said as she struggled to climb out of the ditch, "and Bobby Lee, you hold onto that little girl's hand."

"I don't want to hold hands with him," June Star said. "He reminds me of a pig."

The fat boy blushed and laughed and caught her by the arm and pulled her off into the woods after Hiram and her mother.

Alone with The Misfit, the grandmother found that she had lost her voice. There was not a cloud in the sky nor any sun. There was nothing around her but woods. She wanted to tell him he must pray. She opened and closed her mouth several times before anything came out. Finally she found herself saying, "Jesus. Jesus," meaning, Jesus will help you, but the way she was saying it, it sounded as if she might be cursing.

"Yes'm," The Misfit said as if he agreed. "Jesus thown everything off balance. It was the same case with Him as with me except He hadn't committed any crime and they could prove I had committed one because they had the papers on me. Of course," he said, "they never shown me my papers. That's why I sign myself now. I said long ago, you get you a signature and sign everything you do and keep a copy of it. Then you'll know what you done and you can hold up the crime to the punishment and see do they match and in the end you'll have something to prove you ain't been treated right. I call myself The Misfit," he said, "because I can't make what all I done wrong fit what all I gone through in punishment."

There was a piercing scream from the woods, followed closely by a pistol report. "Does it seem right to you, lady, that one is punished a heap and another ain't punished at all?"

"Jesus!" the old lady cried. "You've got good blood! I know you wouldn't shoot a lady! I know you come from nice people! Pray! Jesus, you ought not to shoot a lady. I'll give you all the money I've got!"

"Lady," The Misfit said, looking beyond her far into the woods, "there never was a body that give the undertaker a tip."

There were two more pistol reports and the grandmother raised her head like a parched old turkey hen crying for water and called, "Bailey Boy, Bailey Boy!" as if her heart would break.

"Jesus was the only One that ever raised the dead," The Misfit continued, "and He shouldn't have done it. He thrown everything off balance. If He did what He said, then it's nothing for you to do but throw away everything and follow Him, and if He didn't, then it's nothing for you to do but enjoy the few minutes you got left the best way you can—by killing somebody or burning down his house or doing some other meanness to him. No pleasure but meanness," he said and his voice had become almost a snarl.

"Maybe He didn't raise the dead," the old lady mumbled, not knowing what she was saying and feeling so dizzy that she sank down in the ditch with her legs twisted under her.

"I wasn't there so I can't say He didn't," The Misfit said. "I wisht I had of been there," he said, hitting the ground with his fist. "It ain't right I wasn't there because if I had of been there I would of known. Listen lady," he said in a high voice, "if I had of been there I would of known and I wouldn't be like I am now." His voice seemed about to crack and the grandmother's head cleared for an instant. She saw the man's face twisted close to her own as if he were going to cry and she murmured, "Why you're one of my babies. You're one of my own children!" She reached out and touched him on the shoulder. The Misfit sprang back as if a snake had bitten him and shot her three times through the chest. Then he put his gun down on the ground and took off his glasses and began to clean them.

Hiram and Bobby Lee returned from the woods and stood over the ditch, looking down at the grandmother who half sat and half lay in a puddle of blood with her legs crossed under her like a child's and her face smiling up at the cloudless sky.

Without his glasses, The Misfit's eyes were red-rimmed and pale and defense-less-looking. "Take her off and throw her where you thrown the others," he said, picking up the cat that was rubbing itself against his leg.

"She was a talker, wasn't she?" Bobby Lee said, sliding down the ditch with a yodel.

"She would of been a good woman," The Misfit said, "if it had been somebody there to shoot her every minute of her life."

"Some fun!" Bobby Lee said.

"Shut up, Bobby Lee," The Misfit said. "It's no real pleasure in life."

Bobbie Ann Mason (b. 1940)

LYING DOGGO

Grover Cleveland is growing feeble. His eyes are cloudy, and his muzzle is specked with white hairs. When he scoots along on the hardwood floors, he makes a sound like brushes on drums. He sleeps in front of the woodstove, and when he gets too hot he creeps across the floor.

When Nancy Culpepper married Jack Cleveland, she felt, in a way, that she was marrying a divorced man with a child. Grover was a young dog then. Jack had gotten him at the humane society shelter. He had picked the shyest, most endearing puppy in a boisterous litter. Later, he told Nancy that someone said he should have chosen an energetic one, because quiet puppies often have some-thing wrong with them. That chance remark bothered Nancy; it could have applied to her as well. But that was years ago. Nancy and Jack are still married, and Grover has lived to be old. Now his arthritis stiffens his legs so that on some days he cannot get up. Jack has been talking of having Grover put to sleep.

"Why do you say 'put to sleep'?" their son, Robert, asks. "I know what you mean." Robert is nine. He is a serious boy, quiet, like Nancy.

"No reason. It's just the way people say it."

"They don't say they put *people* to sleep."

"It doesn't usually happen to people," Jack says.

"Don't you dare take him to the vet unless you let me go along. I don't want any funny stuff behind my back."

"Don't worry, Robert," Nancy says.

Later, in Jack's studio, while developing photographs of broken snow fences on hillsides, Jack says to Nancy, "There's a first time for everything, I guess."

"What?"

"Death. I never really knew anybody who died."

"You're forgetting my grandmother."

"I didn't really know your grandmother." Jack looks down at Grover's face in the developing fluid. Grover looks like a wolf in the snow on the hill. Jack says, "The only people I ever cared about who died were rock heroes."

Jack has been buying special foods for the dog—pork chops and liver, vitamin supplements. All the arthritis literature he has been able to find concerns people, but he says the same rules must apply to all mammals. Until Grover's hind legs gave way, Jack and Robert took Grover out for long, slow walks through the woods. Recently, a neighbor who keeps Alaskan malamutes stopped Nancy in the Super Duper and inquired about Grover. The neighbor wanted to know which kind of arthritis Grover had—osteo- or rheumatoid? The neighbor said he had rheumatoid and held out knobbed fingers. The doctor told him to avoid zucchini and to drink lots of water. Grover doesn't like zucchini, Nancy said.

Jack and Nancy and Robert all deal with Grover outside. It doesn't help that the temperature is dropping below twenty degrees. It feels even colder because they are conscious of the dog's difficulty. Nancy holds his head and shoulders while Jack supports his hind legs. Robert holds up Grover's tail.

Robert says, "I have an idea."

"What, sweetheart?" asks Nancy. In her arms, Grover lurches. Nancy squeezes against him and he whimpers.

"We could put a diaper on him."

"How would we clean him up?"

"They do that with chimpanzees," says Jack, "but it must be messy."

"You mean I didn't have an original idea?" Robert cries. "Curses, foiled again!" Robert has been reading comic books about masked villains.

"There aren't many original ideas," Jack says, letting go of Grover. "They just look original when you're young." Jack lifts Grover's hind legs again and grasps him under the stomach. "Let's try one more time boy."

Grover looks at Nancy, pleading.

Nancy has been feeling that the dying of Grover marks a milestone in her marriage to Jack, a marriage that has somehow lasted almost fifteen years. She is seized with an irrational dread—that when the dog is gone, Jack will be gone too. Whenever Nancy and Jack are apart—during Nancy's frequent trips to see her family in Kentucky, or when Jack has gone away "to think"—Grover remains with Jack. Actually, Nancy knew Grover before she knew Jack. When Jack and Nancy were students, in Massachusetts, the dog was a familiar figure around campus. Nancy was drawn to the dog long before she noticed the shaggy-haired student in the sheepskin-lined corduroy jacket who was usually with him. Once, in a seminar on the Federalist period that Nancy was auditing, Grover had walked in, circled the room, and then walked out, as if performing some routine investigation, like the man who sprayed Nancy's apartment building for silverfish. Grover was a beautiful dog, a German shepherd, gray, dusted with a sooty topcoat. After the seminar, Nancy followed the dog out of the building, and she met Jack then. Eventually, when Nancy and Jack made love in his apartment in Amherst, Grover lay sprawled by the bed, both protective and quietly participatory. Later, they moved into a house in the country, and Nancy felt that she had an instant family. Once, for almost three months, Jack And Grover were gone. Jack left Nancy in California, pregnant and terrified, and went to stay at an Indian reservation in New Mexico. Nancy lived in a room on a street with palm trees. It was winter. It felt like a Kentucky October. She went to a park every day and watched people with their dogs, their children, and tried to comprehend that she was there, alone, a mile from the San Andreas fault, reluctant to return to Kentucky. "We need to decide where we stand with each other," Jack had said when he left. "Just when I start to think I know where you're at, you seem to disappear." Jack always seemed to stand back and watch her, as though he expected her to do something excitingly original. He expected her to be herself, not someone she thought people wanted her to be. That was a twist: he expected the unexpected. While Jack was away, Nancy indulged in crafts projects. At the Free University, she learned batik and macramé. On her own, she learned to crochet. She had never done anything like that before. She threw away her file folders of history notes for the article she had wanted to write. Suddenly, making things with her hands was the only endeavor that made sense. She crocheted a bulky, shapeless sweater in a shell stitch for Jack. She made baby things, using large hooks. She did not realize that such heavy blankets were unsuitable for a baby until she saw Robert—a tiny, warped-looking creature, like one of her clumsily made crafts. When Jack returned, she was in a sprawling adobe hospital, nursing a baby the color of scalded skin. The old song "In My Adobe Hacienda" was going through her head. Jack stood over her behind an unfamiliar beard, grinning in disbelief, stroking the baby as though he were a new pet. Nancy felt she had fooled Jack into thinking she had done something original at last.

"Grover's dying to see you," he said to her. "They wouldn't let him in here."

"I'll be glad to see Grover," said Nancy. "I missed him."

She had missed, she realized then, his various expressions: the staccato barks of joy, the forceful, menacing barks at strangers, the eerie howls when he heard cat fights at night.

Those early years together were confused and dislocated. After leaving graduate school, at the beginning of the seventies, they lived in a number of places— sometimes on the road, with Grover, in a van—but after Robert was born they settled in Pennsylvania. Their life is orderly. Jack is a free-lance photographer, with his own studio at home. Nancy, unable to find a use for her degree in history, returned to school, taking education and administration courses. Now she is assistant principal of a small private elementary school, which Robert attends. Now and then Jack frets about becoming too middle-class. He has become semi-political about energy, sometimes attending anti-nuclear power rallies. He has been building a sun space for his studio and has been insulating the house. "Retrofitting" is the term he uses for making the house energy-efficient.

"Insulation is his hobby," Nancy told an old friend from graduate school, Tom Green, who telephoned unexpectedly one day recently. "He insulates on weekends."

"Maybe he'll turn into a butterfly—he could insulate himself into a cocoon," said Tom, who Nancy always thought was funny. She had not seen him in ten years. He called to say he was sending a novel he had written—"about all the crazy stuff we did back then."

The dog is forcing Nancy to think of how Jack has changed in the years since then. He is losing his hair, but he doesn't seem concerned. Jack was always fanatical about being honest. He used to be insensitive about his directness. "I'm just being honest," he would say pleasantly, boyishly, when he hurt people's feelings. He told Nancy she was uptight, that no one ever knew what she thought, that she should be more expressive. He said she "played games" with people, hiding her feelings behind her coy Southern smile. He is more tolerant now, less judgmental. He used to criticize her for drinking Cokes and eating pastries. He didn't like her lipstick, and she stopped wearing it. But Nancy has changed too. She is too sophisticated now to eat fried foods and rich pies and cakes, indulging in them only when she goes to Kentucky. She uses makeup now—so sparingly that Jack does not notice. Her cool reserve, her shyness, has changed to cool assurance, with only the slightest shift. Inwardly, she has reorganized. "It's like retrofitting," she said to Jack once, but he didn't notice any irony.

It wasn't until two years ago that Nancy learned that he had lied to her when he told her he had been at the Beatles' Shea Stadium concert in 1966, just as she had, only two months before they met. When he confessed his lie, he claimed he had wanted to identify with her and impress her because he thought of her as someone so mysterious and aloof that he could not hold her attention. Nancy, who had in fact been intimidated by Jack's directness, was troubled to learn about his peculiar deception. It was out of character. She felt a part of her past had been ripped away. More recently, when John Lennon died, Nancy and Jack watched the silent vigil from Central Park on TV and cried in each other's arms. Everybody that week was saying that they had lost their youth.

Jack was right. That was the only sort of death they had known.

Grover lies on his side, stretched out near the fire, his head flat on one ear. His eyes are open, expressionless, and when Nancy speaks to him he doesn't respond.

"Come on, Grover!" cries Robert, tugging the dog's leg. "Are you dead?"

"Don't pull at him," Nancy says.

"He's lying doggo," says Jack.

"That's funny," says Robert. "What does that mean?"

"Dogs do that in the heat," Jack explains. "They save energy that way."

"But it's winter," says Robert. "I'm freezing." He is wearing a wool pullover and a goose-down vest. Jack has the thermostat set on fifty-five, relying mainly on the woodstove to warm the house.

"I'm cold too," says Nancy. "I've been freezing since 1965, when I came North."

Jack crouches down beside the dog. "Grover, old boy. Please. Just give a little sign."

"If you don't get up, I won't give you your treat tonight," says Robert, wagging his finger at Grover.

"Let him rest," says Jack, who is twiddling some of Grover's fur between his fingers.

"Are you sure he's not dead?" Robert asks. He runs the zipper of his vest up and down.

"He's just pretending," says Nancy.

The tip of Grover's tail twitches, and Jack catches it, the way he might grab at a fluff of milkweed in the air.

Later, in the kitchen, Jack and Nancy are preparing for a dinner party. Jack is sipping whiskey. The woodstove has been burning all day, and the house is comfortably warm now. In the next room, Robert is lying on the rug in front of the stove with Grover. He is playing with a computer football game and watching *Mork and Mindy* at the same time. Robert likes to do several things at once, and lately he has included Grover in his multiple activities.

Jack says, "I think the only thing to do is just feed Grover pork chops and steaks and pet him a lot, and then when we can stand it, take him to the vet and get it over with."

"When can we stand it?"

"If I were in Grover's shape, I'd just want to be put out of my misery."

"Even if you were still conscious and could use your mind?"

"I guess so."

"I couldn't pull the plug on you," says Nancy, pointing a carrot at Jack. "You'd have to be screaming in agony."

"Would you want me to do it to you?"

"No. I can see right now that I'd be the type to hang on. I'd be just like my Granny. I think she just clung to life, long after her body was ready to die."

"Would you really be like that?"

"You said once I was just like her—repressed, uptight."

"I didn't mean that."

"You've been right about me before," Nancy says, reaching across Jack for a paring knife. "Look, all I mean is that it shouldn't be a matter of *our* convenience. If Grover needs assistance, then it's our problem. We're responsible."

"I'd want to be put out of my misery," Jack says.

During that evening, Nancy has the impression that Jack is talking more than usual. He does not notice the food. She has made chicken Marengo and is startled to realize how much it resembles chicken cacciatore, which she served the last time she had the same people over. The recipes are side by side in the cookbook, gradations on a theme. The dinner is for Stewart and Jan, who are going to Italy on a teaching exchange.

"Maybe I shouldn't even have made Italian," Nancy tells them apologetically. "You'll get enough of that in Italy. And it will be real."

Both Stewart and Jan say the chicken Marengo is wonderful. The olives are the right touch, Jan says. Ted and Laurie nod agreement. Jack pours more wine. The sound of a log falling in the woodstove reminds Nancy of the dog in the other room by the stove, and in her mind she stages a scene: finding the dog dead in the middle of the dinner party.

Afterward, they sit in the living room, with Grover lying there like a log too large for the stove. The guests talk idly. Ted has been sandblasting old paint off a brick fireplace, and Laurie complains about the gritty dust. Jack stokes the fire. The stove, hooked up through the fireplace, looks like a robot from an old science fiction movie. Nancy and Jack used to sit by the fireplace in Massachusetts, stoned, watching the blue frills of the flames, imagining that they were musical notes, visual textures of sounds on the stereo. Nobody they know smokes grass anymore. Now people sit around and talk about investments and proper flue linings. When Jack passes around the Grand Marnier, Nancy says, "In my grandparents' house years ago, we used to sit by their fireplace. They burned coal. They didn't call it a fireplace, though. They called it a grate."

"Coal burns more efficiently than wood," Jack says.

"Coal's a lot cheaper in this area," says Ted, "I wish I could switch."

"My grandparents had big stone fireplaces in their country house," says Jan, who comes from Connecticut. "They were so pleasant. I always looked forward to going there. Sometimes in the summer the evenings were cool and we'd have a fire. It was lovely."

"I remember being cold," says Nancy. "It was always very cold, even in the South."

"The heat just goes up the chimney in a fireplace," says Jack.

Nancy stares at Jack. She says, "I would stand in front of the fire until I was roasted. Then I would turn and roast the other side. In the evenings, my grandparents sat on the hearth and read the Bible. There wasn't anything *lovely* about it. They were trying to keep warm. Of course, nobody had heard of insulation."

"There goes Nancy, talking about her deprived childhood," Jack says with a laugh.

Nancy says, "Jack is so concerned about wasting energy. But when he goes out he never wears a hat." She looks at Jack. "Don't you know your body heat just flies out the top of your head? It's a chimney."

Surprised by her tone, she almost breaks into tears.

It is the following evening, and Jack is flipping through some contact sheets of a series on solar hot-water heaters he is doing for a magazine. Robert sheds his goose-down vest, and he and Grover, on the floor, simultaneously inch away from the fire. Nancy is trying to read the novel written by the friend from Amherst, but the book is boring. She would not have recognized her witty friend from the past in the turgid prose she is reading.

"It's a dump on the sixties," she tells Jack when he asks. "A really cynical look. All the characters are types."

"Are we in it?"

"No. I hope not. I think it's based on that Phil Baxter who cracked up at that party."

Grover raises his head, his eyes alert, and Robert jumps up, saying, "It's time for Grover's treat."

He shakes a Pet-Tab from a plastic bottle and holds it before Grover's nose. Grover bangs his tail against the rug as he crunches the pill.

Jack turns on the porch light and steps outside for a moment, returning with a shroud of cold air. "It's starting to snow," he says. "Come on out, Grover."

Grover struggles to stand, and Jack heaves the dog's hind legs over the threshold.

Later, in bed, Jack turns on his side and watches Nancy, reading her book, until she looks up at him.

"You read so much," he says. "You're always reading."

"Hmm."

"We used to have more fun. We used to be silly together."

"What do you want to do?"

"Just something silly."

"I can't think of anything silly." Nancy flips the page back, rereading. "God, this guy can't write. I used to think he was so clever."

In the dark, touching Jack tentatively, she says, "We've changed. We used to lie awake all night, thrilled just to touch each other."

"We've been busy. That's what happens. People get busy."

"That scares me," says Nancy. "Do you want to have another baby?"

"No. I want a dog." Jack rolls away from her, and Nancy can hear him breathing into his pillow. She waits to hear if he will cry. She recalls Jack returning to her in California after Robert was born. He brought a God's-eye, which he hung from the ceiling above Robert's crib, to protect him. Jack never wore the sweater Nancy made for him. Instead, Grover slept on it. Nancy gave the dog her granny-square afghan too, and eventually, when they moved back East, she got rid of the pathetic evidence of her creative period—the crochet hooks, the piles of yarn, some splotchy batik tapestries. Now most of the objects in the house are Jack's. He made the oak counters and the dining room table; he remodeled the studio; he chose the draperies; he photographed the pictures on the wall. If Jack were to leave again, there would be no way to remove his presence, the way the dog can disappear completely, with his sounds. Nancy revises the scene in her mind. The house is still there, but Nancy is not in it.

In the morning, there is a four-inch snow, with a drift blowing up the back-porch steps. From the kitchen window, Nancy watches her son float silently down the hill behind the house. At the end, he tumbles off his sled deliberately, wallowing in the snow, before standing up to wave, trying to catch her attention.

On the back porch, Nancy and Jack hold Grover over newspapers. Grover performs unselfconsciously now. Nancy says, "Maybe he can hang on, as long as we can do this."

"But look at him, Nancy," Jack says. "He's in misery."

Jack holds Grover's collar and helps him slide over the threshold. Grover aims for his place by the fire.

After the snowplow passes, late in the morning, Nancy drives Robert to the school on slushy roads, all the while lecturing him on the absurdity of raising money to buy official Boy Scout equipment, especially on a snowy Saturday. The Boy Scouts are selling water-savers for toilet tanks in order to earn money for camping gear.

"I thought Boy Scouts spent their time earning badges," says Nancy. "I thought you were supposed to learn about nature, instead of spending money on official Boy Scout pots and pans."

"This is nature," Robert says solemnly. "It's ecology. Saving water when you flush is ecology."

Later, Nancy and Jack walk in the woods together. Nancy walks behind Jack, stepping in his boot tracks. He shields her from the wind. Her hair is blowing. They walk briskly up a hill and emerge on a ridge that overlooks a valley. In the distance they can see a housing development, a radio tower, a winding road. House trailers dot the hillsides. A snowplow is going up a road, like a zipper in the landscape.

Jack says, "I'm going to call the vet Monday."

Nancy gasps in cold air. She says, "Robert made us promise you won't do anything without letting him in on it. That goes for me too." When Jack doesn't respond, she says, "I'd want to hang on, even if I was in a coma. There must be some spark, in the deep recesses of the mind, some twitch, a flicker of a dream—"

"A twitch that could make life worth living?" Jack laughs bitterly.

"Yes," She points to the brilliantly colored sparkles the sun is making on the snow. "Those are the sparks I mean," she says. "In the brain somewhere, something like that. That would be beautiful."

"You're weird, Nancy."

"I learned it from you. I never would have noticed anything like that if I hadn't known you, if you hadn't got me stoned and made me look at your photographs." She stomps her feet in the snow. Her toes are cold. "You educated me. I was so out of it when I met you. One day I was listening to Hank Williams and shelling corn for the chickens and the next day I was expected to know what wines went with what. Talk about weird."

"You're exaggerating. That was years ago. You always exaggerate your background." He adds in a teasing tone, "Your humble origins."

"We've been together fifteen years," says Nancy. She stops him, holding his arm. Jack is squinting, looking at something in the distance. She goes on, "You said we didn't do anything silly anymore. What should we do, Jack? Should we make angels in the snow?"

Jack touches his rough glove to her face. "We shouldn't unless we really feel like it."

It was the same as Jack chiding her to be honest, to be expressive. The same old Jack, she thought, relieved.

"Come and look," Robert cries, bursting in the back door. He and Jack have been outside making a snowman. Nancy is rolling dough for a quiche. Jack will eat a quiche but not a custard pie, although they are virtually the same. She wipes her hands and goes to the door of the porch. She sees Grover swinging from the lower branch of the maple tree. Jack has rigged up a sling, so that the dog is supported in a harness, with the canvas from the back of a deck chair holding his stomach. His legs dangle free.

"Oh, Jack," Nancy calls. "The poor thing."

"I thought this might work," Jack explains. "A support for his hind legs." His arms cradle the dog's head. "I did it for you," he adds, looking at Nancy. "Don't push him, Robert. I don't think he wants to swing."

Grover looks amazingly patient, like a cat in a doll bonnet.

"He hates it," says Jack, unbuckling the harness.

"He can learn to like it," Robert says, his voice rising shrilly.

On the day that Jack has planned to take Grover to the veterinarian, Nancy runs into a crisis at work. One of the children has been exposed to hepatitis, and it is necessary to vaccinate all of them. Nancy has to arrange the details, which means staying late. She telephones Jack to ask him to pick up Robert after school.

"I don't know when I'll be home," she says. "This is an administrative nightmare. I have to call all the parents, get permissions, make arrangements with family doctors."

"What will we do about Grover?"

"Please postpone it. I want to be with you then."

"I want to get it over with," says Jack impatiently. "I hate to put Robert through another day of this."

"Robert will be glad of the extra time." Nancy insists. "So will I."

"I just want to face things," Jack says. "Don't you understand? I don't want to cling to the past like you're doing."

"Please wait for us," Nancy says, her voice calm and controlled.

On the telephone, Nancy is authoritative, a quick decision-maker. The problem at work is a reprieve. She feels free, on her own. During the afternoon, she works rapidly and efficiently, filing reports, consulting health authorities, notifying parents. She talks with the disease-control center in Atlanta, inquiring about guidelines. She checks on supplies of gamma globulin. She is so preoccupied that in the middle of the afternoon, when Robert suddenly appears in her office, she is startled, for a fleeting instant not recognizing him.

He says, "Kevin has a sore throat. Is that hepatitis?"

"It's probably just a cold. I'll talk to his mother." Nancy is holding Robert's arm, partly to keep him still, partly to steady herself.

"When do I have to get a shot?" Robert asks.

"Tomorrow."

"Do I have to?"

"Yes, It won't hurt, though."

"I guess it's a good thing this happened," Robert says bravely. "Now we get to have Grover another day." Robert spills his books on the floor and bends to pick them up. When he looks up, he says, "Daddy doesn't care about him. He just wants to get rid of him. He wants to kill him."

"Oh, Robert, that's not true," says Nancy. "He just doesn't want Grover to suffer."

"But Grover still has half a bottle of Pet-tabs," Robert says. "What will we do with them?"

"I don't know," Nancy says. She hands Robert his numbers workbook. Like a tape loop, the face of her child as a stranger replays in her mind. Robert has her plain brown hair, her coloring but his eyes are Jack's—demanding and eerily penetrating, eyes that could pin her to the wall.

After Robert leaves, Nancy lowers the venetian blinds. Her office is brilliantly lighted by the sun, through south-facing windows. The design was accidental, nothing to do with solar energy. It is an old building. Bars of light slant across her desk, like a formidable scene in a forties movie. Nancy's secretary goes home, but Nancy works on, contacting all the parents she couldn't get during working hours. One parent anxiously reports that her child has a swollen lymph node on his neck.

"No," Nancy says firmly. "That is *not* a symptom of hepatitis. But you should ask the doctor about that when you go in for the gamma globulin."

Gamma globulin. The phrase rolls off her tongue. She tries to remember an odd title of a movie about gamma rays. It comes to her as she is dialing the telephone: *The Effect of Gamma Rays on Man-in-the-Moon Marigolds.* She has never known what that title meant.

The office grows dim, and Nancy turns on the lights. The school is quiet, as though the threat of an infectious disease has emptied the corridors, leaving her in charge. She recalls another movie, *The Andromeda Strain.* Her work is like the thrill of watching drama, a threat held safely at a distance. Historians have to be detached, Nancy once said, defensively, to Jack, when he accused her of being unfriendly to shopkeepers and waiters. Where was all that Southern hospitality he had heard so much about? he wanted to know. It hits her now that historians are detached about the past, not the present. Jack has learned some of this detachment: he wants to let Grover go. Nancy thinks of the stark images in his recent photographs—snow, icicles, fences, the long shot of Grover on the hill like a stray wolf. Nancy had always liked Jack's pictures simply for what they were, but Jack didn't see the people or the objects in them. He saw illusions. The vulnerability of the image, he once said, was what he was after. The image was meant to evoke its own death, he told her.

By the time Nancy finishes the scheduling, the night maintenance crew has arrived, and the coffeepot they keep in a closet is perking. Nancy removes her contact lenses and changes into her fleece-lined boots. In the parking lot, she maneuvers cautiously along a path past a mountain of black-stained snow. It is so cold that she makes sparks on the vinyl car seat. The engine is cold, slow to turn over.

At home, Nancy is surprised to see balloons in the living room. The stove is blazing and Robert's face is red from the heat.

"We're having a party," he says. "For Grover."

"There's a surprise for you in the oven," says Jack, handing Nancy a glass of sherry. "Because you worked so hard."

"Grover had ice cream," Robert says. "We got Häagen-Dazs."

"He looks cheerful," Nancy says, sinking onto the couch next to Jack. Her glasses are fogged up. She removes them and wipes them with a Kleenex. When she puts them back on she sees Grover looking at her, his head on his paws. His tail thumps. For the first time, Nancy feels ready to let the dog die.

When Nancy tells about the gamma globulin, the phrase has stopped rolling off her tongue so trippingly. She laughs. She is so tired she throbs with relief. She drinks the sherry too fast. Suddenly, she sits up straight and announces, "I've got a clue. I'm thinking of a parking lot."

"East or West?" Jack says. This is a game they used to play.

"West."

"Aha, I've got you," says Jack. "You're thinking of the parking lot at that hospital in Tucson."

"Hey, that's not fair going too fast," cries Robert. "I didn't get a chance to play."

"This was before you were born," Nancy says, running her fingers through Robert's hair. He is on the floor, leaning against her knees. "We were lying in the van for a week, thinking we were going to die. Oh, God!" Nancy laughs and covers her mouth with her hands.

"Why were you going to die?" Robert asks.

"We weren't really going to die." Both Nancy and Jack are laughing now at the memory, and Jack is pulling off his sweater. The hospital in Tucson wouldn't accept them because they weren't sick enough to hospitalize, but they were too sick to travel. They had nowhere to go. They had been on a month's trip through the West, then had stopped in Tucson and gotten jobs at a restaurant to make enough money to get home.

"Do you remember that doctor?" Jack says.

"I remember the look he gave us, like he didn't want us to pollute his hospital." Nancy laughs harder. She feels silly and relieved. Her hand, on Jack's knee, feels the fold of the long johns beneath his jeans. She cries, "I'll never forget how we stayed around that parking lot, thinking we were going to die."

"I couldn't have driven a block, I was so weak," Jack gasps.

"You were yellow. *I* didn't get yellow."

"All we could do was pee and drink orange juice."

"And throw the pee out the window."

"Grover was so bored with us!"

Nancy says, "It's a good thing we couldn't eat. We would have spent all our money."

"Then we would have had to work at that filthy restaurant again. And get hepatitis again."

"And on and on, forever. We would still be there, like Charley on the MTA. Oh, Jack, do you *remember* that crazy restaurant? You had to wear a ten-gallon hat—"

Abruptly, Robert jerks away from Nancy and crawls on his knees across the room to examine Grover, who is stretched out on his side, his legs sticking out stiffly. Robert, his straight hair falling, bends his head to the dog's heart.

"He's not dead," Robert says, looking up at Nancy. "He's lying doggo."

"Passed out at his own party," Jack says, raising his glass. "Way to go, Grover!"

POETRY

William Shakespeare (1564–1616)
FEAR NO MORE

Fear no more the heat o' the sun
   Nor the furious winter's rages;
Thou thy worldly task hast done,
   Home art gone and ta'en thy wages:
Golden lads and girls all must,
As chimney-sweepers, come to dust.

Fear no more the frown o' the great,
   Thou art past the tyrant's stroke;
Care no more to clothe and eat,
   To thee the reed is as the oak: 10
The sceptre, learning, physic,° must   medicine
All follow this and come to dust.

Fear no more the lightning-flash
   Nor the all-dreaded thunder-stone,°   bolt
Fear not slander, censure rash;
   Thou hast finished joy and moan:
All lovers young, all lovers must
Consign to° thee and come to dust.   accord with

No exorciser harm thee!
   Nor no witchcraft charm thee!   20
Ghost unlaid forbear thee!
   Nothing ill come near thee!
Quiet consummation have
And renownèd be thy grave!

John Donne (1572–1631)
DEATH, BE NOT PROUD

Death, be not proud, though some have callèd thee
Mighty and dreadful, for thou art not so;
For those whom thou think'st thou dost overthrow
Die not, poor death, nor yet canst thou kill me.

From rest and sleep, which but thy pictures be,
Much pleasure—then, from thee much more must flow;
And soonest our best men with thee do go,
Rest of their bones and soul's delivery.
Thou art slave to fate, chance, kings, and desperate men,
And dost with poison, war, and sickness dwell;   10
And poppy° or charms can make us sleep as well,   opium
And better than thy stroke. Why swell'st thou then?
One short sleep passed, we wake eternally,
And death shall be no more; death, thou shalt die.

John Donne (1572–1631)
HYMN TO GOD MY GOD, IN MY SICKNESS

Since I am coming to that holy room
  Where, with thy choir of saints for evermore,
I shall be made thy music, as I come
  I tune the instrument here at the door,
  And what I must do then, think now before.

Whilst my physicians by their love are grown
  Cosmographers, and I their map, who lie
Flat on this bed, that by them may be shown
  That this is my southwest discovery,[1]
  Per fretum febris,[2] by these straits to die,   10

I joy that in these straits I see my west;
  For though those currents yield return to none,
What shall my west hurt me? As west and east
  In all flat maps (and I am one) are one,
  So death doth touch the resurrectiön.

Is the Pacific Sea my home? Or are
  The eastern riches? Is Jerusalem?
Anyan° and Magellan and Gibraltar,   Bering Strait
  All straits, and none but straits, are ways to them,
  Whether where Japhet dwelt, or Cham, or Shem.[3]   20

Hymn to God My God, in My Sickness
  [1]Term used for the Straits of Magellan.
  [2]Through feverish straits.
  [3]Noah's sons, who, after the Flood, lived in Europe, Africa, and Asia, according to the Old Testament.

We think that Paradise and Calvary,
  Christ's cross and Adam's tree, stood in one place;
Look, Lord, and find both Adams met in me;
  As the first Adam's sweat surrounds my face,
  May the last Adam's blood my soul embrace.

So, in his purple wrapped receive me, Lord;
  By these his thorns give me his other crown;
And as to others' souls I preached thy word,
  Be this my text, my sermon to mine own:
  Therefore that he may raise, the Lord throws down.   30

QUESTIONS

1. As you reread the poem, can you distinguish its main parts?
2. Is the speaker's tone or attitude towards his condition the same throughout?
3. What do the geographical metaphors and symbolism in stanzas 2–4 suggest to you about the speaker's condition?

Robert Herrick (1591–1674)

DIVINATION BY A DAFFODIL

When a Daffodil I see,
Hanging down his head towards me;
Guess I may, what I must be:
First, I shall decline my head;
Secondly, I shall be dead;
Lastly, safely burièd.

Thomas Gray (1716–1771)

ELEGY WRITTEN IN A COUNTRY CHURCHYARD

The curfew tolls the knell of parting day,
  The lowing herd wind slowly o'er the lea,
The plowman homeward plods his weary way,
  And leaves the world to darkness and to me.

Now fades the glimmering landscape on the sight,
   And all the air a solemn stillness holds,
Save where the beetle wheels his droning flight,
   And drowsy tinklings lull the distant folds;

Save that from yonder ivy-mantled tower
   The moping owl does to the moon complain   10
Of such, as wandering near her secret bower,
   Molest her ancient solitary reign.

Beneath those rugged elms, that yew tree's shade,
   Where heaves the turf in many a moldering heap,
Each in his narrow cell forever laid,
   The rude° forefathers of the hamlet sleep.   humble

The breezy call of incense-breathing morn,
   The swallow twittering from the straw-built shed,
The cock's shrill clarion, or the echoing horn,
   No more shall rouse them from their lowly bed.   20

For them no more the blazing hearth shall burn,
   Or busy housewife ply her evening care;
No children run to lisp their sire's return,
   Or climb his knees the envied kiss to share.

Oft did the harvest to their sickle yield,
   Their furrow oft the stubborn glebe° has broke;   earth
How jocund did they drive their team afield!
   How bowed the woods beneath their sturdy stroke!

Let not Ambition mock their useful toil,
   Their homely joys, and destiny obscure;   30
Nor Grandeur hear with a disdainful smile
   The short and simple annals of the poor.

The boast of heraldry,° the pomp of power,   pageantry
   And all that beauty, all that wealth e'er gave,
Awaits alike the inevitable hour.
   The paths of glory lead but to the grave.

Nor you, ye proud, impute to these the fault,
   If Memory o'er their tomb no trophies raise,
Where through the long-drawn aisle and fretted° vault   ornamented
   The pealing anthem swells the note of praise.   40

Can storied° urn or animated bust   inscribed
  Back to its mansion call the fleeting breath?
Can Honor's voice provoke the silent dust,
  Or Flattery soothe the dull cold ear of Death?

Perhaps in this neglected spot is laid
  Some heart once pregnant with celestial fire;
Hands that the rod of empire might have swayed,
  Or waked to ecstasy the living lyre.

But Knowledge to their eyes her ample page
  Rich with the spoils of time did ne'er unroll;   50
Chill Penury repressed their noble rage,
  And froze the genial current of the soul.

Full many a gem of purest ray serene,
  The dark unfathomed caves of ocean bear:
Full many a flower is born to blush unseen,
  And waste its sweetness on the desert air.

Some village Hampden,[1] that with dauntless breast
  The little tyrant of his fields withstood;
Some mute inglorious Milton here may rest,
  Some Cromwell[2] guiltless of his country's blood.   60

The applause of listening senates to command,
  The threats of pain and ruin to despise,
To scatter plenty o'er a smiling land,
  And read their history in a nation's eyes,

Their lot forbade: nor circumscribed alone
  Their growing virtues, but their crimes confined;
Forbade to wade through slaughter to a throne,
  And shut the gates of mercy on mankind,

The struggling pangs of conscious truth to hide,
  To quench the blushes of ingenuous shame,   70
Or heap the shrine of Luxury and Pride
  With incense kindled at the Muse's flame.

Elegy Written in a Country Churchyard
  [1]John Hampden (1594–1643), Parliamentary leader during the Civil War with King Charles I.
  [2]Oliver Cromwell (1599–1658), leader of the Parliamentary forces during the Civil War; Lord
Protector during the Commonwealth.

Far from the madding° crowd's ignoble strife,   frenzied
   Their sober wishes never learned to stray;
Along the cool sequestered vale of life
   They kept the noiseless tenor of their way.

Yet even these bones from insult to protect
   Some frail memorial still erected nigh,
With uncouth rhymes and shapeless sculpture decked,
   Implores the passing tribute of a sigh.   80

Their name, their years, spelt by the unlettered Muse,
   The place of fame and elegy supply:
And many a holy text around she strews,
   That teach the rustic moralist to die.

For who to dumb Forgetfulness a prey,
   This pleasing anxious being e'er resigned,
Left the warm precincts of the cheerful day,
   Nor cast one longing lingering look behind?

On some fond breast the parting soul relies,
   Some pious drops the closing eye requires;   90
Even from the tomb the voice of Nature cries,
   Even in our ashes live their wonted fires.

For thee, who mindful of the unhonored dead
   Dost in these lines their artless tale relate;
If chance, by lonely contemplation led,
   Some kindred spirit shall inquire thy fate,

Haply some hoary-headed swain may say,
   "Oft have we seen him at the peep of dawn
Brushing with hasty steps the dews away
   To meet the sun upon the upland lawn.   100

"There at the foot of yonder nodding beech
   That wreathes its old fantastic roots so high,
His listless length at noontide would he stretch,
   And pore upon the brook that babbles by.

"Hard by yon wood, now smiling as in scorn,
   Muttering his wayward fancies he would rove,
Now drooping, woeful wan, like one forlorn,
   Or crazed with care, or crossed in hopeless love.

"One morn I missed him on the customed hill,
 Along the heath and near his favorite tree;   110
Another came; nor yet beside the rill,
 Nor up the lawn, nor at the wood was he;

"The next with dirges due in sad array
 Slow through the churchway path we saw him borne.
Approach and read (for thou canst read) the lay,
 Graved on the stone beneath yon aged thorn."

The Epitaph

Here rests his head upon the lap of Earth
 A youth to Fortune and to Fame unknown.
Fair Science frowned not on his humble birth,
 And Melancholy marked him for her own.   120

Large was his bounty, and his soul sincere,
 Heaven did a recompense as largely send:
He gave to Misery all he had, a tear,
 He gained from Heaven ('twas all he wished) a friend.

No farther seek his merits to disclose,
 Or draw his frailties from their dread abode
(There they alike in trembling hope repose),
 The bosom of his Father and his God.

QUESTIONS

1. How would you describe the style of this poem? How did you react to the style?
2. What do you hear in the speaker's voice, besides the obvious melancholy?
3. Do you suppose the speaker to be a simple villager?
4. On rereading the poem, can you distinguish its parts? Are their relations to one another clear?

Walter Savage Landor (1775–1864)
ON HIS 75TH BIRTHDAY

I strove with none, for none was worth my strife:
 Nature I loved, and, next to Nature, Art:
I warmed both hands before the fire of Life;
 It sinks; and I am ready to depart.

Percy Bysshe Shelley (1792–1822)
ODE TO THE WEST WIND

I

O wild West Wind, thou breath of Autumn's being,
Thou, from whose unseen presence the leaves dead
Are driven, like ghosts from an enchanter fleeing,

Yellow, and black, and pale, and hectic red,
Pestilence-stricken multitudes: O thou,
Who chariotest to their dark wintry bed

The wingéd seeds, where they lie cold and low,
Each like a corpse within its grave, until
Thine azure sister of the Spring shall blow

Her clarion o'er the dreaming earth, and fill   10
(Driving sweet buds like flocks to feed in air)
With living hues and odors plain and hill:

Wild Spirit, which art moving everywhere;
Destroyer and preserver; hear, oh, hear!

II

Thou on whose stream, mid the steep sky's commotion,
Loose clouds like earth's decaying leaves are shed,
Shook from the tangled boughs of Heaven and Ocean,

Angels of rain and lightning: there are spread
On the blue surface of thine aëry surge,
Like the bright hair uplifted from the head   20

Of some fierce Maenad,[1] even from the dim verge
Of the horizon to the zenith's height,
The locks of the approaching storm. Thou dirge

Of the dying year, to which this closing night
Will be the dome of a vast sepulcher,
Vaulted with all thy congregated might

Ode to the West Wind
[1]In Greek myth, a female worshipper of the god Dionysus.

Of vapors, from whose solid atmosphere
Black rain, and fire, and hail will burst: oh, hear!

III

Thou who didst waken from his summer dreams
The blue Mediterranean, where he lay,   30
Lulled by the coil of his crystálline streams,

Beside a pumice isle in Baiae's bay,[2]
And saw in sleep old palaces and towers
Quivering within the wave's intenser day,

All overgrown with azure moss and flowers
So sweet, the sense faints picturing them! Thou
For whose path the Atlantic's level powers

Cleave themselves into chasms, while far below
The sea-blooms and the oozy woods which wear
The sapless foliage of the ocean, know   40

Thy voice, and suddenly grow gray with fear,
And tremble and despoil themselves: oh, hear!

IV

If I were a dead leaf thou mightest bear;
If I were a swift cloud to fly with thee;
A wave to pant beneath thy power, and share

The impulse of thy strength, only less free
Than thou, O uncontrollable! If even
I were as in my boyhood, and could be

The comrade of thy wanderings over Heaven,
As then, when to outstrip thy skyey speed   50
Scarce seemed a vision; I would ne'er have striven

As thus with thee in prayer in my sore need.
Oh, lift me as a wave, a leaf, a cloud!
I fall upon the thorns of life! I bleed!

A heavy weight of hours has chained and bowed
One too like thee: tameless, and swift, and proud.

---

[2]West of Naples.

V

Make me thy lyre, even as the forest is:
What if my leaves are falling like its own!
The tumult of thy mighty harmonies

Will take from both a deep, autumnal tone,   60
Sweet though in sadness. Be thou, Spirit fierce,
My spirit! Be thou me, impetuous one!

Drive my dead thoughts over the universe
Like withered leaves to quicken a new birth!
And, by the incantation of this verse,

Scatter, as from an unextinguished hearth
Ashes and sparks, my words among mankind!
Be through my lips to unawakened earth

The trumpet of a prophecy! O Wind,
If Winter comes, can Spring be far behind?   70

QUESTIONS

1. When you read the poem aloud, how does it sound?
2. Which images evoke strong responses from you?
3. How do you imagine the speaker? What seems to have been his experience of life?
4. What is the speaker's tone in the concluding section? How do you respond to what he is saying here?

Percy Bysshe Shelley (1792–1822)

OZYMANDIAS[1]

I met a traveller from an antique land
Who said: Two vast and trunkless legs of stone
Stand in the desert . . . Near them, on the sand,
Half sunk, a shattered visage lies, whose frown,
And wrinkled lip, and sneer of cold command,
Tell that its sculptor well those passions read

Ozymadias
[1]Pharaoh of Egypt, also called Ramesses II, who ruled in the thirteenth century B.C.

Which yet survive, stamped on these lifeless things,
The hand that mocked them, and the heart that fed:
And on the pedestal these words appear:
"My name is Ozymandias, king of kings: 10
Look on my works, ye Mighty, and despair!"
Nothing beside remains. Round the decay
Of that colossal wreck, boundless and bare
The lone and level sands stretch far away.

QUESTIONS

1. What purpose is served by having a "traveller" report what remains in the desert?
2. What do you suppose interested the speaker in this report?

John Keats (1795–1821)
TO AUTUMN

Season of mists and mellow fruitfulness,
    Close bosom-friend of the maturing sun;
Conspiring with him how to load and bless
    With fruit the vines that round the thatch-eaves run;
To bend with apples the mossed cottage-trees,
    And fill all fruit with ripeness to the core;
        To swell the gourd, and plump the hazel shells
With a sweet kernel; to set budding more,
    And still more, later flowers for the bees,
    Until they think warm days will never cease,   10
        For summer has o'er-brimmed their clammy cells.

Who hath not seen thee oft amid thy store?
    Sometimes whoever seeks abroad may find
Thee sitting careless on a granary floor,
    Thy hair soft-lifted by the winnowing wind;
Or on a half-reaped furrow sound asleep,
    Drowsed with the fume of poppies, while thy hook
        Spares the next swath and all its twinèd flowers:
And sometimes like a gleaner thou dost keep
    Steady thy laden head across a brook;   20
    Or by a cider-press, with patient look,
        Thou watchest the last oozings hours by hours.

Where are the songs of spring? Ay, where are they?
  Think not of them, thou hast thy music too,—
While barred clouds bloom the soft-dying day,
  And touch the stubble-plains with rosy hue;
Then in a wailful choir the small gnats mourn
  Among the river sallows,° borne aloft   willows
    Or sinking as the light wind lives or dies;
And full-grown lambs loud bleat from hilly bourn;
  Hedge-crickets sing; and now with treble soft
  The red-breast whistles from a garden-croft,°   enclosure
    And gathering swallows twitter in the skies.

Alfred, Lord Tennyson (1809–1892)
ULYSSES[1]

It little profits that an idle king,
By this still hearth, among these barren crags,
Matched with an aged wife, I mete and dole
Unequal laws unto a savage race,
That hoard, and sleep, and feed, and know not me.

I cannot rest from travel; I will drink
Life to the lees. All times I have enjoyed
Greatly, have suffered greatly, both with those
That loved me, and alone; on shore, and when
Through scudding drifts the rainy Hyades[2]   10
Vexed the dim sea. I am become a name;
For always roaming with a hungry heart
Much have I seen and known—cities of men
And manners, climates, councils, governments,
Myself not least, but honored of them all—
And drunk delight of battle with my peers,
Far on the ringing plains of windy Troy.
I am a part of all that I have met;
Yet all experience is an arch wherethrough

Ulysses
[1]Other name for Odysseus. The story of his adventurous journey home to Ithaca after the Trojan War is familiar from Homer.
[2]A group of stars supposed to foretell rain.

Gleams that untraveled world whose margin fades   20
Forever and forever when I move.
How dull it is to pause, to make an end,
To rust unburnished, not to shine in use!
As though to breathe were life! Life piled on life
Were all too little, and of one to me
Little remains; but every hour is saved
From that eternal silence, something more,
A bringer of new things; and vile it were
For some three suns to store and hoard myself,
And this gray spirit yearning in desire   30
To follow knowledge like a sinking star,
Beyond the utmost bound of human thought.

   This is my son, mine own Telemachus,
To whom I leave the scepter and the isle—
Well-loved of me, discerning to fulfill
This labor, by slow prudence to make mild
A rugged people, and through soft degrees
Subdue them to the useful and the good.
Most blameless is he, centered in the sphere
Of common duties, decent not to fail   40
In offices of tenderness, and pay
Meet° adoration to my household gods,   fitting
When I am gone. He works his work, I mine.

   There lies the port; the vessel puffs her sail;
There gloom the dark, broad seas. My mariners,
Souls that have toiled, and wrought, and thought with
    me—
That ever with a frolic welcome took
The thunder and the sunshine, and opposed
Free hearts, free foreheads—you and I are old;
Old age hath yet his honor and his toil.   50
Death closes all; but something ere the end,
Some work of noble note, may yet be done,
Not unbecoming men that strove with Gods.
The lights begin to twinkle from the rocks;
The long day wanes; the slow moon climbs; the deep
Moans round with many voices. Come, my friends,
'Tis not too late to seek a newer world.
Push off, and sitting well in order smite
The sounding furrows; for my purpose holds
To sail beyond the sunset, and the baths   60
Of all the western stars, until I die.

It may be that the gulfs will wash us down;
It may be we shall touch the Happy Isles,[3]
And see the great Achilles, whom we knew.
Though much is taken, much abides; and though
We are not now that strength which in old days
Moved earth and heaven, that which we are, we are—
One equal temper of heroic hearts,
Made weak by time and fate, but strong in will
To strive, to seek, to find, and not to yield.   70

QUESTIONS

1. Did you bring any earlier ideas about Ulysses (or Odysseus) to your reading of this poem?
2. How do you picture the scene as Ulysses speaks here?
3. Why do you suppose this particular moment was chosen for the poem?
4. What ideas about heroism does the poem suggest?

Matthew Arnold (1822–1888)

DOVER BEACH

The sea is calm tonight,
The tide is full, the moon lies fair
Upon the straits;—on the French coast the light
Gleams and is gone; the cliffs of England stand,
Glimmering and vast, out in the tranquil bay.
Come to the window, sweet is the night-air!
Only, from the long line of spray
Where the sea meets the moon-blanched land,
Listen! you hear the grating roar
Of pebbles which the waves draw back, and fling,   10
At their return, up the high strand,
Begin, and cease, and then again begin,
With tremulous cadence slow, and bring
The eternal note of sadness in.

Sophocles long ago
Heard it on the Aegean, and it brought

---

[3]Or Elysium, where those favored by the gods, like the hero Achilles, were thought to dwell after death.

Into his mind the turbid ebb and flow
Of human misery; we
Find also in the sound a thought,
Hearing it by this distant northern sea.   20

The Sea of Faith
Was once, too, at the full, and round earth's shore
Lay like the folds of a bright girdle° furled.   sash
But now I only hear
Its melancholy, long, withdrawing roar,
Retreating, to the breath
Of the night-wind, down the vast edges drear
And naked shingles° of the world.   pebble beaches

Ah, love, let us be true
To one another! for the world, which seems   30
To lie before us like a land of dreams,
So various, so beautiful, so new,
Hath really neither joy, nor love, nor light,
Nor certitude, nor peace, nor help for pain;
And we are here as on a darkling plain
Swept with confused alarms of struggle and flight,
Where ignorant armies clash by night.

QUESTIONS

1. How do you picture the scene and speaker?
2. What do you suppose he means by the Sea of Faith?
3. What mood do the speaker's thoughts arouse in him?
4. Do you suppose an actual war is meant in the last lines?

Walt Whitman (1819–1892)

WHEN LILACS LAST IN THE DOORYARD BLOOM'D[1]

I

When lilacs last in the dooryard bloom'd,
And the great star early droop'd in the western sky in the
  night,

When Lilacs Last in the Dooryard Bloom'd
[1]For President Lincoln, assassinated in April 1865.

I mourn'd, and yet shall mourn with ever-returning spring.
Ever-returning spring, trinity sure to me you bring,
Lilac blooming perennial and drooping star in the west,
And thought of him I love.

II

O powerful western fallen star!
O shades of night—O moody, tearful night!
O great star disappear'd—O the black murk that hides the
 star!
O cruel hands that hold me powerless—O helpless soul of
 me!   10
O harsh surrounding cloud that will not free my soul.

III

In the dooryard fronting an old farm-house near the whitewash'd palings,
Stands the lilac-bush tall-growing with heart-shaped leaves
 of rich green,
With many a pointed blossom rising delicate, with the
 perfume strong I love,
With every leaf a miracle—and from this bush in the
 dooryard,
With delicate-color'd blossoms and heart-shaped leaves of
 rich green,
A sprig with its flower I break.

IV

In the swamp in secluded recesses,
A shy and hidden bird is warbling a song.

Solitary the thrush,   20
The hermit withdrawn to himself, avoiding the settlements,
Sings by himself a song.

Song of the bleeding throat,
Death's outlet song of life, (for well dear brother I know,
If thou wast not granted to sing thou would'st surely die.)

V

Over the breast of the spring the land, amid cities,
Amid lanes and through old woods, where lately the violets
 peep'd from the ground, spotting the gray debris,
Amid the grass in the fields each side of the lanes, passing
 the endless grass,

Passing the yellow-spear'd wheat, every grain from its
    shroud in the dark-brown fields uprisen,
Passing the apple-tree blows° of white and pink in the   blooms
    orchards,   30
Carrying a corpse to where it shall rest in the grave,
Night and day journeys a coffin.

VI

Coffin that passes through lanes and streets,
Through day and night with the great cloud darkening the
    land,
With the pomp of the inloop'd flags with the cities draped
    in black,
With the show of the States themselves as of crape-veil'd
    women standing,
With processions long and winding and the flambeaus of
    the night,
With the countless torches lit, with the silent sea of faces
    and the unbared heads,
With the waiting depot, the arriving coffin, and the sombre
    faces,
With dirges through the night, with the thousand voices
    rising strong and solemn,   40
With all the mournful voices of the dirges pour'd around
    the coffin,
The dim-lit churches and the shuddering organs—where
    amid these you journey,
With the tolling bells' perpetual clang,
Here, coffin that slowly passes,
I give you my sprig of lilac.

VII

(Nor for you, for one alone,
Blossoms and branches green to coffins all I bring,
For fresh as the morning, thus would I chant a song for
    you O sane and sacred death.

All over bouquets of roses,
O death, I cover you over with roses and early lilies,   50
But mostly and now the lilac that blooms the first,
Copious I break, I break the sprigs from the bushes,
With loaded arms I come, pouring for you,
For you and the coffins all of you O death.)

VIII

O Western orb sailing the heaven,
Now I know what you must have meant as a month since I
  walk'd,
As I walk'd in silence the transparent shadowy night,
As I saw you had something to tell as you bent to me night
  after night,
As you droop'd from the sky low down as if to my side,
  (while the other stars all look'd on,)
As we wander'd together the solemn night, (for something I
  know not what kept me from sleep,)   60
As the night advanced, and I saw on the rim of the west
  how full you were of woe,
As I stood on the rising ground in the breeze in the cool
  transparent night,
As I watch'd where you passed and was lost in the
  netherward black of the night,
As my soul in its trouble dissatisfied sank, as where you sad
  orb,
Concluded, dropt in the night, and was gone.

IX

Sing on there in the swamp,
O singer bashful and tender, I hear your notes, I hear your
  call,
I hear, I come presently, I understand you,
But a moment I linger, for the lustrous star has detain'd
  me,
The star my departing comrade holds and detains me.   70

X

O how shall I warble myself for the dead one there I loved?
And how shall I deck my song for the large sweet soul that
  has gone?
And what shall my perfume be for the grave of him I love?

Sea-winds blown from east and west,
Blown from the Eastern sea and blown from the Western
  sea, till there on the prairies meeting,
These and with these and the breath of my chant,
I'll perfume the grave of him I love.

XI

O what shall I hang on the chamber walls?
And what shall the pictures be that I hang on the walls,
To adorn the burial-house of him I love?   80

Pictures of growing spring and farms and homes,
With the Fourth-month° eve at sundown, and the gray   April
    smoke lucid and bright,
With floods of the yellow gold of the gorgeous, indolent,
    sinking sun, burning, expanding the air,
With the fresh sweet herbage under foot, and the pale green
    leaves of the trees prolific,
In the distance the flowing glaze, the breast of the river,
    with a wind-dapple here and there,
With ranging hills on the banks, with many a line against
    the sky, and shadows,
And the city at hand with dwellings so dense, and stacks of
    chimneys,
And all the scenes of life and the workshops, and the
    workmen homeward returning.

XII

Lo, body and soul—this land,
My own Manhattan with spires, and the sparkling and
    hurrying tides, and the ships.   90
The varied and ample land, the South and the North in the
    light,
Ohio's shores and flashing Missouri,
And ever the far-spreading prairies cover'd with grass and
    corn.

Lo, the most excellent sun so calm and haughty,
The violet and purple morn with just-felt breezes,
The gentle soft-born measureless light,
The miracle spreading bathing all, the fulfill'd noon,
The coming eve delicious, the welcome night and the stars,
Over my cities shining all, enveloping man and land.

XIII

Sing on, sing on you gray-brown bird,
Sing from the swamps, the recesses, pour your chant from
    the bushes,   100
Limitless out of the dusk, out of the cedars and pines.

Sing on dearest brother, warble your reedy song,
Loud human song, with voice of uttermost woe.

O liquid and free and tender!
O wild and loose to my soul—O wondrous singer!

You only I hear—yet the star holds me, (but will soon
   depart,)
Yet the lilac with mastering odor holds me.

XIV

Now while I sat in the day and look'd forth,
In the close of the day with its light and the fields of spring,
   and the farmers preparing their crops,
In the large unconscious scenery of my land with its lakes
   and forests,   110
In the heavenly aerial beauty, (after the perturb'd winds
   and the storms,)
Under the arching heavens of the afternoon swift passing,
   and the voices of children and women.
The many-moving sea-tides, and I saw the ships how they
   sail'd,
And the summer approaching with richness, and the fields
   all busy with labor,
And the infinite separate houses, how they all went on,
   each with its meals and minutia of daily usages,
And the streets how their throbbings throbb'd, and the
   cities pent—lo, then and there,
Falling upon them all and among them all, enveloping me
   with the rest,
Appear'd the cloud, appear'd the long black trail,
And I knew death, its thought, and the sacred knowledge of
   death.

Then with the knowledge of death as walking one side of
   me,   120
And the thought of death close-walking the other side of
   me,
And I in the middle as with companions, and as holding the
   hands of companions,
I fled forth to the hiding receiving night that talks not,
Down to the shores of the water, the path by the swamp in
   the dimness,
To the solemn shadowy cedars and ghostly pines so still.

And the singer so shy to the rest receiv'd me,
The gray-brown bird I know receiv'd us comrades three,
And he sang the carol of death, and a verse for him I love.

From deep secluded recesses,
From the fragrant cedars and the ghostly pines so still,   130
Came the carol of the bird.

And the charm of the carol rapt me,
As I held as if by their hands my comrades in the night,
And the voice of my spirit tallied° the song of the bird.   echoed

Come lovely and soothing death,
Undulate round the world, serenely arriving, arriving,
In the day, in the night, to all, to each,
Sooner or later delicate death.

Prais'd be the fathomless universe,
For life and joy, and for objects and knowledge curious,   140
And for love, sweet love—but praise! praise! praise!
For the sure-enwinding arms of cool-enfolding death.

Dark mother always gliding near with soft feet,
Have none chanted for thee a chant of fullest welcome?
Then I chant it for thee, I glorify thee above all,
I bring thee a song that when thou must indeed come,
*   come unfalteringly.*

Approach strong deliveress,
When it is so, when thou has taken them I joyously sing
*   the dead,*
Lost in the loving floating ocean of thee,
Loved in the flood of thy bliss O death.   150

From me to thee glad serenades,
Dances for thee I propose saluting thee, adornments and
*   feastings for thee,*
And the sights of the open landscape and the high-spread
*   sky are fitting,*
And life and the fields, and the huge and thoughtful night.

The night in silence under many a star,
The ocean shore and the husky whispering wave whose
*   voice I know,*
And the soul turning to thee O vast and well-veil'd death,
And the body gratefuly nestling close to thee.

Over the tree-tops I float thee a song,
Over the rising and sinking waves, over the myriad fields
*   and the prairies wide,*   160
Over the dense-pack'd cities all and the teeming wharves
*   and ways,*
I float this carol with joy, with joy to thee O death.

XV

To the tally of my soul,
Loud and strong kept up the gray-brown bird,
With pure deliberate notes spreading filling the night.

Loud in the pines and cedars dim,
Clear in the freshness moist and the swamp-perfume
And I with my comrades there in the night.

While my sight that was bound in my eyes unclosed,
As to long panoramas of visions.   170

And I saw askant° the armies,   anxiously
I saw as in noiseless dreams hundreds of battle-flags,
Borne through the smoke of the battles and pierc'd with
   missiles I saw them,
And carried hither and yon through the smoke, and torn
   and bloody,
And at last but a few shreds left on the staffs, (and all in
   silence,)
And the staffs all splinter'd and broken.

I saw battle-corpses, myriads of them,
And the white skeletons of young men, I saw them,
I saw the debris and debris of all the slain soldiers of the
   war,
But I saw they were not as was thought,   180
They themselves were fully at rest, they suffer'd not,
The living remain'd and suffer'd, the mother suffer'd,
And the wife and the child and the musing comrade
   suffer'd,
And the armies that remain'd suffer'd.

XVI

Passing the visions, passing the night,
Passing, unloosing the hold of my comrades' hands,
Passing the song of the hermit bird and the tallying song of
   my soul,
Victorious song, death's outlet song, yet varying ever-
   altering song,
As low and wailing, yet clear the notes, rising and falling
   flooding the night,
Sadly sinking and fainting, as warning and warning, and
   yet again bursting with joy,   190
Covering the earth and filling the spread of the heaven,

As that powerful psalm in the night I heard from recesses,
Passing, I leave thee lilac with heart-shaped leaves,
I leave thee there in the door-yard, blooming, returning
    with spring.

I cease from my song for thee,
From my gaze on thee in the west, fronting the west,
    communing with thee,
O comrade lustrous with silver face in the night.

Yet each to keep and all, retrievements out of the night,
The song, the wondrous chant of the gray-brown bird,
And the tallying chant, the echo arous'd in my soul,   200
With the lustrous and drooping star with the countenance
    full of woe,
With the holders holding my hand nearing the call of the
    bird,
Comrades mine and I in the midst, and their memory ever
    to keep, for the dead I love so well,
For the sweetest, wisest soul of all my days and lands—and
    this for his dear sake,
Lilac and star and bird twined with the chant of my soul,
There in the fragrant pines and the cedars dusk and dim.

Emily Dickinson (1830–1886)
BECAUSE I COULD NOT STOP FOR DEATH

Because I could not stop for Death—
He kindly stopped for me—
The Carriage held but just Ourselves—
And Immortality.

We slowly drove—He knew no haste
And I had put away
My labor and my leisure too,
For His Civility—

We passed the School, where Children strove
At Recess—in the Ring—   10
We passed the Fields of Gazing Grain—
We passed the Setting Sun—

Or rather—He passed Us—
The Dews drew quivering and chill—
For only Gossamer, my Gown—
My Tippet—only Tulle—[1]

We paused before a House that seemed
A Swelling of the Ground—
The Roof was scarcely visible—
The Cornice—in the Ground—   20

Since then—'tis Centuries—and yet
Feels shorter than the Day
I first surmised the Horses' Heads
Were toward Eternity—

QUESTIONS

1. What details help you to imagine the speaker?
2. How do you respond to this personification of Death?
3. What experience of death is suggested by the poem? How do you react to this view?

Emily Dickinson (1830–1886)

THIS WORLD IS NOT CONCLUSION

This World is not Conclusion.
A Species stands beyond—
Invisible, as Music—
But positive, as Sound—
It beckons, and it baffles—
Philosophy—don't know—
And through a Riddle, at the last—
Sagacity, must go—
To guess it, puzzles scholars—
To gain it, Men have borne   10
Contempt of Generations
And Crucifixion, shown—
Faith slips—and laughs, and rallies—

———————————

Because I could not stop for Death
[1] A tippet is a scarf; tulle a silk netting.

Blushes, if any see—
Plucks at a twig of Evidence—
And asks a Vane, the way—
Much Gesture, from the Pulpit—
Strong Hallelujahs roll—
Narcotics cannot still the Tooth
That nibbles at the soul—   20

Thomas Hardy (1840–1928)
THE MAN HE KILLED

"Had he and I but met
    By some old ancient inn,
We should have sat us down to wet
    Right many a nipperkin!°   half-pint

"But ranged as infantry,
    And staring face to face,
I shot at him as he at me,
    And killed him in his place.

"I shot him dead because—
    Because he was my foe,   10
Just so: my foe of course he was:
    That's clear enough; although

"He thought he'd 'list, perhaps,
    Off-hand like—just as I—
Was out of work—had sold his traps—
    No other reason why.

"Yes; quaint and curious war is:
    You shoot a fellow down
You'd treat if met where any bar is,
    Or help to half-a-crown."   20

QUESTIONS

1. How do you picture the speaker?
2. How has he understood his experience in war?
3. What feelings, if any, does his voice express?

Thomas Hardy (1840–1928)
THE DARKLING THRUSH[1]

I leant upon a coppice° gate   thicket
    When Frost was spectre-gray,
And Winter's dregs made desolate
    The weakening eye of day.
The tangled bine-stems scored the sky
    Like strings of broken lyres,
And all mankind that haunted nigh°   dwelt nearby
    Had sought their household fires.

The land's sharp features seemed to be
    The Century's corpse outleant,   10
His crypt the cloudy canopy,
    The wind his death-lament.
The ancient pulse of germ and birth
    Was shrunken hard and dry,
And every spirit upon earth
    Seemed fervourless as I.

At once a voice arose among
    The bleak twigs overhead
In a full-hearted evensong
    Of joy illimited;   20
An aged thrush, frail, gaunt, and small,
    In blast-beruffled plume,
Had chosen thus to fling his soul
    Upon the growing gloom.

So little cause for carolings
    Of such ecstatic sound
Was written on terrestrial things
    Afar or nigh around,
That I could think there trembled through
    His happy good-night air   30
Some blessed Hope, whereof he knew
    And I was unaware.

The Darkling Thrush
[1]Written on New Year's Eve, 1900. 'Darkling': in the dark.

A. E. Housman (1859–1936)
TO AN ATHLETE DYING YOUNG

The time you won your town the race
We chaired you through the market-place;
Man and boy stood cheering by,
And home we brought you shoulder-high.

To-day, the road all runners come,
Shoulder-high we bring you home,
And set you at your threshold down,
Townsman of a stiller town.

Smart lad, to slip betimes° away   early
From fields where glory does not stay   10
And early though the laurel grows
It withers quicker than the rose.

Eyes the shady night has shut
Cannot see the record cut,
And silence sounds no worse than cheers
After earth has stopped the ears:

Now you will not swell the rout
Of lads that wore their honours out,
Runners whom renown outran
And the name died before the man.   20

So set, before its echoes fade,
The fleet foot on the sill of shade,
And hold to the low lintel up
The still-defended challenge-cup.

And round that early-laurelled head
Will flock to gaze the strengthless dead,
And find unwithered on its curls
The garland briefer than a girl's.

QUESTIONS

1. How much experience of mourning an early death did you bring to your reading of this poem?
2. How consoled by his thoughts does this speaker seem? How much consolation could you borrow from it?

William Butler Yeats (1865–1939)

AN IRISH AIRMAN FORESEES HIS DEATH

I know that I shall meet my fate
Somewhere among the clouds above;
Those that I fight I do not hate,
Those that I guard I do not love;
My country is Kiltartan Cross,[1]
My countrymen Kiltartan's poor,
No likely end could bring them loss
Or leave them happier than before.
Nor law, nor duty bade me fight,
Nor public men, nor cheering crowds,   10
A lonely impulse of delight
Drove to this tumult in the clouds;
I balanced all, brought all to mind,
The years to come seemed waste of breath,
A waste of breath the years behind
In balance with this life, this death.

QUESTIONS

1. How do you picture the speaker, and in which war do you suppose him to be?
2. How patriotic does he seem to be? What is his attitude towards his likely death?
3. How important is it that the poet and speaker are obviously not the same?

William Butler Yeats (1865–1939)

THE SECOND COMING[1]

Turning and turning in the widening gyre[2]
The falcon cannot hear the falconer;
Things fall apart; the centre cannot hold;
Mere anarchy is loosed upon the world,
The blood-dimmed tide is loosed, and everywhere

An Irish Airman Foresees His Death
    [1]Village in County Galway, Ireland. The poem commemorates the death of Major Robert Gregory, heir to a large Irish estate, in action over Italy in January 1918.
The Second Coming
    [1]In the New Testament, Christ is expected to come again, after a period of great tribulation on earth, and to herald the Millenium.
    [2]Spiral. Yeats believed that historic time moved in great spiraling movements, winding and unwinding the ages of civilization.

The ceremony of innocence is drowned;
The best lack all conviction, while the worst
Are full of passionate intensity.

Surely some revelation is at hand;
Surely the Second Coming is at hand.   10
The Second Coming! Hardly are those words out
When a vast image out of *Spiritus Mundi*[3]
Troubles my sight: somewhere in sands of the desert
A shape with lion body and the head of a man
A gaze blank and pitiless as the sun,
Is moving its slow thighs, while all about it
Reel shadows of the indignant desert birds.
The darkness drops again; but now I know
That twenty centuries of stony sleep
Were vexed to nightmare by a rocking cradle,   20
And what rough beast, its hour come round at last,
Slouches towards Bethlehem to be born?

Robert Frost (1874–1963)

FIRE AND ICE

Some say the world will end in fire,
Some say in ice.
From what I've tasted of desire
I hold with those who favor fire.
But if it had to perish twice,
I think I know enough of hate
To say that for destruction ice
Is also great
And would suffice.

Robert Frost (1874–1963)

PROVIDE, PROVIDE

The witch that came (the withered hag)
To wash the steps with pail and rag
Was once the beauty Abishag,[1]

---

[3]The universal soul, or collective memory, in which Yeats believed.

Provide, Provide
[1]In the Old Testament, a lovely concubine chosen for the aged King David. I Kings 1.

The picture pride of Hollywood.
Too many fall from great and good
For you to doubt the likelihood.

Die early and avoid the fate.
Or if predestined to die late,
Make up your mind to die in state.

Make the whole stock exchange your own!   10
If need be occupy a throne,
Where nobody can call *you* crone.

Some have relied on what they knew,
Others on being simply true.
What worked for them might work for you.

No memory of having starred
Atones for later disregard
Or keeps the end from being hard.

Better to go down dignified
With boughten friendship at your side   20
Than none at all. Provide, provide!

Robert Frost (1874–1963)

AFTER APPLE-PICKING

My long two-pointed ladder's sticking through a tree
Toward heaven still,
And there's a barrel that I didn't fill
Beside it, and there may be two or three
Apples I didn't pick upon some bough.
But I am done with apple-picking now.
Essence of winter sleep is on the night,
The scent of apples: I am drowsing off.
I cannot rub the strangeness from my sight
I got from looking through a pane of glass   10
I skimmed this morning from the drinking trough
And held against the world of hoary grass.
It melted, and I let it fall and break.
But I was well
Upon my way to sleep before it fell,
And I could tell

What form my dreaming was about to take.
Magnified apples appear and disappear,
Stem end and blossom end,
And every fleck of russet showing clear.   20
My instep arch not only keeps the ache,
It keeps the pressure of a ladder-round.
I feel the ladder sway as the boughs bend.
And I keep hearing from the cellar bin
The rumbling sound
Of load on load of apples coming in.
For I have had too much
Of apple-picking: I am overtired
Of the great harvest I myself desired.
There were ten thousand thousand fruit to touch,   30
Cherish in hand, lift down, and not let fall.
For all
That struck the earth,
No matter if not bruised or spiked with stubble,
Went surely to the cider-apple heap
As of no worth.
One can see what will trouble
This sleep of mine, whatever sleep it is.
Were he not gone,
The woodchuck could say whether it's like his   40
Long sleep, as I describe its coming on,
Or just some human sleep.

QUESTIONS

1. How do you imagine the speaker? What details suggest his state of mind?
2. Can you say what kind of sleep is coming on him?
3. What is the mood of the poem?

Robert Frost (1874–1963)

THE ROAD NOT TAKEN

Two roads diverged in a yellow wood,
And sorry I could not travel both
And be one traveler, long I stood
And looked down one as far as I could
To where it bent in the undergrowth;

Then took the other, as just as fair,
And having perhaps the better claim,
Because it was grassy and wanted wear;
Though as for that, the passing there
Had worn them really about the same,   10

And both that morning equally lay
In leaves no step had trodden black.
Oh, I kept the first for another day!
Yet knowing how way leads on to way,
I doubted if I should ever come back.

I shall be telling this with a sigh
Somewhere ages and ages hence:
Two roads diverged in a wood, and I—
I took the one less traveled by,
And that has made all the difference.   20

QUESTIONS

1. How do you imagine this "yellow wood"? Do you assume a particular season or time of day?
2. Does any experience of decision-making you have had help you to understand this speaker's?
3. Why does the speaker expect to sigh someday about his choice?

John Crowe Ransome (1888–1974)

BELLS FOR JOHN WHITESIDE'S DAUGHTER

There was such speed in her little body,
And such lightness in her footfall,
It is no wonder her brown study
Astonishes us all.

Her wars were bruited° in our high window.   rumored
We looked among orchard trees and beyond
Where she took arms against her shadow,
Or harried unto the pond

The lazy geese, like a snow cloud
Dripping their snow on the green grass,   10

Tricking and stopping, sleepy and proud,
Who cried in goose, Alas,

For the tireless heart within the little
Lady with rod that made them rise
From their noon apple-dreams and scuttle
Goose-fashion under the skies!

But now go the bells, and we are ready,
In one house we are sternly stopped
To say we are vexed at her brown study,
Lying so primly propped.   20

QUESTIONS

1. How do you imagine the speaker and his relation to the child described?
2. What is the most vivid picture evoked by the poem?
3. What word choices catch your attention, and why?
4. What feeling does the speaker express? Does the poem as a whole convey this same feeling?

Wilfred Owen (1893–1918)

ANTHEM FOR DOOMED YOUTH

What passing-bells for these who die as cattle?
    Only the monstrous anger of the guns.
    Only the stuttering rifles' rapid rattle
Can patter out their hasty orisons.°   prayers
No mockeries now for them; no prayers nor bells,
    Nor any voice of mourning save the choirs,—
The shrill, demented choirs of wailing shells;
    And bugles calling from them from sad shires.°   counties

What candles may be held to speed them all?
    Not in the hands of boys, but in their eyes   10
Shall shine the holy glimmers of good-byes.
    The pallor of girls' brows shall be their pall;
Their flowers the tenderness of patient minds,
And each slow dusk a drawing-down of blinds.

Wilfred Owen (1893–1918)
DULCE ET DECORUM EST

Bent double, like old beggars under sacks,
Knock-kneed, coughing like hags, we cursed through
   sludge,
Till on the haunting flares we turned our backs
And towards our distant rest began to trudge.
Men marched asleep. Many had lost their boots
But limped on, blood-shod. All went lame; all blind;
Drunk with fatigue; deaf even to the hoots
Of tired, outstripped Five-Nines° that dropped behind.   gas shells

Gas! GAS! Quick, boys!—An ecstasy of fumbling,
Fitting the clumsy helmets just in time;   10
But someone still was yelling out and stumbling
And flound'ring like a man in fire or lime . . .
Dim, through the misty panes and thick green light,
As under a green sea, I saw him drowning.

In all my dreams, before my helpless sight,
He plunges at me, guttering, choking, drowning.

If in some smothering dreams you too could pace
Behind the wagon that we flung him in,
And watch the white eyes writhing in his face,
His hanging face, like a devil's sick of sin;   20
If you could hear, at every jolt, the blood
Come gargling from the froth-corrupted lungs,
Obscene as cancer, bitter as the cud
Of vile, incurable sores on innocent tongues,—
My friend, you would not tell with such high zest
To children ardent for some desperate glory,
The old Lie: Dulce et decorum est
Pro patria mori.[1]

Dulce et Decorum Est
  [1]"It is sweet and fitting to die for one's country": from the Roman poet Horace.

e. e. cummings (1894–1962)

MY SWEET OLD ETCETERA

my sweet old etcetera
aunt lucy during the recent

war could and what
is more did tell you just
what everybody was fighting

for,
my sister

isabel created hundreds
(and
hundreds) of socks not to   10
mention shirts fleaproof earwarmers

etcetera wristers etcetera, my
mother hoped that

i would die etcetera
bravely of course my father used
to become hoarse talking about how it was
a privilege and if only he
could meanwhile my

self etcetera lay quietly   20
in the deep mud et

cetera
(dreaming,
et
     cetera, of
Your smile
eyes knees and of your Etcetera)

QUESTIONS

1. What do you supply for each "etcetera"? What is gained by this seemingly offhand
   use of the abbreviation?
2. What effects are gained by the unconventinal capitalization, and punctuation, and by
   the arrangement of lines?
3. What is the speaker's tone?

e. e. cummings (1894–1962)
BUFFALO BILL'S

Buffalo Bill's
defunct
    who used to
    ride a watersmooth-silver
                stallion
and break onetwothreefourfive pigeonsjustlikethat
                             Jesus

he was a handsome man
                and what i want to know is
how do you like your blueeyed boy
Mister Death

Dorothy Parker (1893–1967)
RÉSUMÉ

Razors pain you;
Rivers are damp;
Acids stain you;
And drugs cause cramp.
Guns aren't lawful;
Nooses give;
Gas smells awful;
You might as well live.

Dorothy Parker (1893–1967)
THE LITTLE OLD LADY IN LAVENDER SILK

I was seventy-seven, come August,
  I shall shortly be losing my bloom;
I've experienced zephyr and raw gust
  And (symbolical) flood and simoom.°   desert storm

When you come to this time of abatement,
  To this passing from Summer to Fall,
It is manners to issue a statement
  As to what you got out of it all.

So I'll say, though reflection unnerves me
  And pronouncements I dodge as I can,
That I think (if my memory serves me)
  There was nothing more fun than a man!   10

In my youth, when the crescent was too wan
  To embarrass with beams from above,
By the aid of some local Don Juan
  I fell into the habit of love.

And I learned how to kiss and be merry—an
  Education left better unsung.
My neglect of the waters Pierian[1]
  Was a scandal, when Grandma was young.   20

Though the shabby unbalanced the splendid,
  And the bitter outmeasured the sweet,
I should certainly do as I then did,
  Were I given the chance to repeat.

For contrition is hollow and wraithful,°   spectral
  And regret is no part of my plan,
And I think (if my memory's faithful)
  There was nothing more fun than a man!

Langston Hughes (1902–1967)

SYLVESTER'S DYING BED

I woke up this mornin'
'Bout half-past three.
All the womens in town
Was gathered round me.

The Little Old Lady in Lavender Silk
  [1]In classical myth, a spring sacred to the Muses; hence, poetry and learning.

Sweet gals was a-moanin',
"Sylvester's gonna die!"
And a hundred pretty mamas
Bowed their heads to cry.

I woke up little later
'Bout half-past fo',
The doctor 'n' undertaker's
Both at ma do'.

Black gals was a-beggin',
"You can't leave us here!"
Brown-skins cryin', "Daddy!
Honey! Baby! Don't go, dear!"

But I felt ma time's a-comin',
And I know'd I's dyin' fast.
I seed the River Jerden
A-creepin' muddy past—
But I's still Sweet Papa 'Vester,
Yes, sir! Long as life do last!

So I hollers, "Com'ere, babies,
Fo' to love yo' daddy right!"
And I reaches up to hug 'em—
When the Lawd put out the light.

Then everything was darkness
In a great . . . big . . . night.

10

20

W. H. Auden (1907–1973)
MUSÉE DES BEAUX ARTS[1]

About suffering they were never wrong,
The Old Masters: how well they understood
Its human position; how it takes place

Musée des Beaux Arts
[1]Brussels Museum of Fine Arts. The painting *Landscape with the Fall of Icarus* by Pieter Brueghel the Elder (1520?–1569) is located here. In Greek myth, Icarus and Daedalus, his father, escaped captivity by wings made with wax. But when Icarus flew too near the sun and his wings melted, he plunged into the sea.

While someone else is eating or opening a window or just
   walking dully along;
How, when the aged are reverently, passionately waiting
For the miraculous birth, there always must be
Children who did not specially want it to happen, skating
On a pond at the edge of the wood:
They never forgot
That even the dreadful martyrdom must run its course   10
Anyhow in a corner, some untidy spot
Where the dogs go on with their doggy life and the
   torturer's horse
Scratches its innocent behind on a tree.

In Brueghel's *Icarus,* for instance: how everything turns
   away
Quite leisurely from the disaster; the ploughman may
Have heard the splash, the forsaken cry,
But for him it was not an important failure; the sun shone
As it had to on the white legs disappearing into the green
Water; and the expensive delicate ship that must have seen
Something amazing, a boy falling out of the sky,   20
Had somehwere to get to and sailed calmly on.

Theodore Roethke (1908–1963)
THE WAKING

I wake to sleep, and take my waking slow.
I feel my fate in what I cannot fear.
I learn by going where I have to go.

We think by feeling. What is there to know?
I hear my being dance from ear to ear.
I wake to sleep, and take my waking slow.

Of those so close beside me, which are you?
God bless the Ground! I shall walk softly there,
And learn by going where I have to go.

Light takes the Tree; but who can tell us how?   10
The lowly worm climbs up a winding stair;
I wake to sleep, and take my waking slow.

Great Nature has another thing to do
To you and me; so take the lively air,
And, lovely, learn by going where to go.

This shaking keeps me steady. I should know.
What falls away is always. And is near.
I wake to sleep, and take my waking slow.
I learn by going where I have to go.

William Carles Williams (1883–1963)
TO WAKEN AN OLD LADY

Old age is
a flight of small
cheeping birds
skimming
bare trees
above a snow glaze.
Gaining and failing
they are buffeted
by a dark wind—
But what?
On harsh weedstalks
the flock has rested,
the snow
is covered with broken
seedhusks
and the wind tempered
by a shrill
piping of plenty.

Dylan Thomas (1914–1953)
DO NOT GO GENTLE INTO THAT GOOD NIGHT

Do not go gentle into that good night,
Old age should burn and rave at close of day;
Rage, rage against the dying of the light.

Though wise men at their end know dark is right,
Because their words had forked no lightning they
Do not go gentle into that good night.

Good men, the last wave by, crying how bright
Their frail deeds might have danced in a green bay,
Rage, rage against the dying of the light.

Wild men who caught and sang the sun in flight,   10
And learn, too late, they grieved it on its way,
Do not go gentle into that good night.

Grave men, near death, who see with blinding sight
Blind eyes could blaze like meteors and be gay,
Rage, rage against the dying of the light.

And you, my father, there on the sad height,
Curse, bless, me now with your fierce tears, I pray.
Do not go gentle into that good night.
Rage, rage against the dying of the light.

QUESTIONS

1. How do you imagine the speaker? His father?
2. What do you make of the speaker's demand for "rage"?
3. What connects the first and last stanzas with those between?
4. Why should the speaker demand to be both cursed and blessed with "fierce tears"?
   What sense does the demand make?

Etheridge Knight (b. 1931)

FOR BLACK POETS WHO THINK OF SUICIDE

Black Poets should live—not leap
From steel bridges (like the white boys do).
Black Poets should live—not lay
Their necks on railroad tracks (like the white boys do).
Black Poets should seek—but not search too much
In sweet dark caves, nor hunt for snipe
Down psychic trails (like the white boys do).

For Black Poets belong to Black People. Are
The Flutes of Black Lovers. Are   10
The Organs of Black Sorrows. Are
The Trumpets of Black Warriors.
Let All Black Poets die as Trumpets,
And be buried in the dust of marching feet.

James Wright (1927–1980)

LYING IN A HAMMOCK AT WILLIAM DUFFY'S FARM IN PINE ISLAND, MINNESOTA

Over my head, I see the bronze butterfly,
Asleep on the black trunk,
Blowing like a leaf in green shadow.
Down the ravine behind the empty house,
The cowbells follow one another
Into the distances of the afternoon.
To my right,
In a field of sunlight between two pines,
The droppings of last year's horses
Blaze up into golden stones.   10
I lean back, as the evening darkens and comes on.
A chicken hawk floats over, looking for home.
I have wasted my life.

Alice Walker (b. 1944)

"GOOD NIGHT, WILLIE LEE, I'LL SEE YOU IN THE MORNING"

Looking down into my father's
dead face
for the last time
my mother said without
tears, without smiles
without regrets
but with *civility*

"Good night, Willie Lee, I'll see you
in the morning."
And it was then I knew that the healing
of all our wounds
is forgiveness
that permits a promise
of our return
at the end.

DRAMA

William Shakespeare (1564–1616)
THE TRAGEDY OF HAMLET
PRINCE OF DENMARK

[DRAMATIS PERSONAE

Claudius, King of Denmark
Hamlet, son to the late, and
  nephew to the present King
Polonius, Lord Chamberlain
Horatio, friend to Hamlet
Laertes, son to Polonius
Voltemand ⎫
Cornelius ⎪
Rosencrantz ⎬ courtiers
Guildenstern ⎪
Osric ⎪
A Gentleman ⎭
A Priest
Marcellus ⎫ officers
Barnado ⎭

Francisco, a soldier
Reynaldo, servant to Polonius
Players
Two Clowns, gravediggers
Fortinbras, Prince of Norway
A Norwegian Captain
English Ambassadors
Gertrude, Queen of Denmark,
  mother to Hamlet
Ophelia, daughter to Polonius
Ghost of Hamlet's Father
Lords, Ladies, Officers, Soldiers,
  Sailors, Messengers, Attendants

SCENE: ELSINORE]

[ACT I
SCENE I. A guard platform of the castle.]

Enter Barnardo and Francisco, two sentinels.

Barnardo. Who's there?
Francisco. Nay, answer me. Stand and unfold°[1] yourself.
Barnardo. Long live the King!°
Francisco. Barnardo?
Barnardo. He.   5
Francisco. You come most carefully upon your hour.
Barnardo. 'Tis now struck twelve. Get thee to bed, Francisco.

---

[1]The degree sign (°) indicates a footnote, which is keyed to the text by the line number. Text references are printed in *italic* type; the annotation follows in roman type.
  I.i.2 *unfold* disclose 3 *Long live the King* (perhaps a password, perhaps a greeting)

Francisco. For this relief much thanks. 'Tis bitter cold,
  And I am sick at heart.
Barnardo. Have you had quiet guard?
Francisco.   Not a mouse stirring.   10
Barnardo. Well, good night.
  If you do meet Horatio and Marcellus,
  The rivals° of my watch, bid them make haste.

  Enter Horatio and Marcellus.

Francisco. I think I hear them. Stand, ho! Who is there?
Horatio. Friends to this ground.
Marcellus.   And liegemen to the Dane.°   15
Francisco. Give you° good night.
Marcellus.   O, farewell, honest soldier.
  Who hath relieved you?
Francisco.   Barnardo hath my place.
  Give you good night.

                                                        Exit Francisco.

Marcellus.   Holla, Barnardo!
Barnardo.   Say——
  What, is Horatio there?
Horatio.   A piece of him.
Barnardo. Welcome, Horatio. Welcome, good Marcellus.   20
Marcellus. What, has this thing appeared again tonight?
Barnardo. I have seen nothing.
Marcellus. Horatio says 'tis but our fantasy,
  And will not let belief take hold of him
  Touching this dreaded sight twice seen of us;   25
  Therefore I have entreated him along
  With us to watch the minutes of this night,
  That, if again this apparition come,
  He may approve° our eyes and speak to it.
Horatio. Tush, tush, 'twill not appear.
Barnardo.   Sit down awhile,   30
  And let us once again assail your ears,
  That are so fortified against our story,
  What we have two nights seen.
Horatio.   Well, sit we down,
  And let us hear Barnardo speak of this.

---

  13 *rivals* partners   15 *liegemen to the Dane* loyal subjects to the King of Denmark   16 *Give you* God give you   29 *approve* confirm

Barnardo. Last night of all,   35
  When yond same star that's westward from the pole°
  Had made his course t' illume that part of heaven
  Where now it burns, Marcellus and myself,
  The bell then beating one——

  Enter Ghost.

Marcellus. Peace, break thee off. Look where it comes again.   40
Barnardo. In the same figure like the king that's dead.
Marcellus. Thou art a scholar; speak to it, Horatio.
Barnardo. Looks 'a not like the king? Mark it, Horatio.
Horatio. Most like: it harrows me with fear and wonder.
Barnardo. It would be spoke to.
Marcellus.   Speak to it, Horatio.   45
Horatio. What art thou that usurp'st this time of night,
  Together with that fair and warlike form
  In which the majesty of buried Denmark°
  Did sometimes march? By heaven I charge thee, speak.
Marcellus. It is offended.
Barnardo.   See, it stalks away.   50
Horatio. Stay! Speak, speak. I charge thee, speak.

                                                          Exit Ghost.

Marcellus. 'Tis gone and will not answer.
Barnardo. How now, Horatio? You tremble and look pale.
  Is not this something more than fantasy?
  What think you on't?   55
Horatio. Before my God, I might not this believe
  Without the sensible and true avouch°
  Of mine own eyes.
Marcellus.   Is it not like the King?
Horatio. As thou art to thyself.
  Such was the very armor he had on   60
  When he the ambitious Norway° combated:
  So frowned he once, when, in an angry parle,°
  He smote the sledded Polacks° on the ice.
  'Tis strange.
Marcellus. Thus twice before, and jump° at this dead hour,   65
  With martial stalk hath he gone by our watch.
Horatio. In what particular thought to work I know not;
  But, in the gross and scope° of my opinion,

---

  36 *pole* polestar   48 *buried Denmark* the buried King of Denmark   57 *sensible and true
avouch* sensory and true proof   61 *Norway* King of Norway   62 *parle* parley   63 *sledded
Polacks* Poles in sledges   65 *jump* just   68 *gross and scope* general drift

This bodes some strange eruption to our state.
Marcellus. Good now, sit down, and tell me he that knows,   70
   Why this same strict and most observant watch
   So nightly toils the subject° of the land,
   And why such daily cast of brazen cannon
   And foreign mart° for implements of war,
   Why such impress° of shipwrights, whose sore task   75
   Does not divide the Sunday from the week,
   What might be toward° that this sweaty haste
   Doth make the night joint-laborer with the day?
   Who is't that can inform me?
Horatio.   That can I.
   At least the whisper goes so: our last king,   80
   Whose image even but now appeared to us,
   Was, as you know, by Fortinbras of Norway,
   Thereto pricked on by a most emulate pride,
   Dared to the combat; in which our valiant Hamlet
   (For so this side of our known world esteemed him)   85
   Did slay this Fortinbras, who, by a sealed compact
   Well ratified by law and heraldry,°
   Did forfeit, with his life, all those his lands
   Which he stood seized° of, to the conqueror;
   Against the which a moiety competent°   90
   Was gagèd° by our King, which had returned
   To the inheritance of Fortinbras,
   Had he been vanquisher, as, by the same comart°
   And carriage of the article designed,°
   His fell to Hamlet. Now, sir, young Fortinbras,   95
   Of unimprovèd° mettle hot and full,
   Hath in the skirts° of Norway here and there
   Sharked up° a list of lawless resolutes,°
   For food and diet, to some enterprise
   That hath a stomach in't; ° which is no other,   100
   As it doth well appear unto our state,
   But to recover of us by strong hand
   And terms compulsatory, those foresaid lands
   So by his father lost; and this, I take it,
   Is the main motive of our preparations,   105

---

72 *toils the subject* makes the subjects toil   74 *mart* trading   75 *impress* forced service   77 *toward* in preparation   87 *law and heraldry* heraldic law (governing the combat)   89 *seized* possessed   90 *moiety competent* equal portion   91 *gagèd* engaged, pledged   93 *comart* agreement   94 *carriage of the article designed* import of the agreement drawn up   96 *unimprovèd* untried   97 *skirts* borders   98 *Sharked up* collected indiscriminately (as a shark gulps its prey)   98 *resolutes* desperadoes   100 *hath a stomach in't* i.e., requires courage

The source of this our watch, and the chief head°
Of this posthaste and romage° in the land.
Barnardo. I think it be no other but e'en so;
   Well may it sort° that this portentous figure
   Comes armèd through our watch so like the King   110
   That was and is the question of these wars.
Horatio. A mote it is to trouble the mind's eye:
   In the most high and palmy state of Rome,
   A little ere the mightiest Julius fell,
   The graves stood tenantless, and the sheeted dead   115
   Did squeak and gibber in the Roman streets;°
   As stars with trains of fire and dews of blood,
   Disasters° in the sun; and the moist star,°
   Upon whose influence Neptune's empire stands,
   Was sick almost to doomsday with eclipse.   120
   And even the like precurse° of feared events,
   As harbingers° preceding still° the fates
   And prologue to the omen° coming on,
   Have heaven and earth together demonstrated
   Unto our climatures° and countrymen.   125

Enter Ghost.

But soft, behold, lo where it comes again!
I'll cross it,° though it blast me.—Stay, illusion.

                               It spreads his° arms.

If thou hast any sound or use of voice,
Speak to me.
If there be any good thing to be done   130
That may to thee do ease and grace to me,
Speak to me.
If thou art privy to thy country's fate,
Which happily° foreknowing may avoid,
O, speak!   135
Or if thou hast uphoarded in thy life
Extorted° treasure in the womb of earth,
For which, they say, you spirits oft walk in death,

                               The cock crows.

---

106 *head* fountainhead, origin   107 *romage* bustle   109 *sort* befit   116 *Did squeak . . .*
Roman streets (the break in the sense which follows this line suggests that a line has dropped
out)   118 *Disasters* threatening signs   118 *moist star* moon   121 *precurse* precursor,
foreshadowing   122 *harbingers* forerunners   122 *still* always   123 *omen* calamity   125
climatures regions   127 *cross it* (1) cross its path, confront it (2) make the sign of the cross in
front of it   127 s.d. *his* i.e., its, the ghost's (though possibly what is meant is that Horatio spreads
his own arms, making a cross of himself)   134 *happily* haply, perhaps   137 *Extorted* ill-won

Speak of it. Stay and speak. Stop it, Marcellus.
Marcellus. Shall I strike at it with my partisan°?   140
Horatio. Do, if it will not stand.
Barnardo.   'Tis here.
Horatio.   'Tis here.
Marcellus. 'Tis gone.   *Exit Ghost.*
    We do it wrong, being so majestical,
    To offer it the show of violence,
    For it is as the air, invulnerable,   145
    And our vain blows malicious mockery.
Barnardo. It was about to speak when the cock crew.
Horatio. And then it started, like a guilty thing
    Upon a fearful summons. I have heard,
    The cock, that is the trumpet to the morn,   150
    Doth with his lofty and shrill-sounding throat
    Awake the god of day, and at his warning,
    Whether in sea or fire, in earth or air,
    Th' extravagant and erring° spirit hies
    To his confine; and of the truth herein   155
    This present object made probation.°
Marcellus. It faded on the crowing of the cock.
    Some say that ever 'gainst° that season comes
    Wherein our Savior's birth is celebrated,
    This bird of dawning singeth all night long,   160
    And then, they say, no spirit dare stir abroad,
    The nights are wholesome, then no planets strike,°
    No fairy takes,° nor witch hath power to charm:
    So hallowed and so gracious is that time.
Horatio. So have I heard and do in part believe it.   165
    But look, the morn in russet mantle clad
    Walks o'er the dew of yon high eastward hill.
    Break we our watch up, and by my advice
    Let us impart what we have seen tonight
    Unto young Hamlet, for upon my life   170
    This spirit, dumb to us, will speak to him.
    Do you consent we shall acquaint him with it,
    As needful in our loves, fitting our duty?
Marcellus. Let's do't, I pray, and I this morning know
    Where we shall find him most convenient.   *Exeunt.* 175

---

140 *partisan* pike (a long-handled weapon)   154 *extravagant and erring* out of bounds and
wandering   156 *probation* proof   158 *'gainst* just before   162 *strike* exert an evil influence   163
takes bewitches

[SCENE II. The castle.]

Flourish.° Enter Claudius, King of Denmark, Gertrude the Queen, Councilors, Polonius and his son Laertes, Hamlet, cum aliis° [including Voltemand and Cornelius].

King. Though yet of Hamlet our dear brother's death
    The memory be green, and that it us befitted
    To bear our hearts in grief, and our whole kingdom
    To be contracted in one brow of woe,
    Yet so far hath discretion fought with nature   5
    That we with wisest sorrow think on him
    Together with remembrance of ourselves.
    Therefore our sometime sister,° now our Queen,
    Th' imperial jointress° to this warlike state
    Have we, as 'twere, with a defeated joy,   10
    With an auspicious° and a dropping eye,
    With mirth in funeral, and with dirge in marriage,
    In equal scale weighing delight and dole,
    Taken to wife. Nor have we herein barred
    Your better wisdoms, which have freely gone   15
    With this affair along. For all, our thanks.
    Now follows that you know young Fortinbras,
    Holding a weak supposal of our worth,
    Or thinking by our late dear brother's death
    Our state to be disjoint and out of frame,°   20
    Colleaguèd with this dream of his advantage,°
    He hath not failed to pester us with message,
    Importing the surrender of those lands
    Lost by his father, with all bands of law,
    To our most valiant brother. So much for him.   25
    Now for ourself and for this time of meeting.
    Thus much the business is: we have here writ
    To Norway, uncle of young Fortinbras—
    Who, impotent and bedrid, scarcely hears
    Of this his nephew's purpose—to suppress   30
    His further gait° herein, in that the levies,
    The lists, and full proportions° are all made
    Out of his subject;° and we here dispatch

I.ii.s.d. *Flourish* fanfare of trumpets s.d. *cum aliis* with others (Latin)   8 *our sometime sister* my (the royal "we") former sister-in-law   9 *jointress* joint tenant, partner   11 *auspicious* joyful 20 *frame* order   21 *advantage* superiority   31 *gait* proceeding   32 *proportions* supplies for war 33 *Out of his subject* i.e., out of old Norway's subjects and realm

You, good Cornelius, and you, Voltemand,
For bearers of this greeting to old Norway,   35
Giving to you no further personal power
To business with the King, more than the scope
Of these delated articles° allow.
Farewell, and let your haste commend your duty.
Cornelius, Voltemand. In that, and all things, will we show our duty.   40
King. We doubt it nothing. Heartily farewell.
                                        Exit Voltemand and Cornelius.
And now, Laertes, what's the news with you?
You told us of some suit. What is't, Laertes?
You cannot speak of reason to the Dane
And lose your voice.° What wouldst thou beg, Laertes,   45
That shall not be my offer, not thy asking?
The head is not more native° to the heart,
The hand more instrumental to the mouth,
Than is the throne of Denmark to thy father.
What wouldst thou have, Laertes?
Laertes.   My dread lord,   50
Your leave and favor to return to France,
From whence, though willingly I came to Denmark
To show my duty in your coronation,
Yet now I must confess, that duty done,
My thoughts and wishes bend again toward France   55
And bow them to your gracious leave and pardon.
King. Have you your father's leave? What says Polonius?
Polonius. He hath, my lord, wrung from me my slow leave
By laborsome petition, and at last
Upon his will I sealed my hard consent.°   60
I do beseech you give him leave to go.
King. Take thy fair hour, Laertes. Time be thine,
And thy best graces spend it at thy will.
But now, my cousin° Hamlet, and my son——
Hamlet. [*Aside*] A little more than kin, and less than kind!°   65
King. How is it that the clouds still hang on you?
Hamlet. Not so, my lord. I am too much in the sun.°
Queen. Good Hamlet, cast thy nighted color off,
And let thine eye look like a friend on Denmark.
Do not forever with thy vailèd° lids   70

---

38 *delated articles* detailed documents   45 *lose your voice* waste your breath   47 *native* related   60 *Upon his . . . hard consent* to his desire I gave my reluctant consent   64 *cousin* kinsman   65 *kind* (pun on the meanings "kindly" and "natural"; though doubly related—*more than kin*—Hamlet asserts that he neither resembles Claudius in nature or feels kindly toward him)   67 *sun* sunshine of royal favor (with a pun on "son")   70 *vailèd* lowered

Seek for thy noble father in the dust.
Thou know'st 'tis common; all that lives must die,
Passing through nature to eternity.
Hamlet. Ay, madam, it is common.°
Queen.   If it be,
  Why seems it so particular with thee?   75
Hamlet. Seems, madam? Nay, it is. I know not "seems."
  'Tis not alone my inky cloak, good mother,
  Nor customary suits of solemn black,
  Nor windy suspiration° of forced breath,
  No, nor the fruitful river in the eye,   80
  Nor the dejected havior of the visage,
  Together with all forms, moods, shapes of grief,
  That can denote me truly. These indeed seem,
  For they are actions that a man might play,
  But I have that within which passes show;   85
  These but the trappings and the suits of woe.
King. 'Tis sweet and commendable in your nature, Hamlet,
  To give these mourning duties to your father,
  But you must know your father lost a father,
  That father lost, lost his, and the survivor bound   90
  In filial obligation for some term
  To do obsequious° sorrow. But to persever
  In obstinate condolement° is a course
  Of impious stubbornness. 'Tis unmanly grief.
  It shows a will most incorrect to heaven,   95
  A heart unfortified, a mind impatient,
  An understanding simple and unschooled.
  For what we know must be and is as common
  As any the most vulgar° thing to sense,
  Why should we in our peevish opposition   100
  Take it to heart? Fie, 'tis a fault to heaven,
  A fault against the dead, a fault to nature,
  To reason most absurd, whose common theme
  Is death of fathers, and who still hath cried,
  From the first corse° till he that died today,   105
  "This must be so." We pray you throw to earth
  This unprevailing° woe, and think of us
  As of a father, for let the world take note
  You are the most immediate to our throne,
  And with no less nobility of love   110

---

74 *common* (1) universal (2) vulgar   79 *windy suspiration* heavy sighing   92 *obsequious*
suitable to obsequies (funerals)   93 *condolement* mourning   99 *vulgar* common   105 *corse*
corpse   107 *unprevailing* unavailing

Than that which dearest father bears his son
Do I impart toward you. For your intent
In going back to school in Wittenberg,
It is most retrograde° to our desire,
And we beseech you, bend you° to remain   115
Here in the cheer and comfort of our eye,
Our chiefest courtier, cousin, and our son.
Queen. Let not thy mother lose her prayers, Hamlet.
I pray thee stay with us, go not to Wittenberg.
Hamlet. I shall in all my best obey you, madam.   120
King. Why, 'tis a loving and a fair reply.
Be as ourself in Denmark. Madam, come.
This gentle and unforced accord of Hamlet
Sits smiling to my heart, in grace whereof
No jocund health that Denmark drinks today,   125
But the great cannon to the clouds shall tell,
And the King's rouse° the heaven shall bruit° again,
Respeaking earthly thunder. Come away.

Flourish. Exeunt all but Hamlet.

Hamlet. O that this too too sullied° flesh would melt,
Thaw, and resolve itself into a dew,   130
Or that the Everlasting had not fixed
His canon° 'gainst self-slaughter. O God, God,
How weary, stale, flat, and unprofitable
Seem to me all the uses of this world!
Fie on't, ah, fie, 'tis an unweeded garden   135
That grows to seed. Things rank and gross in nature
Possess it merely.° That it should come to this:
But two months dead, nay, not so much, not two,
So excellent a king, that was to this
Hyperion° to a satyr, so loving to my mother   140
That he might not beteem° the winds of heaven
Visit her face too roughly. Heaven and earth,
Must I remember? Why, she would hang on him
As if increase of appetite had grown
By what it fed on; and yet within a month—   145
Let me not think on't; frailty, thy name is woman—

---

114 *retrograde* contrary   115 *bend you* incline   127 *rouse* deep drink   127 *bruit* announce
noisily   129 *sullied* (Q2 has *sallied*, here modernized to *sullied*, which makes sense and is
therefore given; but the Folio reading, *solid*, which fits better with *melt*, is quite possibly
correct).   132 *canon* law   137 *merely* entirely   140 *Hyperion* the sun god, a model of beauty
141 *beteem* allow

A little month, or ere those shoes were old
With which she followed my poor father's body
Like Niobe,° all tears, why she, even she—
O God, a beast that wants discourse of reason°   150
Would have mourned longer—married with my uncle,
My father's brother, but no more like my father
Than I to Hercules. Within a month,
Ere yet the salt of most unrighteous tears
Had left the flushing° in her gallèd eyes,   155
She married. O, most wicked speed, to post°
With such dexterity to incestuous° sheets!
It is not, nor it cannot come to good.
But break my heart, for I must hold my tongue.

Enter Horatio, Marcellus, and Barnardo.

Horatio. Hail to your lordship!
Hamlet.   I am glad to see you well.   160
   Horatio—or I do forget myself.
Horatio. The same, my lord, and your poor servant ever.
Hamlet. Sir, my good friend, I'll change° that name with you.
   And what make you from Wittenberg, Horatio?
   Marcellus.   165
Marcellus. My good lord!
Hamlet. I am very glad to see you. [*To Barnardo*] Good even, sir.
   But what, in faith, make you from Wittenberg?
Horatio. A truant disposition, good my lord.
Hamlet. I would not hear your enemy say so,   170
   Nor shall you do my ear that violence
   To make it truster° of your own report
   Against yourself. I know you are no truant.
   But what is your affair in Elsinore?
   We'll teach you to drink deep ere you depart.   175
Horatio. My lord, I came to see your father's funeral.
Hamlet. I prithee do not mock me, fellow student.
   I think it was to see my mother's wedding.
Horatio. Indeed, my lord, it followed hard upon.
Hamlet. Thrift, thrift, Horatio. The funeral baked meats   180
   Did coldly furnish forth the marriage tables.
   Would I had met my dearest° foe in heaven

---

149 *Niobe* (a mother who wept profusely at the death of her children)   150 *wants discourse of reason* lacks reasoning power   155 *left the flushing* stopped reddening   156 *post* hasten   157 *incestuous* (canon law considered marriage with a deceased brother's widow to be incestuous)   163 *change* exchange   172 *truster* believer   182 *dearest* most intensely felt

Or ever I had seen that day, Horatio!
My father, methinks I see my father.
Horatio. Where, my lord?
Hamlet.   In my mind's eye, Horatio.   185
Horatio. I saw him once. 'A° was a goodly king.
Hamlet. 'A was a man, take him for all in all,
    I shall not look upon his like again.
Horatio. My lord, I think I saw him yesternight.
Hamlet. Saw? Who?   190
Horatio. My lord, the King your father.
Hamlet.   The King my father?
Horatio. Season your admiration° for a while
    With an attent ear till I may deliver
    Upon the witness of these gentlemen
    This marvel to you.
Hamlet.   For God's love let me hear!   195
Horatio. Two nights together had these gentlemen,
    Marcellus and Barnardo, on their watch
    In the dead waste and middle of the night
    Been thus encountered. A figure like your father,
    Armèd at point exactly, cap-a-pe,°   200
    Appears before them, and with solemn march
    Goes slow and stately by them. Thrice he walked
    By their oppressed and fear-surprisèd eyes,
    Within his truncheon's length,° whilst they, distilled°
    Almost to jelly with the act° of fear,   205
    Stand dumb and speak not to him. This to me
    In dreadful° secrecy impart they did,
    And I with them the third night kept the watch,
    Where, as they had delivered, both in time,
    Form of the thing, each word made true and good,   210
    The apparition comes. I knew your father.
    These hands are not more like.
Hamlet.   But where was this?
Marcellus. My lord, upon the platform where we watched.
Hamlet. Did you not speak to it?
Horatio.   My lord, I did;
    But answer made it none. Yet once methought   215
    It lifted up it° head and did address
    Itself to motion like as it would speak:

---

186 *'A* he   192 *Season your admiration* control your wonder   200 *cap-a-pe* head to foot
204 *truncheon's length* space of a short staff   204 *distilled* reduced   205 *act* action   207
dreadful terrified   216 *it* its

But even then the morning cock crew loud,
And at the sound it shrunk in haste away
And vanished from our sight.
Hamlet.   'Tis very strange.   220
Horatio. As I do live, my honored lord, 'tis true,
    And we did think it writ down in our duty
    To let you know of it.
Hamlet. Indeed, indeed, sirs, but this troubles me.
    Hold you the watch tonight?
All.   We do, my lord.   225
Hamlet. Armed, say you?
All. Armed, my lord.
Hamlet. From top to toe?
All.   My lord, from head to foot.
Hamlet. Then saw you not his face.
Horatio. O, yes, my lord. He wore his beaver° up.   230
Hamlet. What, looked he frowningly?
Horatio. A countenance more in sorrow than in anger.
Hamlet. Pale or red?
Horatio. Nay, very pale.
Hamlet.   And fixed his eyes upon you?
Horatio. Most constantly.
Hamlet.   I would I had been there.   235
Horatio. It would have much amazed you.
Hamlet. Very like, very like. Stayed it long?
Horatio. While one with moderate haste might tell° a hundred.
Both. Longer, longer.
Horatio. Not when I saw't.
Hamlet.   His beard was grizzled,° no?   240
Horatio. It was as I have seen it in his life,
    A sable silvered.°
Hamlet.   I will watch tonight.
    Perchance 'twill walk again.
Horatio.   I warr'nt it will.
Hamlet. If it assume my noble father's person,
    I'll speak to it though hell itself should gape   245
    And bid me hold my peace. I pray you all,
    If you have hitherto concealed this sight,
    Let it be tenable° in your silence still,
    And whatsomever else shall hap tonight,
    Give it an understanding but no tongue;   250

---

230 *beaver* visor, face guard   238 *tell* count   240 *grizzled* gray   242 *sable silvered* black
mingled with white   248 *tenable* held

I will requite your loves. So fare you well.
Upon the platform 'twixt eleven and twelve
I'll visit you.
All.   Our duty to your honor.
Hamlet. Your loves, as mine to you. Farewell.

                                        Exeunt [all but Hamlet].   255

My father's spirit—in arms? All is not well.
I doubt° some foul play. Would the night were come!
Till then sit still, my soul. Foul deeds will rise,
Though all the earth o'erwhelm them, to men's eyes.

                                                            Exit.

[SCENE III. A room]

Enter Laertes and Ophelia, his sister.

Laertes. My necessaries are embarked. Farewell.
   And, sister, as the winds give benefit
   And convoy° is assistant, do not sleep,
   But let me hear from you.
Ophelia.   Do you doubt that?
Laertes. For Hamlet, and the trifling of his favor,   5
   Hold it a fashion and a toy° in blood,
   A violet in the youth of primy° nature,
   Forward,° not permanent, sweet, not lasting,
   The perfume and suppliance° of a minute,
   No more.
Ophelia.   No more but so?
Laertes.   Think it no more.   10
   For nature crescent° does not grow alone
   In thews° and bulk, but as this temple° waxes,
   The inward service of the mind and soul
   Grows wide withal. Perhaps he loves you now,
   And now no soil nor cautel° doth besmirch   15
   The virtue of his will; but you must fear,
   His greatness weighed° his will is not his own.
   For he himself is subject to his birth.
   He may not, as unvalued° persons do,
   Carve for himself; for on his choice depends   20
   The safety and health of this whole state;

---

256 *doubt* suspect   I.iii.3 *convoy* conveyance   6 *toy* idle fancy   7 *primy* springlike   8
Forward premature   9 *suppliance* diversion   11 *crescent* growing   12 *thews* muscles and
sinews   12 *temple* i.e., the body   15 *cautel* deceit   17 *greatness weighed* high rank considered
19 *unvalued* of low rank

And therefore must his choice be circumscribed
Unto the voice and yielding of that body
Whereof he is the head. Then if he says he loves you,
It fits your wisdom so far to believe it   25
As he in his particular act and place
May give his saying deed, which is no further
Than the main voice of Denmark goes withal.
Then weigh what loss your honor may sustain
If with too credent° ear you list his songs,   30
Or lose your heart, or your chaste treasure open
To his unmastered importunity.
Fear it, Ophelia, fear it, my dear sister,
And keep you in the rear of your affection,
Out of the shot and danger of desire.   35
The chariest maid is prodigal enough
If she unmask her beauty to the moon.
Virtue itself scapes not calumnious strokes.
The canker° galls the infants of the spring
Too oft before their buttons° be disclosed,   40
And in the morn and liquid dew of youth
Contagious blastments are most imminent.
Be wary then; best safety lies in fear;
Youth to itself rebels, though none else near.
Ophelia. I shall the effect of this good lesson keep   45
As watchman to my heart, but, good my brother,
Do not, as some ungracious° pastors do,
Show me the steep and thorny way to heaven,
Whiles, like a puffed and reckless libertine,
Himself the primrose path of dalliance treads   50
And recks not his own rede.°

Enter Polonius.

Laertes.   O, fear me not.
I stay too long. But here my father comes.
A double blessing is a double grace;
Occasion smiles upon a second leave.
Polonius. Yet here, Laertes? Aboard, aboard, for shame!   55
The wind sits in the shoulder of your sail,
And you are stayed for. There—my blessing with thee,
And these few precepts in thy memory

---

30 *credent* credulous 39 *canker* cankerworm 40 *buttons* buds 47 *ungracious* lacking
grace 51 *recks not his own rede* does not heed his own advice

Look thou character.° Give thy thoughts no tongue,
Nor any unproportioned° thought his act.　　　　　　　　　　　60
Be thou familiar, but by no means vulgar.
Those friends thou hast, and their adoption tried,
Grapple them unto thy soul with hoops of steel,
But do not dull thy palm with entertainment
Of each new-hatched, unfledged courage.° Beware　　　　　　65
Of entrance to a quarrel; but being in,
Bear't that th' opposèd may beware of thee.
Give every man thine ear, but few thy voice;
Take each man's censure,° but reserve thy judgment.
Costly thy habit as thy purse can buy,　　　　　　　　　　　70
But not expressed in fancy; rich, not gaudy,
For the apparel oft proclaims the man,
And they in France of the best rank and station
Are of a most select and generous, chief in that.°
Neither a borrower nor a lender be,　　　　　　　　　　　　75
For loan oft loses both itself and friend,
And borrowing dulleth edge of husbandry.°
This above all, to thine own self be true,
And it must follow, as the night the day,
Thou canst not then be false to any man.　　　　　　　　　　80
Farewell. My blessing season this° in thee!
Laertes. Most humbly do I take my leave, my lord.
Polonius. The time invites you. Go, your servants tend.°
Laertes. Farewell, Ophelia, and remember well
　　What I have said to you.
Ophelia.　　　　　　　　　'Tis in my memory locked,
　　And you yourself shall keep the key of it.
Laertes. Farewell.　　　　　　　　　　　　　　　*Exit Laertes.*
Polonius. What is't, Ophelia, he hath said to you?
Ophelia. So please you, something touching the Lord Hamlet.
Polonius. Marry,° well bethought.　　　　　　　　　　　　90
　　'Tis told me he hath very oft of late
　　Given private time to you, and you yourself
　　Have of your audience been most free and bounteous.
　　If it be so—as so 'tis put on me,
　　And that in way of caution—I must tell you　　　　　　　95
　　You do not understand yourself so clearly
　　As it behooves my daughter and your honor.

---

59 *character* inscribe　60 *unproportioned* unbalanced　65 *courage* gallant youth　69 *censure* opinion　74 *Are of . . . in that* show their fine taste and their gentlemanly instincts more in that than in any other point of manners (Kittredge)　77 *husbandry* thrift　81 *season this* make fruitful this (advice)　83 *tend* attend　90 *Marry* (a light oath, from "By the Virgin Mary")

What is between you? Give me up the truth.
Ophelia. He hath, my lord, of late made many tenders°
    Of his affection to me. 100
Polonius. Affection pooh! You speak like a green girl,
    Unsifted° in such perilous circumstance.
    Do you believe his tenders, as you call them?
Ophelia. I do not know, my lord, what I should think.
Polonius. Marry, I will teach you. Think yourself a baby 105
    That you have ta'en these tenders for true pay
    Which are not sterling. Tender yourself more dearly,
    Or (not to crack the wind of the poor phrase)
    Tend'ring it thus you'll tender me a fool.°
Ophelia. My lord, he hath importuned me with love 110
    In honorable fashion.
Polonius. Ay, fashion you may call it. Go to, go to.
Ophelia. And hath given countenance to his speech, my lord,
    With almost all the holy vows of heaven.
Polonius. Ay, springes to catch woodcocks.° I do know, 115
    When the blood burns, how prodigal the soul
    Lends the tongue vows. These blazes, daughter,
    Giving more light than heat, extinct in both,
    Even in their promise, as it is a-making,
    You must not take for fire. From this time 120
    Be something scanter of your maiden presence.
    Set your entreatments° at a higher rate
    Than a command to parley. For Lord Hamlet,
    Believe so much in him that he is young,
    And with a larger tether may he walk 125
    Than may be given you. In few, Ophelia,
    Do not believe his vows, for they are brokers,°
    Not of that dye° which their investments° show,
    But mere implorators° of unholy suits,
    Breathing like sanctified and pious bonds,° 130
    The better to beguile. This is for all:
    I would not, in plain terms, from this time forth
    Have you so slander° any moment leisure
    As to give words or talk with the Lord Hamlet.
    Look to't, I charge you. Come your ways. 135
Ophelia. I shall obey, my lord.   *Exeunt.*

---

99 *tenders* offers (in line 103 it has the same meaning, but in line 106 Polonius speaks of
tenders in the sense of counters or chips; in line 109 *Tend'ring* means "holding," and *tender*
means "give," "present")   102 *Unsifted* untried   109 *tender me a fool* (1) present me with a fool
(2) present me with a baby   115 *springes to catch woodcocks* snares to catch stupid birds   122
entreatments interviews   127 *brokers* procurers   128 *dye* i.e., kind   128 *investments* garments
129 *implorators* solicitors   130 *bonds* pledges   133 *slander* disgrace

[SCENE IV. A guard platform.]

Enter Hamlet, Horatio, and Marcellus.

Hamlet. The air bites shrewdly;° it is very cold.
Horatio. It is a nipping and an eager° air.
Hamlet. What hour now?
Horatio.   I think it lacks of twelve.
Marcellus. No, it is struck.
Horatio. Indeed? I heard it not. It then draws near the season   5
　Wherein the spirit held his wont to walk.
　　　　　　　　　A flourish of trumpets, and two pieces go off.
　What does this mean, my lord?
Hamlet. The King doth wake° tonight and takes his rouse,°
　Keeps wassail, and the swagg'ring upspring° reels,
　And as he drains his draughts of Rhenish° down   10
　The kettledrum and trumpet thus bray out
　The triumph of his pledge.°
Horatio.   Is it a custom?
Hamlet. Ay, marry, is't,
　But to my mind, though I am native here
　And to the manner born, it is a custom   15
　More honored in the breach than the observance.
　This heavy-headed revel east and west
　Makes us traduced and taxed of° other nations.
　They clepe° us drunkards and with swinish phrase
　Soil our addition,° and indeed it takes   20
　From our achievements, though performed at height,
　The pith and marrow of our attribute.°
　So oft it chances in particular men
　That for some vicious mole° of nature in them,
　As in their birth, wherein they are not guilty,   25
　(Since nature cannot choose his origin)
　By the o'ergrowth of some complexion,°
　Oft breaking down the pales° and forts of reason,
　Or by some habit that too much o'erleavens°
　The form of plausive° manners, that (these men,   30
　Carrying, I say, the stamp of one defect,

　I.iv.1 *shrewdly* bitterly 2 *eager* sharp 8 *wake* hold a revel by night 8 *takes his rouse*
carouses 9 *upspring* (a dance) 10 *Rhenish* Rhine wine 12 *The triumph of his pledge* the
achievement (of drinking a wine cup in one draught) of his toast 18 *taxes of* blamed by 19
clepe call 20 *addition* reputation (literally, "title of honor") 22 *attribute* reputation 24 *mole*
blemish 27 *complexion* natural disposition 28 *pales* enclosures 29 *o'erleavens* mixes with,
corrupts 30 *plausive* pleasing

Being nature's livery, or fortune's star°)
Their virtues else, be they as pure as grace,
As infinite as man may undergo,
Shall in the general censure° take corruption   35
From that particular fault. The dram of evil
Doth all the noble substance of a doubt,
To his own scandal.°

Enter Ghost.

Horatio.   Look, my lord, it comes.
Hamlet. Angels and ministers of grace defend us!
   Be thou a spirit of health° or goblin damned,   40
   Bring with thee airs from heaven or blasts from hell,
   Be thy intents wicked or charitable,
   Thou com'st in such a questionable° shape
   That I will speak to thee. I'll call thee Hamlet,
   King, father, royal Dane. O, answer me!   45
   Let me not burst in ignorance, but tell
   Why thy canonized° bones, hearsèd in death,
   Have burst their cerements,° why the sepulcher
   Wherein we saw thee quietly interred
   Hath oped his ponderous and marble jaws   50
   To cast thee up again. What may this mean
   That thou, dead corse, again in complete steel,
   Revisits thus the glimpses of the moon,
   Making night hideous, and we fools of nature
   So horridly to shake our disposition°   55
   With thoughts beyond the reaches of our souls?
   Say, why is this? Wherefore? What should we do?
   Ghost beckons Hamlet.

Horatio. It beckons you to go away with it,
   As if it some impartment° did desire
   To you alone.
Marcellus.   Look with what courteous action   60
   It waves you to a more removèd ground.
   But do not go with it.

---

   32 *nature's livery, or fortune's star* nature's equipment (i.e., "innate"), or a person's destiny
determined by the stars   35 *general censure* popular judgment   36–38 *The dram . . . own
scandal* (though the drift is clear, there is no agreement as to the exact meaning of these lines)   40
spirit of health good spirit   43 *questionable* (1) capable of discourse (2) dubious   47 *canonized*
buried according to the canon or ordinance of the church   48 *cerements* waxed linen shroud   55
shake our disposition disturb us   59 *impartment* communication

Horatio.   No, by no means.
Hamlet. It will not speak. Then I will follow it.
Horatio. Do not, my lord.
Hamlet.   Why, what should be the fear?
  I do not set my life at a pin's fee,   65
  And for my soul, what can it do to that,
  Being a thing immortal as itself?
  It waves me forth again. I'll follow it.
Horatio. What if it tempt you toward the flood, my lord,
  Or to the dreadful summit of the cliff   70
  That beetles° o'er his base into the sea,
  And there assume some other horrible form,
  Which might deprive your sovereignty of reason°
  And draw you into madness? Think of it.
  The very place puts toys° of desperation,   75
  Without more motive, into every brain
  That looks so many fathoms to the sea
  And hears it roar beneath.
Hamlet.   It waves me still.
  Go on; I'll follow thee.
Marcellus. You shall not go, my lord.
Hamlet.   Hold off your hands.   80
Horatio. Be ruled. You shall not go.
Hamlet.   My fate cries out
  And makes each petty artere° in this body
  As hardy as the Nemean lion's nerve.°
  Still am I called! Unhand me, gentlemen.
  By heaven, I'll make a ghost of him that lets° me!   85
  I say, away! Go on. I'll follow thee.

                              Exit Ghost, and Hamlet.

Horatio. He waxes desperate with imagination.
Marcellus. Let's follow. 'Tis not fit thus to obey him.
Horatio. Have after! To what issue will this come?
Marcellus. Something is rotten in the state of Denmark.   90
Horatio. Heaven will direct it.
Marcellus. Nay, let's follow him.   *Exeunt.*

---

  71 *beetles* juts out   73 *deprive your sovereignty of reason* destroy the sovereignty of your
reason   75 *toys* whims, fancies   87 *artere* artery   83 *Nemean lion's nerve* sinews of the mythical
lion slain by Hercules   85 *lets* hinders

[SCENE V. The battlements.]

Enter Ghost and Hamlet.

Hamlet. Whither wilt thou lead me? Speak; I'll go no further.
Ghost. Mark me.
Hamlet.   I will.
Ghost.   My hour is almost come,
  When I to sulf'rous and tormenting flames
  Must render up myself.
Hamlet.   Alas, poor ghost.
Ghost. Pity me not, but lend thy serious hearing   5
  To what I shall unfold.
Hamlet.   Speak. I am bound to hear.
Ghost. So art thou to revenge, when thou shalt hear.
Hamlet. What?
Ghost. I am thy father's spirit,
  Doomed for a certain term to walk the night,   10
  And for the day confined to fast in fires,
  Till the foul crimes° done in my days of nature
  Are burnt and purged away. But that I am forbid
  To tell the secrets of my prison house,
  I could a tale unfold whose lightest word   15
  Would harrow up thy soul, freeze thy young blood,
  Make thy two eyes like stars start from their spheres,°
  Thy knotted and combinèd locks to part,
  And each particular hair to stand an end
  Like quills upon the fearful porpentine.°   20
  But this eternal blazon° must not be
  To ears of flesh and blood. List, list, O, list!
  If thou didst ever thy dear father love——
Hamlet. O God!
Ghost. Revenge his foul and most unnatural murder.   25
Hamlet. Murder?
Ghost. Murder most foul, as in the best it is,
  But this most foul, strange, and unnatural.
Hamlet. Haste me to know't, that I, with wings as swift
  As meditation° or the thoughts of love,   30
  May sweep to my revenge.

I.v.12 *crimes* sins   17 *spheres* (in Ptolemaic astronomy, each planet was fixed in a hollow transparent shell concentric with the earth)   20 *fearful porpentine* timid porcupine   21 *eternal blazon* revelation of eternity   30 *meditation* thought

Ghost.   I find thee apt,
   And duller shouldst thou be than the fat weed
   That roots itself in ease on Lethe wharf,°
   Wouldst thou not stir in this. Now, Hamlet, hear.
   'Tis given out that, sleeping in my orchard,   35
   A serpent stung me. So the whole ear of Denmark
   Is by a forgèd process° of my death
   Rankly abused. But know, thou noble youth,
   The serpent that did sting thy father's life
   Now wears his crown.
Hamlet.   O my prophetic soul!   40
   My uncle!
Ghost. Ay, that incestuous, that adulterate° beast,
   With witchcraft of his wits, with traitorous gifts—
   O wicked wit and gifts, that have the power
   So to seduce!—won to his shameful lust   45
   The will of my most seeming-virtuous queen.
   O Hamlet, what a falling-off was there,
   From me, whose love was of that dignity
   That it went hand in hand even with the vow
   I made to her in marriage, and to decline   50
   Upon a wretch whose natural gifts were poor
   To those of mine.
   But virtue, as it never will be moved,
   Though lewdness° court it in a shape of heaven,
   So lust, though to a radiant angel linked,   55
   Will sate itself in a celestial bed
   And prey on garbage.
   But soft, methinks I scent the morning air;
   Brief let me be. Sleeping within my orchard,
   My custom always of the afternoon,   60
   Upon my secure° hour thy uncle stole
   With juice of cursed hebona° in a vial,
   And in the porches of my ears did pour
   The leperous distillment, whose effect
   Holds such an enmity with blood of man   65
   That swift as quicksilver it courses through
   The natural gates and alleys of the body,
   And with a sudden vigor it doth posset°
   And curd, like eager° droppings into milk,
   The thin and wholesome blood. So did it mine,   70

---

33 *Lethe wharf* bank of the river of forgetfulness in Hades   37 *forgèd process* false account   42 *adulterate* adulterous   54 *lewdness* lust   61 *secure* unsuspecting   62 *hebona* a poisonous plant   68 *posset* curdle   69 *eager* acid

And a most instant tetter° barked about
Most lazarlike° with vile and loathsome crust
All my smooth body.
Thus was I, sleeping, by a brother's hand
Of life, of crown, of queen at once dispatched,   75
Cut off even in the blossoms of my sin,
Unhouseled, disappointed, unaneled,°
No reck'ning made, but sent to my account
With all my imperfections on my head.
O, horrible! O, horrible! Most horrible!   80
If thou hast nature in thee, bear it not.
Let not the royal bed of Denmark be
A couch for luxury° and damnèd incest.
But howsomever thou pursues this act,
Taint not thy mind, nor let thy soul contrive   85
Against thy mother aught. Leave her to heaven
And to those thorns that in her bosom lodge
To prick and sting her. Fare thee well at once.
The glowworm shows the matin° to be near
And 'gins to pale his uneffectual fire.   90
Adieu, adieu, adieu. Remember me.   *Exit.*
Hamlet. O all you host of heaven! O earth! What else?
And shall I couple hell? O fie! Hold, hold, my heart,
And you, my sinews, grow not instant old,
But bear me stiffly up. Remember thee?   95
Ay, thou poor ghost, whiles memory holds a seat
In this distracted globe.° Remember thee?
Yea, from the table° of my memory
I'll wipe away all trivial fond° records,
All saws° of books, all forms, all pressures° past   100
That youth and observation copied there,
And thy commandment all alone shall live
Within the book and volume of my brain,
Unmixed with baser matter. Yes, by heaven!
O most pernicious woman!   105
O villain, villain, smiling, damnèd villain!
My tables—meet it is I set it down
That one may smile, and smile, and be a villain.
At least I am sure it may be so in Denmark. [*Writes.*]

---

71 *tetter* scab   72 *lazarlike* leperlike   77 *Unhouseled, disappointed, unaneled* without the
sacrament of communion, unabsolved, without extreme unction   83 *luxury* lust   89 *matin*
morning   97 *globe* i.e., his head   98 *table* tablet, notebook   99 *fond* foolish   100 *saws*
maxims   100 *pressures* impressions

So, uncle, there you are. Now to my word: 110
It is "Adieu, adieu, remember me."
I have sworn't.
Horatio and Marcellus. (Within) My lord, my lord!

Enter Horatio and Marcellus.

Marcellus. Lord Hamlet!
Horatio.   Heavens secure him!
Hamlet. So be it!
Marcellus. Illo, ho, ho,° my lord!   115
Hamlet. Hillo, ho, ho, boy! Come, bird, come.
Marcellus. How is't, my noble lord?
Horatio.   What news, my lord?
Hamlet. O, wonderful!
Horatio. Good my lord, tell it.
Hamlet.   No, you will reveal it.
Horatio. Not I, my lord, by heaven.
Marcellus.   Nor I, my lord.
Hamlet. How say you then? Would heart of man once think it?   120
    But you'll be secret?
Both.   Ay, by heaven, my lord.
Hamlet. There's never a villain dwelling in all Denmark
    But he's an arrant knave.
Horatio. There needs no ghost, my lord, come from the grave   125
    To tell us this.
Hamlet.   Why, right, you are in the right;
    And so, without more circumstance° at all,
    I hold it fit that we shake hands and part:
    You, as your business and desire shall point you,
    For every man hath business and desire   130
    Such as it is, and for my own poor part,
    Look you, I'll go pray.
Horatio. These are but wild and whirling words, my lord.
Hamlet. I am sorry they offend you, heartily;
    Yes, faith, heartily.
Horatio.   There's no offense, my lord.   135
Hamlet. Yes, by Saint Patrick, but there is, Horatio,
    And much offense too. Touching this vision here,
    It is an honest ghost,° that let me tell you.
    For your desire to know what is between us,

---

115 *Illo, ho, ho* (falconer's call to his hawk)   127 *circumstances* details   138 *honest ghost* i.e.,
not a demon in his father's shape

O'ermaster't as you may. And now, good friends,   140
As you are friends, scholars, and soldiers,
Give me one poor request.
Horatio. What is't, my lord? We will.
Hamlet. Never make known what you have seen tonight.
Both. My lord, we will not.
Hamlet.   Nay, but swear't.
Horatio.   In faith,   145
My lord, not I.
Marcellus.   Nor I, my lord—in faith.
Hamlet. Upon my sword.
Marcellus.   We have sworn, my lord, already.
Hamlet. Indeed, upon my sword, indeed.

                                        Ghost cries under the stage.

Ghost. Swear.
Hamlet. Ha, ha, boy, say'st thou so? Art thou there, truepenny?°   150
Come on. You hear this fellow in the cellarage.
Consent to swear.
Horatio.   Propose the oath, my lord.
Hamlet. Never to speak of this that you have seen.
Swear by my sword.
Ghost. [*Beneath*] Swear.   155
Hamlet. Hic et ubique?° Then we'll shift our ground;
Come hither, gentlemen,
And lay your hands again upon my sword.
Swear by my sword
Never to speak of this that you have heard.   160
Ghost. [*Beneath*] Swear by his sword.
Hamlet. Well said, old mole! Canst work i' th' earth so fast?
A worthy pioner!° Once more remove, good friends.
Horatio. O day and night, but this is wondrous strange!
Hamlet. And therefore as a stranger give it welcome.   165
There are more things in heaven and earth, Horatio,
Than are dreamt of in your philosophy.
But come:
Here as before, never, so help you mercy,
How strange or odd some'er I bear myself   170
(As I perchance hereafter shall think meet
To put an antic disposition° on),

---

150 *truepenny* honest fellow   156 *Hic et ubique* here and everywhere (Latin)   163 *pioner*
digger of mines   172 *antic disposition* fantastic behavior

That you, at such times seeing me, never shall
With arms encumb'red° thus, or this headshake,
Or by pronouncing of some doubtful phrase,   175
As "Well, well, we know," or "We could, an if we would,"
Or "If we list to speak," or "There be, an if they might,"
Or such ambiguous giving out, to note
That you know aught of me—this do swear,
So grace and mercy at your most need help you.   180
Ghost. [*Beneath*] Swear.   [*They swear.*]
Hamlet. Rest, rest, perturbèd spirit. So, gentlemen,
    With all my love I do commend me° to you,
    And what so poor a man as Hamlet is
    May do t' express his love and friending to you,   185
    God willing, shall not lack. Let us go in together,
    And still your fingers on your lips, I pray.
    The time is out of joint. O cursèd spite,
    That ever I was born to set it right!
    Nay, come, let's go together.   *Exeunt.* 190

[ACT II
SCENE I. A room.]

Enter old Polonius, with his man Reynaldo.

Polonius. Give him this money and these notes, Reynaldo.
Reynaldo. I will, my lord.
Polonius. You shall do marvell's° wisely, good Reynaldo,
    Before you visit him, to make inquire
    Of his behavior.
Reynaldo.   My lord, I did intend it.   5
Polonius. Marry, well said, very well said. Look you sir,
    Inquire me first what Danskers° are in Paris,
    And how, and who, what means, and where they keep,°
    What company, at what expense; and finding
    By this encompassment° and drift of question   10
    That they do know my son, come you more nearer
    Than your particular demands° will touch it.
    Take you as 'twere some distant knowledge of him,
    As thus, "I know his father and his friends,
    And in part him." Do you mark this, Reynaldo?   15
Reynaldo. Ay, very well, my lord.

_____

174 *encumb'red* folded   183 *commend me* entrust myself   II.i.3 *marvell's* marvelous(ly)   7
Danskers Danes   8 *keep* dwell   10 *encompassment* circling   12 *demands* questions

Polonius. "And in part him, but," you may say, "not well,
    But if't be he I mean, he's very wild,
    Addicted so and so." And there put on him
    What forgeries° you please; marry, none so rank   20
    As may dishonor him—take heed of that—
    But, sir, such wanton, wild, and usual slips
    As are companions noted and most known
    To youth and liberty.
Reynaldo.   As gaming, my lord.
Polonius. Ay, or drinking, fencing, swearing, quarreling,   25
    Drabbing.° You may go so far.
Reynaldo. My lord, that would dishonor him.
Polonius. Faith, no, as you may season it in the charge.
    You must not put another scandal on him,
    That he is open to incontinency.°   30
    That's not my meaning. But breathe his faults so quaintly°
    That they may seem the taints of liberty,
    The flash and outbreak of a fiery mind,
    A savageness in unreclaimèd blood,
    Of general assault.°
Reynaldo.   But, my good lord—   35
Polonius. Wherefore should you do this?
Reynaldo.   Ay, my lord,
    I would know that.
Polonius.   Marry, sir, here's my drift,
    And I believe it is a fetch of warrant.°
    You laying these slight sullies on my son
    As 'twere a thing a little soiled i' th' working,   40
    Mark you,
    Your party in converse, him you would sound,
    Having ever seen in the prenominate crimes°
    The youth you breathe of guilty, be assured
    He closes with you in this consequence:°   45
    "Good sir," or so, or "friend," or "gentleman"—
    According to the phrase or the addition.°
    Of man and country—
Reynaldo.   Very good, my lord.
Polonius. And then, sir, does 'a° this—'a does—
    What was I about to say? By the mass, I was about   50
    to say something! Where did I leave?

---

20 *forgeries* inventions   26 *Drabbing* wenching   30 *incontinency* habitual licentiousness   31 *quaintly* ingeniously, delicately   35 *Of general assault* common to all men   38 *fetch of warrant* justifiable device   43 *Having . . . crimes* if he has ever seen in the aforementioned crimes   45 *He closes . . . this consequence* he falls in with you in this conclusion   47 *addition* title   49 *'a* he

Reynaldo. At "closes in the consequence," at "friend or so," and
    "gentleman."
Polonius. At "closes in the consequence"—Ay, marry!
    He closes thus: "I know the gentleman;   55
    I saw him yesterday, or t'other day,
    Or then, or then, with such or such, and, as you say,
    There was 'a gaming, there o'ertook in's rouse,
    There falling out at tennis"; or perchance,
    "I saw him enter such a house of sale,"   60
    Videlicet,° a brothel, or so forth.
    See you now—
    Your bait of falsehood take this carp of truth,
    And thus do we of wisdom and of reach,°
    With windlasses° and with assays of bias,°   65
    By indirections find directions out.
    So, by my former lecture and advice,
    Shall you my son. You have me, have you not?
Reynaldo. My lord, I have.
Polonius.   God bye ye, fare ye well.
Reynaldo. Good my lord.   70
Polonius. Observe his inclination in yourself.°
Reynaldo. I shall, my lord.
Polonius. And let him ply his music.
Reynaldo.   Well, my lord.
Polonius. Farewell.   *Exit Reynaldo*

                    Enter Ophelia.

            How now, Ophelia, what's the matter?
Ophelia. O my lord, my lord, I have been so affrighted!   75
Polonius. With what, i' th' name of God?
Ophelia. My lord, as I was sewing in my closet,°
    Lord Hamlet, with his doublet all unbraced,°
    No hat upon his head, his stockings fouled,
    Ungartered, and down-gyvèd° to his ankle,   80
    Pale as his shirt, his knees knocking each other,
    And with a look so piteous in purport,°
    As if he had been loosèd out of hell
    To speak of horrors—he comes before me.

---

61 *Videlicet* namely   64 *reach* far-reaching awareness(?)   65 *windlasses* circuitous courses   65
assays of bias indirect attempts (metaphor from bowling; *bias* = curved course)   71 *in yourself*
for yourself   77 *closet* private room   78 *doublet all unbraced* jacket entirely unlaced   80 *down-gyvèd* hanging down like fetters   82 *purport* expression

Polonius. Mad for thy love?
Ophelia.   My lord, I do not know, 85
  But truly I do fear it.
Polonius.   What said he?
Ophelia. He took me by the wrist and held me hard;
  Then goes he to the length of all his arm,
  And with his other hand thus o'er his brow
  He falls to such perusal of my face 90
  As 'a would draw it. Long stayed he so.
  At last, a little shaking of mine arm,
  And thrice his head thus waving up and down,
  He raised a sigh so piteous and profound
  As it did seem to shatter all his bulk 95
  And end his being. That done, he lets me go,
  And, with his head over his shoulder turned,
  He seemed to find his way without his eyes,
  For out o' doors he went without their helps,
  And to the last bended their light on me. 100
Polonius. Come, go with me. I will go seek the King.
  This is the very ecstasy° of love,
  Whose violent property fordoes° itself
  And leads the will to desperate undertakings
  As oft as any passions under heaven 105
  That does afflict our natures. I am sorry.
  What, have you given him any hard words of late?
Ophelia. No, my good lord; but as you did command,
  I did repel his letters and denied
  His access to me.
Polonius   That hath made him mad. 110
  I am sorry that with better heed and judgment
  I had not quoted° him. I feared he did but trifle
  And meant to wrack thee; but beshrew my jealousy.°
  By heaven, it is as proper° to our age
  To cast beyond ourselves° in our opinions 115
  As it is common for the younger sort
  To lack discretion. Come, go we to the King.
  This must be known, which, being kept close, might move
  More grief to hide than hate to utter love.°
  Come. *Exeunt.* 120

---

  102 *ecstasy* madness   103 *property fordoes* quality destroys   112 *quoted* noted   113 *beshrew my jealousy* curse on my suspicions   114 *proper* natural   115 *To cast beyond ourselves* to be overcalculating   117-19 *Come, go . . . utter love* (the general meaning is that while telling the King of Hamlet's love may anger the King, more grief would come from keeping it secret)

[SCENE II. The castle.]

Flourish. Enter King and Queen, Rosencrantz, and Guildenstern [with others].

King. Welcome, dear Rosencrantz and Guildenstern.
Moreover that° we much did long to see you,
The need we have to use you did provoke
Our hasty sending. Something have you heard
Of Hamlet's transformation: so call it, 5
Sith° nor th' exterior nor the inward man
Resembles that it was. What it should be,
More than his father's death, that thus hath put him
So much from th' understanding of himself,
I cannot dream of. I entreat you both 10
That, being of so° young days brought up with him,
And sith so neighbored to his youth and havior,°
That you vouchsafe your rest° here in our court
Some little time, so by your companies
To draw him on to pleasures, and to gather 15
So much as from occasion you may glean,
Whether aught to us unknown afflicts him thus,
That opened° lies within our remedy.
Queen. Good gentlemen, he hath much talked of you,
And sure I am, two men there is not living 20
To whom he more adheres. If it will please you
To show us so much gentry° and good will
As to expend your time with us awhile
For the supply and profit of our hope,
Your visitation shall receive such thanks 25
As fits a king's remembrance.
Rosencrantz.   Both your Majesties
Might, by the sovereign power you have of us,
Put your dread pleasures more into command
Than to entreaty.
Guildenstern.   But we both obey,
And here give up ourselves in the full bent° 30
To lay our service freely at your feet,
To be commanded.
King. Thanks, Rosencrantz and gentle Guildenstern.

II.ii.2 *Moreover that* beside the fact that   6 *Sith* since   11 *of so* from such   12 *youth and havior* behavior in his youth   13 *vouchsafe your rest* consent to remain   18 *opened* revealed   22 *gentry* courtesy   30 *in the full bent* entirely (the figure is of a bow bent to its capacity)

Queen. Thanks, Guildenstern and gentle Rosencrantz.
 And I beseech you instantly to visit   35
 My too much changèd son. Go, some of you,
 And bring these gentlemen where Hamlet is.
Guildenstern. Heavens make our presence and our practices
 Pleasant and helpful to him!
Queen.   Ay, amen!

Exeunt Rosencrantz and Guildenstern [with some Attendants].
                                              Enter Polonius.

Polonius. Th' ambassadors from Norway, my good lord,   40
 Are joyfully returned.
King. Thou still° hast been the father of good news.
Polonius. Have I, my lord? Assure you, my good liege,
 I hold my duty, as I hold my soul,
 Both to my God and to my gracious king;   45
 And I do think, or else this brain of mine
 Hunts not the trail of policy so sure°
 As it hath used to do, that I have found
 The very cause of Hamlet's lunacy.
King. O, speak of that! That do I long to hear.   50
Polonius. Give first admittance to th' ambassadors.
 My news shall be the fruit to that great feast.
King. Thyself do grace to them and bring them in.
                                              [Exit Polonius.]
 He tells me, my dear Gertrude, he hath found
 The head and source of all your son's distemper.   55
Queen. I doubt° it is no other but the main,°
 His father's death and our o'erhasty marriage.
King. Well, we shall sift him.

Enter Polonius, Voltemand, and Cornelius.

                    Welcome, my good friends.
 Say, Voltemand, what from our brother Norway?
Voltemand. Most fair return of greetings and desires.   60
 Upon our first,° he sent out to suppress
 His nephew's levies, which to him appeared
 To be a preparation 'gainst the Polack;
 But better looked into, he truly found
 It was against your Highness, whereat grieved,   65

---

42 *still* always   47 *Hunts not . . . so sure* does not follow clues of political doings with such
sureness   56 *doubt* suspect   56 *main* principal point   61 *first* first audience

That so his sickness, age, and impotence
Was falsely borne in hand,° sends out arrests
On Fortinbras; which he, in brief, obeys,
Receives rebuke from Norway, and in fine,°
Makes vow before his uncle never more   70
To give th' assay° of arms against your Majesty.
Whereon old Norway, overcome with joy,
Gives him threescore thousand crowns in annual fee
And his commission to employ those soldiers,
So levied as before, against the Polack,   75
With an entreaty, herein further shown,

                                               [Gives a paper.]

That it might please you to give quiet pass
Through your dominions for this enterprise,
On such regards of safety and allowance°
As therein are set down.
King.   It likes us well;   80
And at our more considered time° we'll read,
Answer, and think upon this business.
Meantime, we thank you for your well-took labor.
Go to your rest; at night we'll feast together.
Most welcome home!   *Exeunt Ambassadors.*
Polonius.   This business is well ended.   85
My liege and madam, to expostulate°
What majesty should be, what duty is,
Why day is day, night night, and time is time,
Were nothing but to waste night, day, and time.
Therefore, since brevity is the soul of wit,°   90
And tediousness the limbs and outward flourishes,
I will be brief. Your noble son is mad.
Mad call I it, for, to define true madness,
What is't but to be nothing else but mad?
But let that go.
Queen.   More matter, with less art.   95
Polonius. Madam, I swear I use no art at all.
That he's mad, 'tis true: 'tis true 'tis pity,
And pity 'tis 'tis true—a foolish figure.°
But farewell it, for I will use no art.
Mad let us grant him then; and now remains   100
That we find out the cause of this effect,

---

    67 *borne in hand* deceived 69 *in fine* finally 71 *assay* trial 79 *regards of safety and allowance* i.e., conditions 81 *considered time* time proper for considering 86 *expostulate* discuss 90 *wit* wisdom, understanding 98 *figure* figure of rhetoric

Or rather say, the cause of this defect,
For this effect defective comes by cause.
Thus it remains, and the remainder thus.
Perpend.°   105
I have a daughter: have, while she is mine,
Who in her duty and obedience, mark,
Hath given me this. Now gather, and surmise.

                                         [*Reads*] *the letter.*
"To the celestial, and my soul's idol, the most beautified Ophelia"—   110
That's an ill phrase, a vile phrase; "beautified" is a vile phrase. But you
shall hear. Thus:
"In her excellent white bosom, these, &c."
Queen. Came this from Hamlet to her?
Polonius. Good madam, stay awhile. I will be faithful.   115
        "Doubt thou the stars are fire,
            Doubt that the sun doth move;
        Doubt° truth to be a liar,
            But never doubt I love.
O dear Ophelia, I am ill at these numbers.° I have not art to reckon my   120
groans; but that I love thee best, O most best, believe it. Adieu.
    Thine evermore, most dear lady, whilst this machine° is to him,
    HAMLET."
This in obedience hath my daughter shown me,
And more above° hath his solicitings,   125
As they fell out by time, by means, and place,
All given to mine ear.
King.   But how hath she
Received his love?
Polonius.   What do you think of me?
King. As of a man faithful and honorable.   130
Polonius. I would fain prove so. But what might you think,
    When I had seen this hot love on the wing
    (As I perceived it, I must tell you that,
    Before my daughter told me), what might you,
    Or my dear Majesty your Queen here, think,   135
    If I had played the desk or table book,°
    Or given my heart a winking,° mute and dumb,
    Or looked upon this love with idle sight?
    What might you think? No, I went round to work
    And my young mistress thus I did bespeak: 140

---

105 *Perpend* consider carefully   118 *Doubt* suspect   120 *ill at these numbers* unskilled in
verses   124 *machine* complex device (here, his body)   126 *more above* in addition   136 *played
the desk or table book* i.e., been a passive recipient of secrets   137 *winking* closing of the eyes

"Lord Hamlet is a prince, out of thy star.°
This must not be." And then I prescripts gave her,
That she should lock herself from his resort,
Admit no messengers, receive no tokens.
Which done, she took the fruits of my advice,   145
And he, repellèd, a short tale to make,
Fell into a sadness, then into a fast,
Thence to a watch,° thence into a weakness,
Thence to a lightness,° and, by this declension,
Into the madness wherein now he raves,   150
And all we mourn for.
King.   Do you think 'tis this?
Queen. It may be, very like.
Polonius. Hath there been such a time, I would fain know that,
That I have positively said " 'Tis so,"
When it proved otherwise?
King.   Not that I know.   155
Polonius. [*Pointing to his head and shoulder*] Take this from this, if this
be otherwise.
If circumstances lead me, I will find
Where truth is hid, though it were hid indeed
Within the center.°
King.   How may we try it further?
Polonius. You know sometimes he walks four hours together   160
Here in the lobby.
Queen.   So he does indeed.
Polonius. At such a time I'll loose my daughter to him.
Be you and I behind an arras° then.
Mark the encounter. If he love her not,
And be not from his reason fall'n thereon,   165
Let me be no assistant for a state
But keep a farm and carters.
King.   We will try it.

Enter Hamlet reading on a book.

Queen. But look where sadly the poor wretch comes reading.
Polonius. Away, I do beseech you both, away.

Exit King and Queen.

---

141 *star* sphere   148 *watch* wakefulness   149 *lightness* mental derangement   159 *center*
center of the earth   163 *arras* tapestry hanging in front of a wall

I'll board him presently.° O, give me leave. 170
How does my good Lord Hamlet?
Hamlet. Well, God-a-mercy.
Polonius. Do you know me, my lord?
Hamlet. Excellent well. You are a fishmonger.°
Polonius. Not I, my lord. 175
Hamlet. Then I would you were so honest a man.
Polonius. Honest, my lord?
Hamlet. Ay, sir. To be honest, as this world goes, is to be one man picked
out of ten thousand.
Polonius. That's very true, my lord. 180
Hamlet. For if the sun breed maggots in a dead dog, being a good kissing
carrion°—Have you a daughter?
Polonius. I have, my lord.
Hamlet. Let her not walk i' th' sun. Conception° is a blessing, but as your
daughter may conceive, friend, look to't. 185
Polonius. [*Aside*] How say you by that? Still harping on my daughter. Yet
he knew me not at first. 'A said I was a fishmonger. 'A is far gone, far
gone. And truly in my youth I suffered much extremity for love, very near
this. I'll speak to him again.—What do you read, my lord?
Hamlet. Words, words, words. 190
Polonius. What is the matter, my lord.
Hamlet. Between who?
Polonius. I mean the matter° that you read, my lord.
Hamlet. Slanders, sir; for the satirical rogue says here that old men have gray
beards, that their faces are wrinkled, their eyes purging thick amber and 195
plumtree gum, and that they have a plentiful lack of wit, together with
most weak hams. All which, sir, though I most powerfully and potently
believe, yet I hold it not honesty° to have it thus set down; for you yourself,
sir, should be old as I am if, like a crab, you could go backward.
Polonius. [*Aside*] Though this be madness, yet there is method in't. Will you 200
walk out of the air, my lord?
Hamlet. Into my grave.
Polonius. Indeed, that's out of the air. [*Aside*] How pregnant° sometimes his
replies are! A happiness° that often madness hits on, which reason and
sanity could not so prosperously be delivered of. I will leave him and 205
suddenly contrive the means of meeting between him and my daughter.—
My lord, I will take my leave of you.

---

170 *board him presently* accost him at once   174 *fishmonger* dealer in fish (slang for a
procurer)   182 *a good kissing carrion* (perhaps the meaning is "a good piece of flesh to kiss," but
many editors emend *good* to *god,* taking the word to refer to the sun)   184 *Conception* (1)
understanding (2) becoming pregnant   193 *matter* (Polonius means "subject matter," but Hamlet
pretends to take the word in the sense of "quarrel")   198 *honesty* decency   203 *pregnant*
meaningful   204 *happiness* apt turn of phrase

Hamlet. You cannot take from me anything that I will more willingly part withal—except my life, except my life, except my life.

Enter Guildenstern and Rosencrantz.

Polonius. Fare you well, my lord.   210
Hamlet. These tedious old fools!
Polonius. You go to seek the Lord Hamlet? There he is.
Rosencrantz. [*To Polonius*] God save you, sir!

[*Exit Polonius.*]

Guildenstern. My honored lord!
Rosencrantz. My most dear lord!   215
Hamlet. My excellent good friends! How dost thou, Guildenstern? Ah, Rosencrantz! Good lads, how do you both?
Rosencrantz. As the indifferent° children of the earth.
Guildenstern. Happy in that we are not overhappy. On Fortune's cap we are not the very button.   220
Hamlet. Nor the soles of her shoe?
Rosencrantz. Neither, my lord.
Hamlet. Then you live about her waist, or in the middle of her favors?
Guildenstern. Faith, her privates° we.
Hamlet. In the secret parts of Fortune? O, most true! She is a strumpet. What   225
news?
Rosencrantz. None, my lord, but that the world's grown honest.
Hamlet. Then is doomsday near. But your news is not true. Let me question more in particular. What have you, my good friends, deserved at the hands of Fortune that she sends you to prison hither?
Guildenstern. Prison, my lord?   230
Hamlet. Denmark's a prison.
Rosencrantz. Then is the world one.
Hamlet. A goodly one, in which there are many confines, wards,° and dungeons, Denmark being one o' th' worst.
Rosencrantz. We think not so, my lord.   235
Hamlet. Why, then 'tis none to you, for there is nothing either good or bad but thinking makes it so. To me it is a prison.
Rosencrantz. Why then your ambition makes it one. 'Tis too narrow for your mind.
Hamlet. O God, I could be bounded in a nutshell and count myself a king of infinite space, were it not that I have bad dreams.   240

---

219 *indifferent* ordinary   224 *privates* ordinary men (with a pun on "private parts")   233 *wards* cells

Guildenstern. Which dreams indeed are ambition, for the very substance of
   the ambitious is merely the shadow of a dream.
Hamlet. A dream itself is but a shadow.
Rosencrantz. Truly, and I hold ambition of so airy and light a quality that
   it is but a shadow's shadow.   245
Hamlet. Then are our beggars bodies, and our monarchs and outstretched
   heroes the beggars' shadows.° Shall we to th' court? For, by my fay,° I
   cannot reason.
Both. We'll wait upon you.
Hamlet. No such matter. I will not sort you with the rest of my servants,
   for, to speak to you like an honest man, I am most dreadfully attended.
   But in the beaten way of friendship, what make you at Elsinore?   250
Rosencrantz. To visit you, my lord; no other occasion.
Hamlet. Beggar that I am, I am even poor in thanks, but I thank you; and
   sure, dear friends, my thanks are too dear a halfpenny.° Were you not sent
   for? Is it your own inclining? Is it a free visitation? Come, come, deal justly 255
   with me. Come, come; nay, speak.
Guildenstern. What should we say, my lord?
Hamlet. Why anything—but to th' purpose. You were sent for, and there is
   a kind of confession in your looks, which your modesties have not craft
   enough to color. I know the good King and Queen have sent for you.   260
Rosencrantz. To what end, my lord?
Hamlet. That you must teach me. But let me conjure you by the rights of
   our fellowship, by the consonancy of our youth, by the obligation of our
   everpreserved love, and by what more dear a better proposer can charge
   you withal, be even and direct with me, whether you were sent for or no.   265
Rosencrantz. [*Aside to Guildenstern*] What say you?
Hamlet. [*Aside*] Nay then, I have an eye of you.—If you love me, hold not
   off.
Guildenstern My lord, we were sent for.
Hamlet. I will tell you why; so shall my anticipation prevent your discovery,°
   and your secrecy to the King and Queen molt no feather. I have of late,   270
   but wherefore I know not, lost all my mirth, forgone all custom of exercises;
   and indeed, it goes so heavily with my disposition that this goodly frame,
   the earth, seems to me a sterile promontory; this most excellent canopy,
   the air, look you, this brave o'erhanging firmament, this majestical roof
   fretted° with golden fire: why, it appeareth nothing to me but a foul and   275
   pestilent congregation of vapors. What a piece of work is a man, how
   noble in reason, how infinite in faculties, in form and moving how express°
   and admirable, in action how like an angel, in apprehension how like a

---

   246–47 *Then are . . . beggars' shadows* i.e., by your logic, beggars (lacking ambition) are
substantial, and great men are elongated shadows   247 *fay* faith   254 *too dear a halfpenny* i.e.,
not worth a halfpenny   269 *prevent your discovery* forestall your disclosure   275 *fretted*
adorned   277 *express* exact

god: the beauty of the world, the paragon of animals; and yet to me, what
is this quintessence of dust? Man delights not me; nor woman neither, 280
though by your smiling you seem to say so.

Rosencrantz. My lord, there was no such stuff in my thoughts.

Hamlet. Why did ye laugh then, when I said "Man delights not me"?

Rosencrantz. To think, my lord, if you delight not in man, what lenten°
entertainment the players shall receive from you. We coted° them on the 285
way, and hither are they coming to offer you service.

Hamlet. He that plays the king shall be welcome; his Majesty shall have
tribute of me; the adventurous knight shall use his foil and target;° the
lover shall not sigh gratis; the humorous man° shall end his part in peace;
the clown shall make those laugh whose lungs are tickle o' th' sere,° and 290
the lady shall say her mind freely, or° the blank verse shall halt° for't.
What players are they?

Rosencrantz. Even those you were wont to take such delight in, the tragedians
of the city.

Hamlet. How chances it they travel? Their residence, both in reputation and
profit, was better both ways. 295

Rosencrantz. I think their inhibition° comes by the means of the late innovation.°

Hamlet. Do they hold the same estimation they did when I was in the city?
Are they so followed?

Rosencrantz. No indeed, are they not.

Hamlet. How comes it? Do they grow rusty? 300

Rosencrantz. Nay, their endeavor keeps in the wonted pace, but there is, sir,
an eyrie° of children, little eyases, that cry out on the top of question° and
are most tyrannically° clapped for't. These are now the fashion, and so
berattle the common stages° (so they call them) that many wearing rapiers
are afraid of goosequills° and dare scarce come thither. 305

Hamlet. What, are they children? Who maintains 'em? How are they escoted?°
Will they pursue the quality° no longer than they can sing? Will they not
say afterwards, if they should grow themselves to common players (as it
is most like, if their means are no better), their writers do them wrong to
make them exclaim against their own succession?° 310

---

284 *lenten* meager　285 *coted* overtook　288 *target* shield　289 *humorous man* i.e., eccentric
man (among stock characters in dramas were men dominated by a "humor" or odd trait)　290
tickle o' th' sere on hair trigger (*sere* = part of the gunlock)　291 *or* else　291 *halt* limp　296
inhibition hindrance　296 *innovation* (probably an allusion to the companies of child actors that
had become popular and were offering serious competition to the adult actors)　302 *eyrie* nest
302 *eyases, that . . . of question* unfledged hawks that cry shrilly above others in matters of
debate　303 *tyrannically* violently　304 *berattle the common stages* cry down the public theaters
(with the adult acting companies)　305 *goosequills* pens (of satirists who ridicule the public
theaters and their audiences)　306 *escoted* financially supported　307 *quality* profession of
acting　310 *succession* future

Rosencrantz. Faith, there has been much to-do on both sides, and the nation
holds it no sin to tarre° them to controversy. There was, for a while, no
money bid for argument° unless the poet and the player went to cuffs in
the question.
Hamlet. Is't possible?
Guildenstern. O, there has been much throwing about of brains.   315
Hamlet. Do the boys carry it away?
Rosencrantz. Ay, that they do, my lord—Hercules and his load° too.
Hamlet. It is not very strange, for my uncle is King of Denmark, and those
that would make mouths at him while my father lived give twenty, forty,
fifty, a hundred ducats apiece for his picture in little. 'Sblood,° there is 320
something in this more than natural, if philosophy could find it out.

A flourish.

Guildenstern. There are the players.
Hamlet. Gentlemen, you are welcome to Elsinore. Your hands, come then.
Th' appurtenance of welcome is fashion and ceremony. Let me comply°
with you in this garb,° lest my extent° to the players (which I tell you must 325
show fairly outwards) should more appear like entertainment than yours.
You are welcome. But my uncle-father and aunt-mother are deceived.
Guildenstern. In what, my dear lord?
Hamlet. I am but mad north-northwest:° when the wind is southerly I know
a hawk from a handsaw.°   330

Enter Polonius.

Polonius. Well be with you, gentlemen.
Hamlet. Hark you, Guildenstern, and you too; at each ear a hearer. That
great baby you see there is not yet out of his swaddling clouts.
Rosencrantz. Happily° he is the second time come to them, for they say an
old man is twice a child.   335
Hamlet. I will prophesy he comes to tell me of the players. Mark it.—You
say right, sir; a Monday morning, 'twas then indeed.
Polonius. My lord, I have news to tell you.
Hamlet. My lord, I have news to tell you. When Roscius° was an actor in
Rome—

---

312 *tarre* incite   313 *argument* plot of a play   317 *Hercules and his load* i.e., the whole world
(with a reference to the Globe Theatre, which had a sign that represented Hercules bearing the
globe)   320 *'Sblood* by God's blood   324 *comply* be courteous   325 *garb* outward show   325
extent behavior   329 *north-northwest* i.e., on one point of the compass only   330 *hawk from a
handsaw* (hawk can refer not only to a bird but to a kind of pickax; *handsaw*—a carpenter's
tool—may involve a similar pun on "hernshaw," a heron)   334 *Happily* perhaps   339 *Roscius* (a
famous Roman comic actor)

Polonius. The actors are come hither, my lord.   340
Hamlet. Buzz, buzz.°
Polonius. Upon my honor—
Hamlet. Then came each actor on his ass—
Polonius. The best actors in the world, either for tragedy, comedy, history,
    pastoral, pastoral-comical, historical-pastoral, tragical-historical, tragical-   345
    comical-historical-pastoral; scene individable,° or poem unlimited.° Se-
    neca° cannot be too heavy, nor Plautus° too light. For the law of writ and
    the liberty,° these are the only men.
Hamlet. O Jeptha, judge of Israel,° what a treasure hadst thou!
Polonius. What a treasure had he, my lord?   350
Hamlet. Why,
        "One fair daughter, and no more,
        The which he lovèd passing well."
Polonius. [*Aside*] Still on my daughter.
Hamlet. Am I not i' th' right, old Jeptha?   355
Polonius. If you call me Jeptha, my lord, I have a daughter that I love passing
    well.
Hamlet. Nay, that follows not.
Polonius. What follows then, my lord?
Hamlet. Why,
        "As by lot, God wot,"   360
    and then, you know,
        "It came to pass, as most like it was."
    The first row of the pious chanson° will show you more, for look where
    my abridgment° comes.

Enter the Players.

You are welcome, masters, welcome, all. I am glad to see thee well. Wel-   365
    come, good friends. O, old friend, why, thy face is valanced° since I saw
    thee last. Com'st thou to beard me in Denmark? What, my young lady°
    and mistress? By'r Lady, your ladyship is nearer to heaven than when I
    saw you last by the altitude of a chopine.° Pray God your voice, like a
    piece of uncurrent gold, be not cracked within the ring.°—Masters, you   370

---

341 *Buzz, buzz* (an interjection, perhaps indicating that the news is old)   346 *scene individable*
plays observing the unities of time, place, and action   346 *poem unlimited* plays not restricted by
the tenets of criticism   347 *Seneca* (Roman tragic dramatist)   347 *Plautus* (Roman comic
dramatist)   347–48 *For the law of writ and the liberty* (perhaps "for sticking to the text and for
improvising"; perhaps "for classical plays and for modern loosely written plays")   350 *Jeptha,
judge of Israel* (the title of a ballad on the Hebrew judge who sacrificed his daughter; see Judges
11)   363 *row of the pious chanson* stanza of the scriptural song   364 *abridgment* (1) i.e.,
entertainers, who abridge the time (2) interrupters   366 *valanced* fringed (with a beard)   367
young lady i.e., boy for female roles   369 *chopine* thick-soled shoe   369–70 *like a piece . . . the
ring* (a coin was unfit for legal tender if a crack extended from the edge through the ring enclosing
the monarch's head. Hamlet, punning on *ring*, refers to the change of voice that the boy actor will
undergo)

are all welcome. We'll e'en to't like French falconers, fly at anything we see. We'll have a speech straight. Come, give us a taste of your quality. Come, a passionate speech.

Player. What speech, my good lord?

Hamlet. I heard thee speak me a speech once, but it was never acted, or if 375
it was, not above once, for the play, I remember, pleased not the million;
'twas caviary to the general,° but it was (as I received it, and others, whose
judgments in such matters cried in the top of° mine) an excellent play,
well digested in the scenes, set down with as much modesty as cunning.°
I remember one said there were no sallets° in the lines to make the matter 380
savory; nor no matter in the phrase that might indict the author of affectation, but called it an honest method, as wholesome as sweet, and by
very much more handsome than fine.° One speech in't I chiefly loved.
'Twas Aeneas' tale to Dido, and thereabout of it especially when he speaks
of Priam's slaughter. If it live in your memory, begin at this line—let me 385
see, let me see:
"The rugged Pyrrhus, like th' Hyrcanian beast°—"
'Tis not so; it begins with Pyrrhus:
"The rugged Pyrrhus, he whose sable° arms,
Black as his purpose, did the night resemble
When he lay couchèd in th' ominous horse,° 390
Hath now this dread and black complexion smeared
With heraldry more dismal.° Head to foot
Now is he total gules, horridly tricked°
With blood of fathers, mothers, daughters, sons,
Baked and impasted° with the parching streets, 395
That lend a tyrannous and a damnèd light
To their lord's murder. Roasted in wrath and fire,
And thus o'ersizèd° with coagulate gore,
With eyes like carbuncles, the hellish Pyrrhus
Old grandsire Priam seeks." 400
So, proceed you.

Polonius. Fore God, my lord, well spoken, with good accent and good discretion.

Player.   "Anon he finds him,
Striking too short at Greeks. His antique sword,
Rebellious to his arm, lies where it falls, 405
Repugnant to command.° Unequal matched,

---

377 *caviary to the general* i.e., too choice for the multitude   378 *in the top of* overtopping
379 *modesty as cunning* restraint as art   380 *sallets* salads, spicy jests   383 *more handsome than fine* well-proportioned rather than ornamented   386 *Hyrcanian beast* i.e., tiger (Hyrcania was in Asia)   388 *sable* black   390 *ominous horse* i.e., wooden horse at the siege of Troy   392 *dismal* ill-omened   393 *total gules, horridly tricked* all red, horridly adorned   395 *impasted* encrusted 398 *o'ersizèd* smeared over   406 *Repugnant to command* disobedient

Pyrrhus at Priam drives, in rage strikes wide,
But with the whiff and wind of his fell sword
Th' unnervèd father falls. Then senseless Ilium,°
Seeming to feel this blow, with flaming top   410
Stoops to his base,° and with a hideous crash
Takes prisoner Pyrrhus' ear. For lo, his sword,
Which was declining on the milky head
Of reverend Priam, seemed i' th' air to stick.
So as a painted tyrant° Pyrrhus stood,   415
And like a neutral to his will and matter°
Did nothing.
But as we often see, against° some storm,
A silence in the heavens, the rack° stand still,
The bold winds speechless, and the orb below   420
As hush as death, anon the dreadful thunder
Doth rend the region, so after Pyrrhus' pause,
A rousèd vengeance sets him new awork,
And never did the Cyclops' hammers fall
On Mars's armor, forged for proof eterne,°   425
With less remorse than Pyrrhus' bleeding sword
Now falls on Priam.
Out, out, thou strumpet Fortune! All you gods,
In general synod° take away her power,
Break all the spokes and fellies° from her wheel,   430
And bowl the round nave° down the hill of heaven,
As low as to the fiends."
Polonius. This is too long.
Hamlet. It shall to the barber's, with your beard.—Prithee say on. He's for
    a jig or a tale of bawdry, or he sleeps. Say on; come to Hecuba.   435
Player. "But who (ah woe!) had seen the mobled° queen——
Hamlet. "The mobled queen"?
Polonius. That's good. "Mobled queen" is good.
Player. "Run barefoot up and down, threat'ning the flames
    With bisson rheum;° a clout° upon that head   440
    Where late the diadem stood, and for a robe,
    About her lank and all o'erteemèd° loins,
    A blanket in the alarm of fear caught up—
    Who this had seen, with tongue in venom steeped
    'Gainst Fortune's state would treason have pronounced.   445

---

    409 *senseless Ilium* insensate Troy   411 *Stoops to his base* collapses (*his* = its)   415 *painted tyrant* tyrant in a picture   416 *matter* task   418 *against* just before   419 *rack* clouds   425 *proof eterne* eternal endurance   429 *synod* council   430 *fellies* rims   431 *nave* hub   436 *mobled* muffled   440 *bisson rheum* blinding tears   440 *clout* rag   442 *o'erteemèd* exhausted with childbearing

But if the gods themselves did see her then,
When she saw Pyrrhus make malicious sport
In mincing with his sword her husband's limbs,
The instant burst of clamor that she made
(Unless things mortal move them not at all)   450
Would have made milch° the burning eyes of heaven
And passion in the gods."

Polonius. Look, whe'r° he has not turned his color, and has tears in's eyes. Prithee no more.

Hamlet. 'Tis well. I'll have thee speak out the rest of this soon. Good my   455
lord, will you see the players well bestowed?° Do you hear? Let them be well used, for they are the abstract and brief chronicles of the time. After your death you were better have a bad epitaph than their ill report while you live.

Polonius. My lord, I will use them according to their desert.

Hamlet. God's bodkin,° man, much better! Use every man after his desert,   460
and who shall scape whipping? Use them after your own honor and dignity. The less they deserve, the more merit is in your bounty. Take them in.

Polonius. Come, sirs.

Hamlet. Follow him, friends. We'll hear a play tomorrow. [*Aside to Player*]
Dost thou hear me, old friend? Can you play *The Murder of Gonzago?*   465

Player. Ay, my lord.

Hamlet. We'll ha't tomorrow night. You could for a need study a speech of some dozen or sixteen lines which I would set down and insert in't, could you not?

Player. Ay, my lord.

Hamlet. Very well. Follow that lord, and look you mock him not. My good   470
friends, I'll leave you till night. You are welcome to Elsinore.

Exeunt Polonius and Players.

Rosencrantz. Good my lord.

Exeunt [Rosencrantz and Guildenstern].

Hamlet. Ay, so, God bye to you.—Now I am alone.
O, what a rogue and peasant slave am I!
Is it not monstrous that this player here,   475
But in a fiction, in a dream of passion,°
Could force his soul so to his own conceit°
That from her working all his visage wanned,

---

451 *milch* moist (literally, "milk-giving")   453 *whe'r* whether   456 *bestowed* housed   460
God's bodkin by God's little body   476 *dream of passion* imaginary emotion   477 *conceit*
imagination

Tears in his eyes, distraction in his aspect,
A broken voice, and his whole function° suiting   480
With forms° to his conceit? And all for nothing!
For Hecuba!
What's Hecuba to him, or he to Hecuba,
That he should weep for her? What would he do
Had he the motive and the cue for passion   485
That I have? He would drown the stage with tears
And cleave the general ear with horrid speech,
Make mad the guilty and appall the free,°
Confound the ignorant, and amaze indeed
The very faculties of eyes and ears.   490
Yet I,
A dull and muddy-mettled° rascal, peak
Like John-a-dreams,° unpregnant of° my cause,
And can say nothing. No, not for a king,
Upon whose property and most dear life   495
A damned defeat was made. Am I a coward?
Who calls me villain? Breaks my pate across?
Plucks off my beard and blows it in my face?
Tweaks me by the nose? Gives me the lie i' th' throat
As deep as to the lungs? Who does me this?   500
Ha, 'swounds,° I should take it, for it cannot be
But I am pigeon-livered° and lack gall
To make oppression bitter, or ere this
I should ha' fatted all the region kites°
With this slave's offal. Bloody, bawdy villain!   505
Remorseless, treacherous, lecherous, kindless° villain!
O, vengeance!
Why, what an ass am I! This is most brave,°
That I, the son of a dear father murdered,
Prompted to my revenge by heaven and hell,   510
Must, like a whore, unpack my heart with words
And fall a-cursing like a very drab,°
A stallion!° Fie upon't, foh! About,° my brains.
Hum—
I have heard that guilty creatures sitting at a play   515
Have by the very cunning of the scene

---

480 *function* action 481 *forms* bodily expressions 488 *appall the free* terrify (make pale?)
the guiltless 492 *muddy-mettled* weak-spirited 493 *peak/Like John-a-dreams* mope like a
dreamer 493 *unpregnant of* unquickened by 501 *'swounds* by God's wounds 502 *pigeon-
livered* gentle as a dove 504 *region kites* kites (scavenger birds) of the sky 506 *kindless*
unnatural 508 *brave* fine 512 *drab* prostitute 513 *stallion* male prostitute (perhaps one should
adopt the folio reading, *scullion* = kitchen wench) 513 *About* to work

Been struck so to the soul that presently°
They have proclaimed their malefactions.
For murder, though it have no tongue, will speak
With most miraculous organ. I'll have these players   520
Play something like the murder of my father
Before mine uncle. I'll observe his looks,
I'll tent° him to the quick. If 'a do blench,°
I know my course. The spirit that I have seen
May be a devil, and the devil hath power   525
T' assume a pleasing shape, yea, and perhaps
Out of my weakness and my melancholy,
As he is very potent with such spirits,
Abuses me to damn me. I'll have grounds
More relative° than this. The play's the thing   530
Wherein I'll catch the conscience of the King.   *Exit.*

[ACT III
SCENE I. The castle.]

Enter King, Queen, Polonius, Ophelia, Rosencrantz, Guildenstern, Lords.

King. And can you by no drift of conference°
    Get from him why he puts on this confusion,
    Grating so harshly all his days of quiet
    With turbulent and dangerous lunacy?
Rosencrantz. He does confess he feels himself distracted,   5
    But from what cause 'a will by no means speak.
Guildenstern. Nor do we find him forward to be sounded,°
    But with a crafty madness keeps aloof
    When we would bring him on to some confession
    Of his true state.
Queen.   Did he receive you well?   10
Rosencrantz. Most like a gentleman.
Guildenstern. But with much forcing of his disposition.°
Rosencrantz. Niggard of question,° but of our demands
    Most free in his reply.
Queen.   Did you assay° him
    To any pastime?   15

_____

517 *presently* immediately   523 *tent* probe   523 *blench* flinch   530 *relative* (probably
"pertinent," but possibly "able to be related plausibly")   III.i.1 *drift of conference* management of
conversation   7 *forward to be sounded* willing to be questioned   12 *forcing of his disposition*
effort   13 *Niggard of question* uninclined to talk   14 *assay* tempt

Rosencrantz. Madam, it so fell out that certain players
    We o'erraught° on the way; of these we told him,
    And there did seem in him a kind of joy
    To hear of it. They are here about the court,
    And, as I think, they have already order   20
    This night to play before him.
Polonius.   'Tis most true,
    And he beseeched me to entreat your Majesties
    To hear and see the matter.
King. With all my heart, and it doth much content me
    To hear him so inclined.   25
    Good gentlemen, give him a further edge
    And drive his purpose into these delights.
Rosencrantz. We shall, my lord.

                    Exeunt Rosencrantz and Guildenstern.

King.   Sweet Gertrude, leave us too,
    For we have closely° sent for Hamlet hither,
    That he, as 'twere by accident, may here   30
    Affront° Ophelia.
    Her father and myself (lawful espials°)
    Will so bestow ourselves that, seeing unseen,
    We may of their encounter frankly judge
    And gather by him, as he is behaved,   35
    If't be th' affliction of his love or no
    That thus he suffers for.
Queen.   I shall obey you.
    And for your part, Ophelia, I do wish
    That your good beauties be the happy cause
    Of Hamlet's wildness. So shall I hope your virtues   40
    Will bring him to his wonted way again,
    To both your honors.
Ophelia.   Madam, I wish it may.

                        [Exit Queen.]

Polonius. Ophelia, walk you here.—Gracious, so please you,
    We will bestow ourselves. *[To Ophelia]* Read on this book,
    That show of such an exercise may color°   45
    Your loneliness. We are oft to blame in this,

---

    17 *o'erraught* overtook   **29** *closely* secretly   **31** *Affront* meet face to face   **32** *espials* spies
45 *exercise may color* act of devotion may give a plausible hue to (the book is one of devotion)

'Tis too much proved, that with devotion's visage
And pious action we do sugar o'er
The devil himself.
King.   [*Aside*] O, 'tis too true.
How smart a lash that speech doth give my conscience!   50
The harlot's cheek, beautied with plast'ring art,
Is not more ugly to the thing that helps it
Than is my deed to my most painted word.
O heavy burden!
Polonius. I hear him coming. Let's withdraw, my lord.   55

                              [*Exeunt King and Polonius.*]
                                        Enter Hamlet.

Hamlet. To be, or not to be: that is the question:
      Whether 'tis nobler in the mind to suffer
      The slings and arrows of outrageous fortune,
      Or to take arms against a sea of troubles,
      And by opposing end them. To die, to sleep—   60
      No more—and by a sleep to say we end
      The heartache, and the thousand natural shocks
      That flesh is heir to! 'Tis a consummation
      Devoutly to be wished. To die, to sleep—
      To sleep—perchance to dream: ay, there's the rub,°   65
      For in that sleep of death what dreams may come
      When we have shuffled off this mortal coil,°
      Must give us pause. There's the respect°
      That makes calamity of so long life:°
      For who would bear the whips and scorns of time,   70
      Th' oppressor's wrong, the proud man's contumely,
      The pangs of despised love, the law's delay,
      The insolence of office, and the spurns
      That patient merit of th' unworthy takes,
      When he himself might his quietus° make   75
      With a bare bodkin?° Who would fardels° bear,
      To grunt and sweat under a weary life,
      But that the dread of something after death,
      The undiscovered country, from whose bourn°
      No traveler returns, puzzles the will,   80
      And makes us rather bear those ills we have,

---

   65 *rub* impediment (obstruction to a bowler's ball)   67 *coil* (1) turmoil (2) a ring of rope (here
the flesh encircling the soul)   68 *respect* consideration   69 *makes calamity of so long life* (1)
makes calamity so long-lived (2) makes living so long a calamity   75 *quietus* full discharge (a legal
term)   76 *bodkin* dagger   76 *fardels* burdens   79 *bourn* region

Than fly to others that we know not of?
Thus conscience° does make cowards of us all,
And thus the native hue of resolution
Is sicklied o'er with the pale cast° of thought,   85
And enterprises of great pitch° and moment,
With this regard° their currents turn awry,
And lose the name of action.—Soft you now,
The fair Ophelia!—Nymph, in thy orisons°
Be all my sins remembered.

Ophelia.   Good my lord,   90
How does your honor for this many a day?

Hamlet. I humbly thank you; well, well, well.

Ophelia. My lord, I have remembrances of yours
That I have longèd long to redeliver.
I pray you now, receive them.

Hamlet.   No, not I,   95
I never gave you aught.

Ophelia. My honored lord, you know right well you did,
And with them words of so sweet breath composed
As made these things more rich. Their perfume lost,
Take these again, for to the noble mind   100
Rich gifts wax poor when givers prove unkind.
There, my lord.

Hamlet. Ha, ha! Are you honest?°

Ophelia. My lord?

Hamlet. Are you fair?   105

Ophelia. What means your lordship?

Hamlet. That if you be honest and fair, your honesty should admit no discourse to your beauty.°

Ophelia. Could beauty, my lord, have better commerce than with honesty?

Hamlet. Ay, truly; for the power of beauty will sooner transform honesty 110
from what it is to a bawd° than the force of honesty can translate beauty
into his likeness. This was sometime a paradox, but now the time gives it
proof. I did love you once.

Ophelia. Indeed, my lord, you made me believe so.

Hamlet. You should not have believed me, for virtue cannot so inoculate° 115
our old stock but we shall relish of it.° I loved you not.

Ophelia. I was the more deceived.

---

83 *conscience* self-consciousness, introspection   85 *cast* color   86 *pitch* height (a term from
falconry)   87 *regard* consideration   89 *orisons* prayers   103 *Are you honest* (1) are you modest
(2) are you chaste (3) have you integrity   107–08 *your honesty . . . to your beauty* your modesty
should permit no approach to your beauty   111 *bawd* procurer   115 *inoculate* graft   116 *relish
of it* smack of it (our old sinful nature)

Hamlet. Get thee to a nunnery. Why wouldst thou be a breeder of sinners?
I am myself indifferent honest,° but yet I could accuse me of such things
that it were better my mother had not borne me: I am very proud, re- 120
vengeful, ambitious, with more offenses at my beck° than I have thoughts
to put them in, imagination to give them shape, or time to act them in.
What should such fellows as I do crawling between earth and heaven? We
are arrant knaves all; believe none of us. Go thy ways to a nunnery. Where's
your father? 125
Ophelia. At home, my lord.
Hamlet. Let the doors be shut upon him, that he may play the fool nowhere
but in's own house. Farewell.
Ophelia. O help him, you sweet heavens!
Hamlet. If thou dost marry, I'll give thee this plague for thy dowry: be thou 130
as chaste as ice, as pure as snow, thou shalt not escape calumny. Get thee
to a nunnery. Go, farewell. Or if thou wilt needs marry, marry a fool, for
wise men know well enough what monsters° you make of them. To a
nunnery, go, and quickly too. Farewell.
Ophelia. Heavenly powers, restore him! 135
Hamlet. I have heard of your paintings, well enough. God hath given you
one face, and you make yourselves another. You jig and amble, and you
lisp; you nickname God's creatures and make your wantonness your ignorance.° Go to, I'll no more on't; it hath made me mad. I say we will
have no moe° marriage. Those that are married already—all but one— 140
shall live. The rest shall keep as they are. To a nunnery, go.

Exit.

Ophelia. O what a noble mind is here o'erthrown!
The courtier's, soldier's, scholar's, eye, tongue, sword,
Th' expectancy and rose° of the fair state,
The glass of fashion, and the mold of form,° 145
Th' observed of all observers, quite, quite down!
And I, of ladies most deject and wretched,
That sucked the honey of his musicked vows,
Now see that noble and most sovereign reason
Like sweet bells jangled, out of time and harsh, 150
That unmatched form and feature of blown° youth
Blasted with ecstasy.° O, woe is me
T' have seen what I have seen, see what I see!

---

119 *indifferent honest* moderately virtuous   121 *beck* call   133 *monsters* horned beasts,
cuckolds   138–139 *make your wantonness your ignorance* excuse your wanton speech by
pretending ignorance   140 *moe* more   144 *expectancy and rose* i.e., fair hope   145 *The glass
. . . of form* the mirror of fashion, and the pattern of excellent behavior   151 *blown* blooming
152 *ecstasy* madness

Enter King and Polonius.

King. Love? His affections° do not that way tend,
Nor what he spake, though it lacked form a little,   155
Was not like madness. There's something in his soul
O'er which his melancholy sits on brood,
And I do doubt° the hatch and the disclose
Will be some danger; which for to prevent,
I have in quick determination   160
Thus set it down: he shall with speed to England
For the demand of our neglected tribute.
Haply the seas, and countries different,
With variable objects, shall expel
This something-settled° matter in his heart,   165
Whereon his brains still beating puts him thus
From fashion of himself. What think you on't?
Polonius. It shall do well. But yet do I believe
The origin and commencement of his grief
Sprung from neglected love. How now, Ophelia?   170
You need not tell us what Lord Hamlet said;
We heard it all. My lord, do as you please,
But if you hold it fit, after the play,
Let his queen mother all alone entreat him
To show his grief. Let her be round° with him,   175
And I'll be placed, so please you, in the ear
Of all their conference. If she find him not,°
To England send him, or confine him where
Your wisdom best shall think.
King.   It shall be so.
Madness in great ones must not unwatched go.   180

                                                                    Exeunt.

[SCENE II. The castle.]

Enter Hamlet and three of the Players.

Hamlet. Speak the speech, I pray you, as I pronounced it to you, trippingly
on the tongue. But if you mouth it, as many of our players do, I had as
lief the town crier spoke my lines. Nor do not saw the air too much with
your hand, thus, but use all gently, for in the very torrent, tempest, and

---

154 *affections* inclinations   158 *doubt* fear   165 *something-settled* somewhat settled   175
round blunt   177 *find him not* does not find him out

(as I may say) whirlwind of your passion, you must acquire and beget a   5
temperance that may give it smoothness. O, it offends me to the soul to
hear a robustious periwig-pated° fellow tear a passion to tatters, to very
rags, to split the ears of the groundlings,° who for the most part are capable
of° nothing but inexplicable dumb shows° and noise. I would have such
a fellow whipped for o'erdoing Termagant. It out-herods Herod.° Pray   10
you avoid it.
Player. I warrant your honor.
Hamlet. Be not too tame neither, but let your own discretion be your tutor.
Suit the action to the word, the word to the action, with this special
observance, that you o'erstep not the modesty of nature. For anything so
o'erdone is from° the purpose of playing, whose end, both at the first and   15
now, was and is, to hold, as 'twere, the mirror up to nature; to show virtue
her own feature, scorn her own image, and the very age and body of the
time his form and pressure.° Now, this overdone, or come tardy off, though
it makes the unskillful laugh, cannot but make the judicious grieve, the
censure of the which one must in your allowance o'erweigh a whole theater   20
of others. O, there be players that I have seen play, and heard others praise,
and that highly (not to speak it profanely), that neither having th' accent
of Christians, nor the gait of Christian, pagan, nor man, have so strutted
and bellowed that I have thought some of Nature's journeymen° had made
men, and not made them well, they imitated humanity so abominably.   25
Player. I hope we have reformed that indifferently° with us, sir.
Hamlet. O, reform it altogether! And let those that play your clowns speak
no more than is set down for them, for there be of them that will themselves
laugh, to set on some quantity of barren spectators to laugh too, though
in the meantime some necessary question of the play be then to be con-   30
sidered. That's villainous and shows a most pitiful ambition in the fool
that uses it. Go make you ready.

Exit Players.

Enter Polonius, Guildenstern, and Rosencrantz.

How now, my lord? Will the King hear this piece of work?
Polonius. And the Queen too, and that presently.
Hamlet. Bid the players make haste.   *Exit Polonius.*   35
Will you two help to hasten them?

III.ii.7 *robustious periwig-pated* boisterous wig-headed   8 *groundlings* those who stood in the
pit of the theater (the poorest and presumably most ignorant of the audience)   8–9 *are capable of*
are able to understand   9 *dumb shows* (it had been the fashion for actors to preface plays or parts
of plays with silent mime)   10 *Termagant . . . Herod* (boisterous characters in the old mystery
plays)   15 *from* contrary to   18 *pressure* image, impress   24 *journeymen* workers not yet masters
of their craft   26 *indifferently* tolerably

Rosencrantz. Ay, my lord.   *Exeunt they two.*
Hamlet. What, ho, Horatio!

    Enter Horatio.

Horatio. Here, sweet lord, at your service.
Hamlet. Horatio, thou art e'en as just a man   40
    As e'er my conversation coped withal.°
Horatio. O, my dear lord——
Hamlet.   Nay, do not think I flatter.
    For what advancement° may I hope from thee,
    That no revenue hast but thy good spirits
    To feed and clothe thee? Why should the poor be flattered?   45
    No, let the candied° tongue lick absurd pomp,
    And crook the pregnant° hinges of the knee
    Where thrift° may follow fawning. Dost thou hear?
    Since my dear soul was mistress of her choice
    And could of men distinguish her election,   50
    S' hath sealed thee° for herself, for thou hast been
    As one, in suff'ring all, that suffers nothing,
    A man that Fortune's buffets and rewards
    Hast ta'en with equal thanks; and blest are those
    Whose blood° and judgment are so well commeddled°   55
    That they are not a pipe for Fortune's finger
    To sound what stop she please. Give me that man
    That is not passion's slave, and I will wear him
    In my heart's core, ay, in my heart of heart,
    As I do thee. Something too much of this—   60
    There is a play tonight before the King.
    One scene of it comes near the circumstance
    Which I have told thee, of my father's death.
    I prithee, when thou seest that act afoot,
    Even with the very comment° of thy soul   65
    Observe my uncle. If his occulted° guilt
    Do not itself unkennel in one speech,
    It is damnèd ghost that we have seen,
    And my imaginations are as foul
    As Vulcan's stithy.° Give him heedful note,   70
    For I mine eyes will rivet to his face,

---

41 *coped withal* met with   43 *advancement* promotion   46 *candied* sugared, flattering   47
pregnant (1) pliant (2) full of promise of good fortune   48 *thrift* profit   51 *S' hath sealed thee* she
(the soul) has set a mark on you   55 *blood* passion   55 *commeddled* blended   65 *very comment*
deepest wisdom   66 *occulted* hidden   70 *stithy* forge, smithy

And after we will both our judgments join
In censure of his seeming.°
Horatio.   Well, my lord.
If 'a steal aught the whilst this play is playing,
And scape detecting, I will pay the theft.   75

Enter Trumpets and Kettledrums, King, Queen, Polonius, Ophelia, Ro-
sencrantz, Guildenstern, and other Lords attendant with his Guard car-
rying torches. Danish March. Sound a Flourish.

Hamlet. They are coming to the play: I must be idle;°
Get you a place.
King. How fares our cousin Hamlet?
Hamlet. Excellent, i' faith, of the chameleon's dish;° I eat the air, promise-
crammed; you cannot feed capons so.   80
King. I have nothing with this answer, Hamlet; these words are not mine.
Hamlet. No, nor mine now. [*To Polonius*] My lord, you played once i' th'
university, you say?
Polonius. That did I, my lord, and was accounted a good actor.
Hamlet. What did you enact?   85
Polonius. I did enact Julius Caesar. I was killed i' th' Capitol; Brutus killed
me.
Hamlet. It was a brute part of him to kill so capital a calf there. Be the players
ready?
Rosencrantz. Ay, my lord. They stay upon your patience.
Queen. Come hither, my dear Hamlet, sit by me.
Hamlet. No, good mother. Here's metal more attractive.°   90
Polonius. [*To the King*] O ho! Do you mark that?
Hamlet. Lady, shall I lie in your lap?

[*He lies at Ophelia's feet.*]

Ophelia. No, my lord.
Hamlet. I mean, my head upon your lap?
Ophelia. Ay, my lord.   95
Hamlet. Do you think I meant country matters?°
Ophelia. I think nothing, my lord.
Hamlet. That's a fair thought to lie between maids' legs.
Ophelia. What is, my lord?
Hamlet. Nothing.   100
Ophelia. You are merry, my lord.

---

73 *censure of his seeming* judgement on his looks   76 *be idle* play the fool   79 *the*
chameleon's dish air (on which chameleons were thought to live)   90 *attractive* magnetic   96
country matters rustic doings (with a pun on the vulgar word for the pudendum)

Hamlet. Who, I?

Ophelia. Ay, my lord.

Hamlet. O God, your only jig-maker!° What should a man do but be merry? For look you how cheerfully my mother looks, and my father died within's 105 two hours.

Ophelia. Nay, 'tis twice two months, my lord.

Hamlet. So long? Nay then, let the devil wear black, for I'll have a suit of sables.° O heavens! Die two months ago, and not forgotten yet? Then there's hope a great man's memory may outlive his life half a year. But, by'r Lady, 'a must build churches then, or else shall 'a suffer not thinking 110 on, with the hobbyhorse,° whose epitaph is "For O, for O, the hobbyhorse is forgot!"

The trumpets sound. Dumb show follows:

Enter a King and a Queen very lovingly, the Queen embracing him, and he her. She kneels; and makes show of protestation unto him. He takes her up, and declines his head upon her neck. He lies him down upon a bank of flowers. She, seeing him asleep, leaves him. Anon come in another man: takes off his crown, kisses it, pours poison in the sleeper's ears, and leaves him. The Queen returns, finds the King dead, makes passionate action. The poisoner, with some three or four, come in again, seem to condole with her. The dead body is carried away. The poisoner woos the Queen with gifts; she seems harsh awhile, but in the end accepts love.

Exeunt.

Ophelia. What means this, my lord?

Hamlet. Marry, this is miching mallecho;° it means mischief.

Ophelia. Belike this show imports the argument° of the play.

Enter Prologue.

Hamlet. We shall know by this fellow. The players cannot keep counsel; 115 they'll tell all.

Ophelia. Will 'a tell us what this show meant?

Hamlet. Ay, or any show that you will show him. Be not you ashamed to show, he'll not shame to tell you what it means.

Ophelia. You are naught,° you are naught; I'll mark the play.

Prologue. For us, and for our tragedy, 120

---

104 *jig-maker* composer of songs and dances (often a Fool, who performed them) 108 *sables* (pun on "black" and "luxurious furs") 111 *hobbyhorse* mock horse worn by a performer in the morris dance 113 *miching mallecho* sneaking mischief 114 *argument* plot 119 *naught* wicked, improper

Here stooping to your clemency,
    We beg your hearing patiently.   [*Exit.*]
Hamlet. Is this a prologue, or the posy of a ring?°
Ophelia. 'Tis brief, my lord.
Hamlet. As woman's love.   125

Enter [two Players as] King and Queen.

Player King. Full thirty times hath Phoebus' cart° gone round
    Neptune's salt wash° and Tellus'° orbèd ground,
    And thirty dozen moons with borrowed sheen
    About the world have times twelve thirties been,
    Since love our hearts, and Hymen did our hands,   130
    Unite commutual in most sacred bands.
Player Queen. So many journeys may the sun and moon
    Make us again count o'er ere love be done!
    But woe is me, you are so sick of late,
    So far from cheer and from your former state,   135
    That I distrust° you. Yet, though I distrust,
    Discomfort you, my lord, it nothing must.
    For women fear too much, even as they love,
    And women's fear and love hold quantity,
    In neither aught, or in extremity.°   140
    Now what my love is, proof° hath made you know,
    And as my love is sized, my fear is so.
    Where love is great, the littlest doubts are fear;
    Where little fears grow great, great love grows there.
Player King. Faith, I must leave thee, love, and shortly too; 145
    My operant° powers their functions leave to do:
    And thou shalt live in this fair world behind,
    Honored, beloved, and haply one as kind
    For husband shalt thou——
Player Queen.   O, confound the rest!
    Such love must needs be treason in my breast.   150
    In second husband let me be accurst!
    None wed the second but who killed the first.
Hamlet. [*Aside*] That's wormwood.°

---

123 *posy of a ring* motto inscribed in a ring   126 *Phoebus' cart* the sun's chariot   127
Neptune's salt wash the sea   127 *Tellus* Roman goddess of the earth   136 *distrust* am anxious
about   139–40 *And women's . . . in extremity* (perhaps the idea is that women's anxiety is great
or little in proportion to their love. The previous line, unrhymed, may be a false start that
Shakespeare neglected to delete)   141 *proof* experience   146 *operant* active   153 *wormwood* a
bitter herb

Player Queen. The instances° that second marriage move°
　Are base respects of thrift,° but none of love.　　　　　　155
　A second time I kill my husband dead
　When second husband kisses me in bed.
Player King. I do believe you think what now you speak,
　But what we do determine oft we break.
　Purpose is but the slave to memory,　　　　　　　　　　160
　Of violent birth, but poor validity,°
　Which now like fruit unripe sticks on the tree,
　But fall unshaken when they mellow be.
　Most necessary 'tis that we forget
　To pay ourselves what to ourselves is debt.
　What to ourselves in passion we propose,
　The passion ending, doth the purpose lose.
　The violence of either grief or joy
　Their own enactures° with themselves destroy:
　Where joy most revels, grief doth most lament;　　　　　170
　Grief joys, joy grieves, on slender accident.
　This world is not for aye, nor 'tis not strange
　That even our loves should with our fortunes change,
　For 'tis a question left us yet to prove,
　Whether love lead fortune, or else fortune love.　　　　　175
　The great man down, you mark his favorite flies;
　The poor advanced makes friends of enemies;
　And hitherto doth love on fortune tend,
　For who not needs shall never lack a friend;
　And who in want a hollow friend doth try,　　　　　　　180
　Directly seasons him° his enemy.
　But, orderly to end where I begun,
　Our wills and fates do so contrary run
　That our devices still are overthrown;
　Our thoughts are ours, their ends none of our own.　　　185
　So think thou wilt no second husband wed,
　But die thy thoughts when thy first lord is dead.
Player Queen. Nor earth to me give food, nor heaven light,
　Sport and repose lock from me day and night,
　To desperation turn my trust and hope,　　　　　　　　190
　An anchor's° cheer in prison be my scope,
　Each opposite that blanks° the face of joy
　Meet what I would have well, and it destroy:

---

154 *instances* motives　154 *move* induce　155 *respects of thrift* considerations of profit　161 *validity* strength　169 *enactures* acts　181 *seasons him* ripens him into　191 *anchor's* anchorite's, hermit's　192 *opposite that blanks* adverse thing that blanches

Both here and hence pursue me lasting strife,
  If, once a widow, ever I be wife!   195
Hamlet. If she should break it now!
Player King. 'Tis deeply sworn. Sweet, leave me here awhile;
  My spirits grow dull, and fain I would beguile
  The tedious day with sleep.
Player Queen.   Sleep rock thy brain,

                                         [He] sleeps.

And never come mischance between us twain!   *Exit.* 200
Hamlet. Madam, how like you this play?
Queen. The lady doth protest too much, methinks.
Hamlet. O, but she'll keep her word.
King. Have you heard the argument?° Is there no offense in't?
Hamlet. No, no, they do but jest, poison in jest; no offense i' th' world. 205
King. What do you call the play?
Hamlet. *The Mousetrap.* Marry, how? Tropically.° This play is the image 210
  of a murder done in Vienna: Gonzago is the Duke's name; his wife, Bap-
  tista. You shall see anon. 'Tis a knavish piece of work, but what of that?
  Your Majesty, and we that have free° souls, it touches us not. Let the
  galled jade winch;° our withers are unwrung.

                                  Enter Lucianus.

This is one Lucianus, nephew to the King.
Ophelia. You are as good as a chorus, my lord.
Hamlet. I could interpret° between you and your love, if I could see the
  puppets dallying.
Ophelia. You are keen,° my lord, you are keen.   215
Hamlet. It would cost you a groaning to take off mine edge.
Ophelia. Still better, and worse.
Hamlet. So you mistake° your husbands.—Begin, murderer. Leave thy damn-
  able faces and begin. Come, the croaking raven doth bellow for revenge.
Lucianus. Thoughts black, hands apt, drugs fit, and time agreeing,   220
  Confederate season,° else no creature seeing,
  Thou mixture rank, of midnight weeds collected,
  With Hecate's ban° thrice blasted, thrice infected,

---

    204 *argument* plot 207 *Tropically* figuratively (with a pun on "trap") 210 *free* innocent
210–11 *galled jade winch* chafed horse wince 214 *interpret* (like a showman explaining the
action of puppets) 215 *keen* (1) sharp (2) sexually aroused 218 *mistake* err in taking 221
Confederate season the opportunity allied with me 223 *Hecate's ban* the curse of the goddess of
sorcery

Thy natural magic and dire property°
On wholesome life usurps immediately.   225

Pours the poison in his ears.

Hamlet. 'A poisons him i' th' garden for his estate. His name's Gonzago.
  The story is extant, and written in very choice Italian. You shall see anon
  how the murderer gets the love of Gonzago's wife.
Ophelia. The King rises.
Hamlet. What, frighted with false fire?°   230
Queen. How fares my lord?
Polonius. Give o'er the play.
King. Give me some light. Away!
Polonius. Lights, lights, lights!

Exeunt all but Hamlet and Horatio.

Hamlet. Why, let the strucken deer go weep,   235
     The hart ungallèd play:
  For some must watch, while some must sleep;
     Thus runs the world away.
  Would not this, sir, and a forest of feathers°—if the rest of my fortunes
  turn Turk° with me—with two Provincial roses° on my razed° shoes, get 240
  me a fellowship in a cry° of players?
Horatio. Half a share.
Hamlet. A whole one, I.
  For thou dost know, O Damon dear,
     This realm dismantled was   245
  Of Jove himself; and now reigns here
     A very, very—pajock.°
Horatio. You might have rhymed.°
Hamlet. O good Horatio, I'll take the ghost's word for a thousand pound.
  Didst perceive?   250
Horatio. Very well, my lord.
Hamlet. Upon the talk of poisoning?
Horatio. I did very well note him.
Hamlet. Ah ha! Come, some music! Come, the recorders!°
  For if the King like not the comedy,   255
  Why then, belike he likes it not, perdy.°
  Come, some music!

---

  224 *property* nature   230 *false fire* blank discharge of firearms   239 *feathers* (plumes were
sometimes part of a costume)   240 *turn Turk* i.e., go bad, treat me badly   240 *Provincial roses*
rosettes like the roses of Provence (?)   240 *razed* ornamented with slashes   241 *cry* pack,
company   247 *pajock* peacock   248 *You might have rhymed* i.e., rhymed "was" with "ass"   254
recorders flutelike instruments   256 *perdy* by God (French : *par dieu*)

Enter Rosencrantz and Guildenstern.

Guildenstern. Good my lord, vouchsafe me a word with you.
Hamlet. Sir, a whole history.
Guildenstern. The King, sir—— 260
Hamlet. Ay, sir, what of him?
Guildenstern. Is in his retirement marvelous distemp'red.
Hamlet. With drink, sir?
Guildenstern. No, my lord, with choler.°
Hamlet. Your wisdom should show itself more richer to signify this to the 265
    doctor, for for me to put him to his purgation would perhaps plunge him
    into more choler.
Guildenstern. Good my lord, put your discourse into some frame,° and start
    not so wildly from my affair.
Hamlet. I am tame, sir; pronounce.
Guildenstern. The Queen, your mother, in most great affliction of spirit hath 270
    sent me to you.
Hamlet. You are welcome.
Guildenstern. Nay, good my lord, this courtesy is not of the right breed. If
    it shall please you to make me a wholesome answer, I will do your mother's
    commandment: if not, your pardon and my return shall be the end of my
    business.
Hamlet. Sir, I cannot. 275
Rosencrantz. What, my lord?
Hamlet. Make you a wholesome° answer; my wit's diseased. But, sir, such
    answer as I can make, you shall command, or rather, as you say, my
    mother. Therefore, no more, but to the matter. My mother, you say——

Rosencrantz. Then thus she says: your behavior hath struck her into amaze- 280
    ment and admiration.°
Hamlet. O wonderful son, that can so stonish a mother! But is there no
    sequel at the heels of this mother's admiration? Impart.
Rosencrantz. She desires to speak with you in her closet ere you go to bed.
Hamlet. We shall obey, were she ten times our mother. Have you any further 285
    trade with us?
Rosencrantz. My lord, you once did love me.
Hamlet. And do still, by these pickers and stealers.°
Rosencrantz. Good my lord, what is your cause of distemper? You do surely
    bar the door upon your own liberty, if you deny your griefs to your friend.

---

264 *choler* anger (but Hamlet pretends to take the word in its sense of "biliousness") 268
frame order, control   277 *wholesome* sane   281 *admiration* wonder   288 *pickers and stealers*
i.e., hands (with reference to the prayer; "Keep my hands from picking and stealing")

Hamlet. Sir, I lack advancement.°   290
Rosencrantz. How can that be, when you have the voice of the King himself
for your succession in Denmark?

Enter the Players with recorders.

Hamlet. Ay, sir, but "while the grass grows"—the proverb° is something
musty. O, the recorders. Let me see one. To withdraw° with you—why
do you go about to recover the wind° of me as if you would drive me   295
into a toil?°
Guildenstern. O my lord, if my duty be too bold, my love is too unmannerly.°
Hamlet. I do not well understand that. Will you play upon this pipe?
Guildenstern. My lord, I cannot.
Hamlet. I pray you.   300
Guildenstern. Believe me, I cannot.
Hamlet. I pray you.
Guildenstern. Believe me, I cannot.
Hamlet. I do beseech you.
Guildenstern. I know no touch of it, my lord.   305
Hamlet. It is as easy as lying. Govern these ventages° with your fingers and
thumb, give it breath with your mouth, and it will discourse most eloquent
music. Look you, these are the stops.
Guildenstern. But these cannot I command to any utt'rance of harmony; I
have not the skill.
Hamlet. Why, look you now, how unworthy a thing you make of me! You   310
would play upon me; you would seem to know my stops; you would pluck
out the heart of my mystery; you would sound me from my lowest note
to the top of my compass;° and there is much music, excellent voice, in
this little organ,° yet cannot you make it speak. 'Sblood, do you think I
am easier to be played on than a pipe? Call me what instrument you will,   315
though you can fret° me, you cannot play upon me.

Enter Polonius.

God bless you, sir!
Polonius. My lord, the Queen would speak with you, and presently.
Hamlet. Do you see yonder cloud that's almost in shape of a camel?
Polonius. By th' mass and 'tis, like a camel indeed.   320

---

290 *advancement* promotion   293 *proverb* ("While the grass groweth, the horse starveth")
294 *withdraw* speak in private   295 *recover the wind* get on the windward side (as in hunting)
296 *toil* snare   297 *if my duty . . . too unmannerly* i.e., if these questions seem rude, it is because
my love for you leads me beyond good manners.   306 *ventages* vents, stops on a recorder   313
compass range of voice   314 *organ* i.e., the recorder   316 *fret* vex (with a pun alluding to the
frets, or ridges, that guide the fingering on some instuments)

Hamlet. Methinks it is like a weasel.
Polonius. It is backed like a weasel.
Hamlet. Or like a whale.
Polonius. Very like a whale.
Hamlet. Then I will come to my mother by and by. [*Aside*] They fool me to   325
  the top of my bent.°—I will come by and by.°
Polonius. I will say so.   *Exit.*
Hamlet. "By and by" is easily said. Leave me, friends.

                                              [*Exeunt all but Hamlet.*]

  'Tis now the very witching time of night,
  When churchyards yawn, and hell itself breathes out   330
  Contagion to this world. Now could I drink hot blood
  And do such bitter business as the day
  Would quake to look on. Soft, now to my mother.
  O heart, lose not thy nature; let not ever
  The soul of Nero° enter this firm bosom.   335
  Let me be cruel, not unnatural;
  I will speak daggers to her, but use none.
  My tongue and soul in this be hypocrites:
  How in my words somever she be shent,°
  To give them seals° never, my soul, consent!   *Exit.* 340

[SCENE III. The castle.]

Enter King, Rosencrantz and Guildenstern.

King. I like him not, nor stands it safe with us
  To let his madness range. Therefore prepare you.
  I your commission will forthwith dispatch,
  And he to England shall along with you.
  The terms° of our estate may not endure   5
  Hazard so near's° as doth hourly grow
  Out of his brows.
Guildenstern.   We will ourselves provide.
  Most holy and religious fear it is
  To keep those many many bodies safe
  That live and feed upon your Majesty.   10

325–26 *They fool . . . my bent* they compel me to play the fool to the limit of my capacity
326 *by and by* very soon   335 *Nero* (Roman emperor who had his mother murdered)   339 *shent*
rebuked   340 *give them seals* confirm them with deeds   III.iii.5 *terms* conditions   6 *near's* near
us

Rosencrantz. The single and peculiar° life is bound
  With all the strength and armor of the mind
  To keep itself from noyance,° but much more
  That spirit upon whose weal depends and rests
  The lives of many. The cess of majesty°   15
  Dies not alone, but like a gulf° doth draw
  What's near it with it; or it is a massy wheel
  Fixed on the summit of the highest mount,
  To whose huge spokes ten thousand lesser things
  Are mortised and adjoined, which when it falls,   20
  Each small annexment, petty consequence,
  Attends° the boist'rous ruin. Never alone
  Did the King sigh, but with a general groan.
King. Arm° you, I pray you, to this speedy voyage,
  For we will fetters put about this fear,   25
  Which now goes too free-footed.
Rosencrantz.   We will haste us.

                                             Exeunt Gentlemen.

      Enter Polonius.

Polonius. My lord, he's going to his mother's closet.
  Behind the arras I'll convey myself
  To hear the process.° I'll warrant she'll tax him home,°
  And, as you said, and wisely was it said,   30
  'Tis meet that some more audience than a mother,
  Since nature makes them partial, should o'erhear
  The speech of vantage.° Fare you well, my liege.
  I'll call upon you ere you go to bed
  And tell you what I know.
King.   Thanks, dear my lord.

                                        Exit [Polonius].   35

  O, my offense is rank, it smells to heaven;
  It hath the primal eldest curse° upon't
  A brother's murder. Pray can I not,
  Though inclination be as sharp as will.
  My stronger guilt defeats my strong intent,   40
  And like a man to double business bound
  I stand in pause where I shall first begin,
  And both neglect. What if this cursèd hand

---

  11 *peculiar* individual, private   13 *noyance* injury   15 *cess of majesty* cessation (death) of a
king   16 *gulf* whirlpool   22 *Attends* waits on, participates in   24 *Arm* prepare   29 *process*
proceedings   29 *tax him home* censure him sharply   33 *of vantage* from an advantageous place
37 *primal eldest curse* (curse of Cain, who killed Abel)

Were thicker than itself with brother's blood,
Is there not rain enough in the sweet heavens   45
To wash it white as snow? Whereto serves mercy
But to confront° the visage of offense?
And what's in prayer but this twofold force,
To be forestallèd ere we come to fall,
Or pardoned being down? Then I'll look up.   50
My fault is past. But, O, what form of prayer
Can serve my turn? "Forgive me my foul murder"?
That cannot be, since I am still possessed
Of those effects° for which I did the murder,
My crown, mine own ambition, and my queen.   55
May one be pardoned and retain th' offense?
In the corrupted currents of this world
Offense's gilded hand may shove by justice,
And oft 'tis seen the wicked prize itself
Buys out the law. But 'tis not so above.   60
There is no shuffling;° there the action lies
In his true nature, and we ourselves compelled,
Even to the teeth and forehead of our faults,
To give in evidence. What then? What rests?°
Try what repentance can. What can it not?   65
Yet what can it when one cannot repent?
O wretched state! O bosom black as death!
O limèd° soul, that struggling to be free
Art more engaged!° Help, angels! Make assay.°
Bow, stubborn knees, and, heart with strings of steel,   70
Be soft as sinews of the newborn babe.
All may be well.   [*He kneels.*]
Enter Hamlet.
Hamlet. Now might I do it pat, now 'a is a-praying,
And now I'll do't. And so 'a goes to heaven,
And so am I revenged. That would be scanned.°   75
A villain kills my father, and for that
I, his sole son, do this same villain send
To heaven.
Why, this is hire and salary, not revenge.
'A took my father grossly, full of bread,°   80
With all his crimes broad blown,° as flush° as May;

---

47 *confront* oppose   54 *effects* things gained   61 *shuffling* trickery   64 *rests* remains   68
limèd caught (as with birdlime, a sticky substance spread on boughs to snare birds)   69 *engaged*
ensnared   69 *assay* an attempt   75 *would be scanned* ought to be looked into   80 *bread* i.e.,
worldly gratification   81 *crimes broad blown* sins in full bloom   81 *flush* vigorous

And how his audit° stands, who knows save heaven?
But in our circumstance and course of thought,
'Tis heavy with him; and am I then revenged,
To take him in the purging of his soul,   85
When he is fit and seasoned for his passage?
No.
Up, sword, and know thou a more horrid hent.°
When he is drunk asleep, or in his rage,
Or in th' incestuous pleasure of his bed,   90
At game a-swearing, or about some act
That has no relish° of salvation in't—
Then trip him, that his heels may kick at heaven,
And that his soul may be as damned and black
As hell, whereto it goes. My mother stays.   95
This physic° but prolongs thy sickly days.   *Exit.*
King. [*Rises*] My words fly up, my thoughts remain below.
    Words without thoughts never to heaven go.   *Exit.*

[SCENE IV. The Queen's closet.]

Enter [Queen] Gertrude and Polonius.

Polonius. 'A will come straight. Look you lay home° to him.
    Tell him his pranks have been too broad° to bear with,
    And that your Grace hath screened and stood between
    Much heat and him. I'll silence me even here.
    Pray you be round with him.   5
Hamlet. (*Within*) Mother, Mother, Mother!
Queen. I'll warrant you; fear me not. Withdraw; I hear him coming.
                              [*Polonius hides behind the arras.*]
                         Enter Hamlet.
Hamlet. Now, Mother, what's the matter?
Queen. Hamlet, thou hast thy father much offended.
Hamlet. Mother, you have my father much offended.   10
Queen. Come, come, you answer with an idle° tongue.
Hamlet. Go, go, you question with a wicked tongue.
Queen. Why, how now, Hamlet?
Hamlet.   What's the matter now?
Queen. Have you forgot me?
Hamlet.   No, by the rood,° not so!

---

    82 *audit* account   88 *hent* grasp (here, occasion for seizing)   92 *relish* flavor   96 *physic*
(Claudius' purgation by prayer, as Hamlet thinks in line 85)   III.iv.1 *lay home* thrust (rebuke) him
sharply   2 *broad* unrestrained   11 *idle* foolish   14 *rood* cross

You are the Queen, your husband's brother's wife,   15
And, would it were not so, you are my mother.
Queen. Nay, then I'll set those to you that can speak.
Hamlet. Come, come, and sit you down. You shall not budge.
  You go not till I set you up a glass°
  Where you may see the inmost part of you!   20
Queen. What wilt thou do? Thou wilt not murder me?
  Help, ho!
Polonius. [*Behind*] What, ho! Help!
Hamlet. [*Draws*] How now? A rat? Dead for a ducat, dead!
          [*Makes a pass throught the arras and*] *kills Polonius.*
Polonius. [*Behind*] O, I am slain!
Queen.   O me, what hast thou done?   25

Hamlet. Nay, I know not. Is it the King?
Queen. O, what a rash and bloody deed is this!
Hamlet. A bloody deed—almost as bad, good Mother,
  As kill a king, and marry with his brother.
Queen. As kill a king?
Hamlet.   Ay, lady, it was my word.   30
          [*Lifts up the arras and sees Polonius.*]
  Thou wretched, rash, intruding fool, farewell!
  I took thee for thy better. Take thy fortune.
  Thou find'st to be too busy is some danger.—
  Leave wringing of your hands. Peace, sit you down
  And let me wring your heart, for so I shall   35
  If it be made of penetrable stuff,
  If damnèd custom have not brazed° it so
  That it be proof° and bulwark against sense.°
Queen. What have I done that thou dar'st wag thy tongue
  In noise so rude against me?
Hamlet.   Such an act   40
  That blurs the grace and blush of modesty,
  Calls virtue hypocrite, takes off the rose
  From the fair forehead of an innocent love,
  And sets a blister° there, makes marriage vows
  As false as dicers' oaths. O, such a deed   45
  As from the body of contraction° plucks
  The very soul, and sweet religion makes
  A rhapsody° of words! Heaven's face does glow
  O'er this solidity and compound mass

---

19 *glass* mirror   37 *brazed* hardened like brass   38 *proof* armor   38 *sense* feeling   44 *sets a blister* brands (as a harlot)   46 *contraction* marriage contract   48 *rhapsody* senseless string

With heated visage, as against the doom   50
Is thoughtsick at the act.°
Queen.   Ay me, what act,
That roars so loud and thunders in the index?°
Hamlet. Look here upon this picture, and on this,
The counterfeit presentment° of two brothers.
See what a grace was seated on this brow: 55
Hyperion's curls, the front° of Jove himself,
An eye like Mars, to threaten and command,
A station° like the herald Mercury
New lighted on a heaven-kissing hill—
A combination and a form indeed   60
Where every god did seem to set his seal
To give the world assurance of a man.
This was your husband. Look you now what follows.
Here is your husband, like a mildewed ear
Blasting his wholesome brother. Have you eyes?   65
Could you on this fair mountain leave to feed,
And batten° on this moor? Ha! Have you eyes?
You cannot call it love, for at your age
The heyday° in the blood is tame, it's humble,
And waits upon the judgment, and what judgment   70
Would step from this to this? Sense° sure you have,
Else could you not have motion, but sure that sense
Is apoplexed,° for madness would not err,
Nor sense to ecstasy° was ne'er so thralled
But it reserved some quantity of choice   75
To serve in such a difference. What devil was't
That thus hath cozened you at hoodman-blind?°
Eyes without feeling, feeling without sight,
Ears without hands or eyes, smelling sans° all,
Or but a sickly part of one true sense   80
Could not so mope.°
O shame, where is thy blush? Rebellious hell,
If thou canst mutine in a matron's bones,
To flaming youth let virtue be as wax
And melt in her own fire. Proclaim no shame   85
When the compulsive ardor° gives the charge,

48–51 *Heaven's face . . . the act* i.e., the face of heaven blushes over this earth (compounded of
four elements), the face hot, as if Judgment Day were near, and it is thoughtsick at the act   52
index prologue   54 *counterfeit presentment* represented image   56 *front* forehead   58 *station*
bearing   67 *batten* feed gluttonously   69 *heyday* excitement   71 *Sense* feeling   73 *apoplexed*
paralyzed   74 *ecstasy* madness   77 *cozened you at hoodman-blind* cheated you at blindman's
buff   79 *sans* without   81 *mope* be stupid   86 *compulsive ardor* compelling passion

Since frost itself as actively doth burn,
And reason panders will.°
Queen.   O Hamlet, speak no more.
  Thou turn'st mine eyes into my very soul,
  And there I see such black and grainèd° spots   90
  As will not leave their tinct.°
Hamlet.   Nay, but to live
  In the rank sweat of an enseamèd° bed,
  Stewed in corruption, honeying and making love
  Over the nasty sty——
Queen.   O, speak to me no more.
  These words like daggers enter in my ears.   95
  No more, sweet Hamlet.
Hamlet.   A murderer and a villain,
  A slave that is not twentieth part the tithe°
  Of your precedent lord, a vice° of kings,
  A cutpurse of the empire and the rule,
  That from a shelf the precious diadem stole   100
  And put it in his pocket——
Queen.   No more.

Enter Ghost.

Hamlet. A king of shreds and patches—
  Save me and hover o'er me with your wings,
  You heavenly guards! What would your gracious figure?
Queen. Alas, he's mad.   105
Hamlet. Do you not come your tardy son to chide,
  That, lapsed in time and passion, lets go by
  Th' important acting of your dread command?
  O, say!
Ghost. Do not forget. This visitation   110
  Is but to whet thy almost blunted purpose.
  But look, amazement on thy mother sits.
  O, step between her and her fighting soul!
  Conceit° in weakest bodies strongest works.
  Speak to her, Hamlet.
Hamlet.   How is it with you, lady?   115
Queen. Alas, how is't with you,
  That you do bend your eye on vacancy,
  And with the' incorporal° air do hold discourse?
  Forth at your eyes your spirits wildly peep,

---

88 *reason panders will* reason acts as a procurer for desire   90 *grainèd* dyed in grain (fast dyed)   91 *tinct* color   92 *enseamèd* (perhaps "soaked in grease," i.e., sweaty; perhaps "much wrinkled")   97 *tithe* tenth part   98 *vice* (like the Vice, a fool and mischief-maker in the old morality plays)   114 *Conceit* imagination   118 *incorporal* bodiless

And as the sleeping soldiers in th' alarm   120
Your bedded hair° like life in excrements°
Start up and stand an end.° O gentle son,
Upon the heat and flame of thy distemper
Sprinkle cool patience. Whereon do you look?
Hamlet. On him, on him! Look you, how pale he glares!   125
His form and cause conjoined, preaching to stones,
Would make them capable.°—Do not look upon me,
Lest with this piteous action you convert
My stern effects.° Then what I have to do
Will want true color; tears perchance for blood.   130
Queen. To whom do you speak this?
Hamlet.   Do you see nothing there?
Queen. Nothing at all; yet all that is I see.
Hamlet. Nor did you nothing hear?
Queen.   No, nothing but ourselves.
Hamlet. Why, look you there! Look how it steals away!
My father, in his habit° as he lived!   135
Look where he goes even now out at the portal!
                            Exit Ghost.
Queen. This is the very coinage of your brain.
This bodiless creation ecstasy
Is very cunning in.
Hamlet.   Ecstasy?
My pulse as yours doth temperately keep time   140
And makes as healthful music. It is not madness
That I have uttered. Bring me to the test,
And I the matter will reword, which madness
Would gambol° from. Mother, for love of grace,
Lay not that flattering unction° to your soul,   145
That not your trespass but my madness speaks.
It will but skin and film the ulcerous place
Whiles rank corruption, mining° all within,
Infects unseen. Confess yourself to heaven,
Repent what's past, avoid what is to come,   150
And do not spread the compost° on the weeds
To make them ranker. Forgive me this my virtue.
For in the fatness of these pursy° times

---

121 *bedded hair* hairs laid flat   121 *excrements* outgrowths (here, the hair)   122 *an end* on
end   127 *capable* receptive   128–29 *convert/My stern effects* divert my stern deeds   135 *habit*
garment (Q1, though a "bad" quarto, is probably correct in saying that at line 101 the ghost
enters "in his nightgown," i.e., dressing gown)   144 *gambol* start away   145 *unction* ointment
148 *mining* undermining   151 *compost* fertilizing substance   153 *pursy* bloated

Virtue itself of vice must pardon beg,
  Yea, curb° and woo for leave to do him good.   155
Queen. O Hamlet, thou hast cleft my heart in twain.
Hamlet. O, throw away the worser part of it,
  And live the purer with the other half.
  Good night—but go not to my uncle's bed.
  Assume a virtue, if you have it not.   160
  That monster custom, who all sense doth eat,
  Of habits devil, is angel yet in this,
  That to the use° of actions fair and good
  He likewise gives a frock or livery°
  That aptly is put on. Refrain tonight,   165
  And that shall lend a kind of easiness
  To the next abstinence; the next more easy;
  For use almost can change the stamp of nature,
  And either° the devil, or throw him out
  With wondrous potency. Once more, good night,   170
  And when you are desirous to be blest,
  I'll blessing beg of you.—For this same lord,
  I do repent; but heaven hath pleased it so,
  To punish me with this, and this with me,
  That I must be their° scourge and minister.   175
  I will bestow° him and will answer well
  The death I gave him. So again, good night.
  I must be cruel only to be kind.
  Thus bad begins, and worse remains behind.
  One word more, good lady.
Queen.   What shall I do?   180
Hamlet. Not this, by no means, that I bid you do:
  Let the bloat King tempt you again to bed,
  Pinch wanton on your cheek, call you his mouse,
  And let him, for a pair of reechy° kisses,
  Or paddling in your neck with his damned fingers,   185
  Make you to ravel° all this matter out,
  That I essentially am not in madness,
  But mad in craft. 'Twere good you let him know,
  For who that's but a queen, fair, sober, wise,
  Would from a paddock,° from a bat, a gib,°   190
  Such dear concernings hide? Who would do so?

---

155 *curb* bow low   165 *use* practice   164 *livery* characteristic garment (punning on "habits" in line 162)   169 *either* (probably a word is missing after *either*; among suggestions are "master," "curb," and "house"; but possibly *either* is a verb meaning "make easier")   175 *their* i.e., the heavens'   176 *bestow* stow, lodge   184 *reechy* foul (literally "smoky")   186 *ravel* unravel, reveal   190 *paddock* toad   190 *gib* tomcat

No, in despite of sense and secrecy,
Unpeg the basket on the house's top,
Let the birds fly, and like the famous ape,
To try conclusions,° in the basket creep   195
And break your own neck down.
Queen. Be thou assured, if words be made of breath,
And breath of life, I have no life to breathe
What thou hast said to me.
Hamlet. I must to England; you know that?
Queen.   Alack,   200
I had forgot. 'Tis so concluded on.
Hamlet. There's letters sealed, and my two schoolfellows,
Whom I will trust as I will adders fanged,
They bear the mandate;° they must sweep my way
And marshal me to knavery. Let it work;   205
For 'tis the sport to have the enginer
Hoist with his own petar,° and 't shall go hard
But I will delve one yard below their mines
And blow them at the moon. O, 'tis most sweet
When in one line two crafts° directly meet.   210
This man shall set me packing:
I'll lug the guts into the neighbor room.
Mother, good night. Indeed, this counselor
Is now most still, most secret, and most grave,
Who was in life a foolish prating knave.   215
Come, sir, to draw toward an end with you.
Good night, Mother.
              [Exit the Queen. Then] exit Hamlet, tugging in Polonius.

[ACT IV
SCENE I. The castle.]

Enter King and Queen, with Rosencrantz and Guildenstern.

King. There's matter in these sighs. These profound heaves
You must translate; 'tis fit we understand them.
Where is your son?
Queen. Bestow this place on us a little while.
                         [Exeunt Rosencrantz and Guildenstern.]
Ah, mine own lord, what have I seen tonight!   5
King. What, Gertrude? How does Hamlet?

---

195 *To try conclusions* to make experiments   204 *mandate* command   207 *petar* bomb   210
crafts (1) boats (2) acts of guile, crafty schemes

Queen. Mad as the sea and wind when both contend
  Which is the mightier. In his lawless fit,
  Behind the arras hearing something stir,
  Whips out his rapier, cries, "A rat, a rat!"   10
  And in this brainish apprehension° kills
  The unseen good old man.
King.   O heavy deed!
  It had been so with us, had we been there.
  His liberty is full of threats to all,
  To you yourself, to us, to every one.   15
  Alas, how shall this bloody deed be answered?
  It will be laid to us, whose providence°
  Should have kept short, restrained, and out of haunt°
  This mad young man. But so much was our love
  We would not understand what was most fit,   20
  But, like the owner of a foul disease,
  To keep it from divulging, let it feed
  Even on the pith of life. Where is he gone?
Queen. To draw apart the body he hath killed;
  O'er whom his very madness, like some ore   25
  Among a mineral° of metals base,
  Shows itself pure. 'A weeps for what is done.
King. O Gertrude, come away!
  The sun no sooner shall the mountains touch
  But we will ship him hence, and this vile deed   30
  We must with all our majesty and skill
  Both countenance and excuse. Ho, Guildenstern!
           Enter Rosencrantz and Guildenstern.
  Friends both, go join you with some further aid:
  Hamlet in madness hath Polonius slain,
  And from his mother's closet hath he dragged him.   35
  Go seek him out; speak fair, and bring the body
  Into the chapel. I pray you haste in this.
          [Exeunt Rosencrantz and Guildenstern.]
  Come, Gertrude, we'll call up our wisest friends
  And let them know both what we mean to do
  And what's untimely done . . .°   40
  Whose whisper o'er the world's diameter,
  As level as the cannon to his blank°

IV.i.11 *brainish apprehension* mad imagination   17 *providence* foresight   18 *out of haunt* away from association with others   25–26 *ore/Among a mineral* vein of gold in a mine   40 *done . . .* (evidently something has dropped out of the text. Capell's conjecture, "So, haply slander," is usually printed)   42 *blank* white center of a target

Transports his poisoned shot, may miss our name
And hit the woundless° air. O, come away!
My soul is full of discord and dismay.   *Exeunt.*   45

[SCENE II. The castle.]

Enter Hamlet.

Hamlet. Safely stowed.
Gentlemen. (*Within*) Hamlet! Lord Hamlet!
Hamlet. But soft, what noise? Who calls on Hamlet?
   O, here they come.
                Enter Rosencrantz and Guildenstern.
Rosencrantz. What have you done, my lord, with the dead body?   5
Hamlet. Compounded it with dust, whereto 'tis kin.
Rosencrantz. Tell us where 'tis, that we may take it thence
   And bear it to the chapel.
Hamlet. Do not believe it.
Rosencrantz. Believe what?   10
Hamlet. That I can keep your counsel and not mine own. Besides, to be
   demanded of° a sponge, what replication° should be made by the son of
   a king?
Rosencrantz. Take you me for a sponge, my lord?
Hamlet. Ay, sir, that soaks up the King's countenance,° his rewards, his
   authorities. But such officers do the King best service in the end. He keeps   15
   them, like an ape, in the corner of his jaw, first mouthed, to be last
   swallowed. When he needs what you have gleaned, it is but squeezing you
   and, sponge, you shall be dry again.
Rosencrantz. I understand you not, my lord.
Hamlet. I am glad of it: a knavish speech sleeps in a foolish ear.   20
Rosencrantz. My lord, you must tell us where the body is and go with us to
   the King.
Hamlet. The body is with the King, but the King is not with the body. The
   King is a thing——
Guildenstern. A thing, my lord?
Hamlet. Of nothing. Bring me to him. Hide fox, and all after.°   *Exeunt.*   25

---

44 *woundless* invulnerable   IV.ii.12 *demanded of* questioned by   12 *replication* reply   14
countenance favor   25 *Hide fox, and all after* (a cry in a game such as hide-and-seek; Hamlet
runs from the stage)

[SCENE III. The castle.]

Enter King, and two or three.

King. I have sent to seek him and to find the body:
How dangerous is it that this man goes loose!
Yet must not we put the strong law on him:
He's loved of the distracted° multitude,
Who like not in their judgment, but their eyes,   5
And where 'tis so, th' offender's scourge is weighed,
But never the offense. To bear° all smooth and even,
This sudden sending him away must seem
Deliberate pause.° Diseases desperate grown
By desperate appliance are relieved,   10
Or not at all.
                    Enter Rosencrantz, [Guildenstern,] and all the rest.
            How now? What hath befall'n?
Rosencrantz. Where the dead body is bestowed, my lord,
We cannot get from him.
King.   But where is he?
Rosencrantz. Without, my lord; guarded, to know your pleasure.
King. Bring him before us.
Rosencrantz.   Ho! Bring in the lord.   15
                    They enter.
King. Now, Hamlet, where's Polonius?
Hamlet. At supper.
King. At supper? Where?
Hamlet. Not where he eats, but where 'a is eaten. A certain convocation of
politic° worms are e'en at him. Your worm is your only emperor for diet.   20
We fat all creatures else to fat us, and we fat ourselves for maggots. Your
fat king and your lean beggar is but variable service°—two dishes, but to
one table. That's the end.
King. Alas, alas!
Hamlet. A man may fish with the worm that hath eat of a king, and eat of   25
the fish that hath fed of that worm.
King. What dost thou mean by this?
Hamlet. Nothing but to show you how a king may go a progress° through
the guts of a beggar.
King. Where is Polonius?   30
Hamlet. In heaven. Send thither to see. If your messenger find him not there,

---

IV.iii.4 *distracted* bewildered, senseless   7 *bear* carry out   9 *pause* planning   20 *politic*
statesmanlike, shrewd   22 *variable service* different courses   28 *progress* royal journey

seek him i' th' other place yourself. But if indeed you find him not within
this month, you shall nose him as you go up the stairs into the lobby.
King. [*To Attendants*] Go seek him there.
Hamlet. 'A will stay till you come.   35

                                            [*Exeunt Attendants.*]
King. Hamlet, this deed, for thine especial safety,
    Which we do tender° as we dearly grieve
    For that which thou hast done, must send thee hence
    With fiery quickness. Therefore prepare thyself.
    The bark is ready and the wind at help,   40
    Th' associates tend,° and everything is bent
    For England.
Hamlet.   For England?
King.   Ay, Hamlet.
Hamlet.   Good.
King. So is it, if thou knew'st our purposes.
Hamlet. I see a cherub° that sees them. But come, for England! Farewell,
    dear Mother.
King. Thy loving father, Hamlet.   45
Hamlet. My mother—father and mother is man and wife, man and wife is
    one flesh, and so, my mother. Come, for England!   *Exit.*
King. Follow him at foot;° tempt him with speed aboard.
    Delay it not; I'll have him hence tonight.
    Away! For everything is sealed and done   50
    That else leans° on th' affair. Pray you make haste.

                                    [*Exeunt all but the King.*]
    And, England, if my love thou hold'st at aught—
    As my great power thereof may give thee sense,
    Since yet thy cicatrice° looks raw and red
    After the Danish sword, and thy free awe°   55
    Pays homage to us—thou mayst not coldly set
    Our sovereign process,° which imports at full
    By letters conguring to that effect
    The present° death of Hamlet. Do it, England,
    For like the hectic° in my blood he rages,   60
    And thou must cure me. Till I know 'tis done,
    Howe'er my haps,° my joys were ne'er begun.

                                          Exit.

---

37 *tender* hold dear   41 *tend* wait   44 *cherub* angel of knowledge   48 *at foot* closely   51
leans depends   54 *cicatrice* scar   56 *free awe* uncompelled submission   56–57 *coldly set/Our
sovereign process* regard slightly our royal command   58 *present* instant   59 *hectic* fever   62
haps chances, fortunes

[SCENE IV. A plain in Denmark.]

Enter Fortinbras with his Army over the stage.

Fortinbras. Go, Captain, from me greet the Danish king.
  Tell him that by his license Fortinbras
  Craves the conveyance of° a promised march
  Over his kingdom. You know the rendezvous.
  If that his Majesty would aught with us,   5
  We shall express our duty in his eye;°
  And let him know so.
Captain.   I will do't, my lord.
Fortinbras. Go softly° on.
                                        [*Exeunt all but the Captain.*]
                  Enter Hamlet, Rosencrantz, &c.
Hamlet. Good sir, whose powers° are these?
Captain. They are of Norway, sir.   10
Hamlet. How purposed, sir, I pray you?
Captain. Against some part of Poland.
Hamlet. Who commands them, sir?
Captain. The nephew to old Norway, Fortinbras.
Hamlet. Goes it against the main° of Poland, sir,   15
  Or for some frontier?
Captain. Truly to speak, and with no addition,°
  We go to gain a little patch of ground
  That hath in it no profit but the name.
  To pay five ducats, five, I would not farm it,   20
  Nor will it yield to Norway or the Pole
  A ranker° rate, should it be sold in fee.°
Hamlet. Why, then the Polack never will defend it.
Captain. Yes, it is already garrisoned.
Hamlet. Two thousand souls and twenty thousand ducats   25
  Will not debate° the question of this straw.
  This is th' imposthume° of much wealth and peace,
  That inward breaks, and shows no cause without
  Why the man dies. I humbly thank you, sir.
Captain. God bye you, sir.
                                                          [*Exit.*]
Rosencrantz.   Will't please you go, my lord?   30

IV.iv.3 *conveyance of* escort for   6 *in his eye* before his eyes (i.e., in his presence)
8 *softly* slowly   9 *powers* forces   15 *main* main part   17 *with no addition* plainly   22 *ranker*
higher   22 *in fee* outright   26 *debate* settle   27 *imposthume* abscess, ulcer

Hamlet. I'll be with you straight. Go a little before.

                    [Exeunt all but Hamlet.]

How all occasions do inform against me
And spur my dull revenge! What is a man,
If his chief good and market° of his time
Be but to sleep and feed? A beast, no more.   35
Sure he that made us with such large discourse,°
Looking before and after, gave us not
That capability and godlike reason
To fust° in us unused. Now, whether it be
Bestial oblivion,° or some craven scruple   40
Of thinking too precisely on th' event°—
A thought which, quartered, hath but one part wisdom
And ever three parts coward—I do not know
Why yet I live to say, "This thing's to do,"
Sith I have cause, and will, and strength, and means   45
To do't. Examples gross° as earth exhort me.
Witness this army of such mass and charge,°
Led by a delicate and tender prince,
Whose spirit, with divine ambition puffed,
Makes mouths at the invisible event,°   50
Exposing what is mortal and unsure
To all that fortune, death, and danger dare,
Even for an eggshell. Rightly to be great
Is not° to stir without great argument,°
But greatly° to find quarrel in a straw   55
When honor's at the stake. How stand I then,
That have a father killed, a mother stained,
Excitements° of my reason and my blood,
And let all sleep, while to my shame I see
The imminent death of twenty thousand men   60
That for a fantasy and trick of fame°
Go to their graves like beds, fight for a plot
Whereon the numbers cannot try the cause,
Which is not tomb enough and continent°
To hide the slain? O, from this time forth,   65
My thoughts be bloody, or be nothing worth!   *Exit.*

---

   34 *market* profit 36 *discourse* understanding 39 *fust* grow moldy 40 *oblivion* forgetfulness 41 *event* outcome 46 *gross* large, obvious 47 *charge* expense 50 *Makes mouths at the invisible event* makes scornful faces (is contemptuous of) the unseen outcome 54 *not* (the sense seems to require "not not") 54 *argument* reason 55 *greatly* i.e., nobly 58 *Excitements* incentives 61 *fantasy and trick of fame* illusion and trifle of reputation 64 *continent* receptacle, container

[SCENE V. The castle.]

Enter Horatio, [Queen] Gertrude, and a Gentleman.

Queen. I will not speak with her.
Gentleman. She is importunate, indeed distract.
  Her mood will needs be pitied.
Queen.   What would she have?
Gentleman. She speaks much of her father, says she hears
  There's tricks i' th' world, and hems, and beats her heart,   5
  Spurns enviously at straws,° speaks things in doubt°
  That carry but half sense. Her speech is nothing,
  Yet the unshapèd use of it doth move
  The hearers to collection;° they yawn° at it,
  And botch the words up fit to their own thoughts,   10
  Which, as her winks and nods and gestures yield them,
  Indeed would make one think there might be thought,
  Though nothing sure, yet much unhappily.
Horatio. 'Twere good she were spoken with, for she may strew
  Dangerous conjectures in ill-breeding minds.   15
Queen. Let her come in.   [*Exit Gentleman.*]
  [*Aside*] To my sick soul (as sin's true nature is)
  Each toy seems prologue to some great amiss;°
  So full of artless jealousy° is guilt
  It spills° itself in fearing to be spilt.   20
              Enter Ophelia [distracted.]
Ophelia. Where is the beauteous majesty of Denmark?
Queen. How now, Ophelia?
Ophelia. (*She sings.*) How should I your truelove know
              From another one?
            By his cockle hat° and staff   25
              And his sandal shoon.°
Queen. Alas, sweet lady, what imports this song?
Ophelia. Say you? Nay, pray you mark.
            He is dead and gone, lady,   (*Song*)
              He is dead and gone;   30
            At his head a grass-green turf,
              At his heels a stone.
    O, ho!

_____

  IV.v.6 *Spurns enviously at straws* objects spitefully to insignificant matters   6 *in doubt*
uncertainly   8–9 *Yet the . . . to collection* i.e., yet the formless manner of it moves her listeners
to gather up some sort of meaning   9 *yawn* gape (?)   18 *amiss* misfortune   19 *artless jealousy*
crude suspicion   20 *spills* destroys   25 *cockle hat* (a cockleshell on the hat was the sign of a
pilgrim who had journeyed to shrines overseas. The association of lovers and pilgrims was a
common one)   26 *shoon* shoes

Queen. Nay, but Ophelia——

Ophelia. Pray you mark.   35

   [*Sings.*] White his shroud as the mountain snow——

Enter King.

Queen. Alas, look here, my lord.

Ophelia.   Larded° all with sweet flowers (*Song*)

         Which bewept to the grave did not go

           With truelove showers.   40

King. How do you, pretty lady?

Ophelia. Well, God dild° you! They say the owl was a baker's daughter.°
Lord, we know what we are, but know not what we may be. God be at
your table!

King. Conceit° upon her father.   45

Ophelia. Pray let's have no words of this, but when they ask you what it
  means, say you this:

         Tomorrow is Saint Valentine's day.°   (*Song*)

          All in the morning betime,

         And I a maid at your window,   50

          To be your Valentine.

         Then up he rose and donned his clothes

         And dupped° the chamber door,

         Let in the maid, that out a maid

          Never departed more.   55

King. Pretty Ophelia.

Ophelia. Indeed, la, without an oath, I'll make an end on't:

  [*Sings.*] By Gis° and by Saint Charity,

         Alack, and fie for shame!

         Young men will do't if they come to't,   60

          By Cock,° they are to blame.

         Quoth she, "Before you tumbled me,

          You promised me to wed."

  He answers:

         "So would I 'a' done, by yonder sun,   65

          An thou hadst not come to my bed."

King. How long hath she been thus?

Ophelia. I hope all will be well. We must be patient, but I cannot choose but
  weep to think they would lay him i' th' cold ground. My brother shall

---

   38 *Larded* decorated   42 *dild* yield, i.e., reward   43 *baker's daughter* (an allusion to a tale of
a baker's daughter who begrudged bread to Christ and was turned into an owl)   45 *Conceit*
brooding   48 *Saint Valentine's day* Feb. 14 (the notion was that a bachelor would become the
truelove of the first girl he saw on this day)   53 *dupped* opened (did up)   58 *Gis* (contraction of
"Jesus")   61 *Cock* (1) God (2) phallus

know of it; and so I thank you of your good counsel. Come, my coach!   70
Good night, ladies, good night. Sweet ladies, good night, good night.
Exit.

King. Follow her close; give her good watch, I pray you.   [*Exit Horatio.*]
   O, this is the poison of deep grief; it springs
   All from her father's death—and now behold!
   O Gertrude, Gertrude,   75
   When sorrows come, they come not single spies,
   But in battalions: first, her father slain;
   Next, your son gone, and he most violent author
   Of his own just remove; the people muddied,°
   Thick and unwholesome in their thoughts and whispers   80
   For good Polonius' death, and we have done but greenly°
   In huggermugger° to inter him; poor Ophelia
   Divided from herself and her fair judgment,
   Without the which we are pictures or mere beasts;
   Last, and as much containing as all these,   85
   Her brother is in secret come from France,
   Feeds on his wonder,° keeps himself in clouds,
   And wants not buzzers° to infect his ear
   With pestilent speeches of his father's death,
   Wherein necessity, of matter beggared,°   90
   Will nothing stick° our person to arraign
   In ear and ear. O my dear Gertrude, this,
   Like to a murd'ring piece,° in many places
   Gives me superfluous death.   *A noise within.*
Enter a Messenger.

Queen.   Alack, what noise is this?
King. Attend, where are my Switzers?° Let them guard the door.   95
   What is the matter?
Messenger.   Save yourself, my lord.
   The ocean, overpeering of his list,
   Eats not the flats with more impiteous haste
   Than young Laertes, in a riotous head,°
   O'erbears your officers. The rabble call him lord,   100
   And, as the world were now but to begin,
   Antiquity forgot, custom not known,
   The ratifiers and props of every word,
   They cry, "Choose we! Laertes shall be king!"

---

79 *muddied* muddled   81 *greenly* foolishly   82 *huggermugger* secret haste   87 *wonder*
suspicion   88 *wants not buzzers* does not lack talebearers   90 *of matter beggared* unprovided
with facts   91 *Will nothing stick* will not hesitate   93 *murd'ring piece* (a cannon that shot a kind
of shrapnel)   95 *Switzers* Swiss guards   97 *list* shore   99 *in a riotous head* with a rebellious
force

Caps, hands, and tongues applaud it to the clouds,   105
"Laertes shall be king! Laertes king!" *A noise within.*
Queen. How cheerfully on the false trail they cry!
   O, this is counter,° you false Danish dogs!
                   Enter Laertes with others.
King. The doors are broke.
Laertes. Where is this king?—Sirs, stand you all without.   110
All. No, let's come in.
Laertes.   I pray you give me leave.
All. We will, we will.
Laertes. I thank you. Keep the door. [*Exeunt his Followers.*] O thou vile
   King,
   Give me my father.
Queen.   Calmly, good Laertes.
Laertes. That drop of blood that's calm proclaims me bastard,   115
   Cries cuckold° to my father, brands the harlot
   Even here between the chaste unsmirchèd brow
   Of my true mother.
King.   What is the cause, Laertes,
   That thy rebellion looks so giantlike?
   Let him go, Gertrude. Do not fear° our person.   120
   There's such divinity doth hedge a king
   That treason can but peep to° what it would,
   Acts little of his will. Tell me, Laertes,
   Why thou art thus incensed. Let him go, Gertrude.
   Speak, man.   125
Laertes. Where is my father?
King.   Dead.
Queen.   But not by him.
King. Let him demand his fill.
Laertes. How came he dead? I'll not be juggled with.
   To hell allegiance, vows to the blackest devil,
   Conscience and grace to the profoundest pit!   130
   I dare damnation. To this point I stand,
   That both the worlds I give to negligence,°
   Let come what comes, only I'll be revenged
   Most throughly for my father.
King.   Who shall stay you?
Laertes. My will, not all the world's.

---

108 *counter* (a hound runs counter when he follows the scent backward from the prey)
116 *cuckold* man whose wife is unfaithful   120 *fear* fear for   122 *peep to* i.e., look at from a
distance   132 *That both . . . to negligence* i.e., I care not what may happen (to me) in this world
or the next

And for my means, I'll husband them° so well   135
  They shall go far with little.
King.   Good Laertes,
  If you desire to know the certainty
  Of your dear father, is't writ in your revenge
  That swoopstake° you will draw both friend and foe,
  Winner and loser?   140
Laertes. None but his enemies.
King.   Will you know them then?
Laertes. To his good friends thus wide I'll ope my arms
  And like the kind life-rend'ring pelican°
  Repast° them with my blood.
King.   Why, now you speak
  Like a good child and a true gentleman.   145
  That I am guiltless of your father's death,
  And am most sensibly° in grief for it,
  It shall as level to your judgment 'pear
  As day does to your eye.
                 A noise within: "Let her come in."

Laertes. How now? What noise is that?   150
               Enter Ophelia.
  O heat, dry up my brains; tears seven times salt
  Burn out the sense and virtue° of mine eye!
  By heaven, thy madness shall be paid with weight
  Till our scale turn the beam.° O rose of May,
  Dear maid, kind sister, sweet Ophelia!   155
  O heavens, is't possible a young maid's wits
  Should be as mortal as an old man's life?
  Nature is fine° in love, and where 'tis fine,
  It sends some precious instance° of itself
  After the thing it loves.   160
Ophelia.   They bore him barefaced on the bier (*Song*)
        Hey non nony, nony, hey nony
        And in his grave rained many a tear——
        Fare you well, my dove!
Laertes. Hadst thou thy wits, and didst persuade revenge,   165
  It could not move thus.
Ophelia. You must sing "A-down a-down, and you call him a-down-a." O,
  how the wheel° becomes it! It is the false steward, that stole his master's
  daughter.

---

    135 *husband them* use them economically   139 *swoopstake* in a clean sweep
143 *pelican* (thought to feed its young with its own blood)   144 *Repast* feed   147 *sensibly*
acutely   152 *virtue* power   154 *turn the beam* weigh down the bar (of the balance)   158 *fine*
refined, delicate   159 *instance* sample   168 *wheel* (of uncertain meaning, but probably a turn or
dance of Ophelia's, rather than Fortune's wheel)

Laertes. This nothing's more than matter.°

Ophelia. There's rosemary, that's for remembrance. Pray you, love, remem-   170
ber. And there is pansies, that's for thoughts.

Laertes. A document° in madness, thoughts and remembrance fitted.

Ophelia. There's fennel° for you, and columbines. There's rue for you, and
here's some for me. We may call it herb of grace o' Sundays. O, you must
wear your rue with a difference. There's a daisy. I would give you some   175
violets, but they withered all when my father died. They say 'a made a
good end. [*Sings*] For bonny sweet Robin is all my joy.

Laertes. Thought and affliction, passion, hell itself,
She turns to favor° and to prettiness.

Ophelia.   And will 'a not come again?   (*Song*)   180
               And will 'a not come again?
                 No, no, he is dead,
                 Go to thy deathbed,
               He never will come again.

               His beard was as white as snow,   185
               All flaxen was his poll.°
                 He is gone, he is gone,
                 And we cast away moan.
               God 'a' mercy on his soul!
And of all Christian souls, I pray God. God bye you.   190

                                                                    [*Exit.*]

Laertes. Do you see this, O God?

King. Laertes, I must commune with your grief,
Or you deny me right. Go but apart,
Make choice of whom your wisest friends you will,
And they shall hear and judge 'twixt you and me.   195
If by direct or by collateral° hand
They find us touched,° we will our kingdom give,
Our crown, our life, and all that we call ours,
To you in satisfaction; but if not,
Be you content to lend your patience to us,   200
And we shall jointly labor with your soul
To give it due content.

---

169 *This nothing's more than matter* this nonsense has more meaning than matters of
consequence   172 *document* lesson   173 *fennel* (the distribution of flowers in the ensuing lines
has symbolic meaning, but the meaning is disputed. Perhaps *fennel,* flattery; *columbines,*
cuckoldry; *rue,* sorrow for Ophelia and repentance for the Queen; *daisy,* dissembling; *violets,*
faithfulness. For other interpretations, see J. W. Lever in *Review of English Studies,* New Series 3
[1952], pp. 123–29)   179 *favor* charm, beauty   186 *All flaxen was his poll* white as flax was his
head   196 *collateral* indirect   197 *touched* implicated

Laertes.   Let this be so.
His means of death, his obscure funeral—
No trophy, sword, nor hatchment° o'er his bones,
No noble rite nor formal ostentation°—   205
Cry to be heard, as 'twere from heaven to earth,
That I must call't in question.
King.   So you shall;
And where th' offense is, let the great ax fall.
I pray you go with me.   *Exeunt.*

[SCENE VI. The castle.]

Enter Horatio and others.

Horatio. What are they that would speak with me?
Gentleman. Seafaring men, sir. They say they have letters for you.
Horatio. Let them come in.   [*Exit Attendant.*]
  I do not know from what part of the world
  I should be greeted, if not from Lord Hamlet.   5
                    Enter Sailors.
Sailor. God bless you, sir.
Horatio. Let Him bless thee too.
Sailor. 'A shall, sir, an't please Him. There's a letter for you, sir—it came
  from th' ambassador that was bound for England—if your name be Horatio, as I am let to know it is.   10
Horatio. [*Reads the letter.*] "Horatio, when thou shalt have overlooked° this,
  give these fellows some means to the King. They have letters for him. Ere
  we were two days old at sea, a pirate of very warlike appointment° gave
  us chase. Finding ourselves too slow of sail, we put on a compelled valor,
  and in the grapple I boarded them. On the instant they got clear of our   15
  ship; so I alone became their prisoner. They have dealt with me like thieves
  of mercy, but they knew what they did: I am to do a good turn for them.
  Let the King have the letters I have sent, and repair thou to me with as
  much speed as thou wouldest fly death. I have words to speak in thine ear
  will make thee dumb; yet are they much too light for the bore° of the   20
  matter. These good fellows will bring thee where I am. Rosencrantz and
  Guildenstern hold their course for England. Of them I have much to tell
  thee. Farewell.
                    He that thou knowest thine, HAMLET."

---

204 *hatchment* tablet bearing the coat of arms of the dead   205 *ostentation* ceremony
IV.vi.11 *overlooked* surveyed   13 *appointment* equipment   20 *bore* caliber (here, "importance")

Come, I will give you way for these your letters,
And do't the speedier that you may direct me   25
To him from whom you brought them.   *Exeunt.*

[SCENE VII. The castle.]

Enter King and Laertes.

King. Now must your conscience my acquittance seal,
   And you must put me in your heart for friend,
   Sith you have heard, and with a knowing ear,
   That he which hath your noble father slain
   Pursued my life.
Laertes.   It well appears. But tell me   5
   Why you proceeded not against these feats
   So criminal and so capital° in nature,
   As by your safety, greatness, wisdom, all things else,
   You mainly° were stirred up.
King.   O, for two special reasons,
   Which may to you perhaps seem much unsinewed,°   10
   But yet to me they're strong. The Queen his mother
   Lives almost by his looks, and for myself—
   My virtue or my plague, be it either which—
   She is so conjunctive° to my life and soul,
   That, as the star moves not but in his sphere,   15
   I could not but by her. The other motive
   Why to a public count° I might not go
   Is the great love the general gender° bear him,
   Who, dipping all his faults in their affection,
   Would, like the spring that turneth wood to stone,°   20
   Convert his gyves° to graces; so that my arrows,
   Too slightly timbered° for so loud a wind,
   Would have reverted to my bow again,
   And not where I had aimed them.
Laertes. And so have I a noble father lost,   25
   A sister driven into desp'rate terms,°
   Whose worth, if praises may go back again,°

IV.vii.7 *capital* deserving death   9 *mainly* powerfully   10 *unsinewed* weak   14 *conjunctive* closely united   17 *count* reckoning   18 *general gender* common people   20 *spring that turneth wood to stone* (a spring in Shakespeare's county was so charged with lime that it would petrify wood placed in it)   21 *gyves* fetters   22 *timbered* shafted   26 *terms* conditions   27 *go back again* revert to what is past

Stood challenger on mount of all the age
For her perfections. But my revenge will come.
King. Break not your sleeps for that. You must not think   30
That we are made of stuff so flat and dull
That we can let our beard be shook with danger,
And think it pastime. You shortly shall hear more.
I loved your father, and we love ourself,
And that, I hope, will teach you to imagine——   35

        Enter a Messenger with letters.

How now? What news?
Messenger.   Letters, my lord, from Hamlet:
   These to your Majesty; this to the Queen.
King. From Hamlet? Who brought them?
Messenger. Sailors, my lord, they say; I saw them not.
   They were given me by Claudio; he received them   40
   Of him that brought them.
King.   Laertes, you shall hear them.—
   Leave us.   *Exit Messenger.*
   [*Reads.*] "High and mighty, you shall know I am set naked° on your
   kingdom. Tomorrow shall I beg leave to see your kingly eyes; when I shall
   (first asking your pardon thereunto) recount the occasion of my sudden
   and more strange return.   45

                              HAMLET."

   What should this mean? Are all the rest come back?
   Or is it some abuse,° and no such thing?
Laertes. Know you the hand?
King.   'Tis Hamlet's character.° "Naked"!
   And in a postscript here, he says "alone."
   Can you devise° me?   50
Laertes. I am lost in it, my lord. But let him come.
   It warms the very sickness in my heart
   That I shall live and tell him to his teeth,
   "Thus did'st thou."
King.   If it be so, Laertes
   (As how should it be so? How otherwise?),   55
   Will you be ruled by me?
Laertes.   Ay, my lord.
   So you will not o'errule me to a peace.
King. To thine own peace. If he be now returned,
   As checking at° his voyage, and that he means

---

42 *naked* destitute   47 *abuse* deception   48 *character* handwriting   50 *devise* advise   59
checking at turning away from (a term in falconry)

No more to undertake it, I will work him   60
To an exploit now ripe in my device,
Under the which he shall not choose but fall;
And for his death no wind of blame shall breathe,
But even his mother shall uncharge the practice°
And call it accident.
Laertes.   My lord, I will be ruled;   65
The rather if you could devise it so
That I might be the organ.
King.   It falls right.
You have been talked of since your travel much,
And that in Hamlet's hearing, for a quality
Wherein they say you shine. Your sum of parts   70
Did not together pluck such envy from him
As did that one, and that, in my regard,
Of the unworthiest siege.°
Laertes.   What part is that, my lord?
King. A very riband in the cap of youth,
Yet needful too, for youth no less becomes   75
The light and careless livery that it wears
Than settled age his sables and his weeds,°
Importing health and graveness. Two months since
Here was a gentleman of Normandy.
I have seen myself, and served against, the French,   80
And they can° well on horseback, but this gallant
Had witchcraft in't. He grew unto his seat,
And to such wondrous doing brought his horse
As had he been incorpsed and deminatured
With the brave beast. So far he topped my thought   85
That I, in forgery° of shapes and tricks,
Come short of what he did.
Laertes.   A Norman was't?
King. A Norman.
Laertes. Upon my life, Lamord.
King.   The very same.
Laertes. I know him well. He is the brooch° indeed   90
And gem of all the nation.
King. He made confession° of you,
And gave you such a masterly report,
For art and exercise in your defense,

---

64 *uncharge the practice* not charge the device with treachery   74 *siege* rank   77 *sables and his weeds* i.e., sober attire   81 *can* do   86 *forgery* invention   90 *brooch* ornament   92 *confession* report

And for your rapier most especial, 95
That he cried out 'twould be a sight indeed
If one could match you. The scrimer° of their nation
He swore had neither motion, guard, nor eye,
If you opposed them. Sir, this report of his
Did Hamlet so envenom with his envy 100
That he could nothing do but wish and beg
Your sudden coming o'er to play with you.
Now, out of this——

Laertes.   What out of this, my lord?
King. Laertes, was your father dear to you?
Or are you like the painting of a sorrow, 105
A face without a heart?

Laertes.   Why ask you this?
King. Not that I think you did not love your father,
But that I know love is begun by time,
And that I see, in passages of proof,°
Time qualifies° the spark and fire of it. 110
There lives within the very flame of love
A kind of wick or snuff° that will abate it,
And nothing is at a like goodness still,°
For goodness, growing to a plurisy,°
Dies in his own too-much. That we would do 115
We should do when we would, for this "would" changes
And hath abatements and delays as many
As there are tongues, are hands, are accidents,
And then this "should" is like a spendthrift sigh,°
That hurts by easing. But to the quick° of th' ulcer— 120
Hamlet comes back; what would you undertake
To show yourself in deed your father's son
More than in words?

Laertes.   To cut his throat i' th' church!
King. No place indeed should murder sanctuarize;°
Revenge should have no bounds. But, good Laertes, 125
Will you do this? Keep close within your chamber.
Hamlet returned shall know you are come home.
We'll put on those° shall praise your excellence
And set a double varnish on the fame
The Frenchman gave you, bring you in fine° together 130

---

97 *scrimers* fencers   109 *passages of proof* proved cases   110 *qualifies* diminishes   112 *snuff*
residue of burnt wick (which dims the light)   113 *still* always   114 *plurisy* fullness, excess   119
spendthrift sigh (sighing provides ease, but because it was thought to thin the blood and so
shorten life it was spendthrift)   120 *quick* sensitive flesh   124 *sanctuarize* protect   128 *We'll put
on those* we'll incite persons who   130 *in fine* finally

And wager on your heads. He, being remiss,
Most generous, and free from all contriving,
Will not peruse the foils, so that with ease,
Or with a little shuffling, you may choose
A sword unbated,° and, in a pass of practice,°   135
Requite him for your father.
Laertes.   I will do't,
And for that purpose I'll anoint my sword.
I bought an unction of a mountebank,°
So mortal that, but dip a knife in it,
Where it draws blood, no cataplasm° so rare,   140
Collected from all simples° that have virtue°
Under the moon, can save the thing from death
That is but scratched withal. I'll touch my point
With this contagion, that, if I gall him slightly,
It may be death.   145
King.   Let's further think of this,
Weigh what convenience both of time and means
May fit us to our shape.° If this should fail,
And that our drift look through° our bad performance,
'Twere better not assayed. Therefore this project   150
Should have a back or second, that might hold
If this did blast in proof.° Soft, let me see.
We'll make a solemn wager on your cunnings—
I ha't!
When in your motion you are hot and dry—   155
As make your bouts more violent to that end—
And that he calls for drink, I'll have prepared him
A chalice for the nonce,° whereon but sipping,
If he by chance escape your venomed stuck,°
Our purpose may hold there.—But stay, what noise?   160
                    Enter Queen.
Queen. One woe doth tread upon another's heel.
So fast they follow. Your sister's drowned, Laertes.
Laertes. Drowned! O, where?
Queen. There is a willow grows askant° the brook,
That shows his hoar° leaves in the glassy stream: 165
Therewith° fantastic garlands did she make
Of crowflowers, nettles, daisies, and long purples,

---

135 *unbated* not blunted   135 *pass of practice* treacherous thrust   138 *mountebank* quack
140 *cataplasm* poultice   141 *simplex* medicinal herbs   141 *virtue* power (to heal)   148 *shape*
role   149 *drift look through* purpose show through   152 *blast in proof* burst (fail) in
performance   158 *nonce* occasion   159 *stuck* thrust   164 *askant* aslant   165 *hoar* silver-gray
166 *Therewith* i.e., with willow twigs

That liberal° shepherds give a grosser name,
But our cold maids do dead men's fingers call them.
There on the pendent boughs her crownet° weeds   170
Clamb'ring to hang, an envious sliver° broke,
When down her weedy trophies and herself
Fell in the weeping brook. Her clothes spread wide,
And mermaidlike awhile they bore her up,
Which time she chanted snatches of old lauds,°   175
As one incapable° of her own distress,
Or like a creature native and indued°
Unto that element. But long it could not be
Till that her garments, heavy with their drink,
Pulled the poor wretch from her melodious lay   180
To muddy death.
Laertes.   Alas, then she is drowned?
Queen. Drowned, drowned.
Laertes. Too much of water hast thou, poor Ophelia,
And therefore I forbid my tears; but yet
It is our trick;° nature her custom holds,   185
Let shame say what it will: when these are gone,
The woman° will be out. Adieu, my lord.
I have a speech o' fire, that fain would blaze,
But that this folly drowns it.   *Exit.*
King.   Let's follow, Gertrude.
How much I had to do to calm his rage!   190
Now fear I this will give it start again;
Therefore let's follow.   *Exeunt.*

[ACT V
SCENE I. A churchyard.]

Enter two Clowns.°

Clown. Is she to be buried in Christian burial when she willfully seeks her
own salvation?
Other. I tell thee she is. Therefore make her grave straight.° The crowner°
hath sate on her, and finds it Christian burial.
Clown. How can that be, unless she drowned herself in her own defense?
Other. Why, 'tis found so.   5

---

168 *liberal* free-spoken, coarse-mouthed   170 *crownet* coronet   171 *envious sliver* malicious
branch   175 *lauds* hymns   176 *incapable* unaware   177 *indued* in harmony with   185 *trick*
trait, way   187 *woman* i.e., womanly part of me   V.i.s.d. *Clowns* rustics   2 *straight*
straightway   2 *crowner* coroner

Clown. It must be *se offendendo;*° it cannot be else. For here lies the point: if I drown myself wittingly, it argues an act, and an act hath three branches—it is to act, to do, to perform. Argal,° she drowned herself wittingly.

Other. Nay, but hear you, Goodman Delver.

Clown. Give me leave. Here lies the water—good. Here stands the man— 10 good. If the man go to this water and drown himself, it is, will he nill he,° he goes; mark you that. But if the water come to him and drown him, he drowns not himself. Argal, he that is not guilty of his own death, shortens not his own life.

Other. But is this law?

Clown. Ay marry, is't—crowner's quest° law. 15

Other. Will you ha' the truth on't? If this had not been a gentlewoman, she should have been buried out o' Christian burial.

Clown. Why, there thou say'st. And the more pity that great folk should have count'nance° in this world to drown or hang themselves more than their even-Christen.° Come, my spade. There is no ancient gentlemen but 20 gard'ners, ditchers, and gravemakers. They hold up° Adam's profession.

Other. Was he a gentleman?

Clown. 'A was the first that ever bore arms.°

Other. Why, he had none.

Clown. What, art a heathen? How dost thou understand the Scripture? The 25 Scripture says Adam digged. Could he dig without arms? I'll put another question to thee. If thou answerest me not to the purpose, confess thyself—

Other. Go to.

Clown. What is he that builds stronger than either the mason, the shipwright, or the carpenter?

Other. The gallowsmaker, for that frame outlives a thousand tenants. 30

Clown. I like thy wit well, in good faith. The gallows does well. But how does it well? It does well to those that do ill. Now thou dost ill to say the gallows is built stronger than the church. Argal, the gallows may do well to thee. To't again, come.

Other. Who builds stronger than a mason, a shipwright, or a carpenter? 35

Clown. Ay, tell me that, and unyoke.°

Other. Marry, now I can tell.

Clown. To't.

Other. Mass,° I cannot tell.

Enter Hamlet and Horatio afar off.

---

6 *se offendendo* (blunder for *se defendendo*, a legal term meaning "in self-defense")   8 *Argal* (blunder for Latin *ergo*, "therefore")   11 *will he nill he* will he or will he not (whether he will or will not)   15 *quest* inquest   19 *count'nance* privilege   20 *even-Christen* fellow Christian   21 *hold up* keep up   23 *bore arms* had a coat of arms (the sign of a gentleman)   36 *unyoke* i.e., stop work for the day   39 *Mass* by the mass

Clown. Cudgel thy brains no more about it, for your dull ass will not mend 40
his pace with beating. And when you are asked this question next, say "a
gravemaker." The houses he makes lasts till doomsday. Go, get thee in,
and fetch me a stoup° of liquor.

                                              [Exit Other Clown.]
In youth when I did love, did love,   *(Song)*
   Methought it was very sweet   45
To contract—O—the time for—a—my behove,°
   O, methought there—a—was nothing—a—meet.
Hamlet. Has this fellow no feeling of his business? 'A sings in gravemaking.
Horatio. Custom hath made it in him a property of easiness.°
Hamlet. 'Tis e'en so. The hand of little employment hath the daintier sense.° 50
Clown.   But age with his stealing steps   *(Song)*
      Hath clawed me in his clutch,
      And hath shipped me into the land,
      As if I had never been such.

                                     [Throws up a skull.]
Hamlet. That skull had a tongue in it, and could sing once. How the knave 55
jowls° it to the ground, as if 'twere Cain's jawbone, that did the first
murder! This might be the pate of a politician, which this ass now o'erreaches,° one that would circumvent God, might it not?
Horatio. It might, my lord.
Hamlet. Or of a courtier, which could say "Good morrow, sweet lord! How 60
dost thou, sweet lord?" This might be my Lord Such-a-one, that praised
my Lord Such-a-one's horse when 'a went to beg it, might it not?
Horatio. Ay, my lord.
Hamlet. Why, e'en so, and now my Lady Worm's, chapless,° and knocked
about the mazzard° with a sexton's spade. Here's fine revolution, an we 65
had the trick to see't. Did these bones cost no more the breeding but to
play at loggets° with them? Mine ache to think on't.
Clown.   A pickax and a spade, a spade,   *(Song)*
      For and a shrouding sheet;
      O, a pit of clay for to be made   70
      For such a guest is meet.

                              [Throws up another skull.]
Hamlet. There's another. Why may not that be the skull of a lawyer? Where
be his quiddities° now, his quillities,° his cases, his tenures,° and his tricks?
Why does he suffer this mad knave now to knock him about the sconce°

---

43 *stoup* tankard   46 *behove* advantage   49 *in him a property of easiness* easy for him   50
hath the daintier sense is more sensitive (because it is not calloused)   56 *jowls* hurls   58
o'erreaches (1) reaches over (2) has the advantage over   64 *chapless* lacking the lower jaw   65
mazzard head   67 *loggets* (a game in which small pieces of wood were thrown at an object)   73
quiddities subtle arguments (from Latin *quidditas,* "whatness")   73 *quillities* fine distinctions   73
tenures legal means of holding land   74 *sconce* head

with a dirty shovel, and will not tell him of his action of battery? Hum! 75
This fellow might be in's time a great buyer of land, with his statutes, his
recognizances, his fines,° his double vouchers, his recoveries. Is this the
fine° of his fines, and the recovery of his recoveries, to have his fine pate
full of fine dirt? Will his vouchers vouch him no more of his purchases,
and double ones too, than the length and breadth of a pair of indentures?° 80
The very conveyances° of his lands will scarcely lie in this box, and must
th' inheritor himself have no more, ha?

Horatio. Not a jot more, my lord.

Hamlet. Is not parchment made of sheepskins?

Horatio. Ay, my lord, and of calveskins too. 85

Hamlet. They are sheep and calves which seek out assurance° in that. I will
speak to this fellow. Whose grave's this, sirrah?

Clown. Mine, sir.

[*Sings.*]   O, a pit of clay for to be made
            For such a guest is meet. 90

Hamlet. I think it be thine indeed, for thou liest in't.

Clown. You lie out on't, sir, and therefore 'tis not yours. For my part, I do
not lie in't, yet it is mine.

Hamlet. Thou dost lie in't, to be in't and say it is thine. 'Tis for the dead,
not for the quick;° therefore thou liest. 95

Clown. 'Tis a quick lie, sir; 'twill away again from me to you.

Hamlet. What man dost thou dig it for?

Clown. For no man, sir.

Hamlet. What woman then?

Clown. For none neither. 100

Hamlet. Who is to be buried in't?

Clown. One that was a woman, sir; but, rest her soul, she's dead.

Hamlet. How absolute° the knave is! We must speak by the card,° or equiv-
ocation° will undo us. By the Lord, Horatio, this three years I have took
note of it, the age is grown so picked° that the toe of the peasant comes 105
so near the heel of the courtier he galls his kibe.° How long has thou been
a gravemaker?

Clown. Of all the days i' th' year, I came to't that day that our last king
Hamlet overcame Fortinbras.

Hamlet. How long is that since?

Clown. Cannot you tell that? Every fool can tell that. It was that very day 110
that young Hamlet was born—he that is mad, and sent into England.

76–77 *his statutes, his recognizances, his fines* his documents giving a creditor control of a
debtor's land, his bonds of surety, his documents changing an entailed estate into fee simple
(unrestricted ownership)   78 *fine* end   80 *indentures* contracts   81 *conveyances* legal documents
for the transference of land   86 *assurance* safety   95 *quick* living   103 *absolute* positive,
decided   103 *by the card* by the compass card, i.e., exactly   104 *equivocation* ambiguity   105
picked refined   106 *kibe* sore on the back of the heel

Hamlet. Ay, marry, why was he sent into England?

Clown. Why, because 'a was mad. 'A shall recover his wits there; or, if 'a do not, 'tis no great matter there.

Hamlet. Why? 115

Clown. 'Twill not be seen in him there. There the men are as mad as he.

Hamlet. How came he mad?

Clown. Very strangely, they say.

Hamlet. How strangely?

Clown. Faith, e'en with losing his wits. 120

Hamlet. Upon what ground?

Clown. Why, here in Denmark. I have been sexton here, man and boy, thirty years.

Hamlet. How long will a man lie i' th' earth ere he rot?

Clown. Faith, if 'a be not rotten before 'a die (as we have many pocky corses° nowadays that will scarce hold the laying in), 'a will last you some eight 125 year or nine year. A tanner will last you nine year.

Hamlet. Why he, more than another?

Clown. Why, sir, his hide is so tanned with his trade that 'a will keep out water a great while, and your water is a sore decayer of your whoreson dead body. Here's a skull now hath lien you i' th' earth three and twenty 130 years.

Hamlet. Whose was it?

Clown. A whoreson mad fellow's it was. Whose do you think it was?

Hamlet. Nay, I know not.

Clown. A pestilence on him for a mad rogue! 'A poured a flagon of Rhenish on my head once. This same skull, sir, was, sir, Yorick's skull, the King's 135 jester.

Hamlet. This?

Clown. E'en that.

Hamlet. Let me see. [*Takes the skull.*] Alas, poor Yorick! I knew him, Horatio, a fellow of infinite jest, of most excellent fancy. He hath borne me on his back a thousand times. And now how abhorred in my imagination it is! 140 My gorge rises at it. Here hung those lips that I have kissed I know not how oft. Where be your gibes now? Your gambols, your songs, your flashes of merriment that were wont to set the table on a roar? Not one now to mock your own grinning? Quite chapfall'n°? Now get you to my lady's chamber, and tell her, let her paint an inch thick, to this favor° she must 145 come. Make her laugh at that. Prithee, Horatio, tell me one thing.

Horatio. What's that, my lord?

Hamlet. Dost thou think Alexander looked o' this fashion i' th' earth?

Horatio. E'en so.

---

124 *pocky corses* bodies of persons who had been infected with the pox (syphilis)   144 *chapfall'n* (1) down in the mouth (2) jawless   145 *favor* facial appearance

Hamlet. And smelt so? Pah!   [*Puts down the skull.*] 150
Horatio. E'en so, my lord.
Hamlet. To what base uses we may return, Horatio! Why may not imagi-
    nation trace the noble dust of Alexander till 'a find it stopping a bunghole?
Horatio. 'Twere to consider too curiously,° to consider so.
Hamlet. No, faith, not a jot, but to follow him thither with modesty enough,° 155
    and likelihood to lead it; as thus: Alexander died, Alexander was buried,
    Alexander returneth to dust; the dust is earth; of earth we make loam;
    and why of that loam whereto he was converted might they not stop a
    beer barrel?
    Imperious Caesar, dead and turned to clay,
    Might stop a hole to keep the wind away.   160
    O, that that earth which kept the world in awe
    Should patch a wall t' expel the winter's flaw!°
    But soft, but soft awhile! Here comes the King.

*Enter King, Queen, Laertes, and a coffin, with Lords attendant [and a
Doctor of Divinity].*

    The Queen, the courtiers. Who is this they follow?
    And with such maimèd° rites? This doth betoken   165
    The corse they follow did with desp'rate hand
    Fordo it° own life. 'Twas of some estate.°
    Couch° we awhile, and mark. [*Retires with Horatio.*]
Laertes. What ceremony else?
Hamlet.   That is Laertes,
    A very noble youth. Mark.   170
Laertes. What ceremony else?
Doctor. Her obsequies have been as far enlarged
    As we have warranty. Her death was doubtful,°
    And, but that great command o'ersways the order,
    She should in ground unsanctified been lodged   175
    Till the last trumpet. For charitable prayers,
    Shards,° flints, and pebbles should be thrown on her.
    Yet here she is allowed her virgin crants,°
    Her maiden strewments,° and the bringing home
    Of bell and burial.   180
Laertes. Must there no more be done?

---

    154 *curiously* minutely   155 *with modesty enough* without exaggeration   162 *flaw* gust
    165 *maimèd* incomplete   167 *Fordo it* destroy its   167 *estate* high rank   168 *Couch* hide   173
    doubtful suspicious   177 *Shards* broken pieces of pottery   178 *crants* garlands   179 *strewments*
    i.e., of flowers

Doctor.   No more be done.
  We should profane the service of the dead
  To sing a requiem and such rest to her
  As to peace-parted souls.
Laertes.   Lay her i' th' earth,
  And from her fair and unpolluted flesh   185
  May violets spring! I tell thee, churlish priest,
  A minist'ring angel shall my sister be
  When thou liest howling!
Hamlet.   What, the fair Ophelia?
Queen. Sweets to the sweet! Farewell.

                                           [*Scatters flowers.*]
  I hoped thou shouldst have been my Hamlet's wife.   190
  I thought thy bride bed to have decked, sweet maid,
  And not have strewed thy grave.
Laertes.   O, treble woe
  Fall ten times treble on that cursèd head
  Whose wicked deed thy most ingenious sense°
  Deprived thee of! Hold off the earth awhile,   200
  Till I have caught her once more in mine arms.

                                           Leaps in the grave.
  Now pile your dust upon the quick and dead
  Till of this flat a mountain you have made
  T'o'ertop old Pelion° or the skyish head
  Of blue Olympus.
Hamlet.   [*Coming forward*] What is he whose grief 205
  Bears such an emphasis, whose phrase of sorrow
  Conjures the wand'ring stars,° and makes them stand
  Like wonder-wounded hearers? This is I,
  Hamlet the Dane.
Laertes.   The devil take thy soul!

                                           [*Grapples with him.*]°
Hamlet. Thou pray'st not well.   210
  I prithee take thy fingers from my throat,
  For, though I am not splenitive° and rash,
  Yet have I in me something dangerous,
  Which let thy wisdom fear. Hold off thy hand.

---

  199 *most ingenious sense* finely endowed mind   204 *Pelion* (according to classical legend,
giants in their fight with the gods sought to reach heaven by piling Mount Pelion and Mount Ossa
on Mount Olympus)   207 *wand'ring stars* planets   209 s.d. *Grapples with him* (Q1, a bad
quarto, presumably reporting a version that toured, has a previous direction saying "Hamlet leaps
in after Laertes." Possibly he does so, somewhat hysterically. But such a direction—absent from
the two good texts, Q2 and F—makes Hamlet the aggressor, somewhat contradicting his next
speech. Perhaps Laertes leaps out of the grave to attack Hamlet)   212 *splenitive* fiery (the spleen
was thought to be the seat of anger)

King. Pluck them asunder.
Queen.   Hamlet, Hamlet!   215
All. Gentlemen!
Horatio.   Good my lord, be quiet.
[Attendants part them.]

Hamlet. Why, I will fight with him upon this theme
     Until my eyelids will no longer wag.
Queen. O my son, what theme?
Hamlet. I loved Ophelia. Forty thousand brothers   220
     Could not with all their quantity of love
     Make up my sum. What wilt thou do for her?
King. O, he is mad, Laertes.
Queen. For love of God forbear him.
Hamlet. 'Swounds, show me what thou't do.   225
     Woo't weep? Woo't fight? Woo't fast? Woo't tear thyself?
     Woo't drink up eisel?° Eat a crocodile?
     I'll do't. Dost thou come here to whine?
     To outface me with leaping in her grave?
     Be buried quick with her, and so will I.   230
     And if thou prate of mountains, let them throw
     Millions of acres on us, till our ground,
     Singeing his pate against the burning zone,°
     Make Ossa like a wart! Nay, an thou'lt mouth,
     I'll rant as well as thou.
Queen.   This is mere madness;   235
     And thus a while the fit will work on him.
     Anon, as patient as the female dove
     When that her golden couplets are disclosed,°
     His silence will sit drooping.
Hamlet.   Hear you, sir.
     What is the reason that you use me thus?   240
     I loved you ever. But it is no matter.
     Let Hercules himself do what he may,
     The cat will mew, and dog will have his day.
King. I pray thee, good Horatio, wait upon him.
Exit Hamlet and Horatio.

[*To Laertes*] Strengthen your patience in our last night's speech.   245
     We'll put the matter to the present push.°
     Good Gertrude, set some watch over your son.
     This grave shall have a living° monument.

---

   227 *eisel* vinegar   233 *burning zone* sun's orbit   238 *golden couplets are disclosed* (the dove
lays two eggs, and the newly hatched [*disclosed*] young are covered with golden down)   246
present push immediate test   248 *living* lasting (with perhaps also a reference to the plot against
Hamlet's life)

An hour of quiet shortly shall we see;
Till then in patience our proceeding be.   *Exeunt.* 250

[SCENE II. The castle.]

Enter Hamlet and Horatio.

Hamlet. So much for this, sir; now shall you see the other.
   You do remember all the circumstance?
Horatio. Remember it, my lord!
Hamlet. Sir, in my heart there was a kind of fighting
   That would not let me sleep. Methought I lay   5
   Worse than the mutines in the bilboes.° Rashly
   (And praised be rashness for it) let us know,
   Our indiscretion sometimes serves us well
   When our deep plots do pall,° and that should learn us
   There's a divinity that shapes our ends,   10
   Rough-hew them how we will.
Horatio.   That is most certain.
Hamlet. Up from my cabin,
   My sea gown scarfed about me, in the dark
   Groped I to find out them, had my desire,
   Fingered° their packet, and in fine° withdrew   15
   To mine own room again, making so bold,
   My fears forgetting manners, to unseal
   Their grand commission; where I found, Horatio—
   Ah, royal knavery!—an exact command,
   Larded° with many several sorts of reasons,   20
   Importing Denmark's health, and England's too,
   With, ho, such bugs and goblins in my life,°
   That on the supervise,° no leisure bated,°
   No, not to stay the grinding of the ax,
   My head should be struck off.
Horatio.   Is't possible?   25
Hamlet. Here's the commission; read it at more leisure.
   But wilt thou hear now how I did proceed?
Horatio. I beseech you.
Hamlet. Being thus benetted round with villains,
   Or° I could make a prologue to my brains,   30

   V.ii.6 *mutines in the bilboes* mutineers in fetters 9 *pall* fail 15 *Fingered* stole 15 *in fine* finally 20 *Larded* enriched 22 *such bugs and goblins in my life* such bugbears and imagined terrors if I were allowed to live 23 *supervise* reading 23 *leisure bated* delay allowed 30 *Or* ere

They had begun the play. I sat me down,
Devised a new commission, wrote it fair.
I once did hold it, as our statists° do,
A baseness to write fair,° and labored much
How to forget that learning, but, sir, now   35
It did me yeoman's service. Wilt thou know
Th' effect° of what I wrote?

Horatio.   Ay, good my lord.

Hamlet. An earnest conjuration from the King,
As England was his faithful tributary,
As love between them like the palm might flourish,   40
As peace should still her wheaten garland wear
And stand a comma° 'tween their amities,
And many suchlike as's of great charge,°
That on the view and knowing of these contents,
Without debatement further, more or less,   45
He should those bearers put to sudden death,
Not shriving° time allowed.

Horatio.   How was this sealed?

Hamlet. Why, even in that was heaven ordinant.°
I had my father's signet in my purse,
Which was the model° of that Danish seal,   50
Folded the writ up in the form of th' other,
Subscribed it, gave't th' impression, placed it safely,
The changeling never known. Now, the next day
Was our sea fight, and what to this was sequent
Thou knowest already.   55

Horatio. So Guildenstern and Rosencrantz go to't.

Hamlet. Why, man, they did make love to this employment.
They are not near my conscience; their defeat
Does by their own insinuation° grow.
'Tis dangerous when the baser nature comes   60
Between the pass° and fell° incensèd points
Of mighty opposites.

Horatio.   Why, what a king is this!

Hamlet. Does it not, think thee, stand me now upon°—
He that hath killed my king, and whored my mother,
Popped in between th' election° and my hopes,   65
Thrown out his angle° for my proper life,°

---

33 *statists* statesmen   34 *fair* clearly   37 *effect* purport   42 *comma* link   43 *great charge* (1) serious exhortation (2) heavy burden (punning on *as's* and "asses")   47 *shriving* absolution   48 *ordinant* ruling   50 *model* counterpart   59 *insinuation* meddling   61 *pass* thrust   61 *fell* cruel   63 *stand me now upon* become incumbent upon me   65 *election* (the Danish monarchy was elective)   66 *angle* fishing line   66 *my proper life* my own life

And with such coz'nage°—is't not perfect conscience
To quit° him with this arm? And is't not to be damned
To let this canker of our nature come
In further evil?   70
Horatio. It must be shortly known to him from England
What is the issue of the business there.
Hamlet. It will be short; the interim's mine,
And a man's life's no more than to say "one."
But I am very sorry, good Horatio,   75
That to Laertes I forgot myself,
For by the image of my cause I see
That portraiture of his. I'll court his favors.
But sure the bravery° of his grief did put me
Into a tow'ring passion.
Horatio.   Peace, who comes here?   80
                    Enter young Osric, a courtier.
Osric. Your lordship is right welcome back to Denmark.
Hamlet. I humbly thank you, sir. [*Aside to Horatio*]
Dost know this waterfly?
Horatio. [*Aside to Hamlet*] No, my good lord.
Hamlet. [*Aside to Horatio*] Thy state is the more gracious, for 'tis a vice to   85
know him. He hath much land, and fertile. Let a beast be lord of beasts,
and his crib shall stand at the king's mess.° 'Tis a chough,° but, as I say,
spacious° in the possession of dirt.
Osric. Sweet lord, if your lordship were at leisure, I
should impart a thing to you from his Majesty.   90
Hamlet. I will receive it, sir, with all diligence of spirit.
Put your bonnet to his right use. 'Tis for the head.
Osric. I thank your lordship, it is very hot.
Hamlet. No, believe me, 'tis very cold; the wind is northerly.
Osric. It is indifferent cold, my lord, indeed.   95
Hamlet. But yet methinks it is very sultry and hot for my complexion.°
Osric. Exceedingly, my lord; it is very sultry, as 'twere—I cannot tell how.
But, my lord, his Majesty bade me signify to you that 'a has laid a great
wager on your head. Sir, this is the matter——
Hamlet. I beseech you remember.   100
                    [*Hamlet moves him to put on his hat.*]
Osric. Nay, good my lord; for my ease, in good faith. Sir, here is newly come
to court Laertes—believe me, an absolute gentleman, full of most excellent
differences,° of very soft society and great showing. Indeed, to speak feel-

---

67 *coz'nage* trickery   68 *quit* pay back   79 *bravery* bravado   87 *mess* table   87 *chough*
jackdaw (here, chatterer)   88 *spacious* well off   96 *complexion* temperament   103 *differences*
distinguishing characteristics

ingly° of him, he is the card° or calendar of gentry; for you shall find in him the continent° of what part a gentleman would see.   105

Hamlet. Sir, his definement° suffers no perdition° in you, though, I know, to divide him inventorially would dozy° th' arithmetic of memory, and yet but yaw neither in respect of his quick sail.° But, in the verity of extolment, I take him to be a soul of great article,° and his infusion° of such dearth and rareness as, to make true diction° of him, his semblable° is his mirror,   110 and who else would trace him, his umbrage,° nothing more.

Osric. Your lordship speaks most infallibly of him.

Hamlet. The concernancy,° sir? Why do we wrap the gentleman in our more rawer breath?

Osric. Sir?

Horatio. Is't not possible to understand in another tongue? You will to't,°   115 sir, really.

Hamlet. What imports the nomination of this gentleman?

Osric. Of Laertes?

Horatio. [*Aside to Hamlet*] His purse is empty already. All's golden words are spent.

Hamlet. Of him, sir.

Osric. I know you are not ignorant——   120

Hamlet. I would you did, sir; yet, in faith, if you did, it would not much approve° me. Well, sir?

Osric. You are not ignorant of what excellence Laertes is——

Hamlet. I dare not confess that, lest I should compare with him in excellence; but to know a man well were to know himself.   125

Osric. I mean, sir, for his weapon; but in the imputation° laid on him by them, in his meed° he's unfellowed.

Hamlet. What's his weapon?

Osric. Rapier and dagger.

Hamlet. That's two of his weapons—but well.   130

Osric. The King, sir, hath wagered with him six Barbary horses, against the which he has impawned,° as I take it, six French rapiers and poniards, with their assigns,° as girdle, hangers,° and so. Three of the carriages,° in faith, are very dear to fancy, very responsive° to the hilts, most delicate carriages, and of very liberal conceit.°   135

Hamlet. What call you the carriages?

----

104 *feelingly* justly   104 *card* chart   105 *continent* summary   106 *definement* description   106 *perdition* loss   107 *dozy* dizzy   107–108 *and yet . . . quick sail* i.e., and yet only stagger despite all (*yaw neither*) in trying to overtake his virtues   109 *article* (literally, "item," but here perhaps "traits" or "importance")   109 *infusion* essential quality   110 *diction* description   110 *semblable* likeness   111 *umbrage* shadow   113 *concernancy* meaning   115 *will to't* will get there   122 *approve* commend   126 *imputation* reputation   127 *meed* merit   132 *impawned* wagered   133 *assigns* accompaniments   133 *hangers* straps hanging the sword to the belt   133 *carriages* (an affected word for hangers)   134 *responsive* corresponding   135 *liberal conceit* elaborate design

Horatio. [*Aside to Hamlet*] I knew you must be edified by the margent° ere
you had done.

Osric. The carriages, sir, are the hangers.

Hamlet. The phrase would be more germane to the matter if we could carry
a cannon by our sides. I would it might be hangers till then. But on! Six 140
Barbary horses against six French swords, their assigns, and three liberal-
conceited carriages—that's the French bet against the Danish. Why is this
all impawned, as you call it?

Osric. The King, sir, hath laid, sir, that in a dozen passes between yourself
and him he shall not exceed you three hits; he hath laid on twelve for 145
nine, and it would come to immediate trial if your lordship would vouchsafe the answer.

Hamlet. How if I answer no?

Osric. I mean, my lord, the opposition of your person in trial.

Hamlet. Sir, I will walk here in the hall. If it please his Majesty, it is the
breathing time of day with me.° Let the foils be brought, the gentleman 150
willing, and the King hold his purpose, I will win for him an I can; if not,
I will gain nothing but my shame and the odd hits.

Osric. Shall I deliver you e'en so?

Hamlet. To this effect, sir, after what flourish your nature will.

Osric. I commend my duty to your lordship. 155

Hamlet. Yours, yours. [*Exit Osric.*] He does well to commend it himself;
there are no tongues else for's turn.

Horatio. This lapwing° runs away with the shell on his head.

Hamlet. 'A did comply, sir, with his dug° before 'a sucked it. Thus has he,
and many more of the same breed that I know the drossy age dotes on, 160
only got the tune of the time and, out of an habit of encounter,° a kind
of yeasty° collection, which carries them through and through the most
fanned and winnowed opinions; and do but blow them to their trial, the
bubbles are out.°

Enter a Lord.

Lord. My lord, his Majesty commended him to you by young Osric, who 165
brings back to him that you attend him in the hall. He sends to know if
your pleasure hold to play with Laertes, or that you will take longer time.

Hamlet. I am constant to my purposes; they follow the King's pleasure. If
his fitness speaks, mine is ready; now or whensoever, provided I be so able
as now.

---

137 *margent* i.e., marginal (explanatory) comment   150 *breathing time of day with me* time
when I take exercise   158 *lapwing* (the new-hatched lapwing was thought to run around with half
its shell on its head)   159 *'A did comply, sir, with his dug* he was ceremoniously polite to his
mother's breast   161 *out of an habit of encounter* out of his own superficial way of meeting and
conversing with people   162 *yeasty* frothy   164 *the bubbles are out* i.e., they are blown away
(the reference is to the "yeasty collection")

Lord. The King and Queen and all are coming down.   170

Hamlet. In happy time.

Lord. The Queen desires you to use some gentle entertainment° to Laertes
before you fall to play.

Hamlet. She well instructs me.

[*Exit Lord.*]

Horatio. You will lose this wager, my lord.   175

Hamlet. I do not think so. Since he went into France I have been in continual
practice. I shall win at the odds. But thou wouldst not think how ill all's
here about my heart. But it is no matter.

Horatio. Nay, good my lord—

Hamlet. It is but foolery, but it is such a kind of gaingiving° as would perhaps 180
trouble a woman.

Horatio. If your mind dislike anything, obey it. I will forestall their repair
hither and say you are not fit.

Hamlet. Not a whit, we defy augury. There is special providence in the fall
of a sparrow.° If it be now, 'tis not to come; if it be not to come, it will
be now; if it be not now, yet it will come. The readiness is all. Since no
man of aught he leaves knows, what is't to leave betimes?° Let be.   185

*A table prepared. [Enter] Trumpets, Drums, and Officers with cushions;
King, Queen, [Osric,] and all the State, [with] foils, daggers, [and stoups
of wine borne in]; and Laertes.*

King. Come, Hamlet, come, and take this hand from me.

[*The King puts Laertes' hand into Hamlet's.*]

Hamlet. Give me your pardon, sir. I have done you wrong,
But pardon't, as you are a gentleman.
This presence° knows, and you must needs have heard,
How I am punished with a sore distraction.   190
What I have done
That might your nature, honor, and exception°
Roughly awake, I here proclaim was madness.
Was't Hamlet wronged Laertes? Never Hamlet.
If Hamlet from himself be ta'en away,   195
And when he's not himself does wrong Laertes,
Then Hamlet does it not, Hamlet denies it.
Who does it then? His madness. If't be so,

---

172 *to use some gentle entertainment* to be courteous   180 *gaingiving* misgiving   182–83 *the
fall of a sparrow* (cf. Matthew 10:29 "Are not two sparrows sold for a farthing? and one of them
shall not fall on the ground without your Father")   185 *betimes* early   189 *presence* royal
assembly   192 *exception* disapproval

Hamlet is of the faction° that is wronged;
His madness is poor Hamlet's enemy.   200
Sir, in this audience,
Let my disclaiming from a purposed evil
Free me so far in your most generous thoughts
That I have shot my arrow o'er the house
And hurt my brother.
Laertes.   I am satisfied in nature,   205
Whose motive in this case should stir me most
To my revenge. But in my terms of honor
I stand aloof, and will no reconcilement
Till by some elder masters of known honor
I have a voice and precedent° of peace   210
To keep my name ungored. But till that time
I do receive your offered love like love,
And will not wrong it.
Hamlet.   I embrace it freely,
And will this brother's wager frankly play.
Give us the foils. Come on.
Laertes.   Come, one for me.   215
Hamlet. I'll be your foil,° Laertes. In mine ignorance
Your skill shall, like a star i' th' darkest night,
Stick fiery off° indeed.
Laertes.   You mock me, sir.
Hamlet. No, by this hand.
King. Give them the foils, young Osric. Cousin Hamlet,   220
You know the wager?
Hamlet.   Very well, my lord.
Your grace has laid the odds o' th' weaker side.
King. I do not fear it, I have seen you both;
But since he is bettered,° we have therefore odds.
Laertes. This is too heavy; let me see another.   225
Hamlet. This likes me well. These foils have all a length?

Prepare to play.

Osric. Ay, my good lord.
King. Set me the stoups of wine upon that table.
If Hamlet give the first or second hit,
Or quit° in answer of the third exchange,   230

---

199 *faction* party, side   210 *voice and precedent* authoritative opinion justified by precedent
216 *foil* (1) blunt sword (2) background (of metallic leaf) for a jewel   218 *Stick fiery off* stand out
brilliantly   214 *bettered* has improved (in France)   230 *quit* repay, hit back

Let all the battlements their ordnance fire.
The King shall drink to Hamlet's better breath,
And in the cup an union° shall he throw
Richer than that which four successive kings
In Denmark's crown have worn. Give me the cups,   235
And let the kettle° to the trumpet speak,
The trumpet to the cannoneer without,
The cannons to the heavens, the heaven to earth,
"Now the King drinks to Hamlet." Come, begin.

                                              Trumpets the while.

And you, the judges, bear a wary eye.   240
Hamlet. Come on, sir.
Laertes.   Come, my lord.

                                                       They play.

Hamlet.   One.
Laertes.   No.
Hamlet.   Judgment?
Osric. A hit, a very palpable hit.

                  Drum, trumpets, and shot. Flourish; a piece goes off.
Laertes.   Well, again.
King. Stay, give me drink. Hamlet, this pearl is thine.
   Here's to thy health. Give him the cup.
Hamlet. I'll play this bout first; set it by awhile.   245
   Come. [*They play.*] Another hit. What say you?
Laertes. A touch, a touch; I do confess't.
King. Our son shall win.
Queen.   He's fat,° and scant of breath.
   Here, Hamlet, take my napkin, rub thy brows.
   The Queen carouses to thy fortune, Hamlet.   250
Hamlet. Good madam!
King.   Gertrude, do not drink.
Queen. I will, my lord; I pray you pardon me. [*Drinks.*]
King. [*Aside*] It is the poisoned cup; it is too late.
Hamlet. I dare not drink yet, madam—by and by.
Queen. Come, let me wipe thy face.   255
Laertes. My lord, I'll hit him now.
King.   I do not think't.
Laertes. [*Aside*] And yet it is almost against my conscience.
Hamlet. Come for the third, Laertes. You do but dally.
   I pray you pass with your best violence;
   I am sure you make a wanton° of me.   260

---

   233 *union* pearl   236 *kettle* kettledrum   248 *fat* (1) sweaty (2) out of training   260 *wanton*
spoiled child

Laertes. Say you so? Come on.   *[They] play.*
Osric. Nothing neither way.
Laertes. Have at you now!

In scuffling they change rapiers, [and both are wounded].

King. Part them. They are incensed.
Hamlet. Nay, come—again!   *[The Queen falls.]* 265
Osric. Look to the Queen there, ho!
Horatio. They bleed on both sides. How is it, my lord?
Osric. How is't, Laertes?
Laertes. Why, as a woodcock to mine own springe,° Osric.
    I am justly killed with mine own treachery.   270
Hamlet. How does the Queen?
King.   She sounds° to see them bleed.
Queen. No, no, the drink, the drink! O my dear Hamlet!
    The drink, the drink! I am poisoned.   *[Dies.]*
Hamlet. O villainy! Ho! Let the door be locked.
    Treachery! Seek it out.   *[Laertes falls.]* 275
Laertes. It is here, Hamlet. Hamlet, thou art slain;
    No med'cine in the world can do thee good.
    In thee there is not half an hour's life.
    The treacherous instrument is in thy hand,
    Unbated and envenomed. The foul practice°   280
    Hath turned itself on me. Lo, here I lie,
    Never to rise again. Thy mother's poisoned.
    I can no more. The King, the King's to blame.
Hamlet. The point envenomed too?
    Then, venom, to thy work.   *Hurts the King.* 285
All. Treason! Treason!
King. O, yet defend me, friends. I am but hurt.
Hamlet. Here, thou incestuous, murd'rous, damnèd Dane,
    Drink off this potion. Is thy union here?
    Follow my mother.

                                        King dies.

Laertes.   He is justly served.   290
    It is a poison tempered° by himself.
    Exchange forgiveness with me, noble Hamlet.
    Mine and my father's death come not upon thee,
    Nor thine on me!   *Dies.*
Hamlet. Heaven make thee free of it! I follow thee.
    I am dead, Horatio. Wretched Queen, adieu!

---

269 *springe* snare   271 *sounds* swoons   280 *practice* deception   291 *tempered* mixed

You that look pale and tremble at this chance,
That are but mutes° or audience to this act,
Had I but time (as this fell sergeant,° Death,
Is strict in his arrest) O, I could tell you—   300
But let it be. Horatio, I am dead;
Thou livest; report me and my cause aright
To the unsatisfied.°
Horatio.   Never believe it.
I am more an antique Roman° than a Dane.
Here's yet some liquor left.
Hamlet.   As th' art a man,   305
Give me the cup. Let go. By heaven, I'll ha't!
O God, Horatio, what a wounded name,
Things standing thus unknown, shall live behind me!
If thou didst even hold me in thy heart,
Absent thee from felicity° awhile,   310
And in this harsh world draw thy breath in pain,
To tell my story.
                              A march afar off. [*Exit Osric.*]
                    What warlike noise is this?
                                             Enter Osric.
Osric. Young Fortinbras, with conquest come from Poland,
To th' ambassadors of England gives
This warlike volley.
Hamlet.   O, I die, Horatio!   315
The potent poison quite o'ercrows° my spirit.
I cannot live to hear the news from England,
But I do prophesy th' election lights
On Fortinbras. He has my dying voice.
So tell him, with th' occurrents,° more and less,   320
Which have solicited°—the rest is silence.   *Dies.*
Horatio. Now cracks a noble heart. Good night, sweet Prince,
And flights of angels sing thee to thy rest.
                                             [*March within.*]
Why does the drum come hither?

Enter Fortinbras, with the Ambassadors with Drum, Colors, and Atten-
dants.

Fortinbras. Where is this sight?

---

298 *mutes* performers who have no words to speak   299 *fell sergeant* dread sheriff's officer
303 *unsatisfied* uninformed   304 *antique Roman* (with reference to the old Roman fashion of
suicide)   310 *felicity* i.e., the felicity of death   316 *o'ercrows* overpowers (as a triumphant cock
crows over its weak opponent)   320 *occurrents* occurrences   321 *solicited* incited

Horatio.   What is it you would see?   325
  If aught of woe or wonder, cease your search.
Fortinbras. This quarry° cries on havoc.° O proud Death,
  What feast is toward° in thine eternal cell
  That thou so many princes at a shot
  So bloodily hast struck?
Ambassador.   The sight is dismal;   330
  And our affairs from England come too late.
  The ears are senseless that should give us hearing
  To tell him his commandment is fulfilled,
  That Rosencrantz and Guildenstern are dead.
  Where should we have our thanks?
Horatio.   Not from his° mouth,   335
  Had it th' ability of life to thank you.
  He never gave commandment for their death.
  But since, so jump° upon this bloody question,
  You from the Polack wars, and you from England,
  Are here arrived, give order that these bodies   340
  High on a stage° be placèd to the view,
  And let me speak to th' yet unknowing world
  How these things came about. So shall you hear
  Of carnal, bloody, and unnatural acts,
  Of accidental judgments, casual° slaughters,   345
  Of deaths put on by cunning and forced cause,
  And, in this upshot, purposes mistook
  Fall'n on th' inventors' heads. All this can I
  Truly deliver.
Fortinbras.   Let us haste to hear it,   350
  And call the noblest to the audience.
  For me, with sorrow I embrace my fortune.
  I have some rights of memory° in this kingdom,
  Which now to claim my vantage doth invite me.
Horatio. Of that I shall have also cause to speak,   355
  And from his mouth whose voice will draw on° more.
  But let this same be presently performed,
  Even while men's minds are wild, lest more mischance
  On° plots and errors happen.
Fortinbras.   Let four captains
  Bear Hamlet like a soldier to the stage,   360

---

  327 *quarry* heap of slain bodies   327 *cries on havoc* proclaims general slaughter   328 *toward*
in preparation   335 *his* (Claudius')   338 *jump* precisely   341 *stage* platform   345 *casual* not
humanly planned, chance   353 *rights of memory* remembered claims   356 *voice will draw on*
vote will influence   359 *On* on top of

For he was likely, had he been put on,°
To have proved most royal; and for his passage°
The soldiers' music and the rite of war
Speak loudly for him.
Take up the bodies. Such a sight as this   365
Becomes the field,° but here shows much amiss.
Go, bid the soldiers shoot.

Exeunt marching; after the which a peal of ordnance are shot off.
FINIS

QUESTIONS

1. Has any earlier reading of a Shakespeare play been helpful to you with this one?
2. After reading Act I, what sense do you have of the relations among people at the Danish court?
3. Shakespeare's first audience probably relished the ghost scenes of Act I. How do you respond to them?
4. What details give you the strongest sense of Hamlet as a young man? Does anything suggest how he experiences his youth?
5. What seem to be the outstanding traits of Hamlet's character? Do you deduce these from what he says or does or from what the others say about him?
6. Why does the duty to avenge his father pose such a dilemma for him? Does it appear to change him in any way—apart from his acting mad to disguise his purposes?
7. How important does Ophelia seem to be to the play?
8. Do you suppose your sense of Claudius differs from Hamlet's view of the King, as the play proceeds? Explain.
9. How surprised are you by Laertes's readiness to kill Hamlet with a poisoned foil?
10. Since Hamlet has a premonition of his own death, why isn't he more cautious about the invitation to "play" with Laertes? What is Hamlet's mood in the last scene? To what extent is his death a defeat by the power of evil?

---

361 *put on* advanced (to the throne)   362 *passage* death   366 *field* battlefield

Megan Terry (b. 1932)

THE GLOAMING, OH MY DARLING
For My Grandmothers

PRODUCTION NOTES

There is no need for the actresses to be old. Any age will do. If the actresses cannot do a successful Irish accent, they should use whatever they are successful at. The accents of their mothers or grandmothers, or the accent of their native regions. No agony or time should be spent on the technical aspect of this—dwell on the relationships in the play—the relationships of the women to one another, to themselves, to their families, their country, to the past and future.

The scenery can be only two cots, or a nearly complete nursing-home room. If real hospital beds can be used, there is a way of cranking them so that Mr. Birdsong is completely hidden from the audience until he springs from the bed. This is fun, but it isn't necessary to the play.

The transitions should flow one into the other without pause or marking of any kind. The time slides in and out, and the final result should be that it is all the same time. The time can be compressed or extended, but it is all the same time. The intent is to see two lifetimes and certain aspects of the life of a country in one concentrated look.

The backbone of the play is the embrace of life, no matter how little of it is left.

(Two women sit on two chairs in a nursing home. There are two beds in the small sunny room. One of the beds is occupied, but the sheet and blanket are drawn up over the head of the occupant. The two old women speak in Irish accents.)

Mrs. Tweed. Ah yes, Mrs. Watermellon, and the days go by and the days go by and the days go by and the days go by, and by and by the days go by. My God, how the days go by!

Mrs. Watermellon. From where I sit . . . I have to agree with you. But they don't go fast enough by, Mrs. Tweed, not by a half sight, not by a full sight. The world is waiting for the sunrise, and I'm the only one who knows where it begins.

Mrs. Tweed. Why do you keep it a secret?

Mrs. Watermellon. No secret. I've told everyone. I've told and told and told everyone.

Mrs. Tweed. Where does it begin then?

Mrs. Watermellon (Slapping her breast). Here. Right here. Right here it starts! From the old ticker it starts and pumps around and thumps around, co-agulates in my belly and once a month bursts out onto the ground . . . but all the color's gone . . . all but one . . . all but . . . one. . . .

Mrs. Tweed. So that's where the sunrise went.

Mrs. Watermellon. You three-minute egg. You runny, puny twelve week's old, three-minute egg. You're underdone and overripe. What do you know? You only learned to speak when you got mad enough . . . I'm going to sleep. I'd as soon live in the mud with the turtles as to have to converse with the likes of you.

Mrs. Tweed. Don't talk like that. That hurts me.

Mrs. Watermellon. Nothing can hurt you if your mind is on a high plain.

Mrs. Tweed. If you go to sleep on me, then I'll let him go.

Mrs. Watermellon. If you let him go, Mrs. Tweed, then I'll tell you where your daughter is.

Mrs. Tweed. I won't listen.

Mrs. Watermellon. Oh yes, you'll listen. You'll listen to me tell you where she is. It makes you cry and you hate to cry. But once you get started crying you wake up everyone, and then they'll give you an enema.

Mrs. Tweed. I don't care if they do. There's nothing more to come out. They've tubed, and they've squirted, and they've radiated and they've intravened . . . There's nothing more to come out of me. I haven't had reason to pick my nose in two years.

Mrs. Watermellon. Do you think he's awake yet?

Mrs. Tweed. Mrs. Watermellon, what if someone comes to visit him?

Mrs. Watermellon. I won't let them see him.

Mrs. Tweed. You have to let them see him if they're his folks.

Mrs. Watermellon. Nope, you dope, I don't.

Mrs. Tweed. You do have to let folks see him. What else would folks be coming up here for, if not to see him.

Mrs. Watermellon. Perhaps he's passed on—passed over. I'll say he's gone West. ANYWAY, Mrs. Tweed, he's mine now.

Mrs. Tweed. Why, he's ours, Mrs. Watermellon. You can't have him all to yourself!

Mrs. Watermellon. That's what I did in the night. I DIDN'T want you to find out, but since I see what a busybody you finally are, after all these bygone days, I'll tell you once and for all. He's mine!

Mrs. Tweed. But we got him together. I carried the bottom end. You weak old tub, you couldn't even have lifted him from his bed by yourself. You'd have dropped and broken him. They'd have put us in jail for stealing and murder. They'd have electrocuted and hung us . . . they'd have . . .

Mrs. Watermellon. Hush your mouth! Hush up. I won't have him disturbed by your temper.

Mrs. Tweed. I'm going to give him back. Tonight I'll carry him back to the men's ward and tuck him in his crib.

Mrs. Watermellon. No, you won't. He's mine.

Mrs. Tweed. Ours.

Mrs. Watermellon. Mine.

Mrs. Tweed. Ours . . .

Mrs. Watermellon. All right. All right, you pukey squashed robins egg, all right! All right, all right, you leftover maggot mangy mop rag. All right! All right, you dried-up, old snot rag, I'm going to tell you, I'M GOING TO TELL you right here and now. Do you hear me? I'm going to tell you right here and now.

Mrs. Tweed. I don't want to hear. Not here. Not now.

Voice (A recorded voice of a young woman sings. WATERMELLON *and* TWEED *freeze in their places during the song).*[1]

> "In the gloaming, oh my darling,
> When the lights are soft and low,
> Will you think of me and love me
> As you did once long ago?"

Mrs. Watermellon (Coming back to life). I'm hungry for canned rhubarb! Never did get enough. My greedy little sister used to get up in the night when we's all asleep and sneak down to the fruit cellar and eat two quarts of rhubarb, every single night.

Mrs. Tweed. She must a had the cleanest bowels in the whole country.

Mrs. Watermellon. My mother had the best dinner. For her last birthday two days before she died my brother asked her what she wanted. She knew it was her last supper.

Mrs. Tweed. Chicken baked in cream in the oven?

Mrs. Watermellon. Nope, you dope. Pheasant she wanted. Cherrystone clams, six of them, roast pheasant and wild-blackberry pie. She ate every bit of it. We watched her. She ate it all up, every speck of it. Cherrystone clams, six of them, roast pheasant, and wild-blackberry pie. Licked her lips.

Mrs. Tweed. That rings a bell. I had pheasant once. Pheasant under glass. Looked so pretty, I didn't eat it. Where was that?

Mrs. Watermellon. You had it at the old Biltmore. She licked her lips and closed her eyes. She never opened them again.

Mrs. Tweed. That rings a bell. Who'd I have it with? Did I taste it? Under a lovely glass bell. Who was I with?

Mrs. Watermellon. You were with your husband, Mrs. Tweed. Your second husband. You did that on your anniversary. On your wedding anniversary, you dope. You've told me every one of your anniversary stories five hundred times a year.

Mrs. Tweed (Laughs). It's gone from me. All gone from me. Fancy that, but it does ring a bell.

Mrs. Watermellon. You can eat mushrooms under glass too. Don't you know?

---

[1]"In the Gloaming" is a song written c. 1875 by Annie Fortescue Harrison and Meta Orred. 'Gloaming,' originally Scottish dialect, means evening dusk, or twilight.

Mrs. Tweed. Myrtle Classen used to serve them at her bridge luncheons. Mushrooms, under glass. I didn't eat any of those either.

Mrs. Watermellon. What have you done with him, Mrs. Tweed?

Mrs. Tweed. I made him even.

Mrs. Watermellon. WHAT have you done with him?

Mrs. Tweed. What'll you give me if I tell, Mrs. Watermellon?

Mrs. Watermellon. Tell.

Mrs. Tweed. Give.

Mrs. Watermellon. Tell.

Mrs. Tweed. Give.

Mrs. Watermellon. Tell, tell.

Mrs. Tweed. Give, give.

Mrs. Watermellon. Tell, tell, tell!

Mrs. Tweed. Give, give, give!

Mrs. Watermellon (Melting). I give.

Mrs. Tweed. All up?

Mrs. Watermellon. All.

Mrs. Tweed. Say it. Say it all, Mrs. Watermellon.

Mrs. Watermellon. I give it all up. I give it all up to my uncle. My uncle. Uncle.

Mrs. Tweed. Who is he? Who is he, your uncle, uncle?

Mrs. Watermellon (Exhausted). You are. You . . . are . . . Mrs. Tweed.

Mrs. Tweed. Then you've got to tell me what you did to Mr. Birdsong in the night.

Mrs. Watermellon. Now?

Mrs. Tweed. Not a moment too late.

Mrs. Watermellon. I . . . I married him. I married Mr. Birdsong.

Mrs. Tweed. No.

Mrs. Watermellon. In the night, I lifted the covers from his body and I married him. Mrs. Birdsong. Mrs.

Mrs. Tweed. But he was ours. We brought him here together.

Mrs. Watermellon. In the night . . .

Mrs. Tweed. It isn't fair. You didn't do it fair. He was . . .

Mrs. Watermellon. I didn't want to do it, because we've been such good, such only friends. But I didn't want to tell you 'cause I don't want you to stop rubbing my back on rainy days. I didn't want to tell you because I didn't want you to stop cleaning my nails on Sunday mornings. I didn't want to tell you because you eat those hard-cooked carrots for me on Wednesday nights. I didn't want to tell you 'cause you rub a nipple and make me feel sweet sixteen when we play boy friends. I didn't want to tell you because you're all I've got . . . you're all I've been given in this last twenty years. You're all I've seen in this never-never. I didn't want to tell you because you're the only one who can see *me.* I didn't want to tell you because you were all I had. But now I've got Mr. Birdsong. Mr. and Mrs. Birdsong.

Mrs. Tweed. Don't tell me that. You shouldn't have told me that.

Mrs. Watermellon. And you don't even know any good lifetime stories. I've been shut up with a life that never moved at all. The only thing you can remember is how . . .

Mrs. Tweed. . . . Is how I rode out in the Maine snow night with my DOCTOR Father and he held his fur-coat arms around me on his horse and I sat in front of him with his fur-coat arms around me and I held his scratched and leather smelly doctor's bag. Held it tight so's not to drop it in the Maine snow night.

Mrs. Watermellon. That's what I mean, just one sentimental perversion after another.

Mrs. Tweed. There's nothing perverted about father love.

Mrs. Watermellon. There is if there's something perverted about Father.

Mrs. Tweed. Who?

Mrs. Watermellon. You. You. You, Mrs. Tweed.

Mrs. Tweed (Trying to rise). That did it. That did it. That just about did it in, all right.

Mrs. Watermellon. Sit down, you old windbag.

Mrs. Tweed. That did it. That did it, Mrs. Watermellon. That just about did it in, all right.

Mrs. Watermellon. Sit down, you old battle-ax.

Mrs. Tweed (On a rising scale). That did it. That did it. That just about did it. That did it all right.

Mrs. Watermellon. Sit down, you old blister.

Mrs. Tweed (She bursts). THAT DID IT! (*She explodes into a convulsive dance. She sings. As she sings her accent disappears*)

> That's done it, that's better.
> That's done it,
> What ease.
> That's done it,
> That's better.
> What took you so long,
> You tease?

Mrs. Watermellon. Don't leave me. I forbid you to go. Don't leave me, Tweed. Come back. Don't leave me here alone with a man.

Mrs. Tweed (She dances herself down to the age of sixteen). I'm so tired. I'm so tired and so done in. We drank and drank so much grape punch and then that gentle Keith Lewiston took me behind the schoolhouse and you know what he did?

Mrs. Watermellon. He hitched you to his buggy and drove you round the yard.

Mrs. Tweed (Embracing her). He soul kissed me. He kissed my soul. Like this.

Mrs. Watermellon. (*Dodges*) Don't start that mush again.

Mrs. Tweed. (*Still sixteen*) He kissed my soul. Like this. (*She plants a kiss finally on Mrs. Watermellon's neck.*)

Mrs. Watermellon (*She starts to howl in pain, but the howl changes to a kind of gargle and then to a girlish laugh. Her accent leaves also*). Did it make a strawberry? Did you make me a strawberry on my neck? (*Now Mrs. Watermellon is also sixteen.*) Do it again and make a big red strawberry mark. Then we'll have to wear long scarves around our necks, to school, but everyone will know why. They'll think the boys kissed us behind the schoolhouse. Is it red yet? Is it strawberry red yet?

Mrs. Tweed (*Coming back to old age, she knots an imaginary scarf around Mrs. Watermellon's neck and her Irish accent returns*). No—not—yet.

Mrs. Watermellon (*Chokes and laughs as if strangling*). Don't. We're friends. We're best friends. We're girl friends. (*Her Irish accent returns.*) Don't kill me. I'm your mother.

Mrs. Tweed. Save all that for Doctor. I'm on to you. Your smart-assed psycho—hology won't work on me any more. Save it for Mr. Birdsong. If you can find him.

Mrs. Watermellon. What have you done with him?

Mrs. Tweed. Wouldn't you like to know?

Mrs. Watermellon. What have you done with him? What have you done with my . . .

Mrs. Tweed. Your what?

Mr. Birdsong (*He's still in a coma, but speaks out in a voice like W.C. Fields*). Stuck with the cattle through the storm. Dust blew so hard couldn't see yer hand in front of yer face. Twister blew us five hundred miles. Caught us in Illinois and set us down in Nebraska. Dust blew bad, but I never lost a head nor did I even stop to make water.

Mrs. Watermellon. I'm tired of trying to keep alive.

Mrs. Tweed. We'll get off the shelf.

Mrs. Watermellon. Canned beside the hybrid corn.

Mrs. Tweed. And the pickles.

Mrs. Watermellon. And the piccalilli.

Mrs. Tweed. And the bread and butters.

Mrs. Watermellon. Apple butter.

Mrs. Tweed. Watermelon relish.

Mr. Birdsong. We kept right on putting our lives on the line because some fool gave the order.

Mrs. Watermellon. Found a family. All I wanted was to found a great family.

Mrs. Tweed. I worked hard. The wire factory gave me a good pension. I could still run up and down ladders as good as the men.

Mr. Birdsong. The heathens want ours. They've infiltrated us in plain clothes. The heathen emissaries of Satan want to sabotage us. Scorch that earth, boys. That's the ticket. I want to get back to my bride.

Mrs. Tweed. No one cares what we do now, Mrs. Watermellon, we can share him. We can both be Mrs. Birdsongs. The Mormons done it and God didn't get mad at them.

Mrs. Watermellon. In the night I climbed into his bed and married him.

Mrs. Tweed (Begins to cry very quietly). No. No. No. I can't believe it. You promised we'd share him. And to think I trusted you. And to think I loved you like a dear sister. And to think I gave you all my tender feelings for all these whitehouse years. AND TO THINK . . . and to . . .

Mrs. Watermellon. Stop that yipping. It's your own fault. You left me all alone in the night. You went to sleep. You didn't keep watch. You turned out the light and went to sleep. They'd have shot you for that in World War I. You stopped guarding. I had to marry someone! I can't die childless. I refuse!

Mrs. Tweed. Impossible! You have eleven children living, forty-nine grandchildren living, twenty great grandchildren living and three on the way. There's a lot of biscuit in your oven, and your ovens' ovens.

Mrs. Watermellon. I just wanted to make it even with you. You had two husbands, you, you white and wizened shrimp. Two husbands! You knew two cocks of the walk in your time. Why should I take a back seat? Why should you know more than me?

Mrs. Tweed. Is that your fountain of knowledge? I'll never get over this. Never, never. After all the friends we've been through. I'm going to divorce you.

Mrs. Watermellon. I don't care. I'm a newlywed. I have security.

Mrs. Tweed. I'll say! There's nothing more secure than a coma. HE'S BEEN IN THAT COMA FOR EIGHTY DAYS.

Mrs. Watermellon. It'll make our adjustment easier.

Mrs. Tweed. Adjustment?

Mrs. Watermellon (Inordinately satisfied). To married life. Since only one of us has to change his ways, we should become compatible twice as fast.

Mrs. Tweed (Very formal). Mrs. Watermellon, I'm going to ring for the nurse to change my room.

Mrs. Watermellon (Equally formal). Mrs. Tweed, you better ring for the nurse to change your pants. See there, you've messed again.

Mrs. Tweed. You're fooling me.

Mrs. Watermellon. Maybe I am fooling you, but Mother Nature isn't. Ring for the nurse. Ring, ring, ring, ring, ring, ring. Tick a lock, this is a magic spot.

Mrs. Tweed. Don't be mad to me any more.

Mrs. Watermellon. Tick a lock, this is a magic spot.

Mrs. Tweed. Don't be mad to me any more.

Mr. Birdsong. Everywhere you look there's busloads of foreigners. Rats are infiltrating our ranks.

Mrs. Tweed. I hear a man's voice. Listen. Did you hear it?

Mrs. Watermellon. It's your longing. Your longing rising up and talking to you.

Mrs. Tweed. Sounds like my granddad. Just like him when he come back from the war.

Mrs. Watermellon. I don't hear anything but your heart ticks getting fainter and fainter.

Mrs. Tweed. Don't be so nice to me. You know I'm going to die, that's why you're so nice to me.

Mrs. Watermellon. Nonsense. You're not leaving before me. You're not leaving me alone in this hotel.

Mr. Birdsong (MRS. TWEED *and* MRS. WATERMELLON *don't react to* MR. BIRDSONG *when he rises from bed.* BIRDSONG *rises from his bed and stalks around the room, mounts a box to harangue the crowd—his voice now sounds like Teddy Roosevelt*). As U.S. veteran of the Indian Wars, I've come here before you to alarm you. Sons of Liberty unite. Smash the rats of the world. We must cut off their bloody hands. They're bringing this land that I love to wreck and ruin. Wreck and ruin to our God-given America. Murderers of women and children, red rats making balcony speeches. Balcony speeches by the feeble-minded mockers of God. That's the stink of Satan, boys. The stink of the murderers of Americans. The stink smelled is the stink from Satan. Satan who uses the body as a house to live in. The stink of Satan once smelled coming from these bodies is never forgotten. They want to make the United States and Mexico and Canada and Alaska into a death trap. Declare war on these stinking infiltrators. They've made it easy to burn up American bodies in the fiery furnaces of every hospital and prison. American Veterans of foreign wars, boys. Unite to fight. Unite to fight before they drug every one of us with their poisoned needles. Every man has been sexually destroyed by the needle while asleep. Fight the needle, boys. Don't let them burn up our unborn children. Why was Roosevelt murdered? Why was Kennedy murdered? Why was Stevenson[2] murdered? The rat bonecrushers of the world are out to get us, all us American Veterans captive in these hospital jails. Unite to fight the rats, boys. Unite to fight the rats. (*He returns to his bed and his coma.*)

Voice (*The woman's voice is heard again*).

> "In the gloaming, oh my darling,
> When the lights are soft and low,
> Will you think of me and love me
> As you did once long ago?"

Mrs. Watermellon. I love President Kennedy.

Mrs. Tweed. Makes you feel good just to look at him.

---

[2]Probably Adlai Stevenson (1900–1965), Democratic presidential candidate in 1952 and 1956, although his grandfather, also Adlai Stevenson (1835–1914), was Vice-President (1893–1897). Neither Stevenson was murdered; nor was either President Roosevelt.

Nurse (*Enters with a fixed smile.* MRS. TWEED *and* MRS. WATERMELLON *rush to hide the man. They both get on the bed and spread their nightgowns over him. They lapse into their oldest age*). All right, you two—smarten up and look alive. (*She manhandles them—pushing and pulling them into some sort of erect state. They fall back to position like rag dolls—half cackling and half gurgling.*) I said look alive! You're going to have a visit. Your families have come to pay their monthly respects. Look alive, I said, or they'll think we're not taking good care of you.

Mrs. Watermellon (*Frightened of the* NURSE). This woman's molesting me.

Nurse. Hold your head up so I can get some rouge on that pasty cheek.

Mrs. Watermellon. This woman is molesting me.

Nurse. Hold still, you old hag. I got to get some life in your face.

Mrs. Watermellon. I'll tell Dr. Sam on you and Dr. Ben and Dr. Jim, too, and God and everybody.

Nurse (*To* MRS. TWEED). Your turn now, you little old crab.

Mrs. Tweed (*Playfully*). What'll you give me if I let ya?

Nurse. Dirty-minded old ladies. If your family could only hear you.

Mr. Birdsong (*Under the ladies, belches*). I rode five hundred miles with my cattle in the dust storm and never stopped once to make water. (WATER-MELLON *mouths the lines.*)

Nurse. Who said that?

Mrs. Tweed. She did—she always brags about how strong she used to be.

Nurse. Show me a little strength now. Sit up and look out of your eyes.

(MRS. TWEED *bites the nurse; the* NURSE *slaps* TWEED.)

Nurse. Now there's some real color in your cheeks.

Mrs. Watermellon (*Howls*). This woman is molesting us! (*The family enters.*)

Nurse (*Like an overly cheerful demented Katherine Hepburn*). We're feeling very well today. We're glad to see our family today. (*She exits.*) Our family is glad to see us today.

Son Watermellon (*Accompanied by his Son and Daughter*). Mother! (*He goes to her, ultrabeaming.*) You look wonderful! Doesn't she look wonderful, kids?

Son and Daughter (*Flatly*). You look wonderful. Grandma, you look wonderful.

Mrs. Watermellon. Who's there? Is there anyone there? Knock once for yes.

Daughter Tweed (*Accompanied by her Son and Daughter, crosses to* MRS. TWEED). Oh, Mother, you look wonderful. Doesn't she look just wonderful kids? Tell Mother how wonderful she looks.

Son and Daughter (*Run at* TWEED). You look wonderful, Grandma—you look just wonderful. (*They climb all over her.*)

Mrs. Tweed (*Nearly suffocating*). My dear children—my pretty grandchildren. Grandma loves you so much.

Daughter Tweed (*As children swarm all over* TWEED, *kissing and pummeling her*). They love you so much, Mother. Isn't it wonderful for them that you're still alive?

Grandson and Granddaughter Tweed. You feel just wonderful, Grand-mother—just wonderful. (*They kiss and hug* TWEED *while she chokes and gasps.*)

Son Watermellon. Just sign right here, Mother. Here. I'll hold your hand around the pen.

Mrs. Watermellon. What is it? Who are you?

Son Watermellon. I'm so grateful you haven't lost your sense of humor. Mother, you look downright beautiful. Color in your cheeks and every-thing. This isn't such a bad place after all, is it?

Mrs. Watermellon (*Knocks once for yes*). You look a bit familiar around the eyes. I kept company with a young man once had shifty eyes kinda like yours.

Son Watermellon (*Laughs heartily*). Did you hear that, kids?

Kids (*Flat and bored*). Hear what, Father?

Son Watermelon. Same old doll. What a doll my dear old mother was and still is. Just like the gal that married dear old Dad.

Kids (*Flat*). Dear old shifty-eyed Dad.

Son Watermellon. Thanks for signing, honey-love. Makes it a lot easier for me now. Now look, sweetheart—you won't be seeing us for three months or so. Marge and the kids and I are going to Europe, but we'll send you a present from every port. How's about that? Give us a big smile and a kiss goodbye.

Mrs. Watermellon. Then will you go?

Son Watermellon (*Hurt*). Mother! I had to take a day off from work and the kids out of school to drive up here! Marge is stuck with booking the passage.

Mrs. Watermellon (*Turns off—sighs—lies back down*). I'll be all right. Don't worry about me.

Son Watermellon. Mother, don't be like this.

Mrs. Watermellon. Don't worry, son, I won't *be* for much longer.

Son Watermellon (*Kisses her on cheek*). Goodbye, old girl.

Kids. Goodbye, old girl. (*They exit.*)

Mrs. Watermellon. Is there anyone there?

Mrs. Tweed (*To* DAUGHTER). Dorothy, where's your sister, Laura?

Daughter Tweed. She isn't well, Mother. She has a bad cold. She was afraid she'd give it to you—and with your condition you know it could develop into pneumonia and you know . . . (*She makes an explosive gesture.*)

Mrs. Tweed. Well, tell her I thank her for her consideration but I'd like to see her face once in a while.

Daughter Tweed. Well, Mother, we got to be getting back, I guess—got the dogs and cats to feed.

Kids. They sure do get mad at us if they don't get their dinner on time.

Daughter Tweed. It sure was just wonderful to see you and see how good you look and how happy you look. That old lady who shares the room with you looks quiet and nice, too.

Mrs. Tweed. Dorothy—take me home.

Daughter Tweed. You know I'd love to, but you know what I'm up against with Harry.

Mrs. Tweed. Dorothy, your children tire me.

Daughter Tweed (Freezing up). Goodbye, Mother. I'll see you next month. I thought you'd want to see your own grandchildren.

Mrs. Tweed. I've seen enough.

Daughter Tweed (Gathering her children and leaving in a hurt rage). The sun always rose and set on Laura's head and it still does. And she hasn't been to see you in fifty years.

Mrs. Watermellon. Is there anyone here?

Mrs. Tweed. No, thank God. They've gone.

Mrs. Watermellon. They didn't take him?

Mrs. Tweed. I stopped them from it. I told them he'd eloped with a local tramp.

Mrs. Watermellon. Where is he now?

Mrs. Tweed. Under you, you old tub. I hope you haven't smothered him to death.

Mrs. Watermellon (Feeling Mr. Birdsong*).* Here's his head. *(She puts her ear to his chest.)* I hear a beat. Far away—a sweet little beat. *(She lifts the sheet and counts his arms.)* One, two. *(Counts his legs.)* One, two. *(Counts his sex.)* One, two, three. I'm glad it has a handle on it. My husband said he wouldn't accept the baby otherwise.

Mrs. Tweed. Let me see his tiny hands. Oh, oh, the fingernails! *(She kisses the fingernails of* Mr. Birdsong.*)*

Mrs. Watermellon. Why are you crying? A new baby should fill you with joy. Joy!

Mrs. Tweed. These fingernails. Look how tiny, the size of a pin head! And sharp! Oh, oh, the fingernails.

Mrs. Watermellon. God love him. A new life. God love it, God love it, God love it! *(She cuddles* Mr. Birdsong.*)*

Mrs. Tweed. God spelled backwards is dog.

Mrs. Watermellon. A son, a son, we have a son. A son from God. (Mr. Birdsong *gurgles like an infant.*)

Mrs. Tweed. Watch out for the teeth. They grow fast. My left nipple still carries a scar.

Mr. Birdsong. It was scorch the earth . . . scorch the earth of every village we took. After Lieutenant Pike[3] found his brother scalped and his guts strewn across the plain for the wolves to munch, we were ordered to cut down every peach tree, fill every irrigation ditch—burn every lodge and kill every horse, woman, and child of the Navaho.

---

[3]Probably Zebulon Pike (1779–1813), American explorer and army officer, who died in command of troops in the War of 1812.

Mrs. Watermellon. He'll make his mother proud.

Mrs. Tweed. My turn. (*She takes hold of* MR. BIRDSONG. MRS. WATERMEL-LON *holds on and glares.*). You act as if you did it all yourself.

Mrs. Watermellon. I did. It was my idea.

Mrs. Tweed. Not even you and forty million prayers could have raised him.

Mrs. Watermellon. It was my idea. All you were was a pair of arms.

Mrs. Tweed. And a good strong back—which you lack.

Mr. Birdsong (*A young officer returning to Illinois on leave*). Mother! (*To* MRS. WATERMELLON) It's fine to be home.

Mrs. Watermellon. You're thin.

Mr. Birdsong. Not for long. (*To* TWEED) And what have we here—grown up and pretty as a prairie flower.

Mrs. Tweed (*Shyly*). I can still whip you on a fair day, Elijah.

Mr. Birdsong (*Advancing confidently and taking her wrists*). 'Tis fair today, Susan.

Mrs. Tweed (*Wilts and nearly swoons*). Mrs. Watermellon, your son's forgot his manners!

Mrs. Watermellon. Lige! Leave go that gal or marry her.

Mr. Birdsong (*To* TWEED). I stayed with our cattle from here to Nebraska. It was the mightiest dust storm with twisters any man could remember. I rode five hundred miles without stopping to make water. I didn't lose a head. Marry me.

Mrs. Tweed. Marry me. Marry me. (*She goes into a slow-motion waltz with* BIRDSONG—MRS. WATERMELLON *joins them—while the voice of a woman sings a verse of* "In the Gloaming.")

Mr. Birdsong (*They are at a picnic on the grass*). I have my orders, gals— ship out tomorrow. I'll miss your pretty faces—let's have one last roll.

Mrs. Tweed and Mrs. Watermellon. You can't go, Donny—you've only been with us a week.

Mr. Birdsong. Case you didn't hear it, babes, there's a war on. I killed off more than my quota of Huns and now good Old Uncle's sending me against the slants. What a secret weapon to throw at the Japs.

Mrs. Tweed and Mrs. Watermellon (*Leap on him and roll him around in the grass, kissing and stroking him*). The lucky Japs. The lucky Japs. You come back to us, you big, big stud. You hear, you come back to us.

Mr. Birdsong. I rode all night, couldn't see a thing but I heard 'em. The dust so thick I couldn't make out the body of a single cow—but I felt 'em— five hundred miles into the twister and I never lost a head nor did I even stop to make water.

Mrs. Tweed. I go out of my mind over a man in uniform.

Mrs. Watermellon. I go into my mind with a man in my bed. (*She gets* MR. BIRDSONG *back to bed.*)

Mrs. Tweed. They'll catch you.

Mrs. Watermellon. If they catch me—they'll have you too.

Mr. Birdsong (*As he's being put to bed*). The Navaho all got up in their peaked plumed leather caps, blankets draped and heads held high—looked like a battalion of Roman Legionnaires. I felt time had slipped and slided and folded over—there I am in New Mexico fighting Roman warriors.

Mrs. Watermellon. I can see the sunset, can you?

Mrs. Tweed. Filters through.

Mrs. Watermellon. The older I get the hotter I like it.

Mrs. Tweed. You'll love it down below.

Mrs. Watermellon. I'll turn you in. I'll tell the doctor.

Mrs. Tweed. What could you tell the doctor?

Mrs. Watermellon. How you follow him through the hall. How you don't have any pain in your chest and neck. You just crybaby about it so that he'll lift your nightgown and listen to your heartbeat through your dried-up titties.

Mrs. Tweed. Yes, it's true. I like that.

Mrs. Watermellon. No decency.

Mrs. Tweed. Nonsense.

Mrs. Watermellon. Of all the billions of Chinese in the world I have to be incarcerated with you. I served my time in the family way, I earned my arms and legs, I could drive from one town to another and visit New York. You'd think I'd have the right to choose my own cellmate, but no, no, I was placed in a place, it was planned and weighed, and examined, and organized for me. It was arranged. You were arranged for my best interests. I'd kill myself if they'd give me a sharp instrument.

Mrs. Tweed. Your tongue will do.

Mrs. Watermellon. Living with me has done you some improvement.

Mrs. Tweed. You could do worse. You could be with balmy Mary McLemon. She spends every day picking nits off her clothes and her roommates. How'd you like her monkey hands and eyes all over you twenty-four hours a day. Or whining Mary McOrange who complains if it's hot and complains if it's cold and complains if the sun comes up and complains if it don't and complains if she's dry and complains if she's wet and complains if she lives and complains if she dies.

Mrs. Watermellon. Maybe I am fooling you, but old Mother isn't. Tick a lock, this is a magic spot.

Mrs. Tweed. Don't be bad to me any more.

Mrs. Watermellon. Maybe I am fooling you.

Mrs. Tweed. Don't be mean to me any more.

Mrs. Watermellon. Maybe I am fooling you, but I'm not responsible. No, I'm not—not any—any more. I'm not.

Mrs. Tweed. I'm going to call your mother. I'll fly her here on a plane and have you committed. I'm going to phone your son. I'm going to fly him here and have you committed. I am. I will. You'll be committed.

Mrs. Watermellon. Dry up, you old fart. I already am.

Nurse (Entering with tray). Time for cream of wheat. (*She smiles as she says this, but her voice is flat and mechanical.* TWEED *and* WATERMELLON *dive for their beds to hide* BIRDSONG *again.*) Time for your creamy wheat. Time for your wheat. Your cream's all gone. Time for the heap, the wheat's all dry. Sit up like good wrinkled girls and dribble it down your chins. Time for your cream of wheat, the sugar's all gone.

Mrs. Watermellon. I'm tired of being a middleman for that pap. Flush it down the nearest john!

Nurse. I'll eat it myself. I'll eat it all up.

Mrs. Tweed. It's worms. Look at her eat the pail full of worms.

Mrs. Watermellon. You got it all wrong, Tweed. That's the worm and she's eating herself.

Mrs. Tweed. Herself. And so she is. And to think of that.

Mrs. Watermellon (*Laughing and slapping* MRS. TWEED *on a knee*). It's rich and richer and so so rich. I'd not thought it possible, but she's beaten us to it.

Mrs. Tweed. Beaten us to it.

Mrs. Watermellon. Yes, she's beaten us to it. Who'd ever have thought that she'd be the first worm. And she's done it before us.

Mrs. Tweed. And we're so much older.

Mrs. Watermellon. Of course we are. Nobody here could dare to be as old as we are. And look at that. Will you just look at that white worm. She's had the audacity to be a worm before us.

Mrs. Tweed. And we're so much older.

Nurse. Time for your heat, the salve's all spread. Time for your bed, the sheet's all red. Time for the heap, the wheat's all cooked. Time for the deep, the syringe is plunged.

Mrs. Watermellon and Mrs. Tweed. And we're so much older. Nobody would dare to be as old or older. And we're so much older. (*They hold on to one another.*)

Mrs. Watermellon. And older.

Mrs. Tweed. And older.

Mrs. Watermellon. In order.

Mrs. Tweed. And older.

Mrs. Watermellon. Tonight we'll be older still.

Mrs. Tweed. In order.

Mrs. Watermellon. If you'll stay up with me all night, then I'll let you.

Nurse. Time for the . . .

Mrs. Watermellon. Keep right on eating and don't interrupt me.

Nurse. Time for the deep, the syringe is plunged. (*She gives them each a shot.*)

Mrs. Tweed (*Taking* MRS. WATERMELLON'S *hand*). I won't close an eye.

Mrs. Watermellon. Swear?

Mrs. Tweed. I swear by Almighty God and little Lord Jesus asleep in the hay.

Mrs. Watermellon. Then I'll take you back.

Mrs. Tweed. Do you promise?

Mrs. Watermellon. I promise.

Mrs. Tweed. Is he ours?

Mrs. Watermellon. Since we're older together in order, then I do believe that we can now share him.

Mrs. Tweed. Then I'll take *you* back. The two Mrs. Birdsongs!

Nurse. Time for your milk, the white's at night. Time for the drink to put you in the pink. Time for the chalk, you're in the drink.

Mrs. Watermellon (To the NURSE). Will you get out of here? Can't you see you're interfering with a honeymoon?

Nurse (Smiling, leaves). Only a few more to pin, then back to my bin. Time for a sleep, the light's turned out. Time for the deep, the syringe is shoved. (*She's gone.*)

Mrs. Watermellon and Mrs. Tweed (They turn to one another). How do you do, Mrs. Birdsong? How do *you* do, Mrs. Birdsong? (*They begin to laugh and burst out of their age. The Irish accents disappear also.*)

THAT DID IT. THAT DID IT. THANK GOD, THAT DID IT.

(*They jump like young women, leap, float, bump into each other with gaiety, sing and end in a tumble on the floor.*)

> THAT did it, that's better.
> That's done it,
> What ease.
> That did it, that's done it,
> That's better.
> What took you so long,
> What took you so long,
> Whatever on earth took you so long?

Voices (Two women sing very slowly in harmony while MRS. TWEED *and* MRS. WATERMELLON *freeze*).

> "In the gloaming, oh my darling,
> When the lights are soft and low,
> Will you think of me and love me
> As you did once long ago?"

Mrs. Tweed and Mrs. Watermellon.

> YOU TEASE
> YOU TEASE
> YOU TEASE
> WHAT TOOK YOU SO LONG?

(They jump up fiercely on the last line, still laughing. But now they change to a blank stare and say the final line in a singsong—death has grabbed them by the back of the neck)

> WHAT TOOK YOU SO LONG? SO LONG! SO LONG!
>   SO LONG!

(Then happily, saying goodbye—their arms around each other—they look out at the audience and smile)

> SO LONG . . .

CURTAIN

ADDITIONAL QUESTIONS

1. As you read through the poems, which appealed most to you by the attitude towards death expressed in it (or them)? Explain in detail how this attitude is expressed in each poem you choose.
2. Compare Shelley's "Ode to the West Wind" and Keats's "To Autumn". How alike do you find these two poems, in terms of tone, imagery, and meaning?
3. A number of poems in this section are about death in war. Choose two that lend themselves to comparison, and explain the meaning of each. Comment on specific details and use of language.
4. At the end of "Bartleby the Scrivener," we infer that the narrator has drawn some conclusion. At the end of Joyce's "The Dead," Gabriel Conroy appears at least on the verge of doing so. Choose one of these stories, and explain the relation between the preceding events and what you understand of the character's thoughts at the end.
5. An expansion of human sympathy in the face of death is found in different ways in the stories by Melville, Joyce, and O'Connor. How important to the meaning of each story is this sudden access of feeling?
6. The conclusions of both "Barn Burning" and "Lying Doggo" show life going on and convey a sense of renewal. Choose one of these stories, and explain what prepares us to accept its conclusion.
7. Like several poems in this section, Megan Terry's play concerns the meaning of old age. What do Mrs. Tweed and Mrs. Watermellon show us is most important at this final stage of life?
8. "Meaningless tragedy" has no place in literature, since the work of the dramatist imposes some shape on events, thereby enabling us to find meaning. If Hamlet's death does not illustrate the triumph of evil, what does it show?
9. The idea of the "tragic flaw" that causes the protagonist's downfall has been applied to *Hamlet*. For example, his hesitancy throughout the play has been seen as a flaw that eventually leads to his death. How would you assess this view? Is Hamlet a seriously flawed character? If you think so, explain what his flaw is and how it relates to the outcome of this tragedy.

Writing about Literature

Writing an essay about literature means that you will need to explore your responses to your reading further than you would be likely to do, for instance, in a group discussion. You will also examine texts as closely for analytical purposes as if you had written them. Such study should increase your understanding of how creative writers achieve their effects. Planning and working through your essay should also deepen your appreciation of the discipline needed for all writing.

Your instructor may have you write essays in class, in addition to assigning papers due later. A few tips for writing in class under time pressure appear at the end of this chapter. Even with a week or longer to complete an essay, however, you will never have so much time that you do not feel some stress over it. Some method of time management is essential if you wish to do a good job. The best place to begin managing your time is in your reading for the course. Develop the habit of recording your first responses to works—by jotting questions or reactions in the margins, underlining words or passages that strike you, or perhaps by keeping a personal, informal journal. Any such practice will serve you well when you need to begin thinking about an assigned paper.

Make sure you understand what the assignment means. This chapter discusses basic types of development for critical essays, along with style and formal matters, in a way intended to help you; but any stipulations your instructor makes regarding such things as development, length, and format are most important for you to understand clearly. Ask questions if you need clarification, start early, and you will have begun well. Consider your earlier reactions, and note other details that now seem important. Start thinking about what you have noticed, how you have responded, in relation to the type of essay you are planning to write.

Types of Development

Like the questions at the ends of sections in this book, the assignments given you by instructors will usually emphasize one sort of approach. You may combine methods of development, as you do in nonliterary essays; but broadly speaking, you will be reading a work very closely to explain, or "explicate," it in detail; analyzing some part of a work in relation to the whole; or comparing elements in a single work or in two or more works. Each procedure involves assembling and weighing textual detail as supportive evidence for comments you make. Each also involves thinking about how to organize your material before beginning to write.

Explication may be your preferred approach, just because of its focus on one poem or relatively brief passage. Examining the fine detail of a work is a little like studying it under a microscope. Done patiently, it may reward you with similarly surprising discoveries. Explication is really both a method of development and a technique for reading more attentively than most of us customarily do with regard to how details work together. Explication is often necessary to some extent in critical essays emphasizing other approaches. Moreover, this close, careful reading always brings you in touch with the literary uses of language. As you move through a text, you need to ask such questions as: Why this word and not some other? Or why this word order or figure of speech? You should also notice when extra emphasis is achieved by another means, such as repetition, and when the sound of a word or phrase seems as important as the sense.

Explication involves considering the relations of details to one another, especially by observing the sequence in which they appear. An old rule of thumb for explicating any text is to begin at the beginning, proceed through it, with your eye on the details, and when you come to the end, stop. You will make a mishmash out of a sonnet, for example, if you do not recognize that its thought is probably developed in a few sentences, one placed deliberately after another.

Perhaps you can recall hearing someone—maybe in junior high—read an unfamiliar poem without regard to sentences, halting at the end of each line. The result may have been so disastrous that you began, from that occasion, to pay close attention to all punctuation in poetry. You noticed where brief pauses should come and where a reader should pause longer before going on. Remember that lesson now as you reread and prepare to write.

Rereading any work carefully and as often as possible is necessary for writing about it. You need to know it well. Reading the poem or passage aloud to yourself is also a good idea, since hearing what is said may reinforce what you understand from looking at words on a page.

Not every poem (if you are explicating a poem) is composed of several sentences running through the verse lines, but the principle of following the order of details as they have been arranged remains the same. Read Robert Frost's "The Silken Tent," for example, a sonnet consisting of one long sentence. Reading this poem aloud will be especially helpful, since you should pick up in this way the sound effects Frost has built into it. You will need to follow the thought closely, paying attention to its exact wording. Note each clause within the sentence and the complex grammatical construction of the whole, as you consider the figure of speech the speaker elaborates. You should notice such things as the slight jolt probably everyone experiences on first hearing a "she" being compared to a tent—though, notice, a "silken" one. You should take into account the specific time of day, season, and weather mentioned. Perhaps you will wonder whether the lady's age is hinted by such references, or whether "guys" (guise?) may be a pun and, if so, what it means.

THE SILKEN TENT

She is as in a field a silken tent
At midday when a sunny summer breeze
Has dried the dew and all its ropes relent,
So that in guys it gently sways at ease,
And its supporting central cedar pole,
That is its pinnacle to heavenward
And signifies the sureness of the soul,
Seems to owe naught to any single cord,
But strictly held by none, is loosely bound
By countless silken ties of love and thought   10
To everything on earth the compass round,
And only by one's going slightly taut
In the capriciousness of summer air
Is of the slightest bondage made aware.

You will need to ask how many tent poles are of cedar and whether that wood has any significance. What is being said by the references to a "single cord" and the "countless . . . ties"? What would "silken ties" be like, and what sort of woman is bound by "love and thought" to "everything on earth the compass round"? What do you imagine happening when one tie goes "slightly taut"? Beyond how the "capriciousness of summer air" sounds, consider what the phrase means. Consider, too, that the thought builds in any literary work. Therefore, its conclusion, emphatic as such, is always important. In this case, what is being said, finally, about the lady? If the whole poem is complimentary (is it?), perhaps recognition of a particularly important quality is being paid at the end.

As you study all the details of the poem, notice that you must repeatedly consult your responses, the knowledge and personal experience you bring to reading it. The introduction to this book discusses the interaction of reader and text in the reading process. Thinking of it in this way now may be of further help. In reading well, you depend on the text always, but the text also depends on you. When reading closely, you must still contribute to make meaning. You must respect the text as the only reliable evidence of what its author intended— and achieved. You must have the self-reliance to offer your own ideas, as the work elicits them and as they seem to be relevant.

In an explication relevance involves how the details relate to each other to create the meaning of the whole poem or passage. Just as the writer has worked out some idea in setting down the details, so you must work towards a clear idea in planning to comment upon them. When you begin to study a text, you may be puzzled about its meaning. Proceeding carefully, however, while thinking about difficulties that slow you down, should help you develop an overall view. Especially if you are explicating a poem, a few more readings aloud to yourself may be the best step before deciding how to put into your own words what the whole means. You should do so in a single, clear grammatical sentence. If you are working with a passage from a longer work, try putting in one sentence why that passage is important in the whole work. The sentence will both summarize your findings and point the direction your written comments will take. Whether about a poem or passage, such a sentence will provide a basis for checking the relevance of your comments.

Your sentence will be a *thesis statement*. Undoubtedly you are familiar with the need for a thesis from doing other sorts of writing. The same importance attached to it elsewhere applies here. A thesis is a device of unity and clarity. A single, explicit statement is generally best, since wording it forces you to clarify your thought. Putting it down on paper also represents a kind of commitment. As always, if you do not know what you are talking about, who will? A thesis is a means of focusing. It should state what you really believe, not what you suspect someone else, such as an instructor, wants you to say. A thesis need not be startlingly original nor do more than make what you see as the essential point. When you are writing any type of essay about a literary work, your thesis should be about the work. The statement should be broad enough to encompass all the details you wish to discuss and the supporting points you will make. If it is too broad, the details and points will not seem to belong with it. If your thesis is dull or too obvious, what you say about it will also be. So it should be as interesting as you can make it. Word it so that your interest in your subject is clear.

Like an explication, an *analysis* paper may require considerable time for deciding upon a thesis. In explaining the relation of some part of a work to the whole, you will need to have reflected on both the whole and the part about equally. Your purpose really will be to argue your views on both. Since you are not concentrating on all details in a poem or short passage, you must be able to justify your selection of those details upon which you do comment. As in an argument, you must also beware of omitting details that may seem to contradict what you say. In any analysis you take something apart. In a literary analysis you do so scrupulously. You wish to put your perceptions together in a commentary that will inform and persuade a reader.

You may be asked to analyze the imagery of a poem or the tone heard in the speaker's voice. Standard approaches to short stories, as well as novels and plays, involve analyzing a character, the setting, or the progress of the plot. Rather than the approach, the work itself should create the interest in such analyses; but any assignment may involve some specific problem that, as such, prompts thought. For example, you may be asked to analyze a relationship between two characters, or to explain what is happening within a character when only a few details in the text give any direct information concerning this. You may wish to explore the importance of a scene, perhaps a concluding scene, by analyzing what prepares for it. You might also consider some one comment by a character, a repeated phrase in a story or play, or some specific incident as a key to the whole work.

In doing any substantial analysis, plan to spend time assessing and sorting material. At the prewriting stage you may find note cards helpful for recording your ideas and separating particular details from the text. Whatever your system, as you gather material, you must begin to consider how it should be organized. Deciding on your thesis statement—or on a tentative thesis statement—will help you here. A statement with the exact emphasis you want, with just enough detail, and expressing real confidence may take several attempts to achieve. It may take more. Once you have it, however, you should start developing an outline of your ideas.

Place your thesis statement at the top of your outline. Whatever is the focus of your paper should be clear in your statement. Suppose, for example, you were planning to write about "Young Goodman Brown." Depending on your focus, your thesis statement might be like one of the following:

1. In Hawthorne's story Goodman's innocence is itself an illusion.
2. The dark forest through which Goodman journeys represents the terrors of his own mind and heart.
3. The narrator of "Young Goodman Brown" presents his story ironically.

However you word your main idea, it should give you—and your reader—the sense of having somewhere to go from there. As you put together your outline, having your thesis before you is essential. You must not only check your main supporting points against it for relevance. You must also have it in view when considering the order of those points.

The supporting points that become the body of your essay should build towards a conclusion that your thesis indicates. You should marshal your ideas so as to gain, sustain, and finally satisfy your reader's interest. That means in practice that you should begin the body of the essay with a strong point, well worded This is not your thesis statement, which is usually best placed at the end of a brief introductory paragraph. The thesis statement should lead directly and smoothly to the first main supporting point, located at or near the start of the next paragraph. In a paper of only a few pages each supporting point should be developed in a paragraph or two. Development means supplying supportive detail drawn from the text and your comment on it. If you cannot find anything to say about a point, discard it at the outline stage. If you find a great deal, be selective, or consider limiting the subject of your paper to this one interesting area.

Like evidence, the support for your points should make your case in the paper as a whole. The points in the middle of your essay may be less immediately interesting than your first point, but they must be sound. Your last supporting point should be your strongest one. It may involve the most detail or permit the most persuasive commentary. The weight of evidence you present here should confirm your thesis so that a concluding paragraph, if needed, is mostly a formality. In short, in the body of your essay you save your best for last.

Doing so is generally made easy and logical by the fact that the work being analyzed is structured in the same manner. All writers organize material to secure a reader's interest and then counteract the tendency to drift away without a clear sense of significant destination. Creative writers in any form lead off as firmly as they can. They labor over the middle of the story, poem, or play, so that it does not sag. They try to end strongly, tying threads together and showing in one way or another what "all this has been leading to." Whatever the subject of your analysis, therefore, you will rarely go wrong if you organize your comments along the structure of the work. Note the great difference, however, between doing so and committing a most grievous offense—merely retelling the story, summarizing the plot, or paraphrasing the poem.

Whenever you write about a literary work, assume your reader is familiar with it—and will be annoyed by your thinking otherwise. You need to recall details to your reader's mind, especially when you wish to emphasize them or suspect that even a thoughtful reader might overlook them. On the whole, though, picture your reader as possessing average human kindness but, like yourself, having no time to waste. Imagine this reader's tendency to mutter, "what's your point, what's your point?" when anyone tries to retain his or her attention without making one.

Another type of paper in which you need to advance a thesis and make supporting points is a *comparison/contrast* paper. This third type of essay development involves discussing similarities and differences between items within a work or in two or more works. For instance, you might compare two characters within a work, two characters in two works, two poems, and so on. Of course, there must be a clear basis for comparison, and you need a clear reason for making it. You do not just select, say, two characters at random to compare; but you may wish to compare two supporting characters in a play, the heroes of two tragedies by the same author, or the central characters of stories on the same theme. The basis for your comparison need not be obvious, but it must exist. Your purpose in writing may be to make this clear. Most often your purpose will be to clarify the meaning of the work or works by using the comparison/contrast technique.

Writing about *The Taming of the Shrew,* for example, you might wish to compare Kate and Bianca to argue that being women in that time brings out negative qualities in both sisters. Or you might contrast the two as displaying different reactions to having little control over their own lives. Strictly speaking, to contrast means to point out differences between things; to compare to discuss their similarities. More loosely, to compare means to do either. You may emphasize differences or similarities but must usually take both into account, and the mix will provide interest. Whatever your purpose, again an effective arrangement of your main points and supporting evidence is a necessity.

You may already be familiar with the two organizational plans that will serve you as well here as in nonliterary essays. In brief, one involves item-by-item, and the other point-by-point comparison. Using the former plan, you would discuss all you had to say about Bianca before discussing Kate (or vice versa). You would make matching points about the two sisters and not, for example, discuss in detail the attitude of one towards her father and leave that of the other unnoticed or barely discussed. In the other plan you would merely shift your focus and discuss each main point or issue in turn, with reference to each sister.

Suppose that, besides filial attitude, your main points are about receptiveness to courtship and display of willfulness. Using the first plan, a short outline of the paper might look like the following. (Notice that the thesis statement indicates that you will emphasize a similarity underlying obvious differences.)

I. *Thesis.* Although one sister is called a shrew, both Kate and Bianca are shrewd, or sharp-witted, enough in their ways.
- A. Bianca
  1. Plays the loving, submissive daughter.
  2. Is immediately open to courtship.
  3. Once married, is willful towards her enamored husband.
- B. Kate
  1. Taunts her father to arouse his guilt.
  2. Resists being traded like an object.
  3. Once married, learns to curb her tongue.

Using the second plan, a short outline for developing the same thesis might be as follows:
- A. Attitude towards Baptista Minola
  1. Bianca's submissive role
  2. Kate's open anger
- B. Openness to courtship
  1. Bianca's game-playing
  2. Kate's need to battle with Petruchio
- C. Willfulness
  1. Bianca's surprising stubbornness
  2. Kate's surprising about-face

Which of these two plans you should use would depend mostly on the length of the proposed paper. The first plan works best in a relatively short paper and where the material is not very complex. You need to make a firm transition between the two main parts to prevent the paper's seeming to split into two. You should also refer back to the first part of the paper when taking up points in the second half, although only a brief reminder is usually needed.

If you have more than a few main points, fairly detailed supportive material, or are planning more than a few pages, probably you should opt for the second plan. It is more expansible, poses only routine problems of transitions, and may require reminders of points discussed only in a summarizing conclusion.

Whichever plan you choose, however, the guidelines discussed earlier should also be applied here in this type of paper: insofar as possible, organize your comments on the structure of the work(s) being considered. Arrange your material to gain, retain, and satisfy your reader's interest. To emphasize one point more than others, place it last. In either plan for the paper outlined above, if you found Bianca more interesting than Kate for some reason, then your comments on Bianca should follow those on Kate.

Whatever your purposes in a comparison/contrast essay, your organization should help your reader to share your insights. Your two compared items should illuminate each other. Your thesis should illuminate both of them.

Choosing a Topic

An instructor rarely furnishes a thesis but may suggest a broad topic, as well as a type of development. For instance, your assignment may be to write an analysis paper on a particular story. Any such specification is helpful in enabling you to start focusing early. If you have more freedom to choose your topic and approach, you must eliminate options yourself and develop a clear, workable thesis. Generally, it helps to keep in mind the basic types of papers and to consider topics with respect to them. Doing so puts you in a position similar to that of a poet contemplating the requirements of a sonnet on the one hand and total freedom from an established pattern on the other. The problem becomes one of where to begin. In writing about literature, think of types of development so that, once you have decided on your topic, you can concentrate on your ideas.

The most reliable source of topics and ideas is your own response to the material. Always beware of attempting too broad a topic. Two short poems may yield more than enough material for a paper of a few hundred words. Comparable elements in two stories may also, but to treat two entire stories in a few pages would be impossible. To attempt to discuss one good story fully is also likely to be so. Similarly, plays with a number of scenes and characters are far too complex to be treated at all adequately in a short paper. You must be rigorously selective, therefore, in deciding on your specific topic. Start with a limited area that gives you a sense of there being much to say. Then try to narrow your area of concern further, remembering that the best topic may appear at first very small. Having much to say should result from the thinking you do to explain your topic's significance.

When your decision becomes firm, start free-associating ideas in your spare time as you go about other activities and note down any that seem especially promising. Also, try asking yourself specific questions, such as: What is the most important thing to be said about this work? What is the essential nature of this character? What is the main reason for this poem's impact? No matter how vaguely or roughly you start, though, keep trying to say what you think about your topic until that one idea you can use for your thesis becomes clear.

Style

Good ideas deserve to be expressed as effectively as possible. Plan your time so that you will be able to write at least one rough draft. Be sure you have enough supportive evidence in the form of details drawn from the text(s), direct quotations, your comments, and so on. Consider the logic of your main points and other remarks. Work on the transitions from point to point. Check the focus of your introductory paragraph, and consider how much conclusion you need. Probably you will have taken some pains with style all along the way, but now, as you revise, make sure your writing is clear, concise, and suitably polished. Be sure you have established a tone appropriate for your purposes. General rules for effective style you have learned in other contexts apply also to essays on literature. Do not be so formal that you no longer sound at all like yourself. Avoid being too colloquial, but use simple language when it gets the job done. Avoid trite phrasing ("like the plague"). Use more active than passive verbs. Vary the types of sentences you use. Listen to them in your inward ear. Test how they sound by reading them out loud.

Critical essays also have special conventions of style you need to bear in mind. A question often asked when the first paper of a semester is assigned suggests one of them. *"Can we use 'I'?"* someone will ask, recalling a rule laid down hard-and-fast in some earlier classroom. Most often a literature teacher in high school has ruled out the use of 'I'. No doubt his or her reasons for doing so were excellent at the time. Much of education has to do with moving us away from a childlike, egocentric view of things to a more objective, presumably adult attitude. Repeated use of 'I' in writing (other than literature itself) may suggest too much self-absorption. In reading literature, of course, complete objectivity is impossible, and personal response is essential. The introduction to this book has already discussed how you as reader must contribute to make meaning.

But I have also discussed how, in literary discourse, the strictly personal or private response must fall away. To indicate that it has, and to imply that "adult" attitude, use of the first-person singular pronoun generally should be sparing. Note that I have used it above, as in this sentence. Like 'my,' 'me,' or 'you' for that matter, it is a harmless little word, indispensable most of the time, and in writing may actually seem friendly and forthright. In a critical essay it may also strike you as nicely modest or duly cautious in reminders to the effect that, after all, in your opinion, as you see it, this is what you think. Your instructor may still rule out 'I' just to rule out such deprecatory remarks.

They are wordy, as are introductory remarks like: "In this essay I intend to analyze such and such a poem in order to determine this or that." Instead, state your thesis. Throughout your essay, state your other points directly, and do not hedge. A reader expects the thoughts expressed in an essay to be, unless otherwise noted, those of its author. A critical essay also should sound more formal, generally, than a personal essay. When used repeatedly, the personal pronoun may seem too informal. You may even seem not as scrupulous about textual evidence as you need to be. In short, you will create a better impression by keeping your style impersonal. Use "I" if you feel strongly you must at times, but remember that conventions are strong, and that you are dealing with a convention here.

Another convention of the critical essay may be more puzzling. Indeed, use of *the literary present* may strike you at first as childish, too colloquial, or even downright illogical. In reading fiction you will have noticed the use of the past tense for narrative. Thus "Young Goodman Brown *came forth* at sunset"; "We *got up* at four in the morning"; "Old Aunt Nannie *had* a habit." Yet in writing about fiction, as about drama and poetry, you should use mostly the present tense. Use it to describe the contents of a literary work, including what characters say and do. So you may note that Goodman *enters* the forest. The Kentucky boys *hitch* a freight to Saratoga. And Miranda *tries* to wriggle away but cannot. Perhaps the idea is that literature exists in its own sort of eternity. Even events narrated as though in the past occur in some special ever-present continuum.

But earlier and subsequent times still exist—curiously enough—in relation to this time. So you may need to switch from the present tense to the perfect (active or passive voice) or to the future tense, as in the following examples:

1. When the captain walks on the deck, he *has been* in command only a short time.
2. He whispers with Leggatt, whom he *has met* under strange circumstances. (But he *will bid* Leggatt farewell later.)
3. When Nora enters, she *has been shopping.* She appears intimidated by Torvald but later *will leave* him.

Like narrative fiction, drama frequently requires you to switch from the present (used to describe what would occur on stage) to indicate times prior to the action portrayed, or earlier or later within that action.

By its nature, lyric poetry less often requires you to switch from the present tense. The speaker in a poem is always "present" ("on," you might say). As you read the poem, the speaker voices, as though for the first time, thoughts and feelings that a poet wrote perhaps centuries ago. Thus you might note that the speaker in John Donne's poem "The Flea" *tries* to cajole the lady to make love with him. But in "The Canonization" the speaker *demands* to know how his love *has harmed* anyone.

You should extend the literary present, by the way, when referring to Donne's technique in either poem—or to any author's technique in his or her work of any type. You might say, for example, that Donne *demonstrates* his wit in his love poems. Similarly, Dickinson *is* often witty. Thurber *makes* his hero, Jack Smurch, fit his name. Or Hansberry *places* the action of her drama in one room.

When you discuss an author biographically, use the normal past tense. (Donne *wrote* in the seventeenth century. Dickinson *was* reclusive. Thurber once *worked* as a newspaper reporter. Hansberry *scored* a critical success with her first play.) In critical essays, however, you will make much fewer biographical comments than remarks on technique. So you will need to get used to thinking and writing in that odd present tense.

Matters of Form

You must be aware of conventions governing a range of formal matters, including even the way you name authors. Notice the *use of last names* in the preceding paragraph. It is customary to give an author's full name and the title of the work in question early in the introductory paragraph of a paper. After this, you need refer to the author only by his or her last name.

Learn the rules governing the *punctuation of titles*. Remember that a distinction is made between whole books, or works first published alone in book form, and those that have appeared or generally would appear in a collection first. Short stories and most poems fall into this second category. Set their titles off by *quotation marks:* "Out of Place," "The Leap," "A Work of Artifice." *Underline* the titles of plays, novels, short story collections, or volumes of poetry: *Oedipus Rex, Sons and Lovers, Dubliners, The Complete Poems of Emily Dickinson.* In print, as you see, these titles are italicized.

Quoting from literary texts involves a more complex set of rules. You will often wish to quote a word, phrase, line or more in explicating a work or supplying evidence to support a point. The precise way something is said may be crucial, and you may need to draw attention to some language in a text that a reader might overlook. Or you may wish to place before your reader a short passage for reference, if you want to comment upon it in some detail.

Bear in mind that brevity in quoting is best. Most instructors will pounce at once upon long quoted passages as obvious padding. They will also be disturbed if, in quoting for good reason, you do not do so exactly. *Direct quotations* from any text need to be the same, word for word, in your paper as in the text.

Generally speaking, your punctuation of quoted material must also be exactly that found in the original, although you can make some minor adjustments when incorporating quotations into your own text. Note the following rules and examples:

1. Quotation marks go at both ends of material quoted directly, except for longer quotations set off as such.

2. When quoting five or more lines of prose or verse, omit quotation marks. Set off the entire passage from the text by indenting a few spaces from the left and leaving extra space above and below. Single-space, if typing. Longer quotations afford more room for error, so check and double-check your accuracy.

3. In quoting poetry within your text, use a slash (/) with equal space on either side to indicate the original division into lines. Thus in quoting from Wordsworth's "Lines Composed a Few Miles Above Tintern Abbey," you might note the poet's comment that "These beauteous forms, / Through a long absence, have not been to me / As is a landscape to a blind man's eye."

4. A sentence ending with a quotation (as in the example above) must have terminal punctuation that does not distort the sense of the quoted matter. In the above example, a period replaces the semicolon of Wordsworth's text.

5. Use single quotation marks for quotes within quotes. Thus you might write: " 'Then God bless you!' said Faith, with the pink ribbons."

6. You may omit material (usually a very small amount) within a quotation, if doing so does not distort the meaning of the quoted text in any essential

way. Use ellipsis marks (three spaced periods) to indicate such omissions
For example, in quoting from the first paragraph of "Young Goodman
Brown," you might have reason to note only that "Faith . . . thrust her
own pretty head into the street, letting the wind play with the pink ribbons
of her cap." Ellipsis points are generally not used at the beginnings and
ends of quotations, but you must be sure you are not "quoting out of
context" nor changing the meaning of the text in any way.

7. Very rarely, you may wish to insert a comment into a quotation to clarify
a reference, confirm unusual spelling, or supply an omitted verb to make
the sense clear. Place any such addition in brackets [thus], which you may
need to draw in by hand, if typing. Such insertions should always be very
brief and, most often, only a word or two.

Whenever you quote directly, your dual purpose is to be scrupulously faithful
to the text and, at the same time, as clear as possible about your use of the
material.

Furthermore, you must enable your reader to follow your own text easily when
it includes a quotation. Whether this is short or long enough to be set apart,
work it smoothly into your writing. You may be quoting what a character in a
story says or what a narrator comments. In either case, identify him or her in
some way in the sentence that contains the quotation. For example, you might
write: The narrator in "I Want to Know Why" recalls that he and his friends
made their way "with the true instinct of Kentucky boys." Watch the grammar
and syntax of the entire sentence you construct to include quoted matter. The
quotation becomes part of your sentence, and the whole must be acceptable
English. The examples given above will serve once more to illustrate.

For most short essays, you will be expected to develop your own ideas and
not refer to *outside or secondary sources,* such as published biographies or critical
studies. Occasionally, your instructor may suggest you do so, however, or you
may do some background reading to get started or compare your ideas with
others'. Whenever you consult other works besides your *primary source* (the
literary work you are writing about), you must give credit in your paper for any
and all ideas gained in this way.

Plagiarism, a very serious academic offense, means using another person's
ideas—not just that person's exact language—without giving due credit. Especially in searching for the focus you need for an essay, you may absorb someone
else's ideas without realizing you are doing so. Therefore, even though you may
feel that reading some outside source(s) has really given you nothing, it is advisable
to include a page headed *Works Consulted* at the end of the paper. List here any
work you have looked at. Use the same format for entries you would use for an
ordinary bibliography. An English handbook will provide models for all types of
entries you might use, but the following brief list of models may be of help.

1. *Book*

Castillo-Puch, José Luis. *Hemingway in Spain.* Garden City, N. Y.: Doubleday
and Company, 1974.

2. *Book*

   Hemingway, Ernest. *Death in the Afternoon*. New York: Charles Scribner's Sons, 1932.

3. *Short story in collection*

   ———. "The Short Happy Life of Francis Macomber." *The Snows of Kilimanjaro and Other Stories*. New York: Charles Scribner's Sons, 1961.

4. *Essay in book*

   Warren, Robert Penn. "Ernest Hemingway." *Selected Essays*. New York: Random House, 1958.

Notice that such a list is insufficient, however, for acknowledging conscious indebtedness for information and ideas.

Whenever you quote a source directly or summarize information or ideas in it, you must indicate the exact place from which you have borrowed, so that your reader might locate this easily. You may have learned rules for footnoting that have been in use for decades, but more recent rules for citing sources are rapidly making this older style of documentation outdated. What is called the New MLA Style (developed by the Modern Language Association of America) resembles documentation styles of other academic disciplines besides English. The new style relies, first, on an alphabetical list including all your sources, and in the format already illustrated above, at the end of your paper. Then footnotes are kept to a minimum, being used mainly for commentary rather than for locating a source. For the latter purpose, use brief parenthetical references within your text.

When you are using only one outside source by an author—perhaps the essay on Hemingway by Robert Penn Warren listed above—give the full information about it on a final page headed *Bibliography* or *Works Cited* (not underlined in your paper). Then when you wish to cite this work, do so at the appropriate place in your text by giving the page reference in parentheses. Place this reference at the end of a sentence like this (Warren 91). You need give only the page reference, if you identify the author by name within your sentence. For example: Robert Penn Warren remarked on Hemingway's preoccupation with "the despair beyond plenty of money—or beyond all the other gifts of the world" (91). This practice is often preferable, in fact. When using secondary sources, you should acknowledge them as openly as possible. You will be referring far more often, however, to your *primary sources,* the literary works you are discussing.

For longer poems, indicating line numbers after quotations is usually sufficient. When you work shorter quotations into your text, place the numbers in parentheses. In quoting Wordsworth's "Lines Composed a Few Miles above Tintern Abbey," for example: "Nor less, I trust, / To them I may have owed another gift, / Of aspect more sublime" (ll.35–37). If you set off a longer passage by itself, give the line references at the end of it without parentheses.

Treat short stories from this text in the same way as you do outside sources. Plays without line numbers should be treated this way too, although you may wish to mention the act to which you are referring within your text. For Sophocles's and Shakespeare's plays, where both lines and larger divisions are given, citing a combination of these serves most efficiently. For Sophocles, you might give a reference like this (Scene II, 3). A reference to a Shakespeare play—*Hamlet,* for instance—would include the act, scene, and lines in a standard concise form like this (I,ii, 129–30).

Format of the Finished Paper

Your instructor may give you specific guidelines for typing or word-processing, use of a cover sheet, size of margins, and so on. Adapt the following suggestions accordingly. They are meant only as suggestions that may serve your purposes.

1. If you can, type or do your final draft on a word-processor. If typing, use a good medium- or heavyweight paper, *not* the thin kind called "onionskin." Paper with margins in red is not necessary. A good ribbon on your typewriter or printer *is* necessary. So is using plain white paper in a printer—*not* the "continuous feed" type you may have used to print out your rough drafts. Double-space, whether you use a typewriter or computer. If you write your paper in longhand, use white, lined theme paper, *not* pages torn from a notebook. Single-space, unless your handwriting is very small. Write on only one side of each sheet, and work at making your penmanship legible.
2. Whether you write out your essay or not, generally leave margins of at least one inch all around for neatness and your reader's comments. Center your title about two inches from the top of your first page. Do not underline your title, but you will need to punctuate the title of a literary work, if you include it in your title. By the way, your title usually should be short, *not* cute, and indicate what your essay is actually about.
3. Proofread to catch errors in documentation, spelling, grammar, and possible omissions when recopying your final draft. No instructor welcomes a paper that by its appearance alone suggests carelessness.
4. Unless directed to do otherwise, do not enclose your essay in a folder or plastic cover. Do not bother with a title page. Place your name, the number and title of the course, and the date in the upper right-hand corner of your first page. It is helpful also to put your last name in the upper right corner of succeeding pages, in case they should become separated. Number your pages, after the first, just above your name.
5. Use a single staple or paperclip in the upper left corner. Avoid folding down or tearing corners to hold papers together.

Essays Written in Class

If assigned an essay to write in class, you will have to think and write fast. Here are some suggestions that can help you do well.

Read and reread carefully whatever work(s) will provide the subject of the essay. You may wish to review notes taken during a class discussion of the work, but do some serious thinking about it on your own. Do not try to anticipate the exact question that may be given to you; but do not neglect to consider possible questions, especially by recalling the directions class discussions have taken.

When you are given the question or topic, think about it. Make sure, first, that you understand it. If you can ask questions, do so to clarify any uncertainty you may feel about the assignment.

In writing an essay response, decide on a thesis statement before starting to write. Make sure your statement is a direct response to the question or topic given. Keep the thesis fairly brief and simple, since your time is strictly limited. Be sure also that you can support this thesis readily.

Jot down a quick outline. In a fifty-minute class, taking even five minutes for this before writing can ensure an effective, cogent essay and prevent rambling about vaguely. Neatness does not count in such a scratch outline. What does count is your pausing to organize your thoughts. Lay out a bare framework upon which you will build as you write rapidly.

Your thesis statement alone will usually be sufficient introduction for your essay. Probably you can also do without a concluding paragraph. Concentrate on the body of the essay. Develop each point of your outline in a detailed paragraph. A danger is that, under time pressure, you may generalize broadly and omit detailed references to the work in question. If you know the text well, however, you can supply enough detail to make your points effectively.

As in writing essays outside of class, you may discover ideas in the process of writing. But try to stay within your outline—or at least make sure you are reorganizing your thoughts in a coherent way. You should not worry about elegance of style when writing in class under pressure. Be direct, be clear, use simple language, and you should do very well.

Glossary

Allegory A form of extended symbolism in which characters, setting, and incidents in a narrative represent abstract qualities or ideas. Tag names indicating meaning are customary.

> Nathaniel Hawthorne, "Young Goodman Brown," p. 13.

Alliteration Most often, the repetition of an initial consonant sound for effect, especially in a line of poetry.

> When weeds, in wheels, shoot long and lovely and lush—Gerard Manley Hopkins, "Spring," l. 2, p. 100.
> And signifies the sureness of the soul—Robert Frost, "The Silken Tent," l. 7, p. 239.

Allusion A reference within a literary work to something outside it, such as an historic figure or event or a character in another work.

> To say: "I am Lazarus, come from the dead . . .—T. S. Eliot, "The Love Song of J. Alfred Prufrock," l. 94, p. 242.
> He burst from Bessie's crushed black skull—Bob Kaufman, "Blues Note," l. 6, p. 456.

Ambiguity An expression that suggests more than one meaning, often intentionally in poetry.

> Much Madness is divinest Sense—Emily Dickinson, p. 235.
> Flick stands tall among the idiot pumps—John Updike, "Ex-Basketball Player," l. 7, p. 253.

Apostrophe In poetry, a direct address to a person, usually not present, or to an object, abstract quality, or part of the natural world as though it might listen.

> Maxine Kumin, "The Man of Many L's," p. 111.
> John Keats, "Ode on a Grecian Urn," p. 679.
> Percy Bysshe Shelley, "Ode to the West Wind," p. 913.

Aside In drama, the convention by which a character may speak thoughts aloud but unheard by others on stage.

> William Shakespeare, *Hamlet* (II,ii, 207–208), p. 983.

Assonance Repetition of vowel sounds preceded and followed by different consonant sounds, especially for effect in lines of poetry. *See* Consonance.

> I will complain, yet praise—George Herbert, "Bitter-Sweet," l. 5, p. 442.
> For rose-moles all in stipple upon trout that swim—Gerard Manley Hopkins, "Pied Beauty," l. 3, p. 682.

Blank Verse *See* iambic pentameter.

Carpe Diem Latin for "seize the day," usually advice to enjoy youth or life while you may. In a lyric poem the speaker often has a seductive intent in so urging a listener.

> Andrew Marvell, "To His Coy Mistress," p. 443.
> Robert Herrick, "Corinna's Going A-Maying." p. 440.

Catharsis Derived from Aristotle, a problematic term usually thought to mean a purging of strong feelings of pity and fear aroused by Greek tragedy.

Character A person portrayed in a literary work, or the qualities and traits of such a person. Characters are often called *dynamic* when they change in some important way in the work; *static* characters remain the same. A *flat* character is only sketched in with a few details, while a *round* character is presented in more depth. A *stock character* is a familiar or conventional type regularly found in a particular kind of literary work. The Pedant in Shakespeare's *The Taming of the Shrew* is an example of a comic stock character.

Climax In a fictional or dramatic plot the most intense point, or the *turning point*, in the central conflict.

Comedy A broad term for drama meant to amuse and delight, although it may also provoke serious thought by its depiction of human behavior.

> Molière, *The Misanthrope*, p. 261.
> William Shakespeare, *The Taming of the Shrew*, p. 461.

Complication In a plot, those incidents that establish and intensify the *conflict.*

Conceit In poetry, an especially ingenious, elaborate, or striking figure of speech; often called a *metaphysical conceit* in seventeenth-century poems, especially by John Donne.

> John Donne, "A Valediction: Forbidding Mourning," ll. 25–36, p. 439.
> John Donne, "Hymn to God My God, in My Sickness," ll. 6–20, p. 907.

Conflict The struggle, usually of a central character with another person, with an external force, or with his or her own emotions, that creates tension in a plot.

Consonance Repetition of consonant sounds preceded by different vowel sounds, especially for effect in lines of poetry. *See* Alliteration, Assonance.

> So that in guys it gently sways at ease—
> Robert Frost, "The Silken Tent," l. 4, p. 239.

We real cool—Gwendolyn Brooks, "We Real Cool," l. 1, p. 247.

Convention In literature, any way of treating a subject, or handling any type of work, that has become widely accepted in a given period.

Couplet A pair of rhymed lines of poetry.

> So long as men can breathe or eyes can see
> So long lives this, and this gives life to thee—William Shakespeare, Sonnet 18, ll. 13–14, p. 433.

Dénouement *See* Resolution.

Dialogue Conversation between two or more characters in a literary work.

Diction The level of language—formal, colloquial, and so on—or, more narrowly, the choice of particular words in a literary work. An unusual choice of word draws attention to itself and thereby gains emphasis.

> About the lilting house and happy as the grass was green—Dylan Thomas, "Fern Hill," l. 2, p. 108.
> To say we are vexed at her brown study— John Crowe Ransome, "Bells for John Whiteside's Daughter," l. 19, p. 938.

See also Poetic Diction.

Drama A general term for literary works usually meant to be performed on a stage.

Dramatic Monologue A type of poem in which the speaker is a well-defined character addressing another person or persons at some specific moment.

> Robert Browning, "My Last Duchess," p. 96.
> Alfred, Lord Tennyson, "Ulysses," p. 917.

Editorial Omniscience In fiction, when an omniscient narrator expresses a judgment on events or characters. *See* Point of View.

> D. H. Lawrence, "The Horse Dealer's Daughter," p. 380.

Elegy A formal poem of lament for a specific person or, more broadly, of meditation on mortality.

> Thomas Gray, "Elegy Written in a Country Churchyard," p. 908.

Walt Whitman, "When Lilacs Last in the Dooryard Bloom'd," p. 920.

English Sonnet *See* Sonnet.

Epiphany A sudden flash of insight into something, such as a situation. This sense of the term derives from James Joyce.

James Joyce, "The Dead," p. 839.

Exposition In fiction or drama, the presentation of background information at the beginning.

Figurative Language Nonliteral use of language or other departures from customary usage to achieve special effects. *See* Apostrophe, Hyperbole, Irony, Metaphor, Paradox, Personification, Simile, Symbol, Understatement.

Flashback In drama or fiction, any presentation of actions that occurred prior to the opening scene of the work.

Foot A unit of meter in a line of poetry. *See* Meter.

Foreshadowing Intimations within a plot as to what is to come.

Free Verse Usually, unrhymed poetry with no set metrical pattern and with lines of varying length.

Walt Whitman, "I Saw in Louisiana a Live-Oak Growing," p. 234.

Nikki Giovanni, "Nikki-Rosa," p. 259.

Genre A major type or class of literary work, especially drama, poetry, short fiction, the novel.

Hero/Heroine In a literary work, the central character or protagonist; not necessarily a person of noble character or great achievements.

Hubris (or Hybris) In Greek tragedy, the excessive pride often considered responsible for the protagonist's downfall, due to the gods' displeasure. *See* Tragic Flaw.

Hyperbole Exaggeration used to heighten effect or to suggest the opposite of what is said. Same as Overstatement.

Andrew Marvell, "To His Coy Mistress," ll. 3–18, pp. 443–44.

Robert Burns, "A Red, Red Rose," p. 445.

Iambic Pentameter A much-used line of English verse, consisting of five *metrical*

feet, each with an unstressed syllable followed by a stressed syllable. When unrhymed, such lines are called *blank verse. See* Meter, Foot.

Thomas Gray, "Elegy Written in a Country Churchyard," p. 908.

William Shakespeare, *Hamlet,* p. 949.

Image (Imagery collectively) Especially in poetry, language appealing to any of the senses. Imagery may occur in language used literally or figuratively.

Seamus Heaney, "Blackberry-picking," p. 114.

Lucille Clifton, "Miss Rosie," p. 254.

William Shakespeare, Sonnet 73, p. 433.

Robert Hayden, "Those Winter Sundays," p. 452.

Sharon Olds, "Sex without Love," p. 460.

In Medias Res Latin for "in the middle of things," a term used for the device of opening a drama or narrative in the middle of the important action, with previous incidents filled in by flashbacks or other techniques of exposition.

Sophocles, *Oedipus Rex,* p. 116.

Innocent Eye In fiction, the point of view of a child, naïve adult, or other narrator unable to understand much about the events related, although a *participant in them. See* Point of View.

Sherwood Anderson, "I Want to Know Why," p. 22.

Irony An effect created by a contrast or opposition between literal and intended meaning or appearance and actuality. *Verbal irony* includes *hyperbole* and *understatement. Dramatic irony* occurs when the reader or audience knows things important to but hidden from the characters in a drama; also called *tragic* or *Sophoclean irony.*

Sophocles, *Oedipus Rex,* p. 116.

W. H. Auden, "The Unknown Citizen," p. 245.

Italian Sonnet *See* Sonnet.

Lyric Usually a relatively short poem expressing thought and feeling; for the ancient Greeks, a song accompanied by a lyre, and still often songlike. Most of the poems in this book would be classified as lyric poems.

Metaphor An implied comparison achieved by equating two dissimilar items.

> You wet brown bag of a woman—Lucille Clifton, "Miss Rosie," l. 13, p. 255.
>
> Ray Charles is the black wind of Kilimanjaro—Bob Kaufman, "Blues Note," l. 1, p. 456.

Meter The pattern of stressed and unstressed syllables in a line of poetry, which may be described in terms of the predominant kind of *metrical foot* and the number of *feet* in it. The five basic patterns or kinds of metrical feet are:

iambic	an unstressed followed by a stressed syllable
trochaic	a stressed syllable followed by an unstressed one
anapestic	two unstressed syllables followed by a stressed one
dactyllic	a stressed followed by two unstressed syllables
spondaic	two stressed syllables (used mainly for emphasis)

The terms used to describe the lengths of lines are:

monometer	one foot
dimeter	two feet
trimeter	three feet
tetrameter	four feet
pentameter	five feet
hexameter	six feet

See also Foot, Iambic Pentameter, Rhythm.

Motivation In drama or fiction, those details of personality or circumstances that make a character's actions understandable.

Narrative The telling of a story in any literary form and in either prose or verse.

Narrator In fiction, the teller of a story or the point of view from which the story is told. Usually distinguished from the author, and sometimes unreliable owing to limited perspective, naïveté, prejudice, and so on. *See* Point of View.

Neutral Omniscience In fiction, when an omniscient narrator expresses no opinion on events or characters. *See* Point of View.

Richard Wright, "Big Boy Leaves Home," p. 44.

Octave *See* Sonnet.

Ode A lyric poem, usually with a dignified style and serious theme and addressed to some person or thing.

> John Keats, "Ode on a Grecian Urn," p. 679.
>
> John Keats, "To Autumn," p. 916.

Onomatopoeia Use of a word or, more broadly, of language whose sound reinforces the meaning.

> In the capriciousness of summer air—Robert Frost, "The Silken Tent," l. 13, p. 239.
>
> In the tempestuous petticoat—Robert Herrick, "Delight in Disorder," l. 10, p. 677.

Overstatement *See* Hyperbole.

Paradox An apparently contradictory or absurd phrase or statement that nevertheless contains truth.

> Anonymous, "I Sing of a Maiden," p. 85.
>
> John Donne, "Death, Be Not Proud," p. 906.

Persona Literally, "mask." *See* Speaker.

Personification The attribution of human qualities to things in nature, objects, abstract qualities, and so on.

> Michael Drayton, "Since There's No Help," ll. 9–12, p. 432.
>
> George Herbert, "Love," p. 442.

Petrarchan Sonnet *See* Sonnet.

Plot In fiction or drama, the arrangement of incidents in significant relation to each other. *See* Exposition, Complication, Climax, Resolution.

Poetic Diction A specialized diction, distinct from everyday speech and often archaic, once thought proper for poetry.

> Haply some hoary-headed swain may say—Thomas Gray, "Elegy Written in a Country Churchyard," l. 97, p. 911.

Point of View In fiction, any of various relations of the *narrator* to the events described. If a participant in them, the narrator may be a major or minor character.

Participant viewpoints, where the narrator is an "I," are also called *first-person*. *Nonparticipant* narrators refer to characters as "he," "she," "they," and so on, and are called *third-person*. A nonparticipant narrator may appear to know everything about the story, including the thoughts of all the characters, or focus on the mind of one character. The latter two options are often called *omniscience* and *selective omniscience* respectively, and the second is often found in short fiction.

> *Participant* or *first-person* Sherwood Anderson, "I Want to Know Why," p. 22.
>
> *Nonparticipant* or *third-person* Alice Munro, "The Found Boat," p. 76.
>
> *Selective omniscience* Katherine Anne Porter, "The Fig Tree," p. 29. *See also* Editorial Omniscience, Innocent Eye, Narrator, Neutral Omniscience.

Protagonist The central figure in a work of fiction or drama.

Pun Generally a witty play on words with the same sound but different meanings. *See* Ambiguity.

> And the one talent which is death to hide . . .—John Milton, "On His Blindness," l. 3, 677.
>
> Grave men, near death—Dylan Thomas, "Do Not Go Gentle into that Good Night," l. 13, p. 946.

Quatrain A four-line stanza or one of the three groups of four lines in an English sonnet.

Recognition (often with scene) Especially in tragedy, the point at which the protagonist acquires crucial knowledge previously withheld or realizes his or her true situation.

Refrain Repetition of a line or lines at regular intervals in a poem, most often at the ends of stanzas.

> John Skelton, "To Mistress Margaret Hussey," p. 86.

Resolution Especially in a dramatic plot, the outcome of the central conflict; also called the dénouement, meaning literally the unraveling.

Reversal Especially in tragedy, an abrupt change of fortune for the protagonist.

Rhyme Repetition of the final stressed vowel and succeeding consonant, preceded by different consonant sounds, especially in the words of a poem. Depending on where rhyming words appear in a line of poetry, the line is said to have *end rhyme* or *internal rhyme*. The pattern of the end rhyme in a poem or stanza is its *rhyme scheme*.

> *End rhyme* The witch that came (the withered hag)/To wash the steps with pail and rag/Was once the beauty Abishag—Robert Frost, "Provide, Provide," ll. 1–3, p. 934.
>
> *Internal rhyme* Come from the fire, perne in a gyre—William Butler Yeats, "Sailing to Byzantium," l. 19, p. 685.

Rhythm In poetry, the generally regular pattern of stressed syllables comprising the meter, and variations upon this for emphasis or natural effect.

Satire Various kinds of writing that hold aspects of human behavior up to ridicule for the purpose of amending them.

> Countee Cullen, "For a Lady I Know," p. 106.
>
> W. H. Auden, "The Unknown Citizen," p. 245.
>
> Molière, *The Misanthrope*, p. 261.

Scansion Analysis of a poetic line for the kind and number of metrical feet in it.

Sestet *See* Sonnet.

Setting The location of a story in time and place.

Shakespearean Sonnet *See* Sonnet.

Short Story A kind of prose fiction usually focusing on one main incident or a few closely related ones.

Simile An explicit comparison—using "like," "as"—between dissimilar items.

> When the evening is spread out against the sky/Like a patient etherised upon a table—T. S. Eliot, "The Love Song of J. Alfred Prufrock," ll. 2–3, p. 239.
>
> His hands were like wild birds—John Updike, "Ex-Basketball Player," l. 18, p. 254.

Soliloquy In drama, the convention by which a character, alone on stage, speaks his or her thoughts aloud.

William Shakespeare, *Hamlet,* Hamlet's speech (II,ii, 474–531), pp. 991–93.

Sonnet A fourteen-line lyric poem, usually in *iambic pentameter.* An *Italian,* or *Petrarchan sonnet* contains an *octave* and *sestet,* the first eight lines and last six respectively. An *English,* or *Shakespearean sonnet* has three *quatrains* followed by a *couplet.* The *rhyme scheme* in each type of sonnet emphasizes its structure. A *sonnet cycle* or *sequence* is a group of interrelated sonnets by the same poet.

> *Italian sonnet* John Keats, "On First Looking into Chapman's Homer," p. 95.
> John Milton, "On His Blindness," p. 677.
> *English sonnet* William Shakespeare, Sonnets 18, 73, 98, and so on, pp. 432–35.

Sophoclean Irony *See* Irony.

Speaker A term used to distinguish the voice heard in a poem from that of the poet. The speaker may clearly not be the poet or may not be expressing the poet's actual experiences or feelings. *Persona* is sometimes used instead.

> William Blake, "The Little Black Boy," p. 90.
> Ted Hughes, "Hawk Roosting," p. 701.
> Emily Dickinson, "Because I could not stop for Death," p. 928.
> Thomas Hardy, "The Man He Killed," p. 930.

Stage Business The activities indicated for the characters in a play by the author's text.

Stanza One of two or more groups of lines in a poem, each group having the same number of lines and a pattern of meter and rhyme similar to the others.

Story A broad term for the main sequence of events depicted in a work of fiction or drama.

Style A writer's manner of expression, including range of vocabulary, diction, and characteristic sentence or stanza structure.

Symbol An object or action that suggests meanings beyond itself. In and outside literature, a widely recognized symbol is called conventional. *Symbolism* is the use of symbols.

> William Blake, "The Lamb," p. 89.
> William Blake, "The Tyger," p. 89.
> John Keats, "Ode on a Grecian Urn," p. 679.
> D. H. Lawrence, "Snake," p. 687.
> Robert Frost, "The Road Not Taken," p. 936.

Syntax Word order, which may be used for emphasis when it differs from the normal or expected.

> Something there is that doesn't love a wall—Robert Frost, "Mending Wall," ll. 1, 35, pp. 237–38.
> About suffering they were never wrong, / The Old Masters—W. H. Auden, "Musée des Beaux Arts," ll. 1–2, p. 943.

Theme An idea that a literary work illustrates, most often implicitly.

Tone The attitude or feeling present in a literary work and attributable to a narrator, speaker, or the author. Sometimes the poet's tone may be detected behind the speaker's, or the author's behind the narrator's.

Tragedy A broad term for a serious drama in which the central character, often a person of high rank, suffers greatly.

> Sophocles, *Oedipus Rex,* p. 116.
> William Shakespeare, *Hamlet,* p. 949.

Tragic Flaw In tragedy, generally a moral flaw or a mistake leading to the protagonist's downfall. The enormous pride of the Greek tragic protagonist is often considered such a flaw. *See* Hubris.

Tragic Irony *See* Irony.

Turning Point *See* Climax.

Understatement Moderation or weakness of expression used to heighten an effect by suggesting the opposite of what is said.

> The grave's a fine and private place,
> But none, I think, do there embrace—Andrew Marvell, "To His Coy Mistress," ll. 31–32, p. 444.
> And death i think is no parenthesis—e. e. cummings, "since feeling is first," l. 16, p. 451.

Verse A single line of poetry, or metrical speaking or writing generally.

Copyrights and Acknowledgments

The author is grateful to the following publishers and copyright holders for permission to reprint material in this book.

ISABEL BAYLEY For "The Fig Tree" from *The Collected Stories of Katherine Anne Porter* by Katherine Ann Porter. Copyright © 1960 by Katherine Ann Porter. Reprinted by permission of Isabel Bayley, Literary Trustee, estate of Katherine Ann Porter.

BROADSIDE PRESS For "For Black Poets who Think of Suicide" from *Poems from Prison* by Etheridge Knight. Copyright © 1968 by Broadside Press.

GWENDOLYN BROOKS For "We Real Cool" from *Selected Poems* by Gwendolyn Brooks. Copyright © 1963 by Gwendolyn Brooks, The David Company, Chicago, Illinois.

DELACORTE PRESS For "Souvenir" excerpted from the book *Black Tickets* by Jayne Anne Phillips. copyright © 1979 by Jayne Anne Phillips. Reprinted by permission of Delacorte Press/Seymour Lawrence.

DOUBLEDAY AND COMPANY, INC. For "Sonny's Blues" from *Going to Meet the Man* by James Baldwin. Copyright © 1948, 1951, 1957, 1958, 1960, 1965 by James Baldwin. For "Winter Night" by Kay Boyle. Copyright © 1946 by The New Yorker, Inc. from *Fifty Stories* by Kay Boyle. For "The Waking" and "I Knew a Woman." Copyright © 1963 by Beatrice Roethke as administratrix of the estate for Theodore Roethke, all from *The Collected Poems of Theodore Roethke*. For "Good Night, Willie Lee, I'll see You in the Morning" from the book *Good Night, Willie Lee, I'll See You in the Morning* by Alice Walker. Copyright first appeared in *Iowa Review* © 1975 by Alice Walker. For "Light Baggage" from *Good Night, Willie Lee, I'll See You in the Morning* by Alice Walker. Copyright © 1977 by Alice Walker. "Streaking" from *Good Night, Willie Lee, I'll See You in the Morning* by Alice Walker first appeared in *Iowa Review*. Copyright © 1975 by Alice Walker. All reprinted by permission of Doubleday, a division of Bantam, Doubleday, Dell Publishing Group, Inc.

FABER AND FABER LTD. For "Talking in Bed" from *The Whitsun Weddings* by Philip Larkin. Reprinted by permission of Faber and Faber Ltd.

FARRAR, STRAUS AND GIROUX, INC. For "Filling Station" from *The Complete Poems* by Elizabeth Bishop. Copyright © 1983 by Alice Helen Mathfessel. Copyright © 1955 by Elizabeth Bishop. For "Blackberry-Picking" from *Poems, 1965–1975* by Seamus Heaney. Copyright © 1966, 1969, 1972, 1975, 1980 by Seamus Heaney. For "The Skunk" from *Field Work* by Seamus Heaney. Copyright © 1976, 1979 by Seamus Heaney. For "Vers de Société" from *High Windows* by Philip Larkin. Copyright © 1974 by Philip Larkin. For "For the Union Dead" from *For the Union Dead* By Robert Lowell. Copyright © 1956, 1959, 1960, 1961, 1962, 1963, 1964 by Robert Lowell. For "The Magic Barrel" from *The Magic Barrel* by Bernard Malamud. Copyright © 1950, 1951, 1952, 1953, 1954, 1955, 1956, 1958 by Bernard Malamud. All reprinted by permission of Farrar, Straus and Giroux, Inc.

BLANCHE C. GREGORY, INC. For "Out of Place" from *The Seduction and Other Stories* by Joyce Carol Oates. Copyright © by Joyce Carol Oates. Reprinted by permission of the author and her agent Blanche C. Gregory, Inc.

HARCOURT BRACE JOVANOVICH, INC. For "Journey of the Magi" and "The Love Song of J. Alfred Prufrock" from *Collected Poems 1909–1962* by T. S. Eliot, copyright 1936 by Harcourt Brace Jovanovich, Inc., copyright © 1963, 1964 by T. S.

Index of Authors,
Titles,
and First Lines of Poems

A8
B9
C0
D1
E2
F3
G4
H5
I6
J7